D0526599

# The Good Food Guide 2003

## WHICH? BOOKS

Which? Books is the book publishing arm of Consumers' Association, which was set up in 1957 to improve the standards of goods and services available to the public. Everything Which? publishes aims to help consumers, by giving them the independent information they need to make informed decisions. These publications, known throughout Britain for their quality, integrity and impartiality, have been held in high regard for four decades.

Independence does not come cheap: the guides carry no advertising, and no restaurant or hotel can buy an entry in our guides, or treat our inspectors to free meals or accommodation. This policy, and our practice of rigorously re-researching our guides for each edition, helps us to provide our readers with information of a standard and quality that cannot be surpassed.

# The Good Food Guide 2003

Edited by

## Jim Ainsworth

**WHICH?**
BOOKS
**CONSUMERS' ASSOCIATION**

*Which? Books* are commissioned and researched by
Consumers' Association and published by
Which? Ltd, 2 Marylebone Road,
London NW1 4DF

Distributed by The Penguin Group:
Penguin Books Ltd, 27 Wrights Lane,
London W8 5TZ

Copyright © 2002 Which? Ltd

Base mapping © Map Marketing Ltd/
European Map Graphics 2002
Map information © Which? Ltd 2002

**British Library Cataloguing in Publication Data**
A catalogue record for this book is
available from the British Library

ISBN 0 85202 908 X

For a full list of Which? books, please write to:
Which? Books, Castlemead, Gascoyne Way,
Hertford X, SG14 1LH
or access our web site at http://www.which.net

Photoset by Tradespools Ltd, Frome, Somerset
Printed in England by Clays Ltd, St Ives plc

Cover: Price Watkins Design Limited
Cover image: Cephas/Stockfood

# Contents

# *The Good Food Guide* voucher scheme £5

Again this year the Guide includes three £5 vouchers that readers will be able to redeem against the price of meals taken in participating restaurants. (Look for the £5 symbol at the very end of entries to locate those participating.) Only one voucher may be used per booked table, for a minimum of two people. Remember that your intention to use the voucher MUST be mentioned at the time of booking. Some restaurants may restrict use of the voucher at some sessions or for some menus (usually 'special offer' or lower-cost set meals); it is best to ask when booking. Actual vouchers (not photocopies) must be presented. The vouchers will be valid from 1 October 2002 to 30 September 2003, and may not be used in conjunction with any other offers.

## The Guide online

Internet users can find *The Good Food Guide* online at the Which? Online website http://www.which.net. You will need to be a Which? Online subscriber to make full use of the Guide online. See the website for details.

## Update service

Written details of restaurant sales, closures, chef changes and so on since this edition of the Guide was published will be available free of charge from 1 December 2002 to 1 May 2003. Readers should write to: FREEPOST, Update, *The Good Food Guide*, 2 Marylebone Road, London NW1 4DF (no stamp is required if you post your request in the UK). Alternatively, you may email *goodfoodguide@which.net* (remember to include your full name and address when you email), or phone 020-7770 7551. As always, readers who send in reports on meals will be sent an Update Sheet if they request one.

# How to use the Guide

## FINDING A RESTAURANT

**If you are seeking a restaurant in a particular area:** *first go to the maps* at the centre of the book. Once you know the locality (or, for London, the restaurant name), go to the relevant section of the book to find the entry for the restaurant. The Guide's main entries are divided into seven sections: London, England, Scotland, Wales, Channel Islands, Northern Ireland, and Republic of Ireland. In the London section, restaurants are listed alphabetically by name; in all other sections, they are listed by locality (usually the name of the town or village).

In addition to the main entries are the Round-ups (a range of restaurants, cafés, bistros and pubs that are worth a visit but do not merit a full entry): those for London can be found just after the London main-entry section, and those for everywhere else are towards the back of the book just after the Republic of Ireland main-entry section.

**If you know the name of the restaurant:** *go to the index* at the back of the book, which lists both main and Round-up entries.

**If you are seeking award-winning restaurants, those offering a particular cuisine, etc.:** *make use of the lists* starting on page 11, which feature the top-rated restaurants, restaurants with outstanding wine cellars, restaurants of the year, new entries in the Guide, London restaurants by cuisine, budget eating and other helpful groupings.

## HOW TO READ A GUIDE ENTRY

Please see inside front cover for explanation of symbols and cooking marks. At the top of each main entry you will find the restaurant's name, map number, address, telephone and fax numbers, its email address and website if it has these, as well as any symbols that may apply to the establishment. The cuisine style is also given; this is not meant to be a comprehensive assessment of cooking style, but rather to act as a helpful pointer and in many cases has been suggested by the restaurant itself. At the top of entries you will also find the mark, from 1 to 10, awarded by the editor for cooking, and the cost range for one person having a three-course meal including wine. The middle part of the entry describes food, wines, atmosphere and so on, while the final section gives a wealth of additional information, explained below.

## Cost

The price range given is based on the cost of a three-course meal (lunch and/or dinner) for one person, including coffee, house wine, service and cover charge where applicable, according to information supplied by the restaurant. The lower figure is the least you are likely to pay, from either á la carte or set-price menus, and may apply only to lunch. The higher figure indicates a probable maximum cost, sometimes based on a set-price meal of more than three courses, if that is what is offered. This figure is inflated by 20 per cent to reflect the fact that some people may order more expensive wine, extra drinks and some higher-priced 'special' dishes, and that price rises may come into effect during the life-time of this edition of the Guide.

## Meals

At the bottom of entries information on the types of meals offered is given, with any variations for lunch (L) and dinner (D), and details of availability. An á la carte menu is signified by the letters *alc*. This is followed by a range of prices for main courses, rounded up to the nearest 50p. *Set L* denotes a set-price lunch; *Set D* means set-price dinner. Set meals usually consist of three courses, but can include many more. If a set meal has fewer than three courses, this is stated. If there is a cover charge, this is also indicated. Brief details of other menus, such as light lunch or bar snacks, are also given. If there is a cover charge, that is also mentioned here.

## Service

*Net prices* means that prices of food and wine are inclusive of service charge, and this is indicated clearly on the menu and bill; *not inc*, that service is not included and is left to the discretion of the customer; *10%*, that a fixed service charge of 10 per cent is automatically added to the bill; *10% (optional)*, that 10 per cent is added to the bill along with the word 'optional' or similar qualifier; and *none*, that no service charge is made or expected and that any money offered is refused. *Card slips closed* indicates that the total on the slips of credit cards is closed when handed over for signature.

## Other details

Information is also given on *seating, outside seating* and *private parties*. We say *car park* if the restaurant provides free parking facilities for patrons (*small car park* if it has only a few spaces), and say *vegetarian meals* only if menus list at least one vegetarian option as a starter and one as a main course (if this is not noted, a restaurant may still be able to offer vegetarian options with prior notice – it is worth phoning to check).

Any restrictions on children are given, such as *no children* or *no children under 6 after 8pm*; otherwise, it can be assumed that children are welcome. In addition, *children's helpings* are noted if smaller portions are available at a reduced price; *jacket and tie* if it is compulsory for men to wear a jacket and tie to the restaurant; *wheelchair access* if the proprietor has confirmed that the entrance is at least 80cm wide and passages at least 120cm wide in accordance with the Royal Association for Disability and Rehabilitation (RADAR) recommendations, and *also WC* if the proprietor has assured us that toilet facilities are suitable for disabled people (*not WC* means these are not available or the proprietor is not sure). *Music* indicates that live or recorded music is usually played in the dining-room; *occasional music* that it sometimes is; *no music* that it never is. *No mobile phones* means the restaurant requests these are switched off.

## Accommodation

For establishments offering overnight accommodation, the number of rooms, along with facilities provided in the rooms (e.g. bath/shower, TV, phone), is set out. Prices are given usually for bed and breakfast (*B&B*). *D,B&B* indicates that the price also includes dinner. The first figure given is the lowest price for one person in a single room, or single occupancy of a double, the second is the most expensive price for two people in a double room or suite. *Rooms for disabled* means the establishment has stated that its accommodation is suitable for wheelchair-users. Restrictions on children, and facilities for guests with babies, are indicated. *The Which? Hotel Guide* means the establishment is also listed in the 2003 edition of our sister guide to over 1,000 hotels in Britain.

## Miscellaneous information

At the end of London entries, the nearest Underground station is given after the symbol ⊖. For restaurants that have elected to participate in the *Good Food Guide* £5 voucher scheme, a ⑤ symbol appears at the very end of entries (see page 6 for further details).

# The top-rated restaurants

(See inside front cover for explanation of marking system.)

## Mark 10 for cooking

### London
Gordon Ramsay, SW3

## Mark 9 for cooking

### England
Le Manoir aux Quat' Saisons, Great Milton
Waterside Inn, Bray
Winteringham Fields, Winteringham

## Mark 8 for cooking

### London
The Capital, SW3
Pétrus, SW1
Pied-à-Terre, W1
Square, W1
La Tante Claire, SW1

### England
Fat Duck, Bray
Gidleigh Park, Chagford
Merchant House, Ludlow

## Mark 7 for cooking

### London
Foliage, SW1
Le Gavroche, W1
Gordon Ramsay at Claridge's, W1
John Burton-Race at the Landmark, NW1
La Trompette, W4

### England
Castle House, La Rive, Hereford
Le Champignon Sauvage, Cheltenham
Clivedon, Waldo's, Taplow
Fischer's Baslow Hall, Baslow
Hambleton Hall, Hambleton
Harry's Place, Great Gonerby
Hibiscus, Ludlow
Juniper, Altrincham
Monsieur Max, Hampton Hill

Mr Underhill's, Ludlow
L'Ortolan, Shinfield
Paul Heathcote's, Longridge
Pool Court at 42, Leeds
Priory House Restaurant, Stoke sub Hamdon
Sandgate Hotel, La Terrasse, Sandgate
Vineyard at Stockcross, Stockcross
Yorke Arms, Ramsgill

### Scotland
The Creel, St Margaret's Hope

### Wales
Plas Bodegroes, Pwllheli
Ynyshir Hall, Eglywsfach

# The Guide's longest-serving restaurants

The Guide has seen many restaurants come and go. Some, however, have stayed the course with tenacity. (Qualification for this list is that the restaurant has been in each edition of the Guide subsequent to its first entry.)

| | |
|---|---|
| Connaught, W1 | 50 years |
| Gay Hussar, W1 | 46 years |
| Gravetye Manor, East Grinstead | 46 years |
| Porth Tocyn Hotel, Abersoch | 46 years |
| Sharrow Bay, Ullswater | 42 years |
| Walnut Tree Inn, Llandewi Skirrid | 38 years |
| Black Bull Inn, Moulton | 36 years |
| Chez Moi, W11 | 34 years |
| Rothay Manor, Ambleside | 34 years |
| Sundial, Herstmonceux | 34 years |
| Le Gavroche, W1 | 33 years |
| Summer Isles Hotel, Achiltibuie | 33 years |
| The Capital, SW3 | 32 years |
| Miller Howe, Windermere | 32 years |
| Old Fire Engine House, Ely | 31 years |
| Ubiquitous Chip, Glasgow | 31 years |
| Druidstone, Broad Haven | 30 years |
| Peat Inn, Peat Inn | 30 years |
| Plumber Manor, Sturminster Newton | 30 years |
| Waterside Inn, Bray | 30 years |
| White Moss House, Grasmere | 30 years |
| Carved Angel, Dartmouth | 29 years |
| Isle of Eriska, Eriska | 29 years |
| Airds, Port Appin | 27 years |
| Farlam Hall, Brampton | 26 years |
| Hungry Monk, Jevington | 26 years |
| Langan's Brasserie, W1 | 26 years |
| Corse Lawn House, Corse Lawn | 25 years |
| Gidleigh Park, Chagford | 25 years |
| White House, Williton | 25 years |
| Hambleton Hall, Hambleton | 24 years |
| Hunstrete House, Hunstrete | 24 years |
| Sabras, NW10 | 24 years |
| The Pier Hotel, Harbourside Restaurant, Harwich | 24 years |
| Brown's, Worcester | 23 years |
| Cherwell Boathouse, Oxford | 23 years |
| Grafton Manor, Bromsgrove | 23 years |
| Harveys, Bristol | 23 years |
| Magpie Café, Whitby | 23 years |
| Royal Crescent, Pimpernel's, Bath | 22 years |
| Sir Charles Napier, Chinnor | 22 years |
| Drum and Monkey, Harrogate | 22 years |
| Homewood Park, Hinton Charterhouse | 22 years |
| RSJ, SE1 | 22 years |
| Seafood Restaurant, Padstow | 22 years |

# Restaurants with outstanding wine cellars
## Marked in the text with a ▮

### London
Bibendum, SW3
Bleeding Heart, EC1
Brown's Hotel, Restaurant 1837, W1
Chez Bruce, SW17
The Don, EC4
Fifth Floor, SW1
Gordon Ramsay, SW3
Odette's, NW1
Oxo Tower, SE1
Pied-à-Terre, W1
Le Pont de la Tour, SE1
Ransome's Dock Restaurant, SW11
RSJ, SE1
Square, W1
Tate Britain Restaurant, SW1

### England
Birmingham, Hotel du Vin & Bistro
Bolton Abbey, Devonshire Arms,
    Burlington Restaurant
Bowness-on-Windermere,
    Porthole Eating House
Bray, Fat Duck
Bristol, Harveys
Bristol, Hotel du Vin & Bistro
Chagford, Gidleigh Park
Chinnor, Sir Charles Napier
Corse Lawn, Corse Lawn House
Dedham, Le Talbooth
East Grinstead, Gravetye Manor
Faversham, Read's
Grasmere, White Moss House
Great Milton, Le Manoir aux Quat'
    Saisons
Hetton, Angel Inn
Huntingdon, Old Bridge Hotel
Ilkley, Box Tree
Leeds, Leodis
Leeds, Sous le Nez en Ville
Lewdown, Lewtrenchard Manor
Little Bedwyn, Harrow
Lyndhurst, Le Poussin at Parkhill

Marten, Windmill
Moulton, Black Bull Inn
Newton Longville, Crooked Billet
Oxford, Cherwell Boathouse
Padstow, Seafood Restaurant
Petersfield, JSW
Romsey, Old Manor House
Ross-on-Wye, Pheasant at Ross
Sandgate, Sandgate Hotel, La Terrasse
Southwold, Crown Hotel
Stockcross, Vineyard at Stockcross
Tunbridge Wells, Hotel du Vin & Bistro
Ullswater, Sharrow Bay
Williton, White House
Winchester, Hotel du Vin & Bistro

### Scotland
Achiltibuie, Summer Isles Hotel
Anstruther, Cellar
Edinburgh, Valvona & Crolla Caffè Bar
Glasgow, Ubiquitous Chip
Gullane, Greywalls
Kingussie, The Cross
Linlithgow, Champany Inn
Nairn, Clifton House
Peat Inn, Peat Inn

### Wales
Aberdovey, Penhelig Arms Hotel
Llandudno, St Tudno Hotel
Pwllheli, Plas Bodegroes
Reynoldston, Fairyhill

### Republic of Ireland
Kenmare, Park Hotel Kenmare
Kenmare, Sheen Falls Lodge, La
    Cascade
Newport, Newport House

### Channel Islands
St Saviour, Longueville Manor

# Restaurants of the year

This award does not necessarily go to the restaurants with the highest mark for cooking, but rather to ones which have shown particular merit or achievement during the year. It may go to an old favourite or to a new entry, but in either case the places listed below are worth visiting in their own right, and have enhanced the eating-out experience in some way. Although we have looked at all geographical areas, not all have been lucky enough to have such special achievers. This year we have two overall *Restaurants of the year* – one each for England and for Wales – plus, drawn from a wider area, eight *Newcomers of the year* and 16 *Commended* listings.

## Restaurants of the year

### England
Juniper, Altrincham (Greater Manchester)

### Wales
Plas Bodegroes, Pwllheli (Gwynedd)

## Newcomers of the year

### London
Eyre Brothers, EC2

### England
La Cachette, Elland (West Yorkshire)

Old Passage Inn, Arlingham (Gloucestershire)

L'Ortolan, Shinfield (Berkshire)

Restaurant on the Square, Bishop's Waltham (Hampshire)

Seaham Hall Hotel, Seaham (Co Durham)

### Scotland
Seafood Restaurant, St Monans (Fife)

### Wales
Foxhunter, Nant-y-Derry (Monmouthshire)

## Commended

### London
L'Escargot, Picasso Room, W1

Orrery, W1

### England
Arundell Arms, Lifton (Devon)

Harrisons, Kelsale (Suffolk)

Hart's, Nottingham (Notts)

McClements, Twickenham (Greater London)

Quartier Vert, Bristol (Bristol)

Riverside Brasserie, Bray (Berkshire)

Trouble House, Tetbury (Gloucestershire)

Weavers Shed, Golcar (West Yorkshire)

Wickham Vineyard, Shedfield (Hampshire)

Yetman's, Holt (Norfolk)

### Scotland
Crinan Hotel, Westward Restaurant, Crinan (Argyll & Bute)

Darroch Learg, Ballater (Aberdeenshire)

### Wales
Bricklayers Arms, Montgomery (Powys)

Ynyshir Hall, Eglwysfach (Powys)

# London restaurants by cuisine

Boundaries between some national cuisines – British, French and Italian particularly – are not as marked as they used to be. Therefore, the restaurants listed below are classified by the predominant influence, although there may be some crossover. The headings are in many cases more generalised than the brief cuisine descriptions given at the tops of the entries themselves.

## American
Christopher's, WC2

## British
City Rhodes, EC4
Popeseye, W14
Quality Chop House, EC1
Rhodes in the Square, SW1
St John, EC1
Smiths of Smithfield, EC1
Tate Britain Restaurant, SW1
Wiltons, SW1

## Chinese
Ecapital, W1
Four Seasons, W2
Fung Shing, WC2
Golden Dragon, W1
Hakkasan, W1
Mandarin Kitchen, W2
Mr Kong, WC2
Phoenix Palace, NW1
Royal China, E14, NW8, W1
  and W2

## Danish
Lundum's, SW7

## East European/ Eurasian
Baltic, SE1
Gay Hussar, W1
Little Georgia, E8

## Fish/Seafood
Back to Basics, W1
Bibendum Oyster Bar, SW3
Café Fish, SW1
Creelers, SW3
Fish Hoek, W4
J. Sheekey, WC2
Livebait, SE1
Lobster Pot, SE11
Lou Pescadou, SW5
One-O-One, SW1
Rasa Samudra, W1
Two Brothers, N3

## French
Admiralty, WC2
Almeida, N1
Aubergine, SW10
Bleeding Heart, EC1
Brasserie Roux, SW1

Brasserie St Quentin, SW3
The Capital, SW3
Le Chardon, SE22
Club Gascon, EC1
Le Colombier, SW3
Le Coq d'Argent, EC2
The Don, EC4
Drones, SW1
L'Escargot, Ground Floor,
  W1
L'Escargot, Picasso Room,
  W1
L'Estaminet, WC2
Gordon Ramsay, SW3
Gordon Ramsay at
  Claridge's, W1
Le Gavroche, W1
John Burton-Race at the
  Landmark, NW1
Maison Novelli, EC1
Maquis, W6
Mirabelle, W1
One-Seven-Nine, WC2
L'Oranger, SW1
Parisienne Chophouse, SW3
Pétrus, SW1
Pied-à-Terre, W1
QC, WC1
Racine, SW3
Ritz, W1
Roussillon, SW1
Square, W1
La Tante Claire, SW1
Les Trois Garcons, E1
La Trompette, W4
La Trouvaille, W1

## Fusion
e&o, W11
Great Eastern Dining Room,
  EC2
Providores, W1
Sugar Club, W1

## Greek
The Real Greek, N1

## Indian/Pakistani
Babur Brasserie, SE23
Bar Zaika Bazaar, SW3
Café Spice Namaste, E1 and
  SW11
Chor Bizarre, W1
Chutney Mary, SW10
Cinnamon Club, SW1

ginger, W2
Haandi, SW3
Mela, WC2
New Tayyabs, E1
Old Delhi, W2
Parsee, N19
Porte des Indes, W1
Radha Krishna Bhavan,
  SW17
Rasa Travancore, N16
Red Fort, W1
Salloos, SW1
Sarkhel's, SW18
Soho Spice, W1
Tamarind, W1
Vama - the Indian Room,
  SW10
Yatra, W1
Zaika, SW3

## Indian vegetarian
Kastoori, SW17
Rasa, N16 and Rasa W1
Sabras, NW10

## Indonesian/ Straits
Gourmet Garden, NW4
Singapore Garden, NW6

## Italian
Al Duca, SW1
Alloro, W1
Al San Vincenzo, W2
Arancia, SE16
Assaggi, W2
Cecconi's, W1
Connaught, W1
Il Convivio, SW1
Del Buongustaio, SW15
Enoteca Turi, SW15
Il Forno, W1
Green Olive, W9
Ibla, W1
Isola, SW1
Locanda Locatelli, W1
Metrogusto, N1
Neal Street Restaurant, WC2
Olivo, SW11
Passione, W1
Red Pepper, W9
Riso, W4
Riva, SW13
River Café, W6

Rosmarino, NW8
Salusbury, NW6
Sardo, W1
Sartoria, W1
Spiga, W1
Teca, W1
Tentazioni, SE1
Timo, W8
West Street, WC2
Zafferano, SW1

## Japanese/sushi bars

Café Japan, NW11
Itsu, SW3 and Itsu (Soho), W1
Kiku, W1
K10, EC2
Kulu Kulu Sushi, W1

Moshi Moshi Sushi, EC2, EC4 and E14
Nobu, W1
Sumosan, W1
Sushi-Say, NW2
Tsunami, SW4
Ubon, E14
Wagamama, WC1
Zuma, SW7

## North African/ Middle Eastern

Adams Café, W12
Al Hamra, W1
Bel Azur, N12
Istanbul Iskembecisi, N16
Iznik, N5
Noura, SW1
Original Tagines, W1
Tas, SE1

## Peruvian
Fina Estampa, SE1

## Spanish
Cambio de Tercio, SW5
Cigala, WC1
Gaudí, EC1
Moro, EC1

## Thai
Blue Elephant, SW6
Nahm, SW1
Thai Garden, E2

## Vegetarian
Gate, NW3

## Vietnamese
Huong-Viet, N1

# Open credit card slips

According to data provided by the restaurants themselves at the time of going to press, the following places both include a charge for service (sometimes called 'optional') on the bill and leave credit card slips open. This list may help save you paying twice for service.

## London

Back to Basics, W1
Baltic, SE1
Brasserie St Quentin, SW3
Le Chardon, SE22
Coq d'Argent, EC2
Ditto, SW18
Drones, SW1
Electric Brasserie, W11
Eyre Brothers, EC2
Four Seasons, W2
ginger, W2
Golden Dragon, W1V
Gourmet Garden, NW4
Great Eastern Hotel, Aurora, EC2
Iznik, N5
Langan's Brasserie, W1
Maison Novelli, EC1
Maquis, W6
Mirabelle, W1
Nobu, W1
Old Delhi, W2

L'Oranger, SW1
Parisienne Chophouse, SW3
Perseverance, WC1
Phoenix Palace, NW1
Le Pont de la Tour, SE1
Popeseye, W14
QC, WC1
Quo Vadis, W1
Royal China, W1, W2, NW8, E14
Tas, SE1
Le Trois Garcons, E1
Yatra, W1S

## England
Barnet, Mims
Birmingham, Chung Ying
Harrow, Golden Palace
Leamington Spa, Love's
Leeds, Fourth Floor
Leeds, Heathcotes at Rascasse
Leeds, Livebait

Manchester, New Emperor
Manchester, Ocean Treasure
Manchester, Pacific
Penzance, Summer House
Upper Slaughter, Lords of the Manor
Warminster, Bishopstrow House
Wickham, Old House

## Wales
Cardiff, St David's Hotel & Spa, Tides Marco Pierre White

## Republic of Ireland
Dublin, Chapter One
Dublin, L 'Ecrivan
Dublin, Roly's Bistro
Wexford, La Riva

# New entries

These restaurants are new main entries in the Guide this year, although some may have appeared in previous years, or in the Round-ups last year.

## London
Almeida, N1
Aquarium, E1
Baltic, SE1
Bel Azur, N12
Blandford Street, W1
Brasserie Roux, SW1
Chapter Two, SE3
Clerkenwell Dining Room, EC1
Deca, W1
Le Deuxième, WC2
Drapers Arms, N1
e&o, W11
Ecaptial, W1
Electric Brasserie, W11
Embassy, W1
Eyre Brothers, EC2
Fish Hoek, W4
Fox Dining Room, EC2
Gordon Ramsay at Claridge's, W1
Highgate, NW5
Huong-Viet, N1
Light House, SW19
Lightship Ten, E1
Locanda Locatelli, W1
Maquis, W6
Mju, SW1
Nahm, SW1
Oak, W2
One-Seven-Nine, WC2
Parisienne Chophouse, SW3
Perseverance, WC1
Phoenix Palace, NW1
Providores, W1
QC, WC1
Racine, SW3
Red Fort, W1
Sardo, W1
Sumosan, W1
Thyme, SW4
Timo, W8
Les Trois Garcons, E1
La Trouvaille, W1
Tsunami, SW4
Vama–the Indian Room, SW10
West Street, WC2
Zuma, SW7

## England
Abbinger Common, Stephan Langton Inn
Ardington, Boar's Head
Arlingham, Old Passage Inn
Atherstone, Chapel House
Aycliffe, County
Bath, Blinis
Battle, Pilgrims
Birmingham, Chung Ying Garden
Birmingham, Metro Bar & Grill
Bishop's Waltham, Restaurant on the Square

Bispham Green, Eagle & Child
Bowness-on-Windermere, Studio
Bray, Riverside Brasserie
Brighton, Sevendials
Bristol, Brazz
Bristol, Ma Provence
Cheltenham, Chelsea Square
Cheltenham, Daffodil
Chettle, Castleman Hotel
Chipping Camden, Cotswold House
Clipsham, Olive Branch
Crudwell, Old Rectory
Cuckfield, Mansfields
Dorridge, Forest
Elland, La Cachette
Ermington, Plantation House
Frampton Mansell, White Horse
Grimsthorpe, Black Horse
Guildford, Zinfandel
Harrogate, Attic
Harrogate, Kings
Hemingford Grey, Cock
Henley-in-Arden, Edmunds
Holkham, Victoria
Holy Cross, Bell & Cross
Kendal, Déjà-vu
Kibworth Beauchamp, Firenze
Kingsbridge, Ship to Shore
Leamington Spa, Love's
Leeds, Heathcotes at Rascasse
Leeds, Livebait
Lewes, Circa
Little Barrow, Foxcote Inn
Longbridge, Thyme
Lymington, Egan's
Manchester, Zinc
Marten, Windmill
Marton, Appletree
Marton, Sun Inn
Marlow, Danesfield House, Oak Room
Nettlebed, White Hart
Norwich, Tatlers
Nottingham, Restaurant Sat Bains at Hotel des Clos
Odiham, Grapevine
Osmotherley, Golden Lion
Oxford, Branca
Oxford, Chiang Mai Kitchen
Oxford, Gee's
Penzance, Abbey Restaurant
Penzance, Summer House
Romsey, Bertie's
St Ives, Alba
Sapperton, Bell at Sapperton
Seaham, Seaham Hall Hotel
Seaview, Seaview Hotel
Shedfield, Wickham Vineyard

Sheffield, Blue Room Brasserie
Shaftesbury, Wayfarers
Shinfield, L'Ortolan
Southsea, Bistro Montparnasse
Stockbridge, Greyhound
Stow-on-the-Wold, Kings Arms
Stratford-upon-Avon, Margaux
Surbiton, French Table
Totnes, Effings
Totnes, Wills Restaurant
Tunbridge Wells, Thackeray's
Tynemouth, Sidney's
Ullingswick, Three Crowns
Wakefield, Wolski's
Wincanton, Holbrook House
Windermere, Samling
Witney, Fleece Hotel and Brasserie
York, Blue Bicycle
York, Melton's Too

## Scotland
Ayr, Ivy House
Edinburgh, Channings
Edinburgh, Fishers in the City
Edinburgh, Off The Wall
Edinburgh, The Scotsman
Glasgow, Chardon D'Or
Glasgow, Gordon Yuill
Gullane, Golf Inn
Leven, Scotland's Larder
Moffat, Limetree
Oban, Ee-Usk
St Monans, Seafood Restaurant
Strathyre, Creagan House

## Wales
Cardiff, Da Venditto
Llanrhidian, Welcome to Town
Nant-y-Derry, Foxhunter
Skenfrith, Bell at Skenfrith
Tredunnock, The Newbridge

## Channel Islands
St Aubin, Harbour View

## Republic of Ireland
Crookhaven, Out of the Blue
Dublin, Browne's Brasserie
Dublin, Chapter One
Dublin, One Pico
Dublin, Shanahan's on the Green
Galway, Archway
Rathmullen, Rathmullen House
Wexford, La Riva

# Introduction

On the face of it, the past year has not been a good one for the restaurant trade. Foot-and-mouth disease left a trail of destruction in its wake for farmers, but also closed down whole areas of the countryside for a season. In some parts, hotels, country restaurants, bed and breakfast places and pubs alike lost out, as visitors were simply unable to reach their doors.

Then, just as everything was returning to normal, the events of 11 September 2001 shook the world. In the aftermath of the horrifying loss of life most people found themselves affected in some way: emotionally at first, but then economically too, as airlines struggled to survive, the tourist trade collapsed, and businesses around the world faltered.

Finally, financial scandals in America sent the world's stock markets into a tailspin. People who might normally have nothing to do with such matters were affected, as the rug was pulled from under pensions and savings, and confidence ebbed away.

After all that, who wants to go out and spend money in a restaurant?

The answer, remarkably, is that most people still do. For a short time our postbag may not have been quite as full as usual, because people were unable to eat out as often in country restaurants during the long foot-and-mouth epidemic. But things soon returned to normal. There have been fewer transatlantic visitors, which affected London as much as anywhere (remember the London Tourist Board's appeals for British holidaymakers?), and for a time it was possible to walk in off the street and get a table in restaurants that had previously required several months' notice. That situation too is reverting to normal. And the insecurity that we are supposed to feel, as financial markets collapse around us, must be news to those consumers who continue to fuel a high street shopping boom, and whose house prices are rising as never before.

So has it all been as disastrous as it felt at the time? A few restaurants which appeared in the last edition of the Guide have closed, certainly, but the numbers have been no greater than usual. Restaurateurs have not been writing to us bemoaning their bad luck, ready to jack it all in for a nice safe job as an estate agent or accountant. Rather they have hunkered down to weather the storm, the sensible ones offering inducements such as cheaper menus to keep trade going until things pick up again. What we might have expected to happen is that fewer new places would open: but our New Entries for this edition are up slightly on last year, by twenty-five. This may not accurately reflect the number of new openings, but it does indicate a degree of buoyancy in the business.

## Conversions and diversions

Where foot-and-mouth disease is concerned, there seems to have been a sea-change in public opinion. It was perhaps inevitable that the small band of oddballs who have been arguing the merits of organic farming for years would one day swell into the mainstream. They banged on about the dangers of agro-chemicals, from crop sprays to the cocktail of antibiotics in chicken feed, and warned of environmental time bombs ticking away. With each new unfolding disaster, from salmonella in eggs to BSE, they gained a few more converts.

Then, with foot-and-mouth disease, the tide finally turned. Suddenly, even politicians were listening: not, perhaps, because they had been closet Friends of the Earth waiting to come out, but more likely because they could no longer avoid seeing the obvious. If one outbreak of disease could send millions of sheep and cattle up in smoke, destroy the livelihoods of farmers and consign the tourist industry to deep depression, then perhaps it was time someone started looking into this. If it were, by some remote chance, to happen again, then quite a few careers in Whitehall and Westminster would grind to a halt. That is the clincher. That is what has made the difference this time.

It has also sharpened the minds of restaurateurs, who seem to take on board the idea of sustainable agriculture and organic food in greater numbers every year. This is not, as detractors would argue, out of some airy-fairy, namby-pamby 'lifestyle' consideration on the part of 'townies', but because it makes practical sense. Many chefs in areas where foot-and-mouth disease hit hardest, such as the Lake District and the South West, have now taken to buying local produce, particularly meat, in a big way. They are acutely aware that it was the convoluted transport of livestock – which often went from one end of the country to the other, just to gain a few extra pence per kilo – that turned a localised disaster into an almighty country-wide catastrophe. They do not want to be caught in such a situation again, and this is one more reason, to add to the long list, for buying locally.

When it comes to fish, the picture is less clear, although the dilemma is stark enough. If we insist on buying wild fish, we encourage over-fishing and are in danger of depleting stocks to the point where some species reach an unsustainable level. They, and the fishermen who catch them, become endangered, possibly extinct. But if we buy farmed fish, then apparently we sign up for lower quality, and we become responsible, by implication, for the disease the fish suffer, and for the environmental damage they cause when, inevitably, they escape into the wild. There is no easy answer, as Colin Pressdee finds in his exploration of these issues in the pages to follow.

When it comes to ducks, however, there is no more single-minded, obsessive, crazed or hedonistic consumer than Pam Roberts, who is willing to share her passion (though probably not an actual, precious duck) with the world at large: also in the following pages.

## Booze 'n' fags 'n' food

Talking of crazed, the past year has supposedly seen the invention of an 'intelligent' wine glass that, according to one newspaper 'calls over the waiter when it needs refilling', thanks to a microchip and a radio signal. Although the story was probably just an April Fool that some unthinking journalist fell for, it does point up one of the many irritations that concern reporters.

Indeed, just about every aspect of a visit to a restaurant is the source of some frustration or exasperation for somebody. We have highlighted many of these in the past, but one which exercises respondents repeatedly is the business of allowing smoking. It is odd that, throughout the wine trade, the first rule of any wine tasting is that smoking is forbidden: otherwise it is impossible to 'appreciate' a wine (to smell and taste it properly, or get the best out if it). Yet as soon as supposedly professional sommeliers get back from a tasting and into their restaurants, they expect customers to pay high prices for wines that they cannot possibly appreciate fully, thanks to a fug of smoke. I have yet to hear a convincing explanation of this anomaly.

As to the food, and how it strikes people, that is the subject of most of this book. The Guide's strength is you. You are one of the army of amateurs – that is, those who love good food – who express their opinions, often in strident terms, and keep us informed about what is happening in restaurants. You write things such as 'An excellent meal . . . a very enjoyable experience', and score the restaurant 7. Or you may write 'Your "6" is absolutely ridiculous . . . this is a dreary, soulless place . . . an experience not to be repeated . . . we were very badly informed by the Guide', and rate it 2. Or you may write, 'The best value for money in the entire London area, if not the entire SE of England.'

The odd thing about these comments is that they all refer to the same restaurant. It is a random example, but not an isolated one, and makes the business of scoring the cooking a bit tricky. It also makes it difficult to give a fair picture of the restaurant, if indeed there is such a thing. In many other cases, happily, agreement is spot on, making the Guide's job – to reflect, as accurately as possible, the views of its readers – that much easier.

It is, though, little wonder that reporters disagree when comparing the scores of restaurants. Some of you write to say how much better restaurant A is than B, while C on the other hand shouldn't even be in the Guide. According to a mathematician friend, given a nominal 1,000 entries in the Guide, there are some 166,167,000 possible three-way comparisons to be made. Obviously we cannot run them all through our heads just to check, which may be why some anomalies occur. So the more you can do to reduce these 166 million comparisons for us, the more grateful we will be.

But whether you agree or disagree with what you find in the following pages, your voice can be heard. All you have to do is drop us a line at the Freepost address, or e-mail us. Every scrap of information is useful, so even if you can't be bothered to type two sides of A4, a short paragraph or two – telling us about the food you ate, the feel of the place, and what the service was like – will be grist to our mill for the next edition. Thank you for taking the time and trouble to make your experiences available to others, so that eating out for your fellow diners is a less risky and more enjoyable business. We hope that their reports will likewise have helped you, through these pages, to get the greatest pleasure from eating out.

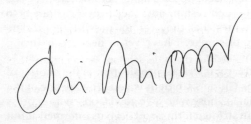

# Have fish had their chips?

**Colin Pressdee** journalist, broadcaster and former restaurateur, who for many years has passionately promoted fish as food and as a resource to be preserved and protected, expresses his concerns over what is happening in the industry today

A century ago the legendary French culinary genius Auguste Escoffier proclaimed that if cod ever were to be the same price as salmon it would gain the culinary recognition it rightly deserves. In the past decade this is precisely what has happened: cod now surpasses salmon in price, and has become a fashionable and highly popular item on restaurant menus everywhere, while salmon has become as familiar on the plate and as affordable as battery chicken.

Behind cod's recently acquired celebrity, as most people by now realise, are some very serious concerns. On the one hand, the enormous growth of fish-farming in recent years has made home-grown salmon – in contrast to its wild cousin – cheap and plentiful, though often at the price of taste and the environment. On the other hand, cod's desirability owes a lot to the fact that it is being fished to nearly unviable limits in the North Sea and elsewhere; its new-found 'rarity value' continues to boost its allure.

## Wild-side worries

A few decades ago the only fish (besides cod) likely to be found on British menus were Dover sole, plaice, brill, turbot and, for those who could afford it, that great fish, the Atlantic salmon. Other native species found in UK waters, such as red mullet, John Dory, monkfish and bass, were largely unknown to British restaurant-goers, though now you will find them on many top restaurants' menus. They are often trendily adorned with salsa, tapénade, wild rocket or wilted spinach, and at prices suited for those with deep pockets, as demand for unfarmed fish regularly outstrips supply.

The story is especially sad for the wild salmon. For a multitude of reasons, numbers have declined catastrophically over the past few decades: the Marine Conservation Society says that stocks have been reduced by 50 per cent in the past 20 years. Great salmon rivers such as the Wye are now virtually empty during the fishing season as a result of the loss of spawning grounds, due in turn to a slew of environmental problems. These include the planting of acidic coniferous forests, which render the waters moribund. And there is still unrelenting fishing in Arctic waters and around the Faeroes – the major feeding grounds of salmon – as well as coastal netting, poaching and pollution.

Pollution is indeed a major worry for wild stocks of all fish. Chemicals such as household cleaning agents in dishwashers pose more danger to fisheries than effluent, though the latter continues to take a major toll. Water run-off from farmland that has been pumped with chemicals or sprayed with farmyard muck can affect coastal waters, raising nitrogen levels, inducing algal and toxic blooms. Nevertheless some progress in combating pollution has been made, demonstrated for example by the revival of invertebrates on the Sussex coast in the ten years since a new treatment plant was installed. The future for Swansea Bay is also more positive after major investment in a state-of-the-art system that filters all solids and chemicals, discharging only fresh water.

'Native' fish are not the only ones under threat. Modern travel and the globalisation of our palates have meant a rise in the popularity of fish from more distant waters, some as far as the Antipodes or Antarctica. Barramundi, hoki, snapper, grouper, mahi mahi, marlin and tuna certainly extend choice on British menus (and on supermarket fish counters) as never before. Moreover, the advent of sushi bars, especially in London, has been in big factor in whetting appetites for a wider range of quality fish.

It seems ironic that, just when the British have taken to fish in a big way after decades of reluctance, we should be subject to a barrage of in-your-face media attention devoted to concerns about species extinction, coastal pollution, the effects that badly run fish farms have on the environment and possibly human health, and the economic ills affecting the fishing industry. Fish, after all, is healthy; in a skilled cook's hands it tastes rather wonderful; and it's a grand alternative to meat and fowl, especially after all the scares they have generated in recent years. The Food Standards Agency indeed advises – despite some recent debate over small amounts of contaminants found in fish – that we should eat two portions of fish a week as part of a healthy, balanced diet, and one of these should be an oily fish.

So fish gives choice and enjoyment: good, wonderful, terrific! And this is not just for consumers in Britain, but in most gastronomic centres of the world, from the Americas to Hong Kong. And if there are problems with the decline of wild species, why worry? There's fish-farming to save us all. Isn't there?

## Nor smooth sailing down on the farm

True enough, thousands of tons of salmon are farmed in sea lochs every year, largely in Scotland, but also in Norway, Ireland, Canada and US, allowing it to be sold at prices most people can afford. Farmed trout has long been an inexpensive fish, and more recently sea bass from Portugal and Greece, recognisable from their uniform 500g size when 'harvested', has become plentiful. Turbot and halibut are also farmed in Scotland, while in the tropics, particularly in parts of China, king prawn farming is in the order of 500,000 tons annually. Bream and tilapia production has become a huge multinational business, and in many economies around the world besides the UK. Chile and Norway are huge producers of salmon and halibut; tuna are now farmed in Spain and Australia; an enormous 180ha facility has just been commissioned in Saudi Arabia for bass and bream; and most notably cod farming in Scotland and Norway produced over 2,000 tons last year, and this is expected to increase 100-fold in the coming decade. All this certainly means there is no shortage of fish generally, even if they normally do not meet the very highest-quality standards.

A case in point is sea bass. The eating quality of farmed bass is in no way comparable to that of large (2 to 3 kilos) wild fish. Bass is naturally a voracious scavenger, eating a widely varying diet that includes all sorts of crustacea, sand worms and other invertebrates, as well as fish ranging from whitebait to pollack. This produces the most wonderful, flavoursome firm textured flesh: not a patch on its puny pellet-fed tame cousin.

Because the fish are farmed at high density, veterinary drugs are necessary to keep disease at bay, giving rise to concerns that the residue from such drugs can end up in our food and in the environment. Some fish farmers use chemicals such as ivermectin and malachite green to treat infections. Although the former is considered harmless to humans, it can cause serious damage to the environment. The second does pose a potential risk to health, though the levels found so far by the Veterinary Medicines Directorate (the body in Britain that runs an annual residue surveillance programme that includes salmon and trout) have been low.

Although few people probably took note of it, the escape of 100,000 farmed salmon from the Orkney islands into natural habitats in spring 2001 increased the risk of passing on farmed pests such as lice to wild species and reducing the potential for genetic diversity.

On a more positive note, the development of vegetable protein, mainly from soya, will take the pressure off industrial fishing for species such as sand-eels, that go to make conventional pellets. Also the huge increase in cod (and haddock) farming may encourage a switch from salmon to these species; a tax on feed for salmon (in force in Norway) provides a further incentive. In addition, the growth rate of cod is encouraging, reaching 2–3 kilos in two years, compared with three to four years for salmon. Furthermore, cod (and turbot) can be farmed in land-based re-circulating water, which greatly decreases environmental concerns.

Despite the fact that farmed fish may not always taste quite as good as wild fish, and that irresponsible and unregulated farming may cause worries for the environment and human health, it is true that farming has relieved some of the pressure on natural fisheries and indeed has allowed consumers a wider – and largely a healthier – choice of protein in their diets.

## Too many chasing too few

Fishermen and their dependants in virtually every fishing port in Britain can relate stories about walking across the harbour on the decks of trawlers in days not long gone. Most of these fleets have disappeared. At Milford Haven, once the premier west coast port, only a handful of boats now work, and most of these are foreign-owned, their catch destined for their own home markets.

The problem throughout Europe is that there are an estimated 30,000 too many fishermen chasing too few fish. Boats, even smaller vessels, are nowadays highly sophisticated and efficient, and grants are still available for new boats under 10m in length. But the real need is to compensate fishermen for giving up. It wasn't long ago that numerous Cornish fishermen sold their quotas to foreign, particularly Spanish boats, and hung up their nets. Having gone this way, it is galling for fishermen to watch others reap the benefits of our waters which, thanks to stringent controls by Sea Fisheries Committees, have remained more prolific than those in other parts of Europe.

In fact, the vast majority of prime species fished around the British coast have long been exported, particularly shellfish. Over 90 per cent of mussels, lobster and crab ends up on Continental markets. It's a little sad, not to mention environmentally unfriendly, that while lorries with seawater tanks transport almost the entire catch of live lobster and crab from our coast, destined for France and Spain, in London we eat lobster air-freighted live from New England and Canada.

Larger offshore boats, over 10m in size (particularly from Spain and Holland, but including some British ones too), have an awesome power and the heftiest gear imaginable. Even though they are not allowed within the six-mile limit, their massive activity is bound to have an effect on inshore stocks. The lack of patrolling vessels makes control difficult, and puts future stocks of many wild fish into question. Large factory trawlers with highly sophisticated sonar equipment and catching gear can suck up an entire shoal of mackerel and other fish in one scoop. These boats now fish to great depths and in remote, hitherto unreachable places, possibly upsetting a natural balance with an effect that is hard to predict.

According to the Marine Conservation Society, among wild fish under threat are: Atlantic cod, Atlantic salmon, European hake, haddock, marlin, monkfish, North Atlantic halibut, sea bass, shark, and tuna (except for skipjack and yellowfin). The society lists some alternatives for consumers to look for: line-caught Icelandic and Norwegian cod; line-caught haddock from Iceland or the Faeroes; line-caught sea bass; pole or line-caught skipjack or yellowfin tuna. For the others it recommends responsibly farmed alternatives.

A new EU regulation will require the labelling of every species for traceability. European waters will be cut up into a patchwork of areas to which every fish can be related. There will be a clear distinction for farmed fish. As yet it is not certain how this can be achieved, or how it will be controlled. It seems unclear to which point in the chain it will be taken – final sale, or actual consumption in catering outlets – but one certainty is that a lot of people in Brussels will be kept busy while the solution is figured out.

Meantime, the reduction in the European fleet is bound to fall heavily on British fishermen as our waters are a most important source of a wide number of species, the envy of much of Europe.

## A responsible view

The British have always undervalued the rich fishery that surrounds their shores, and – as elsewhere – have been slow to realise what steps they should take to protect it. One step, of course, is to be concerned about pollution and to support policies to control it; another is to avoid choosing a species of fish until its sustainability is no longer under threat; yet another is to stay informed about official fishing policy, and to back fair, environmentally sound policies; and finally, one can opt for fish that has been farmed responsibly. A century after Escoffier, farmed cod may become far more important than farmed salmon.

After all, fish is an excellent, exciting, nutritious food that adapts itself to almost any treatment: wrap it around a mousse, douse it with salsa or watercress sauce, chargrill it, poach it, steam it or bake it. Or – especially if it's fresh Dover sole or line-caught wild sea bass – serve it simply on the bone. And so, no, fish have not had their chips if we take the responsible view, and act upon it.

# Confessions of a duckaholic

Pam Roberts, photographic historian, curator and writer, celebrates a lifelong love affair with the duck

If you believe in reincarnation, pray that you do not come back as a duck. For many creatures, including humans, the duck is as tempting a titbit as it gets, at every stage of its life. During the day, wild mallards lounge nonchalantly on the banks of the river running through my garden but live in fear and anxiety at night as foxes prowl, pounce and eviscerate. Magpies, crows, rooks, jackdaws and seagulls love a tasty snack of unprotected duck eggs. Squirrels bury duck eggs in terracotta pots of tulips for a nutritious post-hibernation protein smoothie, only to forget the location. Pike like to snap a young duckling from below, shark-like, as its tiny orange feet skim frantically over the water.

But the duck's greatest predator is undoubtedly the human and this human stands very guilty on all counts. My riverbank chums are safe with me. I no longer eat wild duck at home since I have lived with its close relatives watching through the window, beaks twitching in puzzlement as disconcerting aromas drift from the kitchen. But an endless supply of domestically reared ducks (preferably organic and free range) would have to be my desert island luxury. Roasted with waxy potatoes, garlic and rosemary, or simply roasted Chinese style and served with rice, there are few more satisfying meals in the world to the duckaholic.

## Adventures on Duck Street

The availability of duck has become a major factor in choosing many holiday locations over the last two decades. The first of many magrets de canard I ever cooked were bought 24 years ago from the covered market in Limoux, Languedoc. After we had digested copious instructions from the worried canardier about slashing, judicious salting and peppering of the skin side (he could see we were duck virgins), they were cooked on a tiny barbecue outside our rented gîte under an umbrella in the pouring rain. They were bliss, a livery and deeply satisfying revelation, with a crisp golden skin and so much meat that we were still eating it two days later – in baguettes, in salads etc. Thus began this life-long love affair with the duck.

Over the intervening years, the search for the supreme duck experience has become something of an obsession. Flabby UK supermarket Norfolk or Aylesbury ducks, pale and pasty with pimply-plucked wet skin, bred without care and compassion, never made the grade whatever culinary ingenuity was used on them. Despite dousing them in boiling water, and stringing them up to dry for 24 hours over radiators, Spanish Inquisition-style; or using a strategically placed hairdryer to try to achieve that eventual perfect golden crispy skin, the results were usually disappointing, giving rise to the phrase 'life is too short to blow-dry a duck'.

Therefore any trips to France, business or pleasure, always resulted in empty outward luggage, but heavy return luggage largely comprised of packs of duck legs, magrets and gesiers as well as whole Barbary ducks. God knows what the X-ray scan looked like. Foie gras de canard also crept into the picture and rue Montmartre in Paris, now known to us as 'Duck Street', replete with many produits de canard shops, became a preferred destination. I sprained an ankle there a few years ago, so utterly absorbed in my delicious lunchtime hot duck baguette that I fell off the kerb. A grease spot marks the place.

## Traceable lives

Over the last few years, duck appreciation has finally started to come into its own in the UK. Trelough, Gressingham and Barbary ducks have all winged their way to me by post from committed duck farmers who rear them humanely. Goosnargh ducks, bought fresh in quadruplicate, from Reg Johnson's Lancashire farm where they are bred, achieve that livery hit beloved of any duck afficionado and come with large bagfuls of giblets, a supermarket no-go zone. Websites (now what else would a duck use?) mean that life need never again be duckless, wherever you live in the UK.

Trelough ducks, bred and developed from the French Rouen duck have lean, rich, almost fruity meat and a lower fat-to-meat ratio. Gressingham ducks, beloved of Saint Delia, are bred from a Pekin/wild mallard cross yielding a small frame and a rich gamey flavour.

Increasingly of late, traders at farmers' markets, and even my local butcher in Bath, now sell organic free-range ducks with traceable lives and diets. These taut-skinned, dry-plucked ducks are twice the price of their floppy-skinned, wet-plucked supermarket siblings but worth every extra penny. Apart from the crispy skin, deeply mellow and copious meat, and creamy pure rendered duck fat for future roast potatoes, which runs off the roasting duck like molten honey, the carcasses of these previously contented birds yield the most intense crystal-clear jellied stock. Among other things, this makes a deeply comforting and revivifying duck noodle soup together with chunks of leftover duck, although 'leftover duck' is not a familiar state of affairs for me.

## Chinese alchemy

During these years of dedicated duck research, there has always been one reliable safe haven for an addict with chronic DDS (duck deprivation syndrome). The Chinese can unfailingly cook duck better than anyone else in the world. Peking duck, Cantonese duck, simply roasted duck may all vary in quality from restaurant to restaurant, from country to country, but Chinese roast duck generally has a low disappointment factor. Somehow, they have the alchemy to transmute those unpromising flabby white ducks into crispy gold. I rarely leave London by train at night without a diversion into Chinatown to pick up half a roast duck, which gets messily and satisfyingly slurped and chewed on the journey.

Therefore, logically, the ultimate holiday experience for a duckaholic has to be Hong Kong. Sitting in a comfortable bedroom on the 34th floor of a hotel overlooking Hong Kong Harbour, watching the Star Ferry chug back and forth, with pairs of eagles wheeling at the window, we ate duck practically every day for eight days. This was bought for a few HK dollars from some of the 50 or so roast meat restaurants within 20 minutes' walk of the hotel, ranging from good to exceptionally good.

All washed down with freshly squeezed mango and melon juice – duck for breakfast of course – and so good, and so naughtily decadent, that the experience was repeated most days. Once in the evening too, accompanied by a bottle of very acceptable Chinese red wine, and sometimes a mid-afternoon duck snack.

To tire of roast duck in Hong Kong is to tire of life. At that sad and weary stage however, there is always roast goose to ring the changes. I would love to think there is a Chinese proverb to the effect of 'Every day, eat duck. Every day, much luck.' If there is not, then I claim and copyright this proverb as my own.

*Some useful names and contact details:*

**Trelough ducks:**
English Natural Foods
Wormbridge Court, Wormbridge
Herefordshire HR2 9EN
Tel: (01981) 570600
Email: sales@enf.co.uk
Website: www.englishnaturalfoods.co.uk

**Goosnargh ducks:**
Johnson & Swarbrick
Swainson House Farm
Goosnargh Lane
Lancashire PR3 2JU
Tel: (01772) 865251

**Gressingham ducks:**
Green Label Foods Ltd
Debach, Woodbridge
Suffolk IP13 6JW
Tel: (01473) 735456
Email: sales@greenlabel.co.uk
Website: www.greenlabel.co.uk

Bartlett & Son
10–11 Green Street,
Bath BA1 2JZ
Tel: (01225) 466731

# Neighbourhood restaurants: who needs them?

**David Kenning, independent food writer and regular contributor to the Guide, puts the case for the neighbourhood restaurant**

France: land of gourmets, food capital of the world. Or so the popular myth has always been: gastronomy permeates through every level of society; even the meals served in French school canteens wouldn't disgrace most British restaurants. And the same is true of Italy, as the legions of holidaymakers that descend on Tuscany every year will testify.

Yet in recent years many pundits have claimed that we in Britain have developed an eating-out culture to rival that of France and Italy – and pretty much any other country you may care to mention. Food is now a big deal in Britain. Eating out is more popular than it has ever been.

But if we take a closer look at the evidence, the assertion begins to look a little dubious. It seems that our burgeoning restaurant culture is actually built on media hype, manifested in two predominant forms: the cult of the celebrity chef, and saturation coverage of glitzy new restaurant openings in newspaper columns and magazines.

## A razzle-dazzle food culture

The food-as-entertainment industry cannot claim to promote eating out. Sure, we can all easily name a dozen top chefs of all shapes and sizes, but how many of us have actually eaten in their restaurants? We are more likely to experience their cooking vicariously through television or glossy cookbooks. And apart from Delia – who can fill the aisles of Sainsbury's at the drop of a cranberry – they are cooking to entertain us rather than to educate us. This is not food culture: this is food pornography. It is easy to see why chefs do it: the financial rewards are a powerful lure, and it is easy work compared with running a busy restaurant kitchen. It is not so easy to understand why we, the viewers, let them dazzle us with their skills while we munch on a take-out pizza.

Then there are the glamorous new openings that grab the newspaper headlines. They churn out press packs full of impressive statistics about just how many millions have been spent to recreate, for example, the authentic look of an Indian bazaar, or whatever the latest fad in restaurant design is. To be fair, some of them actually remember to employ someone who can cook – and these places rightly make it into the pages of the Guide – but in too many cases the food is of secondary importance. Menus are dictated by fashion as much as décor: recent years have seen fads for North African and Thai food; this year it's Japanese. It could be Abyssinian shepherd food for all it matters. The various international cuisines that periodically leap into the spotlight of food fashion have much to commend them, but not when they are commoditised, bastardised and reduced to a badly cooked cliché, as they all too often are.

It wouldn't be fair, however, to criticise everything about TV cookery shows and glamorous media-friendly restaurants: they have unarguably done their bit to raise our collective consciousness on matters gastronomic. But if we are to convert this new awareness into a true restaurant culture, we need to look for something a little less capricious and whimsical than fashion to provide the solid foundations that will ensure our new way of life is more than a passing fad.

## Looking close to home

So, where will we find the solid, reliable materials with which to build these foundations? We could look to the French or Italian model for hints, but in fact the answer can be found in small towns everywhere throughout Britain. And often we need look no further than the end of our street: it is our neighbourhood restaurants that we should encourage if we want to establish a lasting restaurant culture in this country.

Decent neighbourhood restaurants are actually a lot more common in Britain than we may realise, though there still aren't enough of them. The best of them will, of course, be found within the democratic pages of The Good Food Guide but because what they do is perceived by many as unglamorous they rarely attract the credit they deserve from the media at large. Perhaps it's about time they got their fair share of the limelight: so step forward the Chiswick in west London, Iznik in north London, Quails in Chobham, Landgate Bistro in Rye, Wig & Mitre in Lincoln, Drum and Monkey in Harrogate, and Bentley's in Shelf (see below for more).

What they have in common may not at first seem apparent, and what makes them – and neighbourhood restaurants generally – so important is not that easy to quantify. But looking through The Good Food Guide at the small-scale bistros, brasseries, cafés, gastropubs and ethnic restaurants that make up this sector of the market, it is easy to recognise some common themes.

**Value for money** is a key factor. The food will be priced to tempt people to visit regularly, not just for birthdays and anniversaries. Too many provincial restaurants try to emulate a more upmarket style that can rarely succeed outside a large city, and they fail because the locals can afford to eat there only on special occasions. When faced with an over-priced, over-elaborate, full three-course menu, many people will go for the convenience and cheapness of fast food instead.

But neighbourhood restaurants can compete with the fast food outlets: cheaper, simpler lunch and early-evening deals bring customers in at times when they are not after a heavy meal. And if they like what they find, they are more likely to come back in the evening for the full dinner menu, so this approach has benefits for both customer and proprietor.

Perhaps the next most important element after price is a **friendly atmosphere**. The best neighbourhood restaurants are usually run by a 'hands-on' proprietor, and are often family businesses. The relationship between the staff and customers will be one of mutual respect, maybe even of friendship, especially when you get to that point where you are known as a regular. And this should extend to all members of the family: a **child-welcoming attitude** is important too, as eating together with the children plays an important part in protecting the future of any eating-out culture. In Britain the evidence is clear to see in areas with large Chinese communities: head into the 'Chinatown' districts of London, Liverpool or Manchester on a Sunday lunchtime to see extended families everywhere tucking into platefuls of dim sum.

If parents feel that their children will be made just as welcome as they are at their favourite neighbourhood restaurant, they are more likely to bring them back again and again, with an obvious knock-on effect when the little ones are grown up. True, children don't always have the most adventurous tastes, but they tend to respond positively to being given the opportunity to join in with mum and dad. Offering smaller, cheaper portions of the regular menu is one of the ways neighbourhood restaurants can encourage both children and parents to enjoy the occasion and each other's company.

## Decent ingredients treated decently

One thing not to expect from a good neighbourhood restaurant is knock-your-socks-off culinary fireworks. Rather than attempting impressively elaborate and highly crafted food, the best will be more likely to concentrate on the fundamentals: sourcing good-quality ingredients, usually from local suppliers, and treating them simply. As long as the ingredients are good, and as long as they are cooked competently, they don't need to be mucked about too much. This is the cornerstone principle on which Raymond Postgate founded The Good Food Guide all those years ago.

Really, it's a case of horses for courses. Although the proprietor at the local bistro may not be as famous as the Gordon Ramsays and Marco Pierre Whites of this world, he or she fills an equally important role. Small, low-key neighbourhood restaurants serve a very real need to their communities. They provide somewhere for groups of friends or families to have informal parties; they can be a little bolt-hole to use when the cupboards at home are bare – just somewhere to get some supper. You will know the best of them because they will be popular and likely to be always busy. They are all doing their bit, whether consciously or otherwise, to promote a genuine culture of eating out that we can be proud of.

## Shift that attitude

Unfortunately, we have a long way to go before we reach the level of other countries, and plenty of neighbourhood restaurants could put in a bit more effort to encourage us along the way. Concentrating on the aspects of value and atmosphere would be a good place to start – these are the areas where too many fall short. Ultimately, though, whatever restaurants do to attract more custom, it is down to us, the restaurant-going public, to use and support our local eateries. If we really want to establish a restaurant culture in Britain, we have to put the effort in where it matters most: at the grass-roots level. We need to shift our collective mentality away from treating restaurants as only appropriate for special occasions, and adopt an attitude that says, 'We're eating out tonight just because we feel like it.'

Of course, good food costs money to produce, and even a good-value restaurant is not necessarily a cheap one. Perhaps one of the reasons we don't eat out so often is having too many other things to spend our money on – mobile phones, satellite TV, computers and so on. Industrially mass-produced 'cheap' food has also done its bit to make us reluctant to spend a larger part of our disposable income on food, though the burgeoning success of farmers' markets indicates the beginnings of a shift in attitude. There are some who genuinely cannot afford the pleasure of eating out, but for many others it is a question of priorities.

The truth is, if there is a little family-run place round the corner that offers simple, unpretentious well-sourced and -cooked food at reasonable prices, served by friendly people in an informal atmosphere, then do you have any excuse for not eating out more often?

And when you do eat out, don't forget to take the kids – they may even thank you for it in the future.

# London

---

## Adams Café ✎ £

map 12

77 Askew Road, W12 9AH
TEL/FAX: (020) 8743 0572

COOKING **3**
NORTH AFRICAN
£23–£28

'Amazingly unpretentious but very authentic' is one verdict on this busy, tightly packed little place festooned with Moroccan posters and artefacts. What it offers is genuine North African cooking that doesn't try to be 'grande cuisine': flavours are boldly aromatic, and prices 'amazingly fair across the board'. Added to this, service is as warm and 'bubbly' as you could wish for.

A selection of hummus, pickled chillies and warm pitta bread sets the mood before lively starters of salades Bedouines or ojja merguez (ratatouille topped with sizzling sausages). The main business, however, is couscous (four kinds, all given classic treatment) and tagines (the version with chicken, pickled lemons, green olives and potatoes has been well received). A new chef is at the helm, and he has extended the menu to include more fish dishes, such as stuffed baby squid in a rich tomato sauce. There are also some Moroccan specialities such as orange fruit salad with orange blossom water and cinnamon; otherwise finish with crepês Berbères (pancakes doused with citrus and honey sauce). The wine list is a short selection of North African and French, beginning at £8.50 a bottle (£2.20 a glass).

CHEF: Sofiene Chahed  PROPRIETORS: Abdel and Frances Boukraa  OPEN: Mon to Sat D only 7 to 11  CLOSED: 25 Dec to 1 Jan, bank hols  MEALS: Set D £10.50 (1 course) to £15.50  SERVICE: not inc  CARDS: Amex, Delta, MasterCard, Switch, Visa  DETAILS: 60 seats. Private parties: 36 main room, 24 private room. Vegetarian meals. Wheelchair access (not WC). Music  ⊖ Ravenscourt Park  £5

---

## Admiral Codrington

map 14

17 Mossop Street, SW3 2LY
TEL: (020) 7581 0005  FAX: (020) 7589 2452

COOKING **4**
MODERN EUROPEAN
£31–£55

Under the same ownership as the Salisbury Tavern in SW6 (see entry), and occupying a Sloaney pub just off Draycott Avenue, 'the Cod' sees itself as a neighbourhood pub-cum-restaurant. The long, thin dining room beyond the bar has a retractable glass roof for fine weather, and a selection of fishy prints on the wall to remind us where the kitchen's heart lies. Treatments range from traditional – moules marinière, smoked haddock with bubble and squeak – to a crisp filo roll containing well-cooked salmon, decorated with nori-like seaweed, brought to life by a drizzle of spicy hoisin-type sauce.

Beyond that come perhaps roast fillet of pork with date confit, or a first-class, juicy, flavourful parcel of braised lamb with parsnip rösti. Desserts are plain and simple, along the lines of chocolate cheesecake, and tangy lemon tart. Muzak can get in the way of enjoyment, but keen young staff deliver cheerful, informed service, and a short, varied if conservative list of wines from Berry Bros is not overpriced for the area. House claret and Sauvignon Blanc are £11.

CHEF: Daniel Pederson  PROPRIETOR: Joel Cadbury  OPEN: all week 12 to 2.30 (3.30 Sat and Sun), 7 to 11 (10 Sun)  CLOSED: 24 to 26 Dec  MEALS: alc (main courses £9 to £16). Cover 50p at D. Bar L menu available  SERVICE: 12.5% (optional), card slips closed  CARDS: Amex, Delta, MasterCard, Switch, Visa  DETAILS: 56 seats. Private parties: 50 main room. Vegetarian meals. Music. No mobile phones. Air-conditioned  ⊖ South Kensington

# Admiralty
map 13

Somerset House, Strand, WC2R 1LA
TEL: (020) 7845 4646  FAX: (020) 7845 4658

COOKING 4
FRENCH
£48–£73

The high-ceilinged room in Somerset House looks like an old-fashioned brasserie, and has an appropriately informal feel, though it clearly has grander ambitions when it comes to food. Morgan Meunier takes an unashamedly French and somewhat conservative stance, though he also makes room for some more modern and cosmopolitan ideas. This is rich and luxurious cooking, and dishes can appear rather elaborate and busy: a starter tian of 'two salmons', for example, with horseradish cream, smoked eel, beetroot bavarois and an apple and cucumber dressing.

Main courses in similar vein might include fish such as wild sea bass fillet with steamed baby leeks, lobster and tarragon ravioli, and a crayfish and saffron velouté, while meat options have included grilled Anjou squab pigeon with braised Puy lentils, pommes Anna, onion soubise and a red wine jus. Desserts are a strength. Fig Tatin was highlighted by one reporter who confessed to not normally enjoying puddings; there may also be 'old-fashioned pain perdu' with apricot confit and nougatine ice cream. Wines are exclusively French, ranging from humble vins de pays to wines of distinguished pedigree and vintage. Prices start around £15.

CHEF: Morgan Meunier  PROPRIETOR: Gruppo Ltd  OPEN: all week L 12 to 2.15, Mon to Sat D 6 to 10.15  MEALS: Set L and D £28 (2 courses) to £42 (whole table only)  SERVICE: 12.5% (optional), card slips closed  CARDS: Amex, Delta, Diners, MasterCard, Switch, Visa  DETAILS: 60 seats. Private parties: 60 main room, 30 private room. Vegetarian meals. Wheelchair access (also WC). Music  ⊖ Temple, Covent Garden

*The 2004 Guide will be published before Christmas 2003. Reports on meals are most welcome at any time of the year, but are particularly valuable in the spring (no later than June). Send them to* The Good Food Guide, *FREEPOST, 2 Marylebone Road, London NW1 4DF. Or email your report to* goodfoodguide@which.net

# Alastair Little

map 15

49 Frith Street, W1D 4SG
TEL: (020) 7734 5183   FAX: (020) 7734 5206

NEW CHEF
MODERN EUROPEAN
£39–£57

Deliberately short on comfort and frills (unless you count prints on the wall and linen tablecloths), this undemonstrative Soho favourite offers a no-nonsense, daily-changing menu, now under the command of Sue Lewis (who has worked at Lola's, the Phoenix and the Cow – see entries, London). She arrived just as the Guide was going to press, too late for us to receive any feedback, but the combination of pleasing inventiveness and often modest ingredients looks set to continue. On offer might be potato pancake with smoked herring, poached ham with petits pois, and gooseberry fool. A compact, well-chosen wine list favours those with £20 to £30 in their pocket, but starts with a brace of house Italians at £14.

CHEF: Sue Lewis   PROPRIETORS: Mercedes André Vega, Kirsten Tormod Pedersen and Alastair Little   OPEN: Mon to Fri L 12 to 3, Mon to Sat D 6 to 11.15   CLOSED: bank hols   MEALS: Set L £27, Set D £35   SERVICE: not inc, 12.5% for parties of 8 or more   CARDS: Amex, Delta, Diners, MasterCard, Switch, Visa   DETAILS: 60 seats. Private parties: 8 to 25 private rooms. Children's helpings. Wheelchair access (not WC). No music. Air-conditioned   ⊖ Tottenham Court Road

# Alastair Little Lancaster Road

map 12

136A Lancaster Road, W11 1QU
TEL: (020) 7243 2220   FAX: (020) 7792 4535

COOKING 3
MODERN ITALIAN
£29–£55

Familiar 'pale and simple' décor, and rows of tightly packed tables down either side, have survived successive refurbishments and rearrangements at this west London stalwart. A reporter who has followed the progress of Alastair Little over two decades, with fond memories of dazzlingly fresh cooking along the way, feels that it might more realistically be called 'Alastair Little Somewhere in Italy', although in his absence the cooking is mostly sound as a bell. It is marked by a commendable orientation towards simplicity, be it a preference for salads over vegetable accompaniments, or a straightforward fixed-price lunch menu that centres on a choice between chicken and chips, and a vegetarian pasta dish.

Successes have included delicately crunchy, deep-fried courgette flowers with aïoli, and a version of Caesar salad tricked out with avocado purée – some spread on the croûtons, some mashed into the dressing – to produce a messy-looking but memorably flavoured starter. New season's lamb is accorded due respect with fattoush and feta salad, together with 'a welter of baby veg bursting with spring virtue'. Creamy, vanilla-flavoured pannacotta makes a pleasantly wobbly finish (though with too little of the advertised aged balsamic vinegar for our inspector); plum crumble with Greek yoghurt might be an alternative. The same wine list as at the Soho branch (see entry above) is offered, and while the selections are very good, prices will certainly jump-start the bill. They open at £14.

CHEF: Tony Abarno   PROPRIETORS: Alastair Little, Mercedes André-Vega and Kirsten Pedersen
OPEN: Mon to Sat L 12 to 2.30 (3 Sat), D 6.30 to 11 (Sun L by arrangement)   CLOSED: bank hols
MEALS: alc (main courses £13.50 to £17). Set L £15 (2 courses) to £18   SERVICE: not inc, 12.5%
for parties of 8 or more   CARDS: Amex, Delta, Diners, MasterCard, Switch, Visa   DETAILS: 45
seats. 12 seats outside. Private parties: 45 main room. Vegetarian meals. Children's helpings.
Wheelchair access (not WC). No music. Air-conditioned   ⊖ Ladbroke Grove

# Al Duca ▼

map 15

4–5 Duke of York Street, SW1Y 6LA
TEL: (020) 7839 3090   FAX: (020) 7839 4050
WEBSITE: www.cuisine-collection.co.uk

NEW CHEF
ITALIAN
£33–£64

A warm atmosphere prevails in this modern, uncluttered dining room – open to
the street when weather permits – and staff are willing and helpful. Michele
Franzolin left just as the Guide went to press, but Antonio Cucchiara seems set to
continue the same style, adding a few dishes of his own along the way: perhaps
crab salad with mango, or rabbit leg with braised beans. Pasta might take in
linguine wtih clams and sweet chilli, while desserts will plough familiar
furrows, in the form of tiramisù, or pannacotta served with grappa and poached
peaches. Wines hail from all over Italy, taking in classic Barolos, pricy Super-
Tuscans and some fresh faces from the South; these last inevitably offer the best
value, although not much else dips below the £20 horizon. Eleven wines by the
glass (£4.50 to £5.50) offer a taste of some of Italy's lesser-known varieties.
Prices start at £16 a bottle.

CHEF: Antonio Cucchiara   PROPRIETOR: Cuisine Collection   OPEN: Mon to Sat 12 to 2.45 (12.30
to 3 Sat), 6 to 10.45   CLOSED: Christmas, bank hols   MEALS: Set L £16.50 (2 courses) to £22.50,
Set D Mon to Wed 6 to 7 and 10.30 to 10.45 £12 (2 courses), Set D £19 (2 courses) to £27
SERVICE: 12.5% (optional), card slips closed   CARDS: Amex, Delta, MasterCard, Switch, Visa
DETAILS: 60 seats. Private parties: 12 main room. Vegetarian meals. No cigars/pipes in dining
room. Wheelchair access (not WC). No music. Air-conditioned   ⊖ Piccadilly Circus

# Al Hamra

map 15

31–33 Shepherd Market, W1J 7HR
TEL: (020) 7493 1954   FAX: (020) 7493 1044
EMAIL: mail@alhamra.co.uk
WEBSITE: www.alhamrarestaurant.com

COOKING 4
LEBANESE
£37–£67

Buzz and hilarity permeate this Mayfair old-stager, where you can either sit in
the rather cramped, elbow-to-elbow dining room or relax outside on the heated
patio and watch the world go by. Meals begin with a harvest festival of salad
vegetables, plus bread and olives (which accounts for the £2.50 cover charge).
The menu does include a sprinkling of French/Continental dishes such as
grilled lamb cutlets with green peppers, but it is the range of Lebanese
specialities that draws the crowds; prices are 'steep', though, and not all dishes
live up to expectations.

Among the long list of hot and cold meze, reporters have singled out star-
quality muhamara (crushed walnuts with chilli, garlic and oil), raheb (roasted
aubergine), 'lively' tabbouleh, and creamy yoghurt-based labneh. Mains tend to
focus on chargrilled lamb and chicken, plus variations on kibbeh, while exotic

fruits are an alternative to the display of traditional sweets. Although staff are at full tilt when the place is humming, service has been 'brusque' and lacking charm. The expense-account wine list is peppered with heavy Bordeaux; house wine is £15.

CHEF: Mahir Abboud   PROPRIETOR: Hassan Fansa   OPEN: all week noon to 11.30   CLOSED: 24 Dec to 2 Jan   MEALS: alc (main courses £13 to £19.50). Set L and D £30. Cover £2.50   SERVICE: not inc   CARDS: Amex, Delta, Diners, MasterCard, Switch, Visa   DETAILS: 65 seats. 24 seats outside. Private parties: 70 main room. Vegetarian meals. Children's helpings. Wheelchair access (not WC). Music. Air-conditioned   ⊖ Green Park  £5

---

# Alloro ▾ ◇

map 15

19–20 Dover Street, W1S 4LU

TEL: (020) 7495 4768   FAX: (020) 7629 5348

COOKING 6
ITALIAN
£38–£75

Although the entrance is through a noisy modern bar, and the design is quite contemporary, something of the staid dignity of an old Mayfair restaurant is still apparent. Service, from black-uniformed staff, is impeccably correct and considerate without being over-solicitous. Marzio Zacchi – who has worked in other kitchens within the A To Z group, including Zafferano and Rosmarino (see entries) – hails from Piedmont, but manages to temper some of the robustness of north-west Italian cooking with a degree of delicacy and refinement. The result is food with a marked 'classical' feel.

Set price menus run the gamut from a summery starter of 'mild and delicate' salt-cod and new potatoes with finely chopped shallots in vinaigrette, to another seasonal dish of mustard-cured pears, broad beans and leaves with lightly salty Tuscan cured ham. An intermediate farinaceous course in the old style might offer linguine with lobster, chilli and garlic, or wild mushroom risotto, and then it's on to the main business: perhaps a hefty leg of wild rabbit, breadcrumbed and set on a pile of balsamic lentils, with red onion marmalade adding a sweet counterpoint. Lightness of touch extends to fish dishes, such as gilt-head bream with spinach and a lemon and thyme sauce, and also to precisely timed beef fillet with ceps and a red wine sauce. Among desserts, the inevitable tiramisù is joined by coconut sorbet with chocolate sauce, and pannacotta spiced with ginger.

The wine list roams the length of Italy, from the Aosta Valley in the north to Sicily and Sardinia in the south. Most space is dedicated to Piedmont and Tuscany, including a whole page on Tuscan 'vini da tavola' that features several vintages of such well-regarded wines as Tignanello and Solaia, as well as ten vintages of Sassicaia. Although there is much here to excite, it comes at a price; there is little below £20 and mark-ups can be stiff. Bottle prices start at £16.50 for Sicilian red and white, and ten wines are sold by the glass (£3.50 to £8).

CHEF: Marzio Zacchi   PROPRIETOR: A To Z Restaurants Ltd   OPEN: Mon to Fri L 12 to 2.30, Mon to Sat D 7 to 10.30 (11 Fri and Sat)   CLOSED: Christmas, bank hols   MEALS: Set L £21 (2 courses) to £23.50, Set D £27.50 (2 courses) to £35. Bar menu available   SERVICE: 12.5% (optional), card slips closed   CARDS: Amex, Delta, Diners, MasterCard, Switch, Visa   DETAILS: 70 seats. Vegetarian meals. No cigars/pipes in dining room. Occasional music. Air-conditioned ⊖ Green Park

# Almeida ♥

30 Almeida Street, N1 1AD
TEL: (020) 7354 4777   FAX: (020) 7354 2777
EMAIL: almeida-reservations@conran-
restaurants.co.uk
WEBSITE: www.almeida-restaurant.co.uk

COOKING **4**
FRENCH BISTRO
£28–£71

The newest restaurant in the Conran stable can be found off Upper Street (also known as 'Supper Street' owing to its high number of eateries) across from the Almeida Theatre, which was still being renovated as the Guide went to press. The restaurant – a large, pale-mustard-coloured room with big windows and an open kitchen at the back – is smart, with clean lines, minimalist décor, a light wood floor and matching tables, some with white cloths. The menu – written in a mixture of French and English – is all French in style, combining sophisticated classics with humble country dishes, all relying on tried-and-tested flavour pairings. It is unpretentious, too, boasting ingredients such as rabbit, pigs' trotters and kidneys, which don't always make their way on to trendy restaurant menus.

Starters, as pretty to look at as they are appetising, might include a generous slice of artichoke tart, or a selection of charcuterie from the wonderfully retro trolley. For mains, navarin of lamb – deemed 'absolutely top drawer' by an inspector – may come bathed in a pool of fine, dark sauce laced with bits of olive, and coq au vin (rather undercooked at the same meal) is served in a small casserole dish. There are also frogs' legs, steak au poivre, and the inevitable Conran crustaceans: oysters, or half a lobster, perhaps.

The trolley of tarts is an appealing selection that may include chocolate, lemon, and almond with apricot; or there may be a 'thick, lightly vanilla' crème brûlée. 'Staff are charming', and the set lunch has been pointed out as a particular bargain. Wines lean heavily towards France, with the south-west contributing some interesting drinking. Italy and Spain join Burgundy and Bordeaux for their turn in the limelight, and the list is rounded out with a short New World section. Mark-ups are generally fair, with house wines starting at £11. Eighteen broad-ranging selections are available by the glass.

CHEF: Ian Wood   PROPRIETOR: Conran Restaurants   OPEN: all week 12 to 3, 6 to 11   CLOSED: 25 and 26 Dec, 1 Jan   MEALS: alc (main courses £11 to £19.50). Set L and D 6 to 7 and 10 to 11 £14.50 (2 courses) to £17.50   SERVICE: 12.5% (optional), card slips closed   CARDS: Amex, Delta, Diners, MasterCard, Switch, Visa   DETAILS: 90 seats. Private parties: 100 main room, 16 private room. Vegetarian meals. No pipes in dining room. Wheelchair access (also WC). No music   ⊖ Angel, Highbury & Islington

# Al San Vincenzo

map 13

30 Connaught Street, W2 2AF
TEL: (020) 7262 9623

COOKING **2**
ITALIAN
£48–£57

This small dining room near the bottom end of Edgware Road divides reporters on just about every count. Short on warmth and cheer for some, it is pleasant and comfortable for others. Detractors single out small portions, high prices (the Borgonzolos ascribe these to their use of all-organic meat and vegetables), and the fact that main courses come with little in the way of vegetables; supporters, meanwhile, talk up the simple rustic nature of the food. Despite smoked salmon, and duck breast with mandarin sauce, there are enough Italian dishes to convince, taking in gnocchi with porcini, fine linguine with clams, osso buco, and a hefty-sounding starter of pig's trotter, cotechino sausage and lentils. Finish perhaps with panettone bread-and-butter pudding, or Vin Santo with cantuccini biscuits. Service varies from 'willing' to 'indifferent', and a tiny Italian wine list starts with Bolla Merlot and Chardonnay at £16.

CHEF: Vincenzo Borgonzolo  PROPRIETORS: Vincenzo and Elaine Borgonzolo  OPEN: Mon to Fri L 12.15 to 1.30, Mon to Sat D 7 to 9.30  CLOSED: 25 and 26 Dec  MEALS: Set L and D £27.50 (2 courses) to £33.50  SERVICE: not inc, 12.5% for groups of 5 or more  CARDS: Delta, MasterCard, Visa  DETAILS: 24 seats. Private parties: 20 main room. Vegetarian meals. No children under 12. No cigars/pipes in dining room. Music  ⊖ Marble Arch

## Anglesea Arms £     map 12

35 Wingate Road, W6 0UR
TEL: (020) 8749 1291  FAX: (020) 8749 1254

COOKING 2
MODERN EUROPEAN
£27–£39

The popularity of this thriving gastro-pub may be merited but it does make it difficult to get a table. When you do get in, allow plenty of time for your meal: the 'Byzantine' ordering system may mean a long wait between sitting down and eating. Indeed, service seems to be a weak link (and an indifferent approach to complaints has been noted), although the food remains an enticing prospect. Dan Evans is an accomplished exponent of the modern eclectic style, even if, in practice, the food does not always live up to expectations. The day's dishes are listed on a blackboard, typically taking in razor clam gratin with chorizo, almonds, and a herb crust, followed by seared gilt-head bream with polenta, peperonata, and black olives, or pot-roast saddle of lamb with white beans, curly kale and rosemary gravy. Finish with poached pear with a matching sorbet, or buttermilk pudding with passion fruit. Most wines on the short global list are under £20, including house French at £10.25. A dozen by the glass start at £2.40.

CHEFS: Dan Evans and Jacky Lelièvre  PROPRIETORS: Dan and Fiona Evans  OPEN: all week 12.30 to 2.45 (3 Sat, 3.30 Sun), 7 to 10.30 (10 Sun)  CLOSED: 24 to 30 Dec, 1 Jan  MEALS: alc (main courses L £7 to £8.50, D £8 to £11)  SERVICE: not inc  CARDS: Delta, MasterCard, Switch, Visa  DETAILS: 70 seats. 24 seats outside. Vegetarian meals. Children's helpings. Wheelchair access (not WC). No music  ⊖ Ravenscourt Park

## Aquarium     [NEW ENTRY]   map 13

Ivory House, St Katharine's Dock, E1W 1AT
TEL: (020) 7480 6116  FAX: (020) 7480 5973
EMAIL: info@theaquarium.co.uk
WEBSITE: www.theaquarium.co.uk

COOKING 3
MEDITERRANEAN
£33–£62

The Aquarium makes the most of its waterside setting, with a large tree-shaded terrace for outdoor eating and, inside, floor-to-ceiling windows giving views over the dock and its moored boats. The design is kept simple, with a tarpaulin-like ceiling, painted metal pillars and industrial-look flooring; table settings are pleasingly straightforward too, with stylish cutlery and interestingly shaped crockery.

Describing itself as a predominantly fish restaurant using seasonal and 'intelligently sourced' ingredients, Aquarium relies heavily on Scandinavian supplies – including freshwater species – flown in daily (Christian Sandefeldt is Swedish). These might turn up as fillet of perch meunière with hazelnut salad and foie gras purée, or roast zander with truffle potatoes, oyster sauce and a red wine glaze. The menu is innovative, dishes are executed and assembled carefully, and timing is spot-on: be it grilled tuna with a crispy shiitake roll and horseradish salad, or roast halibut with mushroom gnocchi, asparagus, turnips, and a grain mustard sauce. Starters may include ballottine of gravad lax with dill salad and smoked cod's roe, while for fish phobics, daube of beef with chorizo, sauté ceps and pommes Maxim may crop up among main courses.

For dessert, a selection of French cheeses may vie with banana sorbet, or raspberry omelette soufflé. Service is generally helpful and demonstrably knowledgeable about the wine list, which is short, rather confusingly arranged, but in possession of some rather smart, pricey bottles from both Old and New Worlds. Prices start at £13.50 for Italian Primitivo and French Chardonnay-Viognier.

CHEF: Christian Sandefeldt   PROPRIETORS: Christian and Kerstin Sandefeldt   OPEN: Mon to Sat L 12 to 3 (4 Sat), Tue to Sat D 6.30 to 11   CLOSED: 25 and 26 Dec, 1 Jan   MEALS: alc (main courses £14.50 to £17). Set L £17.50 (2 courses) to £21. Brunch menu available Sat   SERVICE: 12.5% (optional), card slips closed   CARDS: Amex, Delta, Diners, MasterCard, Switch, Visa   DETAILS: 70 seats. 40 seats outside. Private parties: 100 main room, 30 to 70 private rooms. No children on terrace. Wheelchair access (not WC). Music   ⊖ Tower Hill

# Arancia £     map 13

52 Southwark Park Road, SE16 3RS     COOKING 2
TEL/FAX: (020) 7394 1751     ITALIAN
WEBSITE: www.arancia-london.co.uk     £25–£35

Eagle-eyed locals will have noticed that this neighbourhood Italian restaurant is not in Camberwell, as previously suggested, but in Bermondsey. That apart, little else has changed. The name means 'orange', and that's the colour of the 'designer scruffy' dining room. Floors are wood, tablecloths paper, and net curtains drape the windows. The weekly-changing menu is short and to the point, the food is piled high, and it's not too pricey. Zucchini flowers stuffed with ricotta and Amaretto, or breadcrumbed sardines with pine nuts and sultanas, make invigorating starters, while successful mains might include a skewer of marinated roast pork with beetroot salad and piadina. The kitchen can also deliver Sardinian burrida (fish stew) and peppers stuffed with couscous, followed by a version of chocolate semi-freddo. Service is pleasantly casual, and the list of around two dozen wines has plenty below £15, with house Italian at £8.40.

CHEF: Catherine O'Sullivan   PROPRIETORS: A. Rossi and C. O'Sullivan   OPEN: Wed to Sun L 12.30 to 2.30, all week D 7 to 11   CLOSED: 24 Dec to 3 Jan   MEALS: alc (main courses £9 to £9.50). Set L £7.50 (2 courses) to £10.50   SERVICE: not inc, card slips closed   CARDS: Delta, MasterCard,

Switch, Visa   DETAILS: 46 seats. 10 seats outside. Private parties: 6 to 8 private rooms. Vegetarian meals. No cigars/pipes in dining room. Music. No mobile phones ⊖ Bermondsey £5

# Assaggi

map 13

The Chepstow, 39 Chepstow Place, W2 4TS
TEL: (020) 7792 5501   FAX: (020) 7792 9033

COOKING 3
ITALIAN
£40–£62

Occupying a room over a pub in a smart-looking neighbourhood, Assaggi combines light from large windows with colourful painted panels to make a bright splash. Unfussy to look at, it also has a bare-bones menu, although the fact that the Italian is not translated is a mite pretentious. What it offers, though, is plain but characterful eating, and a meal made up mostly of starters can keep the cost under control as well as bringing plenty of variety. Chickpea soup, a salad of artichoke and bottarga, and stuffed calamari are the sorts of things to expect, and although standards vary a bit, prawn salad on a deep-fried rice cake ('lemon risotto' on the menu) has pleased, as has John Dory with a smear of tomato and olive sauce. A light and fluffy lemon tart stands out among desserts, bread includes thin carta di musica (a bit like a poppadom), and coffee is commended. Sardinian house wine is £11.95, but prices soon escalate.

CHEF: Nino Sassu   PROPRIETORS: Pietro Fraccari and Nino Sassu   OPEN: Mon to Sat 12.30 to 2.30, 7.30 to 11   CLOSED: 2 weeks Christmas, bank hols   MEALS: alc (main courses £11 to £19) SERVICE: not inc, card slips closed   CARDS: Amex, Delta, Diners, MasterCard, Switch, Visa DETAILS: 35 seats. Vegetarian meals. Children's helpings. No music. Air-conditioned   ⊖ Notting Hill Gate

# Atlantic Bar and Grill ♥

map 15

20 Glasshouse Street, W1R 5RQ
TEL: (020) 7734 4888

NEW CHEF
MODERN EUROPEAN
£28–£37

Changes to this vast, marble-pillared, chandeliered basement were afoot as the Guide went to press. The fabric was due for an 'update' (rather than a wholesale refurb), and David Roache was likewise in the process of impressing his own thumbprint on the contemporary menu, offering red mullet escabeche with tapénade and aïoli crostini, spaghetti with lobster, and Trelough duck breast with shallot cream and morels. There are grills too (of Angus or Hereford beef), and desserts such as chilled coconut rice pudding with passion-fruit sorbet. The wine list focuses on the New World as much as Europe, concentrating on modern styles from go-ahead producers; champagne is strongly represented. A dozen well-chosen wines come by the glass (£4.60 to £8.10), but there is little else under £20.

CHEF: David Roache   PROPRIETOR: Gruppo Ltd   OPEN: Mon to Sat 12 to 3, 6 to 11.30   MEALS: alc (main courses £12.50 to £18.50). Set L and D £14.50 (2 courses) to £16.50. Cover £1   SERVICE: 12.5% (optional), card slips closed   CARDS: Amex, Delta, Diners, MasterCard, Switch, Visa DETAILS: 210 seats. Private parties: 300 main room, 55 to 72 private rooms. Wheelchair access (also WC). Music. Air-conditioned   ⊖ Piccadilly Circus

# Aubergine

map 14

11 Park Walk, SW10 0AJ        COOKING **6**
TEL: (020) 7352 3449    FAX: (020) 7351 1770      MODERN FRENCH
£43–£116

Shrubs in tubs, and an aubergine-coloured awning, make this place easy to locate. The oil paintings on the dining room's brushed ochre walls may not be the last word in chic, but William Drabble's food is almost the last word in indulgence. Apart from lobster (tortellini) and scallops (with salsify purée and smoked bacon jus), the kitchen must be knee-deep in foie gras: it comes in a terrine with Madeira jelly, as an assiette (benchmark mousse, boudin and sautéed), and stuffed into seared, rare pigeon breast – 'as good as it gets' for a pigeon (and foie gras) fancier – accompanied by tiny, bitter turnips smeared with caramelised juices.

There is a choice of four items per course on the £25 lunch menu, seven on the £48 dinner version, and dishes are full of interest: braised pig's head comes with root vegetables, while a large, firm piece of accurately roast monkfish arrives on creamed leeks with girolles and chunks of lobster. The kitchen favours assiettes, variations on a theme being applied to foie gras, chicken, duck and lamb: the last consisting of pieces of rare, seared loin (dusted with parsley), tongue, and sweetbread on dauphinoise potato with pungent roast garlic cream and a rosemary reduction.

Desserts may not be quite so turbo-charged, although an assiette of orange has delivered a fine-textured, jelly-like blood orange terrine, an ice cream, and liqueur-soaked sponge cake. Barring a tendency to over-salt, the kitchen's judgement appears sound as a bell. Service varies, but can be short on warmth and charm. The huge wine list concentrates on elite Bordeaux and Burgundies, has comparatively little beyond France, and is generally pricey.

CHEF: William Drabble   PROPRIETOR: A To Z Restaurants Ltd   OPEN: Mon to Fri L 12 to 2.15, Mon to Sat D 7 to 10.15   CLOSED: 2 weeks Christmas, 2 weeks Aug, bank hols   MEALS: Set L £20 (2 courses) to £48, Set D £48 to £65 (whole table only)   SERVICE: 12.5% (optional), card slips closed   CARDS: Amex, Delta, Diners, MasterCard, Switch, Visa   DETAILS: 55 seats. Private parties: 55 main room. Wheelchair access (not WC). No music. No mobile phones. Air-conditioned   ⊖ South Kensington

# Avenue ▼

map 15

7–9 St James's Street, SW1A 1EE       COOKING **4**
TEL: (020) 7321 2111    FAX: (020) 7321 2500    MODERN EUROPEAN
WEBSITE: www.theavenue.co.uk       £27–£58

There is a buzz to this large open-plan dining room and cocktail bar, although customers themselves provide the only real colour in the zealously minimalist, unadorned space. Long brasserie-style menus offer plenty of choice, and the cooking is mostly straightforward and modest, aiming for the wide appeal of watercress soup with smoked haddock cream, Gorgonzola and bacon galette, or a warm salad of wild mushrooms with Brie and truffles. Main courses have a similar modern-classic feel, taking in duck breast with roast apple, roast salmon with minted pea purée, and grilled ribeye with chips and horseradish. Finish with prune and Amaretto crème brûlée, pecan tart, or black cherry and chocolate mousse cake. The cooking may be a bit hit and miss, and service has been considered 'detached', but the wine list is a well-tailored, modern selection from around the globe. Most bottles won't leave much change from £20, although house wines (Argentinean red, French white) start at £14.50 and there is a wide selection by the glass. For those who want to splash out, a small number of wines up for auction at Christie's (next door) are sold here.

CHEF: Dean Carr   PROPRIETOR: Moving Image Restaurants plc   OPEN: all week 12 to 3 (3.30 Sun), Mon to Thur 5.45 to 12 (12.30 Fri and Sat), Sun 7 to 10   CLOSED: 25 and 26 Dec, 1 Jan   MEALS: alc D (main courses £12 to £16.50). Set L and D £17.50 (2 courses) to £19.50. Set D 5.45 to 7.30 and after 10.15 £14.50 (2 courses) to £16.50. Bar menu available all day   SERVICE: 12.5% (optional), card slips closed   CARDS: Amex, Delta, Diners, MasterCard, Switch, Visa   DETAILS: 180 seats. Private parties: 180 main room. Vegetarian meals. Wheelchair access (also WC). Music. Air-conditioned   ⊖ Green Park

## Babur Brasserie £                                        map 12

| 119 Brockley Rise, SE23 1JP | COOKING 2 |
| TEL: (020) 8291 2400   FAX: (020) 8291 4881 | INDIAN |
| WEBSITE: www.babur-brasserie.com | £28–£52 |

Over the white frontage a life-size model tiger greets you with a silent roar; inside all is in contemporary colours. Service may be stretched at busy times, intensifying appetites stimulated by menu descriptions of dishes from several regions of the subcontinent. Some are variations on familiar favourites under different names, such as gilawat ke kebab (minced lamb spiced with mace, cardamom and saffron), or pot-roast raan gulnar (shank of lamb). Breads appreciated by an inspector included fluffy light naan, and grease-free paratha, while the South Indian stuffed pancake, uthappam, made an unconventional starter. Harrey murgh tikka is a beautifully tender tandoori chicken breast covered with a marinade of coriander, tamarind and mint. A dozen vegetable side dishes offer interesting combinations, and desserts likewise range from everyday to highly unusual. The short, modestly priced wine list starts at £8.95. Babur has a new sibling, Planet Spice, Addington (see entry).

CHEF: Enam Rahman   PROPRIETOR: Babur 1998 Ltd   OPEN: Sat to Thur L 12 to 2.15, all week D 6 to 11.15   CLOSED: 25 and 26 Dec   MEALS: alc exc Sun L (main courses £7.50 to £13). Buffet L Sun £8.95   SERVICE: not inc   CARDS: Amex, Delta, Diners, MasterCard, Switch, Visa   DETAILS: 56 seats. Private parties: 30 main room. Vegetarian meals. Children's helpings. No-smoking area. Music. Air-conditioned   (£5)

## Back to Basics £                                        map 15

| 21A Foley Street, W1W 6DS | |
| TEL: (020) 7436 2181   FAX: (020) 7436 2180 | COOKING 3 |
| EMAIL: fishisthedish@aol.com | SEAFOOD |
| WEBSITE: www.backtobasics.uk.com | £26–£52 |

'The name says it all,' summed up one reporter, referring to both décor and food: mostly fresh fish presented without frills. The restaurant consists of a 'homely' interior with bare bulbs, close-together tables, wooden chairs, and a large blackboard listing fish of the day; this usually starts with a dozen items, which get crossed off as supplies run out. The market determines each day's listings, which might include monkfish, gilt-head bream or Dover sole, and the repertoire of treatments tends to be varied but circumscribed, producing sea bass with spring onions and ginger, tuna loin with salade niçoise, and mackerel with a mango and coriander salsa.

A printed menu supplements choice, adding ribeye steak with horseradish and mustard, as well as soups, appetisers (marinated herring with beetroot and sour cream), and salads (rocket, Parmesan and Italian sausage). Desserts run to bread-and-butter pudding with whisky sauce, and apple tart. Wines, as basic as the rest, stay under £20 (house vins de pays are £11.95), but it is worth studying the more ambitious 'alternative cellar', especially for white Burgundy.

CHEFS: Philip Banks and Stefan Pflaumer  PROPRIETOR: Stefan Pflaumer  OPEN: Mon to Fri 12 to 3, 6 to 10  CLOSED: Christmas, last 2 weeks Aug, bank hols  MEALS: alc (main courses £10 to £15.50)  SERVICE: 10% (optional)  CARDS: Amex, Delta, Diners, MasterCard, Switch, Visa  DETAILS: 40 seats. 50 seats outside. Private parties: 40 main room. Vegetarian meals. Children's helpings. Wheelchair access (not WC). Occasional music  ⊖ Oxford Circus, Goodge Street £5

# Baltic

NEW ENTRY    map 13

74 Blackfriars Road, SE1 8HA
TEL: (020) 7928 1111  FAX: (020) 7928 8487
EMAIL: info@balticrestaurant.co.uk
WEBSITE: www.balticrestaurant.co.uk

COOKING 2
EAST/NORTH EUROPEAN
£23–£72

A sleek-looking frontage leads to a long bar, with a walkway down to the dining room, where white walls, blue light, wooden beams and rafters give the place a suitably Nordic feel. Those who like to describe their favourite foods in oceanic terms – such as Mediterranean and Pacific – can now add the Baltic, Adriatic and Black Seas to their repertoire. These are the waters that Nick Pound trawls for ideas, and although the accent may be more Polish than Scandinavian, the focus is on cold-climate, Northern European cooking, the kind where it pays to have a capacity for pork fat, suet and porage, along with beetroot, horseradish, caraway, pickles, sour cream, dill, cabbage, kohlrabi, rye bread and so on.

Familiarity with East European culinary terms might come in handy to translate (or even to pronounce) marchewkowa, barszcz, boczek, mizeria or nalesniki, although some are explained on the menu. If they sound unlikely asylum seekers, don't forget the precedent set by chicken Kiev, here served with braised cabbage and dill. Among more notable successes have been a simple but immensely satisfying sour-creamy stew of sliced mushrooms and kabanos sausage with soft gnocchi-like dumplings, and marinated herrings, of immaculately chewy freshness, served on potato cubes and raw red onion, with chunks of pickled dill cucumber. Finish perhaps with makoviek (poppy seed and honey cake), or with a scoop of intense lemon sorbet in a champagne glass, hovering over a sump of heart-stoppingly strong Polish vodka. There are 36 vodkas to choose from, plus a varied, modern wine list at par-for-the-course prices, starting with a pair of house wines at £10.50.

CHEF: Nick Pound  PROPRIETOR: Jan Woroniecki  OPEN: Sun to Fri L 12 to 3, all week D 6 to 11.30  CLOSED: 25 Dec, L 1 Jan  MEALS: alc (main courses £9.50 to £24). Set L £11.50 (2 courses) to £13.50, Set D £22.50 (2 courses). Bar menu available  SERVICE: 12.5% (optional)  CARDS:

Amex, Delta, Diners, MasterCard, Switch, Visa   DETAILS: 120 seats. 20 seats outside. Private parties: 25 main room. Vegetarian meals. Children's helpings. Wheelchair access (also WC). Music. Air-conditioned   ⊖ Southwark, Waterloo

## Bank Aldwych ♀ 🍴                                                    map 13

1 Kingsway, WC2B 6XF
TEL: (020) 7379 9797   FAX: (020) 7240 7001                        COOKING **4**
EMAIL: aldres@bankrestaurants.com                          MODERN EUROPEAN
WEBSITE: www.bankrestaurants.com                                     £23–£63

The original branch of this expanding group is now 'almost an old friend', having settled into a comfortably dependable routine. This is not damning with faint praise, merely a recognition that the excitable buzz of the early days has somewhat dissipated, although this is still a stylish venue and 'brilliant for breakfast'. Very long brasserie-style menus make choosing difficult: there are plenty of appealing options to suit most tastes, if a slight feeling that the kitchen is playing it safe. Nonetheless, output is 'technically very good': cream of asparagus soup was 'really green and loyal to its vegetable', said one reporter, while artichoke risotto was described as 'perfect, generous and gloopy'. Crab linguini has come with plentiful meat and a zingy bite to the sauce, and chips are fresh and crunchy, although puddings 'sound better in anticipation than to eat'. Service is good natured and polished. The concise wine list, arranged by style, concentrates on fashionable regions and grape varieties. Pricing is fair, with house Pays d'Oc Chardonnay and Merlot £12.90 (£3.40 a glass). For would-be splurgers, the Bank Cellar selection has some good names from Old and New Worlds.

CHEF: Peter Lloyd   PROPRIETOR: Bank Restaurant Group plc   OPEN: all week 12 to 2.45 (11.30 to 3.30 Sat and Sun brunch), 5 to 11.30 (5.30 to 10.30 Sun). Breakfast Mon to Fri 7 to 10.30 CLOSED: Easter Sun, bank hol Mons   MEALS: alc (main courses £11 to £19.50). Set L Mon to Fri £12.50 (2 courses) to £15, Set D 5.30 to 7 and 10 to 11.15 £12 (2 courses) to £15. Brunch and bar menu also available   SERVICE: 12.5% (optional), card slips closed   CARDS: Amex, Delta, Diners, MasterCard, Switch, Visa   DETAILS: 220 seats. Vegetarian meals. Children's helpings. Wheelchair access (also WC). No music. Air-conditioned   ⊖ Holborn  (£5)

## Bank Westminster ♀                                                  map 13

45 Buckingham Gate, SW1E 6BS
TEL: (020) 7379 9797   FAX: (020) 7240 7001                        COOKING **3**
EMAIL: westres@bankrestaurants.com                         MODERN EUROPEAN
WEBSITE: www.bankrestaurants.com                                     £26–£73

The distinguished twenty-first-century design of this bar-brasserie-restaurant sits happily in the Crowne Plaza Hotel, built a century ago as an overflow to accommodate aristocrats and their retinues who were visiting nearby Buckingham Place. The conservatory dining room overlooks, and in summer extends into, a flowery courtyard. The past year's most popular dishes apparently were tart-fine of squid, chorizo and baby spinach to start; and steak and kidney pudding. Exotic ingredients are used imaginatively but not outlandishly, as in dressed crab with gazpacho dressing; or fillet of sea bass with seafood, tomato and thyme risotto. Desserts range from purists' bread-and-butter pudding to a lighter poached melon, papaya and mango with red wine granita.

Wines, from a stylishly put-together list, capitalise on fashionable producers from around the world. Mark-ups are fair, giving good choice in the £20-and-under range. Those marked in bold identify new additions or monthly specials. As at the Aldwych branch there is a more expensive Bank Cellar, and house Chardonnay and Merlot from the Pays d'Oc sell for £12.90 (£3.40 a glass, £9.60 for 50cl).

CHEF: Matt Dawson   PROPRIETOR: Bank Restaurant Group plc   OPEN: Mon to Fri L 12 to 3, Sun brunch 11.30 to 3, all week D 5.30 to 11.30 (10 Sun)   CLOSED: 25 Dec and 1 Jan   MEALS: alc (main courses £10.50 to £24). Set L £12.50 and D 5.30 to 7, 10 to 11.30 (2 courses) to £15. Sun brunch and evening bar menus available   SERVICE: 12.5% (optional), card slips closed   CARDS: Amex, Delta, Diners, MasterCard, Switch, Visa   DETAILS: 180 seats. 25 seats outside. Private parties: 180 main room, 20 to 40 private rooms. Vegetarian meals. Children's helpings. Wheelchair access (also WC). No music. Air-conditioned   ⊖ St James's Park  (£5)

## Bar Zaika Bazaar                          map 14

2A Pond Place, SW3 6DU                                    COOKING 2
TEL: (020) 7584 6655   FAX: (020) 7584 6755                INDIAN
WEBSITE: www.cuisine-collection.co.uk                     £33–£53

The interior of this basement restaurant, a more casual offshoot of the original Zaika (see entry), is draped with colourful Indian fabrics, and each wall is painted a different colour: pink, cream, orange, and black. Recesses hold Indian statuary, ceiling fans rotate slowly above plain wooden tables and chairs, and a few cushions add colour. Apparently 'you can buy everything you see', including the furniture. The menu's offerings have been scaled down quite a bit since opening, but the variety of 'starters and finger food' takes in a minced lamb and smoked cashew nut samosa, and tandoori spiced smoked salmon marinated in honey, mustard and dill. Main courses tend to be along the standard lines of lamb dopiaza, or chicken tikka masala, or perhaps a bright-sounding prawn malabar (with fresh coconut, mango and mangosteen). There are breads, rice and vegetable dishes (though no desserts listed), 'live music by the manager', and a take-away service. Prices on the respectable, globetrotting wine list are mostly under £20. House wines are £13.50, and a handful of wines are sold by the glass from £3.50.

CHEF: Vineet Bhatia   PROPRIETOR: Cuisine Collection   OPEN: Mon to Sat D only 6 to 10.45   CLOSED: bank hols   MEALS: alc (main courses £7.50 to £13). Set D £12.50 (2 courses)   SERVICE: 12.5% (optional), card slips closed   CARDS: Amex, Delta, MasterCard, Switch, Visa   DETAILS: 70 seats. Private parties: 120 main room. Vegetarian meals. No cigars/pipes in dining room. Music. Air-conditioned   ⊖ South Kensington

*The Guide always appreciates hearing about changes of chef or owner.*

# Belair House                                           map 12

Gallery Road, Dulwich Village, SE21 7AB
TEL: (020) 8299 9788    FAX: (020) 8299 9121                    COOKING **4**
EMAIL: belairhouse@aol.com                                  MODERN FRENCH
WEBSITE: www.belairhouse.co.uk                                  £36–£72

Reached up an imposing driveway, this impressively refurbished Georgian house looks out over attractive public parkland dotted with ancient trees. High ceilings and generously spaced tables give the dining room a light, airy feel, and the food's contemporary outlook adds its own sunny dimension. As well as Mediterranean ideas such as provençale fish soup with aïoli, and a tomato and goats' cheese tart flavoured with basil and tapènade, expect to find a cep and snail fricassee, or braised pig's trotter with chicory and morels.

Results can be patchy, but among highlights have been a hearty rabbit terrine with lemon and olives, and confit chicken served with crushed potatoes, wild mushrooms and a herb-flavoured jus. Pineapple provides a variation on the Tatin theme to finish, a fine dark chocolate and cherry tart is accompanied by first-class white and dark chocolate ice creams, and bread is freshly baked. A good range of grape varieties, from Verdicchio to Pinot Gris, from Tempranillo to Sangiovese, characterises the briefly annotated wine list. House Merlot and Chenin Blanc from South Africa are £16.

CHEF: Zak El Hamdou    PROPRIETORS: Gary and Jayne Cady    OPEN: Tue to Sun L 12 to 2.30, Tue to Sat D 7 to 10.30    MEALS: Set L Sun £27, Set L Tue to Sat £18 (2 courses) to £22, Set D £28 (2 courses) to £32    SERVICE: 12.5% (optional), card slips closed    CARDS: Amex, Delta, Diners, MasterCard, Switch, Visa    DETAILS: 85 seats. 30 seats outside. Private parties: 85 main room, 2 to 40 private rooms. Car park. Vegetarian meals. Children's helpings. No cigars/pipes in dining room. Wheelchair access (also WC). No music  ⊖ Brixton  £5

# Bel Azur  £                          NEW ENTRY   map 12

189 Woodhouse Road, N12 9AY                                     COOKING **1**
TEL: (020) 8368 7989                                        NORTH AFRICAN
                                                               £21–£36

For years Laurent Farrugia was – arguably – the couscous king of London in his eponymous Golders Green restaurant. Now his son-in-law has resurrected the formula in this new venue in the outer suburbs. Couscous remains the main event on the tiny menu, accompanied by six versions of his great stew, including royal (vegetables with lamb) and a 'mixed grill' comprising a skewered kebab, lamb chop and merguez sausage. Start with brik à l'oeuf (a classic crisp pastry served with or without tuna) and finish with excellent North African pastries, ice creams or crêpes suzette. Service is amicable, and a handful of punchy Moroccan wines go well with the food. House wine is £9.50.

CHEF/PROPRIETOR: Pasquale Barberio    OPEN: Mon to Sat 12 to 2, 6 to 11    CLOSED: 25 Dec, 1 Jan, first 3 weeks Aug, bank hols    MEALS: alc (main courses £7 to £14.50)    SERVICE: not inc    CARDS: Delta, MasterCard, Switch, Visa    DETAILS: 50 seats. Private parties: 60 main room. Vegetarian meals. Children's helpings. No cigars/pipes in dining room. Wheelchair access (not WC). No music. Air-conditioned

# Belvedere Marco Pierre White     map 13

off Abbotsbury Road, Holland Park, W8 6LU
TEL: (020) 7602 1238    FAX: (020) 7610 4382                    COOKING **5**
EMAIL: sales@whitestarline.org.uk          MODERN BRITISH/MEDITERRANEAN
WEBSITE: www.whitestarline.org.uk                              £34–£89

It may be a bit tricky to find from Kensington High Street; if a wander through
the park doesn't appeal, try coming at it from Abbotsbury Road. The ground-
floor dining room, with its high ceiling (pity the person who has to change the
light bulbs), benefits from natural daylight, fine flower displays, and generously
sized, widely spaced tables. There may be quite a bit of French to the menu, and
to many of the classical techniques – red mullet niçoise with tapénade, or braised
pig's trotter with morels – but there is certainly some British input too, from one
Sunday luncher's thick slice of roast beef with huge hot Yorkshire pudding, to
'well-flavoured but not high' pheasant for a November visitor, the bird moist
with a crisp skin, and presented with trimmings of Brussels sprouts, grilled
sausages wrapped in bacon, roast chestnuts and bread sauce.

Matthew Brown runs a well-disciplined kitchen, and if some dishes (such as
aspic of oysters with watercress) are familiar from other MPW restaurants, at
least they are consistently and impressively rendered. Among highly rated
dishes have been full-flavoured oxtail soup with dumplings, and a rich
chocolate tart made from A1 pastry and covered in dark chocolate shavings.
Otherwise there may be caramel soufflé or pear tart bourdaloue. Those in search
of value should note the three-course lunch at £17.95. 'Pretty well immaculate'
service is overlaid with the calm authority of the head waiter, but prices on the
astutely chosen wine list take much of it out of the realm of ordinary drinkers.

CHEF: Matthew Brown    PROPRIETORS: Marco Pierre White and Jimmy Lahoud    OPEN: all week 12
to 2.30 (3.30 Sun), 6 to 11    CLOSED: Sun D in winter    MEALS: alc (main courses £15.50 to £25).
Set L Mon to Sat £14.95 (2 courses) to £17.95. Set L Sun £19.50    SERVICE: 12.5%, card slips
closed    CARDS: Amex, Delta, Diners, MasterCard, Switch, Visa    DETAILS: 105 seats. 24 seats
outside. Private parties: 60 main room, 24 to 60 private rooms. Occasional music. Air-
conditioned    ⊖ Holland Park, High Street Kensington

# Bibendum 🍾     map 14

Michelin House, 81 Fulham Road, SW3 6RD
TEL: (020) 7581 5817    FAX: (020) 7823 7925                    COOKING **5**
EMAIL: reservations@bibendum.co.uk                              MODERN BRITISH
WEBSITE: www.bibendum.co.uk                                     £34–£100

Everybody should eat here at least once. The unassuming grace and style of the
first-floor dining room – with its etched windows and inimitably curvaceous
glassware – make it a cherished place among the capital's assets, while the food
deftly brings traditional bistro cooking up to date. Jellied ham with parsley
comes with pease pudding and sauce gribiche, deep-fried calves' brains are
given a Thai dipping sauce, and grilled onglet gets a snail, mushroom and onion
suet pudding. That is not to ignore popular taste; indeed, much of the menu
plays to the gallery, generating sheer pleasure in a simple Roquefort tart with
crisp pastry and a light, puffy filling, and in haddock in a light, crisp batter with
French fries and a fine tartare sauce.

This is food to gladden the heart, and what the kitchen does not lose sight of is the significance of good materials straightforwardly presented, be it a fresh crab salad, a properly grilled veal chop, pear and almond tart, or lemon rice pudding with rhubarb compote. The wine list is a dream in terms of depth, scope and clarity. The classic areas of France – Champagne, Burgundy and mature red Bordeaux – are particularly strong, but there are plenty of rising stars from the New World to lend balance. On the downside, mark-ups can be hefty. There is a good selection of half-bottles as well as 21 house wines (starting at £15.95) but only a half-dozen by the glass or 450ml 'pot'.

CHEF: Matthew Harris   PROPRIETORS: Lord Hamlyn, Graham Williams, Simon Hopkinson and Sir Terence Conran   OPEN: all week 12 to 3 (12.30 to 3.30 Sat and Sun), 7 to 11.30 (10.30 Sun) CLOSED: 25 and 26 Dec, 1 Jan   MEALS: alc D (main courses £16.50 to £28). Set L £20   SERVICE: 12.5% (optional), card slips closed   CARDS: Amex, Delta, Diners, MasterCard, Switch, Visa DETAILS: 76 seats. Private parties: 100 main room. Children's helpings. Wheelchair access (not WC). No music. No mobile phones. Air-conditioned   ⊖ South Kensington

## Bibendum Oyster Bar                                           map 14

Michelin House, 81 Fulham Road, SW3 6RD
TEL: (020) 7589 1480   FAX: (020) 7823 7925                          COOKING 4
EMAIL: reservations@bibendum.co.uk                                    SEAFOOD
WEBSITE: www.bibendum.co.uk                                          £29–£77

A North of England couple who ate here one winter lunchtime were so impressed that they returned the next day. 'The food is simple but carefully prepared,' they reckoned, 'and delivers bags of flavour.' Tables in the foyer of the Michelin building are set a bit further apart than in the small Oyster Bar itself, which might be relevant for those sensitive to cigarette smoke. Bivalves naturally receive star billing, with rock oysters and natives served in sixes, nines or dozens, and there are also classic crustacean preparations such as lobster mayonnaise and crab salad.

For the rest, well-dressed salads typically accompany a sweet and creamy cold onion tart, or pink and tender cold roast duck, which also came with an appealing, peppery combination of lentils and watercress. Good renditions of favourites such as Piemontese peppers roasted in garlic and olive oil, or egg mayonnaise with tasty anchovies, also satisfy, and meals might end with crème brûlée, pot au chocolat or cheese. Service is pleasant and efficient, and the wine list does a good job too, ranging from house Sauvignon Blancs from the Tarn or Touraine to a slate of champagnes for high rollers. Prices open at £13.50, or £3.50 a glass.

CHEF: Matthew Harris   PROPRIETORS: Lord Hamlyn, Graham Williams, Simon Hopkinson and Sir Terence Conran   OPEN: all week 12 to 11   CLOSED: 25 and 26 Dec   MEALS: alc (main courses £7 to £32)   SERVICE: 12.5% (optional), card slips closed   CARDS: Amex, Delta, Diners, MasterCard, Switch, Visa   DETAILS: 20 seats. 30 seats outside. Children's helpings. Wheelchair access (also WC). Music

*Report forms are at the back of the book; write a letter if you prefer; or email us at goodfoodguide@which.net*

# Blandford Street

**NEW ENTRY**    map 15

5–7 Blandford Street, W1U 3DB
TEL: (020) 7486 9696   FAX: (020) 7486 5067
EMAIL: bookings@blandford-street.co.uk
WEBSITE: www.blandford-street.co.uk

COOKING 5
MODERN EUROPEAN
£38–£68

Smartened up with a tin or two of red paint since Stephen Bull left for Herefordshire (see entry, Sellack), Blandford Street feels sharply dressed, its bold modern paintings bouncing off large mirrors, its feel as bright and cosmopolitan as one would expect for somewhere that now finds itself part of up-and-coming 'Marylebone Village'. Daniel Ward's food is on the ball too, full of interest at every turn, with seafood and vegetarian options to the fore: perhaps a Moroccan filo strudel with saffron and garlic cream, or a pancake covered in gently spiced scallop slices, seared on top as if cooked Tatin-style, served with a warm vinaigrette. This is a neat idea finely executed, and different from what kitchens normally do with scallops.

Technique is sound, producing, for example, a skilfully pan-fried sea bream fillet, served with a deep-fried courgette flower (the batter 'not of the thin tempura school, more the old fish-and-chip shop stuff'), and with whizzed-up peas and quartered shiitakes. Occasionally the kitchen comes up with 'an inspired combination', such as a thin, well-made UFO-shaped raviolo filled with pounded smoked haddock, served with a sauce made from roasted lobster shells whose affinity with the smoked haddock was considered remarkable. To conclude there may be warm banana cake, and crème fraîche pannacotta with exotic fruits. Service is knowledgeable and well paced, and wines have a penchant for the Old World (and for anything over £20), taking in Pellé's Menetou-Salon 2000, a 1995 Gran Reserva Rioja, and French house varietals at £14.

CHEF: Daniel Ward   PROPRIETORS: Nicholas and Emmaline Lambert   OPEN: Mon to Fri L 12 to 2.30, Mon to Sat D 6.30 to 10.30   CLOSED: Christmas, bank hols   MEALS: alc D (main courses £15 to £20). Set L £21.50 (2 courses) to £25   SERVICE: 12.5% (optional), card slips closed   CARDS: Amex, Delta, Diners, MasterCard, Switch, Visa   DETAILS: 60 seats. 6 seats outside. Private parties: 50 main room. Vegetarian meals. Children's helpings. Wheelchair access (not WC). No music. Air-conditioned   ⊖ Bond Street, Baker Street

# Bleeding Heart ▮

map 13

The Cellars, Bleeding Heart Yard, Greville St,
Hatton Garden, EC1N 8SJ
TEL: (020) 7242 8238   FAX: (020) 7831 1402
EMAIL: enquiries@bleedingheart.co.uk
WEBSITE: www.bleedingheart.co.uk

COOKING 4
FRENCH
£36–£62

Off a side street, down an alleyway, at the back of a hidden courtyard, is a bistro with a flowery patio outside and a cellar restaurant underneath. The latter feels like a lighter version of the English gentlemen's club, its à la carte menu (in English and French, except for desserts) offering a wide choice of almost entirely European ingredients. Typical among starters might be seared scallops on ratatouille with chervil and Chardonnay sauce, or a goats' cheese gâteau with asparagus, morels and a herb tuile.

Classic tastes are catered for in such evening specials as foie gras salad, and chateaubriand with sauce béarnaise, while more contemporary options take in corn-fed chicken and its rillettes on tarragon tagliatelle, with sweetcorn froth; and grilled fillet of sea bass on lobster mash with fennel and chive velouté. One comparatively exotic fixture is rack of New Zealand venison ('tender and beautifully prepared'), reflecting Robyn Wilson's Kiwi origin, as do red and white wines from his Hawkes Bay vineyard that have their own page in the encyclopaedic list. Other New Zealand wines also figure strongly, even if France predominates. High price tags are not uncommon, but poking around in the regional French, Spanish and Australian sections will yield interesting bottles around £20–£25. Twenty-four wines come by the glass, and bottle prices start at £12.75 for South African Chenin Blanc. A sister restaurant, in the City, is The Don (see entry).

CHEF: Andrew Barber   PROPRIETORS: Robert and Robyn Wilson   OPEN: Mon to Fri 12 to 2.30, 6 to 10.30   CLOSED: 24 Dec to 2 Jan   MEALS: alc (main courses £10.50 to £17.95)   SERVICE: 12.5% (optional), card slips closed   CARDS: Amex, Delta, Diners, MasterCard, Switch, Visa   DETAILS: 120 seats. 35 seats outside. Private parties: 50 main room, 35 to 120 private rooms. Vegetarian meals. Children in bistro only. Wheelchair access (not WC). No music. Air-conditioned
⊖ Farringdon

# Bluebird                                                            map 14

350 King's Road, SW3 5UU                                          COOKING 3
TEL: (020) 7559 1000   FAX: (020) 7559 1111            MODERN EUROPEAN
WEBSITE: www.conran.com                                          £29–£73

Sir Terence Conran's multi-purpose gastropolis has obvious appeal, combining cook shop, food store, bustling bar and dining room, all in familiar glamorous Conran style. The kitchen appears not to believe there is such a thing as too much choice: one sample menu offered a bewildering 16 each of starters and main courses, as well as a separate shellfish section featuring three types of oyster, and a three-course set-price deal with four choices at each stage. What is on offer is a blend of classic Mediterranean dishes and old English favourites, some delivered straight, others given a 'modern' twist: crab and avocado tian with lemon and dill, and pressed ham and parsley terrine with piccalilli epitomise starters, while main courses might well include seared haddock with crushed minted peas, and roast rabbit with prosciutto, spinach, and roast garlic. Finish with oeufs à la neige, or white chocolate and lime tart. There is not a great deal of choice under £20 on the wine list, although eight house wines of each colour open with red and white Vin de Pays d'Oc at £12.75 a bottle, £3.75 a glass.

CHEF: Blair Smethurst   PROPRIETOR: Conran Restaurants   OPEN: all week 12.30 to 3, 6 to 11 MEALS: alc (main courses £13 to £22). Set L and D 6 to 7.30 and 10 to 11 £12.50 (2 courses) to £17 SERVICE: 12.5% (optional), card slips closed   CARDS: Amex, Diners, MasterCard, Switch, Visa DETAILS: 200 seats. Private parties: 200 main room, 10 to 32 private rooms. Vegetarian meals. Children's helpings. Wheelchair access (also WC). Music. Air-conditioned   ⊖ Sloane Square

*The Guide is totally independent, accepts no free hospitality, and survives on the number of copies sold each year.*

# Blue Elephant ✎      map 12

3–6 Fulham Broadway, SW6 1AA
TEL: (020) 7385 6595   FAX: (020) 7386 7665     COOKING 1
EMAIL: london@blueelephant.com      THAI
WEBSITE: www.blueelephant.com      £46–£77

A spectacular reproduction of the *Suphannahong*, the Thai royal barge, dominates the Blue Bar at this most lavish and extravagantly appointed of London's Thai restaurants. It is part of an international operation, with prices to match. The menu, quite long, contains some 'splendidly over-the-top descriptions' (chuchi koong: a 'tropical storm of subtle flavours with king prawns and a lightning flash of red curry' has been well received), although results on the plate can taste somewhat westernised. The kitchen delivers creditable versions of dim sim, fish cakes and stir-fried pork with lemon grass and chillies, as well as faithfully 'clumpy' rice and decent noodles. A new convert to the place ('my third visit in two weeks') enthused about the affordable two-course lunches. The wine list is long and global, the mark-ups 'tolerable but not charitable'; house wines start at £12.50.

CHEF: Oula Yodee   PROPRIETOR: Blue Elephant International plc   OPEN: Sun to Fri L 12 to 2.30 (3 Sun), all week D 7 to 11.30 (10.30 Sun)   CLOSED: 3 or 4 days at Christmas   MEALS: alc (main courses £10 to £20). Set L Mon to Fri Jan to Nov £10 (2 courses), Set Sun brunch £19.50. Set D £32 to £37. Cover £1.50. Bar snacks also available   SERVICE: not inc   CARDS: Amex, Diners, MasterCard, Switch, Visa   DETAILS: 230 seats. Private parties: 230 main room. Vegetarian meals. Wheelchair access (also WC). Music. Air-conditioned   ⊖ Fulham Broadway

# Blue Print Café      map 13

1st Floor, Design Museum,
Butlers Wharf, SE1 2YD      COOKING 4
TEL: (020) 7378 7031   FAX: (020) 7357 8810     MODERN EUROPEAN
WEBSITE: www.conran.com      £35–£70

Compared by reporters, perhaps inevitably, to Pont de la Tour, another Conran establishment a short distance away, Blue Print Café competes favourably not only in terms of the view but also in terms of being 'kinder on the pocket'. The dining room is light and bright, the view 'stunning', and the food an appealing contemporary slate of European-inspired dishes. Jeremy Lee seems to take pleasure in deliberately avoiding luxuries in favour of more interesting ingredients, turning out a salad of beetroot and soft-boiled egg spiked with mustard and horseradish, and revelling in such cuts as onglet, ox tongue, and boiled ham served with carrots and parsley sauce.

Pasta features, perhaps as tagliatelle with rabbit, and fish might take the shape of hake with mussels, or John Dory jazzed up with anchovy and chilli. The simplicity that is a welcome feature of the cooking spills over into desserts of gingerbread and custard, and lemon posset with blackcurrant jam. Service divides reporters, varying from 'quick and friendly' for one, to 'incompetent' for another. Those with a ceiling of £20 will find most of the wine list barred to them, those with £30 to spend can drink well. House French is £13.

CHEF: Jeremy Lee   PROPRIETOR: Conran Restaurants   OPEN: all week L 12 to 3, Mon to Sat D 6 to 11   MEALS: alc D (main courses £11.50 to £17.50). Set L £19.50 (2 courses) to £22.50   SERVICE: 12.5% (optional), card slips closed   CARDS: Amex, Delta, Diners, MasterCard, Switch, Visa   DETAILS: 110 seats. Private parties: 110 main room. Vegetarian meals. Children's helpings. Wheelchair access (not WC). No music   ⊖ Tower Hill, London Bridge

## Brackenbury £ map 12

| 129–131 Brackenbury Road, W6 0BQ | COOKING 4 |
| TEL: (020) 8748 0107   FAX: (020) 8741 0905 | MODERN BRITISH |
| EMAIL: brack@placenest.fsnet.co.uk | £22–£48 |

Looking 'wonderfully unchanged' since it first entered the Guide back in 1993, this is the essence of a neighbourhood restaurant. Simple wooden chairs and bare tables fill out its two rooms, and straightforward food is the kitchen's preoccupation: bangers and mash with onion gravy, or smoked haddock with poached egg and mustard sauce for example. But the kitchen generates sufficient variety within this tradition to keep interest going with wild garlic soup, pan-fried chicken livers with broad beans, and grilled onglet served with a potato and bacon pancake. It combines humble materials (farmhouse Cheddar omelette with chips) and more indulgent ones (Dover sole), and might end with rhubarb fool or star anise ice cream. Wines run the gamut from fine Burgundy to everyday Vin de Pays d'Oc which, at £11, is the house offering.

CHEF: Marcia Chang Hong   PROPRIETOR: Christopher Booker   OPEN: Mon to Fri L 12.30 to 2.45, Sun L 12.30 to 3.30, Mon to Sat D 7 to 10.45   CLOSED: Christmas, bank hols   MEALS: alc (main courses £8.50 to £16). Set L £10.50 (2 courses) to £12.50   SERVICE: 12.5% (optional), card slips closed   CARDS: Amex, Delta, Diners, MasterCard, Switch, Visa   DETAILS: 55 seats. 20 seats outside. Vegetarian meals. No cigars/pipes in dining room. Wheelchair access (not WC). No music   ⊖ Hammersmith

## Bradleys ▼ map 13

| 25 Winchester Road, NW3 3NR | COOKING 2 |
| TEL: (020) 7722 3457   FAX: (020) 7435 1392 | ANGLO-FRENCH |
| | £24–£46 |

Feeling more provincial than cosmopolitan, this makes a relaxing place to meet friends and chat. Its Anglo-French offerings take in roast squab pigeon with foie gras and Savoy cabbage, as well as fish soup – thin, dark, fresh-tasting and concentrated – with mild Gruyère and punchy aïoli. Some items lack the deftness required (hard pastry, clumsy saucing, that kind of thing), but the kitchen has produced a fine version of gravad lax, and thick slices of braised shoulder of lamb with flageolets and potato rissoles.

Desserts might include a wintery steamed lemon pudding, a springtime dish of rhubarb three ways, or an all-seasons chocolate fondant. The weekday set-price lunch is reckoned good value. A note on the menu says a 12.5% service charge will be added 'for your convenience'. (Come again ... *whose* convenience?) A stylistically arranged, well-chosen wine list offers good choice at all levels (including an unusual Chasselas Vieilles Vignes 1999 from Schoffit at £23.50), starting with house French at £11.50.

CHEF: Simon Bradley   PROPRIETORS: Simon and Jolanta Bradley   OPEN: Sun to Fri L 12 to 3, all week D 6 to 11   CLOSED: 1 week Christmas   MEALS: Set L Mon to Fri £10 (2 courses) to £14, Set L Sun £15 (2 courses) to £18 (inc wine), Set D Mon to Fri 6 to 7 £10 (2 courses) to £14, Set D £22 (2 courses) to £27   SERVICE: 12.5% (optional), card slips closed   CARDS: Amex, Delta, MasterCard, Switch, Visa   DETAILS: 63 seats. Private parties: 63 main room. Vegetarian meals. Children's helpings. No cigars/pipes in dining room. Wheelchair access (not WC). Music. No mobile phones. Air-conditioned   ⊖ Swiss Cottage  £5

## ▲ Brasserie Roux                     NEW ENTRY   map 15

Sofitel St James Hotel, 8 Pall Mall, SW1Y 5NG                     COOKING 4
TEL: (020) 7968 2900   FAX: (020) 7747 2242                     CLASSIC FRENCH
£25–£68

Brasseries come in all shapes, sizes and styles, but given Albert Roux's involvement, this one can at least claim some sort of link with the classic French kind. The building – once a bank – is as solid as they come, with walls thick enough to keep out traffic noise, and three of the biggest lampshades you are ever likely to see, hanging from the high ceiling. It is a big operation, turning out some 50 savoury dishes grouped into appetisers (hot and cold), pasta, salads, fish and shellfish, and main courses. Apart from a few obscure salads (Camargo, Gabrielle and Surville are explained by the waiter), most of these are as familiar as they are comforting, taking in saucisson lyonnaise with warm potato salad, a headless, firm-fleshed Dover sole on the bone with brown butter, and breadcrumbed pig's trotter with French fries and béarnaise.

In these circumstances we may not expect absolute precision, and we don't get it (some of the accompaniments can be a bit of a letdown), but we do get mostly fine ingredients generally well handled, including a deeply satisfying smoked haddock tartlet, topped with a well-timed poached egg and drizzled with hollandaise, and flavourful veal kidney, cut into smallish pieces, with a mustard-shy stock-based sauce. Finish perhaps with praline tart, or a wedge of dense, rich, smooth, dark chocolate truffle. Professional French service is on the ball, and prices are not too high, making this an attractive venue for its largely affluent middle-aged customers. There are enough wines around the £20 mark on the varietally arranged list to keep bills within reason.

CHEF: John Savage   PROPRIETOR: Accor UK   OPEN: all week 12 to 3, 5.30 to 11.30 (11 Sun) MEALS: alc (main courses £7 to £22). Set D 5.30 to 7 and 10.45 to 11.30 £15   SERVICE: 12.5% (optional), card slips closed   CARDS: Amex, Delta, Diners, MasterCard, Switch, Visa   DETAILS: 90 seats. Private parties: 100 main room, 2 to 12 private rooms. Vegetarian meals. Children's helpings. Wheelchair access (also WC). Music. Air-conditioned   ACCOMMODATION: 186 rooms, all with bath/shower. TV. Phone. Room only £195 to £295. Rooms for disabled. Baby facilities ⊖ Piccadilly Circus

---

*All details are as accurate as possible at the time of going to press, but chefs and owners often change, and it is wise to check by telephone before making a special journey. Many readers have been disappointed when set-price bargain meals are no longer available. Ask when booking.*

---

# Brasserie St Quentin

map 14

243 Brompton Road, SW3 2EP
TEL: (020) 7589 8005   FAX: (020) 7584 6064
EMAIL: reservations@brasseriestquentin
WEBSITE: www.brasseriestquentin.co.uk

COOKING 3
FRENCH
£26–£63

This old stager was reacquired early in 2002 from Groupe Chez Gérard by its founder, Hugh O'Neill, who installed Nana Akuffo – latterly in charge of the River Room at the Savoy Hotel – in the hot seat. Its Parisian tone lives on: small tables with white cloths, mirror-hung cream walls, a wooden floor and an array of chandeliers provide the backdrop to a lively, buzzy atmosphere and 'simple but well-cooked food and pleasant service'.

Many original St Quentin dishes feature (such as feuilleté d'escargots à la crème d'ail), while others are more English than before (including grilled Cranborne traditional-breed pork sausages with mash, for instance). Among dishes that have pleased have been an 'excellent' deep-flavoured soupe de poissons, slow-roast and confit spring lamb with sauce smitane, and apple crumble with vanilla ice cream. The annotated, international wine list has a Francophile bent, with house wines at £11.50 (£3 a glass).

CHEF: Nana Akuffo   PROPRIETORS: Hugh O'Neill and others   OPEN: all week 11 to 11.30   MEALS: alc (main courses £8.50 to £22). Set L £11.75 (2 courses) to £14.50   SERVICE: 12.5% (optional) CARDS: Amex, Diners, MasterCard, Switch, Visa   DETAILS: 55 seats. 4 seats outside. Private parties: 10 main room, 10 to 25 private rooms. Vegetarian meals. Children's helpings. Wheelchair access (not WC). No music. Air-conditioned   ⊖ South Kensington, Knightsbridge

# ▲ Brown's Hotel, Restaurant 1837 ▮

map 15

Albemarle Street, W1S 4BP
TEL: (020) 7493 6020   FAX: (020) 7493 9381
EMAIL: 1837@brownshotel.com
WEBSITE: www.brownshotel.com

COOKING 5
MODERN EUROPEAN
£47–£77

Considered 'a haven of quiet and comfort' just off Piccadilly, 1837 has its own entrance next door to the hotel of which it is a part. A high-ceilinged, oak-panelled dining room with plush gold curtains is all elegant refinement, and service, from a formally dressed brigade, is 'near-impeccable'. One might already guess (correctly) that luxuries will figure prominently, but there is more to Andrew Turner's cooking than merely expensive ingredients. Menu language tends to be brief and to the point, although it takes time out to inform us that it is not just any old scallop that is served with cauliflower purée and a caper and raisin sauce, but a Celtic Sea scallop: so there. But these materials, even down to 'perhaps the best smoked salmon I have eaten', are indeed well sourced.

Central to the operation are seven-, eight- and nine-course Grazing Menus, offering a succession of small portions from the carte. Nothing new in that, perhaps, but their variety is impressive, taking in 'watercress chlorophyll, grey shrimp tortellini', sturgeon parfait with horseradish, and 'rack of English lamb, gribiche, sweetbreads and lambs milk dauphinoise'. Indeed choice on the carte is so generous that it seems churlish not to try as many dishes as possible. To finish, crème brûlée arrives in several little pastry cases, each with a different flavour under the crackle.

Spread over more than 40 pages of a leather-bound list is an amazing array of wines from around the world. Coverage of France is deep, with the Loire, Alsace and other classic areas making the biggest waves, but even Mexico gets a look-in. Mark-ups can be high in some areas, with the New World offering best value, but prices are partially mitigated by a 300-strong selection by the glass, which changes every two months. Bottle prices start at £18 and move upwards swiftly.

CHEF: Andrew Turner   PROPRIETOR: Raffles International Hotels   OPEN: Mon to Fri L 12 to 2.30, Mon to Sat D 7 to 10   CLOSED: 26 Dec to 7 Jan, Easter weekend, bank hols   MEALS: Set L £24 (2 courses) to £31, Set D £38 (2 courses) to £45. Grazing Menu (7 to 9 courses) £37 to £45 available at D   SERVICE: not inc   CARDS: Amex, Delta, Diners, MasterCard, Switch, Visa   DETAILS: 55 seats. Private parties: 70 main room, 4 to 70 private rooms. Wheelchair access (also WC). Occasional music. Air-conditioned   ACCOMMODATION: 118 rooms, all with bath/shower. TV. Phone. Room only £290 to £320 (exc VAT). Rooms for disabled   ⊖ Green Park

## Café du Jardin ♥                                                    map 15

28 Wellington Street, WC2E 7BD
TEL: (020) 7836 8769 and 8760                                       COOKING 1
FAX: (020) 7836 4123                                          MODERN BRITISH
WEBSITE: www.lecafedujardin.com                                     £21–£53

Despite its high ceilings and large windows, the dining room can feel rather cramped and noisy, thanks to small tables and hard surfaces. Its theatreland location explains the evening opening times, and the short set-price menu that might feature sweetcorn and pea risotto, grilled chicken breast on horseradish mash, and creamed rice pudding. Much more ambitious choice on the carte may lead to some inaccuracies, although quite a few of the starters are salad variations: baby spinach, blue cheese, candied walnuts and croûtons impressed one visitor.

Sound materials underpin the operation, although seasoning can be underdone and not all dishes are equally successful. Among those receiving praise have been steak and chips, potato and Parmesan dumplings, and gooseberry crumble with yoghurt sorbet. Service has varied from 'poor' to 'helpful', hardly a ringing endorsement for the 15 per cent 'optional' service charge. Wines range from classic French styles via new-wave Italian to trend-setting New World bottles. Although choice is limited under £20, it opens up substantially beyond the £25 mark. Fourteen wines are available by the glass, including house red and white vin de table for £9.75. A separate 'fine wine' list reads like a 'Who's Who' in the world of wine, taking in top names from France and throughout the world, including many mature vintages. A new branch, Le Deuxième, has opened nearby (see entry).

CHEF: Tony Howorth   PROPRIETORS: Robert Seigler and Tony Howorth   OPEN: Mon to Sat 12 to 3, 5.30 to 12, Sun noon to 11   CLOSED: 24 and 25 Dec   MEALS: alc (main courses £8.50 to £15). Set L and D Mon to Sat 5.30 to 7.30 and 10 to 12, noon to 11 Sun £9.95 (2 courses) to £13.50 SERVICE: 15% (optional), card slips closed   CARDS: Amex, Delta, Diners, MasterCard, Switch, Visa   DETAILS: 100 seats. 20 seats outside. Private parties: 60 main room. Vegetarian meals. Wheelchair access (not WC). Music. Air-conditioned   ⊖ Covent Garden

# Café Fish

map 15

36–40 Rupert Street, W1V 7FR
TEL: (020) 7287 8989   FAX: (020) 7287 8400
EMAIL: lb-cafefish@groupechezgerard.co.uk
WEBSITE: www.santeonline.co.uk

COOKING 2
SEAFOOD
£21–£69

There is no standing on ceremony at this (or indeed at any) branch of Chez Gérard's Livebait operation. Closely packed Formica-topped tables, a bare wooden floor, and basic cutlery and glassware do not preclude a certain sense of style though, and fishy diagrams everywhere help to identify which bit of which species you're about to eat. Rock oysters in threes, sixes and dozens, Atlantic prawns by the pint or half-pint, or – even more demotically – a bowl of whelks, might kick things off. Main-course preparations encompass some lively modern ideas. Setting the pace might be roast cod with herb mash and salsa rossa, sea bass and fantail crevettes with spiced-up linguine, or monkfish wrapped in Bayonne ham and served with wild mushroom risotto and Parmesan. Or you could just as easily go for a Dover sole, simply grilled and anointed with lemon oil. There are mushy peas as well as mash to go with it all, and chocolate brownie, or blackberry and apple crumble to finish. The short wine list, mostly white, opens with house vins de pays at £9.75.

CHEF: Martin Manning   PROPRIETOR: Groupe Chez Gérard   OPEN: Sun 2 to 9, Mon to Sat 12 to 11.30   CLOSED: 25 Dec   MEALS: alc (main courses £9 to £28.50). Set L £10.50 (2 courses) to £12.50, Set D 5.30 to 7 and 10 to 11 £12.50 (2 courses) to £15   SERVICE: 12.5% (optional), card slips closed   CARDS: Amex, Delta, Diners, MasterCard, Switch, Visa   DETAILS: 200 seats. Children's helpings. No-smoking area. Wheelchair access (also WC). Music. Air-conditioned
⊖ Piccadilly Circus, Leicester Square

---

# Café Japan £

map 13

626 Finchley Road, NW11 7RR
TEL: (020) 8455 6854

COOKING 5
JAPANESE
£20–£33

After a period of uncertainty this bright, always busy place (no bookings taken) has become a sushi house, serving real sushi, freshly made to order. All hot dishes, including the old 'special menu', have gone. Sashimi of any fish is also available as are plain rice, and miso soup, the essential accompaniment to sushi. A wide range of fish is supplemented by specials, including seasonal delicacies, and the main list includes exotica such as hand-formed nigiri with turbot fins, or flying fish roe. Specially designed for connoisseurs of slipperiness is sea urchin with raw quail egg. Vegetable ingredients – used mainly in small nori-wrapped rolls – include cucumber, cooked gourd, and wild burdock, as well as pickled specialities such as soya bean (natto), radish, and plum. Shiso, the king of herbs, comes with salmon roe, while inside-out rolls with sesame seeds take in eel and cucumber, and salmon and avocado. Among modern large rolls are California, salmon and avocado with mayonnaise, and 'spider' with soft-shelled crab. Chirashi sushi is good value at £11.80 for a large bowl of rice with raw fish on top, perhaps tuna alone, or salmon and salmon roe. A de luxe version at £14 comes with assorted luxuries including turbot, fresh-water shrimp, salmon roe and sea-urchin. Pickles, Korean style kim-chee or assorted kounomono, contrast wondrously with the sushi. Finish with highly praised ice creams (green tea, red bean or chestnut) or dorayaki (cold pancake filled with sweet red bean paste). Ozeki saké is served hot or cold, or drink Japanese beer.

CHEF/PROPRIETOR: Koichi Konnai   OPEN: Sat and Sun L 12 to 2, Wed to Sun D 6 to 10   CLOSED: Christmas, Easter, 12 Aug to 2 Sept   MEALS: alc (main courses £6 to £12.50). Set L £5.90 to £11.90 (all 2 courses), Set D £12 (2 courses) to £16.50   SERVICE: not inc   CARDS: Delta, MasterCard, Switch, Visa   DETAILS: 40 seats. Music. Air-conditioned   ⊖ Golders Green

## Cafe Spice Namaste                              maps 12 and 13

16 Prescot Street, E1 8AZ
TEL: (020) 7488 9242   FAX: (020) 7481 0508                        COOKING 3
247 Lavender Hill, SW11 1JW                                          INDIAN
TEL: (020) 7738 1717   FAX: (020) 7738 1666                       £28–£65

The red-hot eye-catching colours of these restaurants' décor still startles and pleases first-time visitors, and the friendliness of the service is undoubted, even if its efficiency may vary. Menus are some of London's most enticing, even if Cyrus Todiwala is no longer at the cutting edge of Indian cooking. Nor, in an inspector's opinion, was the cooking at Lavender Hill as exciting as the menu promised. Both the shared ordinary menu, and the weekly speciality list at Prescot Street, offer dishes as familiar as sheikh kebab, and as bizarre as Hungarian wild boar chipolatas ('rarity assured', they say, and we can't disagree). Among vegetarian options is surati undhiu, a curry of raw banana, baby aubergine, sweet potato, broad beans, violet yam and beetroot. If you make it as far as dessert, consider lagan nu custard, a rich, eggy version of crème caramel served with chopped nuts. Both branches share a short, decently priced wine list. For connoisseurs of eccentric drinks, Celis is good: unfiltered Belgian white wheat beer from, of all places, Austin, Texas.

CHEFS: Prescot Street Cyrus Todiwala and Angelo Collaco. Lavender Hill Briston de Sousa PROPRIETOR: Cyrus Todiwala   OPEN: Prescot Street Mon to Fri L 12 to 3, Mon to Sat D 6.15 to 10.30. Lavender Hill Sun L 12 to 3, Tue to Sun D 6 to 11.30 (10.30 Sun)   CLOSED: 25 Dec to 1 Jan, bank hols   MEALS: Prescot Street alc (main courses £10 to £16); Set L and D £30 to £40; light L menu also available. Lavender Hill alc (main courses £8.50 to £13); Set L and D £18 to £25 SERVICE: 12.5% (optional), card slips closed   CARDS: Amex, Delta, Diners, MasterCard, Switch, Visa   DETAILS: Prescot Street 140. Private parties 170 main room; Lavender Hill 86 seats. Private parties. 100 main room. Vegetarian meals. Children's helpings. Wheelchair access (also WC). Music. Air-conditioned   ⊖ Prescot Street: Tower Hill; Lavender Hill: Clapham Common   £5

## Cambio de Tercio                                      map 14

163 Old Brompton Road, SW5 0LJ                                    COOKING 3
TEL: (020) 7244 8970   FAX: (020) 7373 8817              MODERN SPANISH
                                                                 £38–£64

The name is a bullfighting reference, appropriately enough for this thorough-going Spanish restaurant with bold décor, 'bubbling' ambience and lively and interesting food. Presentation can be very straightforward: a plateful of unadorned Ibérico ham makes a first-class if one-dimensional starter. Galician octopus with a smooth, marmalade-like sauce has also been well received: 'I could have eaten this, tapas-style, all night.' Among main courses, Segovianstyle roast suckling pig has impressed for its classy appearance and excellent sweet crackling, while a dish of mixed fresh fish has proved 'pleasingly distinctive', thanks not least to its accompaniments of crunchy asparagus in sea salt, and clams marinière.

To finish, there may be hot chocolate fondant with mint and clotted cream ice cream, a light cinnamon mousse with Rioja sorbet and pear, or a persuasively Spanish selection of cheeses in prime condition, served with quince preserve. Service can be a bit brusque. Unfortunately, a wine list was not made available to us before going to press; if it is anything like last year's, its collection of top-rank producers and bright sparks from throughout Spain (Rioja and Ribera del Duero being particular strengths) and the rest of the vinous world will be worth a detour. The details below are also uncertain – they date from the last edition of the Guide – as they too have not been confirmed by the restaurant.

CHEF: Javier Jimenez   PROPRIETORS: Abel Lusa and David Rivero   OPEN: all week 12.15 to 2.30, 7 to 11.30   CLOSED: 2 weeks at Christmas   MEALS: alc (main courses £13.50 to £15.50) SERVICE: not inc, 12.5% for parties of 6 or more   CARDS: Amex, Delta, MasterCard, Switch, Visa DETAILS: 45 seats. 6 seats outside. Private parties: 20 private room. Wheelchair access (not WC). Music   ⊖ Gloucester Road

## Cantaloupe £                                                              map 13

35–42 Charlotte Road, EC2A 3PD
TEL: (020) 7613 4411   FAX: (020) 7613 4111                      COOKING 3
EMAIL: info@cantaloupe.co.uk                          IBERIAN/SOUTH AMERICAN
WEBSITE: www.cantaloupe.co.uk                                      £26–£44

'Look for the flaming C sign,' advised one visitor. It's a rusted metal logo that hangs over the entrance, and 'sums up the restaurant nicely – no-nonsense, industrial, with a touch of fire (well, chillies)'. There are two bar areas, one a utilitarian space with concrete floor, plain wooden tables and sofas, the other a little more fancy, with tall stools at high tables; the dining area is on a raised section in the latter, decorated colourfully with a modern, informal feel. Culinary influences come from Spain, Portugal and South America, which means an array of dishes from braised hake with asparagus to mussels and judion beans, from pork meatballs with saffron rice and tomato sauce, to a salad of avocado, grapefruit and papaya with a coriander, lime and chilli dressing. Canja, a thin chicken broth from Brazil containing pumpkin, rice and lots of coriander, made a favourable impression at an inspection meal, as did roast salt-cod with mango, rum and chilli salsa, sweet potatoes and fried plantain. To finish, there may be Peruvian dark chocolate and coffee pot, or a savoury alternative of Spanish cheeses with membrillo jelly. Prices on the short wine list open at £11.50.

CHEF: Henry Brereton   PROPRIETORS: Richard Bigg and Nigel Foster   OPEN: Mon to Fri L 12 to 3, Mon to Sat D 6 (7 Sat) to 12   CLOSED: 25 and 26 Dec, 1 Jan, Aug bank hol   MEALS: alc (main courses £9.50 to £12.50). Bar menu available   SERVICE: 12.5% (optional), card slips closed CARDS: Amex, Delta, Diners, MasterCard, Switch, Visa   DETAILS: 50 seats. Private parties: 50 main room. Vegetarian meals. Wheelchair access (also WC). Music. Air-conditioned   ⊖ Old Street, Liverpool Street

# ▲ The Capital ♟

map 14

22 Basil Street, SW3 1AT
TEL: (020) 7591 1202   FAX: (020) 7225 0011
EMAIL: restaurant@capitalhotel.co.uk
WEBSITE: www.capitalhotel.co.uk

COOKING 8
FRENCH
£40–£149

Small, classy and intimate, the Capital offers a luxury retreat from the 'rigours' of Knightsbridge shopping (yes, a male reporter). Its geometric carpets, heavy curtains, and fabrics with autumnal foliage are 'refreshingly out of date' when compared to the metropolitan cool for which so many places aim, but it is comfortable and attracts a flood of enthusiastic reports. The enterprise is precise and professional in all departments, the cooking is assured and confident, and some are convinced that Eric Chavot is performing better than ever. His food is ambitious, he is fearless about tackling complexity, and his shopping list of luxury ingredients includes scallops (with black pudding), pan-fried duck foie gras with Puy lentils and girolles, and pot-roast pigeon with truffle jus.

This is not a place just to admire the cooking and note how clever it is; reporters come away with a feeling of satisfaction that their appetites have been agreeably sated. Sweet, plump, seared langoustines have come on a bed of earthy aïoli potatoes with deep-fried chorizo, accompanied by an unlikely-sounding yet sturdy and flavourful bruschetta with pecorino; and a New Year's Day visitor enjoyed a benchmark tournedos Rossini, with 'excellence all round' from beef fillet, duck foie gras and Périgord truffles. Even the best kitchens can sometimes have an off day, and one meal which got off to a 'stunning' start was followed by a large veal cutlet crudely coated in cheese that was 'like eating a bus'. But that meal has provided the only quibble all year. The consensus – that this remains one of London's finest restaurants – is amply testified by a succession of recommendations, not least among fish dishes: pan-fried turbot with Jerusalem artichokes, accompanied by a ravioli of wild mushrooms and a few garlic crisps; and fresh, beautifully timed sea bass on a bed of boulangère potatoes with a slice of velvety boudin blanc.

Simple, clear flavours are delivered in, for example, a starter of baked goats' cheese on a mix of truffle-oiled leek and endive, and dishes can be 'exhilarating in their execution and combination', judging by a beautifully crafted risotto of 'dazzlingly fresh' king crab with a frothy truffle cappuccino. Even such repertoire standards as tuna niçoise and boeuf bourguignonne are well presented, each a reworking of a traditional idea, the latter deploying a large chunk of beef and a garnish of rich stock containing the obligatory lardons, onions and mushrooms. Café liégeois is another adaptation, this one consisting of a bitter coffee granita and a rich, chocolate-flavoured crème anglaise with some chocolate 'millinery' on top. Bread-and-butter pudding is 'as far from school lunches as can be imagined', and an ace chocolate fondant is accompanied by a fine hazelnut meringue and 'the best pistachio ice cream I've ever tasted'.

Cheeses (from La Fromagerie) are kept in peak condition and knowledgeably served from a domed trolley. Bread is first class, as are the coffee and petits fours, the set-price lunch is considered a bargain, and discreet, efficient and highly skilled service is provided by staff who are relaxed yet utterly professional. The wine list is definite connoisseurs' territory. No surprise that France gets the lion's share of attention, of course. Lovers of fine, mature Bordeaux and Burgundy in particular will find much of interest here, but wines from elsewhere in Europe and the New World are chosen with equal care. The sticking point is prices: mark-ups (on already pricey wines) are high, and there is precious little under £20. Fourteen classy wines by the glass sell for £4 to £9.50, and own-label Gamay and Sauvignon Blanc are £14.50 a bottle.

CHEF: Eric Chavot   PROPRIETORS: Joseph and David Levin   OPEN: all week 12 to 2.15, 7 to 11 CLOSED: D 25 Dec   MEALS: alc D (main courses £25). Set L £27.50, Set D £65   SERVICE: 12.5% (optional), card slips closed   CARDS: Amex, Delta, Diners, MasterCard, Switch, Visa   DETAILS: 35 seats. Private parties: 6 main room, 6 to 24 private rooms. Vegetarian meals. No children under 10. No cigars/pipes in dining room. Wheelchair access (not WC). No music. No mobile phones. Air-conditioned   ACCOMMODATION: 49 rooms, all with bath/shower. TV. Phone. Room only £170 to £375. Baby facilities (*The Which? Hotel Guide*)   ⊖ Knightsbridge

# Le Caprice                                                            map 15

Arlington House, Arlington Street, SW1A 1RT                    COOKING 4
TEL: (020) 7629 2239   FAX: (020) 7493 9040                MODERN BRITISH
EMAIL: reservations@le-caprice.co.uk                            £32–£83

'Not the place for a quiet chat,' reckoned one visitor to this busy, still-trendy sister of the Ivy just around the corner from the Ritz. Although a bit of a walk from Shaftesbury Avenue and Drury Lane, it claims to be a 'theatre restaurant': hence the early and late dinner sittings. Anyone in search of comfort food will not go away disappointed; the roll call includes eggs Benedict, risotto nero, deep-fried haddock with chips and tartare sauce, and grilled rib of beef with tarragon and shallot butter. Sunday brunch is, if anything, even more indulgent. Ideas are plucked from anywhere that suits, taking in anything from Caesar salad to breast of corn-fed chicken in a Szechuan vegetable broth with hoisin.

Seasonal additions bring welcome variety. Springtime, for example, sees asparagus soup with morels and wild garlic, St George's mushrooms with a fillet of halibut, and pea shoots with a pork loin chop. Vegetarians and vegans are catered for, as are lovers of nursery puddings such as Bramley apple crumble, banana sticky toffee pudding, and baked Alaska. Details (such as freshly squeezed orange juice) are well handled, and wines are well chosen at all levels. House Trebbiano is £11.50, Coteaux du Tricastin £13.50.

CHEFS: Kevin Gratton and Tim Hughes   PROPRIETOR: Signature Restaurants plc   OPEN: all week 12 to 3 (3.30 Sun), 5.30 (6 Sun) to 12   CLOSED: 25 and 26 Dec, 1 Jan, Aug bank hol   MEALS: alc (main courses £9 to £22). Cover £1.50. Brunch menu Sun   SERVICE: not inc   CARDS: Amex, Delta, Diners, MasterCard, Switch, Visa   DETAILS: 80 seats. Private parties: 8 main room. Vegetarian meals. Wheelchair access (not WC). Music. Air-conditioned   ⊖ Green Park

---

*'Service was by a Lancashire female helper who didn't pronounce a single French word correctly, and a Frenchman who didn't pronounce a single English word correctly.'*
(On eating in Greater Manchester)

---

# Cecconi's ♟ 🍴

map 15

5A Burlington Gardens, W1X 1LE
TEL: (020) 7434 1500   FAX: (020) 7494 2440
WEBSITE: www.cecconis.co.uk

COOKING 3
ITALIAN
£35–£106

Cecconi's discreet exterior contrasts with the ostentatious splendour of the Royal Academy, the rear of which is directly opposite this Mayfair venue. It has a sleek, understated and sophisticated feel – 'reminiscent of a club' for one reporter – and the bar that runs along one side of the dining room is 'long and thin, attractive and alluring, like much of the clientele'. Food is unmistakably Italian, offering plenty of choice and a range of old favourites, such as veal escalopes with wild mushrooms, or osso buco, alongside some less common items: a salad of scallops and pumpkin, for example, or chargrilled swordfish with wild fennel.

Presentation is a strong point, as in one reporter's starter of supple carpaccio adorned with streaks of delicate mustard mayonnaise and capers dotted artfully about. Flavours also often make a powerful impact: pungently aromatic rosemary to season roast chicken wrapped in Parma ham, for example. To finish, go for tiramisù, or something a bit more interesting like seadas: Sardinian-style pecorino and lemon ravioli with vanilla ice cream. The sommelier is commended as very knowledgeable, which is just as well; unless you have a degree in fine Italian wines you may need his help to negotiate the heavyweight list. It combines Super-Tuscans and Barolos galore with forward-looking producers from throughout the length and breadth of the country (plus a few Bordeaux and New World wines), but the drawback is cost: three-figure prices are not unusual, and there is little under £20. Southern Italy and a short 'sommelier's selection' are the places to look for value. Bottle prices start at £15 and move up swiftly.

CHEF: Pasquale Amico   PROPRIETOR: Hani Farsi   OPEN: all week 12 to 3, 6 to 11   MEALS: alc exc Sun L (main courses £9 to £28.50). Set L Sun £19.50. Cover £1.50. Bar menu available   SERVICE: 12.5% (optional), card slips closed   CARDS: Amex, Delta, Diners, MasterCard, Switch, Visa   DETAILS: 86 seats. Private parties: 10 main room. Vegetarian meals. Children's helpings. Wheelchair access (also WC). Occasional music. No mobile phones. Air-conditioned   ⊖ Green Park, Piccadilly Circus ⓔ5

# Chapter Two

| NEW ENTRY | map 12

43–45 Montpelier Vale, SE3 0TJ
TEL: (020) 8333 2666   FAX: (020) 8355 8399
WEBSITE: www.chaptersrestaurants.co.uk

COOKING 4
MODERN EUROPEAN
£31–£58

Chapter Two is the younger sibling of Chapter One in Farnborough, Kent (see entry). The restaurant occupies a narrow shopfront in Blackheath and is set over two floors, the ground floor giving way to a larger basement via a spiral staircase. Done out in light paint, steel and linen, the look is altogether fresh. This is obviously a popular place for families of all ages to celebrate, and repeat business, so the management informs us, requires a frequently changing menu. Despite a dish of winter fruits (in May) at inspection, the restaurant keeps pretty well to a seasonal rhythm, offering summer truffles (in a risotto) and peas and broad beans (with stuffed breast of chicken) in July.

The modern European range extends as far as Sweden, pulling in gravad lax with sweet mustard and dill sauce, and sweet-cured herrings with potato and horseradish salad. Main courses tend to be substantial, as in honey and mustard pork belly with root vegetables and mash, and roast lamb rump well provisioned with a faggot, lentils and mash. Desserts run from light (lemon tart with mixed berry compote and lemon sorbet) to weighty (blueberry madeleine with strawberry ripple ice cream and a florentine). Service is friendly and helpful. Wines are divided almost evenly between France and the rest of the world, with some decent producers; most are under £25, and seven house wines are £13.50 to £18.

CHEF: Lyndon Edwards  PROPRIETOR: Selective Restaurants Group  OPEN: all week 12 to 2.30 (3.30 Sun), 6.30 to 10.30 (11 Fri and Sat, 9.30 Sun)  CLOSED: 2 to 4 Jan  MEALS: Set L Mon to Sat £14.50 (2 courses) to £18.50, Set L Sun £14.50 (2 courses) to £16.50, Set D Sun to Thur £16.50 (2 courses) to £19.50, Set D Fri and Sat £22.50  SERVICE: 12.5% (optional), card slips closed  CARDS: Amex, Delta, Diners, MasterCard, Switch, Visa  DETAILS: 75 seats. Private parties: 50 main room, 24 to 50 private rooms. Vegetarian meals. Children's helpings. Wheelchair access (also WC). Music. No mobile phones. Air-conditioned  (£5)

# Le Chardon                                              map 12

65 Lordship Lane, SE22 8EP                               COOKING 2
TEL: (020) 8299 1921   FAX: (020) 8693 0959              FRENCH
                                                         £20–£45

'Chardon' means thistle, and images of the eponymous weed appear on the tiled walls of this old-school French bistro. The Gallic theme is emphasised by Parisian street signs and there are paintings for sale. Classic provincial cooking is the order of the day, and the kitchen's fondness for the regions shows in plateaux de fruits de mer, and in dishes such as a stew of queen scallops with wild rice and mushrooms. Meat and game are well represented by marinated lamb shank with flageolet beans, or slow-cooked pheasant with smoked bacon, thyme and cider sauce, while traditional roasts (served till 6 on Sundays) should please English patriots. Around 40 wines keep faith with the provinces, although there are a few bottles from further afield. House wine is £9.95 (£2.80 a glass).

CHEFS: Didier Lemond and Didier Dixneuf  PROPRIETOR: Robert Benayer  OPEN: all week 12 to 11  CLOSED: 1 week from 26 Dec, bank hols  MEALS: alc (main courses £9.50 to £12.50). Set L (to 5pm) £6.95 to £9.95 (both 2 courses), Set L Sun £13.50  SERVICE: 10% (optional)  CARDS: Amex, Delta, Diners, MasterCard, Switch, Visa  DETAILS: 60 seats. 30 seats outside. Private parties: 60 main room. Vegetarian meals. Children's helpings. Wheelchair access (not WC). Occasional music. Air-conditioned  (£5)

# Chez Bruce  ▮ ✦                                         map 12

2 Bellevue Road, SW17 7EG                                COOKING 6
TEL: (020) 8672 0114   FAX: (020) 8767 6648              MODERN BRITISH
                                                         £39–£74

Refurbishment has produced a relaxing setting. Upstairs (non-smoking) may be 'like a tea room … and dimly lit', but natural light from windows over Wandsworth Common illuminates the main room's plain wooden floor, wooden chairs and close-together tables. An appealing three-course set-price menu (with one or two price supplements) oddly doesn't allow a two-course option, even at lunch, but it is stuffed with goodies.

Bruce Poole sets out his contemporary stall with a Beaufort and potato tourte, cauliflower soup with deep-fried mackerel and horseradish cream, and (in winter) some rib-sticking items such as stuffed pig's trotter with saddle of rabbit, or oxtail pappardelle. He also plays to the gallery with deep-fried plaice and tartare sauce, and indulges by adding foie gras and béarnaise to a warm duck confit salad. A few 'careless slips' at inspection took the shine off an otherwise decent meal, but the kitchen can turn out some fine dishes, for example a flavourful, accurately timed free-range chicken breast in a pool of cooking juices, sitting next to a salty fondant turnip topped by Savoy cabbage stuffed with chicken livers and mousse.

Cheeses are a strength – well sourced and described, and served in fine condition – while among desserts the assiettes of chocolate and coffee come in for high praise, the latter taking in a smooth ice cream, a silky cake, a sleek mousse topped by an Irish coffee sabayon, and a delicate meringue layered with crème Chantilly. Service is from a smartly dressed international brigade, and although wine service can leave something to be desired, the wines themselves – 25 pages of carefully chosen bottles from around the world – are well worth a close look. Australia, the Rhône, Burgundy, Bordeaux and Italy are high points, and mark-ups are refreshingly un-greedy. Thirty wines are available by the glass, thirty-six by the half-bottle. Prices start at £16 for red Vin de Pays de Vaucluse.

CHEF/PROPRIETOR: Bruce Poole   OPEN: Sun 12.30 to 3, 7 to 10.30, Mon to Fri 12 to 2, 7 (6.30 Fri) to 10.30, Sat 12.30 to 2.30, 6.30 to 10.30   CLOSED: 24 to 26 Dec   MEALS: Set L £23.50, Set D £30   SERVICE: 12.5% (optional), card slips closed   CARDS: Amex, Delta, Diners, MasterCard, Switch, Visa   DETAILS: 75 seats. Private parties: 65 main room, 12 to 18 private rooms. No babies at D. No smoking in 1 dining room. Wheelchair access (not WC). No music. No mobile phones. Air-conditioned   ⊖ Clapham South, Balham

## Chez Moi                                                                 map 12

1 Addison Avenue, W11 4QS
TEL: (020) 7603 8267   FAX: (020) 7603 3898                         COOKING 3
EMAIL: chezmoi-rest@hotmail.com                                   FRENCH-PLUS
WEBSITE: www.chezmoi-restaurant.co.uk                              £25–£59

Continuing in exactly the same fashion that has seen it through the last 35 years, Chez Moi is a French restaurant from the old school. Reports this year have been mixed – perhaps it is all a little old-fashioned and uncomplicated for some tastes – but one reporter returning 10 years after an earlier visit happily found everything as he remembered and was well satisfied with a meal of oeuf d'amour (poached egg in a tomato with herbs), well-timed seared scallops, venison with celeriac purée, and calves' kidneys in mustard sauce with potato purée, finishing with an intensely flavoured pot au chocolat. The kitchen is not entirely stuck in the French way of thinking, though, and starters might also include tom yum gung, or chicken dhosa, while among main courses might be Moroccan lamb tagine; there are also a few vegetarian options. Service has been variable, but at its best is considered 'on the ball and pleasant'. Some New World wines are tucked away towards the back of the French-dominated wine list. Prices start at £10.75.

CHEF: Richard Walton   PROPRIETORS: Richard Walton and Colin Smith   OPEN: Tue to Fri L 12.30 to 1.45, Mon to Sat D 7 to 10.45   CLOSED: bank hols   MEALS: alc (main courses £13 to £18). Set L £15   SERVICE: not inc   CARDS: Amex, Delta, Diners, MasterCard, Switch, Visa   DETAILS: 45 seats. 16 seats outside. Vegetarian meals. Children's helpings. No babes in arms. No cigars/ pipes in dining room. Wheelchair access (not WC). No music. Air-conditioned   ⊖ Holland Park

# Chinon

map 12

23 Richmond Way, W14 0AS
TEL: (020) 7602 5968   FAX: (020) 7602 4082

COOKING 5
FRENCH-PLUS
£41–£49

Study the map carefully to find this personally run neighbourhood restaurant in a maze of one-way streets, and leave time to find a parking place. Its posters, paintings and ornaments seem to have been collected over the years, rather than picked off a designer's wish list, adding to its sense of individuality so capably fostered by owner Barbara Deane. Classical French cooking may be Jonathon Hayes's jumping-off point, but some offbeat variations add interest, and the bottom line is that he serves up fresh, high-quality ingredients in an attractive format.

Pasta is one of several favourite devices, appearing as a plate of small ravioli of cheese and spinach in a herby, lemony, garlicky, buttery froth, or as a single, whopping raviolo filled with crab and chopped leeks, served with a little bowl of well-balanced bisque. Ideas are sound, if a little unusual from time to time: for example, a large, crisp, filo pastry moneybag with a goats' cheese filling, served with a round of cold, tart and slightly sweet aubergine topped with spicy olives, and a pile of chutney scattered with pine nuts; a dish of pleasingly contrasting tastes, textures and temperatures. Dishes can be elaborate, yet with nothing inappropriate added, as in good-quality calf's liver, cooked just pink, on a pile of hash browns, topped with slices of crisp pancetta.

There is no choice when it comes to cheese (half a dozen French ones, all in good nick), or a plate of four different desserts: perhaps an expertly made rhubarb crème brûlée, a tart raspberry sorbet, rich gooey chocolate cake, and a poached pear. Portions are large, value is good, as is the bread, although service 'with major attitude' is a letdown. Other than house wine (£16), there is virtually nothing on the 50-strong list under £25; some important details are missing, and mark-ups are considered 'outrageous'. As always, the restaurant has not provided any information, so we cannot vouch for the accuracy of the following.

CHEF: Jonathon Hayes   PROPRIETORS: Barbara Deane and Jonathon Hayes   OPEN: Mon to Sat D only 7 to 10.45   CLOSED: phone to check   MEALS: Set D £21 (2 courses) to £25   SERVICE: 12.5% (optional), card slips closed   CARDS: Amex, Delta, MasterCard, Switch, Visa   DETAILS: 60 seats. 6 seats outside. Private parties: 30 main room, 30 private room. No children under 10. No cigars/ pipes in dining-room. Music. Air-conditioned   ⊖ Shepherd's Bush

# The Chiswick £

map 12

131 Chiswick High Road, W4 2ED
TEL: (020) 8994 6887   FAX: (020) 8994 5504
WEBSITE: www.thechiswick.co.uk

COOKING 3
MODERN EUROPEAN
£23–£55

An established part of Chiswick's quasi-Parisian pavement café lifestyle, this is regarded as a 'very enjoyable local restaurant' offering 'exceptional value'. It is hard to argue the point against an early-evening prix fixe that gives change out of £15 for beer-battered monkfish cheeks; gnocchi with chicken livers, bacon and sage butter; and pear and almond tart with crème fraîche ice cream. The main carte continues in similarly imaginative modern European vein, starters ranging from steamed cockles with parsley, chilli and garlic to globe artichoke fritters with trevisse and anchovy dip. Enterprising main-course creations may include steamed turbot with spiced rhubarb and white wine cream, but the kitchen is just as happy with more traditional fare, such as slow-cooked shoulder of lamb with mash and red wine sauce. And on a warm summer's day, with the front of the restaurant open to the world, what a better way to finish than with a granita of ginger beer, lime juice and vodka? The global list of around 50 fairly priced wines opens with six house selections by the glass (from £3), jug (from £9) or bottle (from £11.50).

CHEF: James Garvan   PROPRIETORS: Adam and Kate Robinson   OPEN: Sun to Fri L 12.30 (12 Sun) to 2.45 (3 Sun), Mon to Sat D 7 to 11   CLOSED: 25 and 26 Dec, 1 Jan, bank hols   MEALS: alc (main courses £6.50 to £18.50; not available 14 Feb, 31 Dec). Set L Mon to Fri £9.50 (2 courses) to £12.95, Set L Sun £12.50 (2 courses) to £15.50, Set D 7 to 8 £9.50 (2 courses) to £12.95   SERVICE: 12.5% (optional), card slips closed   CARDS: Amex, Delta, MasterCard, Switch, Visa   DETAILS: 64 seats. 10 seats outside. Private parties: 64 main room. Vegetarian meals. Children's helpings. No cigars/pipes in dining room. No music. Air-conditioned   ⊖ Turnham Green   £5

# Chor Bizarre 🍴

map 15

16 Albemarle Street, W1S 4HW
TEL: (020) 7629 9802 and 7629 8542
FAX: (020) 7493 7756
EMAIL: chorbizarrelondon@oldworldhospitality.com
WEBSITE: www.chorbizarrerestaurant.com

COOKING 1
INDIAN
£44–£80

The name sums up the wacky décor of this plush Indian restaurant, which is cluttered with artefacts and *objets d'art* collected from bazaars around the subcontinent: intricately carved chairs and mismatching tables (including one fashioned from an old four-poster bedstead complete with drapes) are typical of the curio-style furnishings. The cooking has a strong and roving regional accent: rasam is a southern Indian soup, while tandooris from the north range from salmon or king prawns to paneer cheese flavoured with 'a pinch of pickle'. Other intriguing possibilities include duck anarkali in an anise-flavoured red wine sauce, and sarson wali macchi (sole fillet in a whole-grain mustard and green peppercorn masala). Thalis, tiffins and Kashmiri tarami arrive on metal platters or banana leaves. The wine list has been assembled by Charles Metcalfe to match the food, dish by dish. Prices start at £14.50.

CHEF: Deepinder Singh Sondhi  PROPRIETOR: India's Restaurant Ltd  OPEN: Mon to Sat L 12 to 2.45, all week D 6 to 11  MEALS: alc (main courses £6.50 to £15). Set L and D £24  SERVICE: 12.5%, card slips closed  CARDS: Amex, Delta, Diners, MasterCard, Switch, Visa  DETAILS: 76 seats. Private parties: 60 main room, 15 to 30 private rooms. No smoking in 1 dining room. Music. Air-conditioned  ⊖ Green Park  (£5)

## Christopher's

map 15

18 Wellington Street, WC2E 7DD
TEL: (020) 7240 4222  FAX: (020) 7836 3506
EMAIL: info@christophers.uk.net
WEBSITE: www.christophersgrill.com

COOKING 1
CONTEMPORARY AMERICAN
£32–£84

The subtitle – 'American Grill' – will tell you all you need to know about this large-scale Covent Garden eatery, spread over three floors to accommodate the pre- and post-theatre hordes. It was due to undergo refurbishment as the Guide went to press, but the cooking's mix of classic and contemporary modes looks set to continue. Caesar salad, Maryland crab cake with red pepper mayo, and lobster Martini cocktail are typical of starters, while main courses may include grilled swordfish with braised fennel and caper salsa; New England lobster clambake with chorizo, corn and new potatoes; and – for the very hungry – a 10-ounce strip sirloin with béarnaise. Expect to finish with something like New York cheesecake. Wines are not particularly cheap – prices start at £15 – but there is a commendably large selection by the glass. A second branch is at 101 Buckingham Palace Road, tel. (020) 7976 5522, and a third (The Enterprise) at 35 Walton Street, tel. (020) 7584 3148.

CHEFS: Adrian Searing and Francis Agyepong  PROPRIETOR: Christopher Gilmour  OPEN: all week L 12 to 3 (3.30 Sat and Sun), Mon to Sat D 5 to 12  CLOSED: Christmas, New Year  MEALS: alc (main courses £11.50 to £28). Set D 5 to 7 and 10 to £12.50 (2 courses) to £16.50. Brunch menu available Sat and Sun. Cover 50p  SERVICE: 12.5%, card slips closed  CARDS: Amex, Delta, Diners, MasterCard, Switch, Visa  DETAILS: 150 seats. Private parties: 50 main room, 50 private room. Vegetarian meals. Children's helpings. No music. Air-conditioned  ⊖ Covent Garden

## Chutney Mary ▮ ⬠

map 12

535 King's Road, SW10 0SZ
TEL: (020) 7351 3113  FAX: (020) 7351 7694
EMAIL: action@realindianfood.com
WEBSITE: www.realindianfood.com

COOKING 2
INDIAN
£28–£76

Chutney Mary's makeover, after a dozen years, is a great improvement, producing a warm, modern, attractive space divided into three sections (one a conservatory), and a new kitchen presided over by a new chef. The menu has been freshened up too. A few favourites remain, but an emphasis on seafood now brings crab claws in garlic butter, half a dozen Loch Fyne oysters with a lime and chilli salsa, and lobster makhani with lobster tail bhajias.

Start, perhaps, with some Indian street food (Masala Zone in W1 is under the same ownership; see entry): a basket of little potato- and onion-based savouries enlivened with tamarind, cumin, pepper, ginger and coriander. The range takes in tandoori dishes – chicken tikka, lamb chops, and four large, fresh prawns served with a little pot of black dhal – and main courses offer a chance to taste four curry dishes on one plate: Mangalore prawn flavoured with coconut and tamarind; Goan chicken; slow-cooked lamb knuckle with a dark masala sauce; and an aubergine curry in yoghurt.

Although spicing may lack the expected vibrancy, desserts are a strength, offering a dark chocolate fondant with orange blossom lassi, chilled rice pudding with a mango and chilli salsa, and eclairs filled with good-quality shrikand served with chocolate sauce. Service is hard to fault, and the food's claims to be wine-friendly can be put to the test with an up-to-the-minute stylistically grouped list on which Australian wines and new-wave Italians dominate. The selections are an intriguing bunch, and have sensible tasting notes. Mark-ups are reasonable, with a fair proportion of the almost 100 wines priced at or below £20. House Italian starts at £12.50, or £3 per glass.

CHEF: Mr Rubinath   PROPRIETORS: Namita Panjabi and Ranjit Mathrani   OPEN: Sat and Sun L 12 to 2.30 (3 Sun), all week D 6.30 (6 Sun) to 11 (10.30 Sun)   CLOSED: 26 Dec   MEALS: alc (main courses L £13.50 to £17.50, D £13.50 to £24). Set L Sun £16   SERVICE: 12.5% (optional), card slips closed   CARDS: Amex, Diners, MasterCard, Switch, Visa   DETAILS: 150 seats. Private parties: 16 main room, 16 to 28 private rooms. Vegetarian meals. Children's helpings. Wheelchair access (not WC). Occasional music. Air-conditioned   ⊖ Fulham Broadway

# Cigala                                                          map 13

54 Lamb's Conduit Street, WC1N 3LW
TEL: (020) 7405 1717   FAX: (020) 7242 9949                    COOKING 3
EMAIL: info@cigala.co.uk                              SPANISH/MODERN EUROPEAN
WEBSITE: www.cigala.co.uk                                       £27–£58

Given the minimal décor – wooden floor and panels, white paint and tablecloths – it is customers who provide the colour, and indeed the noise when things gets busy. 'Good Spanish cooking' is what Jake Hodges delivers, from a carte that deals in classics from paella to migas (fried breadcrumbs) served with black pudding and a fried egg. Seafood options range from mussels cooked with fino and garlic, via gilt-head bream a la plancha, to a chunk of tender, tasty cuttlefish with green chillies, while meats tend to favour chicken and lamb. The latter might be grilled (with roast root vegetables and quince aïoli) or casseroled with judion beans and chorizo. Desserts are typically rich, along the lines of almond tart with vanilla cream, or chocolate cake with Banyuls, and service is 'well worth the 12.5 per cent'. Aperitifs take in cocktails, sherry and Cava, while the rest of the wine list offers an interesting range based on mostly Spanish grape varieties. Around a dozen wines by the glass might run from Albariño to Monastrell.

CHEF/PROPRIETOR: Jake Hodges   OPEN: Mon to Fri L 12 to 3, all week D 6 to 10.45, Sat L 12.30 to 4.30, D 6 to 10.45 and Sun all day 12.30 to 9.30   CLOSED: 10 days Christmas and New Year, 4 days Easter, bank hols   MEALS: alc exc Sun L (main courses £13 to £16.50). Set L Mon to Fri £15 (2 courses) to £18, Set L Sat and Sun £12 (2 courses) to £15. Tapas bar menu Mon to Sat 6 to 10.30   SERVICE: 12.5% (optional), card slips closed   CARDS: Amex, Delta, Diners, MasterCard, Switch, Visa   DETAILS: 66 seats. 20 seats outside. Private parties: 80 main room, 8 to 40 private rooms. Vegetarian meals. Children's helpings. Wheelchair access (not WC). No music. Air-conditioned   ⊖ Holborn

# Cinnamon Club

map 13

Old Westminster Library,
Great Smith Street, SW1P 3BU
TEL: (020) 7222 2555   FAX: (020) 7222 1333
EMAIL: info@cinnamonclub.com
WEBSITE: www.cinnamonclub.com

COOKING 4
MODERN INDIAN
£36–£79

The old Westminster Library makes a great setting for this contemporary Indian restaurant round the corner from the Abbey. The original identity of the building has been preserved, with a spacious, clubby bar, 'high, high ceilings and a gallery full of books': a surprising location for food that goes all out to break the mould. The full menu calls into play superficially simple yet skilfully balanced ideas such as a filo 'cake' of green peas and corn with stir-fried cauliflower. Meat and fish receive exotic treatment – sandalwood-flavoured chicken breast, for example – and there is also a nod to regional diversity. Sri Lanka is the source of spice-crusted black cod, while biryani of goat is done Hyderabadi-style.

The tandoor oven gets plenty of work, handling everything from halibut with coconut ginger sauce to roasted aubergine 'crush'. Side dishes sound promising, and breads have won approval for their 'variety of subtle flavours'. To finish, there may be warm chocolate mousse, or ice cream. The kitchen thrives on innovation, although results may occasionally fall short. Set lunches seem good value, but wine and extras can send the bill rocketing. Staff are 'very gracious and mostly efficient'. The Club is now open weekdays for breakfast too, where there's a choice of English, Continental, Indian and Anglo-Indian.

A few prestige clarets and burgundies apart, the wine list concentrates on food-friendly New World styles. Prices start at £15 for house red and white, but severe mark-ups mean that they quickly move up to three and even four figures. Five wines of each colour are available by the glass from £3.60.

CHEF: Vivek Singh   PROPRIETOR: Iqbal Wahhab   OPEN: Sun to Fri L 12 to 2.30, Mon to Sat D 6 to 11   CLOSED: 25 to 31 Dec   MEALS: alc (main courses £15 to £25). Set L and D 6 to 7 £19 (2 courses) to £22. Breakfast menu available Mon to Fri 7.30 to 10   SERVICE: 12.5% (optional), card slips closed   CARDS: Amex, Delta, Diners, MasterCard, Switch, Visa   DETAILS: 220 seats. Private parties: 50 main room, 20 to 50 private rooms. Vegetarian meals. No music. Air-conditioned   ⊖ Westminster

# Circus

map 15

1 Upper James Street, W1R 4BP
TEL: (020) 7534 4000   FAX: (020) 7534 4010
EMAIL: circus@egami.co.uk
WEBSITE: www.circusbar.co.uk

COOKING 3
MODERN EUROPEAN
£25–£63

Smack in the middle of Mediaville, amid film companies, Virgin Radio and a style-hungry potential clientele, Circus is a name of ironical aptness. Large tinted picture windows give on to two Soho streets, and the ground-floor restaurant (there is also a basement bar) is an ample, light, modern space with bare-boarded floor and elegant suede-covered chairs. The menu changes at a fairly sedate pace, and is built around modern classics such as risotto with smoked haddock and a poached egg, peppered carpaccio with tomatoes and balsamic, and roasted skate wing with salsa verde. More speculative dishes may end up tasting more tentative than they sound in the descriptions, as was the case with a garlic leaf, orange and vanilla risotto that came with prosciutto-wrapped monkfish. A lime pudding simply didn't taste much of lime at inspection, so maybe Amaretto cheesecake with coffee sauce, or chocolate and hazelnut mille-feuille, may be safer bets. Service won't overdo the courtesies (this is Soho), but manages to keep things rolling. An inspiring, up-to-the-minute wine list is varietally arranged and furnishes plenty of choice for those with money to spend. Loire Chardonnay and Argentine Syrah are both £14.50.

CHEF: Richard Lee   PROPRIETOR: Mirror Image Restaurants plc   OPEN: Mon to Fri L 12 to 3, Mon to Sat D 5.45 to 12   CLOSED: 24 to 26 Dec, 1 Jan   MEALS: alc D (main courses £10 to £18.50). Set L £10.50 (2 courses) to £19.50, Set D 5.45 to 7 and 10.30 to midnight £10.50 (2 courses) to £12.50. Bar menu also available   SERVICE: 12.5% (optional), card slips closed   CARDS: Amex, Delta, Diners, MasterCard, Switch, Visa   DETAILS: 140 seats. Private parties: 14 to 23 private rooms. Vegetarian meals. Children's helpings. Wheelchair access (not WC). No music. No mobile phones. Air-conditioned   ⊖ Piccadilly Circus

## City Rhodes

map 13

1 New Street Square, EC4A 3BF
TEL: (020) 7583 1313   FAX: (020) 7353 1662
WEBSITE: www.rhodesrestaurants.com

COOKING 6
MODERN BRITISH
£48–£86

In a nondescript office block just off Holborn Circus, and with a less-than-exciting tower-block view, the first-floor dining room is done out somewhat anonymously in blues and greys, its blond wood, white walls and comfortable chairs all contributing to an atmosphere of calm. If it is aimed at business lunchers, then it hits the bull's-eye, with discreet, polished and knowledgeable service from a team of French waiters. It is a place to come for confident, well-judged cooking, where classic ideas and often luxurious materials sit comfortably together: lobster minestrone, for example, or a finely executed, well-balanced dish of squab pigeon with caramelised figs and duck foie gras, served with a small white jug of meat juices.

Less expensive ingredients are also given reassuring treatment, producing such items as a lamb kidney sausage, rabbit confit, and thin layers of crisp potato galette acting as a mille-feuille, sandwiching flavourful shallot marmalade and pickled chanterelles, the whole combination 'spot on'. Desserts unsurprisingly take on a very British caste, with bread-and-butter pudding leading the field, followed closely by pistachio baked Alaska, and mulled wine poached pear with an almond sabayon. The wine list is rather conservative, but well chosen, leaning towards the Old World, with a decent New World section. A 'fine wine selection' centres on Bordeaux and Burgundy, with a few offerings from the Rhône, Italy, Spain, Australia and California. The 'sommelier's suggestion' page lists 14 bottles, evidently chosen for interest and value. Prices start at £16.50, and mark-ups are generally fair.

CHEFS: Gary Rhodes and Adam Gray   PROPRIETOR: Sodexho   OPEN: Mon to Fri 12 to 2.30, 6 to 9   MEALS: alc (main courses £14.50 to £23)   SERVICE: 12.5% (optional), card slips closed   CARDS: Amex, Delta, Diners, MasterCard, Switch, Visa   DETAILS: 95 seats. Private parties: 80 main room, 6 to 12 private rooms. Vegetarian meals. No cigars in dining room. Wheelchair access (also WC). Music. Air-conditioned   ⊖ Chancery Lane, Blackfriars

# Clarke's ▼

map 13

124 Kensington Church St, W8 4BH
TEL: (020) 7221 9225   FAX: (020) 7229 4864
EMAIL: restaurant@sallyclarke.com
WEBSITE: www.sallyclarke.com

COOKING **5**
MODERN BRITISH
£38–£60

As psychologists know, if you give people an amorphous ink blot to stare at, what they see tells you more about them than about the ink blot. So it seems to be with Clarke's. For one expert it is 'as good today as 17 years ago' when it opened; for another it is tired and 'running on empty'. From bread to food to service, just about every aspect reflects this divide. Does the bread set the standard in the area (as one says), or is it dry, stale and really not very pleasant (as another sees it)? Is service slick, fast and intrusive, or relaxed, professional and unobtrusive? Perhaps the key lies in reporters' reactions to the restaurant's idiosyncrasies (it serves a no-choice menu at dinner), though responses probably depend mostly on what people are expecting.

What is clear is that the cooking doesn't seek to astound or amaze; rather it focuses on simple, high-quality seasonal ingredients plainly presented. In two rooms – ground floor and basement – of a converted Victorian house, it offers a daily-changing dinner menu (very hard to read, and now offering the option of eating two, three or four courses) featuring a meat main course on some days, seafood on others. Given that prices are 'unforgiving' (although they include service), people want to know why they should be asked to spend so much money on such simple food. The answer goes to the heart of what good food is about.

As one fan put it, if you start with the best possible ingredients, don't overcomplicate matters but maintain balance and season sensitively, then you can hardly go wrong. From this perspective the food is well-judged and precisely rendered. Each ingredient in a plate of San Daniele ham with fried artichoke, grilled leeks and organic bitter leaves dressed in balsamic vinegar appears to have been selected 'at its prime': like many first courses here, it might look like an easy assembly job, but the ham is first-rate and the vegetables might have been picked only minutes ago. Likewise, four plump, moist and accurately timed scallops served with a relish of black olive, pine nuts and celery (together with mushrooms, spinach and Jersey Royals) proved to be a convincing display of 'refreshingly light and healthy cooking'. Desserts, though, may not be quite up to the same standard.

Expectations about wine can be dealt with more straightforwardly. There is much to please and surprise in this lovingly-compiled, California-centred list, from imaginative wines by the glass, via top names from the US's west coast, to some well-chosen European bottles (particularly from Italy and France). This isn't the place to come looking for bargains, even if pricing is un-greedy, but digging around will unearth some interesting bottles in the under-£20 range. House wines are £14, or £4 per glass.

CHEFS: Sally Clarke and Elizabeth Payne   PROPRIETOR: Sally Clarke   OPEN: Mon to Fri L 12.30 to 2 (Sat brunch 11 to 2), Tue to Sat D 7 to 10   CLOSED: 10 days Christmas, Easter weekend, 2 weeks Aug   MEALS: alc (main courses L £14 to D £21). Set D £29 to £48. Brunch menu Sat   SERVICE: net prices, card slips closed   CARDS: Amex, Delta, Diners, MasterCard, Switch, Visa

DETAILS: 85 seats. Private parties: 14 main room. No smoking in dining room at Sat brunch or D. No cigars/pipes. Wheelchair access (not WC). No music. No mobile phones. Air-conditioned ⊖ Notting Hill Gate

## Clerkenwell Dining Room ₤✳   | NEW ENTRY |    map 13

69–73 St John Street, EC1M 4AN
TEL: (020) 7253 9000   FAX: (020) 7253 3322
EMAIL: bookings@theclerkenwell.com
WEBSITE: www.theclerkenwell.com

COOKING **4**
MODERN EUROPEAN
£27–£56

Although the area tends to die a little once the evening rush has subsided, there are enough serious eating options on St John Street to keep the taxis flowing. Almost opposite St John (see entry), this site used to be home to one of Stephen Bull's restaurants. A reception committee of greeters hints that the tone is going to be more formal than EC1 is used to, a feeling underlined by dark walls with modern paintings, and tables covered in white linen.

Andrew Thompson has worked at the Square and at L'Escargot (see entries), as well as having done a stint in New York. His cooking is imbued with a degree of earthiness (not unusual in this part of town), with pig's trotter lyonnaise, an 'exemplary, fantastically crackled' suckling pig with belly pork and sauerkraut, and wild mushrooms all over the place: with braised beef, or partnering a lush terrine of foie gras. There is seafood too, perhaps in the form of langoustine, crab and avocado mayonnaise with a gazpacho dressing, or grilled halibut with mussels. Dessert assiettes are getting more off the wall by the year: the theme at inspection here was lime and coconut, involving lime chibouste, lime sorbet with a coconut tuile, and pannacotta. After the greeting, service tends to be 'pushy' or 'elusive' by turns. The short wine list is a little perfunctory for the circumstances, with most bottles over £20 and a list of fine wines starting at £47. House Chilean is £12.50.

CHEF: Andrew Thompson   PROPRIETORS: Zak Jones and Andrew Thompson   OPEN: Mon to Fri L 12 to 2.30, Mon to Sat D 6 (7 Sat) to 11.30   MEALS: alc (main courses £13.50 to £15). Set L and D 6 to 7 £12.50 (2 courses) to £15.50   SERVICE: 12.5% (optional), card slips closed   CARDS: Amex, Delta, Diners, MasterCard, Switch, Visa   DETAILS: 80 seats. 10 seats outside. Private parties: 80 main room, 60 private room. Children's helpings. No smoking in 1 dining room. No cigars/pipes in dining room. Wheelchair access (not WC). Occasional music. Air-conditioned   ⊖ Farringdon

## Club Gascon     map 13

57 West Smithfield, EC1A 9DS
TEL: (020) 7796 0600   FAX: (020) 7796 0601

COOKING **5**
FRENCH
£26–£66

Close to Smithfield Market and St Bartholomew's Church, Club Gascon flouts most of the rules that seem to underpin other successful restaurants. There is no blond wood or stainless steel, tables are small and close together, there are few concessions to vegetarians (beyond a cassolette of morels and summer truffles, or Pyrenean cheese with tomato confit), and it mostly deals in offal. Its singular character derives from Pascal Aussignac's reliance on the rich food culture of his native south-west France (ducks and geese in particular), and from his decision to serve everything in small portions rather than following a standard three-course format.

Foie gras is the cornerstone of the enterprise, served every which way: in spring rolls, in a bun, as a terrine, and as a Tatin with truffle and turnips. But there are plenty of other diversions, from a kebab of duck hearts with a creamy cake of ceps, via roast rabbit leg with prune chutney, to a 'cappuccino' soup of black pudding with lobster and asparagus. Other fish and seafood options might include smoked zander, fresh sturgeon, and pan-fried tuna with andouille. If the array seems bewildering, a monthly-changing, no-choice, set-price menu takes the pressure off decision-making, and for an extra £20 a glass of wine comes with each of the five courses. If sweet foie gras with iced chestnuts sounds too much, finish with chilled Armagnac parfait with prunes, or a traditional Gascon apple pie. Regional drinks include a range of Armagnacs, floc de Gascogne, sweet wines from Jurançon and Pacherenc du Vic-Bilh, and other wines from Irouleguy, Gaillac, Marcillac, Buzet, Madiran and Cahors.

CHEF: Pascal Aussignac   PROPRIETORS: Vincent Labeyrie and Pascal Aussignac   OPEN: Mon to Fri L 12 to 2, Mon to Sat D 7 to 10.30   CLOSED: 22 Dec to 6 Jan, bank hols   MEALS: alc (main courses £7 to £16). Set L and D £35 (£55 with wine)   SERVICE: 12.5% (optional), card slips closed   CARDS: Amex, Delta, MasterCard, Switch, Visa   DETAILS: 50 seats. Private parties: 60 main room. Vegetarian meals. Children's helpings. Wheelchair access (not WC). Music. Air-conditioned   ⊖ Barbican, Farringdon

# Le Colombier 🍴

**map 14**

145 Dovehouse Street, SW3 6LB                                        COOKING **2**
TEL: (020) 7351 1155   FAX: (020) 7351 0077                      FRENCH
                                                                 £22–£63

Entente is truly cordiale in this converted pub with its spacious terrace, where it is not just the blue décor that recalls an old-style Anglo-French bistro. Service is affably French, and helpful, and while the menu recognises the twenty-first century – in the shape of sea-bass with fennel sauce, or potted leg of duck with rösti – its heart remains in bistro fare: for example, various oysters, oeufs pochés Meurette or chou farçi. The Anglo side appears in grilled Dover sole, poached turbot hollandaise, and hachis Parmentier (translated on the menu as cottage pie). Traditions mingle in desserts, too, as crêpes suzette are juxtaposed with baked Alaska or nougat glacé with honey. The long, (almost) all-French wine list starts at £12.90; it offers useful halves, plus over a dozen by the glass, including old Anglo stalwarts, sherry and port.

CHEF: Frank Schones   PROPRIETOR: Didier Garnier   OPEN: all week 12 to 3.30 (4 Sun), 6.30 to 11 (10 Sun)   MEALS: alc (main courses £10.50 to £20). Set L £13, Set L Sun £15, Set D 6.30 to 7.30 £13 to £16.90   SERVICE: 12.5% (optional), card slips closed   CARDS: Amex, Delta, MasterCard, Switch, Visa   DETAILS: 40 seats. 30 seats outside. Private parties: 45 main room, 6 to 45 private rooms. Vegetarian meals. Wheelchair access (not WC). No music. Air-conditioned   ⊖ South Kensington

*All entries in the Guide are re-researched and rewritten every year, not least because restaurant standards fluctuate. Don't rely on an out-of-date Guide.*

# ▲ The Connaught

map 15

16 Carlos Place, Mayfair, W1K 2AL
TEL: (020) 7499 7070   FAX: (020) 7495 3262
EMAIL: info@the-connaught.co.uk
WEBSITE: www.savoygroup.com

NEW CHEF
MODERN EUROPEAN
£74–£127

Could any change to a restaurant be more dramatic? With this edition the Connaught clocks up 50 years in the Guide, more than half of them under one chef, Michel Bourdin, who was himself only the fifth holder of the post since 1897. Suddenly, in comes a completely new brigade ready to turf out the old Edwardian cooking, the trolleys, the smelly chafing burners, and the unfathomable dishes named after royalty, and replace them with a more relaxed feel (hardly difficult), and with contemporary Italian or Mediterranean food. Even worse for Connaught devotees, Angela Hartnett is, er, a woman. But considering what Gordon Ramsay has done for Claridges (see entry), who wouldn't jump at the chance of seeing the kitchen in the hands of one of his star proteges? We can't wait to see what happens. Since the re-opening was due to take place after the Guide went to press, details below may not be completely accurate.

CHEF: Angela Hartnett   PROPRIETOR: Gordon Ramsay   OPEN: all week 12 to 2.45, 6.30 to 10.45
MEALS: prices and format of menus not known at time of going to press   SERVICE: not included,
card slips closed   CARDS: Amex, Diners, MasterCard, Visa   DETAILS: 65 seats. Private parties:
22 main room, 12 private room. Vegetarian meals. Jacket and tie. Wheelchair access (also WC).
No music. Air-conditioned   ACCOMMODATION: 92 rooms, all with bath/shower. TV. Phone. Room
only £280 to £495. Rooms for disabled. Baby sitter upon arrangement. Baby facilities   ⊖ Bond
Street, Green Park  £5

# Il Convivio

map 13

143 Ebury Street, SW1W 9QN
TEL: (020) 7730 4099   FAX: (020) 7730 4103
WEBSITE: www.etruscagroup.co.uk

COOKING 1
ITALIAN
£32–£71

Just behind Eaton Square, amid some of the most expensive real estate on earth, Il Convivio occupies an elegant Georgian terraced house. Generously sized tables and lots of elbow room are perhaps to be expected in this part of town, but coupled with a spacious dining room and contemporary design they provide a particularly congenial atmosphere for some straightforward Italian cooking. A few items on the set-price menu attract a supplement, including black spaghetti with lobster and spring onions, and veal fillet with wild mushrooms, while the rest of the wide-ranging repertoire might take in swordfish carpaccio with fennel and lemon, a pasta dish such as potato and artichoke gnocchi with crab, and perhaps stuffed rabbit leg, or medallions of wild boar. Finish with a chocolate trilogy, or nougat parfait pyramid with passion-fruit ice cream. Wines made from Falanghina, Inzolia, Nosiola, Grechetto, Aglianico, Cesanese, Lagrein, Sagrantino and Teroldego grapes (as well as more usual Pinot Bianco, Nebbiolo and Sangiovese) feature on an interesting if sometimes pricey list which includes a dozen by the glass.

CHEF: Lucas Pfaff   PROPRIETOR: Etrusca Group   OPEN: Mon to Sat 12 to 2.30, 7 to 11   CLOSED: 25 Dec to 1 Jan   MEALS: alc L (main courses £10 to £14.0). Set L £15.50 (2 courses) to £19.50, Set D £26.50 (2 courses) to £31.50   SERVICE: 12.5%, card slips closed   CARDS: Amex, Delta, Diners, MasterCard, Switch, Visa   DETAILS: 65 seats. Private parties: 65 main room, 6 to 14 private rooms. Vegetarian meals. Cigars and pipes in bar area only. Music. Air-conditioned
⊖ Victoria, Sloane Square  £5

## Coq d'Argent ♥                                    map 13

| | |
|---|---|
| 1 Poultry, EC2R 8EJ | COOKING 3 |
| TEL: (020) 7395 5000   FAX: (020) 7395 5050 | FRENCH |
| WEBSITE: www.coqdargent.com | £39–£78 |

There can be few more impressive locations in London: a dramatic sixth-floor rooftop garden with open-air bar, barbecue for casual diners and viewing gallery; the dining room is indoors, though one side opens up on fine days. The overwhelmingly long menus are written in French with translations in smaller type, which shows where the kitchen's centre of gravity lies: soupe de petits pois au foie gras may be among the ten starter options, along with rillettes de canard, and pissaladière aux poivrons. Main courses are divided into crustacés, poissons, viandes et volailles, and so on. Expect to run into roast halibut with watercress sauce, lemon sole with niçoise dressing, roast rack of Pyrenean lamb with rosemary sauce, and braised pork belly with coco beans and sage jus. As at other Conran establishments, an unenlightened attitude to smoking prevails: cigarettes and cigars are listed on the bar menu. The wine list gravitates towards France; this being the City, champagne scores big here, as does a roll-call of Burgundy, Bordeaux and Northern Rhône stars (with prices to match). Italian and Californian selections are equally well groomed. For those without expense accounts, though, the selection is less appealing: there is precious little under £20.

CHEF: Mickael Weiss   PROPRIETOR: Conran Restaurants   OPEN: Sun to Fri L 11.30 (12 Sun) to 3, Mon to Sat D 6 (6.30 Sat) to 10   MEALS: alc (main courses £10.50 to £25.50). Set L £25 (2 courses) to £29.50. Bar menu also available Mon to Fri   SERVICE: 12.5% (optional)   CARDS: Amex, Diners, MasterCard, Switch, Visa   DETAILS: 148 seats. 217 seats outside. Private parties: 148 main room. Vegetarian meals. Wheelchair access (also WC). Music. No mobile phones. Air-conditioned   ⊖ Bank

## Cotto                                             map 12

| | |
|---|---|
| 44 Blythe Road, W14 0HA | COOKING 4 |
| TEL: (020) 7602 9333   FAX: (020) 7602 5003 | MODERN EUROPEAN |
| EMAIL: bookings@cottorestaurant.co.uk | £30–£56 |

Considered 'an oasis in a very dull area', this modern, welcoming restaurant may be small but it certainly cuts the mustard. Redecoration has resulted in a new red/brown colour scheme and a move towards 'a simpler feel'. An 'irresistible urge to experiment' might be behind some of the dishes – John Dory served with courgette and basil lasagne, white beans and foie gras butter, for example – while others tread a more conventional path: there might be a version of coq au vin, or a 'bonne femme' treatment of corn-fed chicken.

At its heart is some fine technique: the food is cooked correctly and timed well. Ingredients are of a high quality, and for the most part James Kirby's lively way with ingredients is kept under control, producing pan-fried chicken livers with tagliatelle and peas, and a soft-boiled duck egg with shrimp mayonnaise and celeriac rémoulade. Variations on a theme extend to desserts such as baked rhubarb Alaska, while candied blood oranges have come with a coffee and cardamom granita. Half a dozen wines by the large glass, including house Vin de Pays d'Oc at £12.50 (£3.50 a glass), kick off a short, roving list.

CHEF: James Kirby   PROPRIETORS: James and Jane Kirby   OPEN: Mon to Fri L 12 to 2.30, Mon to Sat D 7 to 10.30   CLOSED: 1 week Christmas, bank hols   MEALS: alc (main courses £15.50). Set L and D £15 (2 courses) to £18   SERVICE: 12.5% (optional), card slips closed   CARDS: Amex, Delta, MasterCard, Switch, Visa   DETAILS: 65 seats. 12 seats outside. Private parties: 40 main room, 10 to 40 private rooms. Vegetarian meals. Children's helpings. Wheelchair access (not WC). Music. Air-conditioned   ⊖ Kensington Olympia

## Cow Dining Room

map 13

89 Westbourne Park Road, W2 5QH
TEL: (020) 7221 0021   FAX: (020) 7727 8687
EMAIL: thecow@thecow.freeserve.co.uk

COOKING 4
MODERN EUROPEAN
£27–£60

Hearty food without too much refinement or complication draws a lively young crowd to this simple, relaxed venue over a pub. A large shellfish-themed mural on one wall depicts one of the kitchen's passions: six native oysters with shallot relish and Guinness sausages is a typically full-bodied starter, as are grilled sardines with chermoula, or a salad of roast Jerusalem artichokes, pecorino and rocket. A strongly traditional feel runs through main-course options, from roast leg of lamb with dauphinois potatoes, spinach and rosemary jus, and duck confit with choucroute and mustard sauce, to fillet of sea bream with lentils and salsa verde, and grilled mackerel with ratatouille. Desserts likewise tend to be old favourites, such as crème brûlée, though New York cheesecake with blood orange salad may not be so familiar. A short, varied wine list opens with house French red and white at £12.50.

CHEF: James Rix   PROPRIETOR: Tom Conran   OPEN: Sat and Sun L 12.30 to 3.30, all week D 7 to 11   CLOSED: 25 Dec, 1 Jan   MEALS: alc (main courses £8 to £18)   SERVICE: not inc, 12.5% for parties of 5 or more   CARDS: Amex, Delta, MasterCard, Switch, Visa   DETAILS: 36 seats. Private parties: 28 main room. Vegetarian meals. No children under 18. No music   ⊖ Westbourne Park

## Creelers

map 14

3 Bray Place, SW3 3LL
TEL/FAX: (020) 7838 0788
WEBSITE: www.creelers.co.uk

COOKING 1
SEAFOOD
£25–£70

On a quiet street corner a few minutes' walk from Sloane Square, Creelers is unflashily decorated with plain walls and bare wooden tables. Its preoccupation is seafood, with an especially strong line in smoked salmon, processed at its own smokehouse on the Isle of Arran: as well as cured and hot smoked there is even a blueberry-cured version served with citrus and cucumber yoghurt. Oysters, grilled langoustines, and fish soup with rouille and croûtons make alternative starters, perhaps followed by grilled turbot with spinach and purple potatoes, or Parmesan-crusted cod with mushroom risotto and a saffron sauce. Finish with a well-made, light vanilla pannacotta with a mixed berry compote, or a very sweet chocolate, orange and pistachio mousse. Service is attentive, and a short wine list offers a handful under £20, including three house wines at £12.95.

CHEF: Caroline Campbell   PROPRIETORS: Tim and Fran James, and Dieter Jurgensen   OPEN: Mon to Sat 12 to 2.30, 6 to 10.30   CLOSED: 26 Dec to 2 Jan, 1 week Aug   MEALS: alc (main courses £11 to £20.50). Set L £12 (2 courses) to £15   SERVICE: not inc   CARDS: Amex, Delta, MasterCard, Switch, Visa   DETAILS: 45 seats. Private parties: 20 main room, 12 to 22 private rooms. Vegetarian meals. Children's helpings. No smoking in 1 dining room. Music   ⊖ Sloane Square  £5

## Crowthers

map 12

481 Upper Richmond Road West, SW14 7PU   COOKING 3
TEL/FAX: (020) 8876 6372   MODERN BRITISH/FRENCH
£38–£45

Philip and Shirley Crowther's likeable neighbourhood restaurant has been ploughing an undeviating furrow since 1982. Little changes, including the menu, noted one reporter, who thought it 'a comfortable, quiet venue'. Since Mr Crowther cooks 'the same dishes so often', familiarity breeds confidence, which means that standards are consistent. Classic French is the bedrock of the repertoire, although occasional forays further afield bring back grilled monkfish with toasted sesame seeds, tomatoes and oyster mushrooms. Clean, clear flavours assert themselves in aubergine charlotte topped with pesto, or an accurately timed escalope of salmon with vermouth sauce. The Gallic theme continues in best end of lamb with a provençale herb crust and garlic and rosemary sauce, while pleasing desserts have included 'richly satisfying' glazed sabayon with mixed fruits, and honey ice cream in a brandy-snap basket. Service is friendly and willing. A good choice of sherries and kirs heads the short, well-spread and affordable wine list. House wine is £11.50 (£3 a glass).

CHEF: Philip Crowther   PROPRIETORS: Philip and Shirley Crowther   OPEN: Tue to Sat D 7 to 10 (other times by prior booking only)   CLOSED: 1 week Christmas, 2 weeks Aug   MEALS: Set D £21 (2 courses) to £26   SERVICE: not inc   CARDS: Delta, MasterCard, Switch, Visa   DETAILS: 32 seats. Private parties: 32 main room. Children's helpings. Wheelchair access (not WC). Occasional music. Air-conditioned   ⊖ Richmond  £5

## Cucina

map 13

45A South End Road, Hampstead, NW3 2QB   COOKING 2
TEL: (020) 7435 7814   FAX: (020) 7435 7147   FUSION
EMAIL: enquiries@cucina.uk.com   £27–£43

'One comes away with a glowing feeling,' admits a devotee of this likeable Hampstead restaurant with a food shop attached. Some funky pieces of artwork liven up the windowless dining room, but most attention focuses on the food. Ideas seem a touch less outlandish than in the past, but the kitchen still has its finger firmly on the fusion button, and raids the world larder for kaffir lime leaves, udon noodles, Pecorino cheese and the like. Everything comes together vividly in spiced corn cakes with tortilla crust, gazpacho sauce and crème fraîche, or tandoori spiced swordfish with mango, chilli and mint salsa, or perhaps seared duck breast with baked ginger plums and sesame-fried courgette 'noodles'. Bringing up the rear, you might find cappuccino mousse with Amaretto syrup and almond macaroons. Around 30 wines hold plenty of interest; eight come by the glass, and house wine is £11.95.

CHEF: Andrew Poole   PROPRIETORS: Vernon Mascarenhas and Andrew Poole   OPEN: all week L 12 to 2.30, Mon to Sat D 7 to 10.30   CLOSED: 3 days Christmas   MEALS: Set L £15 (2 courses) to £17.50, Set D £17.50 (2 courses) to £21.50   SERVICE: not inc   CARDS: Amex, Delta, MasterCard, Switch, Visa   DETAILS: 86 seats. Private parties: 90 main room. Vegetarian meals. No cigars/pipes in dining room. No music. No mobile phones. Air-conditioned   ⊖ Belsize Park

# Deca

NEW ENTRY   map 15

23 Conduit Street, W1S 2XS   COOKING 4
TEL: (020) 7493 7070   FAX: (020) 7493 7090   MODERN EUROPEAN
£26–£84

Nico Ladenis's newest venture is muddy brown outside, comfortably appointed, and decked out in blond wood and brown leather. Paul Rhodes, veteran of Chez Nico/cheznico, applies his practised, no-nonsense style to a rather safe menu designed for simple enjoyment. There are no truffles or caviar, just a small amount of foie gras (in a terrine, for example), and the odd lobster sauce (perhaps with lemon sole fillets). There may also be asparagus risotto, charcoal-grilled and spatchcocked quails, and a fine timbale of white crab meat bound in richly seasoned mayonnaise, topped with pulverised brown meat, served with punchy, mustardy celeriac rémoulade.

These are solid, workaday dishes that do what is required, no more, but technique never seems to waver. As at all good brasseries, offal pops up periodically: calf's liver with bacon, perhaps, or veal sweetbreads 'Pojarski' (a fried patty of breaded chopped sweetbreads mixed with ham). Vegetables cost extra. Cheeses (all French) are kept in fine condition and worth the £10.50 charged. Lemon tart is as exquisite as ever, with friable short crust pastry and a curdy-textured filling. Service, 'as strictly stratified as Tsarist Russia', is on the smiley side of formal. Those with £25–£30 to spend can enjoy the sharply chosen wine list, with its one-word descriptions (Ch. Pétrus 1983 – 'divine' – at £825). There are no house wines, but around 15 by the glass.

CHEF: Paul Rhodes   PROPRIETORS: Nico and Dinah-Jane Ladenis   OPEN: Mon to Sat 12 to 3, 5.30 to 11   CLOSED: 10 days Christmas, 4 days Easter, bank hols   MEALS: alc (main courses £12.50 to £18.50). Set L £12.50, Set D 5.30 TO 7 £12.50   SERVICE: 12.5% (optional), card slips closed   CARDS: Amex, Diners, MasterCard, Switch, Visa   DETAILS: 70 seats. Private parties: 10 main room, 11 to 16 private rooms. No pipes in dining room. Wheelchair access (also WC). No music. Air-conditioned   ⊖ Oxford Circus

*The text of entries is based on unsolicited reports sent in by readers, backed up by inspections conducted anonymously. The factual details under the text are from questionnaires the Guide sends to all restaurants that feature in the book.*

# Del Buongustaio ◁ £

map 12

283–285 Putney Bridge Road, SW15 2PT
TEL: (020) 8780 9361   FAX: (020) 8877 0465
EMAIL: mail@theitalianrestaurant.net
WEBSITE: theitalianrestaurant.net

COOKING 1
ITALIAN
£27–£52

In a parade of shops in the heart of Putney, amid a rustic ambience of terracotta tiles, exposed brickwork and a faded tapestry wall-hanging, this unusual Italian restaurant offers a monthly-changing menu that mixes classical, medieval and renaissance influences with more contemporary ideas. For one starter a carefully cooked scallop, prawn and piece of white fish each sat on pastry barchettas, each filled with vegetable purées in one of the colours of the Italian tricolore. Main courses might include a large portion of (clearly freshly made) squid-ink risotto with cuttlefish and tomato confit, or shank of lamb with a purée of broad beans: all cooked with flair, gusto, and a marked enthusiasm for salt. Meals are rounded off with desserts such as meringue-topped lemon tart, or chocolate torta with vanilla ice cream. The wine list covers many of Italy's regions, and opens with four house wines at £11.95 or £12.95.

CHEF: Nicola Ducceschi   PROPRIETOR: Del Buongustaio Ltd   OPEN: all week L 12 (12.30) to 3 (3.30 Sun), Mon to Sat D 6.30 to 11   MEALS: alc (main courses £9 to £11). Set L £12.75 (2 courses), Set D £29.95. Cover 90p   SERVICE: not inc, 10% (optional) for parties of 5 or more, card slips closed   CARDS: Amex, Delta, MasterCard, Switch, Visa   DETAILS: 160 seats. Private parties: 100 main room, 60 private room. Vegetarian meals. Children's helpings. Wheelchair access (also WC). Music. Air-conditioned   ⊖ East Putney (£5)

# Delfina Studio Café

map 13

50 Bermondsey Street, SE1 3UD
TEL: (020) 7357 0244   FAX: (020) 7357 0250
EMAIL: book@delfina.org.uk
WEBSITE: www.delfina.org.uk

COOKING 4
GLOBAL
£33–£50

This former chocolate factory now provides artists with both studio and exhibition space, and they get the bonus of lunch for a pound at the in-house eatery. The Delfina is no cheap canteen, though. Appropriately, its smart, light and spacious dining room has a look of an art gallery: polished wooden floors and white walls hung, of course, with paintings. Hard surfaces boost noise, but this is the happy hum of customers enjoying the 'global eclectic' cooking (their description) rather than the depressing din of loud music.

The gastronomic gamut is wide indeed. Try starting with rabbit and horseradish rillettes with walnut, beetroot and caperberry salad, or perhaps chargrilled orange, chilli, marinated squid and squid ink noodles. A main course of cinnamon and black pepper-crusted belly pork with fennel and orange, 'smashed spuds' and black olives also comes with a well-stamped passport, and other choices range from cosmopolitan-but-familiar (chilli and coconut roasted butternut squash with Asian herbs and jasmine rice) to truly original (venison steak, vanilla mash, chargrilled endive and chocolate oil). Desserts also get in on the act – perhaps as roast quinces with panettone and laurel mascarpone – as does the brief wine list. It is distinguished for variety and value though France, Australia and New Zealand figure strongly. Spanish red, white and rosé start at £12.50, and there are ten wines by the glass.

CHEF: Maria Elia    PROPRIETORS: Digby Squires and Delfina Entrecanales    OPEN: Mon to Fri L only 12 to 3    CLOSED: 24 Dec to 2 Jan    MEALS: alc (main courses £10 to £14)    SERVICE: 12.5% (optional), card slips closed    CARDS: Amex, Delta, Diners, MasterCard, Switch, Visa    DETAILS: 80 seats. Private parties: 260 main room, 80 to 500 private rooms. Vegetarian meals. Wheelchair access (also WC). No music    ⊖ London Bridge  £5

## Le Deuxième ▼                    NEW ENTRY    map 15

65A Long Acre, WC2E 9JH                                        COOKING 3
TEL: (020) 7379 0033    FAX: (020) 7379 0066            MODERN EUROPEAN
                                                              £22–£58

The name is no reflection of a modest aim to be second best; it comes from the fact that this new eating venue in the heart of Covent Garden is an offshoot of the nearby Café du Jardin (see entry). As at its parent establishment, menus offer plenty of choice – a dozen each of starters and main courses – within a broadly modern European style that takes in a few ideas from further afield: starters, for example, might include breaded lambs' sweetbreads on split-pea dhal, or tempura of shrimps with Thai dressing, alongside goose breast on a potato galette, and escargots bourguignonne. Among successes have been a main course of seared tuna with fresh-tasting sesame choi sum and water chestnuts, and a creditable veal dish comprising two thick chunks of meat on a base of rösti and mozzarella garnished with diced red pepper. Finish perhaps with banana crumble with bitter chocolate ice cream, or a selection of French cheeses.

The wine list is Franco-centric, with strong showings from around the regions (as well as Burgundy and Bordeaux). The New World selection is much more than an afterthought, however, with some well-chosen, keenly priced bottles, such as Pikes Polish Hill Riesling from Australia at £21. A list of 'fine and rare' selections centres on fine Burgundy. Twenty wines are available by the glass, and there is a healthy choice by the half-bottle. Four French house wines sell for £11.50 (£3.85 a glass).

CHEF: Geoff Adams    PROPRIETORS: Robert Seigler and Tony Howorth    OPEN: Sat 12 to 12, Sun 12 to 11, Mon to Fri 12 to 3, 5 to 12    CLOSED: 24 and 25 Dec    MEALS: alc (main courses £9 to £16). Set L and D Sat 12 to 7 and 10 to 12, Sun 12 to 11, Mon to Fri 12 to 3, 5 to 7 and 10 to 12 £9.95 (2 courses) to £13.50    SERVICE: 15% (optional), card slips closed    CARDS: Amex, Delta, Diners, MasterCard, Switch, Visa    DETAILS: 55 seats. Private parties: 55 main room. Vegetarian meals. Wheelchair access (not WC). No music. Air-conditioned    ⊖ Covent Garden

## Ditto                                                      map 12

55–57 East Hill, SW18 2QE                                      COOKING 4
TEL: (020) 8877 0110    FAX: (020) 8875 0110            MODERN EUROPEAN
WEBSITE: www.doditto.co.uk                                    £26–£63

Recognisable by its large French windows that open on to the pavement, Ditto is a double shop conversion with a solid wooden bar down one side, and a plank-floored dining room leading to a kitchen at the back. The large, colourful modern paintings are for sale, and a glass-fronted wood-burning stove with a stack of logs lends it a neighbourhood feel. Straightforward contemporary dishes are the mainstay of a kitchen with a strong sense of the comfort that food can bring: in the shape of eggs Benedict, and smoked haddock fishcake with chive butter.

A Mediterranean strand, meanwhile, brings a different kind of reassurance, evident in a goats' cheese and tomato tart, and pan-roasted fillet of black bream with black olives and artichokes. As an alternative to desserts of pannacotta or chocolate tart, there may be Taleggio with walnut toast and a pear and raisin compote. 'Can you not campaign against charging for bread?' asks one reporter, referring to the £2 charge for a 'basket of bread and oil for two'. For an extra £3 you could get a one-course weekday lunch at the bar of fish and chips, or Cumberland sausage and mash. A short wine list keeps prices under control and offers good choice by the glass. House French varietals (Terret and Grenache) are £11.50 (£2.85).

CHEF: Calum Watson   PROPRIETORS: Giles Cooper and Christian Duffell   OPEN: Sun to Fri L 12 to 3 (4 Sun), Mon to Sat D 7 to 11   MEALS: alc (main courses £7.50 to £17). Set L Mon to Fri £10 (2 courses inc wine) to £18.50, Set D £14.50 (2 courses) to £18.50   SERVICE: 12.5% (optional) CARDS: Delta, MasterCard, Switch, Visa   DETAILS: 70 seats. Vegetarian meals. Children's helpings Sun L. Wheelchair access (not WC). No music. No mobile phones  (£5)

## The Don 🍷                                                                      map 13

The Courtyard, 20 St Swithin's Lane, EC4N 8AD
TEL: (020) 7626 2606   FAX: (020) 7626 2616                         COOKING 2
EMAIL: enquiries@thedonrestaurant.co.uk                             FRENCH
WEBSITE: www.thedonrestaurant.co.uk                                £36–£68

Like its stablemate Bleeding Heart in EC1 (see entry), the Don hides in a courtyard, here in Sandeman's one-time office; hence the name, the caped silhouette on the hanging sign, and the sherry and port list. Its bistro espouses wine-cellar style, but the ground-floor restaurant is strikingly modern, with steel ceiling sculptures. The carte, pleasingly varied but without too many voguish ingredients, might include Mediterranean fish soup, or wild mushroom croustade with a quail egg and champagne sabayon to start. Main dishes are mostly classics with a modern touch: calf's liver with braised chicory, champ, and parsley and garlic butter; or roasted monkfish tail with mussel and saffron ragoût. There is proper fillet Rossini with foie gras, sauce Périgord and pommes Parisiennes. Desserts – such as dark chocolate tart with Mandarine eau-de-vie sorbet – are rich but not heavy.

The highly individual wine list offers well-chosen champagnes, and bottles from top names from classic regions of France and around the globe; but there are plenty of surprises too. Nine sherries are available by the glass; ten madeiras are listed (the oldest a 1900), three of them by the glass; and an extensive range of ports can be decanted to order. Reds and whites are organised by price, and mark-ups are generally fair (although if you want to spend expense-account sums, you can). There is plenty of choice by the glass and 'vins du patron' start at £15.95.

CHEF: Matthew Burns  PROPRIETORS: Robert and Robyn Wilson  OPEN: Mon to Fri 12 to 2.30, 6 to 10  CLOSED: 24 Dec to 2 Jan  MEALS: alc (main courses £11 to £22). Bistro menu also available  SERVICE: 12.5% (optional), card slips closed  CARDS: Amex, Delta, Diners, MasterCard, Switch, Visa  DETAILS: 110 seats. Private parties: 50 main room, 24 private room. Vegetarian meals. No music. Air-conditioned  ⊖ Bank

---

# Drapers Arms

[NEW ENTRY]  map 13

44 Barnsbury Street, N1 1ER
TEL: (020) 7619 0348  FAX: (020) 7619 0413

COOKING 3
MODERN BRITISH-PLUS
£28–£47

This new dining room is on the first floor of a pub in a residential part of Islington. It aims for a sophisticated look, with brass chandeliers, and candles on tables, although not a great deal of money seems to have been spent on décor. Considerably more effort has gone into the cooking, which shows a degree of flair. Menus feature some intriguing ideas, have broad appeal, and something of a Mediterranean disposition: seared squid with chorizo and artichoke salad made a simple but effective start to an inspection meal, featuring good-quality ingredients deftly handled, while white gazpacho with chilli tiger prawns has been well balanced, with 'just the right zing of chilli heat'. Among main courses, roast veal chop with blue cheese gratin, beetroot and baby spinach salad is high on flavour, and chicken Kiev is a non-greasy and very garlicky rendition of the old chestnut, served with pea and bean stew and mint aïoli. The list of about three dozen varied wines offers six of each colour by the glass from £3.50, bottle prices starting at £12.

CHEF: Mark Emberton  PROPRIETORS: Paul McElhinney and Mark Emberton  OPEN: all week 12 to 3 (4 Sun), Mon to Sat D 7 to 10.30  MEALS: alc (main courses £8.50 to £14)  SERVICE: 12.5% (optional), card slips closed  CARDS: Delta, Diners, MasterCard, Switch, Visa  DETAILS: 45 seats. Private parties: 10 main room. Vegetarian meals. Children's helpings  ⊖ Angel, Highbury and Islington

---

# Drones

map 14

1 Pont Street, SW1X 9EJ
TEL: (020) 7235 9555  FAX: (020) 7235 9566
EMAIL: sales@whitestarline.org.uk
WEBSITE: www.whitestarline.org.uk

COOKING 5
ANGLO-FRENCH
£31–£86

The combination of David Collins design and Marco Pierre White menu-planning has produced another seemingly effortless success here. Proceed beyond an extensive bar to the dining-area, where walls are done in a coffee cream hue and hung with glamorous portraits of film-stars gone by. You sit on black leather upholstery, at tables crisp with thick white linen, adorned with fresh flowers. The clientele may well be of a certain age, ditto many of the menu offerings. That peculiar, but now extremely popular, MPW blend of classical French and demotic British brings on terrine of foie gras with green peppercorns en gelée de Sauternes, or escargots à la bourguignonne, alongside dressed crab with mayonnaise or kipper pâté with whisky. A wide choice of fish dishes encompasses skate wing with winkles, and there is no excuse for missing the pomme purée, which comes with côte de veau forestière, braised pig's trotter with morels, or beef and snails. Cambridge burnt cream, or red fruit jelly with raspberry syrup, are alternatives to the famous lemon tart. An extensive wine list of obvious class is offered, but there is barely anything below £25. A dozen, plus a couple of champagnes, are available by the glass from £3.40.

CHEF: Joseph Croan   PROPRIETOR: Marco Pierre White   OPEN: all week 12 to 2.30 (3.30 Sun), 6 to 11   CLOSED: 26 Dec   MEALS: alc (main courses £14.50 to £25). Set L Mon to Sat £14.95 (2 courses) to £17.95, Set L Sun £19.50   SERVICE: 12.5% (optional)   CARDS: Amex, Delta, Diners, MasterCard, Switch, Visa   DETAILS: 96 seats. Private parties: 96 main room, 45 private room. No music. Air-conditioned

# e&o

NEW ENTRY   map 12

14 Blenheim Crescent, W11 1NN   COOKING 3
TEL: (020) 7229 5454   FAX: (020) 7229 5522   ASIAN/FUSION
WEBSITE: www.eando.nu   £31–£60

Asian food in an occidental setting is not a new idea, but e&o's dark wood floor, bare white walls, small benches and low-slung chairs make a smart backdrop that sets off the glitterati. 'Studiously informal' table settings include chopsticks, a block containing knives and forks, and a wine bucket hanging off the edge (saves space and keeps the bottle always handy). There is no clear distinction between first and main courses, so meals can be flexible, and the vegetarian menu, unusually, includes chilli salt squid, and swordfish tom kha.

Some dishes are comparatively 'pure': beef bulgogi, and tuna sushi (here called futo maki, but first-class for quality and freshness). Others are fusionary: a curry of aubergine (two types) with pumpkin and lychee, sharp fruit offsetting the creaminess of the rest. Other successes include light prawn and chive dumplings, steamed sea bass in a pool of ginger sauce, and well-made sorbets. Waiters are dressed in black, and the cold soya beans and soy sauce you munch while reading the menu later appear on the bill at £3: 'a bit cheeky'. A global wine list, mostly in the £20 to £40 range, starts with house Vin de Pays d'Oc at £11.

CHEF: Ian Pengelley   PROPRIETOR: Will Ricker   OPEN: all week 12 to 3, 6 to 10.30   CLOSED: Christmas   MEALS: alc (main courses £8 to £19.50). Bar menu available all week   SERVICE: 12.5% (optional), card slips closed   CARDS: Amex, Delta, Diners, MasterCard, Switch, Visa   DETAILS: 82 seats. 12 seats outside. Private parties: 12 to 18 private rooms. Vegetarian meals. No cigars/pipes in dining room. No music. Air-conditioned   ⊖ Ladbroke Grove

# Eagle £

map 13

159 Farringdon Road, EC1R 3AL   COOKING 2
TEL: (020) 7837 1353   MEDITERRANEAN
£22–£43

'In fine fettle', observed a reporter on his way to the ballet. He feasted on penne with an 'unusual combination' of chilli, tomato, kale and spinach, while his partner enjoyed well-timed smoked haddock with potatoes. Single dishes are the order of the day in this noisy, rumbustious gastro-pub (the self-styled godfather of the genre in London). Culinary influences from Iberia and Italy show themselves in pollo ajillo (chicken and garlic casserole with rice), Spanish omelette with mojama (cured tuna loin) and rocket, and in grilled sea bass with a salad of fennel, olive, parsley and orange. To finish, choose between organic Sardinian cheeses with carasau flat bread and quince paste, or pasteis de nata (Portuguese custard tarts). A dozen or so wines (all available by the glass) are chalked on a blackboard, and there are plenty of promising beers and ciders. House wine is £10.50. Michael Belben has opened a second pub, the Fox Dining Room (see entry) in the City.

CHEF: Tom Norrington Davies   PROPRIETOR: Michael Belben   OPEN: all week L 12.30 to 2.30 (3.30 Sat and Sun), Mon to Sat D 6.30 to 10.30   CLOSED: 1 week Christmas, bank hols   MEALS: alc (main courses £8 to £12)   SERVICE: none, card slips closed   CARDS: Delta, MasterCard, Switch, Visa   DETAILS: 70 seats. 24 seats outside. Children's helpings. Wheelchair access (not WC). Music   ⊖ Farringdon

## Ecapital £     NEW ENTRY   map 15

8 Gerrard Street, W1D 5PJ       COOKING 1
TEL: (020) 7434 3838   FAX: (020) 7434 9991       CHINESE
      £25–£75

In among all the Cantonese establishments, this minimalist Chinatown newcomer makes a serious attempt to put Shanghai cuisine on the London gastro-map: 'almost unique' it calls itself. Some familiar noodle dishes and Beijing specialities appear (classic Peking duck mightily impressed a Chinese inspector), but regional specialities provide the real interest. Cold appetisers are a high point, their range of flavours and textures impressive: crunchy jellyfish, 'rustic' vegetarian 'goose' (actually braised bean curd), 'punchy' marinated sliced pig's knuckle and – for the adventurous – the amazing 'thousand layers' (thinly sliced, pressed pigs' ears). Curious names and curious dishes also run to 'lion's head' (fluffy meatballs in hotpot with pak choi greens), and whole 'beggar chicken' (traditionally baked in mud, but here clothed in lotus leaves and dough). The short wine list consists exclusively of high-class burgundies chosen with real care; prices start at £12.

CHEF: David Tam   PROPRIETOR: Mark Chan   OPEN: all week 12 to 12   MEALS: alc (main courses £8 to £20). Set L and D £15 to £20   SERVICE: 12.5% (optional), card slips closed   CARDS: Amex, Diners, MasterCard, Switch, Visa   DETAILS: 60 seats. Vegetarian meals. Wheelchair access (not WC). No music. Air-conditioned

## Electric Brasserie     NEW ENTRY   map 13

191 Portobello Road, W11 2ED
TEL: (020) 7908 9696   FAX: (020) 7908 9595       COOKING 3
EMAIL: reception@electrichouse.com       BRASSERIE
WEBSITE: www.electrichouse.com       £26–£78

The new Electric Cinema complex in the 'scuzzy and smart' middle stretch of Portobello Road includes a private members' club and this smart, clean-cut brasserie, with tables spilling out on to the covered and heated forecourt. Inside is a noisy bar filled with twenty-somethings and, at the back, a dining room with off-white walls, huge bevelled mirrors, a raised kitchen, and leather banquettes. The feel is informal and vaguely 1950s; the atmosphere is buzzy and can be quite loud. Add all-day hours, welcoming staff, a crowd-pleasing menu, and well-handled dishes, and it is not difficult to see the appeal.

The menu, which shows some English and American influence as well as French, is divided into starters, mains, salads and sandwiches, with additional sections for small plates, seafood, side orders and 'trolley' dishes, which is most often a roast (spring lamb, say, or peppered venison). Vegetable soup might turn up as a fine, delicate broth with tarragon, while a spring leaf salad, dressed with hazelnut and raspberry vinaigrette, may come with large chunks of Roquefort, slices of pear, and bacon. Main courses are solidly traditional – sirloin steak, Dover sole, lamb chops, or duck cottage pie topped with thick mashed potato – and there are also some wistfully retro dishes for two, such as chateaubriand with lobster. For dessert, think Eton mess, lemon tart, or torrone molle with chocolate malted ice cream. France dominates the short wine list, which offers few bargains, although prices start at £12.50. Eleven wines by the glass sell for £3.25 to £5.

CHEFS: Jonathan Heath and Adrian Watters    PROPRIETOR: Soho House Ltd    OPEN: all week 12 to 11    CLOSED: 25 and 26 Aug    MEALS: alc (main courses £9.50 to £25). Set L £12 (2 courses) to £15, Set D £24 (2 courses) to £28. Breakfast menu from 8 to 12; 'small plates' menu available from 11 to 11.30    SERVICE: 12.5% (optional)    CARDS: Amex, Delta, Diners, MasterCard, Switch, Visa    DETAILS: 120 seats. 20 seats outside. Vegetarian meals. Wheelchair access (also WC). Music. Air-conditioned    ⊖ Ladbroke Grove, Notting Hill Gate

# Embassy

**NEW ENTRY**    map 15

29 Old Burlington Street, W1S 3AN
TEL: (020) 7437 9933   FAX: (020) 7734 3224
EMAIL: kate@embassylondon.com
WEBSITE: www.embassylondon.com

COOKING **6**
MODERN BRITISH
£32–£80

These premises once housed a nightclub, and some of that ambience lingers in the low ceiling, dim lighting, gold wallpaper and forbidding-looking doorman. The menu is in the hands of Garry Hollihead, whose stint in the Marco empire gave him a taste for nostalgic haute cuisine – lobster thermidor, chicken Rossini, crêpes Suzette – though he brings to it a very contemporary degree of precision. An inspection meal included versions of beef Wellington (made with venison and 'seriously good' pastry) and lobster à l'américaine (with a tomato butter sauce and buttery glazed noodles). Painstaking care with each component of a dish is evident, presentations are original and witty, and flavours strong and true.

More up-to-the-minute dishes have included scallops and artichoke on a bed of intricately cut leeks; salmon tartare with a salad of pea-shoots; and steamed hake with chorizo, curly kale and cherry tomatoes. A delicate dessert of frosted champagne (a kind of crystalline granita) with blackcurrant sorbet on slices of green apple manages to make a lasting impression, and the Suzette pancakes are served traditionally enough with orange and Grand Marnier, though not flamed at the table. Cheeses from La Fromagerie have varied from 'good' to 'tired', and 'service was OK, but some waiters still had their L plates on'. French house wine is £15. Downstairs, music throbs in a private members' club bulging with the young and beautiful.

CHEF: Garry Hollihead   PROPRIETORS: Mark Fuller and Garry Hollihead   OPEN: Mon to Fri L 12 to 3.30, Mon to Sat D 6 to 12 (3 am Thurs to Sat)   CLOSED: bank hols   MEALS: alc (main courses £13 to £25). Set L £16.95 (2 courses) to £19.95   SERVICE: 12.5% (optional), card slips closed   CARDS: Amex, Delta, MasterCard, Switch, Visa   DETAILS: 100 seats. 30 seats outside. Private parties: 100 main room. Vegetarian meals. No children under 8. Wheelchair access (not WC). Occasional music. Air-conditioned   ⊖ Green Park, Piccadilly Circus

## English Garden ⁑✳                                    map 14

10 Lincoln Street, SW3 2TS                              COOKING 4
TEL: (020) 7584 7272   FAX: (020) 7584 1961            ANGLO-FRENCH
                                                        £33–£64

The English Garden is a short wander from the King's Road, on a corner site in a row of residential terraced houses. The interior retains something of the feel of a private residence too, with a conservatory room at the back, and cool, modern, pastel-coloured décor throughout. Malcolm Starmer previously worked alongside Richard Corrigan at the sister establishment, Lindsay House (see entry), and something of his down-to-earth cooking style has clearly rubbed off. Braised stuffed pig's trotter with truffled mash is a robust first course to get stuck into, vigorously salted but 'wonderfully gelatinous and flavourful'. Sound technique and accurate timing have distinguished a grilled leg of rabbit with roast garlic, and a highly accomplished risotto of leeks and pancetta. Those looking for a lighter route through the menu might progress from Cornish crab salad with Cos leaves and Caesar vinaigrette to Indian-spiced scallops with lime-spiked sweet potato and raita. Expect a pre-dessert before the grand finale, which may be a 'rich and wicked' chocolate pot with caramelised oranges and chocolate ice cream, or ginger madeleines with a poached pear. Smiling, hospitable service can be wholeheartedly applauded. Choices on the wine list are mostly laudable too, although with Beaujolais-Villages at £19.50 and Sancerre at £29, the mark-ups won't let you forget you're in Chelsea. House wines open at £15.50.

CHEF: Malcom Starmer   PROPRIETOR: Richard Corrigan   OPEN: Tue to Sun L 12 to 3, all week D 6.30 to 11 (10.30 Sun)   MEALS: Set L £19.50, Set D £27.50   SERVICE: 12.5% (optional), card slips closed   CARDS: Amex, Delta, MasterCard, Switch, Visa   DETAILS: 44 seats. Private parties: 30 main room, 8 to 30 private rooms. Children's helpings. No smoking in 1 dining room. Occasional music. No mobile phones. Air-conditioned   ⊖ Sloane Square   (£5)

## Enoteca Turi ♟ 🍽                                    map 12

28 Putney High Street, SW15 1SQ                         COOKING 3
TEL: (020) 8785 4449   FAX: (020) 8780 5409            ITALIAN
                                                        £32–£59

A few minutes' walk from Putney Bridge, on a busy corner, is this well-run Italian restaurant. Smart but informal, with closely set tables and a buzzy atmosphere, it has a sense of occasion. The menu is classic Italian, and seasonal ingredients abound. Starters might include a traditional platter of marinated and grilled Mediterranean vegetables with fava bean purée, or crab with chickpea purée and baby spinach. Pasta has run to first-rate, freshly made laganelle with roast plum tomatoes, basil and salted ricotta; and black tagliolini with squid, mussels and langoustine. Main courses might take in roast rabbit with olives and roast fennel, or grilled steak of salt marsh lamb with a warm salad of spelt wheat. For afters, tiramisù is tempting, as is the selection of Italian cheeses.

Wine is taken seriously. Dishes on the menu are followed by a number indicating which wine would best match the food (about ten wines are served by the glass). The extensive list is a lavish and largely Italian production, but with some selections from France and Spain and a few bottles from the New World. Sicilian house wines are £12, and there is a good selection of half-bottles. Tasting notes are exhaustive, and producers are well chosen, although wine service is not always hot on recommendations. Best value can be found in central and southern Italy, but all the big names are here too, many with hefty price tags.

CHEF: Luca Lamari   PROPRIETOR: Giuseppe Turi   OPEN: Mon to Sat 12 to 2.30, 7 to 11   CLOSED: 25 and 26 Dec, 1 Jan, L bank hols   MEALS: alc (main courses L £10 , D £10.50 to £17)   SERVICE: 12.5% (optional), card slips closed   CARDS: Amex, Delta, Diners, MasterCard, Switch, Visa   DETAILS: 85 seats. Private parties: 28 main room. Vegetarian meals. No-smoking area. Wheelchair access (also WC). No music. Air-conditioned   ⊖ Putney Bridge

---

# L'Escargot, Ground Floor ♟                            map 15

48 Greek Street, W1D 4EF                                        COOKING 3
TEL: (020) 7439 7474   FAX: (020) 7437 0790                MODERN FRENCH
WEBSITE: www.whitestarline.org.uk                              £31–£60

The ground floor has altered most during the recent David Collins transformation of L'Escargot, the back room now elegant and stylish, its pastel walls covered with paintings by Chagall, Warhol, Miró, Hockney and Matisse. Tables are close together, there are no restrictions on smoking, and piped music adds to the din, but the Franglais menu is full of delights, from omelette Arnold Bennett, and jambon persillé with quince jelly, to a Moroccan treatment of red mullet.

At its best the food achieves crisp, clean flavours – in a mackerel tartare with crushed black beans and a sprinkling of sesame oil – and the kitchen has turned out moist snails, each on a puddle of potato purée, with an expertly made red wine sauce, and an accomplished and flavourful poulet noir well matched with a fine ravioli of wild mushrooms. On the downside, desserts may not be quite up to snuff and, as upstairs, bread is poor, and service is patchy. The wine list is the same as for the Picasso Room (see entry below).

CHEF: Alan Pickett   PROPRIETORS: Jimmy Lahoud and Marco Pierre White   OPEN: Mon to Fri L 12 to 2.30, Mon to Sat D 6 to 11.30   CLOSED: 24 to 26 Dec, 1 Jan, L Good Fri and Easter Mon   MEALS: alc (main courses £13 to £18). Set L and D Mon to Sat 6 to 7 £14.95 (2 courses) to £17.95   SERVICE: 12.5% (optional), card slips closed   CARDS: Amex, Delta, Diners, MasterCard, Switch, Visa   DETAILS: 70 seats. Private parties: 80 main room, 10 to 60 private rooms. Vegetarian meals. Music. Air-conditioned   ⊖ Tottenham Court Road, Leicester Square

---

*The Guide office can quickly spot when a restaurateur is encouraging customers to write recommending inclusion. Such reports do not further a restaurant's cause. Please tell us if a restaurateur invites you to write to the Guide.*

# L'Escargot, Picasso Room ▼

map 15

48 Greek Street, W1D 4EF
TEL: (020) 7439 7474   FAX: (020) 7437 0790
EMAIL: sales@whitestarline.org.uk
WEBSITE: www.whitestarline.org.uk

COOKING **6**
MODERN FRENCH
£37–£99

This old stager, originally opened in 1927, has had a number of makeovers (and chefs) in recent years, latterly being the repository for a splendiferous collection of owner Jimmy Lahoud's artworks, with this first-floor room – small, rather formal and windowless – devoted solely to the work of Picasso, including ceramics, bronzes and lithographs. After its latest transformation, Jeff Galvin remains in the kitchen, making this in effect a showcase for two quite different artists. With the demise of the Oak Room, this is a place to eat some of Marco Pierre White's signature dishes dating from his peak period. At £42 for three courses, prices also recall those heady days. Some dishes may be a bit robust for today's tastes, but there is no denying the appeal of a wonderfully gelatinous braised pig's trotter stuffed with a mousse of chicken, pork and herbs, served with morels and rich and creamy pomme mousseline. But Jeff Galvin's own imprint is also evident, and his food is both impressive and enjoyable, taking in an asparagus risotto garnished with juicy scallops, and a well-sourced and expertly cooked Landes pigeon 'en vessie', served with ceps, root vegetables and a finely judged bouillon.

Coconut crème brûlée, and sablé of rhubarb are among recommended desserts, along with a huge 'floppy hat' of a properly made pistachio soufflé, served with pistachio ice cream. There are one or two minor letdowns (including bread), but the manager is considerate and helpful, although the pace of service echoes the house motto: 'slow but sure'. The wine list focuses on France's classic regions, Burgundy and Bordeaux (Pétrus and Le Pin among them) in particular. New World fans aren't forgotten, though. From Australia, four vintages of Henschke's Hill of Grace Shiraz date back to 1976, while 13 vintages of Penfolds Grange date back to 1965 and there is a range of vintages from California's Château Montelena. Without the luxury of an expense account, though, most people will only be able to look and not touch. Bottle prices start at £14, moving up quickly to four digits.

CHEF: Jeff Galvin   PROPRIETORS: Jimmy Lahoud and Marco Pierre White   OPEN: Tue to Fri L 12.15 to 2.15, Tue to Sat D 7 to 11   CLOSED: last week Dec, first week Jan, 3 weeks Aug   MEALS: Set L £20.50 (2 courses) to £55, Set D £42 to £55   SERVICE: 12.5% (optional), card slips closed   CARDS: Amex, Delta, Diners, MasterCard, Switch, Visa   DETAILS: 30 seats. Private parties: 12 main room. Vegetarian meals. Air-conditioned   ⊖ Tottenham Court Road, Leicester Square

# L'Estaminet

map 15

14 Garrick Street, WC2E 9BJ
TEL: (020) 7379 1432   FAX: (020) 7379 1530

COOKING **1**
FRENCH
£22–£64

Straightforward bistro-style cooking is the style at this theatreland French restaurant: game terrine, Lyons sausage on potato salad, and snails with garlic butter and parsley are typical of starters. Main courses – divided into grills, fish and meat – offer plenty of choice, ranging from simply grilled lamb cutlets or cod fillet with herbs, to poached turbot with spring onions, soy and sesame oil, or roast guinea fowl in red wine sauce. Finish perhaps with crème brûlée or a selection of French cheeses. Wines are exclusively French. Prices on the short list start at £12 but are mostly well above £20.

CHEF: Philippe Tamet  PROPRIETOR: Mr Bellone  OPEN: Mon to Fri L 12 to 2.30, Mon to Sat D 6 to 11.30  CLOSED: Christmas, New Year  MEALS: alc (main courses £10 to £20). Set D 6 to 7 £12  SERVICE: 12.5% (optional), card slips closed  CARDS: Amex, MasterCard, Switch, Visa  DETAILS: 70 seats. Private parties: 50 main room, 6 to 20 private rooms. Children's helpings. Occasional music. No mobile phones. Air-conditioned  ⊖ Leicester Square, Covent Garden

# Eyre Brothers ▼

*LONDON OF THE YEAR NEWCOMER*

70 Leonard Street, EC2A 4BP
TEL: (020) 7613 5346
FAX: (020) 7739 8199
WEBSITE: www.eyrebrothers.co.uk

NEW ENTRY    map 13

COOKING 4
MEDITERRANEAN
£31–£68

At the Eagle on Farringdon Road (see entry), which David Eyre co-founded, the culinary principle was simple: rustic-looking Mediterranean food at tempting prices. His new venture seems to be taking this principle and redefining it from gastro-pub into full-dress restaurant format. Interior design – room-height windows, suspended ceiling, white walls – are simply functional, and front-of-house staff are similarly cool, though confidently responsive to queries.

Spain and Portugal inspire much of the menu, with jamón and piquillos (going into black-bean soup), bacalhau, and membrillo (quince jelly) appearing with Monte Enebro goats' cheese to finish. Three slices of yellow-fin tuna, seared on the surface, blood-red within (spot on for its reporter) come in a marjoram and lemon sauce. Main courses appear to be sparingly sauced in the modern manner: fine when the meat is a moist Barbary duck breast with roast onion wedges and pommes Anna. On-plate salads are favoured: one of fennel and olives accompanying grilled spatchcocked quails marinated with garlic and rosemary. Properly tangy lemon tart is served fashionably with a sorbet of blood orange and Campari, or you could try a cheesecake of sundried cranberries and white chocolate. The final bill is fairly high, but technique is assured and the food confidently rendered.

Along with food-friendly selections from classic French and New World regions, the imaginative wine list favours Mediterranean/Iberian styles, with a good selection from Portugal and some Italian varietals, plus sherries from Emilio Lustau. Prices start at £13, although (Portugal apart) there is limited choice under £20. Fifteen wines are available for £5.25 a glass.

CHEFS: David Eyre and José Pizarro  PROPRIETORS: David and Robert Eyre  OPEN: Mon to Fri L 12 to 5.30, Mon to Sat D 6.30 to 11  CLOSED: 22 Dec to 12 Jan, bank hols  MEALS: alc (main courses £11 to £25). Set L and D 6.30 to 8 £18 (2 courses)  SERVICE: 12.5% (optional)  CARDS: Amex, Delta, Diners, MasterCard, Switch, Visa  DETAILS: 102 seats. Private parties: 20 main room. No children. No-smoking area. Wheelchair access (also WC). Occasional music. Air-conditioned  £5

# Fifth Floor 🍾

map 14

Harvey Nichols,
109–125 Knightsbridge, SW1X 7RJ
TEL: (020) 7235 5250   FAX: (020) 7823 2207
WEBSITE: www.harveynichols.com

COOKING **3**
MODERN BRITISH
£31–£83

Sooner or later, anyone with an interest in food and wine will probably make it up to the Fifth Floor to sample the fresh meat, fish, fruit and vegetables, shelves of tinned and packaged goods, the wine shop, and the coffee bar or sushi bar. It is a whole industry, of which the restaurant is merely a part. As it happens, the dining room and bar were due for a 'face-lift' as the Guide went to press, involving turning the long room into an oval shape, enclosing part of it for private dining, and updating just about every item within: from walls that change colour, and a domed glass ceiling, to Mies van der Rohe chairs.

The style of food, however, is expected to remain as before, replete with up-to-the-minute ingredients such as yuzu (part of a chilli and ginger dressing for rock oysters), and striking a balance between comfort and dynamism. Dorset crab risotto comes with avocado ice cream; roast fillet of Scotch beef with ceps and foie gras. There is, surely, something for everybody, from those who like to toy with a lobster and potato salad, to those for whom savoury dishes are just a prelude to chocolate cake with caramel sauce. The wine list has long been admired for its adventurous nature, and it is hard to find a duff bottle here. Italian Sauvignon Blanc rubs shoulders with Californian Mourvèdre, and Spanish and Italian reds are strong, as are Bordeaux and Burgundy. A more approachable 'house selection' lists wines by price (starting at £13.50); 15 wines are available by the glass. Although there are some expensive bottles, plenty of interesting offerings come in at the £20–£25 mark.

CHEF: Simon Shaw   PROPRIETOR: Dickson Poon   OPEN: all week L 12 to 3 (3.30 Sat and Sun), Mon to Sat D 6.30 to 11.30   CLOSED: 25 and 26 Dec   MEALS: alc D (main courses £16.50 to £23.50). Set L £21.50 (2 courses) to £25, Set D 6 to 7.30 £18.50   SERVICE: 12.5%, card slips closed   CARDS: Amex, Delta, Diners, MasterCard, Switch, Visa   DETAILS: 100 seats. Private parties: by arrangement. Vegetarian meals. Wheelchair access (also WC). No music. Air-conditioned   ⊖ Knightsbridge

# Fina Estampa

map 13

150–152 Tooley Street, SE1 2TU
TEL/FAX: (020) 7403 1342

COOKING **2**
PERUVIAN
£26–£47

Bianca Jones delivers her own version of Peruvian home cooking in this very friendly neighbourhood restaurant: there are photographs of her homeland on the walls, and an interesting collection of plates, mirrors and other artefacts adds to the mood of the place. Many specially imported ingredients appear on the menu, which is helpfully explained by Richard Jones out front: carapulcra is dried potatoes made into a spicy sauce, cooked with pork and chicken, and served with fried cassava and parsley rice, while aji de camarones consists of king prawns in a piquant dry yellow chilli sauce. Cebiche (seafood marinated in citrus juices) makes a refreshing starter, or you might choose causa rellena (potatoes layered with avocado and tuna). Desserts are mostly ice creams and sorbets. The minimal wine list has some gutsy drinking from Chilean and Argentinian producers; prices start at £12.50.

CHEF: Bianca Jones    PROPRIETOR: Richard and Bianca Jones    OPEN: Mon to Fri L 12 to 2.30, Mon to Sat D 6.30 to 10.30    MEALS: alc (main courses £7.50 to £15). Set L and D £22.50    SERVICE: 10%, card slips closed    CARDS: Amex, Delta, Diners, MasterCard, Switch, Visa    DETAILS: 70 seats. Private parties: 70 main room. Vegetarian meals. Children's helpings. Music    ⊖ London Bridge

## First Floor

map 13

186 Portobello Road, W11 1LA
TEL: (020) 7243 0072    FAX: (020) 7221 9440

COOKING 3
MODERN BRITISH
£23–£52

Perched over a pub (called the Ground Floor), but with a separate entrance, the First Floor's large dining room of Georgian proportions has huge sash windows overlooking Portobello Road and a rather Bohemian atmosphere. Colours are unobtrusive, closely packed white-clothed tables are accompanied by antique spoon-backed chairs, and large artificial flower arrangements 'tip menacingly out of elaborate alcoves'; there is an ornate chandelier and splendid wrought-iron candelabras ('dripping with generations of white candle wax'). The menu, though, favours the modern idiom. Keynote fresh ingredients, careful handling and a disciplined approach to flavour combinations ('nothing too brash') are displayed by a starter of crab linguini with 'well-behaved' chilli lemon, and by a roast monkfish main with 'not too aggressive' caponata and zucchini fritti. For meat-eaters, there could be rump of lamb with black pudding, apples and thyme, and for dessert, perhaps a vibrantly fresh-tasting chocolate and mint parfait with raspberry coulis, or light and moist sticky toffee pudding with toffee sauce and crème fraîche. Service is attentive and knowledgeable, while the compact, straightforward wine list is reasonably priced, with house bottles from £10.50 and ten by glass from £3.

CHEF: Simon Hennery    PROPRIETOR: Antony Harris    OPEN: all week L 12 to 3.30 (11 to 4 Sat, 12 to 4 Sun), Mon to Sat D 7 to 11 (11.30 Fri and Sat)    MEALS: alc (main courses £10 to £15.50). Set L £10.50 (2 courses) to £14. Brunch menu available Sat and Sun    SERVICE: 12.5%, card slips closed    CARDS: Delta, MasterCard, Switch, Visa    DETAILS: 45 seats. 12 seats outside. Private parties: 12 main room, 20 to 40 private rooms. Vegetarian meals. No cigars/pipes in dining room. Music    ⊖ Ladbroke Grove

## Fish Hoek

NEW ENTRY   map 12

6–8 Elliot Road, W4 1PE
TEL: (020) 8742 0766    FAX: (020) 8742 3374
EMAIL: info@springbokcafecuisine.com

COOKING 3
SEAFOOD/SOUTH AFRICAN
£33–£82

Just off Chiswick High Street is this new South African fish restaurant, done up in contemporary style, the fishy theme embodied in black and white photographs covering the walls. An informal tone is set by a long menu (nearly 40 dishes) that offers everything in 'half' or 'full' portions, and it's fish and seafood all the way. Many exotic species are on offer, sourced from all over – from Shetland to Falkland, from Cuba to Australia – and the cooking style is equally wide-ranging. There may be Welsh mussels steamed with Chenin Blanc, lime leaves and lemon grass; crisp-fried calamari with tartare sauce; or some fish you may not have seen before, such as musselcracker (grilled and served with sugar snaps, red peppers, roast shallots, mango, chilli and lime), which has a texture 'between swordfish and tuna, with large succulent flakes and a slightly gamey flavour'. The exclusively South African wine list opens with Chardonnay at £14.50 and Cabernet/Cinsault at £14. Fish Hoek is part of the Springbok Café group, which includes nearby Dumela, at 42 Devonshire Road, tel. (020) 8742 3149; described as a 'South African fish and meat restaurant', it operates a menu format not unlike Fish Hoek's.

CHEF/PROPRIETOR: Pete Gottgens   OPEN: Tue to Sun L 12 to 2.15 (Sun 11 to 3), Tue to Sat D 6.30 to 10.30   MEALS: alc (main courses £8 to £20)   SERVICE: not inc, 12.5% for parties of 6 or more CARDS: Delta, MasterCard, Switch, Visa   DETAILS: 54 seats. Private parties: 54 main room. Wheelchair access (not WC). Music   ⊖ Turnham Green

## ▲ Foliage ▼ 🍸 🗒   map 14

Mandarin Oriental Hyde Park,
66 Knightsbridge, SW1X 7LA                                    COOKING 7
TEL: (020) 7201 3722   FAX: (020) 7235 4552          MODERN EUROPEAN
WEBSITE: www.mandarinoriental.com                          £29–£86

Stroll up the steps, cross the marble hallway, go through a bar, and into a split-level dining room that overlooks Hyde Park. The effect is smart yet tranquil, a world away from busy Knightsbridge. After Hywel Jones departed for Lola's (see entry), Chris Stains, who has worked at some top places, arrived to take over what has become a prestigious kitchen. His menus are immediately appealing (lunch offers a glass of wine at each stage for an extra £6), and his food steers its own course, being contemporary without slavishly following fashion. Belly of pork is partnered with a croquant of smoked eel, caramelised pineapple and red wine vinaigrette, and foie gras is served three ways, with the option of sherry three ways (dry manzanilla pasada, amontillado, and sweet oloroso).

Top-quality ingredients lie at the heart of things, and a high level of skill is evident. A ring of five fat, sweet scallops, separated by sweet-and-sour marinated girolles, encircles a tower composed of pea and mint purée, ventreche bacon and salad leaves. Accurately grilled Cornish red mullet fillets are topped with aubergine stuffed with pesto, and served with notably good potatoes, red pepper and a Parmesan tuile. One thing that stands out particularly is that dishes are well balanced and harmonious: a fanned breast of poached Label Anglais chicken, for example, sitting alongside a tower consisting of pea purée, a raviolo of pea and ham hock, and fried chicken liver that was 'dazzling in its flavour', all in a light bath of cooking juices.

Cheese might be improved, but desserts are a highlight, taking in a cylinder of delicate pistachio parfait topped with a scoop of just-melting dark chocolate sorbet, surrounded by spiced cherries and kumquats. Even more impressive has been an intensely flavoured chocolate fondant, served with a round box of cherry tuile containing whole black cherries in jelly, topped with black cherry ice cream: this is cooking of a high standard that takes a mainstream idea and runs with it. The wine list is just what you might expect from an up-market, Francophile restaurant: page upon page of Burgundy, vintage upon vintage of cru classé Bordeaux. The list doesn't stop at France's borders, though. Italian wines are well selected and the New World is not overlooked. House wines start at £17.50 (white) and £19.50 (red), but there is little else below £20. Eight wines sell by the glass from £4.50 to £8.

CHEFS: David Nichols (executive) and Chris Stains    PROPRIETOR: Mandarin Oriental Group    OPEN: all week 12 to 2.30, 7 to 10.30 (10 Sun)    MEALS: Set L £19.50 to £25.50 (inc wine), Set D £42.50 to £55    SERVICE: 12.5%, card slips closed    CARDS: Amex, Delta, Diners, MasterCard, Switch, Visa    DETAILS: 46 seats. Private parties: 150 to 250 private rooms. Children's helpings. No music. Air-conditioned    ACCOMMODATION: 200 rooms, all with bath/shower. TV. Phone. Room only £255 to £3,000. Rooms for disabled. Baby facilities (*The Which? Hotel Guide*)    ⊖ Knightsbridge

## Il Forno 🍴

map 15

63–64 Frith Street, W1V 5TA
TEL: (020) 7734 4545    FAX: (020) 7287 8624
WEBSITE: www.cuisinecollection.com

COOKING 2
MODERN ITALIAN
£24–£46

There is a happy, buzzy young clientele in this informal basement restaurant decorated in (mostly) conventional modern style, with a 'wine cellar' running along one wall, above the tables, as a notable feature. The heart of the menu is a dozen pizze, from a basic tomato, mozzarella and basil version, through Napoli and quattro formaggi, to one that includes olives, artichokes, mushrooms, boiled egg and ham. Pasta, on the firm side of al dente at inspection, might come with peas, pancetta and warm olive oil, while main dishes rely largely on chargrilling and include chicken, tuna, and ribeye steak. Desserts take in good Italian ice creams and a sweet calzone filled with mascarpone, chocolate, pine kernels and Italian biscuits. Service is generally friendly, and a wide-ranging all-Italian wine list is fairly priced, starting at £12.50 for Sicilian white and red.

CHEF: Francesco Sambiase    PROPRIETOR: Cuisine Collection    OPEN: Mon to Sat 12 to 2.45, 6 to 11    CLOSED: 25 Dec to 2 Jan, 18 to 31 Aug    MEALS: alc (main courses £9.50 to £13.50). Set L and D 6 to 8 £10 (2 courses) to £12.50    SERVICE: 12.5% (optional), card slips closed    CARDS: Amex, Delta, MasterCard, Switch, Visa    DETAILS: 70 seats. Private parties: 16 main room. Vegetarian meals. Wheelchair access (not WC). Music. Air-conditioned    ⊖ Tottenham Court Road

## Four Seasons £

map 13

84 Queensway, W2 3RL
TEL: (020) 7229 4320

COOKING 4
CHINESE
£20–£51

Expect crowds lurking outside this 'incredibly popular' Chinese long-runner. The place itself is nothing special, but the food is certainly up to the mark, according to knowledgeable reporters. Cantonese roast meats (especially duck) are displayed in the window and are undoubtedly the stars of the show, but the kitchen's repertoire also extends to minced pork with bean curd and a prodigious list of around 50 chef's specials, ranging from a hotpot of dried shrimps, winter melon and green bean vermicelli to ducks' feet with sea cucumber and fish lips.

In more familiar territory, a long standard menu takes in smoked shredded chicken, and deep-fried squid as appetisers before sizzlers, sliced beef with oyster sauce, diced pork with cashew nuts and the like. Reporters have also noted the emergence of a special 'seafood menu' in line with other local venues: baked eel with black beans comes highly recommended. Vegetables are seriously good: spinach with garlic, and choi sum with oyster sauce have both been notable for their freshness and timing. Service is affable and chatty. Tea is good quality, and the wine list kicks off with house French at £9.

CHEF: Mr Tong    PROPRIETOR: Four Seasons (Queensway) Ltd    OPEN: all week 12 to 11.15 (10.45 Sun)    MEALS: alc (main courses £5.50 to £10.50). Set L and D £12.50 to £17    SERVICE: 12.5% CARDS: Amex, Delta, MasterCard, Switch, Visa    DETAILS: 70 seats. Private parties: 80 main room. Vegetarian meals. Music. Air-conditioned    ⊖ Bayswater, Queensway

## Fox Dining Room £     NEW ENTRY    map 13

28 Paul Street, EC2A 4LB        COOKING 2
TEL: (020) 7729 5708        MODERN EUROPEAN
       £29–£37

Located in what one reporter described as 'the nether regions of the City', the Fox is a modern-style pub (the owners call it a 'scruffy boozer') with a casual atmosphere and a mixed clientele of drinkers and diners. A large communal table dominates the upstairs dining room, and a terrace allows for al fresco eating. If the place is reminiscent of the Eagle (see entry, London), that is because both places are under the same ownership. The cooking is 'based on old-fashioned European tradition', according to the proprietor, which means cosmopolitan and earthy in modern pub fashion: for example, warm lambs' tongues with bobby beans and salsa verde, braised belly pork with peas, broad beans and Jersey Royals, and salmon with spiced lentils. An inspector found mixed degrees of success but was impressed by a simple assembly of beetroot and goats' curd cheese, and by a main course of fine lambs' sweetbreads with white beans in a tarragon-infused broth. Chocolate fondant pudding for one visitor was 'so good we ordered another'. Service is laid back, and the limited wine list is good value, prices starting at £10.50. Almost everything is available by the glass, from £2.50.

CHEFS: Trish Hilferty and Harry Lester    PROPRIETOR: Michael Belben    OPEN: Mon to Fri 12.30 to 2.45, 6.30 to 10    CLOSED: 1 week Christmas, bank hols    MEALS: Set L and D £14 (2 courses) to £18.50. Bar menu available L    SERVICE: not inc, card slips closed    CARDS: Delta, MasterCard, Switch, Visa    DETAILS: 35 seats. 24 seats outside. Vegetarian meals. Children's helpings. No music    ⊖ Old Street, Liverpool Street  (£5)

## Fung Shing        map 15

15 Lisle Street, WC2H 7BE        COOKING 4
TEL: (020) 7437 1539    FAX: (020) 7734 0284        CHINESE
WEBSITE: www.fungshing.co.uk        £32–£74

'An oasis of calm' amid the chaotic bustle of Chinatown is how one reporter described this restaurant next door to one of the busiest supermarkets on Lisle Street. Beyond the blue frontage is a wood-panelled bar leading to a yellow-walled dining area, with a more ornate room at the back. Comfort levels are good, while service is generally helpful.

Fung Shing has long been one of the most respected restaurants of its kind in London, and it has recently come out 'with all guns blazing'. The cooking is mostly Cantonese, seafood is a major strength, and the menu is vast. Some of the more prosaic items can be 'underwhelming', so, to get the best out of the place, it is worth focusing on the chef's specials. Winter melon soup with dried scallops is a classic version, slightly viscous and with a 'benchmark texture'; likewise, aubergine stuffed with pork and black-bean sauce has impressed with its balance of delicacy and richness.

Two very contrasting centrepieces also won over a Chinese inspector: lobster with ginger and spring onions exhibited all the clarity one would expect from a refined dish and 'showed off the true skills of the kitchen'. On the other hand, braised suckling pig was rich, robust and intense, with 'long, deep flavours' and delightfully gelatinous skin. Wines are above the Chinese average, and choice is reasonable, though the majority of bottles are over £20. House wine, however, is £13.50.

CHEF: Fook-On Chung  PROPRIETOR: Forum Restaurant Ltd  OPEN: all week 12 to 11.15  CLOSED: 24 to 26 Dec, bank hol L  MEALS: alc (main courses £8 to £19). Set L £17 to £30, Set D from £34 (for 2 people) to £85 (for 5 people)  SERVICE: 10%, card slips closed  CARDS: Amex, Delta, Diners, MasterCard, Switch, Visa  DETAILS: 120 seats. Private parties: 50 main room, 20 to 30 private rooms. Vegetarian meals. Music. Air-conditioned  ● Leicester Square

# Gate  

map 13

72 Belsize Lane, NW3 5BJ
TEL: (020) 7435 7733  FAX: (020) 7435 3311
EMAIL: belsize@gateveg.co.uk
WEBSITE: www.gateveg.co.uk

COOKING 2
VEGETARIAN
£23–£39

The Gate is that rarity, a serious vegetarian restaurant that treats those who eschew meat as grown-ups and offers them a sophisticated global style of cooking that might tempt even diehard carnivores. Expect starters such as green banana fritters with ginger, garlic, lime and an accompaniment of coconut salsa and chilli coulis, or perhaps a field mushroom tart with mascarpone, tomato and olives, encased in a thyme flavoured pastry. Among main courses, there may be aubergine schnitzel filled with tomatoes, red peppers and smoked mozzarella, served with creamy horseradish sauce, or a tagine of celeriac and sweet potatoes with pomegranate salsa and pistachio couscous. There are also vegan options for each course. Service at lunchtime has disappointed. Prices on the short wine list start at £10.25. A sister establishment is at 51 Queen Caroline Street W6, tel. (020) 8748 6932 (see entry, Round-ups).

CHEFS: Jo Tyrrell and Robin Freeman  PROPRIETORS: Adrian and Michael Daniel  OPEN: Sat to Sun L 12 to 3, all week D 6 to 10.30  MEALS: alc (main courses £7.50 to £11.50)  SERVICE: not inc  CARDS: Amex, Delta, Diners, MasterCard, Switch, Visa  DETAILS: 55 seats. 6 seats outside. Private parties: 60 main room. Vegetarian meals. Children's helpings. Wheelchair access (not WC). No mobile phones. Air-conditioned  ● Belsize Park, Swiss Cottage

# Gaudí 🍴

map 13

63 Clerkenwell Road, EC1M 5NP
TEL: (020) 7608 3220   FAX: (020) 7250 1046
EMAIL: gaudi@turnmills.co.uk
WEBSITE: www.turnmills.co.uk/gaudi

COOKING 3
MODERN SPANISH
£24–£60

This Clerkenwell restaurant pays homage to the Catalan architect via twisted wrought ironwork, extravagantly coloured and patterned tiles, and attractive artwork. Though smells escape from the open-plan kitchen, the dining room is comfortable and spacious, and service by manager María Hernández and her team is 'helpful, friendly and enthusiastic'. The original chef Nacho Martínez has moved on, but his protégé, Josep Carbonell, continues his bold and contemporary style, handling some first-class ingredients with a fine sense of balance.

Menu descriptions are detailed and helpful, given the seemingly endless list of ingredients in some dishes: for example, griddled swordfish with sauté wild mushrooms, soy bean sprouts, green beans with aïoli mousse and red sweet pepper sauce. Notable among starters has been a well-conceived brandy-infused foie gras of duck on grilled peach with citrus syrup. Desserts, meanwhile, might offer refreshing seasonal wild berries and mango mille-feuille with marjoram vinaigrette and clementine-vodka sorbet. The patriotic wine list confines itself to a round-up of Spanish regions, beginning with house wines at £12 and six by glass from £3.

CHEF: Josep Carbonell   PROPRIETOR: John Newman   OPEN: Mon to Fri 12 to 2.30, Mon to Sat 7 to 10.30   CLOSED: bank hols   MEALS: alc (main courses £12 to £17.50). Set L £12.50 (2 courses) to £15   SERVICE: 12.5% (optional), card slips closed   CARDS: Amex, Delta, Diners, MasterCard, Switch, Visa   DETAILS: 35 seats. 10 seats outside. Private parties: 35 main room, 60 private room. Vegetarian meals. No cigars in dining room. Wheelchair access (not WC). Music. Air-conditioned   ⊖ Farringdon

# Le Gavroche ▼

map 15

43 Upper Brook Street, W1K 7QR
TEL: (020) 7408 0881 and 7499 1826
FAX: (020) 7491 4387
EMAIL: bookings@le-gavroche.com
WEBSITE: www.le-gavroche.co.uk and
www.michelroux.co.uk

COOKING 7
FRENCH
£45–£149

Descend from the dark reds and greens of the bar into a cool, comparatively spacious, heavily clubby dining room, with a similarly dark colour scheme and candles. 'I imagine this is the sort of lighting in which women of my age look their best,' volunteered a visitor. Cockerels are a decorative theme (cock-a-doodle-Roux?), and each table is decorated with a silver creature: a crab, a bull, a pheasant, a frog. For those who like to converse during a meal – not always easy in London restaurants – thick carpets and drapes help to absorb the sound and make this possible.

Foie gras, truffles, lobster and caviar all pop up several times on the menu (this is where the rich come to dine), along with a few seasonal items, and old favourites sit cheek by jowl with newer and lighter dishes. All this makes for pleasing variety, as the kitchen offers soft poached gull's eggs on an artichoke heart with smoked salmon and caviar, roast saddle of rabbit, and lobster mousse with a champagne butter sauce. Output wobbles a bit, even during the course of a meal, but usually within acceptable limits. Among highlights have been loin of tuna of impeccable quality and freshness, edged with crushed black peppercorns and briefly seared, sitting on chopped smoked salmon in wasabi dressing, on a broad-bean salad with caviar dressing; 'the flavour was so fresh, so intense, so vibrant and clean that I almost cancelled my main course for another plateful of this'. Even complex dishes are executed with finesse, judging by a plate of organic pork consisting of crisp belly, juicy loin, stuffed trotter and transparent bits of ear (some crunchy, some chewy), all on cheese-flavoured mashed potato.

Lunch is still considered fair value, and desserts can be either 'the strong suit' or 'extremely average' according to taste: omelette Rothschild is an old stager, tarte Tatin is reliable. Staff – 'enough of them to play the crowd scenes in *Gandhi*' – are charming, and wines are in such fulsome abundance that choosing can be difficult. This is highfalutin, big-name territory, a place for premiers crus to rub shoulders with prestige cuvées, Super-Tuscans and others of that ilk. It is as magnificent a collection of fine wines as you will find anywhere. The only problem is, without a kindly rich uncle, it may be difficult to afford them. Prices start at £16.50 for regional French bottles and quickly head to the stratosphere.

CHEF: Michel Roux   PROPRIETOR: Le Gavroche Ltd   OPEN: Mon to Fri 12 to 2, 7 to 11   CLOSED: Christmas, New Year, bank hols   MEALS: alc (main courses £27 to £37). Set L £40, Set D £80 (whole table)   SERVICE: 12.5% (optional), card slips closed   CARDS: Amex, Delta, Diners, MasterCard, Switch, Visa   DETAILS: 60 seats. Private parties: 80 main room. Vegetarian meals. No cigars/pipes in dining room. Jacket. Occasional music. Air-conditioned   ⊖ Marble Arch

## Gay Hussar
map 15

2 Greek Street, W1D 4NB
TEL: (020) 7437 0973   FAX: (020) 7437 4631
EMAIL: eat@gayhussar.co.uk

COOKING 1
HUNGARIAN
£29–£54

For 50 years the Gay Hussar has been plying its trade in traditional Hungarian cooking to the Soho cognoscenti, and, given its distinguished clientele over that time, can be considered as one of the few surviving remnants of Old Labour. The menu may not change much (although a few lighter dishes have been added in recent years), which is just how regulars like it. They come here for wild cherry soup, for pressed boar's head, Transylvanian stuffed cabbage, and of course veal goulash with thimble egg dumplings.

Other Middle European flavour combinations extend to fish terrine with beetroot sauce, fish dumplings with a creamy dill and mushroom sauce, and pork schnitzel cooked with smoked sausage. Pancakes (of sweet cheese, or walnut with chocolate sauce) figure among desserts, service is friendly, courteous and relaxed, and Bulls Blood still features on the Hungarian section of the wine list, along with Tokaji, and house red and white at £10.50.

CHEF: Laslo Holecz   PROPRIETOR: Restaurant Partnership plc   OPEN: Mon to Sat 12.15 to 2.30, 5.30 to 10.45 (11 Fri and Sat)   CLOSED: bank and public hols   MEALS: alc (main courses £10.50 to £16.50). Set L £15.50 (2 courses) to £18.50   SERVICE: 12.5% (optional), card slips closed   CARDS: Amex, Delta, Diners, MasterCard, Switch, Visa   DETAILS: 70 seats. Private parties: 40

main room, 12 to 24 private rooms. Vegetarian meals. Children's helpings. No pipes in dining room. Wheelchair access (not WC). No music. Air-conditioned ⊖ Tottenham Court Road (£5)

## Ginger 🥟                                                                    map 13

115 Westbourne Grove, W2 4UP

TEL: (020) 7908 1990   FAX: (020) 7908 1991                          COOKING 1
EMAIL: info@gingerrestaurant.co.uk                                   BANGLADESHI
WEBSITE: www.gingerrestaurant.co.uk                                    £33–£51

'It is good that a restaurant can offer unashamedly Bangladeshi cooking rather than having to pretend that it is Indian,' noted a reporter familiar with the Subcontinent. There is no mistaking the place, with its turquoise colour schemes, chrome bar, and steel-framed pictures of the eponymous spicy plant. All is bright, brash, loud and modern out front, while the kitchen serves up Bengali equivalents of samosa (shingara) and fishcake (macher borah), as well as an unlikely sounding 'chicken popsicle'. Seafood is capably handled, from skewered king prawns to maachli bhuna (a warmly spiced, rich fish curry). Elsewhere, there may be a dish of spiced lamb cooked with potol (a native root vegetable); there is also kashi mangsho bhuna (goat curry on the bone) if that's your fancy. To finish, mango sorbet has been given the thumbs up. The wine list is a simple, sensible slate with plenty of New World offerings. House wine is £12.

CHEF: Uttam Dey   PROPRIETORS: Ollie Rahman, Alan Hussain and Abdul Quadir   OPEN: all week D only 5.30 to 11 (12 Fri and Sat)   CLOSED: Christmas   MEALS: alc (main courses £8 to £11.50) SERVICE: 12.5% (optional)   CARDS: Amex, Delta, MasterCard, Switch, Visa   DETAILS: 100 seats. Private parties: 70 main room, 10 to 30 private rooms. Vegetarian meals. Music. Air-conditioned ⊖ Notting Hill Gate (£5)

## Golden Dragon                                                               map 15

28–29 Gerrard Street, W1V 7LP                                        COOKING 1
TEL: (020) 7734 2763   FAX: (020) 7734 1073                            CHINESE
                                                                       £28–£55

Dim sum are undoubtedly the crowd-pullers in this lively Chinatown address. You can choose between the standard menu or enquire about the specialities written in Chinese on table cards. Among recent successes have been full-flavoured woo gok (taro dumplings), 'first-class' chicken feet ('as in Hong Kong') and the challenging and pungent delights of congee (rice gruel) with a 100-year-old egg. Reports on the main menu have been less good, and service has varied from 'matter-of-fact' to 'poor'. House French is £9 a bottle (£2.90 a glass).

CHEF: Y.C. Man   PROPRIETOR: Granport Ltd   OPEN: all week 12 to 11.15 (11.45 Fri and Sat) MEALS: alc (main courses £6.50 to £18). Set L and D £12.50 (2 courses) to £22.50 (all min 2 or more)   SERVICE: 10%   CARDS: Amex, Delta, Diners, MasterCard, Switch, Visa   DETAILS: 200 seats. Private parties: 300 main room, 10 to 40 private rooms. Vegetarian meals. Children's helpings. Music. Air-conditioned   ⊖ Leicester Square, Piccadilly Circus

# Gordon Ramsay 🍾

map 14

68–69 Royal Hospital Road, SW3 4HP

TEL: (020) 7352 4441   FAX: (020) 7352 3334

WEBSITE: www.gordonramsay.com

COOKING **10**

FRENCH

£59–£141

It is not easy to secure a booking here. The Editor is not alone in being unable to get a table; one reporter has been trying for over a year without success and wonders if the Guide has any tips that might help. Sorry, we're in the same boat. Those who make it will find a discreet aubergine-coloured canopy leading to a narrow corridor and a tiny bar, opening out into a small dining room. Glass – variously frosted, etched, mirrored, blown and moulded – helps to give it all an elegant and contemporary feel, and, although tables are well distributed, by the time you add pillars and a flurry of staff there isn't much empty space left. Lunch is effectively a choice of two items per course, while dinner expands to around eight options, and there is a seven-course prestige version at £85.

Gordon Ramsay may be spinning a large number of plates, with his enterprises at Claridge's, the Connaught, and in Glasgow (see entries) as well as Dubai, but he is not an absentee chef. He runs a disciplined kitchen, and although dishes have been honed and polished to the nth degree, to the point where most can be considered in the 'signature' category, they still excite: for example, a light, delicate ravioli of Scottish lobster and langoustines in a lobster bisque with a tomato and herb velouté, or roast foie gras with 'superb' caramelised endive and Sauternes jus. Seasoning is accurate to the last grain of salt, and some of the skills are 'breathtaking', producing a knockout, gutsy-flavoured roast Challandais duck with impeccable sauté foie gras and thinly sliced, truffle-infused white radish.

Despite the odd meat and seafood combination, such as a starter of braised belly pork and sauté langoustine, this is not a kitchen that takes risks, and dishes tend not to change greatly year on year. It is, however, cooking at the very highest level, exceeded only by a tiny handful of European restaurants. Simplicity and accuracy, two essential prerequisites, are amply demonstrated in, for example, a pan-fried John Dory fillet served on cabbage and cubes of celeriac, in a coriander nage; it may not sound much, but in the eating it shouts of sheer class. Likewise an 'ethereal' saddle of lamb, harmonised with its accompanying salsify, spinach, and a thyme sauce from a kitchen that is 'on sparkling form'.

The only significant disappointments come from those who try to find fault but are unable to, beyond a little nit-picking about the bread or the size of the tables. Otherwise, the food is characterised by a rare degree of harmony, finesse and poise, not least when it comes to desserts, such as a benchmark chocolate soufflé, perfectly aerated, with just the right level of sweetness, served with an 'inspired' marriage partner in the form of a Tia Maria sauce. Incidentals, from appetisers to pre-dessert to coffee, are as enticing as the rest. In a return to a lost era, sauces are poured on to plates by the waiter, adding to the sense of theatre already engendered by exemplary, well-organised, flawless, world-class service led by Jean-Claude Breton, a master of Franglais. The knowledgeable sommelier 'deserves special praise' for wine service. The majestic and weighty list puts emphasis on France. Loire wines are well selected, but the big guns are saved for Burgundy and Bordeaux. Fans of Domaine de la Romanée-Conti can choose from a number of bottles going back to 1988. The Bordeaux section is dominated by premier cru greats – many mature, including a 1914 Ch. Lafite-Rothschild for £1,400 – with prices to match. A range of Ch. Pétrus includes bottles from 1990 back to 1947. The emphasis on great names inevitably means that choice below £20 is sadly limited; there are in fact six. Seven wines are available by the glass from £5 to £14.

CHEF/PROPRIETOR: Gordon Ramsay   OPEN: Mon to Fri 12 to 2.30, 6.45 to 11   CLOSED: Christmas, bank hols   MEALS: Set L £40, Set D £70 to £85   SERVICE: not inc   CARDS: Amex, Delta, Diners, MasterCard, Switch, Visa   DETAILS: 45 seats. Private parties: 45 main room. Vegetarian meals. No cigars in dining room. Wheelchair access (not WC). No music. No mobile phones. Air-conditioned   ⊖ Sloane Square

## Gordon Ramsay at Claridge's ▼

**NEW ENTRY**   map 13

55 Brook Street, W1A 2JQ
TEL: (020) 7499 0099
WEBSITE: www.gordonramsay@claridges.co.uk

COOKING 7
FRENCH
£39–£86

The Ramsay name, and extensive refurbishment, have brought some sparkle to the hotel's old fashioned, stately opulence. Opened just as the Guide's last edition appeared, the high-ceilinged dining room is spacious and light – elegant and classy to some, dowdy and '1950s Margate' to others – with orange-pink walls, purple chair covers, layered light fittings, and discreet cameras helping the kitchen monitor progress. As this edition of the Guide went to press Mr Ramsay was about to wave his magic wand again, this time over the Connaught (see entry).

The food plays safe, as one might expect in these circumstances, combining top-class materials with classic treatments: a starter of foie gras with caramelised endive, for example, might be followed by breast of black leg chicken with artichoke barigoule. Precise cooking has yielded a plump, juicy Bresse pigeon – lightly and subtly gamey – that had been poached and grilled, served in a rich, gooey, port-based sauce containing caramelised root vegetables and a purée of dates. Fish is deftly handled too: sea bream, 'pan-fried to perfection', is firm yet succulent, accompanied by grilled asparagus and a vanilla sauce. Techniques are well-drilled, and results impressive, even if central ingredients tend to outshine their accompaniments, as in accurately grilled, crisp-skinned red mullet fillets on an assembly of 'fancy stuff', including aubergine caviar and sweet and sour diced vegetables.

Cheeses (on two trolleys, one English, one French) are kept in fine fettle. Desserts do not appear to be a high point, although they might include a Valrhona chocolate fondant, or a prune and Armagnac vanilla tart with mascarpone. Staff are formal, French, and distant rather than engaged, but there is a full complement of sommeliers to help with the massive, Francocentric wine list. This is a predictably stellar collection of big names from Burgundy and Bordeaux; collections of vintages of first growths dominate the claret section, and four-figure prices are not unusual. Even wines from traditional 'good-value' regions like southern France and Beaujolais carry stiff price tags, and there are only four bottles under £20.

CHEF: Mark Sargeant   PROPRIETOR: Gordon Ramsay   OPEN: all week 12 to 3, 5.45 (6 Sun) to 11
MEALS: Set L £25, Set D £50. Prestige tasting menu £60   SERVICE: not inc, card slips closed
CARDS: Amex, Delta, MasterCard, Switch, Visa   DETAILS: 125 seats. Private parties: 25 main
room. Vegetarian meals. No music. No mobile phones. Air-conditioned   ⊖ Bond Street

## Gourmet Garden                                                    map 12

59 Watford Way, Hendon, NW4 3AX                                    COOKING 1
TEL: (020) 8202 9639                               CHINESE/MALAYSIAN/SINGAPOREAN
                                                                   £11–£53

Ignore the traffic and concentrate on the food in this utilitarian, family-run
restaurant beside a busy suburban dual carriageway. The 150-dish menu offers a
broad spread of convincing Malaysian and Singaporean home cooking,
bolstered by a contingent of Chinese specialities. Flavours are bold and there
are no 'compromises for Western taste buds'. Some of the most rewarding stuff is
to be found in the menu's special 'food corner', which promises laksa, claypot
seafood noodles, and tauhu sumbat (crispy stuffed bean curd with peanut
sauce). Elsewhere, there might be braised quail and winter pork, steamed king
prawns with garlic plum sauce and egg white, or 'hearty' eight treasure spring
chicken stuffed with Chinese herbs, carrots, shiitake mushrooms and chestnuts.
Drink Oriental beer or saké; house wine is £7.90.

CHEF: Kia Lian Tan   PROPRIETORS: Annie and Kia Lian Tan   OPEN: Wed to Mon L 12 to 2.15 (2.45
Sun), 6 to 11.15 (10.45 Sun)   CLOSED: 25 and 26 Dec   MEALS: alc (main courses £5 to £18). Set L
Mon, Wed to Fri £5.50, Set D £12.80 to £16.80   SERVICE: 10%   CARDS: Amex, Delta, Diners,
MasterCard, Switch, Visa   DETAILS: 70 seats. Private parties: 70 main room. Vegetarian meals.
Children's helpings. No cigars in dining room. Music. Air-conditioned   ⊖ Hendon Central

## Granita 🍴                                                         map 13

127 Upper Street, N1 1QP                                            COOKING 3
TEL: (020) 7226 3222   FAX: (020) 7226 4833                   MODERN EUROPEAN
WEBSITE: www.granita.co.uk                                          £23–£53

Granita is now owned by Huseyin Ozer, of Ozer (see entry, London) and the
Middle Eastern café chain Sofra. The minimalist look remains unchanged – a
long, thin room; a large plate-glass front window; and cream walls accented by a
single red one – and the food also retains its broadly European focus, with a few
Asian and Middle Eastern embellishments. Straightforward assembly dishes
and salads typically feature among starters: an intriguingly textured asparagus
salad with pear, carrots and courgettes with truffle dressing, or seared tuna
flavoured with sesame oil and garnished with grated mooli.

Materials are impressive, and among main courses a top notch, succulent,
tender rack of lamb has been suitably accompanied by chopped aubergine,
while an ace piece of Alaskan black cod has been served with asparagus
tempura. To finish, a pretty, melted-in-the-middle hot chocolate pudding might
be partnered by a fine pistachio ice cream. Presentation is attractive, although
not all flavour combinations are successful, and portions can be on the small
side. Service is attentive and reasonably professional. The wine list covers New
World and Old, and house red and white start at £11.95; four wines are served by
the glass.

CHEF: Youcef Kaipi  PROPRIETORS: Huseyin Ozer and Bahadir Potukoglu  OPEN: all week noon to 11  MEALS: alc D (main courses £7.50 to £13). Set L and D noon to 7.30 £10 (2 courses) to £12.50. Brunch menu also available  SERVICE: 12.5% (optional), card slips closed  CARDS: Delta, MasterCard, Switch, Visa  DETAILS: 75 seats. Private parties: 100 main room. No-smoking area. Wheelchair access (also WC). No music. Air-conditioned  ⊖ Angel  £5

---

## Great Eastern Dining Room  £ — map 13

54–56 Great Eastern Street, EC2A 3QR

TEL: (020) 7613 4545   FAX: (020) 7613 4137

WEBSITE: www.greateasterndining.co.uk

NEW CHEF
PAN-ASIAN
£27–£48

This busy, minimally decorated bar and dining room draws a mix of refugees from the City, and young style-conscious locals, not least for the atmosphere and cocktails. As the Guide went to press we learned of a change in the kitchen. Out goes the modern Italian cooking, and in comes Paul Day with a penchant for Eastern food (he previously worked at e&o, see entry, which is under the same ownership). Around ten dim sum dishes might offer chilli and garlic squid, or pork and chicken dumplings, and choice extends to sushi, tempura and a few 'house dishes' such as roast chicken ho fun with yellow bean sauce. The southern hemisphere accounts for much of the sharply chosen wine list, although France adds its customary verve to proceedings. Prices start at £11 for vin de pays red and white.

CHEF: Paul Day  PROPRIETOR: Will Ricker  OPEN: Mon to Fri L 12.15 to 3, Mon to Sat D 6.30 to 11  CLOSED: 23 Dec to 3 Jan  MEALS: alc (main courses £9 to £14.50). Set L and D £22.50 (2 courses) to £27 (min 8 people).  SERVICE: 12.5% (optional), card slips closed  CARDS: Amex, Delta, Diners, MasterCard, Switch, Visa  DETAILS: 65 seats. Private parties: 12 main room. Vegetarian meals. Wheelchair access (not WC). No music  ⊖ Old Street

---

## ▲ Great Eastern Hotel, Aurora  ♥ 🗒 — map 13

Liverpool Street, EC2M 7QN

TEL: (020) 7618 7000   FAX: (020) 7618 7001

EMAIL: restaurantres@great-eastern-hotel.co.uk

WEBSITE: www.aurora-restaurant.co.uk

COOKING 4
MODERN EUROPEAN
£49–£90

A stained-glass domed ceiling and handsome Ionic columns are among the features of this period dining room that were restored to their original glory by Sir Terence Conran, who also introduced some of his own ideas, including modern chandeliers, looking like inverted crinolines, constructed from overlapping sheets of sandpaper. Warren Geraghty puts on a thoroughly modern menu, replete with luxury items such as lobster and foie gras, and seems to enjoy a little surf 'n' turf, including rare pigeon with ecrevisse, and a row of three good-quality scallops interspersed with pieces of moist stewed pork belly, accompanied by a smear of cauliflower purée: 'a great combination.'

Materials are sympathetically treated, from a simple seasonal dish of asparagus with a light hollandaise, to an intense and earthy open ravioli of snails and mushrooms. Italian input extends to properly made gnocchi piemontese with artichokes and nettle butter, and to tasty roast guinea fowl with a robustly seasoned walnut risotto. Puddings tend to be rich – even a tropical fruit parcel comes with pastry and lots of cream – but pain perdu, with vanilla ice cream and candied apples, is a light and delicate version. Prices are steep (pea and mint soup is outstanding, but a bit dear at £10.50), and service is patient and good-humoured. An extensive wine list offers plenty of choice (from a Mitchelton Airstrip blend of Marsanne, Roussanne and Viognier to a Montgras Block 144 Syrah from Chile, both 2000) but few bargains. There is much to appeal to wine lovers, but expense-account diners are perhaps best suited to take advantage of areas of keenest interest, such as Bordeaux, Champagne, red Burgundy and reds from Italy and Spain. Ten interesting wines from the sommelier's selection are available by the glass (£4.35 to £8.95) or bottle (£18.50 to £38).

Terminus, at the same address, is a brasserie-style operation offering potted shrimps, Caesar salad, beef rump with chips and béarnaise, and lemon tart; it is open seven days a week from 7am to 10.30pm (half an hour earlier, in each case, at weekends)

CHEF: Warren Geraghty   PROPRIETOR: Great Eastern   OPEN: Mon to Fri 12 to 2.30, 6.45 to 9.30   MEALS: alc (main courses £17.50 to £31.50). Set L £28, Set D £38 to £60 (inc wine). Bar menu available L   SERVICE: 12.5%   CARDS: Amex, Delta, Diners, MasterCard, Switch, Visa   DETAILS: 100 seats. Private parties: 4 to 400 private rooms. Vegetarian meals. Wheelchair access (also WC). Occasional music. Air-conditioned   ACCOMMODATION: 267 rooms, all with bath/shower. TV. Phone. Room only £225 to £515. Rooms for disabled   ⊖ Liverpool Street

---

# Greenhouse
map 15

27A Hays Mews, W1X 7RJ
TEL: (020) 7499 3331   FAX: (020) 7499 5368
EMAIL: reservations@greenhouserestaurant.co.uk
WEBSITE: www.greenhouserestaurant.co.uk

COOKING 5
GLOBAL
£32–£132

Re-launched after a much-hyped makeover by David Collins, the Greenhouse has adopted a 'conservatively modern' style whose best feature is probably a view of exotic shrubbery in a courtyard, lending a tropical feel to proceedings. Staff are welcoming, knowledgeable and efficient, and the bottom line is that this is 'a comforting kind of place, run with friendly professionalism'. Spicing remains a central feature of the cooking, thanks perhaps to Paul Merrett's origins (he was born in Zanzibar), producing a light, refreshing dhal soup spiked with coriander and a kick of chilli, exhibiting 'bags of flavour', and a dish of sea bass with aloo sag, onion bhajia and tomato pickle.

While many dishes have an Eastern bias, other ideas and materials are firmly in European mould, from accurately timed stuffed breast of guinea fowl, served with a truffled leg and a light and tasty smoked sausage pie, to pink roast loin of lamb arranged on sauté discs of sweet potato, with confit aubergine and tomato and a garlicky stock reduction. Desserts cover a similar range, from banana Tatin with honeycomb ice cream, to an impressive plum tarte fine, accompanied by a sharp, spicy ice cream flavoured with lemon grass and black pepper. Cheeses are kept in 'superb condition', and the varietally arranged wine list is a humdinger, though sadly its prices make depressing reading. House Merlot and Sauvignon Blanc are £15.

CHEF: Paul Merrett   PROPRIETOR: The Capital Group   OPEN: Mon to Fri L 12 to 2.30, Mon to Sat D 5.30 to 11   CLOSED: 25 and 26 Dec, bank hols   MEALS: alc (main courses £19.50 to £23.50). Set L Mon to Fri £21, Set D 5.30 to 7 £14 (2 courses) to £18, Set D £55 to £95 (inc wine)   SERVICE:

12.5% (optional), card slips closed   CARDS: Amex, Delta, Diners, MasterCard, Switch, Visa
DETAILS: 70 seats. Vegetarian meals. Children's helpings. No cigars/pipes in dining room. Music.
Air-conditioned   ⊖ Green Park

# Green Olive                                                                    map 13

5 Warwick Place, W9 2PX                                                    COOKING 2
TEL/FAX:  (020) 7289 2469                                                     ITALIAN
                                                                           £27–£49

Under the same ownership as Red Pepper (see entry), Green Olive is a stylish
Italian restaurant that takes a traditional approach in its good-value set-price
menus. Lunch options are restricted to a couple of choices per course, but the
food is felt to be interesting enough to compensate: one reporter praised a lightly
dressed salad of pink chicken livers, and an elegantly presented and carefully
cooked main course of rabbit with broad beans and asparagus. The greater
choice on dinner menus may include tuna carpaccio with green beans, chives
and raspberry vinaigrette among starters, while main courses have taken in sea
bass with sauté potatoes in an artichoke and cherry tomato broth, and roast pork
fillet wrapped in Parma ham served with braised lettuce and lentils. For dessert
there might be white chocolate bavarois with coconut tuille and rhubarb sauce,
or ricotta and cinnamon tart with vanilla sauce; or opt for one of the Italian
cheeses. House wines on the concise, all-Italian list are £14, or £4 per glass.

CHEF: Maurizio Morelli   PROPRIETOR: Red Pepper Group   OPEN: all week 12 to 3, 6 to 11   MEALS:
Set L £11 (2 courses) to £14.50, Set D £21.50 (2 courses) to £27   SERVICE: 12.5% (optional),
card slips closed   CARDS: Amex, Delta, MasterCard, Switch, Visa   DETAILS: 60 seats. Private
parties: 35 main room, 20 private room. Music. Air-conditioned   ⊖ Warwick Avenue

# Haandi                                                                         map 14

136 Brompton Road, SW3 1HY                                                 COOKING 4
TEL:  (020) 7823 7373   FAX:  (020) 7823 9696                                 INDIAN
WEBSITE: www.haandi-restaurants.com                                        £18–£58

In keeping with the traditions of hospitality, the owners of this swish Indian –
right opposite Harrods – have opened a bar called the Black Saffron Lounge.
Down in the basement you can call in anytime for a glass of champagne,
cocktails and some North Indian 'tapas' (vegetable pakoras, monkfish tikka and
the like). Live jazz perks up the mood every evening after 6. The main restaurant
has two entrances, front and back, and once through the door you enter a long
'Tardis-like' room dominated by a kitchen enclosed in glass. Cooking focuses on
the North Frontier, with the tandoori oven delivering benchmark versions of
lamb chops, tikkas and 'fluffy, fresh' naan breads. Even the ubiquitous chicken
tikka masala is taken to high levels of excellence.

Skilled spicing, top-notch ingredients and exact cooking are the kitchen's
trademarks: evident in 'very flavourful' heera panna (stir-fried squid and
monkfish), gosht-e-josh (boneless mutton curry) and murg daraanpur (chicken
with roasted cumin and greens). Dishes are served in eponymous 'haandis'
(wide-bellied, narrow-necked pots), prices are fair for the area, and portions are
'extremely generous'. A longish international wine list has a helpful chart

listing recommended bottles with favourite dishes. Eight wines (plus champagne) are available by the glass, and house wine is £10.95.

CHEFS: Alam Singh Bisht and Ratan Singh   PROPRIETOR: Haandi Restaurants Ltd   OPEN: all week 12 to 3, 6 to 11.30   CLOSED: 25 Dec   MEALS: alc (main courses £6 to £13). Set L £7.95 to £12.50. Bar menu available all day   SERVICE: not inc   CARDS: Amex, Diners, MasterCard, Switch, Visa DETAILS: 80 seats. Private parties: 70 main room, 8 to 15 private rooms. Vegetarian meals. No-smoking area. Music. Air-conditioned   ⊖ Knightsbridge  £5

# Hakkasan                                                              map 15

| 8 Hanway Place, W1P 9DH | COOKING 3 |
| TEL: (020) 7927 7000   FAX: (020) 7436 2929 | CHINESE |
| EMAIL: mail@hakkasan.com | £38–£98 |

You might miss this place completely (it's in a back alley near the junction of Tottenham Court Road and Oxford Street) were it not for the taxis and trendy folk hovering about. A precipitous staircase leads down to a chic, elegant, dark subterranean dining room with black fretwork screens, marble and slate floors, and stark white crockery. It is a seductive place rather than a practical one – tables are a bit small for all the dim sum dishes that can pile up – and the later it gets in the evening the more like a club it becomes. It offers a version of Chinese food for those who want the reassurance of a designery Western ambience and don't mind paying extra for it.

The consensus is that lunch is the better bet for food. Dim sum are suitably varied, although pricier than in Chinatown, and help in choosing them may not be forthcoming. But the spectacularly large and fresh-tasting prawns are worth a go (steamed with coriander and chilli are good), as are grilled chicken and prawn Shanghai dumpling, and roast silver cod with champagne and Chinese honey. Among the 'new' dishes to look out for are century and salted egg congee with bamboo shoots, fried ginger and preserved olive. Western desserts include a fine chocolate and banana fondant with roast almond ice cream, and wines are sharply chosen, but don't expect any bargains.

CHEF: Tong Chee Hwee   PROPRIETOR: Alan Yau   OPEN: all week 12 to 3 (4.30 Sat, Sun and bank hols), 6 to 12 (12.30 Thur, Fri and Sat, 11.30 Sun)   CLOSED: 25 Dec   MEALS: alc (main courses £8.50 to £45)   SERVICE: 13% (optional), card slips closed   CARDS: Amex, Delta, MasterCard, Switch, Visa   DETAILS: 230 seats. Vegetarian meals. Wheelchair access (also WC). Music. Air-conditioned

# Highgate £                              | NEW ENTRY |   map 13

| Highgate Studios, | |
| 53–79 Highgate Road, NW5 1TL | COOKING 3 |
| TEL: (020) 7485 8442   FAX: (020) 7482 0357 | MODERN EUROPEAN |
| EMAIL: kushtibars@aol.com | £27–£47 |

Opened in June 2001, this is a basement restaurant beneath a large, high-ceilinged bar, the whole occupying one end of a warehouse conversion on the Highgate/Kentish Town border. Dimmed lights, leather sofas and potted palms aim at a feeling of intimacy, but the overriding decorative impression is of rough-and-ready functionality. Jamie Polito has cooked at some of London's smarter addresses, including Kensington Place and Odettes (see entries). This shows in starters such as a cep broth of 'full-blown mushroomy character' relying for its salt on a scattering of excellent Parmesan croûtons, and in 'crunchy but not profusely fatty' chunks of deep-fried pork belly served with asparagus in a smooth cidery vinaigrette. Such earthy richness is a feature of the cooking, even when it comes to fish (a strong suit): gilt-head bream arrives on brandade mash and black olives, and salmon with mushroom velouté is highly rated. That much-abused dessert, pannacotta, is well wrought, properly fragile in texture and served with moscatel raisins; summer berry trifle might be an alternative at the appropriate season. Wines – stylistically arranged, from 'fresh' whites to 'rich and elegant' reds – start with house Puglians at £10.50 a bottle (£2.65 a glass/£3.75 a large glass).

CHEF: Jamie Polito   PROPRIETORS: James McDowell, Jamie Polito, Mark Slade and Nick Rouse   OPEN: all week 12.30 to 3 (4 Sun), 6.30 to 10.30 (10 Sun)   MEALS: alc (main courses £9 to £14.50). Bar menu also available   SERVICE: 12.5% (optional), card slips closed   CARDS: Delta, MasterCard, Switch, Visa   DETAILS: 140 seats. 8 seats outside. Private parties: 100 main room. Vegetarian meals. Children's helpings. No children after 8pm. Music. Air-conditioned ⊖ Kentish Town £5

# Holly £

map 12

38 Holly Grove, SE15 5DF
TEL/FAX: (020) 7277 2928

COOKING 2
FRENCH/DUTCH
£25–£40

Just two simple rooms and a small courtyard are all that this very personal restaurant, in the middle of Peckham's one-way system, amounts to. Furnishings are simple, and décor consists of little more than a few quirky photographs, but the congenial atmosphere is helped along by charming, well-trained staff. Given the size of the kitchen, the menu is sensibly pared down to just three choices at each stage (including something for vegetarians). At times the cooking can be 'a bit hit and miss', but there are good things to be had, notably breast of wood pigeon on a bed of apple and beetroot, osso buco ('with plenty of bone marrow'), and ribeye steak with veal jus. Fish is also a reliable bet: a fine fillet of crisp-skinned, pan-fried gilt-head bream on spinach with polenta and beurre blanc has been praised. The chef hails from Holland, so it is no surprise that Dutch apple tart is the real thing; otherwise finish with blackcurrant sorbet with honey cream. House French is £10.50.

CHEF: Norbert van Hest   PROPRIETORS: Norbert and Barbara van Hest   OPEN: Tue to Sat D only 6 to 10   CLOSED: Christmas, New Year, Aug   MEALS: alc (main courses £9 to £15)   SERVICE: not inc, card slips closed   CARDS: Amex, MasterCard, Switch, Visa   DETAILS: 35 seats. 8 seats outside. Private parties: 12 main room. Vegetarian meals. Wheelchair access (not WC). Music

*All entries in the Guide are re-researched and rewritten every year, not least because restaurant standards fluctuate. Don't rely on an out-of-date Guide.*

# Huong-Viet £     | NEW ENTRY |   map 13

An Viet House, 12–14 Englefield Road, N1 4LS     COOKING **1**
TEL: (020) 7249 0877     VIETNAMESE
£19–£33

A Housing, Social Training and Enterprise Centre serving the local Vietnamese community is the unlikely setting for this welcoming little 'canteen-like' restaurant, offering authentic food at very fair prices. Just by the entrance is an impressive chargrill, which is used for satays and other dishes, such as chicken with chilli and lemon grass, and prawns wrapped in pork, while the longish menu also includes classic spring rolls and four versions of pho (a traditional noodle-based soup with coriander). Flavours are delicate, and vegetables are extremely well handled: witness French beans with garlic, and snow peas with black-bean sauce. Unusual-sounding desserts include pineapple leaf cake, and creamy tofu in a sweet ginger 'soup'. It is unlicensed, but you can BYO or try the 'delightfully fresh' home-made lemonade.

CHEF: Thanh Vu   PROPRIETOR: Huong-Viet Ltd   OPEN: Mon to Sat 12 to 3.30 (4 Sat), 5.30 to 11 MEALS: alc (main courses £5 to £7). Set L Mon to Fri £6 (2 courses), Set L Sat £13, Set D £13 (min 4)   SERVICE: L not inc, D 10%, card slips closed, 12% for parties of 5 or more   CARDS: MasterCard, Switch, Visa   DETAILS: 70 seats. Private parties: 32 private room. Vegetarian meals. Children's helpings. No-smoking area. Wheelchair access (also women's WC). Occasional music   ⊖ Angel, Liverpool Street

---

# Ibla      map 15

89 Marylebone High Street, W1U 4QY     COOKING **3**
TEL: (020) 7224 3799   FAX: (020) 7486 1370     ITALIAN
EMAIL: ibla@ibla.co.uk     £30–£59

A relaxed atmosphere pervades this fashionable Marylebone High Street restaurant. There are two dining areas – the front has a green theme, the rear is dark red – and the cooking is broadly Italian, but occasionally features ideas from further afield: unusual ideas may not feature as frequently as they once did, but you may still find paprika frogs' legs, or pea soup with scrambled egg. A salad of artichokes, French beans and apple, and a risotto of peas and broad beans make convincingly Italian starters, while main courses range from pan-fried red mullet with spinach and bacon, to lamb chop with caponata, via sauté sweetbreads with shallots and rocket. Finish on a slightly less than traditional note with Baileys-flavoured pannacotta. Service has shown signs of inexperience at times, and all but a few bottles on the wine list weigh in above the £20 mark, although house white is £14, red £19.

CHEF: Luca Dal Bosco   PROPRIETOR: Luciano Pellicano   OPEN: Mon to Fri L 12 to 2.30, Mon to Sat D 7 to 10.30   CLOSED: Christmas, Easter, bank hols   MEALS: Set L £15 (2 courses) to £18, Set D £26 (2 courses) to £35   SERVICE: not inc, card slips closed, 12.5% for parties of 4 or more CARDS: Amex, Delta, Diners, MasterCard, Switch, Visa   DETAILS: 56 seats. Private parties: 30 main room. Vegetarian meals. No music. Air-conditioned   ⊖ Baker Street

# Incognico

map 15

117 Shaftesbury Avenue, WC2H 8AD
TEL: (020) 7836 8866   FAX: (020) 7240 9525

NEW CHEF
FRENCH
£25–£88

Wooden floorboards, dark panelling and closely packed tables create a bistro atmosphere, while the silver ceiling, Art Deco lights and lavish flower arrangements add a touch of glamour. As the Guide went to press, Darren Bunn (listed in the 2001 edition at Criterion Brasserie) stepped into the kitchen at short notice, although the appealing brasserie-style menu seems set to continue. The broad range takes in cod fillet with pea purée and beurre blanc, roast duck leg with cep sauce, and rice pudding with apricot coulis. Note that the restaurant may require a credit card number when booking, and that prices are comparatively high (although the set lunch and fast-paced early evening deal are considered good value). Wines include a red and white from Uruguay at £20, and some first-class bottles from elsewhere, but most are over £30.

CHEF: Darren Bunn   PROPRIETORS: Nico and Dinah-Jane Ladenis   OPEN: Mon to Sat 12 to 3, 5.30 to 12   CLOSED: 10 days Christmas, 4 days Easter, bank hols   MEALS: alc (main courses £11.50 to £18.50). Set L £12.50, Set D 5.30 to 7 £12.50   SERVICE: 12.5% (optional), card slips closed CARDS: Amex, Diners, MasterCard, Switch, Visa   DETAILS: 85 seats. Vegetarian meals. No pipes in dining room. Wheelchair access (not WC). Music. Air-conditioned   ⊖ Leicester Square

---

# ▲ Inter-Continental, Le Soufflé ♥

map 14

1 Hamilton Place, W1V 0QY
TEL: (020) 7409 3131   FAX: (020) 7491 0926
EMAIL: london@interconti.com
WEBSITE: www.london.interconti.com

COOKING 4
MODERN EUROPEAN
£43–£89

Old-style hotel dining survives in this large rectangular room, complete with its curved white ceiling, tub chairs, patterned carpets, and Friday and Saturday dinner dances that go on till midnight. What *is* new, though, is that Michael Coaker, who succeeded Peter Kromberg in September 2001, seems to be ploughing a more straightforwardly 'modern European' furrow.

A smoked salmon starter, and the roast leg of lamb, are still carved and served from chrome-domed trolleys, and English comfort food – in the shape of Dover sole, or roast beef with Yorkshire pudding and red wine jus – remains central to the kitchen's output. But these traditional items live happily beside red mullet escabèche with coriander and tapénade dressing, or a main-course of roast 'osso bucco' of monkfish with tomato risotto. Desserts might include pan-fried strawberries and raspberries in crisp, thin pastry, or amaretto soufflé. 'Healthy' and vegetarian dishes are clearly marked on the menu.

Service is professional and attentive, and the wine list is suitably posh. Classic French regions are covered (including 1918 Château Latour at £2,000 and three DRC burgundies), and there are good selections from New Zealand, Australia and California. A list of 13 sommelier's suggestions includes wines with more sensible prices, although even here there is nothing below £20.

CHEF: Michael Coaker   PROPRIETOR: Six Continents   OPEN: Tue to Fri and Sun L 12.30 to 3, Tue to Sat D 7 to 10.30 (11.15 Sat)   CLOSED: 26 to 30 Dec, bank hols   MEALS: alc (main courses £19 to £28). Set L £21.50 (2 courses) to £33.50, Set L Sun £33.50, Set D £40 to £47   SERVICE: not inc   CARDS: Amex, Delta, Diners, MasterCard, Switch, Visa   DETAILS: 65 seats. Private parties: 80 main room. Vegetarian meals. Children's helpings. Wheelchair access (also WC). Music. No mobile phones. Air-conditioned   ACCOMMODATION: 458 rooms, all with bath/shower. TV. Phone. Room only £190 to £320 (prices exc VAT). Rooms for disabled. Baby facilities   ⊖ Hyde Park Corner  (£5)

## Isola ♥ 🕮                                                      map 14

145 Knightsbridge, SW1X 7PA                                      COOKING 5
TEL: (020) 7838 1044   FAX: (020) 7838 1099                        ITALIAN
EMAIL: isola@gruppo.co.uk                                          £28–£71

It's all change again at Isola. This year's layout restores a bar area to the ground floor, with the main restaurant occupying a cheery basement filled with natural outdoor light and furnished with cream-upholstered benches and bare wooden tables. Torch songs murmur in the background, and the waiting staff wear monochrome chic.

Now that Bruno Loubet has moved to Australia, a pair of Italian hands is brought to bear on what has always been a modern Italian repertoire. The bilingual menu is supplemented by daily specials, which might include a starter of tagliolini with lobster and tomato, the meat tender and flavourful, the pasta well made, a rich sauce of cooking juices adding depth. Prime Scottish beef is used for carpaccio, which is served with spring onions and Pecorino. That care over the quality of ingredients shows again in a main course of jointed, slow-cooked chicken with peas, shallots and roast potatoes, while the timing of fish, such as a halibut steak on mushrooms with a restrained addition of truffle oil, is impressively precise. Vegetable sides might include a first class dish of roast new potatoes flavoured with rosemary and vanilla. Desserts are classically simple in the Italian way: sublime zabaglione accompanying a slice of chocolate terrine, and a superbly textured, bottomlessly rich version of tiramisù served in a glass.

Wines explore the highways and byways of Italy, from the northern reaches of Trentino-Alto Adige to Sicily and Sardinia. Most attention is lavished on Piedmont (Barolo in particular) and Tuscany (Super-Tuscans galore), although go-ahead producers from the Veneto and Friuli are well chosen, too. In addition to a selection of 32 wines by the glass (£3.50 to £16.70), fans can explore the list via one of the two 'taster trays': five small tasting samples of wines from around the country. Prices start at a reasonable £13.50, but there is plenty for those who want to give their credit cards a work-out.

CHEF: Graziano Bonacina   PROPRIETORS: Oliver Peyton and Gruppo Ltd   OPEN: Mon to Sat 12 to 2.45, 6 to 10.45   MEALS: alc (main dishes £7.50 to £19.50). Set L £14 (2 courses) to £16.50   SERVICE: 12.5% (optional), card slips closed   CARDS: Amex, Delta, Diners, MasterCard, Switch, Visa   DETAILS: 150 seats. Vegetarian meals. Wheelchair access (not WC). Music. Air-conditioned   ⊖ Knightsbridge

# Istanbul Iskembecisi  £

map 12

9 Stoke Newington Road, N16 8BH
TEL/FAX: (020) 72547291
WEBSITE: www.londraturk.com/
istanbuliskembecisi

COOKING 2
TURKISH
£18–£34

'A great way to spend a rather dissolute Sunday afternoon!' noted one visitor after a visit to this 'relatively up-market' venue in an enclave of cheap-and-cheerful cafés and kebab houses. What it offers is sound Turkish cooking without frills. The 'iskembe' of the name is a traditional tripe soup to which you add salt, vinegar, lemon juice and pepper. Otherwise opt for a fistful of more familiar meze: Albanian liver with onion salad, patlican salata (grilled aubergine purée with tahini, lemon and olive oil), and stuffed vine leaves have all been enjoyed. Main courses are mostly grills and slow-cooked dishes (lamb in particular has been 'very tender'). Portions are hefty, but finish with baklava if you have room. Drink raki or Turkish Buzbag, which run in at £8.50 (£2 a glass). Note the noon to dawn opening hours.

CHEFS/PROPRIETORS: Ali Demir and Ahmet Poyraz  OPEN: all week noon to 5am  MEALS: alc (main courses £6.50 to £10)  SERVICE: not inc, 10% for parties of 10 or more  CARDS: none  DETAILS: 90 seats. Private parties: 90 main room. Vegetarian meals. Children's helpings. Music. Air-conditioned  ⊖ Highbury & Islington  £5

# Itsu  ⬦ ⁵✳ £

map 14

118 Draycott Avenue, SW3 3AE
TEL: (020) 7590 2400  FAX: (020) 7590 2403
WEBSITE: www.itsu.co.uk

COOKING 3
JAPANESE
£27–£37

On a large corner site with huge glass windows, the original branch of Itsu still feels contemporary and appealing five years after opening. Informal and funky, it provides 'the sort of fast food that gives the industry a good name' to a background of loud, thumping music. Its two discrete sections consist of a conveyor belt with high stools, and a smaller one with benches, and its highlights are fresh, glossy ingredients that spearhead a well-balanced, inventive and healthy roll call of dishes.

Although the range of fish is limited to salmon, tuna, eel and sea bass (supplemented perhaps by lobster, crab, prawn and crayfish), the fusion approach allows plenty of breadth and choice. Among the better offerings are tender beef carpaccio with citrus dip, fresh crab rolls with chilli dip, sea bass and scallop tartare, and tuna sashimi. Organic salmon comes in several guises: sushi, sashimi, smoked, shiso, chillied, and new-style sashimi with sesame, chives and ginger. Rolls seem to be the least successful group. Hot dishes (made to order) take in grilled chicken teriyaki with a ginger soy sauce, and first-class grilled eel with 'pitch-perfect' sushi rice. Desserts are Westernised – chocolate mousse, for example – and service is friendly and efficient: a press of the red button brings a quick response from enthusiastic and smiling staff. To drink there is saké or Asahi beer, and inventive-sounding fresh fruit drinks; a handful of wines is are also offered.

CHEFS: Angela Baird and Mark Read   PROPRIETORS: Clive Schlee and Julian Metcalfe   OPEN: all week 12 to 11   CLOSED: 24 to 26 Dec   MEALS: alc (sushi £2.50 to £6; sashimi selections £6.50 to £17).   SERVICE: not inc   CARDS: Amex, MasterCard, Switch, Visa   DETAILS: 68 seats. Private parties: 40 main room. Vegetarian meals. No smoking in dining room. Wheelchair access (not WC). Music. Air-conditioned   ⊖ South Kensington

## Itsu (Soho) ✳ £

map 15

103 Wardour Street, W1V 3TD

COOKING 2

TEL: (020) 7479 4794   FAX: (020) 7479 4795

JAPANESE

WEBSITE: www.itsu.co.uk

£27–£37

Seemingly a little bigger and brasher than the Draycott Avenue original (see entry above), the Soho branch is a fun place serving some 'remarkably good stuff' on its conveyor belts. Plate colour indicates the price, starting at £1.50 for white, but silver and gold plates are much more interesting, so it is 'very, very easy to eat far more and spend far more than you intended'. Organic salmon plays a leading role, appearing as tartare, and as a remarkably good 'new-style' sashimi. The range takes in tuna and scallop sushi, and a few more generally Asian dishes, such as bang-bang chicken, as well as hot dishes and made-to-order items, which are not to be ignored. Staff are pleasant and knowledgeable, and Asahi beer makes a good match for much of the food, although there is also saké, green tea and a few wines.

CHEF: Angela Baird   PROPRIETORS: Clive Schlee and Julian Metcalfe   OPEN: all week 12 to 11 (midnight Fri and Sat)   CLOSED: 25 and 26 Dec, 1 Jan   MEALS: alc (sushi £2.50 to £6; sashimi selections £6.50 to £17).   SERVICE: not inc   CARDS: Amex, MasterCard, Switch, Visa   DETAILS: 70 seats. Vegetarian meals. No smoking in dining room. Wheelchair access (also WC). Music. Air-conditioned   ⊖ Piccadilly Circus

## Ivy

map 15

1–5 West Street, WC2H 9NQ

COOKING 5

TEL: (020) 7836 4751   FAX: (020) 7240 9333

MODERN BRITISH

EMAIL: reservations@the-ivy.co.uk

£30–£80

Not everybody sees the Ivy through rose-tinted spectacles, and our reporters in particular take exception to the acres of publicity surrounding what is a very good, though not absolutely top-flight, restaurant. We have explained before that it is noisy and full of celebrities, that unless you are Nicole Kidman or the Prime Minister you have to beg to get a table, and that service can be rushed. If those conditions don't appeal, stay away. But for those prepared to run the gauntlet, the food is definitely worth eating.

An appealing carte seeks to soothe rather than challenge. There is caviar for big spenders, foie gras for the sensuous, Caesar salad for light lunchers, corned beef hash with double fried egg for the unreconstructed, and lots for the nostalgically minded: from potted shrimps to kedgeree, from Mediterranean fish soup to baked Alaska. There is even curried chicken Masala, as well as separate menus for vegans and vegetarians. A few bottles make it under the £20 barrier on a varied and well-chosen wine list that offers a dozen by the glass from £4.50 to £9.75.

CHEFS: Alan Bird and Tim Hughes   PROPRIETOR: Signature Restaurants plc   OPEN: all week 12 to 3 (3.30 Sun), 5.30 to midnight   CLOSED: 25 and 26 Dec, 1 Jan, Aug bank hol   MEALS: alc (main courses £9 to £20). Set L Sat and Sun £17.50. Cover £1.50   SERVICE: not inc   CARDS: Amex, Delta, Diners, MasterCard, Switch, Visa   DETAILS: 100 seats. Private parties: 6 main room, 25 to 60 private rooms. Vegetarian meals. Wheelchair access (not WC). No music. Air-conditioned
⊖ Leicester Square

## Iznik
map 13

| | |
|---|---|
| 19 Highbury Park, N5 1QJ | COOKING 2 |
| TEL: (020) 7704 8099   FAX: (020) 7354 5697 | TURKISH |
| | £21–£32 |

The owners claim this as 'London's most beautiful restaurant', and their years of collecting Turkish artefacts, ancient and modern, certainly make it one of the most gloriously adorned. Daytime and evening menus are nearly identical except for prices, and list all the familiar mezze based on a variety of Mediterranean vegetables and cheeses, plus a few incorporating lamb. Main dishes, again familiar, are mostly skewered grills or stews, with rice and salad. Lamb and chicken are the bases, but there are also swordfish or prawns for the fishy-minded. Anyone wishing to taste Turkish muesli might finish with asure (traditional Turkish dried food compote of cereals, sultanas, nuts, apricots, figs and pomegranates), just one of several alluring desserts, or of course Turkish pastries. A short, varied wine list starts at £9.95 for Turkish red and white.

CHEFS/PROPRIETORS: Adem and Pirlanta Oner   OPEN: all week 10 to 4, 6 to 11   CLOSED: Christmas, Easter   MEALS: alc (main courses £7.50 to £9.50)   SERVICE: 10%   CARDS: Delta, MasterCard, Switch, Visa   DETAILS: 75 seats. Private parties: 75 main room. Vegetarian meals. Wheelchair access (not WC). Music   ⊖ Highbury & Islington

## John Burton-Race at the Landmark ▼
map 13

| | |
|---|---|
| 222 Marylebone Road, NW1 6JQ | |
| TEL: (020) 7723 7800   FAX: (020) 7723 4700 | COOKING 7 |
| EMAIL: jbrthelandmark@btconnect.com | FRENCH |
| WEBSITE: www.landmarklondon.co.uk | £49–£132 |

The Landmark Hotel's atrium is spectacular, and the dining room off it is imposing: a large open space with a high ceiling and rather less intimacy and 'atmosphere' than most reporters would like. Its centrepiece gives an idea of the scale: a huge marble urn on a plinth, sporting eight carved elephants and a vast flower display. As the Guide went to press, we learned that John Burton-Race would be filming in France for much of the coming year, returning intermittently, but Martin Burge has been a trusted and capable lieutenant for some time, so we see no reason why this should adversely affect performance.

What appeals about the cooking is that there is no needless experimentation, no attempt at shock effects, just a succession of fine ingredients that work together harmoniously. Crayfish tails, for example, are flambé in cognac, the flesh arranged in an arc, balanced by a salad that 'could not have been fresher' dressed in walnut oil and sherry vinegar, and by a sliver of pan-fried foie gras resting on a few green beans, the liver firm yet yielding, and full of flavour.

Dishes are labour-intensive and, since combinations are generally unsurprising, rely for effect on finesse: for example, a poussin breast in a pool of cooking juices and eau-de-vie, sharing the plate with a delicate puff pastry box containing half a dozen asparagus tips resting in hollandaise and leek purée, and by a slice of warm foie gras on a pile of spinach, plus creamed morels.

When this highly worked approach is applied to desserts it yields a very fine cylinder of high-quality dark chocolate enclosing two light and delicate mousses, one chocolate, one pistachio, topped with a flawless pistachio ice cream. Even better, perhaps, is the assiette of chocolate, also based on the mousse theme and including a parfait sandwiched between discs of chocolate puff pastry, a mousse containing a few 'perfect cherries', and a sublime chocolate sorbet and white chocolate ice cream in a tuile and caramel cage.

Appetisers and petits fours are also first rate. 'My only reservations would be about the bread, which is ordinary, and the prices, which are not.' Service is exemplary from formally dressed French staff, and the sommelier is both helpful and knowledgeable. As with the cooking, France is the main inspiration for the wine list, with Champagne, Alsace, white and red Burgundy (including 15 wines from the esteemed Domaine de la Romanée-Conti), the Rhône and red Bordeaux commanding the most space. Producers are impeccably sourced for the (rather brief) New World and other European selection, too, but mark-ups are nothing less than greedy. Prices start at £25 for Beaujolais-Villages, and there are only a handful of uninspiring wines at the £25 mark. Four reds and four whites are sold by the glass.

CHEFS: John Burton-Race and Martin Burge   PROPRIETOR: John Burton-Race   OPEN: Mon to Fri L 12 to 2.15, Mon to Sat D 7 to 10.15   CLOSED: first week Jan, bank hols   MEALS: Set L £23 (2 courses) to £65, Set D £65 to £75   SERVICE: not inc   CARDS: Amex, Delta, Diners, MasterCard, Switch, Visa   DETAILS: 85 seats. Private parties: 100 main room, 20 to 150 private rooms. Vegetarian meals. Children's helpings. No cigars/pipes in dining room. Wheelchair access (also WC). No music. No mobile phones. Air-conditioned   ⊖ Marylebone

## J. Sheekey                                                      map 15

28–32 St Martin's Court, WC2N 4AL                    COOKING 5
TEL: (020) 7240 2565   FAX: (020) 7240 8114          BRITISH SEAFOOD
EMAIL: reservations@j-sheekey.co.uk                  £30–£96

The exterior seems to be deliberately drab, and the distressed mirror theme continues inside amid dark oak panelling, 'cracked paint' walls and some large decorative seashells. But this is a sharp operation, confirmed by efficient, pleasant and charming (if not always knowledgeable) service, backed up by 'lots of management' to make sure things are properly organised and smoothly running. Seafood is the kitchen's prime concern, from homely fish pie (mostly salmon for one visitor) to a special, such as salt-baked wild sea bass with fennel hearts.

Along the way are straightforward shellfish, such as lobster mayonnaise and dressed crab, as well as devilled whitebait, caviar with blinis and sour cream, and fresh, flavourful, crisply battered haddock and thin chips with mushy garden (rather than marrowfat) peas. There are meat dishes (braised shin of veal with herb dumplings), vegetarian options (leek and wild mushroom tart), and straightforward desserts of raspberry ripple ice cream, or orange Muscat jelly served with a jug of thick cream. Wines soon hop over the £20 barrier, and don't stop until they reach three figures, but quality is high.

CHEFS: Elliot Ketley and Tim Hughes   PROPRIETOR: Signature Group plc   OPEN: all week 12 to 3 (3.30 Sun), 5.30 to 12   CLOSED: 25 and 26 Dec, 1 Jan, bank hols   MEALS: alc (main courses £10 to £30). Set L Sat and Sun £13.75 (2 courses) to £17.50. Cover £1.50   SERVICE: not inc   CARDS: Amex, Delta, Diners, MasterCard, Switch, Visa   DETAILS: 105 seats. Vegetarian meals. No cigars/pipes in dining room. Wheelchair access (not WC). No music. Air-conditioned ⊖ Leicester Square

## K10 ⁵⅄ £                                          map 13

20 Copthall Avenue, EC2R 7DN
TEL: (020) 7562 8510   FAX: (020) 7562 8515                    COOKING 2
EMAIL: copthall@k10.net                                        JAPANESE
WEBSITE: www.k10.net                                            £19–£34

The main feature of this lively Japanese basement in the heart of the City is a conveyor belt, or kaiten (hence the pun of a name), bearing all kinds of goodies on colour-coded plates. Choose from nigiri sushi (seafood on parcels of vinegared rice), maki (vegetarian, seafood or poultry rolled in seaweed, sometimes inside out), hand rolls, sashimi, udon noodle soups, salads, bento boxes, and a few fusion-style hot dishes. Also note the desserts, such as green tea mousse. Sit at one of the stools by the counter (there is extra seating for larger groups). Water and tea are unlimited; otherwise drink beer, saké or wine from £12.50 a bottle (£2.90 a glass).

The new branch in Soho (102 Wardour Street, W1, tel. (020) 7494 6510, open Mon to Sat 11.30 to 10) is basically a tiny, unlicensed take-away, with three tables if you want to eat in: help yourself to dishes from the refrigerated counter and opt for high-class sushi and sashimi; other items may be a letdown.

CHEFS: Mr Nacer and Miguel Choy   PROPRIETOR: Christopher Kemper   OPEN: Mon to Fri 11.30 to 3, 5 to 10   MEALS: alc (main courses £2 to £4.50)   SERVICE: not inc, card slips closed   CARDS: Amex, Delta, Diners, MasterCard, Switch, Visa   DETAILS: 72 seats. Private parties: 150 main room. No smoking in dining room. Wheelchair access (also WC). Music. Air-conditioned ⊖ Moorgate, Liverpool Street

## Kastoori £                                        map 12

188 Upper Tooting Road, SW17 7EJ                            COOKING 2
TEL: (020) 8767 7027                               GUJARATI VEGETARIAN
                                                               £17–£29

Dinesh and Manoj Thanki have been here since 1987, and their bright restaurant makes just the setting for vividly spiced vegetarian food. The kitchen takes its cue from their native Katia Wahd, a temperate region of Gujarat that is the only part of India where tomatoes grow naturally. The Thankis spent many years in Uganda, and the menu also features some African ingredients and dishes, which tend to show up among the list of specials; here you will find matoki (a green banana curry) and kasodi (sweetcorn in coconut milk with ground peanut sauce), not to mention kontola, karela and the bizarre-sounding 'Thanki européene' (a 'Euroveg' extravaganza involving leeks, rhubarb and much more).

Otherwise, look for such mainstays of the repertoire as samosas, bhel-puris, masala dosa and vegetable koftas. Drink Kingfisher beer or dip into the workaday wine list. House French is £7.95.

CHEF: Manoj Thanki   PROPRIETOR: Dinesh Thanki   OPEN: Wed to Sun L 12.30 to 2.30, all week D 6 to 10.30   CLOSED: 25 and 26 Dec, 1 week mid-Jan   MEALS: alc (main courses £4 to £6). Thalis £8.50 to £16.25   SERVICE: not inc, card slips closed   CARDS: MasterCard, Visa   DETAILS: 82 seats. Private parties: 20 main room. Vegetarian meals. Children's helpings. Wheelchair access (not WC). Music. Air-conditioned   ⊖ Tooting Broadway

# Kensington Place ♟                                    map 13

201–209 Kensington Church Street, W8 7LX                          COOKING 6
TEL: (020) 7727 3184   FAX: (020) 7229 2025                  MODERN BRITISH
                                                                  £29–£68

Floor-to-ceiling windows onto the street, and hard, brightly coloured surfaces (reminding one visitor of a *Dr Who* set) seem to concentrate the congenial conversational noise. The atmosphere is warm, service is a strong point (the mainly antipodean staff are efficient and helpful), and the whole operation is well practised: 'Rowley Leigh, in a dapper purple suit, made a fleeting appearance and toddled off towards Notting Hill Gate, confident that all was well.' His kitchen brigade starts with sound ingredients, and the balance of flavours is well judged, thanks not least to some tried and tested combinations, from chicken and goats' cheese mousse with olives, to cod with lentils and salsa verde.

Temptations to embellish are ably resisted, and this is one restaurant that successfully does what many others claim to do but so rarely achieve: it keeps things commendably simple, serving up omelette fines herbes, unadorned oysters, and grilled sardines. Soups, salads and fish make up the bulk of starters, and main-course meats generally involve slow roasting (shoulder of Highland lamb), or fast grilling (spiced chicken). Daily extras might run to blanquette of veal with chanterelles, and desserts often take their inspiration from Italy, maybe Barolo pears with an almond tart, or a first-class panforte variation on *pain perdu*.

The wine list is refreshingly straightforward too, organised by style and price, and includes a sampling of top producers from around the globe. Mark-ups are not greedy, giving reasonable choice under £20. French house white starts at £13.50, red at £14; around 25 wines are available by the glass, as are five excellent sherries.

CHEF: Rowley Leigh   PROPRIETOR: Place Restaurants Ltd   OPEN: all week 12 to 3, 6.30 to 11.45 (10.15 Sun)   MEALS: alc (main courses £13.50 to £18.50). Set L £16.50   SERVICE: 12.5% (optional), card slips closed   CARDS: Amex, Delta, Diners, MasterCard, Switch, Visa   DETAILS: 140 seats. Private parties: 20 main room, 15 to 45 private rooms. Vegetarian meals. Children's helpings. No pipes in dining room. Wheelchair access (also WC). Occasional music. Air-conditioned   ⊖ Notting Hill Gate

*The Guide always appreciates hearing about changes of chef or owner.*

# Kiku £

map 15

17 Half Moon Street, W1J 7BE
TEL: (020) 7499 4208   FAX: (0200 7409 3259

COOKING 3
JAPANESE
£22–£81

Occupying a spacious site in Mayfair, this may look like a classically luxurious Japanese venue catering for a moneyed crowd. In fact, the smart entrance gives way to a fairly simple establishment with black and chrome chairs, functional black tables, lots of blonde wood and natural blinds. Up some steps is a sushi counter, otherwise progress to the main dining area, where hot towels are brought on arrival.

The a la carte cruises its way through hot and cold appetisers, soups, hot pots, grills, casseroles and the like; alternatively, opt for the full kaiseki works. Sashimi has been 'good and fresh', with squid and marinated mackerel as highlights. Ohitashi (spinach salad) comes with a healthy dose of dried bonito, while uzaku (marinated grilled eel with cool mashed cucumber) is an 'incredibly refreshing' combination. Lunch specials such as noodles, yakitori and tempura are affordably priced, and service is 'generally smiling and willing' despite a few language problems. Corney & Barrow house wines, from £11.50 are a good bet, otherwise stay with saké or beer.

CHEFS: T.Nishimura, Y.Hattori, H.Yamauchi (sushi counter); Y.Hikichi, H.Goto, I.Takahashi (main kitchen)   PROPRIETORS: Hishashi and Mariko Taoka   OPEN: Mon to Sat L 12 to 2.30, all week D 6 to 10.15 (5.30 to 9.45 Sun and bank hols)   CLOSED: 25 and 26 Dec, 1 Jan   MEALS: alc (main courses £5 to £28). Set L £12 to £23, Set D £34 to £51   SERVICE: 12.5%, card slips closed   CARDS: Amex, Delta, Diners, MasterCard, Switch, Visa   DETAILS: 95 seats. Private parties: 50 main room, 8 to 10 private rooms. Wheelchair access (also WC). Music. Air-conditioned  ⊖ Green Park  (£5)

# Kulu Kulu Sushi ✳ £

map 15

76 Brewer Street, W1F 9TX
TEL: (020) 7734 7316   FAX: (020) 7734 6507

COOKING 2
JAPANESE
£21–£39

At peak times you have just 45 minutes to consider and consume what you desire from the conveyor belt in this Soho sushi joint. The small, crowded room may seem a shade makeshift, and there's no ceremony, no fuss, just a rotating help-yourself buffet offering good, fresh Japanese morsels. Salmon is much in evidence: raw on nigiri sushi, its eggs in a sushi roll, teriyaki-style, and as a tempura served in a well-flavoured broth. Tuna, sea eel, octopus and mackerel also feature, along with assorted sashimi, and there are mixed platters covering most of the range. Green tea is free; otherwise have a bottle of beer or house wine at £12 a bottle (£3 a glass.) There is less enthusiasm for the second branch at 39 Thurloe Place, South Kensington, SW7.

CHEF/PROPRIETOR: K. Toyama   OPEN: Mon to Sat 12 to 2.30, 5 to 8   CLOSED: bank hols   MEALS: alc (sushi £5 to £13)   SERVICE: not inc   CARDS: Delta, MasterCard, Switch, Visa   DETAILS: 30 seats. No smoking in dining room. Music. Air-conditioned  ⊖ Piccadilly Circus

# Langan's Brasserie   map 15

Stratton Street, W1J 8LB
TEL: (020) 7491 8822   FAX: (020) 7493 8309
WEBSITE: www.langansrestaurants.co.uk

COOKING **1**
ANGLO-FRENCH
£37–£69

'I was not disappointed,' wrote one visitor, tired of the 'here today, gone tomorrow' food with which the capital is awash, and yearning for something comfortably old-fashioned. For him, Caesar salad and herb-crusted rack of lamb obligingly did the trick. 'I asked for my lamb pink and basically was told that it comes as it comes', which happily turned out to be just right. Old favourites pepper the menu, from asparagus with melted butter to cod and chips, from a Greek-style feta salad to grilled calf's liver and bacon, although Parmesan soufflé won't rise to the first-floor Venetian Room, being available only on the ground floor. Dishes may not require much in the way of skill, but they are competently rendered, and meals might end with rice pudding, or treacle tart. House wine is £14.

CHEFS: Ken Whitehead, Roy Smith and Dennis Mynott   PROPRIETOR: Richard Shepherd   OPEN: Mon to Fri 12.15 to 11.45, Sat D only 7 to 12   CLOSED: bank hols   MEALS: alc (main courses £12.50 to £18.50). Cover £1.50   SERVICE: 12.5% (optional)   CARDS: Amex, Delta, Diners, MasterCard, Switch, Visa   DETAILS: 220 seats. Vegetarian meals. Children's helpings. Wheelchair access (not WC). Music. Air-conditioned   ⊖ Green Park

# Lansdowne £   map 13

90 Gloucester Avenue, NW1 8HX
TEL: (020) 7483 0409
EMAIL: (020) 7586 1723

COOKING **2**
MODERN BRITISH
£26–£52

The Lansdowne is a combination of bustling pub downstairs and more refined restaurant upstairs. Food is served in both, the main difference being that downstairs it is listed on a blackboard and eaten amid a crowd of drinkers. In either case, there is a Mediterranean accent: among starters might be an aubergine, caper, garlic and mozzarella 'pizzetta', or salt cod and morcilla with poached egg and watercress. Main courses have included wild sea bass with saffron mash, prawns and baby fennel; pea and asparagus risotto with Parmesan; and straightforward ribeye steak with chips, watercress and aïoli. Desserts take in old faithfuls such as crème brûlée, as well as polenta and saffron cake with saffron and orange sauce. The wine list is short, varied and fairly priced; house wines start at £11.50 a bottle, £2.90 a glass.

CHEFS: Amanda Pritchett and James Knight   PROPRIETOR: Amanda Pritchett   OPEN: Sun L 12.30 to 2.30, Tue to Sat D 7 to 10.30   MEALS: alc (main courses £8.50 to £16.50). Set L Sun £16.50. Bar menu also available   SERVICE: 12.5%, card slips closed   CARDS: Delta, MasterCard, Switch, Visa   DETAILS: 60 seats. 20 seats outside. Private parties: 80 main room. Vegetarian meals. Music. No mobile phones   ⊖ Chalk Farm

# Launceston Place  ♥

map 14

1A Launceston Place, W8 5RL
TEL: (020) 7937 6912   FAX: (020) 7938 2412

COOKING 3
MODERN BRITISH
£32–£68

Distancing itself from the capital's energy and bustle, Launceston Place prides itself on a quieter rural aspect, helped by leafy environs and by its old-fashioned but tasteful dining room decorated with prints and flower arrangements. The food is lively enough though, the carte changing every six weeks or so, the set menu daily. Bright flavours surface in the shape of seared scallops with Thai curry sauce, and twice-baked goats' cheese soufflé with spicy plums, alongside old favourites such as oxtail stew, and rack of lamb with ratatouille dressing. Diehard traditionalists, meanwhile, can fill up on a mixed grill of minute steak, calf's liver, bacon, chipolatas, grilled tomato, mushrooms, fried egg and chips. The American theme that is evident in clam and sweetcorn chowder is echoed in desserts of blueberry cheesecake, and Mississippi mud pie. Wines are arranged by style and price and lean heavily toward Chardonnay and Cabernet Sauvignon/Merlot. Eight wines are available by the 125ml glass. There is not a great deal under £20, but New World bottlings generally offer better value. House claret starts at £14.50, house Chardonnay at £14.

CHEF: Phillip Reed   PROPRIETOR: Christopher Bodker   OPEN: Sun to Fri L 12.30 to 2.30, all week D 7 to 11.30 (10 Sun)   MEALS: alc (main courses £16 to £18.50). Set L Mon to Fri £15.50 (2 courses) to £18.50, Set L Sun £22.50, Set D 7 to 8 £15.50 (2 courses) to £18.50   SERVICE: 12.5% (optional), card slips closed   CARDS: Amex, Delta, Diners, MasterCard, Switch, Visa   DETAILS: 190 seats. Private parties: 14 private room. Vegetarian meals. No pipes. No music. Air-conditioned   ⊖ Gloucester Road

---

# Light House

NEW ENTRY   map 12

75–77 Ridgway, Wimbledon, SW19 4ST
TEL: (020) 8944 6338   FAX: (020) 8946 4440

COOKING 3
MODERN EUROPEAN
£29–£58

The name alludes to the oceans of daylight the enormous windows let in to this popular neighbourhood restaurant. Its sandy/sprucy-coloured décor creates a monochromatic impression, and a special acoustic ceiling obligingly muffles noise. New incumbent Michael Mannion gleans inspiration from hither and yon, offering chorizo and chargrilled romescu pepper bruschetta to start, and gremolada-crusted salmon with ratatouille to follow on a lunchtime menu. Basil ravioli stuffed with tomatoes, served with Parma ham and a sultana and pine-nut dressing, made 'a pleasing and interesting' starter for one visitor, and an intriguing interplay of complementary flavours has marked a main course of pan-fried halibut with pickled carrots, fennel confit, lime-berry salsa and rocket. Chargrilled wild boar, 'not especially tender', nevertheless has a concentrated taste, its earthiness reflected in the accompanying roast butternut squash. Desserts – in trencherman portions – might muster a fairly dense chocolate Sachertorte with chocolate rum sauce and crème fraîche, or a banana and ginger semifreddo with mango salsa, toasted coconut and candied citrus. The single-page wine list is a model of the contemporary genre, with many stylish bottles, but prices soon leap over the £20 mark. House Italians are £12.50.

CHEF: Michael Mannion   PROPRIETORS: Bob Finch, Ian Taylor and Kate Sim   OPEN: Tue to Sun L 12 (12.30 Sun) to 2.45, Mon to Sat D 6.30 to 10.45   MEALS: alc (main courses £10 to £16.50). Set L Tue to Sat £12.50 (2 courses)   SERVICE: 12.5% (optional), card slips closed   CARDS: Amex, Delta, MasterCard, Switch, Visa   DETAILS: 80 seats. Private parties: 70 main room. Vegetarian meals. Children's helpings. No-smoking area. Wheelchair access (also WC). Music ⊖ Wimbledon £5

## Lightship Ten

**NEW ENTRY**   map 13

5A St Katherine's Way,
St Katherine Docks, E1W 1LP
TEL: (020) 7481 3123   FAX: (020) 7702 0338
EMAIL: info@lightshipten.com
WEBSITE: www.lightshipten.com

COOKING 4
MODERN EUROPEAN
£34–£59

The oldest lightship in the world (built 1877), once stationed in the Baltic off Denmark, having survived two world wars and a sinking, is now a restaurant in St Katherine Docks. The top deck houses bar and kitchen; the wood-lined dining room is below (the tables along each side are the ones to go for – each has its own porthole).

Even with indifferent food such a venue would draw crowds, but David Hart's cooking is far from that. Fittingly, many dishes have a Danish feel: herrings, meatballs, oysters in aquavit vinaigrette, and mussels cooked in Tuborg beer. But the repertoire ranges much wider, taking in, for instance, a superb starter of lightly grilled pigeon breasts with diced pear in a mustardy sweet pickle. At inspection both meat and fish dishes were carefully timed – sea bass fillets on dauphinoise, and lamb on a casserole bed of aubergine, potato and tomato – and the side-dish of pommes sarladaise with goose fat and bacon is a must. A top-drawer selection of smoked, blue and goats' cheeses with Bath Olivers and celery is probably a better bet than dessert. Wines are mainly French, and choice below £20 is severely limited; house vin de pays is £13.50.

CHEF: David Hart   PROPRIETOR: Lightship Restaurant Ltd   OPEN: Mon to Fri 12 to 2.30, Mon to Sat 6 to 10   MEALS: alc (main courses £10 to £18.50). Set L and D £19 (2 courses) to £23. Bar menu also available   SERVICE: 10% (optional), card slips closed   CARDS: Amex, Delta, Diners, MasterCard, Switch, Visa   DETAILS: 60 seats. 60 seats outside. Private parties: 60 main room. Vegetarian meals. Music. No mobile phones. Air-conditioned

## Lindsay House ▼

map 15

21 Romilly Street, W1V 5TG
TEL: (020) 7439 0450   FAX: (020) 7437 7349
WEBSITE: www.lindsayhouse.co.uk

COOKING 6
MODERN BRITISH
£40–£105

Ringing the bell to get in is a reminder that this actually is a house, and an improbably elegant one at that, at least for Soho. Its light, high-ceilinged rooms are simply furnished, with well-spaced tables and crisp white linen cloths, and a bright-sounding menu parades some tempting ideas, among them a 'sublime' dish of green asparagus with a soft-boiled egg and caviar, and a fresh-tasting salad of Cornish crab with globe artichoke. But a closer look at the menu reveals 'no kidneys, no tongue; indeed hardly any offal of any kind', unless you count foie gras. Thus one visitor ruefully observed the sidelining of one of the distinctive aspects of Richard Corrigan's cooking. The innovative, gutsily flavoured food for which he is best known seems to have lost a little of its striking individuality.

At its best the food still shines: for example, in a spot-on dish of poached monkfish wrapped in courgette, served with an impressive ravioli of cockles and mussels, all in a fine bouillabaisse containing pieces of squid, the combination formidable, the dish harmonious. Likewise duck served two ways – slightly rare breast and confit leg – with 'fondue potato' (aka mash), and a little tart of foie gras that was 'vintage Corrigan'. Desserts have produced a warm, autumnal, sweet-and-savoury rosehip soup served hot ('if that's what rosehips taste like, I like them'), with vanilla cream and an almond biscuit, and a pairing of poached figs with a blue cheese bavarois that proved to be a 'really interesting cross between a dessert and a cheese course'. More recent reports are less complimentary, the niggles including long waits, heavy salting, an under-par tasting menu, and prices that no longer make it seem such good value.

Staff are friendly, approachable and generally efficient (with occasional lapses), and wines, which claim to have been selected with the cooking in mind, are an eclectic bunch, arranged by style and taking in good selections from around the wine-making globe. Mark-ups, however, are high, which makes finding something interesting under £20 difficult. There is a good selection of half-bottles, and 12 wines are sold by the glass (£5.30 to £7.70). The 30 bottles in the well-chosen sommelier's selection are a good way to explore the list, but even here prices don't dip below £28.

CHEF/PROPRIETOR: Richard Corrigan    OPEN: Mon to Fri L 12 to 2, Mon to Sat D 6 to 11    CLOSED: 1 week Christmas, 2 weeks summer    MEALS: alc L (main courses £19 to £24). Set L £23, Set pre-theatre D 6 to 7.15 £24 (2 courses) to £29.50, Set D £44 to £65 (whole table only)    SERVICE: 12.5% (optional), card slips closed    CARDS: Amex, Delta, Diners, MasterCard, Switch, Visa    DETAILS: 65 seats. Private parties: 35 main room, 6 to 35 private rooms. Vegetarian meals. Children's helpings. No music. No mobile phones. Air-conditioned    ⊖ Leicester Square, Piccadilly Circus

---

## Little Georgia £                                              map 12

| | |
|---|---|
| 2 Broadway Market, E8 4QJ | COOKING 1 |
| TEL: (020) 7249 9070 | GEORGIAN/RUSSIAN |
| | £22–£38 |

A former pub overlooking Regent's Canal as it wends its way through Hackney is the setting for Georgian food, a homely, comforting and hearty style of cooking characterised by robust and spicy flavours. Chakapuli is lamb in coriander, tarragon and white wine sauce, while satsivi chicken is a whole roast poussin in a tangy walnut sauce, and gupta is a dish of meatballs in a mildly spicy red pepper and tomato sauce. The mixed meze selection remains a popular way to start, and for dessert – if you have room – ledge cake, containing raisins, walnuts and meringue, sounds an interesting prospect. Everything is considered good value, including the wines, which turn up a few Georgian examples. Prices start at £10.

CHEF: Elena Gambashidze   PROPRIETOR: Antony Jones   OPEN: Sun L only 1 to 3.30, Tue to Sat D 6.30 to 10 (10.30 Fri and Sat)   MEALS: alc (main courses £7.50 to £12.50)   SERVICE: not inc CARDS: Delta, MasterCard, Switch, Visa   DETAILS: 45 seats. 12 seats outside. Private parties: 45 main room. Vegetarian meals. Children's helpings. Wheelchair access (not WC). Music. Air-conditioned   ⊖ Bethnal Green

## Livebait                                                                    map 13

43 The Cut, SE1 8LF                                                       COOKING **2**
TEL: (020) 7928 7211   FAX: (020) 7928 2279                                SEAFOOD
                                                                          £27–£71

'Very bright, very clean, very cramped, exceedingly noisy, not comfortable.' So began one missive this year on the original Waterloo branch of the Livebait chain. 'But it is a fun place, excellent for very fresh fish,' continued the same reporter, though it is more of a serious restaurant than the café-style appearance may lead you to expect. The inventive brand of modern fish cookery that has always been Livebait's hallmark might produce sea bass on blue cheese risotto, or swordfish with Asian stir-fried vegetables and black beans. Menus also offer a standard range of shellfish platters, fish and chips and, of course, the catch of the day, which might be chargrilled blue-fin tuna steak with Thai butter or tomato and olive tapénade. Finish, perhaps, with 'excellent' chocolate fondant, or rhubarb and apple crumble. A token half-dozen red wines supplement the choice of about four times that number of whites, many of which are available by the glass or half-bottle. Prices start at £13.50. There are five other branches in London, and more in Leeds, Manchester and Oxford.

CHEF: Richard Gilberd   PROPRIETOR: Groupe Chez Gérard   OPEN: Mon to Sat 12 to 3, 5.30 to 11.30   CLOSED: 25 and 26 Dec, 1 Jan, L bank hols   MEALS: alc (main courses £9 to £28.50). Set L and D 5.30 to 7 and 10 to 11.30 £12.95 (2 courses) to £15.50   SERVICE: 12.5% (optional), card slips closed   CARDS: Amex, Delta, Diners, MasterCard, Switch, Visa   DETAILS: 90 seats. Private parties: 25 main room. Children's helpings. No-smoking area. Wheelchair access (also WC). Music. Air-conditioned   ⊖ Waterloo, Southwark

## Lobster Pot                                                                 map 13

3 Kennington Lane, SE11 4RG                                              COOKING **3**
TEL: (020) 7582 5556                                               FRENCH SEAFOOD
WEBSITE: www.lobsterpotrestaurant.co.uk                                    £23–£67

Very French, very nautical and very eccentric: the Lobster Pot wears its heart on its sleeve, and seems to be an extension of the personality of its owner, Hervé Régent. A good way to sample the cooking for groups with a sense of adventure is the eight-course surprise menu, and the plateau de fruits de mer remains a popular fixture. Otherwise, starters include marinated salmon with cucumber ribbons, and grilled prawns with garlic butter, while main courses range from classic bouillabaisse, or grilled Dover sole with lemon butter, to more modern pan-fried sea bass with Cajun spices, or grilled tuna with a sauce of tomatoes, garlic, chilli and coriander. Meat eaters are not excluded, given confit duck with sweet-and-sour sauce, or roast rack of lamb with mint sauce among the options. Desserts are as straightforward as tarte Tatin, and profiteroles. Prices on the very brief wine list start at £10.50 and stop not far short of £100.

CHEF: Hervé Régent   PROPRIETORS: Hervé and Nathalie Régent   OPEN: Tue to Sat 12 to 2.30, 7 to 10.45   CLOSED: 24 Dec to first week Jan   MEALS: alc (main courses £14.50 to £23.50). Set L £10 (2 courses) to £39.50, Set D £19.50 to £39.50   SERVICE: 12.5% (optional), card slips closed   CARDS: Amex, Delta, Diners, MasterCard, Switch, Visa   DETAILS: 48 seats. Private parties: 30 main room, 14 to 30 private rooms. Vegetarian meals. Children's helpings. No cigars/pipes in dining room. Wheelchair access (not WC). Music. Air-conditioned   ⊖ Kennington  £5

## Locanda Locatelli ♥   [NEW ENTRY]   map 15

8 Seymour Street, W1H 7JZ   COOKING 6
TEL: (020) 7935 9088   FAX: (020) 7935 1149   ITALIAN
WEBSITE: www.locandalocatelli.com   £36–£75

In moving from the A To Z group and from Zafferano (see entry) to new premises, Giorgio Locatelli has made a bid for independence. Designer David Collins has produced a 'dazzling' interior, a James Bond set in glitzy, confident 1970s style, with pillars, fish-eye mirrors, fabric-coated walls and low lighting, whose space is well suited to air-kissing and for checking on celebrities; it can feel rather like a '*Hello!* magazine catwalk'. Service is professional, effortless and exceptionally polite, while the Zafferano-style menu is now longer, with a few more innovative ideas, but still fundamentally Italian. It aspires to please with thinly sliced ox tongue and salsa verde, gnocchetti with goats' cheese and summer truffle, and roast rabbit with polenta, and it often succeeds.

Standards, however, can seesaw within a single meal; indeed, pasta alone (each dish available as a main course for a small supplement) can vary considerably, the best version at an inspection meal combining tagliolini with courgette strands, seasoned with salty flakes of dried tuna roe. Silky-smooth osso buco ravioli has also impressed, and fish has made an impact: in the form of a starkly simple dish of poached skate on fresh rocket leaves with a splattering of balsamic vinegar, as well as a 'stunning' piece of crisp-skinned, just-cooked sea bream, served with an exemplary sweet-sour balsamic sauce that catapulted the dish to another level.

Italian cheeses are kept in first-rate condition, and desserts run from a gratifying almond fondant with milk ice and rhubarb, to a rich yet tangy chocolate parfait, well matched by its accompanying sweet, syrupy blood oranges and jammy apricot garnish. Incidentals include fine bread, from impossibly long grissini to garlic-studded ciabatta. The extensive wine list is an Italian-only zone; none the worse for that, of course, although it helps to know your Lagreins from your Negroamaros. There are scores of palate-pleasing, food-friendly wines here, from many of Italy's top experimentally minded producers. Sadly, wines of this ilk don't come cheap, and there are thin pickings under £20. Fortunately, £12 is the starting point for white Verdicchio and well-made Sicilian red Nero d'Avola.

CHEF: Giorgio Locatelli   PROPRIETORS: Giorgio and Plaxy Locatelli   OPEN: Mon to Sat 12 to 3, 7 to 11   CLOSED: Christmas, 1 week end Aug, bank hols   MEALS: alc (main courses £12 to £28)   SERVICE: not inc   CARDS: Amex, Delta, MasterCard, Switch, Visa   DETAILS: 94 seats. Private parties: 120 main room. Vegetarian meals. Children's helpings. No cigars/pipes in dining room. Wheelchair access (also WC). Occasional music. Air-conditioned   ⊖ Marble Arch

# Lola's ♥ 🍴 map 13

The Mall, 359 Upper Street, N1 0PD
TEL: (020) 7359 1932  FAX: (020) 7359 2209

COOKING 5
MODERN EUROPEAN
£28–£61

The first-floor dining room in this old tram shed has been reinvigorated. Steel girders and glass are still in evidence, but all has been freshened up with a Moorish wall design here, a row of metallic fish there, and a dramatic knife sculpture in the middle. More importantly, the kitchen has been revitalised with the arrival of Hywel Jones from Foliage (see entry), who brings with him a sound culinary intelligence, and produces some fine workmanship. He sets out an appealing menu that might take in fresh, accurately timed, crisp-skinned fillets of gilt-head bream, served with a small nugget of risotto encased in smoky, powerfully flavoured Alsace bacon; or a flavourful dish of lamb combining roast rump with a spring roll-like cannelloni of slow-cooked shoulder, served with roast red pepper and a winy reduction.

Raw materials, timing and production are impressive: in three bouncy scallop halves on a bed of smoked haddock brandade, with marinated beetroot, and in slices of rare seared tuna (accompanied by fresh anchovies deep-fried in a light batter, by an eggy, oily aubergine 'goo', and by finely diced ratatouille vegetables in a well-judged vinaigrette). Equally well-handled desserts have included lemon three ways – a jelly, a sorbet, and a first-class, well-balanced tart – and a ball of mint ice cream sandwiched between mildly flavoured meringue-like macaroons, topped with a scoop of red berry sorbet and surrounded by gently heated seasonal berries. The wine list is designed to encourage experimentation, with 14 wines by the 175ml and 250ml glass (plus half a dozen excellent dry sherries) and five wine flights (£8.50), which may cover grape varieties, regions or other subjects chosen because they are 'fun to try'. The 'offbeat and bin-ends' section is the best place to look for something different, although the rest of the list does its best to pick out interesting wines from around the globe too. House wines start at £11.25.

CHEF: Hywel Jones  PROPRIETOR: Morfudd Richards  OPEN: all week 12 to 2.30 (3 Sat and Sun), 6 to 11 (7 to 10 Sun)  CLOSED: 25 and 26 Dec, 1 Jan, some bank hols  MEALS: alc (main courses £12 to £18). Set L and D Mon to Sat 6 to 7 £17.50  SERVICE: not inc, 12.5% for parties of  CARDS: Amex, Delta, Diners, MasterCard, Switch, Visa  DETAILS: 80 seats. Private parties: 8 to 16 private rooms. Vegetarian meals. No music. Air-conditioned  ⊖ Angel

# Lou Pescadou map 13

241 Old Brompton Road, SW5 9HP
TEL: (020) 7370 1057  FAX: (020) 7244 7545

COOKING 2
SEAFOOD
£19–£60

Behind a large white porthole window in the nautically blue frontage lies an old-fashioned French seafood restaurant. The colour scheme continues inside, the theme underlined with café scenes and ships' hulls, and visitors come for 'straightforward cooking of excellent fresh fish'. It doesn't aim to be trendy but is happy to deal in mussels cooked with cream and garlic (there is a lot of cream about, not always mentioned on the menu), fish soup, and sea bass with fennel.

A wide choice of shellfish runs from oysters and langoustines to crab salad, and a plate of whelks, winkles and crevettes grises with aïoli. Main-course fish tend towards prime species, such as brill and halibut, and there are simple meat alternatives, such as fillet or sirloin steak, plus maybe tripes à la mode de Caen for the more adventurous. Finish with cheese or mousse au chocolat. Incidentals are paid for by a cover charge, and the 'optional' service charge is 15 per cent, both considered 'over the top' by reporters. A short French wine list (around 35 bottles) starts with house red and white at £10.50.

CHEF: Laurent David   PROPRIETORS: Daniel Chobert and Laurent David   OPEN: all week 12 to 3, 7 (6.30 Sat and Sun) to 12   CLOSED: Christmas and New Year   MEALS: alc (main courses £7.50 to £15). Set L Mon to Fri £9.90, Set L Sat and Sun £13.50, Set D Sat 6.30 to 7.45 and Sun £13.50. Cover £1.50   SERVICE: 15% (optional), card slips closed   CARDS: Amex, Delta, Diners, MasterCard, Switch, Visa   DETAILS: 60 seats. 20 seats outside. Private parties: 65 main room, 10 to 50 private rooms. Vegetarian meals. Children's helpings. Wheelchair access (not WC). No music   ⊖ Earl's Court   £5

## Lundum's
map 14

119 Old Brompton Road, SW7 3RN
TEL: (020) 7373 7774   FAX: (020) 7373 4472

COOKING 4
DANISH
£27–£63

Lundum's bills itself as the only Danish restaurant in London. The light, airy late Georgian dining room is sensitively decorated to create an atmosphere of 'Scandinavian vitality', and honesty is the hallmark of the cooking: no unnecessary complications or flourishes, and simple flavours allowed their own voice. An inspector was impressed with the 'unshowy but extremely effective' results at dinner, which included a 'wobbly, ultra-light' white tomato mousse attractively presented with a garnish of tomato segments and mizuna leaves. Masterful handling of fish has produced an 'extremely fresh' halibut steak poached in milk and served with a buttery asparagus sauce and a bundle of asparagus stems; and pan-fried witch parcels: not Hans Christian Andersen's revenge, but rolled fish fillets lightly fried, dusted with sesame seeds and served on excellent rösti. Finish perhaps with a wild berry soup, flavoured with cinnamon and star anise and accompanied by vanilla ice cream, or try the Danish cheeses.

The lunchtime menu makes Lundum's also the place to go for traditional dishes of marinated herrings served with a shot of aquavit, or smørrebrød (open sandwiches) topped with maybe gravad lax, or salt beef and liver pâté. The extensive wine offers little under £20, though house Chardonnay and Merlot are £13.25.

CHEFS: Frank Dietrich and Kay Lundum   PROPRIETORS: the Lundum family   OPEN: all week L 12 to 3, Mon to Sat D 6 to 10   CLOSED: 23 Dec to 4 Jan   MEALS: alc (main courses £7.50 to £16.50). Set L £12.50 (2 courses) to £15.50, Sun brunch £16.50, Set D £17.25 (2 courses) to £21.50 SERVICE: 12.5% (optional), card slips closed   CARDS: Amex, Delta, Diners, MasterCard, Switch, Visa   DETAILS: 40 seats. 12 seats outside. Private parties: 12 main room. Vegetarian meals. Children's helpings. Music. Air-conditioned   ⊖ South Kensington

# Maison Novelli

map 13

29–30 Clerkenwell Green, EC1R 0DU
TEL: (020) 7251 6606   FAX: (020) 7490 1083
EMAIL: maisonnovelli@hotmail.com
WEBSITE: www.whitestarline.org.com

COOKING 4
MODERN FRENCH
£45–£78

A corner site with a panoramic view, just up from Farringdon Tube, makes this a covetable spot, not least when the weather allows tables outside. Novelli trademarks range from the lavender blue paint to such distinctively northern French items as onion soup with glazed Beaufort cheese, or jambon persillé with toasted Poilâne bread. As well as a few comforting, homely staples – salmon fishcake, an 'OK' steak and kidney suet pudding, or a salade tiède of squid and crumbly black pudding topped with a soft-poached egg – the kitchen also goes in for more elaborate flourishes. A poppy-seed pancake of steamed wild mushrooms is served in a port and Madeira reduction with cep oil and Parmesan crackling, while rack of lamb comes with a melted Stilton soufflé, braised Puy lentils and glazed leeks.

Novelli trifle is 'not overpowered with sherry' according to a clergyman, who should know about these things, while another reporter's passion-fruit parfait with cherry ice cream was 'fantastic'. A high-quality roving wine list offers only a handful of bottles under £20, including house Merlot and Chardonnay from southern France at £14.95 (£3.75 a glass).

CHEF: Jean Christophe Novelli   PROPRIETORS: Marco Pierre White and Jean Christophe Novelli
OPEN: Mon to Fri L 12 to 3, Mon to Sat D 6 to 11   MEALS: alc (main courses £14.50 to £23)
SERVICE: 12.5% (optional)   CARDS: Amex, Delta, Diners, MasterCard, Switch, Visa   DETAILS: 80
seats. 15 seats outside. Private parties: 80 main room, 12 to 70 private rooms. Occasional
music. Air-conditioned   ⊖ Farringdon

---

# Mandarin Kitchen £

map 13

14–16 Queensway, W2 3RX
TEL: (020) 7727 9012   FAX: (020) 7727 9468

COOKING 1
CHINESE
£25–£90

Seafood is the main draw at this busy eating house in Queensway's mini-Chinatown. Tables are closely packed, but the food is what counts. 'Wonderfully succulent' lobster with ginger, spring onion and special 'chewy-style' noodles is the number-one bestseller, but reporters have also praised deep-fried soft-shell crabs, steamed sea bass accompanied by top-drawer baby pak choi, and prawns with chilli and garlic. Alternatives to fish come in the shape of aromatic crispy duck, stewed pork with preserved vegetables, and steamed lotus chicken 'with eight treasures in a basket'. Despite the crowds, service is ultra-efficient and works at top speed, although there is no feeling of being rushed. House wine is £10.50.

CHEF: K.W. Man   PROPRIETOR: Steven Cheung   OPEN: all week 12 to 11.30   MEALS: alc (main
courses £6 to £35). Set L and D £10.90 to £20   SERVICE: not inc   CARDS: Amex, Delta, Diners,
MasterCard, Switch, Visa   DETAILS: 110 seats. Private parties: 100 main room. Vegetarian
meals. Wheelchair access (not WC). Music. Air-conditioned   ⊖ Queensway

# Maquis

**NEW ENTRY**   map 12

111 Hammersmith Grove, W6 0NQ
TEL: (020) 8846 3850   FAX: (020) 8846 3855

COOKING **2**
REGIONAL FRENCH
£28–£45

On a street corner at the end of a row of shops, and operating a delicatessen next door, Maquis inhabits a large room with a bare wooden floor, net curtains and a couple of ornate chandeliers, seemingly aiming for an unreconstructed, suburban, neighbourhood feel. It is an offshoot of Moro (see entry), but its preoccupation this time is ostensibly regional French cooking. In this it takes a fairly broad-brush approach, but the food deserves credit for its lack of ostentation, often using modest ingredients, and simple, even homely treatments: in a cracking starter of braised endive with a rich Roquefort sauce, or in a robust, gamey-tasting dish of snails braised with herbs, walnuts and crème fraîche.

The kitchen seems fond of its beans and pulses too, offering a slice of toasted bread with a scattering of braised broad beans and small onions, and a rustic dish of chargrilled lamb chops, just pink inside, with a dollop of flageolet beans. Desserts have included a seasonal rhubarb tart, and a fine-textured, flavourful cake combining chocolate, almonds and Armagnac. Service is amiable and cheerful, and the short Languedoc-Roussillon section of the wine list is a good place to start hunting for value. House red and white are £10.50.

CHEFS: Oliver Rowe and Sam Clark   PROPRIETORS: Sam Clark, Rupert Maunsell and Jason Mitra   OPEN: Sun to Fri L 12.30 to 3, Mon to Sat D 7 to 10.30   MEALS: alc D and Sun L (main courses £12 to £14). Set L £15.50 (2 courses) to £18   SERVICE: 12.5% (optional)   CARDS: Amex, Delta, Diners, MasterCard, Switch, Visa   DETAILS: 85 seats. 15 seats outside. Private parties: 9 main room, 10 to 35 private rooms. Vegetarian meals. No cigars in dining room. Wheelchair access (also WC). No music   ⊖ Hammersmith, Goldhawk Road

# Mash ♟ £

map 15

19–21 Great Portland Street, W1W 8QB
TEL: (020) 7637 5555   FAX: (020) 7637 7333
EMAIL: mash@oxfordcircus.sflife.co.uk

COOKING **3**
MODERN EUROPEAN
£26–£49

This big, brash bar-restaurant has been around quite long enough for any novelty to have worn off, yet it remains popular, especially at weekends. The ground-floor bar is the choice of a young, lively crowd who sip cocktails and home-brewed beers; upstairs the 'unusual, retro-modern' dining room feels more sedate. Maddalena Bonino brings an Italian influence to bear on the long and varied brasserie-style menu: for example, a starter salad of roast courgettes, goats' cheese, roast red peppers and 'carta di musica' (Sicilian flat bread), which impresses for both colour and flavour.

Main courses show scant regard for convention. Pizzas from the wood-fired oven come with unusual toppings including smoked pancetta, French beans, red onion, fromage frais and Gruyère. Other options might include whole roast sea bass with preserved lemon and black olive mayonnaise; and roast beetroot risotto with smoked chicken, cavolo nero and Parmesan. Finish perhaps with pink grapefruit pavlova with blood orange sorbet. Service seems to have improved: 'professional and good-humoured,' thought one reporter; 'pleasant and efficient,' said another. The shortish wine list concentrates on flavourful New World bottles, avoiding the well-worn Chardonnay/Cabernet groove. A dozen wines come by the glass, and house 'Mash series' wines sell for £14.

CHEF: Maddalena Bonino   PROPRIETORS: Oliver Peyton, Gruppo Ltd   OPEN: Mon to Sat 12 to 2.30, 6 to 10.45   MEALS: alc (main courses £9 to £15). Set L £25, Set D 6 to 7.30 £12 (2 courses) to £15   SERVICE: 12.5% (optional), card slips closed   CARDS: Amex, Delta, Diners, Switch, Visa   DETAILS: 165 seats. Private parties: 165 main room, 28 private room. Vegetarian meals. Wheelchair access (also WC). No music. Air-conditioned   ⊖ Oxford Circus

# Mela                                                                      map 15

152–156 Shaftesbury Avenue, WC2H 8HL
TEL: (020) 7836 8635   FAX: (020) 7379 0527
EMAIL: info@melarestaurant.co.uk
WEBSITE: www.melarestaurant.co.uk

COOKING 2
INDIAN
£32–£56

Mere 'colourful' inadequately describes the décor and ambience of this lively place, said to be based on an Indian wedding gathering. On the evening menu there are tandoor, traditional and vegetarian headings with surprises in each. But most original is the tawa section offering street cooking, some items familiar under other names, but including a seafood stir-fry and a Bombay vegetable dish flavoured with dried pomegranate and fenugreek. The good-value 'paratha pavilion' set lunch includes a choice of breads or pancakes plus a curry for £4.95. House wines at £10.90 head a short, interestingly diverse list. A sister restaurant, Chowki, in Denman Street, opened too late for review. Here the menus will change monthly, to feature home-style cooking of no less than 36 Indian regions and of minority communities such as Sindhis, Jains and Marwaris.

CHEF: Kuldeep Singh   PROPRIETORS: Ashraf Rahman and Dinesh Modi   OPEN: all week 12 to 3, 5.30 to 11.30 (Sun 12 to 11)   MEALS: alc (main courses £9 to £12.50). Set L and D (both min 2) £24.95 (vegetarian) to £34.95. Paratha pavilion L menu also available   SERVICE: not inc   CARDS: Amex, Delta, Diners, MasterCard, Switch, Visa   DETAILS: 105 seats. Private parties: 70 main room, 15 to 40 private rooms. Vegetarian meals. Wheelchair access (not WC). Music. Air-conditioned   ⊖ Tottenham Court Road

# Metrogusto Islington                                  map 13

13 Theberton Street, N1 0QY
TEL/FAX: (020) 7226 9400

COOKING 3
MODERN ITALIAN
£32–£50

An experimental and artistic feel to this stylish dining room gives it a great atmosphere; where most restaurants have flowers, here you will find cacti, while walls are hung with 'haunting and strange' paintings. The food is a lot more straightforward, aiming for a rustic Italian style, blending tradition and innovation in equal measure: starters might feature a salad of grilled pears and pecorino, or buffalo mozzarella with spiced aubergines, for example, while main courses typically take in a hearty dish of cod with chickpeas, or guinea fowl with Gorgonzola and aubergine tempura. Pasta is considered a strong suit: the highlight of an inspection meal was a dish of white fish ravioli with broccoli and tomato sauce, delicately flavoured with saffron, and another reporter considered his pasta with wild mushrooms and black truffle shavings 'fit for the gods'. But not all reports have been so enthusiastic, especially when it comes to service. Wines are exclusively Italian; prices start at £14.50.

CHEF: Marco Facco  PROPRIETORS: Susi and Ambro Ianeselli  OPEN: Fri and Sat 12.30 to 3, 6.30 to 11, Sun 12.30 to 3, 7 to 10, Mon to Thur D only 6.30 to 10.30  CLOSED: Christmas, New Year, Easter, bank hols  MEALS: alc D (main courses £9.50 to £14.50). Set L £14.50 (2 courses) to £18.50  SERVICE: 12.5% (optional), card slips closed  CARDS: Delta, MasterCard, Switch, Visa  DETAILS: 50 seats. Private parties: 24 main room, 20 to 24 private rooms. Vegetarian meals. No smoking in 1 dining room. No cigars/pipes in dining room. Wheelchair access (not WC). Music. Air-conditioned  ⊖ Angel, Highbury & Islington  £5

## Mirabelle ▼ 🍴

map 15

56 Curzon Street, Mayfair, W1J 8PA
TEL: (020) 7499 4636  FAX: (020) 7499 5449
EMAIL: sales@whitestarline.org.uk
WEBSITE: www.whitestarline.org.uk

COOKING 6
FRENCH
£35–£74

Beyond the rather anonymous entrance and foyer lies a dining room of character. Despite cheek-by-jowl tables it doesn't feel tightly packed; indeed its mirrors, screens and floral displays have evoked the expansive mood of dining on an ocean liner for more than one visitor. The whole operation is conducted with consummate professionalism and flair. Service from plentiful staff is generally efficient and businesslike, and if it is less than warm it is at least devoid of ersatz amiability.

A colossal laminated menu – mind that glass! – offers masses of choice, much of it appearing to involve truffles, foie gras and wild mushrooms, and much of it written in gastronomic Franglais. Probably more than any other kitchen of its calibre, this is one that believes in doing exactly what it says on the tin. Everything is present and correct, for example in a refined and well-judged main course of moist guinea-fowl breast, served with a spot-on herby risotto scattered with wild mushrooms, and a light and savoury Madeira sauce.

Fine materials are deployed: in a crab salad, and in salmon tartare (salmon fragments sparsely bound in a mustardy, lemony dressing of 'uplifting piquancy'). Painstaking composition is evident too, in a dish of meaty, rare and juicy pigeon breasts, coated in foie gras pâté then wrapped in deep green Savoy cabbage leaves, alongside a mountain ridge of truffle-oiled mash, with a dark, glossy reduction full of pungent black truffle. Or, if you just want rich and comforting, go for the properly runny omelette Arnold Bennett, crammed with flakes of undyed smoked haddock.

Soufflés are a strength; one visitor enjoyed a memorable orange one, another a regally risen raspberry version anointed with intense, blood-red raspberry coulis. Summer fruits in a translucent champagne jelly are also a hit. Bread, though, is very disappointing. France claims the lion's share of the wine list – Bordeaux and Burgundy get most coverage – but there is also a strong showing from the Rhône, and among reds from the south-west. The New World is not overlooked, however, with Australia, New Zealand and California putting in strong showings. Scouting around will reveal a few interesting bottles under £25, some of which can be found among the dozen wines in the 'sommelier's selection', which are also sold by the glass (£4.20 to £8).

CHEF: Phil Cooper   PROPRIETORS: Marco Pierre White and Jimmy Lahoud   OPEN: all week 12 to 2.30 (3 Sat and Sun), 6 to 11.30 (10.30 Sun)   MEALS: alc (main courses £14.50 to £28.50). Set L £16.50 (2 courses) to £19.95, Set L Sun £19.50   SERVICE: 12.5% (optional)   CARDS: Amex, Delta, Diners, MasterCard, Switch, Visa   DETAILS: 120 seats. 40 seats outside. Private parties: 120 main room, 33 to 48 private rooms. Occasional music. Air-conditioned   ⊖ Green Park

# Mr Kong £

map 15

21 Lisle Street, WC2H 7BA

COOKING 3

TEL: (020) 7437 7341 and 9679

CHINESE

FAX: (020) 7437 7923

£23–£45

Since 1984 Mr Kong and his team have maintained this as one of the most reliable addresses in Soho Chinatown. As ever, the cooking is rooted in the Cantonese tradition, with seafood a strong suit. The long list of chef's specials provides plenty of challenging, esoteric stuff in the shape of sauté 'dragon whiskers' (aka pea shoots) with dried scallop, fried cuttlefish cake with garlic sprouts, and deep-fried stuffed pig's intestine with spicy salt; it's also worth enquiring about items not listed on the menu. Alternatively, stay in the mainstream, where there are plenty of such tried-and-tested stalwarts as barbecued spare ribs, baked crab with ginger and spring onion, and beef in oyster sauce. The owners tell us that they plan to increase the number of vegetarian dishes, although non-carnivores are already well served with crispy bean curd and vegetables, and stuffed aubergine in black bean sauce. Drink tea, Chinese beer or something from the minimal wine list (house vin de pays is £7.90).

CHEF: K. Kong   PROPRIETOR: Mr Kong Chinese Restaurant Ltd   OPEN: all week noon to 2.45am (1.45 Sun)   CLOSED: 4 days Christmas   MEALS: alc (main courses £6 to £13). Set D £9.30 (2 courses) to £22   SERVICE: not inc   CARDS: Amex, Delta, Diners, MasterCard, Switch, Visa   DETAILS: 110 seats. Vegetarian meals. No cigars/pipes in dining room. Music Air-conditioned   ⊖ Leicester Square

# ▲ Mju ♥ ⅜

NEW ENTRY   map 14

Millennium Hotel, 17 Sloane Street, SW1 9NU

COOKING 5

TEL: (020) 7201 6330   FAX: (020) 7201 6302

GLOBAL

EMAIL: mju@mill-cop.com

£41–£95

The first thing to get out of the way is the name. Mju (pronounced 'mew') is the Greek letter µ for M, which stands for Millennium Hotel, in which the restaurant is housed. It inhabits a sort of mezzanine floor in the atrium (with good natural light during the day), where a few tables occupy a large area of brown and beige. Japanese-Australian chef Tetsuya Wakuda is the consultant chef and driving force behind it all, and although there is an à la carte menu at lunch, the idea is that no one course should take precedence, so a succession of small dishes best captures the spirit of the cooking.

Sometimes items arrive individually, sometimes in a small group. Fish and meat sometimes succeed each other, sometimes share the same plate, as in a carpaccio of scallops with foie gras, or rare black Angus beef fillet with a salty smudge of sea urchin sauce. Many dishes have an obvious Japanese inspiration, but the question of purity versus crossover is not a particularly fruitful one to pursue since each dish has a logic of its own. Notable in this respect have been some fine lobster dishes: a cocktail glass of intensely flavoured, thick, rich lobster cream with truffle; and thin, supple pasta filled with a light, bouncy, tarragon-flecked lobster mousse, its seaweed vinaigrette and shellfish essence delivering small bursts of gentle heat from chilli and pink peppercorn.

Meals might end with a yuzu sorbet, followed by a take on the floating island theme: a tower of egg white, revealing a smear of intense dark chocolate when cut open, served with both vanilla and praline custards. As to portion size, 'after two or three dishes we began to wonder if we would ever feel as if we had eaten a proper meal, but by the end it all turned out OK'. Although it is not clear who the target audience might be, allergies and dietary requirements are checked, and dishes can be added, subtracted or changed with a commendable degree of flexibility. Casually smart staff don't do anything so vulgar as write down an order, yet register everything more or less accurately. Wines are impeccably chosen but steeply marked up, making £20 the starting point. Alsace and Austria get a look-in, and Australia features prominently. A few sakés (with sensible tasting notes for once) round out the offerings, but also tend to be expensive. Wine by the glass (of which there are half a dozen or so) is one way to proceed.

CHEFS: Tetsuya Wakuda and Chris Behre   PROPRIETOR: Millennium Copthorne Hotels plc   OPEN: Mon to Fri L 12 to 2.30, Mon to Sat D 6 to 10.30   MEALS: alc L (main courses £15 to £22). Set L £25, Set D £55   SERVICE: 12.5% (optional), card slips closed   CARDS: Amex, Diners, MasterCard, Switch, Visa   DETAILS: 100 seats. Private parties: 100 main room. Vegetarian meals. Children's helpings. No smoking in dining room. Wheelchair access (not WC). Music. Air-conditioned   ACCOMMODATION: 222 rooms, all with bath/shower. TV. Phone. B&B £270.25 to £528.75. Rooms for disabled

## ▲ The Montcalm, Crescent Restaurant 🍴 map 15

34–40 Great Cumberland Place, W1H 7TW
TEL: (020) 7402 4288   FAX: (020) 7724 9180
EMAIL: montcalm@montcalm.co.uk
WEBSITE: www.montcalm.co.uk

COOKING 4
MODERN BRITISH
£30–£55

'A welcome calm oasis for London!' admitted one correspondent; 'well-ordered, tasteful surroundings', observed another. This hotel, with its elegant Georgian façade, stands discreetly in a peaceful crescent within walking distance of Marble Arch. 'Outstanding value for money' is another of its attributes, particularly as the fixed-price menus include a half-bottle of house wine.

There is plenty of skill and imagination at work in the kitchen, which comes up with some 'interesting variations of taste and presentation'. Far Eastern influences are obvious in starters of baked scallops and lobster 'on shells' with galangal, spring onions and an intense soy beurre blanc, and in sweet-and-sour squid stuffed with Thai rice and oriental vegetables. Moving westwards, you might encounter 'soft' risotto with scallops and rocket salad, or braised smoked pig's trotter luxuriously stuffed with foie gras and sweetbreads on a truffle jus: 'an exquisite combination', noted the recipient. Meals end on a high note with benchmark versions of tarte Tatin, and chocolate fondant with coffee mousse. Occasionally the cooking doesn't quite live up to expectations, but staff remain 'as pleasant as ever'. A healthy choice of wines by the glass makes the well-annotated list worth exploring. House wine is £17.

CHEF: Stephen Whitney   PROPRIETOR: Nikko Hotels (UK) Ltd   OPEN: Mon to Fri L 12.30 to 2.30, all week D 6.30 to 10.30   MEALS: Set L and D £20 (2 courses) to £25 (all inc wine)   SERVICE: not inc   CARDS: Amex, Diners, MasterCard, Switch, Visa   DETAILS: 60 seats. Private parties: 80 main room, 20 to 80 private rooms. Vegetarian meals. Children's helpings. No smoking in 1 dining room. Wheelchair access (also WC). Occasional music. Air-conditioned   ACCOMMODATION: 120 rooms, all with bath/shower. TV. Phone. Room only £230 to £500. Rooms for disabled. Baby facilities   ⊖ Marble Arch

# Monte's ♥                                                                map 14

164 Sloane Street, SW1X 9QB                                      COOKING 3
TEL: (020) 7245 0896   FAX: (020) 7235 3456         ITALIAN/MODERN EUROPEAN
WEBSITE: www.montes.co.uk                                          £38–£71

Monte's is a curious hybrid: private members' club in the evening and restaurant open to the public at lunch. Ben O'Donoghue may not have been famous for as many minutes as Jamie Oliver (who has now severed his connections with Monte's), but he is no stranger to TV cooking. His menus feature Italian ingredients (buffalo mozzarella, speck from Aosta), and are liberally sprinkled with trendy vegetables; they also home in on some well-sourced meat and fish (some of it organic) including Rossmore oysters, Gloucester Old Spot pork, and Buccleuch beef.

Ideas are bright and lively – organic onion baked in salt with truffled egg and three cheeses – and sometimes incredibly busy: dived Scottish scallops come with lovage salt, orange and chilli, spiced carrot purée, panzotti of scallop roe, coriander and crispy fennel. Desserts, a bit quieter but still intriguing, might offer butternut pumpkin cheesecake with cardamom ice cream. Prices, even for London, are high; the set lunch option, often a bargain elsewhere, is decidedly not so at Monte's. The sophisticated global wine list has its wince-some side: white burgundies are headed 'Burgundy & "That Chardonnay Thang"', non-French Bordeaux-style reds are under 'claret Styl-eee'. If bottles are impeccably sourced, prices, again, are high, starting at £18.50 (for one of two bottles under £20). Fifteen wines come by the glass (£5 to £8.50).

CHEF: Ben O'Donoghue   PROPRIETOR: Jumeirah International   OPEN: Mon to Sat L 12 to 2.30 (and evenings for members only)   MEALS: alc (main courses £15 to £20). Set L £19.50 (2 courses) to £23. Bar menu also available   SERVICE: 12.5% (optional), card slips closed   CARDS: Amex, Delta, Diners, MasterCard, Switch, Visa   DETAILS: 76 seats. Private parties: 24 main room, 14 to 16 private rooms. Vegetarian meals. Children's helpings. Wheelchair access (also WC). Occasional music. Air-conditioned   ⊖ Knightsbridge

---

*Restaurateurs justifiably resent no-shows. If you quote a credit card number when booking, you may be liable for the restaurant's lost profit margin if you don't turn up. Always phone to cancel.*

---

# Moro

map 13

34–36 Exmouth Market, EC1R 4QE
TEL: (020) 7833 8336   FAX: (020) 7833 9338
EMAIL: bookings@moro.co.uk
WEBSITE: www.moro.co.uk

COOKING 5
SPANISH/NORTH AFRICAN
£29–£47

'Noisier and more casual than we expected' is how this double-fronted restaurant in a semi-pedestrianised street struck one couple. A wooden floor, zinc bar and hard edges help to bounce the sound around, but the appeal is not hard to fathom: honest, heart-on-sleeve cooking that is full of interest from its ajo blanco (a chilled, white, garlic- and almond-based 'gazpacho' from Málaga) to its coffee and turron ice cream. The emphasis may have changed a bit over the years, and a book, plus an offshoot in W6 (see Maquis), may have taken away some of the concentration of effort, but there is still much to appeal at this open-hearted and enthusiastic champion of Spanish-inspired food, from hummus with ground lamb and flat bread to deep-fried eel adobo with rocket and lemon.

The wood-fired oven continues to turn out first-class bread, alongside pork belly with white beans and quince aïoli, while the chargrill works hard too: its coals are applied to spicy chicken, and to beef kofta with chickpea and rice pilaff. Nothing is too complicated – a simple but effective dish of leeks and broad beans with goats' cheese was a highlight for one visitor – which is part of the reason for its success. To finish, pomegranate might turn up as a partner for yoghurt cake, or in a sorbet along with blood orange and rosewater. Sherry is one of the stars on a largely southern European wine list, which includes around ten other wines by the glass. Prices start at £10.50.

CHEFS: Samantha and Samuel Clark, and Megan Jones   PROPRIETORS: Mark Sainsbury, and Samuel and Samantha Clark   OPEN: Mon to Fri L 12.30 to 2.30, Mon to Sat D 7 to 10.30   CLOSED: Christmas, bank hols   MEALS: alc (main courses £11 to £16). Tapas menu available Mon to Fri 12.30 to 10.30, Sat 7 to 10.30   SERVICE: not inc, 12.5% for parties of 6 or more   CARDS: Amex, Delta, Diners, MasterCard, Switch, Visa   DETAILS: 90 seats. 15 seats outside. Private parties: 80 main room, 8 to 14 private rooms. Vegetarian meals. No cigars/pipes in dining room. Wheelchair access (also WC). No music. Air-conditioned   ⊖ Farringdon

# Moshi Moshi Sushi 🍴 £

24 Upper Level, Liverpool Street Station,
Broadgate, EC2M 7QH
TEL/FAX: (020) 7247 3227
7–8 Limeburner Lane, EC4M 7HY
TEL: (020) 7248 1808   FAX: (020) 7248 1807
Level 2, Cabot Place East, E14 4QT
TEL: (020) 7512 9911   FAX: (020) 7512 9201
WEBSITE: www.moshimoshi.co.uk

COOKING 2
JAPANESE
£17–£30

When Moshi Moshi opened high above the platforms on Liverpool Street Station in 1994, it was the first restaurant in the UK to serve sushi from a conveyor belt or 'kaiten'. There are now four outlets, including one in Brighton (see Round-ups), and all have distinctive, individual design features. The common denominator is that colour-coded plates pass by on the belt: you sit, watch, and take your pick. Prices remain remarkably low. There are also special set menus served on wooden platters (geta): the 'stamina set' comprises two pieces each of nigiri salmon, tuna, prawn and tamago, plus three salmon rolls and three kappamaki. If you don't see anything you fancy, you can always make a special request to one of the chefs for, say, a hand roll of chilli cod roe and cucumber. Added to all these are hot and cold Japanese 'tapas', ranging from gyoza (deep-fried dumplings) to spinach and sesame salad. Drink saké, beer, or something from the minimal wine list. House French is £11.50.

CHEF: Enrico Venzon  PROPRIETOR: Caroline Bennett  OPEN: Mon to Fri 11.30 to 9.30  CLOSED: Christmas, bank hols  MEALS: alc (plate prices £1.50 to £5). Cover 50p  SERVICE: not inc, card slips closed  CARDS: Diners, MasterCard, Switch, Visa  DETAILS: 83 seats. Vegetarian meals. No smoking in dining room. Wheelchair access (not WC). No music  ⊖ Liverpool Street

## ▲ Nahm  [NEW ENTRY]  map 14

Halkin Hotel, 5 Halkin Street, SW1X 7DJ
TEL: (020) 7333 1000   FAX: (020) 7333 1100
EMAIL: res@halkin.co.uk
WEBSITE: www.halkin.co.uk

COOKING 4
THAI
£40–£89

Beyond the sparkling lobby – a confection of plate glass and marble – the dining room is a spare, sleek, minimalist space, with slatted wooden screens, mosaics, teak furniture, and walls painted a discreet shade of gold. It is a cool, unfussy and calming stage for David Thompson, who seems to have achieved some sort of cult status through his Darley Street Thai restaurant in Sydney. His menu is divided into sections including soups, salads, and pungent nahm prik relishes, with something approximating main courses, although all dishes are small and can be mixed at will. Staff are not as helpful as they might be with recommendations, but for those in doubt a multi-course set meal makes an easy option.

The kitchen is to be congratulated for capturing some of the delicacy and pungency of Thai food, although it tends to be more studied than in its homeland, where exuberance, vitality and freshness are the hallmarks. This is a Western version, and deliberately so as far as some of the materials are concerned: foie gras, venison, John Dory and Longhorn beef are not much used in Bangkok, for example. Among high spots noted by two inspectors (one who has eaten her way around Thailand, another who ate several times at the Sydney restaurant) have been a soup of shredded crab, shiitake and sweetcorn, decked out with coriander, basil and spring onions, in a roast crab-shell stock with egg custard whisked through it all; and a rich, deeply flavoured 'Muslim-style' chicken curry served with santol and peanuts, infused with cardamom.

Well-balanced salads are another strength, including marinated lobster with wild ginger, mint, shredded green mangoes and chilli, and another ebullient, zingily flavoured one of oysters, shredded salt-beef and samphire liberally sprinkled with lemon grass, lemon basil and lime. Desserts, not normally a major part of a Thai meal, have ranged from poor to first class, the latter including palm sugar rice pudding topped by slices of juicily dripping and muskily perfumed mango, and a black liquorice bean jelly full of flavour and interest. Prices are high for both food and wines, although the latter (predominantly white) are varied and well chosen. Prices start at £18.50.

CHEF: David Thompson   PROPRIETOR: Christina Ong   OPEN: Mon to Fri L 12 to 2.30, all week D 7 to 11 (10 Sun)   CLOSED: 25 and 26 Dec, 1 Jan   MEALS: alc (main courses £15 to £22). Set L and D £18 to £47   SERVICE: 12.5% (optional), card slips closed   CARDS: Amex, Delta, Diners, MasterCard, Switch, Visa   DETAILS: 50 seats. Vegetarian meals. No cigars/pipes in dining room. Wheelchair access (also WC). Music. No mobile phones. Air-conditioned   ACCOMMODATION: 41 rooms, all with bath/shower. TV. Phone. Room only £295 to £650   ⊖ Hyde Park Corner

# National Gallery, Crivelli's Garden ⚡✖   map 15

Trafalgar Square, WC2N 5DN                                          COOKING 3
TEL: (020) 7747 2869                                                   ITALIAN
FAX: (020) 7747 2438,                                               £28–£48

In this first-floor restaurant in the Sainsbury Wing, diners at window tables get the bonus of fantastic views over Trafalgar Square. The décor is contemporary: red carpets, recessed lighting and ice-blue and grey walls relieved by large plants and colourful murals. The menu is divided into traditional sections – antipasti, pasta, secondi piatti, salads and side dishes – and there is also a separate pizza menu. A starter of octopus salad with celery and potato may come simply dressed with extra virgin olive oil and balsamic vinegar, while pasta options have taken in a generous portion of triangoli with sun-dried tomato pesto, asparagus and pecorino; and pappardelle with fresh tuna, rocket and cherry tomato. At inspection, however, pasta dishes suffered from both under- and over-cooking. Secondi piatti may feature a pink, flavourful grilled veal chop with cabbage, baby carrots and rosemary dressing. Pizze, from a wood-fired oven, rely on variations on the tomato/mozzarella/vegetable or meat theme, while desserts stick to such classics as light, frothy tiramisù and gelati. Reports about service have varied widely from 'maddeningly slow and incompetent' to 'charming and efficient'. The short, mostly Italian wine list is low on interest. Bottle prices start at £10.95 (£3 a glass).

CHEF: Paolo Zanca   PROPRIETOR: Red Pepper Group   OPEN: all week L 11.30 to 4 (3.30 Wed), Wed D 5.30 to 7.45   MEALS: alc (main courses £7.50 to £14.50). Snack menu also available   SERVICE: 12.5% (optional), card slips closed   CARDS: Amex, Delta, MasterCard, Switch, Visa   DETAILS: 180 seats. Private parties: 160 main room. Vegetarian meals. Children's helpings. No children under 5. No smoking in dining room. Wheelchair access (also WC). No music. Air-conditioned   ⊖ Charing Cross

# National Portrait Gallery, Portrait Restaurant 🍷 ⚡✖   map 15

Orange Street, WC2H 0HE
TEL: (020) 7312 2490   FAX: (020) 7925 0244                   COOKING 3
EMAIL: portrait.restaurant@talk21.com                  MODERN BRITISH
WEBSITE: www.searcys.co.uk                                       £33–£65

Full of buzz and energy, this long, narrow dining space has a spectacular panorama of the London skyline through its huge south-facing picture windows. Hard surfaces tend to ratchet up the noise level, but then it is a meeting place, serving straightforward, unpretentious food under the direction of Brendan Fyldes, last seen in the 2001 edition of the Guide at Paul Heathcote's in Lancashire (see entry, Longridge). The colourful bistro repertoire extends from seared tuna with a Thai salad, via broccoli and Stilton tart, to beer-battered fish and chips with creamed peas. Food arrives quickly, usually in a tower: perhaps a crisply battered goats' cheese fritter (on a salad of beetroot and pine nuts), or a well-balanced salad of endive and walnuts with bacon and blue cheese.

Much of the food seems to consist of a cold assembly in which salad leaves figure prominently, with a (sometimes lukewarm but invariably good-quality) main ingredient cooked to order: perhaps roast skate wing on creamy mash with capers, lemon and a julienne of cucumber, or rump of lamb with a big round of goats' cheese, asparagus stalks and salad leaves. Desserts are an enjoyable part of the package, taking in a lightly textured, golden bread-and-butter pudding, or a crisp-topped crème brûlée with a strong passion-fruit flavour, accompanied by a coconut biscuit. The wine list is to the point, with some good producers and a dozen wines by the glass. Bottle prices start at £13.95 (£3.40 by the glass).

CHEF: Brendan Fyldes   PROPRIETOR: Searcy Tansley and Co Ltd   OPEN: all week L 11.45 to 2.45, Thur and Fri D 5.30 to 8.30   CLOSED: 24 to 26 Dec, 1 Jan   MEALS: alc (main courses £13 to £20). Set D 5.30 to 6.30 £16.95 (2 courses) to £19.95. Brunch menu Sat and Sun 11.30 to 3, light menu Mon to Fri 11.30 to 5, bar menu Thur and Fri 5 to 9   SERVICE: 12.5% (optional), card slips closed   CARDS: Amex, Delta, Diners, MasterCard, Switch, Visa   DETAILS: 90 seats. Private parties: 120 main room. Vegetarian meals. No smoking in 1 dining room. Wheelchair access (also WC). Occasional music. Air-conditioned   ⊖ Leicester Square

# Neal Street Restaurant ✏️ map 15

26 Neal Street, WC2H 9PS
TEL: (020) 7836 8368   FAX: (020) 7240 3964

COOKING 2
ITALIAN
£44–£72

Mushroom man Antonio Carluccio's West End restaurant is a fairly compact space with a cream ceiling and mirrored walls. Fittingly, fungi figure in salads and main courses, or as a mixed sauté of the day. The style is perfectly simple: hand-cut pasta ribbons are expertly timed, and have black truffle shaved over them at the table, and seasonal fruits are served with San Leo ham. Main courses offer three fish and five meats (including veal sweetbreads, veal cutlet and calf's liver at inspection). Roast eel with marinated vegetables has been good, and accompanying salads are crisp and well-dressed. Campari-flavoured passion-fruit sorbet has passionate fans; otherwise, a caramelly pannacotta or Italian cheeses are reliable ways to finish. Service is enthusiastic and mostly efficient, while the largely Italian wine list quickly leaps £20. Prices start at £14.50 (£3.75 a glass) for Montepulciano d'Abruzzo.

CHEF: Andrea Cavaliere   PROPRIETORS: Antonio and Priscilla Carluccio   OPEN: Mon to Sat 12.30 to 2.30, 6 to 11   CLOSED: 23 Dec to 2 Jan   MEALS: alc (main courses £12.50 to £21)   SERVICE: 12.5% (optional), card slips closed   CARDS: Amex, Delta, Diners, MasterCard, Switch, Visa   DETAILS: 65 seats. Private parties: 10 to 24 private rooms. Vegetarian meals. Children's helpings. Wheelchair access (not WC). No music. Air-conditioned   ⊖ Covent Garden

*All entries, including Round-ups, are fully indexed at the back of the Guide.*

# New Tayyabs £

map 12

83 Fieldgate Street, E1 1JU
TEL: (020) 7247 9543 and 6400
EMAIL: info@tayyabs.co.uk
WEBSITE: www.tayyabs.co.uk

COOKING 2
PAKISTANI
£15–£30

An effective makeover has spruced up this utilitarian address in Whitechapel: cream walls decorated with near-abstract pictures, light wooden tables and lilac-purple colours around the ceiling set the tone. The place gets packed, booking may not guarantee a table without joining the queue, and the food is spot-on. What you get is 'well-executed regional cuisine' with its heart in the traditions of the Punjab and Lahore, all at a reasonable price. A laminated, full-colour menu spells out a range of tandooris and karahi dishes, from lamb chops with a chilli-hot marinade to richly flavoured chicken keema. Backup comes in the shape of one or two daily specials: Wednesday brings a curiously original version of lamb korma as well as meat pilau, and there's generally a vegetarian option (pumpkin curry, for example). Breads are good, likewise desserts such as rasmalai. The restaurant is unlicensed, but lassi is served in metal pitchers, or you can BYO and drink from tumblers.

CHEF/PROPRIETOR: Mohammed Tayyab   OPEN: all week D only 5 to 11.30   CLOSED: 1 month during Ramadan   MEALS: alc (main courses £4 to £10)   SERVICE: not inc   CARDS: Amex, Delta, MasterCard, Switch, Visa   DETAILS: 100 seats. Private parties: 70 main room. Vegetarian meals. Wheelchair access (not WC). Music. Air-conditioned   ⊖ Whitechapel, Aldgate East

# Nicole's

map 15

158 New Bond Street, W1Y 9PA
TEL: (020) 7499 8408   FAX: (020) 7409 0381

COOKING 4
MODERN EUROPEAN
£45–£71

'Nicole's on Saturday lunchtime seems to be what it's all about: a civilised chow in between a spot of Bond Street shopping,' observed a reporter. The ladies – and others – who lunch head happily for this monochrome, restful basement below Farhi's designer clothes shop, where legions of waiting staff provide 'professional but good fun service'.

All comers rave about the basket of 'fantastic' breads, and the grill gets plenty of use: its heat is applied to everything from squid ('beautifully presented' with arrocina bean and artichoke salad plus a dollop of aïoli) to calf's liver (with Cumbrian bacon, mustard mash and Savoy cabbage). Elsewhere, a summery soup of fennel with Greek yoghurt, and accurately cooked risotto of red and yellow peppers with goats' cheese have shown plenty of skilful touches and invention. Classic British offerings also follow the seasons (roast rack of spring lamb comes with mint sauce, Jersey Royals and braised peas), while rich chocolate mousse with Chantilly cream and airy 'lace' cookies has been a 'stunner'. The shortish wine list divides equally between Old and New Worlds, with more than half available by the glass. Prices start at £13.25 a bottle.

CHEF: Annie Wayte   PROPRIETOR: Stephen Marks   OPEN: Mon to Sat L 12 to 3.30, Mon to Fri D 6.30 to 10.45   CLOSED: bank hols exc Good Fri   MEALS: alc (main courses £16.50 to £20). Cover £1. Bar menu available 11.30 to 5.30   SERVICE: 15% (optional), card slips closed   CARDS: Amex, Delta, Diners, MasterCard, Switch, Visa   DETAILS: 90 seats. Private parties: 200 main room. Vegetarian meals. No-smoking area. Music. Air-conditioned   ⊖ Green Park

## Noble Rot 　　　　　　　　　　　　　　　　map 15

3–5 Mill Street, W1S 2AU
TEL: (020) 7629 8877   FAX: (020) 7629 8878
EMAIL: noblerot@noblerot.com
WEBSITE: www.noblerot.com

COOKING 4
MODERN EUROPEAN
£32–£79

This stylish venue, near Savile Row, has a members' club beneath. This was unaffected by the fire next door in May 2002, but the smoke-damaged restaurant has been refurbished and put back together again more or less as it was. Since the last edition of the Guide, Matthew Owsley-Brown has left for Norfolk (see entry, Burnham Market), but his successor has taken to the contemporary European style with a will, offering an enterprising foie gras and smoked eel parfait with apple jelly to start, as well as a more straightforward but pleasingly refreshing scallop ceviche with pink peppercorn vinaigrette.

Main courses likewise offer plenty of choice, from steamed cod with beetroot, bacon, quails' eggs and mustard sauce, to a rather uninspiring cannon of lamb at inspection, served with parsnip purée, broad beans and truffles. Finish, perhaps, with sticky toffee pudding accompanied by a glass of something equally sticky. As the name of the place suggests, the wine list features a good selection of botrytised (and other) sweet wines, including several vintages of Ch. D'Yquem, alongside some of the best New World offerings. Prices are highish throughout the list, with little under £20 apart from the six house selections (starting at £15.75).

CHEF: Julian Owen-Mold   PROPRIETOR: Soren Jessen   OPEN: Mon to Fri L 12 to 3, Mon to Sat D 6.30 to 10.30   CLOSED: 25 and 26 Dec, bank hols   MEALS: alc (main courses £11 to £25). Set L £15.95 (2 courses) to £19.50   SERVICE: 12.5% (optional), card slips closed   CARDS: Amex, Delta, Diners, MasterCard, Switch, Visa   DETAILS: 60 seats. 20 seats outside. Private parties: 120 main room, 20 to 120 private rooms. Vegetarian meals. Music. Air-conditioned   ⊖ Oxford Circus

## Nobu ⚡　　　　　　　　　　　　　　　　　　　　map 15

19 Old Park Lane, W1Y 4LB
TEL: (020) 7447 4747   FAX: (020) 7447 4749
WEBSITE: www.nobumatsuhisa.com

COOKING 6
MODERN JAPANESE
£32–£110

The fashionable bareness of this long, rectangular, contemporary space, with its hard chiselled surfaces, is relieved by a view of Hyde Park. Staff (and many customers) wear black; service is attentive and friendly, and provides knowledgeable explanations of dishes and of the components of the eight-course omakase (chef's choice) menu. First-timers generally need a bit of a steer through the menu's various sections – special appetisers, special dishes, sushi rolls, main dishes, and so on – not least because everything sounds tempting. 'New style sashimi' of razor shell, for example, consists of finely cut strips treated like ceviche, served with a salmon-and-bamboo-shoot tempura roll, a roast fig, and a few slices of 'gloriously crisp' Japanese cucumber. Special dishes, meanwhile, offer sea urchin tempura, snow crab with creamy spicy sauce, and grilled black cod ('the great delicacy of the sea') served with a discreet amount of pale miso sauce.

Super-fresh ingredients underlie all this, giving dishes vigour and clear definition, and the sheer variety makes it easy to run up a big bill: sushi for example come in the form of toro, soft-shell crab, sea and freshwater eel, smelt egg, abalone and scallop. Lunch adds donburi and noodle dishes to the list, and desserts include a chocolate bento box with green tea ice cream. Cocktails and sakés feature among the drinks, and some 60 wines (from £20 to £56) are broadly arranged by style, with another 30 top-class 'reserve' bottles, and a hyper-expensive 'favourites' list (fancy J.J. Prum's 1949 Wehlener Sonnenuhr Auslese for £1,260?). House New Zealand Sauvignon is £24, Chilean Merlot £22.

CHEF: Mark Edwards  PROPRIETOR: Nobu Matsuhisa  OPEN: Mon to Fri L 12 to 2.15, all week D 6 to 10.15 (11 Fri and Sat, 9.30 Sun)  CLOSED: 25 and 26 Dec, 1 Jan, Good Fri and Easter Mon L MEALS: alc (main courses £5 to £29.50). Set L £24.50 to £50. Set D £70  SERVICE: 15% (optional) CARDS: Amex, Delta, Diners, MasterCard, Switch, Visa  DETAILS: 205 seats. Private parties: 14 to 40 private rooms. Vegetarian meals. No smoking in 1 dining room. No cigars/pipes in dining room. Wheelchair access (also WC). Air-conditioned  ⊖ Hyde Park Corner

# Noura                                                              map 13

| 16 Hobart Place, SW1W 0HH | COOKING 4 |
| TEL: (020) 7235 9444   FAX: (020) 7235 9244 | LEBANESE |
| WEBSITE: www.noura-brasserie.co.uk | £29–£58 |

Noura has a bright, clean, modish presence and its commodious dining area, done out in pale colours highlighted with mirrors and splashes of pistachio green, can be bustlingly busy. Service, by French-accented all-male staff, is a high point, all professional and solicitous with a side order of flirtation.

The menu is very long, although a specials list can help make lighter work of things. Vegetarians will find plenty to satisfy them among the cold and hot meze, although main courses tend to be meatier affairs. Delicately and accurately flavoured moutabbal (a purée of grilled aubergine with sesame and lemon juice) may be accompanied by a hot meze of wonderfully spiced sfeehah ('described like a small pizza but more like a tartlet' of minced lamb, tomato, onions and pine kernels). Main courses might include several types of kibbeh (minced lamb and cracked wheat) or grills, often of lamb, with a few fish dishes, grilled or fried. Intriguing-sounding ossmallieh (caramelised wheat filled with clotted cream) or karabeej halabi (pistachio-filled shortcrust pastries served with meringue cream) may be among desserts. The wine list includes a rather pricey collection of Lebanese and French bottles, with a few examples from the New World. Prices start at £14 for French house wine, and there is an assortment of arak ('the national drink of Lebanon,' according to the list) for the adventurous.

CHEF: Tony Esper  PROPRIETOR: Nader Bou-Antoun  OPEN: all week 11.30 to 11.45  MEALS: alc (main courses £10 to £18). Set L 11.30 to 6 exc Sun £14, Set L and D £20.50 to £28.50 (all min 2) SERVICE: not inc  CARDS: Amex, Delta, Diners, MasterCard, Switch, Visa  DETAILS: 125 seats. Private parties: 40 main room, 40 to 400 private rooms. Vegetarian meals. Wheelchair access (also WC). Music. Air-conditioned  ⊖ Victoria  (£5)

# No. 6 George Street ✱ £

map 15

6 George Street, W1U 3QX
TEL: (020) 7935 1910   FAX: (020) 7935 6036

COOKING 2
MODERN BRITISH
£29–£52

Subtitled 'restaurant and delicatessen', this is a small, white-painted shop just off increasingly vibrant and bustling Marylebone High Street. At the front is an attractively displayed selection of fruit and vegetables, bread and salamis, which lures you in to the open-plan eating area, a 'pleasingly un-designery' space with bare wooden floorboards, cream walls and scrubbed pine tables. Menus are as unpretentious as the setting, including options as straightforward as herb omelette with salad, and nothing more elaborate than bourride of chicken with mash, or pan-fried Dover sole with tarragon butter and sauté potatoes. Though ambition is modest, the cooking is well served by fresh ingredients, proper skills and the confidence to avoid short cuts. Prices on the short wine list start at £12.50 and remain well under £30 throughout.

CHEF/PROPRIETOR: Emma Miller   OPEN: Mon to Fri L only 12 to 3   CLOSED: bank hols   MEALS: alc (main courses £9.50 to £16)   SERVICE: not inc   CARDS: Delta, MasterCard, Switch, Visa   DETAILS: 30 seats. Private parties: 30 main room. Vegetarian meals. No smoking in dining room. No music. Air-conditioned   ⊖ Bond Street, Baker Street

# Oak

**NEW ENTRY**   map 13

137 Westbourne Park Road, W2 5QL
TEL: (020) 7221 3395   FAX: (020) 7467 0600

COOKING 4
MODERN EUROPEAN
£31–£56

This new gastro-pub on the fringes of Notting Hill occupies a sizeable corner plot. Above the often-heaving pub is a large, square-shaped, high-ceilinged room with ornate cornices and floor-to-ceiling windows. A herringbone floor adds a certain rusticity, as do simple dark wooden chairs and unfinished wooden tabletops, while two chandeliers lend a touch of class. It is a convivial and civilised room to dine in. The daily-changing menu tends towards comfort food, with a focus on good British ingredients, often with a Mediterranean slant. Starters may include a well-judged dish of Cornish crab with avocado, sweet chilli and crisp prosciutto, or Catalan toasted scallops, their accompanying lemon and wood-roasted tinkerbell chillies providing sweet yet spicy flavours.

Slow-roast Old Spot pork belly (with spot-on crackling), soft polenta, and baby carrots, or a robust fillet of Longhorn beef with mash, girolles and foie gras may turn up among main courses. Desserts are of a high standard: warm bitter chocolate financier with buttermilk sherbet, and peach, apricot and almond tart with vanilla ice cream are likely to please. Service is attentive, friendly and proficient. Wines hail from just three countries – France, Italy and Spain – but the range is pleasing, and choice under £20 decent. Wines by the glass (from £3 to £6.50) are also well worth drinking.

CHEF: Mark Broadbent   PROPRIETOR: Jasper Gorst   OPEN: Sat and Sun L 12 to 3, all week D 7 to 10.30   CLOSED: 25 and 26 Dec, 1 Jan, Aug bank hol   MEALS: alc (main courses £10.50 to £17.50)   SERVICE: 12.5% (optional), card slips closed   CARDS: Amex, Delta, Diners, MasterCard, Switch,

Visa   DETAILS: 48 seats. Private parties: 30 main room. Vegetarian meals. No children at D.
Occasional music   ⊖ Westbourne Park

# Odette's 🍷   map 13

130 Regent's Park Road, NW1 8XL                              COOKING 4
TEL: (020) 7586 5486   FAX: (020) 7586 0508                 MODERN BRITISH
                                                            £26–£70

Odette's has occupied this enviable position in a smart shopping street for some
25 years. Tables spill on to the pavement in fine weather, while inside is a
delightful series of contrasting spaces: a dark, formal front room decorated with
gilt-framed mirrors, a light and airy mezzanine room, and a wine bar below, all
acknowledging tradition yet embracing the present. In addition, the 'welcome,
cooking, presentation, care and service are all exemplary', according to one local
supporter.

There is evident skill and enthusiasm in the kitchen, as well as an eye for
interesting combinations, such as slow-braised pork belly with a crab, radish
and pickled pineapple salad. At the same time, there are much more
straightforward ideas – grilled halibut fillet with buttered Savoy cabbage – and
these are generally the ones that work best: a brightly coloured pea soup, for
example, neither too creamy nor too thin, combining sweetness and depth of
flavour, served with chunks of egg in mayonnaise on buttery brioche. Other
uncomplicated successes have included a 'refreshingly straightforward' starter
of rabbit pâté with a well-made and lightly dressed celeriac rémoulade, and
breast of corn-fed chicken with 'satisfyingly creamy' mushrooms, reminiscent of
traditional French cooking but done with a lightness of touch.

Among desserts, it is good to see scoops of richly flavoured and softly textured
yet crunchy walnut praline ice cream unencumbered by the usual irrelevant
strawberries or mint leaves. The lunchtime deal is still one of the best going, and
although service (especially in the absence of the proprietor) has not always
been on top form, an inspector found it friendly and efficient. Imaginative
selection is the key to the broad-ranging and well-priced wine list. It focuses on
food-friendly styles, be they from Italy's Campania region, Spain's Toro region
or New Zealand. Two dozen wines in the 'cellarman's choice' section highlight
the diversity available. There is plenty to choose from under £20, but one could
easily spend more should the mood strike. Twenty-three wines by the glass
range from £3.25 to £6.25; bottle prices start at £11.95.

CHEF: Simon Bradley   PROPRIETOR: Simone Green   OPEN: Sun to Fri L 12.30 to 2.30, Mon to Sat
D 7 to 11   CLOSED: 10 days Christmas, bank hols   MEALS: alc (main courses £10.50 to £18.50).
Set L £12.50 (2 courses) to £15   SERVICE: not inc   CARDS: Amex, Delta, Diners, MasterCard,
Switch, Visa   DETAILS: 60 seats. 8 seats outside. Private parties: 30 main room, 8 to 10 private
rooms. Vegetarian meals. Children's helpings. No cigars/pipes in dining room. No music
⊖ Chalk Farm

---

🍷 *denotes an outstanding wine cellar;* 🍷 *denotes a good wine list, worth travelling for.*

# Old Delhi

map 13

48 Kendal Street, W2 2BP
TEL: (020) 7723 3335   FAX: (020) 7258 0181
WEBSITE: www.old-delhi.com

COOKING 1
INDIAN/IRANIAN
£32–£89

A forerunner of today's sophisticated Indian establishments, this relaxed, comfortably furnished restaurant is well attuned to local requirements. The cooking is a mixture of Indian and Persian, the former involving mainly familiar curry-house and tandoori dishes, the latter providing more temptation for the adventurous. Appetisers are mostly salads or vegetables with yoghurt, and main dishes comprise various grilled kebabs and koresht specialities (lamb or poultry stewed with sometimes exotic vegetables). Rice specialities take in zereshk pollo, white Basmati with berries and saffron, and (on Sunday, or to special order) baghali pollo roasted overnight with lamb shank, broad beans, and dill. A shortish wine list offers house wines at £12.50, some others under £25, and classic bottles up to Château Pétrus 1983 at £1,700. The £2 cover charge applies only twice a week when there is live harp music.

CHEFS: Mohammed Ansar Bhatti and Hossein Jalalvand   PROPRIETOR: Oldelms Ltd   OPEN: all week 12.30 to 3.30 (1 to 4 Fri and Sat), 6.30 to 11 (7 to 11.30 Fri and Sat); Jul to Sept: 1 to 4 and 7 to 11.30   CLOSED: 24 Dec to 2 Jan   MEALS: alc (main courses £14 to £26). Set L £19.50. Cover £2 Wed and Thur D   SERVICE: 15% (optional)   CARDS: Amex, Delta, Diners, MasterCard, Switch, Visa   DETAILS: 60 seats. Private parties: 25 main room. Vegetarian meals. Children's helpings No babies in dining room after 8pm. No-smoking area. Wheelchair access (not WC). Music. Air-conditioned   ⊖ Marble Arch

# Olivo

map 13

21 Eccleston Street, SW1W 9LX
TEL: (020) 7730 2505

COOKING 2
ITALIAN/SARDINIAN
£30–£57

'Olivo is best at the simple things,' commented a regular who values the place like 'an old friend'. Since 1990 Mauro Sanna and chef Marco Melis have been delivering robust Italian food with a pronounced Sardinian accent in a setting of wooden floors and mustard-coloured walls. Chargrilling is applied to everything from marinated lamb (which comes 'smothered with parsley') to sea bass with salt and garlic. There may also be an evocative roast suckling pig, or spaghetti alla bottarga (home-made pasta with grated grey mullet roe and 'an unbelievably rich sauce loaded with mascarpone'). Effective use of good ingredients has resulted in a 'delectable layered pyramid' of mozzarella and cold marinated aubergine, as well as 'exquisite' gnocchi with prawns and baby tomatoes. Rounding things off, there might be pannacotta or sebada (deep-fried pastry filled with cheese and dressed with honey). Service is friendly and efficient, and the all-Italian wine list has a decent fistful from Sardinia. House wine is £14 (£3.50 a glass).

CHEF: Marco Melis   PROPRIETOR: Mauro Sanna   OPEN: Mon to Fri L 12 to 2.30, all week D 7 to 11   CLOSED: Christmas, bank hols   MEALS: alc D (main courses £13 to £15). Set L £15.50 (2 courses) to £17.50. Cover £1.50   SERVICE: not inc   CARDS: Amex, Delta, MasterCard, Switch, Visa   DETAILS: 45 seats. Vegetarian meals. No music. Air-conditioned   ⊖ Victoria

# 1 Lombard Street ♛

map 13

1 Lombard Street, EC3V 9AA
TEL: (020) 7929 6611   FAX: (020) 7929 6622
EMAIL: tg@1lombardstreet.com
WEBSITE: www.1lombardstreet.com

COOKING 4
MODERN EUROPEAN
£50–£93

The former bank – a Grade II listed building – is built on a large scale, its domed skylight hovering over the circular bar, where some slightly less expensive food is on offer. The 'intentionally shabby chic' dining room, with its loads of linen and glassware, is more grown up, just the sort of place one might expect to find financial bigwigs enjoying a discreet lunch. If they have conservative tastes, they are well served by a menu reliant on a well-practised repertoire that soothes with both familiar combinations (feuilleté of smoked haddock with quail's egg and mustard sauce) and luxuries: a warm salad of squab pigeon and foie gras with truffle oil vinaigrette, or a salad of caramelised lobster and scallops.

Dishes appear to have lots of things done to them, be they fish or meat. John Dory is baked in puff pastry with a tomato and black olive confit, accompanied by clams and mussels in a tarragon and citrus velouté, while a mignon of veal is served with caramelised calves' sweetbreads, truffle essence, baby artichokes and pistachio cream. To finish, a caramelised apple feuillantine comes with Guinness ice cream, and a chocolate pyramid with an almond milk granita. Cultish wines from the New World rub shoulders with a range of champagnes and European favourites on the broad-ranging list. A separate 'from the Lombard vault' selection includes top Bordeaux and Burgundies, on which no service charge is levied. Although there is little on the main list under £25, an interesting selection of house wines starts at £14 and there is a good range by the glass.

CHEF: Herbert Berger   PROPRIETOR: Soren Jessen   OPEN: Mon to Fri 12 to 2.30, 6 to 10   CLOSED: Christmas, bank hols   MEALS: alc (main courses £27.50 to £29.50). Set L £32 (2 courses) to £38, Set D £34. Brasserie menu available   SERVICE: 12.5% (optional), card slips closed   CARDS: Amex, Delta, Diners, MasterCard, Switch, Visa   DETAILS: 40 seats. Private parties: 2 to 40 private rooms. No pipes in dining room. Wheelchair access (also WC). Music. Air-conditioned
⊖ Bank

# 192 🍴

map 13

192 Kensington Park Road, W11 2ES
TEL: (020) 7229 0482   FAX: (020) 7229 3300

COOKING 1
MODERN BRITISH
£24–£63

There are two ways to consider this place: either as a busy wine bar with a restaurant attached, or as a bustling neighbourhood restaurant with a bar. Either way, the kitchen pitches its efforts appropriately and makes a success of providing sensibly unfussy dishes in a broad-based modern British style: ceviche of red snapper, bathed in coconut milk and topped with cumin-flavoured tortillas, for example, or perhaps rack of lamb with a herb crust, broad beans and peas, or even squab pigeon with a confit pigeon ravioli, Puy lentils and a truffle jus. Among desserts may be a tasty pine nut and ricotta cheesecake. Wines are a fairly trendy, moderately priced selection. Bottle prices start at £12, and around 20 are served by the glass.

CHEF: Stuart Kennedy   PROPRIETOR: Grove Restaurants   OPEN: all week 12.30 to 3 (3.30 Sat and Sun), 7 to 11.30 (11 Sun)   MEALS: alc (main courses £9.50 to £18). Set L £12.50 (2 courses) to £14.50   SERVICE: 12.5% (optional), card slips closed   CARDS: MasterCard, Switch, Visa   DETAILS: 83 seats. 16 seats outside. Private parties: 8 main room. Vegetarian meals. Children's helpings. No cigars/pipes in dining room. Wheelchair access (not WC). Music at D. Air-conditioned   ⊖ Ladbroke Grove, Notting Hill Gate

# ▲ One-O-One

map 14

101 Knightsbridge, SW1X 7RN

TEL: (020) 7290 7101   FAX: (020) 7235 6196

EMAIL: andrew.morgan@luxurycollection.com

COOKING 5

SEAFOOD

£38–£88

The restaurant forms part of the Sheraton Hotel, fronting on to Knightsbridge, and is a spacious, relaxed environment adorned with a contemporary marine wall sculpture and prints of lobsters and oysters. Pascal Proyart doesn't waver in his mission to bring the best fish and seafood cookery to London. Much of the inspiration comes from his native Brittany, and the food can be as simple or as rich as you fancy. Start with half-a-dozen Marenne d'Olerons oysters on ice, or fish soup with garlic croûtons, rouille and Gruyère, or maybe a salad of poached lobster and king crab with celeriac and apple rémoulade and coriander. There are non-piscine items too, although some of them have been productively paired with fish, as in the open lasagne of duck foie gras and John Dory with jus diable and Puy lentils. Two may dine on a whole sea bass cooked in a crust of Brittany sea-salt, before reclining perhaps into a dessert made of Caribbean Manjari chocolate served with pink grapefruit sorbet. Cheeses with walnut bread are recommended too. Highly polished service keeps things flowing, and there is a list of pedigree wines at mostly uncomfortable prices. Seven wines are available by the glass from £5.25; bottles start at £20.

CHEF: Pascal Proyart   PROPRIETOR: Starwood Hotels and Resorts   OPEN: all week 12 to 2.15, 7 to 10.15   MEALS: alc (main courses £19 to £25). Set L £15.50 (2 courses) to £19.50, Set D £35   SERVICE: not inc, card slips closed   CARDS: Amex, Delta, Diners, MasterCard, Switch, Visa   DETAILS: 86 seats. Private parties: 100 main room. Vegetarian meals. Children's helpings. No-smoking area. Occasional music. No mobile phones. Air-conditioned   ACCOMMODATION: 289 rooms, all with bath/shower. TV. Phone. Room only £204 to £3,200 (exc VAT). Rooms for disabled. Baby facilities   ⊖ Knightsbridge   £5

# One-Seven-Nine ♥

NEW ENTRY   map 15

179 Shaftesbury Avenue, WC2H 8JR

TEL: (020) 7836 3111   FAX: (020) 7836 3888

EMAIL: info@onesevennine.com

WEBSITE: www.onesevennine.com

COOKING 6

MODERN FRENCH

£34–£84

This started life as 'Conrad Gallagher' as the last edition of the Guide was going to press. He left, but his chef Steven Black stayed on, and the restaurant was re-launched with a new name during 2002. The cream-toned dining-room is now on the ground floor, filled with natural light from full-length windows, and the feeling of cool functionality is underlined by waiting-staff in Mao-style grey jackets.

The à la carte moves sedately with the seasons, though fixed-price lunch and pre-/post-theatre dinner menus change fortnightly. There have been letdowns – arising from 'clueless' service of cheese and wine – but fish cookery is particularly impressive: delicate tortellini of salmon with asparagus and baby carrots on a truffled watercress velouté, perhaps, followed by accurately timed brill fillets with garlicky dauphinoise, wild mushrooms and salsify. Although certain dishes seem designed for effect, combinations are never too esoteric: a crab risotto garnished with plum tomato sorbet for example, or a guinea-fowl aromatised with truffle and accompanied by girolles, peas, roast new potatoes and albufera sauce.

Desserts make the most of traditional ideas via impeccable technique and ingredients. The inspection highlight was a square of full-throttle Valrhona chocolate mousse garnished with candied ginger and served with a flawlessly textured lime sorbet. An imaginative selection of 15 by the glass (£3.80 to £7.50) opens a globe-trotting wine list that includes some good producers and interesting grape varieties (some appear under 'favourites from the cellar'). Mark-ups, though, can be hefty, with house wines at £16 and little else under £20.

CHEF: Steven Black   PROPRIETOR: Vince Power, Mean Fiddler Group   OPEN: Mon to Fri L 12 to 2.30, Mon to Sat D 5.30 to 11.30   CLOSED: bank hols   MEALS: alc (main courses £14.50 to £26). Set L and D 5.30 to 7 and 10.30 to 11.30 £14.95 (2 courses) to £18.95, Set D £49.50 (whole table). Bar menu also available Mon to Sat 5.30 to 11.30   SERVICE: 12.5% (optional), card slips closed   CARDS: Amex, Delta, MasterCard, Switch, Visa   DETAILS: 100 seats. Private parties: 100 main room, 10 to 50 private rooms. Vegetarian meals. Wheelchair access (also WC). Music. Air-conditioned   ⊖ Tottenham Court Road, Covent Garden

# L'Oranger                                                    map 15

5 St James's Street, SW1A 1EF                          COOKING 6
TEL: (020) 7839 3774   FAX: (020) 7839 4330       FRENCH/MEDITERRANEAN
                                                            £45–£104

Down at the bottom end of St James's Street, L'Oranger consists of a long, thin room decorated in mushroom colours, with windows looking on to a courtyard. It is a smart restaurant in a smart location, offering set-price menus with a few supplements, mostly for fish and shellfish. The style is appealing, featuring both luxurious and comparatively humble materials, taking in potato salad with a poached egg, caviar and red wine vinaigrette; bone marrow in a veal broth with braised Swiss chard and herbs; and chickpea compote with salted cod and crispy bread.

In this context, lunch (considered a good bet) tends to favour braised rabbit leg, or rump of lamb, while dinner goes in for more upmarket ingredients. Foie gras, for example, might pop up in a sauce for duck magret, or as shavings on a dish of roast corn-fed chicken with morels. Top-of-the-range fish, meanwhile, includes fillet of turbot, and whole sea bass baked in salt. The cooking is technically impressive, and if it doesn't exactly break new ground, nobody is complaining. Desserts might take in roast pineapple sablé, or hazelnut soufflé with chocolate sauce. Service may be formal, but it is friendly too. Drinking wine by the glass is one way to keep the cost down. The French-dominated list is unquestionably well chosen and of high quality, although it seems to believe that anything under £20 is beneath its dignity.

CHEF: Kamel Benamar   PROPRIETOR: A To Z Restaurants Ltd   OPEN: Mon to Fri L 12 to 2.30, Mon to Sat D 7 to 10.45   CLOSED: 24 Dec to 3 Jan   MEALS: Set L £20 (2 courses) to £24.50, Set D £35 (2 courses) to £39.50   SERVICE: 12.5% (optional)   CARDS: Amex, Delta, Diners, MasterCard, Switch, Visa   DETAILS: 50 seats. 8 seats outside. Private parties: 7 main room, 8 to 24 private rooms. Children's helpings. No music. Air-conditioned   ⊖ Green Park

## Original Tagines £

map 15

7A Dorset Street, W1U 6QN
TEL: (020) 7935 1545   FAX: (020) 7935 8279
EMAIL: enquiries@originaltagines.com
WEBSITE: www.originaltagines.com

COOKING 2
MOROCCAN
£17–£47

Bright décor reflects the restaurant's Moroccan roots without falsely exaggerating them, and its attitude to customers is indicated by a note on the menu: 'gratuities to be awarded for good service only'. Start with one of the usual Maghreb vegetable specialities – one of three different ways with aubergines, perhaps, or spinach with garlic and yoghurt – though devoted carnivores will fall on fried or grilled kidneys, or lamb meatballs. Pastry briouattes, stuffed with minced lamb, chicken, goats' cheese or seafood, can be taken as either starters or mains. Fish-lovers are offered only the fish of the day, grilled or in a tagine. There are six sorts of couscous, and nine variations on the tagine theme. Typical desserts include Moroccan pastries or almond briouattes; finally, choose from mint tea, spicy Moroccan, or Turkish coffee. House wines are £11.75, the eight reds all Moroccan except for Lebanese Château Musar.

CHEF: Serif Sepet   PROPRIETOR: Kenan Duran   OPEN: Mon to Fri L 12 to 3, Mon to Sat D 6 to 11   MEALS: alc (main courses £9.50 to £12). Set L £7.95 (2 courses) to £9.95   SERVICE: not inc   CARDS: Delta, MasterCard, Switch, Visa   DETAILS: 37 seats. 16 seats outside. Vegetarian meals. Wheelchair access (also WC). Music. No mobile phones. Air-conditioned   ⊖ Baker Street

## Orrery

map 15

LONDON GFG 2003 COMMENDED

55–57 Marylebone High Street, W1M 3AE
TEL: (020) 7616 8000   FAX: (020) 7616 8080
EMAIL: patrickf@conran-restaurants.co.uk
WEBSITE: www.orrery-restaurant.co.uk

COOKING 6
FRENCH
£37–£112

Perched above the Conran shop, arched windows looking across to Marylebone's Wren church, Orrery has clean concise and stylish lines. The long, thin room feels spacious yet intimate (there is a terrace for al fresco dining when weather permits), and, if the now very serious prices on the Franglais menu make this a special-occasions-only venue, it offers a 'dazzling pit stop for the jaded gourmet'.

Salady starters have included one of crispy duck and warm duck liver with fine green beans and dabs of honey dressing, and another combining nuggets of well-flavoured, herb-stuffed chicken thigh with sweet, moist crayfish. Not all combinations succeed (seared scallops, pork belly and cauliflower left one reporter unconvinced) but the cooking is mostly confident and assured.

Examples include a saddle of venison paired with a rich and flavourful black pudding and pumpkin fondant, and three grilled segments from a monster red mullet, each coated in a sparse bouillabaisse and resting on a bed of garlicky spinach, separated by soft, sweet scallops on potato purée.

The 'classic, exact, no-nonsense cooking' extends to desserts of rich Valrhona chocolate fondant with crème fraîche, and to expertly timed soufflés: blueberry or strawberry, each with vanilla-bean ice cream. Cheeses are well kept. Service can sometimes seem synchronised to a sluggish restaurant clock rather than that of customers, but it is otherwise pleasant and professional, not least from the knowledgeable and unassuming sommelier. His long and expensive list certainly shows an eye for quality, but even the 'sommelier's selection' doesn't include much under £20 a bottle.

CHEF: Chris Galvin   PROPRIETOR: Conran Restaurants   OPEN: all week 12 to 3, 7 to 11 (10.30 Sun) CLOSED: 25 and 26 Dec, 1 Jan, Good Fri   MEALS: alc (main courses £14.50 to £25). Set L £23.50, Set D Mon to Sat £50 to £80 (inc wine). Set D Sun £28.50 to £80 (inc wine). Bar menu available 12 to 3 and 7 to 11 and terrace D menu during summer   SERVICE: 12.5% (optional), card slips closed   CARDS: Amex, Delta, Diners, MasterCard, Switch, Visa   DETAILS: 80 seats. 30 seats outside. Private parties: 80 main room. Vegetarian meals. No pipes in dining room. Wheelchair access (also WC). No music   ⊖ Baker Street, Regents Park

## Oxo Tower ▮ ▧                                                        map 13

Oxo Tower Wharf, Barge House Street, SE1 9PH
TEL: (020) 7803 3888   FAX: (020) 7803 3838                              COOKING 3
EMAIL: oxo.reservations@harveynichols.co.uk                    MODERN BRITISH
WEBSITE: www.harveynichols.co.uk                                        £42–£83

The layout makes it seem like a cruise ship moored on the river, and everyone's abiding memory here is of the tremendous panoramic views over towards St Paul's and beyond. The room itself is simply but stylishly decorated, and the menu is relentlessly fashionable, reading as if a computer had spewed out a list of the latest must-have ingredients. These may be worked up into sweetbread ravioli with Albufera sauce, blue-fin tuna tataki with shiso, or stir-fried crab omelette with enoki and soy-marinated eel. But despite the global larder, this is not fusion food; ingredients on the same plate generally come from the same country.

Although the food seems to try to compete for effect with the setting, proffering small quantities of sometimes exotic or expensive ingredients, there is no shortage of either technical skill or enjoyable dishes. A walnut-whip-sized heap of shredded daikon salad with judiciously flavoured wasabi mayonnaise is topped with a piece of lobster; and well-flavoured sea bass, served on a soothingly soft blini (like a miniature potato soufflé) topped with salty caviar, comes with a 'flavour bomb' of sea urchin. Sauces tend to be minimal, designed more for visual effect than for flavour, and vegetarian options are more thoughtful than usual. Desserts, meanwhile, have included a generous, sweet and obligingly light caramel soufflé with 'just the right amount of wobble'. Service might be more coordinated, but wines are impeccably chosen. Here, the great and the good from classic regions of France and Italy rub shoulders with New World cult wines, such as Torbreck's Run Rig Shiraz from South Australia, and Turley's Dogtown Vineyard Zinfandel from California. Prices are on the high side, but wines in the £20 or under range are at least interesting. House red, white and rosé (from a separate, shorter list) start the bidding at £13.50.

CHEF: Dave Miney   PROPRIETOR: Dickson Poon   OPEN: Sun to Fri 12 to 3, 6.30 to 11.30 (10.30 Sun)   CLOSED: 25 and 26 Dec   MEALS: alc D (main courses £17.50 to £26). Set L £28.50 SERVICE: 12.5%, card slips closed   CARDS: Amex, Delta, Diners, MasterCard, Switch, Visa DETAILS: 130 seats. 75 seats outside. Vegetarian meals. Wheelchair access (also WC). No music. Air-conditioned   ⊖ Blackfriars, Waterloo

## Ozer £         map 15

| 5 Langham Place, W1B 3DG | NEW CHEF |
| TEL: (020) 7323 0505   FAX: (020) 7323 0111 | MODERN OTTOMAN |
| WEBSITE: www.ozer.co.uk | £28–£59 |

Ozer is part of a small international chain (the three other branches in London trade under the Sofra name) and, thanks not least to its almost permanent Happy Hour, has bags of atmosphere and buzz. It also has a new chef to oversee the wide range of mezze, grills and casseroles that form the bedrock of the kitchen's output: anything from falafel or stuffed vine leaves (vegetarian dishes are legion), via Albanian liver, to tuna loin with a red wine and honey sauce. In fact the only changes appear to be the addition of fish and chips to the seafood options, and a more generous selection of dishes for the set-price meals. Service varies between eagle-eyed and forgetful, and a selection of reliable names on the wine list offers choice under £20. Turkish house wine is £12.50.

CHEF: Servet Kilic   PROPRIETOR: Huseyin Ozer   OPEN: all week noon to midnight   MEALS: alc (main courses £7.50 to £19.50). Set L and D Tue to Sat noon to 6 and Sun and Mon noon to midnight £5 (2 courses). Set L and D £6.95 (2 courses) to £8.95, and Meze L and D £9.95 to £11.50 (min 2). Cover £2. Bar menu available   SERVICE: not included   CARDS: Amex, Delta, Diners, MasterCard, Switch, Visa   DETAILS: 110 seats. 10 seats outside. Private parties: 45 main room. Vegetarian meals. Children's helpings. No-smoking area. Wheelchair access (also WC). No music. Air-conditioned   ⊖ Oxford Circus (£5)

## Palais du Jardin         map 15

| 136 Long Acre, WC2E 9AD | COOKING 2 |
| TEL: (020) 7379 5353   FAX: (020) 7379 1846 | FRENCH |
| | £38–£68 |

High French windows open up to the street on fine days. Downstairs has more casual seating and a seafood bar, there is a special afternoon menu for grazers, and an extensive range of cocktails, making it a popular meeting spot at most times of day. A curved wooden bar dominates the restaurant entrance, and colourful modern pictures add to the cheery mood. The gamut runs from crab cake on lemon butter sauce, to a chunk of medium-cooked venison that was 'exceptionally tender, with juicy texture and light, gamey flavour'. A summer lunch produced a fine crisp-skinned sea bass on a creamy mix of cockles, mussels and leeks, followed by white chocolate mousse with dark chocolate sauce, and poached pear with raspberries. Service is rarely put off its stroke, no matter how busy it gets. Three French house wines, Sauvignon, Chardonnay and Merlot, come at £12.

CHEFS: Sam Brown and Jamie Scorer  PROPRIETOR: Le Palais du Jardin Ltd  OPEN: Mon to Sat 12 to 3.30, 5.30 to 11.45, Sun 12 to 10.30  MEALS: alc (main courses £13.50 to £18.50). 'Afternoon menu' 3.30 to 5.30  SERVICE: 12.5% (optional), card slips closed  CARDS: Amex, Delta, Diners, MasterCard, Switch, Visa  DETAILS: 350 seats. 16 seats outside. Private parties: 120 private room. Vegetarian meals. No cigars in dining room. Wheelchair access (also WC). Music. Air-conditioned  ⊖ Covent Garden

## Parade

map 12

18–19 The Mall, W5 2PJ

NEW CHEF

TEL: (020) 8810 0202   FAX: (020) 8810 0404

MODERN EUROPEAN
£24–£53

Looking smart and fashionable, this welcoming restaurant gets marks for its pleasant décor, absence of Muzak, friendly and efficient service, and interesting menu. Related by ownership to Phoenix and Sonny's (see entries), it sets its sights on an appealing mix of both established and contemporary ideas, whose realisation is now under the control of Colin Westal, veteran of Ransome's Dock and Kensington Place (see entries). He arrived as the Guide went to press, but changes were expected to be minor, so straightforward skate wing with beurre noisette, or rib of beef with frites and béarnaise, may sit alongside baked halibut with arrocina beans and leeks in a parsley velouté, and be followed by lemon posset, or chocolate and pear clafoutis. Set-price meals involve a decent saving on à la carte prices, and although the bulk of the sharply chosen wine list is over £20, a couple of vins de pays open the batting at £10.50 (£2.95 a glass).

CHEF: Colin Westal  PROPRIETORS: Rebecca Mascarenhas and James Harris  OPEN: all week L 12.30 to 2.30 (3 Sun), Mon to Sat D 7 to 11  CLOSED: 25 and 26 Dec, bank hols  MEALS: alc (main courses £10.50 to £15.50). Set L £12 (2 courses) to £15. Set L Sun £18.50  SERVICE: 12.5% (optional), card slips closed  CARDS: Amex, Delta, MasterCard, Switch, Visa  DETAILS: 100 seats. Private parties: 100 main room, 10 to 40 private rooms. Vegetarian meals. Children's helpings. No cigars/pipes in dining room. Wheelchair access (also WC). No music. Air-conditioned  ⊖ Ealing Broadway

## Parisienne Chophouse

NEW ENTRY   map 14

3 Yeoman's Row, SW3 3AL

TEL: (020) 7590 9999   FAX: (020) 7590 9900

COOKING 4

EMAIL: sales@whitestarline.org.uk

FRENCH

WEBSITE: www.whitestarline.org.uk

£25–£68

This addition to the MPW repertoire is a large windowless basement, just off Brompton Road, decorated with a 1920s Art Deco theme that one diner thought reminiscent of the Orient Express. Food, likewise, is old-fashioned, with plenty of English and French classics on the long menus: everything, in fact, from frogs' legs à la parisienne to eggs Benedict or Caesar salad among starters, while main courses take in 'haddock and chips à l'anglaise', ribeye of Aberdeen Angus au poivre, and spit-roast duck with honey and Thai spices.

What it may lack in innovation, however, it more than makes up for with a consistently high standard of cooking. Praise has come in for jambon persillé with moist meat, light jelly and deep pink and green colours, and for 'soft, tasty' duck rillettes, while an inspection dinner turned up a main course of precisely timed calf's liver topped with crispy bacon, accompanied by thin, crisp, golden frites. Desserts were the only disappointment of that meal, erring on the rich and sticky side, while service has varied from 'slick and friendly' to 'aloof' and 'lacklustre'. Quality is high throughout the wine list, but so are prices. A couple of Vins de Pays d'Oc open each section at £12.50, and there is an interesting selection of wines by the glass.

CHEF: Adam Clark   PROPRIETOR: Marco Pierre White   OPEN: all week L 12 to 2.30 (3.30 Sun), Mon to Sat D 5.30 to 11   MEALS: alc (main courses £10 to £22). Set L Mon to Sat £12.95 (2 courses) to £14.50, Set L Sun £16.50, Set D 5.30 to 7 £12.95 (2 courses) to £14.50   SERVICE: 12.5%   CARDS: Amex, Delta, Diners, MasterCard, Switch, Visa   DETAILS: 100 seats. Private parties: 120 main room, 24 private room. Music. Air-conditioned   ⊖ Knightsbridge

## Parsee
map 12

34 Highgate Hill, N19 5NL
TEL: (020) 7272 9091   FAX: (020) 7687 1139                    COOKING 3
EMAIL: dining@theparsee.com                                    PARSEE
WEBSITE: www.theparsee.com                                     £35–£52

Simply but brightly decorated, with sepia photos of famous Parsees, this restaurant is where Cyrus Todiwala of Café Spice Namaste (see entry) indulges his nostalgia for Mumbai (Bombay) and its Parsee community. This community is devoted to its highly specialised cooking, and, although Parsee delicacies often share names with other styles, they are very different.

The short menu with full descriptions has a section of chargrills: chicken, salmon or venison. Main dishes include dhaan daar nay kolmi no patio: not a barbecue, but a festive curry, and more exciting than prawn patia. Dhaansaak, made with lamb, lentils and a meatball is the signature dish not just of this restaurant but also of Parsee cooking generally. Supplementary (and frequently changed) specials might include such starters as egg on spiced and sliced potatoes with bread, or pan-grilled chicken livers rolled in chapatti, followed by crisp-fried pomfret, or a palav (pilau) of lamb with rice and unusually prepared lentils. Although vegetables play a comparatively minor role in Parsee cuisine, there are five vegetarian main dishes. Desserts include lagan nu custard, a baked wedding custard. The short, varied wine list starts at £12.90 with few bottles over £20. (The 'Belgian' Celis White, unfiltered wheat beer, is brewed in Austin, Texas.)

CHEFS: Cyrus Todiwala, Chuttan Lal Sain and M. Ali   PROPRIETOR: The Parsee Ltd   OPEN: Mon to Sat D only 6 to 10.45   CLOSED: Christmas and New Year, bank hols   MEALS: alc (main courses £10.50 to £14). Set D £25 (on request or on special Parsee religious occasions)   SERVICE: 10% (optional), card slips closed   CARDS: Amex, Delta, MasterCard, Switch, Visa   DETAILS: 48 seats. Vegetarian meals. Children's helpings. Music. Air-conditioned   ⊖ Archway

---

*The text of entries is based on unsolicited reports sent in by readers, backed up by inspections conducted anonymously. The factual details under the text are from questionnaires the Guide sends to all restaurants that feature in the book.*

# Passione

map 15

10 Charlotte Street, W1P 1HE                                          COOKING 4
TEL: (020) 7636 2833   FAX: (020) 7636 2889               MODERN ITALIAN
WEBSITE: www.passione.co.uk                                          £32–£63

Beyond the unremarkable orange frontage, two small, busy rooms (don't be surprised if smoke gets in your eyes) generate the atmosphere of a 'good, honest local'. The appeal is rustic food that is not tarted up or refined, and doesn't attempt to be smarter than it really is. At the same time, it is sensitively handled: chunks of well-timed rabbit, for example, spiked with rosemary and sitting in a dark brown, stock-based gravy. Gennaro Contaldo's southern Italian upbringing is perhaps responsible for this, as well as for the use of some wild foods. In the countryside you might expect it, but few London chefs bother to source wild sorrel (used in a risotto), or go out and gather their own herbs and mushrooms.

Elsewhere, a humble cannellini and borlotti bean broth might share the menu with truffled tagliatelle, or a fine dish of plump, flavourful sea bream served with endive and a well-balanced honey and vinegar sauce. Some dishes come in two sizes, and anybody counting the pennies can eat just a starter and dessert: the house special is a creamy limoncello and wild strawberry ice cream. Service is low-key and businesslike, and the wine list combines fruity northern whites and characterful southern reds, starting with a pair of house wines from Abruzzo and Umbria at £11.50.

CHEF: Gennaro Contaldo   PROPRIETORS: Gennaro Contaldo, Gennaro D'Urso and Liz Przybylski   OPEN: Mon to Fri L 12.30 to 2.15, Mon to Sat D 7 to 10.15   CLOSED: 1 week Christmas, bank hols   MEALS: alc (main courses £9.50 to £18.50)   SERVICE: 12.5% (optional), card slips closed   CARDS: Amex, Delta, Diners, MasterCard, Switch, Visa   DETAILS: 40 seats. 8 seats outside. Private parties: 44 main room, 6 to 18 private rooms. Vegetarian meals. Children's helpings. Wheelchair access (not WC). No music. Air-conditioned   ⊖ Goodge Street

# Perseverance

NEW ENTRY   map 13

63 Lamb's Conduit Street, WC1N 3NB                                 COOKING 2
TEL: (020) 7405 8278   FAX: (020) 7831 0031              MODERN BRITISH
                                                                     £30–£50

From outside it looks a fairly ordinary pub, the windows etched with 'Beer and Spirits', and the interior doesn't contradict this; but for the young and casually dressed clientele, you might have stepped back into the early twentieth century. The upstairs dining room is a contrast – simple, bright and decorated with modern art – and the food is definitely not pub grub. Expect plenty of eye-catching dishes from an ambitious and inventive repertoire that shows a wide range of influences. For example, after carpaccio of smoked halibut with apple and fennel salsa and citrus crème fraîche, one might have leek-wrapped loin of lamb with pesto couscous and pepper stew, or beef fillet with celeriac fondant, beetroot carpaccio and horseradish sauce. Summer pudding with clotted cream rounds everything off nicely. The short wine list starts at £10.90, and there are eight by the glass.

CHEF: Justin Saunders   PROPRIETOR: Billy Drew   OPEN: Sun to Fri L 12 to 3, Mon to Sat D 7 to 10
MEALS: alc (main courses £9.50 to £16). Bar menu also available   SERVICE: 12.5%   CARDS:
Amex, Delta, Diners, MasterCard, Switch, Visa   DETAILS: 70 seats. 16 seats outside. Vegetarian
meals. No music. Air-conditioned   ⊖ Holborn, Russell Square  £5

# Pétrus

map 14

| | |
|---|---|
| 33 St James's Street, SW1A 1HD | COOKING 8 |
| TEL: (020) 7930 4272   FAX: (020) 7930 9702 | FRENCH |
| WEBSITE: www.petrus-restaurant.com | £44–£98 |

A discreet entrance leads to a small holding area, then to a long, smart, rather
dark dining room with glowering food pictures and well-spaced tables. The
atmosphere is quiet, subdued, businesslike, and although it is not the brightest
or chirpiest of dining rooms these are comforting surroundings in which to enjoy
some stunning contemporary French food. First-rate ingredients are presented
in skilful and exciting ways, and although dishes may be complex, they are
balanced and clearly focused: nothing overwhelms, and nothing is underwhelming. Individual components are spot-on and work convincingly together:
for example, in a deep yellow raviolo, eggy and al dente, stuffed with roughly
chopped wild mushrooms, covered in chopped black truffle and herbs,
partnered by three peeled langoustines, around which the waiter pours an
intense port and foie gras velouté.

Soft textures are contrasted with other carefully managed items on the plate
(there is little to do in the way of struggling with bones here), and dishes
generate sheer pleasure, as in a starter of three pieces of fresh, flavourful red
mullet propped against three fat scallops – dredged in a delicate spice, just
seared, and sticky, as only the freshest ones are – served with bits of artichoke
and beetroot crisps. The star of one meal contrasted the savouriness of a pig's
trotter with the sweetness of its accompanying onion soup, while another
produced an 'unbeatable' dish of Anjou pigeon, the rare roast breasts well rested
and as soft as velvet, by their side a smoked ham tourte that was 'nothing short of
sensational': the pastry pithiviers enclosing a nugget of pink sausage meat,
gamey, slightly smoky, sultry, earthy and sensuous, all in a deeply flavoured
truffley sauce. Braised pork belly comes in for widespread praise too, its deep
flavour and robust chewiness well complemented by a generous and richly
gamey slice of foie gras, set about with roast shallots and crisply fried leeks,
accompanied by a ramekin of truffle-infused potato purée.

Like everything else, desserts are carefully crafted and technically
accomplished. Crème brûlée is served not in a dish but on a plate, sandwiched
between a pool of red berry compote and a similarly flavoured ice cream, while
an iced pistachio parfait is filled with liquid chocolate, with slices of poached
pear fanned around the base, and a thin slice of crisp pineapple parked on top. A
fine cheeseboard adds to the appeal, incidentals (including pre-meal nibbles,
bread and chocolate petits fours) are first-rate, and service is courteous, friendly,
informative, unobtrusive and highly polished. The only cloud on the horizon for
ordinary visitors in the scarily priced wine list – even wines by the glass can add
up fast – although there is no doubting the pedigree, the class or the variety,
especially within France.

CHEF: Marcus Wareing   PROPRIETORS: Gordon Ramsay and Marcus Wareing   OPEN: Mon to Fri
L 12 to 2.30, Mon to Sat D 6.45 to 11   CLOSED: 23 Dec to 5 Jan, bank hols   MEALS: Set L £26 to
£50, Set D £50 to £60   SERVICE: not inc   CARDS: Amex, Delta, Diners, MasterCard, Switch, Visa
DETAILS: 60 seats. Private parties: 50 main room. Children's helpings. No cigars/pipes in dining
room. No music. No mobile phones. Air-conditioned   ⊖ Green Park

## Phoenix 🍳                                                                  map 12

162–164 Lower Richmond Road, SW15 1LY                        COOKING 3
TEL: (020) 8780 3131   FAX: (020) 8780 1114                  MODERN EUROPEAN
EMAIL: phoenix@sonnys.co.uk                                  £25–£58

The art alone is worth a look, reckoned one visitor. Vividly coloured lithographs,
contorted faces in charcoal and pastels, and a pair of intriguingly serene papier-
mâché dolls hovering overhead 'like guardian angels' set the tone. Franco
Taruschio, formerly of the Walnut Tree Inn (see entry, Llandewi Skirrid, Wales),
has been appointed consultant chef, and an Italian spin has naturally been put
on the menus. Trenette with courgette flowers and truffle is a dish of great
power, the al dente pasta an object lesson in timing; a pie of cockles and mussels
with bacon and leeks is a slightly more unexpected first-course proposition.
Boned and rolled roast suckling pig is a triumph, full of 'great, old-fashioned
flavour', and served with rosemary-scented roast potatoes. At inspection, fish
dishes were considerably less successful. A fine rendition of torta della nonna, a
pine-nut cake of cheesecakey texture is a good bet to finish with, or there is semi-
freddo made with ricotta, candied fruits and nuts, or pannacotta with orange
salad. Service can lose its way a little, but manages to exude a 'fun, free-and-easy
atmosphere'. Italian and New World wines leaven French classics on a short list.
Most bottles cost over £20, but prices start with house French Colombard and
Merlot at £10.95.

CHEFS: Franco Taruschio and Chris Parkinson   PROPRIETOR: Rebecca Mascarenhas   OPEN: all
week 12.30 to 2.30 (3 Sun), 7 to 11 (11.30 Fri and Sat, 10 Sun)   CLOSED: 24 to 26 Dec, Good Fri L,
bank hols   MEALS: alc (main courses £10.50 to £16). Set L Mon to Sat £12 (2 courses) to £15, Set
L Sun £18.50, Set D Sun to Thur 7 to 7.45 £12 (2 courses) to £15   SERVICE: 12.5% (optional), card
slips closed   CARDS: Amex, Delta, Diners, MasterCard, Switch, Visa   DETAILS: 100 seats. 40
seats outside. Private parties: 100 main room. Vegetarian meals. Children's helpings. No-
smoking area. Wheelchair access (also WC). Music. Air-conditioned   ⊖ Putney Bridge £5

## Phoenix Palace £                              NEW ENTRY    map 13

3–5 Glentworth Street, NW1 5PG                               COOKING 2
TEL: (020) 7486 3515   FAX: (020) 7486 3401                  CHINESE
                                                             £27–£66

Graceful Chinese calligraphy on the windows marks out this restaurant below a
block of flats not far from Baker Street Tube station. Inside, the open-plan dining
room has a 'water feature', bright panels and raised seating areas along the
walls. The menu of around 200 dishes is predominantly Cantonese with a few
items from Peking and Szechuan. Familiar stuff, such as vegetarian spring rolls
and splendidly good aromatic crispy duck, are skilfully handled, and the
kitchen also shows its paces in more esoteric dishes: minced pork and aubergine
hotpot 'with a pleasant spicy kick', and 'white-cut' shredded chicken with

crunchy strips of jellyfish, for example. Fish shows up strongly (steamed sea bass with ginger and spring onions has been well received), and there is a big contingent of noodles, including 'really well-made' ho fun and yei mein. Daytime dim sum have also been confidently recommended. Service is youthful and ever-so-willing. House French is £9.80.

CHEF: Lam Kwok Wah   PROPRIETOR: City Cuisine Ltd   OPEN: all week 12 to 11.30, Sun 11 to 10.30   CLOSED: 25 Dec   MEALS: alc (main dishes £5.50 to £22), Set meals £9.80 to £19.80 (all min 2)   SERVICE: 12.5%   CARDS: Amex, Delta, MasterCard, Switch, Visa   DETAILS: 250 seats. Private parties: 280 main room. Vegetarian meals. Music. Air-conditioned   ⊖ Baker Street

## Pied-à-Terre ▮ ⍟       map 15

34 Charlotte Street, W1T 2NH
TEL: (020) 7636 1178   FAX: (020) 7916 1171      COOKING 8
EMAIL: p-a-t@dircon.co.uk      FRENCH
WEBSITE: www.pied.a.terre.co.uk      £41–£92

'The redesign is fabulous,' reckoned one visitor, noting the transformation from a rather gloomy cygnet into an exciting swan with comfortable seating; although another found it still too dark for comfort. The dining room is now in two parts, the rear at last non-smoking, a small but significant change that gives those who buy good bottles of wine the chance to appreciate them properly, and everybody the chance to enjoy the food.

Canapés arrive in a neat row, among them a 'ridiculously exquisite' deep-fried snail in salty batter, a chunk of creamy buffalo mozzarella wrapped in Serrano ham, and a crisp filo sandwich encasing a blob of foie gras. This is an early indication that the kitchen revels in minutiae, with the 'twiddly bits' receiving lavish praise. Arrangements may be fiddly but flavours generally ring true and honest, as in a red mullet starter, with a warm, cracklingly crisp-skinned fillet in the centre, the corners of the plate taken up by thin slices of dried cherry tomato stuck into a rich quenelle of sardine mousse, and by slices of cold terrine composed of fresh tomato, red mullet and basil leaves: 'as fine a red mullet dish as I've ever eaten,' concluded our inspector.

At its best the food is inventive yet sensible, taking in an open raviolo of frogs' legs and foie gras with black trumpet mushrooms and a hazelnut emulsion; and roast monkfish with oyster and leek ravioli, an onion crust and a cockle and chive velouté. Highly refined and technically accomplished though it is, the cooking mobilises popular flavours, for example the cumin that infuses both a roast rack of Pyrenean spring lamb and its underpinning purée of aubergine, served with two little turrets of offaly bits wrapped in a cabbage leaf topped with a skinned roast garlic clove and a slice of dried courgette. Soups are intense and velvety (white bean and black truffle with wild mushrooms, for example), and sauces are as impressive as the rest, not least because they taste pleasingly fatty where appropriate, without being greasy.

Quantities and presentation are carefully judged throughout, so desserts are eminently manageable. A small banana split lengthways, roasted and lightly charred, is served with a timbale of hazelnutty praline mousse and a scoop of creamy, buttery, melty butterscotch ice, producing a rich and enveloping finish. Staff in black suits and tunics susurrate a gentle reminder of what you ordered as they lovingly deliver it, and David Moore oversees the generally flawless operation. Wines are taken seriously. The list is predominantly European, with a decent selection of halves and large-format bottles. Burgundy fans will be in their element, but will need a well-padded wallet to enjoy most of the bottles, as basic Mâconnais white starts at £25 before heading decisively up to four figures. Smart Austrian producers are a strength. A bit of poking around will reveal the few bottles under £20; basic French red and white sell for £18, or £4 per glass, although the menu suggests an interesting assortment of wines by the glass to complement various dishes.

CHEF: Shane Osborn   PROPRIETOR: David Moore   OPEN: Mon to Fri L 12.15 to 2.30, Mon to Sat D 7 to 11   CLOSED: 2 weeks Christmas   MEALS: Set L £19.50 (2 courses) to £35 (2 courses), Set D £35 (2 courses) to £55   SERVICE: 12.5% (optional), card slips closed   CARDS: Amex, Delta, Diners, MasterCard, Switch, Visa   DETAILS: 48 seats. Private parties: 8 main room, 6 to 16 private rooms. Vegetarian meals. Children's helpings. No smoking in 1 dining room. Wheelchair access (not WC). Occasional music. Air-conditioned   ⊖ Goodge Street

# Le Pont de la Tour ▮

map 13

36D Shad Thames,
The Butlers Wharf Building SE1 2YE
TEL: (020) 7403 8403   FAX: (020) 7403 0267
WEBSITE: www.conran.com

COOKING 4
MODERN EUROPEAN
£35–£88

Mirrored pillars help even those not facing the windows to enjoy impressive views of the Thames ('we saw Tower Bridge open') from this light, bright room with 'hordes of staff'. A few daily specials supplement a generous carte offering 'uncomplicated food that people like', including perhaps terrine of foie gras with red onion chutney, or shellfish bisque, or grilled Dover sole. Seafood figures prominently, and, although some unchanging starters (half a lobster with fennel and lemon salad, or langoustines mayonnaise) may not take much assembling, the kitchen does make a virtue of simplicity.

It is more than capable with meat, too, judging by first-class peppered beef fillet – 'beautiful piece of meat cooked rare as ordered, tender and full of flavour' – or a huge lump of flavourful, pink-grilled cote de veau on the bone, with a mix of wild mushrooms in a thin brown sauce. Desserts, equally accomplished, include a tarte fine of pears with chocolate caramel sauce, and a notable hot chocolate soufflé with pistachio ice cream. Prices are high (vegetables are charged extra); service is efficient and unobtrusive, but then it should be when credit card slips are left open even though a 'discretionary' service charge has been added. The wine list is a buff's delight, packed full of interesting bottles, with Old World classics alongside rising stars from the New World; it is difficult to find a second-rate producer anywhere. Mark-ups, however, are on the steep side, which means that diners will have to hunt around to find much under £20. Eleven wines are available by the glass (£3.95 to £7.75); bottle prices start at £13.95 and quickly reach four figures.

CHEF: Tim Powell   PROPRIETOR: Conran Restaurants   OPEN: Sun to Fri L 12 to 3, all week D 6 to 11   MEALS: alc (main courses £12 to £25). Set L £28.50. Bar and grill menus also available SERVICE: 12.5% (optional)   CARDS: Amex, Diners, MasterCard, Switch, Visa   DETAILS: 95 seats. 60 seats outside. Private parties: 10 main room, 8 to 22 private rooms. Vegetarian meals. Music ⊖ London Bridge

# Popeseye

map 12

108 Blythe Road, W14 0HD
TEL: (020) 7352 1279

COOKING 1
STEAK AND GRILLS
£23–£60

Popeseye (Scots for rump steak) is a busy neighbourhood restaurant with tightly packed tables and a single-minded devotion to beef, specifically Aberdeen Angus, hung for two weeks or more, and simply but precisely chargrilled. In one corner is an open grill with a single cook loading it with hunks of rump, sirloin and fillet. Priced by weight, they all come with chips; a well-dressed salad is £3.45 extra.

Individual steaks may not be as neat or carefully trimmed as the price warrants, plates may be cold, and relishes (including mustards, béarnaise and horseradish) are from standard-issue bottles, but the quality of the beef is impeccable. Frills, such as starters or bread, are dispensed with, although token desserts on a blackboard take in apple crumble and sticky toffee pudding or cheese. Reds understandably dominate the wine list, including mature clarets as well as Guigal's Gigondas 1998 (£15.50); house wine is £11.50. There is another branch at 277 Upper Richmond Road, London SW15, tel. (020) 8788 7733.

CHEF/PROPRIETOR: Ian Hutchison   OPEN: Mon to Sat D 6.45 to 10.30   MEALS: alc (main courses £9.50 to £30)   SERVICE: 12.5% (optional)   CARDS: none   DETAILS: 34 seats. Private parties: 34 main room. Wheelchair access (not WC). Occasional music   ⊖ Olympia  £5

# Porte des Indes ⚡✳

map 13

32 Bryanston Street, W1H 7EG
TEL: (020) 7224 0055   FAX: (020) 7224 1144
EMAIL: pilondon@aol.com
WEBSITE: www.la-porte-des-indes.com

COOKING 1
INDIAN
£38–£79

An unassuming entrance hides what is probably the grandest of all London's Indian restaurants in terms of décor. Reproduction paintings, spectacular flower displays, giant palm trees and an impressive waterfall contribute to the theme-park atmosphere. Even the food smacks of Disney World, where the rice is always 'fluffy', chicken 'succulent', and rogan josh 'a prince among curries'. Whatever the quasi-French menu may claim, this is entry-level Indian food where even the hottest spicing is mild by most standards. The range includes rasoul (puff pastry stuffed with spiced lamb and peas), pork vindaloo, and crevettes Assadh: large shell-on prawns in a creamy coconutty sauce. Finish perhaps with mango kulfi drizzled with sweet mango coulis. Solicitous staff are friendly and willing, and a wide-ranging wine list starts with 15 by the glass from around £4.

CHEF: Mehernosh Mody   PROPRIETOR: Blue Elephant International plc   OPEN: Sun to Fri L 12 to 2.30 (3 Sun), all week D 7 (6 Sun) to 11.30 (10.30 Sun)   CLOSED: 25 and 26 Dec, 1 Jan   MEALS: alc (main courses £10 to £21). L buffet Mon to Fri £17.50, Sun L buffet £19.90, Set D £30 to £43.50. Cover £1.50   SERVICE: not inc   CARDS: Amex, Diners, MasterCard, Visa   DETAILS: 300 seats. Private parties: 300 main room, 10 to 14 private rooms. Vegetarian meals. Children's helpings. No smoking in 1 dining room. Wheelchair access (not WC). Music. Air-conditioned   ⊖ Marble Arch

# Providores ✸ £

109 Marylebone High Street, W1U 4RX
TEL: (020) 7935 6175   FAX: (020) 7935 6877       COOKING **5**
EMAIL: anyone@theprovidores.co.uk          FUSION
WEBSITE: www.theprovidores.co.uk         £24–£62

Peter Gordon's new roost is an unassuming converted pub with a curved, bow-windowed front. On the ground floor a (singular) Tapa Room – barrel-vaulted ceiling hung with industrial-sized lights, 'cramped as a rush hour tube' on Saturday nights – is open for snacks and light meals virtually all day, serving a big bowl of steamed edamame, a fine salad of tea-smoked salmon, and lip-smacking snails in garlic butter with chorizo mash. This is 'pure fusion' (if such exists) 'without gimmicks': impeccable grazing food based around top-notch ingredients and fired by bags of imagination.

On the floor above, Providores (named after the first Spanish ship to reach Peter's native New Zealand) is a quieter dining room with wooden floor, white walls and close-together tables. It is casual and relaxed, with friendly, well-informed service, and produces the sort of widely sourced, innovative food that 'could not have existed without science, aviation and technology' (nor linguistic licence, judging by feijoa pannacotta with Vampire Spit jelly). Peter Gordon generally handles multiple flavours with assurance, turning out a fresh, lively, well-made coconut laksa with deep-fried shallots, quail's egg and green-tea noodles; and a dish of grilled quail, its cinnamon spicing interacting splendidly with an exotic mixture of coffee-flavoured wattleseed, pomegranate and ginger.

Fusion cooking stands or falls on fresh ingredients and an understanding of what works and what doesn't. This kitchen's sensible use of diverse materials, and the resulting strong flavours, give the food its identity, for example in tender, pink-roast New Zealand venison loin partnered by slightly bitter cavolo nero, roast garlic polenta and a piquillo pepper salsa. Desserts are up to snuff too, taking in a warm, crumbly tart of pear, poached in saffron and ginger, served with pistachio and bee pollen (the combination looking and tasting a bit like spinach), or a small puff-pastry box of chopped Brazil nuts and thin slivers of pink rhubarb, surrounded by a milky rosewater-flavoured cream. The 'gloriously chewy' sourdough bread shouldn't be missed either. New Zealand wines loom large in a sparky, mainly non-European list starting with a page of cocktails.

CHEFS: Peter Gordon and Anna Hansen   PROPRIETORS: Peter Gordon, Anna Hansen, Jeremy Leeming and Michael McGrath   OPEN: Providores: all week 12 to 2.45, 6 to 10.30. Tapa Room: all week 9 to 10.30pm (10 to 10 Sat and Sun)   CLOSED: 24 and 25 Dec, 1 Jan   MEALS: Providores: alc exc Sat and Sun L (main courses £12 to £18.50); Sat and Sun brunch (main courses £6 to £9). Tapa Room: alc (main courses £6 to £10); breakfast menu available Mon to Fri 9 to 11.30   SERVICE: 12.5% (optional), card slips closed. Cover £1.50 Sat and Sun brunch only   CARDS: Amex, MasterCard, Switch, Visa   DETAILS: Providores: 42 seats. 6 seats outside. Private parties: 44 main room; Tapa Room: 46 seats. Vegetarian meals. No smoking in Providores dining room. Wheelchair access (also WC). Music. Air-conditioned   ⊖ Baker Street

# Putney Bridge Restaurant    map 12

Embankment, SW15 1LB
TEL: (020) 8780 1811   FAX: (020) 8780 1211                    COOKING 6
EMAIL: information@putneybridgerestaurant.com              MODERN FRENCH
WEBSITE: www.putneybridgerestaurant.com                          £38–£92

Located in a stunning, wedge-shaped, modern glass and steel structure beside
the Thames, Putney Bridge consists of a ground-floor bar and a calmer first-floor
dining room, its low slanted ceiling supported by steel frames, its vast floor-to-
ceiling windows affording an outstanding view of the river. This is a restaurant
of high ambition, serving French-oriented food with a few Moroccan, Asian and
other influences.

Anthony Demetre has an inventive streak, evident in a trio of scallops (roast,
cooked in red wine, and mi-cuit in nori seaweed); in an oloroso sauce for sea
bass; and in a barley milk ice cream and Jijona turron that accompany a warm
Valrhona chocolate moelleux. There have been disappointments, with
inspectors finding it variously above or below par. But when on song, the
kitchen can produce some dishes of real finesse, including a whole, accurately
cooked lobster, infused with orange and sweet spices, sliced in two and
presented dramatically on a square black plate, with a skewer of claw meat and
butternut squash, in a light cream sauce.

Varied materials are dealt with in appropriate ways: for example, a robust
dish of roast squid stuffed with pieces of marinated octopus, on a large brandade
of salt-cod, garnished with a snail kromeski in an intense parsley purée; and
well-flavoured Trelough duck, the roast breast lacquered with honey and
Szechuan peppercorns, the legs served as a confit, with celeriac purée and
roasted pear. In an effort to shine, the food can be a bit too clever for its own good,
and desserts have failed to impress, but there is a sound collection of cheeses,
and incidentals, including bread and canapés, are generally well rendered. Lots
of staff, mainly French, combine formality with enthusiasm, and a fine list of
wines doesn't offer any bolt holes for modest budgets. House Chilean red is £15,
Touraine white £19.

CHEF: Anthony Demetre   PROPRIETOR: Gerald Davidson   OPEN: Tue to Sun L 12 to 2, Tue to Sat D
6.30 to 10.30   CLOSED: Christmas   MEALS: alc exc Sun L (main courses £18 to £27). Set L Tue to
Sat £22.50, Set L Sun £25.50, Set D £55 (whole table only). Bar menu available   SERVICE: 12.5%
(optional), card slips closed   CARDS: Amex, Delta, Diners, MasterCard, Switch, Visa   DETAILS:
90 seats. Vegetarian meals. Children's helpings at Sun L. Wheelchair access (also WC). No
music. Air-conditioned   ⊖ Putney Bridge  (£5)

# ▲ QC                              NEW ENTRY   map 13

252 High Holborn, WC1V 7EN                                       COOKING 5
TEL: (020) 7829 7000   FAX: (020) 7829 9889                 MODERN FRENCH
WEBSITE: www.renaissancehotels.com/loncc                         £36–£80

Fashioned out of the former banking hall of the Pearl Assurance Company, this
is a hugely spacious, handsome dining room in a swish new hotel complex.
Despite its largely manufactured grandiosity, it is nevertheless a pleasing and
comfortable environment in which to eat, with floor-to-ceiling marble, clean
lines and immaculate table settings. Given its overt appeal to members of the

legal profession, who ply their trade not far away, lunches may well be busier than dinners, when staff can easily outnumber customers.

Jun Tanaka's style is both light and appealing. Red meat is very much in the minority, fish is better represented, and vegetarians might find themselves majoring on a fricassee of Jersey Royals and asparagus, or baked goats' cheese with marinated baby aubergines and red peppers. The cooking is reassuringly skilful, taking in a creamy and delicately flavoured Jerusalem artichoke risotto of 'exactly the right texture and temperature'. The kitchen seems to get the best out of its materials too, judging by tender, flavourful roast quail on a warm salad of couscous flecked with vegetables, and by a light but earthily flavoured celeriac soup containing an accurately timed poached egg covered by a truffle emulsion.

Likewise among desserts, baked vanilla custard tart is 'emphatically not the usually heavy, boring custard tart', but a light, firm custard in a crisp pastry case served with poached rhubarb. Wines are generally well bred but offer little under £20. A page by the glass gives some relief, and house Californian (Fetzer's Coldwater Creek) is £18.

CHEF: Jun Tanaka   PROPRIETOR: Hotel Property Investors   OPEN: Mon to Sat 12 to 3, 5 to 10.30   MEALS: alc D (main courses £14.50 to £21.50). Set L and D 5 to 7 £16.50 (2 courses) to £20.50 (all inc wine)   SERVICE: 12.5% (optional)   CARDS: Amex, Delta, Diners, MasterCard, Switch, Visa   DETAILS: 120 seats. Private parties: 12 main room. Vegetarian meals. No-smoking area. Wheelchair access (not WC). Occasional music. No mobile phones. Air-conditioned   ACCOMMODATION: 356 rooms, all with bath/shower. TV. Phone. Room only £235. Rooms for disabled   ⊖ Holborn

## Quaglino's                                                                map 15

16 Bury Street, SW1Y 6AJ
TEL: (020) 7930 6767   FAX: (020) 7839 2866                          COOKING 2
EMAIL: jaynem@conran-restaurants.co.uk                      MODERN EUROPEAN
WEBSITE: www.conran.com                                            £27–£89

Unashamedly as much about glamour as about food, Quaglino's swaggers through life with its sweeping staircase, its big, brightly coloured pillars, and its large, enticing shellfish counter. It is about as theatrical as a restaurant gets, with cigarette girls in place of dancing ones, and the repertoire brings a diverse menu of brasserie-style food: from fish and chips with tartare sauce to mushroom risotto, from braised pork belly to ribeye steak with béarnaise. Seafood is an undoubted strength, at its simplest in the form of crab, lobster or langoustines with mayonnaise, or (for £30 a head, minimum two people) as a plateau de fruits de mer. Desserts offer a sophisticated take on old favourites, such as prunes with Sauternes custard, and chocolate and kumquat profiteroles. Comparatively few wines come in under £20, and those without financial restrictions can enjoy themselves hugely. For the rest of us, house Domaines Virginie red and white are £13.50.

CHEF: Julian O'Neill   PROPRIETOR: Conran Restaurants   OPEN: all week 12 to 3, 5.30 to 12 (1am Fri and Sat, 11 Sun)   CLOSED: 25 Dec   MEALS: alc (main courses £10 to £30). Set L £13 (2 courses) to £15.50, Set D 5.30 to 6.30 and 11 to 12 Mon to Thur £13 (2 courses) to £15.50. Bar menu available   SERVICE: 12.5% (optional), card slips closed   CARDS: Amex, Delta, Diners,

MasterCard, Switch, Visa  DETAILS: 267 seats. Private parties: 380 main room, up to 40 private rooms. Vegetarian meals. Children's helpings. Wheelchair access (also WC). Music. Air-conditioned  ⊖ Green Park, Piccadilly

## Quality Chop House

map 13

94 Farringdon Road, EC1R 3EA

COOKING 3

TEL: (020) 7837 5093   FAX: (020) 7833 8748

BRITISH

£27–£71

'Another good meal at this reliable old faithful,' reckoned an off-duty inspector who called in for dinner at this 'delightfully unfashionable' restaurant in decidedly voguish Clerkenwell. 'Simple food well done' is the general consensus of reporters, who have enjoyed, among other things, traditional fish soup, artichoke with mustard vinaigrette, steak with bacon and eggs, 'sublime' salmon fishcake with sorrel sauce and – as if to prove the place's anti-fashion credentials – avocado and prawn cocktail, featuring ripe avocado, fresh prawns and a well-balanced Marie-Rose sauce. The multifarious menu ranges from jellied eels to sevruga caviar among starters, from lamb chops to grilled lobster for mains. Service is appropriately friendly for the informality of the setting, and a good selection of Sam Smiths bottled beers offers a viable alternative to the decent wine list (house wines £11).

CHEF/PROPRIETOR: Charles Fontaine   OPEN: Sun to Fri L 12 to 3 (Sun 4), all week D 6.30 (Sun 7) to 11.30   CLOSED: 23 Dec to 2 Jan   MEALS: alc (main courses £6.75 to £24)   SERVICE: not inc CARDS: Amex, Delta, MasterCard, Switch, Visa   DETAILS: 64 seats. Private parties: 10 main room. Vegetarian meals. Children's helpings. No music. Air-conditioned  ⊖ Farringdon

## Quo Vadis

map 15

26–29 Dean Street, W1V 6LL

TEL: (020) 7437 9585   FAX: (020) 7734 7593

COOKING 2

EMAIL: sales@whitestarline.org.uk

ITALIAN/MEDITERRANEAN

WEBSITE: www.whitestarline.org.uk

£32–£74

The emphasis at this venerable address is on comfort, making it something of an oasis amid the more usually noisy Soho competition. Beyond the stained-glass windows are two rooms with parquet floors, cool green walls and some striking animal skeleton artwork by the owner. A long printed carte sets out the kitchen's stall, with a richly creamy mushroom soup, aubergine and zucchini fritters, and copious, meaty chunks of casseroled rabbit with a fine array of winter vegetables. Vegetarians don't get much of a look in, apart perhaps from a well-rendered wild mushroom risotto, while a short daily menu offers straightforward dishes of Caesar salad, potted shrimps, or salmon fishcake. Among desserts, a rich, sweet crème caramel has impressed, not least for the contrast of its pleasantly tart passion fruit accompaniment. On the downside, flavours don't always pack a punch, and service could be improved. Wines aim for the upper end of the market, so there are some fine bottles but little for modest spenders.

CHEF: Curtis Stone   PROPRIETOR: Marco Pierre White   OPEN: Mon to Fri L 12 to 2.30, Mon to Sat D 5.30 to 11.30   MEALS: alc (main courses £10.50 to £22.50). Set L and D 5.30 to 6.45 £14.95 (2 courses)   SERVICE: 12.5% (optional)   CARDS: Amex, Delta, Diners, MasterCard, Switch, Visa DETAILS: 90 seats. Private parties: 90 main room, 8 to 90 private rooms. No cigars in dining room. Wheelchair access (not WC). Occasional music. Air-conditioned   ⊖ Leicester Square, Tottenham Court Road

## Racine                               | NEW ENTRY |   map 14

239 Brompton Road, SW3 2EP                                    COOKING 2
TEL: (020) 7584 4477   FAX: (020) 7584 4900                RUSTIC FRENCH
                                                              £24–£49

Henry Harris (ex-Harvey Nichols' Fifth Floor, see entry), and Eric Garnier (a veteran of Conran and Bank enterprises) opened this unpretentious, neighbourhood outfit in summer 2002. The small, predominantly dark brown room (with lots of enlarging mirrors) seems to have imported its bistro-style décor from Lyons, along with some dishes, including tender, gelatinous tête de veau with ravigote sauce, and salade Lyonnaise.

The cooking – bourgeois with a rustic edge – takes in marmite Dieppoise, earthy-flavoured Jerusalem artichoke soup with a swirl of basil oil, and grilled rabbit with smoked bacon and a well-rendered mustard sauce. Grilling and roasting are favoured, the latter accurately applied to leg of lamb with creamy haricot beans, and to cod fillet in a pool of buttery crab sauce. Desserts are out of the same country-cooking mould – Mont Blanc, or a peach mousse with a macaroon base and top – though vegetables (including chips) and cheese might usefully return to the drawing board. Service is friendly and well-drilled, and prices are not greedy. Wines are predominantly French, with good choice under £20, some juicy burgundies, fair choice of half-bottles, and a dozen available by the 175ml glass for less than £5.

CHEFS: Henry Harris and Chris Handley   PROPRIETORS: Eric Garnier and Henry Harris   OPEN: all week 12 to 3 (3.30 Sat and Sun), 6 to 10.30 (10 Sun)   CLOSED: 25 and 26 Dec   MEALS: alc (main courses £9 to £13). Set L and D 6 to 7.30 £12.50 (2 courses) to £15   SERVICE: 12.5% (optional), card slips closed   CARDS: Amex, Delta, MasterCard, Switch, Visa   DETAILS: 75 seats. 8 seats outside. Private parties: 75 main room, 10 to 18 private rooms. Vegetarian meals. Children's helpings. No music. Air-conditioned   ⊖ South Kensington, Knightsbridge

## Radha Krishna Bhavan  £                              map 12

86 Tooting High Street, SW17 0RN
TEL: (020) 8682 0969   FAX: (020) 8767 3462                COOKING 2
EMAIL: tharidas@aol.com                                    SOUTH INDIAN
WEBSITE: www.mcdosa.com                                       £19–£40

A life-sized statue of a character from the traditional Kathakali dance-dramas of Kerala dominates one corner of this colourful restaurant. Huge tropical murals decorate the walls, Indian film music plays in the background, and fairy lights flicker. The menu has its share of traditional curry-house stalwarts – chicken, lamb and prawns, prepared a dozen ways each – but the real interest is in the South Indian dishes and specialities from Kerala ('God's own country' to the proprietors). Starters are skilfully produced, taking in light-textured uthappam (a kind of pizza embedded with chillies and tomatoes), and Mysore bonda ('lively spiced' lentil and potato balls) with sambar and two coconut sauces. Vegetables are well handled, making use of beetroot, cabbage and green bananas as well as cauliflower and peas. Rice is fine, while breads include star-rated, delightfully fluffy parathas (perhaps flavoured with sweet coconut or garlic). Lassi and beer may be preferable to house wine at £8.95 a bottle.

CHEFS: Mr Salam and Mr Madhu Soodhanan   PROPRIETORS: T. Haridas and family   OPEN: all week 12 to 3, 6 to 11 (12 Fri and Sat)   CLOSED: 25 and 26 Dec   MEALS: alc (main courses £2.50 to £7)   SERVICE: 10%, card slips closed   CARDS: Amex, Delta, Diners, MasterCard, Switch, Visa DETAILS: 50 seats. Private parties: 60 main room. Vegetarian meals. Children's helpings. Occasional music. Air-conditioned   ⊖ Tooting Broadway  £5

# Ransome's Dock  🍶                                    map 12

Unit 29, Ransome's Dock,
35–37 Parkgate Road, SW11 4NP
TEL: (020) 7924 2462 and 7223 1611
FAX: (020) 7924 2614                                     COOKING 4
EMAIL: bookings@ransomesdock.co.uk              MODERN EUROPEAN
WEBSITE: www.ransomesdock.co.uk                        £34–£70

Al fresco eating beside the tiny dock is possible in fine weather, adding to the appeal of Martin and Vanessa Lam's well-run, mature restaurant (they have a decade under their belt). It is friendly, unpretentious, lively, with close-together tables, the food reminding one reporter of good old-fashioned French bistro cooking. Honest materials are turned into some straightforward and generally sound dishes, from Shorthorn sirloin steak with herb butter and chips to Trelough duck with Cumberland sauce and braised chicory.

The broadly based European style also takes in a stew of chicken livers and white beans spiked with oloroso sherry, and cod fillet with grilled sweet potato and tapénade dressing. Although a little of the oomph seems to have gone out of the cooking, the kitchen has nevertheless turned out a first-class cauliflower and cheese soup, a boldly flavoured pork and rabbit terrine, and a light, well-balanced prune and Armagnac soufflé with Armagnac cream sauce that is well worth the 20-minute wait. Prices are sensible, and wines, from an ever-evolving list (it changes every week), are chosen with utmost care. Sparkling reds, Zinfandel and Malbec all earn their own category on the varied list, which champions rising stars from the New World along with Old World classics. The house selection is likely to range from £17 to £24.50; four wines are generally sold by the glass and there is a healthy selection of half-bottles and magnums.

CHEF: Martin Lam   PROPRIETORS: Martin and Vanessa Lam   OPEN: all week L 12 to 6 (3.30 Sun), Mon to Sat D 6 to 11   CLOSED: Christmas, Aug bank hol   MEALS: alc (main courses £10.50 to £20). Set L Mon to Fri £14.25 (2 courses). Brunch menu available Sat and Sun   SERVICE: 12.5% (optional), card slips closed   CARDS: Amex, Delta, Diners, MasterCard, Switch, Visa   DETAILS: 56 seats. 20 seats outside. Private parties: 14 to 50 main room. Car park (evenings and weekends only). Vegetarian meals. Children's helpings. No pipes in dining room. Wheelchair access (not WC). Music. Air-conditioned   ⊖ Sloane Square

# Rasa/Rasa W1 ✳ £

55 Stoke Newington Church Street, N16 0AR
TEL: (020) 7249 0344
6 Dering Street, W1S 1AD                                            COOKING 2
TEL: (020) 7629 1346   FAX: (020) 7491 9540        INDIAN/INDIAN VEGETARIAN
WEBSITE: www.rasarestaurants.com                                  £27–£40

When it comes to the crunch, South Indian vegetarian food has an edge over most other cuisines. Even poppadums, brittle in themselves, can be dipped in a batter of spiced rice flour to make pappadavadai and join achappam and murukku as pre-meal snacks. Dosas, huge rolled pancakes of semolina and rice flour, stuffed with potatoes, exhibit a new dimension of soft-crispness. Vegetable curries (in gravy or dry), various breads and rice dishes, and madhuram – traditional sweets of Kerala – complete the story for vegetarians. At the Dering Street branch a separate, non-vegetarian kitchen on the ground floor offers a life-line for carnivores, with Malabar dishes from the north of Kerala. Lamb puffs, Kaapad chicken cutlet, and crisp-fried hard-boiled eggs are among starters, to be followed by exotic chicken and lamb curries, and a Malabar variation on Hyderabadi chicken biryani. A short, decently priced wine list kicks off at £8.95 at Stoke Newington, £10.95 at Dering Street.

CHEFS: Rajan Karattil (Rasa), Sivaparasad Mahade Van Nair (Rasa W1)   PROPRIETOR: Das Sreedharan   OPEN: Rasa Sat and Sun 12 to 2.45, all week D 6 to 10.30 (11.45 Fri and Sat); Rasa W1 Mon to Sat L 12 to 2.30, all week D 6 to 10.30   CLOSED: several days over Christmas   MEALS: Rasa alc (main courses £3 to £5.50); Set L and D £15. Rasa W1 alc (main courses £6.50 to £10), Set L and D £20   SERVICE: 12.5% (optional), card slips closed   CARDS: Amex, Delta, Diners (not at Rasa), MasterCard, Switch, Visa   DETAILS: 50 seats Rasa, 90 seats Rasa W1. Private parties: 50 Rasa, 55 to 90 Rasa W1. Vegetarian meals. No smoking in dining rooms. Music. Air-conditioned   ⊖ Oxford Circus (Rasa W1)

# Rasa Samudra

map 15

5 Charlotte Street, W1T 1RE
TEL: (020) 7637 0222   FAX: (020) 7637 0224                        COOKING 4
EMAIL: dasrasa@hotmail.com                      INDIAN SEAFOOD/VEGETARIAN
WEBSITE: www.rasarestaurants.com                                  £33–£62

The once purely vegetarian Rasa group now also offers meat (see entries just above and below) and, here, Kerala's seafood cuisine. Vegetarian specialities still feature in the fortnightly-changing menu, though. Newcomers might consider the set-meal 'feasts': one vegetarian, the other seafood. Both incorporate 'pre-meal snacks', variations on the crispest of poppadums, and diverse pickles and chutneys. Vadais and bolis are South Indian tea-shop snacks, such as lentil or bean patties, crisp fried banana or aubergine.

Fishy starters on the carte take in king prawn, mussel, squid and crab. Fully and temptingly explained, but too long to quote, are main fish courses, among them king fish in fresh coconut milk. Vegetarian main courses, meanwhile, consist of dosa pancakes together with curries, such as spinach with beetroot or dhal, or sweet and sour mangoes with green banana. Unusual desserts include banana and cardamom pancakes, and an 'auspicious rice pudding' with cashews and raisins. The décor of the small ground-floor spaces, and the more modern first-floor room, is varied and gloriously colourful, and 60 wines, mainly from the New World, are chosen with a sharp eye (and palate) for interesting matches with food.

CHEF: Ajith Kumar   PROPRIETOR: Das Sreedharan   OPEN: Mon to Sat L 12 to 3, all week D 6 to 10.30   CLOSED: 25 to 30 Dec   MEALS: alc (main courses £5.50 to £13). Set L (2 courses) £10.50 (vegetarian) to £14.50 (seafood), Set D £22.50 (vegetarian) to £30 (seafood)   SERVICE: 12.5% (optional), card slips closed   CARDS: Amex, Delta, Diners, MasterCard, Switch, Visa   DETAILS: 100 seats. Private parties: 50 main room, 10 to 50 private rooms. Vegetarian meals. Children's helpings. No music. Air-conditioned   ⊖ Goodge Street

## Rasa Travancore 🍃 ✸ £     map 12

56 Stoke Newington Church Street, N16 0NB
TEL: (020) 7249 1340   FAX: (020) 7637 0222
EMAIL: dasrasa@hotmail.com
WEBSITE: www.rasarestaurants.com

COOKING 1
INDIAN
£22–£36

Directly opposite the original branch of this group of four (see entries above), Rasa Travancore offers a taste of Syrian Christian cooking from Kerala that takes in meat as well as vegetarian and fish dishes. Pre-meal snacks range from banana chips to murukku (crunchy sticks of roasted rice flour, black sesame seeds and cumin seeds), and come with an astonishing selection of home-made pickles and chutneys. The full menu has stews for the Christmas and Easter festivities, tea shop snacks, classics from the bar menus of the region, and famed dishes from individual families. Ms Mariamma from Trivandrum provides arachu vercha meen: tilapia cooked in a turmeric-coloured coconut sauce with tomatoes, curry leaves and mustard seeds. House vins de pays are £9.50.

CHEF: P. Kotapati   PROPRIETOR: Das Sreedharan   OPEN: Sun L 12 to 3, all week D 6 to 10.45 (11.30 Fri and Sat)   CLOSED: 24 to 31 Dec   MEALS: alc (main courses £5 to £8). Set L and D £20   SERVICE: 12.5% (optional), card slips closed   CARDS: Amex, Delta, MasterCard, Switch, Visa   DETAILS: 42 seats. Private parties: 35 main room. Vegetarian meals. No smoking in dining room. Music. Air-conditioned

## The Real Greek     map 13

15 Hoxton Market, N1 6HG
TEL: (020) 7739 8212   FAX: (020) 7739 4910
WEBSITE: www.therealgreek.co.uk

COOKING 4
GREEK
£29–£58

Just as the bright blue frontage stands out from its neighbours in the square, so Theodore Kyriakou's vivid food contrasts with that of run-of-the-mill Greek restaurants in Britain. Polished floorboards, linen-clad tables, and an open-to-view kitchen combine to produce a relaxed yet on-the-ball atmosphere, while the menu relishes the enormous variety of materials in the Greek larder: from Santorinian capers, via salted cod and tuna, to Metsovone cheese on toast. Part of the appeal lies in the chance to eat comparatively small platefuls, either singly or in pre-set groups. One of the latter takes in cold cabbage, tsatsiki, warm lambs' tongue and a dense chilli-hot sausage, each item good in itself, the ensemble playing off fresh, sour and spicy tastes as well as textural differences.

Meat tends towards innards – grilled lamb's liver with caul fat – or poultry such as a cold dish of saffron-infused duck stuffed with squash and dried figs. As well as preserved fish and roe, there may also be pot-roast crab claws, or poached monkfish cheek with mayonnaise. Desserts are as inventive as the rest, taking in two small cookies topped with a lime and chilli sorbet, in turn with a sweet mango tempura. The mezedes idea extends to the virtually all-Greek wines too, variously available by the glass, 'carafkis' of 250ml and 500ml, as well as by the bottle. Mezedopolio, a wine bar next door, is under the same management.

CHEF: Theodore Kyriakou   PROPRIETORS: Theodore Kyriakou and Paloma Campbell   OPEN: Mon to Sat 12 to 3, 5.30 to 10.30   MEALS: alc (main courses £16 to £17.50). Set L and D 5.30 to 7 £14.50 (2 courses). Meze bar open all day Fri and Sat   SERVICE: not inc, 12.5% for parties of 7 or more   CARDS: Delta, MasterCard, Switch, Visa   DETAILS: 75 seats. 16 outside. Private parties: 8 private room. Vegetarian meals. No cigars/pipes in dining room. Wheelchair access (also WC). Music   ⊖ Old Street

---

# Red Fort
**NEW ENTRY**   map 15

77 Dean Street, W1D 3SH
TEL: (020) 7437 2525   FAX: (020) 7434 0721                              COOKING 4
EMAIL: info@redfort.co.uk                                              NEW-WAVE INDIAN
WEBSITE: www.redfort.co.uk                                                   £46–£88

After a relaunch in late 2001, 'this time they seem to have got it right', thinks an inspector who has followed this establishment's ups and down over the years. A lot of money has gone on décor (there is now a fashionable basement bar), and the jars and statues in niches, and the lighting, are tasteful. Significantly, a new chef and maître d' have come from the New Delhi Sheraton, and it shows.

The shortish menu has a cosmopolitan flavour, and might tempt with Dover sole filled with cottage cheese and pomegranate, or partridge marinated in spiced yoghurt and poppy seeds, or maybe lamb chops in star anise jus. There are no poppadoms – meals begin with an artfully presented vegetable patty – and subtle spicing is a hallmark: salmon tikka marinated with dill is a delicate starter, and tandoori jhingra (mildly spiced jumbo prawns) exhibits freshness and clear flavours. Incidentals are first-rate: fine breads, 'unusually good' cucumber raita, and exceptional baby potatoes stir-fried with curry leaves and mustard seeds. For desserts, the menu boldly offers chocolate fondant as well as pistachio ice cream and raspberry shrikhand. The wine list is classy but pricey; house wine is £16.

CHEF: Mohammed Rais   PROPRIETOR: Amin Ali   OPEN: Mon to Fri L 12 to 2.30, all week D 5.45 (6.30 Sun) to 11.30 (10.30 Sun)   MEALS: alc (main courses L £12 to £17, D £13 to £28). Set L and D before 7.30 £16 (2 courses). Bar menu available   SERVICE: 12.5% (optional), card slips closed   CARDS: Amex, Delta, MasterCard, Switch, Visa   DETAILS: 85 seats. Private parties: 85 main room. Vegetarian meals. No smoking in 1 dining room. Music. Air-conditioned   ⊖ Leicester Square

---

*'When I requested an espresso, the waitress looked at me as if I had proposed something involving warm pannacotta and leather underwear.'* (On eating in East Anglia)

---

# Redmond's ♟ map 12

| | |
|---|---|
| 170 Upper Richmond Road West, SW14 8AW | COOKING 5 |
| TEL: (020) 8878 1922   FAX: (020) 8878 1133 | MODERN BRITISH |
| EMAIL: pippahayward@btconnect.com | £31–£50 |

Redmond's is a neighbourhood restaurant that inspires loyalty: one ex-local still visits regularly, years after moving away. The draw is meals that are of a consistently high standard, 'innovative without being flashy' and good value. Refurbishing the dining room has made the space feel more intimate, and this year has seen the reintroduction of warm duck liver and foie gras tart with fennel salad, a dish Redmond Hayward first conceived 16 years ago, and one that exemplifies a guiding principle of his cooking: 'simple things done properly'. Other starters may include a salad of griddled artichokes with shaved Parmesan, green beans and haricots, or tartare of smoked haddock and sushi ginger with lemon oil.

Main courses can be more involved – perhaps marinated pigeon breast with soft thyme polenta, caramelised endive, seared foie gras and balsamic jus – though there are also more straightforward options such as seared wild salmon with Jersey Royals, asparagus and saffron salsa. To finish, the half-dozen dessert choices may include chocolate meringue with a poached pear, honey and cinnamon ice cream and chocolate sauce. The kids' menu, a cut above the norm, might offer corn-fed chicken with mash and gravy. Wines on a short but wide-ranging list combine quality and value. Trendy regions such as New Zealand's Central Otago and Pic Saint Loup in Languedoc abound, but prices are refreshingly low, starting at £13.75 (£3.75 a glass). There is a good selection of halves.

CHEF: Redmond Hayward   PROPRIETORS: Redmond and Pippa Hayward   OPEN: Sun to Fri L 12 to 2 (2.30 Sun), Mon to Sat D 7 to 10.30   CLOSED: 3 days Christmas, bank hol Mons; closed L Mon to Fri in Aug   MEALS: Set L £16.50 (2 courses) to £19.50, Set L Sun £17.50 (2 courses) to £21, Set D £25 (2 courses) to £28   SERVICE: not inc, 10% (optional) for parties of 6 or more   CARDS: Amex, Delta, MasterCard, Switch, Visa   DETAILS: 52 seats. Private parties: 50 main room. Vegetarian meals. Children's helpings. No cigars/pipes in dining room. Wheelchair access (not WC). No music. Air-conditioned

# Red Pepper 🥪 map 13

| | |
|---|---|
| 8 Formosa Street, W9 1EE | COOKING 3 |
| TEL: (020) 7266 2708 | ITALIAN |
| | £31–£43 |

Red Pepper has acquired a couple of new chefs, but little else has changed at this busy, buzzy Maida Vale stalwart. Tables are as packed – and as tiny – as ever, giving one reporter the feeling that he'd stepped in to an episode of 'Land of the Giants'. The menu is an appealing assortment of pizza and pasta centrepieces, preceded by starters such as chickpea and barley soup with rosemary, or bresaola with Parmesan cream and rocket. Pasta dishes might include a well-flavoured pappardelle of quail and peas, or maltagliati ('badly cut' pasta shapes) with a ragù of guinea fowl and herbs. Sixteen pizze made in the wood-fired oven in the basement feature a range of classics – Margherita, basilico, Napoli, primavera – plus a few others besides. A reporter deemed a pizza rossi, spiced with chilli oil, and a mushroom pizza 'superb, with excellent bases and fine toppings – as good as any pizza in London'. Classic desserts, such as gelati and tiramisù, round out the offerings. Service is friendly and fast, and prices are fair. The short wine list is all Italian, starting at £12 (£3 a glass).

CHEFS: Danilo Bruno and Salvatore Monte   PROPRIETOR: Red Pepper Group   OPEN: Sat and Sun L 12.30 to 3 (3.30 Sun), all week D 6.30 to 11 (10.30 Sun)   MEALS: alc (main courses from £6 to £10)   SERVICE: 12.5% (optional), card slips closed   CARDS: Delta, MasterCard, Switch, Visa DETAILS: 60 seats. 12 seats outside. Private parties: 25 main room. Vegetarian meals. Children's helpings. No cigars/pipes in dining room. Music. Air-conditioned   ⊖ Warwick Avenue

# Rhodes in the Square
map 13

Dolphin Square, Chichester Street, SW1V 3LX
TEL: (020) 7798 6767   FAX: (020) 7798 5685
EMAIL: rhodesinthesquare@sodexho-uk.com
WEBSITE: www.rhodesrestaurants.com

COOKING 6
MODERN BRITISH
£36–£74

A sweeping staircase leads down to this dining room within the Dolphin Square Hotel. 'All royal blue and chrome with millions of tiny lights', its ocean-liner décor conveys a smooth and smart impression, and well-trained staff are both plentiful and friendly. Gary Rhodes made his name updating British classics, and there are some of these around, including calf's liver with streaky bacon, mash and onion gravy, but the net spreads much further, into the realms of a potato, leek and Maroilles risotto, and roast breast of guinea fowl on truffled sauerkraut with its own boudin blanc.

The food has a deep reassurance about it, thanks not least to the indulgence of truffled gnocchi, lobster omelette thermidor, and squab pigeon on a game and foie gras toast, but also because ideas simply make good culinary sense. Herb-flavoured cream sauces with poached meat are one example: milk-poached pork with morels, broad beans and a sage cream, or poached loin of lamb on a shallot tarte Tatin with a marjoram cream sauce.

Where seafood is concerned, the Mediterranean is never far away, so expect tuna niçoise, bouillabaisse, and whiting with crab ravioli. The British influence is most evident among desserts, from the classic bread-and-butter pudding to rhubarb crumble. On its trip round the world the compact wine list picks up a few interesting grape varieties, visits Washington and Oregon, and offers plenty of opportunity to spend lots of money on good bottles. A clutch of 'sommelier's suggestions' ranging from house French at £15 up to £33 are all available by the glass (£3.60 to £7.75).

CHEF: Michael James   PROPRIETOR: Gary Rhodes   OPEN: Tue to Fri L 12 to 2.30, Tue to Sat D 7 to 10   CLOSED: bank hols   MEALS: Set L £17.80 (2 courses) to £19.80, Set D £31.50 (2 courses) to £36.50   SERVICE: 12.5% (optional), card slips closed   CARDS: Amex, Delta, Diners, MasterCard, Switch, Visa   DETAILS: 100 seats. Private parties: 100 main room. Vegetarian meals. No cigars/pipes in dining room. Wheelchair access (also WC). Music. No mobile phones. Air conditioned ⊖ Pimlico

# Riso 🥄 ✺

map 12

76 South Parade, W4 5LF
TEL/FAX: (020) 8742 2121

COOKING 3
MODERN ITALIAN
£29–£51

This orange-fronted restaurant in leafiest Chiswick consists of a pair of dining rooms with terracotta-tiled floors and abstract paintings for sale on the walls. Sardininan-born Piero Fois, who took over the kitchens early in 2002, considers his style to be 'modern Italian', although there are French flourishes in there too. Fregola sarda is one of his specialities: pasta the size of sweetcorn kernels in a riot of colourful vegetables, including peas, aubergine and peppers, scented with saffron, a spanking-fresh dish that makes a good appetiser. This being Riso, it would be odd not to try some form of rice dish, and risotto with tuna, sun-dried tomatoes, and spinach is a generous portion, the grains cooked so as to leave a little bite, and the dish again vibrantly colourful.

Presentations emphasise the culinary skills at work, as a breast of guinea fowl wrapped in prosciutto is sliced to reveal its even stuffing of ricotta, sultanas, pine nuts and leeks, with an enormous mound of mash to accompany. Italian wines are used in fish sauces, maybe Prosecco with roast monkfish, or Vermentino with sea bass, the latter further boozed up with fennel cooked in Pernod. 'Wonderfully light' chocolate cake filled with 'smooth and not too sweet' hazelnut custard is a sophisticated way to finish, or there is the more diverting option of a rice tart sauced with port and zabaglione. Look to the blackboard for the day's specials, or ask the smartly attired waiters. House wines are Tocai Friulano (£12.50) and Montepulciano (£13.50).

CHEF: Piero Fois   PROPRIETORS: Mauro Santoliquido and Maurizio Rimerici   OPEN: Sun L 12 to 2.30, Tue to Sun D 7 to 11   MEALS: alc (main courses £9 to £13.50)   SERVICE: 12.5%, card slips closed   CARDS: Delta, MasterCard, Switch, Visa   DETAILS: 55 seats. Private parties: 60 main room, 10 to 20 private rooms. Vegetarian meals. No smoking in 1 dining room. Wheelchair access (not WC). Music   ⊖ Chiswick Park, Turnham Green   £5

# ▲ Ritz ✺

map 15

150 Piccadilly, W1J 9BR
TEL: (020) 7300 2370   FAX: (020) 7907 2681
EMAIL: enquire@theritzlondon.com
WEBSITE: www.theritzlondon.com

COOKING 3
FRENCH/ENGLISH
£47–£142

Nothing quite prepares those unused to grand hotel dining rooms for the jaw-dropping magnificence of the Ritz. A system of chandeliers is linked with gilded garlands, floor-to-ceiling mirror panels cover one wall, and a tridentigerous Poseidon overlooks all from an alcove at one end. Add to that the highly formal yet unstuffy ministrations of legions of staff (synchronised cloche-raising and at-the-table flambéing live on here), and the fact that each course, including the amuse-bouche, sits not on one plate but on several, and the sense of dining in another era is magically created. The cooking is, almost inevitably, rather more humdrum than the surroundings. Four asparagus spears on a puff pastry base with a soothing lemon and chive butter is the sort of starter that might appear on the fixed-price dinner menu; the carte, meanwhile, offers seared scallops with spring beans in a truffled broth, and a half lobster thermidor. At inspection, both the timing of tiny fillets of sea bass and the partnering of guinea-fowl with Jerusalem artichokes, sautéed girolles and noodles got the nod, while a nicely caramelised tarte Tatin with 'excellent' calvados ice-cream was let down by its impenetrable pastry. Lemon and basil parfait with a coulis of red berries is about as trend-setting as desserts get. House wines, a claret and a Chablis, are £24.

CHEF: Giles Thompson    PROPRIETOR: Ellerman Investments    OPEN: all week 12 to 2.30, 6 to 11 (11.15 Fri and Sat)    MEALS: alc (main courses £25 to £49). Set L £35, Set D £43 to £51    SERVICE: net prices, card slips closed    CARDS: Amex, Delta, Diners, MasterCard, Switch, Visa    DETAILS: 120 seats. 25 seats outside. Private parties: 28 main room, 4 to 70 private rooms. Vegetarian meals. Children's helpings. Jacket and tie. No smoking in 1 dining room. Wheelchair access (also WC). Music. No mobile phones. Air-conditioned    ACCOMMODATION: 133 rooms, all with bath/shower. TV. Phone. Room only £295 to £345. Rooms for disabled. Baby facilities
⊖ Green Park

## Riva
map 12

169 Church Road, SW13 9HR
TEL/FAX: (020) 8748 0434

COOKING 3
NORTH ITALIAN
£33–£62

With its high wooden ceiling, simple painted walls and big bunch of fresh flowers, Riva manages to appear elegant, seemingly without having been designed that way. It has long been held in affection for its easy-going atmosphere and down-the-line, seasonally responsive northern Italian food: perhaps herbed hare ragoût, or roast partridge in winter; at other times spring vegetable risotto, or kid with yellow peppers, olives and artichokes.

Choice is generous, and although a few careless items let down an inspection meal, enough good dishes emerge from the kitchen, including tasty grilled squid with wild herbs, roast best end of lamb with a minty, herby crust, and brill with first-class fava beans. Desserts are highly rated, including a bitter chocolate pudding rather like a pannacotta, and cinnamon ice cream with balsamic and amaretti biscuits. The package is still good value, and the short Italian wine list combines interest and variety, starting with house Merlot and Pinot Bianco from Veneto at £12.

CHEF: Francesco Zanchetta    PROPRIETOR: Andrea Riva    OPEN: Sun to Fri L 12 to 2.30, all week D 7 to 11 (9.30 Sun)    MEALS: alc (main courses £11 to £18.50)    SERVICE: 12.5%, card slips closed    CARDS: Amex, MasterCard, Switch, Visa    DETAILS: 45 seats. 8 seats outside. Private parties: 40 main room. Children's helpings. No cigars/pipes in dining room. Wheelchair access (not WC). No music. No mobile phones. Air-conditioned    ⊖ Hammersmith

## River Café ▼
map 12

Thames Wharf Studios, Rainville Road, W6 9HA
TEL: (020) 7386 4200    FAX: (020) 7386 4201
EMAIL: bookings@rivercafe.co.uk
WEBSITE: www.rivercafe.co.uk

COOKING 6
ITALIAN
£52–£82

Enter through a smoked glass door into a large, big-windowed, table-packed room. Those with a time limit on their table can check progress against a clock face superimposed on the end wall: 'I kept glancing at it and thinking '"We're doing OK, we're doing OK".' In fact, meals are well paced, and staff are friendly and well briefed. A large part of the food's appeal lies in its straightforwardness and lack of embellishment, evident in a simple broad-bean soup with pancetta, or a bruschetta of buffalo mozzarella, violetta artichokes, black olives and herb vinegar.

Fine raw materials and a sense of the seasons also inform the cooking. Allied to this is an ingenuity with humble ingredients, producing for example ravioli filled with turnip tops and sheep's ricotta in a sage butter sauce. The menu is careful to identify the source of its estate-bottled oils and vinegars, some of its meat and fish – organic lamb, or Kelly chicken – and can bring together on a plate materials as diverse as Devon crab, Scottish seakale and shaved Sardinian bottarga.

Treatments vary from chargrilling and pan-frying to pot roasting and poaching, producing a welcome variety of end results within a fairly small compass. Despite an occasional red-blooded dish such as chargrilled sirloin of Aberdeen Angus, there is a pleasing lightness to much of the repertoire thanks to the quota of seafood and vegetables, which might include seabass baked in a bag with Trevise and porcini, or pan-fried Scottish scallops with capers and sage. It is doubtful if chocolate Nemesis could ever be removed from the menu, but there may also be lemon tart, or a polenta, almond and lemon cake served with caramelised blood oranges. Apart from champagne the concise but well-chosen wine list is all slick, new-wave Italian bottles arranged by region. They are not cheap (prices start at £10.50 but most are over £20) but include some relative bargains (Brancaia Chianti Classico 1999 for £27). A dozen come by the glass (£3 to £10.50).

CHEFS: Rose Gray and Ruth Rogers  PROPRIETORS: Rose Gray, Ruth Rogers and Theo Randall  OPEN: all week L 12.30 to 2.30, Mon to Fri D 7 to 9.15  CLOSED: 25 Dec to 1 Jan, bank hols  MEALS: alc (main courses £20 to £30)  SERVICE: 12.5% (optional), card slips closed  CARDS: Amex, Delta, Diners, MasterCard, Switch, Visa  DETAILS: 100 seats. 35 seats outside. Private parties: 100 main room. Car park. Vegetarian meals. Children's helpings. No cigars/pipes in dining room. Wheelchair access (also WC). No music  ⊖ Hammersmith

## Rosmarino ♥                                                     map 13

1 Blenheim Terrace, NW8 0EH                                      COOKING 3
TEL: (020) 7328 5014   FAX: (020) 7625 2639                   MODERN ITALIAN
                                                                  £36–£64

Grand Old Houses such as this take well to conversion, the dining room opening out on to a terrace, the décor modern yet warm. A contemporary menu (virtually the same one operates at a set price at dinner and as a carte at lunchtime) hits all the appropriate buttons, calling not just on buffalo mozzarella and basil oil, but also on finocchiona (pork sausage), served with Parma ham, fennel and thin Sardinian carasau bread. Other antipasti might include chargrilled asparagus with crispy speck and slices of cheese, while the farinaceous section runs from plain old spaghetti with tomato sauce, to rigatoni with green pea cream and quail sauce.

Fish is treated commendably simply – steamed plaice, chargrilled tuna – and served with either a salad or mixed vegetables, while meat might take in pan-fried chicken breast with thyme-flavoured aubergine, or chargrilled leg of lamb with spinach and stewed onion. Finish with apple tart and ice cream (cinnamon and vanilla), or fresh fruit salad. The all-Italian wine list includes many of Italy's top producers, with makers of Super-Tuscan wines such as Sassicaia and Tignanello joined by movers and shakers from southern Italy. House wines start at £14 (£4.50 per glass) but move up swiftly thereafter, with limited choice under £20.

CHEF: Stefano Stecca   PROPRIETOR: A To Z Restaurants Ltd   OPEN: all week 12 to 2.30, 7 to 10.30   CLOSED: 24 Dec to 2 Jan   MEALS: alc L Mon to Fri (main courses £12 to £15). Set L Sat and Sun and all week D £22.50 (2 courses) to £30   SERVICE: 12.5% (optional), card slips closed   CARDS: Amex, Delta, MasterCard, Switch, Visa   DETAILS: 56 seats. 50 seats outside. Private parties: 50 main room. Vegetarian meals. Children's helpings. Music. No mobile phones. Air-conditioned   ⊖ St John's Wood

---

# Roussillon ▼                                          map 14

16 St Barnabas Street, SW1W 8PB                         COOKING 5
TEL: (020) 7730 5550   FAX: (020) 7824 8617             MODERN FRENCH
WEBSITE: www.roussillon.co.uk                           £35–£95

Behind the bow-fronted window of a former pub on a quiet street in Pimlico is a plain but elegant dining room with well-spaced tables and comfortable seating. 'A posh neighbourhood restaurant,' one visitor called it, 'where you can spend lots of money.' The kitchen certainly has high aspirations, its offerings divided into a variety of set menus (with supplements of £8 each for lobster salad and Angus beef), one of them a vegetarian (or Garden) version (£45), another a seasonal one (£60). Lunch, on the other hand, is considered a bargain.

At its best the food is vibrant, carefully balanced and tasty, not because it goes in for exotic spicing or ingredients, but because it uses generally sound techniques to produce, for example, a wild mushroom risotto, a first-rate broad bean soup, and a purée of Jerusalem artichoke with a soft-boiled duck egg and duck jus. Accurate timing has made the most of monkfish, served with herby mash and an impressive fish stock reduction, and of tender and tasty roast wild duck, partnered by a 'hamburger' of apple, foie gras and artichoke heart.

Among desserts, chocolate fondant with cinnamon ice cream is highly rated, or there may be a warm pistachio mille-feuille. Incidentals in abundance are of a high standard, and service is attentive and friendly without being fussy, although a couple of reporters have commented on the fact that some dishes have disappeared from the menu by mid-evening, and that some wines have also been unavailable. Nonetheless, the list is extensive, with southern France playing an important role. Italian wines are also well chosen, and there are some good examples from Austria as well as an impressive list of sherries by the glass. Reports about 'business expense' pricing highlight the list's flaw: finding anything under £25 is very difficult, apart from a selection of 16 wines by the glass (£3.50 to £12).

CHEF: Alexis Gauthier   PROPRIETORS: James and Andrew Palmer, and Alexis Gauthier   OPEN: Wed to Fri L 12 to 2.30, Mon to Sat D 6.30 to 10.30   MEALS: Set L £18 (2 courses) to £21, Set D £29 (2 courses) to £60   SERVICE: 12.5% (optional), card slips closed   CARDS: Amex, MasterCard, Switch, Visa   DETAILS: 48 seats. Private parties: 65 main room. Vegetarian meals. No children. Occasional music. No mobile phones. Air-conditioned   ⊖ Sloane Square

# Royal China £

40 Baker Street, W1V 7AJ
TEL: (020) 7487 4688   FAX: (020) 7935 7893
13 Queensway, W2 4QJ
TEL: (020) 7221 2535   FAX: (020) 7792 5752
68 Queen's Grove, NW8 6ER
TEL: (020) 7586 4280   FAX: (020) 7722 2681
30 West Ferry Circus, E14                                    COOKING 4
TEL: (020) 7719 0888   FAX: (020) 7719 0889                  CHINESE
WEBSITE: www.royalgourment.co.uk                             £20–£85

There are now four branches of this group of Chinese restaurants, all with
signature décor of lacquered wooden panels in shiny black, motifs of golden
flying birds and stylised waves in silver. Staff are generally slim, young and
elegantly dressed, and the menus virtually identical in each place. Front-
runners are the two original branches, Queensway and Baker Street, where
outstanding dim sum are one highlight: expect to queue at weekends, but it's
worth waiting for some of the finest morsels in the business.

Offerings from the main repertoire are equally dependable, and skilfully
wrought from top-notch ingredients. Seafood is a high point, and reporters have
praised fragrant crispy scallops with yam ('a masterpiece'), soft-shell crabs with
red chilli sauce, and steamed sea bass with garlic, ginger and exemplary baby
pak choi. Elsewhere, slow-cooked belly pork with stewed vegetables is a
favourite ('a glorious take on gutsy peasant food', raved one fan) and side orders
such as Chinese broccoli steamed with ginger are 'truly dazzling'. Our rating
applies principally to the Queensway and Baker Street branches; there is less
enthusiasm for the restaurant in Queen's Grove, although the new outlet in West
Ferry Circus shows promise. House wine is £13, or £3 a glass. Only some up-to-
date information was provided, so the details below are approximate.

CHEF: David Pang (Baker Street), Mr Man (Queensway), Mr Nan (Queen's Grove), Chris Chow
(West Ferry Circus)   PROPRIETOR: Royal China Restaurant Group   OPEN: all week 12 to 11 (11.30
Fri and Sat, 10 Sun)   MEALS: alc (main courses £6 to £20). Set meals available   SERVICE: 12.5%
CARDS: Amex, Delta, MasterCard, Switch, Visa   DETAILS: 120 seats. Private parties: 80 main
room, 15 private room. Vegetarian meals. No music. Air-conditioned   ⊖ Baker Street,
Queensway, St John's Wood, Canary Wharf (DLR)

# RSJ 🍶

map 13

33 Coin Street, SE1 8YQ                                      COOKING 3
TEL: (020) 7928 4554   FAX: (020) 7401 2455                  MODERN FRENCH
WEBSITE: www.rsj.uk.com                                      £27–£55

'RSJ clearly deserves its place in the Guide. One only wishes there could be
more restaurants like this.' So concluded a well-travelled inspector, his opinion
reflected in the majority of reports on this old stager in the environs of the South
Bank. It has not moved, incidentally, from 13A to 33, merely been re-numbered.
Some view it as a favourite pre-theatre spot, others come for the wine list, and
most comment on the 'friendly and very professional' service. The varied
modern cooking also receives its share of praise, though some reporters have felt
that the kitchen 'could usefully raise its game'. Nevertheless it has turned out

some impressive dishes, including a delicately flavoured smoked haddock and ricotta tart with thin, buttery pastry; 'moist and wonderfully tender' confit duck leg on Puy lentils with bacon; and a 'generous, fat fillet' of roast cod with gnocchi, spinach and asparagus and a lemon sauce. Finish perhaps with richly flavoured chocolate 'silk' with cappuccino cream, or pannacotta with berries.

The wine list remains a star attraction, with its dedication to the Loire. Light reds, a style overlooked on many lists, are generally food-friendly, as are the crisp whites from Sancerre, Pouilly-Fumé and beyond. Lovers of dessert wines are in for a treat, with 35 to choose from. There are some wines from elsewhere in France and from the New World, but to resist such well-chosen Loire examples would take some doing, especially as pricing is fair. House white and red are £12.50, and there is good choice below £20.

CHEF: Ian Stabler   PROPRIETOR: Nigel Wilkinson   OPEN: Mon to Fri L 12 to 2, Mon to Sat D 5.30 to 11   CLOSED: Christmas, 1 Jan, Good Fri, some bank hols   MEALS: alc (main courses £11 to £18). Set L and D £15.95 (2 courses) to £16.95   SERVICE: 12.5% (optional), card slips closed   CARDS: Amex, Delta, Diners, MasterCard, Switch, Visa   DETAILS: 90 seats. 12 seats outside. Private parties: 8 main room, 10 to 40 private rooms. Vegetarian meals. Children's helpings. No cigars/pipes in dining room. No music. Air-conditioned   ⊖ Waterloo  £5

---

# Sabras  £                                                    map 12

263 High Road, Willesden Green, NW10 2RX                        COOKING 4
TEL: (020) 8459 0340   FAX: (020) 8459 0541                  INDIAN VEGETARIAN
                                                                  £27–£46

The fact that the Desai family have survived and flourished in outer Willesden for some 20 years proves their endurance, faith in and commitment to real Indian vegetarian cooking. Their philosophy revolves around top-quality ingredients (mostly organic), and they are sufficiently flexible to cater for vegans, Jains and strict Hindus.

This is not austere food, though; bright flavours and imaginative ideas abound. The bedrock of the menu is Surati cuisine, although many regions of the Subcontinent are celebrated. Mumbai beach appetisers, such as bhel puri and pani puri, open the account alongside 'farshaan' starters such as samosas, patra and khaman (yellow cubes of ground chickpeas fermented with curd). Beyond are seven variations on the dosa theme, lentil dishes and vegetable bhajias including sakkariya (slow-cooked sweet potato with black pepper, cumin and lemon) and ravaiya (baked aubergine, potato and banana based on a recipe from the owner's mother). Six kinds of lassi, juices and beers are alternatives to the modest wine list, which opens with house French at £10. Mr Desai is a fan of world music and will accept requests.

CHEF: Nalinee Desai   PROPRIETOR: Hemant Desai   OPEN: Tue to Sun D only 6.45 to 10.30   CLOSED: 25 and 26 Dec   MEALS: alc (main courses £4.50 to £7.50). Cover 60p   SERVICE: 12.5%, card slips closed   CARDS: Amex, Delta, Diners, MasterCard, Switch, Visa   DETAILS: 32 seats. Private parties: 16 main room. Vegetarian meals. No cigars/pipes in dining room. Wheelchair access (not WC). Music   ⊖ Dollis Hill  £5

# St John

map 13

26 St John Street, EC1M 4AY
TEL: (020) 7251 0848   FAX: (020) 7251 4090
EMAIL: info@stjohnrestaurant.co.uk
WEBSITE: www.stjohnrestaurant.co.uk

COOKING 5
BRITISH
£37–£69

Spare. Economical. No frills. This bare, white-walled old smokehouse may feel like an army canteen, but it suits the unfussy food. Fergus Henderson's approach is distinguished by its boldness and its commitment: not only to offal, but to the virtue of making meals out of humble ingredients ('a real cook's approach,' reckoned one visitor). The signature dish, roast bone marrow with a lentil and parsley salad, is a fine example of this, but there are plenty more: smoked eel and horseradish; dried, salted pig's liver with radishes and a boiled egg; or a dish of roast chitterlings and radish, neatly combining 'chew and crunch'. If this sounds more casual than normal restaurant fare, it is confirmed by the evening menu's title of 'supper' rather than dinner.

The menu is as thrifty as everything else, listing a starter of 'sea kale' or a main course of 'lemon sole'; so nobody can be disappointed if that is all they get. There are novel variations of familiar ideas (such as salt lamb and caper sauce, or snails with chickpeas and sausage), and sometimes a few rough edges to the cooking, but they go with the peasanty style. Vegetables are well rendered: a bowl of succulent greens for one visitor, young carrots that might have come straight from the garden for another. Plain and simple desserts might take in burnt goats' milk yoghurt, or spotted dick and custard, and the predominantly French wine list has something for most pockets (starting with Pays d'Oc varietals at £14.50) as well as a decent showing by the glass.

CHEF: Fergus Henderson   PROPRIETORS: Trevor Gulliver and Fergus Henderson   OPEN: Mon to Fri 12 to 3, Mon to Sat 6 to 11   CLOSED: Christmas and New Year, Easter bank hol   MEALS: alc (main courses £11 to £23). Bar menu also available   SERVICE: not inc   CARDS: Amex, Delta, Diners, MasterCard, Switch, Visa   DETAILS: 100 seats. Private parties: 130 main room, 1 to 10 private rooms. Vegetarian meals. No music. No mobile phones. Air-conditioned   ⊖ Farringdon

# Salisbury Tavern

map 12

21 Sherbrooke Road, SW6 7HX
TEL: (020) 7381 4005   FAX: (020) 7381 1002

COOKING 3
MODERN BRITISH
£31–£55

Looking unpretentious and ordinary from outside, the well-kept tavern, which attracts an affluent crowd carefully dressed in their best casual clothing, consists of a cheerfully bright and very pubby bar, and a rather mellower dining room that is every inch a restaurant. Under the same ownership as Admiral Codrington (see entry), it knows its market well. The food features many modern favourites (classics, even) as well as a few more experimental ideas, their common denominator being a feeling for comfort: from Caesar salad, or salmon fishcake, to a risotto of chorizo and sun-dried tomatoes.

Cooked items are thin on the ground among starters, but daily dishes add to the variety, taking in fresh, tasty and chilli-spiked langoustine spring rolls on chopped beetroot, followed perhaps by pieces of slowly cooked, moist, flavourful rabbit leg and saddle, on a disc of rösti soaked in a rich, sticky stock reduction. Fish and seafood options might include roast fillet of cod with prawns, or a seafood 'salad' incorporating mussels, clams, prawns, a scallop, tuna and white fish with a mushroom sauce poured over. There is more comfort at pudding stage, with sticky toffee, marbled chocolate mousse, and tarte Tatin with vanilla ice cream. Note the anachronistic 50p cover charge in the evening for poor bread, and – on the plus side – a short wine list that helpfully offers nearly everything by the glass, starting with a brace of non-vintage Berry Bros bottlings at £11 (£2.80 a glass).

CHEF: Micky O'Connor   PROPRIETOR: Joel Cadbury   OPEN: all week 12 to 2.30 (3.15 Sun), 7 to 10.45 (10.15 Sun)   CLOSED: 25 and 26 Dec   MEALS: alc (main courses £10 to £18). Cover 50p at D. Bar menu available Sat and Sun L   SERVICE: 12.5% (optional), card slips closed   CARDS: Amex, Delta, MasterCard, Switch, Visa   DETAILS: 70 seats. Private parties: 85 main room. Vegetarian meals. Children's helpings. Wheelchair access (also WC). Music. Air-conditioned ⊖ Fulham Broadway, Parsons Green

---

# Salloos
map 14

62 Kinnerton Street, SW1X 8ER
TEL: (020) 7235 4444

COOKING 3
PAKISTANI
£27–£62

---

Muhammad Salahuddin ('Salloo' to his friends) set up his long-running restaurant in a Belgravia mews house in 1976. It remains a family affair: his daughters help out front and many of the dishes on the menu are, apparently, based on recipes from his mother. Paintings by Pakistani artists line the walls of the first-floor dining room, which has wooden-latticed windows and corniced ceilings. It is chic without being ostentatious.

Abdul Aziz has been at the helm since day one, and works to a menu that doesn't seem to change much from year to year. What he offers is classic Pakistani cooking fleshed out with a contingent of tandooris (without colourings) and a few old favourites. The clay oven is deployed for marinated lamb chops, quails and king prawns, while items such as chicken jalfrezi and bhuna gosht should be music to the ears of curry house devotees. Explanations of less familiar dishes are helpful: chicken taimuri consists of marinated thighs deep-fried in seasoned batter, while pulao jehangiri comprises Basmati rice cooked in lamb stock plus chicken in 'tomato coulis', almonds and raisins. Chickpeas, aubergines and bhindis keep the vegetable list in safe territory, and desserts include the likes of halva and kulfi. Corney & Barrow house wine is £12.50 (£3.50 a glass).

CHEF: Abdul Aziz   PROPRIETOR: Muhammad Salahuddin   OPEN: Mon to Sat 12 to 2.30, 7 to 11.15   MEALS: alc (main courses £12 to £15). Set L £12 (2 courses) to £16, Set D £25. Cover £1.50   SERVICE: 12.5% (optional), card slips closed   CARDS: Amex, Delta, Diners, MasterCard, Switch, Visa   DETAILS: 60 seats. Private parties: 35 main room. Vegetarian meals. No children under 6 at D. No cigars/pipes in dining room. No music. Air-conditioned   ⊖ Knightsbridge

# Salt House  £

map 13

63 Abbey Road, NW8 0AE

TEL: (020) 7328 6626  FAX: (020) 7625 9168

WEBSITE: www.thesalthouse.co.uk

COOKING 1

MODERN EUROPEAN

£21–£42

Reasonable prices, a trendy no-nonsense menu with a Mediterranean slant and a compact, well-chosen wine list (with most available by glass) await diners in this white building on a corner site in St John's Wood. At the front is a lively, buzzy pub; at the back the high-ceiling, grey-walled restaurant has wooden tables and white napkins, stained-glass windows and subdued lighting (and trestle tables outside for al fresco dining).

Devilled whitebait with aïoli, or goats' cheese bruschetta, is typical of the no-frills starters, while mains move up a gear with a sound dish of middle neck of lamb, grilled aubergine and basil pesto, or pan-fried fillet of sea bass with tabbouleh and baked tomatoes. Desserts – 'very simple, almost an afterthought' – might feature an apple parfait or chocolate brownie with vanilla ice cream. Young staff are friendly and informally dressed, while those wines kick in at £10 (£2.50 a glass).

CHEF: Lee Masters  PROPRIETOR: Adam Robinson  OPEN: all week 12.30 to 3 (Sat and Sun 4), 6.30 to 10.30 (Sat 7 to 10.30, Sun 7 to 10)  CLOSED: 24 to 26 Dec, 1 Jan  MEALS: alc (main courses £5.50 to £12). Set L £8.95 (2 courses) to £11.95  SERVICE: 12.5% (optional), card slips closed  CARDS: Amex, Delta, MasterCard, Switch, Visa  DETAILS: 40 seats. 40 seats outside. Private parties: 15 to 27 private rooms. Vegetarian meals. Children's helpings. Wheelchair access (not WC). No music. Air-conditioned  ⊖ St John's Wood

# Salusbury

map 13

50–52 Salusbury Road, NW6 6NN

TEL: (020) 7328 3286  FAX: (020) 7604 3300

EMAIL: mickrnash@mac.com

COOKING 3

ITALIAN

£23–£45

This is still a pub; so be prepared for a young crowd, plenty of noise, smoke and hubbub in the evening. Of the two doors, take the left if you want to mingle with drinkers; go right if you want the wooden-floored dining room, where a few abstract prints on the plain walls is about all the décor there is.

The owners' description of their food as 'cucina povera' (traditional, peasant-style Italian cooking) is not far off the mark, although there are interlopers in the shape of leek, potato and smoked haddock soup, and 'pure' chocolate torte. Fine ingredients produce correspondingly effective flavours, which have included accurately rendered asparagus risotto, a cartoccio of sea bass (steamed in a fish-shaped envelope with spring vegetables), and a robust and impressively presented dish of grilled swordfish with peas, French beans and cherry tomatoes. Syroppino (soft lemon sorbet with grappa) is 'more of a drink than a dessert', likewise perhaps Cantucci biscuits with Vin Santo. The wine list, favouring France over Italy, provides an affordable and interesting world tour; a dozen house wines start at £10.

CHEF: Enrico Sartor   PROPRIETORS: Nicholas Mash and Robert Claassen   OPEN: Tue to Sun L 12.30 to 3.15, all week D 7 to 10.15   MEALS: alc exc Sun L (main courses £9.50 to £16). Set L £5 (1 course) to £15   SERVICE: not inc   CARDS: Delta, MasterCard, Switch, Visa   DETAILS: 55 seats. Vegetarian meals. No children under 14 after 7pm. No cigars/pipes in dining room. Wheelchair access (also women's WC). No music   ⊖ Queens Park

## Sardo

**NEW ENTRY**    map 15

45 Grafton Way, W1P 5LA
TEL: (020) 7387 2521   FAX: (020) 7387 2559
EMAIL: info@sardo-restaurant.com
WEBSITE: www.sardo-restaurant.com

COOKING 3
SARDINIAN
£31–£55

A wooden floor and trendy artwork and light fittings produce a cool, contemporary dining room (non-smoking at the back) which is comfortable without being fussy. Although not totally Sardinian, the food nevertheless has a strong regional feel, from its thin, brittle carasau bread (a cross between a potato crisp and a poppadom) to finely sliced dried tuna fillet. Fine materials are deployed, including fresh, plump, well-timed mussels sharing a lightly chillied broth with grain-sized pasta (fregula), and a brace of moist, carefully cooked quail, glazed with balsamic and chopped in half, served with prunes and lightly battered courgette batons.

The food is simple but well rendered, taking in a characterful dish of al dente spaghetti sprinkled with bottarga (dried fish roe), and a ring of thin, flavourful, home-made sausage (herby, spicy and gently gamey) on a bed of indifferent cabbage. There appears to be only one Sardinian dessert, sebada, a puffed-up ball of filo-type pastry, its lightly salty cheese filling complemented by a drizzle of dark honey around the edge. Service is well managed, friendly and efficient, and the two dozen or so Sardinian wines are matched by a similar number from the rest of Italy. House wine, from Veneto, is £10.90.

CHEF: Roberto Sardu   PROPRIETOR: Romolo Mudu   OPEN: Mon to Fri L 12 to 3, Mon to Sat D 6 to 11   CLOSED: Christmas, bank hols   MEALS: alc (main courses £9 to £18)   SERVICE: 12.5% (optional), card slips closed   CARDS: Amex, Delta, Diners, MasterCard, Switch, Visa   DETAILS: 60 seats. 9 seats outside. Private parties: 70 main room, 20 to 30 private rooms. No-smoking area. Wheelchair access (not WC). Music. Air-conditioned   ⊖ Warren Street

## Sarkhel's

map 12

199 Replingham Road, Southfields, SW18 5LY
TEL: (020) 8870 1483   FAX: (020) 8874 6603

COOKING 2
INDIAN
£25–£61

Udit Sarkhel made his name at the Bombay Brasserie before opening his own restaurant in Southfields. His menus are a cook's tour of India's regional cuisine, from Assam to Goa: en route you might encounter Bombay and Dehli street snacks such as sev puri and samosa chaat, along with murg ke chaap 'sixer' (Andhra-style hot chicken 'lollipops'). Main dishes range from panthar jhole (a Bengali Sunday lunch special of goat and potato with fresh fried coconut) to slow-roast lamb shank, and a fine showing of vegetables includes puréed spinach with sweetcorn. There are also fortnightly-changing specials from the culinary capitals of the Subcontinent. Two-course express lunches and early-evening thalis (served until 8pm) are bargains. Around 40 wines stay mainly below £20 (house selections are £10.90). A new venture, Dalchini, at 147 Arthur Road, Wimbledon Park SW19, tel. (020) 8947 5966, aims to focus on the tradition of Chinese cooking in India; reports, please.

CHEF: Udit Sarkhel    PROPRIETORS: Udit and Veronica Sarkhel    OPEN: Tue to Sun 12 to 2.30, 6 to 10.30 (11 Fri and Sat)    CLOSED: 25 and 26 Dec    MEALS: alc (main courses £7.50 to £12). Set L Tue to Sat £5 (2 courses) to £9.95, Set D 6 to 8 £9.95 (thali)    SERVICE: not inc    CARDS: Amex, Delta, MasterCard, Switch, Visa    DETAILS: 88 seats. Private parties: 100 main room. Vegetarian meals. Children's helpings. No-smoking area. Wheelchair access (also women's WC). Music. Air-conditioned    ⊖ Southfields

# Sartoria ♥                                              map 15

| | |
|---|---|
| 20 Savile Row, W1X 1AE | COOKING 1 |
| TEL: (020) 7534 7000    FAX: (020) 7534 7070 | ITALIAN |
| WEBSITE: www.conran.com | £36–£70 |

Appropriately, men in suits patronise this handsome restaurant with its tailoring theme, huge pillars, and folding windows opening onto the street. The carte takes Anglo-Italian menuspeak in its stride, offering a starter of saffron tagliorini, mussels and bottarga, and a main course of monkfish with salsiccia, clams and borlotti. Pasta might take in cheese-filled ravioli in an oily dressing with artichoke, and meat options have included poached breast of salt duck with broad beans and other vegetables, topped with a mild horseradish sauce. Finish with ricotta and pear cheesecake (more like fruit tart), or a fine, creamy robbiola cheese with thin, crisp carta di musica bread. Salting can be heavy-handed, but service is very competent. The all-Italian wine list scores points for variety and quality, its strength lying in top modern producers from traditional regions. But wines of such pedigree are not cheap, so there ist little below £20, apart from house red and white (£14.95, £3.25 a glass).

CHEF: Piero Boi    PROPRIETOR: Conran Restaurants    OPEN: Mon to Sat L 12 to 2.30, all week D 6.30 to 11 (Sun 6 to 10)    MEALS: alc (main courses £16 to £19). Set L and D £19.50 (2 courses) to £22.50    SERVICE: 12.5% (optional), card slips closed    CARDS: Amex, Diners, MasterCard, Switch, Visa    DETAILS: 120 seats. Private parties: 120 main room, 10 to 70 private rooms. Vegetarian meals. Wheelchair access (also WC). Occasional music. Air-conditioned    ⊖ Oxford Circus

# Searcy's                                                map 13

| | |
|---|---|
| Level 2, Barbican Centre, Silk Street, EC2Y 8DS | COOKING 4 |
| TEL: (020) 7588 3008    FAX: (020) 7382 7247 | MODERN BRITISH |
| WEBSITE: www.barbican.org.uk | £37–£75 |

Whatever your feelings about the view over the Barbican's green pond, you can't help but feel relaxed in the sedate, simply decorated restaurant, a long, narrow room that struggles for atmosphere. But even if the ambience is less than electrifying, the refined, luxurious modern British cooking certainly raises the excitement level with some interesting and unusual ideas, such as a tarte Tatin of beetroot topped with slices of rare-cooked pigeon breast, and some earthy-sounding offal creations like braised pig's trotter with caramelised sweetbreads and pomme purée. On the whole, though, this is 'posh comfort food', with no shortage of luxury ingredients, and meals are padded out with finely crafted appetisers, pre-desserts and petits fours. An inspector's beef fillet accompanied by foie gras and truffles struck a happy chord, not least for the outstanding quality of the meat and the cooking that rendered it an even pink all the way through, while another reporter's wild duck with potato gratin and roast root vegetables featured a 'good plump breast' of mallard, cooked rare and attractively presented. Results can be uneven, but a dessert of summer berries presented three ways (parfait, sorbet and sweet, delicate pasta) was a 'simply stunning' end to one meal. Wines are not cheap; the 60-strong list opens with Cuvée George Blanc red and white at £17.

CHEF: Chris McGowan    PROPRIETOR: Searcy's    OPEN: Mon to Fri L 12 to 2.30, Mon to Sat D 5 to 10.30    MEALS: alc (main courses £17 to £24.50). Set L and D £19.50 (2 courses) to £22.50    SERVICE: 12.5% (optional), card slips closed    CARDS: Amex, Delta, Diners, MasterCard, Switch, Visa    DETAILS: 90 seats. No-smoking area. Wheelchair access (also WC). Music. Air-conditioned    ⊖ Barbican, Moorgate

## Singapore Garden

map 13

83–83A Fairfax Road, NW6 4DY
TEL: (020) 7328 5314    FAX: (020) 7624 0656

COOKING 2
SINGAPOREAN
£18–£61

'Always very satisfying,' notes a fan of the Lims' long-established, popular restaurant. Behind the wide frontage and dark green awning two narrow dining areas are divided by a partition with windows, their cream and green décor pleasing and understated. The menu has plenty of standard Cantonese dishes, but seek out the Singaporean and Malaysian specialities, some of the most authentic in the capital. Ingredients are the real thing, and flavours pack a punch: unctuously rich Rendang beef is flavoured with specially imported Malaysian curry powder, while Chinese spinach gets a pungent hit from blachan (prawn paste). Also notable are Teo Chow soft-shelled crabs with chillies and garlic, kway pie tee (pastry cups filled with bamboo shoots, prawn and chicken) and fine, subtly flavoured egg tofu with Chinese mushrooms. Service is smooth and polite. Drink Tiger beer or tap into the well-spread wine list. House wines start at £12.

CHEF: Mrs S.K. Lim    PROPRIETORS: the Lim family    OPEN: all week 12 to 2.45, 6 to 10.45 (11.15 Fri and Sat)    CLOSED: 4 days Christmas    MEALS: alc (main courses £6 to £30). Set L £7 (2 courses) to £8.50, Set D £20 to £32.50    SERVICE: 12.5% (optional), card slips closed    CARDS: Amex, Delta, Diners, MasterCard, Switch, Visa    DETAILS: 100 seats. 12 seats outside. Private parties: 60 main room, 6 private room. Vegetarian meals. No cigars. Music. Air-conditioned    ⊖ Swiss Cottage

'They assumed I was unmarried because I'd booked a table for one; in fact, when I booked, [the owner] was so struck by this remarkable fact that she offered to join me at my table in a giggly manner. I sniggered back.' (On eating in Derbyshire)

# Smiths of Smithfield, Top Floor ♥          map 13

67–77 Charterhouse Street, EC1M 4HJ                    COOKING **4**
TEL: (020) 7251 7950   FAX: (020) 7236 5666            MODERN BRITISH
WEBSITE: www.smithsofsmithfield.co.uk                  £36–£83

Thanks to its handsome wrought iron work (vividly painted in mauves, greens and blues), this Victorian warehouse opposite Smithfield Market retains something of an industrial air about it. At ground level is a heaving, club-like atmosphere with communal table-sharing, while upstairs at level 1 is a lounge bar, 2 is a brasserie dealing in British, Thai and Italian food, and at 4 you'll find the comparatively quiet and sophisticated restaurant, where service helps to keep things unstuffy.

Given its location, meat is understandably a strength, perhaps featuring roast venison, or rack of Shropshire lamb, but the menu's big draw is an annotated section labelled 'Fine Meats', which deals in rare breeds, properly hung. Islay rump, supplied by Gilbert McTaggart of Islay Butchers, is aged 26 days, while Shorthorn chateaubriand (for two) comes from Gary Wallace at Chesterton Farm and is aged 31 days. Hanging time really makes a difference to the flavour, further enhanced by commendably straightforward grilling or frying, and a simple accompaniment of béarnaise, red wine butter or creamed horseradish.

Starters explore both European and Far Eastern flavours, in the form of a salad of smoked eel with potato, beetroot and horseradish, and salt and pepper squid with roast chilli dressing, while non-meaty mains run to whole Dover sole with caper butter. Desserts might include Armagnac prunes with Sauternes custard, or fig and honey parfait. The wine list is suitably cosmopolitan, with bottles from Bordeaux and Burgundy alongside others from the French regions, the Americas and South Africa. Australia is particularly strong. Thirteen wines by the glass range from £4.60 (for Chilean Gewurztraminer) to £9 (1996 Bordeaux *cru bourgeois*). Choice is limited below £20.

CHEF: Tony Moyce   PROPRIETOR: John Torode   OPEN: Sun to Fri L 12 to 2.45, all week D 7 to 10.45   MEALS: alc (main courses £13.50 to £28). Sun brunch £25   SERVICE: 12.5% (optional), card slips closed   CARDS: Amex, Delta, Diners, MasterCard, Switch, Visa   DETAILS: 78 seats. 28 seats outside. Private parties: 150 main room, 30 to 50 private rooms. Vegetarian meals. Children's helpings. Wheelchair access (also WC). No music. Air-conditioned   ⊖ Farringdon

---

# Snows on the Green          map 12

164–166 Shepherd's Bush Road, W6 7PB                    COOKING **3**
TEL: (020) 7603 2142                     MODERN BRITISH/MEDITERRANEAN
FAX: (020) 7602 7553                                    £27–£48

Though this is Shepherd's Bush, the green you need to head for is actually Brook Green. After a bout of refurbishment, the draped pillar in the centre of the room has gone, though artistic black and white photographs still adorn the walls. The contemporary cooking achieves the effect of feeling sumptuous without being too heavy. Among enjoyable starters have been a salad of smoked eel with fennel, blood orange and olive dressing; and lobster ravioli with tomato and herb salsa. Main courses might run to 'tender and succulent' confit of pork with creamed cannellini beans, wild garlic, chorizo and an 'excellent' reduced jus, or peppered duck breast, cooked pink, served with pommes Anna and summer vegetables. Fruit compote with Sauternes makes a fine way to finish. Prices on the short, varied wine list open at £11.25 for Vin de Pays d'Oc.

CHEFS: Sebastian Snow and Paul Crescente   PROPRIETOR: Sebastian Snow   OPEN: Mon to Fri L 12 to 3, Mon to Sat D 6 to 11   CLOSED: 4 days Christmas, bank hols   MEALS: alc (main courses £8.50 to £14). Set L and D £10 (2 courses) to £13. Cover 95p   SERVICE: not inc, 12.5% for parties of 6 or more   CARDS: Amex, Delta, Diners, MasterCard, Switch, Visa   DETAILS: 80 seats. 10 seats outside. Private parties: 80 main room, 2 to 30 private rooms. Vegetarian meals. Children's helpings. No-smoking area. Wheelchair access (not WC). Music. Air-conditioned ⊖ Hammersmith

## Soho Spice £ map 15

124–126 Wardour Street, W1F 0TY
TEL: (020) 7434 0808   FAX: (020) 7434 0799
EMAIL: info@sohospice.co.uk
WEBSITE: www.sohospice.co.uk

COOKING 1
INDIAN
£24–£40

Bold colour schemes have replaced the flock wallpaper of old in many of today's new-wave Indian restaurants, and a smart, confident display of orange, purple and gold does its job well in this vibrant West End venue. The menu is a carefully considered selection of starters and main courses, ranging from familiar rogan josh and chicken tikka masala to some promising specialities that are a little bit different. Seafood shows up favourably in the shape of stir-fried squid with peppers and curry leaves, and salmon with mustard and tomatoes; among well-reported vegetable dishes have been cabbage laced with cumin, and Bombay potatoes. Poppadoms come with home-made pickles, and gulab jamun makes a decent finish. Service is capable, if slightly overattentive. The short wine list suits the food. House Vins de Pays d'Oc are £12.95.

CHEF: Suresh Manandhar   PROPRIETOR: Amin Ali   OPEN: all week 11.30 to 12 (3am Fri and Sat, 10.30 Sun)   CLOSED: 25 and 26 Dec   MEALS: alc (main courses £8.50 to £14). Set L and D £14.95 SERVICE: not inc, 10% for parties of 6 or more   CARDS: Amex, Delta, Diners, MasterCard, Switch, Visa   DETAILS: 120 seats. Private parties: 40 main room, 20 to 40 private rooms. Vegetarian meals. No-smoking area. Wheelchair access (also WC). Music. Air-conditioned ⊖ Tottenham Court Road, Oxford Circus

## Sonny's map 12

94 Church Road, SW13 0DQ
TEL: (020) 8748 0393   FAX: (020) 8748 2698

COOKING 4
MODERN EUROPEAN
£25–£54

Pale blues and creams create a naturally soft impression at this long-standing local favourite, which can get animated and jolly at busy times. The menu's modern credentials – squid ink polenta, tomato oil, garlic leaves and so on – are tempered by lots of classical terminology, including sabayon, confit, fricassee, boudin, compote and brandade, all testifying to the kitchen's culinary broad-mindedness. Fish is well handled, judging by a first-class, lightly seared warm tuna loin, served with a niçoise salad featuring quail's eggs, and by firm-textured tasty red mullet on a soft, fluffy butternut squash purée, topped with an unctuous and intense rouille.

Main courses typically appear as tottering towers, which need to be demolished before eating, and there can be more items than necessary on the plate, but their essentials are creditable, from steamed fillet of lemon sole with a broad bean tartlet, to rare roast venison; from 'straight up and down' pot-roast partridge, to tender, flavourful roast rump of lamb paired with merguez sausage and served with a sweet potato version of dauphinois. If a creamy vanilla-flavoured rice pudding (served with poached quince and a thin, flat cantuccini biscuit) doesn't ring your bell, perhaps one of the highly rated chocolate desserts might. A fondant chocolate cake with an unusual but successful savoury mint sauce did it for one visitor; a gooey but light Valrhona chocolate pot with an orange granita proved a highlight for another. Service, though it can be slow, generally holds up under pressure. A short, sharply chosen, up-to-date wine list starts with house French at £10.50.

CHEF: Leigh Diggins   PROPRIETORS: Rebecca Mascarenhas and James Harris   OPEN: all week L 12.30 to 2.30 (3 Sun), Mon to Sat D 7.30 to 11   CLOSED: most bank hols   MEALS: alc (main courses £10.50 to £16). Set L Mon to Sat £13 (2 courses) to £16, Set L Sun £18.50   SERVICE: 12.5% (optional), card slips closed   CARDS: Amex, Delta, Diners, MasterCard, Switch, Visa   DETAILS: 100 seats. Private parties: 20 main room. Vegetarian meals. Children's helpings. Wheelchair access (not WC). Music. Air-conditioned   ⊖ Hammersmith  (£5)

---

# Spiga ⬫                                                                                        map 15

84–86 Wardour Street, W1V 3LF                                                           COOKING 2
TEL: (020) 7734 3444   FAX: (020) 7734 3332                                                ITALIAN
                                                                                           £31–£48

---

Sit at one of the ultra-comfortable leather banquette 'booths' at the front of this modern restaurant, advises a reporter. The menu focuses on pizzas from a wood-fired oven, as well as a range of pasta dishes with interesting combinations of prime ingredients (casareccie with a green sprout of wild garlic, sun-dried tomatoes and smoked ricotta, for example). Starters of delicate minestrone alla Genovese ('very pleasant on a spring evening') and ravioli of salmon with asparagus have pleased visitors, likewise fillet of sea bass baked in a paper bag with clams, mussels and baby fennel (although, as a main course, this seemed rather undersized for its price). 'Exceptionally creamy' lemon tart is a fine dessert, and there are pleasant Italian cheeses in decent condition. Service veers between 'hopeless' and 'couldn't be better'. Around three dozen Italian regional wines offer good value, starting at £12 a bottle (£3 a glass). There is a branch, Spiga Chelsea, at 312–314 King's Road, SW3; tel. (020) 7351 0101.

CHEF: Paolo Barone   PROPRIETOR: A To Z Restaurants Ltd   OPEN: all week 12 to 3, 6 to 12 (11 Sun, Mon and Tue)   CLOSED: 25, 26 and 31 Dec   MEALS: alc (main courses £12.50 to £14)   SERVICE: 12.5% (optional), card slips closed   CARDS: Amex, Delta, Diners, MasterCard, Switch, Visa   DETAILS: 120 seats. Vegetarian meals. Children's helpings. No cigars/pipes in dining room. Wheelchair access (also WC). Music. No mobile phones. Air-conditioned   ⊖ Piccadilly Circus, Tottenham Court Road

# Square 🍾

map 15

6–10 Bruton Street, W1J 6PU
TEL: (020) 7495 7100   FAX: (020) 7495 7150
EMAIL: info@squarerestaurant.com
WEBSITE: www.squarerestaurant.com

COOKING 8
MODERN FRENCH
£44–£128

The discreet frontage masks a spacious dining room with fair-sized tables, exotic-looking flowers and big, bright abstracts on the walls. The Square draws well-dressed, well-heeled customers, and the hubbub and relaxed air show that they enjoy themselves. Lots of staff keep things running smoothly most of the time (occasionally waits can be a little long), and at its best service is professional and solicitous. 'When you book the phone is answered immediately by a real person who handles the details pleasantly and efficiently and doesn't put you on hold' : so rare it's remarkable!

A large menu and heavy wine list take some juggling with, but choice at dinner is generous, talent abundant, and raw materials virtually flawless, judging by a ballotine of chicken enclosing flesh-pink foie gras and white artichoke heart, accompanied by truffled green beans. Moreover, flavours are generally powerful and clear: in a trademark lasagne of crab with a cappuccino of shellfish and basil, or in a classic, virtuoso roast Bresse pigeon with a stuffed cabbage leaf in a rich Madeira sauce. 'Dazzling' appears repeatedly in reports, and dishes often total more than the sum of their parts: for example in a starter of chopped red mullet and aubergine, sautéed, sharpened with a sardine sauce, and inserted between thin discs of puff pastry.

Much effort goes into soothing the clientele and piling on the luxuries, as with a Cornish lobster, unimpeachably fresh, immaculately shelled (even the claws removed without a blemish) and served with a tiny copper pan of risotto dotted with sliced asparagus and more lobster meat. Artfully clever presentations of smallish amounts of very rich food are accompanied by plentiful twiddly bits and high-order incidentals, and there is much velouté-ing, dairy fat, egginess and general opulence, all adding up to a 'bloat' factor unappealing to some. If some extras were cut out, and prices reduced, an inspector ventured, the experience might be improved.

Even so, most make it to dessert: a fine soufflé (of raspberry, or prune and Armagnac), perhaps, or an oozing chocolate fondant partnered by a feuillantine with small poached pears, some boozy cherries and a chocolate sauce. That heavy wine list is a dream, taking in the great and good from all corners of the globe in encyclopaedic fashion. Champagne is particularly well covered as are red and white Burgundy, the Rhône and red Bordeaux. In the New World, California and Australia (including ten vintages of Penfolds Grange) are given plenty of air-time, as are food-friendly areas such as Alsace, Austria and the Loire. A dozen wines by the glass (£4.95 to £18), a smart selection of half-bottles, and an interesting dessert selection round off the list. Prices are not cheap, however, starting at £17.50 for house red, £19.50 for house white, and moving up swiftly thereafter.

CHEF: Philip Howard    PROPRIETORS: Nigel Platts-Martin and Philip Howard    OPEN: Mon to Fri L 12 to 3, all week D 6.30 to 10.45 (10 Sun)    CLOSED: 24 to 26 Dec, L bank hols    MEALS: Set L £20 (2 courses) to £25, Set D £55 to £75 (whole table)    SERVICE: 12.5% (optional), card slips closed    CARDS: Amex, Delta, Diners, MasterCard, Switch, Visa    DETAILS: 70 seats. Private parties: 8 to 18 private rooms. Wheelchair access (also WC). No music. Air-conditioned    ⊖ Green Park

## Stepping Stone                                                            map 12

123 Queenstown Road, Battersea, SW8 3RH
TEL: (020) 7622 0555    FAX: (020) 7622 4230                          | NEW CHEF |
EMAIL: thesteppingstone@aol.com                                      MODERN BRITISH
WEBSITE: www.thesteppingstone.co.uk                                      £28–£51

Standing out from its more downbeat neighbours, Stepping Stone is a light, modern restaurant with large windows, colourful walls and uncluttered tables. It is also undergoing change. Richard Hanson (who previously worked at Foliage, see entry) has moved up from sous-chef into the top job, and may well make some significant alterations to the menu, details of which were unavailable as the Guide went to press. The wine list, meanwhile, appears to have been picked by an enthusiast, offering a Canadian Pinot Blanc, and Italian producers such as Pieropan, Specogna, Haas and Allegrini. Prices start at £11.75.

CHEF: Richard Hanson    PROPRIETOR: Gary Levy    OPEN: Mon to Fri L 12 to 2.30, Mon to Sat D 7 to 11 (10.30 Mon)    CLOSED: 5 days Christmas, bank hols    MEALS: alc (main courses £8.50 to £17). Set L £13 (2 courses)    SERVICE: 12.5% (optional), card slips closed    CARDS: MasterCard, Switch, Visa    DETAILS: 75 seats. Private parties: 75 main room. Vegetarian meals. Children's helpings. No-smoking area. Wheelchair access (not WC). No music. No mobile phones. Air-conditioned    ⊖ Clapham Common

## Sugar Club ✸                                                              map 15

21 Warwick Street, W1R 5RB                                              COOKING 5
TEL: (020) 7437 7776    FAX: (020) 7437 7778                              FUSION
WEBSITE: www.thesugarclub.co.uk                                          £37–£71

The design feels like the distilled essence of minimalism. A huge picture window puts the front tables in full view of Warwick Street, but the rest is pale grey textured walls, hardwood floor, grey banquettes and subtle halogen lighting. The point is to ensure that the food is accorded star status, and Melbourne boy David Selex has proved an indisputably worthy successor to the founder, Peter Gordon, in that respect. Standards of culinary inventiveness – and excursions into odd corners of pan-Pacific cooking – are not one whit diminished.

Squid, for example, seared fast in the wok, is worked into a clever mix of oyster mushrooms, chilli, pak choi and caramelised peanuts, the textures changing with every mouthful. Plantain fritters add crunch, and a sugar and lime dressing zing, to an inspired pairing of 'crispy-steamed' belly pork (some technical achievement, that) and livid pink foie gras. Roast breast of Gressingham duck gets the raciest treatment, a red curry with Thai basil and fresh lychees adding aromatics, and jasmine rice the carbohydrate support. Vegetable side dishes bump up the bill, but both grilled asparagus with lemon and black pepper, and creamy mustard mash, were 'impeccable' at inspection.

Ingenuity doesn't flag at dessert stage either: an ice cream scented with cassia bark and textured with shattered bitter chocolate tastes as complex as it reads, while the richness of a melting dark chocolate fondant is set off by an accompanying granita of green mint tea. Well-drilled, friendly Pacific Rim staff keep things moving efficiently. Cocktails and a good range of wines by the glass kick off a varietally arranged list of sound new-wave bottles; prices start at £12.50, but soon head skywards.

CHEF: David Selex  PROPRIETORS: Ashley Sumner and Vivienne Hayman  OPEN: all week 12 to 2.45, 5.30 to 10.45  CLOSED: 25 and 26 Dec, 1 Jan, Easter Sun  MEALS: alc (main courses £14.50 to £21.50). Set L Sat and Sun £17.50 (2 courses)  SERVICE: 12.5% (optional), card slips closed  CARDS: Amex, Delta, Diners, MasterCard, Switch, Visa  DETAILS: 140 seats. Private parties: 55 main room, 10 to 55 private rooms. Vegetarian meals. No smoking in 1 dining room. No cigars/pipes in dining room. Wheelchair access (not WC). No music. Air-conditioned
⊖ Oxford Circus, Piccadilly Circus

## Sumosan

**NEW ENTRY**  map 15

26B Albemarle Street, W1S 4HY  COOKING **2**
TEL: (020) 7495 5999  FAX: (020) 7356 1247  MODERN JAPANESE
WEBSITE: www.sumosan.com  £29–£88

The large open space at Sumosan (on the former site of Coast) is decked out in shades of beige and brown with some splashes of lilac. Its large tables are highly polished, as are the mostly young clientele. The menu is a long way from the Japanese standard, whereby foods are divided up according to their manner of cooking. Here, a more Western approach is employed, listing appetisers, salads, soup and udon, with sections for fish, meat and vegetarian dishes, and further sections for teppanyaki dishes, sushi and sashimi (for which there are several set menus). There are also some foreign intrusions in the form of Peking duck sushi and sashimi and teppanyaki of foie gras.

Yellowtail has turned in a good account of itself: as a finely chopped and spectacularly presented tartare, topped with sevruga caviar and wasabi-flavoured flying fish roe; and as 'thick and succulent' nigiri sushi. The now-classic black cod with miso is served atop a hoba leaf with three pools of miso sauce. There are meat dishes too, including lamb furikaki, and a warm salad of harusame (glass noodles) generously endowed with chopped beef fillet. On the downside, spicing may sometimes be off-balance – a bit too much chilli here, too little ginger there – and miso soup needs improving. Service is laid back but attentive and very friendly, with a good understanding of the menu. Only one saké is offered on the wine list, along with four fruit-infused ones. Although there are some interesting wines, most of them are in the £25-plus range. Ten are sold by the glass, from £4 to £7, and bottle prices open at £15 for French Chardonnay and Merlot.

CHEF: Vubker Belhit  PROPRIETOR: Janina Wolkow  OPEN: Mon to Fri L 12 to 2.45, Mon to Sat D 6 to 11.30  MEALS: alc (main courses £9.50 to £23.50). Set L £20 to £40, Set D £16.50 to £55  SERVICE: 12.5% (optional), card slips closed  CARDS: Amex, Delta, MasterCard, Switch, Visa  DETAILS: 122 seats. Private parties: 30 main room, 14 to 30 private rooms. Vegetarian meals. No pipes in dining room. Wheelchair access (also WC). Music. Air-conditioned  ⊖ Green Park

## Sushi-Say £      map 12

33B Walm Lane, NW2 5SH      COOKING 3
TEL: (020) 8459 2971 and 7512      JAPANESE
FAX: (020) 8907 3229      £18–£73

It is quite a treat to find a pleasant, family-run Japanese restaurant in the heart of Willesden. This is a thin, small place with 'spartan décor' of pale wood tables, parquet floor and wooden-framed prints on green walls; at the front is a little sushi bar, and there's a tatami room towards the back. The cooking is simple but genuine. Reading the full carte may take time, but ten set dinner menus covering almost all aspects of the cuisine (from tempura to teriyaki) provide an easy way out. Well-reported appetisers have included 'spot-on' agedashi tofu (deep-fried bean curd served with spring onions and seaweed), and a nasu dengaku (grilled aubergine with miso sauce). While the quality of the fish has been a shade variable, turbot and eel have been reported as up to par. Weekly-changing specials are also worth investigating, and the set lunches are fairly priced deals. The restaurant has its own 'dessert wine' (a mixture of vodka and apple juice), otherwise there are sakés, beers and a short list of mainly French wines. House wine is £9.80.

CHEF: Katsuharu Shimizu   PROPRIETORS: Katsuharu and Yuko Shimizu   OPEN: Sat and Sun L 1 to 3.30, Tue to Fri D 6.30 to 10.30, Sat D 6 to 11, Sun D 6 to 10   MEALS: alc (main courses £6 to £19). Set L £7.90 to £12.50 (all 1 or 2 courses), Set D £18.10 to £28.30   SERVICE: not inc   CARDS: Amex, Delta, MasterCard, Switch, Visa   DETAILS: 36 seats. Private parties: 20 main room. Vegetarian meals. No-smoking area. Wheelchair access (also WC). No music. Air-conditioned
⊖ Willesden Green

## Tamarind      map 15

20 Queen Street, W1J 5PR
TEL: (020) 7629 3561   FAX: (020) 7499 5034      COOKING 3
EMAIL: tamarind.restaurant@virgin.net      MODERN INDIAN
WEBSITE: www.tamarindrestaurant.com      £30–£71

The location is a swish Mayfair side street, and this rather opulent Indian restaurant does its best to match the W1 postcode. Refurbishment was under way as the Guide went to press – expect a chocolate-brown lobby, gold and silver walls in the dining room, and more subdued lighting – so it sounds as if it will remain as chic and elegant as ever.

The full menu changes three times a year, and its heart is firmly in the rich traditions of the north-west of the Subcontinent. Tandoori dishes hold centre-stage in the shape of machchi ka sula (salmon and monkfish marinated in mustard and dill) and gobi aur paneer (broccoli and paneer cheese with chilli and ginger marinade), as well as the more familiar chicken and king prawns. The forward-looking intentions of the kitchen are also highlighted in curries of braised lamb with onions and a five-spice mix, or spiced chicken with black pepper and mace. Away from the north-west, you might also encounter meen kari (a South Indian seafood stew), and a vegetable dish of runner beans with water chestnuts. Salads appear among the appetisers, while desserts take in the usual gulab jamun, kulfi and rasmalai. Good-value set lunch menus follow the seasons, although dishes change every few weeks. The wine list seeks to complement the food: France is a strong suit, but there are selections from around the world. House wines start at £14.50.

CHEF: Atul Kochhar   PROPRIETOR: Indian Cuisine Ltd   OPEN: Sun to Fri L 12 to 2.45, all week D 6 to 11.15 (10.15 Sun)   CLOSED: 25 and 26 Dec, 1 Jan, L bank hols   MEALS: alc (main courses £10.50 to £17.50). Set L £16.50, Set D £34.50 to £45   SERVICE: 12.5% (optional), card slips closed   CARDS: Amex, Delta, Diners, MasterCard, Switch, Visa   DETAILS: 90 seats. Private parties: 96 main room. No children under 6 at D after 7.30. Music. Air-conditioned   ⊖ Green Park

# La Tante Claire ♟ map 14

Wilton Place, SW1X 7RL
TEL: (020) 7823 2003   FAX: (020) 7823 2001   COOKING 8
EMAIL: office@latanteclaire.demon.co.uk   FRENCH
WEBSITE: www.latanteclaire.com   £42–£132

Tante Claire may be housed in the Berkeley Hotel, but it is a stand-alone dining room (dark wood and pastel green walls give a sedate, distinguished, understated look) with its own approach to food and cooking. Pierre Koffmann concentrates, as always, on classic French cooking, with an emphasis on his native South-West. The physically huge menu is a sight to see: some seven classically based starters, consisting almost entirely of foie gras and shellfish, are followed by about ten main dishes, including a trademark pig's trotter, perhaps braised in port with a sweetbread and morel stuffing.

But not everything is as traditional as it might appear. A lobster salad includes mango, and one foie gras dish is partnered by chocolate. And, the closer you look, the more the cooking seems lighter than it was. When allied to Pierre Koffmann's customary assurance, this makes for some very fine dishes, among them a tender rack of lamb cut into two thick pieces, served on a ragoût of haricot beans with confit cherry tomatoes; and roast Challans duck on a crescent of baked squash in a herb- and spice-laden sauce.

Materials are top-hole, and dishes are unencumbered by garnish, so flavours are clear, vibrant and precise: as in a langoustine ravioli with a sweet carrot emulsion and drops of basil-flavoured oil, or an exemplary mackerel tartare inside a cucumber stockade, topped with caviar and a poached quail's egg. Cheeses are 'a triumph', and desserts have included a jellied citrus fruit terrine with an Earl Grey sorbet, and thickly sliced bananas under a thin pastry hat with a flavourful rum and raisin ice cream. The fixed-price lunch is recommended, and meals are rounded out with first-rate appetisers, top-quality bread from a trolley, a fine pre-dessert, and 'outstanding' petits fours that come in two waves.

Among staff the English wine waiter, sensitive to customers' needs, is singled out for praise, offering firm but appropriate advice. On the carefully selected wine list France is the main focus, with Alsace and the Loire – along with Bordeaux, Burgundy and the Rhône – providing a plethora of food-friendly styles. There is a hefty price to pay for all of these important names, however; precious little choice can be found under £25, and three-digit prices seem the norm. French regional wines, listed by grape variety, provide the best value, with bottle prices starting at £16.

CHEF/PROPRIETOR: Pierre Koffmann   OPEN: Mon to Fri L 12.30 to 2, Mon to Sat D 7 to 10.45
CLOSED: 22 Dec to 5 Jan, Easter   MEALS: alc (main courses £28 to £40). Set L £29   SERVICE:
12.5% (optional), card slips closed   CARDS: Amex, Delta, Diners, MasterCard, Switch, Visa
DETAILS: 70 seats. Private parties: 60 main room, 8 to 16 private rooms. Jacket and tie. No cigars/
pipes in dining room. Wheelchair access (also WC). No music. No mobile phones. Air-
conditioned   ⊖ Hyde Park Corner

## Tas £

33 The Cut, SE1 8LF                                   COOKING 2
TEL: (020) 7928 1444   FAX: (020) 7633 9686           TURKISH
WEBSITE: www.tasrestaurant.com                        £20–£41

map 13

Stylish, angular, with light wood flooring, pale blue walls, and a few plants, Tas
delivers a fair range of Middle Eastern dishes, including meze, salads, grills,
vegetarian and seafood dishes, and casseroles, traditionally cooked in an
Anatolian cooking pot, or tas. Options run from standard items – such as a plate
of hummus with large coriander-flavoured olives and warm bread, or well-
made vine leaves stuffed with rice and pine kernels – to a skewer of lightly
battered, crisp-coated, deep-fried mussels with a garlic and dill sauce.

Herbs and spices are used to good effect, and slow-cooked dishes are full of
flavour: incik is a large chunk of lamb shoulder cooked in stock with tomatoes,
herbs and onions. Karisik izgara (a mixed grill of lamb meatballs, chicken and
aubergine) is served with a chilli salsa, and rice pudding flavoured with orange
and rose-water makes a fine finish to a spicy meal; or there may be a less typically
Turkish nut cake, marbled with white and dark chocolate, served with a
chocolate ice cream. Staff are attentive and helpful, there may be live music,
prices are reasonable, and a short wine list starts with native Buzbag red and
Villa Doluca white (£10.50 each), which suit the food admirably.

CHEF: Onder Sahan   PROPRIETORS: Onder Sahan, A. Sevim, I. Duman and D. Aslan   OPEN: all
week 12 to 11.30 (10.30 Sun)   MEALS: alc (main courses £6 to £14.50). Set L and D £7.45 to
£18.50 (all min 2)   SERVICE: 10%   CARDS: Amex, Delta, MasterCard, Switch, Visa   DETAILS: 120
seats. 4 seats outside. Private parties: 50 main room. Vegetarian meals. No-smoking area.
Wheelchair access (also WC). Music. Air-conditioned   ⊖ Southwark

## Tate Britain Restaurant  map 13

Millbank, SW1P 4RG
TEL: (020) 7887 8825   FAX: (020) 7887 8902         COOKING 3
EMAIL: tate.restaurant@tate.org.uk                  MODERN BRITISH
WEBSITE: www.tate.org.uk                            £32–£63

The name and the chef may have changed, but Rex Whistler's dynamic mural,
the black leather and wood décor, and high noise levels remain unaffected at this
well-patronised basement dining room. The greeting is friendly, and service by
black-clad staff is 'pleasant and efficient'. While the food may not quite match
the magnificence of its surroundings, the appeal is that you can get a 'well-
executed lunch based on excellent well-sourced ingredients'.

Chris Dines's contemporary repertoire offers a two-choice set option
alongside a more tempting carte that features plenty of seasonal ingredients
and appealing combinations: Gressingham duck breast with spring turnips and

a strawberry tarragon relish, say, or 'well-flavoured' baked Welsh rump of lamb with courgette, vine tomato and marjoram tart. Try sauté of 'robustly-flavoured' wild mushrooms on toasted walnut bread to start, and finish with black fig tart with almond ice cream, or 'a wedge of the richest, darkest, densest' chocolate mousse cake with crème fraîche. Half-bottles, just right for lunchtime drinking, are a feature of an ultra-sophisticated list. There is plenty to please lovers of both classical and modern styles, from top Bordeaux (much of it mature) to up-to-the-minute selections from Argentina, Austria and New Zealand. Pricing, though not cheap, is generally fair. Sixteen sommelier's recommendations start at £15; 13 sell by the glass (£3.75 to £7.50).

CHEF: Chris Dines   PROPRIETOR: Tate Catering Ltd   OPEN: all week L only 12 to 3 (4 Sun)   MEALS: alc (main courses £10 to £18.50). Set L £16.75 (2 courses) to £19.50   SERVICE: not inc, card slips closed   CARDS: Amex, Delta, Diners, MasterCard, Switch, Visa   DETAILS: 100 seats. Private parties: 45 main room. Vegetarian meals. Children's helpings. Wheelchair access (also WC). No music. No mobile phones. Air-conditioned   ⊖ Pimlico

---

# Teatro                                                      map 15

93–107 Shaftesbury Avenue, W1V 8BT
TEL: (020) 7494 3040   FAX: (020) 7494 3050          | NEW CHEF |
EMAIL: info@teatrolondon.co.uk                       MODERN BRITISH
WEBSITE: www.teatrosoho.co.uk                           £26–£75

The past year has seen the opening of a new bar aimed at a young, style-conscious crowd, and the appointment of a new head chef for the restaurant. Jamie Younger has worked at Bibendum and L'Oranger (see entries), and looks set to produce a range of dishes with broad appeal, taking in a tarte fine of tomato and mozzarella, deep-fried haddock with chips and tartare sauce, and sauté rabbit with chorizo and borlotti beans. Among desserts, expect to see passion-fruit bavarois, or peach Melba. A dozen wines by the glass open the ten-page wine list, which offers little choice under £20.

CHEF: Jamie Younger   PROPRIETORS: Lee Chapman and Leslie Ash   OPEN: Mon to Fri L 12 to 3, Mon to Sat D 5.30 to 11.45   CLOSED: 1 week Christmas, bank hols   MEALS: alc (main courses L £6.50 to £35, D £13 to £18.50). Set L £16.50 to £20, Set D 5.30 to 7.15 £11.50 (2 courses) to £14. Bar menu available   SERVICE: 12.5% (optional), card slips closed   CARDS: Amex, Delta, Diners, MasterCard, Switch, Visa   DETAILS: 106 seats. Private parties: 250 main room. Vegetarian meals. Wheelchair access (also WC). Music. No mobile phones. Air-conditioned   ⊖ Leicester Square, Tottenham Court Road   £5

---

# Teca ▼                                                     map 15

54 Brooks Mews, W1Y 2NY                                  COOKING 4
TEL: (020) 7495 4774   FAX: (020) 7491 3545           MODERN ITALIAN
                                                        £38–£79

This lean, clean, cool restaurant comes down on the right side of modernism, its stainless steel and smoked glass mitigated by cream walls and squishy banquettes. A rather well-dressed clientele matches the up-market Italian feel, and the menu takes a fairly classic approach, offering squid-ink risotto with calamari, and pasta shells served with rocket, cherry tomatoes and mozzarella.

There are signs of innovation, though, as in a starter of steamed foie gras with broad beans and beetroot sauce.

Presentation is attractive, with no fiddly blobs and streaks of highly coloured sauces, just thoughtful contrasts instead: perhaps roast fillet of pork with rosemary sauce and shiitake mushrooms. Raw materials are praiseworthy, and if portions are generous, the touch is light, leaving room for desserts of ricotta and pine kernel tartlets with white chocolate sauce, or tiramisù. Service can be fussy, but is solicitous nonetheless. The wine list is almost all Italian – with just a single wine each from Australia, France, Portugal and Spain – and moves from Val d'Aosta to Calabria to Sicily and Sardinia. Many of the wines, particularly from Piedmont and Tuscany, are big names with big prices; southern Italy is usually a source of value, but even here there is little under £20.

CHEF: Marco Torri   PROPRIETOR: A To Z Restaurants Ltd   OPEN: Mon to Fri L 12 to 2.30, Mon to Sat D 7 to 10.30   MEALS: Set L £19.50 (2 courses) to £24.50, Set D £27.50 (2 courses) to £36. Tasting menu £48.50 (whole table)   SERVICE: 12.5% (optional), card slips closed   CARDS: Amex, Delta, MasterCard, Switch, Visa   DETAILS: 50 seats. Private parties: 60 main room. Vegetarian meals. Wheelchair access (also WC). Music. Air-conditioned   ⊖ Bond Street   (£5)

## Tentazioni                                                        map 13

2 Mill Street, SE1 2BD
TEL/FAX: (020) 7237 1100                                       COOKING 4
EMAIL: tentazioni@aol.com                                 MODERN ITALIAN
WEBSITE: www.tentazioni.co.uk                                £32–£65

A new colour scheme and specially commissioned artworks on the theme of temptation have given a fresh feel to the long, narrow dining room at this stylish, intimate venue in a converted warehouse behind Butlers Wharf. Otherwise, it is business as usual, the food continuing to offer an attention-grabbing contemporary take on traditional Italian cuisine: rabbit ravioli with prawns and artichokes, or maybe clam risotto with salmon carpaccio to start, followed by beef fillet with foie gras on radicchio and Asiago cheese pudding. Even grilled ostrich fillet is put through the Italian mill, served with green olives, anchovies, aubergines and courgettes. Finish perhaps with warm wild berry pudding with white chocolate sauce, or Taleggio cheese with fruit mostarda.

The menu changes every three to four weeks to keep up with the seasons; there is also a five-course degustazione option, and a fortnightly-rotating three-course set menu that concentrates on the cooking of one region: the Tuscan version, for example, produces a traditional soup of black cabbage and cannellini beans, spit-roast rack of lamb with roast potatoes and spinach, and ricotta with Vin Santo and cantucci biscuits. Prices on the short, exclusively Italian wine list open at £14.

CHEF: Riccardo Giacomini   PROPRIETORS: Christian di Pierro and Maurizio Rimerici   OPEN: Mon to Fri L 12 to 2.30, Mon to Sat D 6.45 to 10.45   CLOSED: Christmas, bank hols   MEALS: alc (main courses £14 to £19). Set L £15 (2 courses) to £19, Set D £29 to £36   SERVICE: 12.5% (optional), card slips closed   CARDS: Amex, Delta, MasterCard, Switch, Visa   DETAILS: 60 seats. Private parties: 60 main room, 20 to 30 private rooms. Vegetarian meals. Children's helpings. Music   ⊖ London Bridge   (£5)

# Thai Garden ✻ £

map 12

249 Globe Road, E2 0JD
TEL: (020) 8981 5748
EMAIL: thaigarden@hotmail.com
WEBSITE: www.thethaigarden.co.uk

COOKING 1
THAI SEAFOOD AND VEGETARIAN
£20–£33

In an East End enclave of boutiques, this modest looking, family-run café reminded a reader of provincial Thailand, as did the menu shunning meat in favour of vegetables and seafood. The exterior of the building may not encourage the uninitiated to venture inside, but an inspector was glad he took the chance. The menu is divided into separate vegetarian and seafood sections, although there is no bar to choosing dishes from each. 'Good, unpretentious and fairly priced' is how the food comes across, based as it is on fine ingredients, though it downplays the spicing in such dishes as gaeng phed (Thai aubergines, with fresh bamboo shoots in creamy coconut sauce), or hoy ob (steamed mussels with lemon grass, chilli and garlic sauce). Service has been 'laid back to the point of comatose'. House wines are £7.50 (it's not often we can say that!).

CHEF: Naphaphorn Duff   PROPRIETORS: Jack and Suthinee Hufton   OPEN: Mon to Fri L 12 to 2.45, all week D 6 to 10.45   CLOSED: bank hols   MEALS: alc (main courses £4.50 to £7). Set L £7.50 (2 courses), Set D £16 to £20   SERVICE: 10%, card slips closed   CARDS: Delta, Switch, Visa   DETAILS: 32 seats. Private parties: 20 main room, 12 to 14 private rooms. Vegetarian meals. No smoking in 1 dining room. Wheelchair access (not WC). Music   ⊖ Bethnal Green

---

# Thyme

**NEW ENTRY**   map 12

14 Clapham Park Road, SW4 7BB
TEL: (020) 7627 2468   FAX: (020) 7627 2424
EMAIL: adam@thymeandspace.com
WEBSITE: www.thymeandspace.com

COOKING 2
MODERN EUROPEAN
£34–£85

'A bitch of a place to find', according to one visitor, for whom the frosted-up frontage was difficult to spot amid fast-flowing traffic. And parking is another challenge. Beyond the small bar is a long room, plainly and simply decorated in white and burgundy, with only wooden blinds and a single painting of a nude to look at. All dishes are starter-sized, priced between £5 and £10, so three savoury items (out of 18 on offer) and a dessert are roughly equivalent in volume to a normal three-course meal. Alternatively, a tasting menu offers six dishes and four glasses of wine for £60.

Options range from a straightforward, fresh-tasting herb leaf salad with black olive crostini and lemon olive oil, via baby squid stuffed with flavourful oxtail, served on saffron risotto spiked with chopped chorizo, to confit fillet of cod with seared foie gras, truffle mash and morels. For dessert there might be warm banana tart, or roast plum soup with yoghurt pannacotta. There is talent in the kitchen, although not much of it was on display at inspection, when seasoning was variable and flavours were not all they might have been, but the overall idea, the prices, and many of the dishes themselves indicate a sensible foundation. Service is industrious and willing, and a rather traditional, French-dominated wine list starts in the south at £14.50.

CHEF: Adam Byatt    PROPRIETORS: Adam Byatt and Adam Oates    OPEN: Mon to Sat D only 6.30 to 10.30    CLOSED: 2 weeks Christmas, last 2 weeks Aug    MEALS: alc (dishes £5 to £10). Set D £60 (inc wine)    SERVICE: 12.5% (optional), card slips closed    CARDS: Amex, Delta, MasterCard, Switch, Visa    DETAILS: 50 seats. Vegetarian meals. No-smoking area. No cigars/pipes in dining room. Music. Air-conditioned    ⊖ Clapham Common

# Timo

NEW ENTRY    map 13

343 Kensington High Street, W8 6NW    COOKING 5
TEL: (020) 7603 3888    FAX: (020) 7603 8111    ITALIAN
£30–£50

This handsome new restaurant wears its classy credentials with good grace. Although its smart but not flashy exterior is initially difficult to pick out on busy Kensington High Street, the interior oozes Italianate aspiration. Sheet-glass partitions abound, while smart furniture in a pale fawn matches the walls. Customers are likely to receive a warm welcome before sitting down to beautifully set white-clothed tables.

In the Italian fashion, people are encouraged to have four courses – a starter, pasta, main and dessert – from the set-price menus, where some dishes attract the occasional supplement. Starters may include wild boar ham, cut in slices so thin they're transparent, served with rocket and celeriac. Classic dishes, such as linguine con vongole, and tagliatelle with tomato and basil sauce, dominate pasta courses, while mains may centre on fish or meat: 'beautifully seared' sea bream topped with olive paste and red onion, perhaps, or calf's liver with spinach and balsamic sauce. Desserts tend to be straightforward, even slightly retro, as in peach melba with sorbet. The wine list ventures beyond Italy only for champagne, but the concise selection has been chosen with care. Prices start at £9.50 for red and white from the Marches, and there is decent choice under £20.

CHEF: Valerio Daros    PROPRIETOR: A To Z Restaurants Ltd    OPEN: all week 12 to 3, 7 to 11    MEALS: Set L £10 (1 course) to £23.50, Set D £16.50 (2 courses) to £25    SERVICE: 12.5%, card slips closed    CARDS: Amex, Delta, MasterCard, Switch, Visa    DETAILS: 55 seats. Private parties: 9 main room, 8 to 14 private rooms. Vegetarian meals. No-smoking area. No music. Air-conditioned    ⊖ High Street Kensington

# Les Trois Garcons

NEW ENTRY    map 13

1 Club Row, E1 6JX    COOKING 4
TEL: (020) 7613 1924    FAX: (020) 7613 3067    FRENCH
WEBSITE: www.lestroisgarcons.com    £57–£87

The décor here almost defies description: 'high camp' might be a start, volunteered one visitor. The bar area is crammed with antique glassware, and ornate chandeliers drip from the ceilings; table dressings, by contrast, are traditional stiff white linen and plain white china. The cooking can be characterised as 'high French' and rather retro: damn-the-expense ingredients such as foie gras, truffles and ceps abound, highlighted by beurre noisette here and vinaigrette a la Française there. Lobster bisque, from a huge tureen, is 'seriously full of flavour', and meats are sometimes partnered by fruit: perhaps a duck liver terrine layered with black truffles and plum compote, or roast venison fillet with redcurrant sauce.

At its best the food is 'satisfying and full flavoured', as in a braised lamb shank served with a courgette flower stuffed with foie gras and chicken, in an intense rosemary jus. The cheese board sports some fine French examples, and desserts of flambéed crêpes, or crème brûlée of summer fruits, are well executed. Service is formal and French: efficient rather than warm. It is no surprise that wines focus largely on France, especially Bordeaux, but prices and mark-ups are high: a 2000 Cloudy Bay Sauvignon Blanc costs an eye-watering £65. Ouch. House wines start at £19.50, and there are no bargains.

CHEF: Ade Ademola   PROPRIETORS: Michel Lasserre, Stefan Karlson and Hassan Abdullah
OPEN: Mon to Sat D only 7 to 11   CLOSED: 1 week Christmas and New Year   MEALS: alc (main courses £16.50 to £24)   SERVICE: 12.5% (optional)   CARDS: Amex, Delta, Diners, MasterCard, Switch, Visa   DETAILS: 90 seats. Private parties: 10 to 18 private rooms. Vegetarian meals. Music. Air-conditioned   ⊖ Liverpool Street

## La Trompette 🍷 

map 12

5–7 Devonshire Road, W4 2EU
TEL: (020) 8747 1836   FAX: (020) 8995 8097

COOKING 7
FRENCH
£33–£60

A side street in Chiswick might seem an unlikely spot for such a 'swish gem' of a restaurant, but then Chiswick is changing. Welcoming, confident, buzzing with atmosphere and speedy with the service, La Trompette feels like an upmarket neighbourhood place (children are well treated), although reporters understandably come from much further afield. Lunch is considered particularly good value. The draw – 'fine ingredients properly cooked' – is as simple as it is rare, achieved through the medium of an appealingly common-sense menu that is neither too predictable nor too outlandish. The comforting style takes in warm smoked eel with egg-yolk ravioli, accompanied by grain mustard hollandaise; and a 'rich and sonorous' dish of sliced venison with chestnut purée, Jerusalem artichokes and a port and redcurrant sauce.

The word 'stunning' has been applied to several items: cod with mashed potatoes, calf's liver with endive, and partridge served with a potato galette and a reduction of red wine and cooking juices. What shines through is a sense of freshness in the flavours, a set of clean tastes that bear testimony to comparatively simple yet intelligent partnerships, from chargrilled duck hearts with sauce rémoulade, to grilled fillet of sea bream with a ring of provençale vegetables surmounted by crisp, paper-thin sliced potato.

Praiseworthy desserts include a tart with an immaculate fanning of thinly sliced apples and a memorable caramel ice cream. Other ices coming in for praise include a prune and Armagnac version, and the one that replaces cream in Trompette's version of chocolate profiteroles. An exciting 16-strong collection of wines by the glass kicks off the wine list, which uses France as its main pivot but explores Italy, Australia and California in depth. Regional France is the place to look for value, while enthusiasts should check out the well-chosen Austrian and New Zealand selections. Quality is high throughout, even if bottles below £20 are in the minority.

CHEF: Ollie Couillaud   PROPRIETORS: Nigel Platts-Martin and Bruce Poole   OPEN: all week 12 to 2.30 (12.30 to 3 Sun), 6.30 to 10.30 (Sun 7 to 10)   MEALS: Set L Mon to Sat £15 (1 course) to £19.50, Set L Sun £23.50, Set D £30   SERVICE: 12.5% (optional), card slips closed   CARDS: Amex, Delta, MasterCard, Switch, Visa   DETAILS: 72 seats. 20 seats outside. No cigars/pipes in dining room. Wheelchair access (also WC). No music. Air-conditioned   ⊖ Turnham Green

## La Trouvaille ✸

| | |
|---|---|
| | **NEW ENTRY**   map 15 |
| 12A Newburgh Street, W1F 7RR | COOKING 3 |
| TEL: (020) 7287 8488   FAX: (020) 7434 4170 | PROVINCIAL FRENCH |
| | £31–£59 |

This French bistro in a pedestrianised thoroughfare off Carnaby Street has two small rooms, one overlooked by a bar, the other by a metal stork. It has mustard walls, heating ducts running across the ceiling, and tables topped with white linen under a layer of brown paper. The focus is on the kind of French cooking least familiar to British eaters: the rustic, bold, uncompromising fare of the deep south-west. Boudin noir has 'concentrated savoury-sweet flavour and coarse texture', the sweet aspect pointed up with a pear and carrot relish. The French taste for novelty appears in, for example, a summer salad combining dandelion leaves, salsify and cannabis seeds. A startling but successful main course has been brandade of smoked haddock and blue cheese (Fourme d'Ambert) with potato and olive oil, and the establishment's free-range/organic emphasis surfaces in 'cotelettes de mouton Herdwick' with a fresh mint aïoli. Appealing desserts such as a dainty apricot charlotte with raspberry coulis, or crème brûlée made with celery and green apple, all pass muster. Good-humoured service is by 'slinky young Frenchmen'. The wine list concentrates on southern French regions (no claret or burgundy), but choices are sound and prices not bad for central London (starting at £12.50 for vins de pays).

CHEF: Sebastien Gagnebé   PROPRIETOR: Thierry Bouteloup   OPEN: Mon to Sat 12 to 3, 6 to 11   CLOSED: 24 to 30 Dec, bank hols   MEALS: alc D (main courses £12.50 to £17.95). Set L and D 6 to 6.45 £16.95 (2 courses) to £19.75   SERVICE: 12.5% (optional), card slips closed   CARDS: Amex, Delta, MasterCard, Switch, Visa   DETAILS: 35 seats. 20 seats outside. Private parties: 8 main room, 8 to 18 private rooms. Vegetarian meals. Children's helpings. No smoking in 1 dining room. No music. Air-conditioned

## Tsunami

| | |
|---|---|
| | **NEW ENTRY**   map 12 |
| Unit 3, 5–7 Voltaire Road, SW4 6DQ | COOKING 2 |
| TEL: (020) 7978 1610   FAX: (020) 7978 1591 | JAPANESE |
| | £30–£63 |

'A Japanese restaurant in a railway siding between Clapham and Brixton ... unthinkable a decade ago,' observed an inspector, but now this 'worthy and wonderful energetic place' provides 'an oasis of cool' in one of London's darkest reaches. Chef Jimmi Nakamura has worked at Nobu and Ubon (see entries, London) and it shows; if he is trying to 'democratise the élitism' of his rivals (as one visitor reckoned), then he appears to have succeeded, because prices are much less frightening. Sushi disappointed at inspection, but other items scored highly: agedashi tofu with grated daikon and dashi dressing was a traditional dish presented imaginatively; tempura of aubergines could not be faulted; but best of all was a starter of superbly fresh prawns intertwined with 'pastry' made from butternut squash, plus a 'heavenly' butternut squash sauce. Waiting times can be long, but this is a relaxed place run by a charming multi-racial team. Beer or saké may be better bets than house wine (£12).

CHEFS: Antony Tam and Jimmi Nakamura  PROPRIETORS: Ken Sam and Ni Lennette  OPEN: Mon to Sat D only 6 to 10.45 (11.15 Fri and Sat)  CLOSED: 25 and 26 Dec; open bank hols  MEALS: alc (main courses £6.50 to £14). Set D £30 to £35  SERVICE: 12.5% (optional), card slips closed  CARDS: Amex, Delta, MasterCard, Switch, Visa  DETAILS: 100 seats. Private parties: 100 main room. Vegetarian meals. Children's helpings. No-smoking area. Occasional music ⊖ Clapham North

---

# Two Brothers £     map 12

297–303 Regents Park Road, N3 1DP     COOKING 1
TEL: (020) 8346 0469  FAX: (020) 8343 1978     FISH 'N' CHIPS
WEBSITE: www.twobrothers.co.uk     £20–£49

Despite the cosmopolitan streak that nowadays runs through the nation's gastronomic consciousness, there will always be a place for well-made, traditional fish and chips. And as far as north London is concerned, this is it. The unchanging menu offers a standard range of fish, fried in batter or matzo meal – or just steamed or grilled as a concession to the health-conscious – and served with piles of chips and home-made tartare sauce. Jellied eels, cod roe in batter, or avocado with prawns are among starters, and side orders naturally feature mushy peas, gherkins, and pickled onions. Own-label house white from the Côtes de Duras is £9.80, and the rest of the list is a short but varied selection.

CHEFS/PROPRIETORS: Leon and Tony Manzi  OPEN: Tue to Sat 12 to 2.30, 5.30 to 10.15  CLOSED: Christmas, last two weeks Aug, bank hol Mon and Tue  MEALS: alc (main courses £8 to £18.50)  SERVICE: not inc, 10% for parties of 6 or more, card slips closed  CARDS: Amex, Delta, MasterCard, Switch, Visa  DETAILS: 90 seats. Children's helpings. No-smoking area. No cigars/pipes in dining room. Occasional music. Air-conditioned ⊖ Finchley Central

---

# Ubon     map 12

34 Westferry Circus, Canary Wharf, E14 8RR     COOKING 4
TEL: (020) 7719 7800  FAX: (020) 7719 7801     JAPANESE
    £42–£112

The styling in this handsome fourth-floor dining room, just behind the Four Seasons Hotel, is minimal, with dark wooden floors, tall white pillars and a high ceiling. It is spacious, light and comfortable, with a river view adding to the overall pleasure: catch the sunset if you can. Under the same ownership and direction as Nobu (see entry), it goes in for a similar collection of dishes grouped into sushi, sashimi, specials and the like. The menu can be a bit perplexing, since there is no telling whether, for instance, special dishes come in large or small portions (appetisers and mains are listed separately), but staff are on hand to help.

Fine ingredients and some inventive ideas are woven together to produce clear tastes and textures, and the array of dishes is tempting, ranging from lobster ceviche (reminding us that South America is one strand running through

Nobu Matsuhisa's food) to soft-shell crab roll, from spicy sour shrimp to sea urchin tempura. Traditional sushi and sashimi also stand up well, taking in both seawater and freshwater eel, snow crab, and smelt egg as well as toro. Dishes are attractively presented, although the downside is high prices, for both food and wine: the latter well chosen but offering not a single bottle under £20. Half a dozen wines by the glass under £6.50 are one way of getting round the problem.

CHEF: Nobu Matsuhisa  PROPRIETORS: B.S. Ong and Nobu Matsuhisa  OPEN: Mon to Fri L 12 to 2.30, Mon to Sat D 6 to 10.30  CLOSED: bank hols  MEALS: alc (main courses £13.50 to £24). Set L £25 to £40, Set D £70  SERVICE: 12.5% (optional), card slips closed  CARDS: Amex, Delta, Diners, MasterCard, Switch, Visa  DETAILS: 120 seats. Private parties: 130 main room. Car park. Vegetarian meals. No cigars/pipes in dining room. Wheelchair access (also WC). Music. Air-conditioned  ⊖ Canary Wharf, Westferry (DLR)  £5

## The Vale 🕏✗
map 13

99 Chippenham Road, W9 2AB

TEL: (020) 7266 0990  FAX: (020) 7286 7224

EMAIL: valew9@hotmail.com

COOKING 1

MODERN BRITISH

£23–£47

On a corner site, with the main body of the place devoted to drinking, and conservatory-style dining rooms extending out onto the pavement, The Vale embraces the values of a neighbourhood restaurant. Agreeable prices, generous portions and a daily-changing menu are all designed to entice locals in on a regular basis, and reports endorse the strategy: 'I'll certainly be back' is a common conclusion. The draw is a brasserie-type range of offerings – salads, pasta and egg dishes are as numerous as meat and fish main courses – from garbure to deep-fried salt cod fishcakes, from eggs Benedict to Seville orange curd tart. Praise comes in for a fragile buttery tartlet with a well-judged filling of egg and smoked haddock, and for first-class pappardelle with chunks of chicken and rabbit in an unctuous porcini-dominated sauce. Sharply chosen wines at generally reasonable prices starting at £10.50 add to the appeal.

CHEF: Robin Tarver  PROPRIETORS: Francesca Melman and Robin Tarver  OPEN: Tue to Fri L 12.30 to 2.30, Mon to Sat D 7 to 11, Sun brunch 11 to 5  CLOSED: 29 to 31 Dec and Easter weekend  MEALS: alc (main courses L £8 to £12.50 and D £9 to £14). Set L £9.50 (2 courses) to £12, Set D £12 (2 courses) to £15. Sun brunch menu also available  SERVICE: 12.5% (optional), card slips closed  CARDS: Delta, Diners, MasterCard, Switch, Visa  DETAILS: 70 seats. Private parties: 40 main room, 14 to 40 private rooms. Vegetarian meals. Children's helpings. No smoking in 1 dining room. Wheelchair access (not WC). Occasional music. Air-conditioned  ⊖ Maida Vale  £5

## Vama – the Indian Room
NEW ENTRY  map 13

438 King's Road, SW10 0LJ

TEL: (020) 7565 8500  FAX: (020) 7565 8501

WEBSITE: www.vama.co.uk

COOKING 1

PUNJABI

£39–£85

This smart, modern Indian restaurant has a few terrace tables, where you can enjoy the roar of the King's Road traffic. But it is light and airy inside, with a lantern-ceilinged back room and Indian pictures and artefacts offsetting any bareness. The food is neatly presented without straying too far westwards, although flavours rarely match up to menu descriptions, and the symbol on the menu for 'chilli hot' is seldom justified. Ingredients are of excellent quality, especially lamb and vegetables – for example, sag gosht, 'cooked with great care', and rustami khumb bahar, a starter of mushrooms stuffed with home-made cheese and pomegranate – and meticulous cooking is shown in cracklingly crisp, dry poppadoms, 'perfect' steamed basmati rice, and soft, thin roomali bread. Europeanised desserts are best avoided. Service is friendly and helpful, and the short, international wine list starts at £12.95 and includes a dozen by the glass.

CHEF: Andy Varma   PROPRIETORS: Andy and Arjun Varma   OPEN: all week 12 to 3, 6.30 to 11.30   CLOSED: 25 and 26 Dec, 1 Jan   MEALS: alc (main courses £6.50 to £26). Set L Mon to Sat £5 (2 courses), Buffet L Sun £11.95. Cover £1   SERVICE: not inc, 12.5% for parties of 6 or more   CARDS: Amex, Delta, Diners, MasterCard, Switch, Visa   DETAILS: 90 seats. 8 seats outside. Private parties: 30 main room. Vegetarian meals. Wheelchair access (not WC). Music. Air-conditioned   ⊖ Sloane Square

## Villandry ⅔✱                                                         map 15

170 Great Portland Street, W1W 5QB                                      COOKING 3
TEL: (020) 7631 3131   FAX: (020) 7631 3030                    MODERN EUROPEAN
                                                                        £32–£56

A broad glass frontage tempts passers-by in to this multi-purpose foodie haven that combines a deli, a florist, a café-bar and a restaurant. 'You cannot help but browse' as you pass through the food hall on the way to the simple dining room at the rear, which has a laid-back and convivial atmosphere. 'Simplicity is key' is the mantra of the kitchen, as typified by starters of marinated organic salmon with cucumber and dill salad, or wild mushrooms on toast with garlic and thyme butter, and by main courses such as grilled chicken breast with pesto, or fillet of cod with leek and potato gratin and tapénade. A reporter praised 'tender and pink' roast pigeon breast with green beans, almonds and sultanas, and pan-fried cod fillet with leek and potato broth and crayfish velouté, but concluded that prices are on the high side for cooking that can occasionally take simplicity too far into the realms of ordinariness. A short but well-chosen wine list spans a wide price range but offers fair choice under £20. Prices start at £12.50.

CHEF: Steve Evenett-Watts   PROPRIETOR: Martha Greene   OPEN: all week L 12 to 3.30 (11 to 4 Sun), Mon to Sat D 6 to 10.30   MEALS: alc (main courses £10 to £18.50). Bar menu available Mon to Sat   SERVICE: 12.5% (optional), card slips closed   CARDS: Amex, Delta, Diners, MasterCard, Switch, Visa   DETAILS: 100 seats. Private parties: 12 to 80 private rooms. Vegetarian meals. No smoking in dining room. Wheelchair access (not WC). No music. Air-conditioned   ⊖ Great Portland Street

## Wagamama ⅔✱ £                                                        map 15

4A Streatham Street, WC1A 1JB                                          COOKING 1
TEL: (020) 7323 9223                                            JAPANESE-STYLE
WEBSITE: wwww.wagamama.com                                              £16–£27

The Wagamama brand is stronger than ever, with branches carefully placed in key locations around the capital; Soho, Leicester Square, Covent Garden and Camden among them. The fact that they remain wholly owned – only the branches outside the UK are franchised – has helped ensure that standards have been maintained. The formula has not changed since their mid-'90s opening here at Streatham Street, and people still queue (although with so many branches you stand a better chance than before of walking straight in) for bowls of ramen or teppan-fried noodles. An inspector was satisfied with amai udon, the soft-fried tofu and plump prawns demonstrating that good ingredients are handled correctly, while ebi gyoza (deep-fried dumplings) are a good accompaniment. Desserts, listed on the paper table mats, are somewhat incidental. Service is cheerful and friendly, although the computerised ordering system means that the safe completion of your order is in the hands of Bill Gates. Tables are basic and communal, but that's the point. Drink house wine (£10.35) and green tea, or choose from a selection of raw juices.

CHEF: Mon Khadraoui   PROPRIETOR: Graphite   OPEN: all week 12 to 11 (Sun 12.30 to 10) CLOSED: 25 and 26 Dec   MEALS: alc (main courses £5 to £8). Set L and D £9.95 (2 courses) to £10.95 (2 courses)   SERVICE: not inc   CARDS: Amex, MasterCard, Switch, Visa   DETAILS: 136 seats. Vegetarian meals. No smoking in dining room. No music. Air-conditioned   ⊖ Tottenham Court Road

# Wapping Food                                        map 12

Wapping Hydraulic Power Station,
Wapping Wall, E1W 3ST
TEL: (020) 7680 2080   FAX: (020) 7680 2081                        COOKING 3
EMAIL: wappingfood@wapping-wpt.com   MODERN EUROPEAN/MEDITERRANEAN
WEBSITE: www.wapping-wpt.com                                      £36–£54

Hydraulic electricity-generation may be a thing of the past, but this former power station's cavernous shell lives on as a stylish venue for contemporary food and art. The setting rates highly for atmosphere, with the remains of old machinery redeployed as decorative sculpture and juxtaposed against displays of performance and video art. A similarly eclectic note rings through the cooking, which takes the Mediterranean as its centre of gravity but roams further afield for some ideas. For starters, toasted goats' cheese is partnered with watercress, pear and walnut salad, while deep-fried oysters are accompanied by cod 'chitterlings', onion rings, lemon and aïoli. Main courses range from roast stuffed chicken breast with Jerusalem artichokes and creamed leeks, to monkfish saltimbocca with Puy lentils and green beans, via slow-roast belly of pork with braised Savoy cabbage, mash and 'mustard fruits'. To finish there may be Sauternes crème caramel, or rhubarb cheesecake. The wine list is all-Australian (apart from champagne) and features some well-chosen producers and reasonable mark-ups. Wines are divided by style, with ten by the glass (£3.60 to £6.15). Bottle prices start at £14.75

CHEF: Justin Aubrey   PROPRIETOR: Wapping Restaurants Ltd   OPEN: all week L 12 to 3, Mon to Sat D 7 to 10.30   CLOSED: 25 to 28 Dec, Good Fri   MEALS: alc (main courses £11.50 to £16) SERVICE: 12.5% (optional), card slips closed   CARDS: Amex, Delta, Diners, MasterCard, Switch, Visa   DETAILS: 150 seats. 30 seats outside. Private parties: 150 main room. Car park. Vegetarian meals. Wheelchair access (also WC). Occasional music   ⊖ Wapping  £5

# Waterloo Bar and Kitchen  map 13

131 Waterloo Road, SE1 8UR                    COOKING 2
TEL: (020) 7928 5086                              GLOBAL
                                                  £26–£37

This cavernous open-plan space gets its name from its location (close to Waterloo Station, behind the Old Vic), the small bar area in one corner where drinkers congregate, and the open-plan kitchen at the back. The atmosphere is lively and informal, with plenty of hubbub created by a varied clientele who all seem to be having a good time. Food is generally straightforward and not too challenging, though there is plenty to appeal in the global style: strong, richly flavoured boar terrine set off by a sharp redcurrant sauce is from the classical end of the spectrum, while Asian-style prawn cocktail with naan suits more modern tastes. Main courses might be as rustic and hearty as wood-roasted chicken breast with flageolet beans and chorizo, or as refined as grilled halibut with sauté spinach, new potatoes and hollandaise. Finish perhaps with 'gloriously and unashamedly calorific' Eton mess. A blackboard lists two dozen or so wines, all but one under £20. Prices start at £10.50.

CHEF: Bruce Miller   PROPRIETOR: Clive Watson   OPEN: Mon to Fri L 12 to 2.45, Mon to Sat D 5.30 to 10.30   CLOSED: bank hols   MEALS: alc (main courses L £8 to £10, D £10 to £12). Set L £11.95 to £13.95 (both 2 courses), Set D £13.95 to £15.95 (both 2 courses)   SERVICE: not inc, 10% for parties of 6 or more   CARDS: Amex, Delta, Diners, MasterCard, Switch, Visa   DETAILS: 60 seats. 9 seats outside. Private parties: 50 main room. Vegetarian meals. Music   ⊖ Waterloo

---

# ▲ West Street ♥          NEW ENTRY   map 15

13–15 West Street, WC2H 9NE                    COOKING 4
TEL: (020) 7010 8600   FAX: (020) 7010 8601       ITALIAN
EMAIL: office@westreet.net                        £23–£64

A big glass frontage leads to a ground-floor eating area with a wood-fired oven, a basement bar, and a first-floor dining room done mostly in black and white. Casual eating appears to be one of the operation's main targets, given pizzas on the ground floor and a long menu in the main room that deals in salady starters, pasta that can be eaten as a first or main course (cubes of spinach and ricotta gnocchi doused in butter and sprinkled with finely grated Parmesan), and a handful of fish dishes. There are some interesting cheese options too, including artichoke with smoked Provolone, spicy chorizo with mozzarella, and a generously sized crisp pastry tart filled with a moist, creamy mix of endive and Gorgonzola, its richness countered by a pile of salad leaves.

Scope for more substantial meals is evident from braised beef in Barolo, and pink veal kidney, sliced into tiny pieces, served with a few chanterelles. Vegetable side dishes are a prominent feature, taking in pumpkin with toasted almonds, baked tomatoes with cream and basil, and well-judged green lentils mixed with pinhead-sized diced vegetables. The Italian thrust continues into desserts of lemon polenta cake with amaretti ice cream, Vin Santo with biscotti, and a rich mousse-like chocolate semi-freddo with the texture of velvet, accompanied by an even better espresso sorbet. Service is a strength: accommodating, charming, properly trained and well managed. Wines lean heavily to Italians, and Italian varietals from the New World, rounded out with French offerings. The result is some interesting drinking, thankfully at prices that are not too difficult to swallow (a large proportion of the bottles cost less than £25). Twenty-four imaginative selections are available by the glass; bottle prices start at £12.

CHEF: Lawrence Keogh   PROPRIETOR: Mirror Image Restaurants plc   OPEN: all week L 12 to 3, Mon to Sat D 5.45 to 12   CLOSED: 25 and 26 Dec, Easter Sun and Mon   MEALS: alc (main courses £7 to £17.50). Set L £10.50 (2 courses) to £17.50, Set D 5.45 to 7.15 and 10.15 to 12 £10.50 (2 courses) to £12.50. Bar menu available   SERVICE: 12.5% (optional), card slips closed   CARDS: Amex, Delta, Diners, MasterCard, Switch, Visa   DETAILS: 160 seats. Private parties: main room 35. Vegetarian meals. Wheelchair access (also WC). Music. Air-conditioned   ACCOMMODATION: 3 rooms, all with bath/shower. TV. Phone. B&B £250 to £450. Rooms for disabled (*The Which? Hotel Guide*)

## William IV 🍴 £   map 12

786 Harrow Road, NW10 5JX   COOKING 2
TEL: (020) 8969 5944   FAX: (020) 8964 9218   MODERN EUROPEAN
WEBSITE: www.william-iv.co.uk   £25–£43

The location on a stretch of the Harrow Road not far from Kensal Green Tube may not be the most auspicious around, but this roomy Victorian pub is in confident mood. Bar and restaurant are separate, and the place also has the advantage of a big garden for fine-weather eating. Sensibly tight menus that follow the seasons have a sunny Mediterranean feel. Starters are simple assemblages such as chorizo, tomato and Gruyère bruschetta, or rare spiced duck with noodle salad (one of a couple of interlopers from the Orient). The Mediterranean theme is continued in seared swordfish with ratatouille and Jerusalem artichoke purée, and in kleftiko with aromatic rice and olives. Among half a dozen desserts might be prune and Armagnac tart, or good old-fashioned greengage crumble. Serving staff are young, neat and competent. Single-course lunches include a pint of beer or a glass of wine. The full wine list is organised by style and priced from £10.75.

CHEF: Sarah Farrell   PROPRIETORS: Carlos Horrillo, Patrick Morcas and Nick Daniel   OPEN: all week 12 to 3 (4 Sat and Sun), 6 to 11 (10.30 Mon to Wed, 10 Sun)   CLOSED: 25 and 26 Dec   MEALS: alc (main courses £7.50 to £13.50). Set L £7.75 (1 course), Set D 6 to 8 £9 (2 courses). Bar menu also available   SERVICE: 10% (optional), card slips closed   CARDS: Amex, Delta, Diners, MasterCard, Switch, Visa   DETAILS: 70 seats. 50 seats outside. Private parties: 45 main room. Vegetarian meals. Music. No mobile phones   ⊖ Kensal Green  (£5)

## Wiltons   map 15

55 Jermyn Street, SW1Y 6LX
TEL: (020) 7629 9955   FAX: (020) 7495 6233   | NEW CHEF |
EMAIL: wiltons@wiltons.co.uk   TRADITIONAL ENGLISH
WEBSITE: www.wiltons.co.uk   £42–£108

Jerome Ponchelle was groomed to take over from Michel Bourdin when the latter retired from the Connaught (see entry), but that plan went out the window with the arrival of Gordon Ramsay and Angela Hartnett. The only other restaurant as remotely conservative and traditional as the Connaught is this 'living national treasure', under the same ownership now for 60 years; so perhaps it is no surprise that this is where Ponchelle should fetch up. The last thing that Wiltons customers are likely to want is change, so rest assured that the à la carte's range of hors d'oeuvres (from potted shrimps to Beluga caviar) remains, as do the grills and the Dover sole meunière. Only the odd dish – such as a terrine of duck, pork and foie gras 'Michel Bourdin' – betrays a shift, and that is hardly seismic. Wines will contribute substantially to an already hefty food bill, with nothing on the list under £25.

CHEF: Jerome Ponchelle   PROPRIETORS: the Hambro family   OPEN: Sun to Fri 12 to 2.30, 6.15 to 10.30   MEALS: alc (main courses £8 to £30). Cover £1.50   SERVICE: not inc   CARDS: Amex, Delta, Diners, MasterCard, Switch, Visa   DETAILS: 75 seats. Private parties: 20 main room. Jacket and tie. Wheelchair access (not WC). No music. No mobile phones. Air-conditioned
⊖ Green Park

---

## Yatra

map 15

34 Dover Street, W1S 4NF
TEL: (020) 7493 0200   FAX: (020) 7493 4228                          COOKING 3
EMAIL: yatra@lineone.net                                                   INDIAN
WEBSITE: www.yatra.co.uk                                             £27–£70

Cast in the chic mould of new-wave Indian restaurants, this smart venue has lots of up-to-the-minute touches – a black tiled floor, some tables fashioned from black stone, subdued spotlighting – while downstairs is a bar/disco where the music often throbs. The menu has been condensed since last year (more 'user friendly', say the owners), but still mixes traditional and contemporary cooking with influences from across the Subcontinent. There is a classical ring to aloo tikki (spiced mashed potato cakes), rogan josh and Malabar prawn curry, but much of the interest is in more modern ideas. Steamed rock lobster with ginger and lime on a gram flour crêpe is a typically adventurous starter, while main courses might range from tandoori salmon on coriander risotto with Parmesan shavings to Railway lamb (an Anglo-Indian speciality from track-laying days). Vegetables also show touches of invention. Prices are by no means cheap, and there is a minimum charge for food of £19.50 per head, although affordable set menus are available up to 7.30pm. Wines include a sizeable contingent from the New World, as well as trio from India; house French is £14 (£3.50 a glass).

CHEF: Krishna Bal Negi   PROPRIETOR: Cafe Bollywood (UK) Ltd   OPEN: Mon to Fri L 12 to 2.45, all week D 6 to 11 (11.30 Thur to Sat)   CLOSED: 25 and 26 Dec, 1 Jan   MEALS: alc (main courses £6.50 to £18.50). Set L and D 6 to 7.30 £9.50 (1 course) to £14.50, Set L and D £23.50 (2 courses) to £32.50. Min charge £19.50 after 7.30. Bar menu also available   SERVICE: 12.5% (optional)   CARDS: Amex, Delta, MasterCard, Switch, Visa   DETAILS: 155 seats. Private parties: 106 main room. Vegetarian meals. No cigars/pipes in dining room. Wheelchair access (also WC). Music. Air-conditioned   ⊖ Green Park  £5

---

*The Guide relies on feedback from its readers. Especially welcome are reports on new restaurants appearing in the book for the first time. All letters to the Guide are acknowledged.*

---

# Zafferano

map 14

15 Lowndes Street, SW1X 9EY
TEL: (020) 7235 5800   FAX: (020) 7235 1971

COOKING 6
ITALIAN
£36–£83

A couple of rooms, fashioned from an odd-shaped space behind the long frontage, captivatingly combine smartness and informality. The bare brick walls, tiled floor and small tables don't put off the affluent locals, who make a beeline for this place. Success rests on a succession of flawless ingredients: maybe a simple May-time pea and broad bean salad with a first-class dressing, or a deconstructed pigeon, breast pink and flavourful, served with a gentle garlic purée and a superb stock-based sauce. The food soothes, with silky risottos skilfully made 'the old-fashioned, proper way': perhaps a Parmesan and black truffle version, with a pool of stock and red wine sauce, or a yet more indulgent one of foie gras and truffle.

Not everything is from the luxury end of the spectrum, however, as the kitchen also comes up with a calf's trotter and artichoke salad, oxtail ravioli, and knobbly chunks of veal sweetbread in a Marsala-injected sauce of dried morels. Much of the food has a northern Italian bias – a dish of light gnocchi with melted Taleggio and smoky speck, for instance, constituting 'a perfect marriage of flavours' – but there are simple, sunny, Mediterranean presentations too, including a slice of moist and palpably fresh halibut, served with black olives and cherry tomatoes, full of colour and vitality. Tiramisù is a decent version; sensual chocolate fondant is even better, epitomising the kitchen's quiet skill and professionalism. Breads come with good olive oil for dipping, service is well drilled, and from a selection of around 300 wines, house red and white start at £14.50, or £3.50 a glass.

CHEF: Andy Needham   PROPRIETOR: A To Z Restaurants Ltd   OPEN: all week 12 to 2.30, 6.30 to 10.45   CLOSED: 25 Dec, 1 Jan   MEALS: Set L Mon to Fri £19.50 (2 courses) to £28.50, Set L Sat and Sun and Set D £29.50 (2 courses) to £41.50   SERVICE: not inc   CARDS: Amex, Delta, Diners, MasterCard, Switch, Visa   DETAILS: 45 seats. Vegetarian meals. Children's helpings. No cigars/pipes in dining room. Occasional music. Air-conditioned   ⊖ Knightsbridge

# Zaika

map 13

1 Kensington High Street, W8 5NP
TEL: (020) 7795 6533   FAX: (020) 7937 8854
WEBSITE: www.cuisine-collection.co.uk

COOKING 5
MODERN INDIAN
£26–£81

In this former bank, transformed into a smart, attractive, stylish dining room by means of a few statues and drapes of silk, Vineet Bhatia's new-wave cooking can take you by surprise. 'We are all regular curry eaters, and none of us has ever experienced anything like it.' You won't find grilled lobster with curry leaf and broccoli risotto on a typical High Street Indian menu.

Some items are familiar – butter chicken, lamb biryani – but much of Zaika's appeal lies in combining Eastern and Western ideas into novel dishes, interesting and subtly spiced. Bhatia's sound culinary intelligence gives results a pleasing sense of inevitability; tandoori-spiced smoked salmon may be the most obvious example, but one might also come across scallops poached in coconut milk flavoured with mangosteen and spices, served with chilli mash. The repertoire runs from tandoori pheasant with Punjabi spices, to vegetarian items such as pineapple soup with peppercorns and coriander, or a sweet-and-sour potato salad incorporating sweetened yoghurt and tamarind chutney. Desserts take in carrot halva with cardamom sorbet, and tandoori saffron pineapple.

Lunch is considered 'great value'. The cover charge pays for poppadoms and chutneys, and staff are friendly, chatty and anxious to please. The wine list has plenty of 'important' wines from Bordeaux, Burgundy and Tuscany, though good selections from Alsace and the Loire add a note of food-friendliness; Australia and New Zealand also shine. Mark-ups are not greedy, and there are some gems, including Grüner Veltliner Alte Reben from Austria (£24.50). Prices start at £14.50, and 13 come by the glass (£4.50 to £6.75).

CHEF: Vineet Bhatia  PROPRIETOR: Cuisine Collection  OPEN: Sun to Fri L 12 to 2.45, all week D 6.30 to 10.45 (10 Sun)  CLOSED: Christmas  MEALS: alc (main courses £11 to £24.50). Set L £11.95 (2 courses) to £13.95, Set D £33.50 to £75 (inc wine). Cover £1.50  SERVICE: 12.5% (optional), card slips closed  CARDS: Amex, Delta, MasterCard, Switch, Visa  DETAILS: 85 seats. Private parties: 20 main room. Vegetarian meals. No cigars/pipes in dining room. Wheelchair access (not WC). Music. Air-conditioned  ⊖ Kensington High Street

## Zuma ▼ ✳

NEW ENTRY    map 14

5 Raphael Street, SW7 1DL
TEL: (020) 7584 1010   FAX: (020) 7584 5005
EMAIL: info@zumarestaurant.com
WEBSITE: www.zumarestaurant.com

COOKING 5
MODERN JAPANESE
£33–£80

Despite the slightly forbidding exterior of this Knightsbridge office block, Zuma inhabits a large, high-ceilinged space, its layout based on that of a Zen garden: floors are pale grey stone, and walls are covered in highly polished wood. The effect is remarkable, even if the noise level suggests something other than a Zen-like peace. On one side of the restaurant is a bar, while centre stage is dedicated to a sushi bar and a robata (a trench-like chargrill).

The long, often inventive, menu is not divided up traditionally, by methods of cooking, but into vegetables, seafood, meat, and a few specials. It starts with 'small dishes and salads', including charcoal-grilled vegetables rolled in yuba (tofu 'skin') with soy mustard sauce; and home-made tofu, with a pleasantly grainy texture, served with ginger, spring onion, bonito flakes, miso, and chopped pickled daikon. Sushi and sashimi are based on superbly fresh fish: hand-rolled sushi include the intriguing-sounding dynamite spider roll, consisting of soft-shell crab, cucumber and jalapeño peppers. From the robata may come chicken wings with sea salt accentuated by lime juice, or ayu, a Japanese river fish served with kinome (young sansho leaf) vinegar. 'Zuma dishes' may take in marinated black cod, or nasudengaku (grilled aubergine with sweet miso). Desserts, such as Granny Smith sorbet and lychee wine gelée, are not in the same class.

Service is well timed, order-taking is skilled, and knowledge of menu and drinks list is excellent. Wines are a globetrotting collection, dominated by forward-looking New World producers and food-friendly styles from Austria, Alsace and the Loire. Twenty-one sakés, sold in various sizes, round out the inventive list. Wine prices start at £16, and in addition ten wines are sold by the glass from £4.75.

CHEFS: Colin Clague and Takemi Tanaka  PROPRIETORS: Rainier Becker, Divia Lalvani and Arjun Waney  OPEN: all week L 12 to 2.30, Mon to Sat D 6.30 to 11  MEALS: alc (dishes from £3 to £18.50). Set L £11.50 to £14.50  SERVICE: 12.5%, card slips closed  CARDS: Amex, MasterCard, Switch, Visa  DETAILS: 108 seats. Private parties: 24 main room, 8 to 24 private rooms. Vegetarian meals. No smoking in 1 dining room. Wheelchair access (also WC). Music. Air-conditioned  ⊖ Knightsbridge

# London Round-ups

With so many venues vying for attention, finding a place to eat out in London that offers the right blend of food, location, style and price to suit the occasion can often be very much down to potluck. This section aims to make choosing easier by providing details of a broad range of restaurants, bistros, cafés, hotel dining rooms, and so on, that are deserving of attention, though they do not merit a full entry. There are also one or two rising stars, well worth keeping an eye on, and in some cases establishments have been included here rather than in the main entries because of significant late changes or a lack of positive feedback. Reports on these places are particularly welcome. Brief details of opening times and prices are given in each entry where available.

**Adam Street Restaurant**   WC2
9 Adam Street   map 15
(020) 7379 8000
A private members' club in the evening, at lunchtime this stylish, spacious and informal newcomer in an historic Robert Adam building opens to the public. Chef Alastair Ross moved on as the Guide was going to press, and his number-two Chris Keil now holds the culinary reins. Expect a typical metropolitan menu bolstered by some classics (main courses £9 to £18) and backed up by a ravishing wine list: each bottle has been carefully chosen, the range is global and prices are fair. Eight 'club selections' from £13.50 to £19.50 also come by the glass (£3.50 to £5). Reports please. Open Mon to Fri L.

**Aka**   WC1
18 West Central Street   map 15
(020) 7836 0110
Groovy cocktails, thumping music and a giant screen for sports addicts set the clubby tone of this Covent Garden joint. Food seems almost incidental, but there are up-to-the-minute ideas on the main menu: chargrilled squid and black pudding with spring onion and Cheddar mash (£5.50), or confit of corn-fed chicken with sauté ceps and Savoy cabbage (£9.50), for example, with spiced banana tarte Tatin to finish (£4.50). Light dishes – tempura prawns, or unleavened bread with chorizo and hummus – are served in the bar. The short, sharp wine list, starting at £12.50, includes six by the glass. Open Tue to Sat D only.

**Asakusa**   NW1
265 Eversholt Street   map 13
(020) 7388 8399
This cramped eating house might have been transplanted straight from Tokyo, along with many of its clientele. Untranslated special dishes on wall posters are no more help for non-Japanese than the friendly but mostly monoglot staff, so a set meal may be a wise choice. To compose your own menu, remember the importance of varied cooking methods rather than ingredients. Sashimi, grilled salmon, yakitori, with a tempura set were the choice of a satisfied reporter. Alternatively, point to a wall poster and see what comes – the surprise may be a pleasant one, and the cost minimal. Main courses £5.30–£8.50. Open Mon to Sat D.

**L'Auberge**   SW15
22 Upper Richmond Road   map 12
(020) 8874 3593
The name befits this re-creation, between Putney and Wandsworth, of a rural French village restaurant, run by Madame in front, and Monsieur in the kitchen. An inspector found escargots in crisp flaky pastry cases on creamy garlic sauce (£4.95) – a novel twist on a classic combination – and also approved the 'vibrant mushroom flavour' of a terrine of petits legumes, including French beans

and asparagus (£4.75). 'Juicy and tasty' guinea-fowl breast (£11.50) was lifted by green olives, just as the brill fillet (£14.50) was enhanced by whole, deep-fried capers. Short, all-French wine list; champagne £5 a glass. Open Tue to Sat for D.

**L'Aventure**      NW8
3 Blenheim Terrace      map 13
(020) 7624 6232
This restaurant, with its attractive terrace garden, is true to its French roots in offering only set-price menus (dinner £29.50), but seven dishes at each course provide plenty of choice. A reporter found service slow and far from overattentive, and diners' knowledge of classical menu French is assumed: feuilleté d'escargots aux pleurots, and salade d'artichaut aux pignons have featured as starters; and filet de boeuf poêlé, sauce Bercy, or lotte rôtie, sauce au pistou, as main courses. Finish with tarte fine aux pommes, or île flottante for nostalgia, and note that the menu's wine 'recommendations' are treats, not house wines. Open Mon to Fri L, Mon to Sat D.

**Azou**      W6
375 King Street      map 12
(020) 8563 7266
At this small, brightly coloured restaurant the cooking plays variations on Moroccan, Algerian and Tunisian themes. Start perhaps with baba ghanoush (£3.95). The centrepiece couscous and tagine dishes include Algerian couscous royale (with lamb shank, chicken breast and merguez; £14.50), and Moroccan chicken tagine with olives and preserved lemon (£8.95). Parties of up to 12 can pre-order mechoui: whole spiced roast lamb served buffet-style. A tiny wine list starts at £9.70. Open Mon to Fri for L, all week for D.

**Balzac Bistro**      W12
4 Wood Lane      map 12
(020) 8743 6787
Choose from a set menu, £12.90 for two courses, or à la carte, for the bistro cooking we have long known and loved. Try

calamari in garlic butter, or pappardelle with rabbit compote (£5.50), then chicken breast wrapped in Parma ham with goats' cheese and rösti (£10.90). After that tribute to the Italian owner, further consider Tatin of caramelised red onion and fresh goats' cheese (£5.20), boeuf bourguignon (£10.90), or rabbit casserole with olives (£11.90) – dishes as French as the simple décor or the vin maison (blanc or rouge at £10.90). Closed Sat D and Sun.

**Belgo Centraal/Noord**
50 Earlham Street (Centraal)      WC2
(020) 7813 2233

72 Chalk Farm Road (Noord)      NW1
(020) 7267 0718      maps 15/13
Mussels, frites, and beer made Belgo famous, but the menus now range far and wide. Start with borscht, duck terrine, cheese croquettes with piccalilli, or mixed charcuterie. Continue with roast cod with clams, roasted peppers and a basil-flavoured cream (£10.95), spit-roast chicken basted in blond beer (£8.95), or wild boar sausages with stoemp (Belgian bubble and squeak) (£8.95). But in the end can you resist one of the ten mussel platters or pots? Express lunch and beat-the-clock menus are good value, and in either you can choose between mussels, or slow-roast pork belly with sticky rice and pak choi. Drink Belgian beer. Open all week. Belgo Zuid in Ladbroke Grove, W10, has closed.

**Bellamys Dining Room**      SE11
332 Kennington Lane      map 13
(020) 7582 9569
This rather elegant little modern restaurant certainly stands out in deepest Vauxhall. Its menu (main courses £9.95 to £12.95) is more down to earth than before and the high point of a reporter's meal was chicken livers with Parmentier potatoes; rabbit and tagliatelle was acceptable but the kitchen's limits were exposed by cottage pie with buttered vegetables. Finish with rhubarb and custard or Eton mess. Jurançon sec and Vouvray Brut stand out in a short, interesting wine list from £11.50. Closed Mon D, Sun and Sat.

### Bertorelli's                                    WC2
44A Floral Street                                  map 15
(020) 7836 3969

Convenient for a post-Puccini supper or a pre-Verdi high tea, Bertorelli's has an Italian menu and an equally patriotic wine list. Smoked salmon comes with herb potato salad, beetroot, crispy pancetta and a salsa verde dressing, but more typical is bresaola with truffled artichokes, minestrone, or a selection of cured meats. Pasta or risotto may precede, or replace, modish main courses, such as monkfish tail with blackeye beans, rocket, salami, and mustard sauce (£13.95), or calf's liver with pancetta, sage, red onions and parsnip purée (£12.50). Wines, from £10.50, include 12 by the glass. Closed Sun. Other branches are at 19 Charlotte Street, W1, tel. (020) 7636 4174, and 11 Frith Street, W1, tel. (020) 7494 3491.

### Boisdale                                        SW1
15 Eccleston Street                                map 13
(020) 7730 6922

The Boisdale package is pure Belgravia club, complete with dark panelling, leather armchairs, a huge choice of whiskies and cigars plus after-dinner jazz. Ingredients come direct from Scotland where possible, whether it be beef, venison, haggis, hand-dived scallops or cheese. Two-course lunches (billed as The Flying Scotsman; £14) give way to The '1745' menu in the evening, and the kitchen delivers dishes such as marinated Orkney herrings, braised beef olives with spinach and horseradish mash, and 'crofter's pie'. Desserts such as cranachan and Scotch tart are 'particularly noteworthy'. There is a new branch, Boisdale of Bishopsgate, at 202 Swedeland Court, EC2, tel. (020 7283 1763). Open Mon to Sat L and D.

### Brady's                                         SW18
513 Old York Road                                  map 12
(020) 8877 9599

'It does one thing, one thing only and does it well,' observed a fan of this long-running utilitarian place. The 'thing' in question is, of course, fish and chips, and

'the interior takes London diners to the seaside in one hit'. Choice runs from battered cod and haddock to grilled red bream, brill and monkfish (all £6.50), with a splendid tray of accompaniments including home-made basil, tarragon and dill mayonnaise. Freshness and simplicity are the keys to its success. Start with salmon fishcakes or prawn cocktail (from £2) and finish with steamed treacle pudding (£1.95). House wine is £8.75. Open Mon to Sat D only.

### Bush                                            W12
45A Goldhawk Road                                  map 12
(020) 8746 2111

A bright spark in Goldhawk Road, this contemporary bar/grill occupies a huge space with an open kitchen at the back. The chargrill comes into its own for swordfish with mizuna and lentil salad (£13.50) as well as Aberdeen Angus ribeye steaks (£14.75); the modern menu also features the likes of prawn and vegetable tempura with chilli sauce (£7.50), poached salmon with pak choi, lime and lemon-grass broth (£10.50), and vegetarian tagine (£9). Snazzy cocktails are alternatives to the well-considered list of Old and New World wines, which leads off with house French at £11 (£2.80 a glass). Open all week L and D.

### Cafe Grand Prix, La Rascasse                    W1
50A Berkeley Street                                map 15
(020) 7629 0808

A well-worn racing Jaguar in a glass case is the first thing you notice in this gargantuan venture that comprises a bar, a brasserie as well as a 'fine-dining' restaurant, La Rascasse, at the back of the place. The décor is 'grand and completely over the top' with half-moon shaped windows, columns and a vast Venetian chandelier. The menu is a fancy Mediterranean-style tome, taking in smoked cod brandade with scallops and leek vinaigrette, excellent mixed charcuterie, and such as sauté of sole with little gems, peas, carrots and roast chicken jus, while desserts include lemon tart. The huge wine list has generous offerings by the glass. Not cheap. Open Mon to Fri L and D, Sat D only.

## Café Portugal                          SW8
6A Victoria House                          map 13
(020) 7587 1962

The trans-ethnic menu of this modest café in one of London's Portuguese quarters includes a soup of the day, cockles with garlic and white wine, Spanish-style octopus, and prawns piri-piri to start. Mains run to three paellas, Portuguese-style seafood rice, crab and seafood in fennel gratin, skewered monkfish and scallops with bacon, and salt-cod with fried potatoes, onions and eggs. Carnivores might choose lamb in pastry, steak with Parma ham topped with a fried egg, or chicken Kiev. Main courses £7 to £12. Open all week.

## Carluccio's Caffé                       W1
8 Market Place                             map 15
(020) 7636 2228

Italian empire builder Antonio Carluccio has opened ten branches of his eponymous caffés (including some outside London), and we're still counting as we go to press. The formula is the same in all outlets: superb bread 'tins', olives and other specially imported native ingredients, 'heart-burstingly good' espresso and cappuccino, and a flexible menu that takes in antipasti (including Sicilian arancini), plus salads, pasta and main courses ranging from calzone to osso buco Milanese. Prices stay below £10. Regional cheeses, desserts and ice creams round things off. There's also a short list of well-chosen and fairly priced Italian wines. Open all week.

## Chapel                                  NW1
48 Chapel Street                           map 13
(020) 7402 9220

The daily-changing menu at this popular pub takes in starters (£3.50–£5) including chilled watercress soup, fish croquettes with roast vegetable salad, or goats' cheese terrine with braised celery. Among main dishes (£8–£12.50), seared marlin steak with anchovy chive dressing, and bison

steak with roasted parsnips and mustard, are as unusual as it gets, while roasted lamb chump with baby ruby chard and juniper, or vegetarian gnocchi with artichoke hearts and Parmesan cream, are more typical. Thirty wines from £9.90 are offered, eight by the glass. Open all week.

## Che                                     SW1
23 St James's Street                       map 14
(020) 7747 9380

Che is a luxurious cigar-bar/restaurant set in a former bank, and though the cigars are an important feature they do not influence a menu that balances solidity against lightness in its options. Seared scallops with lentils and curried cream, or chicken consommé with julienne of chicken and spring onions, might precede lobster risotto, assorted roast fish with baby fennel, fish and chips, a mixed grill, braised pork belly cassoulet, or Thai green curry. None of this comes cheap: even spaghetti carbonara is £9/£14; and house wines are £20, although 40 in the 600-strong list are served by the glass. Closed Sat L and Sun.

## China City                             WC2
White Bear Yard                            map 15
(020) 7734 3388

Tucked away in a courtyard off Lisle Street, this is a warren of a place on three floors with a mass of tables outside. The kitchen works to a menu of around 150 dishes (main dishes £6–£10.50) that holds few surprises (apart from baked lobster with cheese and garlic), and the choice ranges from appetisers such as grilled meat dumplings (£3) to a decent batch of rice and noodles. Beancurd soup is a good version, Chinese broccoli is 'delicately steamed', and the repertoire extends to deep-fried duck with yam paste, and abalone with seasonal vegetables at £20 a throw. Service is polite and pleasant. Open all week.

**Chuen Cheng Ku**                    W1
17 Wardour Street                    map 15
(020) 7734 3281

A veteran of Soho Chinatown (complete with a totem pole landmark), this is one of the premier league addresses for dim sum. It is run by agreeable and watchful staff: a constant stream of trolley-girls pass by, stop, tempt, dispense, then move on. Recently reported favourites have included slithery cheung fun filled with scallops, knuckly steamed spare ribs with chilli and black beans, beef dumplings topped with Chinese mushrooms, and a bowl of soup noodles with 'excellent' roast duck. Portions are generous, prices very fair: 'it is very hard to spend much more than £10 on your lunch.' Open all week 11am to around midnight.

**Como Lario**                       SW1
18–22 Holbein Place                  map 14
(020) 7730 2954

Ten years down the line, this Chelsea Italian still manages to be a crowd-puller. The kitchen deals in staples such as fish soup with saffron, veal chop with butter and sage, and calf's liver 'cooked as you like', but there are plenty of modern twists too: for example, carpaccio of salmon with fresh crab, linguine with red mullet sauce, and roast rabbit with vegetables and beer, while side orders might run to grilled radicchio with balsamic sauce. Main courses £10 to £14. Apart from champagne, the wine list never strays over the Italian border; house wine is £11. Closed all day Sat and Sun.

**Daquise**                          SW7
20 Thurloe Street                    map 14
(020) 7589 6117

'Looking like a time-warp café from the '60s', Daquise had already been going for a dozen years when that decade began. The Polish (but not exclusively so) menu has produced some good borscht and blinis with smoked salmon to start, while potato pancake with Hungarian goulash has been a successful main course (prices £5.50 to £12.50). Polish vodka is a natural accompaniment to the hearty food, or try the beer. Open all week.

**Diwana Bhel Poori**                NW1
121 Drummond Street                  map 13
(020) 7387 5556

'The best of the bunch in the neighbourhood,' notes a regular visitor to this long-running Indian vegetarian place across the road from Euston Station. Although the café-style décor may seem rather dated, the food remains fresh and interesting. Top-of-the-range bhel pooris (£2.30) tend to steal the show, but there have also been votes for samosas, aloo papri chat and dosas (£2.80). Curries (£2.40 to £3) such as channa masala and mattar paneer are fine and thalis are an affordable way of working through the full range. Lunchtime buffets are also 'easy on the pocket'. Unlicensed, but lassi is 'supremely good'. Open all week noon to midnight.

**Ebury Wine Bar**                   SW1
139 Ebury Street                     map 13
(020) 7730 5447

A ground-breaker when it opened in 1959, this wine bar/restaurant has always moved with the times and new head chef Trevor John is proving to be no slouch. His recently introduced two-course lunch menu (£12.50) has been particularly well received: starters of vegetable tempura or a market salad 'full of Mediterranean flavours' might be followed by pork with pumpkin and onion jus, or leek, crab and saffron tart. The atmosphere is 'very comfortable' and the wine list is a must: 30 come by the glass, plus there are special monthly promotions. House wines start at £12. Open all week L and D.

**Efes Kebab House**                 W1
80 Great Titchfield Street           map 15
(020) 7636 1953

'It is as good as ever,' comments a regular visitor, 'and even the waiters are cheerful these days.' This Turkish stalwart has been turning out meze and hearty kebabs for nigh on 30 years. The former is an ideal way to explore the range of cold dips, plus some cooked options such as arnavut cigeri (diced liver) and borek. Main courses are mostly variations on kebabs, with good-quality meat chargrilled and served with rice and salad, as well as ubiquitous pitta bread (charged for). A second branch is just around the corner at 175 Great Portland Street, W1, tel. (020) 7436 0600. Closed Sun.

### Esarn Kheaw W12

314 Uxbridge Road                    map 12
(020) 8743 8930

This basic eating house specialises in the cuisine of Esarn in north-eastern Thailand. The genuine chilli-hotness is toned down for Westerners, but try asking for your meal to be 'real Thai-style' if you like it hot. The menu varies little from those of ordinary Thai places, for many have adopted Esarn specialities. These include laab (salads of minced meat with papaya and other flavourings), and Esarn sausages. Sticky rice, in the bamboo stem in which it is steamed, is the staple to accompany these dishes, and there are curries of various colours. Dishes range from £4 to £15. Open Mon to Fri L, all week D.

### fish! SE1

Cathedral Street                    map 13
(020) 7407 3803

As the Guide went to press the fish! group was in receivership, and the days of rapid expansion had ended. Eleven of the branches had closed, although nine, including this branch (the first), were still operating. The future is uncertain, but for now things remain the same here in Cathedral Street. Expect the day's fish (£6.50 to £16.95) simply steamed or grilled, with a choice of five sauces including salsa and red wine gravy. The vegetable garnish is not up to much, while starters include devilled whitebait and a classic rendition of prawn cocktail. Open all week.

### Fish Central EC1

151 King's Square                    map 13
(020) 7253 4970

To see how a simple fish and chip shop, in the same ownership for 35 years, can become a fish restaurant, look at the menu's head and tail. Start with grilled sardines with tomato coulis (£3.45), or scallops with rocket salad (£4.50). To finish, choose espresso, cappuccino, filter or cafetière coffee. In between there is fried cod, haddock, skate, plaice, even rock salmon (£4.95–£5.75); chips are extra. 'Gourmet's choices' (£7.95–£10.90) include skate with capers and brown butter; and the chargrill provides steaks or chicken breast with creole sauce. Wines from a basic list start at £7.95. Credit cards attract a 5% surcharge. Closed Sun.

### Frederick's N1

Camden Passage                    map 13
(020) 7359 2888

This attractive restaurant, 'an epitome of urban chic' with white painted brick walls bearing 'electrically bright' modern paintings in the main dining room, also has a splendid conservatory, and in fine weather you can dine outside too. Simpler dishes, the large (16oz) steak, or chicken with sarladaise potatoes, tend to succeed better than elaborate 'modern London' ideas, while desserts highlight such retro British classics as rhubarb crumble, Bakewell tart and knickerbocker glory. Wines from well-known names offer reasonable value, with Duboeuf Morgon 2000 and Sancerre Henri Bourgeois around the £20 mark. Closed Sun.

### Gate W6

51 Queen Caroline Street                    map 12
(020) 8748 6932

Brothers Adrian and Michael Daniel started out in this converted artist's studio in 1989 and their venture has been so successful that a sibling is now open in Belsize Lane, NW3 (see London, main entry). Their philosophy is simple: make vegetarian food as inventive as possible, keep faith with organic ingredients, and look worldwide for inspiration. The result is an eclectic menu that takes in wild mushroom spring rolls, chargrilled halloumi with butter-bean salad and harissa, and root vegetable tagine with pomegranate salsa, plus sweets like chocolate brownie with caramelised kumquats. Main courses £7.50 to £11. The short wine list has ten by the glass; house wine is £10.25. Closed Sat L and all day Sun.

## Gilbeys                           W5

77 The Grove                    map 12
(020) 8840 7568

French wines which they ship, are the *raison d'être* of this restaurant. Of 60 listed, 40 are priced from £9 to £20 and all are good value. They are supported in the pleasant conservatory and at garden and pavement tables by a set two-course menu, £7 for lunch, £11.50 for dinner. Start perhaps with whitebait and lemon and herb mayonnaise, or chicken liver and Calvados parfait, continue with pasta or roast mackerel fillet with new potatoes and carrots. These and a similarly imaginative à la carte, are served as speedily, or calmly, as required, by 'friendly, efficient staff'. Closed all day Mon and Sun D.

## Golborne House                   W10

Golborne Road                   map 13
(020) 8960 6260

Although Golborne House sells tip-top cocktails and decent food, it is still very much a pub. The unprepossessing location makes it seem all the more appealing inside: an open-plan layout, wooden floors and uncomplicated décor strike the right note. On the international menu starters have included Thai sweet potato and coconut soup (£4.45), and a tapas plate (£6.75), while mains run to fettuccine with potatoes, pesto and green beans (£7.50), and duck confit with herbed green lentils (£9.50). Over 40 varied wines start at £9.90; eight by the glass. Open all week.

## Great Nepalese                    NW1

48 Eversholt Street             map 13
(020) 7388 6737

Gopal Manandhar may greet regulars with a traditional Nepalese 'salute' in this useful venue near Euston station. Refurbishment (including air conditioning) was under way in mid-2002, but little changes on the menu. The kitchen continues to deliver authentic dishes with intense, forthright flavours: look for momo (steamed meat pastries), hask ko bhutuwa (duck with green herbs), gundruko tarkari (Tibetan dry vegetables), and aloo kerau ko achar (a cold dish of potatoes, peas and sesame seeds). Main courses £5 to £10, and ask about the 'remarkable value' £6.50 special lunch. House wine is £8.50. Open all week.

## Harry's Social Club               W2

30 Alexander Street             map 13
(020) 7229 4043

Although it was set up as a private club (members have their own key), this trendy newcomer is happy to admit non-members – tables are apparently like gold dust. Two bed heads in pink Toile de Jouy flank the entrance to the first-floor dining room, where salacious newspaper headlines are plastered on the backs of chairs. The kitchen works to a modern menu that promises rustic chicken liver and foie gras terrine, tomato, basil and ricotta risotto, and sea bass fillets with a 'luscious' sauce and young spinach. Finish with passion-fruit sorbet or summer pudding 'stack'. Main courses £12–£14.75. House wines from £12.50. Open Tue to Sat D only.

## Havelock Tavern                   W14

57 Masbro Road                  map 12
(020) 7603 5374

Order and pay at the bar in this buzzy gastro-pub behind Olympia. Menus change every session, and it's worth checking the blackboard, as dishes can disappear quickly. Salt cod fishcakes with tartare sauce, and curried onion, spinach and potato in filo represent the lighter dishes, while those wanting something more filling might go for grilled Italian sausages with lentils, or crispy roast loin of pork with mash, mustard sauce and apple. Conclude with rhubarb fool, or chocolate and hazelnut torte. Main courses £6 to £12. The seasonally changing wine list starts at £9.50. No bookings, no credit cards. Open all week.

### Ichi-Riki                                    SW1
17 Strutton Ground                       map 13
(020) 7233 1701
A bright little basement not far from Westminster Abbey is the setting for this modest Japanese eating house. Sushi (£2.60–£5) is the main theme: nigiri runs to sea urchin, turbot and surf clams, while maki rolls include fatty tuna with spring onion, eel with cucumber, sour plum and herb. Added to this are side dishes ranging from wakame salad to yako (silken tofu with dry fish flakes and ginger). To finish there might be rice cakes or green tea ice cream. Saké is served cold or warm, or drink beer or house wine (£10.90 a litre). Closed Sat and Sun.

### Joe Allen                                   WC2
13 Exeter Street                          map 15
(020) 7836 0651
'Simplicity on a plate' is how one reporter described the food in this long-running Covent Garden bolthole. 'Succulent' burgers are the big hit, although they don't appear on the menu; otherwise the transatlantic offerings dishes up black-bean soup (£5), Caesar salad (£5.50/£7.50), and gut-busters such as barbecued ribs with rice, wilted spinach, black-eyed peas and corn muffin (£12). Desserts (£5) are – predictably – ice creams, New York cheesecake and pecan pie, as well as apricot and frangipane tart. Service is 'brisk and professional' and the wine list doesn't stray far from the USA; prices start at £14. Open all week from about noon to midnight.

### Kandoo                                       W2
458 Edgware Road                         map 13
(020) 7724 2428
The location may be nothing to write home about, but this modest restaurant offers a taste of genuine, reasonably priced Persian cooking. In the window is an authentic, mosaic-glazed kandoo and the place is colourfully decked out with ethnic artefacts. The menu divides equally between meze starters and main courses mostly along the lines of grills of lamb or chicken (£4.50 to £8.50). There's also a special of the day: Thursday is 'abgoosht' (a bowl of soup plus a mixture of mashed potatoes, lamb, chickpeas and white beans with bread). Unlicensed, but you can drink yoghurt-based 'doogh' or BYO (no corkage). Open all week L and D.

### Konditor & Cook                              SE1
Young Vic Theatre, 66 The Cut       map 13
(020) 7620 2700
Start the day with a full English fry-up or opt for toasted brioche with butter and jam at this handy venue housed in the Young Vic. From noon till 8pm the menu offers heartier dishes ranging from foie gras croque monsieur via smoked haddock pie, to French-style casserole of sausage with roast new potatoes (main courses £6–£8). Leave room for the hand-made cakes and pastries. Six wines from £11.75. Open Mon to Sat L and D. Other branches at Gray's Inn Road, Waterloo and Borough Market.

### Lahore Kebab House                           E1
2 Umberston Street                        map 13
(020) 7488 2551
This basic eating house gets no smarter, or more expensive, but continues to satisfy, especially with its mixed starter that comprises sheekh kebab, grilled lamb, chicken, and lamb cutlets, all enlivened by fresh herbs and well-judged spices. Vegetarians will have a thin time, although there is spinach, potatoes and dhal in various combinations. The short list of curries rises to £6, and there is just one dessert, home-made kheer (rice

pudding). Unlicensed: BYO. Open all week.

## Lemonia                                    NW1
89 Regents Park Road                     map 13
(020) 7586 7454

Bargain-basement weekday set lunches are the prime deal at this long-running taverna: £6.75 might pay for tabbouleh or grilled courgettes with pitta bread before grilled sea bass or kotopoulo (chicken burgers), with coffee to finish. Daily specials are also worth a punt: perhaps gavros (deep-fried anchovies), bakaliaros (baked cod with olive oil and herbs) or anginares (artichokes stuffed with mincemeat, pine kernels, dill and spinach). The main menu runs from meze to moussaka, with stifado, kleftiko and pork afelia along the way. Main courses £8 to £10. Quaffable Greek-Cypriot wines, although house wine is French, £12 a litre. Closed Sat L and Sun D.

## LMNT                                         E8
316 Queensbridge Road                    map 13
(020) 7249 6727

An extravagant mix of over-the-top artefacts, including Sphinx fireplaces, raised opera boxes, a giant classical urn and a huge Greek-style mask, set the tone in this converted Dalston pub. The menu has plenty of up-to-the-minute offerings at keen prices: grilled mackerel, sweet potatoes and lime pickle is a typical starter, while mains could encompass free-range chicken breast with lentils, chorizo and artichoke velouté, or grilled ribeye steak with oxtail pie and green beans. Caramelised banana bavarois might be a suitable finish. Main courses £8, desserts £3. The short wine list has some decent offering by the glass; house wine is £10.95. Open all week.

## Lomo                                       SW10
222 Fulham Road                          map 14
(020) 7349 8848

In warm weather, when the windows are opened right out, those perching on high stools at high tables can watch the comings and goings along this part of the Fulham Road. Inside, it is light and bright, with a dark-red ceiling and metal fixtures giving a modern look. Tapas (£2.95 to £4.95) and raciones (£4.95 to £7.95) are the thing – patatas bravas, and sizzling scallops among the former, and salt-cod brandada, and rocket and Manchego salad among the larger-portioned raciones. The eponymous lomo (cured loin of pork) is among the charcuterie, which also includes chorizo and jamón Serrano. Paella is available at weekends, but you'll need a friend to share it with. A range of sherries confirm the Iberian credentials. Open Sat L, all week D.

## Lucky Seven                                 W2
127 Westbourne Park Road                 map 13
(020) 7727 6771

Tom Conran's latest venture is a re-creation of an American diner, serving burgers every which way, fries three ways, plus malts and thick shakes – along with Maryland crab burgers (£7.95) and bowls of 'flavourful' clam chowder (£4.50) if you want to push the boat out. Breakfast 'for builders' (and everyone else, £4.95) brings eggs 'any style', hash browns, omelettes and pancakes, while desserts are things like triple chocolate brownie (£3.95). Seating is in red leather booths, which you are expected to share. No bookings, so expect queues. Open all week.

## Mango Tree                                 SW1
46 Grosvenor Place                       map 14
(020) 7823 1888

Located on the ground floor of an office block right behind Buckingham Palace, this Thai restaurant is a bright, serene 'oasis of calm'. It has a 'great-looking interior', laid out in a symmetrical and minimalist style. The menu is splendid to behold, bound in tactile shantung silk, with coloured illustrations of various dishes: giant prawns 'that would frighten a baby lobster' are one of the high points, but the kitchen can also deliver competent renditions of satays, deep-fried shrimp cakes, stir-fried bean sprouts with tofu, and classic pad thai noodles. Prices are steep. Open all week for L and D.

## Manzi's                              WC2
1–2 Leicester Street          map 15
(020) 7734 0224

'How refreshing to be able to have a good-sized Dover sole, plain-grilled – on the bone – with no frills,' commented one happy soul who was first taken here by his father some 50 years ago. This venerable, family-run institution is not about to change its ways or follow fashion, so expect fish cookery of the old school in the shape of fried cod fillet (£11.50), scallops Mornay (£16.95), lobster Thermidor (£28.95) and so on. Conveniently placed a stone's throw from theatreland and the West End nightspots – and there's the bonus of affordable accommodation if you fancy staying over. Open all week for L and D.

## Masala Zone                         W1
9 Marshall Street             map 15
(020) 7287 9966

Handy for a quick, Subcontinental lunchtime fix in the West End. Customers sit at rows of refectory tables, against a background of graffiti-style cityscapes, and dip into a mixed bag of street snacks (£2.50–£4), one-dish curry and rice meals (£4.75–£6), noodles and thalis (£7–£9; including an ayurvedic version for diabetics), supplemented by lunchtime salads, burgers and, perhaps, a chicken tikka sandwich. Open all week, and there is a take-away counter.

## Mem Saheb                           E14
65–67 Amsterdam Road          map 15
(020) 7538 3008

In the depths of the Isle of Dogs is this plain, bare-boarded Indian restaurant/wine bar with a modern attitude. 'Old favourites' such as chicken korma and lamb dopiaza show up on the menu, but the most interesting prospects are regional specialities such as Goan lamb xacuti, South Indian konju papas (prawns cooked with tamarind, mustard seeds and coconut), and Bengali roast chicken. Beer

is probably a better bet than wine: the minuscule list kicks off with house French at £7.95.

## Mezzanine                           SE1
National Theatre              map 13
(020) 7452 3600

The evening star performance for one reader was her brother miming 'fish with new potatoes' for the nice Chinese waiter with limited English. The buzz of the restaurant continues to please, and the menu, with its vegetarian and fishy emphasis, is seemingly planned to avoid post-prandial drowsiness. Lift the curtain on soft herb risotto, roasted red pepper soup, or Thai shellfish, enjoy a second act of smoked paprika duck breast; cardamom and rosemary lamb rump; or whole sea bass en papillote. Passion-fruit and yoghurt mousse with mango coulis, or chocolate, rum and coconut parfait, might make a happy ending. Two courses £17.95, three £19.95. Open Mon to Sat L and D.

## Mirch Masala                        SW16
1416 London Road              map 12
(020) 8679 1828

'You wish it – we cook it' is the motto of this highly popular suburban Indian. Expect queues, great value and laid-back service. The menu kicks off with 'warmers' (samosas, masala steamed spring chicken, fish bhajias) and concludes with 'coolers' (rice, breads and sweets such as falooda and ras malai). In between are 'steamers' (karahi specialities, chicken jalfrezi, 'deigi' sag ghost and chana dhal). Dishes from 60p to £10. Unlicensed, but you can drink lassi, mango shake or bring your own wine. Open all week.

## Miyama                              W1
38 Clarges Street             map 15
(020) 7499 2443

'A first-class Japanese restaurant with traditional food and excellent service' was one reporter's verdict on this long-running Mayfair establishment. Mr Miyama has been at the helm since 1982 and his repertoire spans all aspects of the cuisine; here you will find zensai appetisers from kanisu (crabmeat and cucumber marinated in rice vinegar) to asari sakamushi (clam saké), as well as dobinmushi soup served in a pot, a full quota of sushi and sashimi, grilled salmon with salt, and black cod with sweet miso. Set menus make ordering stress-free: L £7 to £22, D £26 to £40. House wine is £13. Closed Sat and Sun L.

## Momo                                         W1
25 Heddon Street                          map 15
(020) 7434 4040

Billed as a 'restaurant familial', this atmospheric venue actually peddles Moroccan excitement to a trendy young crowd. Couscous and tagines (£11–£16) are at the heart of the menu, which also branches out for fillet of sea bass with confit of tomatoes and artichokes (£19.50), and skewers of marinated duck with chive mash, quince and orange sauce (£15.50). Start with, say, filo pastry filled with chicken, prunes and almonds (£7) and round off with sweet Maghrebi pastries (£5.50). A few North African wines show up on the lively list; prices start at £14.50. Open all week. Next door is Mô, a shop serving teas and light meals.

## New Diamond                            WC2
23 Lisle Street                              map 15
(020) 7437 2517

A soup of salted eggs with pork and 'algae' (actually black sea moss), and a glazed steamed custard of three kinds of egg (hen's, salted duck, and 100-year-old) are among the obscure treasures to be unearthed in this Soho Chinatown establishment. Braised ducks' webs with fish lips throw down the gauntlet to Westernised palates, but there's also comfort in sweet-and-sour pork. The main menu and additional folder of specialities promise great stuff such as 'gloriously tender' lamb with green scallions, garlic and ginger. Beware of the deep-brown, seriously potent chilli oil! Main courses £6.80–£14.80. Long opening hours all week.

## New World                               W1
1 Gerrard Place                             map 15
(020) 7434 2508

A devotee of this huge, basic, Cantonese restaurant finds it gives him either cool and calm relief or a rush of adrenaline. At lunchtime a flotilla of dim sum trolleys is propelled by ladies who knowledgeably put together ingredients and trimmings for such delicacies as vegetable cheung fun (soft noodle rolls) with warm oil and soya dressing, or 'tender and rich' roast duck with noodles in soup. Other dishes approved have included 'spiky, bristly' pieces of nicely chewy, but not tough, tripe with chunks of red chilli and black beans, and deep-fried yam cakes. Main courses £4.65 to £15.80. Open all week.

## Orsino                                      W11
119 Portland Road                        map 12
(020) 7221 3299

What you get here is 'Italian food by way of Notting Hill'. In a setting of ochre-coloured walls with black-and-white photos, this lively place delivers sound cooking to a mostly local clientele. Pizzas and pastas come every which way and the kitchen also turns out a fair minestrone, buffalo mozzarella with sweet tomatoes and basil, and more ambitious-sounding dishes like roast John Dory with braised onions, pancetta and wild garlic. Set lunches and early-evening menus keep prices in check (£14.50 to £18.50), and the decent all-Italian wine list includes eight by the glass. House wine is £13.50 a litre. Open all week.

## Philpott's Mezzaluna                  NW2
424 Finchley Road                        map 13
(020) 7794 0455

David Philpott's Italian menus, changed monthly (weekly for Sunday lunch), allow just a single 'foreign' incursion: lemon-grass butter to accompany black-banded bream with spinach. More typical are cream of red lentil and tomato soup, mushroom budino with herbs and green raisins, a dish highly praised by a reader, and pea risotto. Main courses might include stuffed lemon sole with wild mushrooms, or lamb stinco with potato purée and ratatouille. Desserts could be caramelised pears with granita, or frozen orange parfait with poached plums. A page of Italian wines from £11.50 precedes a few from elsewhere. Two courses £19, three £23. Closed all day Mon and Sat L.

**Pizza Metro**      SW11
64 Battersea Rise      map 12
(020) 7228 3812
'Pizzas by the metre' is the claim-to-fame of this brash, boisterous Battersea joint, where it always seems to be party time. The prized offerings themselves are brought from the wood-fired oven on huge communal trays: the standard size is 50cm for two people (£11.50 to £16.50). Meals start with Neapolitan antipasti such as arancini (rice balls in breadcrumbs) Parmesan, and there are pastas aplenty plus a few substantial main courses like grilled swordfish (£11) or baked sea bream (£10.50). Drink Peroni beer or delve into the short Italian wine list; house wine is £9.95. Open Sat and Sun L and Tue to Sun D.

**Pomegranates**      SW1
94 Grosvenor Road      map 13
(020) 7828 6560
Patrick Gwynn-Jones just keeps on running in this clubby Pimlico basement, and his kitchen is forever seeking out new ideas for a long menu that covers virtually every corner of the globe. Take a world tour, from Danish pickled herrings with rye bread, via West Indian curried goat with fried plantain, to crispy breast of lamb with Szechuan sauce. Otherwise, stay at home for Welsh salt duck, poached chicken with parsley sauce, or treacle tart. Main courses £13 to £20. The mammoth list of 200 wines also covers a lot of territory; house wines from £13.50 to £29. Closed Sat L and all day Sun.

**Poons**      W2
Unit 205 Whiteleys,      map 13
151 Queensway
(020) 7792 2884
Unpromisingly situated on an upper floor in the shopping mall, this serious Chinese restaurant devotes two pages of its menu to dim sum. Set meals (from £16) are more adventurous than usual, and with a long à la carte the whole repertoire would not be out of place in Soho's Chinatown. Scallops stir-fried with asparagus (£8.50), quick-fried shredded eel (£7.50), and stir-fried chicken with white fungi (£5) are among imaginative possibilities. The long, varied wine list has house selections at £11, plus enterprising choices from distinguished vintners. There is a long, equally varied, list of fine beers and malt whiskies. Open all week for L and D.

**Prospect Grill**      WC2
4–6 Garrick Street      map 15
(020) 7379 0412
Lunch and pre-theatre menus offer the best prospects at this dimly lit Covent Garden venue. As its name suggests, the chargrill holds centre stage (for steaks, burgers and even vegetables), but the full carte provides plenty of variety in the shape of salmon fishcakes with parsley sauce (£12) and pan-fried duck breast with gratin dauphinois (£13.95). Start the old-fashioned way with potted shrimps and finish with spiced poached pear, or Roquefort cheese with organic Italian honey (£6). Glamorous cocktails and aperitifs, plus a decent choice of sharply chosen wines from £11.50. Open Mon to Sat L and D.

**Ragam**      W1
57 Cleveland Street      map 15
(020) 7636 9098
'Nothing changes here,' notes a regular. This congenial, box-like dining room in the shadow of Telecom Tower makes an informal and often 'smoky' setting for remarkably good-value cooking. The menu divides equally between Keralan and South Indian specialities and homespun renditions of curry-house favourites; paper dosai, uthappam (a kind of chilli pizza) and vadai (gram-flour doughnuts) get good reports, as do 'pungent' fish curry made with tilapia, chicken Malabar and lamb dopiaza. Vegetables such as dhal with spinach are

spot on, and rice is 'always just right'. Dishes range from £2 to £8. Drink lassi, Cobra beer or house wine (£9). Open all week.

## Randall & Aubin                      W1
16 Brewer Street                        map 15
(020) 7287 4447

Somehow the impressive décor survived through the twentieth century intact, and now this former butcher's shop with its marbled table-tops and tiled walls is a stylish restaurant. Sitting on high stools at high tables may not encourage a long stay, although the display of seafood on ice and the meats on the rotisserie will surely tempt. The menu extends to starters such as Japanese fishcakes (£5.95) and main courses of grilled sea bass (£12.95) and calves' liver with mash (£15.50). Finish with white chocolate cheesecake. A second branch at 329–331 Fulham Road, SW10, tel. (020) 7823 3515, is as 'Fulham' as the original is 'Soho'.

## Rani                                 N3
7 Long Lane                             map 12
(020) 8349 4386

The Pattni family's long-serving Finchley address is devoted to the vegetarian cuisine of the Kathiawadi region in Gujarat. Home-made pickles and chutneys are the real stars of the show, but hot and cold starters (£3–£3.50) range from bhel pooris and chana chat to potato bhajias and bhakervelli (spiced vegetables rolled and fried in pastry). More substantial slow-cooked 'sak' curries take in sakaria (sweet potatoes with ginger and coconut milk, £4.90) and chola (black-eyed beans with coriander, £4.30). Good-value thalis (£9.80) and an enterprising children's menu. Lassi, herb teas and juices are alternatives to house wine at £9.70. Open Sun L and all week D.

## Rebato's                             SW8
169 South Lambeth Road                  map 12
(020) 7735 6388

The grand senõrita of London tapas bars shows no signs of giving up the ghost. In the front area of this Hispanic institution,

with its dark wood and tiled floor, you can graze your way through chorizo served hot, Serrano ham, artichoke hearts and grilled sardines (tapas from £2 to £7). The formal dining room at the back serves Spanish-Continental stalwarts like paella, calf's liver and bacon and grilled Dover sole (3 courses at D £16.95). Roast suckling pig is a special treat when it's on. Start proceedings with sherry, then get stuck into the Riojas; Torres house wine is £9.75. Closed Sat L and all day Sun.

## Rules                                WC2
35 Maiden Lane                          map 15
(020) 7836 5314

Reputedly London's oldest restaurant (dating from 1798), this bastion of tradition is a Mecca for tourists. The décor is 'a cross between an auction house and a Victorian dining room', and the menu seems set in 'tablets of stone'. Main dishes patriotically focus on 'game', 'grass-fed beef and lamb' and fish. Start with Stilton and celeriac soup (£6.25), move on to steak and kidney pudding with oysters (£18.95), and finish with treacle sponge (£6.50). This is indeed a venerable institution, but there have been comments about inconsistent cooking and sloppy service of late. French house wines come by the glass, jug or bottle (£13.95). Open all week 12 to 11.30 (10.30 Sun).

## Saga                                 W1
43–44 South Molton Street               map 15
(020) 7408 2236

Thanks to last year's refurbishment, passers-by can now peep into this modern-looking Japanese restaurant just off Bond Street. A new chef is at the helm, but there's still a broad scope to the menu and the kitchen turns its hand to almost all essential aspects of the cuisine, from sushi and sashimi to tempura and teriyaki. Otherwise look for affordable bowls of udon and soba noodles (£6 to £9) and specials of the week such as butabara kimuchi itame (stir-fried belly pork with fiery pickled Chinese cabbage). House wine is £13. Open all week L and D.

**Selasih** W1
114 Seymour Place map 13
(020) 7724 4454
A busy little eating house which promises 'exotic Malaysian cuisine', and also embraces Chinese and Thai dishes, such as sweetcorn soup, tom yum, Singapore fried vermicelli, and even sweet-and-sour and kurma chicken. Enthusiasts for 'real' Malaysian food can dive into soup Selasih with mixed vegetables, bean curd and egg; chicken or prawn satay; or one of four nasi goreng (fried rice) dishes, which include 'village-style' rice flavoured with balachan (dried shrimp paste), incorporating prawns and chicken, and topped with fried egg. Salmon features heavily in the fish section; one surprise is hot-and-sour tamarind fish soup with salmon. Main courses £3.95 to £17.95. Closed Sun L.

**So.Uk** SW4
165 Clapham High Street map 12
(020) 7622 4004
Expect smoke, noise, DJs and elbow-to-elbow communal tables at this fun joint in Clapham. Food is almost incidental, but it's reasonably priced and serves its purpose. Mixed plates (£12.50) comprise large round platters loaded with nibbles from the global melting pot: marinated goats' cheese toasts, spring rolls with chilli sauce, satay, grilled couscous salad and more. The main business, however, is drinking, whether champagne cocktails, bottled beers, obscure liqueurs or wacky teas and coffees. The short wine list covers the globe with prices from £12.50. Under the same ownership as Teatro (see main entry, London). Open Mon and Tue 5pm to midnight, Wed and Thur 5pm to 1am, Fri 5pm to 2am, Sat 3pm to 2am, Sun noon to midnight.

**Sofra** WC2
36 Tavistock Street map 15
(020) 7240 3773
Huge menus, fast service and modest prices in this bright, lively Turkish café-restaurant attract revelling parties. Hot and cold mezes (£2.95 each) include many traditional items; meat main dishes are either from the charcoal grill (lamb fillet with oregano, £7.95) or guvechs (casseroles: chicken and vegetables with garlic and paprika, £7.45). There are also plenty of fish options, including drunken kalamar (£7.50), and (for vegetarians) pasta with feta and dill, or spinach, leek and potato stew (£6.95). Turkish house wines are £11, many others under £20. Branches are at 1 St Christopher's Place, W1, tel. (020) 7224 4080, and 18 Shepherd Street, W1, tel. (020) 7493 3320; and there are outlets in Istanbul, Ankara and Helsinki if you are passing.

**Sotheby's, The Café** W1
34–35 New Bond Street map 15
(020) 7293 5077
Bidders and Bond Street shoppers can take advantage of this café attached to the auction rooms as a handy weekday refuelling point. Breakfast opens proceedings Continental-style with juices, croissants, pain au chocolat, teas and coffees, while the daily-changing lunch menu might offer duck and rosemary rösti with blackberry sauce (£8), roast fillet of salmon with braised leeks (£15), or spanakopitta with Greek salad (£12) before pistachio and vanilla crème brûlée. Hand-made chocolate truffles will provide the final kick before resuming business. Afternoon teas are also worth noting. Sotheby's champagne comes by the glass (£6.75) and the short list is peppered with classy stuff. Open Mon to Fri L and D.

**La Spighetta** W1
43 Blandford Street map 15
(020) 7486 7340
Pizzas from a wood-fired oven (£7.50–£9.50) and pastas (£6.90–£9.80) are the main players in this bare-floored, windowless Italian joint. Ravioli of smoked swordfish with fresh tomato sauce (£8) has been enjoyed and the menu also extends to chargrilled tuna with fennel and tomato salad (£11.90) and pan-fried calf's liver with spinach and balsamic sauce (£12.90). Start with warm goats' cheese, French beans and shallot

dressing, or wild boar fillet with rocket, carasau bread and truffle oil, and finish with tiramisù or apple strudel. Service is 'slick'. Closed Sun L.

### Spread Eagle · SE10
1–2 Stockwell Street · map 12
(020) 8853 2333

Part tourist attraction, part gastro-pub, this atmospheric seventeenth-century inn opposite the Greenwich Theatre continues to pull in the crowds. Former sous-chef Richard Munn has stepped into Bernard Brique's shoes, although reports suggest that he is not as consistent as his predecessor. However, there have been successes, notably a tiny scallop and spring vegetable risotto, a timbale of red mullet with couscous, and canon of lamb on a bed of leeks with dauphinoise potatoes. Desserts, such as pineapple tarte Tatin, have also passed muster. Main courses £13 to £19.50, and Set L and D £16.75. Good coffee, moderately priced wines from £11.50. Closed Sun D.

### Star of India · SW5
154 Old Brompton Road · map 14
(020) 7373 2901

A long-serving, ornately decorated restaurant providing Indian food for the denizens of Kensington. The menu is peppered with unfamiliar dish names, but detailed descriptions help. 'Star specialities' include such things as dum ka jhinga (tiger prawn casserole in a creamy sauce with root vegetables, £14.50), and duck varuval (braised with Chettinad spices and served with aniseed and curry leaves, £13). Added to this are tandooris, biryanis and some promising vegetables like new potatoes pan-roasted with cumin, ground mango and pomegranate (£4.95). 'Indifferent' service took the edge off an otherwise sound meal for one reporter. Open all week.

### Tate Modern · SE1
Bankside · map 13
(020) 7401 5020

Café 7, high up on the seventh floor of the Gallery, now accepts reservations, so book your table to avoid the queues and enjoy the panoramic vistas over the Thames towards St Paul's. Breakfast brings croissants, pain au chocolat and a wide choice of drinks, while the lunch menu takes in a range of mostly light dishes along the lines of salt cod fritters with smoked paprika aïoli, and Parma ham with marinated artichokes and pickled tomatoes. Desserts might include organic ice creams, and caramelised lemon tart. A similar menu is available in the café on Level 2. Open all week L, Fri and Sat D.

### Tbilisi · N7
91 Holloway Road · map 13
(020) 7607 2536

Starter combination plates have been replaced by a choice of 12 individually priced dishes at this north London Georgian restaurant. There are fried aubergines with garlic, fried liver and heart, or traditional breads with egg, beans or cheese. Approved soups include borscht with sausage, bacon and black olives. Main dishes are more basic despite exotic names such as ostry (spicy beef stew with tomatoes, onions and other vegetables), or monastic trout (baked with mushrooms, egg, yoghurt and cheese). Main courses £6.50 to £8. Open all week L only.

### Thai Bistro · W4
99 Chiswick High Road · map 12
(020) 8995 5774

Consistent cooking and authentic ingredients make this Chiswick local a reliable address for sound Thai cooking. Tom yung goong (£4.50) is the real thing 'with a full set of spices, including holy basil'; also coming in for praise have been green papaya salad with a well-balanced chilli sauce (£4.95) and skilfully timed potatoes with ginger and copious amounts of other vegetables including snow peas. Old faithfuls like pad Thai noodles (£5.95) have also been endorsed. Service remains 'courteous'. Open all week.

### 3 Monkeys
SE24
136–140 Herne Hill
map 12
(020) 7738 5500

'Trying desperately NOT to be a local curry house' is one view on this highly popular 'contemporary restaurant serving modern Indian food'. The menu spans the Subcontinent with the emphasis on renditions of regional dishes: from plump shammi kebabs with cumin-flavoured dipping sauce (£4.95) via crab Malabari (£6.25) to Parsee-style lamb kumani with dried apricots (£9.50). 'Sticky sweet' carrot halwa studded with pistachio nuts is the real thing and makes a fine finish. Service is willing and informed. Eight wines by the glass open the short list; house wine is £12.95. Open all week D only.

### Tokyo Diner
WC2
2 Newport Place
map 15
(020) 7287 8777

The appeal of this converted Chinatown laundrette is obvious: the location is convenient for theatreland, prices are rock bottom, and the atmosphere zings. What the kitchen aims for is streetwise authenticity and the kind of up-front flavours you might find in urban Japanese cafés. Best sellers are arty lacquered bento boxes (£8.30–£12.90) with their compartments of cold noodles, rice, sashimi and other goodies. Also look for miso soup, bowls of udon and soba noodles (£5.10–£5.90), and katsu curries (£7.50); there's also sushi if you don't mind waiting. Drink tea, beer or saké; house wine is £6.90. No bookings, no tipping. Open all week noon to midnight.

### Truc Vert
W1
42 North Audley Street
map 15
(020) 7491 9988

This deli-cum-restaurant offers an appealing French/Mediterranean menu. Soups (including bread) are £4.50 or £4.95; light dishes or starters, such as grilled squid or fishcakes, start at £7.25, while main courses run from £10.50 for pasta up to £13.75 for chargrilled veal loin steak with vegetables. There are selections of cheese or charcuterie, and desserts like warm pumpkin pie with coffee ice cream. Vegetable and salad extras include a mysterious 'salade très verte'. Very short wine list from £8. Closed D Sat and Sun.

### Vasco & Piero's Pavilion
W1
15 Poland Street
map 15
(020) 7437 8774

This family-run Umbrian restaurant evokes happy memories of old Soho, where – as one reporter noted – substance was more important than style. Nonetheless the 'light menu' of two courses for £12.50 suits today's smaller appetites. Dinner is £22.50 for three courses. Salami with garlic crostino, zucchini and fennel is a typical starter; pasta dishes might include fusilli with beef ragù; while main courses are mostly grills, perhaps including cod, rare tuna or guinea fowl with juniper berries. Desserts are as authentically Italian as the wine list. Closed Sat L and Sun.

### Village Bistro
N6
38 Highgate High Street
map 12
(020) 8340 5165/0257

'Nouvelle moderne' is one reporter's description of the cooking at this high street bistro. Smoked haddock mousse served on poppadoms makes a sprightly starter, otherwise you might opt for a baked field mushroom with garlic and herb crust (£4.95). Confit of duck has been well received, and other mains run to cod on leek mash with prawns and capers, and pot-roast rabbit with olives, rosemary and garlic. Main courses £10 to £15.50. Finish with an apricot crêpe with warm Grand Marnier ice cream, if it's on. Service is pleasantly international. Closed Sun.

### Vrisaki
N22
73 Myddleton Road
map 13
(020) 8889 8760

The main surprise in the wine list of this simple Greek-Cypriot kebab house, established for 20 years, may be the inclusion of Liebfraumilch in the Greek section. In the menu, feta is noted as 'from Greece' but the provenance of avocado with prawns remains undisclosed. The charcoal grill provides simple steaks and lamb as well as various kebabs (£8.50 to £14), while kleftiko, souvla and moussaka are listed as specialities (all £9), and there is a sweets trolley to round things off. Closed Sun.

### Yoshino                                        W1
3 Piccadilly Place                          map 15
(020) 7287 6622

Mr Yoshino's eponymous restaurant is a useful venue if you are looking for affordable Japanese food around Piccadilly. Lunchtime specials are great value for, say, seared tuna sashimi with potato salad (£6.80) or teriyaki eel fillet (£8.50), which come with the classic trinity of rice, miso soup and pickles; there's also a choice of bento boxes. The full menu runs to sushi, oden hotpots and side dishes of home-made bean curd, mackerel with miso, and vinegared mooli and carrots. Tea is free, otherwise investigate the choice of sakés, beers and oddities like potato vodka. The minimal wine list starts at £15. Closed Sun.

### Zilli                                          W11
210 Kensington Park Road                map 13
(020) 7792 1066

The western outpost of the Zilli group (see entry below for a sibling) offers a marine-based menu in a matching décor, and its Italian parentage is apparent, although a few dishes escape, mostly towards their British home. Grilled king scallops marinated in ginger, coriander, lime and basil oil even shows an oriental influence, and there are salmon and crab fishcakes, as well as roasted wild salmon with mustard mash and beetroot vinaigrette. Squid is offered in three styles, and among

eight pasta dishes pappardelle bolognese is the only concession to carnivores. Main courses £8 to £19. Open all week.

### Zilli Fish Too                                 WC2
145 Drury Lane                          map 15
(020) 7240 0011

A reporter found this a fun place, although noisy. Italian origins are evident in the 12 pizze, including seafood calzone, and a Zilli fish version with scallops, shrimps, calamari, and cherry tomatoes. Meat eaters are not neglected, with platters of salami, or Parma ham and asparagus among starters, and steak, or chicken Caesar salad among main dishes. Oriental touches appear in tuna sushi, or ginger-baked salmon with soy, star anise, pak choi and noodles. But pasta, risotto and Italian ways with fish predominate – unless you order beer-battered cod with chips. Main courses £6.90 to £23. Closed Sat L and all day Sun.

### Zinc                                           W1
21 Heddon Street                        map 15
(020) 7255 8899

This Conran bar and grill offers seafood specialities and main dishes ranging in sophistication from Cumberland sausages and mash (£9.50) to pan-fried salmon with tom kah and Asian greens (£12.95). Bar food at £5 per item, or £12 for three, might include Thai fishcakes, Turkish flatbread with three dips, and crisply fried balls of wild mushrooms. Other examples of the menu's international outlook are duck spring roll with hoisin sauce, chargrilled swordfish with panzanella (an Italian bread-based salad), and cappuccino crème brûlée. The short wine list, from £13, includes eight by the glass. Closed Sun.

# England

## ABINGER COMMON Surrey                                    map 3

# Stephan Langton Inn ✗ £                    **NEW ENTRY**

Friday Street, Abinger Common RH5 6JR
TEL: (01306) 730775
from A25 Dorking to Guildford road after Wotton
take Hollow Lane signed Friday Street, then
sharp left turn also signed Friday Street and                    COOKING 3
follow very narrow road; turn right just before             MODERN BRITISH
lake; pub is after cottages                                      £27–£38

Unpretentious enough for walkers to call in, this former pub – down tiny, winding roads in rural, sylvan Surrey – is named after the Archbishop of Canterbury who was mainly responsible for drafting the Magna Carta, of which there is a translation at the entrance to the bar. The large dining room is painted yellow, without frills or fancies, just assorted wooden tables and chairs, big dressers filled with china, and a small, daily-changing menu.

Jonathan Coomb cut his teeth in a few well-known London restaurants, and knows how to put an enticing yet straightforward selection of dishes together, offering chargrills and roasts of anything from sardines to rump of lamb with sumac, from lightly seared tuna surrounded by ratatouille and rocket to onglet with chips and horseradish cream. Slow roasts also feature, perhaps a large piece of tender pork surrounded by masses of cannellini beans and rounds of chorizo.

First courses are equally appealing, taking in a smoked haddock and saffron risotto with Cheddar cheese melting over it, and light, crisply browned goats' cheese gnocchi with sun-dried tomatoes and pesto. Finish, perhaps, with buttermilk pudding and al dente rhubarb, or light chocolate brownies with white chocolate chips in them, served with crème fraîche. Service is friendly and informative, though it can be a little slow. A lively single-page wine list packs in plenty of variety, starts with house vin de pays at £10.75, and stops at about £30.

CHEF: Jonathan Coomb   PROPRIETORS: Jonathan Coomb and Cynthia Rajabally   OPEN: Sun L 12.30 to 3, Tue to Sat D 7 to 10   CLOSED: 2 weeks Jan   MEALS: alc (main courses £10 to £12.50). Bar menu available Tue to Sun L   SERVICE: not inc, card slips closed   CARDS: Delta, MasterCard, Switch, Visa   DETAILS: 50 seats. 50 seats outside. Private parties: 80 main room. Car park. Children's helpings. No smoking in dining room. Wheelchair access (not WC). Music £5

---

*All entries, including Round-ups, are fully indexed at the back of the Guide.*

# Drakes on the Pond

Dorking Road, Abinger Hammer RH5 6SA          COOKING **6**
TEL/FAX:  (01306) 731174                       MODERN EUROPEAN
                                                      £31–£54

This is an unostentatious restaurant, attractive in its simplicity and restraint, whose smartly dressed tables and comfortable chairs exhibit none of the usual decorative excesses. Its priorities are with the food, and Steve Drake's cooking seems to be steadily gaining in confidence as it settles into a style that suits both himself and the rest of Surrey. Seafood (from Brixham) is a strength, evident in one reporter's langoustine ravioli followed by steamed sea bass on crab risotto, and in another's moist salmon fillet with a simple but winning sauce of sweet organic vine tomatoes and shredded basil leaves.

Dishes are prepared with accuracy and handled deftly; they are well rehearsed, displaying balance and undemonstrative skills: for example in a pair of tender roast wood pigeon breasts on a raft of buttery mashed potato, with a full-flavoured shallot and balsamic sauce. Parfaits are praised, whether savoury to start or sweet to finish – perhaps a chocolate version with orange sauce anglaise – and the kitchen's sympathy for seasons has produced an uncomplicated but effective autumnal dish of briefly roasted quartered figs with a creamy-textured honey ice cream.

Well-crafted incidentals run from a clear-tasting starter soup of chicken with noodles and herbs, to a pre-dessert of rosemary ice cream with diced pear. Service from Tracey Honeysett radiates relaxed professionalism, and the well-sourced wine list, with a good spread of styles and prices, is now augmented by 20 half-bottles. A six-strong house selection starts with Vin de Pays Merlot at £10.30.

CHEF: Steve Drake  PROPRIETORS: Tracey Honeysett and John Morris  OPEN: Wed to Fri L 12 to 1.30, Tue to Sat D 7 to 9.30  CLOSED: Christmas to New Year, 2 weeks Aug  MEALS: Set L £16 (2 courses) to £19, Set D £28 (2 courses) to £32.50  SERVICE: not inc  CARDS: Amex, MasterCard, Switch, Visa  DETAILS: 34 seats. Private parties: 34 main room. Car park. No children under 10. No smoking before 9.30pm. Wheelchair access (not WC). No music. Air-conditioned  £5

# Planet Spice  £

88 Selsdon Park Road, Addington CR2 8JT          COOKING **2**
TEL:  (020) 8651 3300  FAX:  (020) 8651 4400              INDIAN
WEBSITE:  www.planet-spice.com                          £18–£45

Planet Spice could equally be named Planet Colour in honour of its eye-catching modern décor, with white-clothed tables, some set against green and beige semi-circular banquettes, and pale green, yellow and crimson walls. The menus offer a Subcontinent-wide survey of many cooking styles. Unconventional starters might include calamari balchao (strips of squid stir-fried in a hot-sour Goan sauce); malai murgh tikka, bringing together chargrilled chicken and cottage cheese marinated in yoghurt and cashew nut purée; ros-tos crab, the white meat cooked in white wine and mango juice and topped with cheese; and goats' cheese and mozzarella samosa. Main courses are equally varied, and among the vegetable dishes are crisp-fried okra tossed with onion and tomato, courgettes with turmeric, Keralan avial, and diced apple with sweet potato. Desserts take in viceroy's banana pie, and more conventional carrot halva. Decently priced wines start at £8.95, and six are sold by the glass.

CHEF: Dulal Pal   PROPRIETOR: Planet Spice Ltd   OPEN: all week 12.30 to 2.15 (3 Sun), 6.30 to 11.15   CLOSED: 25 and 26 Dec   MEALS: alc exc Sun L (main courses £7.50 to £12). Set L Mon to Sat £9.95 (2 courses), Set L Sun £9.95, Set D Sun to Thur £9.95 (2 courses)   SERVICE: 10% (optional), card slips closed   CARDS: Amex, Delta, Diners, MasterCard, Switch, Visa   DETAILS: 90 seats. Private parties: 50 main room. Car park. Vegetarian meals. Children's helpings. No-smoking area. Wheelchair access (also WC). Music. No mobile phones. Air-conditioned  £5

## ALDEBURGH Suffolk                                                          map 6

# Lighthouse 🍷 ✳ £

| 77 High Street, Aldeburgh IP15 5AU | COOKING 3 |
| --- | --- |
| TEL/FAX: (01728) 453377 | MODERN BRITISH-PLUS |
| | £22–£47 |

Everyone seems to have a great time at this exceedingly popular bistro-style restaurant by the seaside. It gets packed – especially during the Aldeburgh Festival – but cheery young staff cope admirably with the crush. 'A very happy birthday was had by all,' commented a satisfied party, while another felt it was as if you had 'gate-crashed a private function with the great show of familiarity to regulars'. Despite the cramped conditions, the holiday atmosphere and no-frills food continue to work their magic.

Menus change daily to take account of availability, although some dishes are fixtures, and the value for money is undeniable. This year's postbag is bulging with recommendations, particularly for fish: potted Norfolk shrimps, and warm salad of scallops and Alsace black bacon for starters, then skate, sea bass (perhaps with a 'lovely' risotto) and – that perennial favourite – haddock in beer batter with chips. Meat eaters and vegetarians have tucked into goose rillettes with pickled figs, spaghetti bolognese, mighty bangers and mash, and mushroom pancakes. Desserts could range from walnut tart with ice cream to lemon posset with amaretti biscuits, and the keenly priced wine list wanders off the beaten track to deliver an intriguing mix of grape varieties and wine styles from throughout the Old and New Worlds. Value is evidently important, as mark-ups are low. Seven house wines, all £10.95, sell for £2.50 a glass, and there's plenty of choice below £20, including many food-friendly styles.

CHEFS: Sara Fox, Guy Welsh and Gavin Battle   PROPRIETORS: Sara Fox and Peter Hill   OPEN: all week 12 to 2 (2.30 Sat and Sun), 6.30 to 10   CLOSED: 1 week Oct, 2 weeks Jan   MEALS: alc L (main courses £6.50 to £13). Set D £13.95 (2 courses) to £17.50   SERVICE: not inc, card slips closed   CARDS: Amex, Delta, MasterCard, Switch, Visa   DETAILS: 95 seats. 25 seats outside. Private parties: 45 main room, 20 to 25 private rooms. Vegetarian meals. No smoking in 1 dining room. No cigars/pipes in dining room. Wheelchair access (also WC). No music. Air-conditioned  £5

# Regatta £

171 High Street, Aldeburgh IP15 5AN
TEL: (01728) 452011 FAX: (01728) 453324
WEBSITE: www.regattaaldeburgh.com

COOKING 3
SEAFOOD/EUROPEAN
£24–£47

Behind the neat blue and yellow façade of this popular local restaurant is a cheerful nautical-themed interior, also blue and yellow. The simple, unpretentious menu, which leans towards fish and bistro favourites rather than flaunting great ambitions, is reinforced by a blackboard listing fresh fish dishes as well as specials: often from the restaurant's own smoker. Starters of zingy Mediterranean fish soup with rouille and croûtons, or smoked Aldeburgh sprats, are generally well received. Main courses may be fish-based – skate with black butter and capers, for example – or not: say, grilled marinated breast of Gressingham duck. Desserts are indulgent, as evidenced by banana bread-and-butter pudding with sticky sauce, or a dense piña colada sorbet. Cooking isn't always as accurate as it might be, but service is generally competent and very friendly. Crayons are provided for children. The wine list is not particularly imaginative (and omits vintages), but prices are quite low, starting at £10.50, and most bottles are under £20.

CHEFS: Robert Mabey and Christopher Murray  PROPRIETORS: Robert and Johanna Mabey
OPEN: all week 12 to 2, 6 to 10 (later from June to Aug)  CLOSED: Mon to Tue and Sun D during
Nov to Mar  MEALS: alc (main courses £7.50 to £18)  SERVICE: not inc  CARDS: Amex, Delta,
MasterCard, Switch, Visa  DETAILS: 95 seats. Private parties: 35 main room. Vegetarian meals.
No children at Sat D. Children's helpings. Wheelchair access (also WC). Occasional music. Air-
conditioned

## ALTRINCHAM Greater Manchester

map 8

# Juniper

21 The Downs, Altrincham WA14 2QD
TEL: (0161) 929 4008 FAX: (0161) 929 4009
EMAIL: reservations@juniper-restaurant.co.uk

COOKING 7
MODERN FRENCH
£33–£73

'By far the best restaurant in the North West' is a typical summary, all the more unexpected given Juniper's suburban location in a parade of shops amid a welter of estate agents and a sprinkling of themed pubs, cafés, brasseries and bars. And given Paul Kitching's Geordie background (he is a 'delightfully unpretentious bloke'), his intricate food can come as something of a surprise too. The first thing that generally strikes visitors – after the smart downstairs bar, and the aquamarine dining room with its interpretation of Uccello's *The Battle of San Romano* – is the menu's playful way with ingredients. What do you make of roast saddle of Cumbrian hare with foie gras, watercress, yoghurt, Horlicks powder, sugared cashews and melon syrup sauce, or roast best end of lamb accompanied by, among other things, kidney, sweetbreads, jumbo sultanas, Weetabix and double espresso coffee sauce, other than to note a penchant for weird ideas and proprietary brands?

Some of these could be a real dog's breakfast in less skilful hands, but Kitching's undoubted technical accomplishment ensures, for the most part, that they hang together. A winter ragoût combining moist, steamed sea bass and a nugget of sauté chicken liver achieves a fine contrast, as does another starter of courgette squares topped with fried banana, each covered variously with a morsel of sea bass, cod, turbot, salmon and scallop, with parsnip purée and a lemon cream forming geometrical lines of sauce with dabs at each corner. For one visitor this amounted to a 'plethora of extras', for another the dishes are 'reassuringly spare' since many of the ingredients are no more than slicks, blobs or froths.

Dessert seems to please everybody, be it a classic glazed lemon tart, or a remarkable fruitcake soufflé with caramel ice cream. Bread and incidentals are impressive too, from an opening glass of cauliflower purée with parsley and truffle oil, to the flavoured milk (rosewater for one couple, apricot for another) that precedes dessert. Portions are small, but so well judged that there is a feeling of satisfaction without surfeit. Service is overseen with consummate skill by Kate O'Brien, and wines are well chosen, although mark-ups can be a bit daunting. Red and white Bordeaux house wines are £16.50.

CHEF: Paul Kitching   PROPRIETORS: Paul Kitching, Kate O'Brien and P. and D. Keeling   OPEN: Tue to Fri L 12 to 2.15, Tue to Sat D 7 to 10   CLOSED: first week Jan, 2 weeks Aug   MEALS: alc D (main courses £17 to £21). Set L £15 (2 courses) to £19, Set D £32. Gourmet menus also available for whole tables   SERVICE: not inc, card slips closed   CARDS: Amex, Delta, MasterCard, Switch, Visa   DETAILS: 34 seats. Private parties: 32 main room. Children's helpings. No smoking in dining room; smoking in bar only. Music. Air-conditioned  £5

## ALVECHURCH Worcestershire                                    map 5

# Mill ♥ ✸

| Radford Road, Alvechurch B48 7LD | COOKING 3 |
|---|---|
| TEL: (0121) 447 7005   FAX: (0121) 447 8001 | MODERN BRITISH £27–£41 |

The setting is an old redbrick watermill, a three-storey edifice with windows diminishing in size as the gaze travels upwards. Chintz and decorative china dominate the décor, and walls are hung with copies of Impressionism's greatest hits. Carl Timms has been cooking here as long as the McKernons have owned it, which is to say a decade, and his monthly-changing menus do their best to please a loyal band of regulars with deftly realised homespun cooking. Chicken liver parfait with red onion marmalade or a pancake filled with cod, salmon and prawns might set you up, and be followed by roasted pork fillet with wholegrain mustard sauce, or salmon with spinach and watercress. Finish with white chocolate marquise or a cheese plate. Note that the price for a three-course Saturday dinner is £7 more than the weekday menu for exactly the same choice: a good reason to get out of the house midweek. France is the main focus of the wine list, although New World selections do get more than a passing glance. Mark-ups are quite low, and there's plenty to choose from under £20: quite a feat for a French-focused list. House wines, however, could easily be more exciting. Prices for the dozen house selections range from £9.75 to £16.95.

CHEF: Carl Timms   PROPRIETORS: Stefan, Geoffrey and Vivienne McKernon   OPEN: Tue to Sat D only 7 to 8.30 (9 Fri & Sat)   CLOSED: first week Jan, first 2 weeks Aug   MEALS: Set D Tue to Fri £17.50 (2 courses) to £19.50, Set D Sat £26.50   SERVICE: not inc   CARDS: Amex, Delta, MasterCard, Switch, Visa   DETAILS: 24 seats. Private parties: 20 main room. Car park. Vegetarian meals. No smoking in dining room. Music  £5

# Glass House ▼ ◇ ✺

Rydal Road, Ambleside LA22 9AN                                    COOKING 3
TEL: (01539) 432137   FAX: (01539) 433384                 MODERN EUROPEAN
EMAIL: enquiries@theglasshouserestaurant.co.uk                     £29–£52

The bright pink advertising board that speaks of all the fun things going on
inside may not look very Ambleside, but the place is usually buzzing with
custom. Extending over three floors, with a mezzanine level overlooking the
ground floor, it occupies the same building as a glass studio and a working
watermill. The aim is to bring bright, modern cooking to locals and visitors
alike. Tomato and Parmesan tart with marinated red onion is thin, crisp and full
of flavour, and in a neat variation on a familiar theme, black pudding is served
with a crêpe of caramelised apple and pancetta. A restraining hand is needed on
main-course sauces and dressings, which can overwhelm: a shame when the
main item is a generous piece of grilled John Dory on chargrilled vegetables. A
meat alternative might be roast guinea fowl with cauliflower and sweet potato
purée.

Desserts are where the kitchen really dazzles, as in lemon tart with raspberry
coulis and raspberry sorbet of 'arrestingly clear flavour', or a skewer of honey-
glazed fruits with hazelnut ice cream. Service can struggle to cope. New and Old
Worlds rub shoulders on the diverse wine list, with clever selections from South
America and Australia offering the best value. About two-thirds of the 100 or so
wines are priced below £20. The eight house selections are a snip at £11 to £13,
all sold by the large and small glass. Diners may find a list of clearance specials
ranging from Cloudy Bay to the Super-Tuscan Solaia. There are a good number
of half-bottles, and an amazing Armagnac selection dating back to 1900.

CHEF: Richard Collins   PROPRIETOR: Neil Farrell   OPEN: Wed to Mon 12 to 3, 6.30 to 10 (10.30
Sat, 9 Sun)   CLOSED: 24 to 26 Dec, 6 Jan to 1 Feb   MEALS: alc (main courses £10 to £16). Set D
£9.95 (2 courses) to £12.50   SERVICE: not inc   CARDS: Delta, MasterCard, Switch, Visa
DETAILS: 100 seats. 34 seats outside. Private parties: 100 main room, 25 to 40 private rooms.
Vegetarian meals. No children under 5 at D. No smoking in dining room. Wheelchair access (not
WC). Music  £5

# ▲ Rothay Manor ▼ ✺

Rothay Bridge, Ambleside LA22 0EH
TEL: (015394) 33605   FAX: (015394) 33607
EMAIL: hotel@rothaymanor.co.uk
WEBSITE: www.rothaymanor.co.uk                                    COOKING 3
off A593 to Coniston, ¼m W of Ambleside                    MODERN BRITISH
                                                                   £26–£50

This charming hotel just outside Ambleside was considered by one satisfied
customer to be 'a delightful place to luxuriate in understated nostalgia'. Despite
a slightly formal appearance, the atmosphere is relaxed and homely, and the
latter term could also be used to describe the cooking, which takes a
traditionalist approach livened up with a few modern touches. At one meal, a
starter salad of grilled sardines with tomato and basil salsa showed 'lively
flavours' and overall had a 'pleasing summery feel', while a main course of

salmon fillet, on a potato pancake with a topping of spring onions and crème fraîche, and with a herb oil dressing, proved a well-judged and enjoyable dish. The conservative streak that runs through the food has let the side down on occasion – overcooked meat and unsuitable vegetable accompaniments have been noted – but there is nothing wrong with a traditional dessert of crêpes suzette, or a crisp brandy-snap basket of summer berries with vanilla ice cream. The wine list is a serious tome, slightly Franco-centric but with well-chosen selections from elsewhere in Europe and throughout the New World too. Mark-ups are thoroughly reasonable, and there's the added option of enjoying most of the wines by the half-bottle. 'Suggested wines' to accompany various dishes are listed on the menu. Five house wines are £13 per bottle, £3 per glass.

CHEFS: Jane Binns and Colette Nixon  PROPRIETORS: Nigel and Stephen Nixon  OPEN: all week 12.30 to 2 (12.45 to 1.30 Sun), 7.30 to 9  CLOSED: 3 Jan to 9 Feb  MEALS: alc L Mon to Sat (main courses £9.50). Set L Sun £15 to £18.50, Set D £28 to £31. Light L available Mon to Sat  SERVICE: not inc  CARDS: Amex, Delta, Diners, MasterCard, Switch, Visa  DETAILS: 70 seats. Private parties: 34 main room. Car park. Vegetarian meals. Children's helpings. No children under 8 at D. No smoking in dining room. Wheelchair access (also WC). No music. Air-conditioned ACCOMMODATION: 18 rooms, all with bath/shower. TV. Phone. B&B £75 to £130. Rooms for disabled. Baby facilities (*The Which? Hotel Guide*)

## APPLETHWAITE Cumbria                                      map 10

# ▲ Underscar Manor ✦✶

Applethwaite CA12 4PH                                    COOKING 6
TEL: (01768) 775000  FAX: (01768) 774904                 ANGLO-FRENCH
off A66, ½m N of Keswick                                  £39–£75

This Italianate Victorian villa on Skiddaw's lower slopes has spectacular views down Derwentwater. A chalet-style time-share development alongside is somewhat intrusive, but the garden's colony of red squirrels doesn't seem to mind. Despite a degree of eccentricity – orders are taken in a large sitting room, in the middle of what appears to be a Teddy Bears' picnic – the house feels natural, the atmosphere convivial. Lace tablecloths and chandeliers in the conservatory dining room create a sense of occasion, and the kitchen's strength lies in its assured technique and lack of gimmickry.

Well-sourced raw materials are at the heart of things, including Angus beef fillet, and organic poultry, perhaps in the shape of a duck breast with crisp, honeyed skin, served with a light samosa of minced duck, in a lemony, honeyed sauce. Lunch is more straightforward than dinner, but dishes are equally well executed, including a mousse-like mound of crabmeat, prawns and avocado bound with crème fraîche, with slices of mango, grapefruit and orange making an effective contrast. Part of Robert Thornton's success stems from his way with vegetables and accompaniments: for example a roast saddle of lamb partnered by a miniature moussaka, tomato-stuffed courgette, and dauphinoise potato, in a well-judged port sauce.

Desserts, stronger on quality than excitement, take in a light, citrussy lemon cheesecake on a crumbly base, professionally made sticky toffee pudding, and rhubarb tart in a fine short-crust pastry case. Cloche-wielding staff are friendly and efficient, service is unstuffy, and wines – although mostly over £20 and including comparatively few non-French Europeans – include some very sound bottles.

CHEF: Robert Thornton   PROPRIETORS: Pauline and Derek Harrison, and Gordon Evans   OPEN: all week 12 to 1, 7 to 8.30 (9 Sat)   CLOSED: 2 or 3 days after New Year   MEALS: alc (main courses L £14, D £20 to £25). Set L £20 to £28, Set D £33   SERVICE: not inc, card slips closed   CARDS: Amex, Delta, MasterCard, Switch, Visa   DETAILS: 50 seats. Private parties: 30 main room. Car park. Vegetarian meals. No children under 12. Jacket. No smoking in dining room. Occasional music. No mobile phones   ACCOMMODATION: 11 rooms, all with bath/shower. TV. Phone. D,B&B £125 to £360. No children under 12. Swimming pool (*The Which? Hotel Guide*)

## ARDINGTON   Oxfordshire                                                       map 2

## ▲ Boar's Head ⑤✳                                    | NEW ENTRY |

| Church Street, Ardington OX14 8QA | COOKING 3 |
| TEL/FAX: (01235) 833254 | MODERN EUROPEAN |
| EMAIL: brucebuchan@theboarshead.freeserve.co.uk | £27–£58 |

An arresting tableau of English heartland can be seen from the grounds of the church at Ardington. It is part of an 'almost eerily well-manicured village' with a shop, 'ye olde conference centre' and the Boar's Head. Maintained to a level of restoration so high as to make it appear repro, this country pub is nonetheless the genuine article, evident at once from its venerable beams.

Bruce Buchan, who took over in 2001, looks to be aiming high. Aberdeen Angus beef, Newlyn fish, dry-cured bacon, organic vegetables and his own bread all play their parts, and the menu of seven each of starters and main courses (together with a separate bar menu) seems in itself ambitious for the size of the place. A version of bouillabaisse at inspection was praised for the juicy freshness of its chunks of fish and its creamy consistency. A starter of various ways with salmon is intelligently garnished with a deep-fried oyster, but melon balls in Sauternes that come with smoked goose seem to be from a less discerning era. Main-course meats are classically prepared, with rack of salt-marsh lamb herb-crusted and partnered with duxelles and a cake of fried potato, or there may be a more voguish combination of sweetbreads, chorizo and monkfish in an agreeably viscous gravy. A hot Grand Marnier soufflé into which is ladled melting chocolate ice cream and some more of the liqueur is worth deciding on at the outset. France is the main thrust of the wine list, with some clarets in three figures, but there are some well-chosen, more affordable bottles too. House wines start at £10.50.

CHEF: Bruce Buchan   PROPRIETORS: Bruce Buchan, Terry Chipperfield and Richard Douglas   OPEN: all week 12 to 2.15, 7 to 9.30 (10 Fri and Sat)   CLOSED: 4 days at Christmas   MEALS: alc (main courses £11.50 to £19). Set L Sun £16.95. Bar menu available exc Sat D and Sun L   SERVICE: not inc   CARDS: Amex, Delta, MasterCard, Switch, Visa   DETAILS: 45 seats. 20 seats outside. Private parties: 26 main room. Car park. Children's helpings. No smoking in 1 dining room. Wheelchair access (also WC). Occasional music. No mobile phones   ACCOMMODATION: 3 rooms, all with bath/shower. TV. Phone. B&B £75 to £120   £5

---

*Report forms are at the back of the book; write a letter if you prefer; or email us at goodfoodguide@which.net*

## ARLINGHAM  Gloucestershire                                           map 2

# ▲ Old Passage Inn ⠀

**NEW ENTRY**

Passage Road, Arlingham GL2 7JR
TEL: (01452) 740547    FAX: (01452) 741871
EMAIL: oldpassageinn@ukonline.co.uk
WEBSITE: www.fishattheoldpassageinn.co.uk

COOKING 5
SEAFOOD
£28–£76

The name refers to the fact that, for hundreds of years, this location has been the lowest crossing point on the River Severn. It's an isolated spot, but the deep-green building is hard to miss, and the panoramic views across the river towards the Forest of Dean are a joy. Inside is bright and airy, with terracotta tiles, mint-green walls and palms in the dining room.

Fish and seafood are the specialities, and the stated philosophy is 'to treat the best ingredients simply'. That certainly seems to be registered by reporters, who have praised sauté scallops on minted pea purée with red wine jus, and daily specials such as a medley of eloquently fresh oysters, mussels, cockles and Atlantic prawns, baked and dressed with nothing more than lemon, garlic, herbs and olive oil. Corpulent lobsters are on display in a tank, and may turn up later grilled with garlic butter or with lobster sauce and Gruyère. A similar lobster sauce added resonant depth to a piece of crisp-skinned, 'perfectly timed' sea bass served on a bed of spinach leaves for an inspector. Meat eaters can enjoy organic sirloin steak, while a vegetarian main course might offer baked goats' cheese pie with tomato and pesto. An inch-deep slice of lemon tart with fine shortcrust is one way of finishing, but freshly made raspberry sorbet in a brandy-snap basket is considered a triumph as well, and hot-weather diners may well encounter a memorable version of summer pudding served with crème fraîche. A visitor on whom the place made a big impression described the service as 'intelligent, cheerful, relaxed, obliging and observant'. An imaginative wine list favours France and the southern hemisphere. Prices are fair, and it all kicks off with French white and Chilean red house wines at £10.60.

CHEFS: Patrick Le Mesurier and Raoul Moore    PROPRIETOR: Inn Fish ltd    OPEN: Tue to Sun L 12 to 2, Tue to Sat D 6.45 to 9    MEALS: alc (main courses £10.50 to £33)    SERVICE: not inc, card slips closed    CARDS: Amex, Delta, MasterCard, Switch, Visa    DETAILS: 60 seats. 20 seats outside. Private parties: 60 main room, 6 to 14 private rooms. Car park. Vegetarian meals. Children's helpings. No smoking in dining room. Wheelchair access (also WC). Occasional music. No mobile phones. Air-conditioned    ACCOMMODATION: 3 rooms, all with bath/shower. TV. Phone. B&B £50 to £90

## ARNCLIFFE  North Yorkshire                                           map 8

# ▲ Amerdale House ⠀

Arncliffe, Littondale BD23 5QE
TEL: (01756) 770250    FAX: (01756) 770266
WEBSITE: www.amerdalehouse.co.uk

COOKING 4
MODERN EUROPEAN
£43–£51

A peaceful spot in which to relax and unwind, Amerdale House is well cared for, inside and out. It feels like a family home, with well-spaced, neatly set tables, where four-course meals pass at a leisurely pace. The style is thankfully not too ambitious, which ensures a high degree of success, from a ramekin of creamed oyster mushrooms with bacon, to a terrine of oranges set in a Campari and orange jelly (not a dessert but a starter).

A no-choice second course (such as plump asparagus spears with melted butter and Parmesan shavings) might be followed by a fresh, tasty turbot fillet with a topping of prawns and a lemon butter sauce, or pink lamb fillet studded with garlic and rosemary, the meat coming from a butcher in Grassington. Finish with a platter of local Dales cheeses, a poached pear with a chocolate sauce and melting vanilla ice cream, or a wedge of gooey, toffee-flavoured pie packed with walnuts and pecans. Incidentals include good bread (especially the apricot and hazelnut), less good coffee, and an agreeably priced roving wine list: nothing from Italy but enough from France and Australia. Prices start at £12.95.

CHEF: Nigel Crapper  PROPRIETORS: Paula and Nigel Crapper  OPEN: all week D only 7.30 to 8 CLOSED: mid-Nov to mid-Mar  MEALS: Set D £32.50  SERVICE: none, card slips closed  CARDS: MasterCard, Switch, Visa  DETAILS: 24 seats. Private parties: 6 main room. Car park. No children under 8. No smoking in dining room. No music  ACCOMMODATION: 11 rooms, all with bath/ shower. TV. Phone. D,B&B £82.50 to £155. Baby facilities (*The Which? Hotel Guide*)

## ASENBY  North Yorkshire                                     map 9

## ▲ Crab & Lobster  🍴✳

Dishforth Road, Asenby YO7 3QL
TEL: (01845) 577286   FAX: (01845) 577109
EMAIL: reservations@crabandlobster.co.uk
off A168, between A19 and A1

COOKING 2
FISH/MODERN EUROPEAN
£24–£60

'A gem of a place and a real one-off,' summed up a visitor to this thatched pub and its quirky hotel (each room is modelled on a famous original from around the world, and breakfast includes boiled eggs with Marmite soldiers). The restaurant has been enlarged to include a conservatory ('the Pavilion'), and the eccentric but endearing décor continues to intrigue with its profusion of bric-à-brac. Despite a change of ownership Stephen Dean remains in the kitchen, where seafood is the main suit, in just about every guise one could imagine, from plain oysters to fishcakes, from mussels with chilli, garlic, coriander, lemon grass and coconut to a rich, appetising lobster, scallop and king prawn thermidor, served with new potatoes and well-dressed leaves.

Among main courses, a Moroccan-style tagine of mixed fish rubs shoulders with 'posh fish and chips' (chips are good, incidentally), and there is beef fillet with mushroom pudding for anyone who really can't stand seafood. The assiette of desserts combines quality and quantity, typically including a properly made crème brûlée with a thin, crisp topping, a simple lemon mousse, a soft and creamy tiramisù, a compote of summer fruits, a rich sticky toffee pudding, and an even richer chocolate brownie. Service appears to have been tightened up and is professional and unobtrusively attentive, and fair pricing characterises the lively wine list, which starts with house Duboeuf at £13, or £2.80 per glass.

CHEF: Stephen Dean  PROPRIETORS: Vimac Leisure  OPEN: all week 12 to 2.30, 6.30 to 10 MEALS: alc (main courses £12.50 to £17.50). Set L £11.50 (2 courses) to £13.50, Set L Sun £14.50 (2 courses) to £16.50, Set D Sun to Thur £19.50  SERVICE: not inc  CARDS: Amex, Delta, MasterCard, Switch, Visa  DETAILS: 140 seats. 100 seats outside. Private parties: 120 main room, 8 to 52 private rooms. Car park. Vegetarian meals. Children's helpings. No smoking in 1 dining room. Wheelchair access (also WC). Occasional music. No mobile phones. Air-conditioned ACCOMMODATION: 11 rooms, all with bath/shower. TV. Phone. B&B £85 to £150. Rooms for disabled

## ASHBOURNE  Derbyshire                                                                    map 8

## ▲ Callow Hall  ♥ ⁵⨯

Mappleton, Ashbourne DE6 2AA
TEL: (01335) 300900   FAX: (01335) 300512
EMAIL: reservations@callowhall.co.uk
WEBSITE: www.callowhall.co.uk
from Ashbourne marketplace, take A515; at top
of hill turn W at crossroads with Bowling Green          COOKING 3
pub on left; Mappleton road is first on right after      MODERN BRITISH-PLUS
bridge                                                   £29–£61

For those who don't already own a large country mansion, a visit to Callow Hall is probably the next best thing. Its 44 acres on the edge of the Peak District National Park give a sense of its scale, echoed by antlered heads in the hallway, big windows with large draped curtains in the drawing room, and a warm red dining room. A brochure notes that the Spencer family (owners here for 20 years) have been master bakers in Ashbourne since 1724, so it comes as no surprise that breads, pastries, jams and marmalades are all made in-house, nor perhaps that local materials (such as game and cheese) figure among the kitchen's materials.

A combination of traditional and more up-to-date ideas produces starters of asparagus in puff pastry with tomato fondue, and a salmon, crab and spinach fishcake served with red onion marmalade and beurre blanc. Beef and lamb are regulars to follow, and fish gets interesting treatment, appearing as baked Whitby cod with couscous and basil oil, or perhaps halibut steak with a rich onion gravy. Finish with a raspberry mousse gâteau, or a warm bread and almond pudding. Wines are quite traditional, with the classic regions of France featuring prominently. Lovers of fine German wine will find some excellent and keenly priced bottles, while Australian addicts are well catered for too; in addition, there is a decent selection of half-bottles. Six house wines range from £11.95 to £14.75.

CHEFS: David and Anthony Spencer   PROPRIETORS: David, Dorothy, Anthony and Emma Spencer
OPEN: Sun L 12.30 to 1.45, Mon to Sat D 7.30 to 9 (Sun D residents only)   CLOSED: 25 and 26 Dec
MEALS: alc D (main courses £16.50 to £20). Set L £20.50, Set D £38.50   SERVICE: not inc   CARDS:
Amex, Delta, Diners, MasterCard, Switch, Visa   DETAILS: 80 seats. Private parties: 40 main
room, 20 to 30 private rooms. Car park. Vegetarian meals. Children's helpings. No smoking in
dining room. No music. No mobile phones   ACCOMMODATION: 16 rooms, all with bath/shower.
TV. Phone. B&B £85 to £165. Rooms for disabled. Baby facilities. Fishing (*The Which? Hotel Guide*)  £5

---

Net prices *in the details at the end of an entry indicates that the prices given on a menu and on a bill are inclusive of VAT and service charge, and that this practice is clearly stated on menu and bill.*

---

## ASHBURTON Devon                                    map 1

# Agaric ✬✳

30 North Street, Ashburton TQ13 7QD                  COOKING 4
TEL: (01364) 654478                              MODERN BRITISH-PLUS
WEBSITE: www.agaricrestaurant.co.uk                      £32–£50

Easily found in the middle of Ashburton, Agaric is the vocation of a husband-and-wife team: Nick Coiley does the cooking, drawing on some years' experience at the Carved Angel in Dartmouth (see entry), while Sophie Coiley provides a warm welcome and a friendly presence front-of-house. Reporters have commented that the dining room lacks atmosphere and that staff could be more relaxed, but the food is attraction enough in itself. Nick Coiley's aim is to blend traditional and contemporary, hitching tried and tested techniques to an innovative approach, and basing menus on what is seasonal and locally available: crabs from Dartmouth and fish from Brixham, for example. On the one hand starters may include fish soup with croûtons, Parmesan and rouille, or a terrine of pork with sweetbreads and pistachios, and on the other pan-fried mackerel with garlic and smoked paprika. Main courses, meanwhile, range from brochette of marinated Devon lamb with vegetable couscous to pan-fried fillet of sea bass with tomato and lime salsa and coriander dressing; venison braised with shallots, red wine and bacon is for the more traditionally minded. Quince parfait with toasted brioche and quince compote makes a temptingly unusual way to finish. The list of two dozen wines is not perhaps the most inspired selection, but prices are fair, starting at £10.

CHEF: Nick Coiley    PROPRIETORS: Nick and Sophie Coiley    OPEN: Wed to Sun L 12 to 2.30, Wed to Sat D 7 to 9.30    CLOSED: 2 to 18 Oct, 25 Dec to 1 Jan    MEALS: alc exc Sun L (main courses £11 to £18.50). Set L Sun £19.50 (2 courses) to £22.50. Light L available    SERVICE: not inc, card slips closed    CARDS: Delta, MasterCard, Switch, Visa    DETAILS: 32 seats. 22 seats outside. Private parties: 32 main room. Vegetarian meals. Children's helpings. No smoking in dining room. Wheelchair access (also WC). Occasional music

## ASHFORD Derbyshire                                 map 9

# ▲ Riverside House ✬✳

Fennel Street, Ashford in the Water,
nr Bakewell DE45 1QF
TEL: (01629) 814275    FAX: (01629) 812873            COOKING 4
EMAIL: riversidehouse@enta.net                        FRENCH-PLUS
WEBSITE: www.riversidehousehotel.co.uk                   £38–£63

A 'soothing and civilised ambience' reports one, a 'luxurious country house atmosphere' says another of this stylishly furnished Georgian house a couple of miles from Bakewell. John Whelan's cooking owes much to France, though it also embraces Szechuan peppered salmon with a pineapple and red onion salsa, and tops off a cannelloni of courgette and roasted Mediterranean vegetables with curried halloumi cheese.

He cooks a sensibly short set-price menu and deals in generally straightforward combinations of ingredients, such as grilled lemon sole with herb butter and new potatoes, and a well-executed salad of moist quail with slices of boudin blanc. Although not all reporters have been equally happy with results, the food is mostly delivered with assurance, from rare roast partridge with roast vegetables, to first-class roast sea bass with a creamy, sticky, expertly made chive risotto. Desserts might include warm cherry and almond tart, cheese is pre-cut and pre-selected, and meals are rounded out with good appetisers, pre-dessert and petits fours. A new wine list was in preparation as the Guide went to press.

CHEF: John Whelan  PROPRIETOR: Penelope Thornton  OPEN: all week 12 to 2, 7 to 9.30  MEALS: Set L £26.95 (Sun £28.95), Set D £39.95. Brasserie menu also available  SERVICE: not inc  CARDS: Amex, Delta, Diners, MasterCard, Switch, Visa  DETAILS: 60 seats. 12 seats outside. Private parties: 60 main room, 16 to 32 private rooms. Car park. Vegetarian meals. No children under 12. No smoking in dining room. Wheelchair access (also WC). No music. No mobile phones  ACCOMMODATION: 15 rooms, all with bath/shower. TV. Phone. D,B&B £120 to £235. Rooms for disabled. No children under 12. Fishing  £5

---

**ATHERSTONE Warwickshire**                                                              map 5

## ▲ Chapel House ⁵✳                                    NEW ENTRY

Friar's Gate, Atherstone CV9 1EY                                            COOKING 1
TEL: (01827) 718949  FAX: (01827) 717702                          MODERN EUROPEAN
                                                                              £33–£54

Secluded, yet right in the town centre, the former dower house is half-hidden behind a high wall next to the parish church. It is deeply old-fashioned, with 'forgettable prints' on the walls, but exudes an air of enthusiasm, thanks not least to the amiable and unpretentious Keith Hawes. Ambition on the monthly-changing menu runs from a twice-baked Roquefort soufflé partnered by smoked salmon, to fresh-tasting, crusty calves' sweetbreads served with an unlikely pairing of pistachio dressing, and mustard and honey sauce. Although better sourcing of raw materials, and a drive for simpler, clearer flavours would go some way towards improving output, the cooking makes an honest impression: for example, in a tower of roast loin and slow-cooked shoulder of lamb, layered with aubergine purée, in a decent stock-based sauce. Likewise a respectable orange and Grand Marnier soufflé, with an ace chocolate ice cream, rounded off one meal. Incidentals include first-class springy bread, and a roving wine list offers plenty of choice under £20.

CHEF: Adam Bennett  PROPRIETOR: Keith Hawes  OPEN: Mon to Sat D only 7 to 9.15  CLOSED: 25 and 26 Dec  MEALS: alc (main courses £14 to £17.50)  SERVICE: not inc, card slips closed  CARDS: Amex, Diners  DETAILS: 40 seats. Private parties: 30 main room, 15 private room. Vegetarian meals. No children under 12. No smoking in dining room. Wheelchair access (not WC). Music. No mobile phones  ACCOMMODATION: 13 rooms, all with bath/shower. TV. Phone. B&B £35 to £90. No children under 12 (The Which? Hotel Guide)  £5

---

*If 'vegetarian meals' is noted in the details at the end of an entry, this means that a restaurant routinely lists at least one vegetarian starter and main course on menus. Other restaurants, however, may offer good vegetarian choices if you let them know in advance, so it is worthwhile phoning to enquire.*

---

## AYCLIFFE  Co Durham                                    map 10

# County ✦

**NEW ENTRY**

13 The Green, Aycliffe DL5 6LX
TEL: (01325) 312273   FAX: (01325) 308780
WEBSITE: www.the-county.co.uk

COOKING **3**
MODERN EUROPEAN
£23–£51

Just off the main road that runs through the village, this cream-painted pub, its name written up in smart blue script, faces a large green. Bar lunches and daily specials are chalked on a couple of boards, dinner is a generous carte, and between them they run the gamut from bangers and mash, via salmon spring rolls with a ginger and lime dipping sauce, to baked corn-fed chicken with roast winter vegetables. The menu is not averse to a bit of comfort food, in the form of eggs Benedict, or crayfish tails with tarragon and lemon mayonnaise, and the cooking is straightforward and carefully managed, using good materials.

Fish and seafood items feature prominently, including a bowl of smooth, creamy-textured saffron, mussel and smoked cod chowder, and a prime piece of haddock in a light, crisp batter with a sharp tartare sauce. Desserts are in equally soothing vein, perhaps offering chocolate torte with a Grand Marnier crème anglaise, or redcurrant cheesecake with blackcurrant sorbet. Service is personable, and a short wine list (mostly under £20) starts with house vin de pays at £10.95 (£2.85 a large glass, £3.75 for a third of a bottle).

CHEF/PROPRIETOR: Andrew Brown   OPEN: restaurant Sun L 12 to 3, Mon to Sat D 6.45 to 9.15; bar Mon to Sat L 12 to 2, Mon to Fri D 6 to 9   CLOSED: 25 Dec, 1 Jan   MEALS: alc (main courses £11 to £16.50). Set L Sun £11.95 (2 courses) to £13.95.   SERVICE: not inc, card slips closed   CARDS: Amex, Delta, Diners, MasterCard, Switch, Visa   DETAILS: 85 seats. Private parties: 10 to 30 private rooms. Car park. Vegetarian meals. Children's helpings. No smoking in 1 dining room. Music. Air-conditioned

## AYLESBURY  Buckinghamshire                             map 3

# ▲ Hartwell House ✦

Oxford Road, Aylesbury HP17 8NL
TEL: (01296) 747444   FAX: (01296) 747450
EMAIL: info@hartwell-house.com
WEBSITE: www.hartwell-house.com
on A418, 2m from Aylesbury towards Oxford

COOKING **5**
BRITISH
£32–£64

Hartwell House is one of the few establishments in the Guide that still requires male diners to wear jacket and tie, a practice as archaic as the magnificent Grade I listed mansion itself. Luxury and ornament are abundant throughout, and tables in the dining room are so well spaced that you may not even be able to overhear your neighbour's conversation.

Bucking the country-house trend, Daniel Richardson avoids the clutter of appetisers, intermediary courses and so on. Although luxury ingredients are not eschewed altogether, dishes are kept conceptually simple, avoiding excessive combinations of flavours and garnishes. A likeable unpretentiousness shows up in pumpkin soup with ginger and crème fraîche, for example, or pot-roast pork cutlets on sage-flavoured potatoes with leeks and confit shallots. Results can be impressive, as in an inspector's 'spanking-fresh' scallops cooked 'immaculately à point' and served on a diced tomato with purée shallots and crisp curls of deep-fried sweet potato. Meat dishes are equally well rendered: rack of Aylesbury lamb comes on intensely flavoured confit onions with smooth rosemary-infused mash and 'silky' spinach mixed with wild mushrooms.

You might finish with passion-fruit soufflé with its own sorbet, but the cheeseboard deserves special mention: ten varieties are listed with detailed tasting notes, and are served with home-made chutney and apricot and pecan bread. Service is 'extremely well drilled but not at all pompous', while wines are an imposing collection of heavyweights with big numbers attached. The house selection of five bottles are £14.90 and £21.

CHEF: Daniel Richardson   PROPRIETOR: Historic House Hotels Ltd   OPEN: all week 12.30 to 1.45, 7.30 to 9.45   CLOSED: dining room closed to non-residents Christmas and New Year   MEALS: Set L £22 to £29, Set D £46   SERVICE: net prices, card slips closed   CARDS: Amex, Delta, MasterCard, Switch, Visa   DETAILS: 60 seats. 25 seats outside. Private parties: 60 main room, 12 to 60 private rooms. Car park. Vegetarian meals. No children under 8. Jacket and tie at D. No smoking in dining room. Wheelchair access (also WC). Occasional music. No mobile phones   ACCOMMODATION: 46 rooms, all with bath/shower. TV. Phone. Room only £145 to £235. Rooms for disabled. No children under 8. Swimming pool. Fishing (*The Which? Hotel Guide*)

---

**BAKEWELL Derbyshire**                                                                 map 8

# Renaissance ⅍

Bath Street, Bakewell DE45 1BX                                      COOKING 4
TEL: (01629) 812687                                                       FRENCH
                                                                          £23–£52

---

Renaissance is an attractive conversion of a stone-built barn hidden away in a quiet corner of this bustling market town. Its air of lively informality is well received, as is the unmistakably Gallic atmosphere: this is an unashamedly French restaurant offering accomplished traditional cooking of a fairly sophisticated nature, and consistency appears to be a strong point. A starter of black pudding with a soft-boiled egg and a leek sauce impresses for the craft in its construction and the harmonising combination of flavours and textures, while a tureen of bright green broccoli soup has had a satin-like texture and plenty of flavour. Among main courses, braised lamb shank in white wine sauce has made a strong impact, the sweet-flavoured juicy meat falling from the bone into a full-flavoured broth-like sauce. Alternative options typically run to beef tournedos on a wild mushroom galette with green pepper sauce, or sea bass fillet with fennel sauce. Finish perhaps with glazed rice pudding and vanilla ice cream, or strawberries on lemon meringue. The list of around 50 wines is extensively annotated and offers a good range of prices and styles, starting with three house wines at £10.99.

CHEF: Eric Piedaniel   PROPRIETORS: Mr and Mrs Eric Piedaniel, and Mrs Béraud   OPEN: Tue to Sat and first and second Sun of month L (bookings only) 12 to 1.30, Tue to Sat D 7 to 9.30   CLOSED: 3 weeks Christmas, first two weeks Aug   MEALS: Set L Sun £14.95, Set L Tue to Sat £22.95, Set D Tue to Thur £14.95, Set D £22.95   SERVICE: not inc   CARDS: Delta, MasterCard, Switch, Visa   DETAILS: 70 seats. Private parties: 50 main room, 1 to 25 private rooms. Vegetarian meals. Children's helpings. No smoking in dining room. Wheelchair access (also women's WC). Music

## BARNET Hertfordshire      map 3

# Mims ⚡ £

63 East Barnet Road, Barnet EN4 8RN      COOKING 6
TEL/FAX: (020) 8449 2974      MEDITERRANEAN
EMAIL: enquiries@mims-restaurant.co.uk      £24–£33

Despite its unprepossessing location in a nondescript parade of shops, Mims continues to impress with its innovative take on Mediterranean-inspired dishes. Chef Ali Al-Sersy puts together brief, well-focused menus that emphasise strong flavours, among them a light and 'amazing' cappuccino-style smoked mushroom soup, and an open raviolo of aubergine (made of thin pasta) with a smoked tomato dressing. Reports have praised a main course of tender shank of lamb with 'beautifully presented and flavoured vegetables'. Main-course options may also include grilled chicken with penne, lemon, chilli and smoked garlic, or wood-roasted beef with roast vegetables and rosemary jus.

Pan-roasting is a favoured technique: sea bass with basil oil, or calf's liver with roast potatoes and sage, for instance. Presentation is 'smart', and towers are popular. Desserts may sound uncomplicated, but the likes of pear and almond tart, and strawberry cheesecake win plaudits. There is a short wine list of ten largely uninspired bottles (£8.50 to £19.95), but a BYO policy means that you can take along the wine of your choice (there is no corkage charge), making a visit even more of a bargain.

CHEFS: Ali Al-Sersy and M. Shaheen   PROPRIETOR: Ali Al-Sersy   OPEN: Tue to Sun 12.30 to 3, 6.30 to 11, Sat and Sun 12.30 to 11 (10.30 Sun)   MEALS: Set L £10.50 (2 courses) to £15, Set D £14 (2 courses) to £18.50. Snack menu available exc Sat D   SERVICE: 10%   CARDS: Diners, MasterCard, Switch, Visa   DETAILS: 45 seats. Private parties: 60 main room. No children under 7. No smoking in 1 dining room. Wheelchair access (not WC) £5

## BARNSLEY Gloucestershire      map 2

# ▲ Village Pub ⚑

Barnsley, Cirencester GL7 5EF
TEL: (01285) 740421   FAX: (01285) 740142      COOKING 3
EMAIL: reservations@thevillagepub.co.uk      MODERN BRITISH
WEBSITE: www.thevillagepub.co.uk      £29–£43

This place is full of atmosphere and feels like an old-fashioned pub, although in fact it goes in for up-market dining. It can get very crowded (and noisy), so that sometimes service can be over-stretched, though at others it is 'efficient'.

Food and drink orders are taken at the bar and followed up with table service. The cooking has an attractive heartiness, and the general impression is of good materials handled with skill and 'a lack of fussy goings-on'. Among enticing starters might be suckling pig and cabbage terrine with mustard celeriac, or pan-fried chicken livers with grilled polenta and mushrooms. Main courses might include Barnsley chop with sauté potatoes and rosemary roast carrots, or whole lemon sole with new potatoes, asparagus and morels. For afters, choose from farmhouse cheeses with home-made bread and chutney, or rice pudding with apple jelly. The annotated wine list is arranged by style. Italian wines – especially reds – are a strength, and 18 wines come by the 175 and 250ml glass. Bottle prices start at £10.95, and mark-ups are fair, most of the wines coming in under £20.

CHEF: Dominic Blake  PROPRIETORS: Tim Haigh and Rupert Pendered  OPEN: all week 12 to 2.30 (3 Sat and Sun), 7 to 9.30 (10 Fri and Sat)  CLOSED: 25 Dec  MEALS: alc (main courses £8 to £14.50)  SERVICE: not inc, 12% for parties of 8 or more  CARDS: Delta, MasterCard, Switch, Visa  DETAILS: 100 seats. 50 seats outside. Private parties: 20 main room. Car park. Vegetarian meals. Children's helpings. No music. No mobile phones  ACCOMMODATION: 6 rooms, all with bath/shower. TV. B&B £65 to £125  (£5)

## BARNSLEY  South Yorkshire                                          map 9

# Armstrongs  ♥ ⁵⁄✻

102 Dodworth Road, Barnsley S70 6HL
TEL/FAX:  (01226) 240113                                              COOKING 1
WEBSITE: www.armstrongsrestaurant.co.uk                       MODERN BRITISH
1½m from junction 37 of M1 towards Barnsley                          £37–£52

Robert and Elizabeth Crookes have made themselves at home in this large detached Victorian residence on the edge of town, and continue to welcome customers with good humour, while white-gloved waitresses usher visitors to the impeccably set dining room. The cooking still has a noticeable European slant, although some oriental influences might surface in, say, sesame chicken with peanut sauce, or Thai spiced mussels. Inconsistencies have been noted, and the kitchen appears to have lost some of its edge. Even so, there are good things to be had, notably pan-fried pork fillet with yellow peppers and sugar snap peas, and venison pudding with herb mash (although the 'hard' suet crust did not impress). Desserts might include a trio of rhubarb sweets, or warm apple pie with cider sorbet and crème anglaise. The wine list takes a quick spin around the winemaking globe; mark-ups are sensible, so there is plenty to choose below £20. A separate list of the fine and rare offers some good wines from classic French regions, as well as a couple of Italians and New World bottles. Five house wines sell for £12.50 or £14.50 (£3.30 or £3.50 a glass).

CHEF: Robert Crookes  PROPRIETORS: Robert and Elizabeth Crookes  OPEN: Wed to Fri L 12 to 2, Wed to Sat D 7 to 9.30  MEALS: Set L £14.50, Set D Wed to Fri £24.95, Set D Sat £29.95  SERVICE: not inc  CARDS: MasterCard, Switch, Visa  DETAILS: 40 seats. Private parties: 40 main room. Car park. Vegetarian meals. No children under 9. No smoking in dining room. Music

## BARWICK  Somerset                                                  map 2

# ▲ Little Barwick House  ♥ ⁵⁄✻

Barwick BA22 9TD
TEL:  (01935) 423902  FAX:  (01935) 420908
EMAIL:  reservations@barwick7.fsnet.co.uk
WEBSITE:  www.littlebarwickhouse.co.uk                           COOKING 6
turn E off A37 at roundabout 1m S of Yeovil; Little           MODERN ENGLISH
Barwick House ¼m on left                                              £26–£56

In a serene setting just outside Yeovil, this listed Georgian building is quietly decorated, its small, high-ceilinged rooms including a comfortable lounge and an uncluttered dining room with well-spaced tables, plus a conservatory extension. Tim Ford's food may be 'quite technical' but this isn't showy cooking; indeed, it comes over as quite conventional, though none the worse for that. He centres on prime cuts and species, the main item generally coming roasted with a straightforward accompaniment: squab pigeon with braised lentils, Cornish sea bass with baby fennel and girolles, or saddle of roe deer with beetroot purée and port sauce.

Local suppliers of patently good-quality materials provide an underpinning, and the fixed-price dinner menu might start with a warm salad of grilled red mullet with a tapénade dressing, or a pressed terrine of duck confit and foie gras served with spiced fruits, followed by pan-fried calves' sweetbreads on wild mushroom risotto. Desserts are as impressive as everything else, taking in a hot plum soufflé, banana tarte Tatin with a star anise ice cream, and 'exemplary' bread-and-butter pudding with vanilla custard and ice cream. Service from Emma Ford is friendly and professional, and the wine list features well-chosen bottles, arranged by style, and sensible pricing. At the upper end of the price spectrum, Australian reds are a strong point. Four house wines are £12.50 or £13.50, and there is plenty of interesting choice under £20.

CHEFS: Tim Ford and Maxime Perrier   PROPRIETORS: Tim and Emma Ford   OPEN: Wed to Sun L 12 to 2, Tue to Sat D 7 to 9   CLOSED: 1 Jan, 2 weeks Jan   MEALS: alc L (main courses £15 to £17). Set L £12.95 (2 courses) to £14.95, Set D £24.95 (2 courses) to £29.95   SERVICE: not inc, card slips closed   CARDS: Amex, MasterCard, Switch, Visa   DETAILS: 56 seats. 14 seats outside. Private parties: 35 main room. Car park. Children's helpings. No smoking in dining room. No music. No mobile phones. Air-conditioned   ACCOMMODATION: 6 rooms, all with bath/shower. TV. Phone. B&B £60 to £103. Baby facilities (The Which? Hotel Guide)

## BASLOW Derbyshire                                                    map 9

## ▲ Cavendish Hotel, Gallery Restaurant 🏵✖

Church Lane, Baslow DE45 1SP
TEL: (01246) 582311   FAX: (01246) 582312                COOKING 3
EMAIL: info@cavendish-hotel.net                         MODERN EUROPEAN
WEBSITE: www.cavendish-hotel.net                            £35–£58

Staff at this congenial hotel overlooking the Chatsworth Estate are 'without exception, welcoming, helpful, considerate and obviously enjoy their work'. Proprietor Eric Marsh is very much hands on, and the Cavendish also serves as a gallery for his varied collection of 300-odd paintings, some of them, naturally enough, hung from the high green walls of the grand and aptly named Gallery Restaurant. Antique chairs and well spaced tables add to the sense of comfort.

Adaptable modern menus offer plenty of choice, and there is no need to follow the usual three-course structure. Dishes are categorised under 'soups', 'meat', 'fish' and 'vegetarian', with several available as both starter and main: perhaps pan-seared calf's liver with balsamic red onions on scallion mash in a Maderia and truffle oil sauce. Begin perhaps with an open ravioli of tiger prawns, scallops and pak choi in a lobster bisque, followed by tender fillet of Castlegate beef with a mustard and peppercorn crust, and end with homely apple Bakewell tart ('crisp, light pastry') with Calvados ice cream and vanilla sauce. The compact wine list, organised by price, has a commendable range of halves, plus 'bin ends'. House wine is £12.95 (£3.50 a glass).

CHEF: Chris Allison   PROPRIETOR: Eric Marsh   OPEN: all week 12 to 2, 6 to 10   MEALS: alc (main courses £13 to £18). Garden Room menu also available   SERVICE: not inc   CARDS: Amex, Delta, Diners, MasterCard, Switch, Visa   DETAILS: 50 seats. Private parties: 50 main room, 18 private room. Car park. Vegetarian meals. Children's helpings. No smoking in dining room. Music. No mobile phones   ACCOMMODATION: 23 rooms, all with bath/shower. TV. Phone. Room only £95 to £145. Baby facilities. Fishing (*The Which? Hotel Guide*)

## ▲ Fischer's Baslow Hall 🍷 ✳

Calver Road, Baslow DE45 1RR
TEL: (01246) 583259   FAX: (01246) 583818
EMAIL: m.s@fischers-baslowhall.co.uk
WEBSITE: www.fischers-baslowhall.co.uk

COOKING 7
MODERN EUROPEAN
£37–£80

Baslow lies where the Derbyshire hills give way to softer countryside, a fine spot for an Edwardian house that looks older than it is. The place conveys a feeling of comfort and 'relaxed quality', its cosseting emphasised by a menu that delights in lobster, truffles, foie gras and wild mushrooms.

Materials include Label Anglais chicken and outdoor-reared Derbyshire Texel lamb, but sourcing here involves also picking the best materials from the lowlier rungs of the gastronomic ladder, and such humbler materials as pig's trotter, belly pork and rabbit form a central plank of the repertoire. Main courses often present two contrasting cuts, one prime, one less so: perhaps saddle of lamb beside a charlotte of the shank, or pink saddle of venison ('singularly high-quality', wild, from the Forest of Dean) paired with a deep mahogany venison osso buco. Sauces favour the sticky end of the spectrum, and dishes may be complex, but all the elements have a point – and, in these cases, a counterpoint.

It all sounds very meaty, and vegetarians do indeed get short shrift. Seafood lovers, though, have a choice of daily specials, such as a fresh-tasting, accurately timed turbot fillet on a sharp red wine sauce, surrounded by fondant potatoes topped with quartered artichoke hearts, and scattered with chanterelles and shallots. An inspection meal found bland flavours, inaccuracies in seasoning and timing, and little of the excitement or flair that has characterised the food in the past, but others have found the cooking on song and 'impressive without ostentation'. Successes have included a layered, ham-wrapped rabbit terrine set in jellied stock, served with a dense gribiche sauce and a small mound of sharply dressed leaves, plus a slew of well-executed desserts. A fig platter, for example, incorporated a scoop of ice cream in a roast fig, a fig Tatin, and a beignet of rice pudding with fig sauce. If the style sounds elaborate, Max's menu (£30, available Monday to Friday) dispenses with intricate appetisers and offers rather simpler dishes. Susan Fischer manages front-of-house with cool efficiency, aided by a team of young staff, and wines, from a clearly laid-out list, reflect the same level of professionalism. Tasting notes are concise, and the wines themselves centre on food-friendly styles from the Old and New Worlds at prices that won't break the bank. Three house wines sell for £13 and £15 (£3 and £3.75 per glass).

CHEF: Max Fischer   PROPRIETORS: Max and Susan Fischer   OPEN: all week 12 to 1.30, 7 to 9.30 (Sun D residents only)   CLOSED: 25 and 26 Dec   MEALS: Set L £20 (2 courses) to £24, Set L Sun £30. Set D Mon to Fri £25 (2 courses) to £30, Set D all week £48   SERVICE: not inc   CARDS: Amex, Delta, Diners, MasterCard, Switch, Visa   DETAILS: 68 seats. Private parties: 40 main room, 12 to 16 private rooms. Car park. Children's helpings. No children under 12 after 7pm. Jacket and tie.

No smoking in dining room. Wheelchair access (not WC). No music. No mobile phones ACCOMMODATION: 11 rooms, all with bath/shower. TV. Phone. B&B £100 to £180. Baby facilities (*The Which? Hotel Guide*)

## BATH  Bath & N. E. Somerset                                        map 2

## ▲ Bath Priory  ⅚✳

| | |
|---|---|
| Weston Road, Bath BA1 2XT | COOKING 6 |
| TEL: (01225) 331922   FAX: (01225) 448276 | MODERN FRENCH |
| WEBSITE: www.thebathpriory.co.uk | £40–£91 |

In a quiet road about a mile from the city centre, this house's clean architectural lines incline towards Georgian elegance. But internally its décor is a riot of late Victoriana: brocaded armchairs, sofas 'with so many cushions you scarcely know where to sit', and a dining room with swirly beige wallpaper and sporting prints. Robert Clayton's mission statement mentions simple foods but not humble ones, and his menu (a hefty set price with a few supplements) groans with foie gras, scallops, wood blewits and langoustines.

There is, though, a refreshing lack of richness or elaboration. Flavours are more conservative than bold, and if the cooking seems a little lacking in passion it is refined and balanced. Pared-down modern dishes are deftly flavoured: a scallop salad gaining a warming, oriental tang from a ginger velouté, for example. Good technique is applied to high-quality ingredients (including locally reared organic lamb), and fish is 'accurately cooked down to the last second', taking in 'stunning' sea bass with provençale couscous, and brill with a langoustine risotto.

Desserts also resist the temptation to gild the lily, judging by a top-notch apple tart (a simple round of flaky pastry with sharp apples and a rich, honeyed glaze) served 'at the ideal temperature – just warm', its flavours shrewdly balanced by an apple sorbet and crème anglaise. Service is from good-humoured, attentive French waiters. Few wines give change from £20, but another tenner brings plenty more within range; those with over £100 to spend can do so. House wine is £15.50.

CHEF: Robert Clayton   PROPRIETOR: Andrew Brownsword   OPEN: all week 12 to 1.45, 7 to 9.45 CLOSED: first week Jan   MEALS: Set L £25, Set D £47.50   SERVICE: not inc   CARDS: Amex, Delta, Diners, MasterCard, Switch, Visa   DETAILS: 55 seats. 12 seats outside. Private parties: 60 main room, 6 to 60 private rooms. Car park. Vegetarian meals. Children's helpings. No children under 7. No smoking in dining room. Wheelchair access (also WC). Occasional music. No mobile phones  ACCOMMODATION: 28 rooms, all with bath/shower. TV. Phone. B&B £140 to £330. Rooms for disabled. Baby facilities. Swimming pool (*The Which? Hotel Guide*)

## Blinis  ⅚✳                                              | NEW ENTRY |

| | |
|---|---|
| 16 Argyle Street, Bath BA2 4BQ | |
| TEL: (01225) 422510   FAX: (01225) 421764 | COOKING 5 |
| EMAIL: info@blinisbath.co.uk | ANGLO-FRENCH |
| WEBSITE: www.blinisbath.co.uk | £34–£82 |

Martin Blunos has run a small restaurant in suburban Bristol, a country-house-style operation outside Bath, and now operates a Blini Bar and restaurant in central Bath. Plush and padded, with saffron, primrose and pumpkin-coloured walls, and scenes of bucolic jollity on curtains and drapes, Blinis has an air of sparkle and freshness.

The long-standing scrambled-duck-egg signature dish is served in a shell in a leggy metal egg-cup, heated by a blue vodka flame, accompanied by Sevruga caviar, buckwheat pancakes and a glass of chilled flavoured vodka. The cooking – individual without being outlandish – takes in roast monkfish with oak-smoked bacon on a fricassée of peas, beans and asparagus, and a pressed terrine consisting of ham surrounded by butter beans set with jellied ham stock, served with pickled girolles and basil oil.

Portions are not all large – roast breast and stuffed thigh of poussin disappeared in a few mouthfuls – but the food is satisfying; a cube of braised belly pork comes with a silky-textured raviolo of herby sausage meat. Desserts might include bitter chocolate marquise with bay-leaf ice cream, or a little prune-filled frangipane tart with an almond top, served with a heap of spicy mashed prunes and a dollop of armagnac ice cream. Traditional French regions predominate on a wine list offering little under £20, bar some house wines (from £14, or £3.50 a glass).

CHEF: Martin Blunos  PROPRIETORS: Sebastian and Phillipa Hughes  OPEN: Tue to Sun L 12.30 to 1.30, Tue to Sat D 7.15 to 9.30  MEALS: Set L £14.50 (2 courses) to £20, Set D £44.50 to £55 (whole table). Bar menu also available all day  SERVICE: not inc, card slips closed  CARDS: MasterCard, Switch, Visa  DETAILS: 32 seats. Private parties: 16 main room. Vegetarian meals. Children's helpings. No smoking in dining room. Music ⓔ5

# Le Clos

1 Seven Dials, Saw Close, Bath BA1 1EN
TEL/FAX: (01225) 444450
EMAIL: reservations@leclos.co.uk
WEBSITE: www.leclos.co.uk

COOKING 3
MODERN FRENCH
£30–£56

Everything about Le Clos suggests style and confidence. Overlooking Kingsmead Square at the heart of Bath, the restaurant is next door to the Theatre Royal. Its dining room makes a favourable impression – done out elegantly in primrose yellow, tables laid smartly with crisp white cloths and sparkling glassware and cutlery – but doesn't overshadow Peter Quinion's assured, accomplished cooking.

Menus have a predominantly French accent and, although techniques are largely traditional, plenty of modern ideas are taken on board: loin of lamb on spicy couscous with tomato and basil jus, for example. Otherwise, the wide-ranging options may offer pan-fried salmon with garlic mash and horseradish cream sauce, alongside caramelised duck breast with kumquat confit and Grand Marnier sauce. Well-balanced flavours and careful cooking are commonly noted in reports, as is perfectly judged portion control. Service is 'superb – young, enthusiastic, knowledgeable', while wines are a well-chosen selection at reasonable prices, starting at £11.50.

CHEF: Peter Quinion  PROPRIETOR: David J. Gerhardt  OPEN: all week L 12 to 2.30, Mon to Sat D 6 to 10  MEALS: alc (main courses £11 to £19.50). Set L and D 6 to 7.30 £15.95 (2 courses) to £19.95, Set D £19.50 (2 courses) to £24.50  SERVICE: not inc, card slips closed  CARDS: Amex, Delta, Diners, MasterCard, Switch, Visa  DETAILS: 65 seats. Vegetarian meals. Children's helpings. No cigars/pipes in dining room. Wheelchair access (not WC). Music

# FishWorks ❧✳

| | |
|---|---|
| 6 Green Street, Bath BA1 2JY | COOKING 3 |
| TEL: (01225) 448707   FAX: (01225) 447562 | SEAFOOD |
| WEBSITE: www.fishworks.co.uk | £29–£59 |

A bright blue awning and paintwork pinpoint this combined seafood café and fishmonger just off Bath's main shopping street. The upstairs dining room has modern pale-wood furniture, blackboards announcing specials from daily landings and wine of the week, and a buzzy, cosmopolitan atmosphere.

Head chef Gary Rosser follows FishWorks philosophy (there are sibling branches in Bristol and Christchurch, see entries), cooking high-quality materials simply: thin slices of octopus tossed with salt and olive oil to start for example. To follow, try whole sea bass baked in sea salt, or (from the specials board) roast monkfish with baby fennel and shellfish. Crustacea contribute such delights as oysters, lobster, mussels, clams and crab, and vegetables are 'as top-class as the seafood'; desserts, though (perhaps Sicilian lemon tart with mascarpone) play second fiddle. The compact wine list majors on whites, but has a few light reds, and five house bottles from £12 (£3 a glass). Service is quick but can be variable.

CHEF: Gary Rosser   PROPRIETOR: FishWorks plc   OPEN: Tue to Sun 12 to 3, Tue to Sat 6 to 10   MEALS: alc (main courses £8.50 to £20)   SERVICE: not inc, card slips closed   CARDS: Amex, Delta, Diners, MasterCard, Switch, Visa   DETAILS: 40 seats. 16 seats outside. Private parties: 30 main room. Vegetarian meals. Children's helpings. No smoking in dining room. Music  £5

---

# Moody Goose ❧✳

| | |
|---|---|
| 7A Kingsmead Square, Bath BA1 2AB | |
| TEL/FAX: (01225) 466688 | COOKING 5 |
| EMAIL: enquiries@moody-goose.com | ENGLISH |
| WEBSITE: www.moody-goose.com | £28–£62 |

The Goose is in a row of identical honey-coloured stone buildings, and newcomers might note that it is easy to pass the entrance a couple of times before spotting it. Two dining rooms – one small, one tiny – are in the basement under vaulted ceilings, decorated in understated style and with good white table linen. 'Highly specialised and very forward-looking' is how one report characterised Stephen Shore's culinary philosophy. A set lunch and a pre-theatre menu give way to fixed-price and à la carte dinners, when creativity takes wing.

Cannelloni of confit wild rabbit plus roast apple and a herb broth is one way to start, or there may be an unusual terrine: say, spring lamb with sweetbreads and mint with a chickpea and chilli salsa. At inspection a complex main course married caramelised duck breast, a jambonnette of the leg, and a blueberry chutney 'sharp and bursting with flavour'; the final garnish was a stack of vegetables topped with a 'tiny grilled rasher of excellent pancetta'. This layering continues in desserts such as a small tart of fine short-crust pastry housing a poached half-peach masked with a sabayon strewn with chopped pistachios, plus a scoop of 'speckled and creamy' vanilla ice cream to one side. Lily-gilding maybe, but technique is so accomplished that reporters are won over. Service can appear to suffer stage-fright, but generally gets things right. A broad-minded and commendable wine list centres on France; nine house wines start at £13 (£3.30 a glass).

CHEF: Stephen Shore PROPRIETORS: Stephen and Victoria Shore OPEN: Mon to Sat 12 to 1.30, 6 to 9.30 (10 Sat) CLOSED: 1 week Jan, 1 week May, bank hols (exc Good Friday) MEALS: alc D (main courses £18 to £19.50). Set L and D 6 to 7 £12 (2 courses) to £16, Set D £25 SERVICE: not inc, card slips closed CARDS: Amex, Delta, Diners, MasterCard, Switch, Visa DETAILS: 30 seats. Private parties: 20 main room, 8 private room. Vegetarian menu available with notice. No children under 8. No smoking in dining room. Music

## ▲ Queensberry Hotel, Olive Tree

Russel Street, Bath BA1 2QF
TEL: (01225) 447928 FAX: (01225) 446065 COOKING **4**
EMAIL: reservations@batholivetree.com ANGLO-FRENCH-PLUS
WEBSITE: www.batholivetree.com £27–£57

Occupying a basement – in fact, three basements under neighbouring houses, whose floor levels step down, following the road's incline – the Olive Tree is warmly decorated in pinky beige, with fresh flowers and reasonably spaced tables. Although the kitchen claims its blend of English and French ideas to be modern, the repertoire takes in some fairly traditional dishes too, such as provençale fish soup with rouille and croûtons, and coq au vin, alongside maybe asparagus with herb risotto cakes, or a stir-fry of cuttlefish, mussels, cockles and clams with coriander.

Seafood gets its fair share of attention, perhaps in the form of home-smoked haddock with a poached egg and spiced potato, or a light and delicately flavoured crab soufflé spiked with saffron and Gruyère, while meat dishes have included moist, tender shank of lamb with assorted vegetables, and partridge (served well done rather than the advertised pink, for one reporter) with lentils, ceps and roast vegetables. Portion sizes, by the way, are on the small side. Finish perhaps with cherry and Kahlùa soufflé, or orange cake with clotted cream. Service is attentive and friendly, and the wine list, though fairly brief, packs in plenty of interest without sacrificing value. France is the main focus of attention, although Italy and Australia feature among the eight house selections (up to £12.50), and some well-chosen bottles from Argentina, Spain and South Africa make their way into the 'recommended' section.

CHEF: Jason Horn PROPRIETORS: Stephen and Penny Ross OPEN: Mon to Sat L 12 to 2, all week D 7 (6.45 Fri and Sat) to 10 CLOSED: 4 days Christmas, L bank hols MEALS: alc (main courses £12.50 to £18). Set L £13.50 (2 courses) to £15.50, Set D exc Sat £26 SERVICE: not inc CARDS: Delta, MasterCard, Switch, Visa DETAILS: 60 seats. Private parties: 30 main room, 2 to 30 private rooms. Vegetarian meals. Children's helpings. No smoking in dining room. Wheelchair access (also WC). Music. Air-conditioned ACCOMMODATION: 29 rooms, all with bath/shower. TV. Phone. B&B £95 to £210. Rooms for disabled. Baby facilities (*The Which? Hotel Guide*)

*'They do not appear to know what Pommes de terre Dauphinoise are, no crime unless you claim to serve them. They do.'* (On eating in Scotland)

# Richmond Arms £

7 Richmond Place, Bath BA1 5PZ

TEL: (01225) 316725

COOKING 2
FUSION
£19–£33

An 'extraordinary location' in a venerable Georgian terrace sets the mood for this bow-windowed, two-room pub. Over the years, the Cunninghams have maintained its identity as a local hostelry, although the smoke-laden atmosphere in the drinkers' bar is not to everyone's taste. However, you can always escape to the south-facing patio for a breath of fresh air and some al fresco dining in good weather.

The kitchen's roll call of dishes may not be large, but it spans the globe. Sharp, modern ideas abound and there's a 'very pleasing simplicity' about the food: warm salad of squid with chickpeas, coriander, chilli and lemon juice has been notable for well-balanced flavours and spot-on timing. Duck breast with tamarind sauce has also made a good impression, and other dishes might include Thai pork curry, and chicken breast poached in mango, rum and ginger, as well as the ever-popular kangaroo steak. Home-made ice creams are the stars of desserts. Service is unpretentious. The wine list is a modest, fashionable selection chalked on boards behind the bar, kicking off with house French at £8.

CHEF: Marney Cunningham   PROPRIETORS: John and Marney Cunningham   OPEN: Tue to Sun L 12 to 2, Tue to Sat D 6 to 8.30 (9 Fri and Sat)   CLOSED: no food served 25 Dec to 1 Jan; 2 weeks owners' holiday later in year (phone to check)   MEALS: alc (main courses Tue to Sat L £4 to £5.50, D and Sun L £7.50 to £11)   SERVICE: not inc   CARDS: none   DETAILS: 35 seats. 30 seats outside. Vegetarian meals. No children under 14. Music

---

# ▲ Royal Crescent, Pimpernel's ✱

16 Royal Crescent, Bath BA1 2LS

TEL: (01225) 823333   FAX: (01225) 339401

EMAIL: reservations@royalcrescent.co.uk

WEBSITE: www.royalcrescent.co.uk

COOKING 5
FUSION
£42–£84

The hotel, slap in the middle of the crescent, is grand without being stuffy, and blessed with helpful staff. Pimpernel's, 'with an air of Jane Austen about it', is in the dower house at the back, reached along a garden path. While service at Pimpernel's has been described as 'patchy', the food by contrast is button-bright and often exotic, thanks to a significant Asian input. This may appear at odds with the surroundings – anyone expecting florid hotel presentation or a mid-meal sorbet will be disappointed – but it certainly provides a welcome breath of fresh air.

There are, to be sure, a few luxuries, such as marbled foie gras with Sauternes jelly, but the cooking generally makes its impact with sound technique, prime materials and astute judgement. Flavours tend to be pointed up with a sparky accompaniment, such as sherry vinegar jus (with sauté pigeon on Puy lentils) or a gribiche dressing (with baked codling), while at the more straightforward end of the spectrum might be a starter salad of crab and sauté scallops.

Even the lunch menu enters into the spirit of things, producing Jerusalem artichoke soup with chicken and tarragon dumplings, and roast salmon in a coconut and coriander froth. Desserts, meanwhile, take in a vanilla and blackcurrant trifle, peppermint parfait, and a dark chocolate soufflé with crunchy toffee ice cream. In so far as prices are a bone of contention, the stylistically arranged wine list doesn't help; there is much of interest, but little under £20. House Anjou Blanc is £18.50, Saumur-Champigny £27.50.

CHEF: Steven Blake   PROPRIETOR: Cliveden Ltd   OPEN: all week 12.30 to 2, 7 to 10   MEALS: alc D (main courses £19.50 to £26.50). Set L £18 (2 courses) to £25   SERVICE: not inc   CARDS: Amex, Delta, Diners, MasterCard, Switch, Visa   DETAILS: 60 seats. 45 seats outside. Private parties: 40 main room, 40 to 100 private rooms. Car park. Vegetarian meals. Children's helpings. No smoking in dining room. Wheelchair access (not WC). Occasional music. Air-conditioned ACCOMMODATION: 45 rooms, all with bath/shower. TV. Phone. Room only £230. Baby facilities (*The Which? Hotel Guide*)

## BATTLE  East Sussex                                                    map 3

# Pilgrims ✱ £                                              NEW ENTRY

1 High Street, Battle TN33 0AE                                    COOKING 2
TEL: (01424) 772314   FAX: (01424) 775547            MODERN EUROPEAN
WEBSITE: www.foodrooms.co.uk                                  £26–£73

Formerly a tea-room and, rather longer ago, a rest house for pilgrims to Battle Abbey, this is an architectural gem. Its lofty, many-timbered entrance hall leads to a more comfortably domestic dining area, with armchair and sofa seating and abstract artwork. The menu structure may look a little complicated, but there's striking food for those who get the hang of it. Sliced pigeon breast with mashed potato and a red wine and balsamic reduction made a full-flavoured starter at inspection, while real skill at timing shows in a main course of loin of spring lamb with artichoke hearts. Offbeat ideas can work well: a pairing of brill and turbot accompanied by mash topped with a thick emulsion flavoured with chilli and pepper, the plate slicked with bouillabaisse sauce. Portions can seem generous, witness a large sundae glass of syllabub trifle piled with more whipped cream. A separate list of chocolate desserts gives addicts agonising choices: the ice-cream alone is superb, 'correctly bitter and rich'. Assured and friendly service complements the food, and the wine list offers a skilfully chosen selection at generally agreeable prices. Five house wines (including one from Sussex) are £10.50.

CHEFS: Neil Sadler and Glenn Keen   PROPRIETOR: Food Rooms Ltd   OPEN: all week L 12 to 2.45, Mon to Sat D 7 to 9.30   CLOSED: 25 and 26 Dec   MEALS: alc (main courses £7.50 to £24.50). Set L Mon to Fri £12.75 (2 courses) to £17.20. Set L Sun £13.75 (2 courses) to £17.25. Set D Mon to Thur £12.75 (2 courses) to £17.20. Light menu also available 12 to 10.45   SERVICE: 12.5% (optional), card slips closed   CARDS: Amex, MasterCard, Switch, Visa   DETAILS: 68 seats. 60 seats outside. Private parties: 50 main room, 8 to 14 private rooms. Vegetarian meals. Children's helpings. No smoking in dining room. Occasional music  £5

---

*'We were not privy to the jokes that made the partying coven at another table screech every ten seconds for half an hour, and might have enjoyed ourselves more had we been.'*
(On eating in Scotland)

## BEESTON Nottinghamshire                                    map 5

# La Toque ✽

| | |
|---|---|
| 61 Wollaton Road, Beeston NG9 2NG | COOKING 3 |
| TEL: (0115) 922 2268   FAX: (0115) 922 7979 | FRENCH |
| | £33–£58 |

After a dash of redecorating, creams and browns now dominate this very French restaurant, its tables clothed in trendy brown and black, its seasonally changing menu a combination of both traditional ideas and more contemporary offerings. Expect to find foie gras accompanied by a compote of grapes, apples and raisins in a Sauternes jus, as well as a salmon fillet served unusually with a ragoût of bacon and mushrooms, watercress purée and a crab and guinea fowl jus.

A few other luxuries find their way on to the plate – a truffled celeriac rémoulade, for example, to accompany a peppered, seared loin of tuna – and meat and fish tend to favour prime cuts and species: such as Dover sole with asparagus in a champagne velouté, or Scottish beef fillet with a red onion and shiitake galette in a port sauce. Variations on classic ideas also appear among desserts, perhaps an apple version of clafoutis, or crème brûlée served with a caramelised pear cake. A compact list of reasonably priced wines is supplemented by a short fine wine section and four French house wines at £12.50 (£4.50 for a very large glass).

CHEF: Mattias Karlsson   PROPRIETOR: La Toque Ltd   OPEN: Mon to Sat 12 to 2, 6.45 to 10.45 (booking advisable at L)   CLOSED: 26 to 30 Dec, second week Aug   MEALS: alc (main courses £14.50 to £17). Set L £14.95 (2 courses) to £19.95   SERVICE: 10%, card slips closed   CARDS: Amex, Delta, Diners, MasterCard, Switch, Visa   DETAILS: 44 seats. Private parties: 30 main room. Car park. Vegetarian meals. No children under 8. No smoking in 1 dining room. Wheelchair access (also WC). Music. Air-conditioned £5

## BIRCH VALE Derbyshire                                      map 8

# ▲ Waltzing Weasel ✽

| | |
|---|---|
| New Mills Road, Birch Vale SK22 1BT | |
| TEL/FAX: (01663) 743402 | |
| EMAIL: w-weasel@zen.co.uk | COOKING 2 |
| WEBSITE: www.w-weasel.co.uk | ANGLO-EUROPEAN |
| on A6015, ½m W of Hayfield | £26–£43 |

Rooms and a restaurant extension help to make this stone-built country inn more than just a pub. The kitchen works on three fronts, starting with a combination of traditional English dishes (roast duck with apple sauce) and what it calls 'European casseroles', such as Spanish pollo al chilindron (chicken with pork and bacon). It also has a penchant for Italian food, perhaps in the shape of lamb, marinated and cooked with anchovies, garlic, rosemary and wine. Thirdly, just under half the items are vegetarian, ranging from griddled aubergine with chilli and garlic to Moroccan vegetable casserole. Desserts take in treacle tart (with custard or cream) and cold lemon soufflé. Prices are ambitious, and a predominantly French wine list stays commendably under £20 for the most part, starting with a quartet of house wines at £11.95.

CHEF: Tracy Young   PROPRIETORS: Michael and Linda Atkinson   OPEN: all week 12 to 2, 7 to 9
MEALS: alc L (main courses £8.50 to £15.50). Set D £22.50 (2 courses) to £26.50   SERVICE: not
inc, card slips closed   CARDS: Amex, Delta, MasterCard, Switch, Visa   DETAILS: 36 seats. 20
seats outside. Private parties: 36 main room. Car park. Vegetarian meals. Children's helpings.
No children under 5 at D. No smoking in dining room. Wheelchair access (not WC). No music. No
mobile phones. Air-conditioned   ACCOMMODATION: 8 rooms, all with bath/shower. TV. Phone.
B&B £45 to £105 (*The Which? Hotel Guide*)

## BIRMINGHAM West Midlands

map 5

# Bank ▼

4 Brindleyplace, Birmingham B1 2JB
TEL: (0121) 633 7001   FAX: (0121) 633 4465                          COOKING 3
EMAIL: birres@bankrestaurants.com                          MODERN EUROPEAN
WEBSITE: www.bankrestaurants.com                               £24–£63

One of the big players in Birmingham's revitalised restaurant scene, this vibrant
venue is part of the cool, fashionable development now entitled Brindleyplace.
Through a revolving door you are ushered politely along a corridor, and past the
bar and kitchen: 'it must be the longest route to any dining room in Britain.'
There is 'design' everywhere, from serried ranks of glass slats suspended from
the ceiling, to watercolours depicting dreamy images of seaside holidays. Staff
are supremely keen, eager to serve and eager to please.

The place caters for all comers with breakfasts, express lunches and pre- and
post-theatre deals (it's just a few minutes' walk from Symphony Hall and the
New Rep), as well as a full carte. The owners describe their cooking as 'liberated
French' (in fact it spans everything from crispy duck won tons to sausage and
mash), and the kitchen goes about its business with methodical professionalism, delivering first-division pea and Gorgonzola risotto, and supremely
good scallops, seared to perfection, with a salad of new potatoes, artichoke
hearts and strips of roasted red pepper. Elsewhere, there are specials, such as
slow-roast belly pork with soba noodles. A shot of Australian Botrytis Semillon
fits comfortably with desserts such as pannacotta with apricot 'nectar', and
sticky apple toffee pudding. The wine list suits the contemporary setting and is
scattered with trendy producers from Australia to Canada, all organised by style.
Prices are generally fair: house Chardonnay and Merlot from France's pays d'Oc
start at £11 a bottle (£2.90 a glass, £8.05 for 50cl) and there is good choice below
£20. For those feeling more flush, the 20-strong Bank Cellar list is the place to
look.

CHEF: David Colcombe   PROPRIETOR: Bank Restaurant Group Plc   OPEN: Mon to Sat L 12 (11
Sat) to 3, Sun L 11.30 to 3.30, D 5 to 10, Mon to Sat D 5.30 to 11 (11.30 Fri and Sat)   CLOSED: 1
and 2 Jan   MEALS: alc (main courses £9.50 to £20). Set L and D 5.30 to 7 and 10 to 11 £11.50 (2
courses) to £14. Bar menu, Sat and Sun brunch available   SERVICE: 12.5% (optional), card slips
closed   CARDS: Amex, Delta, Diners, MasterCard, Switch, Visa   DETAILS: 150 seats. 100 seats
outside. Private parties: 150 main room, 50 to 100 private rooms. Vegetarian meals. Children's
helpings. No-smoking area. Wheelchair access (also WC). No music. Air-conditioned  (£5)

---

*All entries, including Round-ups, are fully indexed at the back of the Guide.*

# Chung Ying £

16–18 Wrottesley Street, Birmingham B5 4RT
TEL: (0121) 622 5669   FAX: (0121) 666 7051          COOKING 2
EMAIL: chungying@aol.com                              CHINESE
WEBSITE: www.chungying.co.uk                         £26–£62

At the heart of Birmingham's rejuvenated Chinese quarter, this long-serving warhorse opposite the Arcadian Centre is still – arguably – the most consistent venue of its kind in the city. Like most of its oriental neighbours, it has been given a few licks of colourful paint, but the dining room remains resolutely traditional. Don't expect new-wave minimalism or effete interpretations of classic dishes here: what you get are mighty portions of authentic, peasant-style Cantonese food that are big on flavour and punch. The monumental menu kicks off with more than 50 dim sum, and reporters have singled out scallops cheung fun, deep-fried shredded squid, and a benchmark version of glutinous rice packed with luscious meaty titbits wrapped in lotus leaves. For those with even bigger appetites, there are casseroles, hotpots (braised brisket with spices has been authentically fatty and 'wonderfully tender'), and a host of one-plate rice and noodle dishes, not to mention esoteric specialities, such as steamed pork pie with fresh squid. An army of waiters keeps up with the kitchen and the turnover. House French is £11.

CHEF: T.C. Tsang   PROPRIETOR: Siu Chung Wong   OPEN: all week 12 to 11.30 (10.30 Sun)
CLOSED: 25 Dec   MEALS: alc (main courses £7.50 to £17.50). Set D £28 (2 people) to £80 (5 people)   SERVICE: 10% (optional)   CARDS: Amex, Delta, Diners, MasterCard, Switch, Visa
DETAILS: 250 seats. Private parties: 120 main room. Vegetarian meals. Wheelchair access (not WC). Music. Air-conditioned .

# Chung Ying Garden £          | NEW ENTRY |

17 Thorp Street, Birmingham B5 4AT
TEL: (0121) 666 6622   FAX: (0121) 622 5860          COOKING 2
EMAIL: chungyinggarden@aol.com                       CHINESE
WEBSITE: www.chungying.co.uk                         £25–£59

Like its elder sibling, Chung Ying (see entry above), this city-centre Chinese is a vast place with a gargantuan menu. It stands just round the corner from the Hippodrome and you can't miss the huge red and silver sign or the pennants with calligraphy blowing in the wind. Inside, it reminded one reporter of a European hotel dining room with solid-looking pillars and patterned carpets, but there's no denying the legitimacy of the food. The 400-dish menu is staunchly Cantonese with a huge assortment of dim sum, one-plate rice and noodle dishes, hotpots and casseroles. Steamed beef dumplings sitting on a bed of watercress impressed at inspection, although the real highlight was a superb dish of rich stewed belly pork with sliced yams, which oozed intensity and depth of flavour. Also recommended are stuffed bean curd with black-bean sauce, and braised noodles with king prawns, and there are a few unusual crossovers among the chef's specials: deep-fried chicken stuffed with banana, for example. Service is on the ball. House French is £9.50.

CHEF/PROPRIETOR: Siu Chung Wong  OPEN: all week noon to 11.30 (10.30 Sun)  CLOSED: 25 Dec
MEALS: alc (main courses £7.50 to £13). Set D £28 (2 people) to £80 (5 people)  SERVICE: not inc
CARDS: Amex, Delta, Diners, MasterCard, Switch, Visa  DETAILS: 350 seats. Private parties: 250
main room, 10 to 250 private rooms. Vegetarian meals. Wheelchair access (also WC). Music. Air-
conditioned  £5

---

## ▲ Hotel du Vin & Bistro 🍷

25 Church Street, Birmingham B3 2NR
TEL/FAX: (0121) 200 0600                              COOKING 3
EMAIL: reservations@birmingham.hotelduvin.com        MODERN EUROPEAN
WEBSITE: www.hotelduvin.com                          £33–£54

'There is so much to enjoy here' enthused one reporter, citing the atmosphere,
wines, friendly service and of course the food; as at other branches of this small,
individual chain (see entries in Bristol, Tunbridge Wells and Winchester), it is
the ensemble that wins fans. The building has been 'joyfully restored' with a
bold sweeping staircase, handsome marble columns and wonderful limestone
walls.

A few 'simple classics' from the bistro repertoire, common to all four outlets,
include foie gras and chicken liver parfait, and ribeye steak with frites and
béarnaise, while the regular menu might offer roast black pudding with celeriac
purée, and risotto of smoked salmon with broad beans and mint. Variety is
ensured with braises of pork cheek or heel of beef sitting alongside whole
grilled plaice, or roast cod with mussel sauce. Finish with a French cheese
selection, rice pudding, or pannacotta. The wine list delights with its broad
range and fair mark-ups. Famous names from Burgundy and Bordeaux rub
shoulders with less-well-known ones from around France, as well as Austria,
Switzerland and the New World (California is particularly well represented).
Producers are well chosen throughout and the reasonable mark-ups encourage
experimentation. A short list of 'sommelier's selections' of wines by the glass is
listed on the menu, and three house wines, two whites and a red, start at £12.95,
or £3.65 per glass.

CHEF: Eddie Grey  PROPRIETOR: Hotel Du Vin Ltd  OPEN: all week 12 to 1.45, 7 to 9.45  MEALS:
alc exc Sun L (main courses £12.50 to £15.50). Set L Sun £23.50  SERVICE: not inc  CARDS:
Amex, Delta, Diners, MasterCard, Switch, Visa  DETAILS: 90 seats. 20 seats outside. Private
parties: 70 main room, 10 to 24 private rooms. Vegetarian meals. Children's helpings. No cigars/
pipes in dining room. Wheelchair access (also WC). No music  ACCOMMODATION: 66 rooms, all
with bath/shower. TV. Phone. Room only £110 to £395. Rooms for disabled. Baby facilities (*The
Which? Hotel Guide*)

---

## Metro Bar & Grill                    `NEW ENTRY`

73 Cornwall Street, Birmingham B3 2DF                COOKING 2
TEL: (0121) 200 1611  FAX: (0121) 200 1911           MODERN EUROPEAN
WEBSITE: www.themetrobar.co.uk                       £32–£56

Set up in 1997, this pre-dates much of the Birmingham bar/brasserie revolution.
The building is deep in the city's commercial centre, although the narrow
entrance is easily missed ('look for the crowds of suited-and-booted city slickers
outside on their mobile phones,' observed one reporter). Inside, the bar heaves

when happy hour comes around: beyond is the restaurant with its mirrored walls, spot-lit glass roof and curious abstract artwork. The menu changes regularly, but the chargrill and rotisserie are given plenty of exercise turning out calf's liver with pea mash, onion jam and pancetta; and spit-roast chicken with artichoke, smoked bacon and rocket boulangère. Rustic breads with olives and Feta are fine (although they do not come cheap); starters include lively combos such as citrus-marinated sardine fillets with courgette and sweet potato rösti; while the crustacean constituency is represented by, for example, lobster and giant prawn kebab with samphire and chorizo salad. Service is as effusive and willing as you could wish for in this regenerated city. Six house wines on a short, fairly priced, global list start at £10.95, or £2 per glass.

CHEF: Jenny Clarke   PROPRIETORS: Chris Kelly and Paul Salisbury   OPEN: Mon to Fri L 12 to 2.30, Mon to Sat D 6 to 9.30   CLOSED: 24 Dec D, all 25 Dec, 26 Dec L, 31 Dec D, all 1 Jan   MEALS: alc (main courses £10 to £19)   SERVICE: not inc   CARDS: Amex, Delta, MasterCard, Switch, Visa   DETAILS: 100 seats. 6 seats outside. Private parties: 80 main room. Vegetarian meals. No cigars/ pipes in dining room. Wheelchair access (also WC). Music. Air-conditioned  (£5)

## Le Petit Blanc  £

9 Brindleyplace, Birmingham B1 2HS
TEL: (0121) 633 7333   FAX: (0121) 633 7444
EMAIL: birmingham@lepetitblanc.co.uk
WEBSITE: www.lepetitblanc.co.uk

NEW CHEF
MODERN FRENCH
£24–£54

It is perhaps inevitable with this sort of enterprise that chefs move around, and Anthony Brown was appointed just as the Guide went to press. This coincided with a couple of other changes to the Petit Blanc chain. Clive Fretwell, who used to cook at HQ (see entry Great Milton), has returned to take executive charge of the four branches (see entries Cheltenham, Manchester and Oxford), and the same menu is now in operation at each. This means that Anthony Brown will be serving up a range of options – including children's and fixed price menus – and dishes such as a coconut, vegetable, lime and coriander soup, a rather more French chicken liver and foie gras parfait, followed perhaps by fillet of sea bream with squid fricassee and bouillabaisse jus, and then caramelised tarte Tatin. Three dozen wines, grouped by variety, start at £11.

CHEF: Anthony Brown   PROPRIETOR: Raymond Blanc   OPEN: all week 12 to 3, 5.30 to 11 CLOSED: 25 Dec   MEALS: alc (main courses £8.50 to £16). Set L and D 5.30 to 7 £12.50 (2 courses) to £15   SERVICE: not inc, 10% for parties of 8 or more   CARDS: Amex, Delta, Diners, MasterCard, Switch, Visa   DETAILS: 180 seats. 40 seats outside. Private parties: 40 main room, 10 to 20 private rooms. Vegetarian meals. Children's helpings. Wheelchair access (also WC). Music. Air-conditioned

'The waiter ... poured the entire bottle of water into each of our glasses right up to the brim. He smiled as if to express his joy in managing to pour the whole bottle into our glasses without any spillage. I showed it to the English manager who looked in horror but said nothing.'
(On eating in London)

# La Toque d'Or

27 Warstone Lane, Hockley,
Birmingham B18 6JQ
TEL/FAX: (0121) 233 3655                    COOKING 3
EMAIL: didier@latoquedor.co.uk          FRENCH
WEBSITE: www.latoquedor.co.uk          £26–£63

Down an alleyway some 300 yards from the Clock Tower, and surrounded by jewellery shops, is a relaxed, rectangular dining room with tables down the sides. Despite the industrial décor of bare brick, wooden beams and metal girders, it feels 'quite Parisian', as indeed it should given Didier Philipot's determinedly French approach to the food. Not content with simple renditions of the classics, he is keen to add a personal stamp: fish soup comes with an unusual mackerel and aïoli crostini, and a ham and parsley terrine is accompanied by a soft-boiled egg and a salad of ratte potatoes in a mustard dressing.

Fish from Devon (supplemented by Skye scallops) might include Brixham cod with creamed leeks, while foie gras hails from Périgord, and beef comes from Hereford cattle: perhaps braised in red wine with onion and bacon and served with a parsnip mousseline. Customary diligence is applied to desserts, giving cherry clafoutis a chocolate spin, for example, and the soufflé of the day is worth a punt. A short, mostly French wine list incorporates three house wines at £12.50.

CHEF: Didier Philipot    PROPRIETOR: SSPG Consulting Ltd    OPEN: Tue to Fri L 12.30 to 2, Tue to Sat D 7 to 9.30    CLOSED: Christmas and New Year, Easter, 2 weeks Aug    MEALS: Set L £12.50 (2 courses) to £15.50, Set D £23.50    SERVICE: not inc    CARDS: Amex, Delta, MasterCard, Switch, Visa    DETAILS: 32 seats. Private parties: 40 main room. Vegetarian meals. Children's helpings. Wheelchair access (1 step; also WC). Music. Air-conditioned

---

**BISHOP'S WALTHAM Hampshire**                               **map 2**

# Restaurant on the Square        NEW ENTRY

The Square, Bishop's Waltham SO32 1AR             COOKING 5
TEL: (01489) 891515    FAX: (01489) 896928        FRENCH
                                             £26–£60

This corner site in the heart of the old town, formerly known as Peppers, was re-launched under new owners in June 2002 with a new name and a new look. The design is stylish, with a floor of polished wood, and sleek, high-backed, armless chairs in the split-level dining room, where subdued jazz sets the tone for an unshowy but impressive operation.

The cooking is in the hands of Peter Reffell, previously head chef at the Criterion Brasserie in London. He has retained the essentially French orientation of Marco Pierre White's formula, but the level of skill involved in its execution is anything but formulaic. Brandade of smoked cod makes a clever foil for a trio of roast scallops surrounding a heap of quality leaves dressed with leek vinaigrette, and a classically conceived terrine pairs duck and foie gras, accompanied by pear chutney. French treatment is also accorded to a roast breast of flavourful chicken, served with a colourful medley of vegetables and strips of ventrêche bacon, a combination commended as 'accomplished simplicity, light and perfectly proportioned'. A discreet note of tarragon in a red wine reduction gives powerful support to a small fillet of expertly timed brill, and that earthy way with fish shows up again in another main course, of roast cod with clams, white beans, chorizo and romesco sauce.

Well-chosen, lesser-known artisan cheeses are a possible alternative to desserts such as poached saffron pears with orange-flower ice cream, or a well-made spiced pineapple tarte Tatin. Breads are of good quality, appetisers – perhaps pea and mint soup with truffle oil – add to the pleasure, and service is slick, polite and unstuffy. French classics and their New World counterparts stand shoulder to shoulder on the modern wine list. Fans will find a number of well-known names here, but the majority of wines cost £25-plus. Bottle prices start at £11.50 for red and white vin de pays.

CHEF: Peter Reffell   PROPRIETOR: Maine Castle Ltd   OPEN: Tue to Sat 12 to 2.30, 7 to 10.30   CLOSED: 25 Dec to 1 Jan, bank hols   MEALS: alc (main courses L £9 to £14, D £11 to £18). Set L £12.95 (2 courses) to £15.50. Bar menu available L   SERVICE: 12.5%, card slips closed   CARDS: Amex, Delta, MasterCard, Switch, Visa   DETAILS: 55 seats. Private parties: 22 main room, 4 to 12 private rooms. Vegetarian meals. Children's helpings. No-smoking area. Music  (£5)

## BISPHAM GREEN  Lancashire                                    map 8

# Eagle & Child  £                                    | NEW ENTRY |

Malt Kiln Lane, Bispham Green L40 3SG
TEL:  (01257) 462297   FAX:  (01257) 464718
from M6 junction 27, take A5209 over Parbold                    COOKING 1
Hill, right on B5246, fourth left signposted                    MODERN EUROPEAN
Bispham Green; pub is ½m on right                               £21–£37

This long, low building, facing the green in a quiet hamlet, offers country pub grub off undressed tables with music churning around you. The only concession to restaurant eating is in the quality of the cooking. Neil McKevitt used to cook at the relocated and re-fashioned Ziba (now called the Racquet Club) in Liverpool; here the menu is much less ambitious but done with panache. An inspector's substantial starter of hand-made al dente tagliatelle with Parma ham and asparagus was excellent, as was a superbly tender loin of lamb with roast aubergine and new potatoes. Lighter starters include grilled sardines on turmeric-yellow couscous, or a tomato and goats' cheese tart, while battered cod, chips and mushy peas reminds you you're in Lancashire. Desserts range from apple crumble with custard to tiramisù with coffee sauce. Hand-pumped, cask-conditioned ales supplement a wine list that doesn't stick to pub standards but even includes Ch. Beychevelle 1982 (at £120 – weep, ye Londoners!), though prices start at £10.50.

CHEF: Neil McKevitt   PROPRIETOR: Martin Ainscough   OPEN: all week 12 to 2, 6 to 8.30 (9 Fri/Sat)   CLOSED: D 25 Dec   MEALS: alc (main courses £6.50 to £10)   SERVICE: not inc, card slips closed   CARDS: Delta, MasterCard, Switch, Visa   DETAILS: 60 seats. 40 seats outside. Private parties: 50 main room, 30 to 60 private rooms. Car park. Vegetarian meals. Children's helpings. Wheelchair access (also WC). Occasional music

# September Brasserie

15–17 Queen Street, Blackpool FY1 1NL
TEL: (01253) 623282   FAX: (01253) 304882

COOKING 1
MODERN BRITISH
£22–£42

Restaurant reviews serve as wallpaper up the stairs from the street to the first-floor dining room, and after more than a dozen years nobody, it seems, would object if the décor were smartened up a bit. The place has a masculine feel: no flowers, just manly service and robust flavours to match. A gratin of queen scallops comes in a pungent, oniony, fishy sauce smothered in melting cheese, and goats' cheese soufflé is served with chunky plum chutney, while main courses take in braised pork knuckle with mushy peas and mustard sauce: lunch might even offer a seaside staple of gammon and fried eggs. Finish with a brittle-topped crème brûlée, or a slice of light date sponge with a powerful peanut butter and toffee sauce. The wine list was due for a revamp as the Guide went to press.

CHEF/PROPRIETOR: Michael Golowicz   OPEN: Tue to Sat 12 to 2, 7 to 9.30   CLOSED: 2 weeks winter, 2 weeks summer   MEALS: alc (main courses L £6 to £10, D £10.50 to £14.50). Set L £10 (2 courses) to £13, Set D £16.90 (2 courses) to £19.90   SERVICE: not inc, 10% for parties of 6 or more   CARDS: Amex, Delta, Diners, MasterCard, Switch, Visa   DETAILS: 40 seats. Private parties: 35 main room. Vegetarian meals. Music   £5

# ▲ White Horse Hotel ⁵⚹

4 High Street, Blakeney NR25 7AL
TEL: (01263) 740574   FAX: (01263) 741303
WEBSITE: www.blakeneywhitehorse.co.uk
off A149 between Cley and Morston

COOKING 1
MODERN BRITISH-PLUS
£28–£48

Although Blakeney is technically on the coast, the sea is a fair distance away, and it is bird-life and the coastal path that seem to attract most visitors. Happily the White Horse – a pub first and foremost, full of different rooms, bars and dining areas – serves up large portions that make 'good walkers' fare'. The menu in the bright yellow dining room covers a range from grilled halloumi cheese with salsa, via chargrilled steak, to a creamily sauced dish of turbot with local mussels. 'They deserve credit for not piling too many unnecessary items on the plate,' reckoned one visitor, and also for desserts such as steeped purple figs with vanilla ice cream, or a large splodge of rich, thick chocolate mousse. A modestly priced wine list starts with house Australian at £9.95.

CHEF: Christopher Hyde   PROPRIETORS: Daniel Rees and Sue Catt   OPEN: Tue to Sat D only 7 to 9   CLOSED: 2 weeks mid-Jan   MEALS: alc (main courses £9 to £17). Bar menu available all week L and D   SERVICE: not inc   CARDS: Amex, Delta, MasterCard, Switch, Visa   DETAILS: 100 seats. 60 seats outside. Private parties: 40 main room. Car park. Vegetarian meals. Children's helpings. No smoking in dining room. Wheelchair access (not WC). Occasional music. No mobile phones   ACCOMMODATION: 10 rooms, all with bath/shower. TV. Phone. B&B £30 to £90. Baby facilities (*The Which? Hotel Guide*)

# ▲ Devonshire Arms, Burlington Restaurant 🍷 ✤

Bolton Abbey BD23 6AJ
TEL: (01756) 710441   FAX: (01756) 710564
EMAIL: sales@thedevonshirearms.co.uk
WEBSITE: www.thedevonshirearms.co.uk                    COOKING **6**
5m NW of Ilkley, on B6160 250 yards N of              MODERN BRITISH
junction with A59                                        £30–£69

Walks and open countryside in this part of Wharfedale help to make it a 'rural idyll', and the Devonshire Arms plays the role of country-house hotel with all the attendant pomp and ceremony. Accomplished, confidence-building service permeates all the small rooms (including a conservatory extension) that help to make the dining area feel quite intimate. Sound materials underpin the operation, including local or salt marsh lamb, game from the Devonshire estate (perhaps fashioned into a terrine and served with a salad of baby vegetables and pickled girolles), and herbs and vegetables from the hotel's own garden.

Among more straightforward results have been a well-constructed pressing of ham hock and foie gras with a truffle salad, and a first-class piece of gilt-head bream with shredded, marinated potatoes. But the kitchen is not short of bright ideas, particularly among first courses, partnering seared langoustines with an artichoke pannacotta and shellfish dressing, serving home-cured venison with beetroot jelly, and pairing brown lentil soup with seared duck liver. Not all ingredients shine with as much flavour as they might, but among successes have been a pavé of salmon with stewed chicory and mushroom duxelle, a smooth banana parfait with crisp slices of deep-fried pineapple, and a steamed lemon sponge 'as light as a fairy', served with crème anglaise and a flavourful marmalade sorbet.

The wine list is a compendium of the great and the good from around the world. Barely a region goes unnoticed among the 5,000-plus selections, but most attention is lavished on red Bordeaux: here there are old vintages galore, including 'verticals' (a collection of vintages from a single producer) from the likes of Châteaux Palmer and Margaux, as well as a number of large-format bottles. None of this comes cheap (there are many four-figure price tags); nonetheless mark-ups are generally sensible and there is much to choose from at the less expensive end. Prices for house wines (there are 70 of them) start at £14; about ten wines are available by the glass, starting at £2.50.

CHEF: Steve Williams   PROPRIETORS: the Duke and Duchess of Devonshire   OPEN: Sun L 12 to 2.30, all week D 7 to 10   MEALS: Set L Sun £19.95, Set D £45   SERVICE: not inc, card slips closed   CARDS: Amex, Delta, Diners, MasterCard, Switch, Visa   DETAILS: 70 seats. Private parties: 90 main room, 10 to 90 private rooms. Car park. Vegetarian meals. Children's helpings. No smoking in dining room. Wheelchair access (not WC). Occasional music   ACCOMMODATION: 41 rooms, all with bath/shower. TV. Phone. B&B £145 to £345. Rooms for disabled. Swimming pool. Fishing (*The Which? Hotel Guide*)

---

*'No olives, no pianist, no pole-dancers, nothing.'* (On payment of a cover charge)

---

# Dining Room 🍷 ⅗✕

| | |
|---|---|
| 20 St James's Square, Boroughbridge YO51 9AR | COOKING 4 |
| TEL/FAX: (01423) 326426 | MODERN BRITISH |
| | £27–£45 |

Until recently, the Bronze Age megalithic monuments known as the Devil's Arrows were Boroughbridge's nearest approximation to a tourist attraction. Lisa and Chris Astley may not aim to draw hordes of camera-toting sightseers, but they have certainly put the town on the gastronomic map with their comfortable, relaxed and welcoming restaurant, situated on the main square.

They run a tight ship, both front-of-house, where Lisa is in charge (praise for service is a common theme in reports), and behind the scenes, where contemporary pan-European cooking is Chris's modus operandi. The scope of his repertoire is demonstrated by starters such as straightforward bresaola with shaved Parmesan and white truffle oil, and a more complex parcel of smoked salmon, cream and chives with marinated cucumber, dill and Avruga caviar. Main courses, meanwhile, might take in a rustic-sounding pan-fried breast of corn-fed chicken with boudin noir, apple and Calvados sauce, alongside fillet of sea bass with a simple accompaniment of olive oil, tomatoes, peppers and basil. For dessert there might be praline crème brûlée, and banana milkshake with bitter chocolate sorbet. The wine list kicks off with eight house selections, six from the Southern Hemisphere, one from France and one from Romania, starting at £12.50. After that, modern styles mix with French classics, resulting in a diverse list in which value figures highly. A 'connoisseurs selection' focuses on Burgundy and Bordeaux.

CHEF: Christopher Astley  PROPRIETORS: Christopher and Lisa Astley  OPEN: Wed to Fri and Sun L 12.15 to 2 (booking essential), Tue to Sat D 7 to 9.30  CLOSED: 25 Dec, first 2 to 3 weeks July, bank hols; open Thur to Sat only in Jan  MEALS: alc (main courses L £8 to £10, D £8.50 to £15). Set D £19.95 (2 courses) to £23.50  SERVICE: not inc, card slips closed  CARDS: Delta, MasterCard, Switch, Visa  DETAILS: 30 seats. 6 seats outside. Private parties: 35 main room. Vegetarian meals. Children's helpings. No smoking in dining room. Wheelchair access (not WC). Music. No mobile phones

# ▲ Linthwaite House ⅗✕

| | |
|---|---|
| Crook Road, Bowness-on-Windermere LA23 3JA | |
| TEL: (015394) 88600  FAX: (015394) 88601 | |
| EMAIL: admin@linthwaite.com | |
| WEBSITE: www.linthwaite.com | COOKING 5 |
| off B5284, ¾m S of Bowness, near Windermere | MODERN BRITISH |
| golf club | £31–£68 |

On a promontory just outside Bowness, off the road to Newby Bridge, Linthwaite House welcomes with a comfortable dining room and well-drilled but pleasant service. One of the four courses at dinner is an intermediate soup, served after a starter of chicken liver parfait with apple purée and truffle butter, or perhaps smoked salmon and chive risotto with a 'crispy' poached egg.

Part of the appeal is the range of materials the kitchen deploys on a comparatively short menu (four options per course), taking in anything from a sweet chilli dressing (with a salad of crab, avocado and tomato), to a black pudding beignet, served alongside thyme mash and a sage sauce with pancetta-wrapped pork fillet. Ideas are borrowed from near and far, as the kitchen turns out a pesto-crusted loin of lamb with Mediterranean vegetables, and soy-seared salmon with a vegetable spring roll and trompette purée. One of the main courses is usually vegetarian: perhaps crispy polenta with ratatouille and Parmesan cream.

The food doesn't aim to break any moulds, though, and desserts embrace the familiar territory of vanilla crème brûlée, chocolate fondant, and glazed lemon tart. Cheeses, on the other hand, are something of a speciality. Totally British and Irish, they might include Allerdale (semi-soft ewes' milk), Deepdale (hard, fat buffalo milk), or Pant Ysgawn (soft goats'). Wines, arranged by style, take more than a passing interest in the southern hemisphere, although relatively few make it under the £20 barrier. House Tempranillo and Sauvignon Blanc, both from Argentina, are £17.95 and £16.50 respectively.

CHEF: Andy Nicholson   PROPRIETOR: Mike Bevans   OPEN: Sun L 12.30 to 1.30, all week D 7 to 9
MEALS: Set L Sun £16.95, Set D £39. Light L available   SERVICE: not inc, card slips closed
CARDS: Amex, Delta, Diners, MasterCard, Switch, Visa   DETAILS: 60 seats. 20 seats outside.
Private parties: 45 main room, 16 to 45 private rooms. Car park. Vegetarian meals. Children's helpings. No children under 7 in dining room. No smoking in dining room. Wheelchair access (also WC). Music. No mobile phones   ACCOMMODATION: 26 rooms, all with bath/shower. TV. Phone. B&B £85 to £260. Rooms for disabled. Baby facilities. Fishing (*The Which? Hotel Guide*) (£5)

# Porthole Eating House ▮

3 Ash Street, Bowness-on-
Windermere LA23 1AU
TEL: (015394) 42793   FAX: (015394) 88675                     COOKING 4
EMAIL: gianni.berton@which.net                                 ANGLO-ITALIAN
WEBSITE: www.porthole.fsworld.co.uk                            £20–£55

In a short, pedestrian side street in the heart of Bowness, the Porthole competes with cafés offering chips with everything and three-course lunches for £3.50. But it ploughs its own furrow with a confidence born of three decades, its small dining areas, stone floors and wooden tables giving it 'atmosphere in spades'. The kitchen's forte is homely food, much of it as traditional as prawn cocktail, spaghetti bolognese and beef stroganoff. Even when dishes are as simple as fresh asparagus, or pasta with pesto (containing masses of freshly chopped basil), they have an honesty about them which is appealing.

Given the national obsession to make dishes more elaborate than they need to be, the directness of deep-fried, breadcrumbed scampi with tartare sauce, or accurately timed Dover sole, is welcome. A few Oriental ideas surface (turbot fillet Thai-style, perhaps) but not among desserts, which tend towards raspberry pavlova, or sticky toffee pudding. The lengthy, pleasantly idiosyncratic wine list has numerous treasures, including what must be one of the broadest ranges of fine German wines in the country. Food-friendly bottlings from Alsace are another speciality, with Spain, the Rhône, Australia, Bordeaux – and, of course,

Italy – rounding out the offerings. A separate 'collection and rarity' list features some real gems. One can spend a great deal on wine here, but rooting around will reward efforts to find something of interest below £20.

CHEF: Andy Fairchild  PROPRIETORS: Gianni and Judy Berton  OPEN: Wed to Fri and Sun L 12 to 2, Wed to Mon D 6.30 to 10.30  MEALS: alc (main courses L £5 to £11.50, D £11.50 to £16.50). Set L £12.50  SERVICE: not inc, card slips closed  CARDS: Amex, Diners, MasterCard, Switch, Visa  DETAILS: 40 seats. 24 seats outside. Private parties: 40 main room, 20 to 40 private rooms. Vegetarian meals. Music

## Studio ▾ 　　　　　　　　　　　　　　　　　　NEW ENTRY

21 Lake Road, Bowness-on-　　　　　　　　　　COOKING 2
Windermere LA23 3DE　　　　　　　　　MODERN EUROPEAN
TEL/FAX: (015394) 44065　　　　　　　　　　　　£19–£50

With its mustard-coloured walls and red ceiling, the Studio aims at a modern feel, as does the balanced menu. Bold, no-nonsense flavours are evident – in a pleasingly rustic, rough-textured terrine of pork and chicken, served with Cumberland sauce – while a traditional combination of pan-fried chicken livers, bacon and mushrooms is served Italian style: on toasted ciabatta with balsamic jus.

Main courses are equally straightforward – perhaps including Cumberland sausages with mustard mash, or loin of Mansergh Hall lamb in a herb crust – while desserts are as traditional as bread-and-butter pudding and crème brûlée. There may be a tendency to over-cook meat, and the kitchen could put more faith in its quality ingredients, but overall this newcomer is a 'lovely find'. Service is 'friendly and attentive', and the customary difficulties of communicating with French-speaking staff are dealt with good-naturedly. The wine list is laudable for both quality and reasonable pricing. About half of it is under £20 (including eight under £12), and bargains abound.

CHEF: Chris Davies  PROPRIETORS: Lynn And Russell Beddoe  OPEN: Tue to Sun 12 to 2.30, 6.30 (6 Sat) to 9.30 (10.30 Sat)  MEALS: alc (main courses L £5 to £8.50, D £7.50 to £15.50). Set D (not Sat after 7.30) £12.95 (2 courses) to £16.50  SERVICE: not inc  CARDS: Delta, MasterCard, Switch, Visa  DETAILS: 60 seats. Private parties: 75 main room. Vegetarian meals. Children's helpings. Wheelchair access (not WC). Music. No mobile phones. Air-conditioned £5

### BRADFORD West Yorkshire　　　　　　　　　　　　map 8

## Akbars ⅚✖ £

1276 Leeds Road, Thornbury, Bradford BD3 8LF　　COOKING 2
TEL: (01274) 773311　　　　　　　　　　　　　　INDIAN
WEBSITE: www.akbars.co.uk　　　　　　　　　　　£14–£26

Part of the crowd-pulling attraction of this Indian is its wildly OTT décor, which comes complete with a brilliantly coloured tented ceiling, brazier wall lights and even a mock fountain. The place gets jam-packed, but everything runs with military precision, thanks to an army of friendly, accommodating waiters. There are no surprises on the menu and nothing that inhabits new-wave territory: baltis and karahi dishes show up forcefully alongside old stalwarts such as chicken dhansak, but there are a few less familiar dishes, too, such as chicken liver tikka, fish pakoras, chamgidar (three different meats cooked together), and lamb lumbet (with home-made cheese). Fluffy nans are served suspended from metal frames, which are left on the table (choose between the standard or huge 'family' version). Jugs of lassi and beer suit the food; otherwise house wine is a modest £6.95 per bottle.

CHEF: Talab Hussain    PROPRIETOR: Shabir Hussain    OPEN: Sun all day 1 to 12, Mon to Sat D only 5 to 12    MEALS: alc (main courses £4.50 to £8)    SERVICE: not inc    CARDS: not inc    DETAILS: 270 seats. Private parties: 60 main room. No smoking in dining room. Wheelchair access (not WC). Music

## BRAMPTON  Cambridgeshire                                        map 6

# ▲ Grange Hotel ▉ ⁵⤬

115 High Street, Brampton PE28 4RA
TEL: (01480) 459516    FAX: (01480) 459391                     COOKING 3
EMAIL: nsteiger@grangehotelbrampton.com              MODERN EUROPEAN
WEBSITE: www.grangehotelbrampton.com                          £26–£48

Once HQ for the US air force during the Second World War (RAF Brampton is nearby), this comfortable Victorian hotel on the main street of a pretty village doubles as a pub and restaurant. Nowadays it strikes an informal pose, with stripped wooden floorboards, candles on tables, and a picture window overlooking the garden. The restaurant menu, which changes every ten days to a fortnight, takes a sensible, broadly European line, offering beetroot risotto with sour cream and beetroot fritters, and grilled sea bass with crispy pasta and clam minestrone.

Herbs are well used, cropping up in courgette and marjoram soup, in saltimbocca of rabbit with onion and bay purée, and in a peach Tatin with thyme ice cream. Other interesting-sounding puddings include liquorice pannacotta with cappuccino anglaise, and rhubarb charlotte with eggnog ice cream. The bar menu, meanwhile, runs to omelette and chips, smoked haddock fishcakes, and sticky toffee pudding. The wine list is thoughtfully chosen and sensibly arranged. The 15 wines by the glass (from £2; £4.75 for champagne) are rather unexciting, but there's a lot more to grab one's interest in the main list. Here, £20 is certain to get you a bottle of something interesting, particularly if you're a fan of aromatic whites or spicy reds.

CHEFS: Nick Steiger and Mark Caffrey    PROPRIETORS: Susanna and Nick Steiger    OPEN: all week L 12 to 2 (2.30 Sun), Mon to Sat D 7 to 10    CLOSED: first week Jan    MEALS: alc (main courses £8.50 to £16.50)    SERVICE: not inc    CARDS: Amex, Delta, MasterCard, Switch, Visa    DETAILS: 40 seats. 15 seats outside. Private parties: 40 main room, 16 private room. Car park. Vegetarian meals. Children's helpings. No smoking in dining room. Wheelchair access (not WC). No music ACCOMMODATION: 8 rooms, all with bath/shower. TV. Phone. B&B £55 to £85. Baby facilities  (£5)

Card slips closed *in the details at the end of an entry indicates that the total on the slips of credit cards is closed when handed over for signature.*

# ▲ Farlam Hall

Brampton CA8 2NG
TEL: (016977) 46234   FAX: (016977) 46683
EMAIL: farlamhall@dial.pipex.com
WEBSITE: www.farlamhall.co.uk                          COOKING 3
on A689, 2½m SE of Brampton (not in Farlam      ENGLISH COUNTRY HOUSE
village)                                                £43–£53

At this plain Victorian House, in well-maintained grounds in a comparatively quiet corner of Cumbria, the Quinion and Stevenson families continue to maintain their welcoming and 'familiar but gracious' style. A couple of comfortably furnished sitting rooms in sumptuous 'period' style, and a large and equally well-appointed dining room, provide the backdrop for a 'dinner party' atmosphere. The country-house approach involves seasonal game, from pheasant terrine to well-flavoured venison in a juniper and red wine sauce, and well-reported fish: perhaps a small, moist red mullet fillet with dressed salad to start, or grilled salmon with dill butter on a smoked salmon risotto. It is the sort of place that offers a sorbet before the main course, a free jug of tap water (regularly replenished) and cheese (with sliced apple, grapes and celery) before a dessert such as iced crème chiboust with plum compote, or a dark chocolate bavarois with white chocolate ice cream. The wine list sticks largely with familiar names, at prices to suit all pockets, starting with house Chileans and Australians at £13.75.

CHEF: Barry Quinion   PROPRIETORS: the Quinion and Stevenson families   OPEN: all week D only 8 to 8.30   MEALS: Set D Sun to Fri £32.50, Set D Sat £33.50   SERVICE: not inc, card slips closed   CARDS: MasterCard, Switch, Visa   DETAILS: 46 seats. Private parties: 24 main room. Car park. No children under 5. No cigars/pipes in dining room. Wheelchair access (not WC). No music   ACCOMMODATION: 12 rooms, all with bath/shower. TV. Phone. D,B&B £127.50 to £265. No children under 5 (The Which? Hotel Guide)

# Fat Duck ▮

High Street, Bray SL6 2AQ                              COOKING 8
TEL: (01628) 580333   FAX: (01628) 776188          MODERN EUROPEAN
WEBSITE: www.fatduck.co.uk                             £46–£118

Well-spaced tables, eggshell blues, and a soothing and tranquil setting might lull some customers into thinking that this is an ordinary restaurant. But they would be wrong. Heston Blumenthal is a highly individual, imaginative chef who produces 'technically stunning, brilliant-tasting food'. His infectious enthusiasm and passion 'should be bottled and prescribed to the depressed'. The principle underlying his approach is that we should think more about what we eat and cook, and why, and this has enabled him to filter out much of the nonsense and folklore from cooking, and replace it with 'seemingly bonkers ideas which translate into fabulous food on the plate'. It may not be rocket science, but it is 'molecular gastronomy'.

Those interested in chip technology, for example, might be interested to know that they lose their crunch because steam evaporates from the inside. After trials involving starch powder, and pricking holes in them with a pin, the latest method of preparation entails blanching them in unsalted water, placing them in a desiccator, creating a vacuum which sucks the moisture out, then cooking them in warm groundnut oil, refrigerating them, and finally cooking them in kidney fat. This method, apparently, 'works brilliantly'. As do lots of other things, including a 'wonderfully satisfying' starter of silky pumpkin velouté, with a fine layer of crushed hazelnuts pressed into it, accompanied by a fricassee of ceps and pig's cheek; and snail porridge, dense with parsley, full of chopped chewy snails, topped with shredded Jabugo ham: 'very good in a weird sort of way.'

Blumenthal insists that he is not simply trying to be wacky for the sake of it; he is just following the logic produced by scientific answers to his simple questions. Even so, this can lead to some unusual dishes, such as sardines on buttered toast ice cream, or soft, creamy sweetbreads, crusted with pollen and cooked in a salt crust with hay, accompanied by half a dozen sweet and juicy cockles piled into a shell. The bottom line, however, is that the food tastes good. A plate of huge, succulent roast scallops comes on a bed of caramelised cauliflower purée with oloroso jelly: 'I could have eaten buckets of it.' A degree of sweetness is often applied to meat dishes too, perhaps a result of Blumenthal's research with flavour perception, or of his penchant for nostalgia food, reckoning that the smells and tastes of childhood can be among the most exciting, and therefore worth trying to recapture.

Despite his involvement in other ventures – not just the Brasserie (see entry below), but a book, a short television series, and other projects – standards have remained vertiginously high. Among desserts, 'bacon and egg ice cream much pleased the person who had spent the whole meal waiting for this'. Chocolate has been partnered by blue cheese (together with a fromage blanc sorbet and Szechuan pepper), and has appeared as a délices containing space dust 'which exploded in the mouth, to the astonishment of the person who ordered it'. Staff are attentive and knowledgeable, although a reporter's suggestion to employ one fluent English speaker to deal with reservations seems a good one.

In its own way, the wine list is as adventurous as the cooking. Austria, Germany, south-west France, Alsace and the Loire round out the big names from Bordeaux, Burgundy, Piedmont and Tuscany that are the mainstay. The Californian selection lists some of the west coast's brightest stars. An enlightened by-the-glass policy (staff will open any bottle on the list, apart from the oldest and rarest, to serve by the glass) and one of the best sherry selections in the country round out the diverse offerings. Prices aren't cheap, however, with little below £20.

CHEF: Heston Blumenthal  PROPRIETORS: Heston and Susanna Blumenthal  OPEN: Tue to Sun L 12 to 2 (3 Sun), Tue to Sat D 7 to 9.30 (10 Fri and Sat)  CLOSED: 24 Dec to 7 Jan  MEALS: Set L Tue to Sat £27.75 to £75, Set L Sun £58 to £75, Set D £58 to £75  SERVICE: 12.5% (optional), card slips closed  CARDS: Amex, Delta, Diners, MasterCard, Switch, Visa  DETAILS: 50 seats. Private parties: 50 main room. Children's helpings. No cigars/pipes in dining room. No music

*See inside the front cover for an explanation of the symbols used at the tops of entries.*

# Riverside Brasserie

BERKSHIRE GFG 2003 COMMENDED

**NEW ENTRY**

Bray Marina, Monkey Island Lane,
Bray SL6 2EB
TEL: (01628) 780553    FAX: (01628) 674312

COOKING **6**
MODERN EUROPEAN
£31–£52

Follow the signs to Bray Marina and the Water Treatment Works. The Thin Duck, as it has been called, is under the same ownership as its portlier relative (see entry above), and inhabits an unassuming café-like building that also serves as a lavatory block for some of the floating gin palaces with which the Thames around here is rife. Tables outside on the deck have a view of the river, while, inside, the Formica, MDF and distressed metals are reminiscent of the parent restaurant in its earlier days. Eating the food, too, is 'like rediscovering the Fat Duck all over again'. Heston Blumenthal is applying his 'molecular gastronomy' to what he calls simple rustic cooking, returning in a way to his starting point, yet informed by years of chemistry lessons in the kitchen.

Instead of the Fat Duck's quail jelly, pea purée and crab cream, this kitchen goes in for a smooth and silky Jerusalem artichoke and smoked haddock soup, and a meaty rabbit terrine bound together with a lip-smacking winy jelly, accompanied by a first-class sauce gribiche. The upshot is confident, approachable food, such as a clean, light and refreshing escabèche of red mullet, the lozenge of perky fish parked on lightly pickled and gently cooked carrot and onion, with a small pile of pinky-purple tapénade intense enough 'to stop your taste-buds in their tracks'. The appeal to popular tastes is evident, for example, in a 'perfect' ribeye steak, marbled and juicy, scattered with chopped marrow and served with 'the best chips in the world ever', and in salted, cured belly pork with velvet-textured strips of fat, served with huge, creamy, mealy butter beans, peppery shredded cabbage, small chorizo sausages and soft, spicy black pudding.

Simple desserts are presented starkly without garnish of any sort, but still pack a punch. Tarts are served warm, be they a deeply satisfying dark chocolate one, or an accurately judged lemon version, while crème brûlée is infused with aromatic bay leaves and vanilla, its surface of unrefined sugar burnt to a conker brown and cracking like thin ice. Service is cheerful, although numbers can put pressure on the operation, and a roving wine list offers some opportunity for those on a modest budget to enjoy themselves. House Côtes de Duras white is £13.50, Bordeaux red £14.50.

CHEF: Derek Creagh    PROPRIETOR: Bookdawn Ltd    OPEN: Sun 12 to 10, Mon to Sat 12 to 3, 6.30 to 10    MEALS: alc (main courses £11 to £14). Snack menu available 3.30 to 6.30    SERVICE: 10% (optional), card slips closed    CARDS: Amex, Delta, Diners, MasterCard, Switch, Visa    DETAILS: 38 seats. 60 seats outside. Car park. Children's helpings. No cigars/pipes in dining room. Wheelchair access (not WC). Music

---

*The Guide relies on feedback from its readers. Especially welcome are reports on new restaurants appearing in the book for the first time. All letters to the Guide are acknowledged.*

---

# ▲ Waterside Inn

Ferry Road, Bray SL6 2AT
TEL: (01628) 620691   FAX: (01628) 784710
EMAIL: reservations@waterside-inn.co.uk
WEBSITE: www.waterside-inn.co.uk

COOKING 9
FRENCH
£50–£180

This is not a pretentious place. Without much of a lounge for pre-meal drinks, most people are led straight to a table in the mirrored dining room, looking out through the branches of a willow onto the Thames. Flurries of waiters ('real professionals') whirl around and excuse themselves, proffer a menu, something resembling a Bible (the wine list), and bring a tray of appetisers. As the menu swims into focus, some prime ingredients begin to register – foie gras in a terrine, lobster cooked in a bouillon with a sauce vierge, and Bresse pigeon breasts with crushed potato and cabbage – and humbler materials too: snails (sautéed with morels and smoked bacon), a provençale vegetable flan, and grilled rabbit fillets with glazed chestnuts. In sum, within the confines of high French cooking, there is something for most tastes.

In the kitchen, the original Roux brothers' double act is turning into the cousins' double act, as Michel's son Alain here follows Albert's son Michel (see Le Gavroche, London) in taking on the family business. The key to the cooking remains rare refinement applied to impeccable ingredients. Lobsters from their tank are turned perhaps into pan-fried medallions, carefully timed and tender, in a pale brown sauce made from white port, decorated with julienne strips of carrot, fennel and ginger. And three large, lightly seared scallops, still 'natural and sticky' in the middle, have impressed, served with sliced baby artichokes dressed with citrus and honey, and with rocket leaves sprinkled with white crab meat.

Seasonal dishes encompass a springtime saddle of pale pink, milk-fed lamb stuffed with morels, cut into rounds, partnered by strips of leek, white and green asparagus, broad beans and other tiny vegetables, and served with a first-class hollandaise. A selection of miniature desserts is perhaps the best way for two to sample the variety: maybe dark chocolate mousse, chocolate crème brûlée, an inverted rhubarb crumble, caramelised pear tart, passion-fruit ravioli, vanilla ice cream, and a chocolate soufflé flavoured with stem ginger.

If, after all that, petit fours seem de trop, they can be wrapped in a box and taken home. This place generally lives up to people's expectations, especially those happy to spend a lot of money. Ladies' menus still come unpriced; only a Frenchman, one feels, could get away with such discrimination for so long. The thumping tome of a wine list is unstintingly Francophile, with not a single bottle listed from outside France (apart from Port and Madeira in the 'vins fortifiés' section). Prices are fearsome: if finances can stretch to four figures, diners can enjoy splendid old vintages of the likes of Pétrus, Cheval-Blanc and Latour. Those without expense accounts or wealthy uncles won't be able to partake of much, although the good news is that the under-£20 selection has quadrupled since 2001: there are now four.

CHEFS: Michel Roux and Alain Roux   PROPRIETOR: Michel Roux   OPEN: Wed to Sun 12 to 2 (2.30 Sun), 7 to 10; from 1 June to 31 Aug also open Tue D   CLOSED: 26 Dec to 30 Jan   MEALS: alc (main courses £32.50 to £49.50). Set L Wed to Sat £36 to £76, Set L Sun £52. Set D £76 SERVICE: 12.5% (optional), card slips closed   CARDS: Amex, Delta, Diners, MasterCard, Switch,

Visa DETAILS: 75 seats. Private parties: 80 main room, 6 to 10 private rooms. Car park. Vegetarian meals. Children's helpings. No children under 12. No cigars in dining room. Wheelchair access (not WC). No music. No mobile phones ACCOMMODATION: 9 rooms, all with bath/shower. TV. Phone. B&B £160 to £290. No children under 12

**BRIGHTON & HOVE East Sussex** map 3

# Black Chapati

12 Circus Parade, New England Road, COOKING **4**
Brighton BN1 4GW GLOBAL
TEL: (01273) 699011 £32–£49

Stephen Funnell deserves to be 'a national treasure', according to one who loves this weirdly named but totally innovative restaurant. Appearances have changed little, although there are now more comfortable chairs and lights that 'you no longer hit your head on'. What it offers is seriously nonconformist, maverick cooking with assertive flavours and real power.

This kitchen was delivering its own version of global fusion cooking well before the term became *de rigueur* in London. It is also an intelligent view of things, where exotic ideas and influences are married with local and seasonal ingredients: seared Cornish scallops come with a complex assemblage of glass noodles, bean sprouts and other flavourings. A new dish appears from time to time on the short menu, but much of the repertoire benefits from fine-tuning and regular practice. The Far East dominates proceedings, whether it be a high-flavour, forceful dish of grilled duck breast with Chinese sausage, polenta cake, mange-tout and rice wine sauce, or 'wonderfully gelatinous' braised belly pork with caramelised garlic, steamed rice and pak choi. Elsewhere, expect a salad of shredded chicken with Thai basil and roasted peanuts, as well as cauliflower pilau with chana dhal, minted salad and spiced yoghurt (a rare throwback to the restaurant's earlier Indian-influenced days).

Desserts offer European comfort in the shape of pine nut and almond tart with crème fraîche, or 'majestically' realised ice creams (raisin and Montilla, coffee and walnut, blood orange). Service 'has never been a priority here', but it remains pleasant. The wine list is nothing grand, although it has been carefully chosen, and there are French ciders too. House wine is £10.50.

CHEFS/PROPRIETORS: Stephen Funnell and Lauren Alker OPEN: Tue to Sat D only 7 (6.30 Sat) to 10 CLOSED: 3 weeks Christmas, 2 weeks July MEALS: alc (main courses £12 to £15.50) SERVICE: 10%, card slips closed CARDS: Amex, Delta, MasterCard, Switch, Visa DETAILS: 32 seats. Vegetarian meals. No children under 6. Wheelchair access (not WC). Music

# ▲ La Fourchette

101 Western Road, Brighton BN1 2AA COOKING **2**
TEL/FAX: (01273) 722556 FRENCH
£31–£38

Tables are shoehorned into this small room, quirkily decorated with painted brickwork, wall-mounted wheat sheaves and a jumble of random adornments. It takes itself seriously, judging by some contorted menuspeak, its printed offerings supplemented by a generous blackboard of daily fish dishes; among them pan-fried sea bass with braised fennel, or a big bowl of palpably fresh mussels in a thin red broth fired up with chilli and coriander.

Despite some under-par dishes and a feeling of 'making do' about things, the kitchen has turned out accurately timed beef fillet, lamb chartreuse – a single chop in a cabbage package, with a tangy, meat-rich stuffing – and a convincing rendition of duck confit, the meat shreddy and appealingly greasy, the skin cooked so that it crackled with bacony crispness. Finish, perhaps, with a lemon tart with a soft, eggy and intensely flavoured filling, served with vanilla ice cream. Service is not a strength, and, although the restaurant claims to close card slips after adding a 10% service charge, our evidence suggests that this is not always the case. A short wine list stays mostly under £20, starting with a brace of house wines at £9.75. Accommodation was planned as the Guide went to press.

CHEF/PROPRIETOR: Pascal Madjoudj OPEN: all week L 12 to 2.30, Mon to Sat D 7 to 10.30 MEALS: Set L £7.50 (2 courses), Set D £18.50 (2 courses) to £22.50 SERVICE: 10%, card slips closed CARDS: Amex, Delta, Diners, MasterCard, Switch, Visa DETAILS: 35 seats. Private parties: 30 to 40 private rooms. Wheelchair access (not WC). Music. No mobile phones

## ▲ Gingerman

21A Norfolk Square, Brighton BN1 2PD
TEL/FAX: (01273) 326688

COOKING 4
MODERN EUROPEAN
£25–£41

A small, cream-coloured room that seems to fill up most nights with a chattery, enthusiastic crowd is the setting for Ben McKellar's food. His menus are never less than interesting, and although there has been a move to introduce more robust ingredients (pig's cheek and lamb's brain), the style remains undaunting. Even the more hearty-sounding dishes – braised oxtail stuffed with wild mushrooms served with swede and a red wine sauce, or grilled venison with apples and allspice and a potato and celeriac gratin – achieve proper balance on the plate. Fish is sensitively handled too, producing Thai-seasoned steamed mussels to start, and maybe roast skate wing with leeks and sauce Choron to follow. Classic French items, such as prune and Armagnac tart, or orange and Grand Marnier soufflé, form the backbone of the dessert list, but a spin on an old English favourite, like spotted dick with sun-dried cranberries and rum custard, may well show up too. A shortish wine list could do with a bit of an overhaul – the more affordable whites in particular look dull – but bottles such as Palliser Estate Sauvignon Blanc from New Zealand, or Edwards and Chaffey McLaren Vale Shiraz, add flashes of interest. House Vins de Pays d'Oc are £10.95.

CHEF: Ben McKellar PROPRIETORS: Ben McKellar and Pamela Abbott OPEN: Tue to Sat 12.30 to 2, 7.30 to 10 CLOSED: 2 weeks winter, 2 weeks summer MEALS: Set L £9.95 (1 course) to £14.95, Set D £21 (2 courses) to £23.50 SERVICE: not inc, 10% for parties of 6 or more CARDS: Amex, Delta, Diners, MasterCard, Switch, Visa DETAILS: 32 seats. Private parties: 36 main room. Children's helpings. No cigars/pipes in dining room. Music

NEW CHEF is shown instead of a cooking mark where a change of chef occurred too late for a new assessment of the cooking.

# Kooky at New Whytes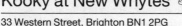

33 Western Street, Brighton BN1 2PG COOKING **3**
TEL: (01273) 776618 MODERN EUROPEAN
WEBSITE: www.whytesrestaurant.com £32–£47

Hidden away in a side-street near the seafront, the re-named New Whytes occupies a trim, white-fronted terraced house. The sense of a quart in a pint pot is emphasised by having tables in both ground-floor and basement rooms, but the tone is cheery and the cooking tends to impress. It may not be particularly polished or refined, but the manner in which strongly flavoured ingredients are used ('controlled boldness' is one way of putting it) demonstrates real skill. Spinach and wild mushrooms combine to make a successful soup, a first-course fillet of sea bass on a potato cake is judiciously topped with caviar, and crisply roasted loin of lamb comes with turnip dauphinoise and a parcel of chopped cabbage, smoked bacon and garlic. These are good ideas, well-executed. The mid-meal sorbet is probably superfluous, being generally too sweet to fulfil its purpose, especially when desserts are worth waiting for in themselves. Lime and tequila tart with sweet chilli sorbet should turn heads, or there may be a chocolate ice cream sandwich cake with chopped pistachios. Service can seem nervous, but is efficient and friendly. The wine list has gradually developed into quite an attractive little collection. All it lacks now is vintages. House Australian is £10.95.

CHEFS: Jordan White and Simon Harris PROPRIETORS: Jordan White, Jack Brabham and Simon Harris OPEN: Tue to Sat D only 7 to 9.30 MEALS: alc (main courses £12.50 to £14) SERVICE: not inc CARDS: Amex, MasterCard, Switch, Visa DETAILS: 40 seats. Private parties: 20 main room. Vegetarian meals. No cigars/pipes in dining room. Music

# One Paston Place

1 Paston Place, Brighton BN2 1HA COOKING **6**
TEL: (01273) 606933 FAX: (01273) 675686 MODERN EUROPEAN
£29–£62

The décor doesn't change in this 'pleasant and classy' dining room. Tables are spaced at civilised intervals, the floor is bare-boarded, and the feel is bright and airy. Mark Emmerson has been cooking here for 15 years and the food is 'as consistently good as ever' according to one visitor, confirming its pole position on the Brighton grid. The style is contemporary and sophisticated, underpinned by top-quality materials such as poulet de Bresse with spring vegetables and a pearl barley risotto, or new season cannon of lamb with mint and rocket pesto.

This is clearly focused cooking, where dishes have a recognizable centre of gravity, as in stuffed quail with a green bean salad, or roast veal sweetbreads with fresh morels. At the same time, intelligent combinations of two or more ingredients can make dishes that total more than the sum of their individual parts. Pan-fried foie gras, for instance, might come with rhubarb and crisp beetroot, and Dover sole fillets have been served in a Thai-spiced nage with crab dim sum. Deserts are equally appealing, taking in tarte Tatin with a coconut sorbet, and an almond and apricot crème brûlée with caramelised almonds. Prices are 'very London', although note that service is included; and the set lunch still offers good value. Nicole Emmerson runs front of house with brisk efficiency, and a French-dominated wine list, though well chosen, doesn't offer much under £20 outside the quartet of house wines at £15 to £16.50.

CHEF: Mark Emmerson   PROPRIETORS: Mark and Nicole Emmerson   OPEN: Tue to Sat 12.30 to 1.45, 7.30 to 9   CLOSED: 3 weeks Dec/Jan, 2 weeks Aug   MEALS: alc (main courses £21 to £22). Set L £16.50 (2 courses) to £19   SERVICE: net prices, card slips closed   CARDS: Amex, Delta, Diners, MasterCard, Switch, Visa   DETAILS: 45 seats. Vegetarian meals on request. No cigars/pipes in dining room. Wheelchair access (not WC). Music. No mobile phones. Air-conditioned

## Sevendials                                        NEW ENTRY

| | |
|---|---|
| 1 Buckingham Place, Brighton BN1 3TD | COOKING 2 |
| TEL: (01273) 885555   FAX: (01273) 888911 | MODERN BRITISH |
| WEBSITE: www.sevendialsrestaurant.co.uk | £23–£51 |

After stints in several big-name London restaurants, Sam Metcalfe has set up on his own in a converted bank. The building, with its stone fascia and large windows, still looks rather grand in a low-key sort of way: 'smart but not stuffy' sums it up. Pan-fried foie gras on crushed new potatoes, and grilled tuna niçoise are typical of the now-familiar range of modern British dishes on offer: there's nothing too revolutionary, ingredients are sound and results have pleased across the board. A 'comforting' dish of carefully poached plaice fillets with fresh noodles and a mussel and saffron broth has topped the list of recent recommendations; otherwise there are colourful 'combos', such as soft goats' cheese salad with green lentils, mint and roasted beetroot. Puddings have drawn a more muted response, although apple and hazelnut crumble has been fine. The contemporary wine list kicks off with house wines from £12.

CHEF/PROPRIETOR: Sam Metcalfe   OPEN: Wed to Sun L 12 to 2.30, Tue to Sat D 7 to 10   CLOSED: Christmas and New Year   MEALS: Set L £10 (2 courses) to £12.50, Set D £19.50 (2 courses) to £22.50   SERVICE: 12% (optional), card slips closed   CARDS: Amex, Delta, Diners, MasterCard, Switch, Visa   DETAILS: 55 seats. 45 seats outside. Private parties: 55 main room, 10 to 18 private rooms. Vegetarian meals. Children's helpings. Wheelchair access (also WC). Music

## Terre à Terre  ⁵⋇

| | |
|---|---|
| 71 East Street, Brighton BN1 1HQ | COOKING 4 |
| TEL: (01273) 729051   FAX: (01273) 327561 | GLOBAL VEGETARIAN |
| EMAIL: mail@terreaterre.co.uk | £31–£42 |

This packed and 'stunningly original' place exudes a lively café atmosphere, and a new extension has given it a roomier feel. Its high-octane blend of integrity and passion shows not just in the cooking and sourcing of ingredients, but also in 'the care taken to ensure that everybody is comfortable and having a nice time'. The kitchen grabs vegetarian cooking and gives it a good shake, its 'heroic inventiveness' producing, for example, Lipstick pimento stingo: a complex but triumphant salad of fava and squeaky green beans with Manchego, a mousse of Sussex Slipcote cheese, a smoked paprika cigarillo and gribiche sauce.

The dinner menu opens with nibbles (roasted and salted pumpkin and sunflower seeds, say), tasters (turmeric and onion bhaji with coconut chutney and sour mango relish) and starters (perhaps congee shiso yuzu puff cluster). Underpinning the creativity, consistent craftsmanship shows in everything from a twice-baked Jerusalem artichoke soufflé main, to crisp-fried cakes of potato, apple, onion and cheese with sour and horseradish creams and red and yellow pickled beetroot.

Desserts include a sharp, dense rhubarb and rose-hip sorbet served with custard-filled batter pillows, and 'gugelhopf': this version a dark chocolate sponge with a melting interior, served with baby Williams pears and matching ice cream. Also noteworthy are the children's menu, take-away service, and organic wines and beers. House French red and white are £11.50 (£3.65 a large glass).

CHEFS: Lawrence Glass, Amanda Powley and Philip Taylor   PROPRIETORS: Amanda Powley and Philip Taylor   OPEN: Tue to Sun L 12 to 6, all week D 6 to 10.30   CLOSED: 25 and 26 Dec   MEALS: alc (main courses £10.50 to £12)   SERVICE: not inc, 10% for parties of 6 or more   CARDS: Amex, Delta, Diners, MasterCard, Switch, Visa   DETAILS: 112 seats. 18 seats outside. Private parties: 40 main room. Vegetarian meals. Children's helpings. No smoking in 1 dining room. Wheelchair access (also WC). Music. Air-conditioned

## BRIMFIELD  Herefordshire                                                    map 5

# ▲ Roebuck Inn  🌟  £

Brimfield SY8 4NE
TEL: (01584) 711230   FAX: (01584) 711654
EMAIL: dave@theroebuckinn.com
WEBSITE: www.theroebuckinn.demon.com                          COOKING 3
just off A49 Leominster to Ludlow road, 4m W of              MODERN BRITISH
Tenbury Wells                                                    £25–£50

Visitors to this country pub just south of Ludlow, in a pleasant village near the Shropshire-Herefordshire border, generally start with a drink by the inglenook fireplace in the comfortable bar. Another bar dates back to the fifteenth century, while a more modern dining room with cane furniture has a bright, conservatory-garden feel to it. An industrious kitchen services a carte that offers such homely favourites as fish pie (in a dill sauce with leek mash), and steamed steak and mushroom suet pudding, alongside perhaps a Gary Rhodes idea of rack on black: a combination of lamb fillet and black pudding.

Starters might include home-cured gin-soused salmon, or duck spring rolls with a Thai dressing, while the Roebuck's take on fillet steak is to stuff it with Stilton, wrap it in bacon, and serve it with a Madeira sauce. Not all dishes live up to expectations, but spot-on Dover sole meunière pleased one reporter, as did a lemon tart with crisp pastry; alternatively there might be bread-and-butter pudding, or British cheeses that could include Hereford Yop, Worcester Gold or Ragstone. Some three dozen varied wines are grouped by style and sympathetically priced, starting with Santa Rita Chardonnay and Cabernet Sauvignon at £10.

CHEFS: Jonathan Waters and David Willson-Lloyd   PROPRIETORS: David and Susan Willson-Lloyd   OPEN: all week 12 to 2.15, 7 to 9.30   CLOSED: 25 Dec   MEALS: alc (main courses £8 to £20)   SERVICE: not inc, card slips closed   CARDS: Delta, MasterCard, Switch, Visa   DETAILS: 50 seats. Private parties: 50 main room, 20 private room. Car park. Vegetarian meals. Children's helpings. No smoking in dining room. No music. No mobile phones   ACCOMMODATION: 3 rooms, all with bath/shower. TV. Phone. B&B £45 to £70 (The Which? Hotel Guide)

## BRISTOL Bristol

map 2

# Bell's Diner ✸

1–3 York Road, Montpelier, Bristol BS6 5QB

TEL: (0117) 924 0357   FAX: (0117) 924 4280

WEBSITE: www.bellsdiner.co.uk

COOKING 5

MODERN EUROPEAN

£26–£56

Though York Road is not in one of the more fashionable parts of Bristol, this friendly, inviting restaurant is reason enough for a visit. Christopher Wicks has bought the freehold and invested in some improvements: the kitchen has been extended and the lavatories brought inside. He remains as dedicated as ever to sourcing wild and organic foods: wood sorrel, sea beet, wild garlic, nettles and assorted seasonal mushrooms are among the many ingredients to feature regularly in the repertoire. All this makes for a cooking style that takes its influences mainly from France and Italy: start with crab taglierini with chilli and gremolata, for example, or seared scallops with parsnip purée and pancetta salad. Main courses continue in similar vein: poached turbot with globe artichoke, cherry tomatoes, thyme ragoût and crispy sea beet may be among the more unusual choices, balanced by the more classic appeal of roast loin of Somerset Levels lamb with thyme and rosemary crumbs, spring vegetables, crushed Jersey Royals and roast garlic jus. Strawberry soup with mascarpone sorbet makes a novel way to round off a meal. The set-price three-course menu is excellent value and a viable alternative to the carte, and a short but well-chosen wine list opens with ten house selections from £10.50 a bottle, £2.70 a glass. Of particular interest is a vertical list of organic Provençal wines from Dom. de Trevallon, going back to 1988.

CHEF/PROPRIETOR: Christopher Wicks   OPEN: Tue to Fri L 12 to 2.30, Mon to Sat D 7 to 10.15 MEALS: alc (main courses £9.50 to £18.50). Set L and D £17.50   SERVICE: not inc, 10% for parties of 6 or more   CARDS: Amex, Delta, MasterCard, Switch, Visa   DETAILS: 50 seats. Private parties: 30 main room. Vegetarian meals. Children's helpings. No smoking in dining room. Music ⓔ⑤

# Brazz ✸

NEW ENTRY

85 Park Street, Bristol BS1 5PJ

TEL: (0117) 925 2000   FAX: (0117) 929 0225

EMAIL: bristol@brazz.co.uk

WEBSITE: www.brazz.co.uk

COOKING 2

MODERN BRASSERIE

£24–£57

The third member of this chain (see entries, Taunton and Exeter) opened in May 2002, bringing its trade-mark décor of a sky-blue barrel-vaulted roof set with hundreds of twinkly fibre-optic lights, a large tank full of darting silver dollar fish, ceramic fish-shaped dishes in bright primary colours on the walls, and 'Christine Keeler-type' chairs. The place has energy and drive, its typically large brasserie menu divided into Classical (salads and pastas, grills, fish and seafood), Seasonal, and a two-course Market option, as well as a few lighter dishes and appetisers to nibble while ordering.

The populist range takes in salmon fishcakes, ribeye steak with béarnaise, and bangers and mash with onion gravy. Over-salting across the board made an inspection meal difficult to enjoy, although the better dishes included a couple of sourdough doorsteps covered in buttery mushrooms, and a poussin cut into chunks, served with baby leeks and a 'sledgehammer' red wine sauce. Cathedral pudding has made the pilgrimage from Exeter (with 45p a time going to the Bristol Cathedral Choral Foundation), or there may be lemon tart, or Clifton puffs with clotted cream. Service is cheery, amenable and unpretentious, and some three dozen wines are pitched to meet the requirements of interest and affordability. House French is £10.95.

CHEF: Andy Turner   PROPRIETOR: Brazz plc   OPEN: all week noon to 11, reduced menu from 3 to 6   CLOSED: 25 Dec   MEALS: alc (main courses £8 to £16). Set L and D £12.95 (2 courses)   SERVICE: 10% (optional), card slips closed   CARDS: Amex, Delta, Diners, MasterCard, Switch, Visa   DETAILS: 80 seats. Private parties: 80 main room. Vegetarian meals. Children's helpings. No smoking in dining room. Wheelchair access (also WC). Music. Air-conditioned

# Deason's ♥ ✳

43 Whiteladies Road, Clifton, Bristol BS8 2LS
TEL: (0117) 973 6230   FAX: (0117) 923 7394   COOKING 3
EMAIL: enquiries@deasons.co.uk   MODERN BRITISH
WEBSITE: www.deasons.co.uk   £22–£51

A stylish modern house conversion has produced a bright, clean restaurant with wooden floors, cigar-shaped ceiling lights and upholstered banquettes. Allied to this is a confident and sympathetic approach to service from Jodie Deason, and dishes that are interesting and well designed: perhaps spring vegetable minestrone with goats' cheese crostini, sauté scallops with rhubarb butter sauce, or roast suckling pig on creamed choucroute and peas, with Toulouse sausage.

Frequently changing menus keep up interest for regular visitors, and choice is nothing if not generous. The repertoire takes in a wide range of ideas, from mustard- and honey-marinated rump of lamb with hummus and truffled peaches, via griddled swordfish with couscous and baba ganoush, to vegetarian options such as a main course of baked Jerusalem artichoke and wild mushroom 'Wellington'. If you don't fancy honeycomb and dark chocolate tartlet with pineapple sorbet, then 'Clockwork Orange' sounds an intriguing way to finish. A trio of Emilio Lustau sherries kicks off the compact wine list, which picks its way carefully through some interesting bottles. Mark-ups are fair, with the majority of wines coming in well under the £25 mark. House Vin de Pays des Côtes du Tarn is £10.95.

CHEF: Jason Deason   PROPRIETORS: Jason and Jodie Deason   OPEN: Sun to Fri L 12 to 2.30, Mon to Sat D 6.30 to 10 (10.30 Fri and Sat)   MEALS: alc exc Sun L (main courses L £5.50 to £11.50, D £13 to £19.50). Set L Sun £10.50 (2 courses) to £13.50, Set D Mon to Fri £15.50 (2 courses) to £19.50   SERVICE: 10% (optional), card slips closed   CARDS: Amex, Delta, Diners, MasterCard, Switch, Visa   DETAILS: 80 seats. 25 seats outside. Private parties: 40 main room, 11 to 40 private rooms. Vegetarian meals. Children's helpings. No smoking in dining room. Music. Air-conditioned   (£5)

*Dining rooms where music, either live or recorded, is never played are signalled by* No music *in the details at the end of an entry.*

# FishWorks ✸

128–130 Whiteladies Road, Clifton,
Bristol BS8 2RS                                    COOKING 4
TEL: (0117) 974 4433   FAX: (0117) 974 4933        SEAFOOD
WEBSITE: www.fishworks.co.uk                       £28–£59

With three lively and popular branches to supply (the others are in Bath and
Christchurch; see entries), the only thing threatening the successful formula of
fishmonger-cum-restaurant-cum-cookery school is the dire prognosis for world
fish stocks. If this problem can be overcome, then the future looks bright for the
crowds of happy piscivores that regularly fill this lively, informal eatery. One
popular option has been a tapas-style selection of appetisers, comprising
taramasalata, brandade, anchovies and octopus, served with brown bread and
olive oil on a wooden platter, a dish characteristic of FishWorks' style: keep
things simple to get the best out of top-quality materials. Other successes have
included spaghetti with crab, chilli, coriander and mint, skate grilled with
capers, and whole lemon sole with black butter. It is also possible to cast the
menu aside and opt for whatever you fancy from the shop display, cooked to
your liking. Unsurprisingly, wines are chosen according to their suitability for
fish. Prices start at £12.

CHEF: Matthew Prowse   PROPRIETOR: FishWorks plc   OPEN: Tue to Sun 11 to 11 (3 Sun)   MEALS:
alc (main courses £8.50 to £20)   SERVICE: not inc, card slips closed   CARDS: Amex, Delta,
MasterCard, Switch, Visa   DETAILS: 50 seats. Private parties: 40 main room, 1 to 16 private
rooms. Vegetarian meals. Children's helpings. No smoking in dining room. Wheelchair access
(not WC). Music  £5

---

# Harveys ▮

12 Denmark Street, Bristol BS1 5DQ                 COOKING 5
TEL: (0117) 927 5034   FAX: (0117) 927 5003       MODERN EUROPEAN
EMAIL: harveys@adswev.com                          £33–£83

Denmark Street may not be the city's most salubrious walkway, but entering
this cavernous basement restaurant is like 'stepping into a different world'. Its
white-painted brick walls are covered in oil paintings, Bristol blue glass is much
in evidence, and its formal, old-fashioned feel is highlighted by attentive, highly
polished and choreographed French service. Expensive ingredients and flowery
descriptions pepper the pricey menu, but Daniel Galmiche's confident and
assured cooking sweeps all before it. The style may not be ground-breaking, but
standards are high, and neither fashion nor exuberance is allowed to nudge it off
course. A warm tomato tart made with flaky pastry comes with an expertly
produced crab salad, while a well-balanced and finely tuned starter of three
plump and 'supremely fresh' scallops is accompanied by asparagus and candied
tomato.

   Timings (of fish, for example) can be conservative, but there is no doubting
the quality of raw materials, nor the thoughtful way that dishes are put together:
an admirable piece of sea bass served with a beguiling spinach ravioli and a
discreet balsamic dressing, or a rich and gutsy Anjou pigeon breast, cooked
pink, its equally delectable leg meat served over first-class sauté potatoes, all in a
light and well-integrated jus. Outsized plates and odd-shaped vessels

contribute to the vivid presentation, and desserts are a match for the rest, taking in a beautifully crafted spiced crème brûlée of unimpeachable texture, served with raspberry coulis and a muesli biscuit, and an impressive hot lavender soufflé with a harmonious accompaniment of basil syrup and peach sorbet.

The classic regions of France – Bordeaux and Burgundy in particular – are the biggest strengths of the impressive wine list. The rest of the wine-making world isn't overlooked, however, with regional France (Alsace, Rhône and Loire especially), Austria, Germany and the New World (New Zealand and California are the high points) all making a good showing. Given Harveys' wine trade connections, it is no surprise to see that sherry, port and Madeira are also well represented. Prices for some of the more stellar wines are hefty, but pricing is fair throughout, and there is good, interesting drinking at the under-£20 end of the scale too, reinforced by a good selection of half-bottles. Prices start at £14 for Argentinian Chardonnay.

CHEF: Daniel Galmiche   PROPRIETOR: Allied Domecq plc   OPEN: Mon to Fri L 12 to 2, Mon to Sat D 7 to 10   MEALS: alc (main courses £21 to £24). Set L £20   SERVICE: not inc   CARDS: Amex, Delta, Diners, MasterCard, Switch, Visa   DETAILS: 60 seats. Private parties: 60 main room, 8 to 24 private rooms. Vegetarian meals. Children's helpings. No cigars/pipes in dining room. Music. Air-conditioned

## ▲ Hotel du Vin & Bistro ▮

The Sugar House, Narrow Lewins Mead,
Bristol BS1 2NU
TEL: (0117) 925 5577   FAX: (0117) 925 1199                          COOKING 3
EMAIL: reservations@bristol.hotelduvin.com                  MODERN EUROPEAN
WEBSITE: www.hotelduvin.com                                          £33–£54

A pleasant change from the standard corporate hotel, this branch of a small chain (see entries in Birmingham, Tunbridge Wells and Winchester) occupies the historical Sugar House, a Grade II listed warehouse dating from the eighteenth century. Its spacious dining room with wood-panelled fireplace, aged-effect ochre walls and dark, stained floorboards help to make it (for most, though not all, reporters) a 'sociable and relaxing place for dinner', while the food appeals for its honesty and simplicity, taking in starters of devilled sweetbreads, ham hock terrine, and a neat and tidy frisée salad with smoked eel and lardons.

Seafood is a strong suit, including bistro favourites of salmon fishcake with sorrel beurre blanc, and poached smoked haddock with chive velouté, while the kitchen's use of fresh ingredients, its sound judgement and sensitive seasoning are apparent in, for example, one reporter's pan-fried sea bass with braised fennel and red wine jus. Finish in the comfort zone with a triple chocolate bavarois, banana tarte Tatin with caramel sauce, or steamed blueberry pudding with crème fraîche. Service is helpful and friendly, particularly from the sommelier, who presides over a globe-trotting list with knowledge and enthusiasm. Although France is understandably given much room, there is lots more to choose from. New World wines are very well selected and, for novelty seekers, something from Luxembourg, Switzerland, Israel or Thailand might fit the bill. Mark-ups are commendably fair, encouraging experimentation. 'Sommelier's suggestions' by the glass are listed on the menu, from £4 to £6.50. Monthly-changing house wines are around £11.50 to £16.

CHEF: Rob Carr   PROPRIETOR: Hotel du Vin Ltd   OPEN: all week 12 to 1.45, 6 to 10   MEALS: alc
exc Sun L (main courses £12.50 to £15.50). Set L Sun £23.50   SERVICE: not inc   CARDS: Amex,
Delta, Diners, MasterCard, Switch, Visa   DETAILS: 85 seats. Private parties: 70 main room, 8 to
30 private rooms. Car park. Vegetarian meals. Children's helpings. No cigars/pipes in dining
room. Wheelchair access (also WC). No music   ACCOMMODATION: 40 rooms, all with bath/
shower. TV. Phone. Room only £110 to £225. Rooms for disabled. Baby facilities (*The Which?*
*Hotel Guide*)

# Ma Provence

| NEW ENTRY |
| --- |

| 2 Upper Byron Place, Clifton, Bristol BS8 1JY | COOKING 3 |
| TEL: (0117) 926 8314 | FRENCH |
| WEBSITE: www.table42.net | £33–£58 |

The two interconnecting rooms of this back-street restaurant are done out in
green and yellow, with 'bright and brash' paintings of Provence landscapes. If
that seems assertive in these monochrome/minimalist times, remember that
bright and brash is just how restaurants look in Provence. For once, the menu
French has been written by a native, and the kitchen delivers a convincing
version of the most Mediterranean of France's regional cuisines. Excellent fish
soup with rouille and croûtons uses red mullet for a deep, rich flavour
underscored by saffron and an aniseedy note, and vividness characterises a
terrine of roast provençale vegetables and mozzarella with red pepper coulis and
coriander oil. Southern summers are evoked by a roast fillet of sea bass on
mashed potato with chorizo and basil in it and an intense sundried tomato sauce.
For a finisher, try a 'truly substantial' wedge of walnut and pine-nut tart with a
fanned poached pear and a soft, orange mass of pumpkin cream, or a selection of
seasonal sorbets for lighter appetites. On occasion, service can be erratic under
pressure. The wine list isn't hefted to Provence, but does confine itself to France.
Its choices are sound, and reasonable prices start at £10.50.

CHEF: David Margas   PROPRIETOR: Elli and Philippe Quemard   OPEN: Tue to Fri 12 to 2, Mon to
Sat 7 to 10   CLOSED: Most bank hols   MEALS: alc (main courses £14 to £28). Light L menu also
available   SERVICE: not inc   CARDS: Amex, Delta, MasterCard, Switch, Visa   DETAILS: 30 seats.
Private parties: 30 main room. Wheelchair access (not WC). Music

# Markwicks ♥

| 43 Corn Street, Bristol BS1 1HT | COOKING 5 |
| TEL/FAX: (0117) 926 2658 | MODERN BRITISH |
| EMAIL: markwicks@amserve.net | £34–£64 |

Amid Corn Street's bars and clubs, with people spilling out of them on busy
evenings, it is a surprise to descend a discreet marble staircase and find a calm,
'quietly classy' basement dining room with a low-key, conservative
atmosphere. This long-standing Bristol star reflects its owners' dedication,
treating food seriously but not pompously: 'real food, real flavours, real talent'.
Markwicks' cuisine – not flashy, certainly not trendy – looks and tastes like the
work of a craftsman. It is modern with traditional roots, delivering carefully
considered textures and occasionally 'big, hearty tastes': thin sheets of pasta, for
example, generously layered with ceps in a creamy sauce seasoned with truffle
oil. A hand-written menu is supplemented by a list of daily fish specials, which

may illustrate that even a fish ragout – monkfish, scallops, crab and prawns in a creamy, fish-stocky, dill-freshened sauce – can be 'a thing of joy'.

Although dishes are sometimes a little short on thrill, their components complement each other well. An inspection meal's show-stopper was a tender, pink breast of Trelough duck with a deeply flavourful crust, combined with sweet-tart apple and celeriac purée, and caramelised bitter-sweet chicory in a dark, intense sauce: 'I can't imagine anything more harmonious.' Desserts – a little quirkier – take in hot chocolate tortellini, an apple and Lancashire cheese tart, and a deconstructed rhubarb fool (sticks of poached rhubarb, a blob of sweetened cream and a couple of first-rate almond biscuits). Service is professional, discreet and courteous, but quite relaxed, and the wine list is put together with one eye on quality and the other on value. The main list runs the gamut from Bordeaux (favouring lesser-known but more keenly priced bottles, rather than big names) to New Zealand, while 11 house wines range from £4 to £20. Bin-ends, listed at the back, reveal a few gems.

CHEF: Stephen Markwick   PROPRIETORS: Stephen and Judy Markwick   OPEN: Mon to Fri L 12 to 2, Mon to Sat D 6 to 10   CLOSED: 1 week Christmas to New Year, 1 week Easter, last 2 weeks Aug   MEALS: alc (main courses £18 to £19.50). Set L and D 6 to 7 £17.50 (2 courses) to £21.50   SERVICE: not inc   CARDS: Amex, Delta, MasterCard, Switch, Visa   DETAILS: 45 seats. Private parties: 8 main room, 6 to 20 private rooms. Vegetarian meals. Children's helpings. No music

---

## Quartier Vert ♥

85 Whiteladies Road, Bristol BS8 2NT
TEL: (0117) 973 4482   FAX: (0117) 974 3913
EMAIL: quartiervert@netscapeonline.co.uk
WEBSITE: www.quartiervert.co.uk

BRISTOL
GFG
2003
COMMENDED

COOKING 4
MEDITERRANEAN
£27–£54

Straightforward, well organised, with an unfussy attitude and accessible food, Quartier Vert serves up a blackboard menu of Spanish-inspired 'little dishes' in the bar, and more substantial and wide-ranging food in the dining room. In an age when many restaurants pay lip service to the principles underlying good food, QV is at pains to address the questions of where food comes from and how it is grown, as well as how it is cooked. It is not 100 per cent organic, but with meat from Eastbrook Farm, fish and game from Heritage Fine Foods, flour from Shipton Mill, and Spanish supplies from Brindisa it certainly knows where to shop.

Such careful sourcing does not guarantee good results, but here a confidence and lightness of touch produce unequivocal, clean flavours. The kitchen sets its sights on traditional dishes of provincial Europe, from provençale fish soup to pigeon breast with butter bean purée, from a salad of serrano ham with quail eggs and piquillo peppers, to duck confit with roast winter vegetables. French and Spanish cheeses with in-house biscuits (baking is a strength) offer an alternative to desserts of honey and lavender ice cream with shortbread, or a bitter chocolate and almond torte.

Given the high principles on which the restaurant operates it is all the more strange that smoking is allowed (unless everybody is puffing organic tobacco). The short but sensible wine list favours Europe, with some interesting choices from Italy and the French regions. Pricing is fair, there's a decent selection of half-bottles, and a dozen house wines (five organic) are available by the glass or carafe, as well as bottle. Bottle prices start at £11.95 for Spanish red and white.

CHEF: Barny Haughton   PROPRIETORS: Barny Haughton and Mrs C. Coombes   OPEN: all week 12 to 3, 6 to 10.30.   CLOSED: 1 week Christmas, Sun after 4 in winter   MEALS: alc (main courses £10.50 to £19.50). Set L and D before 3 and after 6 £14.50 (2 courses) to £17.50. Light snacks available Mon to Sat 10 to 11, Sun 10 to 4   SERVICE: not inc, 10% for parties of 5 or more CARDS: Delta, MasterCard, Switch, Visa   DETAILS: 80 seats. 25 seats outside. Private parties: 50 main room, 5 to 25 private rooms. Vegetarian meals. Children's helpings. Wheelchair access (not WC). Music

---

## riverstation

| | |
|---|---|
| The Grove, Bristol BS1 4RB | COOKING 3 |
| TEL: (0117) 914 4434   FAX: (0117) 934 9990 | MODERN BRITISH-PLUS |
| WEBSITE: www.riverstation.co.uk | £23–£51 |

Views over the river are one of the attractions in this first-floor restaurant, which sports a big bar, leatherette banquettes, steel-framed chairs, and veneered wooden tables. Local vegetables, meat and eggs contribute to a lively menu that runs from soupe au pistou, via griddled asparagus with red pepper vinaigrette, to fillet steak with pommes sarladaise. Given its location, seafood under-standably gets serious treatment, including 'textbook' plump scallops with a restrained pesto sauce, roast halibut with cockles and beurre blanc, and roast hake with judión beans, chorizo and aïoli.

Despite wide-ranging materials and ideas, dishes have a pleasing simplicity, from smoked haddock chowder to lambs' sweetbreads with tartare sauce, from risi e bisi to a whole roast sea bass with couscous salad. Desserts, meanwhile, take in hot chocolate pithiviers with vanilla ice cream, and a saffron, honey and pistachio tart with raspberry sauce. Not all reports are equally enthusiastic, with 'inexcusably pedestrian' service among the problems, but the stylistically arranged wine list has plenty of interest, with a Canadian Pinot Noir at £19.75 among the house selection of ten bottles. Prices start around £11.

CHEFS: Peter Taylor and Simon Green   PROPRIETORS: Peter Taylor, John Payne, Shirley Anne Bell and Mark Hall   OPEN: open all week 12 (10.30 Sat) to 2.30 (3 Sun), 6 to 10.30 (11 Fri and Sat, 9 Sun)   CLOSED: Christmas, 1 Jan   MEALS: alc exc Sat and Sun L (main courses £10 to £16.50). Set L Mon to Sat £11.50 (2 courses) to £13.75, Set L Sun £12 (2 courses) to £15. Brunch menu available Sat   SERVICE: not inc   CARDS: Delta, Diners, MasterCard, Switch, Visa   DETAILS: 120 seats. 24 seats outside. Private parties: 120 main room. Vegetarian meals. Children's helpings. No-smoking area. No music

---

## Severnshed ⚡✳

| | |
|---|---|
| The Grove, Harbourside, Bristol BS1 4RB | |
| TEL: (0117) 925 1212   FAX: (0117) 9251214 | COOKING 3 |
| EMAIL: info@severnshed.co.uk | MODERN ORGANIC |
| WEBSITE: www.severnshed.co.uk | £27–£48 |

At one time this really was a boatbuilding shed (with great views over the harbour basin), though you probably wouldn't recognise its origins now: the exterior is eau-de-nil clapperboard, and inside it is all white walls, timber roofing, a zinc bar and metal fittings. The huge expanse also includes a café area serving light dishes throughout the day (including 'the best steak sarnie' in ciabatta bread).

The kitchen is driven by a crusading commitment to well-sourced organic produce, and the restaurant menu shows off lots of trendy twists, Oriental spicing and other worldwide influences, alongside simple things like grilled Torbay sole with new potatoes and salad. Among starters, an accurately made risotto of lobster and asparagus has garnered plenty of votes, and side orders of roasted Mediterranean vegetables have been well received. The quality of raw materials also shines through: in fillet of Somerset lamb coated with pesto and wrapped in filo pastry, and in wood-oven roasted fillet of salmon ('full of earthy taste') marinated in black bean sauce. To finish, raspberry crème brûlée has been a fine version. Service is deft and cheerful. An assorted list of around 30 wines includes a fistful of organics; house wine is £9.95.

CHEF: James Brown   PROPRIETOR: Organic Ventures Ltd   OPEN: all week 12 to 6, 6.30 to 11   MEALS: alc (main courses £8 to £15). Café menu also available   SERVICE: 10% (optional), card slips closed   CARDS: Amex, Delta, Diners, MasterCard, Switch, Visa   DETAILS: 150 seats. 100 seats outside. Private parties: 400 main room. Car park. Vegetarian meals. Children's helpings. No smoking in dining room. Wheelchair access (also WC). Music. Air-conditioned

---

**BRITWELL SALOME  Oxfordshire**                                    map 2

# The Goose ⅚✗

Britwell Salome OX49 5LG
TEL: (01491) 612304   FAX: (01491) 614822                     COOKING 4
on B4009, just outside Watlington, 5 min from                 ENGLISH
M40 junction 6                                                £22–£62

This brick-and-flint pub looks unremarkable outside, but bar and dining room are decorated with vibrant colours and enough modern paintings for a small art gallery. Chris Barber and Michael North split their time between here and the White Hart at Nettlebed (see entry), but format and style at the Goose remain much as before. Simplicity seems to be the key to the operation, and sound technical skills and good ingredients (some local) are evident: in a starter of plump, squeaky-fresh scallops, accurately timed, on a bed of St George's mushrooms, and in slices of tender, pink-roast venison on a first-class purée of potato and parsnip, topped with paper-thin parsnip tuiles.

Clear, well-defined flavours show in a lightly peppery wild rocket soup made with good stock, and in a smooth, dense yet spreadable duck liver and foie gras parfait with a lightly tart pear and apple chutney. Cheeses come pre-portioned, and desserts might include a gently shivering, vanilla-flavoured pannacotta with a jumble of exotic fruits and a drizzle of mint coulis. The no-choice lunch looks good value, service is friendly and informative (no pomp or ceremony) and a compact, well-chosen, helpfully priced wine list starts with a handful by the glass from £2.65 (£11.50 a bottle).

CHEFS: Chris Barber and Michael North   PROPRIETOR: Chris Barber   OPEN: Tue to Sun L 12 to 2 (2.45 Sun), Tue to Sat D 7 to 9   MEALS: alc (main courses £14 to £22). Set L Tue to Sat £12.50, Set D £17.50   SERVICE: not inc, 10% for parties of 8 or more   CARDS: MasterCard, Switch, Visa   DETAILS: 50 seats. Private parties: 12 main room, 8 to 12 private rooms. Car park. Children's helpings. No smoking in dining room. Music. No mobile phones   £5

## BROADHEMBURY Devon                                         map 2

# Drewe Arms ⁵⨯

Broadhembury EX14 3NF                                         COOKING 2
TEL: (01404) 841267   FAX: (01404) 841118                    SEAFOOD
off A373, between Cullompton and Honiton                     £30–£59

From outside, this looks the quintessential, centuries-old English village pub, but inside it has more of a bistro feel: there are oilcloths on the tables and prints of fish on the walls: a reminder that seafood is indeed the kitchen's main business. Blackboard menus are backed up by daily specials, and descriptions could not be briefer: 'tuna loin – seared – garlic', 'fillet of plaice – béarnaise', 'sea bass – basil and chilli oil', and so on. Gravlax and marinated herrings are produced on the premises (Kerstin Burge hails from Sweden), while meat eaters might be offered confit of duck salad, or tenderloin of venison with mushroom sauce. To finish, there are traditional favourites like lemon posset, or bread pudding with whisky sauce. Service is all on chatty, first-name terms. House wines from £11.75 head the list, there are several half-bottles, and prices throughout are reasonable.

CHEFS: Nigel and Andrew Burge   PROPRIETORS: Nigel, Kerstin and Andrew Burge   OPEN: all week L 12 to 2, Mon to Sat D 7 to 9.30   CLOSED: 25 and 31 Dec   MEALS: alc (main courses £10 to £25). Bar menu available   SERVICE: not inc   CARDS: Delta, MasterCard, Switch, Visa   DETAILS: 40 seats. 100 seats outside. Private parties: 25 main room. Car park. Children's helpings. No smoking in dining room. Wheelchair access (also WC). No music

## BROADWAY Worcestershire                                    map 5

# ▲ Dormy House ⁵⨯

Willersey Hill, Broadway WR12 7LF
TEL: (01386) 852711   FAX: (01386) 858636
EMAIL: reservations@dormyhouse.co.uk                          COOKING 3
WEBSITE: www.dormyhouse.co.uk                   MODERN EUROPEAN-PLUS
just off A44, 1m NW of Broadway                              £30–£65

There is no shortage of modern facilities at this seventeenth-century Cotswold house at the top of a steep climb just outside Broadway: everything from a putting green and croquet lawn to a sauna and gym. Weddings, banquets and conferences are the focus of attention, but the Tapestries restaurant – housed in a modern conservatory extension and named after a wine-themed wall hanging – is open to all comers, as is the Barn Owl Bar, where simpler meals are served.

Options in the restaurant include a carte, and a set-price and a six-course 'gourmet' menu, though canapés and a mid-meal sorbet are served whichever you take. The elaborate cooking style aims towards making a strong visual impact: witness a starter of thinly sliced sauté scallops arranged on a rough purée of broad beans, topped with deep-fried 'spaghetti' of vegetables and surrounded by a moat of red pepper sauce. Main courses are similarly busy: steamed turbot with prawn and crab beignets and a coriander and lime sauce, or roast beef fillet with a ragoût of oxtail and wild mushrooms on a red wine sauce, for example. At inspection, some good ideas and fine raw materials were let down by poor execution, but when the food hits the mark it can be impressive. Wines are fairly priced and include a good choice by the glass. The house selection starts at £12.75.

CHEF: Alan Cutler   PROPRIETOR: Jorgen Philip-Sorensen   OPEN: Sun L 12 to 2, all week D 7 to 9.30 (9 Sun)   CLOSED: 24 to 26 Dec   MEALS: alc (main courses £17 to £23). Set L £20.50, Set D £33.50 to £37.50. Bar menu available   SERVICE: not inc   CARDS: Amex, Delta, MasterCard, Switch, Visa   DETAILS: 80 seats. 30 seats outside. Private parties: 160 main room, 2 to 160 private rooms. Car park. Vegetarian meals. No children under 16 after 7pm in dining room. Jacket and tie. No smoking in dining room. Wheelchair access (also WC). No music. Air-conditioned   ACCOMMODATION: 48 rooms, all with bath/shower. TV. Phone. B&B £110 to £195. Rooms for disabled. Baby facilities (*The Which? Hotel Guide*)

## BROCKENHURST Hampshire                                     map 2

# Simply Poussin ✸

The Courtyard, Brookley Road,
Brockenhurst SO42 7RB
TEL: (01590) 623063   FAX: (01590) 623144                   COOKING 3
EMAIL: sales@simplypoussin.co.uk                            MODERN BRITISH
WEBSITE: www.simplypoussin.co.uk                             £25–£50

Under the same ownership as Le Poussin at Parkhill (see entry Lyndhurst), Simply Poussin is a one-roomed operation with bare tables, a welcoming atmosphere and professional service. Part of the draw is a two-course menu for £10, available at both lunch and dinner, which might offer smoked salmon filled with smoked salmon mousse, baked cod on pea purée, or haunch of venison braised in red wine, followed by cheese.

The repertoire ranges from a fine, silky, flavourful wild mushroom ravioli agreeably infused with truffle oil, to chicken in a coconut broth spiked with chilli and coriander, served with a ginger and lime leaf pilaff, but ambition is largely kept under control. Twice-baked cheese soufflé, or a salad of chargrilled wood pigeon, might be followed by breast of duck with beetroot sauce, or pot roast New Forest pork, first brined in beer and then basted with honey. Hot passion-fruit soufflé is a regular among desserts, or there may be an iced hazelnut nougatine. A selection of well-chosen wines at reasonable prices adds to the appeal; 18 are available by the glass, including house Touraine Sauvignon Blanc and Cabernet Franc at £10 (£2.50 a glass).

CHEF: Karl Wiggins   PROPRIETOR: Le Poussin Ltd   OPEN: Tue to Sat 12 to 2, 7 to 10   CLOSED: 25 December, 6 to 20 Jan   MEALS: alc (main courses £10.50 to £16). Set L and D Tue to Fri £10 (2 courses)   SERVICE: 10% (optional), card slips closed   CARDS: Amex, Delta, MasterCard, Switch, Visa   DETAILS: 36 seats. 4 seats outside. Private parties: 30 main room. Car park. Vegetarian meals. No smoking in dining room. Music

*The Guide office can quickly spot when a restaurateur is encouraging customers to write recommending inclusion. Such reports do not further a restaurant's cause. Please tell us if a restaurateur invites you to write to the Guide.*

## BROMSGROVE Worcestershire                    map 5

# ▲ Grafton Manor ✱

Grafton Lane, Bromsgrove B61 7HA
TEL: (01527) 579007   FAX: (01527) 575221                    COOKING 4
WEBSITE: www.graftonmanorhotel.co.uk              MODERN INDIAN/EUROPEAN
off B4091, 1½m SW of Bromsgrove                              £31–£53

Mellow and half-crumbling, this red-brick pile (tricky to find, so ask for directions) comes with a carved sandstone porch, a grand staircase, moulded plaster ceilings, and strong colours everywhere, from the lounge's red and blue to the dining room's green and gold. It exudes the atmosphere of an upper-class English family home, complete with portraits of soulful-looking spaniels, although anyone expecting a traditionally British country-house approach to the food will be in for a bit of a surprise. True, some dishes fit the bill – ballottine of salmon, or Caesar salad with white pudding and poached egg – but it is the Indian ones that reflect Simon Morris's real passion.

Indeed, it would seem that the more the kitchen concentrates on Indian food, the better the results. Although not all reporters have been equally impressed, spicing is generally deftly handled, flavours are interesting, and textures carefully considered, the repertoire taking in crab and cottage cheese chaat with tomato raita, and Bengal lamb with chickpeas, aubergine and apple. Even desserts join in, perhaps offering semolina halva, or chocolate and cardamom mousse. The wine list's scope and reasonable pricing are also cause for cheer. Eight house wines start the ball rolling, from £9 to £14.10.

CHEF: Simon Morris   PROPRIETORS: the Morris family   OPEN: Sun to Fri L 12 to 2, Mon to Sat D 7 to 9   CLOSED: 31 Dec, first week Jan, bank hols   MEALS: Set L Mon to Fri £20.50, Set L Sun £18.50, Set D £27.85 to £32.75   SERVICE: not inc, card slips closed   CARDS: Amex, Diners, MasterCard, Switch, Visa   DETAILS: 60 seats. Private parties: 150 main room, 40 private room. Car park. Vegetarian meals. Children's helpings. No smoking in dining room. No music. No mobile phones   ACCOMMODATION: 9 rooms, all with bath/shower. TV. Phone. B&B £85 to £165. Rooms for disabled (The Which? Hotel Guide)

## BRUTON Somerset                               map 2

# Truffles

95 High Street, Bruton BA10 0AR                         COOKING 3
TEL/FAX: (01749) 812255                                      BRITISH
EMAIL: TRUFFLESBRUTON@tinyworld.co.uk                    £26–£49

'Small, uncluttered and serene' is how one visitor described this terraced, grey-stone building on a bend at the bottom of a hill. It is an 'old-fashioned neighbourhood restaurant' done out in warm lemon-yellow, apricot and terracotta, that benefits enormously from the presence of Denise Bottrill. Laughing and smiling, she is just the sort of genuinely friendly person to encourage a loyal following of local regulars. A few upbeat ingredients add interest to an otherwise conventional repertoire whose monthly-changing menu might feature hot-smoked salmon with chive vermouth sauce, and breast of pigeon with black pudding and a wild mushroom sauce.

Not all the fusion ideas fuse, and a lack of clarity in flavours rather let down an inspection meal, but there is still plenty to enjoy: for example a prawn and dill mayonnaise 'castle' amounting to a well made, old fashioned prawn cocktail garnished with a seared scallop. Other fine raw materials include English lamb: for one visitor three thick pink cutlets accurately roasted to the required degree, resting on a round, flat cake of herby polenta. Desserts might include an orange and Cointreau pudding in a thin clear syrup with tangy strips of marmaladey zest. Outside France the wine list stays comfortably under £20, offering a good range of half-bottles, and starts with house Chilean Chardonnay and Merlot at £11.95 and £12.50.

CHEF: Martin Bottrill   PROPRIETORS: Denise and Martin Bottrill   OPEN: Tue to Sat D only 7 to 9.30 (weekday L by arrangement; open for Mothering Sun and Good Fri L)   MEALS: Set D Tue to Thur £15 (2 courses). Set D £25.95.   SERVICE: not inc, card slips closed   CARDS: MasterCard, Switch, Visa   DETAILS: 30 seats. Private parties: 20 main room, 10 private room. No children under 8. No smoking while others eat. Wheelchair access (not WC). No music. Air-conditioned  (£5)

## BUCKLAND Gloucestershire

map 5

## ▲ Buckland Manor 🍷 ⅹ

Buckland WR12 7LY
TEL: (01386) 852626   FAX: (01386) 853557
EMAIL: enquire@bucklandmanor.com
WEBSITE: www.bucklandmanor.com
off B4632, 2m SW of Broadway

COOKING 5
MODERN BRITISH
£38–£90

Both the manor and the adjacent church, built from matching honey-coloured stone, date from the thirteenth century. The electronic gates, of more recent provenance, swish slowly open, and ranks of begonias attend your ascent to the front door. Inside, the floral theme runs riot all over carpets, curtains, upholstery, in fireplaces and on occasional tables, and in the dining room you will sit on a William Morris fabric design and be gazed on by portraits in oils.

The cooking, led by Kenneth Wilson, aims forthrightly enough to match the surrounding grandeur. Home-made bread rolls flavoured with pesto or smoked salmon, Echiré butter and an intermediate sorbet that might be made from something unusual such as crème fraîche announce as much. When it comes to the main business, a strong streak of inventiveness runs through the dishes on a fixed-price menu that manages to avoid supplements. A firm mousse of langoustine and scallop is packed into a tortellino parcel, sauced with an admirably intense langoustine froth, and accompanied by a couple of spoonfuls of lemon risotto and a small bundle of herby salad. Asparagus in season is given strong support from Parmesan cream and garlic vinaigrette. Meat main courses get glazed and crusted – honey and cloves for duck, a herb mixture for lamb – and the sauces are old-school, sticky reductions with a slug of alcohol in them: sweet Banyuls in the case of duck, perhaps champagne with morels for chicken. Fine technique ensures balance in desserts, such as a banana tarte Tatin with translucent cardamom syrup and Indian-spiced ice cream, or hot cherry soufflé with its own sorbet and mint anglaise. Service is utterly formal, and utterly charming.

The impressive wine list includes a good number of great producers from Italy (Super-Tuscans are a strong point), Bordeaux, Alsace, Burgundy, and across the

New World. Mark-ups can be on the high side, but a list of 18 interesting house wines (£17.50 to £33.50) holds up the value end of the spectrum, as does a list of country wines from France.

CHEF: Kenneth Wilson   PROPRIETORS: Roy and Daphne Vaughan   OPEN: all week 12.30 to 1.45, 7.30 to 9   MEALS: Set L £24.50, Set D £45.50   SERVICE: not inc   CARDS: Amex, Delta, Diners, MasterCard, Switch, Visa   DETAILS: 40 seats. 25 seats outside. Private parties: 36 main room. Car park. No children under 8. Jacket and tie. No smoking in dining room. Wheelchair access (not WC). No music. No mobile phones   ACCOMMODATION: 13 rooms, all with bath/shower. TV. Phone. B&B £205 to £350. Rooms for disabled. No children under 12. Swimming pool (*The Which? Hotel Guide*)

## BUCKLAND  Oxfordshire                                                   map 2

# ▲ Lamb at Buckland  ✷  £

| Lamb Lane, Buckland SN7 8QN | COOKING 2 |
| TEL: (01367) 870484   FAX: (01367) 870675 | BRITISH |
| | £23–£56 |

'There are lambs as ornaments, a lamb motif on the bar's carpet and lambs' kidneys on the menu,' observed a visitor to this eighteenth-century Cotswold-stone pub. Food is served in the beamed bar or in the 'slightly chintzy' dining room, and one blackboard menu is operational throughout. Paul Barnard's cooking ranges far and wide, although it is most convincing when it stays safely within Northern European boundaries. Successful dishes also tend to be the ones that are least fussy: a warming bowl of flavourful mushroom soup shows 'a tasteful hand in the kitchen', although there has been something earthier about the viscous cep gravy accompanying pork en croûte. Elsewhere, the kitchen might tackle anything from warm goats' cheese salad to seafood risotto. As a finale, a 'splendid' version of junket apparently 'sends many regulars into fits of nostalgia'. Six house wines from France, Italy and the New World start at £11.95 on a wide-ranging list of around 50; nine wines are served by the glass, from £2.35.

CHEF: Paul Barnard   PROPRIETORS: Paul and Peta Barnard   OPEN: all week 12 to 2 (2.30 Sun), 6.30 to 9.30   CLOSED: D 24 Dec, 25 and 26 Dec, D 1 Jan   MEALS: alc (main courses £6.50 to £19). Set L Sun £21.95   SERVICE: not inc, card slips closed   CARDS: Amex, Delta, MasterCard, Switch, Visa   DETAILS: 70 seats. 36 seats outside. Private parties: 58 main room, 8 to 18 private rooms. Car park. Vegetarian meals. Children's helpings. No smoking in dining room. Music   ACCOMMODATION: 4 rooms, all with bath/shower. TV. Phone. B&B £42.50 to £59.50  £5

---

*'I did not know whether to laugh or cry as I watched the [restaurant] manager hack away at our whole roast duck in an attempt to carve the bird. It took him seven minutes to complete the hacking. This was already an achievement as another, less experienced waiter not only took longer, but as he could not find the right places to carve, he gave up and served [all the] pieces to another group of diners ... It was pitiful to have to experience death by carving in a restaurant.'* (On eating in London)

---

map 2

# ▲ Master Builder's House Hotel, Riverview Restaurant

Bucklers Hard SO42 7XB
TEL: (01590) 616253   FAX: (01590) 616297                    COOKING 3
EMAIL: res@themasterbuilders.co.uk                       MODERN EUROPEAN
WEBSITE: www.themasterbuilders.co.uk                          £30–£55

Bucklers Hard, an eighteenth-century shipbuilding village, stands on the estuary of the Beaulieu river, within the estate of Lord Montagu. Views over the water from the light and airy dining room give it a tranquil feel, and large paintings in the style of Rothko add a touch of class to the décor. Despite that, and a collection of David Bailey prints, there is an unpretentious feel to the place, which applies not least to the food. Menus plough a fairly safe, not too ambitious modern European furrow: start, for example, with fish soup with aïoli, or pan-fried mozzarella wrapped in Parma ham with balsamic dressing. Characteristic main-course options include calf's liver and bacon with spring onion mash, grilled pork chop with polenta and apple sauce, and pan-roast red snapper with a crab cake and parsley dressing, while those looking for a comforting way to finish might try coffee mousse with coffee sauce, or poached pear with rice pudding and chocolate sauce. Around a dozen house selections at £12.50, split fairly evenly between the New World and Europe, including a bottle from the local estate, open the well-chosen wine list.

CHEF: Dennis Rhoden   PROPRIETORS: Jeremy Willcock and John Illsley   OPEN: all week 12 to 3, 7 to 10   MEALS: alc (main courses £15 to £18). Set L £16.95 (2 courses) to £19.50, Set D £29.50 SERVICE: not inc, card slips closed   CARDS: Amex, Delta, MasterCard, Switch, Visa   DETAILS: 70 seats. 20 seats outside. Private parties: 80 main room, 10 to 40 private rooms. Car park. Vegetarian meals. No cigars in dining room. No music   ACCOMMODATION: 25 rooms, all with bath/shower. TV. Phone. B&B £120 to £215

map 5

# ▲ Jonathan's at the Angel ✼

14 Witney Street, Burford OX18 4SN
TEL: (01993) 822714   FAX: (01993) 822069                     COOKING 5
EMAIL: jo@theangel-uk.com                          MODERN EUROPEAN/BRASSERIE
WEBSITE: www.theangel-uk.com                                  £31–£54

Describing itself as a brasserie-with-rooms, this sixteenth-century coaching inn down a narrow street nevertheless goes in for flowery curtains, and flickering candles in the evening. Josephine Lewis generates a happy atmosphere out front, while husband Jonathan oversees a lively carte that seems equally at home with asparagus and hollandaise as it does with lemon, lime and coriander flavours in a marinated loin of marlin.

Meat and game are sourced from local suppliers, perhaps appearing as sirloin or T-bone steaks, or roast pheasant with pear sauce, and seafood also strikes a populist note. Cornish lobster can be served grilled or cold, and sea bass might come with roast leeks and Cinzano sauce. Finish with fruit – pineapple marinated in saffron syrup, served with pistachio ice cream – or more indulgent baked banana and toffee crumble with clotted cream. A pithy wine list starts with eight house recommendations from £12.75 to £14.75, including northern Italian Pinot Grigio and Argentinian Merlot.

CHEFS: Jonathan Lewis and Greig Palmer   PROPRIETORS: Jonathan and Josephine Lewis   OPEN: Thur to Sun L 12 to 2, Tue to Sat D 7 to 9.30 (later Fri and Sat)   CLOSED: 26 Dec, 1 Jan, 12 Jan to 8 Feb   MEALS: alc (main courses £8.50 to £17). Light L menu Thur to Sat   SERVICE: not inc, card slips closed   CARDS: Delta, MasterCard, Switch, Visa   DETAILS: 36 seats. 24 seats outside. Children's helpings. No smoking in dining room. Occasional music. No mobile phones   ACCOMMODATION: 3 rooms, all with bath/shower. TV. Phone. B&B £85. No children under 9 (*The Which? Hotel Guide*)  (£5)

## BURNHAM MARKET  Norfolk                                          map 6

# Fishes'

| Market Place, Burnham Market PE31 8HE | COOKING 3 |
|---|---|
| TEL: (01328) 738588   FAX: (01328) 730534 | SEAFOOD |
| EMAIL: buzzmatt@eggconnect.net | £24–£59 |

Previous owner Gillian Cape sold up in 2001 after three decades of culinary service to this attractive Norfolk market town (the restaurant overlooks the green), and Matthew Owsley-Brown stepped into her shoes. Having cooked with Rick Stein at the Seafood Restaurant (see entry, Padstow) he is more than qualified to continue specialising in the type of cookery for which the place is famed, and so no name change has been necessary either. 'An enjoyable, summery mix of flavours' was the verdict on a July dish of marinated anchovies with beetroot salsa and a potato and chive salad in good mayonnaise, while traditional fish soup with rouille, croûtons and Gruyère has been appreciated for its subtlety and freshness. Admired main-course fish dishes have included oatmeal-crusted plaice with rosemary and walnut butter, and fillet of turbot with celeriac purée and a creamy sauce of wild mushrooms, while one reporter applauded the appearance of local marsh samphire to accompany lightly cooked smoked haddock in hollandaise with a poached egg. To finish, lemon tart – 'a perfect balance between creaminess, sweetness and tartness' – seems a good bet, or there may be fine bread-and-butter pudding, or chocolate nemesis served in a glass. The fairly sizeable wine list concentrates mainly on white wines, and starts with a French Colombard-Chardonnay blend at £10.95.

CHEF: Matthew Owsley-Brown   PROPRIETORS: Matthew and Caroline Owsley-Brown   OPEN: Tue to Sun L 12 to 2, Tue to Sat D 7 to 9.30   CLOSED: 23 to 27 Dec, 6 to 31 Jan   MEALS: Set L £15.50, Set D £20 (2 courses) to £25   SERVICE: not inc, card slips closed   CARDS: Amex, Delta, MasterCard, Switch, Visa   DETAILS: 42 seats. Private parties: 12 main room. Children's helpings. No children under 5 after 8.30pm. No smoking in dining room. Music

---

*Prices quoted in the Guide are based on information supplied by restaurateurs. The prices quoted at the top of each entry represent a range, from the lowest meal price to the highest; the latter is inflated by 20 per cent to take account of likely price rises during the year of the Guide.*

## ▲ Hoste Arms ♀ ✕

The Green, Burnham Market PE31 8HD
TEL: (01328) 738777  FAX: (01328) 730103
EMAIL: reception@hostearms.co.uk
WEBSITE: www.hostearms.co.uk
on B1155, 5m W of Wells

COOKING 2
MODERN BRITISH
£26–£59

A welcoming bar and a big working fireplace greet customers to this large yellow-fronted inn facing the green. Fish features prominently in the dining room and conservatory beyond, in the shape of Brancaster mussels, grilled sardines, and for one visitor baked cod with a more-than-generous accompaniment of potatoes, broccoli and spinach. Standards appear to seesaw, due in no small measure to its popularity, judging by reports of a busy and sometimes pressed operation, but praise has been heaped on best end of lamb, partridge, and stewed plums with mascarpone. Young staff are keen and helpful, although organisation does not appear to be their strongest point. Wines are arranged by both style and country, with Bordeaux, South Africa and Tuscany given top billing. Two shorter lists – white and red – make choosing easier, while buffs can go straight for the 'wines of special interest' categories. There are five reds and five whites by the glass, served in two sizes. Prices start at £10.25 and go up to £355 for 1979 and 1981 Pétrus.

CHEF: Andrew Mcpherson  PROPRIETOR: Paul Whittome  OPEN: all week 12 to 2, 7 to 9  MEALS: alc (main courses £8.50 to £16)  SERVICE: not inc  CARDS: Delta, MasterCard, Switch, Visa  DETAILS: 140 seats. 70 seats outside. Private parties: 80 main room, 12 to 24 private rooms. Car park. Vegetarian meals. Children's helpings. No smoking in dining room. Wheelchair access (also WC). No music. Air-conditioned  ACCOMMODATION: 36 rooms, all with bath/shower. TV. Phone. B&B £66 to £120. Rooms for disabled (*The Which? Hotel Guide*)

## BURNSALL  North Yorkshire                                      map 8

## ▲ Devonshire Fell ✕ £

Burnsall BD23 6BT
TEL: (01756) 729000  FAX: (01756) 729009
WEBSITE: www.devonshirehotels.co.uk

COOKING 3
MODERN BRITISH
£27–£43

'Idiosyncratic' was one reporter's description of this tall stone hotel, which is set into a hillside on the main road out of one of the most idyllic villages in the Dales. The modern interior may be out of keeping with the building, but it is stylishly done and 'just what the place needs'. Menus offer a range of brasserie mainstays: everything from smoked salmon with rosemary mayonnaise to pan-fried sea bass with 'real chips', or liver and bacon with parsnip mash. A blackboard of daily specials enhances the choice, and dishes are arranged informally under headings such as 'considerable', 'tapas' and 'simple'. In the tapas section have been Chinese-style crispy duck pancakes featuring moist, well-flavoured meat and impressively thin pancakes, while successes in the 'substantial' range have included tender lamb shank in a wine jus with a generous serving of roast potatoes, 'perfect for soaking up the gravy'. Thai fishcakes have also been praised, despite being somewhat light on chilli. Staff are a hard-working, friendly young bunch. Wines are arranged by price with ten

283

each of red and white in the 'under £18.50' category. Spanish house wines are £11.50 a bottle, £1.85/£2.50 a glass.

CHEFS: Steve Williams and Neil Waterfield   PROPRIETORS: The Duke and Duchess of Devonshire
OPEN: all week 12 to 2.30, 6.30 to 10   MEALS: alc (main courses £9 to £13)   SERVICE: not inc, card
slips closed   CARDS: Amex, Delta, Diners, MasterCard, Switch, Visa   DETAILS: 60 seats. 24
seats outside. Private parties: 70 main room, 2 to 20 private rooms. Car park. Vegetarian meals.
Children's helpings. No smoking in 1 dining room. Music. No mobile phones   ACCOMMODATION:
12 rooms, all with bath/shower. TV. Phone. B&B £70 to £160 (*The Which? Hotel Guide*)

---

## BURRINGTON  Devon                                                    map 1

## ▲ Northcote Manor 🍴

Burrington EX37 9LZ
TEL: (01769) 560501   FAX: (01769) 560770
EMAIL: rest@northcotemanor.co.uk
WEBSITE: www.northcotemanor.co.uk                          COOKING 3
on A377 between Umberleigh and Crediton, 4m              MODERN BRITISH
NW of Chulmleigh.                                              £36–£59

If the prospect of dining in a stone-built house in pretty countryside, with woodland, lawns and a terrace for drinks in fine weather, is an enticing one, then Northcote Manor lives up to expectations. Dinner is the main event: three courses that make use of some local materials, including duck and beef from just a few miles away (a fillet of the latter perhaps served with Savoy cabbage, oyster mushrooms and a red wine jus), as well as organic fruit and vegetables and West Country seafood. Grilled red mullet fillet, for example, might come with a basil risotto, or Dover sole with prawn tempura and a parsley and caper sauce.

Chris Dawson is obviously happy to borrow ideas from far and wide, although Europe is a preferred hunting ground, producing game terrine with celeriac rémoulade, breast of chicken with smoked bacon and chive risotto, and pear Tatin, or pannacotta with apples, to finish. New Zealand wines (try the Peregrine Pinot Gris from Central Otago) take pride of place on a wide-ranging list. Five house wines are among the handful that make it under £20.

CHEF: Chris Dawson   PROPRIETOR: D.J. Boddy   OPEN: all week 12 to 1.30, 7 to 9   MEALS: Set L
£18.50 (2 courses) to £25.50, Set D £35. Light L menu available   SERVICE: not inc, card slips
closed   CARDS: Amex, Delta, Diners, MasterCard, Switch, Visa   DETAILS: 37 seats. Private
parties: 80 main room, 2 to 26 private rooms. Car park. Vegetarian meals. Children's helpings.
No smoking in dining room. Music   ACCOMMODATION: 11 rooms, all with bath/shower. TV.
Phone. B&B £90 to £220. Baby facilities (*The Which? Hotel Guide*)  (£5)

---

*The 2004 Guide will be published before Christmas 2003. Reports on meals are most welcome at any time of the year, but are particularly valuable in the spring (no later than June). Send them to* The Good Food Guide, *FREEPOST, 2 Marylebone Road, London NW1 4DF. Or email your report to* goodfoodguide@which.net

# Langs ✦✶

Horse Leys Farm, 147 Melton Road,
Burton on the Wolds LE12 5TQ
TEL/FAX: (01509) 880980
EMAIL: langsrestaurant@amserve.net
WEBSITE: www.langsrestaurant.com

COOKING 4
MODERN EUROPEAN
£24–£48

This low red-brick building, once a farmhouse, is surrounded by flat, open countryside (yet close enough to the M1 to make it a viable lunch stop), and fronted by a well-organised car park. Its spacious, relaxed and comfortable dining room, with orangey terracotta walls and ivory-cream furnishings, may strike a rather conservative note, but the food has integrity, and workmanship is meticulous. Ideas range from a starter of oriental marinated beef with tiger prawns and pickled ginger, to a boned quail stuffed with wild mushrooms, sitting on strips of red and yellow pepper, topped with a rough green pesto mix.

Attempts to be modern and original may be outshone by more classically simple ideas, such as a 'dead straightforward' plate of lamb incorporating juicy rack, tasty chump (both cooked pink as ordered), and a well-made shepherd's pie. Flavours are clear and straightforward, and properly cooked vegetables are a strength: eight different ones involving four different methods of preparation at inspection, yet all full of flavour. Texture and flavour contrasts are well managed: for example, in a painstakingly made sticky banana pudding, served with a coconut-crusted white chocolate truffle, and surrounded by artistic streaks of caramel sauce. Other pluses include bread, value, and well-trained service that operates smoothly. A French-dominated wine list, most of it over £20, starts with four house wines from £12.50 to £14.50.

CHEFS: Gordon Lang and Steven Taylor    PROPRIETORS: Gordon Lang and Paul Simms    OPEN: Tue to Fri and Sun L 12 to 2 (2.30 Sun), Tue to Sat D 7.15 to 9.45 (10 Sat)    MEALS: alc exc Sun L (main courses £10 to £15.50). Set L Tue to Fri £12.75 (2 courses) to £15.95, Set L Sun £13.95    SERVICE: not inc, card slips closed    CARDS: Amex, Delta, MasterCard, Switch, Visa    DETAILS: 50 seats. 20 seats outside. Private parties: 50 main room, 12 private room. Car park. Vegetarian meals. Children's helpings. No smoking in dining room. Wheelchair access (also WC). Occasional music. No mobile phones

# St James ✦✶

30 High Street, Bushey WD23 3HL
TEL: (020) 8950 2480    FAX: (020) 8950 4107

COOKING 2
MODERN ENGLISH
£27–£47

'Praise the Lord! A minor miracle in the gastro-wilderness called Hertfordshire,' exclaimed our inspector. This local asset is a neatly designed modern venue with wooden floors, exposed brickwork and red pillars, whose big picture window looks out on the church of St James (who else?). The mood is easy-going but business-like.

A broadly European repertoire, strongly French-accented, takes in potato and onion soup with Toulouse sausage, and duck breast with dauphinoise potatoes and herb garlic jus. Good raw materials are sympathetically treated, producing seared scallops with a timbale of crunchily textured roast fennel and apple salad, and chargrilled calf's liver on a mound of comforting garlic and leek mash with a sticky, smoked bacon-flavoured jus. Results look appealing (stacking is clearly the order of the day), and desserts are a familiar bunch, running from raspberry brûlée (in March!) to chocolate torte with toffee ice cream. Italian and French wines feature strongly on a list that makes brief forays into the New World too, and is supplemented by wines of month. House red and white are £11.95 (£3.10 per glass).

CHEF: Simon Trussel  PROPRIETORS: Simon Trussel and Alfonso la Cava  OPEN: Mon to Sat 12 to 2, 6.30 to 9.30  CLOSED: 25 and 26 Dec, 1 Jan, bank hols  MEALS: alc (main courses £14.50 to £20). Set L £13.95 (2 courses), Set D £14.50 (2 courses) to £18.95  SERVICE: 10%, card slips closed  CARDS: Amex, Delta, MasterCard, Switch, Visa  DETAILS: 86 seats. Private parties: 50 main room, 30 to 40 private room. Vegetarian meals. No smoking in 1 dining room. Wheelchair access (also WC). Occasional music. No mobile phones. Air-conditioned

## CAMBRIDGE Cambridgeshire                                                map 6

# Midsummer House ✸✸

Midsummer Common, Cambridge CB4 1HA
TEL: (01223) 369299   FAX: (01223) 302672                         COOKING 5
EMAIL: reservations@midsummerhouse.co.uk          FRENCH/MEDITERRANEAN
WEBSITE: www.midsummerhouse.co.uk                           £38–£96

The bright, airy conservatory has not altered much over the years. Colourful paintings, natural light and padded chairs combine to make it an attractive room in which to dine. Since last year, however, the kitchen seems to have embarked on a radical change of direction, now producing a stream of dishes based around ideas familiar to anybody who has eaten at the Fat Duck (see entry, Bray). To those who have not, these appear original and arresting; to those who have, they are not quite in the same league, but are interesting nonetheless.

Excitement starts straight away, with a palate-cleansing foam of lemon and fennel sour, followed by a glass colourfully layered with olive purée, red pepper mousse and yellow tomato jelly, topped with a thin foam of garlic, rosemary and yoghurt. Foams are obviously 'in', as are risotti: of smoked haddock with grain mustard ice cream, or one of smoked bacon with parsley ice cream to accompany three little Scotch egg-like balls of deep-fried snails. Other intriguing combinations include a dish of just-cooked salmon partnered by an almond purée and a sauce of white chocolate and caviar, with its contrasting sweet, salt and bitter components. In this context, a pig's trotter stuffed with veal sweetbreads, black pudding and caramelised onion becomes a comparatively conventional dish.

Ambition may run slightly ahead of skill, but at least it all makes people sit up and take notice, and successes can be delightful, as with a first-class orange and Grand Marnier soufflé, served with an orange sauce and sorbet, or a pineapple mousse accompanied by a fennel and anise sorbet, pineapple jelly and a Pernod foam. Service includes lots of 'fussy attention', perhaps in an effort to assess how the new style is going down, and the wine list has been substantially expanded since last year. The range of Australian reds has increased to include 13 vintages of Penfolds Grange going back to 1966; California, Bordeaux, Burgundy and

Italy have also seen a substantial jump in quality bottles, while Austria is a newcomer to the list. All this activity would normally merit the award of a Glass or Bottle symbol. The bad news, however, is that the mark-ups are just as swingeing as they have been in the past, including a 2001 Cloudy Bay Sauvignon Blanc for a gob-smacking £63. To compensate, there are a few more options in the £20-a-bottle league, but only a few. Prices start at £13.95 for Sicilian white and move up pretty sharpish.

CHEF: Daniel Clifford   PROPRIETOR: Midsummer House Ltd   OPEN: Tue to Sat 12 to 2, 7 to 10   CLOSED: 26 Dec to 9 Jan, 19 Aug to 3 Sept   MEALS: Set L £18 (2 courses) to £24, Set D £42 to £60 (latter preferably for whole table)   SERVICE: not inc, card slips closed   CARDS: Amex, Delta, MasterCard, Switch, Visa   DETAILS: 50 seats. Private parties: 50 main room, 10 to 22 private rooms. Vegetarian meals. No smoking in dining room. Wheelchair access (not WC). No music. No mobile phones   (£5)

---

# 22 Chesterton Road ♥ ⅍

22 Chesterton Road, Cambridge CB4 3AX

TEL: (01223) 351880   FAX: (01223) 323814                              COOKING 4

EMAIL: davidcarter@restaurant22.co.uk                       MODERN EUROPEAN

WEBSITE: www.restaurant22.co.uk                                         £35–£48

Heading anti-clockwise around the ring road, you will drive right past the door of this green-shuttered Victorian house; driving the other way you will miss it completely. Then there's parking to worry about. And remember to book in advance: this is a popular place. But don't be put off by any of these small hurdles, for this is a restaurant worth seeking out, combining a formal but friendly atmosphere, tasteful, slightly old-fashioned décor, and attractively presented modern European cooking that caters for all tastes while showing an adventurous streak.

Among starters, traditional themes appear in novel combinations such as smoked pigeon breast on pear tarte Tatin with celeriac and port jus, or a spiced fish sausage on yellow split pea purée with coriander and coconut sauce. An optional fish course follows – maybe seafood risotto with Parmesan crisps and squid ink sauce – before the main course: choices tend towards rustic-sounding dishes like roast cod with plum tomatoes and Welsh rarebit, daube of beef with roast vegetables in red wine jus, or pan-fried chicken with sweetcorn fritters in tomato and chilli salsa. Tempting desserts might include poached pear in mulled wine syrup with brown bread ice cream. France predominates on the well-annotated wine list, although New World countries are given more than a passing glance. The 'choice selection' at the front highlights 'wines which people might neglect in favour of traditional favourites'. Four house wines sell for £10.75 and £11.95 (£3 and £3.25 per glass).

CHEF: Martin Cullum   PROPRIETOR: David Carter   OPEN: Tue to Sat D only 7 to 9.45   CLOSED: 1 week Christmas to New Year   MEALS: Set D £24.50   SERVICE: not inc   CARDS: Amex, Delta, Diners, MasterCard, Switch, Visa   DETAILS: 38 seats. Private parties: 26 main room, 12 private room. Vegetarian meals. No children under 10. No smoking in dining room. Occasional music. No mobile phones. Air-conditioned

## CARLISLE Cumbria                                                      map 10

# Number 10

10 Eden Mount, Stanwix, Carlisle CA3 9LY
TEL/FAX: (01228) 524183

COOKING 2
MODERN BRITISH
£27–£46

Just to the north of the city centre, Number 10 is a small restaurant run by a husband-and-wife partnership. It has a reassuringly light and friendly atmosphere, with a seasonally changing menu that likewise is not too challenging but not dull either. Use of good local produce gives a distinctly British feel to Geoff Ferguson's cooking, though ideas are brought in from all over: among starters may be potted shrimps, or Thornby Moor goats' cheese baked in filo with caramelised onions, served on a tomato and chive salad. Main courses take in classics such as roast rack of lamb with Shrewsbury sauce, and fillet steak with pepper sauce, alongside more modern chargrilled marlin with salsa verde and noodles. Two dozen or so wines open with a pair of house Australians at £10.75.

CHEF: Geoff Ferguson   PROPRIETORS: Geoff and Isabel Ferguson   OPEN: Tue to Sat D only 7 to 9.30   CLOSED: Feb, last week Oct   MEALS: alc (main courses £10 to £17.50)   SERVICE: not inc, card slips closed   CARDS: Amex, Delta, MasterCard, Switch, Visa   DETAILS: 24 seats. Private parties: 24 main room. Vegetarian meals. No smoking while others eat. Music

## CARTERWAY HEADS Northumberland                                        map 10

# ▲ Manor House Inn ⅙✳ £

Carterway Heads, Shotley Bridge DH8 9LX
TEL/FAX: (01207) 255268
on A68, 3m W of Consett

COOKING 1
MODERN BRITISH
£20–£42

'Run as a country inn ought to be,' concluded one reporter after visiting Chris and Moira Brown's modest pub/restaurant overlooking the Derwent Valley. Log fires warm the place in winter, and there are real ales on tap. Menus are on a blackboard, and choice is abundant, from starters such as warm salad of smoked bacon and mange-tout, or spicy mushrooms with rosemary and tomato, to honey and ginger sponge, or up to 16 local cheeses. In between, you might encounter calf's liver with black pudding and rocket and garlic mash, pigeon breast with Madeira and braised shallots, or ribeye steak with tomato, red wine and tarragon. More than 60 malt whiskies are available, and the 50-strong wine list has plenty of decent drinking at fair prices. House wine is £8.95.

CHEF: Peter Tiplady   PROPRIETORS: Chris and Moira Brown   OPEN: Mon to Thur 12 to 2.30, 5.30 to 9.30, Fri to Sun and bank and school hols 12 to 9.30   CLOSED: D 25 Dec   MEALS: alc (main courses £6.50 to £17)   SERVICE: not inc, card slips closed   CARDS: Amex, Delta, MasterCard, Switch, Visa   DETAILS: 58 seats. 40 seats outside. Private parties: 50 main room. Car park. Vegetarian meals. Children's helpings. No smoking in dining room. No music. No mobile phones   ACCOMMODATION: 4 rooms, all with bath/shower. TV. B&B £33 to £65 (£5)

---

▮ *denotes an outstanding wine cellar;* ▼ *denotes a good wine list, worth travelling for.*

## ▲ Aynsome Manor £✳

Cartmel LA11 6HH
TEL: (015395) 36653   FAX: (015395) 36016
EMAIL: info@aynsomemanorhotel.co.uk                    COOKING 3
WEBSITE: www.aynsomemanorhotel.co.uk          ENGLISH COUNTRY-HOUSE
off A590, ½m N of village                                £22–£43

An air of gentility pervades the Georgian manor, thanks not least to its views of
rolling countryside, its elegant curved stairway and ornate ceilings. Cumbria
was particularly badly scarred by foot-and-mouth disease and, since the
movement of livestock was one of the main factors contributing to its virulent
spread, one consequence has been that more attention is now paid to local
supplies: in this case including roast fillet of Cumbrian pork wrapped in air-
dried ham, and saddle of Holker Estate venison with pot-roast vegetables.

Such dishes form the centrepiece of a menu that might start with a poached
boudin of monkfish and lobster, or a risotto of chorizo, apple and tarragon.
Obviously, not everything comes from the locality, but nobody can complain if
the kitchen moves with the times. Regular visitors who may remember the
cream-laden dessert trolley (it was referred to in Aynsome Manor's first entry in
the Guide in 1984) will now be struck by its absence. In its place, a menu offers
the likes of vanilla crème brûlée with caramelised pear and rhubarb compote, or
hot apricot bread-and-butter pudding, along with a range of local ice creams,
from honey and treacle ripple, to cinnamon and cider. Members of the Varley
family still amiably patrol front-of-house, and the wide-ranging wine list
continues to offer lots of choice at a fair price (Bellingham Merlot from South
Africa, and Matua Valley Sauvignon Blanc from New Zealand, for example, both
£14.50), while half a dozen house wines weigh in at £11.75.

CHEFS: Nicholas Stopford, Julian Wright and David Sloman   PROPRIETORS: Tony, Margaret,
Christopher and Andrea Varley   OPEN: Sun L 12.30 to 1, Mon to Sat D 7 to 8.30 (residents only
Sun D)   CLOSED: 2 to 30 Jan   MEALS: Set L £14.25, Set D £19 to £25   SERVICE: not inc   CARDS:
Amex, Delta, MasterCard, Switch, Visa   DETAILS: 30 seats. Private parties: 30 main room. Car
park. Vegetarian meals. Children's helpings. No children under 5 at D. No smoking in dining
room. No music   ACCOMMODATION: 12 rooms, all with bath/shower. TV. Phone. D,B&B £62 to
£135. Baby facilities (*The Which? Hotel Guide*)  £5

## ▲ Uplands £✳

Haggs Lane, Cartmel LA11 6HD
TEL: (015395) 36248   FAX: (015395) 36848
EMAIL: uplands@kencomp.net
WEBSITE: www.uplands.uk.com                            COOKING 4
2½m SW of A590, 1m up road opposite Pig and            BRITISH
Whistle                                               £24–£47

Set on a hillside just outside Cartmel, Uplands is a country-house hotel with a
domestic feel. After aperitifs in the comfortable lounge, everyone sits down to
dinner at 8: those lucky enough to get the window table have views over the
valley to Morecambe Bay. The style may be more Lakeland colloquial than

cutting edge – four courses, large portions, elaborate garnishes – but superior skills keep it all afloat: home-baked bread fresh from the oven is commendable, and asparagus soup has been noted for its depth of flavour and thick, smooth texture. Despite a tendency to sweeten savoury dishes, successful main courses have included baked turbot of exemplary freshness with a delicately flavoured, frothy and buttery lemon and tarragon sauce, and tender medallions of venison with a bittersweet blackcurrant and juniper sauce. Main dishes are all adorned with the same five vegetables (among them, accomplished gratin dauphinois, crunchy minted carrots, and tangy beetroot with lime) although a tailored selection would surely be more appropriate. Desserts are highly calorific – spiced apricot pie with warm butterscotch sauce, for example – and wines are a concise but eclectic and reasonably priced selection. Six house wines are £11.50.

CHEF: Tom Peter   PROPRIETORS: Tom and Diana Peter   OPEN: Fri to Sun L 12.30 for 1 (1 sitting), Tue to Sun D 7.30 for 8 (1 sitting)   CLOSED: 2 Jan to 1 Mar   MEALS: Set L £16, Set D £29.50   SERVICE: not inc, card slips closed   CARDS: Amex, Delta, MasterCard, Switch, Visa   DETAILS: 28 seats. Private parties: 28 main room. Car park. No children under 8 at D. No smoking in dining room. No music   ACCOMMODATION: 5 rooms, all with bath/shower. TV. Phone. D,B&B £140 (double room) to £162. No children under 8 (*The Which? Hotel Guide*)  £5

---

## CASTLE COMBE  Wiltshire                                    map 2

# ▲ Manor House, Bybrook Restaurant ⚡✶

Castle Combe SN14 7HR
TEL: (01249) 782206   FAX: (01249) 782159
EMAIL: enquiries@manor-housecc.co.uk                          COOKING 3
WEBSITE: www.exclusivehotels.co.uk                             ENGLISH
on B4039, 3M NW of junction with A420                          £32–£79

The huge Georgian manor is surrounded by greensward, and the restaurant – reached through a baronial oak-panelled hall with a large fireplace – occupies an L-shaped room with windows along two sides affording fine views of the gardens. Mark Taylor's cooking is in the grand style, 'borrowing unashamedly from other cultures', as he puts it, to produce a diverting first-course 'bonbon' of duck confit and foie gras (like a Scotch egg) with rhubarb and a peppered caramel sauce. Indeed the combination of savoury and sweet flavours seems to be a charatceristic: three tail fillets of monkfish have been served with capers and sultanas, and Quantock duck breast has come with prunes, while one reporter felt the sweet mid-meal sorbet made with rose-water needed only a Turkish cigarette to complete the picture.

Those looking for a respite from sweetness might turn to loin of lamb with artichoke relish and garlic potatoes, and thence perhaps to a copious plate of cheeses. Desserts, for the otherwise inclined, run to chocolate praline mousse with bitter chocolate sorbet, and pear poached in Cassis with anise-spiced pannacotta. Chocolate truffles come with fine cafetière coffee, and a classical, aggressively priced French-led wine list includes the likes of Sauzet's Le Montrachet at £450. Otherwise, start with one of the half dozen house wines at £19.95.

CHEF: Mark Taylor   PROPRIETOR: Manor House Hotel (Castle Combe) Ltd   OPEN: all week 12.15 to 2 (12.30 or 1.30 Sun), 7 to 9 (9.30 Fri and Sat)   MEALS: Set L Mon to Sat £12.95 (1 course) to £18.95, Set L Sun £24.50, Set D Sun to Thur £35, Set D Fri and Sat £45. Bar menu available

SERVICE: not inc, card slips closed   CARDS: Amex, Delta, Diners, MasterCard, Switch, Visa
DETAILS: 100 seats. 20 seats outside. Private parties: 100 main room, 2 to 30 private rooms. Car
park. Vegetarian meals. Children's helpings. No smoking in dining room. Wheelchair access (not
WC). No music   ACCOMMODATION: 47 rooms, all with bath/shower. TV. Phone. Room only £145
to £450. Rooms for disabled. Baby facilities. Swimming pool. Fishing (*The Which? Hotel Guide*)

## CAUNTON Nottinghamshire                                     map 5

# Caunton Beck £

| | |
|---|---|
| Main Street, Caunton NG23 6AB | COOKING 2 |
| TEL: (01636) 636793   FAX: (01636) 636828 | MODERN EUROPEAN/PACIFIC RIM |
| | £20–£49 |

Flexibility is at the core of the ideology at this sixteenth-century pub-restaurant,
on a river bank next to the village church. It bills itself as 'meeting house,
reading room, watering hole and restaurant', and you can call in for a meal at any
time from 8am to around 11pm, either in the bar, which can be a bit noisy, or in
the 'pleasantly relaxed' restaurant. The main menu is a gastronomic lucky dip:
delve in and pluck out anything from Thai-spiced fishcakes with ginger and
lime mayonnaise to Mrs Beeton's mulligatawny soup for starters, followed by
slow-roast lamb shank with bubble and squeak, or linguine with roast red
onions, oven-dried tomatoes, chilli, basil and ciabatta croûtons. Sandwiches,
good-value set menus and breakfasts are also available. Wines are as diverse as
the food. Half a dozen house selections start at £10.50 a bottle and are also sold
by the small or large glass.

CHEFS: Paul Vidic and Andrew Pickstock   PROPRIETORS: Valerie and Michael Hope   OPEN: all
week 8 to 11   MEALS: alc (main courses £9.50 to £17). Set L and Sun to Fri D £9 (2 courses) to
£12 . Breakfast and sandwich menu available   SERVICE: not inc   CARDS: Amex, Delta, Diners,
MasterCard, Switch, Visa   DETAILS: 120 seats. 40 seats outside. Private parties: 55 main room,
30 private room. Car park. Vegetarian meals. Children's helpings. No-smoking area. Wheelchair
access (also WC). No music  £5

## CHADDESLEY CORBETT Worcestershire                          map 5

# ▲ Brockencote Hall ✻

| | |
|---|---|
| Chaddesley Corbett DY10 4PY | |
| TEL: (01562) 777876   FAX: (01562) 777872 | |
| EMAIL: info@brockencotehall.com | |
| WEBSITE: www.brockencotehall.com | COOKING 4 |
| on A448, Bromsgrove to Kidderminster road, just | MODERN FRENCH |
| outside village | £25–£81 |

The Hall's two linked buildings overlook a lake and are surrounded by
parkland. When a sign asks you to go carefully along the drive to avoid injuring
the wildfowl, it's hard to believe you're just half an hour from Birmingham.

Jérôme Barbançon's cooking emphasises lightness and the use of herbs to add
aromatic lustre, and local suppliers include a shiitake mushroom grower. The
main carte deals in the likes of sauté foie gras with an exotic fruit salsa, a potato
tuile and fig chutney; sea bass with scallop ravioli, leek fondue and a crab bisque
sauce; and roast peppercorned beef fillet. A labour-intensive game medley

comprises venison brochette, poached wood pigeon, roast pheasant and a wild boar sausage, all sauced with red wine and orange. Parsnip soup with garlic oil dribbled into the middle is well-reported, as is a poached pear served with sorbet (more daring desserts include roast pineapple with banana tortellini in a Sauternes and saffron soup).

Reports agree on the professionalism and friendliness of the service, and the comfort that envelops you. Claret-lovers in particular will enjoy the very classical Francophile wine list (other countries get a perfunctory nod); house selections start with two Languedocs at £12.80 (£3.30 a glass).

CHEF: Jérôme Barbançon   PROPRIETORS: Joseph and Alison Petitjean   OPEN: Sun to Fri L 12 to 1.30, all week D 7 to 9.30   MEALS: alc (main courses £13.50 to £22.50). Set L £12 (2 courses) to £18.20, Set Sun L £22.50, Set D £27.50, Set D 7 to 9 £55 (whole table)   SERVICE: net prices, card slips closed   CARDS: Amex, Delta, Diners, MasterCard, Switch, Visa   DETAILS: 50 seats. 10 seats outside. Private parties: 50 main room, 10 to 36 private rooms. Car park. Vegetarian meals. Children's helpings. No smoking in dining room. Wheelchair access (also WC). Occasional music   ACCOMMODATION: 17 rooms, all with bath/shower. TV. Phone. B&B £88 to £170. Rooms for disabled. Baby facilities. Fishing (*The Which? Hotel Guide*)   (£5)

## CHAGFORD Devon                                                                             map 1

# ▲ Gidleigh Park ▮ ⅗

Chagford TQ13 8HH
TEL: (01647) 432367   FAX: (01647) 432574
EMAIL: gidleighpark@gidleigh.co.uk
WEBSITE: www.gidleigh.com

| from Chagford Square turn right at Lloyds Bank | COOKING 8 |
| into Mill Street, take right fork after 150 yards, | MODERN EUROPEAN |
| follow lane for 1½m | £49–£98 |

This black-and-white timbered building seems too big to call a 'house', but the Hendersons, their front-of-house team (under polished and professional hostess Catherine Endacott), and their Siamese cats stretched before the hall fire, make it feel comforting and relaxing. Lunch offers a couple of items per course, but dinner is the showcase, its luxurious feel starting with the truffles that might appear in three out of six first courses. Soft textures also promise inudulgence: perhaps (in spring) a moulded circle of finely textured, truffle-flecked chicken mousse enclosing morels and asparagus, or (in autumn) a cocktail glass of 'ravishing' lobster jelly set on tangy soured cream to offset its rich intensity.

As for combinations, there is nothing here to frighten the horses, and yet the cooking is not formulaic. Roast partridge comes with braised chicory, quince and walnuts in a Gewürztraminer sauce; and four shelled and carefully pan-fried langoustines lying on sautéed leeks alternate with tasty frogs' legs, all separated by a frothy pea velouté, surrounding a pile of penne mixed with truffle cream. Technique is hard to fault: witness a stupendous fillet of local beef, tasty and accurately timed, served with tiny mushrooms, roast shallots and pools of garlic purée; and roast best end of local lamb – tender, well trimmed and tasty – with a few pieces of sweetbread, the components of a ratatouille layered in a timbale, some broad beans and a flavourful stock-based sauce.

A varied selection of cheeses is kept in immaculate condition, and desserts sound fiddly but deliver clear flavours, typically variations on a theme: maybe layers of light, refreshing apple mousse separated by apple slices, topped with caramelised apple and accompanied by chocolate-piped vanilla ice cream; or a thin, crisp tuile basket of poached cherries, accompanied by cherries dipped in dark chocolate, and a first-rate Kirsch ice cream. The wine list is a delight. Producers are impeccably chosen from Alsace to Germany's Rhine and Mosel, and on to Italy and the USA, where big names dominate. Naturally, classic French regions are well represented too, and prices are sensible (they include service). Eight wines come by the glass (£5.50 to £13), and bottle prices start at £22.

CHEF: Michael Caines   PROPRIETORS: Paul and Kay Henderson   OPEN: all week 12.30 to 2, 7 to 9 MEALS: Set L £26 (2 courses) to £72.50, Set D £67.50 to £72.50. Light L menu also available SERVICE: net prices, card slips closed   CARDS: MasterCard, Switch, Visa   DETAILS: 35 seats. Private parties: 22 main room. Car park. Children's helpings by arrangement. No children under 7 in dining room. No smoking in dining room. Wheelchair access (not WC). No music. No mobile phones   ACCOMMODATION: 15 rooms, all with bath/shower. TV. Phone. D,B&B £260 to £500. Baby facilities. Fishing

## ▲ 22 Mill Street ⁵⋇

| | |
|---|---|
| 22 Mill Street, Chagford TQ13 8AW | COOKING **6** |
| TEL: (01647) 432244   FAX: (01647) 433101 | MODERN EUROPEAN |
| | £29–£48 |

Green outside, yellow inside, the simply furnished dining room of this converted shop looks directly on to the street. It is an unassuming setting for some deceptively simple and beguiling cooking. Everybody has a good word to say about it; indeed, thanks to its unpretentious approach and appealingly soothing food, there is 'no place quite like it'.

A few luxury materials, and a few bright flavours, help things along – pickled ginger and coriander consommé with sauté scallops for example – but the essence of the operation is utterly sound technique allied to a fine sense of culinary balance. Many ideas are quite straightforward, such as sauté foie gras with braised endive and Sauternes, or roast sea bass fillet with basil, tomato and olive oil. But it is this very clarity that makes for success: you won't find unnecessary extras on the plate. Reporters compliment the freshness of fish, the roast loin of Dartmoor lamb, the value (especially at lunch), and desserts, including hot raspberry soufflé and iced passion-fruit parfait in a warm fruit salad.

Duncan Walker pops out from the kitchen now and again, happy to talk to customers about other chefs, restaurants, and the food world in general. Those who stay overnight can enjoy a fine breakfast, as well as the full benefit of a well-chosen and fairly priced wine list. Kloovenburg Chardonnay from South Africa is recommended, and house wines (which are not simply the cheapest bottles in the list) take in examples from Australia, New Zealand and California in the £15 to £18 range (£4.25 to £4.50 per glass). If you feel the need, for £10 corkage you can bring your own wine.

CHEFS: Duncan Walker, Stephen Langstone and Dexter Fuller   PROPRIETOR: Duncan Walker OPEN: Wed to Sat L 12.30 to 1.45, Mon to Sat D 7.30 to 8.45; also open bank hol Suns   CLOSED: bank hol Mons   MEALS: Set L £17.50 (2 courses) to £19.50, Set D £26.50 (2 courses) to £32.50

SERVICE: net prices, card slips closed   CARDS: Delta, MasterCard, Switch, Visa   DETAILS: 22 seats. Vegetarian meals on request. No smoking in dining room. Music. No mobile phones
ACCOMMODATION: 2 rooms, both with bath/shower. TV. B&B £30 to £45

## CHEESDEN  Greater Manchester                                            map 8

# Nutters ✦

Edenfield Road, Cheesden,
nr Rochdale OL12 7TY                                               COOKING 6
TEL/FAX: (01706) 650167                                          MODERN BRITISH
on A680, between Norden and Rochdale                             £28–£47

A friendly welcome is normal at this large, stone-built former pub, although the chandeliers, busily patterned carpet, swagged curtains and gastronomic memorabilia are perhaps a little 'chintzy' for Andrew Nutter's imaginative modern menus, which include a vegetarian version and lots of specials. The restless kitchen can push the boundaries a bit in its search for novelty – medallions of lamb with a ginger ale dressing as a starter, perhaps – although things often turn out better than they sound. The dolly mixture sauce, for example, that accompanies accurately timed beef fillet on a chorizo and potato rösti is merely a way of describing finely cubed vegetables.

Few northern restaurants nowadays can get away without a black pudding dish of some sort, in this case light, crispy won tons filled with the soft pudding and served with a sweet chilli dip. Complex dishes can mean that good-quality ingredients sometimes have to compete with lots of other flavours. This high-risk strategy can be very good when it works, which it does more often than not, although at these prices consistency matters too. The kitchen nevertheless deploys evident skill, and the cooking is deft where it needs to be, for example in a first-class warm pear and frangipane tart with poire William ice cream. The 'specialist local and regional cheeses' may range as far as French ones, but if they're this good, who's complaining about geography? A traditionally based wine list offers fair variety and something for most pockets; outside France, look to Australia and New Zealand for greatest variety. Own-label Aussie house wine is £11.50.

CHEF: Andrew Nutter   PROPRIETORS: Rodney, Jean and Andrew Nutter   OPEN: Wed to Mon 12 to 2 (4 Sun), 6.45 (6.30 Sat and Sun) to 9.30 (9 Sun)   CLOSED: first 2 weeks Aug   MEALS: alc (main courses L £10.50 to £15, D £15 to £16.50). Set L Sun £19.95, Set D £29.95   SERVICE: not inc, 10% for parties of 10 or more   CARDS: Amex, Delta, MasterCard, Switch, Visa   DETAILS: 84 seats. Private parties: 44 main room, 40 private room. Car park. Vegetarian meals. Children's helpings. No smoking in dining room. Wheelchair access (also WC). Music

---

*'The boldly named assiette de deserts comprised some extremely sad leftovers.... The worst culprit was three small lumps of something blackened and rock hard that could not be cut. When the waiter was called over, neither he nor two of his colleagues could identify the items, or dissect them.'* (On eating in East Anglia)

---

map 5

# Le Champignon Sauvage ▼

| | |
|---|---|
| 24–26 Suffolk Road, Cheltenham GL50 2AQ | COOKING 7 |
| TEL: (01242) 573449   FAX: (01242) 254365 | FRENCH |
| | £31–£75 |

Hanging baskets of flowers announce this (somewhat hidden) 'gem' a short walk from the town centre. Comfortable and intimate, its striking blue and yellow décor is further enlivened by some large modern pictures. This is the backdrop for some elaborate and heavily worked cooking in contemporary French mode, much of it beguiling: tortellini of eel with a watercress cream, for example, or a pig's trotter croquette with Puy lentils and smoked ham hock. It is the simple ingenuity inherent in some of the partnerships that gives the food its vitality: an oyster and leek emulsion to accompany a pressed skate and leek terrine, or a velouté of horseradish and onion that comes with rabbit confit.

Elsewhere, Chinese spices are applied to a two-part dish of roe deer and belly pork, and one reporter's duck confit with dried fig purée made a 'rather Middle Eastern' impression. Not everything in the garden is rosy, judging by one disappointed reporter's overcooked lamb and uninspiring vegetables, but generally the food is attractively presented and powerfully flavoured, be it wood pigeon on a cumin-flavoured cauliflower risotto, or skate wing with a pea purée. Lunch provided 'the bargain of the year' for one visitor, who ate salmon and wild garlic ravioli with peas and morels, pink roast lamb with crushed aubergine and black olives, and an iced, roasted strawberry parfait. Desserts from the carte, meanwhile, might include an iced chicory root parfait with juniper berry ice cream, or a hot fig tart with a honey and spice bread ice cream.

High-order incidentals include appetisers – perhaps an earthy soup of chickpeas flavoured with vanilla – and pre-dessert, while low-key, friendly, unobtrusive service from Helen Everitt-Matthias is a bonus. France is the main focus of the annotated wine list. Although no wines from elsewhere in Europe are listed, there are some decent selections from California, Australia, South Africa and New Zealand. Prices are generally fair, kicking off at £10.50 for French vins de table, the house red and white.

CHEF: David Everitt-Matthias   PROPRIETORS: David and Helen Everitt-Matthias   OPEN: Tue to Sat 12.30 to 1.30, 7.30 to 9   CLOSED: 1 week Christmas, 3 weeks June   MEALS: Set L £16.50 (2 courses) to £19.95, Set D Tue to Fri £17.95 (2 courses) to £48, Set D Sat £35 (2 courses) to £48   SERVICE: not inc   CARDS: Amex, Diners, MasterCard, Switch, Visa   DETAILS: 28 seats. Private parties: 22 main room. No smoking at L and before 10 at D. Wheelchair access (not WC). No music. No mobile phones at L   (£5)

# Chelsea Square ⅍ £   | NEW ENTRY |

| | |
|---|---|
| 60 St George's Place, Cheltenham GL50 3PN | COOKING 3 |
| TEL/FAX: (01242) 269926 | MODERN BRITISH |
| | £20–£35 |

Tony Amos believes wholeheartedly in the informal approach. No bookings are taken, except for large parties, and no advertising is placed for this quietly located restaurant that opened in February 2002. Bright blue walls and a pitched glass ceiling make up for the lack of view, although a long quotation from a wistful German author painted along two walls is barely worth craning one's neck for.

Ryan Bell has devised a modern menu, scoring plenty of hits as he goes. A starter special of three giant scallops on squid ink risotto with pesto makes an impressive dish, the timing of the shellfish just right. Another trio – of oysters – might come with red wine and shallot vinaigrette, while a warm potato salad makes a comforting accompaniment to marinated salmon. Care in preparation is evidenced by the slow, overnight cooking of lamb, served with roast shallots and puréed carrot and swede, and by honey-glazed breast of duck with braised red cabbage and a spicy stock-based sauce. Finish with a boozy dessert, such as caramelised banana crumble with rum ice cream, iced Baileys and Kahlúa parfait with espresso sauce, or an immaculately presented tarte Tatin of pineapple with Galliano sorbet. Black-clad waiting staff tell you to 'Enjoy!' The functional wine list is competitively priced, opening with house French at £6.95 and Australian at £8.95.

CHEF: Ryan Bell   PROPRIETOR: Tony Amos   OPEN: Mon to Sat 12 to 2 (2.30 Fri and Sat), 6 to 10 (10.30 Fri and Sat)   CLOSED: 25 Dec, 1 Jan   MEALS: alc (main courses £7 to £10)   SERVICE: not inc, 10% for parties of 6 or more   CARDS: Delta, MasterCard, Switch, Visa   DETAILS: 90 seats. Private parties: 100 main room. Vegetarian meals. Children's helpings. No smoking in dining room. Music  £5

---

# Daffodil ⅝

**NEW ENTRY**

18–20 Suffolk Parade, Montpellier,
Cheltenham GL50 2AE
TEL: (01242) 700055   FAX: (01242) 700088
EMAIL: daffodilrest@cs.com
WEBSITE: www.thedaffodil.co.uk

COOKING 3
MODERN EUROPEAN
£23–£53

For 40 years this was a cinema, and if you didn't know that already you would guess the minute you walked through the door. A sweeping staircase leads from the vast, chic, art deco auditorium up to a mezzanine bar; there are giant projectors, and black and white photographs of vintage film stars. Chefs beaver away in full view where the screen was. Marcel Frichot (who last appeared in the Guide in 1998 as co-owner of Elms near Worcester, with Andrew Palmer as chef), runs a big, relaxed, brasserie-style operation with a sharp, modern menu and some smart, clued-up staff who have tasted the dishes and can talk sensibly about them.

The dinner menu changes every three months, lunch every three weeks, and the repertoire runs from twice-baked goats' cheese soufflé to calf's liver with mash and smoked bacon. Dinner, it has to be said, is the superior meal by a long chalk, and among the more interesting ideas is a sweetly roasted flavourful rabbit leg served with a creamy and accurately timed leek risotto and a well-made, stock-based port sauce. Good raw materials and fine technical skills have also produced a first-class cannon of lamb on a small mound of Puy lentils, with a well-balanced grain mustard sauce, and an intensely flavoured tart of poached pineapple pieces and crushed almonds, served with a scoop of coconut ice cream and a pool of thin custard. A short, functional wine list starts at £12.90 and offers around a dozen by the large glass.

CHEF: Andrew Palmer  PROPRIETOR: Marcel Frichot  OPEN: Mon to Sat 12 to 2.30, 6.30 to 10
MEALS: alc D (main courses £9.50 to £17). Set L £10 (2 courses) to £12.50  SERVICE: not inc, card
slips closed, 10% for parties of 6 or more  CARDS: Amex, MasterCard, Switch, Visa  DETAILS:
150 seats. 12 seats outside. Private parties: 120 main room. Vegetarian meals. Children's
helpings. No smoking in dining room. Wheelchair access (also WC). Music. Air-conditioned

## Lumière ▼ ⁵✗

| | |
|---|---|
| Clarence Parade, Cheltenham GL50 3PA | COOKING 5 |
| TEL: (01242) 222200 | GLOBAL |
| EMAIL: lumiere@globalnet.co.uk | £47–£66 |

Artful design has made the dining-room at the Chapmans' central Cheltenham
restaurant seem more spacious than it really is, with restful, muted colours and
stylish abstracts lending the place a pleasing air of cosmopolitan minimalism.
Geoff Chapman blends old and new in his cooking, mixing the skills of a
classical saucier with ingredients from the southern-hemisphere repertoire:
fillet of springbok has become something of a signature main course, usually
chargrilled and served maybe with a truffle and mushroom potato cake and an
emulsion of leeks. Nearer home, seared scallops might be presented on herb
noodles with truffled mascarpone and a saffron-scented reduction to start,
followed by baked breast and slow-roast leg of guinea-fowl, accompanied by a
sauce spiked with chilli and ginger.

First-course listings always begin with a 'soup creation' that's worth
enquiring about, and if desserts such as lemon, herb and maple yoghurt sorbet,
or dark chocolate torte with espresso cream don't tempt, the alternative is 'one
perfect cheese'. Good coffee rounds things off in style. The wine list is dedicated
to cutting-edge modern styles, whether from New World or Old (California and
Italy are very strong). Prices are not cheap (most are in the £20 to £30 range) but
they're not bad value, either, given the quality. The list changes frequently to
accommodate 'guest wines'; house offerings start around £14.50 to £16.95.

CHEF: Geoff Chapman  PROPRIETORS: Lin and Geoff Chapman  OPEN: Tue to Sat D only 7 to 8.45
CLOSED: first 2 weeks Jan, 2 weeks late summer  MEALS: Set D Tue to Thur £25.50 (2 courses),
Set D £30  SERVICE: not inc  CARDS: Amex, MasterCard, Switch, Visa  DETAILS: 30 seats.
Private parties: 34 main room. No children under 9 in dining room. No smoking. No music. Air-
conditioned

## Mayflower

| | |
|---|---|
| 32–34 Clarence Street, Cheltenham GL50 3NX | COOKING 2 |
| TEL: (01242) 522426  FAX: (01242) 251667 | CHINESE |
| | £17–£62 |

For more than 20 years the Kong family have been pleasing the citizens of
Cheltenham and beyond with their consistent Chinese cooking. Mother and son
run the kitchen, and work to a repertoire of familiar Cantonese, Pekinese and
Szechuan dishes with no detours into the esoteric world of ducks' tongues or
goose feet. Among starters you might find deep-fried crab claws in prawn paste,
and fruity Mandarin spare ribs, while the remainder is a mix of favourites such
as crispy aromatic duck, sizzling chicken with ginger and onions, and beef with
cashew nuts in yellow-bean sauce. There are also plenty of vegetarian options

like 'mock duck' egg foo yung, and sauté celery with black beans and chilli. The list of around 70 wines is a carefully chosen slate, with house French at £11.75.

CHEFS: Mrs M.M. Kong and Mr C.F. Kong   PROPRIETORS: the Kong family   OPEN: Mon to Sat L 12 to 1.45, all week D 6 to 10 (10.30 Fri and Sat)   CLOSED: 24 to 26 Dec   MEALS: alc (main courses £6.50 to £12.50). Set L £6.95, Set D £19 to £22   SERVICE: not inc   CARDS: Amex, Delta, MasterCard, Switch, Visa   DETAILS: 120 seats. Private parties: 80 main room, 20 to 45 private rooms. Vegetarian meals. Music. Air-conditioned £5

## Le Petit Blanc ✸ £

The Queens Hotel, The Promenade,
Cheltenham GL50 1NN
TEL: (01242) 266800   FAX: (01242) 266801

| NEW CHEF |
EMAIL: cheltenham@lepetitblanc.co.uk   MODERN FRENCH
WEBSITE: www.lepetitblanc.co.uk   £24–£54

A new chef was about to be appointed at this brasserie, tacked on to the side of the smart-looking Queen's Hotel, just as the Guide went to press. Clive Fretwell, who used to cook at Le Manoir aux Quat' Saisons (see entry Great Milton), is now in executive charge of the group (see entries, Birmingham, Manchester and Oxford), and the same menu and format are now in operation at all four branches. Among its offerings might be a twice-baked Roquefort soufflé with pears and walnut dressing, roast chicken breast with braised leeks and morel sauce, and lemon tart with raspberry sorbet. As if the kitchen weren't busy enough (with some two dozen savoury items), there are also menus for children, vegetarians and vegans, as well as for those who don't eat nuts or dairy produce, plus a fixed-price and a quick menu. Three dozen varietally arranged wines start at £11.

CHEF: Clive Fretwell (executive)   PROPRIETOR: Raymond Blanc   OPEN: all week 12 to 3, 6 to 10.30 (10 Sun)   CLOSED: 25 Dec   MEALS: alc (main courses £8.50 to £16). Set L and D 5.30 to 7 £12.50 to £15   SERVICE: not inc, 10% for parties of 8 or more   CARDS: Amex, Delta, Diners, MasterCard, Switch, Visa   DETAILS: 160 seats. 20 seats outside. Private parties: 80 main room, 80 private room. Vegetarian meals. Children's helpings. No smoking in dining room. Wheelchair access (not WC). Music. Air-conditioned £5

## CHESTER Cheshire                                                    map 7

## ▲ Chester Grosvenor, Arkle ♥ ✸

Eastgate, Chester CH1 1LT
TEL: (01244) 324024   FAX: (01244) 313068   COOKING 6
EMAIL: c_b@chestergrosvenor.co.uk   TRADITIONAL EUROPEAN
WEBSITE: www.chestergrosvenor.co.uk   £41–£94

An enormous gabled and turreted façade, in the heart of the city's traffic-free shopping centre, fronts a hotel, a ground-floor brasserie and, up a few steps past a doorman in top hat and tails, a bar lounge lined with books, and a dining room decorated with horsy paintings. Despite the 'posh hotel' mode, Simon Radley's dishes show originality without resorting to extremes, taking in, for example, a starter of chilled, sweet pickled tuna tail, with oysters and foaming watercress, and oxtail ravioli paired with langoustine tails.

The kitchen allows itself plenty of opportunity for practice, since the menu changes only seasonally, but the cooking is accomplished and results are impressive, as one might reasonably expect at these prices. Although the food can appear 'clever', everything on the plate is there for a reason, a sure sign of culinary intelligence, as in a round stack of crabmeat, mixed with a langoustine emulsion and layered with a couple of Parmesan crisps, surrounded by a shallow moat of bright, frothy cucumber coulis set with five fat, accurately timed half-scallops.

Raw materials and timing are beyond reproach. Five fat cubes of duck breast, each topped with crisp skin and fat, come with caramel-roasted shallots and foie gras, the dish 'an interesting study in stickiness' thanks not least to its apple and fig chutneys. Flavour combinations are strikingly successful throughout, as, for example, in a hot praline soufflé lightly flavoured with ginger, into which the waiter pours a lime sauce, with a creamy ginger sorbet on the side. Extras include a well-crafted appetiser, and service is male, formal, foreign and knowledgeable. The wine list, with its pages of big names from Burgundy and Bordeaux (many of the vintages are mature), will appeal to serious oenophiles, but there is little to mitigate the hefty prices these command. Wines under £20 are few and far between, with regional France providing the best choice, starting at £13.75.

CHEF: Simon Radley   PROPRIETOR: Grosvenor Estate   OPEN: Tue to Sun L 12 to 2.30, Tue to Sat D 7 to 9.30   CLOSED: 25 Dec to 20 Jan exc 31 Dec, third week Aug   MEALS: Set L £30 to £52, Set D £45 (2 courses) to £60   SERVICE: not inc, 12.5% for parties of 6 or more   CARDS: Amex, Delta, Diners, MasterCard, Switch, Visa   DETAILS: 45 seats. Private parties: 45 main room, 18 to 240 private rooms. Vegetarian meals. Children's helpings. Jacket and tie. No smoking in dining room. Wheelchair access (not WC). Music. Air-conditioned   ACCOMMODATION: 83 rooms, all with bath/shower. TV. Phone. Room only £170 to £282. Rooms for disabled. Baby facilities

# Brasserie 10/16 ⁵⅄ £

| Brookdale Place, Chester CH1 3DY | COOKING 3 |
| TEL: (01244) 322288   FAX: (01244) 322325 | MODERN EUROPEAN |
| WEBSITE: www.brasserie1016.com | £21–£40 |

'An excellent addition to the Chester gastronomic scene,' noted one couple who mingled with pre-Christmas party-goers at this lively, modern venue. Like the owners' original outlet in Hawarden (see entry, Wales), the menu here is a familiar run through the modern brasserie catalogue, although there are a few unexpected twists and turns along the way. A salad of chicken, penne pasta and chorizo receives a dressing of sweet chilli crème fraîche, while seared salmon comes with garden pea mash, lobster and tarragon dressing. Vegetarians also get a good look-in with goats' cheese crostini, or filo parcels filled with wild mushrooms, ricotta, shallots and tarragon. Cheesecakes (perhaps vanilla, or passion fruit) are skilfully crafted, and chocolate caramel mousse cake has been well received. Standards may have slipped after a promising start, but this is still a place worth supporting. The wine list runs to around three dozen keenly priced bins, including six house wines by the glass: prices start at £9.95 (£2.40 a glass).

CHEF: Mark Jones and Ian Derbyshire   PROPRIETORS: Neal Bates and Mark Jones   OPEN: all week 12 to 10   MEALS: alc (main courses £7 to £16). Set L and D 12 to 7pm £9.95 (2 courses). Light meals also available from 12 to 6   SERVICE: not inc   CARDS: Amex, Delta, MasterCard, Switch, Visa   DETAILS: 130 seats. Private parties: 70 main room. Vegetarian meals. Children's helpings. No smoking in 1 dining room. Wheelchair access (also WC). Music

## CHETTLE Dorset                                                    map 2

## ▲ Castleman Hotel  ♥ ✸ £                    | NEW ENTRY |

Chettle DT11 8DB
TEL: (01258) 830096   FAX: (01258) 830051
EMAIL: chettle@globalnet.co.uk
WEBSITE: www.castlemanhotel.co.uk                        COOKING 2
6m NE of Blandford Forum turn N off A354 for             ENGLISH
Chettle                                                   £23–£40

'One of those eccentric places found only in Britain', this serene dower house is run with unassuming, ungrasping friendliness by the family that has owned it and the village for some 150 years. Owner Edward Bourke reminds one visitor of Wodehouse's Lord Emsworth, and all the staff treat customers like old friends. The food has a traditional feel, usually offering a soup, pâté, tart or salad to start, and smoked meats and fish feature: maybe smoked duck breast with quail egg salad and Roquefort dressing.

Using local raw materials, and sensibly sticking to what it can handle, the kitchen produces 'enjoyable and thoroughly decent home cooking'. Typical main courses – simple grilled or roast meat, fowl or fish, such as top-quality seared scallops in a flavoured butter, accurately sauté lamb kidneys, or tasty guinea-fowl breast – come with a generous assortment of vegetables. Highly rated ice creams include a creamy brown bread version served with pears in red wine, or try a wedge of frangipane tart made with quince jelly. Cheeses are kept in good condition, bread is first-rate, and the food is good value, as is the wine list. Deceptively simple at first glance, it offers a number of excellent producers whose wares are sold at very fair prices (£16.50 for Seresin Chardonnay from New Zealand, for example). Three house wines sell for £9 a bottle or £2.25 a glass.

CHEFS: Barbara Garnsworthy and Richard Morris   PROPRIETORS: Edward Bourke and Barbara Garnsworthy   OPEN: Sun L 12 to 1.30, all week D 7 to 10   CLOSED: 25 and 26 Dec, Feb   MEALS: alc D (main courses £8 to £14.50). Set L Sun £16   SERVICE: not inc, card slips closed   CARDS: Delta, MasterCard, Switch, Visa   DETAILS: 40 seats. Private parties: 40 main room. Car park. Vegetarian meals. No smoking in dining room. Wheelchair access (also WC). No music ACCOMMODATION: 8 rooms, all with bath/shower. TV. Phone. B&B £45 to £80. Baby facilities (*The Which? Hotel Guide*)

---

*'The puddings were without exception lathered in cream. There was a Monty Python feel to them – for Spam read ''Whipped Cream''. ''I'll have the whipped cream with whipped cream, with a side order of whipped cream please.'' Grotesquely, they offered pouring cream with them! Benecol would have been more appropriate.'* (On eating in Scotland)

## CHINNOR Oxfordshire

map 2

# Sir Charles Napier

Sprigg's Alley, Chinnor OX39 4BX
TEL: (01494) 483011   FAX: (01494) 485311
from M40 junction 6 take B4009 to Chinnor, at
mini-roundabout in Chinnor turn right and
continue up hill for 2m to Sprigg's Alley

COOKING 4
MODERN ANGLO-FRENCH
£40–£68

This flint and brick building is set in a large, well-kept garden amid the Chiltern beech woods. Through a discreet front door, guests walk straight into the comfortable, warm bar area. In the dining room, tables are old and wooden and an enthusiasm for sculpture is evident (summer lunches are served on the terrace overlooking the gardens).

Chef Eric de Vaux took over in October 2001 and continues the Anglo-French vein of his predecessor. Combinations are skilfully and intelligently handled, despite a few inconsistencies. For starters, moist scallops may come with minted pea purée and watercress, and herb risotto has been jazzed up with chorizo and squid. Fillet of turbot with a chard and celeriac 'cake', and sea bream fillets with butternut squash risotto have both drawn praise, and the turning year is marked by the move from spring dishes of guinea fowl and rabbit to autumn's woodcock, mallard and roast partridge. Desserts might include chocolate fondant with 'excellent deep flavour' accompanied by pistachio ice cream.

Service can show signs of stress at busy lunch-times. The wine list, carefully chosen and clearly annotated, ranges across Old World and New picking out top producers. Mark-ups are lowish, although there are some expensive bottles. A 'house selection' of eight wines, from £17.95 to £26.50, also comes by the glass, but the house wines proper – concealed amid the main list – are well-chosen and sell for a tasty £12.95.

CHEF: Eric de Vaux   PROPRIETOR: Julie Griffiths   OPEN: Tue to Sun L 12 to 2.30 (3.30 Sun), Tue to Sat D 7 to 10   CLOSED: 3 or 4 days Christmas   MEALS: alc (main courses £13.50 to £19.50). Set L Tue to Sat £14.50 (2 courses), Set D Tue to Fri £16.50 (2 courses). Light L menu available Tue to Fri   SERVICE: 12.5% (optional), card slips closed   CARDS: Amex, Delta, Diners, MasterCard, Switch, Visa   DETAILS: 70 seats. 70 seats outside. Private parties: 45 main room, 12 to 24 private rooms. Car park. Children's helpings. No children under 7 at D. No smoking in 1 dining room. Wheelchair access (not WC). Music. No mobile phones. Air-conditioned

## CHIPPING CAMPDEN Gloucestershire

map 8

# ▲ Cotswold House

NEW ENTRY

The Square, Chipping Campden GL55 6AN
TEL: (01386) 840330   FAX: (01386) 840310
EMAIL: reception@cotswoldhouse.com
WEBSITE: www.cotswoldhouse.com

COOKING 5
MODERN BRITISH
£53–£64

A severe, symmetrical façade of ochre-coloured Cotswold stone faces the town square, and three arched French windows overlook formal gardens at the back. Inside, by contrast, the décor is dramatic, with ornate plasterwork, and a restaurant ceiling done in throbbing tomato red. Its two dining rooms, the Garden Restaurant and Hicks' Brasserie, share one kitchen: since spring 2002 the domain of Simon Hulstone, whose polished, elegant cooking has made an immediate impact.

In the Restaurant he offers a seasonally changing modern British menu at a fixed price without supplements (except for cheese). A simple risotto uses butternut squash and girolles, enriched with chive mascarpone and lubricated with an emulsion of coriander. A single large raviolo of oxtail, topped with an equally mighty seared scallop, rests on an 'amazingly light and smooth' bed of shallot puree. Main courses also pursue robust, four-square flavours, as in John Dory with parsnip purée, roast salsify and wilted spinach, all sharpened with verjuice; and venison loin (three slices of 'superb, wild-tasting' meat) with a crusty-brown pheasant sausage, sweet potato mash and beetroot marmalade. Portions may look lightish, but every bite packs a punch. Among desserts, passion-fruit crème, apple carpaccio, warm banana pudding and apple syrup is just one option. Service has been short-handed, but on the whole does justice to some remarkable cooking. The Restaurant wine list gallops quickly through Old and New Worlds, gathering good selections from France, Italy and Australia. Fair mark-ups afford good choice under £20; bottle prices start at £14.50 for German white.

CHEF: Simon Hulstone   PROPRIETORS: Christa and Ian Taylor   OPEN: restaurant Sun L 12 to 2.30, all week D 7 to 9.45; brasserie all week 9.30 to 9.30   MEALS: restaurant alc Sun L (£10 to £14), Set D £30 (2 courses) to £38; brasserie alc (main courses £10 to £25). Set L and D £11.95 (2 courses)   SERVICE: not inc   CARDS: Amex, Delta, MasterCard, Switch, Visa   DETAILS: 46 seats. 35 seats outside. Private parties: 25 main room, 12 to 24 private rooms. Car park. Vegetarian meals. Children's helpings. No smoking in dining room. Wheelchair access (not WC). Music. No mobile phones   ACCOMMODATION: 20 rooms, all with bath/shower. TV. Phone. B&B £115 to £350. Baby facilities (*The Which? Hotel Guide*)

## CHOBHAM Surrey                                                            map 3

# Quails

1 Bagshot Road, Chobham GU24 8BP                              COOKING 3
TEL/FAX: (01276) 858491                                  MODERN EUROPEAN
WEBSITE: www.quailsrestaurant.co.uk                              £27–£53

In late 2001 the Wale family expanded their culinary operation and set up a new venture called Zinfandel in Guildford (see entry). The family's hands-on involvement in both places means that Quails is no longer open for lunch, though otherwise it is business as usual.

The modern European cooking has an oriental slant, and is noteworthy for high-quality raw materials and accurate timing, whether it be rump of lamb (with a toasted hazelnut crumb), fillet of Scotch beef, or sea bass with crab and lemon-grass fettucine. The eclectic style also runs to sweet chilli squid with risotto nero; saddle of roe deer with celeriac purée, Cassis and juniper; and a strudel of monkfish, salmon and scallops with wilted rocket, saffron and Chardonnay. Desserts range from baked raspberry cheesecake with mascarpone to iced passion-fruit parfait. The tidy wine list, arranged by style, features several halves and some useful drinking by the glass. House wine is £10.95.

CHEF: Christopher Wale   PROPRIETORS: The Wale family   OPEN: Tue to Sat D only 7 to 9.30
CLOSED: 25 and 26 Dec   MEALS: alc (main courses £14 to £18). Set D Tue to Fri £13.95 (2 courses)
to £16.95   SERVICE: not inc   CARDS: Amex, Delta, Diners, MasterCard, Switch, Visa   DETAILS:
50 seats. Private parties: 50 main room. Car park. Vegetarian meals. No cigars/pipes in dining
room. Wheelchair access (not WC). Music. Air-conditioned  £5

## CHRISTCHURCH Dorset                                              map 2

# FishWorks �><

10 Church Street, Christchurch BH23 1BW
TEL: (01202) 487000   FAX: (01202) 487001                    COOKING 4
EMAIL: fishworks.christchurch@virgin.net                     SEAFOOD
WEBSITE: www.fishworks.co.uk                                 £28–£59

The winning FishWorks formula has gone multimedia, and is now available as a
couple of cookery books, a TV series, and a slick website. But still the best way to
sample what FishWorks has to offer is to visit one of the three outlets: as well as
Christchurch, there are branches in Bath and Bristol (see entries). The approach
is the same across the group: a fishmonger's with a dining room where you can
sample anything in the display fridges, cooked as you like. There is also a
'classic' menu offering maybe crab salad with tarragon mayonnaise, smoked
haddock with poached egg, or spaghetti with clams, chilli, garlic and parsley;
plus a range of simple seafood platters that take in anything from oysters and
lobster to cockles and winkles. Note that vegetarians are catered for, but not
carnivores. A short wine list is helpfully divided into categories including
'unusual but brilliant with fish' and 'classic fine wines with fish', the latter
aimed at big spenders. House wines start at £12.

CHEFS: Abbie Bennett and Nick Davies   PROPRIETOR: FishWorks plc   OPEN: Tue to Sat 11 to 11
MEALS: alc (main courses £8.50 to £20)   SERVICE: not inc, card slips closed   CARDS: Amex, Delta,
Diners, MasterCard, Switch, Visa   DETAILS: 45 seats. 4 seats outside. Private parties: 30 main
room. Vegetarian meals. Children's helpings. No smoking in dining room. Music. Air-
conditioned  £5

# Splinters ✦><

12 Church Street, Christchurch BH23 1BW
TEL: (01202) 483454   FAX: (01202) 480180                    COOKING 5
EMAIL: eating@splinters.uk.com                          FRENCH/INTERNATIONAL
WEBSITE: www.splinters.uk.com                                £33–£60

Splinters stands in a cul-de-sac that leads to the cemetery of the town's
exceptionally beautiful Priory, so if you've turned up a little early for your
booking it's worth having a potter about. Inside is a bar, together with three
contrastingly decorated dining areas, one of which – the Cellar Room – will
prove a magnet to serious wine lovers, with its floor-to-ceiling bottle racks.

A slight tendency towards brash culinary novelty has been productively
curbed of late, and the cooking is more than capable of impressing without it. A
cake of smoked haddock with tomato and rocket salad and a chervil butter sauce
is the kind of first course that might appear on a weekday set-price menu, while
the main menu deals in the likes of roast celeriac soup with wild mushroom and
mozzarella ravioli, or – something of a long stayer – a warm salad of calf's liver

and crostini topped with pancetta and tapénade. Fillet of Herefordshire beef (served with cabbage and bacon purée, mushrooms, and mashed potato) has been a textural triumph, the intensity of its white truffle sauce supporting an assemblage of fine ingredients. Cappuccino brûlée with a star anise-flavoured tuile, or lemon tart with clotted cream, is the kind of dessert to leave room for. Service may struggle to cope at busy times but is willing enough. The wine list has been thoughtfully composed, although prices may feel a touch uncomfortable. A good house selection, ranging from £12.95 to £14.50, covers France, Australia and Argentina.

CHEF: Jason Davenport   PROPRIETORS: Robert Wilson and Tim Lloyd   OPEN: Tue to Sat (and Sun D bank hols) 12 to 2, 7 to 10   CLOSED: 26 and 27 Dec, 1 and 2 Jan   MEALS: alc L (main courses £10.50 to £11). Set D Tue to Fri £24.50, Set D Tue to Sat £27 (2 courses) to £34. Bar menu available L   SERVICE: not inc   CARDS: Amex, Delta, Diners, MasterCard, Switch, Visa   DETAILS: 40 seats. Private parties: 24 main room, 8 to 10 private rooms. Vegetarian meals. Children's helpings. No smoking in dining room. Music  (£5)

## CLAYGATE  Surrey                                                             map 3

# Le Petit Pierrot

4 The Parade, Claygate KT10 0NU                                    COOKING 4
TEL: (01372) 465105   FAX: (01372) 467642             MODERN FRENCH
                                                                      £22–£51

The Brichots' intimate, compact little French bistro – hidden away in a parade of shops in leafy suburbia – justifiably continues to draw the crowds after some 13 years. Under a tented ceiling, bright pink cloths cover small tables while large mirrors, French pictures and masks decorate the walls, and Madame oversees some excellent service. The appealing fixed-price Francophile menu (with the odd supplement, a choice of seven dishes at each course, and an interesting sprinkling of assiettes) makes skilful use of first-class ingredients and attractive presentation. Veal and bacon terrine delivered with a herb salad and spicy plum sauce, or an assiette of marinated cod and prawns (served with a young spinach leaf salad and confit tomato dressing), may be among the starters, followed perhaps by roast partridge with girolles, or pan-fried calf's liver layered with bacon and crisp celeriac wafers. To finish, expect an assiette of hot and cold chocolate desserts, or passion-fruit pudding (served hot with a marmalade cheesecake cream). The all-French wine list is reasonably priced, including plenty of half- bottles and house vin de pays at £11.75 (£3 a glass).

CHEFS: Jean-Pierre Brichot and Eric Plantureux   PROPRIETORS: Annie and Jean-Pierre Brichot OPEN: Mon to Fri L 12.15 to 2, Mon to Sat D 7.15 to 9.30   CLOSED: 1 week Christmas, last week Aug   MEALS: Set L £12.25 (2 courses) to £21.75, Set D £24.50   SERVICE: not inc   CARDS: Amex, Diners, MasterCard, Visa   DETAILS: 32 seats. Private parties: 32 main room. No children under 9. Wheelchair access (not WC). Music. Air-conditioned  (£5)

---

*All details are as accurate as possible at the time of going to press, but chefs and owners often change, and it is wise to check by telephone before making a special journey. Many readers have been disappointed when set-price bargain meals are no longer available. Ask when booking.*

---

## CLIPSHAM  Rutland

# Olive Branch ⅚ £

**NEW ENTRY**

map 6

Main Street, Clipsham LE15 7SH
TEL: (01780) 410355
FAX: (01780) 410000

COOKING 3
MODERN AND TRADITIONAL BRITISH
£26–£49

The old stone farmhouse in a tiny hamlet is the picture of a modern English country pub, with a relaxed, informal atmosphere, quirky décor, and a long menu of contemporary classics. It is run by three friends, one of whom does the cooking, while another oversees front-of-house, and it is evidently popular: on a sunny day you may see the entire population of the village filling up the outside tables as well as those in the restaurant. By and large, the formula is a successful one: an inspector was impressed by the skills evident in a starter of tuna niçoise in the form of a confit of the fish mixed with a strongly garlicky mayonnaise, and by an inventive dessert of coconut parfait with strawberry and mango salsa. In between, main courses might feature poached trout with tomato risotto and asparagus, roast duck breast with fondant potato and sauerkraut, or perhaps warm chicken salad with spiced aubergine and a sweet yoghurt dressing. To drink, the choice is real ale or something from the short but varied wine list, priced from £9.95. At the time of going to press, a second pub was due to open under the same ownership: the Red Lion, Stathern.

CHEF: Sean Hope  PROPRIETOR: Rutland Inn Company  OPEN: all week L 12 to 2 (3 Sun), Mon to Sat D 7 to 9.30  CLOSED: 26 Dec, 1 Jan  MEALS: alc (main courses L £9 to £15, D £9 to £17). Set L Mon to Sat £11.50, Set L Sun £14.50. Bar menu available Mon to Sat L  SERVICE: not inc, card slips closed  CARDS: Delta, Diners, MasterCard, Switch, Visa  DETAILS: 50 seats. 25 seats outside. Private parties: 20 main room. Car park. Vegetarian meals. Children's helpings. No smoking in 1 dining room. Wheelchair access (not WC). Occasional music

## CLITHEROE  Lancashire

# Auctioneer ⅚

map 8

New Market Street, Clitheroe BB7 2JW
TEL: (01200) 427153
EMAIL: henk@auctioneer-clitheroe.co.uk
WEBSITE: www.auctioneer-clitheroe.co.uk

COOKING 2
MODERN EUROPEAN
£22–£55

Over the years, Henk and Frances Van Heumen's old stager on the edge of Clitheroe's open market has become renowned for its globetrotting monthly menus and themed evenings. This intriguing cook's tour can take in everywhere from Catalonia to New Zealand, and visitors can choose to sample the results in the rustic, stone-walled dining room or on the more modern wooden verandah.

During March it is Portugal's turn to hold centre stage, when the kitchen might produce caldo verde (green vegetable soup), lampatana (roast loin of lamb), and highly enjoyable arroz doce bairradinho (creamy rice pudding flavoured with cinnamon and lemon). There are also events for vegans and vegetarians, as well as a brief carte offering more conventional European fare in the shape of provençale fish soup, medallions of pork in herb breadcrumbs with grain mustard sauce, and apple and mincemeat strudel. Service is 'civil and well paced'. Ten house wines at £12 a bottle kick off the good-value list, which contains plenty of interesting, varied drinking. Parking is available in the adjacent market car park and is free on Sundays and evenings.

CHEF: Henk Van Heumen   PROPRIETORS: Henk and Frances Van Heumen   OPEN: Fri to Sun L 12 to 1.30, Wed to Sat D 7 to 8.30 (9.45 Sat)   MEALS: alc (main courses £14 to £19). Set L £9.95 (2 courses) to £11.95, Set D £19.75   SERVICE: not inc   CARDS: Amex, Delta, MasterCard, Switch, Visa   DETAILS: 48 seats. Private parties: 24 main room. Vegetarian meals. Children's helpings. No babies in dining room. No smoking in dining room. Music

## COCKERMOUTH Cumbria                                            map 10

# Quince & Medlar ✸

13 Castlegate, Cockermouth CA13 9EU                       COOKING 2
TEL: (01900) 823579                                       VEGETARIAN
                                                          £30–£40

Near the top of a short, steep hill just off the main street, on the way to the town's fourteenth-century castle, this three-storey Georgian building uses dark reds, pinks and greens to create a warm, homely feeling that is somewhere between Victorian and Art Nouveau in style. The owners (Louisa Le Voi heads up 'competent and helpful' service) are relaxed vegetarians who take an 'adventurous and interesting' line in cooking, skilfully coping with one diner's non-gluten diet, and unfussily meeting a child's penchant for plain pasta. Vegetable combinations are well thought out, and if some of them sound unlikely, they do seem to work: a coconut pancake filled with butternut squash (accompanied by chilli oil, crème fraîche and lemon grass) for example, and grilled cheesy polenta with sweet red pepper, water chestnuts, bamboo shoots and a garnish of fried onion and asparagus tips. Desserts might include sturdy spiced-apple cheesecake, or brown bread ice cream with light toffee sauce. Drink English country wine, local beer, or organic wine, mostly vegetarian or vegan, from £10.50.

CHEFS/PROPRIETORS: Colin and Louisa Le Voi   OPEN: Tue to Sat D 7 to 9.30 (earlier by arrangement)   CLOSED: 24 to 26 Dec, two weeks Feb/Mar   MEALS: alc D (main courses £12) SERVICE: not inc, card slips closed   CARDS: MasterCard, Switch, Visa   DETAILS: 26 seats. Private parties: 16 main room. Vegetarian meals. No children under 6. No smoking in dining room. Music

## COLCHESTER Essex                                               map 6

# Lemon Tree

48 St Johns Street, Colchester CO2 7AD
TEL/FAX: (01206) 767337                                   COOKING 1
EMAIL: reservations@the-lemon-tree.com                    MODERN BRITISH
WEBSITE: www.the-lemon-tree.com                           £18–£46

A terrace for al fresco dining is an enjoyable bonus at this town-centre venue. Otherwise, eat in the large, airy dining room with its stripped floorboards and creamy yellow walls; stencilled frescoes of a lemon tree echo the restaurant's name. Daily blackboards supplement the printed menus, and the repertoire encompasses everything from American crab and potato salad with a lime and ginger dressing, to roast duck breast with pak choi, hoisin and plum sauce, followed by desserts such as lemon parfait with shortbread. Note that the excellent-value lunch menu runs through to 5pm every day and there are pre-theatre evening meals too. The short wine list keeps its prices in check: house French is £10.50 (£2.25 a glass).

CHEF: Patrik Minder   PROPRIETORS: Joanna and Patrik Minder   OPEN: Mon to Sat 12 to 9.30 (10 Fri and Sat)   MEALS: alc (main courses £8 to £16). Set L Mon to Fri £5.95 (1 course) to £9.95, Set D Mon to Thur 5 to 9 £6.95 (1 course) to £12.95   SERVICE: not inc, card slips closed   CARDS: Amex, Delta, Diners, MasterCard, Switch, Visa   DETAILS: 90 seats. 45 seats outside. Private parties: 60 main room, 20 to 35 private rooms. Vegetarian meals. Children's helpings. Wheelchair access (also women's WC). Music  £5

## COOKHAM  Berkshire                                          map 3

# Manzano's

19–21 Station Hill Parade, Cookham SL6 9BR                COOKING **4**
TEL:  (01628) 525775                                      MEDITERRANEAN
                                                          £21–£66

Following the retirement of Alfonso and Maria Baena, chef Richard Manzano and his wife Deena took over the running of this long-established and popular venue, changing its name from Alfonso's to Manzano's. The place has had a decorative makeover too, and while they may not be able to do much about the unprepossessing location in a row of shops, the welcome remains as warm as ever.

Food continues in the same vein, Mediterranean themes holding sway over a fairly refined style: seared sea bass with crackling skin is served on a purée of tomatoes, peppers and saffron with anchovy- and Amontillado-flavoured oil, while a delicate guinea-fowl mousseline gâteau comes with wild mushrooms, sherry cream and a drizzle of chorizo oil. Simpler (and sometimes less Mediterranean) options are available in the shape of loin of pork with a light cider cream and buttered apples, or breast of Barbary duckling marinated in citrus and rosemary, pan-fried and served with its juices. An inspection meal began with a skilfully made terrine of suckling pig and chorizo wrapped in Serrano ham with sweet chilli and onion marmalade, and ended with an enjoyable apple and cinnamon lattice tart with chilled vanilla custard. A pair of vins de pays at £11.95 a bottle, £3 a glass, open a well-chosen list.

CHEFS: Richard Manzano and Adam Savage   PROPRIETORS: Richard and Deena Manzano   OPEN: Mon to Fri L 12 to 2, Mon to Sat D 7 to 10   CLOSED: 2 weeks Aug, bank hols   MEALS: alc (main courses £15 to £20). Set L £7.50 (2 courses)   SERVICE: 12.5%, card slips closed   CARDS: Amex, Delta, MasterCard, Switch, Visa   DETAILS: 34 seats. 12 seats outside. Private parties: 34 main room. Car park. Vegetarian meals. Children's helpings. Wheelchair access (not WC). Occasional music. Air-conditioned

£  *means that it is possible to have a three-course meal, including coffee, half a bottle of house wine and service for £30 or less per person, at any time the restaurant is open, i.e. at dinner as well as lunch. It may be possible to spend considerably more than this, but by choosing carefully you should find £30 or less achievable.*

## CORSCOMBE Dorset                                                        map 2

# ▲ Fox Inn ✻ £

Corscombe DT2 0NS
TEL/FAX:  (01935) 891330
EMAIL:  dine@fox-inn.co.uk                                          COOKING 2
WEBSITE:  www.fox-inn.co.uk                                  MODERN BRITISH
off A356, 6m SE of Crewkerne                                        £24–£47

Low, rambling, thatched, and set in delightful rolling countryside, the cream-painted building is healthily covered in summer flowers climbing energetically out of their tubs, troughs, baskets and pots. The kitchen is pretty vigorous too, with a large blackboard menu supplementing the already perfectly adequate carte: this proudly lists local suppliers, while the inn itself fills in the gaps by growing herbs, making chutneys and conjuring up a few drinks, from elderflower cordial to sloe gin. 'Good pub food' is what it deals in, with a strong line in fish, from whole roast bream or sea bass, via home-cured salt-cod, to salmon and haddock kedgeree. There is plenty more besides, though, including wild garlic soup, a Somerset goats' cheese salad, Dorset lamb, local venison, roast partridge, and perhaps a green Thai chicken curry. Puddings are traditional, offering treacle tart and apple crumble, while the short, annotated wine list stays helpfully under £20; a page of finer wines, and another of half-bottles, are equally accommodating. House Spanish red and white are £10.50.

CHEF: George Marsh   PROPRIETORS: Martyn and Susie Lee   OPEN: all week 12 to 2, 7 to 9 (9.30 Fri and Sat)   CLOSED: 25 Dec   MEALS: alc (main courses £8.50 to £18)   SERVICE: not inc, card slips closed   CARDS: Amex, Delta, MasterCard, Switch, Visa   DETAILS: 80 seats. 40 seats outside. Private parties: 32 main room, 16 to 20 private rooms. Car park. Vegetarian meals. Children's helpings. No smoking in 1 dining room. Wheelchair access (not WC). No music. No mobile phones   ACCOMMODATION: 4 rooms, all with bath/shower. TV. B&B £55 to £100 (*The Which? Hotel Guide*)

## CORSE LAWN Gloucestershire                                              map 2

# ▲ Corse Lawn House ▮ ✻

Corse Lawn GL19 4LZ
TEL:  (01452) 780771   FAX:  (01452) 780840
EMAIL:  hotel@corselawnhouse.u-net.com                            COOKING 2
WEBSITE:  www.corselawnhousehotel.co.uk                       ANGLO-FRENCH
on B4211, 5m SW of Tewkesbury                                      £29–£58

Something of a cross between a pub and a country-house hotel, this Grade II listed Queen Anne building has been run by the Hines for 25 years. The spacious dining room is not at all flashy or smart; indeed, it feels distinctly 'how hotels used to be', with relaxed, friendly and attentive service to match. A long carte (from which the shorter set-price menu is derived) gives the kitchen plenty of opportunity to flex its hearty Anglo-French muscles, taking in a daube of beef with horseradish mash, and haunch of venison with port sauce. Salmon and chicken are smoked in-house, crab is potted, and alcohol is used more liberally in savoury sauces than in desserts, which might include hot butterscotch sponge pudding, or passion-fruit soufflé with matching sorbet.

There is a French accent to the carefully selected, well-annotated wine list too, though other parts of Europe and the New World get a fair look-in. Mark-ups are quite low, giving decent choice under £20, and half-bottles number an admirable 59. Ten house wines start at £11; five are available by the glass, although one, a Muscadet, has received less than glowing reports. All in all, however, the list has plenty to keep wine lovers' interest.

CHEFS: Baba Hine and Andrew Poole   PROPRIETORS: the Hine family   OPEN: all week 12 to 2, 7 to 9.30   CLOSED: 24 to 26 Dec   MEALS: alc exc Sun D (main courses £15 to £18). Set L £16.50 (2 courses) to £18.50, Set D £27.50   SERVICE: not inc, card slips closed   CARDS: Amex, Delta, Diners, MasterCard, Switch, Visa   DETAILS: 50 seats. 30 seats outside. Private parties: 80 main room, 35 to 60 private rooms. Car park. Vegetarian meals. Children's helpings. No smoking in dining room. Wheelchair access (also WC). No music. No mobile phones   ACCOMMODATION: 19 rooms, all with bath/shower. TV. Phone. B&B £80 to £160. Rooms for disabled. Baby facilities. Swimming pool

## CRAYKE  North Yorkshire — map 9

# ▲ Durham Ox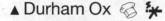

Westway, Crayke YO61 4TE
TEL: (01347) 821506   FAX: (01347) 823326
EMAIL: enquiries@thedurhamox.com
WEBSITE: www.thedurhamox.com

COOKING 3
MODERN EUROPEAN
£25–£54

Crayke, with its medieval church and castle, is rather hidden from the outside world, although the Foss Walk passes through the village, making the old inn a handy stop for hungry ramblers. It is a friendly place, with a flagged floor, oak settles and a log fire in winter, and combines the roles of pub and restaurant well. The carte, which changes every four weeks or so, is available throughout, while a blackboard lists the daily-changing dishes.

Reporters come for 'uniformly excellent' food, based on palpably fresh materials. Salads are prominent among first courses, perhaps of crisp belly pork with a sweet sesame soy dressing, or a Waldorf with a goats' cheese beignet. Main courses, supplemented by a couple of grilled steaks, might take in braised lamb shank in a red wine sauce, or seared salmon with chorizo and black olives, while vegetarian options have included a spicy vegetable pancake topped with mozzarella and pesto. A plate of ten different desserts for two to share is 'a real treat'. Children are welcome in the bar (but not the restaurant) 'provided they are accompanied by well-behaved parents'. Wines focus on choice under £20, with a few special bottles for those with something to celebrate, and start with three house wines at £10.50.

CHEF: Jason Moore   PROPRIETOR: Michael Ibbotson   OPEN: all week 12 to 2.30, 6 to 9.30 (10 Fri and Sat, 8.30 Sun)   CLOSED: 25 Dec   MEALS: alc (main courses £7.50 to £18). Set L Sun £10.95 (1 course) to £16.95. Light lunch menu available Mon to Sat   SERVICE: not inc, 10% for parties of 10 or more, card slips closed   CARDS: Amex, Delta, MasterCard, Switch, Visa   DETAILS: 60 seats. 20 seats outside. Private parties: 16 private room. Car park. Vegetarian meals. No children in restaurant. No smoking in dining room. Wheelchair access (not WC). Music   ACCOMMODATION: 8 rooms, all with bath/shower. TV. B&B £49.95 to £120 (The Which? Hotel Guide)  £5

## CROSTHWAITE  Cumbria                                           map 8

# ▲ Punch Bowl Inn  ⁙× £

Crosthwaite LA8 8HR
TEL: (015395) 68237   FAX: (015395) 68875
EMAIL: enquiries@punchbowl.fsnet.co.uk                    COOKING 4
WEBSITE: www.punchbowl.fsnet.co.uk                    MODERN BRITISH
in village, next to church                                    £19–£46

This may look like an ordinary country pub, but not much solo drinking goes on.
The bar counter is effectively a reception desk, with the rest of the room (warmed
by a couple of log fires) given over to tables for eating, some on a small balcony;
but the whole place remains pleasingly informal. Some ideas are out of the
familiar brasserie mould (smoked haddock with poached egg and grain mustard
sauce, for example, or ribeye steak with sauté potatoes) but the repertoire also
encompasses plump, tasty mussels in a powerful curry sauce, and slow-cooked
shank of lamb with a stew of potatoes, leeks and white beans.

First courses tend to include assemblies – perhaps Caesar salad with
Cumbrian pancetta, or roast peppers with crumbled goats' cheese and pesto –
while desserts range from Tunisian orange cake to steamed sponge pudding
with custard, by way of local Lyth Valley damsons in a pancake with toasted
almonds. The wines, from Old world and New and none over £25, fit on a single
sheet, but 20 can be had by the glass; house red and white are £9.75 (£2.65 a
glass). Bargain-seekers should consider the set lunch and early-evening deals.

CHEF: Steven Doherty   PROPRIETORS: Steven and Marjorie Doherty   OPEN: Tue to Sun L 12 to 2,
Tue to Sat D 6 to 9   CLOSED: last week Nov, first week Dec, 1 week Jan   MEALS: alc (main
courses £8.50 to £14). Set L £8.50 (2 courses) to £10.95, Set L Sat £9.95 (2 courses) to £12.95,
Set L Sun £12.95 (2 courses) to £14.95, Set D 6 to 7 £13.95 (2 courses) to £15.95   SERVICE: not
inc, card slips closed   CARDS: MasterCard, Switch, Visa   DETAILS: 60 seats. 20 seats outside.
Private parties: 18 main room. Car park. Vegetarian meals. Children's helpings. No smoking in
dining room. No music. No mobile phones   ACCOMMODATION: 3 rooms, all with bath/shower. TV.
B&B £37.50 to £55 (The Which? Hotel Guide)

## CRUDWELL  Wiltshire                                           map 2

# ▲ Old Rectory  ⁙×                              [ NEW ENTRY ]

Crudwell SN16 9EP
TEL: (01666) 577194   FAX: (01666) 577853              COOKING 2
EMAIL: office@oldrectorycrudwell.co.uk                 MODERN BRITISH
WEBSITE: www.oldrectorycrudwell.co.uk                         £29–£57

The Old Rectory has had a change of name (it was formerly Crudwell Court,
which last appeared in the Guide in 2000) as well as new owners and chef (Peter
Fairclough used to cook at the Greenway in Shurdington). It is a charming,
serene and 'very English' place (apart from a geometrically formal walled garden
and lawns at the back), with a view of the village church, and a dining room with
stripped wooden panelling from floor to ceiling. Menus read straightforwardly,
although the food is labour-intensive and can be very elaborate.

Perfectly good raw materials have included three giant scallops, first
marinated then paired with a layered cake of crab, red pepper and tomato, as

well as little mounds of spicy, herby mango salsa, a cheesy pesto and a small tuft of well-dressed leaves. Mains might run to roast rack of lamb (you aren't asked; it comes medium), or calf's liver with smoked bacon and wild mushrooms. The simplest dish at inspection proved to be the best: wafer-thin slices of pineapple, sparingly marinated in pepper and chilli, with a scoop of intensely strawberry-flavoured ice cream. A roving wine list offers choice under £20 and starts with house French at £12.95.

CHEF: Peter Fairclough  PROPRIETORS: Derek and Karen Woods  OPEN: all week 12 to 1.45, 7 to 9.30  MEALS: alc D (main courses £15.50 to £19). Set L Mon to Sat £14.50 (2 courses) to £17.95, Set L Sun £13.95 (2 courses) to £16.50, Set D £24.95. Light menu available  SERVICE: not inc  CARDS: Amex, Delta, Diners, MasterCard, Switch, Visa  DETAILS: 60 seats. 20 seats outside. Private parties: 40 main room, 2 to 30 private rooms. Car park. Vegetarian meals. Children's helpings. No children under 7 in dining room. No smoking in dining room. Wheelchair access (not WC). Occasional music. No mobile phones  ACCOMMODATION: 12 rooms, all with bath/shower. TV. Phone. B&B £65 to £125. Baby facilities (*The Which? Hotel Guide*)

## CUCKFIELD  West Sussex                              map 3

# Mansfields 🍴                              [ NEW ENTRY ]

1 Broad Street, Cuckfield RH17 5LJ                    COOKING 2
TEL: (01444) 410222  FAX: (01444) 410333             MODERN EUROPEAN
                                                     £33–£48

Small tables laid with linen, candles and flowers give an impression of warm nostalgia in the dining room of this white-painted house, close to the centre of the village. Despite some unevenness in the cooking the plus points are considerable, including a kitchen that demonstrates 'genuine skill and sensitivity' in what it delivers to the plate. Among starters, fish soup with a side dish of light and lemony rouille, grated cheese and croûtons has impressed for its clear, well-balanced flavours, while an individual Roquefort tart has featured light, buttery pastry and a delicately flavoured filling. Good-quality ingredients and careful technique are evident – in grilled sea bass fillet with caramelised chicory and red Rioja sauce, and in saddle of venison with mushrooms – while a well-judged Belgian chocolate tart with crème anglaise combines yet more first-class pastry with a richly flavoured filling. Service is 'efficient and friendly', and wines are a fairly standard range, starting with house vins de pays at £9.95.

CHEF: Günther Schlender  PROPRIETORS: Günther and Patricia Schlender  OPEN: Tue to Sat D only 7 to 10; also open L 25 Dec  CLOSED: bank hols  MEALS: alc (main courses £10 to £15)  SERVICE: not inc, 10% for parties of 6 or more, card slips closed  CARDS: Delta, MasterCard, Switch, Visa  DETAILS: 32 seats. Private parties: 12 main room, 8 to 15 private rooms. Vegetarian meals. Children's helpings. No smoking in 1 dining room. Music  (£5)

---

*If customers are asked to switch off mobile phones while in a restaurant, this is noted in the details at the end of an entry.*

*New main entries are listed near the front of the book. Some may have appeared in earlier years (though not in the previous edition) or as a Round-up entry last year.*

# ▲ Ockenden Manor ♀ ⅝

Ockenden Lane, Cuckfield RH17 5LD
TEL: (01444) 416111   FAX: (01444) 415549
EMAIL: ockenden@hshotels.co.uk                    COOKING 4
WEBSITE: www.hshotels.co.uk                    MODERN FRENCH
off A272, 2m W of Haywards Heath                    £35–£83

Occupying a sixteenth-century manor house in a picturesque village near the
South Downs, Ockenden goes in for elaborate ceilings, plush carpets, and a
serious oak-panelled dining room with heavy white cloths on decent-sized
tables. Two basic set-price menus (called Cuckfield and Sussex) come with
more than a £10 difference in price, but are in fact quite similar in style; there is
also a vegetarian and a seven-course tasting menu. For the most part the cooking
is highly competent and well presented, delivering anything from red mullet
fillets with mussels and saffron, to braised oxtail with buttered Savoy cabbage.

Pasta appears in a few guises – with a fricassee of oysters and leeks, and as a
boudin blanc ravioli to accompany breast of corn-fed chicken in a wild
mushroom sauce – and ideas rarely stray far from the mainstream: sliced fillet of
beef comes with a horseradish potato pancake, tarte Tatin with a cinnamon ice
cream, and caramelised lemon tart with a blackcurrant sauce. Service appears to
be a weak link in the operation. Wines range from grand red Bordeaux and
Super-Tuscans to well-chosen producers from the New World, with the
emphasis on Europe. A dozen house wines range from £15.50 to £18.50 a bottle,
but elsewhere pricing can be stiff.

CHEF: Steve Crane   PROPRIETORS: Sandy and Anne Goodman   OPEN: all week 12 to 2, 7.15 to
9.30 (9 Sun)   MEALS: Set L and D £10 (2 courses) to £47, Set gourmet L and D £55 (whole table),
Set L Sun £24.50. Bar menu available   SERVICE: not inc   CARDS: Amex, Delta, Diners,
MasterCard, Switch, Visa   DETAILS: 45 seats. 20 seats outside. Private parties: 75 main room, 8
to 16 private rooms. Car park. Vegetarian meals. Children's helpings. No smoking in dining
room. Wheelchair access (also WC). No music. No mobile phones   ACCOMMODATION: 22 rooms,
all with bath/shower. TV. Phone. B&B £99 to £270 (The Which? Hotel Guide)

## DARGATE Kent                                          map 3

# Dove £

Plum Pudding Lane, Dargate ME13 9HB                    COOKING 3
TEL: (01227) 751360                                        FRENCH
                                                        £28–£42

Is it a pub? Is it a restaurant? No, it's the Dove. The atmosphere is pubby – lively,
noisyish and occasionally smoky – and service from friendly bar staff doesn't go
in for the usual restaurant formalities. It looks like a pub, too, with bare wooden
floor and simple wooden furnishings, but the food is well above the public
house norm. The style is mostly heartily rustic: maybe rillettes of rabbit infused
with tapénade and served with a chunky, fresh-tasting spicy apple and tomato
chutney, perhaps followed by a hefty chunk of braised lamb shank on a large
mound of exemplary smooth mash. More refined options may include tempura
of fat, juicy prawns and red peppers attractively arranged on a cylinder of
couscous flecked with chunks of spicy chorizo: 'an inspired combination,'

thought a reporter, who followed it with 'spanking fresh' roast wild sea bass on tapénade-flavoured crushed potatoes. Finish with a selection of English and Irish cheeses or a soufflé-like hot chocolate fondant. Drink Shepherd Neame beers or try one of the twenty-odd Old and New World wines listed from £10.95; most are under £20.

CHEF: Nigel Morris   PROPRIETORS: Nigel and Bridget Morris   OPEN: Tue to Sun L 12 to 2, Wed to Sat D 7 to 9   MEALS: alc (main courses £12.50 to £17). Snack menu also available at L   SERVICE: net prices, card slips closed   CARDS: MasterCard, Switch, Visa   DETAILS: 20 seats. 20 seats outside. Car park. Children's helpings. Music

---

## DARTMOUTH Devon                                                        map 1

# Carved Angel

2 South Embankment, Dartmouth TQ6 9BH
TEL: (01803) 832465   FAX: (01803) 835141                     COOKING 4
EMAIL: enquiries@thecarvedangel.com              MODERN BRITISH-PLUS
WEBSITE: www.thecarvedangel.com                               £43–£88

The exuberantly carved half-timbered building is right on the estuary, facing a steeply rising hillside on the other side of the Dart, with bobbing boats in between. A rather misleading 'sample menu' is pinned up outside, but an open kitchen adds to the glass-fronted dining room's appeal. Darren Prideaux, listed last year at the Feathers in Woodstock, has made a few changes – the à la carte menu has gone, for example – but he still benefits from strong supply lines: among seasonal highlights has been an early-summer dish of well-timed veal sweetbreads with fresh morels, peas and asparagus in a frothy sauce.

A degree of complexity has crept into the food, and, while greater attention to more basic matters might not go amiss, the menu's sense of adventure is a plus, producing, for example, a lobster salad with apple, confit tomato and fennel pannacotta. Although there have been problems with seasoning and inaccurate timing, much remains impressive, including a main course at inspection that combined a first-class, rough-textured, attractively browned oyster boudin on a simplified pesto, with a couple of stiff John Dory fillets on a jumble of vegetables in a creamy smoked salmon sauce.

Desserts are well rendered too. The sharpness of roast plums on toasted brioche contrasts well with the rich creaminess of its crackingly good honey and yoghurt ice cream, an idea echoed in roast figs with goats' cheese ice cream. Meals are rounded out with decent bread and a fine appetiser (foie gras terrine with Madeira jelly for one visitor). After a brief lapse, the 'smooth, solicitous, obliging' service seems to be picking up again. Prices are considered high, not helped by a wine list that offers, for example, Louis Roederer Brut Premier champagne (retailing around the £20–£25 mark) at a hefty £71. Otherwise, the list ranges across the Old and New Worlds, although most time is spent in classic French regions. That said, New World selections (California aside) arguably offer the best value and are well chosen. Seven house recommendations are priced between £14.75 and £31.25 (£2.50 to £6.50 a glass).

CHEF: Darren Prideaux  PROPRIETORS: Paul and Andie Roston, and Peter Gorton  OPEN: Tue to Sun L 12.30 to 2.30, Mon to Sat D 7 to 9.30  MEALS: Set L £25.50 (2 courses) to £29.50, Set D £39.50 to £55  SERVICE: not inc  CARDS: Amex, Delta, MasterCard, Switch, Visa  DETAILS: 50 seats. Private parties: 35 main room, 6 to 16 private rooms. Vegetarian meals. Children's helpings. No children under 10 at D. No smoking in dining room. Music  (£5)

---

## Carved Angel Café 🍞 ⅙✶ £

7 Foss Street, Dartmouth TQ6 9DW
TEL: (01803) 834842                                          COOKING 3
EMAIL: enquiries@thecarvedangel.com                          GLOBAL
WEBSITE: thecarvedangel.com                                  £22–£41

Foss Street is good for browsing, amply provided as it is with boutiques, galleries and cafés, 'touristy in a quiet, genteel sort of way' in the opinion of a reporter. She went on to have a rather good lunch at this particular café, enjoying a window table and the open-armed feeling of a place that caters for everyone, from nonagenarians to her own baby. Baguettes, omelettes and sandwiches are available at lunchtime, alongside more substantial dishes of gravad lax with a cucumber and dill salad, and coarse-textured sausages with creamy mash and airily battered onion rings. A superior rendition of chunky banoffi pie has also excelled. In the evenings it gets more sophisticated, along the lines of asparagus flamiche with duxelles-stuffed eggs, fillets of red mullet with tomato and pepper tagliatelle and beurre blanc, and cold grapefruit and brandy soufflé with kiwi-fruit sauce. Service is full of solicitous good cheer. Seven each of red and white wines comprise the modest list, which begins with house Spanish at £9.95.

CHEF: Myles Hogarth  PROPRIETORS: Paul Roston and Peter Gorton  OPEN: Mon to Sat L 12 to 3, Thur to Sat D (Tue to Sun D July to Sept) 7 to 9  MEALS: alc (main courses L £5.50 to £6.50, D £9 to £11)  SERVICE: not inc, card slips closed  CARDS: Amex, Delta, Diners, MasterCard, Switch, Visa  DETAILS: 38 seats. Private parties: 38 main room. Vegetarian meals. Children's helpings. No smoking in dining room. Wheelchair access (also WC). Music. No mobile phones

---

## ▲ Gunfield

Castle Road, Dartmouth TQ6 0JN
TEL: (01803) 834571  FAX: (01803) 834772          | NEW CHEF |
EMAIL: enquiry@gunfield.co.uk                            GLOBAL
WEBSITE: www.gunfield.co.uk                              £29–£45

Readers may remember new chef Nick Crosley, who last appeared in the 2000 edition of the Guide at Cutter's Bunch. The hotel is also for sale, so more changes may be in the pipeline, but in the meantime a short menu still deals in upbeat ideas, from crab nachos, via prawn and monkfish nori rolls, to merguez sausage with moutabal and tsatsiki. Fish varies by the day, and while fillet steak is simply peppered, duck might be twice-cooked, Vietnamese style, and served with an orange and ginger sauce. Finish with lemon tart, or sticky toffee pudding. Reports are welcome.

CHEF: Nick Crosley  PROPRIETORS: Mike and Lucy Swash  OPEN: Sat and Sun L (all week L summer school hols) 12.30 to 2.30, all week D 7.30 to 9  MEALS: alc (main courses £10 to £16). Bar menu available at L  SERVICE: not inc  CARDS: Amex, MasterCard, Switch, Visa  DETAILS: 50

seats. 100 seats outside. Private parties: 50 main room. Car park. No children under 10. Music
ACCOMMODATION: 10 rooms, 7 with bath/shower. TV. B&B £47.50 to £145. Fishing (*The Which?*
*Hotel Guide*)

## DEDHAM  Essex                                                                    map 6

# ▲ milsoms ⅚✳ £

| | |
|---|---|
| Stratford Road, Dedham CO7 6HW | COOKING 1 |
| TEL: (01206) 322795   FAX: (01206) 323689 | BISTRO |
| WEBSITE: www.talbooth.com | £25–£45 |

No bookings are taken, and you need to order at the bar in Gerald and Paul
Milsom's young and buzzy venture. Like their other properties, Le Talbooth (see
below) and Pier Hotel, Harbourside Restaurant at Harwich (see entry), this
Georgian house is also a hotel, in this case with wide-ranging food designed for
all comers. Fish from the Harwich boats might show up in salt and pepper squid
with sweet chilli sambal, while Suffolk-reared mutton goes into 'Mr G's
shepherd's pie'. The rest is a mix of home and away, from Caesar salad with
pancetta to Thai glass noodles with poached tiger prawns, and Malaysian
chicken curry. As a finish, fresh-fruit fondue with warm chocolate sauce and
house-made marshmallow sounds worth an investment. House vin de pays is
£10.75, £2.80 a glass.

CHEF: Stas Anastasiades   PROPRIETORS: Paul and Gerald Milsom   OPEN: all week 12 to 2.15, 6 to
9.30 (10 Fri and Sat)   CLOSED: 24 Dec   MEALS: alc exc Sun L (main courses £8 to £12). Set L Sun
£15.45 (2 courses) to £19.45. Light L available   SERVICE: not inc, card slips closed   CARDS:
Amex, Delta, Diners, MasterCard, Switch, Visa   DETAILS: 80 seats. 60 seats outside. Private
parties: 8 to 16 private rooms. Car park. Vegetarian meals. Children's helpings. No smoking in 1
dining room. Wheelchair access (also WC). Music. Air-conditioned   ACCOMMODATION: 14 rooms,
all with bath/shower. TV. Phone. Room only £67.50 to £120. Rooms for disabled. Baby facilities
(*The Which? Hotel Guide*)

# ▲ Le Talbooth 🍴

| | |
|---|---|
| Gun Hill, Dedham CO7 6HP | |
| TEL: (01206) 323150   FAX: (01206) 322309 | COOKING 4 |
| EMAIL: talbooth@talbooth.co.uk | MODERN EUROPEAN |
| WEBSITE: www.talbooth.com | £35–£74 |

The attractive beamed building has been extended and rearranged over the
years, as the Milsom family restaurant (now 50 years old) has kept pace with
changing times. Since last year a new face has arrived in the kitchen, and the set
price dinner has departed, but a welcome straightforwardness still pervades the
cooking, which might offer local asparagus with first-class hollandaise, Dover
sole meunière, or chateaubriand for two. In the same spirit, lunch offers a daily
roast from the trolley (leg of lamb on Tuesday, rib of beef on Thursday), while
choice on the carte is generous to a fault.

Materials are well sourced, taking in fine, accurately seared foie gras with
toasted brioche and a dollop of sweet plum chutney, and a trio of veal –
sweetbreads, liver and kidney – of impeccable quality and lightly cooked,
served with sliced potatoes, spinach and port sauce. An occasional dish fails to
shine, and seasoning can be variable, but the basics are sound. A star among

desserts has been a hot banana napped with caramel, served with an intense cappuccino parfait (coffee ice, vanilla ice, and a dusting of powdered chocolate), fudge sauce and a banana crisp. Service by young (mostly foreign) staff is thoughtful, friendly and efficient, and the wine list has wide appeal. Claret lovers will be impressed with the range of mature red Bordeaux, many of which offer exceptional value, while fans of New World wines will find much to choose from, particularly in the South African section. Mark-ups are sensible, allowing good choice under £20. Twelve house wines (all available by the glass from £4) are priced between £13.50 and £19.75 per bottle.

CHEFS: Terry Barber and Ian Rhodes   PROPRIETORS: Gerald and Paul Milsom   OPEN: all week L 12 to 2.30, Mon to Sat D 7 to 9.30 (and Sun D in summer for barbecue)   MEALS: alc Mon to Sat (main courses £15.50 to £26.50). Set L £18.50 (2 courses) to £21.50   SERVICE: 10%, card slips closed   CARDS: Amex, Diners, MasterCard, Switch, Visa   DETAILS: 75 seats. 60 seats outside. Private parties: 84 main room, 8 to 34 private rooms. Car park. Vegetarian meals. Children's helpings. Occasional music   ACCOMMODATION: 10 rooms, all with bath/shower. TV. Phone. B&B £95 to £210. Rooms for disabled (*The Which? Hotel Guide*)

## DERBY Derbyshire                                                          map 5

# Darleys ✚✗

Darley Abbey Mill, Darley Abbey,
Derby DE22 1DZ
TEL: (01332) 364987   FAX: (01332) 541356                          COOKING 3
WEBSITE: www.darleys.com                                        MODERN BRITISH
off A6 2m N of city centre                                            £27–£60

Soak up the historical surroundings as you cross a former toll bridge to enter this converted mill by a weir. Once inside, 'you leave the past behind'; a huge coffee machine stands on the bar, the walls are ice blue with patches of wood panelling, some luxurious textiles have appeared after recent refurbishment, and the lights are dim.

Kevin Stone has a new partner at the stoves, although the thrust of the cooking remains largely unchanged. 'A few niggles' – particularly about timing – have coloured recent reports, but the kitchen can still deliver ambitious modern dishes, such as seared scallops on creamy leeks with crispy crab risotto cakes, and confit of duck on a cassoulet of white beans, chorizo and foie gras. The assiette of pork is a north-country-sized plateful of pork loin, slow-roast belly pork, home-made sausage, black pudding, and mustard mash with a glazed apple and honey jus. Finish with, say, spiced poached pear beside a pear brûlée with shortbread biscuits and vanilla ice cream. Service seems to have regained its professionalism, and the extensive wine list still offers good drinking at very reasonable prices, starting with a dozen 'personal recommendations' from £14 a bottle (£3.50 a glass).

CHEF: Kevin Stone   PROPRIETOR: David Pinchbeck   OPEN: all week L 12 to 2, Mon to Sat D 6.30 to 10 (10.30 Fri and Sat)   CLOSED: bank hols (exc Good Friday)   MEALS: alc (main courses £14.50 to £18.50). Set L £13.50 (2 courses) to £17.50   SERVICE: 10% (optional), card slips closed CARDS: Amex, Delta, Diners, MasterCard, Switch, Visa   DETAILS: 70 seats. 20 seats outside. Private parties: 70 main room. Car park. Vegetarian meals. Children's helpings. No smoking in dining room. Wheelchair access (not WC). Music. No mobile phones. Air-conditioned  £5

## DINTON Buckinghamshire · map 3

# La Chouette ♀ ✴

Westlington Green, Dinton HP17 8UW
TEL/FAX: (01296) 747422
3½SW of Aylesbury off A418, follow signs to
Westlington and Ford

COOKING 4
BELGIAN
£21–£61

This well-preserved former village pub may announce itself as a Belgian restaurant, but it is the sort of idiosyncratic place we tend to feel is uniquely British, perhaps because we cherish the eccentric and extraordinary. The food seems to inhabit its own time bubble, and the menu (in French with English subtitles) is devoted to variations on themes that have occupied Frédéric Desmette for over a decade: from scallops in a saffron sauce to slices of briefly marinated Scottish salmon on a jumble of sharply dressed leaves tossed with apple and pine nuts.

Ingredients are of a generally high quality, and, if their excellence is sometimes overlaid by pepper or cream (a favourite ingredient here), they have shone with, for example, a Périgueux duck breast, cooked pink as requested, served in an expertly made sauce spiked with crisp, sharp green peppercorns. Vegetables are served on the main-course plate, although they are effectively a 'side plate selection', while desserts typically include a soufflé, crêpes (Comédie Française as well as the more familiar Suzette) and sorbets and ice creams. An 'astoundingly well made' creamy-textured sorbet was one visitor's 'surprise' dessert. M. Desmette often takes charge of service as well as the cooking.

Many of France's great and good are on the wine list, including notable selections from Alsace and the Rhône (as well as the requisite Burgundy and Bordeaux, of course). Two Loire whites from Savennières are bargains at £22 and £25.50, and a selection from the underrated south-west will put a smile on oenophiles' faces. A handful of non-French wines appears on the last page, almost as an afterthought. More half-bottles and by-the-glass options would be good, though. House red and white are £11.50.

CHEF/PROPRIETOR: Frédéric Desmette  OPEN: Mon to Fri L 12 to 2, Mon to Sat D 7 to 9  MEALS: alc (main courses £14 to £16.50). Set L £11 (weekdays only) to £36.50, Set D £29.50 to £36.50  SERVICE: 12.5% (optional), card slips closed  CARDS: Delta, MasterCard, Visa  DETAILS: 40 seats. 12 seats outside. Private parties: 40 main room. Car park. Children's helpings. No smoking in dining room. Occasional music. No mobile phones

## DORRIDGE West Midlands · map 5

# ▲ Forest ✴    NEW ENTRY

25 Station Approach, Dorridge B93 8JA
TEL: (01564) 772120   FAX: (01564) 732680

COOKING 4
MODERN FRENCH
£27–£54

To the south-east of Birmingham, near the M42, where suburbia gives way to rolling Warwickshire countryside, and just opposite Dorridge Station, is this large Victorian pile, formerly a pub. Full of bay windows, gable ends and ornate woodwork, it has had a serious makeover, now featuring a bar, hotel, banqueting suite and conference centre as well as a restaurant. 'Contemporary neutral chic' is how one visitor saw the restaurant's simple, clean lines, highly polished wooden floors, pastel walls, and dark veneered tables.

Ian Mansfield, listed last year at the Sir Edward Elgar restaurant in Birmingham's Marriot Hotel (see Round-up entry), and before that at Eastwell Manor in Kent (see Round-up entry, Boughton Lees), puts on a savvy menu of appealing dishes, from a smooth, putty-coloured ballottine of foie gras with a delicate fringe of crumbled Monbazillac jelly, to deep-fried lambs' sweetbreads with mustard oil and capers. Oversized plates and huge deep bowls, all in plain white, provide the background for some fine cooking, taking in first-class roast scallops partnered with crisp, lightly salty pancetta on a smooth pea purée, and a firm, flavourful breast of guinea fowl, served with shelled broad beans, bacon and sage. Vegetables need to be ordered separately, but include runner beans with aïoli, and a velvety celeriac purée sprinkled with crunchy hazelnuts.

Recommended desserts have included blackberry crème brûlée, pannacotta with pineapple and peppercorns, and a wedge of light, open-textured, hot Bakewell tart served with clotted cream. Service is attentive, and the Tuesday evening deal (any two courses for £12.50) sounds a good one. Wines, grouped by style, include a couple of organic Californian varietals (Viognier and Sangiovese) from Fetzer, offer plenty of choice under £20, and start with ten by the glass.

CHEF: Ian Mansfield  PROPRIETORS: Gary and Tracy Perkins  OPEN: Tue to Sun L 12 to 2, Tue to Sat D 6.30 to 10  CLOSED: 25 Dec  MEALS: alc exc Sun L (main courses £10 to £17.50). Set L Tue to Sat £10 (2 courses), Set L Sun £17.50, Set D Tue £12.50 (2 courses, inc wine). Bar menu available Tue to Sat L  SERVICE: not inc, card slips closed  CARDS: Amex, Delta, MasterCard, Switch, Visa  DETAILS: 68 seats. Private parties: 68 main room, 12 to 40 private rooms. Car park. Vegetarian meals. Children's helpings. No smoking in dining room. Wheelchair access (also WC). Music. Air-conditioned  ACCOMMODATION: 4 rooms, all with bath/shower. TV. Phone. B&B £70.50 to £97

## DORRINGTON Shropshire                                        map 5

## ▲ Country Friends ▼ ⅚✳

Dorrington SY5 7JD
TEL: (01743) 718707                                              COOKING 6
EMAIL: countryfriends@ukonline.co.uk               MODERN BRITISH
on A49, 6m S of Shrewsbury                                  £41–£49

The black and white building on the main road through Dorrington has a lawn with a pool, a rockery, and a tarmac car park. Gardening does not appear to be a high priority, though, any more than interior decoration is in the compact bar and plain but spacious dining room. The term 'sedate pace' seems to apply to most things, including the evolution of the menu, but that does not mean it lacks interest. Far from it. Among the sharper flavours to appear might be a green olive salsa, accompanying a first-course baked goats' cheese with roast cherry tomatoes, and an old English favourite: horseradish, which partners smoked salmon on a potato cake, and forms a crust on a fillet steak that comes with Madeira sauce.

A twice-baked vegetable and cheese soufflé often features (leek and Llanboidy, or broccoli and Gruyère), while risotto might come with smoked haddock or wild mushrooms. Main-course seafood varies by the day and is not listed on the menu, but among starters might be crab ravioli with a tomato and lemon dressing, or chargrilled marinated salmon on spiced aubergine. For those not wanting to go the whole hog, lighter lunches might include confit duck leg with an orange salad, or fish quenelles in a herb sauce, while desserts run to chocolate tart with raspberry sorbet, and praline and white chocolate ice cream with coffee-bean sauce. The wine list is brief but imaginatively put together, grouped by style and price. New and Old Worlds are equally well represented, and there is plenty to please those who are bored with Cabernet and Chardonnay. Sixteen half-bottles round out the list; and bottle prices start at £12.75 for house Australian red and white.

CHEF: Charles Whittaker   PROPRIETORS: Charles and Pauline Whittaker   OPEN: Wed to Sat 12 to 2, 7 to 9 (9.30 Sat)   CLOSED: 2 weeks mid-July   MEALS: Set L and D £28.50 (2 courses) to £30.90. Light lunch menu available   SERVICE: not inc   CARDS: Delta, Diners, MasterCard, Switch, Visa DETAILS: 40 seats. Private parties: 40 main room. Car park. Vegetarian meals. No smoking in dining room. No music. No mobile phones   ACCOMMODATION: 1 room with bath/shower. D,B&B £75 to £130

## DRYBROOK Gloucestershire         map 5

# Cider Press

The Cross, Drybrook GL17 9EB
TEL/FAX: (01594) 544472
EMAIL: info@ciderpress.org.uk
WEBSITE: www.ciderpress.org.uk

COOKING 2
MODERN EUROPEAN
£25–£44

A strong blue-purple façade makes this small restaurant by a crossroads at the centre of the village stand out from its neighbours. Inside, honey-coloured walls are adorned with numerous prints and artefacts in a very homely style. Helen Short, one of the new owners who took over last autumn, is in charge of the kitchen. There is less emphasis on fish than before, but the cooking is otherwise in a fairly similar modern vein. A starter of mushroom ravioli, featuring an intensely flavoured duxelles filling, comes scattered with pieces of 'sweet and tasty' roast red pepper and flakes of Parmesan, and a main course of pan-fried Gressingham duck breast on potato galette with raspberry and red wine sauce has been described as 'decent home cooking'. Light lunch menus offer a cheaper alternative to the carte. Three Chilean house wines at £9.95 open the short but varied wine list.

CHEF: Helen Short   PROPRIETORS: Jon Whateley and Helen Short   OPEN: Fri to Sun L 12 to 2, Wed to Sat D 7 to 10   MEALS: alc exc Sun L (main courses £12.50 to £17). Set L Sun £12.95 (2 courses) to £15.95. Light L menu available   SERVICE: not inc, card slips closed   CARDS: MasterCard, Switch, Visa   DETAILS: 24 seats. 4 seats outside. Private parties: 20 main room. Vegetarian meals. No smoking in dining room. Music

*Dining rooms where music, either live or recorded, is never played are signalled by* No music *in the details at the end of an entry.*

*Card slips closed in the details at the end of an entry indicates that the total on the slips of credit cards is closed when handed over for signature.*

## DURHAM  Co Durham                          map 10

# Bistro 21  🍴 ✳ £

Aykley Heads House, Aykley Heads,                 COOKING 2
Durham DH1 5TS                                    MEDITERRANEAN
TEL: (0191) 384 4354   FAX: (0191) 384 1149       £24–£55

'Thank goodness for the Laybournes,' summed up a visitor, pleased to have
found somewhere good to eat in the area. The former farmhouse has an open
courtyard within, rustic chic décor, and a new chef, although the crowd-pleasing
menu remains in the same vein as before, offering food along the lines of Caesar
salad, fishcakes with parsley cream and chips, and a warm potato pancake with
black pudding, bacon and a poached egg.

Soups are well reported, be it pea and mint with slices of crusty bread, or
garlicky broad bean, and the kitchen generally delivers the flavours expected:
for example in a hefty piece of chargrilled pork loin with 'splendid-tasting'
mustard mash. Desserts are equally pleasing, judging by apple and almond tart
with cinnamon ice cream, and by a triple chocolate mousse layered in a cocktail
glass and topped with whipped cream. Staff seem to be not only as friendly as
ever, reckons a regular, but a bit faster and more professional; another adds that
'they have cheered up considerably'. House Duboeuf at £11 heads up a short,
serviceable wine list.

CHEF: Mark Anderson   PROPRIETOR: Terence Laybourne   OPEN: Mon to Sat 12 to 2, 7 (6 Sat) to
10.30   CLOSED: 25 and 26 Dec, bank hols   MEALS: alc (main courses £10 to £18.50). Set L £12 (2
courses) to £14.50   SERVICE: not inc   CARDS: Amex, Delta, Diners, MasterCard, Switch, Visa
DETAILS: 100 seats. 24 seats outside. Private parties: 50 main room, 10 to 30 private rooms. Car
park. Vegetarian meals. Children's helpings. No smoking in dining room. Wheelchair access
(also WC). Music

## EASTBOURNE  East Sussex                      map 3

# ▲ Grand Hotel, Mirabelle  🍷 ✳ 🍴

Jevington Gardens, Eastbourne BN21 4EQ            COOKING 6
TEL: (01323) 435066   FAX: (01323) 412233         MODERN EUROPEAN
WEBSITE: www.grandeastbourne.com                  £27–£76

Gerald Röser's Hastings restaurant closed last autumn, but in spring 2002 he
moved along the coast to join Keith Mitchell at these rather smarter premises.
Meals are eaten in an expansive, bay-windowed dining room with plush
carpets, great swags of curtain and a fine view of the seafront. Dinner offers two
three-course set-price menus, plus a seven-course tasting menu with
recommended wines by the glass for each dish; and if the cost seems high,
don't forget that prices are net.

The highly worked cooking features stuffings, mousselines and purées, but
still keeps its eye on the main business. Contrasts are effective, as in a
straightforward but appetising juxtaposition of moist, pungent smoked salmon
on a blini with a single scallop sliced wafer-thin and dressed with lemon and
vanilla; and the balance of dishes is typified by a tightly rolled, firm brill fillet
wrapped in appealingly salty pancetta, the crisp skin parked on top,
accompanied by a truffly fennel cream. Tops at inspection was a roast squab

pigeon – breast, wings, legs and liver, all cooked to a nicety and robustly gamey – served with Puy lentils and savoury baby onions bound in a strongly reduced sauce.

Textures are gentle right through to desserts: Kirsch pannacotta, warm chocolate fondant, or creamy unmoulded mango crème brûlée with a thin crisp topping, served with a smooth, intense raspberry sorbet. In-house breads and incidentals are excellent. Service is from informed European staff (including Scouse), and prices are high. Wines too are pricey: a glass of Moët & Chandon Brut Imperial, for example, costs £11.50 when a bottle costs under £20 in the high street. That said, this is an extremely fine list – particularly for lovers of Burgundy and mature Bordeaux – offering a few wines under £20 for non-expense-account drinkers. Best value is found in French regional wines (where bottle prices start at £16.50 for Vin de Pays d'Oc), in Australia and in the Italian whites section.

CHEFS: Gerald Röser and Keith Mitchell  PROPRIETOR: Elite Hotels  OPEN: Tue to Sat 12.30 to 2, 7 to 10  CLOSED: first 2 weeks Jan  MEALS: Set L £12.50 (1 course) to £19, Set D £35 to £55  SERVICE: net prices, card slips closed  CARDS: Amex, Delta, Diners, MasterCard, Switch, Visa  DETAILS: 50 seats. Private parties: 56 main room. Car park. Vegetarian meals. Children's helpings L, no children D. Jacket and tie at D. No smoking in dining room. Wheelchair access (also WC). Music. No mobile phones. Air-conditioned  ACCOMMODATION: 152 rooms, all with bath/shower. TV. Phone. B&B £125 to £410. Rooms for disabled. Baby facilities. Swimming pool (*The Which? Hotel Guide*)  (£5)

---

**EAST CHILTINGTON** East Sussex                                    **map 3**

# Jolly Sportsman ★

Chapel Lane, East Chiltington BN7 3BA
TEL/FAX: (01273) 890400
EMAIL: jollysportsman@mistral.co.uk
WEBSITE: www.thejollysportsman.com
from B2116 ½m E of Plumpton, turn N                    COOKING **2**
(signposted East Chiltington), and after 1½m turn      MODERN EUROPEAN
left (pub is signposted)                               £23–£56

As beaten tracks go, the Sportsman is certainly off one, but cool-headed navigators will be pleased they persevered. This is indeed a jolly place, 'a country pub with unusual flair' to one of its regulars. A modest extension of the dining area and a patio for summer eating are now installed, and the seriousness of intent is shown in the ample list of top-notch suppliers that the kitchen draws on. A simple approach means that dishes such as artichoke heart with mushrooms and quails' eggs in hollandaise, or seafood risotto generously crammed with lobster and mussels, speak for themselves without need of 'the prinking and fussing you find elsewhere'. Rabbit is bound in bacon to keep it moist and served with Puy lentils, while fish from Cornwall might take in grilled halibut with lemon and chives. Lavender honey ice cream with turrón, or raspberry champagne jelly accompanied by grappa pannacotta, will keep the changes ringing at dessert stage. An imaginative international list of fairly priced wines kicks off with vins de pays at £10.85.

CHEF: Richard Willis  PROPRIETORS: Bruce and Gwyneth Wass  OPEN: Tue to Sun L 12.30 to 2 (3 Sun), Tue to Sat D 7 to 9.30 (10 Fri and Sat)  CLOSED: 5 days at Christmas, D bank hol Mons  MEALS: alc (main courses £8 to £20). Set L Tue to Sat £10 (2 courses) to £13.75. Bar menu available  SERVICE: 10%, card slips closed  CARDS: Delta, MasterCard, Switch, Visa  DETAILS: 80 seats. 30 seats outside. Private parties: 35 main room. Car park. Vegetarian meals. Children's helpings. No smoking in dining room. Wheelchair access (also WC). No music

## EAST END  Hampshire                                                   map 2

# East End Arms

Main Road, East End SO41 5SY
TEL/FAX: (01590) 626223
EMAIL: jennie@eastendarms.co.uk
WEBSITE: www.eastendarms.co.uk                         COOKING 3
2m E of Lymington turn SE off B3054 and          MODERN BRITISH/SEAFOOD
continue 2m                                                £26–£43

It may sound like a Londoner's local, but this comfortable, unpretentious pub is actually secreted away on the edge of the New Forest. The wall over the bar is hung with black-and-white photographs of '60s stars, a nod perhaps to owner John Illsley of rock band Dire Straits (who also owns the George at Yarmouth, see entry). Tables and chairs are a mishmash of sturdy pub styles, and there are attractive prints and a welcoming log fire for winter days.

The weekly-changing menu looks to cater for all tastes, with locally sourced fish and shellfish representing about half the kitchen's output; perhaps grilled halibut with tomato oil and Parmesan fries, or sea bass with creamed spinach and coriander risotto. These might follow an asparagus, Parma ham and bantam egg terrine, and precede homely desserts (chalked on the blackboard) of warm brownie, treacle tart, or bread-and-butter pudding. Lighter lunch options could take in a well-received fresh fish pie, or a variety of filled baguettes. Service is 'amiable and good-natured', while the 20-bottle wine list keeps all under £20 (except champagne), with four house wines at £11 (£2.50 a glass).

CHEFS: Stuart Kitcher and Paul Sykes  PROPRIETOR: John Illsley  OPEN: Tue to Sun L 12 to 2, Tue to Sat D 7 to 9  CLOSED: 25 and 26 Dec, 1 Jan  MEALS: alc (main courses £6.50 to £15). Light lunch menu also available exc Mon  SERVICE: not inc, card slips closed  CARDS: Delta, MasterCard, Switch, Visa  DETAILS: 34 seats. 60 seats outside. Private parties: 25 main room. Car park. Children's helpings. Wheelchair access (not WC). Music

## EAST GRINSTEAD  West Sussex                                           map 3

# ▲ Gravetye Manor  ▮ ✳

Vowels Lane, East Grinstead RH19 4LJ
TEL: (01342) 810567  FAX: (01342) 810080
EMAIL: info@gravetyemanor.co.uk                        COOKING 6
WEBSITE: www.gravetyemanor.co.uk                  TRADITIONAL ENGLISH
off B2110, 2m SW of East Grinstead                         £39–£89

'Ye Olde England' and *House & Garden* are invoked to convey readers' impressions of this stone-built Elizabethan mansion and its gardens and grounds. With a large hall, wood panelling, log fire, antique furniture and magnificent flower arrangements, it attracts all sorts – a lady 'dripping with diamonds' next to a table of tie-less Welsh rugby players in shirtsleeves – and cossets them with some soothing cooking. Luxury materials are the first thing to catch the eye: a trio of crab, scallops and langoustines, a ballottine of foie gras with truffled leeks, plain Dover sole with herb butter, and fillet of Angus beef with Roquefort tortellini.

The food is not all rich, though. A provençale vegetable salad comes with goats' cheese won tons, and a light tempura of codling arrives on a bed of couscous and Indian-spiced cream sauce. In fact, the menu's diversity reflects the kitchen's appropriate response to its varied ingredients, producing a lasagne of forest mushrooms with a cappuccino of Scottish ceps, a fricassee of red mullet with cockles and mussels, and a pairing of young pigeon and local venison with braised Savoy cabbage in a powerful-tasting sauce. Although desserts may not be numerous, they are certainly appealing, taking in a hot plum crumble soufflé, and a warm chocolate fondant with cinnamon ice cream.

Wines are a well-bred collection of bottles. Peter Herbert's recent forays to Western Australia and New Zealand have added to the New World offerings, but France (Burgundy and Bordeaux in particular) remains at the forefront. Although prices for many bottles are high, mark-ups are not unreasonable and value can be found, particularly in the New World and Alsace sections; service is also included in the bottle price. Nine house suggestions range from £19 to £33, but prices start at £16.

CHEF: Mark Raffan   PROPRIETORS: the Herbert family   OPEN: all week 12.30 to 1.45, 7 to 9.30   CLOSED: D 25 Dec (residents only)   MEALS: Set L £27 to £52, Set D £37 to £52   SERVICE: net prices, card slips closed   CARDS: MasterCard, Switch, Visa   DETAILS: 45 seats. Private parties: 8 to 20 private rooms. Car park. Vegetarian meals. No children under 7. Jacket and tie. No smoking in dining room. Wheelchair access (not WC). No music. No mobile phones   ACCOMMODATION: 18 rooms, all with bath/shower. TV. Phone. Room only £90 to £320. No children under 7. Fishing (*The Which? Hotel Guide*)

---

**EAST WITTON** North Yorkshire                                              map 8

## ▲ Blue Lion  £

East Witton DL8 4SN
TEL: (01969) 624273   FAX: (01969) 624189
EMAIL: bluelion@breathemail.net                              COOKING 3
WEBSITE: www.thebluelion.co.uk                          MODERN BRITISH
on A6108 between Masham and Leyburn                        £27–£56

A late eighteenth-century coaching inn that once catered for travellers and drovers on their way through Wensleydale, the Blue Lion is now every inch the Yorkshire country pub. Flagstoned floors and an open fire, together with a candlelit dining room hung with many pictures, establish the mood. The cooking acknowledges current trends, as well as offering tried-and-true pub dishes on the bar menu, so whether you're in the mood for a suet-crusted game pie, or chicken breast stuffed with blue Wensleydale served with smoked bacon risotto, you won't put the kitchen off its stroke.

Apart from Sunday lunch, the restaurant proper is only open for dinner. Here, foie gras lightly smoked over apple wood and served with an apple and orange salad made a diverting opener at inspection, and the tenderness of meat has been praised, from beef fillet rolled in cep powder to flash-roasted local venison, served with potato rösti and sauced with juniper and bilberries. Half a dozen vegetarian options add to the allure. For the indecisive, a generous dessert selection consists of no fewer than seven items, perhaps including lemon mousse on lemon shortbread, steamed apple and blackberry sponge, and superb raspberry sorbet in a tuile basket. A trim list of well-chosen wines opens with house French at £10.50, or £2.65 a glass.

CHEF: John Dalby  PROPRIETORS: Paul and Helen Klein  OPEN: Sun L 12 to 2, all week D 7 to 9.15  CLOSED: 25 Dec  MEALS: alc (main courses £8.50 to £18). Bar menu also available all week L (exc Sun) and D  SERVICE: not inc  CARDS: Delta, MasterCard, Switch, Visa  DETAILS: 100 seats. 50 seats outside. Private parties: 50 main room, 10 to 15 private rooms. Car park. Vegetarian meals. Children's helpings. No music  ACCOMMODATION: 12 rooms, all with bath/shower. TV. Phone. B&B £53.50 to £89. Baby facilities (*The Which? Hotel Guide*)

## ELLAND  West Yorkshire

map 8

# La Cachette ♥ £

**NEW ENTRY**

31 Huddersfield Road, Elland HX5 9AW
TEL: (01422) 378833  FAX: (01422) 327567

COOKING 3
MODERN EUROPEAN
£19–£49

Having relocated from just around the corner to occupy the former Bertie's Supper Rooms, David and Maureen Gault have created a place with a relaxed, intimate yet bustling French brasserie atmosphere. The large, airy room has a central bar, walls – painted in clean, bright but subtle colours – are hung with posters and modern art, while white-linen-dressed tables have paper covers that emphasise the informal tone.

Lee Marshall (ex-Dining Room, Boroughbridge; see entry) heads up a new kitchen brigade, and offers a contemporary brasserie menu that is both extensive and appealing, with a number of dishes available in two sizes. Sauté king scallops with sticky rice and deep-fried crab spring rolls makes an adventurous starter, with Caesar or Greek salads among other options. The menu changes every three or four weeks, but main courses might take in well-executed beef fillet (on a bed of spinach with sweet roast shallots, wild mushrooms, toasted pine nuts and red wine jus), or whole grilled sea bass with lemon and herb butter and new potatoes. Close with a 'brilliant' rum and raisin creamed rice pudding with glazed banana. The welcome is friendly and waiting staff are 'well trained, observant and pleasant' The wine list satisfies seekers of quality in the French and Spanish sections, and predominantly comes in under £20. Eight house wines are £9.95 to £12.95 (£2 to £2.60 a glass).

CHEF: Lee Marshall  PROPRIETOR: CGL Partnership  OPEN: Mon to Sat 12 to 2.30, 6 to 9.30 (10 Fri and Sat)  CLOSED: 25 Dec to 4 Jan, 2 weeks Aug, bank hols  MEALS: alc (main courses £8 to £16). Set L £7.95 (2 courses), Set D £15.55 (inc wine)  SERVICE: not inc  CARDS: Delta, MasterCard, Switch, Visa  DETAILS: 80 seats. Private parties: 25 main room. Vegetarian meals. Children's helpings. Wheelchair access (not WC). Music. Air-conditioned £5

*To find a restaurant in a particular area use the maps at the centre of the book.*

## ELY Cambridgeshire
map 6

# Old Fire Engine House ✻

25 St Mary's Street, Ely CB7 4ER  COOKING **1**
TEL: (01353) 662582  FAX: (01353) 668364  TRADITIONAL ENGLISH FARMHOUSE
on A10 in centre of Ely  £30–£47

Within a stone's throw of the cathedral, this eighteenth-century brick-built former farmhouse doubles as an art gallery. Start with a drink in a small bar, then walk through the kitchen into a tile-floored dining room set with bare wooden tables and church-pew seating. It is a family restaurant with an English country style of cooking, offering dishes that don't often surface elsewhere: mittoon of pork (an old-fashioned coarse-textured terrine), lovage soup, pike or zander in season, and jugged hare likewise. Generosity rather than finesse distinguishes the output, and one of the attractions is that seconds are usually offered. A reporter who enjoyed pigeon in a game sauce felt particularly hungry, so 'had another pigeon and some more vegetables'. Finish with apple and blackberry pie, Cambridge burnt cream, or sherry trifle. France is the wine list's favourite country, although house wines come from Chile and Germany.

CHEF: Terri Baker  PROPRIETORS: Ann Ford and Michael Jarman  OPEN: all week L 12.15 to 2, Mon to Sat D 7.15 to 9  CLOSED: 24 Dec to 5 Jan, bank hols  MEALS: alc (main courses £13 to £16)  SERVICE: not inc  CARDS: Delta, MasterCard, Switch, Visa  DETAILS: 55 seats. 20 seats outside. Private parties: 35 main room, 10 to 22 private rooms. Car park. Vegetarian meals. Children's helpings. No smoking in 1 dining room. No music. No mobile phones

## EMSWORTH Hampshire
map 2

# Spencers £

36–38 North Street, Emsworth PO10 7DG  COOKING **1**
TEL/FAX: (01243) 372744  MODERN BRITISH
£26–£46

Spencers has expanded, taking over the ground floor of the next-door bakery. The same food is served in both downstairs brasserie and upstairs dining room (and indeed in the branch at nearby Petersfield), with fish much to the fore: perhaps monkfish with olives, tomatoes and Moroccan spices, or grilled Dover sole with a seaweed version of tartare sauce. There are few frills or extras, and although the food rarely sets the pulse racing, it is wholesome with no-nonsense presentation and fair prices, satisfying one couple with main courses of sauté oak-smoked fillet steak (served with whole-grain mustard mash), and venison and wild mushroom bourguignonne. Finish with a glazed lemon tart, or fresh fruit vacherin with glazed zabaglione cream, and drink from a short list that starts with French and Australian house wines at £11.50 (£2.30 a glass).

CHEF: Denis Spencer  PROPRIETORS: Denis and Lesley Spencer, and Mike and Sue Mulchrone  OPEN: Mon to Sat 12 to 2, 6 to 10.30  CLOSED: 25 and 26 Dec  MEALS: alc (main courses £8 to £14). Set L and D 6 to 7 £7.45 (2 courses)  SERVICE: not inc  CARDS: Amex, Delta, Diners, MasterCard, Switch, Visa  DETAILS: 64 seats. Private parties: 30 main room, 8 to 10 private rooms. Vegetarian meals. No-smoking area. Music. Air-conditioned (£5)

# 36 on the Quay ♥ ⅋✻

47 South Street, Emsworth PO10 7EG
TEL: (01243) 375592   FAX: (01243) 375593
WEBSITE: www.36onthequay.co.uk

COOKING **6**
MODERN EUROPEAN
£34–£72

Down by the water's edge, amid a lemon-yellow and slaty greyish-blue colour scheme, the Farthings continue to serve up their intricate and appealing food. 'I was amazed at the complexity his dishes have now achieved,' summed up one who had not tasted them for some time. Local fish and game feature, perhaps as sliced loin of rabbit with wild mushrooms and a cep sauce, or as pan-fried sea bass on stir-fry vegetables with curry oil and mussel cream.

Saucing is a strength, helping to draw the elements of a dish together: a chicken reduction, for example, to accompany seared dived scallops with their salad of crisp Parma ham, caramelised apple, pesto potato and aubergine caviar. Other engaging partnerships include veal medallion and sweetbread with a potato and truffle oil risotto, and steamed cannelloni of crab and salmon served with tempura langoustines and a vanilla-flavoured shellfish sauce.

Hot mango and lime soufflé with fresh raspberries and sweet biscuit spirals gets the thumbs up, as does genial service from Karen Farthing and her team. The wine list shouts 'serious' with its preponderance of big names from Bordeaux and Burgundy. There are some good bottles from south-west France, an interesting (but pricey) selection of 'rare American finds' and a fair selection of dessert wines. The house selection of a dozen, all below £20, is certainly cheaper but won't set pulses racing.

CHEFS: Ramon Farthing and Steven Midgley   PROPRIETORS: Ramon and Karen Farthing   OPEN: Tue to Fri L 12 to 1.45, Mon to Sat D 7 to 9.45   CLOSED: 1 week end Oct, 25 and 26 Dec, first 3 weeks Jan   MEALS: Set L £16.95 (2 courses) to £36.95, Set D £36.95 to £44.95   SERVICE: not inc CARDS: Amex, Delta, Diners, MasterCard, Switch, Visa   DETAILS: 41 seats. 8 seats outside. Private parties: 37 main room, 8 to 11 private rooms. Car park. Children's helpings. No smoking in dining room. Wheelchair access (not WC). Occasional music

## EPWORTH  North Lincolnshire                                   map 9

# Epworth Tap ♥ ⅋✻ £

9–11 Market Place, Epworth DN9 1EU
TEL: (01427) 873333   FAX: (01427) 873333 and 872135
EMAIL: epworthtap@which.net
WEBSITE: www.theepworthtap.co.uk
3m S of M180 junction 2

COOKING **3**
MODERN EUROPEAN
£23–£46

For years, this converted private residence has been doing great service as a little village wine bar with church pew seating and candles on wooden tables. On the food front, the menu follows a broadly European path, although there are occasional influences from the Orient in, say, duck spring roll with spicy dressings. Otherwise, expect starters such as game terrine with chutney, or modern-sounding pan-fried scallops with cauliflower compote and a white raisin and caper dressing. To follow, you might go for traditional liver with onions, fisherman's pie, or perhaps loin of lamb with ratatouille vegetables, tomato farci and rosemary. Finish with classic lemon tart, or pear and almond clafoutis with honey and whisky ice cream. Arrive before 7.15 on Wednesday or Thursday to take advantage of reduced 'early-call prices'.

Many of the wines are priced under £25, making the eclectic list a fertile hunting ground for diners on the lookout for value. Quality is pretty high too, and a short 'fine wine selection' lists some well-chosen bottles from France, Italy, Spain and California. Bottle prices start at £11.50 for French Colombard and £12 for Spanish Garnacha.

CHEF: Christopher Randle-Bissel   PROPRIETORS: Gail Perry and Simon Cliff   OPEN: Wed to Sat D only 6.30 to 9.30   MEALS: alc (main courses £9.50 to £16). Set D Wed and Thur 6.30 to 7.15 £10 (1 course) to £17.50   SERVICE: not inc, card slips closed   CARDS: Delta, MasterCard, Switch, Visa   DETAILS: 56 seats. Private parties: 20 main room, 2 to 26 private rooms. Vegetarian meals. No smoking in dining room. Music   £5

## ERMINGTON Devon                                                         map 1

## ▲ Plantation House, Matisse ⅚✳            NEW ENTRY

Totnes Road, Ermington PL21 9NS
TEL: (01548) 831100   FAX: (01548) 831248
EMAIL: enquiries@plantationhousehotel.com
WEBSITE: www.plantationhousehotel.com

COOKING 5
MODERN EUROPEAN
£33–£56

The dining room of this eighteenth-century rectory turned small yellow hotel is named after Matisse, who would surely approve of the riot of colour his prints create on the walls. Add to that classical music overlaid with marine sound-effects (breaking waves, gulls crying in a howling gale), and clearly this restaurant sees itself as not quite run-of-the-mill. Faultlessly knowledgeable staff add gravitas.

Many of the kitchen team, including senior chef David Jones, came from the Carved Angel at Dartmouth (see entry). The cooking style is old-school fine dining, with plenty of extras, including the cup-o'-soup taster (velouté of Jerusalem artichoke at inspection). Dishes look intricate, julienne vegetables and skinned broad beans accompanying a first course of crunchy-topped scallops, the corals battered and deep-fried, all resting in a pool of deep-flavoured creamy fish sauce. Crab from Start Bay is dressed and pressed, then served with avocado, calamari and red pepper cream. Seasoning is vigorous, threatening to unbalance an otherwise well-executed main course of Gressingham duck with its mousse of foie gras, roasted pear and sherry vinegar jus. A tartlet topped with a batter-based clafoutis mixture incorporating peach struck one reporter as a good idea, well-served by the contrasting honey and ginger ice cream and surrounding wreath of raspberry coulis and lime honey.

The wine list is divided into Plantation, Classic and New World Connoisseurs' selections, the last group being where most excitement lies. Prices are on the high side, but the Plantation selection (effectively house wines) offer a good choice between £14.50 and £21.

CHEFS: David Jones and Ashley Hatton   PROPRIETOR: Helen Coby   OPEN: all week 12 to 2.30, 7 to 9.30   MEALS: alc L (main courses £9 to £13). Set D £26.50 (2 courses) to £33   SERVICE: not inc, card slips closed   CARDS: Amex, Delta, MasterCard, Switch, Visa   DETAILS: 40 seats. 20 seats outside. Private parties: 40 main room. Car park. Vegetarian meals. Children's helpings. No smoking in dining room. Wheelchair access (not WC). Music ACCOMMODATION: 12 rooms. TV. Phone. B&B £60 to £120. Rooms for disabled. Baby facilities (£5)

---

## EXETER Devon                                                          map 1

# Brazz 🍴 £

10–12 Palace Gate, Exeter EX1 1JA
TEL: (01392) 252525    FAX: (01392) 253045                        COOKING 2
EMAIL: enquiries@brazz.co.uk                              BRITISH BRASSERIE
WEBSITE: www.brazz.co.uk                                         £26–£49

Stylish Brazz takes up two floors, linked by a huge winding staircase, with a vast aquarium full of brightly coloured fish set into a central pillar. It pulls in a hip crowd of 20-, 30- and even 40-somethings and is modern, bright, jazzy, fun and comfortable, with a happy atmosphere. The food is an appealing brasserie mix, taking in Caesar salad, calf's liver, braised lamb shank, bangers and mash, salmon fishcakes with creamed leeks, and many more dishes in like vein. Although the cooking can be patchy, it has a hearty, likeable and enthusiastic streak. What it lacks in sophistication it makes up for in simple enjoyment, producing the sort of things people might knock up at home for supper, such as soft, flavourful mushrooms in a rich creamy sauce, piled on to small rounds of toasted baguette, or half a dozen big, fresh, moist sardines, with a gremolata-type sauce full of tiny capers spooned over, and some flavour-packed buttered new potatoes.

Cathedral pudding, with its 45p donation to Exeter Cathedral Music Foundation, is worth having: light, fluffy and creamy, it consists of layers of chocolate mousse and different shades of sponge built into a square tower, with thin, crisp biscuit 'windows' poked into the sides. Service is efficient and friendly, wines are well treated – check out the selection by the glass – and other drinks include a wheat beer blended with mangoes and peaches (try it with dessert). House French is £10.95.

CHEF: Craig Gray    PROPRIETOR: The English Brasserie Company    OPEN: all week 12 to 3, 6 to 10.30 (11 Fri and Sat)    CLOSED: 25 Dec    MEALS: alc (main courses £9 to £15). Set D £12.95 (2 courses)    SERVICE: 10% (optional), card slips closed    CARDS: Amex, Delta, Diners, MasterCard, Switch, Visa    DETAILS: 160 seats. Private parties: 100 main room. Vegetarian meals. Children's helpings. Wheelchair access (also WC). Music. Air-conditioned

---

# ▲ Michael Caines at Royal Clarence 🍷 ⁎✶

Cathedral Yard, Exeter EX1 1HD
TEL: (01392) 310031    FAX: (01392) 310032                        COOKING 5
EMAIL: tables@michaelcaines.com                                     FRENCH
WEBSITE: www.michaelcaines.com                                  £31–£69

Modern, comfortable and quiet, despite an often bustling cathedral green outside, this smartly appointed yet informal restaurant brings a sense of cosmopolitan assurance to its food. Comparisons with Gidleigh Park, where Michael Caines cooks (see entry, Chagford), are hardly valid given the different set-ups, but the kitchen here is not short on ambition. Its contemporary French-inspired repertoire, based on fine materials, is loyal to some classic combinations: roast pheasant with lentils and boudin noir, calf's liver with sage and onion purée, and pan-fried sea bass on braised fennel.

Although reports are mixed, positive ones outweigh the rest, and among highlights have been duck terrine, steak and chips, and 'impeccable' honeyed duck. Despite a few minor excursions – into wild mushroom risotto with white truffle oil, or scallop and crab mousse with lemon-grass and ginger sauce – it is the classic French foundation that seems to keep the cooking on course, including fine pastry work, for example in an onion tartlet with poached egg and balsamic.

Desserts are good enough to 'put many places to shame', taking in a dark chocolate tart with coffee ice cream, and a mille-feuille of walnut nougatine and chestnut mousse, served with preserved fruits in a spicy syrup. Service continues to have its ups and downs, value is considered good, and a varietally organised wine list offers much of interest for those with a little over £20 to spend. As well as a short fine wine section, there are French and Chilean house varietals for £13.50 (also available in two glass sizes).

CHEF: Jean-Marc Zanetti   PROPRIETOR: Michael Caines   OPEN: all week 12 to 2.30, 7 to 10 MEALS: alc D (main courses £14 to £22). Set L £16.50 (2 courses) to £19.50   SERVICE: not inc CARDS: Amex, Delta, Diners, MasterCard, Switch, Visa   DETAILS: 76 seats. Private parties: 76 main room, 30 to 120 private rooms. Vegetarian meals. Children's helpings. No smoking in dining room. Wheelchair access (also WC). No music. No mobile phones. Air-conditioned ACCOMMODATION: 56 rooms, all with bath/shower. TV. Phone. Room only £65 to £150. Baby facilities  (£5)

---

# ▲ St Olaves Hotel  ⅝✳

Mary Arches Street, Exeter EX4 3AZ
TEL: (01392) 217736   FAX: (01392) 413054
EMAIL: info@olaves.co.uk
WEBSITE: www.olaves.co.uk

COOKING 4
MODERN BRITISH
£31–£47

This is an intimate venue in the centre of Exeter, the sort of place to cherish for a peaceful romantic night out, or perhaps even a discreet business meal. The carte has been replaced with set-price menus, a sacrifice of breadth for depth that allows the kitchen to focus on detail, although there is still a good range of appealing dishes on offer. Starters take in grilled trout with pesto potato salad, alongside sweetbread and chicken terrine with red cabbage, or steamed crab sausage with couscous and caviar. 'Classic cuisine with a modern twist' is how they describe their style: a fair assessment of main courses such as pan-fried duck breast with sweetcorn potato cakes, or black bream with saffron mash, cherry tomatoes and basil cream. Treacle tart with lemon-curd ice cream, or white chocolate parfait with broken-hazelnut sugar are typical desserts. A light menu of simpler fare is offered as an alternative at lunchtime. Four house selections at £14.50 are among the few offerings under £20 on the largely French wine list.

CHEF: Michael Davies   PROPRIETORS: Sebastian and Philippa Hughes   OPEN: all week 12 to 2, 7 to 9.30   MEALS: Set L £15 (2 courses) to £19, Set D £21 (2 courses) to £25. Light L menu also available all week   SERVICE: not inc, card slips closed   CARDS: Amex, Delta, MasterCard, Switch, Visa   DETAILS: 40 seats. 20 seats outside. Private parties: 50 main room, 2 to 12 private rooms. Car park. Vegetarian meals. Children's helpings. No smoking in dining room. No music. No mobile phones  ACCOMMODATION: 15 rooms, all with bath/shower. TV. Phone. B&B £60 to £115. Rooms for disabled. Baby facilities (*The Which? Hotel Guide*)  £5

## FARNBOROUGH Kent                                          map 3

# Chapter One

Farnborough Common, Locksbottom,
Farnborough BR6 8NF                                          COOKING 4
TEL: (01689) 854848   FAX: (01689) 858439                    MODERN EUROPEAN
WEBSITE: www.chaptersrestaurants.co.uk                       £32–£62

A former pub in the Locksbottom district of Farnborough, Chapter One (for sibling Chapter Two, in London, see entry) serves a diverse menu to an enthusiastic local following. The half-timbered building might need a lick of paint inside, but there's nothing flaky about Andrew McLeish's cooking. He does rely rather a lot on foie gras and truffles for effect, and the menu's price supplements are not endearing, but presentations are painstaking, with stacks and drizzles prominent.

Underpinning all is a culinary intelligence that delivers a pumpkin and vanilla soup of come-hither texture, a 'meltingly creamy and well-seasoned' ballottine of salmon on a bed of buttery leeks, and main courses such as pancetta-wrapped saddle of rabbit, with a confit of the leg and a sauce made with Gewurztraminer. Vegetarian dishes are well conceived – witness a mousse-stuffed globe artichoke heart with layered vegetables and pasta, offered in May – while roast brill with ceps, Jerusalem artichoke and onion purée shows a successfully nerveless approach to fish cookery. Desserts have included a beautifully loose-textured pannacotta with chocolate dentelle and alcohol-soaked griottines, and the Continental cheeses (no waiting staff could identify them) served with chutney and warm raisin bread are kept in excellent condition.

Wines are listed in no particular order, not even price, which makes things rather confusing, but perseverance reveals some good growers and vintages; prices are toughish, though. House Italian is £13.50.

CHEF: Andrew McLeish   PROPRIETOR: Selective Restaurants Group   OPEN: all week 12 to 2.30 (3 Sun), 6.30 to 10 (9.30 Sun)   CLOSED: 1 to 3 Jan   MEALS: alc D (main courses £14.50). Set L £16 (2 courses) to £19.50. Brasserie menu available Mon to Sat L   SERVICE: 12.5% (optional), card slips closed   CARDS: Amex, Delta, Diners, MasterCard, Switch, Visa   DETAILS: 120 seats. Private parties: 20 to 55 private rooms. Car park. Vegetarian meals. Children's helpings. No cigars/pipes in dining room. Wheelchair access (not WC). Music. Air-conditioned  £5

---

*'Not being a vegetarian, I wasn't sure what to expect. I thought that, since the main course consisted of vegetables, they might give us a side dish with a tiny bit of grilled steak or a small lamb chop, but they didn't. We just got more vegetables.'*
(On eating in a vegetarian restaurant)

---

# ▲ Museum Inn

Farnham DT11 8DE
TEL: (01725) 516261   FAX: (01725) 516988
EMAIL: themuseuminn@supanet.com
WEBSITE: www.museuminn.co.uk                                    COOKING 5
from A354, 6m NE of Blandford Forum, turn N for          MODERN EUROPEAN
Farnham                                                                   £27–£58

This restaurant seems to have a clear and unusual philosophy: encourage customers to enjoy themselves. The trick is worked by treating them with happy, unforced politeness, making them feel at home in an interesting and friendly architectural space, and feeding them good food and wine cheerfully, knowledgeably and at a reasonable price. It may seem astonishing that such an obviously sensible approach needs comment, but sadly it does.

The dining room of the seventeenth-century building is a converted stable block, opened up into a white and airy space that operates only three sessions a week (though the main pub operates normal hours, and bar food is always available). There is much overlap between the two menus, and anybody stumbling innocently on food of this quality in a bar will be more than pleasantly surprised. A substantial cube of lush, caramelly foie gras comes with a well-balanced apple compote (on garlic-rubbed brioche), and a terrine of ham knuckle, duck and mushroom has a scoop of mustardy grated celeriac and a chutney relish.

There is no stinting on protein, either: from a huge, rare, marbled chargrilled ribeye, to even huger duck breasts (40DD by one estimate) served in chunks (not sliced and fanned) to preserve the juices, with 'great crispy skin' peppered and lightly honeyed. Desserts may be nurseryish – creamed rice pudding, steamed syrup sponge – but have also included plum fritters in a light batter with Christmas pudding ice cream and Bailey's custard. Varied, well-chosen, sensibly priced wines starts with French house red and white at £9.95.

CHEF: Mark Treasure   PROPRIETORS: Vicky Elliot and Mark Stephenson   OPEN: Sun L 12 to 3, Fri and Sat D 7 to 9.30   CLOSED: 25 Dec and D 31 Dec   MEALS: alc D Fri and Sat (main courses £13 to £18). Set L Sun £14.95 (2 courses) to £17.95. Bar menu available all week   SERVICE: not inc, card slips closed   CARDS: MasterCard, Switch, Visa   DETAILS: 40 seats. 44 seats outside. Private parties: 40 main room. Car park. Vegetarian meals. No children under 5. No smoking before 10pm. Wheelchair access (also WC). No music. No mobile phones   ACCOMMODATION: 8 rooms, all with bath/shower. TV. Phone. B&B £55 to £120. Rooms for disabled. No children under 5 (The Which? Hotel Guide) £5

*If customers are asked to switch off mobile phones while in a restaurant, this is noted in the details at the end of an entry.*

£5 *indicates that the restaurant has elected to participate in the* Good Food Guide *voucher scheme. For full details, see page 6.*

# ▲ Read's 🍾

Macknade Manor, Canterbury Road,
Faversham ME13 8XE
TEL: (01795) 535344   FAX: (01795) 591200                    COOKING 6
WEBSITE: www.reads.com                                    MODERN BRITISH
on A2 Canterbury road, ½m E of Faversham                      £33–£70

Reached along a short gravel driveway, the Georgian house stands above the road, fronted by a large green with magnificent trees. Uncluttered décor and low-key creams and yellows set the tone for some distinctly un-trendy cooking, based around a wordy menu that gives a fair idea of just how busy some of the dishes can be. There is usually a three-way starter, for example, perhaps of duck consommé, a well-balanced smoked duck salad (with apple, celery and hazelnuts), and a smooth, rich duck parfait.

The gardens include half an acre given over to vegetables, herbs, salads and fruits; other vegetables come from a local farm shop, and fish from Whitstable and Hythe: perhaps 'outstanding' sea bass, precisely timed, on a bed of shredded leeks. Smoked fish is a favoured ingredient, with eel, salmon and haddock all providing starters for a summer menu. And the combination of smoked haddock with cheese is another leitmotif, perhaps appearing as a rich, expertly made Montgomery Cheddar soufflé on a smoked haddock sauce.

Seasonal fare includes a spring dish of well-trimmed and remarkably tender Kentish lamb cutlets, the plate strewn with morels and accompanied by asparagus, spinach, an artichoke heart stuffed with minced lamb, creamy dauphinois potato and a rich sauce. Another visitor, in summer, enjoyed a dish of lamb, lamb, lamb, lamb and lamb, combining best end, saddle, fillet, rump and kidneys. The food can be more elaborate than it needs to be, and while individual components of dishes are typically well rendered, the whole may not always amount to more than the sum of its parts. This is nevertheless accomplished cooking, deploying a wide range of skills, not least among desserts. The selection plate might bring an intense blackcurrant sorbet, a wobbly vanilla and rum pannacotta with stewed fruits, a crisp-topped lemon crème brûlée, a chocolate marquise and a meringue swan.

Service is 'very formal, very French', and a tail-coated sommelier oversees the wines, which appear on a rather formal but clearly laid out list. French wines – red Bordeaux and red and white Burgundy in particular – get top billing. The claret is fairly priced, although more mature bottles can be expensive. New World producers are carefully selected, and there's plenty to choose from beyond Cabernet Sauvignon and Chardonnay. A 'best buys' section lists 63 wines, all but one under £25, for those who want to keep an eye on the purse strings. Six house wines sell for £16.

CHEF: David Pitchford   PROPRIETORS: Rona and David Pitchford   OPEN: Tue to Sat 12 to 2, 7 to 9.30   CLOSED: bank hols   MEALS: Set L £19.50 to £42, Set D £42   SERVICE: not inc, card slips closed   CARDS: Amex, Delta, Diners, MasterCard, Switch, Visa   DETAILS: 40 seats. 12 seats outside. Private parties: 60 main room, 4 to 30 private rooms. Car park. Children's helpings. No cigars/pipes in dining room. Wheelchair access (also WC). No music. No mobile phones   ACCOMMODATION: 6 rooms, all with bath/shower. TV. Phone. B&B £95 to £150. Baby facilities (*The Which? Hotel Guide*)  £5

## FERRENSBY  North Yorkshire                                              map 9

## ▲ General Tarleton  ✸

Boroughbridge Road, Ferrensby HG5 0PZ
TEL: (01423) 340284   FAX: (01423) 340288                    COOKING 5
EMAIL: gti@generaltarleton.co.uk                            MODERN BRITISH
WEBSITE: www.generaltarleton.co.uk                             £24–£54

This 250-year-old coaching inn comes in two parts. One is a white-painted brick
and pebbledash pub, the other a stone-built dining room with beams, prints and
sharp lighting; both are relaxed, informal and full of people enjoying
themselves. Several dishes appear on the menus in each, from the long-
running seafood-filled filo pastry 'moneybags' to Goosnargh duckling and
Aberdeen Angus ribeye steak, although where the bar-brasserie might offer a
plate of Lishman's pork and chive sausages and mash, the restaurant prefers
roast leg of Yorkshire Dales lamb with roast garlic and thyme jus.

The kitchen comes up with some interesting combinations, such as black
pudding with smoked haddock and grain mustard sauce, alongside more
traditional slow-braised pork on parsnip mash. The cooking standard has
wobbled a bit over the year, but John Topham is now back cooking full time.
Sticky toffee pudding and crème brûlée confirm the traditional approach to
desserts; service is efficient and courteous, and an early-bird set dinner menu
helps to cut the cost. A dozen or so wines by the glass (house Vin de Pays d'Oc is
£11.50, or £2 a glass) introduce a French-dominated list (try Dagueneau's
Pouilly-Fumé 2000) that has something for most pockets and tastes.

CHEF: John Topham   PROPRIETORS: John Topham and Denis Watkins   OPEN: Sun L 12 to 1.45,
Mon to Sat D 6 to 9.30   MEALS: alc D (main courses £9.75 to £17.50). Set L Sun £17.50, Set D
Mon to Fri 6 to 7pm £10 (2 courses, £14 with wine) to £14 (£17.50 with wine). Bar/brasserie menu
also available   SERVICE: not inc   CARDS: Amex, MasterCard, Switch, Visa   DETAILS: 150 seats.
30 seats outside. Private parties: 30 main room, 15 to 40 private rooms. Car park. Vegetarian
meals. Children's helpings. No smoking in dining room. Wheelchair access (not WC). No music
ACCOMMODATION: 14 rooms, all with bath/shower. TV. Phone. B&B £75 to £85. Rooms for
disabled

## FOTHERINGHAY  Northamptonshire                                        map 6

## Falcon  ♟ ✸  £

Fotheringhay PE8 5HZ
TEL: (01832) 226254                                           COOKING 2
FAX: (01832) 226046                        MODERN EUROPEAN/MEDITERRANEAN
off A605, 4m NE of Oundle                                      £25–£49

Built of pale stone, like most of this neat, well-kept village, the Falcon aims to
keep a wide range of customers happy with its combination of bar, dining room,
conservatory and garden. The 'eat whatever you like' approach certainly helps,
as does the upbeat treatment of materials. Few opportunities are lost to add a
vibrant dash of flavour: a spicy fishcake with chilli, spring onion and coriander
salsa, or crispy duck spring rolls with Asian coleslaw in a sweet-and-sour
dressing. Elsewhere mustard (in a sauce for chicken) and horseradish (in the
mash for daube of beef) do a similar job.

The search for popularity takes in beer-battered fish and chips with tartare sauce, and grilled rump steak, also with chips, while desserts range from a conventional caramelised lemon tart to a less usual chocolate pot with pear chutney. The wine list successfully aims to offer 'wines of character and individuality'. Organised by style, there is a wide-ranging selection of grape varieties from quality producers throughout the winemaking world. Mark-ups are sensible and there is plenty of choice at £20 or below. A selection of 'top class' reds and whites includes classics from the Old and New Worlds. A dozen or so well-chosen house wines sell for £11.50 to £23 (£2.80 to £5.75 per glass). The Falcon is a member of the Huntsbridge Group, which also includes the Old Bridge at Huntington, the Pheasant at Keyston and the Three Horseshoes at Madingley (see entries).

CHEF: Ray Smikle   PROPRIETORS: John Hoskins and Ray Smikle   OPEN: all week 12 to 2.15, 6 to 9.30 (7 Sun)   MEALS: alc (main courses £9.50 to £16.50). Set L Mon to Sat £11 (2 courses) to £14.75   SERVICE: not inc   CARDS: Amex, Diners, MasterCard, Switch, Visa   DETAILS: 60 seats. 30 seats outside. Private parties: 60 main room, 10 to 34 private rooms. Car park. Vegetarian meals. Children's helpings. No smoking in dining room. No music

## FRAMPTON MANSELL  Gloucestershire                              map 2

# White Horse  £                                    | NEW ENTRY |

Cirencester Road, Frampton Mansell GL6 8HZ
TEL:  (01285) 760960                                             COOKING 2
on A419 7m W of Cirencester, beside turning to              MODERN ENGLISH
Frampton Mansell                                                 £25–£44

An old stone building on the A419 beside a filling station, the White Hart – a new venture by Emma and Shaun Davis (ex Hare and Hounds, Foss Cross) – has a relaxed, food-based gastro-pub tone, and chef Howard Matthews's short, contemporary, daily-changing menu 'combines trad and trendy'. Pigeon breast with pea purée, crisp bacon and mint and caper dressing might open proceedings, with lamb's sweetbreads and well-timed kidneys with chorizo, roast garlic and thyme jus to follow. For a simple finish, try poached rhubarb with vanilla ice cream.

The interior has been revamped on an open plan – so non-smokers beware, especially as cigars are sold at the bar – and walls are hung with a mix of paintings and sepia photographs of India. Tables with upholstered chairs are attended by Emma, who runs front of house with 'much efficiency and charm'. A simple, reasonably-priced wine list, organised by style, starts with Spanish Tempranillo at £10.75 (£2.90 a glass).

CHEF: Howard Matthews   PROPRIETORS: Emma and Shaun Davis   OPEN: all week L 12 to 2.30, Mon to Sat D 7 to 9.45   MEALS: alc (main courses £9 to £14). Light L menu also available   SERVICE: not inc   CARDS: Delta, MasterCard, Switch, Visa   DETAILS: 45 seats. 40 seats outside. Private parties: 45 main room. Car park. Vegetarian meals. Children's helpings. No music

*If a restaurant is new to the Guide this year (did not appear as a main entry in the last edition),* NEW ENTRY *appears opposite its name.*

## FRITHSDEN  Hertfordshire
map 3

# Alford Arms  £

Frithsden HP1 3DD
TEL: (01442) 864480   FAX: (01442) 876893

COOKING **2**
MODERN BRITISH
£24–£44

Frithsden amounts to little more than a few pretty houses around a small green, much of which can be taken up with parked cars when this cream-painted pub gets busy. Relaxed, casual and plainly decorated, it is 'the kind of place you'd be more than happy to take anyone, from your mum to your best mate', with a board advertising daily specials to supplement the printed menu. 'Small plates' enable anyone to make a meal of dolcelatte and fig tart, or crab and coriander cakes with sweet chilli relish, while main meals take in anything from halloumi and vegetable kebabs, through roast cod with chorizo, to braised lamb shank or oxtail. Desserts run to lemon crème brûlée, and warm chocolate brownie, and most of the wines on the short, reasonably priced list are available in two glass sizes, starting with house Vin de Pays de l'Aude at £9.75 (£2.45 and £3.25 a glass).

CHEF: Damien Ng   PROPRIETORS: David and Becky Salisbury   OPEN: all week 12 to 2.30 (3 Sun), 7 to 10   CLOSED: 25 and 26 Dec   MEALS: alc (main courses £9 to £13)   SERVICE: not inc   CARDS: Amex, Delta, MasterCard, Switch, Visa   DETAILS: 67 seats. 82 seats outside. Car park. Vegetarian meals. Children's helpings. Music

## FUNTINGTON  West Sussex
map 3

# Hallidays  ⚡✗

Watery Lane, Funtington PO18 9LF
TEL: (01243) 575331

COOKING **2**
MODERN BRITISH
£24–£49

It feels like 'the sitting room of a Victorian farm worker's cottage', observed a correspondent after eating at these low-ceilinged, centuries-old thatched premises. Green china bunnies are neatly arranged on a windowsill, but the short menu is a little more contemporary, taking in tempura of Thai prawns with peppery jam and sour cream, as well as honey-glazed duck with orange and five-spice. Chef Andy Stephenson seeks out local produce assiduously, and the restaurant now has its own smokehouse for hickory-cured salmon (served with cucumber pickle and a dill and horseradish mayonnaise). Reporters have also enjoyed 'healthy-looking' nettle soup, and confit of duck with braised red cabbage, while puddings, such as poached pear in pastry 'leaves' with hazelnut butterscotch sauce, are 'pleasant enough'. Service is 'earnest and hard-working', rather than friendly. Around 80 wines keep prices within most people's budgets, but investigate the 'premiere selection' if you're feeling flush. House wines start at £9.75.

CHEF: Andy Stephenson   PROPRIETORS: Andy Stephenson and Peter Creech   OPEN: Wed to Fri and Sun L 12 to 1.30, Wed to Sat D 7 to 9   CLOSED: first 2 weeks Mar, first week Sept   MEALS: alc (main courses £13 to £16.50). Set L Wed to Fri £12.50 (2 courses) to £14.50, Set L Sun £16.50

SERVICE: not inc   CARDS: Delta, MasterCard, Switch, Visa   DETAILS: 28 seats. Private parties: 20 main room. Car park. No smoking in dining room. Wheelchair access (also women's WC). No music

## GATESHEAD  Tyne & Wear                                           map 10

## ▲ Eslington Villa  ⚡✕

8 Station Road, Low Fell, Gateshead NE9 6DR
TEL: (0191) 487 6017   FAX: (0191) 420 0666
leave A1(M) at Team Valley Trading Estate,                  COOKING 3
approach Gateshead along Team Valley; at top              ANGLO-FRENCH
of Eastern Avenue, turn left into Station Road               £23–£49

Head north on the A1 out of town, making sure you don't miss Antony Gormley's *Angel of the North* as you go, and in the Low Fell area of town this rather imposing hotel set in its own grounds looms before you. As well as the dining room in the original house, there is another in a glassed-in veranda with good views across the Team Valley. The new head chef is David Kennedy, who worked at 21 Queen Street, Newcastle, but Barry Forster continues to oversee the menus. These deal in tried and tested favourites, such as roast lamb with potato gratin, and chargrilled sirloin with béarnaise, but there are one or two more inventive touches too. A tian of crab is appealingly partnered with a gazpacho dressing and a Parmesan crisp for one first course, while the oriental notes in spiced breast of duck include sesame, coriander and a crisp spring roll filled with leg meat. Espresso granita adds raciness to an otherwise run-of-the-mill chocolate mousse served in a glass, vanilla pannacotta is accompanied by blueberry compote, and pink grapefruit sorbet is sloshed with Campari. A kindly priced wine list is judiciously spread between Old and New Worlds. France, Australia and Chile provide the house wines, the first £11.50, the other two £13.50.

CHEFS: Barry Forster and David Kennedy   PROPRIETORS: Nick and Melanie Tulip   OPEN: Sun to Fri L 12 to 1.45, Mon to Sat D 7 to 9.45   CLOSED: Christmas, bank hols   MEALS: alc (main courses £13 to £17). Set L £11.50 (2 courses) to £13.50, Set D Mon to Fri £18.50   SERVICE: not inc   CARDS: Amex, Delta, Diners, MasterCard, Switch, Visa   DETAILS: 85 seats. 15 seats outside. Private parties: 85 main room, 2 to 36 private rooms. Car park. Vegetarian meals. Children's helpings. No smoking in dining room. Wheelchair access (not WC). Music   ACCOMMODATION: 17 rooms, all with bath/shower. TV. Phone. B&B £54.50 to £69.50. Baby facilities (*The Which? Hotel Guide*)

---

*The Guide always appreciates hearing about changes of chef or owner.*

*All details are as accurate as possible at the time of going to press, but chefs and owners often change, and it is wise to check by telephone before making a special journey. Many readers have been disappointed when set-price bargain meals are no longer available. Ask when booking.*

## ▲ Stock Hill 🍴✦

Stock Hill, Gillingham SP8 5NR
TEL: (01747) 823626   FAX: (01747) 825628
EMAIL: reception@stockhillhouse.co.uk
WEBSITE: www.stockhillhouse.co.uk
off B3081, 1m W of Gillingham

COOKING 5
MODERN EUROPEAN
£34–£57

A life-sized statue of a wild boar amid tall trees is the first indication of the Hausers' unusual taste, followed soon afterwards by their very personal and sometimes whimsical approach to décor. Powder-pink walls are covered in ornate gold-framed mirrors and paintings, and there are lots of warm, floral fabrics, as well as colourfully painted wooden carvings of animals.

Peter Hauser's Austrian background is recognisable (one couple enjoyed wiener schnitzel), although he doesn't aim to, as it were, force it down people's throats. Rather he takes an international approach, happy to deal in such modern staples as seared scallops with black pudding and minted pea purée, or to take a detour via North Africa into black bream fillet on fennel tagine spiked with cumin and harissa. Among other interesting materials are home-cured ox tongue filled with horseradish, then breadcrumbed and shallow-fried, and Dorset roe deer served with a Bohemian bread dumpling.

'We are very heavy on game during the winter months,' write the Hausers, 'and Viennese desserts all year round', among which might be kalter schönbrunner reis mit hollerester, or malakoff torte auf beeren zaft. Not all reports on the food are complimentary, and the atmosphere has varied from 'friendly and cheerful' to 'glacial', but most find Nita Hauser pleasant and courteous, and service well regulated. The wine list is in the process of being overhauled, step by step, and has plenty to offer those with a budget of £20 to £30 (a trio of Austrian wines falls into this category). Otherwise, house wines start around £16.

CHEFS: Peter Hauser and Lorna Connor   PROPRIETORS: Peter and Nita Hauser   OPEN: Sun to Fri L 12.15 to 1.30, all week D 7.15 to 8.30   MEALS: Set L £22 to £25, Set D £35   SERVICE: not inc, card slips closed   CARDS: MasterCard, Switch, Visa   DETAILS: 24 seats. 8 seats outside. Private parties: 24 main room, 6 to 12 private rooms. Car park. Vegetarian meals. Children's helpings. No smoking in dining room. No music. No mobile phones   ACCOMMODATION: 9 rooms, all with bath/shower. TV. Phone. D,B&B £120 to £290 (*The Which? Hotel Guide*)

## ▲ Combe House 🍴✦

Gittisham EX14 3AD
TEL: (01404) 540400
EMAIL: stay@thishotel.com
WEBSITE: www.thishotel.com
1½m off A30, 2m SW of Honiton

COOKING 3
MODERN BRITISH
£32–£57

Playing the 'romantic' card for all it's worth, and with facilities for weddings, meetings and corporate hospitality, this Elizabethan manor house on a 3,500-acre estate makes a pretty picture indeed. It feels 'warts and all' old (not just modernised old, despite a revamped Victorian cooking range in the old kitchen, to be used for special events), the dining room boasting a moulded ceiling, elaborately carved fireplace and splendid views over the fields. Philip Leach's style is beguiling, neatly contrasting some ingenuity in starters with more straightforward treatment of main courses. Begin, perhaps, with a black truffle boudin, tortellini of eel with watercress sauce, or a warm salad of tempura fried oysters with a vierge dressing.

Some country-house luxuries are evident, but so are modest materials, for example roast stuffed saddle of rabbit with Jerusalem artichoke, and braised shank of lamb with colcannon potatoes. Materials are conscientiously sourced – from day-boat fish to local beef, pork and West Country cheeses – while desserts take in poached pear with amaretto filling, and pineapple Tatin with crème fraîche ice cream. Chablis is a house favourite (it has its own list), and the traditional French range is balanced by a decent showing from the southern hemisphere. Half-bottles are plentiful, helped along by a handful of wines by the (large) glass.

CHEF: Philip Leach   PROPRIETORS: Ken and Ruth Hunt   OPEN: all week 12 to 2, 7 to 9.30   MEALS: Set L £15 (2 courses) to £19.50, Set L Sun £22.50, Set D £32.50   SERVICE: not inc, card slips closed   CARDS: Amex, Delta, Diners, MasterCard, Switch, Visa   DETAILS: 50 seats. 20 seats outside. Private parties: 30 main room, 2 to 48 private rooms. Car park. Vegetarian meals. Children's helpings. No smoking in dining room. Wheelchair access (also WC). No music. No mobile phones   ACCOMMODATION: 15 rooms, all with bath/shower. TV. Phone. B&B £75 to £265. Baby facilities. Fishing (*The Which? Hotel Guide*)

## GOLCAR  West Yorkshire                                                  map 8

## ▲ Weavers Shed  ♥ ✳ £

Knowl Road, Golcar HD7 4AN
TEL: (01484) 654284   FAX: (01484) 650980
EMAIL: info@weaversshed.co.uk
WEBSITE: www.weaversshed.co.uk
on B6111, 2m W of Huddersfield via A62

W. YORKSHIRE
GFG
2003
COMMENDED

COOKING 5
MODERN BRITISH
£20–£55

This converted cloth-finishing mill – a handsome, cleverly restored building – provides an atmospheric setting, with its flag floors, stone walls and church pew seating. It sets high standards and reaches them and, being tranquil and friendly, proved a 'therapeutic' package for one visitor. One of its strengths is the owners, whose commitment and genuine love of their job are notable, summed up as 'good Yorkshire hospitality'. Another is the slew of top-notch ingredients, including vegetables, herbs and fruit from the kitchen garden, orchard and greenhouses, and a (recently introduced) henhouse for the supply of chicken, bantam and duck eggs.

Such local sourcing is in the service of a more wide-ranging contemporary approach to cooking, which produces fulsome, highly enjoyable results with plenty of northern generosity and vigour. A substantial slice of fresh rabbit terrine, for example, is effectively partnered by pickled butternut squash, and a rich, creamy, well-rendered wild mushroom risotto is served with deep-fried sage. Accurate timing is applied across the board: to calf's liver with braised chicory and a mushroom reduction, and to beef fillet with a savoury oxtail reduction, accompanied by aligot: smooth, creamy mashed potato topped with melted cheese. Cheeses themselves are kept in good condition, and desserts have included first-rate rhubarb crumble with vanilla ice cream, and an equally successful lemon soufflé covering a base of lemon compote, served with a tingly lime sorbet. In keeping with the philosophy of the kitchen, the wine policy here is to 'concentrate on finding smaller, less well-known producers who make excellent wines in small quantities'. Bottles from south-west France take pride of place on an enterprising list that combines interest and value throughout, starting with half a dozen house wines at £10.95 (try the Italian Riesling).

CHEFS: Stephen Jackson, Robert Jones, Ian McGunnigle and Cath Sill   PROPRIETORS: Stephen and Tracy Jackson   OPEN: Tue to Fri L 12 to 2, Tue to Sat D 7 to 9 (10 Sat)   CLOSED: 25 Dec to 3 Jan   MEALS: alc (main courses £10 to £18). Set L £9.95 (2 courses) to £12.95   SERVICE: not inc   CARDS: Delta, MasterCard, Switch, Visa   DETAILS: 60 seats. Private parties: 38 main room, 26 private room. Car park. Vegetarian meals. No smoking in dining room. Music. No mobile phones   ACCOMMODATION: 5 rooms, all with bath/shower. TV. Phone. B&B £45 to £75. Rooms for disabled (*The Which? Hotel Guide*)

---

**GORING** Oxfordshire                                                          **map 2**

# Leatherne Bottel

The Bridleway, Goring RG8 0HS
TEL: (01491) 872667   FAX: (01491) 875308
EMAIL: leathernebottel@aol.com                          COOKING **4**
WEBSITE: www.leathernebottel.co.uk                    MODERN EUROPEAN
on B4009 out of Goring, 5m S of Wallingford                      £30–£59

---

A secluded riverside spot just upstream from Goring, with little but meadows and the Thames to gaze at, provides an enviable setting for this simple and amenable cottage restaurant. In fine weather there can be few more enticing places to eat than on the terrace, much improved with new decking and hardwood tables and chairs by the water's edge; at other times, the cottage-style dining room, for which redecoration is planned in early 2003, is the place to be.

Although European-based, the cooking takes naturally to some lively Eastern flavourings, including salmon and wasabi ravioli with kaffir lime sauce, and marinated venison liver with sweet-and-sour onions and a chilli and raisin jam. Slow-cooked dishes from the winter repertoire take in roast lamb shank and osso buco, the latter given a novel twist with vanilla-seed risotto and gingered sweet potato crisps, while desserts run to pistachio pannacotta, lemon tart with passion-fruit sorbet, and sticky toffee pudding. A fair quota of young antipodeans under the smooth control of Annie Bonnet help to make service relaxed and efficient, and although wines under £20 are scant, another tenner will open up the possibilities significantly. House wines from John Armit are £14.50.

CHEF: Julia Storey   PROPRIETOR: Croftchase Ltd/Annie Bonnet   OPEN: all week L 12 to 2 (3.30 Sun), Mon to Sat D 7 to 9   CLOSED: 3 weeks Jan   MEALS: alc (main courses £16.50 to £20). Set D Mon to Fri £19.50   SERVICE: 10%, card slips closed   CARDS: Amex, Delta, MasterCard, Switch, Visa   DETAILS: 50 seats. 80 seats outside. Private parties: 36 main room. Car park. Vegetarian meals. No children under 10. Wheelchair access (not WC). No music. No mobile phones   £5

# ▲ Borrowdale Gates Hotel ▼ ✺

Grange in Borrowdale CA12 5UQ
TEL: (017687) 77204   FAX: (017687) 77254
EMAIL: hotel@borrowdale-gates.com
WEBSITE: www.borrowdale-gates.com                    COOKING 3
off B5289, about 3m S of Keswick, ¼m N of           ANGLO-FRENCH
Grange                                                £27–£65

Take a long drive down a lane by the edge of Derwent Water to reach this old-fashioned country-house hotel. Evening guests may not get the benefit of dramatic views from the dining room windows that residents enjoy: a good reason, perhaps, to stay the night and catch the scenery in daylight at breakfast.

Menus are firmly set in traditional mould, complete with a less than impressive soup or sorbet before the main course, and choice is wide. A terrine of Tuscan vegetables served on crostini with tapénade has made a colourful starter, while a mousse of lemon sole in saffron sauce has been considered delicate and aromatic. Among main courses to make a favourable impact have been duck breast with prunes and celeriac mash, and the repertoire extends from pan-fried monkfish with lemon aïoli and a vermouth nage, to chargrilled ribeye with a mini steak and kidney pudding, dauphinois potatoes, and a red wine glaze. Ice creams – pecan, coffee, strawberry, and orange – get high praise, and there may also be lemon tart with raspberry coulis, or dark chocolate terrine.

Service is generally regarded as 'courteous and helpful', and the wine list proves that one can focus on France and still offer good value. Bordeaux, the Rhône and Burgundy rub shoulders with up-and-coming names from the New World. Pricing is ungreedy, leaving plenty of choice around £20 or under. Vin de table is £13.50, and a decent selection of half-bottles rounds out the list.

CHEF: Michael Heathcote   PROPRIETORS: Terry and Christine Parkinson   OPEN: all week 12.15 to 1.30, 7 to 8.45   CLOSED: Jan   MEALS: alc L Mon to Sat (main courses £7.50 to £12). Set L Sun £15.75, Set D £32.50   SERVICE: not inc   CARDS: Amex, Delta, MasterCard, Switch, Visa   DETAILS: 60 seats. 15 seats outside. Private parties: 24 main room. Car park. Vegetarian meals. Children's helpings. No children under 7 at D. No smoking in dining room. Wheelchair access (also WC). No music. No mobile phones   ACCOMMODATION: 29 rooms, all with bath/shower. TV. Phone. D,B&B £65 to £175. Rooms for disabled. Baby facilities (*The Which? Hotel Guide*)  £5

# ▲ White Moss House ▮ ✺

Rydal Water, Grasmere LA22 9SE
TEL: (015394) 35295   FAX: (015394) 35516
EMAIL: sue@whitemoss.com                            COOKING 6
WEBSITE: www.whitemoss.com                   TRADITIONAL BRITISH
on A591, at N end of Rydal Water                      £38–£46

White Moss House has been in the Guide for 30 years, and so little alters that it seems 'set in aspic'. The biggest changes, perhaps, are seasonal: those who go in winter can expect warm, welcoming fires, and help with wet boots, while spring and summer visitors can enjoy the terrace and gardens. Its colourful, high-ceilinged lounge contrasts with the cottagey dining room's bare wooden tables, and although the style (and indeed the cooking) may not be everybody's cup of tea, essentials are carefully managed. Dinner is at 8pm, and the five courses (with no choice before dessert) are well judged for quantity. The format is soup, fish, meat, pudding, and cheese.

Among soups, fennel and apple comes in for praise, and the fish course is well received, perhaps a soufflé of peat-cured haddock, or a praiseworthy trio of salmon: poached, smoked, and oak-roast. The repertoire is not large, but is likely to take in roast rack of Mansergh Hall lamb, ale-marinated fillet of Fell-bred beef, and crisp-skinned Lakeland mallard, served with a purée of salsify, celeriac, parsnip and honey, in a damson, port and Pinot Noir sauce. Steamed puddings don't change much but still get rave reviews: cabinet, huntsman's and guardsman's (combining lemon and strawberries) feature regularly. Service from Sue Dixon is efficient and friendly. Wines are equally well bred, with mature red Bordeaux being a great strength. The list is cleverly laid out, with European wines (red Bordeaux, Italian reds, etc.) as the main entries, with New World equivalents listed beneath. Producers are well chosen and mark-ups are fair, resulting in good potential for interesting drinking under £20. A 'personal selection' of seven wines (£10.95 to £19.50) is available by the glass (£2.50 to £4.75).

CHEF: Peter Dixon   PROPRIETORS: Sue and Peter Dixon   OPEN: Mon to Sat D only 8 (1 sitting) CLOSED: Dec and Jan   MEALS: Set D £29.50   SERVICE: not inc, card slips closed   CARDS: MasterCard, Switch, Visa   DETAILS: 18 seats. Private parties: 18 main room. Car park. Vegetarian meals. Children's helpings. No smoking in dining room. Wheelchair access (not WC). No music   ACCOMMODATION: 6 rooms, all with bath/shower. TV. Phone. D,B&B £65 to £184. Baby facilities. Fishing (*The Which? Hotel Guide*) (£5)

# Harry's Place ✸✳

17 High Street, Great Gonerby NG31 8JS                          COOKING 7
TEL: (01476) 561780                                             MODERN FRENCH
on B1174, 1m N of Grantham                                      £56–£84

Once a farm, this Georgian house on the main street, now with a sky-blue pebbledash façade, is a highly personal enterprise, from its tomato-red walls and miniature scale – just three pine tables – to its antique furniture and collection of old china plates. Everything about it speaks of individuality, in particular the lengths to which the Hallams go in their diligent search for quite exceptional raw materials: wild salmon from the North Esk, Orkney king scallops from a supplier in Grimbister, and live lobsters from the south Yorkshire coast. Lamb and beef come from a small West Country cooperative, the Real Meat Company, with its own abattoir, and game birds are hand-picked in feather. Throughout all dishes runs a trade mark leitmotif of exhilaratingly fresh herbs.

Such sourcing perhaps helps to justify the pricing, while Harry Hallam's single-handed approach goes a long way towards explaining the choice of just two items per course. He must spend a lot of time thinking about the composition of dishes: each item is clearly recognisable, and yet plays its part in a unified and clear-tasting whole, for example in a thickly sliced, soft-textured and full-flavoured loin of young roe deer, cooked rare (without asking), served with a light, thin sauce of white wine and Madeira pepped up with thyme and tarragon. Supporting this centrepiece at inspection were a small flat cake of onion and herb stuffing, a slice of herby black pudding, a mound of vegetables including red Camargue rice and sliced mushrooms, and a small but perfectly formed salad. That may seem excessive, but the dish turns out to be well balanced, another hallmark of the style.

The boldness of spicing and peppering, and the complexity of the cooking, can all sail close to the wind, but this gives it an edge of excitement without any suggestion that the boat will capsize. Among successes have been pink sauté chicken livers coated with a layer of sherry jelly spiked with black pepper, on a small pool of translucent Cumberland sauce flecked with minute shreds of orange zest. Also sharing the plate was a lively and highly successful salad of crunchy peas, sweetcorn, spring onions, mint, basil and lemon zest. Pepper has surfaced among desserts too: a generous sprinkling on a long white blob of yoghurt that accompanies a small round mould of clear, very wobbly, red cherry brandy jelly, served with a lightly spiced pink sauce echoing the flavour of the jelly. Everything is helped along by personable service from Caroline Hallam, and by extras such as the crusty and impeccably professional bread straight from the oven. Wine prices, as ever, come as a bit of a shock. The cheapest red on the dozen-strong list is a Chilean Pinot Noir at £29.50; wines by the glass range from £4.50 to £8.50.

CHEF: Harry Hallam   PROPRIETORS: Harry and Caroline Hallam   OPEN: Tue to Sat 12.30 to 2, 7 to 9.30   CLOSED: 25 and 26 Dec, bank hols   MEALS: alc (main courses £22.50 to £27.50)   SERVICE: not inc   CARDS: Delta, MasterCard, Switch, Visa   DETAILS: 10 seats. Private parties: 10 main room. Car park. Children's helpings. No children under 5. No smoking in dining room. Wheelchair access (not WC). No music  (£5)

---

## GREAT MILTON  Oxfordshire                          map 2

## ▲ Le Manoir aux Quat' Saisons  🍷 ✳

Church Road, Great Milton OX44 7PD
TEL: (01844) 278881   FAX: (01844) 278847
EMAIL: lemanoir@blanc.co.uk                          COOKING 9
WEBSITE: www.manoir.co.uk                          MODERN FRENCH
off A329, 1½m from M40 junction 7                  £64–£138

Throughout years of expansion and refurbishment the fifteenth-century Cotswold manor house and its grounds have always retained their composure. This is a serene environment in which to eat. Although a large amount of theatre is involved in a restaurant such as this, there is also an openness to the operation. The organic garden is a delight to stroll through, and visitors can take a tour of the kitchen. Given the elegant lounges, top-class fixtures and fittings, and a vista of manicured lawns from the brace of dining rooms, one visitor wondered if the high life could get much better.

The food itself flatters with luxuries, from appetisers of caviar, or a truffle-sauced wedge of baby leek terrine, to turbot with morels, or roast Trelough duck breast with a foie gras sauce. But there is a pleasing balance between richness and lightness, as the menu offers a starter of clear tomato essence with pressed tomatoes, and heftier main dishes of roast loin, braised cheek and belly of suckling pig, or a partnership of veal kidney with snails in red wine sauce. High-quality ingredients are precisely handled, including an exceptionally fine roast loin of venison with a deeply flavoured aigre-doux sauce containing bitter chocolate, served with braised celery hearts and caramelised chicory, and freshness is a notable characteristic, not just when it comes to vegetables from the garden. 'I wouldn't be surprised if they were caught that day,' volunteered one visitor of the pan-fried langoustines that accompanied his macaroni in a truffle cream.

Items also work together harmoniously in a dish, as in a large ravioli containing a purée of herbs and a lightly truffle-scented poached egg, served with wild mushrooms, toasted hazelnuts, small triangles of poached celery and a buttery sauce of poultry juices. Desserts are often a highlight, combining a high degree of skill with stunning presentation and some exotic flavours (mango soup with peppermint and a passion-fruit sorbet), but equally at home with a poached pear, half of it chopped into bite-sized pieces and placed in a hollowed-out brioche, the other half resting on top, served with two ice creams: vanilla, and honey and ginger. Service by 'youthful Continentals' can involve some long waits; those without a pressing schedule appear to be least troubled by the pace of things.

Any disappointments, of which there are a few, are compounded by 'stratospheric' prices, while wines reflect the 'très sérieux' nature of proceedings, both in scope and price. The great and the good of Bordeaux are a strong point, with a choice of vintages of Lafite, Latour and Mouton-Rothschild, as well as some well-known 'super-seconds', but less celebrated regions such as the south-west and Provence get a look-in too, and there are some good selections from Spain, Italy and California. Mark-ups, however, are steep, so you'll need to dig around to find much under £20 (bottle prices start at £15 for a Moscato d'Asti) . A meagre five wines are available by the glass, from £5 to £8.

CHEFS: Raymond Blanc and Gary Jones   PROPRIETOR: Raymond Blanc   OPEN: all week 12.15 to 2.45, 7.15 to 9.45   MEALS: alc (main courses £32 to £36). Set L £45 to £95, Set D £95   SERVICE: not inc   CARDS: Amex, Delta, Diners, MasterCard, Switch, Visa   DETAILS: 100 seats. Private parties: 8 main room, 50 private room. Car park. Vegetarian meals. Children's helpings. No smoking in dining room. Wheelchair access (also WC). No music. No mobile phones. Air-conditioned   ACCOMMODATION: 32 rooms, all with bath/shower. TV. Phone. B&B £245 to £825. Rooms for disabled. Baby facilities (*The Which? Hotel Guide*)

---

**GREAT MISSENDEN** Buckinghamshire                                              map 3

# La Petite Auberge

107 High Street, Great Missenden HP16 0BB                          COOKING **4**
TEL: (01494) 865370                                                        FRENCH
                                                                      £37–£52

The name conjures up an image of rural France rather than the Home Counties, an impression reinforced by the long, narrow dining room adorned with light-hearted French country scenes. Whether or not Hubert Martel's cooking will transport you back to his homeland is a question that has divided reporters, but there is no disputing the provenance of such dishes as fish soup with rouille and croûtons, coquilles Saint Jacques with sauce vierge, or noisettes of venison with red cabbage and chestnuts. At its best, the food makes a very favourable impression: John Dory with tapénade has struck a happy chord, as has a seasonal special of 'wonderfully tender' young grouse. To finish, rich chocolate mousse, caramelised lemon tart, or iced nougat with chocolate sauce might tempt. Service is generally attentive and friendly but has occasionally cracked under pressure when the restaurant is busy. Wines are exclusively from the major French regions, with reasonable choice under £20, including a Muscadet at £11.50 and a Brouilly at £14.80.

CHEF: Hubert Martel   PROPRIETOR: Mr and Mrs H. Martel   OPEN: Mon to Sat D only 7.30 to 10.30; also open L Mothering Sun   CLOSED: 2 weeks Christmas, 2 weeks Easter, bank hols   MEALS: alc (main courses £15 to £17)   SERVICE: not inc   CARDS: Delta, Diners, MasterCard, Switch, Visa   DETAILS: 30 seats. Private parties: 30 main room. Children's helpings. Wheelchair access (also WC)

## GREAT YELDHAM  Essex                                    map 3

# White Hart ▼ ✳ £

Poole Street, Great Yeldham CO9 4HJ
TEL: (01787) 237250   FAX: (01787) 238044
EMAIL: reservations@whitehartyeldham.co.uk
WEBSITE: www.whitehartyeldham.co.uk

COOKING 2
ANGLO-FRENCH-PLUS
£28–£50

The centuries-old timbered building, with large fireplaces, exposed brickwork and 'all its ribs showing' is a delight. Two menus serve both bar and more formal, non-smoking dining room; the lighter version covers salads and sandwiches, cod and chips with tartare sauce, and grilled Lincolnshire sausages with mash and gravy, while the main menu is more ambitious.

Ingredients are good-quality, presentation attractive, and, if results don't match John Dicken's personal best (he is also chef/proprietor at Dicken's in Wethersfield, see entry), the kitchen has produced a decent beef and onion pudding with mash, roast root vegetables and cabbage; and calf's liver (requested very pink, served well done) on a jumble of leeks and lentils garnished with first-class pancetta. To finish, perhaps raspberry trifle, chocolate and pecan nut tart, or a couple of sorbets with a fine, crisp tuile. Espresso is as good as it comes, and wines on the stylistically arranged list fulfil the range and value criteria admirably. Mark-ups are low and careful sleuthing can reveal some remarkable finds, particularly in the 'top class red wines' section. Thirteen house wines range in price from £9.95 to £19.50, and most are available by the glass, for £1.95 to £3.95.

CHEF/PROPRIETOR: John Dicken   OPEN: all week 12 to 2, 6.30 to 9.30   CLOSED: Christmas (phone to check)   MEALS: alc (main courses £9 to £16). Light menu also available   SERVICE: not inc   CARDS: Amex, Delta, Diners, MasterCard, Switch, Visa   DETAILS: 100 seats. 40 seats outside. Private parties: 80 main room, 36 private room. Car park. Vegetarian meals. Children's helpings. No smoking in dining room. Wheelchair access (not WC). No music. No mobile phones

---

*Report forms are at the back of the book; write a letter if you prefer; or email us at goodfoodguide@which.net*

## GRIMSTHORPE Lincolnshire

map 6

## ▲ Black Horse ▼ ✸ £

NEW ENTRY

Grimsthorpe PE10 0LY
TEL: (01778) 591247   FAX: (01778) 591373
EMAIL: dine@blackhorseinn.co.uk

COOKING 1
MODERN BRITISH
£26–£46

Built in 1717 as a coaching inn, the Black Horse still has the look and feel of an old-fashioned pub. In other ways it is more up to date, the long menu offering a diverse range of dishes from pan-fried halloumi cheese with a lime and caper dressing, via sauté lamb kidneys, to roast cod with parsley mash and creamed pea sauce. An inspector was greatly encouraged by the honest and straightforward approach. Home-baked breads, and carefully made sauces are plus-points, and a starter of peppery fried squid, accompanied by rocket and lemon vinaigrette, was timed with 'split-second accuracy', while a dessert of Turkish Delight pannacotta with clementine and mint salad proved a successful invention. The wine list will cheer those with an eye for a bargain. A globe-trotting, well-selected range is organised by style, and mark-ups are kept commendably low. Particular bargains can be found in the champagne section, where prices aren't much higher than retail. Elsewhere, the excellent Tuscan Cepparello (100 per cent Sangiovese) from Isole e Olena is a steal at £31. There is also an organic wine selection and a good collection of half-bottles. Prices start at £8.95; five wines by the small/large glass sell for £3/£4.

CHEF: Brian Rey   PROPRIETORS: Brian and Elaine Rey   OPEN: Tue to Sun 12 to 2, 7 to 9.30 (9 Sun)
MEALS: alc (main courses £9 to £16). Bar menu available   SERVICE: not inc, card slips closed
CARDS: Amex, Delta, Diners, MasterCard, Switch, Visa   DETAILS: 60 seats. 30 seats outside.
Private parties: 34 main room, 12 private room. Car park. Vegetarian meals. Children's helpings.
No children under 10 in dining room. No smoking in dining room. Occasional music
ACCOMMODATION: 6 rooms, all with bath/shower. TV. Phone. B&B £45 to £95. No children under
10

## GRIMSTON Norfolk

map 6

## ▲ Congham Hall ▼ 🍴 ✸

Lynn Road, Grimston PE32 1AH
TEL: (01485) 600250   FAX: (01485) 601191
EMAIL: reception@conghamhallhotel.co.uk
WEBSITE: www.conghamhallhotel.co.uk
off A148 or B1153, 7m E of King's Lynn and at W
edge of Grimston

COOKING 5
MODERN BRITISH/FRENCH
£28–£63

Set in extensive parkland, beside the village cricket ground, this elegant eighteenth-century manor looks out over expansive lawns that lead to a meadow dotted with old trees and grazed by horses: sit on the terrace at dusk for best effect. The dining room is discreetly themed, with prints of exotic fruits and decorative plates depicting orange trees, and since November 2001 Fraser Miller has been making an impact, producing balanced dishes of real technical accomplishment.

Top-notch canapés and good breads get things off to a fine start, swiftly followed in one case by a Gressingham duck trio: three slices of breast, a terrine of concentrated flavour and a fine, earthy rissole served with sweet onion chutney. 'Exquisitely fresh and expertly seared' fillets of brill have come with braised fennel, Avruga and a slightly puddingy herb risotto. Great pains are taken with presentation too, evident in a tarragon- and truffle-stuffed chicken breast topped with a crown of puff pastry on a deftly made rösti. Nor are vegetarian options mere standbys: main courses have included a bean sprout and tofu filo wrap with roasted provençale vegetables marinated in soy.

A dessert assiette might play tunes on the theme of rhubarb, or there could be 'densely textured, intensely flavoured' chocolate pavé with walnut ice-cream and coffee anglaise. Service has seemed a little inexperienced, but eager with it. The wine list – impressively wide-ranging, organised by style, and with good descriptions – takes in food-friendly styles from good producers in Italy, the Loire, Bordeaux and the New World. There are six house recommendations (£19.50–£22.50, or £3.50–£3.75 a glass), and reasonable choice at or below £20.

CHEF: Fraser Miller   PROPRIETOR: Von Essen Hotels   OPEN: all week 12 to 2, 7 to 9.30   MEALS: Set L £11.50 (2 courses) to £29.95. Set D £27.50 (2 courses) to £39.95. Bar menu also available L and D, and light L menu in summer   SERVICE: not inc, card slips closed   CARDS: Amex, Delta, Diners, MasterCard, Switch, Visa   DETAILS: 60 seats. 20 seats outside. Private parties: 60 main room, 4 to 20 private rooms. Car park. Vegetarian meals. Children's helpings; no children under 7 at D. No smoking in dining room. Wheelchair access (not WC). No music. No mobile phones ACCOMMODATION: 14 rooms, all with bath/shower. TV. Phone. B&B £99 to £230. Swimming pool (*The Which? Hotel Guide*)  (£5)

---

map 3

# Zinfandel £ NEW ENTRY

4–5 Chapel Street, Guildford GU1 3UH   COOKING 3
TEL: (01483) 455155   FAX: (01483) 455144   CONTEMPORARY AMERICAN
WEBSITE: www.zinfandel.org.uk   £28–£51

Napa Valley, home of the eponymous grape variety, is the source of culinary inspiration at this shop conversion in the town centre, under the same ownership as Quails in Chobham (see entry). With its minimalist decorative theme, it is a good place for an informal meal of pizza and a glass of wine, thought one visitor, who also praised the 'excellent value'. The 'gourmet brick-fired pizzas' are indeed inviting, topped with combinations like chorizo, roasted red onions, jalapeños and Monterey Jack cheese, or caramelised pear, soufflé Gorgonzola, prosciutto and pistachios. Starters, salads and main courses 'from the rotisserie and chargrill' are not run-of-the-mill either: hits at an inspection meal included breadcrumbed mushrooms stuffed with a mixture of dolcelatte and oregano, and served with caramelised bell pepper relish; and corn-fed chicken cooked on the rotisserie with garlic and tarragon, topped with bourbon-cured bacon and accompanied by lemon aïoli. Star anise pink-stemmed rhubarb and figs with wattle seed cream has made a refreshing way to round off a meal. Around 30 mainly American wines, including half a dozen Zinfandels, are mostly priced under £20. Sicilian Arpeggio Bianco and Rosso open the list at £10.95.

CHEF: Kevin Grove  PROPRIETORS: the Wale family  OPEN: Mon to Sat 12 to 3, 6 to 10  CLOSED: 25 and 26 Dec, 1 Jan  MEALS: alc (main courses £8 to £14). Light L Mon to Sat £7.25 (1 course)  SERVICE: 10% (optional), card slips closed  CARDS: Amex, Delta, MasterCard, Switch, Visa  DETAILS: 60 seats. Vegetarian meals. Children's helpings. No-smoking area. No cigars/pipes in dining room. Wheelchair access (also WC). Music. Air-conditioned  (£5)

## HAMBLETON  Rutland                                            map 6

# ▲ Hambleton Hall  ♥ ⅝✱

Upper Hambleton LE15 8TH
TEL: (01572) 756991  FAX: (01572) 724721
EMAIL: hotel@hambletonhall.com                    COOKING 7
WEBSITE: www.hambleton.hall.com              MODERN BRITISH
off A606, 3m SE of Oakham                       £35–£108

Set high above Rutland Water, with the date 1881 over the porch, Hambleton is a rambling place overseen by the hands-on Harts. It is friendly, unstuffy, smart and relaxed, with a dining room overlooking the lake. A longish carte changes twice a year, while other menus respond to the market, and sourcing is impressive: herbs and saladings – an interesting collection in prime condition – come from the hotel's garden, and meat from Northfield Farm.

The intricate style is evident in, for example, first-class, perfectly timed lamb sweetbreads, given a light crumb coating and built into a tower in a crisp filo pastry basket, along with wild mushrooms in a sticky, dark, sweet-sour sauce, and blobs of pea purée, topped with a slice of deep-fried Parma ham; all suffused with a gentle orange flavour. Poultry and game tend to feature, perhaps as a rabbit trio: succulent loin wrapped in crisp-roasted Parma ham; a whole rack on pearl barley 'like a wet risotto' flavoured with wild mushrooms; and a sturdy roast leg coated in glistening sweet-sour sauce; all around are strewn girolles, skinned broad beans and tiny spears of asparagus in a grain mustard sauce. Seafood, too, is skilfully handled: witness a starter of poached langoustine tail, served cold on tomato flesh and creamy goat cheese, around which is poured a colourless, flavour-packed tomato essence.

Workmanship is detailed, and the food 'very work of art'. With so many bells and whistles however (typical of a large and skilled brigade), dishes can miss their main target: the 'wow' comes from admiring technical achievement rather than from any direct hit on the palate. Sauces tend to be slicks rather than useful liquids, combinations good rather than striking, a passion fruit soufflé at inspection lacked the necessary oomph, and not all the bread is equally good (take the sourdough if it's there). Nonetheless, this remains a seriously good restaurant, delivering an experience exceeding the sum of its parts.

The wine list's roll call of prestige producers from Bordeaux, Burgundy, Italy, Spain and California is impressive and (as they say) reassuringly expensive. Prices start at £15, but there is little under £20; however the 20 'wines of the moment' highlight some interesting bottles under £35. Five or six wines – or more, if a number of bottles have been opened – are served by the glass.

CHEF: Aaron Patterson  PROPRIETORS: Tim and Stefa Hart  OPEN: all week 12 to 1.30, 7 to 9.30  MEALS: alc (main courses £27.50 to £34). Set L £16.50 (2 courses) to £21.50, Set D £29.50 (2 courses) to £35  SERVICE: not inc, card slips closed  CARDS: Amex, Delta, MasterCard, Switch  DETAILS: 60 seats. Private parties: 40 main room, 14 to 20 private rooms. Car park. Vegetarian meals. Children's helpings. No smoking in dining room. Wheelchair access (also WC). No music ACCOMMODATION: 17 rooms, all with bath/shower. TV. Phone. B&B £185 to £335. Rooms for disabled. Baby facilities. Swimming pool (*The Which? Hotel Guide*)

## HAMPTON HILL  Greater London                                        map 3

# Monsieur Max ▼

| | |
|---|---|
| 133 High Street, Hampton Hill TW12 1NJ | COOKING 7 |
| TEL: (020) 8979 5546   FAX: (020) 8979 3747 | FRENCH |
| EMAIL: monsmax@aol.com | £39–£64 |

'Bienvenue à Hampton Hill' announces the restaurant, setting the thoroughgoing French tone succinctly. It is neither trendy nor pretentious, decorated in browns and deep reds, with mirrored glass panels here, a selection of historical menus there, and plainly but smartly set tables. After half a dozen years, the place is in fine fettle; indeed, despite the departure of Max Renzland, and the possibility of a further change in ownership, Alex Bentley's cooking has shifted up a gear or two over the past year, to become 'of a far higher standard than one has a right to find in Hampton Hill'.

His cuisine bourgeoise has a reassuringly down-to-earth feel: from a 'sybaritic and flawless' terrine of foie gras and coq au vin, with Monbazillac jelly and green beans, to a comforting moist pork fillet en crépinette served with boudin blanc, creamy dauphinois and earthy beetroot purée. Despite their sometimes complex nature, dishes are nevertheless artfully composed and finely balanced: for example, honey-roast Barbary duck with Savoy cabbage and pancetta, a cep and sorrel risotto, and a pepper and chestnut sauce. 'Over the top? Maybe. Do we want it again? At once!' Likewise a starter of grilled quail on a guinea fowl boudin, set about with purées and sauces (including pesto, tomato, herbed olive oil, and white haricots spiked with lemon peel), which could easily have been a dog's breakfast in lesser hands, proved to be carefully considered so that each item related to every other 'like the genealogical table of some vast extended family'.

Despite the rib-sticking nature of much of the output, seafood also turns up trumps. A rich lobster and basil ravioli with briny braised oysters manages to be both unctuous and refreshing at the same time, while pieces of squid flesh and lobster, all smokily grilled, come in a buttery, vanilla-perfumed orange sauce, served with thick slices of grilled, truffle-studded mozzarella that 'exploded with flavour'. Even the flashbacks to earlier days show a respect for materials, as in a generous cocktail of tasty brown shrimps with rich Marie-Rose sauce and crisp cos lettuce, and in a 'triumphant' Aberdeen fillet en croûte with mushroom mousseline.

Desserts are generally a match for the rest, and attractively presented. Pineapple tarte Tatin is accompanied by a scoop of nutty, smooth, rum-flavoured ice cream, and soufflés are invariably successful: for example, a tangy, rich, impeccable mango and lime version with apricot coulis. Cheeses are kept in prime condition, and service is warm, precise, knowledgeable and attentive. Wines, in keeping with the leanings of the place, are largely French – and classic to boot – with a few concessions to Europe and the New World. The south of France and Chile are the most likely places to find value, but there is little below

£20, with prices starting at £14.50 for house red and white and moving up swiftly from there.

CHEF: Alex Bentley   PROPRIETOR: Sunbow Ltd   OPEN: Sun to Fri L 12 to 2, all week D 7 to 10
MEALS: Set L £20 (2 courses) to £25, Set D £37.50   SERVICE: 12.5% (optional), card slips closed
CARDS: Amex, Delta, Diners, MasterCard, Switch, Visa   DETAILS: 70 seats. No children under 8.
No music. Air-conditioned

## HAROME  North Yorkshire                                               map 9

# ▲ Star Inn 🍴 £

| High Street, Harome YO62 5JE | COOKING 5 |
|---|---|
| TEL: (01439) 770397   FAX: (01439) 771833 | MODERN BRITISH |
| off A170, 3m SE of Helmsley | £26–£56 |

In a pretty village close to the North York Moors, this thatched pub looks a picture. Most people come to eat, either in the bar or in the unpretentious dining room with its bare wooden tables and chairs. Andrew Pern's food, responding to the seasons, offers rich, warming, flour-thickened, stock-based beef broth with a weighty herb dumpling in November, and asparagus salad with Cotherstone cheese and scallion dressing in early summer. Likewise risottos might be made with organic beetroot and Irish cheese in March, or new season black truffle and fairy ring mushrooms in June.

Sourcing is a strength – honey, poultry, game, beef, lamb, eggs, organic vegetables and smoked products all come from within three miles – and the kitchen takes a lively approach to whatever comes its way, turning out a starter of mussels steamed in dark beer, and a casserole of rabbit with a faggot of black pudding and lovage mash. Combinations are interesting without being outlandish: witness a salad-filled Parmesan cup topped with three or four partridge breasts, served with a sweetly fruity and lightly acidic sauce of Californian huckleberries. Cheeses are served at room temperature, and desserts have included a wedge of caramelised lemon tart served with a bramble purée. Service is friendly, helpful and attentive.

The wine list balances France against the New World, the latter accounting for most of the under-£20 bottles (bar house Languedocs at £11.95) There is a bakery/deli in Cross House Lodge, just opposite the inn, where new accommodation is due to open by the time the Guide appears.

CHEF: Andrew Pern   PROPRIETORS: Andrew and Jacquie Pern   OPEN: all week L 11.30 (12 Sun) to 2 (6 Sun), Mon to Sat D 6.30 to 9.30   CLOSED: 1 week Nov, 25 Dec, 2 weeks Jan, bank hols
MEALS: alc (main courses £8.50 to £14.95)   SERVICE: not inc, card slips closed   CARDS: Delta, MasterCard, Switch, Visa   DETAILS: 60 seats. 40 seats outside. Private parties: 35 main room. Car park. Vegetarian meals. Children's helpings. No smoking in 1 dining room. No music. No mobile phones   ACCOMMODATION: 3 rooms, all with bath/shower (plus 8 further rooms planned for late 2002). TV. B&B £90 to £110 (The Which? Hotel Guide)

---

'The least creamy offering was a Sherry Trifle. It was not a Sherry Trifle. There was more Sherry in the waitress than in the Trifle. It was a trifling Trifle; I trifled with it then left it.'
(On eating in Scotland)

---

# Attic ⬛ NEW ENTRY

62A Union Street, Harrogate HG1 1BS
TEL: (01423) 524400 FAX: (01423) 523191 COOKING 3
EMAIL: info@attic-harrogate.co.uk MODERN EUROPEAN
WEBSITE: www.attic-harrogate.co.uk £24–£48

Set in a restored warehouse, down a small side street near the Exhibition Centre, this new venture is slick and modern, done up in restful shades of cream and mushroom, with a profusion of pale wood. Downstairs is a flagstoned bar with low tables and comfortable seating. The short menu might take in a simple salad of leaves and sweet herbs with lemon oil and aged balsamic, the quality of the dressing shining through at inspection. Other starters might include a moist, meaty terrine of rabbit and foie gras with French beans and shallots, followed by main courses of moistly seared fillet of salmon with beetroot, crème fraîche and pineapple salsa, or a generous portion of fall-off-the-bone Moroccan-spiced lamb shank with herbed yoghurt and couscous. For dessert, queen of puddings, or a trio of British cheeses might tempt. Service is welcoming, professional and knowledgeable. The wine list is a relatively brief affair with a sharp selection of mainly New World wines, chosen with an eye to value and food-friendliness. Six house wines sell for £11.50 a bottle.

CHEF: Robert Craggs PROPRIETOR: Chris Patchett OPEN: Mon to Sat 12 to 2, 6.30 to 10 CLOSED: 25 and 26 Dec, 1 Jan, bank hols MEALS: alc (main courses L £5.50 to £14.50, D £11 to £14.50). Set L and D Mon to Thur 6.30 to 7.30 £11.50 (2 courses) to £14.50 SERVICE: not inc CARDS: Amex, Delta, MasterCard, Switch, Visa DETAILS: 56 seats. Private parties: 56 main room. Vegetarian meals. No-smoking area. No cigars in dining room. Wheelchair access (not WC). Music (£5)

# Drum and Monkey £

5 Montpellier Gardens, Harrogate HG1 2TF COOKING 2
TEL: (01423) 502650 FAX: (01423) 522469 SEAFOOD
£19–£55

Book well ahead or be prepared to queue at this loyally supported local venue, because devotees are known to make reservations months in advance. Downstairs is the bar area, where tables are so highly prized that they almost have the regulars' nameplates attached. Above is a more formal dining room, slightly reminiscent of 'a Parisian neighbourhood restaurant'.

This is a set-up that resolutely offers nothing for meat eaters and confines vegetarians to cheese salad, avocado and melon. Seafood is its business, supplies arrive daily from Fleetwood, Brixham and Whitby, and value for money is a plus. Doubters might argue that the style is 1970s fish cookery, lavishly doused with cream and cheese sauces. Some dishes are undoubtedly very rich (croustade of seafood Mornay, for example), but elsewhere there is sensitive treatment of fine raw materials: a generous hot shellfish platter, and sea bass with herb butter and wild mushrooms, have both been keenly judged. Vegetables are many and varied, while ice creams and sorbets are alternatives to substantial nursery puddings. Pleasant waitresses know the ropes. The fairly priced wine list favours piscine-friendly whites. House Duboeuf is £8.65.

CHEFS: Keith Penny and Selina Leamy   PROPRIETOR: William Fuller   OPEN: Mon to Sat 12 to 2.30, 6.30 to 10.15   CLOSED: D 24 Dec to 2 Jan   MEALS: alc (main courses £5.50 to £17.50)   SERVICE: not inc   CARDS: Delta, MasterCard, Switch, Visa   DETAILS: 56 seats. No music

## Kings ⅝✳

**NEW ENTRY**

24 Kings Road, Harrogate HG1 5JW
TEL: (01423) 568600   FAX: (01423) 531838

COOKING 3
MODERN BRITISH
£23–£40

The Maineys opened a restaurant called Spice Box in Boston Spa, followed by a branch in Harrogate. They sold Boston Spa (and, crucially, the name), so have renamed their Harrogate enterprise after the address. Lively and buzzy, it stands opposite the Conference Centre, its bistro atmosphere boosted by plain walls, modest furniture, paper table covers, and daily dishes – mostly fish – chalked not just on blackboards but all over the walls. The written menu is a bit of a scrawl too, and a bit corny, but full of lively ideas; again mostly fish, but with calf's liver, duck breast, and beef fillet to balance things out.

Successes have included wholesome fishcakes rolled in polenta, served with peanut sauce and a well-dressed salad, and an 'off-the-wall' dish of top-quality oysters served two ways: fresh, and in an impressively light, tempura-like batter. Cream and brandy can make their presence felt, lending a rather old-fashioned air to some of the dishes – a deep-flavoured Whitby crab soup for example – and bouillabaisse at inspection came with lots of salmon, mussels, cream, and a plate of vegetables, rendering it a less-than-authentic version. Finish, perhaps, with lemon tart or 'chocolate oblivion', and drink from a 50-strong wine list that starts with house red and white at £10.75.

CHEFS: Karl Mainey and Stephen Ardern   PROPRIETORS: Karl and Amanda Mainey   OPEN: Tue to Sat L 12 to 2, Mon to Sat D 6 to 10   CLOSED: 1 week after Christmas, first week Jan   MEALS: alc (main courses L £7 to £11, D £13 to £13.50). Set L £8.50 (2 courses), Set D 6 to 7.30 £12.50 to £16.95   SERVICE: not inc   CARDS: Amex, Delta, MasterCard, Switch, Visa   DETAILS: 120 seats. 15 seats outside. Private parties: 45 main room, 45 private room. Vegetarian meals. Children's helpings. No smoking in 1 dining room. Wheelchair access (also WC). Music

## HARROW  Greater London

map 3

## Golden Palace  £

146–150 Station Road, Harrow HA1 2RH
TEL: (020) 8863 2333

COOKING 4
CHINESE
£25–£78

The Palace was about to celebrate its tenth anniversary as the Guide went to press, and it continues to 'deliver the goods and perform miracles'. A fan who fancied celebrating Christmas Eve in the colourfully decorated dining room found it riotously festive and the kitchen on cracking form. Even when it is in mundane, familiar territory (sizzling sliced chicken with black-bean sauce for example) it excels: there is delicacy and finesse here as well as plenty of big-hearted gusto. Every classic cooking technique is just about spot-on, from supremely good deep-frying (huge crispy won tons, and sliced aubergines in grease-free, crisp batter) to steaming (succulent scallops in their shells topped with a crust of finely chopped garlic and 'eaten with a teaspoon').

Beyond the basic menu, there are 'wondrously challenging' specialities, hotpots (braised bean curd with shredded pork that was 'rich, unctuous and heart-warming on a bitterly cold winter's night'), and a whole section of vegetarian options. Queues form (especially at weekends) for the prospect of top-drawer dim sum. Service is cheery, helpful and smooth. House wine is £9.50.

CHEF/PROPRIETOR: Mr G. Ho   OPEN: all week 12 to 11.30   CLOSED: 25 Dec   MEALS: alc (main courses £5 to £28). Set L and D £14.50 to £22.50 (min 2)   SERVICE: 10%   CARDS: Amex, Delta, Diners, MasterCard, Switch, Visa   DETAILS: 150 seats. Private parties: 150 main room, 10 to 70 private rooms. Vegetarian meals. Wheelchair access (also WC). Occasional music. Air-conditioned

---

## HARWICH Essex                                                    map 6

## ▲ Pier Hotel, Harbourside Restaurant ▼ ⁵✳

The Quay, Harwich CO12 3HH
TEL: (01255) 241212   FAX: (01255) 551922                      COOKING 1
EMAIL: reception@thepierhotelharwich.co.uk                    SEAFOOD/ENGLISH
WEBSITE: www.milsomhotels.co.uk                                   £29–£70

Although the name has undergone a small change, everything else remains as before at this cheery fish restaurant not far from the quay. Given the ships passing by, the local catch, and their own lobster tanks, it is easy to see the appeal. Just about every kind of traditional seafood dish is listed, from dressed crab, and rock and native oysters, via fish and chips, to Cullen skink, fish pie, and deep-fried oriental tiger prawns in filo pastry. Meat eaters might be offered calf's liver, or chargrilled sirloin steak, and there are vegetarian options too. Straightforward desserts have included banana crème brûlée and white chocolate cheesecake. The wine list is small but perfectly formed, and good value to boot, split evenly between European and New World selections (South Africa is very strong), with good producers evident throughout. Mark-ups are low, and there is wide choice around £20 or below. Eight house wines range from £11.95 to £14.50.

CHEF: Chris Oakley   PROPRIETOR: Mr Milsom   OPEN: all week 12 to 2, 6 to 9.30   MEALS: alc exc Sun L (main courses £9.50 to £30). Set L £15 (2 courses) to £17.50   SERVICE: 10%, card slips closed   CARDS: Amex, Delta, Diners, MasterCard, Switch, Visa   DETAILS: 80 seats. 20 seats outside. Private parties: 90 main room, 2 to 16 private rooms. Car park. Vegetarian meals. Children's helpings. No smoking in dining room. Music. No mobile phones   ACCOMMODATION: 14 rooms, all with bath/shower. TV. Phone. B&B £57.50 to £150. Baby facilities (The Which? Hotel Guide)

---

*All details are as accurate as possible at the time of going to press, but chefs and owners often change, and it is wise to check by telephone before making a special journey. Many readers have been disappointed when set-price bargain meals are no longer available. Ask when booking.*

## HAWORTH  West Yorkshire

map 8

# ▲ Weavers ⅗⋇ £

13/17 West Lane, Haworth BD22 8DU

TEL: (01535) 643822   FAX: (01535) 644832

EMAIL: weavers@amserve.net

WEBSITE: www.weaversmallhotel.co.uk

COOKING 3

MODERN BRITISH

£23–£45

Weavers backs onto the Brontë Parsonage car park, its bar covered in eccentric paraphernalia from bobbins to tin cans, its green and mustard dining room upstairs decorated with books, plates, pot plants and an old radio. After 25 years changes are few, although there is now greater emphasis on local and seasonal produce. Blackboard specials supplement the printed carte, and commendably modest ingredients include corned beef hash with a free-range egg, and griddled purple sprouting broccoli and cauliflower with herb butter.

The repertoire aims for wide appeal, taking in accurately timed dishes of crisp haddock goujons with a pleasantly chunky tartare sauce, and well-trimmed ribeye steak with skin-on chips and battered onion wedges. A dish of pork, meanwhile, exploits the contrasts between roast fillet and a piece of belly with crisp crackling, all served with a tasty kale and potato cake. To finish, warm chocolate cake with a dark chocolate sauce and marmalade ice cream comes recommended. The wine list is wide-ranging and fairly priced, the bulk of the bottles under £20 (try the Lievland Estate Shiraz 1998 from South Africa at £15.50); eight house wines start at £10.45.

CHEFS: Jane, Colin and Tim Rushworth   PROPRIETORS: Jane and Colin Rushworth   OPEN: Sun L 12 to 2.30, Tue to Sat D 6.30 to 9   CLOSED: last week Dec, last week Jun   MEALS: alc (main courses £7.50 to £16.50). Set L £10.50 (2 courses) to £14, Set D Tue to Fri 6.30 to 7.30 £10.50 (2 courses) to £14   SERVICE: not inc, 10% for parties of 6 or more   CARDS: Amex, Delta, Diners, MasterCard, Switch, Visa   DETAILS: 65 seats. Private parties: 14 main room, 14 private room. Vegetarian meals. No smoking in dining room. Music. Air-conditioned   ACCOMMODATION: 3 rooms, all with bath/shower. TV. Phone. B&B £55 to £85 (The Which? Hotel Guide)  (£5)

## HAYDON BRIDGE  Northumberland

map 10

# General Havelock Inn ⅗⋇

9 Ratcliffe Road, Haydon Bridge NE47 6ER

TEL: (01434) 684376   FAX: (01434) 684283

EMAIL: generalhavelock@aol.com

WEBSITE: www.northumberlandrestaurants.co.uk

on A69, 8m W of Hexham, 100yds from junction with B6319

COOKING 2

MODERN EUROPEAN

£23–£35

This 200-year-old roadside inn functions as a traditional, friendly pub at the front, with a converted barn for dining at the back, overlooking the South Tyne River; it even has a sheltered, tranquil patio area down by the river bank. It is run in suitably unpretentious style by a well-practised husband and wife team whose local supplies take in Northumberland meat, from either the village butcher or a nearby farm: perhaps appearing as rack of lamb on ratatouille, or grilled sirloin steak with mushrooms and tomato. Start with wild mushroom risotto or home-made gravlax, look at the board to find the 'catch of the day', and finish with glazed lemon tart or regional cheese. Calm, friendly service prevails, and a modest wine list stays commendably under £20, starting with house Duboeuf red and white at £9.50.

CHEF: Gary Thompson   PROPRIETORS: Gary and Joanna Thompson   OPEN: Tue to Sun L 12 to 2, Tue to Sat D 7 to 9   CLOSED: Tue during Jan   MEALS: alc (main courses £5.50 to £11). Set L £12.75 (2 courses) to £14.75, Set D £17.25 (2 courses) to £22. Bar menu also available Tue to Sun L and D   SERVICE: not inc, card slips closed   CARDS: Amex, MasterCard, Switch, Visa DETAILS: 50 seats. 20 seats outside. Private parties: 50 main room. Vegetarian meals. Children's helpings. No smoking in dining room. Wheelchair access (also WC). No music   £5

## HAYWARDS HEATH  West Sussex                                    map 3

# Jeremy's ⅝✳

Borde Hill, Balcombe Road, Haywards
Heath RH16 1XP
TEL: (01444) 441102   FAX: (01444) 443936                    COOKING 5
EMAIL: jeremys.bordehill@btinternet.com               MODERN EUROPEAN
WEBSITE: www.homeofgoodfood.com                          £32–£54

Borde Hill Gardens, the principal tourist attraction of this well-heeled commuter settlement, are well signposted from the centre of town. They make a fittingly stylish setting for this well turned-out restaurant where the food is as vivacious as the dining room's vibrant yellow colour scheme. Among Jeremy Ashpool's stated aims is the imaginative use of 'lesser cuts and non-luxury items' in order to maintain a balance of quality and value. Terrine of local rabbit with prunes and shallot compote, and warm salad of local pigeon, chorizo and beetroot with sauce vierge exemplify this approach among starters, while veal kidneys with mustard mash, spinach and dry-cure bacon, and roast new season lamb with gratin dauphinoise and a warm bean salad pick up the baton for the main-course leg.

On the other hand, grilled spiced turbot with Moroccan vegetables and saffron rice, and organic Scottish salmon on petit pois purée with new potatoes and watercress sauce show that there is no skimping on quality materials, and in any case, Jeremy's accomplished technique and stylish presentation make a favourable impression across the board. Desserts range from traditional tiramisù to ultra-modern carpaccio of pineapple with mint and chilli syrup, and the short wine list covers a good range of styles and prices, starting with a pair of house Italians at £12 a bottle, £2.85 a glass.

CHEFS: Jeremy and Vera Ashpool and Dominic Stanton   PROPRIETORS: Jeremy and Vera Ashpool OPEN: Tue to Sun L 12.30 to 2.30, Tue to Sat D 7.30 to 9   CLOSED: 1 week after Christmas MEALS: alc exc Sun L (main courses £13.50 to £18.50). Set L Tue to Sat £10 (1 course inc wine) to £24, Set Sun L £19.50 (2 courses) to £24. Set D Tue to Thur £16.50 (2 courses) to £20.50 SERVICE: not inc, 10% for parties of 8 or more   CARDS: Amex, Diners, MasterCard, Switch, Visa DETAILS: 55 seats. 120 seats outside. Private parties: 60 main room. Car park. Vegetarian meals. Children's helpings. No smoking in dining room. Wheelchair access (also WC). Music   £5

*Subscribers to Which? Online can access* The Good Food Guide *on www.which.net.*

## HEMINGFORD GREY Cambridgeshire

map 6

# Cock 🍴 £

NEW ENTRY

47 High Street, Hemingford Grey PE28 9BJ
TEL: (01480) 463609
EMAIL: oliver.thain@condorpubs.com

COOKING 2
MODERN BRITISH
£18–£44

Two separate entrances emphasise the fact that both a pub and a restaurant occupy the same building in this delightful Cambridgeshire village. A designer makeover has given it a clean-looking contemporary feel, where pale yellow walls, sage-green paintwork and bare boards set the tone in the simple, airy restaurant. The full menu is Anglo-French by inclination, with a few detours for baked duck parcel with sweet-and-sour cucumber, and roasted aubergine layered with tomato, basil and mozzarella. Two blackboards also list daily fish dishes (skate wing with anchovy, garlic and caper butter has been simply but stylishly executed), while a mix-and-match selection of local sausages comes with a choice of flavoured mash. The kitchen works competently across the board, from seared asparagus with a poached egg and mustard dressing to individual beef Wellington in a 'generous lake' of rich port sauce. Among desserts, cardamom pannacotta with luscious summer fruits has been 'a real winner'. Lunch menus are a bargain, service is smart and friendly. The wine list was being revamped as the Guide went to press.

CHEFS: Richard Bradley and Chris Brading   PROPRIETORS: Oliver Thain and Richard Bradley
OPEN: Tue to Sun L 12 to 2.30 (3 Sun), Tue to Sat D 7 to 9.30   CLOSED: 25 and 26 Dec   MEALS: alc
D (main courses £9 to £17). Set L Tue to Sat £6.95 (2 courses) to £9.95, Set L Sun £10.95 (1
course) to £16.95   SERVICE: not inc   CARDS: Delta, MasterCard, Switch, Visa   DETAILS: 63
seats. 30 seats outside. Private parties: 40 main room. Car park. Vegetarian meals. Children's
helpings. No smoking in dining room. Wheelchair access (not WC). No music

## HENLEY-IN-ARDEN Warwickshire

map 5

# Edmunds 🍴

NEW ENTRY

64 High Street, Henley-in-Arden B95 5BX
TEL/FAX: (01564) 795666

COOKING 5
MODERN BRITISH
£51–£36

Andy and Beverley Waters set up shop in this steeply roofed, half-timbered house in the summer of 2002, close enough to the international magnet of Stratford-upon-Avon to benefit from some of its business, and yet distant enough not be overrun by the tourist hordes. The ground floor has been knocked through and done in coral tones, with copper table decorations and fresh flowers everywhere. Despite its being early days when our inspector visited, the kitchen is already very much on form, and presentations are diverting: a triangular slab of terrine standing an inch proud of the plate combines chicken, foie gras and shiitake mushrooms, its fine flavours drawn out by dabs of dark mushroom jus and parsnip purée.

There may not be a dish on the menu with whose conception you are not already familiar, and yet the precision and dexterity with which it is all handled is what enthrals. Fanned slices of Loch Fyne salmon are served alongside a tian of Cornish crab and prawns with a sparing quantity of gazpacho dressing to make the best kind of seafood starter. Main courses run the gamut from baked hake fillet on a bed of spinach with a creamy St-Emilion sauce, to a fatless and sinewless rosette of Scotch beef served with button mushrooms, caramelised baby onions and lardons in a Madeira jus: 'a feast of flavours, textures and aromas'. Desserts evoke memories of schooldays, with strawberry jelly and ice cream, or bread-and-butter pudding made with brioche and flavoured with orange. Cheeses are well kept, and properly strong espresso comes with excellent petits fours. The modestly proportioned wine list doesn't really live up to the expectations created by the food, but prices are agreeable enough. Four house wines come from France (£10.95) and Chile (£11.50).

CHEF: Andy Waters PROPRIETORS: Andy and Beverley Waters OPEN: Tue to Fri L 12 to 2, Tue to Sat D 6.45 to 9.45 CLOSED: 25 Dec, bank hols MEALS: Set L £5 (1 course) to £19.50, Set D Tue to Thur £12.50 (2 courses) to £19.50, Set D Fri and Sat £17.50 (2 courses) to £19.50 SERVICE: not inc, card slips closed CARDS: Delta, MasterCard, Switch, Visa DETAILS: 42 seats. Vegetarian meals. Children's helpings. No smoking in dining room. Music (£5)

## HEREFORD Herefordshire — map 5

### ▲ Castle House, La Rive

Castle Street, Hereford HR1 2NW
TEL: (01432) 356321 FAX: (01432) 365909 — COOKING **7**
EMAIL: info@castlehse.co.uk — ANGLO-FRENCH
WEBSITE: www.castlehse.co.uk — £32–£77

Under the same Dutch ownership as Left bank Village (a cluster of shops and a brasserie near the Wye a few hundred yards away), this elegant Georgian town house is a small, outstandingly well-run luxury hotel in a quiet location close to the cathedral. La Rive is the 'fine dining' arm of the enterprise: a serious, dimly lit dining room overlooking what remains of the moat of long-vanished Hereford Castle. The food is as modern as it comes: start perhaps with a cappuccino of watercress and pear, with tortellini of confit snails, Gruyère cheese and cep oil, or with a pavé of sweet blackened cod, wilted pak choi with pickled ginger, truffled cauliflower, and lemon-grass foam.

There is a bit of 'fuss and tra la la' about things – the dinner menu is written rather unnecessarily (and often inaccurately) in French and then translated, the length of descriptions serving only to highlight the sometimes diminutive portions – but the essentials are more than convincing. The Heijn estate supplies a few materials, such as Hereford beef and Gloucester Old Spot pork (the fillet perhaps on sweet-sour red onions, with black pudding, apple, and a crisp beignet of bean sprouts). This is accomplished, complex and ambitious food handled with assurance. Satisfying combinations of flavour and texture abound, from a starter of roast red mullet accompanied by a langoustine tempura, to a tender rabbit and foie gras 'mosaic' with a fine, wobbly Gewürztraminer jelly.

Techniques are impeccable, flavours spot on, right through to desserts, which are sometimes presented in themed trios: an orange one incorporates a soufflé, a cold parfait with a sorbet, and a wobbly jelly topped with mousse. British and French cheeses are well kept, lunch is good value, and service is solicitous and generally efficient. A classically styled and well-chosen wine list concentrates on Bordeaux and Burgundy before venturing to other French regions, the rest of Europe and the New World. Prices are sensible although 'important' French wines, particularly those from mature vintages, may not be cheap. For choice under £20, look either to South America or to the five house wines at £16.95.

CHEF: Stuart McLeod  PROPRIETORS: Dr and Mrs A. Heijn  OPEN: all week 12.30 to 2, 7 to 10  MEALS: Set L £18.95, Set D £32.95 to £46.95 (whole table)  SERVICE: not inc  CARDS: Amex, Delta, MasterCard, Switch, Visa  DETAILS: 34 seats. Private parties:Car park. Vegetarian meals. Children's helpings. No smoking in dining room. Wheelchair access (also WC). Music. Air-conditioned  ACCOMMODATION: 15 rooms, all with bath/shower. TV. Phone. B&B £90 to £210. Rooms for disabled. Baby facilities (*The Which? Hotel Guide*)  (£5)

## HERSTMONCEUX  East Sussex                                  map 3

## ▲ Sundial  ⁙

| Gardner Street, Herstmonceux BN27 4LA | COOKING 5 |
| TEL: (01323) 832217   FAX: (01323) 832909 | FRENCH-PLUS |
|  | £33–£84 |

Frenchness runs through every aspect of the Sundial: from smart service ('we were welcomed as old friends') to menu descriptions (translations are provided) and Vincent Rongier's cooking. He brings a few contemporary ideas to an unashamedly traditional style, turning out crab mousse on avocado salad with lemon vinaigrette, followed perhaps by brill fillet with crayfish tail and lobster sauce, or roast loin of lamb with marjoram jus.

Reporters have commended starters of lobster bisque, and 'feuilleté asperge' with a 'mere wisp of the lightest puff pastry decorating a fan of tender asparagus', and main courses such as thinly sliced calf's liver cooked à point and served on 'light, creamy' potato purée with an intense raspberry-flavoured reduction. The predominantly enthusiastic correspondence has been countered by the occasional disappointment, but coffee is the only element that repeatedly comes in for criticism.

The weekday bistro menu offers simpler, cheaper fare along the lines of coq au vin with pasta, and grilled lamb cutlets with herbs. Wines, unsurprisingly, are mostly French. A selection of good-value house wines from £13.50 opens the list.

CHEF: Vincent Rongier  PROPRIETORS: Vincent and Mary Rongier  OPEN: Tue to Sun L 12 to 2, Mon to Sat D 7 to 9.30  MEALS: alc (main courses £16.50 to £28.50). Set L Tue to Sat £20.50, Set L Sun £24.50, Tue £20.50, Set D Mon and Wed to Sat £26.50. Bistro menu available Tue to Sat L and Sun D  SERVICE: 10%, card slips closed  CARDS: Amex, Delta, Diners, MasterCard, Switch, Visa  DETAILS: 50 seats. 28 seats outside. Private parties: 50 main room, 10 to 20 private rooms. Car park. Children's helpings. No smoking in dining room. Wheelchair access (not WC). Music  ACCOMMODATION: 1 room, with bath/shower. TV. B&B £55 to £85  (£5)

---

*The 2004 Guide will be published before Christmas 2003. Reports on meals are most welcome at any time of the year, but are particularly valuable in the spring (no later than June). Send them to* The Good Food Guide, *FREEPOST, 2 Marylebone Road, London NW1 4DF. Or email your report to* goodfoodguide@which.net

---

# Angel Inn ▮ ✼✕

Hetton BD23 6LT
TEL: (01756) 730263   FAX: (01756) 730363
EMAIL: info@angelhetton.co.uk                                    COOKING 5
WEBSITE: www.angelhetton.co.uk                               MODERN BRITISH
off B6265, 5m N of Skipton                                          £25–£57

You can see why this place is popular. It combines informal eating with food that
would not look out of place in a classier establishment, all the time keeping
prices more gastro-pub than city dining. It can be thought of as a gentrified pub
in two parts – a bar-brasserie, and a comfortable dining room – with a relaxed yet
orderly feel: lunchtime bookings are now taken for the bar, which avoids the 12
o'clock scramble for seats. The kitchen's feeling for comfort food is finely tuned,
as it seeks out smoked haddock fishcakes with whole-grain mustard sauce, and
a first-rate, in-house black pudding with a melting texture and delicate flavour
(more like Continental versions, without the lumps of fat), served with Puy
lentils and crisp pancetta.

Ye olde favourite, moneybags of seafood, is still going strong, while main
courses offer chargrilled ribeye steak with Yorkshire Blue polenta, roast haunch
of venison, and pan-roast Whitby cod with leeks and a pleasingly salty caviar-
flecked cream sauce. A lightness of touch pervades the cooking, and
presentation is appealing, especially when it comes to desserts. Crème brûlée
is a fine version, silky and creamy with a wafer-thin topping, flavoured with
rhubarb for an April visitor; otherwise there may be Bakewell tart ice cream, or
sticky toffee pudding with caramel sauce. Service is friendly and professional,
and wines reflect the care taken elsewhere. France is well represented, with a
number of surprisingly good-value (if not necessarily cheap) red and white
Burgundies. From the New World, Australia, Chile, California, South Africa,
Argentina and New Zealand all get a look-in. House wines start at £11.95 for
house Vin de Pays d'Oc. Nineteen wines by the glass, including two
champagnes, are complemented by a good selection of half-bottles.

CHEFS: Denis Watkins and Bruce Elsworth   PROPRIETORS: Denis Watkins and John Topham
OPEN: Sun L 12 to 1.45, Mon to Sat D 6 to 9   CLOSED: 25 Dec   MEALS: alc D Mon to Fri (main
courses £11.50 to £18.50). Set L Sun £21, Set D 6 to 7 Mon to Fri £14.50 (2 courses) to £17.50
(inc wine), Set D Sat £31. Bar menu available   SERVICE: not inc   CARDS: Amex, MasterCard,
Switch, Visa   DETAILS: 110 seats. 45 seats outside. Private parties: 40 main room. Car park.
Vegetarian meals. Children's helpings. No smoking in 1 dining room. Wheelchair access (not
WC). No music. No mobile phones. Air-conditioned

*'[We ordered] assiette of rabbit with grain mustard creamed potatoes, spinach and tarragon
liquorice jus. I queried the liquorice and was told firmly that it was another word for
"liquor".'* (On eating in Sussex)

*The Guide's longest-serving restaurants are listed near the front of the book.*

## HINDON Wiltshire                                        map 2

# ▲ Angel Inn ✻ 🥧 £

Angel Lane, Hindon SP3 6DJ
TEL: (01747) 820696   FAX: (01747) 820869
EMAIL: eat@the-angel.co.uk

COOKING 3
MODERN EUROPEAN
£25–£46

Ignore the Grosvenor Arms sign outside this re-named Georgian coaching inn at the village crossroads; that is from its pre-October 2001 incarnation. A hotel/restaurant/pub, the Angel has been 'sympathetically modernised with some style' to make just 'the kind of hostelry we'd all crave in our home village'. The bar has real atmosphere: bold red walls, flagstone floor and welcoming log fire (try for the two fireside armchairs over aperitifs). While the bar dining area has polished floorboards and wooden tables and chairs, the long, narrow restaurant has much lighter, contemporary country décor. Walls are hung with historic photographs of local country scenes and a glass-fronted kitchen offers fleeting glimpses of 'chefs on show'.

Matthew Laughton's extensive modern menu, with nods to the Mediterranean and beyond, is a wide-ranging and robust affair and serves both bar and restaurant. Among dishes that have pleased are baked brioche filled with wild mushrooms and asparagus with béarnaise sauce; roast cod in a 'generous volume' of clam, potato and sweet-corn chowder with Toulouse sausage; and 'excellent' warm compote of Agen prunes, orange, vanilla and tea with vanilla ice cream. Service is informal, polite and friendly, while the wine list – a globe-trotting, reasonably-priced affair – starts with South Africans at £10 (£2.55 a glass).

CHEF: Matthew Laughton   PROPRIETORS: Penny Simpson, Bill Laret and Jeff Fergus   OPEN: all week L 12 to 2, Mon to Sat D 7 to 9   CLOSED: early Jan   MEALS: alc (main courses £7 to £14). Set L Sun £14 (2 courses) to £16.50   SERVICE: not inc   CARDS: Delta, MasterCard, Switch, Visa   DETAILS: 65 seats. 30 seats outside. Private parties: 14 main room, 8 to 14 private rooms. Car park. Vegetarian meals. No smoking in dining room. Wheelchair access (not WC). No music   ACCOMMODATION: 7 rooms, all with bath/shower. TV. Phone. B&B £45 to £85  (£5)

## HINTON CHARTERHOUSE Bath & N.E. Somerset          map 2

# ▲ Homewood Park ✻

Hinton Charterhouse BA2 7TB
TEL: (01225) 723731   FAX: (01225) 723820
EMAIL: res@homewoodpark.com
WEBSITE: www.homewoodpark.com
off A36, 6m SE of Bath

COOKING 4
MODERN ENGLISH
£35–£74

In a pleasant, out-of-the-way corner of Somerset, Homewood Park is a 'homely' country house. Its chintzy décor makes it feel 'more posh B&B than grand hotel', which is fitting, considering the stated aim to create 'a sense of elegance without undue formality'.

Nigel Godwin's cooking, on the other hand, is highly refined, characterised by elaborate presentation: among starters, 'a study of winter tastes' brings together a 'mosaic' of game, ballotine of foie gras, chicory Tatin and a Maury reduction. Main courses – poached smoked haddock with crushed potatoes and a lightly poached egg, or braised oxtail with creamed potatoes in red wine jus – demonstrate skill and care in the cooking, though portions tend to be on the small side. Desserts bring 'a welcome bit of fun': for example, a roast pear tasting of mulled wine, with 'lusciously wobbly' pannacotta sandwiched between two biscuits, and a 'deliciously alcoholic' Poire William ice cream spiked with a vanilla pod.

Service is formal in style but friendly in manner, and the wine list runs to a dozen or so pages, most of them preoccupied with major French regions. Apart from house French at £17, only a handful of bottles are under £20.

CHEF: Nigel Godwin   PROPRIETOR: Alan Moxon   OPEN: all week 12 to 1.30, 7 to 9.30   MEALS: Set L £19.50, Set D £39.50 to £47.50 (min 2)   SERVICE: not inc   CARDS: Amex, Delta, Diners, MasterCard, Switch, Visa   DETAILS: 50 seats. Private parties: 40 main room, 2 to 50 private rooms. Car park. Vegetarian meals. Children's helpings. No smoking in dining room. Wheelchair access (also WC). No music   ACCOMMODATION: 19 rooms, all with bath/shower. TV. Phone. B&B £109 to £139. Rooms for disabled. Baby facilities. Swimming pool (*The Which? Hotel Guide*)

## HOLKHAM  Norfolk                                                     map 6

## ▲ Victoria ⁵⁕                                          NEW ENTRY

Park Road, Holkham NR23 1RG                              COOKING 2
TEL: (01328) 711008   FAX: (01328) 711009              MODERN EUROPEAN
WEBSITE: www.victoriaatholkham.co.uk                        £25–£47

The Coke family, which has owned the open fields of Holkham Estate for hundreds of years, also lays claim to this strikingly attractive, flint-stoned cube of a pub. Sandwiches are served in the colonial-style bar, but the main business is in the restaurant, which one reporter thought was done out like 'a baronial Mediterranean manor' complete with ancient wooden doors, bare boards and rough-hewn furniture. Although the food is modern European, there are forays far and wide for rabbit and ginger won tons with rhubarb salsa, Thai fishcakes, and lamb steak with couscous. Beef is supplied by the estate, while crabs are from nearby Wells-next-the-Sea. Fish has also impressed, in the shape of roast salmon with saffron mash and red pepper coulis, while successful desserts have included syrup sponge, and intensely rich chocolate pot served in an espresso cup. The serviceable wine list is arranged by style and offers plenty of decent drinking under £20. House wines start at £10.50.

CHEF: Henry Cumming   PROPRIETOR: Viscount Coke   OPEN: all week 12 to 2.30 (3 Sat and Sun), 7 to 9.30 (10 Sat and Sun)   MEALS: alc (main courses L £5 to £15, D £9 to £15.50). Bar menu available weekdays   SERVICE: not inc   CARDS: Delta, MasterCard, Switch, Visa   DETAILS: 70 seats. 100 seats outside. Private parties: 45 main room. Car park. Vegetarian meals. Children's helpings. No smoking in 1 dining room. Wheelchair access (also WC). Music   ACCOMMODATION: 11 rooms, 10 with bath/shower. TV. Phone. B&B £50 to £170. Rooms for disabled. Baby facilities

---

*'The manager wanted to know if I was a restaurant inspector. My questions about the changes in the kitchen had naturally aroused his suspicions, plus I stood out from the crowd because I was dressed in more than just my underwear and didn't put a mobile phone beside my plate.'*
(On eating in Berkshire)

---

## HOLT Norfolk
map 6

# Yetman's ▼

37 Norwich Road, Holt NR25 6SA
TEL: (01263) 713320
WEBSITE: www.yetmans.net

COOKING 5
MODERN BRITISH
£45–£65

This 'delightful little cottage' in town is simply yet stylishly decorated, with a determinedly informal approach. Peter Yetman, in his (always very fresh and clean) rugby shirt and trainers, welcomes in his usual way – 'Well, hello, you guys' – and monitors progress with 'How are you guys coping?'. 'Anybody who has lived through the 1960s will find him endearing.' What stands out about Alison Yetman's cooking is that it is not too ambitious. The food is simply prepared from first-class ingredients: a just-as-described, heart-on-sleeve dish of local cockles poached in white wine with olive oil, chilli, garlic and pasta, or leg of local lamb, swimming in a liquid heady with lamb juices, cumin and other spices, served with a couple of slices of gently acidic quince.

'I liked the straightforwardness of the food, its lack of pretension, and the skill with which it was done,' summed up a visitor. By this means, quite ordinary dishes are made special without the need for any frills, whether savoury (a fine, upstanding, light-textured twice-baked cheese soufflé with a simple but effective creamy cheese sauce) or sweet: a first-class, vanilla-speckled pannacotta is well paired with figs poached in red wine, while a thick but light and friable pastry case is filled with Victoria plums and ground almonds, and comes with a small jug of single cream. The pretty, annotated wine list exhibits the same lack of pretension, delivering clean, modern styles that complement the cooking. New World Sauvignon Blanc figures largely, but there are also some well-chosen bottles from France and Italy. In lieu of house wines are 'current favourites', which appear at the bottom of the menu and are sold by the glass. Mark-ups are reasonable, with a decent under-£20 selection starting at £16.75.

CHEF: Alison Yetman   PROPRIETORS: Alison and Peter Yetman   OPEN: Sun L 12.30 to 2, Wed to Sat D (Wed to Sun and bank hols late July to end Aug) 7 to 9.30   MEALS: Set L and D £25 (2 courses) to £35   SERVICE: not inc   CARDS: Amex, Delta, MasterCard, Switch, Visa   DETAILS: 32 seats. Private parties: 20 main room. Vegetarian meals. No smoking while others eat. No music

## HOLY CROSS Worcestershire
map 5

# Bell & Cross ⁂✳ £

**NEW ENTRY**

Holy Cross DY9 9QL
TEL: (01562) 730319   FAX: (01562) 731733
off A491, SE of West Hagley

COOKING 1
MODERN EUROPEAN
£23–£45

On a crossroads at the centre of a tiny village, this pub's custard-coloured paintwork makes it hard to miss. Here Paul Mohan cooks a menu overseen by executive chef Roger Narbett (the man who feeds the England Football team). Production has been rather uneven, but good dishes have included a burly-flavoured lobster and crayfish mousse with an asparagus salad copiously dressed in lemon oil. Simpler dishes work best, as so often: perhaps whole lemon sole with lemon and herb butter; calf's liver with smoked bacon, red onion confit and mash; or poached salmon with hollandaise and crushed new potatoes. An individual glazed passion-fruit tart, properly caramelised and crackly, comes with passion-fruit cream and the fresh juice of the fruit. The resolute might tackle the house treacle tart served with ice cream made from clotted cream. Staff present each dish with a reminder of its name, and the command 'Enjoy!' A short wine list includes some vivid southern-hemisphere varietals, with prices opening at £10.50.

CHEFS: Roger Narbett and Paul Mohan   PROPRIETOR: Roger and Jo Narbett   OPEN: all week L 12 to 2 (2.30 Sun), Mon to Sat D 6.30 to 9.30   CLOSED: 25, 26 Dec and 31 Dec D, 1 Jan D, 2 Jan MEALS: alc exc Sun L (main courses £9.50 to £16). Set L Sun £12.75 (2 courses) to £14.75 SERVICE: not inc, card slips closed   CARDS: MasterCard, Visa   DETAILS: 64 seats. 40 seats outside. Private parties: 30 main room, 10 to 15 private rooms. Car park. Vegetarian meals. Children's helpings. No smoking in 1 dining room. Wheelchair access (not WC). Occasional music

## HONLEY  West Yorkshire                                                    map 8

# Mustard & Punch  ▼

6 Westgate, Honley HD9 6AA                                               COOKING 4
TEL: (01484) 662066                                                     ANGLO-FRENCH
EMAIL: (01484) 660742                                                      £23–£50

In March 2001 Rick Dunn joined brother Chris in the kitchen here; in November they took the place over, and much has changed. The décor is now restaurant rather than bistro; chairs are upholstered in a subtle rare beef colour, tables wear white cloths, and service, led by a calm restaurant manager, is pleasant if somewhat tentative. The à la carte partners pan-fried wood pigeon with potato gnocchi and veal jus, and deep-fried frog's leg with cauliflower risotto, which an inspector found a 'fantastic combination'. More predictable seared calf's liver with chive mash and pancetta has been 'perfectly executed'. An assiette of Gressingham duck breast, rillettes and foie gras has come with fondant potato and Puy lentils – 'a great treat for duck-lovers' – while roast peaches with honeycomb ice cream, pain d'épice and bay-scented anglaise has made an agreeably spicy dessert.

The wine list is extensive and well annotated, with a good range of producers from New and Old Worlds, including a Greek white for £16.75. Prices are very reasonable, and most bins are under £20, apart from some big names from Bordeaux and Burgundy. Six house wines cost £8.75 to £13.95 (£1.75 to £2.75 a glass), while an inspector found a Corbières red at £10.95 'very good indeed'.

CHEFS/PROPRIETORS: Chris and Rick Dunn   OPEN: Sun to Fri L 12 to 2 (4 Sun), Mon to Sat D 7 (6 Fri and Sat) to 10   MEALS: alc exc Sun (main courses £11 to £17). Set L Tue to Fri £7.95 (2 courses) to £14.95, Set L Sun £14.95, Set D Tue to Thur £17.95 (2 courses, inc half-bottle house wine) SERVICE: not inc   CARDS: Amex, Delta, MasterCard, Switch, Visa   DETAILS: 66 seats. Private parties: 70 main room. Vegetarian meals. Children's helpings. Music  (£5)

▲ *means accommodation is available.*

## HORNCASTLE Lincolnshire                                    map 9

# Magpies ⚞✸

| | |
|---|---|
| 71–75 East Street, Horncastle LN9 6AA | COOKING 2 |
| TEL: (01507) 527004 | MODERN BRITISH |
| EMAIL: magpies@fsbdial.co.uk | £19–£45 |

Reasonably spacious and very pink, Magpies is a family-run enterprise in a low cottagey building, sporting images of farmyard animals on fabrics and walls. Old favourites may pop up now and again – a hot and cold salad of scallops and smoked salmon, or goats' cheese with red pepper – but the menu also takes a broad sweep, offering guinea fowl breast with apricots and couscous, and loin of lamb with Puy lentils and Madeira sauce.

The kitchen has an eye for native produce in the shape of local asparagus with hollandaise, and Lincoln red fillet steak with béarnaise, while seafood might take the form of stir-fried tiger prawns with garlic and chilli, or monkfish with rosemary and bacon. Traditional desserts, meanwhile, typically include lemon tart, crème brûlée, and sticky toffee pudding. Lunch (a choice of three items per course) is the bargain option, and good-value drinking adds to the appeal: house French white and Australian red are £12 (£3.20 a large glass).

CHEFS: Simon and Matthew Lee   PROPRIETORS: the Lee family   OPEN: Mon to Fri L 12 to 2, Wed to Sat D 7.30 to 9.30   CLOSED: Christmas, 3 weeks Aug, bank hols   MEALS: Set L £8.50 (2 courses) to £9.95, Set D £24   SERVICE: not inc   CARDS: Delta, MasterCard, Switch, Visa   DETAILS: 40 seats. Private parties: 40 main room. No smoking in dining room. Music. Air-conditioned

## HORNDON ON THE HILL Essex                                    map 3

# ▲ Bell Inn ⚑ ⚞✸ £

| | |
|---|---|
| High Road, Horndon on the Hill SS17 8LD | |
| TEL: (01375) 642463   FAX: (01375) 361611 | COOKING 2 |
| EMAIL: info@bell-inn.co.uk | MODERN EUROPEAN |
| WEBSITE: www.bell-inn.co.uk | £24–£41 |

This has been a coaching inn since 1445. Few coaches call today, but, close to the M25, it is still popular with travellers as well as being a favourite haunt of locals. The daily-changing menu has a varied, modern style with 'excellent presentation, distinct flavours' and plenty of quirky touches: among starters, for example, bacon knuckle terrine with deep-fried egg and gherkin dressing, and oyster and apple jelly with apple sabayon and tarragon sauce. Main courses might include grilled red mullet with oxtail-stuffed pepper and a parsley and truffle sauce, or grilled ribeye of beef with bacon fritter and cep purée. Service is 'attentive and professional'. The main menu is also available in the bar along with a list of snacks and lighter dishes. Wines are 50 per cent French; of the rest, New World producers in particular are well chosen. All are available for off-sale at commendably low mark-ups; in fact at the higher price levels there is virtually no mark-up at all, making for excellent value. Prices for on-premises consumption start at £9.10 for French house white, £10 for Australian red.

CHEF: Finlay Logan   PROPRIETOR: John and Christine Vereker   OPEN: all week 12 to 1.45 (2.15 Sun), 6.45 to 9.45   CLOSED: 25 and 26 Dec, bank hols   MEALS: alc (main dishes £9.50 to £13.50). Set L £13.95 (2 courses) to £15.95. Bar and sandwich menus also available   SERVICE: not inc, card slips closed   CARDS: Amex, Delta, MasterCard, Switch, Visa   DETAILS: 80 seats. 36 seats outside. Private parties: 12 main room, 14 to 36 private rooms. Car park. Vegetarian meals. Children's helpings. No smoking in dining room. No music   ACCOMMODATION: 15 rooms, all with bath/shower. TV. Phone. Room only £50 to £100. Rooms for disabled. Baby facilities (*The Which? Hotel Guide*)

## HUDDERSFIELD  West Yorkshire                                          map 9

# Bradley's ✹ £

84 Fitzwilliam Street, Huddersfield HD1 5BB
TEL: (01484) 516773   FAX: (01484) 538386                               COOKING 2
EMAIL: enquiries@bradleysrestaurant.co.uk   MEDITERRANEAN/MODERN BRITISH
WEBSITE: www.bradleysrestaurant.co.uk                                   £15–£48

Andrew Bradley's enthusiasm and bouncy presence help to ensure that this bistro-style restaurant behind the station runs like a well-oiled machine. Crowds pack the neatly appointed, split-level dining room for food that provides quality and excellent value for money. The kitchen takes an eclectic approach to all things gastronomic, offering everything from tempura of Cajun-spiced chicken with celeriac rémoulade and satay dressing, to sirloin steak accompanied by a kidney pie.

Good raw materials are handled with confidence, and there is plenty to admire on the plate. Pan-fried duck breast, cooked slightly pink, appears with a crisp-skinned confit, a small tower of fondant potato and some not-too-sweet red cabbage, while moist fillets of John Dory sit on a pile of saffron mash with an intensely rich crab and prawn bisque beneath. To finish, iced dark chocolate and strawberry soufflé with five-spice syrup sounds a lively idea. Set lunches are a bargain; likewise the 'primetime' evening menu, where the price of three courses includes a half-bottle of wine. An affordable slate of around fifty wines includes eight by the glass. House French is £9.95.

CHEF: Eric Paxman   PROPRIETOR: Andrew Bradley   OPEN: Mon to Fri L 12 to 2, Mon to Sat D 6 to 10 (10.30 Fri and Sat)   CLOSED: bank hols exc Christmas   MEALS: alc (main courses £9 to £16). Set L £5 (2 courses) to £6.95, Set D £10.50 (2 courses) to £15.50 (inc wine)   SERVICE: not inc   CARDS: MasterCard, Switch, Visa   DETAILS: 130 seats. Private parties: 130 main room, 60 to 130 private rooms. Car park (D only). Vegetarian meals. Children's helpings. No smoking in 1 dining room. Wheelchair access (also WC). Music. No mobile phones. Air-conditioned

# ▲ Lodge Hotel ♟ ✹

48 Birkby Lodge Road, Birkby,                                           COOKING 2
Huddersfield HD2 2BG                                            MODERN EUROPEAN
TEL: (01484) 431001   FAX: (01484) 421590                               £22–£47

Extended and decorated by an Art Nouveau enthusiast at the beginning of the twentieth century, the Lodge's interior is covered with patterned fabrics in dark, warm colours. Family-run, it is a place whose commendable ambition seems to be 'to deliver a decent meal at a decent price', according to one visitor. Four-course dinners include a mid-meal soup, but apart from dome-lifting there are few extraneous gestures. The food takes a varied approach to both materials and treatments, offering a smoked haddock and leek risotto with poached egg, chargrilled calf's liver with red onion compote, and a vegetarian option such as Roquefort cheesecake with wilted spinach and black olive dressing. Finish with rhubarb, strawberry and ginger crumble, or cheese. Service is friendly and cheery, and the wine list is likely to keep a smile on your face. It has some excellent producers and a generous number of half-bottles (although only two house wines, and seven dessert wines, are available by the glass). Mark-ups are low, starting at £10.95 for house Vin de Pays d'Oc red and white, and there's much to choose from in the £20–£25 range.

CHEF: Richard Hanson  PROPRIETORS: Garry and Kevin Birley  OPEN: Sun to Fri L 12 to 1.45, Mon to Sat D 7.30 to 9.45  MEALS: Set L £10.95 (2 courses) to £14.95, Set D £23.95 to £26  SERVICE: not inc, card slips closed  CARDS: Amex, Delta, Diners, MasterCard, Switch, Visa  DETAILS: 60 seats. Private parties: 60 main room, 6 to 20 private rooms. Car park. Vegetarian meals. Children's helpings. No smoking in dining room. Wheelchair access (also WC). Music ACCOMMODATION: 12 rooms, all with bath/shower. TV. Phone. B&B £55 to £80. Rooms for disabled. Baby facilities (*The Which? Hotel Guide*)

# Thorpe Grange Manor

Thorpe Lane, Almondbury, Huddersfield HD5 8TA
TEL/FAX: (01484) 425115
EMAIL: enquiries@thorpegrangemanor.com
WEBSITE: www.thorpegrangemanor.com
off A629, 3m E of Huddersfield

COOKING **4**
ANGLO-FRENCH
£22–£60

This is an impressive stone-built eighteenth-century house, now with the air of a conference hotel in need of rejuvenation, its dining room kitted out with varnished floorboards, potted palms and well-spaced tables. The menu reads interestingly, promising modern food with a penchant for the sunny south – perhaps a tartlet of Mediterranean vegetables and black olives topped with goats' cheese and pesto – although the ambitious cooking hits the spot only some of the time: patently fresh fish at inspection suffered from over-cooking and 'clumsy' presentation.

Among more successful items have been a moist, juicy pork terrine, bound in mushroom purée and bacon, and a couple of sweet, well-timed langoustines baked in a crisp filo shell, accompanied by a salad whose strongly mint-flavoured dressing 'went surprisingly well with the shellfish'. Cheeses are well kept, and desserts have included exotic poached fruits on rice pudding under a glazed sabayon, and a chocolate fondant 'like large amaretti stuffed with runny dark chocolate'. Service from an efficient team of young waitresses is on the ball, and wines embrace a fair range of styles and prices, starting with six house wines up to £13.50.

CHEF: Jason Neilson  PROPRIETORS: Ronald, Gillian, Jason and Ruth Neilson  OPEN: Tue to Fri and Sun L 12 to 1.45, Tue to Sat D 6 (7 Fri and Sat) to 9  MEALS: alc (main courses £15.50 to £22.50). Set L Tue to Fri £12.50 (2 courses) to £14.95, Set L Sun £14.95, Set D Tue to Thur 6 to 7.30 £14.95, Set D £19.95  SERVICE: not inc  CARDS: Delta, MasterCard, Switch, Visa  DETAILS: 60 seats. 20 seats outside. Private parties: 19 main room, 40 to 50 private rooms. Car park. Vegetarian meals. Children's helpings. No children under 5 after 7.30pm Sat. No cigars/pipes in dining room. Wheelchair access (also WC). Music. Air-conditioned £5

# ▲ Hunstrete House 🍷 🌟

Hunstrete, Pensford BS39 4NS
TEL: (01761) 490490   FAX: (01761) 490732
EMAIL: user@hunstretehouse.co.uk
WEBSITE: www.hunstretehouse.co.uk
off A368, 4m S of Keynsham

COOKING **4**
MODERN BRITISH/EUROPEAN
£31–£81

Seen in the right light, this is a mellow, golden-stone building, with deer grazing outside the windows. Comfort is something of a priority, given four lounges, all replete with squashy sofas and interesting chairs, while the pale green and peach dining room looks out through tassel-curtained windows on to a small courtyard. The menu appears not to change very often, but materials are sound, particularly seafood: fat, juicy, tasty scallops for one visitor, served with a risotto redolent with the flavour of langoustine shells, and with a thin, frothy fish cream. Also enjoyed has been a baked, earthily sweet and chunky fillet of brill, with a buttery breadcrumb crust and a mild mustard sauce.

Dishes tend to involve quite a bit of workmanship: for example, in a tender saddle of white rabbit meat, sliced into collops, served with a crispy boudin blanc of appealing livery gaminess, and some shredded carrot in a deep-fried puff pastry parcel, the latter perhaps a tongue-in-cheek gesture since it is the favourite food of all rabbits from Peter to Bugs Bunny. The kitchen has an eye for presentation and colour – 'everything we ate looked beautiful' – and taste often lives up to appearance: for example, in a pale green iced apple parfait that was the 'vibrant essence of Granny Smith', stuck with apple crisps and surrounded by a bright green clear syrup and a crescent of raspberry juice. High prices provide a bit of a hurdle, but service is friendly and good-natured, while wines are chosen with care. France gets top billing on the globe-trotting list, with Italy and Spain providing interest elsewhere in Europe. A selection of six French house wines starts at £15.95 (£3.75 per 175ml glass).

CHEF: Phil Hobson   PROPRIETOR: North American Country Inns   OPEN: all week 12 to 2, 7 to 9.30   MEALS: alc exc Sun L (main courses £23.50 to £25.50). Set L £15.95 (2 courses) to £19.95, Set L Sun £25   SERVICE: not inc   CARDS: Amex, Delta, Diners, MasterCard, Switch, Visa   DETAILS: 50 seats. 20 seats outside. Private parties: 50 main room, 2 to 30 private rooms. Car park. Vegetarian meals. Children's helpings. No smoking in dining room. Wheelchair access (also WC). Occasional music. No mobile phones   ACCOMMODATION: 25 rooms, all with bath/shower. TV. Phone. B&B £135 to £350. Rooms for disabled. Swimming pool (*The Which? Hotel Guide*)

# ▲ Old Bridge Hotel 🍸 🌟 £

1 High Street, Huntingdon PE29 3TQ
TEL: (01480) 424300   FAX: (01480) 411017
EMAIL: oldbridge@huntsbridge.co.uk

COOKING **4**
MODERN BRITISH
£24–£55

Part of the Huntsbridge Group (with the Falcon, Fotheringhay; Pheasant, Keyston; and Three Horseshoes, Madingley – see entries), this creeper-covered hotel overlooks the Great Ouse. Its menu ranges from sandwiches and light dishes to interesting creations of fashionable ingredients. Many dishes have an

Italian accent. A starter of spinach and ricotta gnudi (like gnocchi) comes with sage butter, Parmesan and oil, while a large raviolo of Portland crab may be spiced with ginger, lemon-grass and coriander bisque. A perfectly cooked roast salmon steak with flageolet beans and braised fennel may follow, or a rustic seared breast of tender wood pigeon with garlic polenta, spinach and red wine sauce. There may be delicately flavoured cherry and camomile compote with lemon mousse to finish, or perhaps macaroons with warm apricots and coconut ice cream.

Service is smart and pleasant, if less proficient than it was. The wine list, organised by style, runs the gamut of well-chosen producers from Old World and New, classic and new wave. Mark-ups are low, and lower on more expensive wines, making the big guns of Burgundy, Bordeaux, Italy and the New World comparatively better value. There is much choice under £20, a good selection of halves, and 13 house wines starting at £11.50 (£2.80 a glass).

CHEF: Martin Lee  PROPRIETORS: John Hoskins and Martin Lee  OPEN: all week 12 to 2.15, 6.30 to 10 (7 to 10 Sun)  MEALS: alc (main courses £9.50 to £18.50). Set L Mon to Sat £11 (2 courses) to £14.50  SERVICE: not inc  CARDS: Amex, Diners, MasterCard, Switch, Visa  DETAILS: 100 seats. 25 seats outside. Private parties: 90 main room, 10 to 50 private rooms. Car park. Vegetarian meals. Children's helpings. No smoking in dining room. Wheelchair access (not WC). No music. No mobile phones  ACCOMMODATION: 24 rooms, all with bath/shower. TV. Phone. B&B £80 to £175

---

**ILKLEY  West Yorkshire**　　　　　　　　　　　　　　　　　　　　**map 8**

# Box Tree

35–37 Church Street, Ilkley LS29 9DR
TEL: (01943) 608484　FAX: (01943) 607186　　　　　　　　　COOKING 5
EMAIL: info@theboxtree.co.uk　　　　　　　　　　　　　MODERN FRENCH
WEBSITE: www.theboxtree.co.uk　　　　　　　　　　　　　　£39–£71

The cottage, on a corner in the centre of town, looks much as it has always done: a series of low-ceilinged rooms in dusty pink with lots of artwork on display. There are some changes, though. The two statues guarding the dining room entrance have gone, and, after Toby Hill left for Lords of the Manor (see entry, Upper Slaughter), young Shane Goodway (who has worked in a few prestigious kitchens) boldly stepped into a kitchen that has seen some remarkably good cooking over the years.

Varied materials bring diversity to the menus, which might take in lobster ravioli, terrine of ham with roast parsnips, and roast rabbit with tarragon and wild mushrooms. Not all ingredients are top notch but, despite a few inconsistencies in timing and seasoning, the cooking shows much promise: in a well-flavoured boudin blanc served with wild mushrooms and potato crisps, and in scallops coated with crushed peanuts, well seared outside, soft within, arranged around a cold tian of lightly crunchy cauliflower, garnished with tomatoes and aubergines. Foie gras works its way into a number of dishes, including pink duck breast with braised Little Gem, and plainly cooked pink lamb cutlets with a crisp, almond pastry basket of seasonal vegetables.

Cheeses are served with good prune bread, and a well-executed pear Tatin has made a fine finish, accompanied by a creamy vanilla ice cream and a pool of sweet caramel sauce. Champagne is a big story on the wine list, with luxury cuvées aplenty, along with well-chosen selections from Bordeaux (including a number of vintages from all five premiers crus) and Ch. d'Yquem going back to 1957. Good New World selections from Australia, the USA and Chile round out the wide-ranging list. House red and white Burgundy are £14, although bottle prices (from Alsace and Germany) start at £11.50.

CHEF: Shane Goodway   PROPRIETOR: The Box Tree Restaurant (Ilkley) Ltd   OPEN: Tue to Sun L 12 to 2.30, Tue to Sat D 7 to 9.30   CLOSED: Christmas to New Year, 1 to 15 Jan   MEALS: alc (main courses £14 to £21.50). Set L and D £19.50 (2 courses)   SERVICE: not inc, card slips closed   CARDS: Amex, Delta, MasterCard, Switch, Visa   DETAILS: 50 seats. Private parties: 30 main room, 16 private room. Vegetarian meals. No smoking in dining room. Wheelchair access (not WC). Occasional music. No mobile phones

# Farsyde £

38A The Back Grove, Ilkley LS29 9EE
TEL: (01943) 602030
WEBSITE: www.thefarsyde.com

COOKING 4
MODERN BRITISH
£19–£38

Bright, primary colours welcome visitors to this cheerful ground-floor restaurant underneath Betty's tearooms: enter it via the town's main car park. Value for money is considered good, and staff are welcoming and friendly; indeed, 'it is most pleasing to find such a restaurant where ... customers are truly valued and looked after so well'. A gently inventive approach pervades the cooking, producing dishes such as smoked haddock clafoutis – 'light as a feather ... packed with flavour' – and the balance of tastes also impresses, for example in a dish of pink duck served with sweet potato rösti and a spicy green lentil salsa.

Wednesday is fish night (seafood successes include a generous-sized skinless fillet of salmon on a well-made herb risotto), and early-evening opening is welcomed not just for its early-bird prices but also because shoppers don't have to hang around for another hour and a half waiting for somewhere to eat; one couple enjoyed a duck stir-fry and a marinated tuna salad, followed by rump of lamb, finishing with pannacotta and a trio of sorbets. Three dozen well-chosen wines contrive to stay mostly under £20, and start with house French at £7.75.

CHEF/PROPRIETOR: Gavin Beedham   OPEN: Tue to Sun L 11.30 to 2, Tue to Sat D 6 to 10   CLOSED: closed Sun L Apr to end Sept   MEALS: alc (main courses L £4 to £8, D £11 to £14). Set L £11.95, Set D Tue to Thur 6 to 7.15 £11.95 (2 courses)   SERVICE: not inc   CARDS: Delta, MasterCard, Switch, Visa   DETAILS: 55 seats. Vegetarian meals. No cigars/pipes in dining room. Wheelchair access (not WC). Music

## IPSWICH Suffolk                                                          map 6

# Mortimer's ⚡✳ £

1 Duke Street, Ipswich IP3 0AE
TEL/FAX: (01473) 230225

COOKING 1
SEAFOOD
£20–£57

Mortimer's is no longer on the quay, having moved to new premises about 400 yards from the original site, which the Amblers and their team have outgrown after 16 successful years. Everything else remains as before, including the daily-changing menu format. Starters can be as simple as chargrilled sardines with garlic butter and are never more elaborate than scallops parisienne (cooked in vermouth, garlic and cream with a breadcrumb topping) or grilled skewered prawns with a satay dip. Alternatively, go for the oysters or one of the platters of smoked fish, before moving on to salmon fillet on mushroom duxelles with a puff pastry topping and a watercress and cream sauce, or perhaps chargrilled red snapper on noodles and stir-fried vegetables with a Thai-style dressing. A few meat and vegetarian options ensure that all comers are catered for. Wines, understandably, are mostly white and have a French bias. House selections are £10.50 and £12.25.

CHEFS: Kenneth Ambler, Alison Mott and Reda A. Irain    PROPRIETORS: Kenneth and Elizabeth Ambler    OPEN: Mon to Fri L 12 to 2, Mon to Sat D 6.30 to 9 (8.30 Mon)    CLOSED: 24 Dec to 5 Jan, bank hol Mons    MEALS: alc (main courses £5 to £19)    SERVICE: not inc    CARDS: Amex, Delta, Diners, MasterCard, Switch, Visa    DETAILS: 125 seats. Private parties: 125 main room, 20 private room. Car park. Vegetarian meals. Children's helpings. No smoking in dining room. Wheelchair access (also WC). Occasional music  (£5)

---

**IXWORTH Suffolk**                                                                      map 6

# Theobalds ▾ ⅍

| | |
|---|---|
| 68 High Street, Ixworth IP31 2HJ | COOKING **3** |
| TEL/FAX: (01359) 231707 | ANGLO-FRENCH |
| WEBSITE: www.theobaldsrestaurant.co.uk | £27–£51 |

'A long-standing favourite of all the family', one East Anglian reporter called this village restaurant. The building is centuries old, with a log fire in the inglenook, and beams and timbers separating the warren of little dining areas. Geraldine Theobald oversees front-of-house, and service generally runs smoothly.

Our inspector describes Simon Theobald's cooking as 'very English with Continental drift'. Well-tried dishes on the seasonal menus seem to work best, from an enthusiastically received twice-baked cheese soufflé with a crusty top, to a 'wonderfully rich' chocolate and walnut mousse with orange flavoured crème anglaise. In between, the kitchen might turn its hand to roast breast of Gressingham duck with caramelised figs and port sauce, or rump of lamb on diced courgettes and pimentos with a rosemary, tomato and sherry sauce. Sea bass or scallops might form the basis of seafood alternatives, the latter perhaps grilled on a bed of smoked salmon risotto. Technique and saucing occasionally go awry but, overall, this is a 'very pleasant' place. A number of very good producers appear on the varied, annotated wine list, and there is plenty under £20 (prices start at £11.75). Five wines come by the glass, and 25 half-bottles are listed.

CHEF: Simon Theobald    PROPRIETORS: Simon and Geraldine Theobald    OPEN: Tue to Fri and Sun L 12.15 to 1.30, Tue to Sat D 7 to 9    MEALS: alc D (main courses £12.50 to £17). Set L Tue to Fri £12.95 (2 courses) to £16.95, Set L Sun £18.95, Set D Tue to Thur £21    SERVICE: not inc, card slips closed    CARDS: MasterCard, Switch, Visa    DETAILS: 42 seats. Private parties: 50 main room, 10 to 20 private rooms. Vegetarian meals. Children's helpings. No children under 6 at D. No smoking in dining room. Wheelchair access (not WC). No music

## JEVINGTON East Sussex     map 3

# Hungry Monk ♥ ✕

Jevington BN26 5QF
TEL/FAX: (01323) 482178     COOKING **2**
WEBSITE: www.hungrymonk.co.uk     ENGLISH/PROVINCIAL FRENCH
on B2105, off A22 between Polegate and Friston     £39–£53

'It is reassuring to find that little has changed over 33 years at this small cottagey restaurant,' noted one visitor in admiration. Walls have been repainted at intervals, carpets replaced periodically, and the pictures of monks have gone, but otherwise it is business as usual. Loyal customers return time and again for a succession of dishes that are gently updated, and yet which remain comfortingly familiar: crispy chorizo on potato and chive salad perhaps, or a mould of thin bread filled with creamed leeks, baked, and given a Gruyère sauce.

Meat predominates among main courses – accurately roast Hereford beef for Sunday lunch, or a choice of duck breast (Norfolk or Barbary) – although fish might turn up as roast cod with black pudding, sherry vinegar sauce and frîtes. The family staple, 'The Original Hungry Monk Banoffi Pie', is 'very good and fattening but worth the calories'. For a change, try the goats' cheese and blue Brie savoury. Service is 'pleasant and helpful', and regional French wines get fair billing on the good value list, helping to balance the customary Bordeaux and Burgundy sections. For those who prefer to drink by the glass, two selections of three wines each (one per course) are available at £12.50 or £15.50. Six house wines range from £12 to £18.

CHEFS: Gary Fisher and Nick Sharman   PROPRIETORS: Sue and Nigel Mackenzie   OPEN: Sun L 12 to 2.30, all week D 6.45 to 9.45   CLOSED: 24 to 26 Dec, bank hol Mons   MEALS: Set L £26.50, Set D £28.50   SERVICE: not inc, 12.5% for parties of 8 or more, card slips closed   CARDS: Amex, MasterCard, Switch, Visa   DETAILS: 40 seats. Private parties: 38 main room, 4 to 16 private rooms. Car park. Vegetarian meals. Children's helpings. No children under 4. No smoking in dining room. Occasional music. No mobile phones. Air-conditioned (£5)

## KELSALE Suffolk     map 6

# Harrisons ✕ £

Main Road, Kelsale IP17 2RF
TEL/FAX: (01728) 604444
on A12 outside Kelsale village; going N look for
sign for 'Carlton Industrial Estate' and then turn
left at layby after sharp bend

SUFFOLK
GFG
2003
COMMENDED

COOKING **4**
MODERN BRITISH
£22–£42

This white-painted thatched cottage just outside Kelsale village is a 'real find'. It has a pretty, timbered dining room on the ground floor, with more tables upstairs, and the operation has a sincere and unpretentious air. Through his links with the Suffolk Smallholders Society and the Rare Breeds Survival Trust, Peter Harrison uncovers interesting ingredients, maybe roast belly of Gloucester Old Spot pork, Red Poll ribeye steak with chunky chips, or accurately timed Dexter beef fillet ('bags of flavour') with Caesar salad.

His range extends to spiced aubergine with mint and yogurt, Aldeburgh asparagus with hollandaise, and an unusual starter of braised oxtail with horseradish and Stilton. Seafood takes in fish from Southwold, Aldeburgh oysters, and dived Scottish scallops with lentils and coriander. The three-course lunchtime deal is appreciated, and dishes ranging from whole sea bass to a translucent elderflower jelly with a fine shortbread biscuit have attracted plaudits. The first Tuesday of the month is Starters and Sweets night (choice of around eight and six respectively); order four, in any order you like, for £16.95. Bread is good, service friendly and efficient, and a short wine list, mostly under £20, starts with house Italian Inzolia and Sangiovese at £9.95.

CHEF: Peter Harrison   PROPRIETORS: Peter and Melanie Harrison   OPEN: Tue to Fri and Sun L 12 to 2, Tue to Sat D 7 to 10   CLOSED: 24 Dec to 7 Jan   MEALS: alc (main courses £10 to £14). Set L Tue to Fri £11.50 (2 courses) to £13.50   SERVICE: not inc, card slips closed   CARDS: Delta, MasterCard, Switch, Visa   DETAILS: 50 seats. 12 seats outside. Private parties: 22 main room. Car park. Vegetarian meals. Children's helpings. No children under 8. No smoking in dining room. Wheelchair access (not WC). No music. No mobile phones

## KENDAL Cumbria                                                                map 8

# Déjà-vu £                                                 | NEW ENTRY |

124 Stricklandgate, Kendal LA9 4QG                               COOKING 2
TEL: (01539) 724843   FAX: (01539) 739323                      MEDITERRANEAN
                                                                  £16–£48

'A glimmer of southern warmth in the home of the walker's/climber's vademecum, Kendal mint cake' is how one visitor characterised this relaxed town-centre eatery. What décor there is is van Gogh-influenced, and everything is done with great goodwill and pleasantness. The chef is from Spain (Spanish evenings are a regular feature), but the cooking is more broadly Mediterranean. Lunch menus are 'fantastic' value, even though many dishes carry supplements: reporters have greatly enjoyed pan-fried king prawns with fettucine and red pepper coulis; crostini with roasted vegetables and a Parmesan crust; and Toulouse sausage with garlic mash and red wine jus. Ambition and prices rise in the evening, when the kitchen tackles the likes of chargrilled chorizo with cassoulet, Cornish sea bass with grape and coriander fish broth, and dark chocolate and organic raspberry tart with damson and plum sorbet. House wines are from £8.95 (1.95 a glass), and there's good choice under £20.

CHEFS: José González López and Fabien Bellouère   PROPRIETOR: François Bellouère   OPEN: Mon to Sat 12 to 2, 7 to 9 (9.30 Fri, 10 Sat); bank hol Sun 7 to 9   CLOSED: 25 and 26 Dec, 1 and 2 Jan   MEALS: alc exc on 'Spanish nights' (main courses L £4.50 to £8.50, D £10 to £16). Set L £5.95 (2 courses) to £8.50. Paella/tapas menu Wed D (main courses £8.50 to £10)   SERVICE: not inc, 10% for parties of 6 or more   CARDS: Amex, Delta, Diners, MasterCard, Switch, Visa   DETAILS: 34 seats. Private parties: 40 main room. Vegetarian meals. Music ⓔ5

*Prices quoted in the Guide are based on information supplied by restaurateurs. The prices quoted at the top of each entry represent a range, from the lowest meal price to the highest; the latter is inflated by 20 per cent to take account of likely price rises during the year of the Guide.*

# Restaurant Bosquet ▼

97A Warwick Road, Kenilworth CV8 1HP
TEL/FAX: (01926) 852463

COOKING 5
FRENCH
£39–£57

The uninitiated could be forgiven for not expecting great things of this 'unobtrusive' terraced house on the main Warwick Road (it's hard to pick out, driving past in a car). Nonetheless, it harbours some fine French cooking. Inside, it feels rather 'like being in someone's front room'; the décor evokes a 'bygone era', and starched white-clothed tables are well spaced, the atmosphere 'homely, relaxed and laid-back'. After some 22 years here the Ligniers' double act still draws in the visitors: Jane providing a 'warm and genuine' welcome out front, Bernard behind the stove dedicated to a repertoire steeped in traditional French cuisine.

Classic ingredients and luxuries pop up right from the start: pâté de foie gras with sweet chestnuts and ginger, coquilles St Jacques served with crab and lemon-flavoured rice in a saffron and squid-ink sauce, or 'smooth and silky' asparagus soup with truffles. Poultry might run to duck breast with spicy fig sauce, or guinea fowl breast (marinated in pomegranate and spices) with a carrot juice sauce, while fresh market fish could see a fillet of turbot teamed with a well-balanced mustard sauce. To finish, there is classic lemon tart with 'crisp buttery pastry' and strawberry coulis. Vegetables, an integral part of dish compilation, are all top-notch, and 'decent' ciabatta rolls and 'good strong' coffee with petit fours confirm the obvious 'love and care that goes into the cooking'. All the wines on the 90-strong list are, naturally enough, French, and give fair choice under £20. Four house wines kick off at £13.50, or £3.50 per glass, and a splattering of half-bottles is welcome too.

CHEF: Bernard Lignier   PROPRIETORS: Bernard and Jane Lignier   OPEN: Tue to Fri L (bookings only) 12 to 1, Tue to Sat D 7 to 9.15   MEALS: alc (main courses £17 to £18). Set L and D Tue to Fri £26   SERVICE: not inc   CARDS: Amex, Delta, MasterCard, Switch, Visa   DETAILS: 26 seats. Private parties: 30 main room. Children's helpings on request. Wheelchair access (not WC). No music. No mobile phones

# Simpson's ⚡

101–103 Warwick Road, Kenilworth CV8 1HL
TEL: (01926) 864567   FAX: (01926) 864510

COOKING 5
MODERN FRENCH
£33–£79

Green awnings and floor to ceiling windows announce this chipper restaurant on the main road, which celebrates a decade here in 2003. Light bounces from ceiling spots off bright white linen tablecloths, walls are covered with colourful landscapes, cartoons, and menus from well-known restaurants, and smokers are well segregated, making it all the easier to appreciate the kitchen's lively output. Set price options offer just a couple of items per course, while the carte comes up with a more generous half a dozen or so, and a degree of experimentation characterises the cooking. House specialities, for example, include roast squab pigeon with truffled pineapple and sweet potato fondant.

Much, though, is in more familiar contemporary mould, taking in seared foie gras with roast fig, scallops with black pudding, and slow braised belly pork with turnips, girolles and marjoram sauce. Desserts likewise offer both conservative and more enterprising choices. Profiteroles come, conventionally enough, with hot chocolate sauce, but a dome of strawberries in champage jelly is served with cheese ice cream, and a white chocolate mousse is partnered by (wait for it) aromatic Puy lentils and Kirsch sauce. The globe-trotting wine list combines variety and interest, with fair choice for those with £25 to spend; there are some 20 half-bottles, and 14 house wines starting at £13.50.

CHEFS: Andreas Antona and Luke Tipping  PROPRIETORS: Andreas and Alison Antona  OPEN: Tue to Sat 12.30 to 2, 7 to 10  CLOSED: 24 to 26 Dec, last 2 weeks Aug, bank hols  MEALS: alc (main courses £19.50 to £22). Set L £15 (2 courses) to £20, Set D £28 (2 courses) to £34. Tasting menu (6 courses) L and D £49.95  SERVICE: not inc, 10% for parties of 6 or more  CARDS: Amex, Delta, Diners, MasterCard, Switch, Visa  DETAILS: 70 seats. Private parties: 40 main room, 10 to 40 private rooms. Car park. Vegetarian meals. Children's helpings. No smoking in 1 dining room. Occasional music. No mobile phones. Air-conditioned

## KEW  Greater London

map 3

# Glasshouse ♥

14 Station Parade, Kew TW9 3PZ

TEL: (020) 8940 6777   FAX: (020) 8940 3833

COOKING 5
MODERN BRITISH
£32–£78

A reporter noted with surprise the relative paucity of good eating places in Kew, which only goes to make the Glasshouse shine all the more luminously. The interior is enlivened with abstract paintings, though if that should change – refurbishment was ongoing as the Guide went to press – Anthony Boyd's menus are sure to catch the eye: 'the mere sight of what was on offer led us to celebrate by ordering champagne'. The tendency to trio presentations noted last year continues, producing a first course of crab three ways: dressed with mayonnaise, in a tart topped with a grilled cherry tomato, and as a little cup of 'stratospherically good' smooth bisque. A lunch-time starter of pigeon and its liver in a warm salad has been equally highly praised. The cooking is nothing if not earthy, using a variety of vegetables to build depth into the dishes. Roast sea bass might come with butternut squash broth, provençale vegetables and sage beurre noisette, or cod with leeks, cauliflower and salsify, while duck breast is well served by caramelised endive tart and potato purée. Trifle served in a glass seems, in the circumstances, an oddly (perhaps ironically) old-fashioned notion. An assortment of apple desserts, however, has garnered approval for beautifully executed pie, purée in filo, and a first-rate sorbet. Service is commended for its warmth and eagerness to please.

The wine list is a fine collection of bottles from quality-minded, cutting-edge producers throughout the Old and New Worlds, rather than the predictable big names. Food compatibility seems to have been a criterion for inclusion too. Good value comes as part of the package, even if the wines are not necessarily cheap. There is plenty to choose from around £20, and, with a couple of exceptions, prices keep below the £100 mark. Prices start at £13.50.

CHEF: Anthony Boyd   PROPRIETOR: Larkbrace Ltd   OPEN: all week 12 (12.30 Sun) to 2.30, 7 (6.30 Fri and Sat, 7.30 Sun) to 10.30   CLOSED: Christmas   MEALS: Set L Mon to Sat £19.50, Set L Sun £23.50, Set D £30   SERVICE: 12.5% (optional), card slips closed   CARDS: Amex, Delta, MasterCard, Switch, Visa   DETAILS: 60 seats. Private parties: 65 main room. Vegetarian meals. Children's helpings. No children under 5 exc at weekends. No music. Air-conditioned

## KEYSTON  Cambridgeshire                                                    map 6

# Pheasant ▼ ⅝✳

Loop Road, Keyston PE18 0RE                                      COOKING 5
TEL: (01832) 710241   FAX: (01832) 710340        MODERN EUROPEAN/BRITISH
on B663, 1m S of junction with A14                                £27–£55

The Huntsbridge formula has proved its worth over the years, and the shared philosophy of all four listed establishments (see the Falcon, Fotheringhay; the Three Horseshoes, Madingley; and the Old Bridge, Huntingdon) in no way diminishes their individuality. The Pheasant looks every inch the village pub, with its thatched roof, oak beams and log fire; its easy-going approach is just the ticket too, allowing options of just drinking, or snacking, or eating a big hearty meal. The lively menu picks up ideas from all over, taking in South Coast crab with chilli, lime and caviar on cucumber jelly, beside pan-fried ox tongue with Italian lentils and horseradish dressing; its flexibility is extended by offering some items, such as salads, in two sizes.

Output can be variable, and flavour partnerships sometimes erratic, but Clive Dixon is a talented chef who can charm with both traditional and more up-to-date ideas, from salmon with hollandaise to sausage and mash, from a terrine of pheasant, chicken and foie gras – a generous portion of rustic simplicity – to a hot apricot soufflé. This is all backed up by a good-value set-price lunch, by 'welcoming and cheerful attention' from staff, and a by a well-chosen wine list that's easy to navigate through. Organised by style, it offers some excellent selections from Austria, Alsace and Tasmania, as well as old favourites from France and Italy. Mark-ups are sensible, as are tasting notes. A selection of 'top class' reds and whites is particularly appealing. A dozen house wines sell for £11.50 to £20 (£2.90 to £5 a glass).

CHEF: Clive Dixon   PROPRIETOR: Huntsbridge Ltd   OPEN: all week 12 to 2, 6.30 (7 Sun) to 9.30   MEALS: alc (main courses £10 to £18.50). Set L Mon to Sat £11.75 (2 courses) to £14.95   SERVICE: not inc, 10% for parties of 10 or more   CARDS: Amex, Delta, Diners, MasterCard, Switch, Visa   DETAILS: 80 seats. 20 seats outside. Private parties: 40 main room. Car park. Vegetarian meals. Children's helpings. No smoking in dining room. Wheelchair access (not WC). No music. No mobile phones

---

*The 2004 Guide will be published before Christmas 2003. Reports on meals are most welcome at any time of the year, but are particularly valuable in the spring (no later than June). Send them to The Good Food Guide, FREEPOST, 2 Marylebone Road, London NW1 4DF. Or email your report to goodfoodguide@which.net*

# Firenze ✺

**NEW ENTRY**

9 Station Street, Kibworth Beauchamp LE8 0LN
TEL: (0116) 279 6260   FAX: (0116) 279 3646
WEBSITE: www.firenze.co.uk

COOKING 3
MODERN ITALIAN
£32–£52

Serious Italian restaurants have a problem. If they work at the cutting edge of modern cooking, the food might not be recognisable as Italian at all; and if they don't, it is hard for the good ones to stand out from the crowd. This one – a single room in a white pebbledash building on a roundabout in the centre of the village – certainly sticks out. The Florence theme is hammered home pretty thoroughly, via prints, photographs, a couple of Leonardo da Vinci drawings, and a detail from Uccello's *Journey of the Magi* turned into a large and striking wall hanging. But Lino Poli doesn't specialise in food from any particular region; his forte is simply cooked food with forthright flavours.

Behind this lies a sound grasp of techniques, for example in the split-second timing applied to a piece of first-class tuna, to produce a moist, supple, grill-striped fillet, served classically on a loose bed of butter beans and raw onion strands; the olive oil in which it is bathed, and the minute quantities of other flavourings, demonstrate the kitchen's talent for getting a dead simple dish just right. Saucing is expertly done too, judging by the large pool of brick-red lamb stock and tomato sauce that comes with a generous rack of pink, tasty lamb and its accompanying stack of aubergine slices sandwiched with pesto and tomato sauce.

A tangy, sweet lemon and almond polenta cake, with a small scoop of mascarpone, proved an object lesson in how to deal with polenta: 'I had no idea it could be this interesting.' Service from Sarah Poli and her team is notably well informed and unpretentious, and an all-Italian wine list celebrates the diversity of the country's viticulture while remaining reasonably priced. House white is £11, red £12.50.

CHEF: Lino Poli   PROPRIETORS: Lino and Sarah Poli   OPEN: Tue to Fri L 12 to 2, Tue to Sat D 7 to 10   CLOSED: 1 week Christmas, 1 week Easter, 2 weeks Aug   MEALS: alc (main courses £12.50 to £18). Set L £10 (1 course)   SERVICE: not inc   CARDS: Delta, MasterCard, Switch, Visa   DETAILS: 60 seats. Private parties: 70 main room. Vegetarian meals. Children's helpings. No smoking in 1 dining room. Wheelchair access (not WC). Music. No mobile phones   (£5)

# ▲ Ship to Shore ✺

**NEW ENTRY**

45 Church Street, Kingsbridge TQ7 1BT
TEL: (01548) 854076   FAX: (01548) 857890
EMAIL: enquiries@ship-to-shore.co.uk
WEBSITE: www.ship-to-shore.co.uk

COOKING 4
MODERN BRITISH
£28–£58

The Stanton family left Ludlow for the gastronomically calmer waters of Kingsbridge in the summer of 2000. Home is now a Victorian end-terrace restaurant-with-rooms at the heart of the town's one-way system. Look for the 'patrons only' car park, and, if there are no spaces left, the quayside is the next best option, barely five minutes' walk away. The beamed dining room is done out in maroon and white, with brocade curtains and reproductions on the walls, and Roger Stanton runs front-of-house with infectious good cheer.

Eldest son Richard heads an industrious kitchen that aims to produce as much as possible in-house. Home-made breads set the tone: three kinds at inspection, including an excellent mini-brioche. The short menus change every few weeks, and are built around a few stalwart dishes that regular customers insist on retaining, supplemented by daily specials. Tender squid in a salad with pancetta in a balsamic dressing demonstrates a good combination of flavours and textures, and the cooking is not without a certain boldness, as suggested by stuffing quail with apricots and serving it on Puy lentils and a chocolate-enriched sauce. That same assertiveness shows up again in a Gressingham duck breast crusted with cardamom and sauced with redcurrants, and in the garlic and ginger butter that accompanies salmon. Essentially, though, simplicity is the watchword, as in a main course of two fillets of halibut sandwiching a layer of spinach. 'Everything on the pud menu looked interesting,' wrote a visitor who opted for a light clafoutis, its griottine cherries 'copiously drenched with Kirsch'. The bedrock of the wine list is French, but there are some well-chosen southern hemisphere bottles too, and prices are generally pretty keen. Six house selections are all £10.25 a bottle, £2.75 a glass.

CHEFS: Richard and Rosamund Stanton PROPRIETORS: Roger, Rosamund and Richard Stanton OPEN: Tue to Sat and Sun in Aug D only 7 (6.30 June to Aug) to 9 MEALS: alc (main courses £10 to £25) SERVICE: not inc, card slips closed CARDS: Delta, MasterCard, Switch, Visa DETAILS: 36 seats. Private parties: 40 main room, 4 private room. Car park. Vegetarian meals. Children's helpings. No smoking in dining room. Wheelchair access (not WC). Music ACCOMMODATION: 3 rooms, all with bath/shower. TV. B&B £25 to £50. Baby facilities

## KING'S CLIFFE  Northamptonshire                              map 6

# King's Cliffe House ▮ ⅙✷

31 West Street, King's Cliffe PE8 6XB
TEL: (01780) 470172
EMAIL: kchr@onetel.net.uk

COOKING 4
MODERN EUROPEAN
£28–£48

After a friendly welcome, 'a most enjoyable meal' is typical of what reporters experience at this curious rambling house in the north-east corner of the county. Although the restaurant is open only four sessions a week, Emma Jessop and Andrew Wilshaw put the rest of their time to good use, diligently sourcing their free-range poultry and eggs, and Dexter beef and Gloucester Old Spot pork from a local butcher with a small abattoir. Above all, the food has a strong seasonal input: Abbey Parks asparagus might be deep-fried in beer batter, and soups may have something of the hedgerow about them, based variously on nettles or wild garlic.

A plate of charcuterie or fish normally features among first courses (perhaps smoked salmon, gravlax, potted shrimps and a salt-cod beignet with pickled samphire), while mains might take in roast loin of lamb with aubergine and tarragon sauce, or sea trout in champagne sauce. As for vegetables, 'a large bowl of cheesy potato was placed on the table for all to share'. The food may not aim for excitement, but it does achieve consistency, and seasonal desserts are well reported: for example, a 'plate of blackberries' incorporating jelly, crème brûlée, and ice cream. With just the owners in attendance, service is necessarily abbreviated: wine is opened, but not poured, which in any case suits most people down to the ground. The varied wine list is packed with good producers from around the wine-making globe, the bottles ordered according to price. The focus seems to be on quality, food-friendly styles; sensible pricing encourages experimentation, as does a very good selection of half-bottles. Six imaginative house wines sell for £9.95 to £13.

CHEFS/PROPRIETORS: Emma Jessop and Andrew Wilshaw   OPEN: Wed to Sat D only 7 to 9.30   CLOSED: 2 weeks autumn, Christmas, 2 weeks spring, bank hols   MEALS: alc (main courses £11 to £15.50)   SERVICE: not inc   CARDS: none   DETAILS: 16 seats. Private parties: 16 main room. Car park. Vegetarian meals. Children's helpings. No smoking in dining room. No music

## KINGTON Herefordshire                                                    map 5

## ▲ Penrhos Court ✻

Kington HR5 3LH
TEL: (01544) 230720   FAX: (01544) 230754
EMAIL: martin@penrhos.co.uk                                          COOKING 3
WEBSITE: www.penrhos.co.uk                                       MEDITERRANEAN
on A44, ½m E of Kington                                              £43–£58

An evening at Penrhos Court is often memorable, not least for the ancient manor farm's medieval atmosphere, with its cruck-beamed dining hall, flagstone floor, and long, bare, communal wooden tables lit by candles. Only organic produce is used, salt is reduced to an absolute minimum, and red meat is banned from the kitchen, although chicken and fish are allowed. Part of the mini-industry includes a well-stocked half-acre 'demonstration garden', developed for the 'green cuisine' courses Daphne Lambert runs, an indication of the importance attached to timely harvesting of herbs, fruit and vegetables. An inspector admired the way in which every item made a 'spankingly freshly prepared impression'. Technical skills are considerable, notable particularly when it comes to bread and pastry (in a caramelised onion tart, for example); and Daphne Lambert 'can execute a really good sauce and a lovely dressing'.

The repertoire advances slowly; roast red pepper sauce has long been a kitchen favourite, while a Thai marinade for chicken seems a comparatively recent development, and very welcome for its fine balance of flavours. Four-course dinners end with a choice of desserts that might take in a flavourful, rough-textured blood orange sorbet, or white chocolate terrine with raspberry sauce. Service bumbles along good-naturedly, and wines, while seemingly not of utmost importance here, are at least reasonably priced, with most under £20.

CHEF: Daphne Lambert   PROPRIETORS: Daphne Lambert and Martin Griffiths   OPEN: all week D only 7.30 to 9.30 (L by arrangement)   CLOSED: 1 Jan to 14 Feb   MEALS: alc (main courses £12 to £20). Set D £31.50   SERVICE: not inc, card slips closed   CARDS: Delta, MasterCard, Switch, Visa DETAILS: 80 seats. 120 seats outside. Private parties: 80 main room, 20 private room. Car park. Vegetarian meals. Children's helpings. No smoking in dining room. Wheelchair access (also WC). No music   ACCOMMODATION: 15 rooms, all with bath/shower. TV. Phone. B&B £65 to £115. Rooms for disabled. Baby facilities (The Which? Hotel Guide)   £5

# Cromwellian

16 Poulton Street, Kirkham PR4 2AB
TEL/FAX: (01772) 685680

COOKING 3
MODERN BRITISH
£29–£45

Since 1986, Peter and Josie Fawcett have worked as a team in this modest converted terrace cottage. He maintains a relaxed, chatty presence in the low-ceilinged dining room, she is the diligent, unflustered cook. The whole place has a reassuring feel of domestic intimacy and it works to a well-tried formula that pleases everyone.

Dinner is fixed-price for two or three courses, with a few supplements. Meals generally kick off with a homely soup (say, mushroom, apple and Calvados), or filo pastry parcels with various fillings. Over the years, fillet of Aberdeen Angus steak has been a best seller and remains a fixture. However, other dishes are beginning to make their presence felt, thanks to the possibilities offered by new suppliers. In the fish department, there might be sea bass with roasted peppers and warm herb vinaigrette, while game could appear in the guise of baked suprême of pheasant with a bubble and squeak 'scone' and Madeira sauce. Desserts are in the old-fashioned mould of mincemeat and apricot crumble, or upside-down chocolate and pear sponge. The wine list is a well-chosen slate with good bottles from around the world. House wine is £10.50 (£2.75 a glass).

CHEF: Josie Fawcett   PROPRIETORS: Peter and Josie Fawcett   OPEN: Tue to Fri 7 to 9   MEALS: Set D £16 (2 courses) to £19.50   SERVICE: not inc, card slips closed   CARDS: Amex, Delta, MasterCard, Switch, Visa   DETAILS: 20 seats. Private parties: 10 main room, 10 to 12 private rooms. Vegetarian meals. No music. No mobile phones

# ▲ Langar Hall ▼ ⅝✳

Langar NG13 9HG
TEL: (01949) 860559   FAX: (01949) 861045
EMAIL: langarhall-hotel@ndirect.co.uk
WEBSITE: www.langarhall.com
between A46 and A52, 4m S of Bingham; Langar
Hall in middle of village next to the church

COOKING 3
ENGLISH
£23–£66

At the end of a long drive, this deep-orange, symmetrical building, dating from 1837, backs on to the village church. Staff help to create a homely atmosphere, and previous descriptions of its individuality and mild eccentricity have apparently hit the nail on the head. The cooking follows no particular school, taking in a wide range of ideas, from Stilton fritters with Cumberland sauce, via sea bass with champagne sauce, to chargrilled leg of Langar lamb with minted gravy.

Fine raw materials stand out particularly, including a first-class, pink roast duck breast with a tangy, citrus-flavoured stock sauce; although the roast potatoes and tartare sauce that come with it may not be everyone's idea of an appropriate accompaniment, the simple seasonal vegetables that partner main courses are top quality. There have been some ups and downs in the cooking, from a 'bedsit-level' starter of scallops with garlic butter, to a trendily presented frozen banana parfait with an intense, dark chocolate sorbet 'tasting of about 500 per cent cocoa solids'. Imogen Skirving sources wines from specialists and aims to keep mark-ups low, offering Isabel Estate's Marlborough Sauvignon Blanc at £17.95, for example, and starting with ten house wines from John Armit between £11 and £18. There's a wealth of choice under £20, while 'Imogen's selection' at the front of the list is a good starting point for lively styles from around the world.

CHEF: Toby Garratt  PROPRIETOR: Imogen Skirving  OPEN: all week 12 to 1.45, 7 to 10 (8.30 Sun)  MEALS: alc D (main courses £12.50 to £20). Set L Mon to Thur £12.50 (2 courses) to £15, Set L Fri £15 (2 courses) to £17.50, Set L Sat £17.50, Set L Sun £22.50, Set D Mon to Thur £25 (2 courses) to £30, Set D Fri and Sat £30 (2 courses) to £35  SERVICE: 5% (optional), card slips closed  CARDS: Amex, Delta, Diners, MasterCard, Switch, Visa  DETAILS: 30 seats. 20 seats outside. Private parties: 22 main room, 8 to 22 private rooms. Car park. Vegetarian meals. Children's helpings. No smoking in dining room. Wheelchair access (also WC). No music  ACCOMMODATION: 10 rooms, all with bath/shower. TV. Phone. B&B £65 to £175. Baby facilities. Fishing (The Which? Hotel Guide)

---

**LANGFORD BUDVILLE Somerset**　　　　　　　　　　　　　　　　map 2

# ▲ Bindon Country House, Wellesley Restaurant ⅚✳

Langford Budville TA21 0RU
TEL: (01823) 400070　FAX: (01823) 400071　　　　　　　COOKING 3
EMAIL: stay@bindon.com　　　　　　ANGLO-FRENCH COUNTRY-HOUSE
WEBSITE: www.bindon.com　　　　　　　　　　　　　　　　£31–£61

Bindon is a most unusual-looking place, the seventeenth-century house having been given a Gothic makeover by one of its Victorian owners. Otherwise it is familiar grand country-house territory: oak panelling, chandeliers, and so on. As might be expected, menus show a classical inclination but do so without being too fuddy-duddy: witness starters of foie gras terrine with duck breast, pear and mango, and blue cheese soufflé with mint potato and balsamic dressing. Reporters are generally liberal with their praise: a main course of 'impeccably cooked' quail accompanied by confit of celery stood out at one meal, and choice may extend to seared monkfish on a mussel and smoked haddock risotto with red wine sauce, or pan-fried rack of lamb with sarladaise potatoes, vegetable 'noodles' and thyme sauce. Desserts show an inventive streak: pink grapefruit and basil soufflé with champagne and basil sorbet, for example. Around a dozen house wines by the glass (from £3.85) or bottle (from £15) open a list whose centre of attention is everything that is fine and French.

CHEF: Patrick Roberts  PROPRIETORS: Lynn and Mark Jaffa  OPEN: all week 12 to 1.30, 7.30 to 9  MEALS: alc L (main courses £10 to £17.50). Set L £12.95 (2 courses) to £16.95, Set L Sun £18.95, Set D £29.95 TO £36  SERVICE: not inc  CARDS: Amex, Delta, Diners, MasterCard, Switch, Visa  DETAILS: 50 seats. 30 seats outside. Private parties: 50 main room, 2 to 30 private rooms. Car park. Vegetarian meals. Children's helpings. No smoking in dining room. Wheelchair access (not WC). Occasional music  ACCOMMODATION: 12 rooms, all with bath/shower. TV. Phone. D,B&B £95 to £205. Rooms for disabled. Baby facilities. Swimming pool (The Which? Hotel Guide) £5

# ▲ Northcote Manor ▼ ⅜⚹

Northcote Road, Langho BB6 8BE
TEL: (01254) 240555   FAX: (01254) 246568
EMAIL: sales@northcotemanor.com                          COOKING 6
WEBSITE: www.northcotemanor.com                       MODERN BRITISH
on A59, 9m E of M6 junction 31                               £26–£82

In 2003 Craig Bancroft and Nigel Haworth notch up 20 years at this Edwardian country-house hotel, where a comfortable lounge welcomes with sofas and a real fire, and the minimalist but tasteful dining room contrasts with the traditional feel elsewhere (watch for wobbly tables, though). The kitchen moves with the times while ensuring that, at least in part, the food reflects its north-western setting: witness a Lancashire hotpot salad (just-warm chargrilled lamb fillet on a salad of new potatoes, with carrot vinaigrette and lightly pickled red cabbage), or an apple crumble soufflé with a tangy Lancashire cheese ice cream. Chips are traditionally wrapped in newspaper hereabouts; hence the tongue-in-cheek presentation of fat chips (with roast beef fillet) in an origami basket fashioned from the *Financial Times*.

But not everything evokes Lancashire. The menu keeps up to date not by following the herd, but by making its own gently innovative way forward, taking in tender West Coast scallops with black macaroni and a creamy girolle sauce, and corn-fed Goosnargh duckling breast with a salsify beignet and an open ravioli of mulled pears. Chargrilled calf's liver has impressed too, served with a 'tour de force' sweetbread sausage on potato purée with a red wine sauce. To finish, Stilton is served with stem ginger, and a 'terrific dish' of Pimms jelly containing raspberries and nectarines comes with a cucumber sorbet and mint ice cream. The set lunch is considered 'a real bargain', and the service, friendly and professional, creates a notably relaxing atmosphere.

The wine list – a good-sized collection of styles and producers – gives more or less equal billing to New and Old Worlds. Lovers of champagne, white burgundy, port (six available by the glass) and Madeira are well-cared for, as are fans of Australian wine. Mark-ups can be steep (£45.25 for Cloudy Bay Chardonnay from New Zealand), but there are five house wines for £15 (£2.75 per glass), as well as an excellent selection of half-bottles.

CHEFS: Nigel Haworth and Warwick Dodds   PROPRIETORS: Craig Bancroft and Nigel Haworth   OPEN: Sun to Fri L 12 to 1.30 (Sun 2), all week D 7 to 9.30 (Sat 10)   CLOSED: 25 Dec and 1 Jan   MEALS: alc (main courses £16 to £26.50). Set L £16.50, Set D £45   SERVICE: 10% (optional), card slips closed   CARDS: Amex, Delta, MasterCard, Switch, Visa   DETAILS: 70 seats. Private parties: 70 main room, 8 to 35 private rooms. Car park. Vegetarian meals. Children's helpings. Jacket and tie. No smoking in dining room. Wheelchair access (not WC). Music. No mobile phones   ACCOMMODATION: 14 rooms, all with bath/shower. TV. Phone. B&B £100 to £150. Rooms for disabled. Baby facilities (*The Which? Hotel Guide*)

---

*If 'The Which? Hotel Guide' is noted at the end of an entry, this means that the establishment is also in the 2003 edition of our sister guide, published in September 2002.*

---

## LAVENHAM Suffolk　　　　　　　　　　　map 6

# ▲ Great House ✸

Market Place, Lavenham CO10 9QZ
TEL: (01787) 247431　FAX: (01787) 248007
EMAIL: info@greathouse.co.uk
WEBSITE: www.greathouse.co.uk

COOKING 2
FRENCH
£27–£57

'The best of England combined with the best of France.' So enthused one reporter after feasting on foie gras on Christmas day in this Gallic outpost in Lavenham's half-timbered market square. Régis Crépy, proudly French, makes regular trips to Rungis market to replenish his larder, though menus yo-yo happily between Anglais and Français. Most lunchtimes you can snack on an omelette or a bowl of mussels, but the full menu earns high praise. Eye-catching starters include pan-fried gâteau of Beaufort cheese, layered with potato, wrapped in Parma ham and finished with a 'sticky' balsamic dressing. Mains too pack visual punch: thick slices of pink calf's liver with local bacon and raspberries, say, or (startlingly colourful) halibut fillets on a beetroot purée. To finish, saffron crème brûlée and iced Grand Marnier soufflé have both drawn drools. Excellent service from 'charming' French staff. Wines give France pride of place, but don't exclude alternatives from elsewhere; house wines from £10.25 a bottle.

CHEF: Régis Crépy　PROPRIETORS: Régis and Martine Crépy　OPEN: Tue to Sun L 12 to 2.30, Tue to Sat D 7 to 9.30 (10 Sat)　CLOSED: Jan　MEALS: alc D (main courses £14 to £18). Set L £13.95 (2 courses) to £16.95, Set L Sun £21.95, Set D Tue to Fri £21.95. Light L menu available Tue to Sat SERVICE: not inc　CARDS: Amex, Delta, MasterCard, Switch, Visa　DETAILS: 45 seats. 30 seats outside. Private parties: 60 main room. Children's helpings. No smoking in dining room. Music ACCOMMODATION: 5 rooms, all with bath/shower. TV. Phone. B&B £60 to £140. Baby facilities (The Which? Hotel Guide)

## LEAMINGTON SPA Warwickshire　　　　　　map 5

# Love's ✸

| | NEW ENTRY |

15 Dormer Place, Leamington Spa CV32 5AA
TEL/FAX: (01926) 315522
EMAIL: lovesrestaurant@aol.com

COOKING 4
MODERN BRITISH
£30–£67

In a row of old houses facing a stretch of greensward, this restaurant, which used to be Amor's and, before that, Les Plantagenêts, was taken over by Steve Love, previously at Mallory Court in nearby Bishop's Tachbrook, in October 2001. The setting is 'plain and simple': a small basement room, with warm, custard-coloured walls and ceiling and a few foodie prints. The cooking is ambitious, and aspirations are usually met with immaculately timed good-quality raw materials, along with sound judgement and some skilful saucing. A light, frothy wild mushroom soup 'startled with its depth of flavour', while a 'superb' shellfish sauce accompanies another starter of seared red mullet with brandade and black olives.

Presentation is intricate – or 'leans toward beauty rather than bounty', as one reporter put it – and dishes tend to have a multitude of components. A main course of tasty, well-hung roast rump of beef comes on shredded Savoy cabbage, and its accompanying pig's trotter – with a 'beautifully made' stuffing – on pease pudding, with various other vegetables and an exemplary red wine jus, while a column of shoulder of lamb has impressed as much for its artistically arranged vegetables as for its tender, tasty meat and gravy.

Desserts may consist of 'an extraordinary Dali-esque creation' of a praline-topped tower of chocolate, or a rich, clearly flavoured dish of caramelised banana and gingerbread mousse with banana and passion-fruit sorbet and citrus caramel. Service is efficient and courteous, although things tend to collapse when the pace gets too fast. The wine list keeps things simple, with its shortish, fairly priced collection of bottles. Four house wines sell for £12.50 and £13.95 (£3.25 and £3.65 a glass).

CHEF/PROPRIETOR: Steve Love   OPEN: Tue to Sat 12 to 2, 7 to 10   CLOSED: Christmas, first week Jan, last 2 weeks Aug   MEALS: Set L £14.50 (2 courses) to £18.50, Set D £23.50 (2 courses) to £29. Menu gourmand £37.50   SERVICE: 10% (optional)   CARDS: Delta, MasterCard, Switch, Visa   DETAILS: 30 seats. Private parties: 35 main room. Vegetarian meals. Children's helpings. No smoking in dining room. Music. No mobile phones. Air-conditioned

## LEEDS  West Yorkshire · map 8

# Brasserie Forty Four

44 The Calls, Leeds LS2 7EW
TEL: (0113) 234 3232   FAX: (0113) 234 3332
EMAIL: brasserie44@onetel.net.uk
WEBSITE: www.dine-services.com

COOKING 4
MODERN EUROPEAN
£23–£51

With wooden floors and polished tables lit by candles and spotlights, this warehouse near the waterfront feels 'casual and professional'. Jeff Baker's team espouses broadly based cosmopolitan cooking with a few bistro classics: imam bayaldi, say, and calf's liver with creamed Savoy cabbage. The signature paella with chorizo, baby squid, mussels and smoked prawns was distinctly under-par at inspection, but there is excellence elsewhere, for example some 'brilliant' meat dishes: a well-hung sirloin steak with large, mustardy watercress leaves, or high-quality, pink-grilled duck breast, crisp-skinned, served in a soup bowl with a 'garbure' of duck confit and Toulouse sausage. Vegetables need ordering separately but are worth it.

Desserts might include steamed chocolate pudding with candied stem ginger, chocolate sauce and whipped mascarpone, or a light, moist, sticky toffee pudding with butterscotch sauce and cinnamon ice cream. The early-bird set dinner (order by 7.15, leave by 8.15) is a good one, but even those eating from the carte at this time can be affected by the rush (our inspector's starter of deep-fried fishcakes 'hadn't been deep-fried since we ordered it', arriving in less than a minute from being ordered). Uniformed staff are good at what they do, and there is choice under £20 on the generally safe wine list, which starts at £13.95.

CHEF: Jeff Baker   PROPRIETOR: Michael Gill   OPEN: Mon to Fri L 12 to 2, Mon to Sat D 6 to 10.30 (11 Fri and Sat)   CLOSED: bank hols   MEALS: alc (main courses £10 to £16). Set L and D 6 to 7 £10 (2 courses) to £12.50   SERVICE: 10% (optional), card slips closed   CARDS: Amex, Delta, Diners, MasterCard, Switch, Visa   DETAILS: 110 seats. Private parties: 110 main room, 12 to 50 private rooms. Vegetarian meals. Children's helpings by prior arrangement. No cigars/pipes in dining room. Wheelchair access (also WC). Music. Air-conditioned

# Guellers ✸✕

3 York Place, Leeds LS1 2DR
TEL: (0113) 245 9922   FAX: (0113) 245 9965
EMAIL: dine@guellers.com
WEBSITE: www.guellers.com

COOKING **6**
FRENCH/MEDITERRANEAN
£29–£71

Tricky to find in the one-way 'loop system' near the railway station, Guellers is a stylishly furnished modern restaurant. The long, narrow room, with two rows of smartly laid tables, has the feel of a 'posh brasserie', and the food is up to date too. A set-price menu with rather a lot of supplements, often for quite ordinary-sounding dishes, such as a gâteau of crab with cucumber gazpacho, or an admittedly labour-intensive pig's trotter stuffed with ham hock and morels, is not the most user-friendly way of setting out the stall; and vegetables are charged extra too. In the end, though, value is considered fair.

First courses typically include a terrine or pavé in some form – perhaps a substantial slab of foie gras terrine, served with well-dressed frisée, orange segments and Poilâne bread – and a salad, such as lobster with mango and avocado. Fish tends to be given a simple and traditional butter sauce – maybe roast turbot with deep-fried anchovies and beurre noisette – and materials are well timed: for example, pink-roasted, skinless breast of Barbary duck, sliced and topped with a purée of sweet potato, served with a vegetable-strewn stock reduction containing green peppercorns.

Among desserts, apricot soufflé comes in for high praise, and the enigmatic 'pyramid' is an impressive construction, its sides formed from sheets of thin toffee, its core made of smooth passion-fruit sorbet. Service is attentive and efficient, and a varietally arranged wine list offers some choice under £20 but generally favours deeper pockets. House Vin de Pays d'Oc is £12.50 (£3.50 a glass).

CHEF: Simon Gueller   PROPRIETOR: FMC Ltd   OPEN: Tue to Sat 12 to 2, 6.30 to 10   CLOSED: 2 weeks after Christmas, first 2 weeks Aug   MEALS: Set L £14.50 (2 courses) to £26.50, Set D 6.30 to 7.30 £14.50 (2 courses) to £18.50, Set D £19.50 (2 courses) to £43.50   SERVICE: 10% (optional), card slips closed   CARDS: Amex, Delta, MasterCard, Switch, Visa   DETAILS: 52 seats. Private parties: 52 main room. No smoking in dining room. Wheelchair access (also WC). Music. Air-conditioned

# Fourth Floor

Harvey Nichols, 107–111 Briggate,
Leeds LS17 6AZ
TEL: (0113) 204 8000   FAX: (0113) 204 8080
WEBSITE: www.harveynichols.com

COOKING **4**
MODERN BRITISH
£28–£54

Calling itself a café and bar rather than a restaurant, Harvey Nick's northern outpost strikes a contemporary pose with its open kitchen, long lacquered bar and rooftop views over the city. By day it is more of a canteen for shoppers, while at night candles summon up a different mood. The food is modern too, but good sourcing and intelligent cooking lend substance to the operation. Whitby fish might run to crisp-skinned, firm-fleshed mackerel, served with squid and egg noddles in a gingery, fishy Thai broth, while Lishman's butcher's in Ilkley provides a pork and black pudding sausage, accompanied by crushed potato and caramelised onions. Black pudding has also partnered roast breast of duck, and other successes include ham hock and parsley terrine, and gnocchi with wild mushrooms in a creamy sauce. Puddings aim for the comfort zone with chocolate fudge cake (with pear ice cream) and treacle tart (with vanilla ice). Service is attentive and efficient, and wines include interesting reds from Spain, Italy and Tunisia, plus a fair few by the glass. House French red and white are £12.50.

CHEF: Richard Allen  PROPRIETOR: Harvey Nichols & Co  OPEN: all week L 12 to 3 (4 Sat and Sun), Thur to Sat D 5.30 (7 Sat) to 10  CLOSED: 25 and 26 Dec, 1 Jan, Easter Sun  MEALS: alc (main courses £9.50 to £16.50). Set L £14 (2 courses) to £17, Set D £10.95 (2 courses) to £14.95. Bar menu Mon to Wed 3 to 5, Thur and Fri 3 to 8 and Sat 4 to 6; breakfast Mon to Sat 10 (9 Sat) to 12  SERVICE: 10% (optional)  CARDS: Amex, Delta, Diners, MasterCard, Switch, Visa  DETAILS: 85 seats. 16 seats on balcony in summer. Private parties: 90 main room (evenings only). Vegetarian meals. Children's helpings Sun only. No-smoking area. Wheelchair access (also WC). Occasional. Air-conditioned

---

# Heathcotes at Rascasse ⍣

| NEW ENTRY |

Canal Wharf, Water Lane, Leeds LS11 5PS
TEL: (0113) 244 6611  FAX: (0113) 244 0736
EMAIL: leeds@heathcotes.co.uk
WEBSITE: www.heathcotes.co.uk

COOKING 2
MODERN BRITISH
£24–£51

Only brave Lancashiremen open restaurants in the heart of Yorkshire, but the Leeds–Liverpool canal alongside this old warehouse provides Paul Heathcote with an umbilical connection to his outlets on the other side of the Pennines. Little has changed physically since he took over Rascasse from Nigel Jolliffe: there's a new lounge on the first floor, but the dining room still has wooden floors and light oak tables.

Classical aspirations have, however, yielded to less ambitious output such as ham hock terrine with Lancashire cheese and brown sauce, and braised lamb shank with root vegetables. Now it's a Heathcote operation, there's black pudding (typically with crushed potatoes and baked beans), and trademark Goosnargh poultry also features: perhaps crisp-skinned, pink roast duckling breast with bittersweet honey-glazed turnip and shredded Savoy cabbage. Chocolate-lovers are treated to a segment of moist tart with a scoop of 'real' chocolate-chip ice cream, while vanilla-bean ice cream comes with a first-rate Pedro Ximenez sauce. Service is friendly and efficient, and wines come in a range of styles from £12.

CHEF: Philip Bowen  PROPRIETOR: Paul Heathcote  OPEN: all week 12 to 2.30, 6 to 10 (10.30 Sat) CLOSED: 25 and 26 Dec, 1 and 2 Jan  MEALS: alc (main courses £10.50 to £15). Set L and Set D 6 to 7 £13.50 (2 courses) to £15.50  SERVICE: 10% (optional)  CARDS: Amex, Delta, Diners, MasterCard, Switch, Visa  DETAILS: 120 seats. Private parties: 120 main room. Car park. Vegetarian meals. Children's helpings. No smoking in dining room. Wheelchair access (also WC). Music. No mobile phones. Air-conditioned

---

⍣ *indicates that smoking is either banned altogether or that a separate dining room (not just an area) is maintained for non-smokers.*

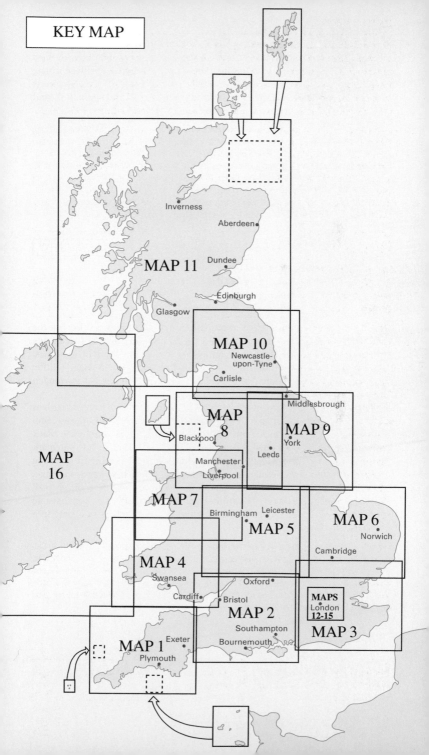

# KEY MAP

# MAP 1

- ■ Restaurant
- ▲ Restaurant with accommodation
- ○ *Round-up entry*
- ▣ Combined main and round-up entries
- △

```
0          5        10 miles
0                   15 kms
        © Copyright
```

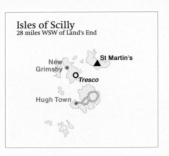

Lundy Islar

### Isles of Scilly
28 miles WSW of Land's End

New Grimsby • **St Martin's** ▲

○ *Tresco*

Hugh Town •

*B u d
B a*

*Port Isaac Bay*

A39

Bo

**Padstow** ▲ ○ *Rock*

▲ Wadebridge

A39

R. Camel

*Watergate Bay*

Bodn

A30

Newquay ● C O R N W A L

A392

*Ligger Bay*

A30

A39

R. Fal

St Austell ●

A390

*St Austel*

**Portreath** ■

A30

A390

Truro ●

A39

*St Ives Bay*

**St Ives** ▣

*Treen* ○

A30

A394

A39

*Veryan Bay*

St Just

▲ **Penzance**

A394

*Constantine* ○

**St Mawes** ▲

Falmouth ●

○ *Mousehole*

**Porthleven** ■

Helston ◉

*Falmouth Bay*

*Lands
End*

*M o u n t ' s
B a y*

*Gillan* ○

*Lizard Point*

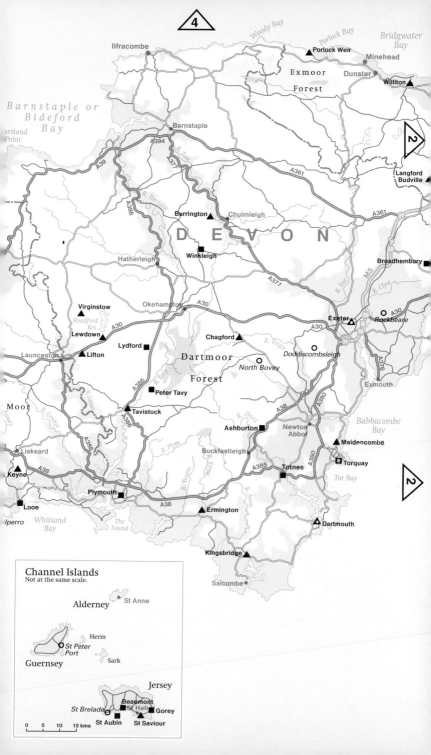

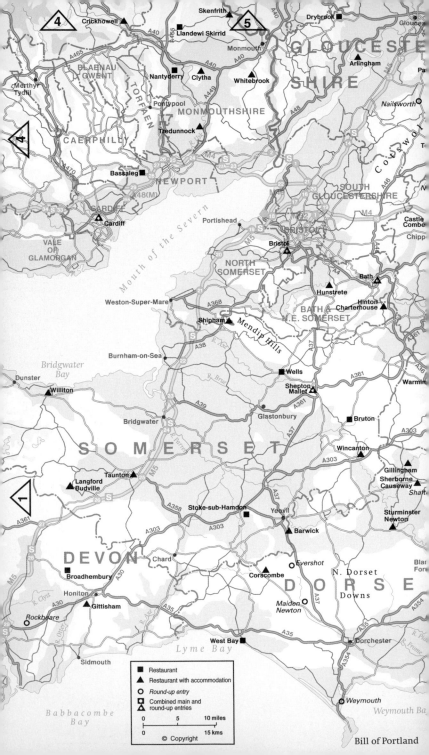

MAP 2

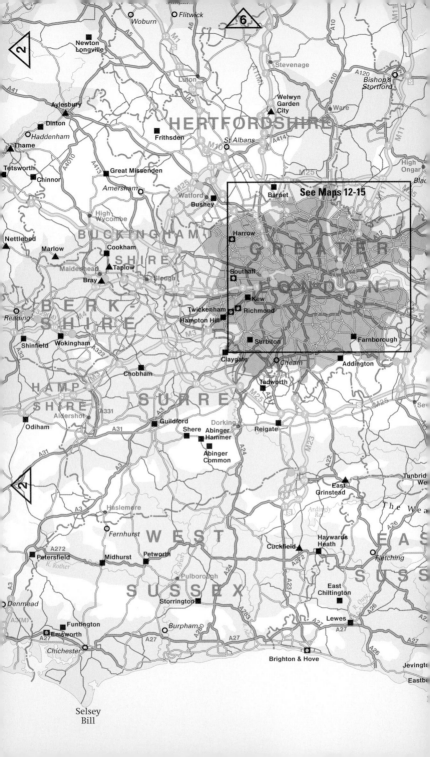

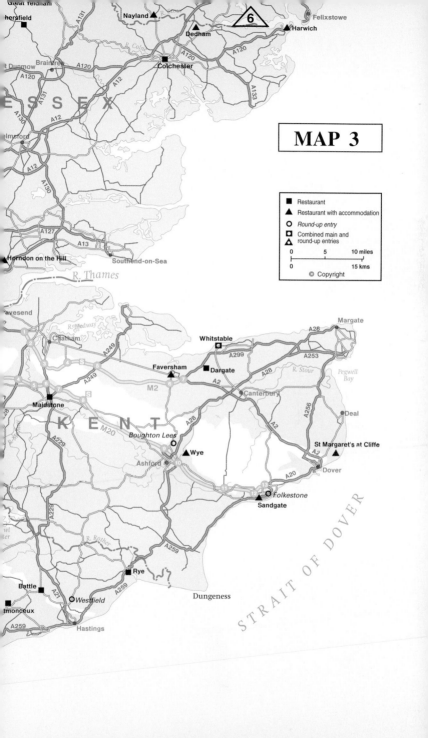

MAP 3

Restaurant
Restaurant with accommodation
Round-up entry
Combined main and
round-up entries

| 0 | | 5 | | 10 miles |
| 0 | | | | 15 kms |

© Copyright

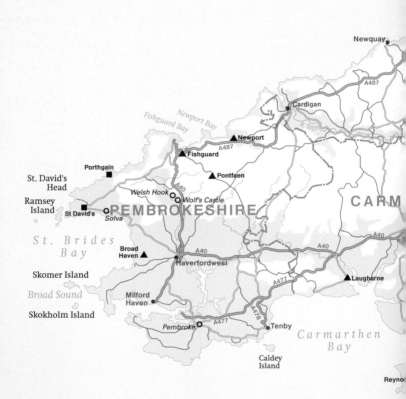

## MAP 4

■ Restaurant
▲ Restaurant with accommodation
○ Round-up entry
▢ Combined main and round-up entries
△

0        5        10 miles
0                 15 kms
© Copyright

CARDIGAN

BAY

Newquay

A487

Cardigan

R. Teifi

Newport Bay

Fishguard Bay

▲ Newport

A487

▲ Fishguard

Porthgain ■

▲ Pontfaen

St. David's
Head

Welsh Hook ○○ ● Wolf's Castle

A40

CARM

Ramsey
Island

■ St David's

○ PEMBROKESHIRE

Solva

CAR

A40

A40

A487

St. Brides
Bay

Broad
Haven ▲

A40

Skomer Island

Haverfordwest

A477

▲ Laugharne

Broad Sound

Milford
Haven ●

Skokholm Island

A478

Pembroke

A477

● Tenby

Carmarthen
Bay

Caldey
Island

Reyno

BRISTOL

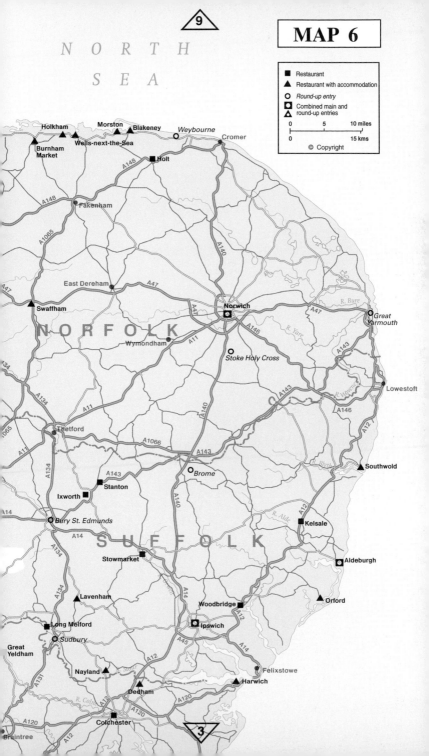

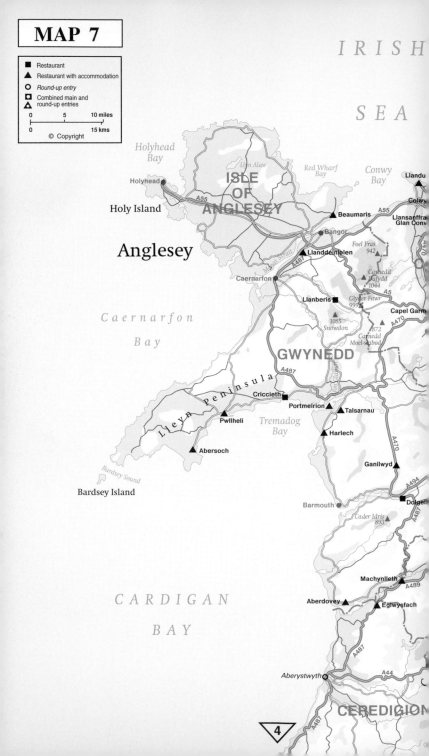

# MAP 7

**Legend:**
- ■ Restaurant
- ▲ Restaurant with accommodation
- ○ *Round-up entry*
- ◻ Combined main and
- △ round-up entries

| 0 | 5 | 10 miles |
| 0 | | 15 kms |

© Copyright

*IRISH*

*SEA*

*Holyhead Bay*

*Llyn Alaw*

*Red Wharf Bay*

*Conwy Bay*

Llandu

Holyhead

**ISLE OF ANGLESEY**

Colw

A55

▲ Beaumaris

A55

Llansanffra
Glan Conw

**Holy Island**

● Bangor

# Anglesey

▲ Llanddeiniolen

*Foel Fras*
942

● Caernarfon

A5

*Carnedd
Dafydd*
1044

A5

*Caernarfon*

■ Llanberis

*Glyder Fawr*
999

**Capel Garm**

A470

*Bay*

1085
*Snowdon*

872
*Carnedd
Moel-siabod*

**GWYNEDD**

A487

■ Criccieth

● Portmeirion ▲

▲ Talsarnau

*Lleyn Peninsula*

▲ Pwllheli

*Tremadog Bay*

▲ Harlech

▲ Abersoch

Ganllwyd ▲

*Bardsey Sound*

A494

**Bardsey Island**

Barmouth ●

A470

*Cader Idris*
893

■ Dolgel

A487

*CARDIGAN*

Machynlleth ▲

A489

Aberdovey ▲

▲ Eglwysfach

*BAY*

A487

*Aberystwyth* ○

A44

④

**CEREDIGION**

# MAP 8

- ■ Restaurant
- ▲ Restaurant with accommodation
- ○ Round-up entry
- ◻ Combined main and round-up entries
- △

| 0 | 5 | 10 miles |
| 0 | 15 kms |

© Copyright

Whitehaven
Ennerdale Water
10
Grange in Borrowdale
CUMBRIA
Scafell Pike 977
West Water
▲ Grasmere
Ambleside ▲
Windermere ▲
Windermere
Hawkshead
Bowness-on-Windermere ▲
R. Esk
R. Duddon
Near Sawrey ▲
Crosthwaite ▲
Ke
Witherslack ▲
A5092
Ulverston ▲
Cartmel ▲
A590
A595

Barrow-in-Furness
Isle of Walney

Morecambe
Heysham
Lanc
Morecambe Bay
Forton ○
Fleetwood ▲
A585
Poulton-le-Fylde ▲
R. Wyre
Blackpool ◻
Kirkham ■
A583
Pres
M55

Point of Ayre
Ramsey Bay
Ramsey
Kirk Michael
Isle of Man
Laxey Bay
Glenmaye
Douglas
Port Erin
Port St Mary
Calf of Man

Southport ■
A570
A565
Wright
Bispham Green ■
Ormskirk
Skelmersdale
M58

MERSEYSIDE
Wallasey
Liverpool ■
Birkenhead ○
M57
A580 St H

7
Conwy Bay
Colwyn Bay
▲ Llandudno
Prestatyn
Rhyl
■ Colwyn Bay
▲ Llansantffraid Glan Conwy
A55
CONWY
Foel Fras
A470
Denbigh
7 FLINTSHIRE
Hawarden
Chester
CH
Runcorn
R. Mersey
M56
Little Barrow

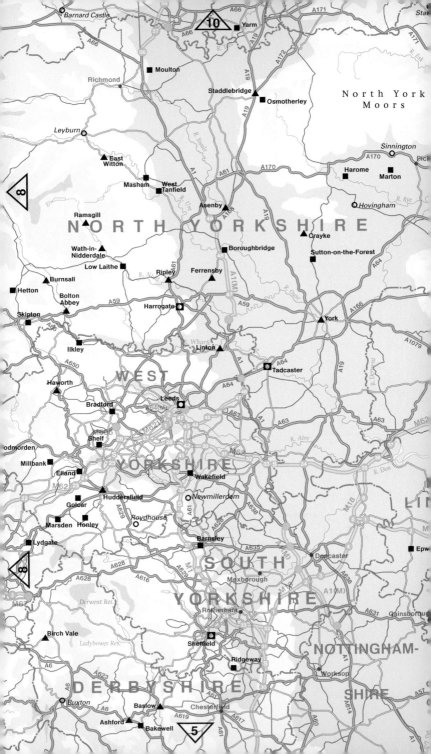

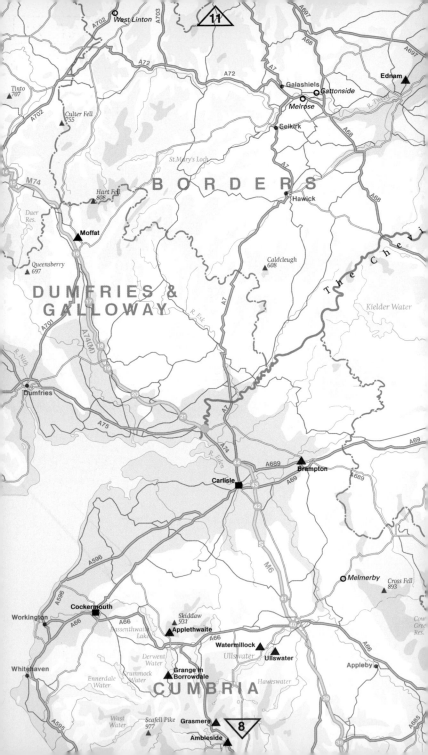

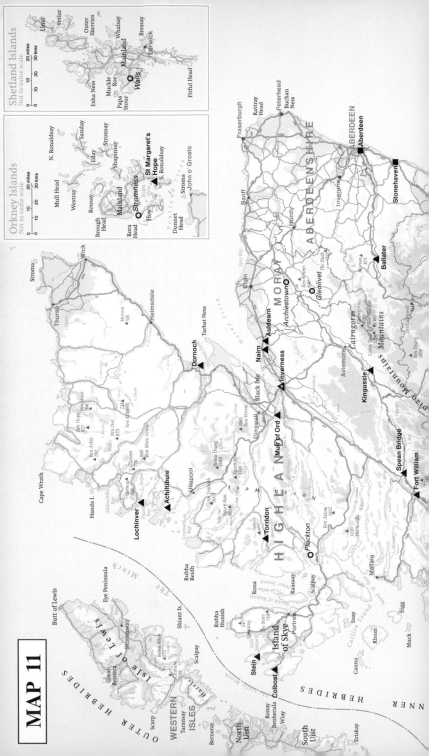

**MAP 11**

Shetland Islands
Not to same scale

Unst
Fetlar
Outer Skerries
Whalsay
Bressay
Mainland
Lerwick
Esha Ness
Muckle Roe
Papa Stour
Walls
Fitful Head

0   10   20   30 kms
0      10      20 miles

Orkney Islands
Not to same scale

N. Ronaldsay
Westray
Sanday
Eday
Stronsay
Rousay
Shapinsay
Mull Head
Brough Head
Mainland
Stromness
St Margaret's Hope
Hoy
S. Ronaldsay
Rora Head
Dunnet Head
Stroma
John o'Groats

0   10   20   30 kms
0      10      20 miles

Fraserburgh
Rattray Head
Peterhead
Buchan Ness
ABERDEENSHIRE
ABERDEEN
Stonehaven
Banff
Huntly
Inverurie
Elgin
MORAY
Archiestown
Glenlivet
The Buck
Ballater
Morven 871
Cairngorm
Cairn Toul
Cairngorm Mountains
Ben Macdui 1309
Aviemore
Kingussie
Grampian Mountains
Ben Nevis 1344
The Cairnwell
Ben Dearg 1008
Spean Bridge
Fort William

Wick
Stroma
Thurso
Helmsdale
Morven 705
Dornoch
Tarbat Ness
Nairn
Auldearn
Black Isle
Inverness
Cape Wrath
Handa I.
Ben Hope 927
Ben Loyal 764
Ben Klibreck 873
Ben More Assynt 998
Lochinver
Achiltibuie
Suilven 731
Ben Dearg 1084
Ullapool
Dingwall
Muir of Ord
H I G H L A N D
Torridon
Plockton
Ben Attow 1032
Kintail
Rubha Reidh

Butt of Lewis
Eye Peninsula
ISLE OF LEWIS
Stornoway
Great Bernera
Beinn Mhor 572
Shiant Is.
Scalpay
The Minch
WESTERN ISLES
Taransay
Scarp
Ronay
Benbecula
Wiay
North Uist
Berneray
South Uist
Eriskay
OUTER HEBRIDES
Rona
Raasay
Sound of Raasay
Rubha Hunish
Stein
Colbost
Island of Skye
Portree
The Storr 719
Scalpay
Soay
Cuillin Sound
Canna
Rhum
Muck
Eigg
INNER HEBRIDES

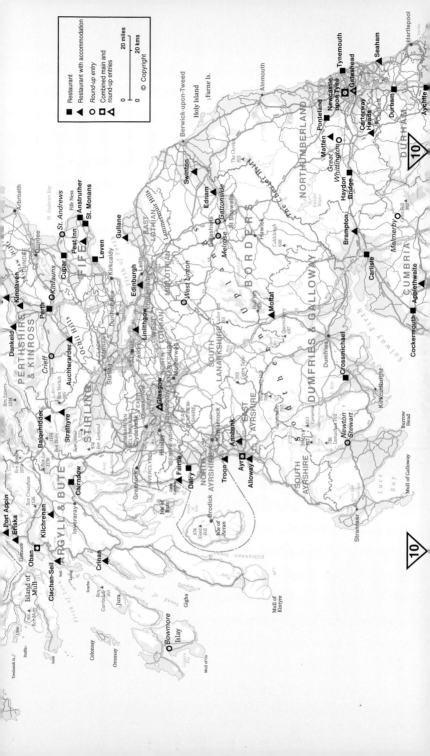

CHIGWELL

EDMONTON

Woodford

Hainault

A112

A10

A1010

A112

A406

A1112

A123

4

A503

Walthamstow

REDBRIDGE

A12

WALTHAM
FOREST

A104

ILFORD

A124

Rasa Travancore

Istanbul Iskembecisi

HACKNEY

A11

A118

A123

Little
Georgia

NEWHAM

Barking

A13

Thai Garden

A102(M)

BARKING &
DAGENHAM

HACKNEY

A114

East Ham

A11

TOWER
HAMLETS

A13

New
Tayyabs

R.Thames

A13

Poplar

Wapping Food

Ubon

Royal China

Moshi Moshi Sushi

Thamesmead

Mem Saheb

UTHWARK

A2

Woolwich

A206

A202

Greenwich

A102(M)

A205

A209

Spread
Eagle

GREENWICH

A2

Holly

Chapter Two

A2

Lewisham

A20

MBETH

A210

Le Chardon

Babur Brasserie

Eltham

Dulwich

A205

Catford

A20

A222

A205

LEWISHAM

A211

Sidcup

A2212

A21

Crystal Palace

A208

BROMLEY

## MAP 12

Beckenham

■ Restaurant
▲ Restaurant with accommodation
○ Round-up entry

A21

0           5km

BROMLEY

0        4 miles

A232

© Copyright

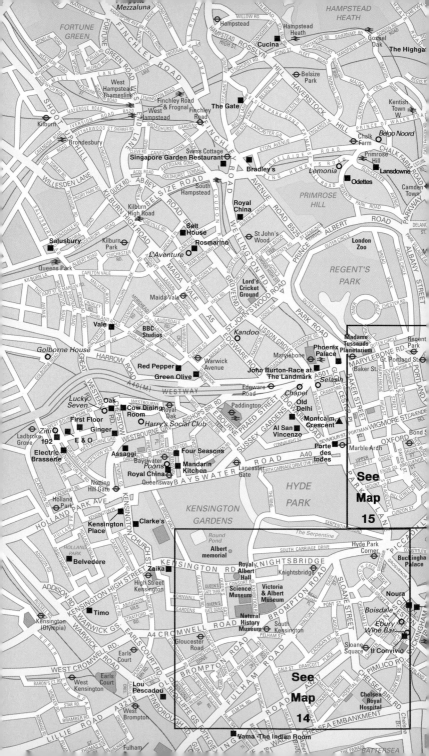

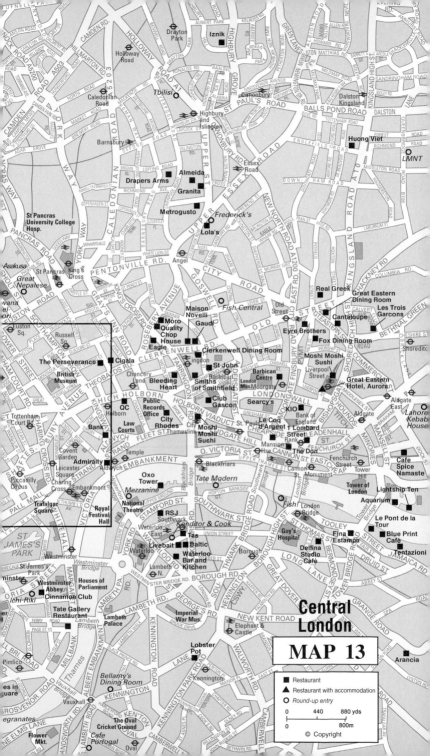

Central
London

MAP 13

- ■ Restaurant
- ▲ Restaurant with accommodation
- ○ Round-up entry

| 0 | 440 | 880 yds |
| 0 | | 800m |

© Copyright

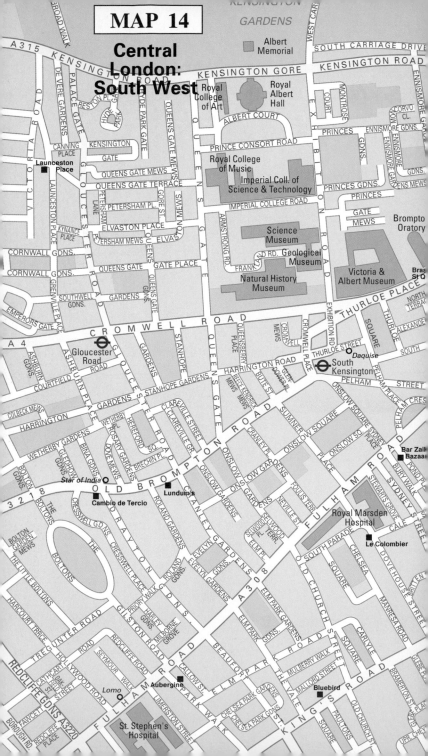

# MAP 14

## Central London: South West

KENSINGTON GARDENS

A 315

Albert Memorial

KENSINGTON GORE

SOUTH CARRIAGE DRIVE

KENSINGTON ROAD

Royal College of Art

Royal Albert Hall

WEST CAR

ENNISMORE

MONTROSE

CORVO CL.

ALBERT COURT

PRINCES

ENNISMORE GDNS.

ENNISMORE GARDENS

ENNISMORE GDNS

PRINCE CONSORT ROAD

KENSINGTON GATE

Royal College of Music

PRINCES GDNS.

PRINCES

QUEENS GATE MEWS

Imperial Coll. of Science & Technology

GATE MEWS

Brompto Oratory

IMPERIAL COLLEGE ROAD

Launceston Place

CANNING PLACE

KENSINGTON GATE

QUEENS GATE MEWS

QUEENS GATE TERRACE

PETERSHAM PL.

PETERSHAM LANE

ELVASTON PLACE

Science Museum

Geological Museum

Victoria & Albert Museum

Bras St Q

ARMSTRONG RD

FRANK

KYNANCE PLACE

ERSHAM MEWS

ELVAS

Natural History Museum

THURLOE PLACE

NORTH TERRAC

CORNWALL GDNS.

QUEENS GATE

GATE PLACE

EXHIBITION ROAD

THURLOE SQUARE

ALEXANDE

CORNWALL GDNS.

SOUTHWELL GDNS.

GARDENS

GDNS

NORTH TERRAC

EMPERORS GATE

CROMWELL ROAD

CROMWELL

THURLOE STREET

SOUTH

A 4

Gloucester Road

Daquise

A 4

ASHBURN GDNS.

STANHOPE

QUEENSBERRY PLACE

CROMWELL PLACE

South Kensington

PELHAM STREET

COURTFIELD

ASHBURN PLACE

STANHOPE ROAD

HARRINGTON ROAD

BUTE ST.

GREEN MEWS

CORNWA

PELHAM PLACE

PELHAM CRES

COLBECK MEWS

GARDENS

STANHOPE GARDENS

CLAREVILLE STREET

REECE MEWS

SUMNER PLACE

ONSLOW SQUARE

HARRINGTON

WETHERBY

HEREFORD SQ.

CLAREVILLE GR.

CRANLEY P

ONSLOW SQ.

SYDNEY

Bar Zaik Bazaar

WETHERBY GARDENS

BINA GDNS.

ROSARY GARDENS

BRECHIN PL.

CRANLEY GARDENS

ONSLOW GARDENS

FOULIS TERR

STEWART'S GROVE

SYDNEY

BURY WALK

POND P

BOLTON GDNS.

Star of India

OLD BROMPTON ROAD

Lundum's

NEVILLE'S T

CALE

3 2 1 8

Cambio de Tercio

ROLAND GARDENS

STANLEY

ONSLOW GARDENS

Royal Marsden Hospital

DOVEHOUSE

THE BOLTONS

CRESSWELL GDNS.

DRAYTON GDNS.

CRESSWELL PLACE

EVELYN GARDENS

SELWOOD PL. TERR.

SELWOOD TERR.

SOUTH PARADE

Le Colombier

CHELSEA

MANRESA ROAD

BOLTON GARDEN MEWS

THE BOLTONS

PRIORY WALK

HARLEY GDNS.

MILBORNE GROVE

ELM PARK GARDENS

OLD CHURCH STREET

CARLYLE

THE LITTLE BOLTONS

GILSTON ROAD

ELM P

MULBERRY WALK

HARCOURT TERCE

TREGUNTER ROAD

HOLLYWOOD ROAD

REDCLIFFE ROAD

ROLAND GDNS.

BEAUFOR PAR

THE VALE

MALLORD STREET

Bluebird

REDCLIFFE GDNS. A 3220

CATHCART

OAK

SEYMOUR WALK

Lomo

Aubergine

FULHAM ROAD

LIMERSTON STREET

CHELSEA PARK GARDENS

CHELSEA PARK GDNS.

PAULTONS

BRAMERTON ST.

OLD CHURCH

BRITTEN STRE

FAWCETT ST.

REDCLIFFE PLACE

BOROUGH RD

St. Stephen's Hospital

FULHAM

A 308

ELM PARK

ROAD

KING'S ROAD

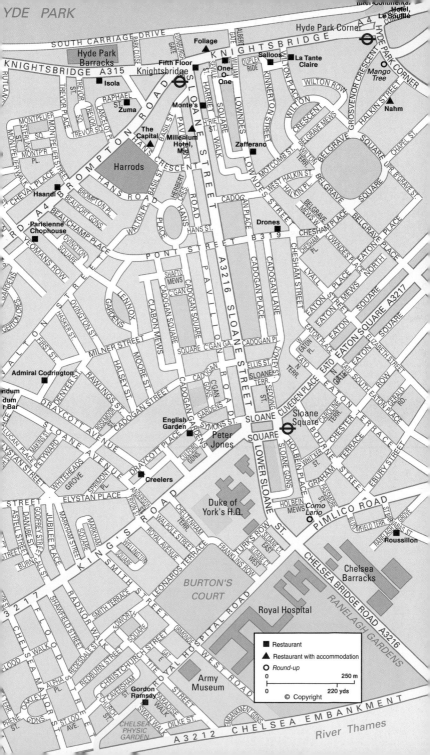

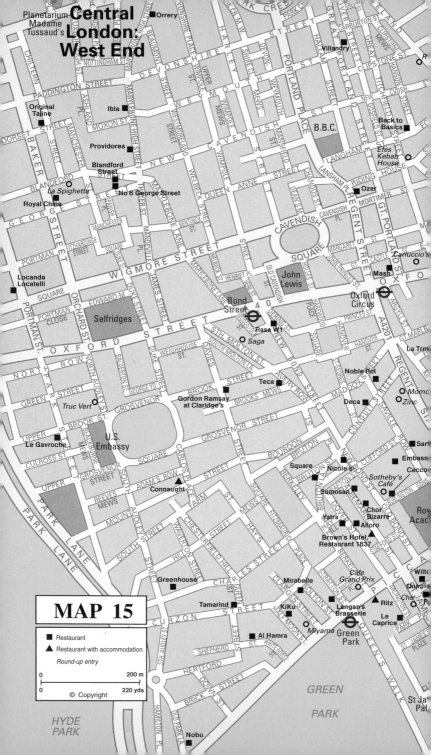

**Central London: West End**

Planetarium
Madame Tussaud's

Orrery

Villandry

B.B.C.

Back to Basics

Efes Kebab House

Original Tajine

Ibla

Providores

Langham

Ozer

Blandford Street

La Spighetta

No 6 George Street

Royal China

CAVENDISH SQUARE

Carluccio's

Mash

John Lewis

Locanda Locatelli

WIGMORE STREET

Oxford Circus

Selfridges

Bond Street

Rasa W1

La Tro

OXFORD STREET

Saga

Teca

Noble Rot

Momo

Truc Vert

Zinc

GROSVENOR STREET

Gordon Ramsay at Claridge's

Deca

Sar

U.S. Embassy

Le Gavroche

Embass

Square

Cecco

Nicole's

Sotheby's Café

Connaught

Sumosan

Chor Bizarre

Yatra

Alloro

Brown's Hotel, Restaurant 1837

Greenhouse

Café Grand Prix

Wilto

Mirabelle

Ouagli

Ritz

Cha

Tamarind

KiKu

Langan's Brasserie

Le Caprice

Al Hamra

Miyama

Green Park

**MAP 15**

■ Restaurant
▲ Restaurant with accommodation
*Round-up entry*

0 ———— 200 m
0 ———— 220 yds
© Copyright

HYDE PARK

GREEN PARK

Nobu

St Ja
Pal

# MAP 16

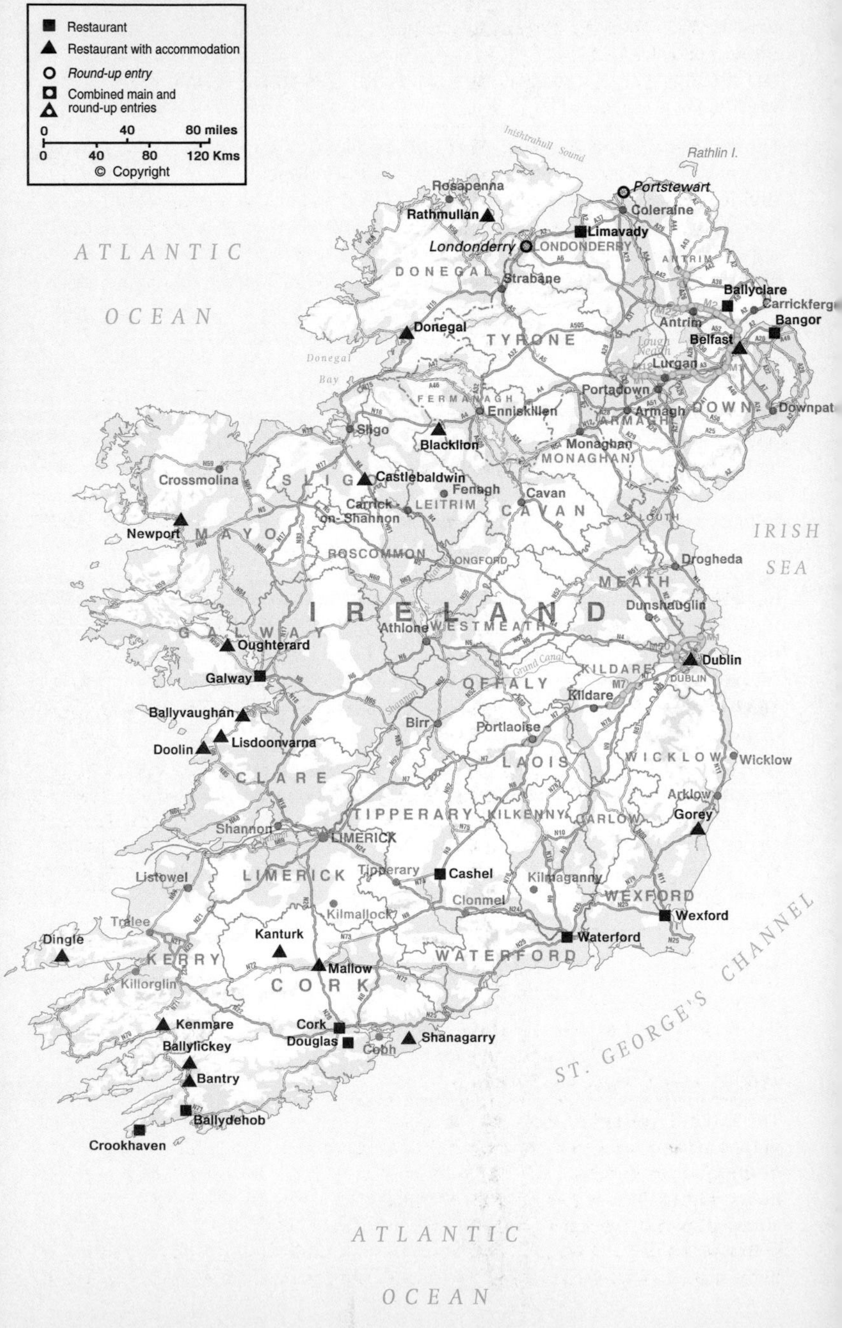

**Legend:**
- ■ Restaurant
- ▲ Restaurant with accommodation
- ○ Round-up entry
- ▣ Combined main and round-up entries
- △

```
0        40        80 miles
0    40    80   120 Kms
© Copyright
```

ATLANTIC

OCEAN

*Inishtrahull Sound*

*Rathlin I.*

Rosapenna

**Rathmullan** ▲

*Londonderry* ○ LONDONDERRY

DONEGAL

Strabane

■ Limavady

○ *Portstewart*
● Coleraine

ANTRIM

**Ballyclare** ■
Carrickferg.

Antrim
**Belfast** ▲

**Bangor** ▲

**Donegal** ▲

TYRONE

M2

Lurgan

Portadown

Armagh ▲

DOWN

● Downpat.

*Donegal Bay*

FERMANAGH

Enniskillen ▲

Sligo ●

**Blacklion** ▲

Monaghan ●

MONAGHAN

Crossmolina ●

SLIGO

**Castlebaldwin** ▲

Carrick-on-Shannon

LEITRIM

Fenagh ●

Cavan

CAVAN

LOUTH

**Newport** ■

MAYO

ROSCOMMON

LONGFORD

● Drogheda

MEATH

I R E L A N D

Athlone WESTMEATH

Dunshauglin

G A L W A Y

**Oughterard** ▲

**Galway** ■

OFFALY

KILDARE

● Dublin

DUBLIN

Kildare ●

M7

**Ballyvaughan** ▲
**Lisdoonvarna** ▲
**Doolin** ■

CLARE

Birr ●

Portlaoise ●

LAOIS

WICKLOW

● Wicklow

Shannon ●

TIPPERARY KILKENNY

CARLOW

Arklow

**Gorey** ▲

Listowel ●

LIMERICK

LIMERICK

Tipperary ●

**Cashel** ■

Kilmaganny

WEXFORD

Tralee ●

Kilmallock ●

Clonmel ●

**Wexford** ■

Dingle ▲

KERRY

**Kanturk** ▲

**Mallow** ▲

WATERFORD

**Waterford** ■

Killorglin ●

C O R K

**Kenmare** ▲
**Ballylickey** ▲

**Cork** ■
Douglas ■

Cobh ●

**Shanagarry** ▲

**Bantry** ▲

ST. GEORGE'S CHANNEL

**Ballydehob** ▲

Crookhaven ●

IRISH SEA

ATLANTIC

OCEAN

# Leodis 🍾

Victoria Mill, 4 The Embankment, Sovereign
Street, Leeds LS1 4BJ
TEL: (0113) 242 1010   FAX: (0113) 243 0432
WEBSITE: www.leodis.co.uk

COOKING 3
BRASSERIE/MODERN BRITISH
£27–£56

On the ground floor of a converted mill beside the River Aire, the brasserie
occupies one big room with bare brick walls and stripped-wood floor, its space
divided up by curved glass panels. It is relaxed and generally bustling with a
varied crowd of people, from large parties to couples, and all ages. There is lots to
appeal on the tersely worded menu: from skate terrine, via steak and kidney
sausages and mash, to chicken and goats' cheese mousse with 'just the right level
of wobble to keep it standing'. Other successes have included such brasserie
staples as calf's liver with bacon and rösti (plus a huge portion of caramelised
onions).

The menu's very lack of description, however, can disconcert when
ingredients it omits to mention play a key role on the plate. A unexpectedly
powerful pesto, for example, anointed our inspector's wild mushroom risotto,
and an unannounced ice cream and chocolate sauce accompany a dessert of
rhubarb and custard in a filo pastry basket. Service has been reported as rushed,
impersonal and inattentive, although it has also been seen as skilled and well
managed. The well-considered wine list goes way beyond the usual heartlands
of Bordeaux and Burgundy. A separate section of fine wines is rounded out by
modern classics such as Mas La Plana from Spain and a range from modern
Italian master Jermann. Mark-ups are fair, with good choice under £20, and
there are 22 half-bottles; six house wines are listed at £13.95.

A sister restaurant called Paris (Calverley Lane, Rodley, Leeds, tel. (0113) 258
1885) offers a generous and broad-minded selection of straightforward brasserie
dishes, backed up by 150 wines.

CHEFS: Steven Kendell and John Wilks   PROPRIETORS: Martin Spalding, Steven Kendell and
Philip Richardson   OPEN: Mon to Fri L 12 to 2, Mon to Sat D 6 to 10 (11 Sat)   CLOSED: 26 Dec, 1
Jan, L bank hols   MEALS: alc (main courses £8 to £16). Set L and D (exc after 7.15 Sat) £15.95
SERVICE: 10% (optional), card slips closed   CARDS: Amex, Delta, Diners, MasterCard, Switch,
Visa   DETAILS: 180 seats. 48 seats outside. Private parties: 100 main room. Car park. Vegetarian
meals. No cigars/pipes in dining room. Wheelchair access (also WC). Music

# Livebait                                            NEW ENTRY

Shears Yard, The Calls, Leeds LS2 7EY
TEL: (0113) 244 4144   FAX: (0113) 243 7933
EMAIL: gcg_lb_leeds@groupechezgerard.co.uk
WEBSITE: www.santeonline.co.uk

COOKING 3
SEAFOOD
£23–£52

The Livebait operation continues to expand, the London branches joined by
outlets in Manchester and now Leeds. This one is opposite a hotel near the heart
of the city, unobtrusive from outside, with redbrick walls and stone-flagged
floors within. Warm and informal service complements the group's widely
admired specialist seafood cookery, here entrusted to Stuart Tattersall, formerly
of Brasserie Forty Four (see entry, above). Seared scallops with a salad of spring
herbs makes a fresh and invigorating starter, and the timing of main-course fish

such as roast turbot with thyme-seasoned Mediterranean vegetables, and sea bass with wilted spinach, have been flawless; the latter arriving with an enterprising salsa of broad beans, pine-nuts, peas and apricot, lifted with a touch of mint. If the mood takes, various head-turning, if expensive, mixed shellfish platters run the gamut from lobster to winkle, and the blackboard specials (perhaps whole roast John Dory with saffron mash and chargrilled asparagus) are worth a look too. Chocolate orange pots with tuiles, or caramel pannacotta with raspberries, are dessert options. The short, intelligently composed wine list (mostly white, of course) opens with house French at £10.25 and offers a dozen by the glass.

CHEF: Stuart Tattersall   PROPRIETOR: Groupe Chez Gerard   OPEN: all week 12 to 3, 5.45 to 11 (1 to 9.30 Sun and bank hols)   CLOSED: 25 and 26 Dec, 1 Jan   MEALS: alc (main courses £9.50 to £17). Set L and D £11.50 (2 courses) to £14. Shellfish bar menu also available   SERVICE: 10% (optional)   CARDS: Amex, Delta, Diners, MasterCard, Switch, Visa   DETAILS: 62 seats. 40 seats outside. Private parties: 70 main room. Vegetarian meals. Children's helpings. No cigars/pipes in dining room. Wheelchair access (also WC). Music. Air-conditioned  £5

---

# Pool Court at 42 ⁵✳

44 The Calls, Leeds LS2 7EW

TEL: (0113) 244 4242   FAX: (0113) 234 3332                              COOKING 7
EMAIL: poolcourt@onetel.net.uk                       CLASSIC FRENCH/MODERN BRITISH
WEBSITE: www.dine-services.com                                            £42–£83

Inhabiting a prime canal-side spot, this 'real Yorkshire gem', with its cool 'city chic' mood, would not look out of place in any major city around the world. Its wavy lines, chrome and blond wood, and its oval dish hanging (seemingly precariously) from the ceiling can strike visitors as 'mildly eccentric'. Not so Jeff Baker's considered, articulate, restrained and refined cooking. His ambitious and seductive ideas include an oxtail and celeriac pie, and jellied rock oysters infused with beetroot and served with a cauliflower pannacotta. Fine materials underpin the operation, the cooking is never less than proficient, and seafood is notably well handled, from outstandingly fresh griddled scallops – moist, plump and sweet – on a ragoût of oysters, to three cold, juicy langoustine tails topped with fine spears of white asparagus and decorated with drizzles of mascarpone.

Seasoning is spot on, presentation is vivid, and every component is considered and carefully rendered. Duck emerged triumphant at an inspection meal, its quality beyond reproach, the skin crisp, the breast pink and flavourful, the croustade of leg meat and liver infused with aged sherry. Sometimes the food may lack its customary seasonality and spark of originality, while at other times it can be superlative, thanks to an undoubted streak of creativity and invention. Cheeses – all in fine fettle – come with a slice of rich fruitcake (the result 'a revelation'), and highly recommended desserts have included a well-considered Cassis-flavoured crème brûlée, and a rhubarb and orange compote ('a kind of Eton mess') topped with cinnamon-flavoured yoghurt. Courteous, well-mannered service from a youthful team is backed up by an experienced manager, and although white wines offer more choice under £25 than reds, quality across the board is commendable. Chilean Chardonnay and Californian Cabernet Franc start the ball rolling at £15.50.

CHEF: Jeff Baker   PROPRIETOR: Michael Gill   OPEN: Mon to Fri L 12 to 2, Mon to Fri D 7 to 10 and Sat 7 to 8.30   CLOSED: bank hols   MEALS: Set L and D £25 (2 courses) to £55   SERVICE: 10%, card slips closed   CARDS: Amex, Delta, Diners, MasterCard, Switch, Visa   DETAILS: 38 seats. 18 seats outside. Private parties: 38 main room. Vegetarian meals. Children's helpings by arrangement. No children under 3. No smoking in dining room. Wheelchair access (also WC). Music. No mobile phones. Air-conditioned

## Sous le Nez en Ville ▮ £

| | |
|---|---|
| The Basement, Quebec House, Quebec Street, | COOKING **4** |
| Leeds LS1 2HA | MODERN EUROPEAN |
| TEL: (0113) 244 0108   FAX: (0113) 245 0240 | £27–£52 |

This restaurant is in the basement of a central Leeds office building. Everything is bistro style: so no tablecloths, but plenty of lively chatter, especially early evening when the set-price supper draws the crowds. The food mixes old favourites with a smattering of new ideas in step with culinary fashion: deep-fried brie, and gâteau of fillet steak with peppercorn sauce are old friends, while fish casserole with crab claws and scallops, and salad of rare peppered beef fillet represent modernity. Interesting desserts might include lemon curd tart with confit lemons and coriander sorbet, or iced nougat parfait with pineapple and lime salsa. Young English and French staff are impressively hard-working, well-organised and pleasant.

The wine list is stuffed with bottles from top-drawer producers. The Rhône, Burgundy and Spain are Old-World highlights, while California, Australia and South Africa lead for the New World. Mark-ups are sensible and 11 house wines, at £9.95–£19.95 (£2–£3.95 a glass) pick out a range of styles.

CHEFS: Andrew Carter and Andrew Lavendar   PROPRIETOR: Sous Le Nez Ltd   OPEN: Mon to Sat 12 to 2.30, 6 to 10 (11 Fri and Sat)   CLOSED: 25 to 27 Dec, bank hol Mons   MEALS: alc (main courses £9 to £15.50). Set L Sat 12 to 2 and Set D 6 to 7.30 (7 Sat) £17.95 (inc wine). Bar menu also available   SERVICE: not inc   CARDS: Delta, Diners, MasterCard, Switch, Visa   DETAILS: 85 seats. Private parties: 120 main room, 4 to 20 private rooms. Vegetarian meals. Music. Air-conditioned £5

**LEWDOWN** Devon                                                                    map 1

## ▲ Lewtrenchard Manor ▮ ✳

| | |
|---|---|
| Lewdown EX20 4PN | |
| TEL: (01566) 783256   FAX: (01566) 783332 | |
| EMAIL: stay@lewtrenchard.co.uk | |
| WEBSITE: www.lewtrenchard.co.uk | COOKING **5** |
| off A30 Okehampton to Launceston road; turn | MODERN BRITISH |
| left at Lewdown | £25–£54 |

Leopard-skin rugs (and the owner's tartan trews) add an exotic note to the more traditional feel of dark panelled walls and heavy furniture in this old house. A log fire roars away in winter, flowers brighten it up in summer, and Jason Hornbuckle's contemporary food follows the seasons too. West Country suppliers are central to the operation, although ideas are much more broadly based. At first sight these may seem striking – a smoked salmon and chicken boudin with artichoke and truffle purée, in a pea and foie gras sauce – but most turn out to be some sort of variation on a familiar theme. French onion soup, for example, comes with shredded duck confit and goats' cheese on sourdough croûtons, and peppered loin of venison with chestnut purée.

In short, the food treads a successful path between the adventurous and the familiar, taking its cue from tried and tested partnerships: ravioli of squab pigeon is served with beetroot consommé and horseradish cream, and roast loin of veal is partnered by sweetbread and kidney on smoked garlic mash with a morel sauce. The pattern continues in desserts of banana Tatin with a vanilla banoffi sauce, and hot chocolate tart with confit kumquats and an orange and cardamom ice cream. Bordeaux and South Africa are the strong points of the wine list, although there are good selections from other countries around the wine-making globe too. Mark-ups are fair, and producers have obviously been well researched, resulting in a delightfully duff-free list. Ten house selections are £12 to £13 a bottle, six of which are sold by the glass for £2.75.

CHEF: Jason Hornbuckle   PROPRIETORS: James and Sue Murray   OPEN: all week 12 to 1.30, 7 to 9   MEALS: Set L Mon to Sat £10 (2 courses) to £35, Set D £35. Bar menu available 12 to 3, 6 to 9   SERVICE: not inc, card slips closed   CARDS: Amex, Delta, Diners, MasterCard, Switch, Visa   DETAILS: 30 seats. 30 seats outside. Private parties: 60 main room, 8 to 24 private rooms. Car park. Vegetarian meals. Children's helpings. No children under 8. No smoking in dining room. Wheelchair access (not WC). Music. No mobile phones   ACCOMMODATION: 9 rooms, all with bath/shower. TV. Phone. B&B £95 to £180. No children under 8. Fishing (*The Which? Hotel Guide*)  (£5)

## LEWES  East Sussex                                                    map 3

# Circa ᑊ✳                                                    NEW ENTRY

145 High Street, Lewes BN7 1XT
TEL: (01273) 471777   FAX: (01273) 488416                    COOKING 3
EMAIL: eat@circacirca.com                                    FUSION
WEBSITE: www.circacirca.com                                  £29–£43

It is a while since Lewes had a main entry in the Guide. The estimable Kenwards last appeared in the 1990 edition, when some of the items served here – feta won ton dippers, salted squid with beer sorbet, or kangaroo cottage pie – would barely have been imaginable. On a corner site, away from the busiest part of the High Street, this is a large, appealing space, its contemporary design emphasised by curved lines and a solid-stone floor. Primary ingredients are generally straightforward – cod, duck, beef, lamb, sea bass, calf's liver – but their treatments are certainly eye-catching.

At its best, the cooking has turned out an accomplished starter of moist and tender quail, accompanied by a bowl of gently spiced mung-bean soup flavoured with coconut, the spoon standing upright in it, held in place by a disc of fried chapati-like bread acting as a roof; this might sound fussy, but every element is well judged. Not all dishes achieve the balance that fusion food (like any other) requires, while sometimes the fusion element is understated, as in roast rump of lamb served with a small pile of chillified ratatouille, with an artily turned out potato looking like a bone, with Brie oozing out from its centre as if it were marrow.

Desserts tend to be more mainstream, along the lines of puffed rice topped with a dense and creamy chocolate marquise, with a blood orange ice cream.

Service is smart and attentive yet relaxed. A short, varied wine list (supplemented by an even shorter selection of special bottles) starts with house French at £11.95.

CHEF: Marc Bolger  PROPRIETOR: Ann Renton  OPEN: Tue to Sun L 12 to 2.30, Tue to Sat D 6 to 10 MEALS: alc (main courses L £9, D after 7pm £14). Set D 6 to 7 £20  SERVICE: 10% (optional), card slips closed  CARDS: Amex, Delta, Diners, MasterCard, Switch, Visa  DETAILS: 80 seats. Private parties: 80 main room. Vegetarian meals. Children's helpings. No smoking in 1 dining room. Wheelchair access (also WC). Music. Air-conditioned

## LIFTON Devon                                                                      map 1

# ▲ Arundell Arms ⅍

Lifton PL16 0AA
TEL: (01566) 784666  FAX: (01566) 784494
EMAIL: reservations@arundellarms.com
WEBSITE: www.arundellarms.com                          COOKING 5
just off A30, 3m E of Launceston                        MODERN BRITISH/FRENCH
                                                               £32–£60

The interconnecting rooms that form the bar of this welcoming, eighteenth-century, ivy-covered coaching inn are lined with hunting, shooting and fishing prints, testifying to its sporting credentials: Anne Voss-Bark MBE is the recipient of a Lifetime Achievement Award for Services to Angling. An elegant, restful dining room, meanwhile, done in mustard yellow, with decorated panels and a chandelier, looks as if it could host a party of Jane Austen characters at the drop of a hat. The butcher and fishmonger are among suppliers listed on the menu, testament to careful sourcing that duly yields faultlessly fresh and flavourful ingredients, including five fat scallops in a thin, crisp, tempura batter accompanied by an orientally dressed rocket salad, and a combination of organic chicken and Gressingham duck, both reminiscent of poultry as it used to be, each with a crisp, aromatic crust, surrounded by a pool of pungent peppercorn sauce.

   Dishes are also carefully devised, be they a roast rack of mint-crusted lamb on a bed of sharp rhubarb in a strongly flavoured white wine sauce, or a simple but 'totally satisfying' salad of baby turnips, carrots and beetroot on a mound of interesting leaves, served with mayonnaise lightly flavoured with roast garlic and Parmesan. Main courses are accompanied by 'enterprising' vegetables, and desserts have included a passion-fruit délice (consisting of sponge, mousse and a jelly topping) with a matching coulis, the balance of sweetness and sharpness 'spot on'. A balanced wine list, with choice under £20, takes in a South African Sauvignon Blanc from Neil Ellis, and an Australian Durif (from Campbell's of Rutherglen), and starts with seven house wines up to £16.50.

CHEFS: Philip Burgess and Nick Shopland  PROPRIETOR: Anne Voss-Bark  OPEN: all week 12.30 to 2, 7.30 to 9.30  CLOSED: 24 and 25 Dec, D 26 Dec  MEALS: Set L £18.75 (2 courses) to £23, Set D £31 to £38.75. Bar menu available  SERVICE: not inc  CARDS: Amex, Delta, Diners, MasterCard, Switch, Visa  DETAILS: 70 seats. 30 seats outside. Private parties: 80 main room, 30 private room. Car park. Vegetarian meals. Children's helpings. No smoking in dining room. Wheelchair access (also WC). Music  ACCOMMODATION: 27 rooms, all with bath/shower. TV. Phone. B&B £48 to £150. Baby facilities. Fishing (The Which? Hotel Guide)  £5

## LINCOLN Lincolnshire       map 9

# Wig & Mitre ✸

| | |
|---|---|
| 30/32 Steep Hill, Lincoln LN2 1TL | COOKING 3 |
| TEL: (01522) 535190   FAX: (01522) 532402 | MODERN BRITISH |
| EMAIL: reservations@wigandmitre.co.uk | £21–£50 |

Occupying two floors near the top of the accurately named Steep Hill (on the way up for pilgrims to the cathedral), the present incarnation of this fourteenth-century building goes out of its way to be flexible: not the least advantage is that it is open 15 hours a day, 365 days a year. Food changes as the day unfolds, with the option of breakfast, sandwiches and, from noon to 6pm, a set menu; the main à la carte menu is available at all times throughout the premises, and a blackboard lists daily specials: red mullet with pink fir potatoes for one visitor.

It should come as no surprise that there is something to suit most tastes: a soup containing butternut squash, crab, lemon grass and coconut; a twice-baked cheese soufflé with bacon and leeks, sitting in a pool of cream; and steamed syrup sponge with crème anglaise. Standards vary (tender roast duck and tough pigeon at the same meal), but service is up to the job, and wines provide an obliging array of styles with good choice under £20, starting with house French at £10.50.

CHEFS: Peter Dodd and Robbie Borst   PROPRIETORS: Valerie and Michael Hope   OPEN: all week 8am to 11pm   MEALS: alc (main courses £6 to £18). Set L £9.75 (2 courses) to £12.75 (served from 12 to 6). Breakfast, sandwiches and snacks also available   SERVICE: not inc   CARDS: Amex, Delta, Diners, MasterCard, Switch, Visa   DETAILS: 135 seats. Private parties: 65 main room, 20 private room. Vegetarian meals. Children's helpings. No smoking in dining room. No music (£5)

## LINTON West Yorkshire       map 8

# ▲ Wood Hall  ✸

| | |
|---|---|
| Trip Lane, Linton LS22 4JA | |
| TEL: (01937) 587271   FAX: (01937) 584353 | |
| EMAIL: events.woodhall@arcadianhotels.co.uk | |
| WEBSITE: www.arcadianhotels.co.uk | |
| from Wetherby take A661 N for ½m, turn left for | |
| Sicklinghall and Linton, then left to Linton and | COOKING 3 |
| Wood Hall; turn right in Linton opposite Windmill | MODERN EUROPEAN |
| pub, and continue 2m along single-track road | £24–£67 |

This secluded, imposing hotel set in a prime countryside enjoys plenty of peace and quiet, which might well be down to the condition of the road you take to reach it: bumpy and narrow enough to deter casual visitors. The décor could do with a bit of updating, some have felt, but there is nothing old-fashioned about the health spa and leisure facilities.

Unsurprisingly in this setting, a rather classic style prevails, and richness is a dominant trait: smooth chicken liver parfait with toasted brioche, or perhaps cream of asparagus soup to start, followed by a fricassee of well-timed, fresh-tasting fish with a champagne and herb sauce, or maybe pan-fried medallions of pork with potato purée, creamed cabbage and glazed apple. A couple of visitors have written in praise of Sunday lunch: roast Aberdeen Angus with Yorkshire pudding, carved at table from a large rib joint, cooked pink and 'extremely tender with a good matured taste'. Dessert might include 'really sticky' toffee pudding, or glazed lemon tart with raspberry sorbet. The 140-bin wine list has global scope, but limited choice under £20, although eight house wines start at £14.50, £3.80 a glass.

CHEF: Lee Parsons   PROPRIETOR: Hand Picked Hotels   OPEN: Sun to Fri L 12 to 2.30, all week D 7 to 9.45 (9.30 Sun)   MEALS: alc D (main courses £16.50 to £22). Set L Mon to Fri £12.50 (2 courses) to £14.50, Set L Sun £16, Set D £29.50   SERVICE: not inc, card slips closed   CARDS: Amex, Delta, Diners, MasterCard, Switch, Visa   DETAILS: 80 seats. Private parties: 80 main room, 2 to 80 private rooms. Car park. Vegetarian meals. Children's helpings. No smoking in dining room. Wheelchair access (also WC). Occasional music. No mobile phones ACCOMMODATION: 43 rooms, all with bath/shower. TV. Phone. B&B £90 to £190. Rooms for disabled. Baby facilities. Swimming pool. Fishing

## LITTLE BARROW Cheshire      map 8

# Foxcote Inn     | NEW ENTRY |

Station Lane, Little Barrow CH3 7JN
TEL: (01244) 301343   FAX: (01244) 303287
EMAIL: thefoxcote@hotmail.com
WEBSITE: www.thefoxcote.com

COOKING 2
SEAFOOD
£24–£50

Nominally a pub, this is more a restaurant with a bar, though it maintains pubby practices, such as displaying the menu on a blackboard and taking orders at the bar. Fish is the focus of the kitchen's attention, and there are some interesting ideas among the huge list of dishes on offer (one visitor counted no fewer than 27 main courses), including accurately seared scallops with cauliflower purée, pesto and roast yellow pepper coulis; and roast monkfish tail with asparagus tempura, morsels of salmon and a plum sauce, which exhibited prime ingredients and sound treatment. Specialities include paella (give 24 hours' notice) and mussels, served in one-kilo portions with a choice of sauces such as dry cider and apples, or fresh orange and chicory. There is also plenty of choice for meat eaters and vegetarians: roast lamb shank with spiced apricot and sultana chutney, for example. Wine service has been found wanting: a wide choice is offered by the glass (from £2.50) but the opened bottles from which they are served could be better looked after. Still, prices are fair throughout the wide-ranging list, starting at £9.95.

CHEFS: Leigh Parry, Kelvin Ward, and John and Emma Evans   PROPRIETORS: Leigh Parry and Cathy Goulding   OPEN: Sun 12 to 9.30, Mon to Sat 12 to 2.30, 6 to 9.30 (10 Fri and Sat)   MEALS: alc (main courses L £8 to £9.50, D £10 to £17). Set D 6 to 7 £12 (2 courses) to £17.50 (inc wine) SERVICE: not inc, card slips closed   CARDS: Delta, MasterCard, Switch, Visa   DETAILS: 64 seats. 12 seats outside. Car park. Vegetarian meals. Children's helpings. No-smoking area. Music

Net prices *in the details at the end of an entry indicates that the prices given on a menu and on a bill are inclusive of VAT and service charge, and that this practice is clearly stated on menu and bill.*

**LITTLE BEDWYN Wiltshire** map 2

## Harrow

Little Bedwyn SN8 3JP
TEL: (01672) 870871
EMAIL: dining@harrowinn.co.uk
WEBSITE: www.harrowinn.co.uk
off A4, 4m SW of Hungerford

COOKING **4**
MODERN BRITISH
£45–£69

That 'Inn' has been dropped from the name confirms that this one-time village hostelry is now a full-fledged restaurant. The interlinked small dining rooms have a cheery, bistro feel, with bright curtains and prints of seafood, and service is very friendly, polite and observant. Roger and Sue Jones' reputation hinges on serious food and an excellent wine cellar. The kitchen's success lies in sourcing fine ingredients across the board, with seafood a major strength: shellfish are delivered live, other fish is from day boats or line-caught where possible. This has resulted in some of the finest scallops an inspector had ever tasted, lightly seared with a jumble of squid tentacles and chilli jam. Elsewhere fillet of turbot might be served with spinach, ceps and fresh truffle oil, while a tempura of 'native' lobster and sole is given a wasabi and ginger dressing.

Beef is Welsh Black or Aberdeen Angus (perhaps a carpaccio with shaved Périgord truffles); otherwise Roger Jones seeks out salt-marsh lamb, squabs and venison (paired with crispy duck and 'bashed neeps'). Desserts are in the more traditional mould of bread-and-butter pudding, but it would be criminal to ignore the outstanding cheeses (from Jeroboams) which come with a 'fantastic' tasting of three wines. The list itself is a delight, with Australia, France, Italy and Spain providing most interest. Besides notable red and white Riojas, including López de Heredia's, there are five vintages of Moss Wood Pinot Noir from Australia, ten sherries by the glass and an imaginative selection of dry and sweet Italian wines. Prices are commendably fair (Cloudy Bay Sauvignon Blanc for £16), and 'recommended wines' start at £15 per bottle (£4 a glass).

CHEF: Roger Jones PROPRIETORS: Roger and Sue Jones OPEN: Wed to Sun L 12 to 2, Wed to Sat D 7 to 9 CLOSED: 23 Dec to 14 Jan, last 2 weeks Aug MEALS: alc (main courses £18). Set L and D £45 to £75 (inc wine) SERVICE: not inc, card slips closed CARDS: Amex, MasterCard, Switch, Visa DETAILS: 36 seats. 32 seats outside. Private parties: 36 main room. Vegetarian meals. Children's helpings. No smoking in dining room. Wheelchair access (also WC). No music. No mobile phones

**LITTLE SHELFORD Cambridgeshire** map 6

## Sycamore House

1 Church Street, Little Shelford CB2 5HG
TEL: (01223) 843396

COOKING **3**
MODERN BRITISH
£34–£41

Michael and Susan Sharpe's neat, cream-painted detached house is as understated as they come, giving the impression of a tasteful and fairly select eating place, complete with a neatly tended garden. It may feel rather conservative but, equally, 'nothing goes far wrong'. Don't expect fusion or fireworks in this Cambridgeshire backwater, because here is a kitchen that relies on quiet confidence (and operates only four nights a week). Michael Sharpe works to a fixed-price menu of four courses, with limited options at each stage, but results are both comforting and professionally wrought: 'your taste-buds are certainly in safe hands,' noted an inspector.

Dinner might begin with a neat rectangle of smoked haddock served with grilled cheesy mashed potato and chives, before a palate-cleansing salad spiked with pickled ginger. Mains are attractive and generous: perhaps venison braised with red wine, shallots and chestnuts, or that well-tried Sycamore House favourite (listed half a dozen years ago in the Guide), seared scallops on pea purée with mint vinaigrette. Desserts are in the pleasantly traditional mould of Bakewell tart with vanilla cream sauce, and 'velvety' chocolate nemesis. Susan Sharpe is the model of a professional hostess, 'eagle-eyed, but kindly attentive'.

Despite its forest of over-excited exclamation marks, the wine list is short and pleasing. Every bottle seems to have been hand-picked and the quality shows. Pricing is fair, giving plenty of choice under £20. More in the by-the-glass range wouldn't hurt, though, as – excepting dessert wines – only the two house selections (£10.50 a bottle) are sold by the glass (£2.50).

CHEF: Michael Sharpe   PROPRIETORS: Michael and Susan Sharpe   OPEN: Wed to Sat D only 7.30 to 9   CLOSED: Christmas   MEALS: Set D £25   SERVICE: not inc, card slips closed   CARDS: Delta, MasterCard, Switch, Visa   DETAILS: 24 seats. Private parties: 24 main room. Car park. Vegetarian meals. No children under 12. No smoking in dining room. No music  £5

---

**LIVERPOOL  Merseyside**                                                      map 8

# Chung Ku  £

Riverside Drive, Columbus Quay,
Liverpool L3 4DB                                                    COOKING 4
TEL: (0151) 726 8191   FAX: (0151) 726 8190                          CHINESE
WEBSITE: www.chungku-restaurant.co.uk                              £18–£79

Superb riverside views are one of the great assets at this stunningly designed, contemporary Chinese restaurant by Columbus Quay. You can view the sights from the windows of the two dining areas: noise levels can be high when the downstairs dining room is in full swing, although things are less frenetic upstairs. A formidable contingent of dim sum running to some 70 items is one of the kitchen's trademarks: choice extends from familiar sui mai to Peking fried dumplings with Chinese chives, pot sticker dumplings with red vinegar and shredded ginger dip, and deep-fried custard buns.

The main carte is an extensive and thorough-going trawl through the Cantonese repertoire with a few additions; and there are set banquets if you don't fancy choosing. Appetisers such as salt and pepper spare ribs, braised mussels in spicy sauce and Vietnamese spring rolls precede roast meats, sizzlers, one-plate rice and noodle dishes and a decent selection for vegetarians. Aficionados, however, tend to home in on the challenging 'Chinese-only' menu; if you fancy experimenting, staff should be able to help. House French is £10.50.

CHEF: Au Tung   PROPRIETOR: Mrs T.L. Shum   OPEN: all week 12 to 11 (10 Sun and bank hols) CLOSED: 25 Dec   MEALS: alc (main courses £7.50 to £30). Set L 12 to 2 £9.50, Set D until 10.30 £18 to £28 (min 2 to 4). Dim sum menu available 12 to 6 all week   SERVICE: not inc   CARDS: Amex, Delta, MasterCard, Switch, Visa   DETAILS: 375 seats. Private parties: 200 main room, 30 to 200 private rooms. Car park. Vegetarian meals. Music. Air-conditioned

# Shangri-La

37 Victoria Street, Liverpool L1 6BQ

TEL: (0151) 255 0708 and 227 2707

FAX: (0151) 236 6560

COOKING **2**

CHINESE

£25–£49

A long-serving fixture of Liverpool's Chinese scene, this old-stager still looks in good shape, with its three-level tiered dining room decked out in flag-waving colours of the Orient: black, green and red. Banquets and starter platters no doubt please office parties and the business crowd, but the long menu also promises some more serious dishes, a few 'pottery' hotpots such as diced chicken with aubergine and salted fish, and proper Chinese vegetables like 'kai lan' cooked with crushed garlic and dressed in hot chicken fat. Elsewhere, chilli and salt frog's legs, and shredded chilli beef in a bird's nest have been competently executed. Portions are hearty and presentation may seem a touch rough-and-ready, but the kitchen's heart is in the right place. Staff are pleasant and helpful. House wine is around £10, although we cannot confirm that, nor any of the details below, because the restaurant has declined to send back its wine list, menus and requested information about personnel, opening times and so on.

CHEF: Mr Chan   PROPRIETOR: Mr Ho   OPEN: all week noon to midnight   CLOSED: 25 Dec   MEALS: alc (main courses £5.50 to £24). Set L 12 to 2.30 £5.30, Set D 2.30 onwards £14 to £24 (min 2) SERVICE: not inc, card slips closed   CARDS: Amex, Delta, Diners, MasterCard, Switch, Visa DETAILS: 400 seats. Private parties: 200 main room, 100 private room. Vegetarian meals. Music. Air-conditioned

# Simply Heathcotes ✱

Beetham Plaza, 25 The Strand, Liverpool L2 0XL

TEL: (0151) 236 3536   FAX: (0151) 236 3534

EMAIL: liverpool@simplyheathcotes.co.uk

WEBSITE: www.heathcotes.co.uk

COOKING **3**

MODERN ENGLISH

£25–£47

As chef-branded mini-chains go, Paul Heathcote's is one of the better efforts. The maestro's style – described as 'modern British cooking with a northern English edge' (or 'class without pomposity' as one reporter put it) – is clearly stamped on the menu. Tatin of Cumberland sausage with cider glaze and mustard and onion compote takes its place among starters, while main courses might feature honey-roast ham with mustard mash, butter and broad beans, and herb butter sauce; or paprika-roasted cod fillet with carrot and lime salad, chickpeas and a parsley and lemon dressing. 'Exciting' architecture and décor – curved plate-glass walls and lots of polished black granite – help to give the place a 'really lively buzz', and service is 'among the best we've had anywhere: efficient, intelligent and truly Liverpudlian'. Ten wines are sold by the glass from a list that mostly represents good value, though a few big numbers are thrown in for good measure. House French is £12.

CHEF: Andrew McGuinness   PROPRIETOR: Paul Heathcote   OPEN: all week 12 to 2.30, 6 to 10 (11 Sat)   CLOSED: 25 and 26 Dec, bank hol Mon   MEALS: alc (main courses £10 to £15). Set L and D Mon to Sat 6 to 7 and Sun 6 to 10 £13.50 (2 courses) to £15.50   SERVICE: 10% (optional), card slips closed  CARDS: Amex, Delta, MasterCard, Switch, Visa  DETAILS: 96 seats. Private parties: 80 main room, 8 to 28 private rooms. Vegetarian meals. Children's helpings. No smoking in dining room. Wheelchair access (also WC). Music. Air-conditioned

# 60 Hope Street ♀ 🍳

60 Hope Street, Liverpool L1 9BZ
TEL: (0151) 707 6060   FAX: (0151) 707 6016
EMAIL: info@60hopestreet.com
WEBSITE: www.60hopestreet.com

COOKING 4
MODERN EUROPEAN
£24–£63

'The standard continues to be excellent' at this dual-purpose eatery in a Georgian terrace at the Anglican cathedral end of Hope Street. The choice is basement café-bar or ground-floor restaurant, the latter only slightly more formal; both are in simple modern style with plenty of polished bare wood and plain pale-coloured walls.

The kitchen aims for a recognisably contemporary cooking style – with culinary influences from here, there and everywhere – but is powered by a sense of adventure. Hence, it partners kidneys wrapped in pancetta with sweet and sour shiitakes, and complements roast breast of duck with crushed sweet potatoes, chorizo and a balsamic jus; roast salmon is given a soft crab crust and served with noodles and a herb velouté. Inventive desserts have included cannelloni of lemon curd with yoghurt sorbet, honey and sunflower seeds. The long café menu offers a range of salads and sandwiches, and main dishes ranging from fish and chips with mushy peas to Madras curry.

Service is 'attentive but not pushy'. Wines come from a collection of good producers from Old World and New, and many seem to have been chosen for food compatibility. Mark-ups are generally fair, with decent choice in the under-£20 bracket; prices start at £11.95.

CHEF: Gary Manning   PROPRIETORS: Colin, Gary and Holly Manning   OPEN: Mon to Fri L 12 to 2.30, Mon to Sat D 7 to 10.30   CLOSED: bank hols   MEALS: alc (main courses £13 to £19). Set L £10.95 (2 courses) to £13.95. Café-bar menu also available Mon to Sat noon to 10.30   SERVICE: not inc, 10% for parties of 8 or more   CARDS: Delta, MasterCard, Switch, Visa   DETAILS: 90 seats. Private parties: 90 main room. Vegetarian meals. Children's helpings. No-smoking area. Music. Air-conditioned

# Tai Pan £

W.H. Lung Building, Great Howard Street,
Liverpool L5 9TZ
TEL: (0151) 207 3888   FAX: (0151) 207 0100

COOKING 4
CHINESE
£16–£50

The location – above a supermarket overlooking the dockside hinterland – may be nothing to write home about, but this kitchen is capable of producing some of the most convincing Chinese food in the north-west. Chef Tommy Chan came here from the New Emperor (see entry, Manchester) and has quickly found his feet. A standard menu offers chicken wings with salt and chilli, sliced beef in oyster sauce, and duck in plum sauce, but the treasures – and the real reason for coming here – are in the 'Chinese only' menu, which has its own versions of set dinners as well as authentic specialities. Seafood is a major strength: not only delicate steamed scallops, but also a signature dish of lobster with ginger and spring onions on a bed of noodles and deep-fried crispy oysters with seasoned salt and Worcester sauce for dipping.

More obscurities can be found in the shape of deep-fried pig's intestine stuffed with prawn mousse ('an absolute hit' with a 'sublime combination of textures and flavours', observed an inspector). The kitchen also excels at dim sum and it's worth queuing on Sunday lunchtime when the trolleys are wheeled round with their array of steamed dumplings, cuttlefish cakes, seafood balls with almond flakes and much more besides. House wine is £8.80.

CHEF: Tommy Chan   PROPRIETOR: Tai Pan Restaurants   OPEN: all week 12 to 11 (9.30 Sun and bank hols)   MEALS: alc (main courses £6 to £11.50). Set L (12 to 2 Mon to Fri but not bank hols) £5.45 to £8.45, Set D £15 to £25 (all min 2). Dim sum menu available 12 to 6 all week, dim sum trolley service Sun 12 to 2.30   SERVICE: not inc   CARDS: Amex, MasterCard, Switch, Visa   DETAILS: 250 seats. Private parties: 250 main room, 10 to 80 private rooms. Car park. Vegetarian meals. Music. Air-conditioned

---

## LLANFAIR WATERDINE Shropshire                                    map 5

# ▲ Waterdine ♥ ⅗✳

Llanfair Waterdine LD7 1TU                                          COOKING 5
TEL: (01547) 528214   FAX: (01547) 529992                      MODERN BRITISH
                                                                     £24–£48

Towards the head of the Teme Valley, in Offa's Dyke country, this peaceful old pub lies in a village surrounded by rolling fields. Beyond the bar, with its huge blackened stone chimney, is a residents' lounge with a fine view, and a small, ancient cottagey dining room with a wobbly stone floor. Ken Adams offers a regularly changing three-course menu built on fine materials, including roe deer from nearby Mortimer Forest, Wiltshire hare with braised celeriac, and an enterprisingly sourced trimmed, pink rack of Manx Loghtan lamb accompanied by a skewer of chargrilled spring lamb and kidney.

Dishes are well judged and balanced, taking in a tower of fresh, rare salmon topped with a spoonful of white crabmeat in mayonnaise (spiked with tomato and caper), surmounted by a swirl of fine smoked salmon. Although the kitchen seems to have an aversion to seasoning, stock-based saucing is properly handled and timing is generally accurate, producing pink slices of Hereford beef fillet served with horseradish sauce and some comprehensively fried spätzli. Meals might end with a crisp lemon tart in good pastry, or a slice of layered terrine (gâteau Marjolaine) incorporating dark and white chocolate, praline, almond meringue and a well-judged coffee sauce. The wine list turns up some well-considered bottles, many of which take a welcome detour from the beaten path, such as reds and whites from Austria as well as some good examples from New Zealand. Pricing isn't at all painful, and a separate list of six red and six white 'especially recommended' wines starts at £10.50; six wines are offered by the glass from £2.25.

CHEF/PROPRIETOR: Ken Adams   OPEN: Tue to Sun L 12.15 to 1.45, Tue to Sat D 7.15 to 9   CLOSED: 1 week early winter, 1 week early summer   MEALS: alc exc Sat D and Sun L (main courses £9.50 to £15.50). Set L Sun £15, Set D Sat £25. Bar menu available exc Sat D and Sun L   SERVICE: not inc, card slips closed   CARDS: Delta, MasterCard, Switch, Visa   DETAILS: 31 seats. 10 seats outside. Private parties: 22 main room, 12 to 16 private rooms. Car park. No children under 8 at D. No smoking in dining room. No music   ACCOMMODATION: 3 rooms, all with bath/shower. TV. B&B £45 to £80. No children under 12

## LONG CRENDON  Buckinghamshire                                                    map 2

# ▲ Angel Restaurant ♥ ⁵⚹

| | |
|---|---|
| 47 Bicester Road, Long Crendon HP18 9EE | COOKING 3 |
| TEL: (01844) 208268   FAX: (01844) 202497 | SEAFOOD/FUSION |
| WEBSITE: www.angelrestaurant.co.uk | £29–£68 |

For years this was the Angel Inn, until the gastronomically oriented name change. The sixteenth-century building exudes affluent comfort, and proceedings begin in the beamed bar, which has a couple of Chesterfields for good measure. Then you move through to one of the dining areas, each of them very different in style: there's even a patio for al fresco eating. Fish is the kitchen's forte, and the specials board is the thing to watch: here you might see steamed Scottish rope mussels with saffron and herbs, roast fillet of halibut on hot green vegetable salad in a tomato and clam chowder or – if you fancy a touch of fusion – lightly curried codling on wild mushroom risotto with coriander sabayon. Printed menus cater adequately for meat eaters and vegetarians ('saltimbocca' of Highland venison with roast garlic mash, or ricotta and spinach lasagne, for example), and there are also crostinis at lunchtime. Finish with 'good-looking' fig tarte Tatin or sticky toffee pudding, otherwise the assiette of Angel desserts is a showcase for some of the kitchen's best efforts.

Sensibly, the wine list features more whites than reds. France and Australia figure most strongly, although the list covers most of the winemaking world. Pricing isn't as keen as it could be, but there is plenty to choose from under £20 nonetheless. Seven house wines are £13.50, or £3.25 by the glass.

CHEFS: Trevor Bosch and Donald Joyce   PROPRIETORS: Trevor and Annie Bosch   OPEN: all week L 12 to 3, Mon to Sat D 7 to 10   MEALS: alc exc Sun L (main courses £12.50 to £22). Set L Sun £13.95 (2 courses) to £16.95. Light L menu also available   SERVICE: not inc   CARDS: Delta, MasterCard, Switch, Visa   DETAILS: 75 seats. 30 seats outside. Private parties: 35 main room, 7 to 15 private rooms. Car park. Vegetarian meals. Children's helpings. No smoking in 1 dining room. Music. Air-conditioned   ACCOMMODATION: 3 rooms, all with bath/shower. TV. Phone. B&B £55 to £65. Baby facilities (The Which? Hotel Guide)  £5

## LONG MELFORD  Suffolk                                                            map 6

# Scutchers Bistro ⁵⚹

| | |
|---|---|
| Westgate Street, Long Melford CO10 9DP | COOKING 3 |
| TEL: (01787) 310200   FAX: (07000) 785443 | MODERN BRITISH |
| WEBSITE: www.scutchers.com | £31–£54 |

This brightly lit and cheery bistro in what was once a pub has a 'smart-but-casual restaurant' atmosphere. Vibrant primary colours – red, yellow and blue – add a modern feel to the open-plan, multi-level interior, with its wood panelling, pine tables and chairs, and open log fire in the lounge. The kitchen's forte is simple but stylish modern British cooking, with flavours that shine through, illustrated by such starters as a 'perfectly cooked and very enjoyable' combination of sauté foie gras on black pudding, haggis and pea purée in a rich wine gravy; likewise a 'balanced' dish of seared scallops comes with a risotto given 'a little oomph' from spring onion and pickled ginger. Grilled fillet of turbot with lime hollandaise, or pan-fried Scottish fillet of beef with béarnaise, offer a more straightforward approach to mains perhaps, while a simply presented crème brûlée with a compote of cherries in Kirsch, or raspberry trifle, rounds things off. Service proves smart and professional, while the wine list, grouped by grape variety, has a commendable number of half bottles and a 13-strong house selection from £11.50, plus a welcome choice by the glass from £2.20.

CHEFS: Nicholas Barrett and Guy Alabaster   PROPRIETORS: Nicholas and Diane Barrett   OPEN: Tue to Sat 12 to 2, 7 to 9.30   CLOSED: Christmas, 1 to 10 Jan   MEALS: alc (main courses £11.50 to £17.50)   SERVICE: not inc   CARDS: Amex, Delta, MasterCard, Switch, Visa   DETAILS: 70 seats. Car park. Vegetarian meals. Children's helpings. No smoking in dining room. Wheelchair access (also WC). No music. Air-conditioned

## LONGRIDGE  Lancashire                                                        map 8

# Paul Heathcote's ✸✖

104–106 Higher Road, Longridge PR3 3SY
TEL: (01772) 784969   FAX: (01772) 785713
EMAIL: longridge@heathcotes.co.uk
WEBSITE: www.heathcotes.co.uk

from Preston, follow Town Centre signs, drive                    COOKING 7
uphill though centre of Longridge, then turn left,            MODERN BRITISH
following signs for Jeffery Hill                                    £26–£99

Three cottages house Paul Heathcote's flagship operation. Exposed stone, cream walls and wooden panelling line the small, interlinked rooms, which can have 'the air of being in church', with everybody whispering. The décor might now benefit from a makeover, but spacious tables are smartly set with heavy linen and glistening glassware. Despite his multitude of business interests (including brasseries in Preston, Liverpool and Leeds, see entries), Paul Heathcote remains very much involved here. His food has a personal stamp, be it a humble potato cake supporting a piece of moist black pudding and an accurately poached egg, surrounded by an inspirational ginger jus; or roast Goosnargh chicken (juicy and tender, with 'a terrific taste') served with marjoram mash and a generous sprinkling of wild mushrooms in cream.

Menu descriptions can be mildly misleading, but quality materials and technical prowess are evident: in a fresh-tasting pressed terrine of vegetables (serried rows of aubergine, courgette and asparagus lightly bound in aspic), and in a light duck consommé flecked with tiny dice of red pepper and tomato, containing a thin tortellino of shredded duck and apple. Although there are some bold-sounding ideas (such as poached Scottish lobster with passion-fruit risotto), quite a few dishes are elevated into haute cuisine without losing sight of their country roots: for example a pile of haricot beans and Toulouse sausage supporting pink slices of well-flavoured Goosnargh duck breast, served with an intense, sticky reduction of duck stock infused with beetroot and ginger, with mushrooms adding to its robust earthiness.

Highlights among desserts include glazed raspberry tart with a contrasting strong chocolate sorbet, and 'the aristocrat of bread-and-butter puddings' spiked with sharp apricot, and accompanied by clotted cream. Cheeses were not very impressive at inspection, although incidentals are impeccable. Lunch is considered a bargain, though service, just the right side of formal, could do with a dash more brio and confidence. Wines won't suit those of modest means (little but house wine makes it under £20), but the quality is undoubted.

CHEFS: Paul Heathcote and Matthew Harris   PROPRIETOR: Paul Heathcote   OPEN: Wed to Fri and Sun L 12 to 2.15, Wed to Sun D 7 to 9.45   CLOSED: 1 and 2 Jan   MEALS: alc Wed to Sat D (main courses £19 to £24). Set L £16.50, Set D Wed to Sat £38 to £65 (latter whole table), Set D Sun £25 SERVICE: 10% (optional), card slips closed   CARDS: Amex, Delta, Diners, MasterCard, Switch, Visa   DETAILS: 70 seats. Private parties: 10 to 18 private rooms. Car park. Vegetarian meals. Children's helpings. No smoking in dining room. Wheelchair access (not WC). Music

## Thyme 🍴 £                                    NEW ENTRY

1–3 Inglewhite Road, Longridge PR3 3JR                        COOKING 3
TEL/FAX: (01772) 786888                              MODERN EUROPEAN
WEBSITE: www.thyme-restaurant.co.uk                           £16–£42

Paul Heathcote put Longridge on the map (see entry above), but since November 2001 local epicureans have had a choice. At a T-junction in the centre two knocked-through terraced cottages house a smart, split-level restaurant with boarded floor, decorated in light green, deep purple and brown. The menus' obvious puns ('Thyme for Indulgence', etc.) don't undermine the culinary skill that informs a multi-influenced style. Local roots are celebrated – via roast Goosnargh duckling sauced with mulled wine and plum, or pork escalope filled with black pudding and apple – and a May special was Lancashire fishcake (white fish, prawns, capers and Lancashire cheese) with tartare sauce and a crisp salad. But some dishes are more cosmopolitan: tempura-battered asparagus in sweet-and-sour dressing, Mediterranean fish soup, or tuna with scallops, saffron risotto and Parmesan. Salting can seem heavy, and not every unusual idea comes off as well as a 'knickerbocker glory' with all the attendant cream, custard and ice cream, as well as a hot centre of gingery sticky toffee pudding. Service is well-paced and friendly. The shortish, annotated wine list is high-class, generally fairly priced and good value, with most bottles well under £20. House vins de pays are £9.75 (or £1.95/£2.60 a 125ml/175ml glass), Schloss Vollrads Riesling is a bit of a steal at £16.25, and six wines come by the glass.

CHEF/PROPRIETOR: Alex Coward   OPEN: Tue to Sat 11 to 4, 6.30 to 9.30; Sun 1 to 8   CLOSED: 1 week New Year, bank hol Mons   MEALS: alc (main courses £12 to £15). Set L £6.95 (2 courses) to £7.95, Set L Sun £9.95 (2 courses) to £11.95. Light L menu also available   SERVICE: not inc CARDS: Amex, Delta, MasterCard, Switch, Visa   DETAILS: 45 seats. Private parties: 45 main room. Vegetarian meals. No smoking in 1 dining room. Wheelchair access (also WC). Occasional music. No mobile phones

*The Guide relies on feedback from its readers. Especially welcome are reports on new restaurants appearing in the book for the first time. All letters to the Guide are acknowledged.*

## LOOE  Cornwall                                                                map 1

# Trawlers ✸✺

Buller Quay, East Looe PL13 1AH
TEL: (01503) 263593                                                    COOKING 2
EMAIL: trawlerslooe@aol.com                      CAJUN/PROVENÇALE SEAFOOD
WEBSITE: www.trawlersrestaurant.co.uk                              £29–£50

Among the fishing sheds, fish shops and smokeries on the quayside, the aptly
named Trawlers proves quite a catch, thronging with regulars who flock here to
enjoy a daily-changing menu that ebbs with the seasons and tides. It's an
unpretentious, relaxed and friendly kind of place, where seafood is the order of
the day; fishing pictures and memorabilia line the room, with its view over the
harbour's bobbing boats. Chef Todd Varnedoe, from Louisiana, adds a few
Creole and provençale twists to proceedings, and, while some may contest that
the freshest fish simply prepared may be hard to beat, his flavour combinations
don't overpower. One visitor judged her local mussels cooked in Thai spices
(chilli, ginger, lime and coconut) the most enjoyable for 20 years. A blackboard
supplements the card menu with perhaps a duo of monkfish and John Dory with
lime and coriander, while vegetables come individually plated and are as
generous as the service. Cholesterol-challenging desserts might feature a hot
bread-and-butter pudding with rum and raisins, and wines on the simple list
come in predominantly under £20 (house French is £10.50).

CHEF: Todd Varnedoe  PROPRIETORS: Roger Stamp and Cathy Styche  OPEN: Tue to Sat D only
6.30 to 9.30  CLOSED: 24 to 26 Dec  MEALS: alc (main courses £12.50 to £19.50). Set D £15.50 (2
courses)  SERVICE: not inc  CARDS: Amex, Delta, MasterCard, Switch, Visa  DETAILS: 30 seats.
Private parties: 20 main room. Vegetarian meals. Children's helpings. No children under 7. No
smoking in dining room. Wheelchair access (not WC). Music  £5

# Water Rail ✸✺

Lower Market Street, Looe PL13 1AX                                  COOKING 2
TEL/FAX: (01503) 262314                                                SEAFOOD
                                                                   £27–£61

'Fish fresh from the quay' is the enticing message chalked up on a blackboard
outside this atmospheric seventeenth-century house; and apart from a few more
exotic specimens, it is nearly all to be found swimming in waters off the shores of
this historic fishing village. Indeed, most produce, from bread through to wines,
comes from local suppliers. Lobsters are a speciality, and, as the Guide went to
press, a lobster tank was due to be installed in the dining room: it will need to be
a large one to accommodate the purple-shell deep-sea lobsters that come big
enough for up to four people to share. Otherwise, the menu goes in for classic
fish cookery along the lines of sauté scallops in garlic butter with prawns and
parsley, or poached skate wing with creamy caper sauce; plus a few more
unusual items such as crab and anchovy cakes with yoghurt, garlic and
cucumber sauce. A few meat and pasta dishes offer a viable alternative to fish,
and puddings are straight from the nursery. Seven house selections from £9.50
open the list of two dozen varied wines, nearly all under £20.

CHEF: Richard Maior-Barron  PROPRIETORS: Richard and Denise Maior-Barron  OPEN: Thur to Sat L (June to Sept only) 12 to 2, Wed to Mon D (all year) 7 to 10  CLOSED: 25 Dec, 1 to 31 Jan  MEALS: alc (main courses £12 to £30). Set D £14.95 (2 courses). 'Summer lunch' menu also available  SERVICE: not inc, card slips closed  CARDS: Delta, MasterCard, Switch, Visa  DETAILS: 40 seats. Private parties: 28 main room, 2 to 12 private rooms. Vegetarian meals. No children under 10. No smoking in dining room. Music. No mobile phones  (£5)

## LOW LAITHE  North Yorkshire                                    map 9

# Dusty Miller

Low Laithe, Summerbridge HG3 4BU                         COOKING 4
TEL: (01423) 780837                                    ANGLO-FRENCH
on B6165, 2m SE of Pateley Bridge                          £36–£57

In 2003 the Dennisons celebrate 20 years at this stone-built restaurant on the edge of the Dales. Their tiny, split-level dining room is like 'an old-fashioned living room,' complete with flock wallpaper and a giant palm in an earthenware pot. The food, too, smacks of a bygone era. A half-lobster thermidor is nostalgic enough, and while a starter of ripe melon is perked up with a prawn salsa, the general thrust is of tried and tested combinations such as roast duckling with apples and Calvados, lamb shank with mint gravy, and Aberdeen Angus beef with bordelaise sauce.

Perhaps the most positive legacy of such tradition is the combination of well-sourced, high-quality materials, and the skills necessary to do them justice. Brian Dennison's cooking is technically accomplished, even if the dishes sound easy to prepare. Soups usually separate the men from the boys – here perhaps a choice of asparagus or scampi – while alternatives might include a roasted vegetable terrine or a plate of black pudding with bacon and foie gras. Finish with a tuile basket of raspberries, or a plate of cheeses. A short, well-chosen list of wines is backed up by a page of fine French wines and a trio of house wines at £12.90 (£3.50 a glass).

CHEF: Brian Dennison  PROPRIETORS: Brian and Elizabeth Dennison  OPEN: Tue to Sat D 7 to 11  CLOSED: 24 to 28 Dec, 2 weeks July  MEALS: alc (main courses £18). Set D £24  SERVICE: not inc  CARDS: Amex, MasterCard, Switch, Visa  DETAILS: 44 seats. Private parties: 30 main room, 14 private room. Car park. Children's helpings. No children under 9. Wheelchair access (not WC). Music

## LUDLOW  Shropshire                                             map 8

# ▲ Dinham Hall  ⁵⅍

Dinham, Ludlow SY8 1EJ
TEL: (01584) 876464  FAX: (01584) 876019                   COOKING 3
EMAIL: info@dinhamhall.fsnet.co.uk                           FRENCH
WEBSITE: www.dinhamhall.co.uk                              £44–£53

Barely a slingshot from the castle, Dinham Hall is a small, old-fashioned hotel with an ancient wooden fire surround in the lounge, squishy sofas, and a deep-pink dining room. A French menu deals in such items as quenelle de brochet, an aumônière de chèvre, and cannon of lamb flavoured with réglisse (a sweetish liquorice sauce with a pleasing depth of flavour). Although materials such as asparagus in January, uneven timing, and some old-fashioned cooking (a mix of pasta and seafood topped with cream and melted cheese) tend to take the edge off things, the kitchen also tries hard with some interesting combinations, some of which are more effective than others: salmon fillet with a cumin-flavoured beurre blanc works well, for example. To finish, a blackcurrant and sage sorbet makes an unusual gateway to desserts of, for example, hot chocolate and raspberry pudding served with an aniseed ice cream and pistachio sauce. An 80-strong French-dominated wine list starts with around half a dozen house wines up to £15.50.

CHEF: Olivier Bossut   PROPRIETORS: J.P. and J.E. Mifsud   OPEN: all week 12.30 to 2, 7 to 9 MEALS: Set L and D £30.50 to £39.50   SERVICE: not inc, card slips closed   CARDS: Amex, Delta, Diners, MasterCard, Switch, Visa   DETAILS: 24 seats. 10 seats outside. Private parties: 36 main room, 2 to 26 private rooms. Car park. Children's helpings. No children under 8. No smoking in dining room. Wheelchair access (not WC). No music. No mobile phones   ACCOMMODATION: 15 rooms, all with bath/shower. TV. Phone. B&B £55 to £180. Baby facilities (*The Which? Hotel Guide*)

---

# Hibiscus ⁵⁄ₓ

17 Corve Street, Ludlow SY8 1DA                      COOKING 7
TEL: (01584) 872325   FAX: (01584) 874024                FRENCH
                                                      £39–£69

Ancient wooden panels combine with grey stonework and creamy coffee-coloured fabric to produce an uncluttered air of 'restrained opulence' here. Neatness and order mark the cooking too; dishes look appealing without lily-gilding extras (important components are simply well arranged). Ideas and combinations can be startling and original, but they are soundly based, even when they bring together some strange bedfellows: plump farmed Hereford snails in a bright green, deeply flavoured broth of wild garlic, with slivers of black olive and a waft of lemon, say, or moist, accurately timed Dover sole, cooked on the bone but presented filleted, with a drizzle of passion-fruit juice and slices of pumpkin.

Dishes are technically demanding, raw materials impeccable in quality, and flavours typically gentle yet effective and balanced. One springtime meal, for example, peaked with milk-fed lamb, its skin infused with cumin, cooked pink and rested ('a joy to eat'); it came with minted breadcrumbs, a macedoine of vegetables and a slick of date purée: halfway to Africa, yet as French as can be. Be prepared for some slight undercooking, and for some dishes not tallying exactly with their menu description, but otherwise this is a polished, well-rehearsed and disciplined kitchen, producing firm, sweet, perky, just-seared scallops with sliced ceps and a swirl of thyme-flavoured walnut oil, and a tranche of foie gras impaled on two skewers of liquorice and partnered by a thick slice of pear and a scoop of lemon sauce.

The warm tarte au chocolat – spongy, cakey, melting chocolate on crisp biscuity pastry – comes with a powerful star anise ice cream; and a warm peanut-butter soufflé is successfully partnered by banana ice cream. Incidentals, such as an appetiser cheese puff, and a pre-dessert of gingery ice cream in a hazelnut 'soup', are ineffably light, and bread (including one made from roasted white flour) is also first-class. Claire Bosi is a skilful hostess – welcoming, efficient, smiling and friendly – and the wine list handsomely rewards anyone with up to £30 to spend. House French is £14.

CHEF: Claude Bosi   PROPRIETORS: Claire and Claude Bosi   OPEN: Wed to Sat L 12.30 to 1.30, Mon to Sat D 7 to 10   CLOSED: 3 weeks Jan, 1 week Aug   MEALS: Set L £19.50 (2 courses) to £25, Set D £32.50 to £42.50   SERVICE: not inc, card slips closed   CARDS: Delta, MasterCard, Switch, Visa   DETAILS: 28 seats. Private parties: 30 main room. Car park. Children's helpings. No smoking in dining room. Wheelchair access (not WC). No music. No mobile phones

# Merchant House ❧✲

Lower Corve Street, Ludlow SY8 1DU
TEL: (01584) 875438
EMAIL: shaunhill@merchanthouse.org
WEBSITE: www.merchanthouse.co.uk

COOKING 8
MODERN BRITISH
£35–£50

The sign outside the black and white timbered house is discreet, and so is the setting. A couple of rooms with bare wooden tables are decorated with Shaker-like simplicity: just a few prints and bits of fabric on the walls. If you're looking for a no-nonsense approach without frills – no lounge in which to take an aperitif or coffee, no tablecloths, no waves of extras, no flunkies, no spun sugar – this is the place for you. Such an absence of airs and graces lies at the heart of Shaun Hill's cooking, although it is anything but austere. Indeed, it seems to be most people's idea of excellence and good value. There are chefs with larger brigades serving more complex dishes, but is there anything better coming out of a single-handed kitchen? Not so far as we know.

Several things contribute to success. Materials are first-rate and cooked with precision, producing a juicy rack of rose-pink lamb, and springy-textured monkfish, as fresh as a daisy, teamed with aromatic gingery tomato. Flavours are emphatic too: for example, in a well-judged, generously endowed basil and artichoke risotto with an appetising savoury sharpness to it. Shaun Hill understands the idea of balance as well as anyone, so that dishes taste complete and harmonious. Lobster is combined with coriander, chickpeas and olive oil to make a cracking first course, and hare has made a fine seasonal appearance, the saddle neatly sliced, the leg meat marinated, minced and made into a little hareburger, served with celeriac and quince.

Dishes are uncluttered in flavour and presentation, such apparent simplicity disguising careful workmanship. A piece of sea bass 'as fresh as you could wish for', its skin scored and seared, rests in a pool of beurre blanc containing diced shallot. You can't get much less showy than this. And sauces are executed with finesse, not over-reduced or laboured. A deconstructed pigeon, all of it pink, tender and flavourful, is plainly served with small brown lentils and diced bacon, in a natural-tasting red wine sauce. Desserts are no less impressive, at their best perhaps in a chocolate pithiviers made with light, crisp puff pastry, and in a concentrated yet light and clean Muscat crème caramel served with prunes soaked in Armagnac.

'Spot-on' service from Anja Hill and helper is friendly, efficient and unobtrusive. Another example of the common-sense approach is found in the comparatively short and mostly European wine list, which is not greedily priced. It offers Zind-Humbrecht's Riesling Herrenweg 1998 at £23.50, Felton Road Pinot Noir 2000 from Central Otago at £32.50, and starts with house

Aquileia del Friuli white (£13.50) and Tenuta del Ornellaia's Le Volte red (£15.50).

CHEF: Shaun Hill   PROPRIETORS: Shaun and Anja Hill   OPEN: Fri and Sat L 12.30 to 1.45, Tue to Sat D 7 to 8.45   CLOSED: 1 week Christmas, 1 week spring   MEALS: Set L £26, Set D £32   SERVICE: net prices, card slips closed   CARDS: Delta, MasterCard, Switch, Visa   DETAILS: 24 seats. No smoking in dining room. Wheelchair access (not WC). No music

## ▲ Mr Underhill's ♀ ✲

| Dinham Weir, Ludlow SY8 1EH | COOKING 7 |
| TEL: (01584) 874431 | MODERN EUROPEAN |
| WEBSITE: www.mr-underhills.co.uk | £42–£56 |

Mr Underhill's occupies a peacefully romantic spot by the river beneath Ludlow Castle. Now the Teme is back to its gentle ways after severe flooding a while back, all looks serene, and the garden comes into its own for aperitifs in fine weather. The comfortable dining room, meanwhile, conveys a pleasing air of conviviality, and a three-course menu (no choice before dessert) typically starts with a fish or vegetable dish, then something meaty or gamy. One meal began with gleaming curds of undyed smoked haddock on a bed of spinach and creamed potato, served with an accurately poached quail's egg and a beurre blanc made with champagne; that was followed by fillet of distinctively flavoured Marches venison, sliced onto a puddle of peppery sauce, served with roast root vegetables and diced celeriac baked in cream.

This is assured, accomplished cooking. Chris Bradley has the knack of using first-class ingredients to best advantage and producing harmonious dishes. Lemon sole 'at the peak of freshness' is cooked to the right degree of springiness, balanced on a tiny raft of shredded, crisply cooked cabbage with a thread of wild lime sauce, while pink slices of Barbary duck breast are fanned around a 'still-life study' of autumn vegetables, with little dabs of quince cream adding sweetness, and hints of cinnamon and cumin contributing an extra dimension. Desserts (usually half a dozen) are a high point, light and carefully crafted, including pears poached with lemongrass and vanilla, with pistachio ice cream; and a Highland parfait with a pleasingly rough texture from the porage oats incorporated into its praline mix, plus a dash of malt whisky in the caramel sauce.

Some find the no-choice menu a pleasant relief; others feel that simple economics require such a meal to be a little cheaper than it is. Service from Judy Bradley and helpers is welcoming, efficient and helpful; although one reporter confessed to feeling 'managed rather than served', another praised the way he was integrated with other guests yet treated individually. Wines are carefully chosen, with value and quality both much in evidence. Most are French, but there are excellent selections from Italy, Spain and Australia, too. A good selection of halves adds interest, and thoroughly reasonable mark-ups send the right signals; prices start at £13.50.

CHEF: Christopher Bradley   PROPRIETORS: Chris and Judy Bradley   OPEN: Wed to Mon D 7.30 to 8.30   MEALS: Set D £30 to £32   SERVICE: not inc   CARDS: MasterCard, Switch, Visa   DETAILS: 24 seats. 36 seats outside. Private parties: 8 main room. Car park. Children's helpings. No smoking in dining room. No music. No mobile phones   ACCOMMODATION: 6 rooms, all with bath/shower. TV. Phone. B&B £65 to £120. Fishing (The Which? Hotel Guide)

# ▲ Overton Grange 🍷 ⁵⁄✳

Hereford Road, Overton, Ludlow SY8 4AD
TEL: (01584) 873500   FAX: (01584) 873524
EMAIL: dartudor@globalnet.co.uk
WEBSITE: www.overtongrangehotel.co.uk
on B4361, 1½m S of Ludlow

COOKING 5
ANGLO-FRENCH
£40–£65

Sitting in parkland just outside town, the house looks as if it was built for a well-to-do merchant or entrepreneur around the 1920s. Solid, unshowy, it offers a pleasant bar and lounge, an unremarkable panelled dining room, and a kitchen with a modicum of innovation and plenty of ambition. Tempura of langoustine is served in a miso soup, and scallops come with a cassoulet of white beans, while main courses take in steamed pigeon with confit turnips, and rabbit loin with watercress purée and a tarragon and mustard sauce.

The seven-course tasting menu gets the thumbs-up (highlights have included lobster with a mango and cucumber dressing, and cod with a red wine sauce). There is no desire to upset the apple cart with outlandish combinations; rather the food stands on its own simple merits, producing recommendable dishes of seared turbot with peas and bacon, and poached peach on a passion fruit and raspberry coulis. Service is friendly, though not the last word in professionalism, and with a change of ownership the effervescent Igi Gonzalez is sadly missed. A selection of eight house wines (£16 to £23 per bottle, £4 to £6 per glass) kicks off the globe-trotting wine list, which starts in the French regions before heading off to other European countries and the New World. New-wave Spanish reds are particularly well covered, as are classics from Australia. Prices can be quite high, but South America offers most scope below £20.

CHEF: Wayne Vickerage   PROPRIETOR: F. Choblet   OPEN: Sun to Wed L 12 to 1.45, all week D 7 to 9.30   CLOSED: 23 Dec to 6 Jan   MEALS: Set L £25, Set L Sun £28, Set D £25 to £35. Tasting menu £60   SERVICE: not inc, card slips closed   CARDS: Delta, MasterCard, Switch, Visa   DETAILS: 50 seats. Private parties: 78 main room, 8 to 50 private rooms. Car park. No children under 8. No smoking in dining room. Wheelchair access (also WC). No music. No mobile phones   ACCOMMODATION: 14 rooms, all with bath/shower. TV. Phone. B&B £65 to £135

## LUND East Riding of Yorkshire   map 9

# Wellington Inn 🍷

19 The Green, Lund YO25 9TE
TEL: (01377) 217294   FAX: (01377) 217192

COOKING 3
MODERN BRITISH
£30–£49

A reporter eating here in late November wondered if the experience might be more enjoyable in summer, when the surrounding countryside was visible. But at least winter visitors are greeted with a crackling log fire, for this is a country pub run in traditional style, and by 'friendly and knowledgeable' staff too. The kitchen works to a gentle pace, but the cooking is worth waiting for, as demonstrated by a daily special that was the centrepiece of that November evening: halibut with leeks in an 'amazingly light' cream sauce. Others have commended the decent rendition of French onion soup; sole with asparagus and lemon hollandaise; and rice pudding with golden syrup dripped into it. Choice is wide, the meat options running to venison with Yorkshire pan haggerty and juniper; or duck breast sauced with port, orange and honey, alongside ginger and spring onion couscous. Finish with iced chestnut parfait and coffee crème anglaise or a cheese selection. The well-annotated wine list keeps one eye on value and the other on imaginative drinking, neatly blending Old and New World styles. South Africa is a particular strength. Prices start at £10.95, and there is plenty under £20.

CHEFS: Sarah Jeffery and Toby Greensides  PROPRIETORS: Russell and Sarah Jeffery  OPEN: Tue to Sat D only 7 to 9.30  MEALS: alc (main courses £13 to £16)  SERVICE: not inc, card slips closed  CARDS: Delta, MasterCard, Switch, Visa  DETAILS: 42 seats. Private parties: 30 main room, 8 to 12 private rooms. Car park. Vegetarian meals. No children under 14. Music

## LYDFORD Devon                                                                map 1

# Dartmoor Inn ✳ £

Moorside, Lydford EX20 4AY                                    COOKING 4
TEL: (01822) 820221   FAX: (01822) 820494              MODERN BRITISH-PLUS
on A386 Tavistock to Okehampton Road                         £21–£51

Sitting on the busy A386 just outside Lydford, the Inn nonetheless projects more than a touch of *Country Living* ambience. Work by artists is more exhibition than decoration, there are needlework samplers and dried flowers everywhere, and the tables are dressed in stiff white linen. Karen Burgess, the whole place in the palm of her hand, leads the service with cheerful composure. Local suppliers are listed proudly, so you know the name of the man who provided the beef fillet that is chargrilled, and served with mushrooms, fried onions, chips and herb butter. Presentation avoids frills and fripperies and concentrates on the tastebuds; a risotto of black pudding, chicken livers and red wine was a brown study, but full of fine combinations. Cornish crab might come simply dressed with mayonnaise and avocado, while a medley of seafood – red mullet, scallops, clams and crab claws – might make a casserole cooked in a mildly curried cream sauce. Quantities will test digestion to the limit, even in desserts such as baked peaches with marsala and almonds, or strawberry fritters with vanilla sauce and clotted cream. Well-chosen wines start at £9.50, and house selections include South African Sauvignon Blanc and Chilean Merlot.

CHEFS: Philip Burgess and Ian Brown  PROPRIETORS: Karen and Philip Burgess, Anne Voss-Bark  OPEN: Tue to Sun L 12 to 2.15, Tue to Sat D 6.30 to 10  CLOSED: bank hols  MEALS: alc (main courses £10 to £19). Set L £13.50 (2 courses) to £15.75, Set L Sun £15 (2 courses) to £17.50, Set D £14.50 (2 courses) to £19.75. Bar L menu also available  SERVICE: not inc, card slips closed  CARDS: Delta, MasterCard, Switch, Visa  DETAILS: 65 seats. 20 seats outside. Private parties: 20 main room. Car park. Vegetarian meals. Children's helpings. No babies Fri and Sat D. No smoking in dining room. Occasional music. No mobile phones

---

Occasional music *in the details at the end of an entry means live or recorded music is played in the dining room only rarely or for special events.* No music *means it is never played.*

---

## ▲ White Hart ✹

51 Stockport Road, Lydgate OL4 4JJ                                COOKING **5**
TEL: (01457) 872566   FAX: (01457) 875190                      ANGLO-FRENCH
on A6050, 3m E of Oldham                                              £25–£48

A modern-day Proteus, the White Hart – situated on the edge of the Pennines
overlooking Oldham – succeeds at the difficult task of being simultaneously a
restaurant with serious aspirations, a relaxed, pubby brasserie, a bustling bar,
and a place to lay your head. In the brasserie, vibrant red walls and wooden
tables provide the backdrop for a lengthy repertoire covering the likes of
haddock fillet in 'crisp and golden' beer batter with fried potatoes, tarragon peas
and caper beurre blanc. A stalwart of the menu, the in-house Saddleworth
Sausage Company's bangers (ranging from maize-fed chicken and smoked
bacon to Cumberland or wild boar with apple and sage) are served with mash of
your choice.

The restaurant moves up a gear in both repertoire and décor: stylish
furnishings, wood floor and yellow walls combine with a more sophisticated
approach. Curried glazed oysters with coriander salad might provide the
accompaniment for seared scallops, while pan-seared Welsh Black beef fillet
could team up with sauté sweetbreads and a balsamic onion jus. Homely,
comforting desserts, such as steamed blackberry sponge with sauce anglaise,
bring things to a close. Service is efficient, espresso generous, and breads home-
made; an enterprising wine list that travels the globe is fairly priced (from
£13.75), and offers an admirable selection by half-bottle and glass.

CHEF: John Rudden   PROPRIETORS: Charles Brierley and John Rudden   OPEN: all week 12 to
2.30, 6 to 9.30 (Sun 1 to 8.30)   MEALS: alc (main courses £10.50 to £16.50). Set L and D Mon to
Fri 6 to 7 £14.25. Set L Sun £16.50   SERVICE: not inc, card slips closed   CARDS: Amex, Delta,
MasterCard, Switch, Visa   DETAILS: 50 seats. 25 seats outside. Private parties: 55 main room, 12
to 24 private rooms. Car park. Vegetarian meals. Children's helpings. No smoking in 1 dining
room. Wheelchair access (also WC). Music. Air-conditioned   ACCOMMODATION: 12 rooms, all
with bath/shower. TV. Phone. B&B £72 to £100. Baby facilities (*The Which? Hotel Guide*)

## Egan's ✹                                                   | NEW ENTRY |

24 Gosport Street, Lymington SO41 9BE                            COOKING **2**
TEL: (01590) 676165   FAX: (01590) 670133                    MODERN BRITISH
                                                                     £21–£50

Just off the bustling high street, behind a picket fence and a dark blue front door
set in a white frontage, is this vibrantly coloured dining room, which has an
informal bistro-type atmosphere and a Mediterranean feel. Fish is the thing to go
for: a long carte is supplemented by a blackboard of daily specials that might
offer seared scallops and bacon with rocket and Parmesan, or skate with capers
and shrimps, while non-fish options might include lamb noisettes with pesto-
roasted vegetables and minted couscous, or calf's liver with lardons, mushrooms
and shallots. The emphasis is more on value for money than finesse, though
dishes benefit from attractively colourful presentation and first-rate local

produce. A starter of deeply-flavoured Cornish lobster bisque was a highlight at inspection, and there was also praise for a perfectly timed halibut fillet given a piquant edge with Thai spices, served on a bed of spicy vegetable 'spaghetti' and garnished with a crab samosa. Desserts are not quite up to the same standard. The long wine list has a French bias but prices are fair; five house recommendations are £10.95, or £2.90 per glass.

CHEF: John Egan   PROPRIETORS: John and Debbie Egan   OPEN: Tue to Sat 12 to 2, 6.30 to 10   MEALS: alc (main courses £13 to £16.50). Set L £8.95 (2 courses) to £10.95   SERVICE: not inc   CARDS: Amex, MasterCard, Switch, Visa   DETAILS: 50 seats. 12 seats outside. Private parties: 20 main room. Vegetarian meals. Children's helpings. No smoking in dining room. Music

---

## LYNDHURST  Hampshire                                       map 2

# ▲ Le Poussin at Parkhill  🍷 ✕

Beaulieu Road, Lyndhurst SO43 7FZ
TEL: (023) 8028 2944   FAX: (023) 8028 3268
EMAIL: sales@lepoussin.co.uk
WEBSITE: www.lepoussin.co.uk                             COOKING 6
from Lyndhurst take B3056 for Beaulieu; Le            MODERN BRITISH
Poussin is on right after 1m                               £33–£68

The bigger chicken (its sibling Simply Poussin is in Brockenhurst, see entry) is a large custard-coloured building of indefinable age with a rather conventional feel, though the conservatory dining room has the advantage of looking out over lawns and trees. This year an à la carte has been introduced, which changes less frequently than the set menus, and all benefit from the kitchen's use of outstanding raw materials: for example, three griddled, dived scallops (crusty outside, barely past translucent in the middle), each on a bed of creamed cauliflower purée, with tiny blobs of a jam-like red-wine reduction.

Dishes often sound busy, and the style is more conservative than venturesome, but admirable technical skills (apart from a tendency to over-season) set the cooking apart. A saddle of venison, for example – 'fabulous meat' served blue as requested – is wrapped in the thinnest prosciutto, given a well-reduced Banyuls-based sauce, and served with sweet, honey-coated walnuts, a spiced wine-poached pear, a fondant potato and a jumble of baby vegetables. Wild fungi are likely to crop up: girolles with a ballottine of quail, or a creamy morel sauce with breast of corn-fed chicken. The à la carte has suggestions for accompanying wines (available by the glass at extra cost), such as a Jurançon to partner a pyramid of crisp praline enclosing an orange sorbet, which in turn harbours a scoop of hazelnut ice cream, all surrounded by orange flesh in a thin custard.

Wine-wise, Alex Aitken admits that he favours the classics from France and from older vintages. The intelligently put-together list does indeed focus on top producers across Bordeaux, Burgundy, the Rhône and Champagne as well as Alsace and the Loire. Elsewhere, California is worth a look, as is the selection of half-bottles. Mark-ups are lower on fine wines, making them better value; prices start at £14.50 in southern France and move up quickly thereafter. Wine service is pleasantly flexible, and will happily offer glass sizes larger that the advertised 125ml size.

CHEFS: Alex Aitken and Neil Dore   PROPRIETORS: Alex and Caroline Aitken   OPEN: all week 12 to 2, 7 to 10   MEALS: alc (main courses £16 to £20). Set L £15 (2 courses) to £25, Set D £20 (2 courses) to £35   SERVICE: 10% (optional), card slips closed   CARDS: Amex, Delta, MasterCard, Switch, Visa   DETAILS: 50 seats. 20 seats outside. Private parties: 100 main room, 6 to 40 private rooms. Car park. Vegetarian meals. Children's helpings. No smoking in dining room. No music. No mobile phones   ACCOMMODATION: 19 rooms, all with bath/shower. TV. Phone. B&B £60 to £150. Rooms for disabled. Baby facilities. Swimming pool. Fishing (The Which? Hotel Guide)

## MADINGLEY Cambridgeshire                                               map 6

# Three Horseshoes ♥ ⅍

High Street, Madingley CB3 8AB
TEL: (01954) 210221   FAX: (01954) 212043                           COOKING 4
off A1303, 2m W of Cambridge, close to M11            MEDITERRANEAN/GLOBAL
junction 13                                                          £29–£61

Occupying a pretty thatched building in a picture-book village, Three Horseshoes is part of the Huntsbridge group (Falcon, Fotheringhay; Old Bridge, Huntingdon; and Pheasant Inn, Keyston; see entries). The shared philosophy embraces an informal approach to food – the same menu is available in both bar and conservatory dining room – while its individual interpretation is up to each chef/patron. Richard Stokes's wide-ranging menu makes some dishes sound very busy: 'too many "additions" adding little to the whole' is how it struck one reporter, while another found the food 'thoughtful, interesting and tasty'. It is certainly not a place to come for plainly prepared food, judging by a dish of teriyaki chicken with wok-fried pak choi, black vinegar, oyster sauce, chilli, shiso cress, and tempura of sweet potato and avocado. Even the gravy that comes with half a roast pheasant (plus cabbage, bacon, caramelised apple, boudin noir and château potatoes) is spiked with Madras curry oil.

Portions are generous (extra vegetables come with a small charge), which may explain why desserts are rarely reported, although they may include tamarillo crumble with a white chocolate ice cream, or lemon-grass and lime leaf jelly with roast mango and a chillied mango sorbet. One other thing shared by all Huntsbridge operations is a bravura wine list, selected in each case by Master of Wine John Hoskins. Wines are arranged by style and/or grape variety, with a few helpful notes about choosing food-friendly examples. There is a fine selection under £20 – starting at £11.50 for South African Cabernet Shiraz and Italian Garganega – as well as 'top class' selections for the aficionado. Dessert wines and sherries are also strong points in this well-balanced list.

CHEF: Richard Stokes   PROPRIETOR: Huntsbridge Ltd   OPEN: all week L 12 to 2, Mon to Sat D 6.30 to 9.30   MEALS: alc (main courses £11 to £19)   SERVICE: not inc, 10% for parties of 10 or more, card slips closed   CARDS: Amex, Delta, Diners, MasterCard, Switch, Visa   DETAILS: 95 seats. 40 seats outside. Private parties: 60 main room. Car park. Vegetarian meals. Children's helpings. No smoking in dining room. Wheelchair access (not WC). No music

## MAIDENCOMBE Devon                                        map 1

# ▲ Orestone Manor ✸

Rockhouse Lane, Maidencombe TQ1 4SX
TEL: (01803) 328098   FAX: (01803) 328336
EMAIL: enquiries@orestone.co.uk                         COOKING 2
WEBSITE: www.orestone.co.uk                          MODERN ENGLISH
on A379 between Torquay and Teignmouth                  £24–£61

Within reach of Torquay and Babbacombe, and yet in a secluded tree-sheltered
spot, Orestone Manor plays on its selected pachydermal and Indian motifs with
a degree of ingenuity. In the comfortable dining room, meanwhile, an English
garden theme predominates, mirroring the kitchen's contemporary English
approach with its customary international borrowings. Dinner might take in
Thai crab soup with shiitake mushrooms, smoked salmon with dill blinis, and
grilled calf's liver with pancetta. Wild mushroom risotto again is well reported,
ambition runs to grilled red mullet fillet with smoked haddock ravioli, and
desserts have included baked cranberry cheesecake with lime sauce, and
hazelnut pancake with caramelised pear and dark chocolate sauce. House wines
start at £11.50 on a fair-value list that takes in a Sharpham red and white from
Devon; a supplementary list of unusual or rare wines is available on request.

CHEF: Anthony Hetherington   PROPRIETOR: Orestone Ltd   OPEN: all week 12.30 to 2.30, 7 to 9
MEALS: alc L Mon to Sat (main courses £8.50 to £12.50). Set L Sun £16.50, Set D Sun to Thur
£27.50, Set D Fri and Sat £32.50   SERVICE: not inc   CARDS: Amex, Delta, MasterCard, Switch,
Visa   DETAILS: 45 seats. 25 seats outside. Private parties: 65 main room. Car park. Vegetarian
meals. Children's helpings. No smoking in dining room. Wheelchair access (also WC). No music
ACCOMMODATION: 12 rooms, all with bath/shower. TV. Phone. B&B £52 to £170. Swimming pool
(The Which? Hotel Guide)  £5

## MAIDSTONE Kent                                          map 3

# Soufflé

31 The Green, Bearsted, Maidstone ME14 4DN              COOKING 2
TEL/FAX: (01622) 737065                                ANGLO-FRENCH
                                                        £28–£57

Bearsted is the 'posh end of Maidstone', a trim, neat suburb that feels like a
separate village, complete with its own green. Standing on the edge of it is this
sixteenth-century cottage with a terrace for outdoor eating. Inside, skeletal
timber frames, exposed brickwork and an old bread oven give away the age of
the place. Nick Evenden's ambitious, elaborate cooking has something of a
French accent and features plenty of luxury ingredients. At inspection, not every
dish achieved the desired impact – flabby tiger prawns came with a sweet chilli
sauce lacking bite – but others were more successful: half a dozen briefly seared
scallops with a scattering of crisp lardons and a sweet balsamic dressing, for
example, showed good technique. Among main courses, rare pan-fried calf's
liver with confit limes and caramelised onions is a happy combination of
flavours, and a large chunk of flavoursome beef fillet comes topped with
parsnips cooked dauphinois-style with truffles. For dessert, hot chocolate
fondant with five-spice is a good idea that works well, and there might also be

lemon tart, or caramel mousse. Wines are mostly French, with vins de pays opening the list at £12.50.

CHEF: Nick Evenden   PROPRIETORS: Nick and Karen Evenden   OPEN: Tue to Fri and Sun L 12 to 2, Tue to Sat D 7 to 9.30   MEALS: alc exc Sun L (main courses £16.50 to £18.50). Set L £13.50 (2 courses) to £16.50, Set D Tue to Fri £22.50   SERVICE: 10% (optional), card slips closed   CARDS: Amex, Delta, MasterCard, Switch, Visa   DETAILS: 65 seats. 30 seats outside. Private parties: 50 main room, 10 to 25 private rooms. Car park. Vegetarian meals. Children's helpings. No children under 8 Sat D. No cigars/pipes in dining room. Wheelchair access (also men's WC). Music. No mobile phones  (£5)

---

## MALMESBURY Wiltshire                                     map 2

## ▲ Old Bell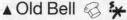

Abbey Row, Malmesbury SN16 0AG
TEL: (01666) 822344   FAX: (01666) 825145                         COOKING 3
EMAIL: info@oldbellhotel.com                            MODERN BRITISH/FRENCH
WEBSITE: www.oldbellhotel.com                                    £24–£60

The 'old' part of the moniker is certainly well deserved: this hostelry dates from 1220, when it was built as a guesthouse for people visiting the next-door abbey. Its grey Cotswold-stone walls are heavily creeper clad, and its warren of lounges and bars, complete with log fires, offers a welcome haven. The main dining room is high-ceilinged, with tall mullioned stone windows and two stone fireplaces.

The kitchen makes use of good raw materials, which are generally well timed, and the menu features a number of trendy items. Duck galantine may be given an 'escabèche' of vegetables, while a main course of pan-fried salmon may come with artichoke ravioli, a courgette clafoutis, and a sauce of cabbage and ginger. The effect is well intentioned and honest, even if not all combinations are carried off with equal panache. To finish, farmhouse cheeses, served with home-made bread, vie for attention with puddings such as honey and lavender parfait, or champagne jelly with mango compote. The atmosphere is relaxed and unpretentious, and service, though formal, is 'cheerful and well trained'. The wine list roams the globe, plucking out keenly priced bottles from Old and New Worlds. A short 'director's bin' includes some good – and good-value – selections. Six house wines sell for £11.95 to £15, and there's decent choice under £20, with six half-bottles.

CHEF: Susan Bell   PROPRIETOR: Simon Hughes   OPEN: all week 12.30 to 2, 7 to 9.30   CLOSED: 23 Dec to 2 Jan   MEALS: Set L £10 (2 courses) to £13.50, Set D £23 to £30. Light menu available SERVICE: not inc, card slips closed   CARDS: Amex, Delta, MasterCard, Visa   DETAILS: 80 seats. 25 seats outside. Private parties: 24 main room, 6 to 24 private rooms. Car park. Vegetarian meals. Children's helpings. No smoking in dining room. Wheelchair access (not WC). No music. No mobile phones   ACCOMMODATION: 31 rooms, all with bath/shower. TV. Phone. B&B £85 to £200. Baby facilities (*The Which? Hotel Guide*)  (£5)

---

*'Service was (initially) a bit unsmiling and uninterested, but as the evening progressed we bonded with our waitress due to the fact that the man at the table next to us was wearing a George Bush mask which he kept on throughout his (solo) meal.'* (On eating in London)

# ▲ Crowne Plaza Midland, French Restaurant

Peter Street, Manchester M60 2DS
TEL: (0161) 236 3333   FAX: (0161) 932 4100
EMAIL: sales@basshotels-uknorth.co.uk                 COOKING 4
WEBSITE: www.manchester-                                       FRENCH
themidland.crowneplaza.com                              £43–£84

At first glance this resembles any corporate-style hotel dining room (striped, dusty pink wallpaper, dull chandeliers, overlooking a huge, impersonal lobby); it seems to recall the intimidating formality of 50 years ago, when waiters carved and flambéed at table: and there are 1980s echoes in the synchronised dome-lifting. But despite appearances this place is thoroughly up to date, with a lightness of cooking and a willingness to incorporate a few non-European influences into its classically derived food.

Well-thought-out modern variations on repertoire standards include French onion soup with home-made muffins, and beef fillet with a suet pudding of pancetta, mushrooms and shallots. Fish is particularly good, judging by a thick tranche of lightly grilled yellow-fin tuna on chickpeas with an intense tomato, garlic and salt-cod sauce, and by fresh, accurately timed turbot in a fish consommé dotted with clear-flavoured spring vegetables and fish-stuffed tortellini.

Desserts indulge with hot Black Forest fondant, or flavourful 'espresso' steamed pudding with rich chocolate sauce and pistachio ice cream. Seasoning and pastry work might be improved, but rolls and loaves are good, and cheeses are kept in good condition (though they might be better sourced). A stylistically arranged wine list doesn't offer much below £20, but does include some first-rate bottles for a few pounds more. French house varietals start at £13.50.

CHEFS: Simon Holling and André Matter   PROPRIETOR: Six Continents Hotels plc   OPEN: Mon to Sat D 7 to 10.30 (11 Fri and Sat)   CLOSED: bank hols   MEALS: alc (main courses £17 to £30). Set D Mon to Thur £29 to £38   SERVICE: not inc   CARDS: Amex, Delta, Diners, MasterCard, Switch, Visa   DETAILS: 40 seats. Private parties: 60 main room. Vegetarian meals. No smoking before 10. Wheelchair access (also WC). Occasional music. No mobile phones. Air-conditioned ACCOMMODATION: 303 rooms, all with bath/shower. TV. Phone. Room only £165. Rooms for disabled. Baby facilities. Swimming pool (*The Which? Hotel Guide*)  £5

# Greens £

43 Lapwing Lane, West Didsbury,                        COOKING 1
Manchester M20 2NT                              GLOBAL VEGETARIAN
TEL: (0161) 434 4259   FAX: (0161) 448 2098             £13–£28

Greens occupies a single room with a large front window, a wooden floor, a couple of striking paintings on its cream-coloured walls, and tables overlaid with solid easy-wipe plastic covers. As so often with vegetarian restaurants, large platefuls are the norm, perhaps to compensate for a lack of animal protein in the diet, and this may be one reason why the slightly smaller first courses here seem to be more successful: for example, a crisp, Thai-spiced potato cake on a flavourful, fresh-tasting crunchy coleslaw spiked with wasabi and lime leaf.

Main courses might include Lancashire cheese 'sausages' on whole-grain mustard mash with a fine onion gravy, or ojja, an African stew containing okra, broad beans and sweet potato in a tasty smoked paprika sauce. Finish perhaps with a wedge of banana cheesecake with a swirl of chocolate sauce, and bring your own wine, for which there is no corkage charge.

CHEFS: Simon Connolly, Simon Rimmer and Darren Chapman   PROPRIETORS: Simon Connolly and Simon Rimmer   OPEN: Tue to Fri and Sun L 12 to 2 (2.30 Sun), all week D 5.30 to 10.30   MEALS: alc (main courses £9 to £10.50). Set L £6.95 (2 courses), Set L Sun £10.95, Set D Sun and Mon, and Tue to Sat 5.30 to 7, £10.95. Unlicensed: BYO, no corkage   SERVICE: not inc, card slips closed   CARDS: Delta, MasterCard, Switch, Visa   DETAILS: 34 seats. 6 seats outside. Private parties: 34 main room. Vegetarian meals. Children's helpings. No cigars/pipes in dining room. Music

## Koreana  £

40A King Street West, Manchester M3 2WY    COOKING 2
TEL: (0161) 832 4330   FAX: (0161) 832 2293    KOREAN
£19–£57

This welcoming, family-run, basement restaurant demonstrates the link between Korean and Japanese cuisines. Everything comes at once in traditional-style banquets (£15 per head), including soup of the day, rice, miniature potato and beef pancakes, and of course kim-chee (cabbage pungently pickled with garlic and chilli), which is one of Korea's gifts to world gastronomy. The other, hidden away in the à la carte appetisers, is yook hwae, its version of steak tartare, with sesame seeds and strips of oriental pears. New to the menu is shabu shabu, a hotpot cooked at the table, either with seafood or beef and vegetables, while another popular Japanese speciality (as British now as chicken tikka masala) is sushi. As well as modestly priced wines there are Korean saké, soju, plum wine and ginseng liqueur.

CHEFS: Mrs H. Kim and Cheung Hong   PROPRIETOR: Koreana Ltd   OPEN: Mon to Fri L 12 to 2.30, Mon to Sat D 6 (5.30 Sat) to 10.30 (11 Sat)   CLOSED: Christmas and New Year   MEALS: alc (main courses £5.50 to £14). Set L £3.95 (1 course) to £4.50 (2 courses), Set D £9.90 (2 courses) to £17.90. Business lunch menu also available   SERVICE: not inc, 10% for parties of 8 or more, card slips closed   CARDS: Amex, Delta, Diners, MasterCard, Switch, Visa   DETAILS: 60 seats. Private parties: 60 main room. Vegetarian meals. Children's helpings. Music  (£5)

## Lime Tree  ♥ ✳ £

8 Lapwing Lane, West Didsbury,
Manchester M20 8WS    COOKING 2
TEL: (0161) 445 1217   FAX: (0161) 445 8166    GLOBAL
WEBSITE: www.thelimetree.com    £22–£47

Car-crowded suburban streets fan out in all directions from this tasteful house conversion, which offers a choice between a light conservatory and a darker dining room with bare wood, terracotta decorations, a big zinc work station and a fireplace full of candle wax. Service is happy, friendly and efficient, and the menu wanders amiably around the world, starting close to home with locally smoked salmon, and extending to roast monkfish with curried sweet potatoes and Thai coconut sauce.

Seafood and vegetable dishes are apt to predominate, from a warm potato pancake with wild mushrooms, to dived scallops with sweet chilli and ginger sauce, while meats are likely to include crispy roast duckling, or pan-fried calf's liver. Finish perhaps with velvet chocolate torte, or apple and almond crumble. The wine list tends to be Franco-centric, although there's a good selection from the New World, as well as selections from Italy, Spain and Portugal. Four house wines are £10.95, eight wines are available by the 175ml or 250ml glass, and mark-ups generally are low enough to encourage experimentation.

CHEFS: Jason Parker and Jason Dickenson    PROPRIETOR: Patrick Hannity    OPEN: Tue to Fri and Sun L 12 to 2.30, 6 to 10.30 (10 Sun)    CLOSED: 25 and 26 Dec, 1 Jan    MEALS: alc (main courses L £6.50 to £14.50, D £10 to £14.50). Set L Tue to Fri £14.95, Set L Sun £12.95, Set D 6 to 7 £14.95    SERVICE: not inc, 10% for parties of 6 or more    CARDS: Amex, Delta, MasterCard, Switch, Visa    DETAILS: 95 seats. 20 seats outside. Vegetarian meals. Children's helpings. No smoking in 1 dining room. No cigars/pipes in dining room. Wheelchair access (not WC). Music

## Lincoln £

| 1 Lincoln Square, Manchester M2 5LN | COOKING 2 |
| TEL: (0161) 834 9000    FAX: (0161) 834 9555 | GLOBAL |
| WEBSITE: www.thelincolnrestaurant.com | £24–£49 |

Just off Deansgate in the city centre, this restaurant offers a stylishly upmarket setting with a relaxed and informal atmosphere. A cosmopolitan philosophy defines the cooking: starters range from risotto primavera to Moroccan beef salad with couscous and harissa; while main courses include tandoori monkfish with Indian-style chickpeas, and five-spiced duck breast with udon noodles and Chinese greens, as well as things like fillet steak au poivre with grilled mushrooms and chips. Desserts have a more domestic and old-fashioned feel, taking in sticky toffee pudding and knickerbocker glory. Wines are a varied mix with a bias towards France, annotated and arranged by price. A Chilean Cabernet Sauvignon and a French Sauvignon Blanc kick off at £11.65.

CHEF: Jem O'Sullivan    PROPRIETORS: Nicola and Fred Done    OPEN: Sun to Fri L 12 to 2.30 (4 Sun), Mon to Sat D 5.30 to 10.30 (11 Fri and Sat)    MEALS: alc exc Sun L (main courses £10 to £17). Set L Mon to Fri and D 5.30 to 7 £12.50 (2 courses) to £14.50, Set L Sun £16.95    SERVICE: 10%, card slips closed    CARDS: Amex, Delta, MasterCard, Switch, Visa    DETAILS: 100 seats. Private parties: 100 main room. Vegetarian meals. Children's helpings. Wheelchair access (also WC). Music. Air-conditioned

## Livebait ✸ £

| 22 Lloyd Street, Albert Square, | |
| Manchester M2 5WH | COOKING 2 |
| TEL: (0161) 817 4110    FAX: (0161) 817 4111 | SEAFOOD |
| WEBSITE: www.santeonline.co.uk | £23–£64 |

This lively city-centre bistro, an outpost of the London-based chain (see entries, London and Leeds), sports lots of green and white, and has an elegant, airy feel. It handles quality ingredients with some skill, and, apart from chargrilled sirloin steak, concentrates exclusively on seafood. A starter of whelks, served by the bowl, or whole Whitby crab, may be followed by roast monkfish tail with shellfish risotto and deep-fried ginger, or chargrilled sea bass with either garlic butter or tomato salsa. The Livebait platter (£49.50) – with a whole Dorset crab, a whole lobster, Madagascan crevettes, Atlantic prawns and Saudi white crevettes – is 'gargantuan' and was well received by its reporter. Desserts are simple affairs of perhaps vanilla crème brûlée, or rice pudding flavoured with orange and cardamom. Service is 'fine and professional but not gushing'. Given the focus, wines tend to white rather than red, and are grouped according to style. Mark-ups are fair, with most bottles under £20, starting at £9.95 for vin de pays. A dozen are sold by the large and small glass.

CHEF: Steven Dray  PROPRIETOR: Groupe Chez Gérard  OPEN: Mon to Fri 12 to 3, 5.30 to 10.30, Sat 12 to 11  CLOSED: bank hols  MEALS: alc (main courses £10 to £25.50). Set L and D 5.30 to 7 and 10 to 10.30 £10.50 (2 courses) to £14  SERVICE: 10% (optional), card slips closed  CARDS: Amex, Diners, MasterCard, Switch, Visa  DETAILS: 150 seats. Private parties: 40 main room, 8 to 40 private rooms. Children's helpings. No smoking in 1 dining room. Wheelchair access (also WC). Music. Air-conditioned

---

# Moss Nook

Ringway Road, Moss Nook,
Manchester M22 5WD                                                    COOKING 6
TEL: (0161) 437 4778  FAX: (0161) 498 8089                  MODERN BRITISH
on B5166, 1m from Manchester Airport                              £28–£79

The décor here (throbbing reds, gilded putti and fairy-lights) does tend to divide readers, some finding it oppressively old-school, others appreciating its slightly OTT quality. Those needing a respite might ask to be seated on the newly refurbished terrace, which has an awning and heating in case the weather threatens to get a little too Manchester.

The cooking, in Kevin Lofthouse's experienced hands, is also a touch rococo: luxury ingredients and complex presentations are the norm. Seared scallops come with a 'tagliatelle' of vegetables and diced tomatoes in lime butter sauce; the inevitable foie gras is sautéed and enthroned on a potato rösti, with Madeira and truffle sauce for extra posh. Sturdy appetites may be needed to tackle the richness of many dishes (breast of duckling is glazed with honey, then sauced with orange and Grand Marnier), but there is light relief too, perhaps in one of the verbally announced fish specials. An array of fresh berries with a brandy-snap basket of ice cream might well be the lightest thing on the pudding menu; for determined hedonists there's a chocolate medley, or perhaps tiramisù laced with Tia Maria. The elevated tone (although slightly undermined by a menu strewn with spelling errors) is maintained with a wine list in which Bordeaux and Burgundy lead the charge, prices stiffening with the pedigree, though there are other European and southern hemisphere options as well. Half-bottles are reasonably plentiful, and the house selection includes a useful Australian Shiraz-Cabernet at £14.

CHEF: Kevin Lofthouse  PROPRIETORS: Pauline and Derek Harrison  OPEN: Tue to Fri L 12 to 1.30, Tue to Sat D 7 to 9.30  CLOSED: 2 weeks Christmas  MEALS: alc (main courses £19.50 to £29). Set L £18.50, Set D £36 (both whole tables only)  SERVICE: not inc, card slips closed  CARDS: Amex, Delta, MasterCard, Switch, Visa  DETAILS: 65 seats. 20 seats outside. Private parties: 55 main room. Car park. No children under 12. Jacket and tie. Occasional music. No mobile phones

# New Emperor ⚡✹

52–56 George Street, Manchester M1 4HF
TEL: (0161) 228 2883    FAX: (0161) 228 6620
EMAIL: reservation@newemperor.co.uk
WEBSITE: www.newemperor.co.uk

COOKING 2
HONG KONG CANTONESE
£16–£56

There is competition aplenty in Manchester's Chinatown, but this big restaurant continues to pack them in. Its long menu focuses on all the major aspects of Cantonese cuisine, from dim sum (steamed spare ribs with garlic, and roast pork buns, for example) to a host of noodle dishes. In between there are soups and casseroles with mostly familiar ingredients, although specials promise a few more esoteric offerings, such as steamed minced pork with salted egg. There are also a few geographical detours for Peking hot-and-sour soup, Shanghai-style pork chops, and straw mushrooms with baby sweetcorn in Szechuan sauce. Banquet menus are a feature, and here the choice might extend to steamed salmon in black-bean sauce, or stewed lamb with black pepper. Note that the ten per cent service charge is billed as an 'eat-in charge' and credit card slips are left open. House wines start at £9.90 a bottle, £2.20 a glass.

CHEF: Master Fong    PROPRIETORS: John Lee and Patrick Ng    OPEN: all week noon to midnight (12.45 Sat)    MEALS: alc (main courses £7 to £16.50). Set L Mon to Sat £8, Set D £16 to £35.50 SERVICE: 10%    CARDS: Amex, Delta, Diners, MasterCard, Switch, Visa    DETAILS: 350 seats. Private parties: 350 main room, 8 to 16 private rooms. Vegetarian meals. No smoking in 1 dining room. Wheelchair access (also WC). Music. Air-conditioned

# Ocean Treasure £

1/F Greenside Way, Middleton,
Manchester M24 1SW
TEL: (0161) 653 6688    FAX: (0161) 653 3388

COOKING 2
CHINESE
£16–£53

To track down this brightly-coloured, pagoda-like Chinese restaurant on a trading estate towards the outskirts of Oldham, 'Get an A to Z and hope for the best'. Seafood is the main theme, tanks of live creatures providing a decent selection when the markets are closed, and an adjoining supermarket no doubt keeps the kitchen topped up. What it offers is straightforward Cantonese cooking, plus lots of banquet menus and the prospect of karaoke in (sound-proof) private rooms. A limited dim sum selection has produced very acceptable steamed spicy pork and prawn dumplings, and deep-fried king prawn 'packets' with a Worcestershire sauce dip (all the rage these days); otherwise there are sizzlers and stir-fries aplenty (king prawns with Szechuan sauce have been well received), and a few 'roasties': good versions of crispy aromatic duck and the like. The wine list roams the world, with house Duboeuf from £9.90.

CHEF: Mr Wong    PROPRIETORS: Stewart Yip and Jack Lui    OPEN: all week 12 to 10.30    MEALS: alc (main courses £6.50 to £12). Set L £4.90 to £11.90, Set D £16 to £35 (all min 2)    SERVICE: 10% CARDS: Amex, Delta, Diners, MasterCard, Switch, Visa    DETAILS: 300 seats. Private parties: 250 main room, 8 to 50 private rooms. Car park. Vegetarian meals. Occasional music. Air-conditioned

# Pacific

58–60 George Street, Manchester M1 4HF
TEL: (0161) 228 6668   FAX: (0161) 236 0191
EMAIL: enquiries@pacific-restaurant-manchester.co.uk
WEBSITE: www.pacific-restaurant-manchester.co.uk

COOKING 2
CHINESE/THAI
£18–£64

Two cuisines under one roof are what you can expect in this colourfully decorated terraced building in the ethnic heart of the city. On the first floor is the Chinese restaurant, with a long selection of dim sum, a host of chef's specials, and a system whereby you can choose your own cooking method (stir-frying, steaming, deep-frying), sauces (among them black bean and Szechuan chilli) and accompaniments (seasonal vegetables, etc.).

If you are looking for Thai food, head up to the next floor. Here, the menu is similarly extensive and the same basic principles apply. A dry red curry of duck has been appreciated; likewise crisp-skinned, deep-fried sea bass (tasting much better than it looked), and sensitively spiced fried noodles with vegetables. Service (at least in the Thai restaurant) has been 'outstandingly attentive and courteous'. The wine list is long and serious, and prices don't seem too grasping even if you hit the heavyweight vintages in the 'connoisseur list'. House wines range from £9.90 to £14.95.

CHEFS: Tim Wong (China) and Vunnee Kitruksa (Thailand)   PROPRIETOR: Special Charms Ltd
OPEN: all week (China) 12 to 10.45, (Thailand) 12 to 2.30, 6 to 10.45   MEALS: alc (main courses £7.50 to £18). Set L £5.50 (2 courses) to £9, Set D £18 to £38   SERVICE: 10%   CARDS: Amex, Delta, Diners, MasterCard, Switch, Visa   DETAILS: 200 seats. Private parties: 200 main room, 10 to 35 private rooms. Vegetarian meals. No babes in arms. No-smoking areas. Wheelchair access (also WC). Music. Air-conditioned

# Le Petit Blanc 🍽 £

55 King Street, Manchester M2 4LQ
TEL: (0161) 832 1000   FAX: (0161) 832 1001
EMAIL: manchester@lepetitblanc.co.uk
WEBSITE: www.lepetitblanc.co.uk

COOKING 2
MODERN FRENCH
£24–£51

Dark tables, red and blue seating, and long windows overlooking the street produce a relaxed, cosmopolitan air. The Petit Blanc format (see entries Birmingham, Cheltenham and Oxford) covers a fixed-price option with about three items per course, a children's menu, vegetarian, vegan, nut-free and dairy-free menus, and a brasserie-type carte. At its best the food is simply prepared, using fresh, well-timed ingredients, as in a first-class piece of roast cod – fat, pearly flakes just cooked – on mushrooms, sauté potatoes and smoked lardons in red wine sauce.

Chefs change, and some 'Maman Blanc' dishes have gone, but the French feel is still exemplified in a large ramekin of livery-tasting, shredded, potted duck under a thick layer of truffle butter, or in a wedge of Grand Marnier tart with a slightly sweet orangey filling and a small splodge of blood-orange granita. Three dozen varietally arranged wines include a couple of Viogniers, a Pinot Grigio, three Pinot Noirs and a Tempranillo; prices from £11 (£2.90 a glass).

CHEF: Simon Stanley   PROPRIETOR: Raymond Blanc   OPEN: all week 12 to 3, 5.30 to 11 (10.30 Sun)   CLOSED: 25 Dec   MEALS: alc (main courses £8.50 to £16). Set L and D 5.30 to 7 £12.50 (2 courses) to £15   SERVICE: not inc, 10% for parties of over 8   CARDS: Amex, Delta, Diners, MasterCard, Switch, Visa   DETAILS: 130 seats. 10 seats outside. Private parties: 48 main room, 8 to 48 private rooms. Vegetarian meals. Children's helpings. Wheelchair access (also WC). Music. Air-conditioned  (£5)

# The Restaurant Bar & Grill  £

14 John Dalton Street, Manchester M2 6JR
TEL: (0161) 839 1999   FAX: (0161) 835 1886

COOKING 2
MODERN EUROPEAN
£22–£47

In only its second year, this ground-floor bar and first-floor restaurant continues to draw the crowds with its modern good looks and vibrant atmosphere. Up the open, suspended staircase, the restaurant is a vast room with Wenge wood tables and leather chairs, glass partitions, sympathetic lighting and large windows. Staff, trendily clad in black, are well-schooled, and service is slick and polite.

The printed contemporary (i.e. no-caps) menu, and the wine list on the reverse, are globally inspired and affordably priced. Kick off with fried chilli squid and Thai noodle salad, or perhaps linguine with crab, chilli, lime and mint, or maybe wild mushroom risotto with Parmesan wafer. Mains run from marinated and grilled sea bass with citrus and sesame on Chinese greens, to chargrilled ribeye with béarnaise. Close with the likes of warm chocolate pudding and good espresso. Wines are mostly under £20, with house selections from £10.95 (£2.60 by the glass).

CHEF: James Gingell   PROPRIETOR: Derek Lilley   OPEN: Mon to Fri 12 to 3, 6 to 11, Sat noon to 11, Sun noon to 10.30   CLOSED: 25 and 26 Dec   MEALS: alc (main courses £5 to £15). Bar and Sun brunch menu also available   SERVICE: not inc, 10% for parties of 6 or more   CARDS: Amex, Delta, Diners, MasterCard, Switch, Visa   DETAILS: 200 seats. Private parties: 60 main room. Vegetarian meals. Wheelchair access (also WC). Music. Air-conditioned

# Rhodes & Co

Waters Reach, Trafford Park,
Manchester M17 1WS
TEL: (0161) 868 1900   FAX: (0161) 868 1901
WEBSITE: www.rhodesrestaurants.com

COOKING 3
MODERN BRITISH
£31–£53

In the heart of the regenerated Trafford Park development, just a free kick away from Manchester United's North Stand, this is one place where Gary Rhodes – or his representatives on earth – can truly feel at home (Mr R is a keen supporter). Perhaps understandably, there is no lunch service on match days, but otherwise they set out to cater for the whole family, with a separate kids' menu on offer. Dishes are a mix of crowd-pleasing and novel, including a well-timed risotto of tomato, spinach and Parmesan; grilled asparagus with soft-boiled eggs; and main courses such as lasagne made with beef and red wine, or superbly tender and flavourful braised lamb with crushed celeriac. Despite the odd curiosity – shallots cooked in blackberry liqueur with sea bass – the kitchen avoids unnecessary complexity. At inspection, puddings let the side down a bit, so consider opting instead for the imaginative and well-kept cheese selection.

Service is enthusiastic, if not always as knowledgeable as it might be, and a thoroughly modern wine list opens with house French at £12.75.

CHEF: Ian Morgan   PROPRIETOR: Sodexho   OPEN: Mon to Fri L 12 to 2.30, all week D 6.30 to 9.45   CLOSED: closed some sessions football match days: phone to check   MEALS: alc (main courses £9 to £16). Bar menu also available   SERVICE: 10% (optional), card slips closed   CARDS: Amex, Delta, Diners, MasterCard, Switch, Visa   DETAILS: 120 seats. Private parties: 90 main room. Car park. Vegetarian meals. Children's helpings. Wheelchair access (also WC). Music. Air-conditioned  £5

## Simply Heathcotes ✴

Jacksons Row, Manchester M2 5WD
TEL: (0161) 835 3536   FAX: (0161) 835 3534
EMAIL: manchester@simplyheathcotes.co.uk
WEBSITE: www.heathcotes.co.uk

COOKING 2
MODERN ENGLISH
£25–£48

Starry ceiling lights and curvy chairs contribute to the contemporary feel of this first-floor dining room near the city centre. Like other branches in Preston, Liverpool and Leeds (see entries), it puts a commendably northern spin on things, serving lively, gutsy, characterful food with the Heathcote signature all over it, from black pudding with crushed potatoes and baked beans, to terrine of ham hock with Lancashire cheese and piccalilli. Mediterranean ideas also feature, and roasting is a favoured way with main courses, applied to chump of lamb with couscous, to cod fillet with curried leek dumplings, and to the famous Goosnargh poultry: breast of duckling with honey-glazed turnip and spring cabbage, or chicken breast with baby leeks and truffle.

The food's wide appeal is evident in deep-fried cod in beer batter, and in desserts such as the Heathcote version of bread-and-butter pudding, and a melting chocolate tart with chocolate chip ice cream. Wines offer choice under £20, plus some fine bottles (at a price), and around a dozen by the glass, starting with own-label French and Chilean varietals at £12 and £13.50 a bottle respectively.

CHEF: Dave Aspin   PROPRIETOR: Paul Heathcote   OPEN: all week 12 to 2.30, 5.30 to 10 (11 Sat)   CLOSED: bank hol Mons   MEALS: alc (main courses £10 to £15). Set L and D 5.30 to 7 £13.50 (2 courses) to £15.50   SERVICE: 10%, card slips closed   CARDS: Amex, Delta, Diners, MasterCard, Switch, Visa   DETAILS: 150 seats. Private parties: 150 main room, 10 to 60 private rooms. Vegetarian meals. Children's helpings. No smoking in dining room. Wheelchair access (also WC). Music. Air-conditioned

## Yang Sing ▼

34 Princess Street, Manchester M1 4JY
TEL: (0161) 236 2200   FAX: (0161) 236 5934
EMAIL: info@yang-sing.com
WEBSITE: www.yang-sing.com

COOKING 5
CANTONESE
£26–£66

An international household word among Chinese restaurants, this famous basement owes much to the efforts of the Yeung family and, in particular, Harry Yeung, who has overseen the kitchens here since 1977. His 'specials' (many created to order) show an inventive spirit and an eagerness to absorb from other cultures and cuisines, and here you will probably need to discuss the possibilities with his well-trained staff. Dim sum are 'terrific'; indeed, much of the restaurant's high reputation rests on the supreme quality of these fascinating morsels. A veteran of Manchester's Chinatown scene noted the superb spring onion pancakes and a sort of samosa filled with barbecued pork, and eulogised scallop dumplings, turnip cake, chillies stuffed with prawn meat, and salt and pepper spare ribs.

At the other end of the gastronomic scale, Yang Sing is also famous for its banquets: 'tell them what you like and they make up a set dinner', as one reporter described the process. Some of the kitchen's gestures are deliberately aimed at Western customers (duck comes off the bone unless you request otherwise), although its heart is still faithful to its Cantonese roots. The repertoire may not be as anatomically challenging as some (no fish lips or goose feet on the standard menu), but it does promise braised brisket with spices, steamed chicken with Chinese sausages, and shredded pork with winter bamboo shoots, alongside a good crop of vegetarian dishes, such as stir-fried celery with 'vegetarian globes' and glazed walnuts.

The wine list is distinctly Francophile, its largest sections covering clarets and burgundies (many mature, some good value), plus some fine bottles from Spain and the New World filling the gaps. There are few selections under £20, most coming from outside Bordeaux and Burgundy. Five house wines are £10.95 (£3.50 a glass).

CHEF: Harry Yeung   PROPRIETOR: Yang Sing Ltd   OPEN: all week noon to 11.45 (12.15 Fri and Sat, 10.45 Sun)   CLOSED: 25 Dec   MEALS: alc (main courses £5.50 to £12). Set D from £16.50 (min 2 people). Banquets from £20 per person   SERVICE: not inc   CARDS: Amex, Delta, MasterCard, Switch, Visa   DETAILS: 250 seats. Private parties: 20 to 250 private rooms. Vegetarian meals. Children's helpings. Wheelchair access (also WC). Music. Air-conditioned

## Zinc £                                              | NEW ENTRY |

The Triangle, Hanging Ditch, Manchester M4 3ES                      COOKING 1
TEL: (0161) 827 4200   FAX: (0161) 827 4212                  MODERN EUROPEAN
WEBSITE: www.conran.com                                            £28–£55

The bar spills out on to the pavement facing the Triangle, a meeting place for local and visiting youth, while the restaurant can also be accessed from the Corn Exchange shopping mall. Zinc and brushed aluminium are trade-mark Conran, as is much of the single-page menu. Seafood takes the form of prawns with mayo, grilled lobster, and a big chunk of rare tuna loin with a drizzle of herb butter. The food is well suited to snacking, offering anything from a spring roll with a meaty duck filling, to Caesar salad, by way of a burger ('made from real meat') topped with melted cheese. A few protein-rich mains, for the really hungry, are grilled and served with a choice of sauce, from mint to harissa to a little pot of well-made béarnaise that might come with strip-loin of beef, cooked 'bloody as ordered'. Neapolitan parfait, or coconut rice pudding might round things off, and over half the 20 or so wines are served by the glass. House Vin de Pays d'Oc Domaines Virginie is £10.50 (£2.75 a glass).

CHEF: Nick Male   PROPRIETOR: Conran Restaurants   OPEN: all week 12 to 10   MEALS: alc (main courses £8.50 to £29.50). Set L and D £12.50 (2 courses) to £15   SERVICE: 12.5%, card slips closed   CARDS: Amex, Delta, Diners, MasterCard, Switch, Visa   DETAILS: 80 seats. 20 seats outside. Private parties: 60 main room. Vegetarian meals. Wheelchair access (also WC). Music. Air-conditioned

## MARSDEN  West Yorkshire                                                map 8

# ▲ Olive Branch

Manchester Road, Marsden HD7 6LU
TEL: (01484) 844487
EMAIL: reservations@olivebranch.uk.com                          COOKING 2
WEBSITE: www.olivebranch.uk.com                            MODERN ENGLISH
on A62, between Slaithwaite and Marsden                          £28–£51

Scrubbed wooden tables and small, open-plan rooms contribute to the homely, unpretentious atmosphere of this stone-built, family-run Pennine pub. The menu – sometimes on a blackboard, sometimes printed – is mustard-keen to please, offering a terrine of young rabbit with cep oil, and a ragoût of veal sweetbreads with chanterelles and truffle mash. Nobody could quibble with the ambition of its snail ravioli in aniseed broth, or of a coffee-bean and Gamay jus to accompany roast Gressingham duck breast.

The kitchen's willingness to take risks also runs from a chilled almond and hazelnut soup with a milk mousse, to roast cod with a Granny Smith compote, while desserts tend to be more mainstream, perhaps including glazed lemon tart with honey ice cream. Results on the plate may not always evoke the same excitement as the descriptions, but reporters have enjoyed undyed smoked haddock on a pleasingly sticky herb risotto, simply prepared vegetables, and friendly, laid-back service. Wine service is refreshingly unfussy too, delivering an enterprising range of bottles from a New Zealand Syrah to a Uruguayan Tannat at user-friendly prices.

CHEF: Paul Kewley   PROPRIETORS: John and Ann Lister   OPEN: Wed to Fri L 12 to 1.45, Tue to Sat D 6.30 to 9.30, Sun 1 to 8.30   CLOSED: first 2 weeks Jan, second week Aug   MEALS: alc (main courses £10 to £17). Set L £12.95 (2 courses), Set D Tue to Thur 6.30 to 7.30 £12.95   SERVICE: not inc, card slips closed   CARDS: Delta, MasterCard, Switch, Visa   DETAILS: 70 seats. 16 seats outside. Private parties: 40 main room, 40 private room. Car park. Vegetarian meals. Children's helpings. Music   ACCOMMODATION: 3 rooms, all with bath/shower. TV. Phone. B&B £45 to £71 (The Which? Hotel Guide)  £5

## MARSH BENHAM  Berkshire                                               map 2

# Red House  ⬢ ✳

Marsh Benham RG20 8LY                                           COOKING 2
TEL: (01635) 582017   FAX: (01635) 581621                   MODERN BRITISH
just off A4 between Newbury and Hungerford                       £30–£55

The Red House is a handsome, thatched, red-brick pub in an attractive hamlet close to the A4. At the front is a bar-cum-bistro with vibrant red-painted walls; at the rear is a light and airy extension that houses the dining room. The same menu is offered in both areas: a seamless blend of British, French and Italian ideas, both classic and contemporary, and choice is augmented by a blackboard of daily specials. Portions are generous, and presentation creative: an inspector was impressed by an artfully arranged plate of smoked seafood (salmon and haddock) garnished with tzatziki, and by a colourful warm squab pigeon salad with grapes and truffle dressing. Main courses might run to pan-fried cod fillet on pesto tagliatelle with spring onion and crème fraîche, or medallions of pork on sage and garlic mash with Madeira and green peppercorn sauce. Desserts range from tarts (of lemon or chocolate) to poached apricot in vanilla syrup with lemon sorbet. The short wine list opens with four house offerings at £12.95 a bottle, £3 a glass.

CHEF: Yves Girard   PROPRIETOR: Tricane Ltd   OPEN: Tues to Sun L 12 to 2.15, Tue to Sat D 7 to 10   CLOSED: 25 and 26 Dec, bank hol Mons   MEALS: alc exc Sun L (main courses £10 to £15.50). Set L Sun £15.95 (2 courses) to £18.95. Bistro menu also available   SERVICE: not inc, 10% for parties of 6 or more   CARDS: Amex, Delta, MasterCard, Switch, Visa   DETAILS: 75 seats. 30 seats outside. Private parties: 60 main room, 8 to 16 private rooms. Car park. Vegetarian meals. Children's helpings. No children under 6 in dining room. No smoking in dining room. Wheelchair access (also WC). Occasional music

## MARTEN  Wiltshire                                    map 2

# Windmill  🍷                                    NEW ENTRY

Salisbury Road, Marten SN8 3SH                      COOKING 5
TEL: (01264) 731372   FAX: (01264) 731284         MODERN EUROPEAN
EMAIL: thewindmill@whsmithnet.co.uk                    £29–£64

Named after the Wilton windmill, this large, spruce-looking, custard-coloured building is on a main road in the middle of green fields and downs. Apart from the old oak floorboards, everything seems to have had a revamp. Walls are covered in antique prints and gilt-framed mirrors, and a dusky-rose and grey colour scheme adds a degree of sophistication. Seasonality is given a high priority, helped by a kitchen garden and a penchant for organic and free-range materials. Some bolder flavours might not go amiss, but what the cooking may lack in bravura it more than makes up for in technical accomplishment: evident in a fresh-tasting, sweet pea risotto (made with fish stock), surmounted by a couple of small but high-quality scallops.

The classical and regional cooking of France and Italy have provided some of the inspiration, which perhaps explains why skate wing with black butter, and a three-part dish of pork incorporating a slice of sticky trotter enclosing a thick, eggy morel mousse; a tiny, conservatively timed loin on potato purée; and a cube of luscious, crusty, confit belly on a smear of apple purée. Where flavours are pronounced, they delight: for example, in an intense, tangy lemon tart made with crunchy shortcrust pastry, with a sweet caramelised top, surrounded by a pool of orangey, marmaladey syrup. Extras – appetiser and bread particularly – are 'immaculate'. Chris Ellis 'messes around making customers feel welcome', although it is odd, for an owner who was in the wine trade, not to ban smoking in at least part of the restaurant. Wines are sensibly arranged by price within style categories. Good value is apparently a priority here, as there is much eminently good drinking under £20. Producers, be they from classic French regions or trendy New World ones, are chosen with care. A 'fine and rare' list is where to look for big names, from Bordeaux to Super Tuscans, and for New

World classics such as Penfolds Grange. Bottle prices start at £12.50; 15 wines are sold by the glass.

CHEF: Peter Brewer   PROPRIETOR: Chris Ellis   OPEN: Tue to Sun L 12 to 2.30, Tue to Sat D 7 to 10 MEALS: alc D (main courses £14 to £18.50). Set L £14.95 (2 courses) to £17.95. Light L menu available Tue to Sat 11.30 to 2.30   SERVICE: not inc   CARDS: Delta, MasterCard, Switch, Visa DETAILS: 35 seats. 30 seats outside. Private parties: 24 main room, 6 to 12 private rooms. Car park. Vegetarian meals. Children's helpings. No cigars in dining room. Wheelchair access (also WC). Music  (£5)

## MARTON  North Yorkshire                                                                   map 9

# Appletree ⸙✳                                                      | NEW ENTRY |

Marton, nr Pickering YO62 6RD                                                  COOKING 3
TEL: (01751) 431457   FAX: (01751) 430190                              MODERN BRITISH
WEBSITE: www.appletreeinn.co.uk                                             £23–£49

This traditional old country inn in a tiny village changed dramatically following the arrival of chef T.J. Drew and Melanie Thornton, who runs front-of-house, in the spring of 2001. Though it still has the look and feel of an inn, it now offers sophisticated country cooking of a sort that won't often be found in pubs. Unusual but successful ideas among starters have included smoked salmon ice cream with avocado, prawns and caviar, while less daring appetites are catered for by the likes of crispy duck and bacon salad with garlic croûtons. Among main courses, haunch of venison with parsnip dauphinois and lavender gravy was one of the highlights of an inspection meal, while roast suckling pig was 'as sweet as you can get' and came with a fresh, chunky apple sauce, herby mash and sage-flavoured jus. First-class home-baked breads also merit special mention, and desserts run the gamut from cherry clafoutis to a black rice, banana and coconut pudding. The pub credentials are enhanced by up to three cask ales, usually from local breweries, and wine drinkers have the choice of eight by the glass in addition to a short but well-chosen list of bottles priced from £9.50.

CHEF: T.J. Drew   PROPRIETOR: Orchard Inns Ltd   OPEN: Wed to Mon 12 to 2 (3 Sun), 6.30 to 10 (7 to 9 Sun)   CLOSED: 2 weeks Oct, 25 Dec, Feb   MEALS: alc (main courses L £7 to £15.50, D £10.50 to £16.50)   SERVICE: not inc, card slips closed   CARDS: Delta, MasterCard, Switch, Visa DETAILS: 55 seats. 16 seats outside. Private parties: 10 private room. Car park. Vegetarian meals. Children's helpings. No smoking in dining room. Music

## MARTON  Shropshire                                                                        map 7

# Sun Inn ⸙✳ £                                                      | NEW ENTRY |

Marton SY21 8JP                                                                COOKING 4
TEL: (01938) 561211                                                    MODERN BRITISH
on B4386, 13m SW of Shrewsbury                                               £16–£41

In what is little more than a hamlet just the English side of the Welsh border, the MacCallum family run a very traditional country pub. Mum and one son run the bar, while the other son – who gained something of a reputation at Airds Hotel in Scotland (see entry, Port Appin) – cooks for the small, plainly decorated dining-room. The food treads an attractive, modern and not overambitious line, pairing hot-smoked salmon with marinated cucumber, dressing baked goats' cheese with onion marmalade, and adding deep-fried prawns, spinach, samphire and mustard sauce to a sautéed fillet of turbot. Honey-roast breast of duck looks like being a stayer, accompanied by whatever veg are in season; these were spring cabbage, beetroot and broad beans when our inspector visited, and the fresh flavours were underpinned by apple and sage, while the meat was tenderly pink. Puddings are clearly a strong suit: pears poached in champagne with shortbread and caramel sauce; strawberry and Drambuie ice cream with ginger biscuits; and iced toffee (a cross between crème brûlée and parfait) with rum-soaked sultanas and apples, have all had rave reviews. The pub-sized wine list offers a good variety of styles, opening with house blends from Australia at £10.25.

CHEF: Steve MacCallum   PROPRIETORS: Ian and Rosie MacCallum   OPEN: Wed to Sun L 12 to 2, Tue to Sat D 6 to 9   MEALS: alc (main courses £8.50 to £13.50). Set L Sun £9.50. Bar menu also available   SERVICE: not inc, card slips closed   CARDS: MasterCard, Switch, Visa   DETAILS: 20 seats. Private parties: 30 main room. Car park. Vegetarian meals. Children's helpings. No smoking in dining room. Music  (£5)

## MASHAM  North Yorkshire                                                map 9

# Floodlite  £

7 Silver Street, Masham HG4 4DX                                    COOKING 5
TEL:  (01765) 689000                                              ANGLO-FRENCH
                                                                      £20–£46

Tired of dining amid blond wood, glass and shiny steel? Find solace at this quirkily decorated former shop, with its old clock, chandelier, and display cabinet full of crockery. Nor does Charles Flood's cooking follow the crowd; not many chefs these days bother to make pike quenelles, for example, and a carrot and Gruyère gâteau provides another interesting starter. And yet the food is mainstream enough for wide appeal, taking in shredded, tasty duck confit, with bits of crisp skin, salad leaves and a spicy plum dressing, and a moist grilled salmon fillet with a honey and ginger sauce.

Saucing is a strength, be it a straightforward hollandaise for half a dozen seasonal asparagus stems, or a rich and creamy thermidor sauce poured over carefully cooked lobster and grilled (a local promotion of Nova Scotia lobsters takes place annually in early summer). Game – another forte – takes in roast saddle of roe deer with wild mushrooms; desserts, too, are a highlight, judging by lemon tart with crisp, buttery shortcrust pastry (served with summer berries, a raspberry coulis and custard), or by a light-textured, deep-flavoured bitter chocolate pudding with vanilla ice cream and chocolate fudge sauce. Coffee and bread, on the other hand, might be improved. Fair prices characterise the roving wine list; try Natter's Sancerre (£16); a Cabernet blend called Julia from South Africa's Avondale Estate (£14.95); or one of six house wines under £10.

CHEF: Charles Flood   PROPRIETORS: Charles and Christine Flood   OPEN: Fri to Sun L 12 to 1.45, Tue to Sat D 7 to 9   MEALS: alc (main courses £9.50 to £17.50). Set L £11.50 (2 courses) to £13.50, Set D £13.50 (2 courses) to £16   SERVICE: not inc, card slips closed   CARDS: Amex, MasterCard, Visa   DETAILS: 36 seats. Private parties: 30 main room, 10 private room. Children's helpings. Wheelchair access (not WC). No music

## ▲ Matfen Hall ⁑

Matfen NE20 0RH
TEL: (01661) 886500   FAX: (01661) 886055
EMAIL: info@matfenhall.com                                                 COOKING 3
WEBSITE: www.matfenhall.com                                          MODERN BRITISH
off B6318, just S of Matfen village                                        £27–£55

Near Hadrian's Wall, where vistas are measured not in hundreds of acres but in thousands, this enormous 1830 pile has its own 18-hole golf course, plus Great Hall, tall windows and chimneys, and public rooms each the size of a small house. No wonder it does conferences, banquets and weddings. Dinner, in the Library, brings a choice between set-price and à la carte menus, the latter offering a little more interest. Ambition is not too high, but the appealing repertoire takes in a sweetcorn and spring onion risotto, baked Cheddar and spinach soufflé, and confit duck leg with braised cabbage.

The cooking shows skill, although seasoning and flavour matching leave something to be desired. A pairing of pan-fried sea bass and haddock brandade is served on a fine bed of ratatouille, while thin, just pink, chargrilled calf's liver has come with caramelised onions in a thick, sweet, glossy reduction. Desserts are simple classics: creamed rice pudding with Armagnac prunes, or baked custard tart with nutmeg ice cream. Refreshingly, the wine list isn't as long, fancy and full of expensive clarets as the surroundings might suggest; creditably, Matfen keeps it comparatively short and unfussy, and there is choice under £20. House vin de pays Sauvignon Blanc and Syrah are £13.45.

CHEF: Craig McMeeken   PROPRIETORS: Sir Hugh and Lady Blackett   OPEN: Sun L 12 to 2.30, all week D 7 to 9.30   MEALS: alc D (main courses £9.50 to £18.50). Set L Sun £15.95, Set D £22.50   SERVICE: not inc, card slips closed   CARDS: Amex, Delta, MasterCard, Switch, Visa   DETAILS: 60 seats. Private parties: 120 main room, 8 to 120 private rooms. Car park. Vegetarian meals. Children's helpings. No smoking in dining room. Wheelchair access (also WC). Music. Air-conditioned   ACCOMMODATION: 31 rooms, all with bath/shower. TV. Phone. B&B £98 to £225. Rooms for disabled. Baby facilities (The Which? Hotel Guide)

## ▲ Danesfield House, Oak Room ⁑   | NEW ENTRY |

Henley Road, Marlow SL7 2EY
TEL: (01628) 891010   FAX: (01628) 484115
EMAIL: sales@danesfieldhouse.co.uk                                         COOKING 4
WEBSITE: www.danesfieldhouse.co.uk                                     ANGLO-FRENCH
on A4155 between Marlow and Henley                                          £38–£85

The present house, the third on this site, dates from the late Victorian era. Sitting in 65 acres overlooking the Thames, it feels more stately home than country house, an impression reinforced when you enter the stunning Grand Lounge, with its distant carved wooden ceiling, gallery and tall, elaborately draped windows.

Damian Broom cooks a contemporary version of Anglo-French cuisine, building on seasonal game and fine supplies, some of them local. That might translate into large pieces of poached lobster with chestnuts, carrots and samphire in a lobster bisque sauce, perhaps followed by breast of corn-fed chicken with creamed celeriac and asparagus, or accurately timed Scottish beef fillet topped with spinach on a potato rösti. Rich sauces underpin many dishes – sea bass is poached in a truffle bouillon, while veal cutlet gets Madeira – and demonstrable skill is brought to bear on desserts such as Beaumes-de-Venise parfait with a peppered jelly and compote of roasted pineapple. Beside all that, nibbles and petits fours seem a touch ordinary in the context.

France is royally treated on the wine list, with champagnes, clarets and burgundies showing up strongly, and there is a decent slate of Californian wines, but prices are inevitably tough. House vins de pays – Chardonnay and Grenache – are £19.50.

CHEF: Damian Broom    GENERAL MANAGER: Brian Miller    OPEN: all week 12 to 1.45, 7 to 10 MEALS: alc (main courses £24 to £28.50). Set L £18.50 (2 courses) to £24.50, Set D £39.50. Orangery brasserie menu also available    SERVICE: not inc, card slips closed    CARDS: Amex, Delta, Diners, MasterCard, Switch, Visa    DETAILS: 39 seats. 20 seats outside. Private parties: 8 main room, 4 to 110 private rooms. Car park. Vegetarian meals. Children's helpings. No smoking in dining room. Wheelchair access (also WC). No music. No mobile phones    ACCOMMODATION: 87 rooms, all with bath/shower. TV. Phone. B&B £185 to £300. Rooms for disabled. Baby facilities. Swimming pool  (£5)

## MELBOURN  Cambridgeshire                                               map 6

# Pink Geranium 🍴✦

| | |
|---|---|
| 25 Station Road, Melbourn SG8 6DX | NEW CHEF |
| TEL: (01763) 260215   FAX: (01763) 262110 | MODERN BRITISH |
| WEBSITE: www.pinkgeranium.co.uk | £31–£88 |

Late changes in the kitchen meant that there was insufficient time for the Guide to receive any feedback about new chef Gordon Campbell. But he has worked at some good addresses (including the Vineyard at Stockcross and L'Escargot in London; see entries), and his largely classical style of cooking looks inviting. Expect to start with a salad of beetroot and goats' cheese, or seared foie gras with sherry dressing, followed perhaps by sea bass with creamed leeks, or pot-roast guinea fowl. Finish with a strawberry and vanilla crème brûlée, or pineapple tarte Tatin with Baileys ice cream, and drink from a balanced and wide-ranging list of wines that includes a fair sprinkling of halves, and starts with house Chardonnay and Merlot at £14.

CHEF: Gordon Campbell    PROPRIETOR: Lawrence Champion    OPEN: Tue to Sun L 12 to 2, Tue to Sat D 7 to 9.30    MEALS: alc exc Sun L (main courses £18.50 to £26). Set L Mon to Sat £14 (2 courses) to £18, Set L Sun £22.50, Set D £30 to £60    SERVICE: 10% (optional), card slips closed    CARDS: Amex, Delta, MasterCard, Switch, Visa    DETAILS: 60 seats. Private parties: 50 main room, 4 to 14 private rooms. Car park. Vegetarian meals. Children's helpings. No smoking in dining room. Occasional music

---

*'You will be really excited to hear that the crêpes flambés were made from beginning to end at table, in full view of all the diners – I kept hoping they'd burn the place down.'*
(On eating in Worcestershire)

---

## ▲ Sheene Mill

Station Road, Melbourn SG8 6DX
TEL: (01763) 261393   FAX: (01763) 261376
EMAIL: mail@stevensaunders.co.uk
WEBSITE: www.stevensaunders.co.uk

COOKING 3
GLOBAL
£24–£66

This small hotel is a converted water-mill, and its conservatory extension overlooks the mill pond. The publicity leaflet, which offers a multilingual welcome, could be a metaphor for Steven Saunders' many-faceted cooking, which is described as 'modern trendy'. Tom yum soup with prawns and lemon grass seems a pretty accurate rendition of a Thai favourite, down to the unapologetic smoulder of chilli running through it, while a salad of seared rare tuna with basil oil is topped off with grilled halloumi. Despite their polyglot nature, most dishes are kept reasonably straightforward, with herb-crusted rack of lamb on rosemary-seasoned mash and baby vegetables offering plenty of savoury satisfaction. Red snapper is carefully timed, benefiting from the richness of its accompanying Parmesan polenta and the asperity of a watercress sauce. Side-dishes of organic veg are elegantly presented and dressed with just the right quantity of butter or oil. Striking presentation extends to a 'mellow yet tangy' two-tone bavarois of gooseberry and strawberry, or there might be warm cranberry tart with chestnut caramel sauce. The properly international wine list includes a red from Suffolk (for which grandiose claims are made), Bonterra Californian organic varietals, and a decent show of halves. Prices open at £11.50.

CHEFS: Steven Saunders and Tristian Welch   PROPRIETORS: Steven and Sally Saunders   OPEN: all week L 12 to 2, Mon to Sat D 7 to 10   CLOSED: 26 Dec, 1 Jan   MEALS: alc (main courses £13.50 to £19.50). Set L Mon to Sat £12 (2 courses) to £16. Set L Sun £21. Set D Mon to Fri £30. Light L menu also available   SERVICE: 10% (optional), card slips closed   CARDS: Amex, Delta, MasterCard, Switch, Visa   DETAILS: 110 seats. 30 seats outside. Private parties: 110 main room. Car park. Vegetarian meals. Children's helpings. No smoking before 2.30 at L, 9.30 at D. Music. Air-conditioned   ACCOMMODATION: 9 rooms, all with bath/shower. TV. Phone. B&B £80 to £130 (The Which? Hotel Guide)  £5

---

**MIDHURST West Sussex**                                                       map 3

## Maxine's ⅚✳

Elizabeth House, Red Lion Street,
Midhurst GU29 9PB
TEL: (01730) 816271
EMAIL: maxines@lineone.net

COOKING 2
EUROPEAN
£25–£44

Sharing an island in the centre of town with the Red Lion pub, Maxine's is not large. Indeed, behind the old oak door of the black and white timbered house the scale seems to be that of a doll's house: just one room with five tables, laid with starched white linen and polished glasses. Despite an occasional interloper such as a Thai sauce, Robert de Jager's repertoire is staunchly European, featuring a Dutch pea soup, bœuf bourguignon and, the star of the evening for one party, a fluffy double-baked garlic and Gruyère soufflé oozing a punchy, creamy filling.

Portions vary from a trencherman-sized duck leg salad to a pair of small, crisply fried, flavourful crab cakes, fish tends to be cooked well rather than

427

lightly, and desserts have included a first-class, rich yet sharp lime and ginger crème brûlée. The house speciality, a spicy Dutch apple pie, comes with a good pastry crust. Service can be a bit on edge, while a French-dominated wine list starts with house Vin de Pays d'Oc at £11.50.

CHEF: Robert de Jager   PROPRIETORS: Robert and Marti de Jager   OPEN: Wed to Sun L 12 to 1.30, Wed to Sat D 7 to 9   MEALS: alc exc Sun L (main courses £10.50 to £18). Set L £17.95, Set D Wed to Fri £17.95   SERVICE: net prices, card slips closed   CARDS: Amex, Delta, MasterCard, Switch, Visa   DETAILS: 26 seats. Private parties: 30 main room. Children's helpings. No smoking in dining room. No music

## MILFORD ON SEA  Hampshire                                        map 2

# Rouille ⅚✳

69–71 High Street, Milford on Sea SO41 0QG
TEL: (01590) 642340                                            COOKING **4**
EMAIL: rouille@ukonline.co.uk                            MODERN FRENCH
WEBSITE: www.rouille.co.uk                                      £28–£50

Refurbishment of this double-fronted house has produced a dining room of primrose yellow and dark beetroot red, with artificial flowers and a busy swirly carpet. Menus (including a less expensive daily version) are ambitious and wide ranging, taking in anything from butternut squash and Kirsch soup, via wild partridge, to grilled sea bass and scallops served with red pepper and a saffron and tomato sauce. Menu descriptions don't always predict what is to come with much accuracy, however. Freshwater Bay crab with mayonnaise, for example, consists of a layered cake of mashed avocado, topped with white crabmeat mixed with mayonnaise and diced peppers, in turn by crème fraîche, fromage frais and fish roe.

Among the kitchen's better dishes have been a wodge of puff pastry filled with scrambled duck egg, topped with spears of local Hinton asparagus, and served with a truffley sauce, although an inspection meal found several dishes quite unworthy of the kitchen's previous output. Finish perhaps with a passion-fruit mousse cake, or ginger sponge pudding. The two pages of wines hail from France, the Mediterranean and the New World, with choice under £20. House Chilean is £13.50.

CHEF: Lui Hollomby   PROPRIETORS: Nicola and Lui Hollomby   OPEN: Tue to Sat 12 to 2, 7 to 9.30 (booking essential at L)   MEALS: Set L £14.95, Set D Tue to Thur £14.95 to £27.95. Set D Fri and Sat £23.95 (2 courses) to £27.95   SERVICE: not inc, card slips closed   CARDS: Amex, Delta, Diners, MasterCard, Switch, Visa   DETAILS: 24 seats. Private parties: 30 main room. No smoking in dining room. Occasional music. No mobile phones. Air-conditioned  (£5)

*All details are as accurate as possible at the time of going to press, but chefs and owners often change, and it is wise to check by telephone before making a special journey. Many readers have been disappointed when set-price bargain meals are no longer available. Ask when booking.*

## MILL BANK  West Yorkshire                                 map 9

# Millbank ✓⨯ £ 🍷

Millbank HX6 3DY
TEL: (01422) 825588   FAX: (01422) 822080
EMAIL: millbankph@ukonline.co.uk
WEBSITE: www.themillbank.com

COOKING **5**
MODERN EUROPEAN
£22–£45

This 'stylish, slick and professional' gastro-pub has a city feel despite being set in the middle of the countryside. It has a bar and a pub area with a flagstoned floor, a fireplace, bench seating and stools. In contrast, the dining room has wood flooring and doors that lead out on to a decked area for outdoor eating, from which there are spectacular views. The menu is short but makes imaginative use of ingredients. Starters might include properly seared scallops with light, crisp Jerusalem artichoke fritters; crab cannelloni with vine tomato and Asian pesto; or a ballottine combining chunks of moist chicken with cep mousse.

Among main courses, tender, crisp-skinned suckling pig, served with potatoes cooked in cider and mixed with sage and onion, has been a hit, as has an assiette of duck comprising sliced breast, seared foie gras, and spicy pan-fried shredded meat. Yorkshire Blue and Swaledale might be among the local cheeses on offer, while desserts have included a high quality hot chocolate fondant with pistachio ice cream. Service is relaxed, pleasant and professional, and the short wine list is organised by style. All but a few of the 40 bottles are under £20, and there are some good (and good-value) selections among them. Prices start at £9.10 for Italian white, and eight wines are sold by the glass (£2.50 to £3).

CHEF: Glen Futter   PROPRIETORS: Paul and Christine Halsey   OPEN: Wed to Sun L 12 to 2 (12.30 to 3.30 Sun), Tue to Sat D 5.30 to 9.30 (6 to 10 Fri and Sat)   MEALS: alc (main courses £9 to £15). Set L and D 5.30 to 7 £10.50 (2 courses) to £13.50. Bar menu available   SERVICE: not inc   CARDS: Delta, MasterCard, Switch, Visa   DETAILS: 32 seats. 32 seats outside. Private parties: 32 main room. Vegetarian meals. Children's helpings. No smoking in dining room. Wheelchair access (not WC). Music

## MILTON ERNEST  Bedfordshire                               map 6

# Strawberry Tree ✓⨯

3 Radwell Road, Milton Ernest MK44 1RY
TEL: (01234) 823633   FAX: (01234) 825976
on A6 5 miles N of Bedford

COOKING **6**
MODERN BRITISH
£40–£61

It is 'a real joy' to eat at this charming, eighteenth-century thatched cottage a few miles from Bedford. Simple tasteful décor – an inglenook fireplace, wooden beams, plentiful prints – produces a restful atmosphere, and furniture and table settings add to the sense of comfort. This is a family enterprise (parents out front, brothers in the kitchen) where a short yet varied menu might offer twice-baked goats' cheese soufflé, or a crab salad to rival the best, followed by roast loin of venison with a tarte fine of celeriac and pear.

Ideas don't stray far from the mainstream, and yet are full of interest: perhaps smoked haddock with a mild potato curry and poached egg, or roast saddle of rabbit with a black pudding gâteau. Sauces are well-flavoured, portions are well-judged, and presentation is neat and pleasing. Desserts proved the highlight for one couple, who ate a white chocolate and lime parfait with mascarpone sorbet, and a bitter chocolate délice with vanilla ice and marinated prunes. Incidentals from appetiser soup to petits fours are on a par, and the short, predominantly French wine list offers some bottles under £20.

CHEFS: Jason and Andrew Bona   PROPRIETORS: John and Wendy Bona   OPEN: Wed to Fri L 12 to 1.45, Wed to Sat D 7.30 to 8.30   CLOSED: 2 weeks Jan, 2 weeks summer   MEALS: alc L (main courses £14 to £18). Set D £38   SERVICE: not inc, 10% optional for parties of 10 or more, card slips closed   CARDS: Delta, MasterCard, Switch, Visa   DETAILS: 22 seats. Private parties: 18 main room, 4 to 8 private rooms. Car park. Children's helpings. No smoking in dining room. Wheelchair access (not WC). No music  (£5)

---

**MORETON-IN-MARSH Gloucestershire**                        map 5

# Annie's

3 Oxford Street, Moreton-in-Marsh GL56 0LA                  COOKING 2
TEL/FAX:  (01608) 651981                                     ANGLO-FRENCH
EMAIL:  anniesrest@easicom.com                               £36–£59

For some, this is 'a very, very old-fashioned and decent operation', which is, perhaps, why American visitors are seduced by its singular virtues: a couple from the Big Apple were charmed by the dining room, 'bathed in the warmth of candlelight', with cricketing mementoes dotted around the walls. Raw materials are 'frightfully good' and 'fresh as the morning', fine home-baked rolls arrive with starters, and a cornucopia of up to six different vegetables embellishes every main course. There is a comforting familiarity about a warm salad of chicken livers, mushrooms and bacon, or fillet of venison with brandy and green peppercorn sauce, but it is also worth exploring the fish specials: sea bass baked en papillote with white wine, herbs and a touch of ginger has been well received. To finish, sunken chocolate soufflé with Armagnac prunes may 'bring tears to your eyes!' Plenty of halves show up on the serviceable wine list. Four house wines, all from France, are £12.95.

CHEF: David Ellis   PROPRIETORS: David and Anne Ellis   OPEN: Mon to Sat D only 7 to 9.30 (L by arrangement)   MEALS: alc (main courses £16 to £22)   SERVICE: not inc, card slips closed   CARDS: Amex, Delta, Diners, MasterCard, Switch, Visa   DETAILS: 30 seats. Private parties: 30 main room. Vegetarian meals. No smoking while others eat. Music. No mobile phones  (£5)

---

**MORSTON Norfolk**                                          map 6

# ▲ Morston Hall ♥ ⁵⁄✳

Morston NR25 7AA
TEL:  (01263) 741041   FAX:  (01263) 740419
EMAIL:  reception@morstonhall.com                            COOKING 6
WEBSITE:  www.morstonhall.com                                MODERN BRITISH
on A149, 2m W of Blakeney                                    £34–£57

The seventeenth-century brick and flint house is surrounded by pretty, well-kept gardens, its décor 'old country house' in a very English provincial way, with an inglenook fireplace, William Morris-patterned pelmets, china plates on the walls, and good white napery on the tables. Tracy and Galton Blackiston celebrated their first decade here last year with a larger and better-equipped kitchen, although the format remains as before. Four-course no-choice dinners are served at a single sitting (which in a full dining room can mean at a moderate pace) with a meat main course typically preceded by an intermediate fish dish: perhaps grilled red snapper on Puy lentils with parsley beurre blanc.

Among materials might be corn-fed chicken served with pasta and roast salsify, or organic lamb from Devon, perhaps seared noisettes rather conservatively timed, with a first-class béarnaise. Generally, this is refined cooking, not hearty fare, and while it can strike reporters as rather affected, with its purées, mousses and tiny portions of vegetables, others find meals thoroughly enjoyable, attractively presented and well judged for quantity. First courses might embrace a seductive ballottine of foie gras with truffled leeks and Sauternes jelly, or pan-fried locally smoked eel on potato pancake with horseradish and crème fraîche.

Desserts hit the comfort zone with a soufflé Rothschild, or chocolate fondant with mascarpone sorbet; as an alternative, small pieces of cheese are served ready-plated. Wines are arranged by grape variety, making it easy to find one's way around the offerings from France, Spain, South Africa, California and New Zealand. The list is well-annotated and thoughtfully chosen, with reasonable mark-ups. A dozen wines by the glass (plus sparkling and dessert) range from £3.50 to £9.

CHEFS: Galton Blackiston and Samantha Wegg   PROPRIETORS: Tracy and Galton Blackiston
OPEN: Sun L 12.30 for 1 (1 sitting), all week D 7.30 for 8 (1 sitting)   CLOSED: 25 and 26 Dec, 1 Jan to 1 Feb   MEALS: Set L £24, Set D £36   SERVICE: not inc, card slips closed   CARDS: Amex, Delta, Diners, MasterCard, Switch, Visa   DETAILS: 36 seats. 32 seats outside. Private parties: 40 main room, 10 to 16 private rooms. Car park. Children's helpings. No smoking in dining room. Wheelchair access (also men's WC). No music. No mobile phones   ACCOMMODATION: 6 rooms, all with bath/shower. TV. Phone. D,B&B £130 to £220. Baby facilities (*The Which? Hotel Guide*)

---

**MOULSFORD Oxfordshire**                                                    **map 2**

## ▲ Beetle & Wedge ▮ ✳

Ferry Lane, Moulsford OX10 9JF
TEL: (01491) 651381   FAX: (01491) 651376
EMAIL: katesmith@beetleandwedge.co.uk                          COOKING 4
WEBSITE: www.beetleandwedge.co.uk                            ANGLO-FRENCH
off A329, down Ferry Lane to river                              £37–£72

The Thames here is wide and placid, an understandable lure for Jerome K. Jerome (of *Three Men in a Boat* fame), who once lived here. Al fresco dining in the small garden is an added summer attraction, although most eating takes place either in the Boat House (chargrilling of all sorts) or in the conservatory dining room of the main house. Deep sofas and chairs in varied fabrics help to make it feel 'very English', every table has a view, and the rather static repertoire's Anglo-French thrust is evident throughout: for example, in artichoke heart with wild mushrooms and hollandaise, or in seared squid and scallops with lamb's lettuce and salsa.

Main courses might run to turbot fillet in a champagne saffron sauce, or a small rack of roast lamb sliced into four cutlets on a bed of chargrilled Mediterranean vegetables; they arrive with a side plate of half a dozen or more vegetables, among them perhaps a flavourful swede purée, and broccoli coated in hollandaise. Timings might be improved, and sauces – even a chive tomato salsa and a rosemary stock sauce – tend to be creamy and under-herbed, while desserts run from a hot Cointreau soufflé to an indulgent treacle sponge with thin vanilla custard and vanilla ice cream. The 'personal selection' of wines concentrates on the classic regions of France and Italy; wines from other areas – New Zealand, Spain, Chile and the like – are listed at the back. A minority dip below the £20 horizon, but 11 house wines start at £15.

CHEFS: Richard Smith and Olivier Bouet  PROPRIETORS: Kate and Richard Smith  OPEN: Dining Room Tue to Sun L 12 to 1.45, Tue to Sat D 7 to 9.45; Boat House all week 12 to 1.45, 7 to 9.45  MEALS: alc (main courses Dining Room £18 to £22.50; Boat House £12.50 to £18.50; no alc Dining Room Sun L). Set L Sun (Dining Room) £37.50. Cover £1 (Boat House)  SERVICE: not inc  CARDS: Amex, Delta, Diners, MasterCard, Switch, Visa  DETAILS: Dining Room 35 seats, Boat House 60 seats. 50 seats outside. Private parties: 30 Dining Room, 20 to 35 Boat House, 64 private room. Car park. Vegetarian meals. Children's helpings. No smoking in Dining Room. Wheelchair access (also WC). Occasional music. No mobile phones  ACCOMMODATION: 10 rooms, all with bath/shower. TV. Phone. B&B £99 to £175 (D,B&B on Sat, double room, £250). Rooms for disabled. Baby facilities (*The Which? Hotel Guide*)

## MOULTON  North Yorkshire

map 9

# Black Bull Inn  ▮

Moulton DL10 6QJ
TEL: (01325) 377289    FAX: (01325) 377422
EMAIL: sarah@blackbullinn.demon.co.uk
1m SE of Scotch Corner

COOKING 4
SEAFOOD/MODERN BRITISH
£25–£60

Audrey Pagendam continues 'casting her spell' at this long-running North Country inn a short drive from Scotch Corner. There's plenty of buzz and bustle in the bar, but there's also the comfortable dining room in the now-legendary converted Pullman railway carriage. The long carte and specials board are liberally peppered with seafood: creamy curried prawn and pea risotto revived a pair of inspectors after a long walk, and choice extends to roast cod on pak choi with chilli jam, and grilled Dover sole.

Meat dishes, such as a trio of lamb (kidney, cutlets and leg steak in filo pastry), also receive 'masterful treatment', according to one regular. Others have praised juicy tournedos of beef with a luxurious complement of trompette mushrooms, foie gras and Madeira sauce, while those with vegetarian inclinations should approve of the exemplary spinach and Cheddar soufflé. Desserts include a full quota of home-made ice creams, as well as correctly 'wobbly' pannacotta with caramelised banana. The weightier areas of France – Bordeaux, Burgundy and the Rhône – are the main focus of the wine list: a number of mature clarets are certainly worth a look. Wines from other European countries and the New World are carefully selected. Good producers characterise the list throughout, but high prices do not. House recommendations start at £11.95, while five house wines sell for £9.95 to £10.95.

CHEF: Paul Grundy  PROPRIETOR: A.M.C. Pagendam  OPEN: Mon to Fri L 12 to 2, Mon to Sat D 6.30 to 10.15  CLOSED: 24 to 26 Dec  MEALS: alc (main courses £15.50 to £20). Set L £15.50. Bar menu available Mon to Sat L  SERVICE: not inc  CARDS: Amex, Delta, Diners, MasterCard, Switch, Visa  DETAILS: 100 seats. 20 seats outside. Private parties: 10 main room, 10 to 30 private rooms. Car park. Vegetarian meals. No children under 7. No music

## NAYLAND  Suffolk                                                map 6

# ▲ White Hart

11 High Street, Nayland CO6 4JF
TEL: (01206) 263382   FAX: (01206) 263638                    COOKING 2
EMAIL: nayhart@aol.com                                  MODERN EUROPEAN
WEBSITE: www.whitehart-nayland.co.uk                         £23–£56

Tables are closely packed but smartly laid in this restaurant-with-rooms just
inside the Suffolk border. The set-price 'countryside menu' at lunch might take
in pork terrine en croûte, or an Alsace-style salad to begin, followed by either
bouillabaisse, or Lancashire hotpot, while fixed-price dinners aim a little
higher, offering quail stuffed with foie gras, and grilled veal chop with wild
mushroom sauce. There is a carte as well, and among successes have been roast
breast of wood pigeon served with Mediterranean vegetables in a first-class
olive jus, and moist, flavourful seared salmon with red peppers and baby
vegetables. Accompanying vegetables are also commended. The White Hart is
not without shortcomings though: some dishes are below par, service is a
distinct letdown, and prices are high for the quality. More wines under £20
would be appropriate too, on a wide-ranging list that stretches to Canada and
Uruguay. House Duboeuf is £11.

CHEF: Carl Shillingford   PROPRIETOR: Michel Roux   OPEN: all week 12 to 2.30, 6.30 to 9.30
MEALS: alc (main courses £10 to £16). Set L £9.95 (2 courses) to £12.95, Set D Tue to Fri £16.10 (2
courses) to £21.50   SERVICE: 12.5% (optional), card slips closed   CARDS: Amex, Delta, Diners,
MasterCard, Switch, Visa   DETAILS: 50 seats. 35 seats outside. Private parties: 70 main room, 10
to 36 private rooms. Car park. Vegetarian meals. Children's helpings. Wheelchair access (not
WC). Music   ACCOMMODATION: 6 rooms, all with bath/shower. TV. Phone. B&B £69 to £82. Baby
facilities (The Which? Hotel Guide)   £5

## NEAR SAWREY  Cumbria                                            map 8

# ▲ Ees Wyke ⁵⚡

Near Sawrey LA22 0JZ
TEL/FAX: (015394) 36393
EMAIL: eeswyke@aol.com                                       COOKING 2
WEBSITE: www.eeswyke.co.uk                                    BRITISH
on B5285 2m S of Hawkshead                                   £34–£40

A conservatory dining room has been added to the back of this small Georgian
country-house hotel that was once Beatrix Potter's holiday home, its character
now determined by the personalities of the owners. Mrs Williams, 'call me
Margaret', greets visitors by name on arrival and introduces everybody, while
husband John beavers away at a repertoire of mostly traditional dishes ranging
from leek and potato soup, via grilled halibut with lemon and parsley butter, to
calf's liver with Dubonnet and orange sauce. The five courses include an
intermediate one (perhaps a soufflé, or maybe Thai-style crab cakes with chilli
mayonnaise), and cheese to finish. Helpings are generous, seven vegetables are
served, and desserts are recited, taking in old favourites such as French apple tart
and crème brûlée. Forty-plus wines rarely stray above £25 and start with a
handful of house wines at £11 (£3 a glass).

CHEF: John Williams   PROPRIETOR: Margaret and John Williams   OPEN: all week D only 7.30 (1 sitting)   MEALS: Set D £25 for non-residents, included in accommodation price for residents   SERVICE: not inc, card slips closed   CARDS: Amex   DETAILS: 20 seats. Private parties: 20 main room. Car park. Children's helpings. No children under 8. No smoking in dining room. No music. No mobile phones   ACCOMMODATION: 8 rooms, all with bath/shower. TV. D,B&B £65 to £130. No children under 8 (*The Which? Hotel Guide*)

## ▲ Sawrey House ⁵⅍

Near Sawrey LA22 0LF
TEL: (015394) 36387   FAX: (015394) 36010
EMAIL: mail@sawreyhouse.com
WEBSITE: www.sawreyhouse.com
on B5285 S of Hawkshead

NEW CHEF
MODERN BRITISH-PLUS
£40–£48

Originally a clergyman's house, this stone-built Victorian property lies in three acres west of Lake Windermere, overlooking Esthwaite Water. As the Guide went to press a new chef was announced, although the style of cooking was not expected to change. The format is a six-course dinner (soup, appetiser, starter, sorbet, main, and cheese or dessert) that might take in cod fishcake with pea purée, loin of venison with a liquorice sauce, and summer pudding with meringue and cream. The wine list does not always divulge vintages, but starts with house wine at £11.95.

CHEF: Bryan Parsons   PROPRIETOR: Shirley and Colin Whiteside   OPEN: all week D only 7.15 to 8   CLOSED: Jan   MEALS: Set D £32   SERVICE: none, card slips closed   CARDS: MasterCard, Switch, Visa   DETAILS: 35 seats. Private parties: 15 main room. Car park. No children under 8. No smoking. Music. No mobile phones. Air-conditioned   ACCOMMODATION: 11 rooms, all with bath/shower. TV. Phone. D,B&B £65 to £170. Rooms for disabled. No children under 8. Fishing (*The Which? Hotel Guide*)

## NETHER ALDERLEY  Cheshire                                   map 8

## The Wizard ⁵⅍

Macclesfield Road, Nether Alderley SK10 4UB
TEL: (01625) 584000   FAX: (01625) 585105

COOKING 3
MODERN BRITISH
£21–£52

A 'slick, professional provider of good food in a privileged community' is one visitor's summing-up of this beamed roadside pub near the lush, well-wooded slopes of Alderley Edge. Flagstone floors and scrubbed wooden tables convey a casual yet smart feel, staff are young, friendly and efficient, and the menu lays on a display of contemporary ideas, from the nowadays obligatory wild mushroom risotto, and sweet chilli dressing (here applied to crab and coriander linguine), to more homely pork and leek sausages with mash and onion gravy.

Raw materials are sound, and although seasoning may not always be given the attention it deserves, ideas are both sensible and enticing. Caesar salad is made with fresh anchovies, grilled black pudding comes with a poached egg and brown sauce, and chargrilled swordfish with shrimp and dill cream. Desserts favour tradition, in the shape of bread-and-butter and sticky toffee puddings, and a wide-ranging list of wines grouped by style (Capel Vale unoaked Chardonnay at £16.50 is an example of a 'dry, full-flavoured white') starts with eight house wines at £12 to £13.

CHEF: Mark Wilkinson   PROPRIETOR: Ainscoughs   OPEN: Tue to Sun L 12 to 2, Tue to Sat D 7 to 9.30   MEALS: alc exc Sun L (main courses L £7 to £9.50, D £9.50 to £15.50). Set L Tue to Sat £10.50 (2 courses) to £13.50, Set L Sun £12.95 (1 course) to £18.95   SERVICE: not inc, card slips closed   CARDS: Amex, Delta, MasterCard, Switch, Visa   DETAILS: 90 seats. 20 seats outside. Private parties: 45 main room, 10 to 45 private rooms. Car park. Vegetarian meals. Children's helpings. No smoking in 1 dining room. Music

## NETTLEBED Oxfordshire                                                    map 2

## ▲ White Hart ⅚✳                                          NEW ENTRY

Nettlebed RG9 5DD
TEL: (01491) 641245   FAX: (01491) 649018                          COOKING 4
EMAIL: info@whitehartnettlebed.com                        TRADITIONAL ENGLISH
WEBSITE: www.whitehartnettlebed.com                                  £37–£79

Chris Barber and Michael North (who split their time between here and the Goose at Britwell Salome, see entry) opened this new venture in early 2002. The classic seventeenth-century brick and flint building in the centre of the village combines a hotel with a smart brasserie and the more ambitious Nettlebed Restaurant, the latter's brown colour scheme, metal sculptures, and vast stark paintings contributing to its slick and uncompromisingly modern feel. The menu is up to date too, offering such delights as a ravioli of braised pig cheek with pea purée and white truffle, or roast breast of duck with smoked bacon gnocchi.

A preference for small and specialist suppliers pays dividends in the quality of ingredients, producing crisp pastry layered with lightly cooked wild mushrooms, served with an accurately poached Maran egg, and fillet of well-hung Orkney beef, cooked rare as requested. Fish is well treated too, judging by precisely roast sea bass, its flesh firm yet springy, and by poached turbot surrounded by a gang of top-class langoustines. 'Billy Bunter's ideal nursery pudding', according to one visitor, is a moist, slightly tart Bramley apple crumble with a crisp topping, served with vanilla ice cream and butterscotch sauce, while a well-risen, fluffy prune and Armagnac soufflé has come with caramel ice cream tasting of expensive toffee.

If prices sound steep, a no-choice menu of the day offers three courses for barely more than the price of a main course on the carte. Service from young women in baggy pants and T-shirts is friendly and efficient, and wines cover a lot of ground at fair prices, starting with ten house wines under £16.

CHEFS: Chris Barber and Michael North   PROPRIETOR: Chris Barber   OPEN: Tue to Sat 12 to 2, 7 to 9   MEALS: alc (main courses £21 to £24). Set L and D £25. Brasserie and bar menus available   SERVICE: 12.5% (optional), card slips closed   CARDS: MasterCard, Switch, Visa   DETAILS: 90 seats. Private parties: 40 main room, 20 private rooms. Car park. Vegetarian meals. No children under 12 in dining room. No smoking in dining room. Wheelchair access (also WC). No music. No mobile phones   ACCOMMODATION: 12 rooms, all with bath/shower. TV. Phone. B&B £105 to £145. Rooms for disabled  (£5)

## ▲ Newbury Manor ♟ ⚒

London Road, Newbury RG14 2BY
TEL: (01635) 528838   FAX: (01635) 523406                COOKING 6
EMAIL: enquiries@newbury-manor-hotel.co.uk              MODERN EUROPEAN
WEBSITE: www.newbury-manor-hotel.co.uk                      £31–£87

The nine serene acres of grounds in which the hotel sits do a good impression of being in the country, when if fact they are on the edge of a town, and just a small stretch of lawn and some huge trees separate the dining room from the A4. Nicholas Evans puts on a suitably grand menu with the help of some original ideas. Duos and trios are a favourite device, sometimes including two cuts from the same species, such as pork fillet and belly, or a combination of boned, rolled shoulder of lamb with tiny loin fillets, in a strongly reduced and powerfully flavoured rosemary sauce, the dish scattered with small broad beans, roast garlic and baby onions.

Materials are generally well sourced, although dishes tend to be elaborate, with little bundles of this, small piles of that, and dabs of sauce, which tends to reduce their impact. Contrasts may be interesting rather than thrilling, but they produce some enjoyable dishes: for example, mounds of crusted scallop on a bed of creamed leek, together with small, square John Dory fillets on buttery stewed spinach, all sharing the plate with minuscule asparagus spears tied with a strip of leek, some black wild mushroom filaments and a butter sauce.

Desserts are as intricate as the rest, judging by a tower of salted butter caramel stuffed with pine nuts, topped with a thin layer of popcorn, and then by two small scoops of creamy Guinness ice cream separated by first-class, fragile filigree biscuit wafers. Disappointments have been registered during the course of the year in several departments, although an inspection meal found much to commend. In line with the grandeur of the surroundings, service is extremely formal and the wine list includes plenty of mature claret (often at quite stratospheric prices), three vintages of Château d'Yquem, and so on. That said, the New World, Italian and regional France selections are much more than an afterthought and generally offer better value for money, but don't expect to find much under £25. A house selection of eight wines starts at £14.50; 13 wines are sold by the half-bottle.

CHEF: Nicholas Evans   PROPRIETOR: Robert Rae   OPEN: Sun to Fri L 12 to 2, Mon to Sat D 7 to 9.30 (10 Fri and Sat)   CLOSED: 26 to 30 Dec   MEALS: Set L Mon to Fri £16 (2 courses) to £22.50, Set L Sun £12.95 (2 courses) to £17.95, Set D £31 (2 course) to £55   SERVICE: not inc, card slips closed   CARDS: Amex, Delta, Diners, MasterCard, Switch, Visa   DETAILS: 60 seats. 12 seats outside. Private parties: 85 main room, 6 to 85 private rooms. Car park. Vegetarian meals. Children's helpings. No smoking in dining room. Wheelchair access (also WC). Music. No mobile phones. Air-conditioned   ACCOMMODATION: 33 rooms, all with bath/shower. TV. Phone. B&B £115 to £275. Rooms for disabled. Baby facilities. Fishing

---

*Restaurateurs justifiably resent no-shows. If you quote a credit card number when booking, you may be liable for the restaurant's lost profit margin if you don't turn up. Always phone to cancel.*

# Café 21 ✝✷

| | |
|---|---|
| 19–21 Queen Street, Princes Wharf, Quayside, | COOKING **6** |
| Newcastle upon Tyne NE1 3UG | BISTRO |
| TEL: (0191) 222 0755   FAX: (0191) 221 0761 | £24–£58 |

Close to the quayside, and both the Tyne and Gateshead Millennium Bridges, the flagship of Terence Laybourne's reduced empire (Sunderland has gone, but Durham and Ponteland are still going strong; see entries) is set incongruously amid solid, imposing nineteenth-century banking buildings, its logo picked out in green on the etched window. Industrial-size lamps hang from the ceiling, and tables are laid with starched cloths, providing a smart, cosmopolitan setting for some fine populist cooking.

Blackboard menus (one with the day's specials, the other vegetarian) supplement a printed carte, and the kitchen knows how to press all the right crowd-pleasing buttons while conveying a sense that this is more than just ordinary café food. It offers fishcakes with parsley cream and chips, grilled calf's liver with smoky bacon, and the long-standing terrine of ham knuckle and foie gras with pease pudding. A few minor errors creep in (serving temperature at inspection), but mostly the cooking is reassuring, for example in a restaurant presentation of pork shoulder – rolled, slowly cooked and neatly sliced – with semi-crisp crackling, served with black pudding mash, shredded Savoy cabbage and a clear, stock-based gravy.

Some desserts have a seasonal ring to them, including a white chocolate mousse accompanied in springtime by rhubarb and Sauternes, and (in autumn) a variation on trifle incorporating layers of blackberry jelly, fruit, custard, sponge and more jelly in a knickerbocker glory glass, with a blackberry crisp poking out of the top. Service is polite, professional and businesslike, and a soundly chosen, fairly priced wine list (which includes La Segreta Planeta from Sicily and Starve Dog Sauvignon Blanc from Australia) starts with house Duboeuf at £11.

CHEF: Christopher Dobson   PROPRIETORS: Terence and Susan Laybourne   OPEN: Mon to Sat 12 to 2.30, 6 to 10.30   MEALS: alc (main courses £10 to £19.50). Set L £12.50 (2 courses) to £14.50   SERVICE: not inc, 10% for parties of 10 or more   CARDS: Amex, Delta, Diners, MasterCard, Switch, Visa   DETAILS: 60 seats. Vegetarian meals. Children's helpings. No smoking in 1 dining room. No pipes in dining room. Wheelchair access (not WC). Music

# Fisherman's Lodge ✝✷

| | |
|---|---|
| Jesmond Dene, Jesmond, Newcastle upon | |
| Tyne NE7 7BQ | |
| TEL: (0191) 281 3281   FAX: (0191) 281 6410 | COOKING **4** |
| EMAIL: enquiries@fishermanslodge.co.uk | SEAFOOD/MODERN BRITISH |
| WEBSITE: www.fishermanslodge.co.uk | £33–£93 |

Built in leafy Jesmond Dene in 1870, and under the same ownership as Seaham Hall, Seaham, and Samling, Windermere (see entries), the lodge takes a strong line in seafood. The carte offers most choice in this respect, starting maybe with a plate of fresh crab, half a dozen oysters, or sauté king prawns with a Thai-style chilli and garlic dressing. Main-course fish tend to be prime species, such as turbot (with shellfish bouillabaisse), or grilled Dover sole (with lemon and herb butter). But there are meat options too, such as foie gras terrine to start, followed by chargrilled beef fillet with boulangère potatoes.

Set-price menus are no less interesting, judging by a cep fritter with buffalo mozzarella, by roast pheasant breast with merguez sausage, and by iced mandarin soufflé with orange 'sushi'. Other ways to finish might include blackcurrant vacherin, or a plate of caramel desserts. Good names pepper the well-chosen wine list (which includes a couple from Canada), and prices reflect the quality. House vin de pays is a shade under £15 (£3.50 a glass).

CHEF: Paul Amer   PROPRIETOR: Tom Maxfield   OPEN: Mon to Fri L 12 to 2, Mon to Sat D 7 to 10.30 CLOSED: bank hols   MEALS: alc (main courses £19.50 to £36.50). Set L £19.50, Set D £34.50 SERVICE: not inc   CARDS: Amex, Delta, MasterCard, Switch, Visa   DETAILS: 70 seats. Private parties: 70 main room, 14 to 40 private rooms. Car park. Vegetarian meals. No smoking in dining room. Occasional music

---

## NEW MILTON  Hampshire                                                    map 2

# ▲ Chewton Glen  ♥ ⅝✳

Christchurch Road, New Milton BH25 6QS
TEL: (01425) 275341   FAX: (01425) 272310
EMAIL: reservations@chewtonglen.com
WEBSITE: www.chewtonglen.com
from A35 follow signs to Walkford and Highcliffe;                      COOKING 6
take second turning on left after Walkford down              MODERN EUROPEAN
Chewton Farm road                                                     £33–£92

Despite the large scale – there is a health club, pool, gym, and bedrooms 'as big as a cricket pitch' – nothing intimidates. The dining room has a light, airy feel to it, and top-notch service makes every effort to ensure comfort and enjoyment. Indeed, after a stay here people have to relearn how to make and pour their own tea. The only real whinge concerns the difficulty of finding the car park and entrance; otherwise everything is hunky-dory. Fine materials are at the heart of things, as the menu's roll-call of suppliers indicates, and the repertoire incorporates low-calorie and vegetarian options without in any way compromising taste or quality.

The food is reassuring, and dishes are well balanced, with interesting flavours, textures and colours. Indeed, presentation is something of an art form. Foie gras terrine comes on a frosted-glass platter (with crushed peppercorns along one edge, sea salt along another), the accompanying lightly dressed salad leaves and grape chutney assembled into a decorative vegetable composition. Pale-pink organic salmon, looking for all the world like a boat, arrives with white crabmeat 'waves' splashing over it, and lobster claws for oars, and is served with an 'exquisite' tarragon-flavoured sauce. Such artistic flourishes (which can easily get out of hand) make sense thanks to the kitchen's precise and meticulous way with materials, including accurately seared scallops and sliced avocado arranged in a starfish shape, with a first-class dill butter sauce, and rich, dark, moist, top-quality duck, splayed and briefly grilled, on a bed of potato and ceps that was 'a joy to eat'.

Desserts are as soothing as the rest – taking in chocolate fondant, twice-baked raspberry soufflé, and bread-and-butter pudding – and come with a recommended wine by the glass. Elsewhere on the wine list are innumerable important names, particularly from France and Italy. Mature red Bordeaux is a strong point, including a range of Latour vintages and Lafite-Rothschild from the legendary 1961 vintage (for £1,800). Wines like these don't come cheap, it's true, but there is precious little to mitigate the high prices. Organic wines are picked out with a green cloverleaf symbol. Bottle prices start at £17 and rise quickly.

CHEF: Pierre Chevillard  PROPRIETORS: Martin and Brigitte Skan  OPEN: all week 12.30 to 1.45, 7.30 to 9.30  MEALS: alc L exc Sun (main courses £9 to £16.50). Set L Sun £36, Set D £55. Light L menu available  SERVICE: net prices, card slips closed  CARDS: Amex, Delta, Diners, MasterCard, Switch, Visa  DETAILS: 120 seats. Private parties: 120 main room, 6 to 120 private rooms. Car park. Vegetarian meals. Children's helpings. No smoking in dining room. Wheelchair access (also WC). No music. No mobile phones. Air-conditioned  ACCOMMODATION: 59 rooms, all with bath/shower. TV. Phone. Room only £250 to £380. Rooms for disabled. No children under 6. Swimming pool (*The Which? Hotel Guide*)

---

**NEWTON LONGVILLE Buckinghamshire**                    **map 3**

# Crooked Billet ▮ ⅝✳

---

2 Westbrook End, Newton Longville MK17 0DF
TEL: (01908) 373 936   FAX: (01908) 631 979
WEBSITE: www.thebillet.co.uk
off B4034 S of Milton Keynes; from centre of                    COOKING 3
village turn W on Whaddon Road (church on                    MODERN BRITISH
corner) and then left into Westbrook End                    £27–£56

---

'Swearing will not be tolerated' reads a sign over the door. Another prohibits the wearing of vests. You wonder what kind of rough trade rolls up here. In the event, everybody looks respectable enough, happy to be enjoying the friendly service and homely décor of this sixteenth-century pub close to Milton Keynes. It still has the feel of a local, but the dining room is serious. The menu (which names and thanks suppliers, not forgetting the services of 'Eileen the Cleaner') includes elaborate dishes of pan-fried scallops with cauliflower purée, Avruga caviar cream and deep-fried leeks; and salt-and-pepper-roasted duck breast with a cucumber and spring onion roll, special fried rice (containing prawns, chicken and peas) and deep-fried Savoy cabbage.

At its best the kitchen has produced an assured combination of herbs and wild mushrooms, with poached egg and hollandaise, in a filo pastry tart, and another impressive starter of smoked salmon and smoked eel with potato pancake and pickled cucumber. Timing is accurate too: in a dish of roast cod with Cromer crab mash and a sweetcorn and courgette fritter, and in 'meltingly sweet' venison fillet with prune stuffing. Alongside lemon tart, or caramel ice cream sandwiched in meringue, note the well-stocked and expertly served cheese selection. Some dishes may be too ambitious for their own good, and bar food does not appear to be in the same class. Wines, on the other hand, are noteworthy. Each of the almost 300 wines is available by the glass (at one-quarter the full-bottle price). The list (starting with regional France and finishing in South America) spans the wine-making world, spending a lot of time in Burgundy (for red and white) and Bordeaux. Bottle prices start at £13.50 for vins de pays, and there is a good selection of half-bottles.

CHEF: Emma Gilchrist   PROPRIETORS: John and Emma Gilchrist   OPEN: Tue to Sun L 12 to 2 (3 Sun), Tues to Sat D 7 to 10   CLOSED: 2 weeks Sept, 25 and 26 Dec, 2 weeks Jan   MEALS: alc (main courses L £6.50 to £12, D £10 to £20). Bar L menu available   SERVICE: not inc, card slips closed   CARDS: MasterCard, Switch, Visa   DETAILS: 60 seats. 60 seats outside. Car park. Children's helpings. No smoking in dining room. No music. No mobile phones  £5

---

## NORTON  Shropshire                                                                map 5

## ▲ Hundred House Hotel  ⁵⨉

Bridgnorth Road, Norton TF11 9EE
TEL: (01952) 730353   FAX: (01952) 730355
EMAIL: hundredhouse@lineone.net
WEBSITE: www.hundredhouse.co.uk
on A442, 6m S of Telford

COOKING 3
MODERN EUROPEAN
£29–£60

The tall Georgian house of mellow red brick – its name derives from the 'hundreds' into which shires have been divided since medieval times – is blessed with a particularly fine herb garden, and an informative card on every table highlights a 'herb of the month'. Warm, rich colours splattered with gold permeate the three linked dining rooms, and a generous menu points to some quite complex cooking. Flavour and texture combinations can work extremely well, for example in a first course of grilled scallops served with a ginger-flavoured red pepper coulis and a crusty rice cake topped with a bird's nest of bean sprouts.

Nobody would accuse the dishes of being neat or pared down to essentials – portions are large, and unnecessary extra vegetables are served in profusion – but what stands out above all else is the high quality of ingredients throughout, some of them local, including a pink, juicy, flavourful rack of Shropshire spring lamb with a tapénade crust (plus sliced potatoes cooked in cream and garlic, and an aubergine 'tian'). Fish specials vary by the day, from grilled halibut fillet to a casserole of sea bass and mussels. Desserts don't appear to be a strong suit. A short, sensibly priced wine list starts with a dozen house wines at £12.50, all available in large or extra-large glass sizes.

CHEF: Stuart Phillips   PROPRIETORS: the Phillips family   OPEN: all week 12 to 2.30, 6 (7 Sun) to 9.30 (9 Sun)   MEALS: alc (main courses £9.50 to £19). Set L Sun £14.95 (2 courses) to £17.95. Brasserie menu available   SERVICE: 10% (optional), card slips closed   CARDS: Delta, MasterCard, Switch, Visa   DETAILS: 70 seats. 30 seats outside. Private parties: 30 main room. Car park. Vegetarian meals. Children's helpings. No smoking in 1 dining room. Wheelchair access (also WC). No music. No mobile phones   ACCOMMODATION: 10 rooms, all with bath/ shower. TV. Phone. B&B £75 to £125. Baby facilities (The Which? Hotel Guide)  £5

---

*Prices quoted in the Guide are based on information supplied by restaurateurs. The prices quoted at the top of each entry represent a range, from the lowest meal price to the highest; the latter is inflated by 20 per cent to take account of likely price rises during the year of the Guide.*

---

# Adlard's

79 Upper St Giles, Norwich NR2 1AB
TEL: (01603) 633522   FAX: (01603) 617733
EMAIL: info@adlards.co.uk
WEBSITE: www.adlards.co.uk

COOKING **5**
MODERN BRITISH
£32–£63

A calm and easy-going atmosphere pervades this 'civilised and welcoming' dining room where cream, taupe and grey predominate, colour coming from bold, bright paintings. While David Adlard ambles about talking to customers, service is calm, smiley, personable and efficient. Choice may be limited on each menu, but options are enticing, and the food impressive and enjoyable. Simplicity is a point in its favour, yet dishes involve fine workmanship and good judgement: for example in a velvety, deeply creamy mussel and saffron soup, and in a well-executed starter of two fat seared scallops, prime specimens, each on a small disc of potato, on a pool of pea purée, with a drizzle of citrussy dressing to balance the sweetness of the shellfish.

This is 'classy cooking', according to one couple who praised a chunk of accurately timed monkfish, spot on for flavour and texture, served with a small pile of risotto and an artichoke velouté. Meat might range from loin of venison with red cabbage, to pink flavourful loin of lamb on a bed of 'energetically grilled' aubergine, courgette and red peppers, in a translucent stock-based sauce. To finish, prune soufflé comes with Earl Grey tea ice cream, and tarte Tatin with a honey ice cream. Lunch value is commended. Wine prices reflect the sharply chosen, high-quality selection, but a few bottles under £20 are helpfully picked out at the beginning (Babich's Pinot Gris 2000 from Marlborough, and a Valdepeñas Gran Reserva from 1993 are both £19). House wine is £14 (£3.75 a glass).

CHEF: Roger Hickman   PROPRIETOR: David Adlard   OPEN: Tue to Sat L 12.30 to 1.45, Mon to Sat D 7.30 to 10.30   MEALS: alc (main courses £15 to £19.50). Set L £15 (2 courses) to £19, Set D Sat (and occasionally other evenings) £25   SERVICE: not inc   CARDS: Amex, Delta, Diners, MasterCard, Switch, Visa   DETAILS: 42 seats. Private parties: 42 main room. Vegetarian meals. Children's helpings. Wheelchair access (not WC). No music. Air-conditioned

# Tatlers ✦

NEW ENTRY

21 Tombland, Norwich NR3 1RF
TEL: (01603) 766670   FAX: (01603) 766625
EMAIL: sam@tatlers.com
WEBSITE: www.tatlers.com

COOKING **3**
MODERN BRITISH
£28–£55

This attractive Georgian town house near the cathedral is blessed with several dining rooms of varying size, all with unfussy and unobtrusive décor. Tables are set far enough apart to allow privacy, but not so far that you feel isolated; lunchtime is generally 'business-y, but not in an intimidating way', and in the evenings it tends to feel more intimate. Sam Clifford acknowledges the experience gained at Adlard's (see entry above), which has produced, among other things, a penchant for Norfolk produce: buttered Blakeney samphire, perhaps, or Cromer crab, fashioned either into a cocktail, or into deep-fried 'puffers' with tomato salsa.

This diligent approach to sourcing also shows in the use of organic salmon (turned into ceviche with the help of lime, coriander and chilli), wild sea bass (pan-fried with dill beurre blanc) and skate wing served simply with lemon and parsley, careful treatment making the most of its flavour and texture. But this is not a seafood restaurant. Vegetarian options might include an enterprising beetroot and scallion tarte Tatin with horseradish, while meats have offered poached Gressingham duck with white beans and foie gras in a herb broth, and filet of well-hung Aberdeen Angus beef cooked rare, as ordered, served (on request) with a salad dressed with first-class olive oil. Finish perhaps with lemon tart, or with a cinnamon and hazelnut bombe and a glazed pear. Service is friendly rather than dazzlingly efficient – 'the first course took an age to arrive but was accompanied by the chef himself apologising for the delay' – and the wine list aims for quality (Austrian wine-maker Willi Opitz is well represented), offering a fair selection of half-bottles and ten house wines under £20.

CHEFS: Eden Derrick and Sam Clifford   PROPRIETORS: Sam Clifford and Keith Roberts   OPEN: Mon to Sat 12 to 2, 6.30 to 10   CLOSED: 23 to 28 Dec   MEALS: alc (main courses £11 to £15). Set L £14 (2 courses) to £17.50, Set D £25 to £30   SERVICE: not inc, 10% for parties of 10 or more   CARDS: Amex, Delta, Diners, MasterCard, Switch, Visa   DETAILS: 54 seats. Private parties: 35 main room, 15 to 20 private rooms. Vegetarian meals. Children's helpings. No smoking in 1 dining room. Music  (£5)

## NOTTINGHAM Nottinghamshire                                    map 5

# Hart's ▼

1 Standard Court, Park Row,
Nottingham NG1 6GN
TEL: (0115) 911 0666   FAX: (0115) 911 0611                    COOKING 6
EMAIL: ask@hartsnottingham.co.uk                               MODERN ENGLISH
WEBSITE: www.hartsnottingham.co.uk                             £24–£59

*NOTTS GFG 2003 COMMENDED*

'Nottingham is lucky to have somewhere of this quality,' sums up the gist of favourable reports. Close to the city centre, yet in a comparatively quiet backwater on the edge of a residential development, it is modern, spacious and attractively decorated, its cosmopolitan style considered a model for others to emulate. Mark Gough's confident food completes the sense of easy-going sophistication, taking in brightly flavoured dishes of duck won ton with borscht consommé and soured cream, and steamed mussels and clams with a sweet chilli dressing.

It is not difficult to appreciate the menu's wide appeal, as it hops from old-fashioned deep-fried whitebait (with a jazzy salsa), or a satisfyingly fresh-flavoured parsnip soup, to the indulgence of souffléd haddock omelette with an Emmental glaze, or the contrast of pan-fried sea bass with its mini chorizo sausages. While a few luxury materials add to the sense of extravagance, the kitchen never forgets that it is there to please, turning out calf's liver to equal the best, and serving up deep-fried halibut with minted peas and chips.

The simplicity of desserts is another plus, judging by 'sublime' pear Tatin with vanilla ice cream, or a straightforward partnership of coconut ice cream with chocolate sauce. Service has been praised as 'attentive but not intrusive', and there's terrific value on the wine list of 43 reds and whites (the vast majority below £20), with nary a duff bottle in sight, enabling wine lovers to keep out of the Chardonnay/Cabernet rut. Four are sold by the glass (starting at £3), and in addition there are 20-plus fine wines, predominantly French. Hart's Hotel is planned to open next door during the spring of 2003.

CHEF: Mark Gough   PROPRIETOR: Tim Hart   OPEN: all week 12 to 2, 7 to 10.30 (9 Sun)   CLOSED: 24 to 26 Dec, 1 Jan   MEALS: alc (main courses £10.50 to £18.50). Set L Mon to Sat £11 (2 courses) to £14.95, Set L Sun £18, Set D Sun £16 (2 courses) to £21   SERVICE: 10% (optional), card slips closed   CARDS: Amex, Delta, MasterCard, Switch, Visa   DETAILS: 80 seats. 20 seats outside. Private parties: 80 main room, 6to 110 private rooms. Car park. Vegetarian meals. Children's helpings. No-smoking area. Wheelchair access (also WC). No music. Air-conditioned

## ▲ Restaurant Sat Bains at Hotel des Clos ✸

**NEW ENTRY**

Old Lenton Lane, Nottingham NG7 2SA
TEL: (0115) 986 6566   FAX: (0115) 986 0343
EMAIL: info@hoteldesclos.com
WEBSITE: www.hoteldesclos.com

COOKING 5
MODERN EUROPEAN
£21–£68

Near the A52, but sitting peacefully just yards from the River Trent, Hotel des Clos occupies a set of brick-built Victorian farm buildings with well-tended gardens. Menus in the comfortable, stylish (dark beams, cream walls, good-quality tableware) dining room – renamed in autumn 2002 in honour of its chef – are set, rather than à la carte, but full of thought and interest. One starter combines roast scallop with a salad of raw cauliflower and caramelised cauliflower purée; another partners a terrine of duck breast and lightly cooked foie gras with small pools of sweet carrot purée, topped with a disc of black pudding in light, crispy batter.

Portions can be small: two slices of pink, crisp-skinned duck breast for a main course, with asparagus and green beans, a cranberry-filled samosa triangle, a properly done fondant potato, and a spicy red-wine sauce. And ingredients may sometimes seem too many, as in a fine dessert of chocolate fondant with both lemon jelly and sweet marzipan ice cream. A more straightforward dessert might be a light-textured chocolate marquise with blood orange sorbet. Cheese comes with first-class oatkcakes; appetisers, breads and petits fours are well done; and service is friendly and attentive. A heavily annotated wine list aims for both quality and interest; those on a tight budget may wince, but five house wines come in under £16.50.

CHEF: Satwant Bains   PROPRIETORS: the Ralley family   OPEN: Mon to Fri L 12 to 2, Mon to Sat D 7 to 9.45 (10.15 Sat)   CLOSED: bank hols   MEALS: Set L £10 to £28.50, Set D £30 (2 courses) to £40   SERVICE: not inc, card slips closed   CARDS: Amex, Delta, Diners, MasterCard, Switch, Visa   DETAILS: 40 seats. 20 seats outside. Private parties: 40 main room, 4 to 14 private rooms. Car park. Vegetarian meals. No children under 8. No smoking in dining room. Wheelchair access (also women's WC). Music. No mobile phones   ACCOMMODATION: 9 rooms, all with bath/shower. TV. Phone. B&B £79.50 to £129.50. Rooms for disabled. No children under 8. Fishing (*The Which? Hotel Guide*)

# Sonny's ✎

3 Carlton Street, Hockley, Nottingham NG1 1NL  | NEW CHEF |
TEL/FAX: (0115) 947 3041                            GLOBAL
                                                   £23–£54

The name Sonny's on the glass frontage may be discreet and perhaps occasionally missed by the uninitiated, but this contemporary, airy, city-centre brasserie still draws the informed crowd with its cool, clean lines, vibrant atmosphere. As the Guide was about to go to press, new chef John Melican arrived, and early menus indicate he will be maintaining the kitchen's modern repertoire while making a few tweaks of his own. Expect starters along the lines of warm quail and onion tartlet, or wild mushroom and bacon risotto with shredded pig's trotter, and main courses of roast monkfish with pak choi, mango salsa and sweet potato, or roast loin of lamb with ratatouille and polenta. Staff are polite, helpful and friendly, while the compact wine list comes sensibly priced with plenty to drink under £20 and a good selection by the glass from £2.85. House vin de pays kicks in at £10.45 a bottle.

CHEF: John Melican  PROPRIETORS: Rebecca Mascarenhas and James Harris  OPEN: all week 12 to 2.30, 7 to 10.30  MEALS: alc (main courses £10.50 to £15.50). Set L Mon to Sat £10 (2 courses) to £13.50, Set L Sun £17.95  SERVICE: 10% (optional), card slips closed  CARDS: Amex, Delta, MasterCard, Switch, Visa  DETAILS: 80 seats. Private parties: 30 main room. Vegetarian meals. Wheelchair access (not WC). Music. No mobile phones. Air-conditioned

# World Service ♥ ⁵✳

Newdigate House, Castle Gate,
Nottingham NG1 6AF                               COOKING 4
TEL: (0115) 8475587  FAX: (0115) 8475584        MODERN BRITISH
WEBSITE: www.worldservicerestaurant.com          £22–£57

In a narrow street below the castle, what sounds like a BBC canteen is in fact a spacious Georgian house, reached through an oriental garden. Its exotic décor (lacquered coconut-shell tables for example) is well integrated, creating a relaxing, informal, aesthetically pleasing effect. The 'service' part of the name comes from the United Services Club, whose building it occupies; 'world' evokes the globe-scouring menu (in small italic type on a beige background, so not easy reading in low light).

Main materials may be typically up-market cuts and species such as halibut, turbot, beef fillet, and calf's liver, but treatments are wide-ranging. Moist, briefly cooked and crispy sea bass might come with Thai vegetables in a coconut and coriander sauce, while monkfish has been given a Moroccan-style accompaniment of chickpeas and green beans. The kitchen gets timings and textures right, producing a fine spinach, ricotta and wild mushroom tart made with first-class pastry, on a bed of creamed cauliflower: and braised, herb-crusted shoulder of lamb (the consistency of smooth pâté) served with fondant swede. Side dishes of extra vegetables (charged separately) may be unnecessary.

To finish, banana mousse with caramel sauce is 'a real treat', praise has been heaped on a warm chocolate fondant with pistachio ice cream, and a trio of chocolate desserts – steamed pudding with a rich praline sauce, an ice cream, and a marquise – has been drooled over. The set-price lunch (two choices per course) is considered good value, and service is friendly and efficient. Note, however, the two-hour limit on tables for two. The wine list is short and sweet, taking a quick trot through the food-friendlier regions of the New and Old Worlds. Mark-ups on the 'fine wine' list can be greedy (£46 for 1999 Cloudy Bay Chardonnay), making the main section a better place to look for value. Bottle prices start at a reasonable £10.90, while a page of interesting sakés will appeal to the more adventurous.

CHEFS: Chris Elson and Preston Walker   PROPRIETORS: Ashley Walter, Philip Morgan and Chris Elson   OPEN: all week 12 to 2.30 (3 Sun), 7 (6.30 Sat) to 10 (10.30 Sat, 9 Sun)   CLOSED: 1 and 2 Jan   MEALS: alc (main courses £12 to £18.50). Set L Mon to Sat £9.50 (2 courses) to £13. Set L Sun £12.50 (2 courses) to £17. Set D Sun £9.50 (2 courses) to £13   SERVICE: not inc, 10% for parties of 10 or more   CARDS: Amex, MasterCard, Switch, Visa   DETAILS: 80 seats. 40 seats outside. Private parties: 8 to 32 private rooms. Car park at D and weekends only. Vegetarian meals. Children's helpings. No smoking in dining room. Music (£5)

## ODIHAM Hampshire                                                    map 2

# Grapevine                                                   [ NEW ENTRY ]

121 High Street, Odiham RG29 1LA                                  COOKING 3
TEL: (01256) 701122                                           ENGLISH/ITALIAN
WEBSITE: www.info@grapevine-gourmet.co.uk                          £24–£48

Odiham is an attractive Georgian village with a broad high street, at one end of which, in a double-fronted bow-windowed property, is this bright, modern bistro. The menu has been described variously as 'resolutely Mediterranean' and 'rustic modern English with Italian influences' (chef David Bennett previously worked at the Walnut Tree Inn, Llandewi Skirrid; see entry). Either way, among the many attractive options might be scallops with Puy lentils, chargrilled red mullet niçoise, and boneless quail stuffed with lemon and skewered on a branch of thyme. Though the style is easily recognisable, some dishes are fairly unusual: poached beef fillet with wild mushrooms and a Gorgonzola risotto, for example, or salmon with rhubarb, ginger, leeks, green olives, peppers and fennel. The last, at inspection, turned out to be less weird than it might sound, the rhubarb complementing the richness of the good-quality salmon. A starter salad of chargrilled pear, soft goats' cheese and watercress has also met with approval, though an interesting-sounding dessert of basil crème brûlée fared less well. The short wine list offers plenty of choice under £20, including house Vin de Pays d'Oc at £11.

CHEFS: David Bennett and David Bailey   PROPRIETOR: Matthew Fleet   OPEN: Mon to Fri L 12 to 2, Mon to Sat D 6 to 10   CLOSED: 1 week Christmas, bank hols   MEALS: alc (main courses £10 to £16). Set L £8.95 (2 courses) to £12.95, Set D 6 to 7 £14.95 (inc wine)   SERVICE: not inc, 10% for parties of 8 or more   CARDS: Amex, Delta, Diners, MasterCard, Switch, Visa   DETAILS: 40 seats. Private parties: 50 main room. Vegetarian meals. Children's helpings. Music. Air-conditioned

*The Guide is totally independent, accepts no free hospitality, and survives on the number of copies sold each year.*

## OLD BURGHCLERE Hampshire  map 2

# Dew Pond ▼ ✻

Old Burghclere RG20 9LH
TEL: (01635) 278408 FAX: (01635) 278580  COOKING **5**
WEBSITE: www.dewpond.co.uk  ANGLO-FRENCH
off old A34, 3m W of Kingsclere  £40–£53

A couple of buildings have been linked together and plastered in a pale custard colour. Peaceful views from the dining room on to green fields and hills soon make you forget the busy A34 nearby, and perhaps the rather routine décor, while the cooking promises solid delivery ('a very good even standard', one visitor concluded). The starting point is tip-top ingredients – from line-caught fish, via Welsh lamb, to free-range poultry – assembled into a three-course menu that might offer wild mushroom risotto, steamed fish of the day (sea bass for one reporter) with vermouth sauce, and glazed Gressingham duck breast with a honey and ginger sauce.

It is not innovation or excitement that this rather conservative kitchen seeks; it prefers workable combinations of ingredients and flavours, finding them in starters of pan-fried scallops with lentils and pancetta, and a Roquefort and leek tartlet, as well as in main dishes such as beef fillet with a cep and Madeira sauce. Workmanlike desserts, meanwhile, typically include vanilla crème brûlée, caramelised lemon tart, and layered dark and white chocolate terrine with a coffee-bean sauce. The wine list is thoughtfully put together, its wares organised by style. Producers are generally well chosen, and there's plenty to be found under £20. House wines from France and Australia are £11.95, and four wines are available by the glass (£3).

CHEF: Keith Marshall PROPRIETORS: Keith and Julie Marshall OPEN: Tue to Sat D only 7 to 10 CLOSED: 2 weeks Christmas, 2 weeks Aug MEALS: Set D £28 SERVICE: not inc CARDS: Delta, MasterCard, Switch, Visa DETAILS: 45 seats. 25 seats outside. Private parties: 50 main room, 10 to 25 private rooms. Car park. No children under 5. Children's helpings. No smoking in dining room. No music £5

## OMBERSLEY Worcestershire  map 5

# Venture In ✻

Main Road, Ombersley WR9 0EW  COOKING **3**
TEL: (01905) 620552  MODERN BRITISH/FRENCH
  £27–£52

In a quiet village, striped window awnings set this place apart from its black-and-white half-timbered fellows. It has an inglenook fireplace and mellow timbers, service is professional, informed and alert, and value (particularly at lunchtime) is good. Sound technique has produced a starter of local asparagus coated in a thick beurre blanc emulsion, accompanied by a small pile of tangily dressed leaves; and two glossy white sea bream fillets (Birmingham fish market is handy) on first-class leek risotto.

Combinations are carefully considered. A seared fillet of gently home-smoked salmon, attractively browned yet just cooked within ('a lovely piece of non-oily fish'), is matched with tomato- and caper-flecked slippery noodles dressed in a mild horseradish velouté, while moist but crip-skinned Gressingham duck breast in a puddle of golden-brown pan juices comes with a thin pastry case of celeriac and apple purée. Vegetables might include strips of carrot, courgette and celeriac, coated in a cumin 'crumb' and deep-fried.

Desserts are equally accomplished. An assiette of lemon features contrasts of texture and taste, ranging from a delicately flavoured ice cream in a sweet pastry case to a sharply piquant mousse in a thin, crisp meringue. Wines have doubled in number, and, although some mark-ups seem high, there is fair choice up to £25. Five house wines come in at £11 each.

CHEF/PROPRIETOR: Toby Fletcher   OPEN: Tue to Sun L 12 to 2, Tue to Sat D 7 to 9.45   CLOSED: 25 and 26 Dec, bank hols   MEALS: Set L £15.95 (2 courses) to £18.95, Set L Sun £18.95, Set D £28.95. Every second Wed L and D gourmet fish menu £30.95   SERVICE: not inc, card slips closed   CARDS: MasterCard, Switch, Visa   DETAILS: 35 seats. Private parties: 35 main room. Car park. Vegetarian meals. Children's helpings. No children under 9 at D. No smoking in dining room. Music. No mobile phones. Air-conditioned

## ORFORD  Suffolk                                                    map 6

# ▲ Crown and Castle, Trinity  £

Orford IP12 2LJ
TEL: (01394) 450205                                                COOKING 4
EMAIL: info@crownandcastlehotel.co.uk               MODERN BRITISH-PLUS
WEBSITE: www.crownandcastlehotel.co.uk                          £27–£48

In this brick-and-pebbledash inn near the Norman keep, the succession of interlinked rooms (with beams, wooden floors and antiques) is bright, airy and sophisticated and done largely in buttermilk yellow. A no-nonsense menu, subdivided into raw, cold and hot items, offers appealing and flexible ideas. Some sound straightforward, but conceal skilful work: notably an 'immensely enjoyable' salad of feta cheese, roast beetroot and mint, with all kinds of bits and bobs maintaining interest to the last mouthful, or a silky smooth butternut squash soup enriched with coconut milk.

Seafood and vegetarian options add to the sense of lightness: perhaps a chunk of notably fresh roast cod dotted with brown shrimps in a caper-strewn blackened butter, or a rich, just-cooked quiche combining cubes of buffalo ricotta in savoury custard with thin, buttery pastry. Contrasting textures also feature in desserts such as a slice of expertly made treacle fondant scattered with crunchy coconut, served with a mellow yogurt ice cream.

Service is amiable and enthusiastic, and the colour-coded wine list is organised by grape variety (grape descriptions at the back help to disentangle Pinot Gris from Primitivo) with sub-sections for bin ends, half bottles, house wines and so on. House Sicilian comes in litres (£15), half-litres (£7.50) or large glasses (£2.75).

CHEF: Brendan Ansbro   PROPRIETORS: David and Ruth Watson   OPEN: all week 12 to 2, 7 to 9 (9.30 Sat)   CLOSED: Sun D from 1 Nov to Easter (except Christmas and school hols)   MEALS: alc (main courses L £7.50 to £15.50, D £9.50 to £15.50). Set L £14.50 (2 courses) to £21.50 SERVICE: not inc   CARDS: Delta, MasterCard, Switch, Visa   DETAILS: 50 seats. 36 seats outside. Private parties: 12 main room, 8 to 12 private rooms. Car park. Vegetarian meals. No children

under 9 at D or weekends. Children's helpings. Wheelchair access (not WC). No music
ACCOMMODATION: 18 rooms, all with bath/shower. TV. Phone. B&B £68 to £125 (*The Which? Hotel Guide*)

## OSMOTHERLEY North Yorkshire       map 9

# Golden Lion ░✳ £     | NEW ENTRY |

6 West End, Osmotherley DL6 3AA          COOKING 3
TEL: (01609) 883526   FAX: (01609) 884000     ENGLISH/FRENCH/ITALIAN
                           £22–£44

This newcomer in an ever-so-pretty village used to be a pub, and still has wooden floors, painted stone walls, a fireplace and beamed ceiling to prove it. Outside are a few wooden tables overlooking the village green. Having undergone a conversion, it is now a hikers' bar (the village is located at the start of the Lyke Wake Walk) and high-class restaurant rolled into one.

The menu offers a bit of something for everyone and is divided up into sections for fish, soup, vegetarian, pasta and risotto, meat and salads. Sardines may be grilled in olive oil and served with lemon; deep-fried calamari and prawn cocktail may turn up too, along with a main course of firm, flaky cod with home-made chips. At inspection, a creamy-textured lemon risotto topped with caramelised onions impressed, as did a rich lamb casserole containing lambs' kidneys: an unpretentious dish described as 'real hikers' food'. The long dessert menu may feature chocolate cake, strawberry tart, or 'very sherry trifle'. Wines are a good-natured, if short, collection of bottles, mostly under £20. House Vin de Pays d'Oc is £11.50, St-Emilion £13.50.

CHEF: Giorgiu Nicholas   PROPRIETORS: Christie Connelly, Peter McCoy and Belal Radwan
OPEN: all week 12 to 3.30, 6 to 10   MEALS: alc (main courses £6 to £14)   SERVICE: not inc, card slips closed   CARDS: Delta, MasterCard, Switch, Visa   DETAILS: 90 seats. 20 seats outside. Private parties: 50 main room. Vegetarian meals. Children's helpings. No smoking in 1 dining room. Wheelchair access (not WC). Music

## OSWESTRY Shropshire       map 7

# ▲ Sebastians ░✳

45 Willow Street, Oswestry SY11 1AQ
TEL: (01691) 655444   FAX: (01691) 653452        COOKING 3
EMAIL: sebastians.rest@virgin.net              FRENCH
WEBSITE: www.sebastians-hotel.co.uk          £39–£51

The building may seem like pure English tea shop – a chintzy sixteenth-century cottage complete with beams, wood panelling and uneven, carpeted floors – though the food on offer is anything but scones and crumpets. As a family-run set-up, it earns Brownie points for sheer effort and hard work across the board: not least in the kitchen, where Mark Sebastian Fisher has adopted a simple, fine-tuned approach to what is resolutely old-style French provincial cooking.

This is one of those restaurants that still describes dishes in French with English subtitles: potage du jour (perhaps pumpkin), magret de canard au poivre, and so forth. Ingredients are allowed to shine, and timing is generally spot-on, as in a fillet of lamb rolled in a thick layer of chicken mousse, served with fondant potato and lamb jus. Elsewhere, a salad of seared tuna niçoise is the real thing, complete with waxy new potatoes, while fillet of cod comes on a bed of vegetables with parsley and garlic butter. Desserts might include an old-fashioned steamed pudding flavoured with toffee, bananas and pecan nuts. France is naturally the main player on the list of around 50 wines. House Chilean is £11.95.

CHEFS: Mark Sebastian Fisher and Richard Jones  PROPRIETORS: Mark Sebastian Fisher and Michelle Fisher  OPEN: Tue to Sat D only 6.45 to 9.45  CLOSED: 25 and 26 Dec, 1 Jan  MEALS: Set D £22.95 (2 courses) to £26.95  SERVICE: not inc, card slips closed  CARDS: Amex, Delta, MasterCard, Switch, Visa  DETAILS: 40 seats. 35 seats outside. Private parties: 50 main room. Car park. Vegetarian meals. Children's helpings. No smoking in dining room. Wheelchair access (not WC). Music  ACCOMMODATION: 8 rooms, all with bath/shower. TV. Phone. Room only £50 to £60. Rooms for disabled. Baby facilities (£5)

---

**OXFORD Oxfordshire**　　　　　　　　　　　　　　　　　　**map 2**

# ▲ Al-Shami £

| | |
|---|---|
| 25 Walton Crescent, Oxford OX1 2JG | COOKING 1 |
| TEL: (01865) 310066  FAX: (01865) 311241 | LEBANESE |
| WEBSITE: www.al-shami.co.uk | £19–£39 |

In a quiet Victorian terrace just off the main drag of Jericho, this 15-year-old Lebanese restaurant remains a popular haunt for university types. It's an attractively bright place, with a tiled floor, an abundance of greenery, and Eastern-style prints on the walls; the atmosphere is busy, although staff can seem rather complacent. Hone your appetite with ayran (a yoghurt drink with a kick of garlic), then the best advice is to stay with the extensive list of hot and cold meze: among recent successes have been juicy grilled chicken wings with garlic sauce, moutabel (creamy baked aubergine purée), and maqaniq (bite-sized Lebanese sausages). Main courses are mostly predictable grills, although baked cod fillet with a hot sesame sauce sounds like an interesting alternative. Desserts may be more limited than the menu suggests. Drink Almaza beer or check out the vintages of Ch. Musar on the short wine list. House Lebanese is £9.99.

CHEF: Mimo Mahfouz  PROPRIETOR: Al-Shami Cuisine  OPEN: all week 12 to 12  MEALS: alc (main courses £6.50 to £12). Cover £1  SERVICE: not inc, 10% for parties of 6 or more  CARDS: MasterCard, Switch, Visa  DETAILS: 100 seats. Private parties: 100 main room, 50 private room. Vegetarian meals. Wheelchair access (also WC). Music  ACCOMMODATION: 12 rooms, all with bath/shower. TV. B&B £35 to £45 (£5)

---

# Branca ⁵⁄✳ £　　　　　　　　　　　　　　　| NEW ENTRY |

| | |
|---|---|
| 111 Walton Street, Oxford OX2 6AJ | COOKING 3 |
| TEL: (01865) 556111  FAX: (01865) 556501 | MODERN ITALIAN |
| EMAIL: brancarestaurant@aol.com | £23–£44 |

The atmosphere at this newcomer to the Jericho area is lively and cosmopolitan. Décor is contemporary, with a glass and steel entrance and a large bar area curving along two-thirds of the room's width. Rows of dark-wood tables and red-seated chairs run to the back of the long room, and cutlery and napkins placed in beakers on the tables underline its informality. The menu is divided into sections: antipasti, salads, risotto, pizza, pasta, meat, fish, and so forth, and there is a dedicated children's menu.

A superb risotto with butternut squash, Gorgonzola and caramelised onions has made a great starter, while main courses might turn up tender and flavourful slow-roast belly pork with aubergine caponata, topped with a separate rectangle of crisp crackling. For dessert, a tasting plate of tiramisù, lemon tart with crème fraîche, panettone bread-and-butter pudding, and hazelnut and praline semifreddo accentuates the modern Italian approach of the kitchen. Service is bright, cheery and attentive. The all-Italian wine list has a run-of-the-mill pizza-joint selection of ten wines sold by the bottle (£9.95 to £19.95), 500ml pot, or 175ml glass (£2.45 to £5.25).

CHEF: Michael MacQuire   PROPRIETOR: Branca Ltd   OPEN: all week 11 to 11 (11.30 Fri and Sat) MEALS: alc (main courses £8 to £12). Set L Mon to Fri 12 to 5 £5 (1 course inc wine), Set D Mon to Fri 5 to 7 £10 (2 courses inc wine)   SERVICE: not inc, 10% (optional) for parties of 5 or more, card slips closed   CARDS: Amex, Delta, Diners, MasterCard, Switch, Visa   DETAILS: 120 seats. Private parties: 50 main room. Vegetarian meals. Children's helpings. No smoking in dining room. Wheelchair access (also WC). Music. Air-conditioned

# Cherwell Boathouse 🍷 ⁵⁄✳ £

50 Bardwell Road, Oxford OX2 6ST
TEL: (01865) 552746   FAX: (01865) 553819
EMAIL: info@cherwellboathouse.co.uk
WEBSITE: www.cherwellboathouse.co.uk

COOKING 2
MODERN ENGLISH/FRENCH
£25–£38

Located on the bank of the River Cherwell, where punts tie up and relaxation beckons, this site has been a pleasure spot for generations. Recently, the place has undergone something of a renaissance. The genteel shabbiness of yore has been replaced by a glitzy but not overdone look: the old boathouse remains but is now joined by a brightly lit conservatory with a light wood floor and arty photos.

A short, set-price menu relies on sensible, rather traditional flavour combinations with the odd surprise (such as garlic and almond soup). Breast of wood pigeon on a bed of warm red lentils makes a satisfying starter, and there might be couscous-stuffed tomato topped with melted mozzarella. A simple sirloin steak, pink and meltingly tender, with mustard sauce and new potatoes might crop up among main courses alongside grilled sea bass with a yellow pepper and saffron sauce. Puddings are not fancy and may feature cheesecake and ice creams. The wine list is a treat: 13 pages of top selections from across the globe, at prices that get the mouth watering in anticipation. Fine burgundies and Bordeaux underpin the list, but there's plenty from Spain, California and other New World countries to balance. Twenty house wines (£9 to £22) cover a wide range of styles, and many of these are sold by the glass.

CHEF: Wayne Cullen   PROPRIETOR: Anthony Verdin   OPEN: all week 12 to 2, 6.30 to 9   CLOSED: 25 to 30 Dec   MEALS: Set L Mon to Fri £9.75 (2 courses) to £18.50, Set L Sat and Sun £19.50, Set D £21.50   SERVICE: not inc, 10% for parties of 6 or more   CARDS: Amex, Delta, MasterCard, Switch, Visa   DETAILS: 75 seats. 90 seats outside. Private parties: 50 main room, 10 to 20 private rooms. Car park. Vegetarian meals. Children's helpings. No smoking in dining room. Wheelchair access (also WC). No music. No mobile phones £5

# Chiang Mai Kitchen ⚡✻

| | |
|---|---|
| Kemp Hall Passage, 130A High Street, | COOKING **2** |
| Oxford OX1 4DH | THAI |
| TEL: (01865) 202233 | £29–£51 |

**NEW ENTRY**

Popular with 20 to 40 somethings, this Thai restaurant is down a tiny alleyway off the High Street. The building doesn't look much from outside, but it's a 'lovely old place' where the mood is happy and relaxed. A few westernised crowd-pleasers show up on the menu, although ingredients are bona fide and flavours all 'present and correct': witness stir-fried venison with red curry paste, baby aubergines and clumps of young green peppercorns. The kitchen's dedication to the real thing shows in a classic tom yum soup, meaty khanom jeep (pork dumplings), and superb scallops steamed in their shells with chilli, garlic and soy. Noodles and salads are creditable, and there are (unusually) a couple of genuine desserts, including a gelatinous block of Thai custard topped with strips of carrot. Drink beer or delve into the affordable wine list. House French is £10.50.

CHEF: Pun Bua-In   PROPRIETOR: Helen O'Malley   OPEN: all week 12 to 2.30 (3 Sun), 6 to 10.30
MEALS: alc (main courses £5.50 to £10.50)   SERVICE: not inc, 10% for parties of 5 or more
CARDS: Amex, Delta, Diners, MasterCard, Switch, Visa   DETAILS: 80 seats. Private parties: 33
main room. Vegetarian meals. No smoking in 1 dining room. Wheelchair access (not WC). No
music  £5

# Gee's ⚡✻

**NEW ENTRY**

| | |
|---|---|
| 61 Banbury Road, Oxford OX2 6PE | |
| TEL: (01865) 553540   FAX: (01865) 310308 | COOKING **2** |
| EMAIL: info@gees-restaurant.co.uk | MODERN EUROPEAN |
| WEBSITE: www.oxford-hotels-restaurant.co.uk | £26–£58 |

About ten minutes from the centre, towards moneyed north Oxford, Gee's is 'the whole dining experience'. A capacious Victorian conservatory filled with light and greenery lifts the spirits on a luminous summer's evening; then, as darkness falls, discreet theatrical spotlighting of each table creates an intimate feel. Michael Wright's cooking is comfortingly domestic, with seafood specialities prominent. Starters might include firm-cooked seasonal asparagus with a hard-boiled quail's egg and well-made hollandaise, or top-quality goats' cheese served in a tower with marinated aubergine and tomato. Fish specials have included moistly meaty chargrilled swordfish on buttery noodles bursting with coriander flavour. Chargrilled, too, was a veal cutlet, served with roast squash and rosemary butter, and marination extends into desserts, such as peaches in Muscat wine with clotted cream. Attention to detail characterises the well-drilled service, and the short wine list, starting at £11.85, offers adequate choice below £20, plus seven wines by the glass from £3.

CHEF: Michael Wright   PROPRIETOR: Jeremy Mogford   OPEN: all week 12 to 2.30, 6 to 11
CLOSED: 25 and 26 Dec   MEALS: alc (main courses £10.50 to £19). Set L £12.50 (2 courses) to
£16, Set D £25.95   SERVICE: not inc, 10% for parties of 6 or more, card slips closed   CARDS:
Amex, Delta, MasterCard, Switch, Visa   DETAILS: 85 seats. 20 seats outside. Private parties: 85
main room. Car park. Vegetarian meals. Children's helpings. No smoking in dining room.
Wheelchair access (also WC). Music. Air-conditioned  £5

# La Gousse d'Ail ✳

268 Woodstock Road, Oxford OX2 7NW
TEL: (01865) 311936   FAX: (01865) 516613
EMAIL: info@lagoussedail.co.uk                    MODERN FRENCH
WEBSITE: www.lagoussedail.com                     £39–£125

*As the Guide went to press this restaurant closed.*

CHEF: Jonathan Wright   PROPRIETORS: Jayne and Jonathan Wright   OPEN: Tue to Sun L 12 to 2, Tue to Sat D 7 to 10.30   CLOSED: first 2 weeks Jan   MEALS: Set L £24 to £60, Set D £45 to £60   SERVICE: 10% (optional), card slips closed   CARDS: Delta, MasterCard, Switch, Visa   DETAILS: 75 seats. 35 seats outside. Private parties: 100 main room, 24 private room. Car park. Children's helpings. No smoking in dining room. Wheelchair access (also WC). No music. No mobile phones

## ▲ Parsonage Restaurant & Bar

1 Banbury Road, Oxford OX2 6NN
TEL: (01865) 310210   FAX: (01865) 311262              COOKING 3
EMAIL: info@oldparsonage-hotel.co.uk          ENGLISH/MEDITERRANEAN
WEBSITE: www.oldparsonage-hotel.co.uk                  £30–£47

'Established 1660' on the menu masthead refers to the original building, of which only the heavy oak door, and the stone fireplace in the entrance hall remain. The bar is modern but the restaurant wears 'olde Englishe attire' – oil paintings, and newspapers on poles – and has the comfort and warmth of a shooting lodge. The menu is a twenty-first century roll-call of global dishes that might feature gingered chicken cakes; monkfish and prawn green curry; or chargrilled quail with rösti, Savoy cabbage and bacon. Highest praise has gone to a 'light, moist and cheesy' twice-baked spinach and Parmesan soufflé; and to pan-fried scallops – 'barely cooked to near-perfection' – with coriander pesto. Simpler fare might take the form of rack of lamb with crushed new potatoes, or calf's liver and bacon with sage and onion mash. Approved desserts have included 'dense, luxurious, creamy New York cheesecake' and chocolate tart with a 'grown-up' bitter chocolate sorbet. Unrushed service is generally friendly and well-informed. The wine list is short but geographically diverse, with half the bottles under £20 and a dozen by the glass; but note that corkage for BYO is £10.

CHEF: Alison Watkins   PROPRIETOR: Jeremy Mogford   OPEN: all week 12 to 3 (12.30 to 3 Sun), 6 to 10.30   CLOSED: 23 to 27 Dec   MEALS: alc (main courses £10 to £14)   SERVICE: not inc
CARDS: Amex, Delta, Diners, MasterCard, Switch, Visa   DETAILS: 30 seats. 30 seats outside. Car park. Vegetarian meals. Children's helpings. No cigars/pipes in dining room. Music. Air-conditioned   ACCOMMODATION: 30 rooms, all with bath/shower. TV. Phone. B&B £130 to £200. Rooms for disabled. Baby facilities (*The Which? Hotel Guide*)

# Le Petit Blanc ❧✻

71–72 Walton Street, Oxford OX2 6AG
TEL: (01865) 510999   FAX: (01865) 510700                    | NEW CHEF |
EMAIL: oxford@lepetitblanc.co.uk                                   FRENCH
WEBSITE: www.lepetitblanc.co.uk                                  £24–£55

As the Guide went to press, the Oxford branch of this small chain became the third out of four (see entries, Cheltenham, Birmingham and Manchester) to get a last-minute change of chef. The shake-up has involved the appointment of Clive Fretwell, who used to cook at Le Manoir aux Quat' Saisons (see entry Great Milton), as over-all executive chef, and the standardising of the menus. These are tailored for speedy meals, lunch and early-evening deals, and for children, with all-day coffee and cakes available, plus a range of alcohol-, dairy-, gluten-, and nut-free menus. The rest takes in vegetarian and 'signature' dishes such as twice-baked Roquefort soufflé with pears and walnut dressing, and roast chicken breast with braised leeks and morel sauce, plus desserts such as lemon tart or chocolate fondant. A dozen wines by the glass are a useful part of the well-chosen, varietally arranged list that starts with a brace of French country wines at £11.

CHEF: Graham Corbett   PROPRIETORS: Raymond Blanc/Orient Express Hotels   OPEN: all week 11 to 11   CLOSED: 25 Dec   MEALS: alc (main courses £9.50 to £16). Set L and D 5.30 to 7 and 10 to 11 £12.50 (2 courses) to £15. Light L menu available 12 to 7   SERVICE: not inc, 10% for parties of 8 or more   CARDS: Amex, Delta, Diners, MasterCard, Switch, Visa   DETAILS: 135 seats. Private parties: 8 to 16 private rooms. Vegetarian meals. Children's helpings. No smoking in dining room. Wheelchair access (also WC). Music. No mobile phones. Air-conditioned

£   *means that it is possible to have a three-course meal, including coffee, half a bottle of house wine and service for £30 or less per person, at any time the restaurant is open, i.e. at dinner as well as lunch. It may be possible to spend considerably more than this, but by choosing carefully you should find £30 or less achievable.*

# Margot's ⚡✳

11 Duke Street, Padstow PL28 8AB
TEL: (01841) 533441
EMAIL: oliveradrian@hotmail.com
WEBSITE: www.margots.co.uk

COOKING **3**
MODERN BRITISH
£28–£47

Margot's is a cheerful, welcoming little place that puts on a happy face: 'even the loo is shared by males and females,' observed one reporter. Coiled lamps dangle from the ceiling, and there are framed pictures of the chef on the two-tone walls. This is just up the street from the harbour, so seafood is a big player on the menu. Fish soup has real depth of flavour, while spot-on timing is a feature of dishes such as mussels with ginger, coriander and coconut milk, and spanking-fresh fillet of turbot coated in sesame seeds with asparagus and a skilfully made chive butter sauce.

The kitchen also pleases carnivores and vegetarians with a warm salad of black pudding and bacon topped with a poached egg, rack of lamb on spring onion mash with another good sauce (this time red wine and rosemary), and a salad of roast aubergine, feta and cherry tomatoes. Meals end on a high note with perfectly textured lemon tart, or saffron-poached pears with shortbread. The short wine list is a well-chosen, reasonably priced slate with five house selections from £9.95 a bottle (£3.25 a glass).

CHEFS: Adrian Oliver and David Amaglo   PROPRIETORS: Adrian and Julie Oliver   OPEN: Wed to Sun 12 to 2, 7 to 9.30   CLOSED: 2 weeks Nov, Jan   MEALS: alc L (main courses £11 to £17). Set D £19.95 (2 courses) to £24.95   SERVICE: not inc   CARDS: Amex, Delta, MasterCard, Switch, Visa   DETAILS: 22 seats. Private parties: 22 main room. Vegetarian meals. Children's helpings. No smoking in dining room. Wheelchair access (not WC). Music. No mobile phones

## ▲ Rick Stein's Café ⚡✳

10 Middle Street, Padstow PL28 8AP
TEL: (01841) 532700   FAX: (01841) 532942
EMAIL: reservations@rickstein.com
WEBSITE: www.rickstein.com

NEW CHEF
GLOBAL/SEAFOOD
£28–£40

The café has acquired a new bar, a wall has been removed to make it all look bigger, and stainless steel, chrome, granite and wood are now in evidence alongside the white-painted wooden walls that help to make this a bright, airy dining room. The kitchen also acquired a new chef, just as the Guide went to press. Paul Harwood is no stranger to Rick Stein enterprises, having worked for the organisation for a number of years, and should have no difficulty turning his hand to Thai fishcakes with a sweet and sour dressing, gurnard with sage and garlic butter, or simply grilled sole. Straightforward desserts (chocolate pot, or lime posset) round things off, and a tiny, well-chosen list of wines strays over £20 only for champagne, and starts with house French white at £13.50 and Italian red at £15.95.

CHEF: Paul Harwood and Roy Brett (executive chef)   PROPRIETORS: Rick and Jill Stein   OPEN: Mon to Sat 12 to 2.30, 7 to 9.30   MEALS: alc (main courses L £6 to £8, D £10.50). Set D £19.50   SERVICE: not inc   CARDS: Delta, MasterCard, Switch, Visa   DETAILS: 40 seats. 10 seats outside.

Private parties: 16 private room. Vegetarian meals. Children's helpings. No smoking in dining room. Music  ACCOMMODATION: 3 rooms, all with bath/shower. TV. Phone. B&B £75 (double room) to £95. Baby facilities (*The Which? Hotel Guide*)

---

## ▲ St Petroc's Bistro ⭐

4 New Street, Padstow PL28 8EA

TEL: (01841) 532700   FAX: (01841) 532942

EMAIL: reservations@rickstein.com

WEBSITE: www.rickstein.com

COOKING 2
BISTRO
£40–£53

Up a short hill, away from the usually thronged harbour, this busy, hard-edged, smart but informal spin-off from the Seafood Restaurant (see following entry) is simply decorated, with wooden floors and modern pictures. Alistair Clive's easygoing, straightforward style of cooking suits the materials well, taking in deep-fried squid with aïoli, Thai mackerel salad, and a whole grilled lemon sole with sea salt and lemon. The enterprise is not entirely devoted to fish, however, and offers Cornish chicken with thyme, and steak-frîtes with béarnaise, by way of variety. Finish perhaps with baked chocolate mousse and clotted cream, or lemon posset with cranberry compote. Attentive and knowledgeable staff are also commended for their wine advice: a compact list of cannily chosen bottles keeps an eye on value, with prices starting at £10.75.

CHEFS: Alistair Clive and Roy Brett (executive chef)  PROPRIETORS: Rick and Jill Stein  OPEN: Tue to Sun 12 to 1.30, 7 to 9.30  CLOSED: 22 to 26 Dec  MEALS: alc (main courses £13.50 to £16.50)  SERVICE: not inc  CARDS: Delta, MasterCard, Switch, Visa  DETAILS: 50 seats. Children's helpings. No smoking in dining room. Music. Air-conditioned  ACCOMMODATION: 12 rooms, all with bath/shower. TV. Phone. B&B £100 to £160. Baby facilities (*The Which? Hotel Guide*)

---

## ▲ Seafood Restaurant 🍴

Riverside, Padstow PL28 8BY

TEL: (01841) 532700   FAX: (01841) 532942

EMAIL: reservations@rickstein.com

WEBSITE: www.rickstein.com

COOKING 6
SEAFOOD
£50–£100

Mirrors enlarge, and pictures enliven, this fresh, white-painted dining room. A new executive chef, Roy Brett, now oversees all three kitchens (see entries above for St Petroc's Bistro and Rick Stein's Café), plus the bakery and deli. This leaves Rick himself free to develop new recipes and source supplies. More fish now comes from dayboats; he has also managed to find elvers (to one reporter's delight), and might serve ormers (abalone) with cuttlefish, shiitake and enoki mushrooms.

The kitchen has no difficulty balancing innovation against the simple treatment that the best fish so often deserves. First courses tend to be dealt with more imaginatively; mussels, for example, stir-fried with black beans, garlic, ginger, coriander and spring onions is a well-rehearsed combination with a sense of integrity. Other dishes may be more straightforward: a well-rendered Dover sole meunière, served on or off the bone, perhaps, or a sizeable chunk of accurately timed crisp-skinned turbot fillet with excellent hollandaise.

For shellfish-lovers it's always Christmas here. An appetising starter of notably fresh and lightly cooked shellfish, served warm, has included mussels, oysters, langoustines, cockles, winkles, spider crab, razor clams and a large scallop, all drizzled with a mix of olive oil, lemon juice, garlic and parsley. Desserts can be plain (vanilla ice cream with a glass of Pedro Ximenez to pour over) or fancy (a triangle of light-textured, deep-flavoured, flourless chocolate cake with a pool of orange syrup and an orange sorbet). Service varies from relaxed to rushed depending on circumstances – 'at these prices, I want to linger' – and the wine list proves that Mr Stein knows a thing or two about wine. Tasting notes are spot-on and selections impeccable, from Austria to France to new-wave Italy and the New World. White wines, understandably, are favoured, but for those who want to pull the cork on a quality Bordeaux or an Italian red, there's plenty of scope there too. Eighteen house selections hover at about the £20 mark, offering some of the best value on the list. Prices start at £16 for vin de pays; 11 wines are available by the glass (£3.50 to £4.50).

CHEFS: Stéphane Delourme and Roy Brett (executive chef)   PROPRIETORS: Rick and Jill Stein   OPEN: all week 12 to 2 (1.30 low season), 7 to 10   CLOSED: 22 to 26 Dec, 31 Dec, 1 May   MEALS: alc (main courses £16.50 to £39)   SERVICE: not inc   CARDS: Delta, MasterCard, Switch, Visa   DETAILS: 109 seats. Private parties: 16 to 18 private rooms. Vegetarian meals. Children's helpings. No children under 3. No music. Air-conditioned   ACCOMMODATION: 35 rooms, all with bath/shower. TV. Phone. B&B £100 to £210. Baby facilities (*The Which? Hotel Guide*)

## PAINSWICK  Gloucestershire                             map 2

## ▲ Painswick Hotel ▐ ✱

Kemps Lane, Painswick GL6 6YB
TEL: (01452) 812160   FAX: (01452) 814059                   COOKING 5
EMAIL: reservations@painswickhotel.com                      BRITISH
WEBSITE: www.painswickhotel.com                             £28–£65

On a winding narrow lane in a village set on a steep hillside, this grey Cotswold-stone building, with its classical façade, is traditionally English, from the croquet lawn in the garden to the carved plaster ceiling in the bar. The dining room is well-to-do without being ostentatious, with stripped wood panelling and white linen.

Kevin Barron makes use of local materials, sourcing ingredients from the farmers' market in Stroud as well as from nearby shoots, while fish is delivered from Brixham. Bread, pasta, rolls and biscuits are all made on the premises. Home-smoked quail may appear as a starter in a large raviolo, accompanied by braised chicory and a roast quail breast, while home-cured salmon comes with cucumber pickle and crème fraîche. Main-course portions are generous: a beautifully textured marinated rump of Cotswold lamb served with chive mash, salsify and roast sweetbreads, for instance, or slow-cooked belly pork partnered with pea and bacon risotto, creamed celeriac and a caper gravy.

Proprietor Gareth Pugh's involvement in sourcing is such that he commissioned a local dairy farmer to make traditional Double Gloucester, which might appear on the cheeseboard alongside Sharpham and Exmoor Blue. Alternatively, consider the well-executed hot strawberry soufflé with strawberry compote and clotted cream ice cream. The atmosphere is polite and fairly formal, yet still relaxed and convivial, and service is well paced and observant. Wines are a pedigree collection from Burgundy and Bordeaux, with some snappy selections from Italy, Spain and the New World as well. There's a healthy assortment of half-bottles too. Six house wines sell for £13.75 to £17.50, and an eight-strong 'cellarman's choice' flags up a number of interesting styles.

CHEF: Kevin Barron   PROPRIETORS: Gareth and Helen Pugh   OPEN: all week 12 to 2, 7 to 9.30 MEALS: alc D (main courses £19 to £23.50). Set L Mon to Sat £14 (2 courses) to £17, Set L Sun £19.50, Set D £26 (2 courses) to £29.50.Light L available Mon to Sat   SERVICE: not inc, card slips closed   CARDS: Amex, Delta, MasterCard, Switch, Visa   DETAILS: 30 seats. 20 seats outside. Private parties: 60 main room, 2 to 18 private rooms. Car park. Vegetarian meals. Children's helpings. No smoking in dining room. Occasional music   ACCOMMODATION: 19 rooms, all with bath/shower. TV. Phone. B&B £75 to £190. Baby facilities  (£5)

## PAULERSPURY Northamptonshire                                      map 5

## ▲ Vine House ⅍✷

| | |
|---|---|
| 100 High Street, Paulerspury NN12 7NA | COOKING 3 |
| TEL: (01327) 811267   FAX: (01327) 811309 | ENGLISH-PLUS |
| off A5, 2m SE of Towcester | £41–£49 |

The Springetts' 300-year-old cottage of local limestone continues to run pleasingly as a modest country restaurant with six bedrooms attached. Marcus cooks, and offers three-course lunches and dinners, the same price for each. The style is 'traditional English with a modern twist', according to the owners, which might translate into local rabbit and Tamworth pork pâté with home-made winter walnut chutney, or marinated aubergine with cannellini beans and a sweet roast garlic dressing. Mains show the same diversity, ranging from roast saddle of local venison with smoked bacon, braised cabbage and a port and cep sauce, to fillet of sea bass with mash and a basil and red pepper butter sauce. To finish, farmhouse cheeses sit alongside desserts such as toffee banana mousse with passion-fruit sauce and toasted sesame seeds. Vegetarians are asked to give 24 hours' notice of their requirements. Julie and her small team set out to please customers 'by constant attention', noted one visitor. The wine list is a predominantly French slate, opening with house wines from £11.25 a bottle (£2.70 a glass).

CHEF: Marcus Springett   PROPRIETORS: Marcus and Julie Springett   OPEN: Thur and Fri L 12.30 to 1.45, Mon to Sat D 7 to 9   MEALS: Set L and D £28.95   SERVICE: not inc   CARDS: MasterCard, Visa   DETAILS: 45 seats. Private parties: 45 main room. Car park. Children' helpings. No smoking in dining room. Wheelchair access (not WC). No music   ACCOMMODATION: 6 rooms, all with bath/shower. TV. Phone. B&B £49 to £79 (The Which? Hotel Guide)  (£5)

## PAXFORD Gloucestershire                                           map 5

## ▲ Churchill Arms £

| | |
|---|---|
| Paxford GL55 6XH | |
| TEL: (01386) 594000   FAX: (01386) 594005 | COOKING 4 |
| EMAIL: info@thechurchillarms.com | MODERN EUROPEAN |
| WEBSITE: www.thechurchillarms.com | £23–£46 |

This old pub, built of honey-coloured Cotswold stone, is diagonally opposite the village church. Outside are a few trestle tables front and back, while the open-plan interior is plain, with bare wooden floors, painted tongue-and-groove walls and sepia prints. The constituency is a mix of locals and people who have made a detour to come here, and the now familiar gastro-pub format remains true to its roots: dishes and wines are chalked up on blackboards, food and drinks are ordered and paid for at the bar and then delivered to tables. 'Brilliant' flavour combinations, as in breast of guinea fowl with a saffron, sage and Parmesan risotto, are a trade mark. Medallions of venison may come with 'delectable' saffron mash, while a starter salad of duck may be served with grapefruit and fennel. For dessert, sticky toffee pudding may turn up beside polenta and almond cake. Wines tend towards the New World, and prices of virtually all are below £20. Laudably, most are sold by the glass (£2.45 to £4.90). Bottle prices start at £9.95.

CHEF: Ivan Reid   PROPRIETORS: Sonya and Leo Brooke-Little   OPEN: all week 12 to 2, 7 to 9 MEALS: alc (main courses £7.50 to £15)   SERVICE: not inc   CARDS: Delta, MasterCard, Switch, Visa   DETAILS: 60 seats. 60 seats outside. Vegetarian meals. Wheelchair access (not WC). No music   ACCOMMODATION: 4 rooms, all with bath/shower. TV. Phone. B&B £40 to £70 (*The Which? Hotel Guide*)

---

## PENZANCE Cornwall                                                    map 1

# Abbey Restaurant 🍴✳                                 [NEW ENTRY]

Abbey Street, Penzance TR18 4AR
TEL/FAX: (01736) 330680                                              COOKING 3
EMAIL: info@theabbeyonline.com                               MODERN EUROPEAN
WEBSITE: www.theabbeyonline.com                                      £23–£54

In a narrow lane near the harbour, next to the unrelated Abbey Hotel, is this tastefully refurbished former nightclub, now a popular restaurant run in a very hands-on way by a husband-and-wife team. A video screen in the bar area gives a view of Ben Tunnicliffe at work in the kitchen, while the light and airy dining room has views over the harbour. 'Simple, modern food' is what Ben aims for, using local materials that include fish from Newlyn market and meat from a long-established local butcher. The daily-changing menus offer good choice and plenty of variety: crisp-fried squid with chorizo and cucumber chutney, alongside grilled aubergine with oven-dried tomatoes and marinated feta among starters, for example, as well as classics such as 'the best tuna niçoise I have had for a long time'. For main courses, there may be tender, well-flavoured pork fillet with grilled polenta, caramelised shallots and salsa verde, or perhaps beef fillet with roasted peppers and anchovy compote. Finish perhaps with gooseberry soufflé, or a light, nutty chocolate brownie with marmalade ice cream. Wines are a well-chosen global selection including some Cornish examples. House French is £9.50, Australian £10.50.

CHEF: Ben Tunnicliffe   PROPRIETORS: Ben and Kinga Tunnicliffe   OPEN: Tue to Sat 12 to 2, 7 to 10 MEALS: alc (main courses L £7.50 to £15, D £10 to £20)   SERVICE: not inc   CARDS: Delta, Diners, MasterCard, Switch, Visa   DETAILS: 26 seats. Private parties: 22 main room. Vegetarian meals. Children's helpings. No children at D. No smoking in dining room. Music. No mobile phones. Air-conditioned  (£5)

---

*The Guide's longest-serving restaurants are listed near the front of the book.*

---

# Harris's ✽✻

46 New Street, Penzance TR18 2LZ
TEL: (01736) 364408
EMAIL: harriss.restaurant@lineone.net

COOKING 3
ANGLO-FRENCH/SEAFOOD
£40–£64

For some, the dining room is simply pink; others have evocatively described the colour as 'cream of tomato soup' or even 'burnt lobster'. Whatever the case, the ubiquitous rosy hues lend a warmth to Roger and Anne Harris's backstreet fish restaurant, which celebrated its thirtieth anniversary in 2002. Cooking is largely traditional and not over-ambitious, but 'what they do, they do well'. Parsnip and pear soup garnished with parsnip crisps, and a generous salad of smoked duck have been well-received starters. Main courses are likely to include Dover sole grilled with chive butter, or something more modern such as roast cod with ginger and lime mash and a lime and olive oil dressing, while non-fish options have run to noisettes of Cornish lamb on roast fennel with rosemary jus. Finish with an old favourite, such as treacle tart or crème brûlée; local cheeses offer an alternative. Service has been commended for its attention to detail. A preference for France shows up on the well-chosen wine list, where there is plenty of choice under £20 and a page of half-bottles. House selections start at £12.50.

CHEF: Roger Harris PROPRIETORS: Roger and Anne Harris OPEN: Tue to Sat and bank hol Suns L 12 to 2, D (inc Mon in summer) from 7 CLOSED: 3 weeks winter, 25 and 26 Dec, 1 Jan MEALS: alc (main courses £15 to £24.50). Light L menu available SERVICE: 10%, card slips closed CARDS: Amex, MasterCard, Switch, Visa DETAILS: 40 seats. Private parties: 20 main room, 20 private room. No smoking in 1 dining room. Music. No mobile phones

# ▲ Summer House

**NEW ENTRY**

Cornwall Terrace, Penzance TR18 4HL
TEL: (01736) 363744 FAX: (01736) 360959
EMAIL: summerhouse@dial.pipex.com
WEBSITE: www.summerhouse-cornwall.com

COOKING 2
MEDITERRANEAN
£33–£40

Ring the doorbell to get into this small, hexagonal, Grade II listed hotel, found down a side street close to the seafront. It consists of an elegant lounge with antique furniture, a courtyard-style garden for al fresco eating and drinking, and a small, light-yellow dining room. Its Mediterranean colours anticipate a menu that might take in linguine with pesto, risotto al Valpolicella, or cod livornese, and seafood is an understandable strength. Fresh-tasting, lightly cooked scallops come with samphire; salmon is baked and served cold with asparagus as a starter; and a moist brill fillet gets a light langoustine sauce.

Rack of lamb with a Provençal-inspired mustard and herb crust is typical of the meat output, while desserts have included a warm apple tart with crème Chantilly, and a spongeless tiramisù made with Tia Maria-flavoured mascarpone, layered with a mousse powerfully infused with espresso. Service is friendly and efficient, with Ciro Zaino much in evidence, and an all-Italian, 40-bottle wine list doesn't stint on quality. House Montepulciano d'Abruzzo and Marche Trebbiano are £12.

CHEF: Ciro Zaino   PROPRIETORS: Ciro and Linda Zaino   OPEN: Mon to Sat D only 7.30 to 9 (7 to 9.45 midsummer)   MEALS: Set D £22.50   SERVICE: 10%   CARDS: Delta, MasterCard, Switch, Visa   DETAILS: 22 seats. 20 seats outside. Private parties: 25 main room. No smoking before 10pm. Music   ACCOMMODATION: 5 rooms, all with bath/shower. TV. B&B £60 to £85. No children under 13 (*The Which? Hotel Guide*)

## PETERSFIELD Hampshire                                                    map 2

# JSW ▮

1–3 Heath Road, Petersfield GU31 4JE                              COOKING **5**
TEL: (01730) 262030                                              MODERN BRITISH
                                                                       £32–£51

Although JSW's initials are etched into the windows of this long, two-tiered restaurant, it is an unpretentious place, elegantly yet simply decorated. The confidence and expertise of the husband-and-wife team (with little in the way of assistance) come through loud and clear, from the friendly, well-organised front-of-house to the kitchen's concise, contemporary style of cooking. Local materials surface in the shape of chicken, pork and South Downs lamb, while seasonal items run to hare, grouse, grey-leg partridge, mallard, woodcock, sea trout and wild mushrooms.

Choice is sensibly limited to four options at each stage, and straightforward main courses, such as roast cod with crab risotto, or loin of veal with truffled mash, add to the sense of focus and precision. First courses might play on the theme of smoked fish and pasta (smoked eel lasagne, or an open ravioli of smoked haddock), or offer a pigeon and endive tarte Tatin with bacon. Among desserts, rhubarb feuillantine has drawn applause, or there may be an apple and cinnamon beignet. Since the last edition the wine list has been expanded substantially. South Africa is a newcomer, as are big names such as (in Italy) Angelo Gaja and a number of Super Tuscans. Australia and Bordeaux have also been upgraded, as have some of the prices. Nonetheless, there's much here to attract, with a scattering of well-chosen wines under £20, and half-bottles, ports and dessert wines particularly strong. Six wines by the glass range from £3.50 to £4.50.

CHEF/PROPRIETOR: Jake Watkins   OPEN: Tue to Sat 12 to 1.30, 7 to 10   CLOSED: 2 weeks Jan, 2 weeks Aug   MEALS: Set L £15 (2 courses) to £19.50, Set D £25 (2 courses) to £29.50   SERVICE: not inc   CARDS: Delta, MasterCard, Switch, Visa   DETAILS: 22 seats. Private parties: 28 main room. Vegetarian meals. Wheelchair access (not WC). No music. No mobile phones

---

*Some restaurants leave credit card slips open even though they also make a fixed (or 'optional') service charge. The Guide strongly disapproves of this practice as it may result in consumers unknowingly paying twice for service. A list of restaurants that have told us they do this, or that were found by our inspectors to do so, can be found at the front of the book.*

*Report forms are at the back of the book; write a letter if you prefer; or email us at goodfoodguide@which.net*

---

## PETER TAVY  Devon

map 1

# Peter Tavy Inn ⅙ £

Peter Tavy PL19 9NN
TEL: (01822) 810348  FAX: (01822) 810835
EMAIL: peter.tavy@virgin.net
off A386 Tavistock to Okehampton road, 2m NE
of Tavistock

COOKING 1
MODERN EUROPEAN
£19–£39

Down a country lane by the village church, this down-to-earth fifteenth-century hostelry really looks the part, although the interior hasn't been over-quaintified. In a setting of beams and flagstones you can sample real ales and a workmanlike version of honest pub cooking. Menus are written on blackboards: simple stuff for lunch, a touch more elaboration in the evening. Much of the repertoire has a cosmopolitan feel, be it mozzarella balls with crispy bacon and a snappy balsamic dressing, or Thai tiger prawn stir-fry, although more robust dishes such as game casserole with a Stilton dumpling also win votes. Round things off with an old favourite in the sticky toffee pudding mould. 'Smashing' staff do a grand job: 'the landlord played with our baby for 20 minutes while we ate in peace', reported one grateful couple. An affordable list of around three dozen wines starts at £8 and includes seven by the glass (from £2.20).

CHEF: Steve Byrne  PROPRIETORS: Graeme and Karen Sim  OPEN: all week 12 to 2, 7 (6.30 Fri and Sat) to 9  CLOSED: 25 Dec and D 31 Dec  MEALS: alc (main courses L £5.50 £10, D £7 to £16) SERVICE: not inc, card slips closed  CARDS: Delta, MasterCard, Switch, Visa  DETAILS: 70 seats. 100 seats outside. Private parties: 45 main room. Car park. Vegetarian meals. No children in bar areas. Children's helpings. No smoking in 1 dining room. Music  (£5)

## PETWORTH  West Sussex

map 3

# Soanes ⅙

Grove Lane, Petworth GU28 0HY
TEL/FAX: (01798) 343659
WEBSITE: www.soanes.co.uk

COOKING 2
MODERN BRITISH
£46–£61

Set in acres of open fields, this old grey-stone farmhouse is a hive of industry. Soanes' boxed and bottled luxuries, from chocolates to flavoured vinegars, are for sale throughout: in the modern conservatory extension, and in the spacious and civilised (no music, no smoking) dining room, with its combination of traditional and artistic décor. The kitchen goes in for some ambitious cooking, taking in a poached fillet of smoked haddock with bubble and squeak, a poached egg and hollandaise (a starter, this), and including a few old-fashioned touches: a mid-meal sorbet, and dishes that are 'finished with' their dressing or sauce.

Although the food can be fussy, extras do not always enhance the item they are garnishing, and some essential skills, such as soufflé-making, can be below par. On the plus side some first-class raw materials are deployed: for example, accurately roasted loin of venison (pink, as requested), served with crispy shreds of Savoy cabbage, carrot and swede batons, rocket leaves, grilled bacon, toasted hazelnut, a pitted prune, a poached pear, sweet potato, ordinary potato, and a pool of dark, opaque sauce made with cognac. Pacing can be brisk, and wines on the French-dominated list are a bit pricey, although house Chilean varietals are £14.

CHEFS: Gregory and Allison Laskey  PROPRIETORS: Gregory and Allison Laskey, and Gillian St Quintin  OPEN: Tue to Sat D only 7 to 9.30; also Sun L once every 3 weeks  CLOSED: 2 weeks beginning Jan  MEALS: alc (main courses £17 to £20)  SERVICE: not inc  CARDS: Delta, MasterCard, Switch, Visa  DETAILS: 26 seats. Private parties: 38 main room. Car park. Vegetarian meals. Children's helpings. No children under 7 at D. No smoking in dining room. Wheelchair access (not WC). No music. No mobile phones. Air-conditioned

## PLYMOUTH Devon                                                    map 1

# Chez Nous ▼

13 Frankfort Gate, Plymouth PL1 1QA                        COOKING 4
TEL/FAX: (01752) 266793                                         FRENCH
                                                              £48–£58

A discreet, tidy, blue and white frontage helps first-time visitors pick out this evocative Gallic restaurant from more clamorous neighbouring shops. Adverts for Pernod and Gauloises, menus from Moulin des Mougins, and Art Nouveau prints give a clear indication where Jacques Marchal is coming from, indeed has been coming from for the past 20-odd years. He makes full use of his close proximity to the covered market – fish comes from a stall just three minutes' walk away – and sources meat, poultry and game from local butchers. Treatments, though, are as French as soupe à l'oignon, pigeon and foie gras en gelée, and porc aux pruneaux. A catalogue of successes takes in crab salad with orange, calmars provençale, and duck breast with Puy lentils. 'There is not a bad dish to be had,' according to one regular visitor, who has also enjoyed venison (from Hatherleigh in north Devon), the cheeseboard, and a black and white chocolate dessert.

Wines are suitably French-accented, with some very good Bordeaux and Burgundy (notably Chablis) making up most of the list, and a smattering of wines from 'autres pays' (Australia, New Zealand, South Africa, Italy and Spain among them) thrown in. Prices are fair, there's a good selection of half-bottles, and six house wines are all £12.50. Note that the restaurant is no longer open for lunch.

CHEF: Jacques Marchal  PROPRIETORS: Jacques and Suzanne Marchal  OPEN: Tue to Fri D only 7 to 10.30  MEALS: Set D £37.50  SERVICE: not inc  CARDS: Amex, Delta, Diners, MasterCard, Switch, Visa  DETAILS: 28 seats. Private parties: 28 main room. No children under 12. Wheelchair access (not WC). Music

---

*All entries in the Guide are re-researched and rewritten every year, not least because restaurant standards fluctuate. Don't rely on an out-of-date Guide.*

*The text of entries is based on unsolicited reports sent in by readers, backed up by inspections conducted anonymously. The factual details under the text are from questionnaires the Guide sends to all restaurants that feature in the book.*

## PONTELAND Northumberland    map 10

# Café 21  £

35 The Broadway, Darras Hall,
Ponteland NE20 9PW
TEL/FAX: (01661) 820357

NEW CHEF
MODERN EUROPEAN
£25–£52

News of a new chef reached the Guide too late for us to secure any feedback, although the lively style of broadly European cooking looks set to remain. Bright-sounding flavours are the norm, taking in a plate of chillied, wok-fried scallops, prawns and calamari, followed by chargrilled chicken breast with lemon couscous. There are simple crowd pleasers too, in the form of fishcakes with parsley cream, sirloin steak with chips and salad, and sticky toffee pudding with butterscotch sauce. A short, varied wine list, mostly under £20, starts with house Duboeuf (red and white) at £11.

CHEF: David Ward   PROPRIETOR: Terence Laybourne   OPEN: Sat L 12 to 2, Mon to Sat D 5.30 to 10.30   CLOSED: Christmas, bank hols   MEALS: alc (main courses £8.50 to £18.50)   SERVICE: not inc   CARDS: Amex, Delta, Diners, MasterCard, Switch, Visa   DETAILS: 70 seats. Private parties: 70 main room. Car park. Vegetarian meals. Children's helpings. No-smoking area. No pipes. Wheelchair access (also WC). Music

## POOLE Dorset    map 2

# ▲ Mansion House ♥ ⅚✖

Thames Street, Poole BH15 1JN
TEL: (01202) 685666   FAX: (01202) 665709
EMAIL: enquiries@themansionhouse.co.uk
WEBSITE: www.themansionhouse.co.uk

COOKING 3
MODERN BRITISH
£27–£53

An elegant sweeping staircase sets the tone for this gracious hotel just off Poole Quay. It has been a fixture of the local scene for many years and manages to sustain a 'happy balance of quality food, informal but good and helpful service and attractive ambience', according to one reporter who has frequented the place for more than a decade.

Gerry Godden's cooking is in tune with the times, delivering a dish of Chinese-style beef slices on a noodle and watercress salad, or tempura of tiger prawns with mango salsa and chilli jam. In more robust European vein, there might be lamb and black pudding sausage with lentils, or peppered ribeye steak. All of this relies on good raw materials: fish from the Poole boats, game from the New Forest, organic vegetables, and West Country cheeses. Desserts are mostly classics (rhubarb and custard vacherin, bread-and-butter pudding) and none the worse for that. The lengthy, well-annotated wine list is sensibly divided into three sections: house recommendations, good value, and some fine wines to top things off. Carefully chosen, they offer plenty of interest from both Old World and New. House selections start at £12.95 for whites and reds from Catalonia.

CHEF: Gerry Godden   PROPRIETORS: Jackie and Gerry Godden   OPEN: Sun to Fri L 12 to 2, Mon to Sat and bank hol Sun D 7 to 9.30   MEALS: alc L exc Sun (main courses £9 to £10). Set L Sun £18.50, Set D £20.75 (2 courses) to £29   SERVICE: not inc   CARDS: Amex, Delta, Diners,

MasterCard, Switch, Visa  DETAILS: 85 seats. Private parties: 100 main room, 14 to 36 private rooms. Car park. Vegetarian meals. Children's helpings. Under-5s must eat at 7pm at D. No smoking in 1 dining room. Occasional music. Air-conditioned  ACCOMMODATION: 32 rooms, all with bath/shower. TV. Phone. B&B £70 to £120. Baby facilities (*The Which? Hotel Guide*) (£5)

## PORLOCK WEIR  Somerset                                                    map 1

# ▲ Andrew's on the Weir  ♥ ✸✕

Porlock Weir TA24 8PB
TEL: (01643) 863300   FAX: (01643) 863311                      COOKING 5
EMAIL: information@andrewsontheweir.co.uk          MODERN ENGLISH/EUROPEAN
WEBSITE: www.andrewsontheweir.co.uk                          £29–£54x

A large, cream-coloured Victorian villa sits on a low rise near Porlock harbour. Inside are voluminous swags, a moulded dado of Chinese design and huge log sculptures; if all this seems a bit much, bay-windows in bar and dining-room offer calming views of the attractive garden and the sea.

Menus teem with West Country produce: fish from Porlock and Minehead, game from Taunton, smoked products from a fine Bristol smokehouse. The style is highly modish. Smoked Exmoor lamb plumps out a first-course ravioli on steamed mange-tout in a garlic velouté, while a cabbage-wrapped gâteau of salmon and sole comes in a casserole of mussels and clams. Multi-layered dishes can create effects of substantial richness: as in Ruby Devon beef fillet, for example, partnered with braised oxtail, and served on truffled creamed parsnips and cooking juices dosed with Madeira. Similarly, vegetarians might go from a warm goats' cheese pithiviers on a salad of plum tomatoes and basil, to truffled-up wild mushroom risotto. For those with room, a délice in three shades of chocolate comes with an orange sorbet and Grand Marnier sauce; alternatives include a savoury (perhaps a cheese soufflé with mustard dressing), or there is a full, elaborately annotated cheese menu. The highlight of the short wine list, arranged by style, is five vintages of Penfolds Grange (£235–£275 a bottle – under 'heavyweight reds'), but other prices are much less frightening. Seven house wines are £10.25–£12.50 a bottle (£3.10–£5.50 a glass).

CHEF: Andrew Dixon  PROPRIETORS: Andrew Dixon and Rodney Sens  OPEN: Tue to Sun L 12 to 2.30, Tue to Sat D 7 to 9.30  CLOSED: Jan  MEALS: alc D (main courses £18). Set L and D Tue to Thu £10.50 (2 courses) to £17  SERVICE: not inc  CARDS: Amex, Delta, MasterCard, Switch, Visa  DETAILS: 35 seats. Private parties: 25 main room, 10 private room. Car park. Vegetarian meals. No children under 12. No smoking in dining room. Wheelchair access (not WC). Music. No mobile phones  ACCOMMODATION: 5 rooms, all with bath/shower. TV. B&B £45 to £100. No children under 12 (*The Which? Hotel Guide*) (£5)

*The 2004 Guide will be published before Christmas 2003. Reports on meals are most welcome at any time of the year, but are particularly valuable in the spring (no later than June). Send them to* The Good Food Guide, *FREEPOST, 2 Marylebone Road, London NW1 4DF. Or email your report to* goodfoodguide@which.net

## PORTHLEVEN Cornwall | map 1

## ▲ Critchards ⁙

Harbourside, Porthleven TR13 9JA
TEL: (01326) 562407   FAX: (01326) 564444
EMAIL: stevecritchard@aol.com
WEBSITE: www.critchards.com

COOKING 1
SEAFOOD
£31–£57

This 300-year-old converted mill house by the harbour does many people very nicely, as our postbag attests. Old-fashioned, country-pub décor adorns the interior, but the cooking is by no means backward-looking, using Far Eastern seasonings to good effect, and offering deep-fried squid with garlic dip, or goats' cheese and apple tartlet with crispy bacon dressing to start, and maybe vanilla pannacotta with red berries to finish. It's the seafood cookery in between that attracts people, though: crab and ginger filo bake with fresh tomato and coriander sauce, Dover sole with a strong langoustine sauce, or perhaps an Indian treatment for monkfish and prawns served with basmati rice and raita. (There's a vegetarian menu, and pork fillet, or fillet steak, for carnivores.) Service is 'friendly and efficient'. The shortish wine list is 50% French (including house wines at £12.95); the other 50 per cent includes a Cornish white and a couple of Californian organics.

CHEF: Jo Critchard   PROPRIETORS: Steve and Jo Critchard   OPEN: Mon to Sat D only 6.30 to 9.30
MEALS: alc (main courses £9 to £20)   SERVICE: not inc, card slips closed   CARDS: MasterCard,
Switch, Visa   DETAILS: 44 seats. Vegetarian meals. Children's helpings. No children under 6. No
smoking. Music   ACCOMMODATION: 2 rooms, both with bath/shower. TV. B&B £50 to £60. No
children under 6  £5

## PORTREATH Cornwall | map 1

## Tabb's ⁙

Tregea Terrace, Portreath TR16 4LD
TEL: (01209) 842488

COOKING 2
MODERN BRITISH-PLUS
£23–£53

Portreath may not be Cornwall's most picturesque seaside village, but it does have a beach, a small harbour, and this small but enterprising restaurant whose stone-walled dining room lends it a pleasingly rustic air. Given its location, seafood (from Newlyn market) is an understandable preoccupation, taking in anything from sardines with tapénade and chilli, via scallops with lemon grass and ginger, to grilled turbot fillet with sesame seed and onion sauce. Otherwise there might be rabbit, wild pigeon, or pan-fried sirloin steak. Vegetables are organic, and include some interesting combinations: stir-fried spring greens with cumin seeds, and diced baked potatoes with tomatoes and horseradish. Desserts might run to steamed black treacle pudding, or lemon and honeycomb ice cream, and chocolate lovers are indulged with chocolate marquise, chocolate and cardamom ice cream, and handmade chocolates to accompany coffee. A straightforward roving wine list stays mostly under £20 and starts with a couple of French country wines at £9.95.

CHEF: Nigel Tabb   PROPRIETORS: Melanie and Nigel Tabb   OPEN: Sun L 12.15 to 1.45, Wed to Mon D 7 to 9   CLOSED: 2 weeks Nov, 2 weeks Jan   MEALS: alc D (main courses £11.50 to £20). Set L Sun £13.50, Set D £16.50   SERVICE: not inc, card slips closed   CARDS: Delta, MasterCard, Switch, Visa   DETAILS: 30 seats. 4 seats outside. Private parties: 35 main room. Vegetarian meals. Children's helpings. No smoking in dining room. Wheelchair access (not WC). Music  £5

## POULTON-LE-FYLDE Lancashire                              map 8

# ▲ River House

Skippool Creek, Thornton-Le-Fylde, Poulton-le-
Fylde FY5 5LF
TEL: (01253) 883497   FAX: (01253) 892083
EMAIL: enquiries@theriverhouse.org.uk
WEBSITE: www.theriverhouse.org.uk                          COOKING 4
from roundabout junction of A585 and B5412                 FRENCH-PLUS
follow signs to Skippool Creek                             £34–£60

'Idiosyncratic is an understatement,' thought one reporter, without specifying how far beyond the pale he thought it went. Victorian fittings and furnishings lend charm to the setting, and tables are decently spaced in the pleasant dining room, while menus continue in much the same vein as they have done for nearly half a century. Soufflé suissesse is one of many long-stayers among starters; there may also be salmon in white wine and cream sauce, or fusilli pasta in Mediterranean sauce with 'tomato, garlic and things' (according to the menu). Bill Scott has dispensed with the practice of allowing diners to choose the sauce to go with their main course, instead trusting his own judgement, finely honed over the years. It may be safe and traditional, but there is no denying the classic appeal of rare roast venison with port and blueberry sauce, chateaubriand with béarnaise, or baked mixed seafood in a herby sauce; and the strength of the food lies in fine ingredients cooked with care. Finish with old-fashioned hot chocolate pudding, or crème brûlée. Wines are chiefly French but other countries are fairly represented; house wines are £12.50 a bottle, £3.50 a glass.

CHEF/PROPRIETOR: Bill Scott   OPEN: Mon to Sat 12 to 2, 7.30 to 9.30   CLOSED: 25 and 26 Dec, 1 Jan   MEALS: alc (main courses £16 to £22). Set L and D £25   SERVICE: not inc   CARDS: Delta, MasterCard, Switch, Visa   DETAILS: 40 seats. Private parties: 40 main room. Car park. Vegetarian meals. No children under 7. Music   ACCOMMODATION: 4 rooms, all with bath/shower. TV. Phone. B&B £70 to £90 (*The Which? Hotel Guide*)  £5

---

*'At the table of six nearest us were three couples ... , one of whom had a very high opinion of his own wit and spoke loudly and often enough to share it with the rest of us. His wit was of the racist and chauvinist school. I was glad to see he had ordered the dried-up duck.'*
(On eating in Hampshire)

🍾 *denotes an outstanding wine cellar;* 🍷 *denotes a good wine list, worth travelling for.*

# ▲ White House

New Road, Prestbury SK10 4DG
TEL: (01625) 829376   FAX: (01625) 828627
EMAIL: info@thewhitehouse.uk.com           COOKING 2
WEBSITE: www.thewhitehouse.uk.com      MODERN BRITISH
on A538, 4m N of Macclesfield            £27–£67

The hotel occupies a Georgian manor house in 'Manchester's poshest dormitory village', while the restaurant (once a farmhouse) is some five minutes' walk away. The original incumbents would not recognise the interior now, with its beams in limed wood, handsome stone fireplace and a conservatory tacked on at the back.

Ryland Wakeham's wide-ranging cooking matches the contemporary look of the place: although some of it is 'pedestrian', much is bright and professionally executed. A starter of seared scallops with peeled broad beans and an orange, vanilla and cardamom sauce is typical of his ambitious outlook, and the exotic approach continues with Thai chicken breast with chilli jam and a timbale of coconut-scented rice. There are also restyled old favourites such as calf's liver with Wilmslow smoked bacon, mash and a sage jus, and 'Mr Pugh's suckling pig' is apparently a winner, served with roast winter root vegetables. Some dishes (whole grilled Dover sole with sea salt and lime, for example) are highlighted as low-fat 'spa cuisine', while desserts bump up the calories with the likes of chocolate samosas with banana sorbet. The list of around 50 wines covers a lot of territory. House wines are £13.95, and ten are available by the glass.

CHEFS: Ryland Wakeham and Mark Cunniffe  PROPRIETORS: Mr and Mrs Ryland Wakeham, and Judith Wakeham  OPEN: Tue to Sun L 12 to 2, Mon to Sat D 7 to 10  CLOSED: 25 Dec  MEALS: alc exc Sun L (main courses £11.50 to £18). Set L Tue to Sun £14.50, Set D Mon to Fri £15.95 (2 courses) to £18.95. Bar menu available Tue to Sat L  SERVICE: not inc, card slips closed  CARDS: Amex, Delta, Diners, MasterCard, Switch, Visa  DETAILS: 75 seats. 12 seats outside. Private parties: 28 main room, 8 to 40 private rooms. Car park. Vegetarian meals. Children's helpings. No smoking in dining room before 2pm and 10pm. Wheelchair access (not WC). Music ACCOMMODATION: 11 rooms, all with bath/shower. TV. Phone. Room only £40 to £120. No children under 10

# Simply Heathcotes ⁵⁄✳

23 Winckley Square, Preston PR1 3JJ
TEL: (01772) 252732   FAX: (01772) 203433        COOKING 3
EMAIL: preston@simplyheathcotes.co.uk         BRASSERIE
WEBSITE: www.heathcotes.co.uk            £23–£49

This converted Georgian terraced property is divided into two: a basement café-bar serving snacks, and a large, airy, plainly decorated dining room with clean lines, natural wood veneers and a relaxed feel. All branches (see entries, Manchester, Liverpool and Leeds) share a similar quarterly-changing menu, which is supplemented by daily specials. The food is not too ambitious, and the kitchen more than capably does what it sets out to do, judging by the clearly defined flavours of a terrine of artichoke and wild mushrooms, bound together with savoury ricotta and edged with vivid green leeks.

Ideas range from black pudding with crushed potatoes and baked beans, via goats' cheese hash brown with mustard butter, to good-quality sea bass fillet with herb risotto and plum tomato fritters. Goosnargh chicken is a stalwart, its breast perhaps served with new potatoes, oyster mushrooms and baby leeks. Side orders of vegetables might include cauliflower hollandaise, and ribbons of spring cabbage, while among desserts Malteser parfait with malted chocolate sauce has been declared a winner. Around 40 wines (plus champagnes and a few special bottles) are tailored to the job, with good choice under £20, starting with house French at £12.

CHEF: Matt Nugent   PROPRIETOR: Paul Heathcote   OPEN: Sun 12 to 3, 6 to 9.30, Mon to Sat 12 to 2.30, 7 to 10 (6 to 10.30 Fri and Sat)   CLOSED: 25 and 26 Dec, bank hol Mons   MEALS: alc (main courses £10 to £15). Set L and D 7 to 8 (6 to 7 Sat, 6 to 9.30 Sun) £11.50 (2 courses) to £13.50   SERVICE: 10% (optional), card slips closed   CARDS: Amex, Delta, Diners, MasterCard, Switch, Visa   DETAILS: 80 seats. Private parties: 60 brasserie, 70 bistro. Vegetarian meals. Children's helpings. No smoking in dining room. Wheelchair access (not WC). Occasional music. Air-conditioned

## RAMSBOTTOM  Greater Manchester                                map 8

# Ramsons ⅝✳ £

18 Market Place, Ramsbottom BL0 9HT
TEL: (01706) 825070   FAX: (01706) 822005
EMAIL: chris@ramsons.org.uk
off A56/M66, 4m N of Bury

COOKING 4
ITALIAN
£21–£53

Although still occupying a couple of terraced cottages at the northern end of the village, Ramsons continues to evolve. Refurbishment has involved not just renovation of the church pews, but also the introduction of hand-printed fabrics, including an eight-foot-high 'Tree of Life', in recognition of the chef's cultural background in the Maldives. A new kitchen is also planned, courtesy of a grateful customer, but the indebtedness to Italy remains uppermost: in the Enoteca, Caffetteria e Bar (in the basement) and in the espousal of the aims of the Slow Food movement, which originated in Rome in opposition to fast food.

Expect salads, plates of cold meats and variously topped bruschette in the basement, and more substantial fare in the ground-floor dining room: perhaps seared Shetland scallops with stir-fried chard and a saffron sauce, or breast of corn-fed chicken with gratin potatoes and Calvados sauce. Vegetarian items run from truffled fontina crostini with roast San Marzano tomato, to porcini and wild rocket risotto, while desserts might take in hot chocolate soufflé with clotted cream ice cream. Sadly, as Chris Johnson writes, 'Our lovely cellar of wines has been largely sold to pay for our refurbishment.' What remains are just over 30 'house wines', all Italian, eight of which are available by the glass. Bottle prices start at £9.95.

CHEF: Abdullah Naseem   PROPRIETORS: Ros Hunter and Chris Johnson   OPEN: Wed to Sun L 12 (1 Sun) to 2.30 (3.30 Sun), Tue to Sat D 6 to 10   CLOSED: 2 weeks May, 1 week Sept   MEALS: alc exc Sun L (main courses £9.50 to £16.50). Set L Wed to Sat £9.95 (2 courses) to £12.95, Set L Sun £15.95 (2 courses) to £19.95, Set D 6 to 8.30 £9.95 (2 courses) to £12.95. Café bar menu

available   SERVICE: not inc, card slips closed   CARDS: Delta, MasterCard, Switch, Visa
DETAILS: 40 seats. Private parties: 16 main room, 8 to 12 private rooms. Vegetarian meals. No
smoking in dining room. Music. No mobile phones  £5

## RAMSGILL  North Yorkshire                                                        map 8

## ▲ Yorke Arms  ⁵⁄₊

Ramsgill HG3 5RL
TEL: (01423) 755243   FAX: (01423) 755330                              COOKING 7
EMAIL: enquiries@yorke-arms.co.uk                                     MODERN BRITISH
WEBSITE: www.yorke-arms.co.uk                                            £36–£60

Backing on to the river, facing the village green, Yorke Arms occupies a
'charming backwater' of the Nidd Valley. It has moved in its six years from being
a pub with food to a restaurant-with-rooms, although behind the creeper-
covered frontage it feels like an old pub, with a flag-floored bar, and a big
fireplace and impressive antique dresser in the dining room. Tables are smartly
set with gleaming glassware, and the varied offerings are supplemented by a
special fish menu on Tuesdays and Thursdays, as the kitchen plays to one of its
strengths. Accurately cooked lemon sole has come with asparagus, fennel, peas
and artichokes, and fillet of sea bass on a sweet-tasting parsnip purée with
oyster and shiitake mushrooms.

Shellfish is if anything even more notable, judging by one reporter's mille-
feuille of pounded crabmeat in a light mayonnaise, accompanied by a sauté lobe
of foie gras, together with an acidulated, mustardy vinaigrette containing Puy
lentils and rocket. This is deft, sophisticated cooking, whose complexities are
well handled. Pasta demonstrates the point: a thin casing enclosing a tarragon-
flavoured chicken mousse in a pool of sauce vierge made all the more impressive
by the quality of its diced tomato flesh; and a 'soft and delicate' lobster raviolo
accompanied by fennel confit and sun-dried tomatoes in a beurre blanc.

Poultry and game also feature prominently, perhaps in the form of pink,
flavourful seared wood pigeon with pineapple relish and foie gras, or as skinless
slices of wild duck served with cabbage and lardons in a sticky game jus. British
cheeses are expertly described by the waiter, and desserts have included a
vanilla rice pudding brûlée topped with caramelised banana, and slices of hot
pear on accurately cooked puff pastry, served with a grainy butterscotch syrup
and first-class gingerbread ice cream. Portions are well judged, and staff are,
without exception, efficient, welcoming and knowledgeable; 'one instinctively
feels in safe hands', reckoned one visitor, although another found service
altogether 'rushed'. Nine house wines from £12.95 to £14.95 kick off a balanced
list that combines interest, value and wide choice.

CHEFS: Frances Atkins and Michael Taylor   PROPRIETORS: Gerald and Frances Atkins   OPEN: all
week 12 to 1.45 (2.15 Sun), 7 to 9 (9.30 Sat); Sun D residents only   CLOSED: last 2 weeks Jan
MEALS: alc exc Sun L (main courses £15 to £17.50). Set L Sun £20 (2 courses) to £27. Light L
menu available all week   SERVICE: not inc   CARDS: Amex, Delta, Diners, MasterCard, Switch,
Visa   DETAILS: 70 seats. 30 seats outside. Private parties: 40 main room, 10 to 20 private rooms.
Car park. Vegetarian meals. No smoking in dining room. Wheelchair access (not WC). Music. No
mobile phones   ACCOMMODATION: 14 rooms, all with bath/shower. TV. Phone. D,B&B £80 to
£300 (The Which? Hotel Guide)  £5

# Dining Room 🍴

59A High Street, Reigate RH2 9AE                          COOKING 5
TEL/FAX: (01737) 226650                                MODERN BRITISH
                                                          £28–£56

Slap bang in the middle of the High Street, the first-floor dining room is reached up a narrow flight of stairs. 'Serious but pleasing', its smart, cosmopolitan air is tempered by warm peachy-beige tones and an elegant fireplace, its lively menus incorporating both a fixed-price version and a carte where all dishes at a given stage are the same price. And there is hardly a one without an oriental spicing or unusual ingredient, so it helps to know your orzo from your yuzu. Just to take a couple of examples: cumin-roast quail has come with a lemon and fennel confit, and citrus-marinated 'capitaine' (a tropical fish) with a green mango and noodle salad. Exotic oils and emulsions add yet more colour.

Good raw materials are more often than not improved by the treatment they receive: a thick slab of spiced rib of beef, with a deep-red blob of cold tomato 'kasundi' (chutney to the rest of us), has been accurately chargrilled, and a risotto cooked successfully with coconut milk, mixed with strongly spiced mussels and garnished with crispy fried shallots (battered onion rings to the rest of us). Sometimes lots of busy additions get in the way, which is partly why a simple, neat, traditional apple and pear crumble makes such a favourable impression, its rough topping providing just the sort of contrast in taste and texture with the fruit that makes this dish a classic. A short, user-friendly wine list (supplemented by some finer bottles) starts with four Chilean varietals at £11.95 (£4.50 a glass). There is another branch, Dining Room 2, in Haywards Heath.

CHEFS: Tony Tobin and Robert Gathercole   PROPRIETOR: Elite Restaurants Ltd   OPEN: Sun to Fri L 12 to 2.30, Mon to Sat D 7 to 10   CLOSED: Christmas, Easter, first 2 weeks Aug   MEALS: alc exc Sun L (main courses £16.50). Set L Mon to Fri £13 (2 courses) to £16.50, Set L Sun £25, Set D £16.95 (2 courses)   SERVICE: 12.5% (optional), card slips closed   CARDS: Amex, Diners, MasterCard, Switch, Visa   DETAILS: 50 seats. Private parties: 50 main room. Vegetarian meals. Children's helpings. No smoking in dining room. Occasional music. No mobile phones. Air-conditioned  (£5)

# Burnt Chair 🍷 🍴 ✉

5 Duke Street, Richmond TW9 1HP
TEL: (020) 8940 9488                                      COOKING 2
EMAIL: connect1@burntchair.com                             GLOBAL
WEBSITE: www.burntchair.com                               £33–£60

Done up in shades of peach, with a terracotta floor, high ceilings and large windows, Burnt Chair is a narrow converted shop in the centre of Richmond. Weenson Oo continues to tread the same global fusion path he set out on in 1991, and the menu rounds up Eastern and Western flavours and influences. Perhaps start with oriental vegetable bonbons with wasabi mayonnaise, or marinated wood pigeon and chicken liver terrine with redcurrant dressing. Main courses are equally ambitious in their flavourings: a tian of salmon ceviche may be served with mango, clams, lavender and tomato hollandaise, while a breast of chicken is accompanied by chèvre and sweet pepper pesto, Serrano ham and fennel-scented mash. Some dishes pull off the flavour balancing act with more assurance than others, although desserts, such as date and mocha pudding with butterscotch sauce, or ginger-crisped roasted pears with Cointreau raisins, are generally well received. The wine list focuses on American producers, taking in imaginative selections based on Cabernet Sauvignon and Chardonnay, as well as more unusual varieties such as Mourvèdre and Zinfandel. Burgundy and Bordeaux, with other French wines and a handful from the New World, appear at the back of the list. Prices are not cheap, starting at £18 and leaving little scope under £20.

CHEFS: Weenson Andrew Oo, Mark Frees and Harry Perez   PROPRIETOR: Weenson Andrew Oo   OPEN: Tue to Sat D only 6 to 11   CLOSED: 2 weeks Christmas, 10 days Aug   MEALS: alc (main courses £11.50 to £19). Set D 6 to 7 £15 (2 courses). Set D Tue to Fri £18 (2 courses) to £20. Cover £1   SERVICE: not inc, 10 to 12.5% for parties of 5 or more   CARDS: Delta, MasterCard, Switch, Visa   DETAILS: 36 seats. Private parties: 36 main room. Vegetarian meals. No smoking in dining room. Music  £5

## Chez Lindsay  £

| 11 Hill Rise, Richmond TW10 6UQ | COOKING 1 |
|---|---|
| TEL: (020) 8948 7473 | BRETON |
| | £21–£62 |

Traditional Breton cooking is the furrow that Lindsay Wotton has ploughed for the last 15 years. Two menus are offered, one exclusively devoted to the Breton specialities of galettes and crêpes, which come with various savoury fillings, such as cheese, ham and spinach, or cheese and ratatouille. The other menu mainly goes in for seafood: platters of winkles with aïoli, oysters or clams, and simple starters such as grilled sardines with thyme and parsley butter, followed by a pastry case of scallops and leeks with a cider butter sauce, or perhaps a gratin of Camembert with red snapper, prawns and crème fraîche. Meat eaters might opt for lamb leg steak with rosemary jus and gratin dauphinois. The traditional choice of drink with Breton food is cider, and there are some good examples on the drinks list, including Loïc Raison. For wine drinkers there is a choice of reasonably priced bottles, virtually all French, from £10.95.

CHEFS: Lindsay Wotton and Olivier Cauvin   PROPRIETOR: Lindsay Wotton   OPEN: Sun 12 to 10, Mon to Sat 11 to 3, 6 to 11 (crêperie menu also available 3 to 6 Sat)   MEALS: alc (main courses £5.50 to £18.50). Set L Mon to Sat exc bank hols £5.99 (2 courses) to £14.99, Set L Sun £14.99, Set D Sun to Fri £14.99   SERVICE: not inc   CARDS: Delta, MasterCard, Switch, Visa   DETAILS: 48 seats. Private parties: 50 main room, 36 private room. Vegetarian meals. Children's helpings. No cigars/pipes while others eat. Wheelchair access (not WC). Music  £5

*The Guide office can quickly spot when a restaurateur is encouraging customers to write recommending inclusion. Such reports do not further a restaurant's cause. Please tell us if a restaurateur invites you to write to the Guide.*

# Old Vicarage 🍷 ⚘

Ridgeway Moor, Ridgeway S12 3XW
TEL: (0114) 247 5814    FAX: (0114) 247 7079
EMAIL: eat@theoldvicarage.co.uk
WEBSITE: www.theoldvicarage.co.uk
from A616, ¾m NW of Mosborough, turn W on                           COOKING 6
B6054/B6388; in Ridgeway, turn S; restaurant is           MODERN BRITISH-PLUS
½m on L, nearly opposite village church                              £49–£75

Inside this typically sturdy stone-built Derbyshire house, surrounded by neat lawns and a well-tended herb and vegetable garden, a dark red and gold entrance hall leads to a light, airy dining room with pale oak flooring, casement windows overlooking manicured lawns, and deep-yellow walls hung with stunning floral paintings. It is a very personal operation, with Tessa Bramley spending much of her time front-of-house these days, and the cooking has a degree of individuality about it: in a cumin-spiced potato cake served with poached egg and Gruyère soldiers, or in the cobnut stuffing that accompanies roast fillet of honey-glazed pork.

Some demur at the prices (there are no concessions at lunch), some at what they see as small portions, others at what they consider a rather unadventurous menu with standard composition and preparation, but our inspector found fine ingredients, accurate timing, and 'spot-on' textures. Seafood illustrates what the kitchen can accomplish: for example, a puddle of glossy basil butter flanked by a just-cooked fillet of chargrilled salmon, and by two thin triangles of spinach-flecked frittata supporting slices of dill-marinated salmon, the flavours emphatic, the counterpoint well considered.

Variations on traditional themes might include four plump sweet scallops, mother-of-pearl inside, their surfaces crisped to a pale toasty brown, partnered by diced smoky pancetta swirled into a tangle of thin noodles. Likewise a pairing of lightly pan-fried calf's liver and a minute slice of satiny-textured foie gras, served with prosciutto and first-class mashed potato liberally mixed with tiny dice of spring onion.

Cheeses in good condition come neatly portioned, and desserts have included chunky slices of roasted plum, apple, pear and pineapple, served with a doll's house portion of creamy rice pudding and a pineapple sorbet. Although not huge, the wine list abounds with quality producers across the globe. The New World seems to offer better value, and food compatibility is given priority. There is plenty of interesting drinking at the £20 mark or below, although a number of wines will please those with more money to spend. Bottle prices start at £16.50 for Vin de Pays d'Oc.

CHEFS: Tessa Bramley, Andrew Gilbert and Nathan Smith    PROPRIETOR: Tessa Bramley    OPEN: Tue to Fri and Sun L 12.30 to 2.30, Tue to Sat D 7 to 10    CLOSED: 26 and 31 Dec, 1 Jan, bank hol Mons    MEALS: Set L and D £33 to £45    SERVICE: not inc, card slips closed    CARDS: Amex, Delta, MasterCard, Switch, Visa    DETAILS: 50 seats. 20 seats outside. Private parties: 50 main room, 24 private room. Car park. Vegetarian meals. Children's helpings. No smoking in dining room. Wheelchair access (not WC). No music

## ▲ Boar's Head ♥ ⚞

Ripley HG3 3AY
TEL: (01423) 771888   FAX: (01423) 770152      COOKING **3**
EMAIL: reservations@boarsheadripley.co.uk      MODERN BRITISH
WEBSITE: www.boarsheadripley.co.uk      £24–£42

Life in this small, picturesque nineteenth-century village, just off the main road,
at least in the tourist season, revolves largely around the castle and its visitors.
Hotel residents have the run of the Ingilbys' walled gardens, which include the
English National Hyacinth Collection, while the chirpy bistro ('boaring it's not,'
har har) deals in hearty lamb's liver and bacon, and venison sausage and mash.
In the richly appointed dining room, meanwhile, with its red walls, gilt frames
and heavy curtains, the menu goes in for modifications of tried and trusted
favourites, producing main courses of breast and confit leg of duck with spiced
vegetable couscous, and grilled fillet steak with deep-fried oysters.

    The gamut runs from tuna niçoise to Thai steamed mussels, and the variations
from Black Forest sponge with sozzled cherries to queen of puddings tart with
strawberry jam ice cream. France is the main anchor for the lengthy wine list,
with Italy, Spain, Germany and the New World adding variety. There's
something to suit every pocket, from Chilean house red (£12.75) to mature claret
(although most red Bordeaux listed are still quite young).

CHEF: Jason Main   PROPRIETORS: Sir Thomas and Lady Ingilby   OPEN: all week 12 to 2, 7 to 9.30
MEALS: Set L £11 (2 courses) to £15, Set D £18.50 to £25.50. Bistro menu available   SERVICE: not
inc   CARDS: Amex, Delta, Diners, MasterCard, Switch, Visa   DETAILS: 80 seats. Car park.
Vegetarian meals. Children's helpings. No smoking in dining room. Wheelchair access (also
WC). Music   ACCOMMODATION: 25 rooms, all with bath/shower. TV. Phone. B&B £99 to £140.
Rooms for disabled. Baby facilities. Fishing (*The Which? Hotel Guide*)

## ▲ Roade House ⚞

16 High Street, Roade NN7 2NW
TEL: (01604) 863372   FAX: (01604) 862421
EMAIL: info@roadehousehotel.co.uk      COOKING **5**
WEBSITE: www.roadehousehotel.co.uk      MODERN BRITISH
off A508, 4m S of Northampton      £27–£52

'Absolutely delightful as a place to eat and stay, thanks largely to the personable,
caring and genuinely helpful atmosphere created by Chris and Sue Kewley.' So
runs one ringing endorsement of this unpretentious restaurant-with-rooms that
the Kewleys have run for 20 years. Start with a drink in an airy bar underneath a
clerestory roof, and proceed to a dark-beamed dining room where presentation
is clear and simple and the cooking is precise, well thought out and admirably
executed. Among the delights are a starter of poached egg with chorizo, oyster
mushrooms and tomato concassé, and calf's liver is highly rated, thanks to its
quality and accurate timing, perhaps served with an onion compote, bacon and a
pepper sauce.

Materials include corn-fed chicken, Scottish beef, and prime fish such as turbot or sea bass, the last served with a well-rendered prawn risotto. Combinations are by no means humdrum, taking in seared foie gras on spiced honey bread with wilted chicory and sultanas, and braised belly of pork with spiced sauerkraut and a grain mustard sauce. A few disappointments are registered (puddings for one visitor, service for another), but most reporters come away happy. Wine prices are fair at all levels (even for expense-account drinkers), and choice is pleasingly varied. House wines (two French, two South African) are £12.

CHEFS: Chris Kewley and Steve Barnes   PROPRIETORS: Chris and Sue Kewley   OPEN: Tue to Fri and Sun L 12.15 to 1.45, Mon to Sat D 7 to 9.30   CLOSED: bank hols   MEALS: alc D (main courses £14.50 to £19). Set L Tue to Fri £15 (2 courses) to £16.50, Set L Sun £20   SERVICE: not inc, card slips closed   CARDS: Amex, Delta, MasterCard, Switch, Visa   DETAILS: 50 seats. Private parties: 16 main room. Car park. Children's helpings. No smoking in dining room. Wheelchair access (also WC). No music. Air-conditioned   ACCOMMODATION: 10 rooms, all with bath/shower. TV. Phone. B&B £58 to £80. Rooms for disabled. Baby facilities

## ROCHDALE  Greater Manchester                                   map 8

# After Eight  ⅝✗

| 2 Edenfield Road, Rochdale OL11 5AA | COOKING 3 |
| TEL/FAX: (01706) 646432 | ANGLO-FRENCH |
| WEBSITE: www.aftereight.uk.com | £27–£43 |

Geoffrey and Anne Taylor take trouble to look after customers in their converted wool merchant's house on a corner with the Blackburn road. He runs the stoves, she keep things happy out front. Their enterprise is built on a personable approach and sheer dedication. Buying locally sustains what they do. Home-farmed venison from York appears on spring onion, bacon and sliced potatoes with cherry brandy sauce, while piglets from Garstang are roasted and served on apple mash with whole-grain mustard sauce. Choice is sensibly restricted, but vegetarians have their own mini-menu, promising twice-baked cauliflower cheese soufflé, and roast red pepper plait, for example.

A handful of internationally inclined desserts might range from mango sorbet with caramelised oranges to apricot and brandy trifle with ratafia biscuits. The Taylors' loyalty to the north also shows in their informatively described cheese selection, which lists Chris Sandham's Lancashire and Judy Bell's Yorkshire Blue from Thirsk, among others, accompanied by Oldham pickles. A well-spread, carefully annotated list of more than 80 wines roams the world picking up affordable bottles from Argentina to Australia. House wine is £10.90, £2.50 a glass.

CHEF: Geoffrey Taylor   PROPRIETORS: Geoffrey and Anne Taylor   OPEN: Tue to Sat D only 7 to 9.30 (L party bookings only)   CLOSED: 25 and 26 Dec, 1 Jan, 17 to 24 Mar   MEALS: alc (main courses £10.50 to £17)   SERVICE: not inc, 10% for parties   CARDS: Amex, Delta, Diners, MasterCard, Switch, Visa   DETAILS: 45 seats. Private parties: 30 main room, 10 to 20 private rooms. Vegetarian meals. Children's helpings. No smoking in dining room. Wheelchair access (not WC). Music  £5

## ROMALDKIRK  Co Durham                                        map 10

# ▲ Rose & Crown 🗡

Romaldkirk DL12 9EB
TEL: (01833) 650213   FAX: (01833) 650828
EMAIL: hotel@rose-and-crown.co.uk
WEBSITE: www.rose-and-crown.co.uk
on B6277, 6m NW of Barnard Castle

COOKING 3
TRADITIONAL ENGLISH
£21–£44

Far from the business end of the Tees, in an unspoilt village just underneath the moors, and with the Tees-side path running nearby, Rose & Crown combines the roles of pub (there is a separate room for bar snacks) and restaurant, its partly oak-panelled dining room decorated with china plates. Here the deal is a set-price, daily-changing dinner menu of four courses, with first and main separated by a soup of the day: a rustic celeriac, leek and apple for one visitor.

Ambition is realistic, which helps to keep everything on course: from a moist, creamy and accurately cooked leek and spinach risotto at inspection, to a pink fillet of roast Teesdale lamb sitting in a first-class broth, its potato, mushrooms and black pudding given extra zing from smoky bacon. Vegetables are served separately, and while they may not always be appropriate they are expertly done. Among desserts, a generous portion of dark chocolate marquise beats the Irish coffee ice cream. A varietally arranged wine list has much to offer under £20, plus a few special bottles, a dozen halves, and four house wines starting at £10.95 for Chilean Sauvignon Blanc and Cabernet.

CHEFS: Christopher Davy and Dawn Stephenson   PROPRIETORS: Christopher and Alison Davy
OPEN: Sun L 12 to 1.30, Mon to Sat D 7.30 to 9   CLOSED: 24 to 26 Dec   MEALS: Set L £13.95, Set D £25. Bar menu available   SERVICE: not inc, card slips closed   CARDS: Delta, MasterCard, Switch, Visa   DETAILS: 24 seats. 24 seats outside (bar meals only). Private parties: 20 main room. Car park. Vegetarian meals. Children's helpings. No children under 6. No smoking in dining room. Wheelchair access (not WC). No music. No mobile phones   ACCOMMODATION: 12 rooms, all with bath/shower. TV. Phone. B&B £65 to £110. Rooms for disabled. Baby facilities (*The Which? Hotel Guide*)  (£5)

## ROMSEY  Hampshire                                           map 2

# ▲ Bertie's 🗡                              [NEW ENTRY]

80 The Hundred, Romsey SO51 8BX
TEL: (01794) 830708   FAX: (01794) 507507
WEBSITE: www.berties.co.uk

COOKING 2
MODERN EUROPEAN
£26–£50

The brother of Bertie's in Winchester (see entry), this has been a coaching inn and workhouse in its time, but is now artfully designed with a splendid set of gastronomic murals produced, as at Winchester, by Jenny Muncaster. Expansion into an adjacent building has provided a brighter, airier, if rather more formal space. Simon Lakey moved here from Winchester in 2001, bringing his vibrant, Mediterranean-accented repertoire with him. Seared scallops with chilli-fried spinach and balsamic syrup was a spring blackboard special, the chilli zipping up an otherwise straightforward dish. Fish dishes may be complex, as was the case with an inspector's fillet of halibut on a salad of butter beans and sun-dried tomatoes, the crisp skin matched by a rasher of crisp-cooked Parma ham and a couple of razor clams in tempura batter. Nor are meat dishes simple: a roast wood pigeon, stuffed with roast garlic and pears, comes on a potato rösti with game stock sauce. Miss the cheese and head perhaps for a chocolate tart with mascarpone cream and raspberry marmalade. Ten house wines from £10.50 to £15.50 begin a list of dependable bottles from across the world.

CHEF: Simon Lakey   PROPRIETOR: David Birmingham   OPEN: Mon to Sat 12 to 2, 6.30 to 10   CLOSED: 26 to 30 Dec, bank hols   MEALS: alc (main courses L £7 to £13, D £11 to £18). Set L and D Mon to Fri £14.95 (2 courses) to £16.95   SERVICE: not inc   CARDS: Amex, Delta, Diners, MasterCard, Switch, Visa   DETAILS: 66 seats. 15 seats outside. Private parties: 40 main room, 40 private room. Car park. Vegetarian meals. No smoking in 1 dining room. Wheelchair access (not WC). Music   ACCOMMODATION: 7 rooms, all with bath/shower. TV. B&B £49.50 to £65   (£5)

# Old Manor House ▮

21 Palmerston Street, Romsey SO51 8GF   
TEL/FAX: (01794) 517353

COOKING 5   
ITALIAN   
£37–£54

The Bregolis have run this distinctive and characterful restaurant for over 20 years. Their gabled, brick and timber building (on the market as the Guide went to press) houses a dining room with a low ceiling, exposed beams, and a log fire in winter, and the whole place exudes a rather domestic feel. Mauro Bregoli is an avuncular kind of figure, and it may be 'difficult to envisage him shooting deer', but that is one of the many things he does in order to keep the kitchen well supplied. He picks mushrooms too, cures beef fillet, and makes an 'out of this world' cotechino sausage, served simply and traditionally with lentils.

Such industrious preparation and unfussy presentation are typical, and the resulting clear focus much appreciated. A barbecued eel steak comes with salsa verde, duck breast is served with a red wine and walnut sauce, and pasta might feature among first courses: perhaps as part of a Tuscan bean soup, or as tagliatelle with Poole cockles. Recent reports, however, suggest that results are not as impressive as they were, although an 'incredible' honey parfait with pine nuts wowed one visitor. Service also seems to have had its ups and downs, and despite the restaurant's Italian focus, venerable premier cru red Bordeaux – including a bottle from the late nineteenth century – makes up the heart of the wine list (although reports suggest that not all vintages listed are available). Elsewhere, Alsace is well represented and there are some top Italians, taking in three vintages of Sassicaia. Many New World selections are under £20 and around 18 house wines sell for £12.50 to £18.50.

CHEF: Mauro Bregoli   PROPRIETORS: Mauro and Esther Bregoli   OPEN: Tue to Sun L 12.15 to 2, Tue to Sat D 7.15 to 9.30   MEALS: alc (main courses £14.50 to £18.50)   SERVICE: not inc   CARDS: Amex, Delta, MasterCard, Switch, Visa   DETAILS: 28 seats. Private parties: 28 main room. Car park. No cigars/pipes in dining room. No music. No mobile phones

*The cuisine styles noted at the tops of entries are only an approximation, often suggested to us by the restaurants themselves. Please read the entry itself to find out more about the cooking style.*

# Pheasant at Ross ▌ ⁵⋇

52 Edde Cross Street, Ross-on-Wye HR9 7BZ
TEL: (01989) 565751   FAX: (01989) 763069

COOKING 2
COUNTRY COOKING
£38–£45

The single front room, with large windows overlooking the street, combines traditional wooden beams and an old stone fireplace with 1920s-accented wallpaper and light fittings. A self-proclaimed country restaurant, open only three sessions a week, the Pheasant clearly targets out-of-towners with its homely and well-intentioned cooking. Simple menu descriptions translate into equally straightforward dishes – rather a blessing these days – as Eileen Brunnarius single-handedly produces baked wild sea trout fillet with buttered samphire and mustard sauce, or goats' cheese gnocchi (poached then sautéed) with watercress and roast cherry tomatoes.

Although promised spicing may not always make itself felt, there are no frothy or pretentious flourishes, just half a dozen spears of local asparagus (for a May visitor) accurately cooked under a veil of hollandaise, followed perhaps by roast fillet of beef (from the Forest of Dean), or slow-cooked Middle White pork. Desserts, just as domestic, take in poached figs with crème fraîche, or bread-and-butter pudding. Taster menus offer glasses of suggested wines to accompany each course, and front-of-house man Adrian Wells brings the already interesting wine list to life with his recommendations and knowledgeable patter (although this can lengthen the evening considerably). The list eschews what the proprietors call the 'classic' approach, grouping wines by style instead, although you can also select by grape variety or by food choice. There is also a broad by-the-glass selection. Although lovers of red Bordeaux may feel left out (they are actively excluded from the list), there is more than enough choice to satisfy most cravings. A 'try before you buy' policy helps customers avoid unwelcome surprises. Pricing is fair and bottle prices start at £12.60, a small price to pay for quality German Riesling.

CHEF/PROPRIETOR: Eileen Brunnarius   OPEN: Thur to Sat D 7 to 9.30 (and other evenings for booked groups)   CLOSED: 22 Dec to 2 Jan, first week June   MEALS: Set D £22.50 (2 courses) to £27. Taster menus inc wine £28.50 (2 courses) to £36   SERVICE: not inc   CARDS: Amex, Delta, MasterCard, Switch, Visa   DETAILS: 20 seats. Private parties: 20 main room, 8 private room. Vegetarian meals. Children's helpings. No smoking in dining room. Wheelchair access (not WC). No music   (£5)

# George & Dragon ⁵⋇ £

High Street, Rowde SN10 2PN
TEL: (01380) 723053   FAX: (01380) 724738
EMAIL: gd-rowde@lineone.net

COOKING 3
SEAFOOD
£21–£51

This mustard-coloured pub, with steep steps up to the front door, and some tables outside at the back, has an engagingly rural air about it, and while the wood-panelled bar and beamed dining room might do with a bit of a face-lift, the kitchen continues to major on seafood. Reports this year register everything from disappointment to satisfaction, and conclusions range from 'going steadily downhill' to 'consistently good' (both from regulars), so it is difficult to be definitive about standards.

Highlights have included a generous serving of accurately cooked langoustines with a splendid lemony mayonnaise, and notably fresh turbot accompanied by scallops and a first-class orange hollandaise. Whole grilled Dover sole on the bone has been both a triumph and a letdown. Among non-fishy items might be a rich and creamy twice-baked cheese soufflé, and a fine chocolate pot with preserved kumquats. A savvy wine list that combines good quality and fair pricing is backed up by half a dozen house wines at £10 and a short but well-chosen selection of bottled beers.

CHEFS: Tim Withers and Kate Patterson   PROPRIETORS: Tim and Helen Withers   OPEN: Tue to Sat 12 to 2, 7 to 10   CLOSED: 25 Dec, 1 Jan   MEALS: alc (main courses L £6.50 to £18, D £9 to £18). Set L £10 (2 courses) to £12.50   SERVICE: not inc, card slips closed   CARDS: Delta, MasterCard, Switch, Visa   DETAILS: 35 seats. 20 seats outside. Private parties: 12 main room. Car park. Vegetarian meals. Children's helpings. No smoking in dining room. No music. No mobile phones

## RYE  East Sussex                                                            map 3

# Landgate Bistro ✸ £

5–6 Landgate, Rye TN31 7LH                                          COOKING 4
TEL: (01797) 222829                                            MODERN BRITISH
WEBSITE: www.landgatebistro.co.uk                                    £23–£36

'Rye ought to be a World Heritage Site,' thought one visitor. It's certainly an atmospheric place: a mix of Tudor, Georgian, and Victorian buildings clustered on a clifftop around a network of narrow cobbled streets, and the Landgate fits in agreeably, occupying two knocked-through old houses just outside the ancient town walls. It is something of a fixture in these parts and would be celebrating its twenty-first successive appearance in the Guide but for a temporary closure in the mid-1980s.

During their long tenure, owners Nick Parkin and Toni Ferguson-Lees have built up an enviable network of first-rate local suppliers, whose produce is put to good use in a largely traditional cooking style. An eye for what is seasonal and fresh and a firm grasp of culinary techniques were all evident at an inspection meal: for starters, a broad bean and pecorino tart featured warm, thin shortcrust pastry and a well-judged filling, while warm, wobbly scallop mousse was 'meltingly light', delicately flavoured and complemented by a light, lemony fish sauce. Among main courses, baked sea bass with hollandaise has made a favourable impression, and the half-dozen or so choices might also run to calf's liver with sage and balsamic vinegar, or marinated chump of Romney Marsh lamb with onions and thyme. To finish, rhubarb compote with orange crème, and lemon and sherry syllabub have drawn enthusiastic comments. Wines are varied and fairly priced, starting at £8.90 for house French. Eight are offered by the glass from £2.

CHEF: Toni Ferguson-Lees   PROPRIETORS: Nick Parkin and Toni Ferguson-Lees   OPEN: Tue to Sat D only 7 to 9.30   CLOSED: 1 week Christmas, 2 weeks summer   MEALS: alc (main courses £9 to £12). Set D Tue to Thur £16.90   SERVICE: net prices, card slips closed   CARDS: Amex, Delta, Diners, MasterCard, Switch, Visa   DETAILS: 30 seats. Vegetarian meals. Children's helpings. No smoking in dining room. Music

## ST IVES  Cornwall                                              map 1

# Alba 🌟

**NEW ENTRY**

Old Lifeboat House, St Ives TR26 1LF
TEL: (01736) 797222  FAX: (01736) 798937

COOKING 2
MODERN BRITISH
£23–£52

Opened in the spring of 2002, Alba occupies two floors of the old St Ives lifeboat house. On the ground floor is a deli-cum-coffee bar, with a split-level restaurant upstairs. A glass frontage provides panoramic views of the harbour, and the light wood floor, abstract paintings and recessed lighting make a suitably muted backdrop for some accomplished cooking. The kitchen team includes a Japanese sushi chef, and oriental modes are much in evidence. A Chinese bowl of crab and noodles in parsley broth is a light starter full of fresh flavours, or there might be seared tuna crusted with Szechuan peppercorns served with tuna tartare, mizuna, sanga radish and a curry vinaigrette. Two moist, fresh fillets of brill at an inspection meal gained from being served on a large piece of prosciutto, with asparagus, peas and mint to accompany.

While the menu chiefly centres around fish, there is meat too (corn-fed chicken poached in Gewurztraminer broth, perhaps), or maybe a compromise dish of monkfish paired with braised oxtail and served with deep-fried leeks. A 20-minute wait seems a small price to pay for a thoroughly satisfying hot chocolate pudding with Glenmorangie ice cream and a coffee and vanilla syrup. The less patient might forge ahead with poached tamarillo with pain perdu and passion-fruit ice cream. Given Isolation Ridge Riesling and Toasted Head Chardonnay, it is clear that the wine list is doing its best to offer a voguish selection. Interesting wines at fair prices make up the bulk of it. House offerings – an Italian white and a Spanish red – are £10.50.

CHEFS: Grant Nethercott, Neil Carrie, Paul Hearn and Hiro Itami  PROPRIETOR: The Harbour Kitchen Company  OPEN: all week 12 to 3, 6.30 to 10  CLOSED: 26 Dec  MEALS: alc (main courses L £7 to £9.50, D £12 to £18.50)  SERVICE: not inc  CARDS: Delta, MasterCard, Switch, Visa  DETAILS: 40 seats. Private parties: 46 main room. Vegetarian meals. Children's helpings. No smoking in dining room. Music. Air-conditioned

# Porthminster Beach Café 🌟

Porthminster Beach, St Ives TR26 2EB
TEL/FAX: (01736) 795352
EMAIL: pminster@btopenworld.com

COOKING 4
GLOBAL
£19–£51

'Café' hardly seems an appropriate name for this slick, fast-moving beachside restaurant, although you can still drop in during the morning for a mug of hot chocolate and a toasted teacake. By lunchtime the place has moved into gear, and during the evening its allegiance to Mediterranean, Pacific Rim and fusion food is there for all to see.

Daily deliveries of fresh fish form the bedrock of the menu, and the owners are now smoking their own as well. The results might take in smoked haddock with wasabi mash, salt-cod and corn chowder, Japanese marinated sea bass with soba noodles, pak choi and cilantro broth, or baked Newlyn cod with celeriac and fennel confit. Supplies of organic meat and poultry also find their way into the kitchen: fillet of Cornish beef might be served with poached pear, goats' cheese rösti and basil gremolata, for example. Desserts include equally lively ideas, such as caramelised baby bananas with brandy, nougat parfait and black pepper. Seafood barbecues are held on Sunday evenings in high season. The wine list is short and to the point, with plenty of decent drinking under £15. House wine is £10.50.

CHEFS: Simon Pellow and Andy Grant   PROPRIETORS: W.J. Woolcock, D. Fox, T. Symons and S. Symons   OPEN: all week 12 to 4, 6.30 to 10   MEALS: alc (main courses L £5 to £14, D £10 to £18) SERVICE: not inc   CARDS: MasterCard, Switch, Visa   DETAILS: 57 seats. 45 seats outside. Vegetarian meals. No smoking in dining room. Music

---

## ST KEYNE  Cornwall                                          map 1

## ▲ Well House ♚ ⚔

St Keyne PL14 4RN
TEL: (01579) 342001   FAX: (01579) 343891
EMAIL: enquiries@wellhouse.co.uk
WEBSITE: www.wellhouse.co.uk                                 COOKING 4
on B3254, 3m S of Liskeard; at end of village near          MODERN BRITISH
church, follow sign to St Keyne Well                         £34–£56

---

This grey-stone Victorian building, standing in three acres of grounds just outside the small village of St Keyne, has a 'very English' feel: it is small-scale, and more comfortable than grand, despite some ambitious work going on in the kitchen. The cooking style is broad-ranging, taking in ideas as diverse as ham and herb terrine with caramelised pineapple tart (an interesting take on an old standby), and breast of corn-fed chicken with crisp goats' cheese polenta and black truffle cream. Despite the evident technical skills there is a feeling that some dishes are more complicated than they need to be: boudins, risottos, soufflés, tortellini and tarts are often called upon to play supporting roles.

That said, a starter of turbot fillet with shallot confit and thyme oil combines top-class raw materials and 'absolutely perfect' preparation, and a main course of pan-fried duck breast with fig tart, pink peppercorn sauce and foie gras butter has been 'superbly executed'. Pear Tatin with liquorice ice cream, and cherry clafoutis with caramel balsamic ice cream are typically unconventional desserts. Service, overseen by Nick Wainford, is 'friendly and attentive'. The wine list proves that restaurants can focus on France and still deliver good value. A shorter New World selection is dominated by Australia, New Zealand and California, and sensible mark-ups mean that there is a wealth of good drinking under £20. House red and white are £10.50, £2.50 per glass.

CHEF: Matthew Corner   PROPRIETORS: Nick Wainford and Ione Nurdin   OPEN: all week 12.30 to 1.30, 7 to 9   MEALS: Set L £18.50 (2 courses) to £23.50, Set D £29.50   SERVICE: not inc, card slips closed   CARDS: Delta, MasterCard, Switch, Visa   DETAILS: 30 seats. 16 seats outside. Private parties: 26 main room. Car park. Vegetarian meals. No children under 8 at D. No smoking in dining room. Wheelchair access (not WC). No music. No mobile phones   ACCOMMODATION: 9 rooms, all with bath/shower. TV. Phone. B&B £70 to £160. Baby facilities. Swimming pool (*The Which? Hotel Guide*)

## ST MARGARET'S AT CLIFFE  Kent map 3

# ▲ Wallett's Court ⚡✕

Westcliffe, St Margaret's at Cliffe CT15 6EW
TEL: (01304) 852424   FAX: (01304) 853430
EMAIL: dine@wallettscourt.com
WEBSITE: www.wallettscourt.com                                    COOKING 3
on B2058, off A258 Dover to Deal road, 3m NE of                  ANGLO-FRENCH
Dover                                                            £30–£69

A plaque on the wall outside designates this seventeenth-century farmhouse as a Historic Building of Kent. Outbuildings have been sympathetically converted to provide modern leisure and business facilities, but the main house still has an old-world feel, both in the bar, with its huge inglenook, and in the intimate, beamed dining room. Stephen Harvey's cooking is inventive but founded on classical techniques, with Kentish ingredients a feature: lobster from nearby St Margaret's Bay was a hit at an inspection meal, baked with thyme and vanilla and served with almond risotto. There may also be lamb from Romney Marsh, its roasted rack served on sweet potato fondant with a fricassee of beans and a rosemary jus. There is plenty of choice, with maybe a dozen main-course options at dinner, and some creative vegetarian dishes, such as a tian of avocado and goats' cheese with Bloody Mary granita. Desserts are a strong suit whose sophisticated creations may include a fine coconut mousse with liquorice ice cream and Malibu-infused crème anglaise. The wine list offers a good range and reasonable prices. House Bourgogne Aligoté and Pinot Noir are £15.

CHEF: Stephen Harvey   PROPRIETORS: the Oakley family   OPEN: Tue to Fri and Sun L 12 to 2, all week D 7 to 9   MEALS: Set L £15 (2 courses) to £17.50, Set D £27.50 (2 courses) to £42.50   SERVICE: not inc   CARDS: Amex, Delta, Diners, MasterCard, Switch, Visa   DETAILS: 70 seats. Private parties: 40 main room, 6 to 60 private rooms. Car park. Vegetarian meals. Children's helpings. No children under 8 after 8pm. No smoking in dining room. Wheelchair access (not WC). Music. No mobile phones   ACCOMMODATION: 16 rooms, all with bath/shower. TV. Phone. B&B £75 to £150. Baby facilities. Swimming pool (*The Which? Hotel Guide*)

## ST MARTIN'S  Isles of Scilly map 1

# ▲ St Martin's on the Isle ⚡✕

Lower Town, St Martin's TR25 0QW
TEL: (01720) 422092   FAX: (01720) 422298                        COOKING 5
EMAIL: stay@stmartinshotel.co.uk                            MODERN EUROPEAN
WEBSITE: www.stmartinshotel.co.uk                               £50–£77

Regular flights and a passenger ferry put the small archipelago within easy reach of Penzance; some even pilot their own planes in the search for peace and quiet. Arrival at St Martin's is by boat, to a warm welcome from hotel staff (they can see you coming), and the stone-built hotel makes the most of its panoramic potential. The light and airy dining room, done in blue and yellow, affords 'magnificent' views over the water, and Stewart Eddy's three-course menus offer four options per course, two of them changing daily to provide variety for long stayers. The scope of the cooking is evident from materials ranging from Serrano ham (with goats' cheese fondant) to nori seaweed (wrapped around yellow-fin tuna), and from sauces that might include a lemon sabayon (with Cornish turbot) or a coconut and lime sauce (with a potage of seafood).

In addition, there is a proper, full-length vegetarian menu, and a shellfish menu using only Scillonian lobster and crabs. This needs to be ordered 24 hours in advance, but might take in smoked lobster with chive beurre blanc, or a fricassee of lobster with summer vegetables in a ginger and shellfish broth. Calvados parfait, and white chocolate mousse, are recommended, service comes in for special praise, breakfast is highly rated, and the wine list's emphasis on whites (with plenty of choice under £20) reflects the preponderance of seafood.

CHEF: Stewart Eddy   PROPRIETOR: Peter Sykes   OPEN: all week D only 7 to 9.30   CLOSED: 25 Oct to 13 Mar   MEALS: Set D £37.50. Bar menu available   SERVICE: not inc, card slips closed   CARDS: Amex, Delta, Diners, MasterCard, Switch, Visa   DETAILS: 60 seats. Private parties: 90 main room, 2 to 24 private rooms. Vegetarian meals. No children under 12 in dining room. No smoking in dining room. Wheelchair access (also WC). No music. No mobile phones   ACCOMMODATION: 30 rooms, all with bath/shower. TV. Phone. D,B&B £95 to £260. Rooms for disabled. Baby facilities. Swimming pool. Fishing (*The Which? Hotel Guide*)

## ST MAWES  Cornwall                                                                    map 1

## ▲ Rising Sun ⚡✳

The Square, St Mawes TR2 5DJ                              COOKING 3
TEL: (01326) 270233   FAX: (01326) 270198               MODERN ENGLISH
EMAIL: therisingsun@btclick.com                          £22–£45

'Unrivalled' views of the harbour, and across the water to the Roseland peninsula, are one of the special claims of this small inn at the centre of St Mawes. Menus in the 'pleasantly decorated, very comfortable' dining room change daily, partly to reflect the catch from local boats, though choice is divided roughly half and half between fish and non-fish dishes: crabmeat and bacon tartlet set against duck salad with orange dressing among starters, for example. Reports this year have differed quite markedly in their opinions, suggesting some inconsistency in standards, but at its best the cooking is simple and effective: 'perfectly steamed' sea bass, spiced monkfish tails in a filo case on a colourful mixed salad, and rare roast beef with mushroom pâté in pastry have all been praised. Raspberry oatmeal meringue was a 'memorable' dessert for one visitor. Ten house wines by the bottle or glass (from £10 and £2.60 respectively) open an unpretentious and varied list.

CHEF: Ann Long   PROPRIETOR: R.J. Milan   OPEN: Sun L 12 to 2, all week D 7 to 9   MEALS: Set L £14.95, Set D £29. Bar menu available   SERVICE: not inc, card slips closed   CARDS: Delta, MasterCard, Switch, Visa   DETAILS: 50 seats. 70 seats outside. Private parties: 50 main room. Car park. Vegetarian meals. No children under 14. No smoking in dining room. Wheelchair access (also WC). No music   ACCOMMODATION: 8 rooms, all with bath/shower. TV. Phone. B&B £39.50 to £109 (*The Which? Hotel Guide*)

---

*If 'vegetarian meals' is noted in the details at the end of an entry, this means that a restaurant routinely lists at least one vegetarian starter and main course on menus. Other restaurants, however, may offer good vegetarian choices if you let them know in advance, so it is worthwhile phoning to enquire.*

# ▲ Tresanton Hotel ☒

Lower Castle Road, St Mawes TR2 5DR
TEL: (01326) 270055   FAX: (01326) 270053
EMAIL: info@tresanton.com
WEBSITE: www.tresanton.com

COOKING 4
MODERN EUROPEAN
£36–£54

Well back from the road, Tresanton is where 'rich Chelsea types might escape to: knowing they're on holiday because of the view, relaxed colours and informal surroundings, but not having to rough it'. The food is correspondingly modern yet conservative: no risks, no fireworks, but satisfying with well-handled ingredients and successful combinations.

The four options per course give priority to fish: perhaps a large white bowl filled with tomato (more sauce than soup) and plump mussels, clams, cockles, a prawn and a langoustine, all impressively fresh. So, too, were a dish of skinned, sauté fillets of Dover sole with grilled artichoke, turned potatoes and black olives, and a fried John Dory fillet on artichoke purée with new potatoes and tomatoes.

Vegetarians might be offered wild mushroom risotto, and meat options have included pink-grilled, flavourful rump of lamb with white beans, red peppers and a simple reduction. Cheeses are well kept – Menallack, Cropwell Bishop and Polmesk for one visitor, with crumbly oatcakes and a sweet chutney – while desserts might take in a slice of pear and frangipane tart (good short-crust pastry) with a powerful almond ice cream. Service is well paced, and the mainly Franco-Italian wines are well chosen, though they soon top £20.

CHEF: Paul Wadham   PROPRIETOR: Olga Polizzi   OPEN: all week 12.30 to 2.30, 7 to 9.30   MEALS: Set L £20 (2 courses) to £25, Set D £33. Light L menu also available   SERVICE: not inc, card slips closed   CARDS: Amex, Delta, MasterCard, Switch, Visa   DETAILS: 50 seats. 60 seats outside. Private parties: 40 main room. Car park. Vegetarian meals. Children's helpings. Wheelchair access (not WC). No music   ACCOMMODATION: 26 rooms, all with bath/shower. TV. Phone. B&B £200 to £235. Baby facilities (*The Which? Hotel Guide*)

## SALE  Greater Manchester                                                          map 8

# Hanni's £

4 Brooklands Road, Sale M33 3SQ
TEL: (0161) 973 6606   FAX: (0161) 972 0469

COOKING 2
EASTERN MEDITERRANEAN
£23–£50

The yellow and maroon colours, and closely packed tables complete with ash-trays, are not unusual in Middle Eastern establishments. But the menu certainly is. Kleftiko, osso buco (a lamb steak here), couscous Marocaine, Tbilisi kebab (kofta and shish kebab) are just some of a wide range of Mediterranean lamb dishes, and a number of specialities are from the Maghreb. Meze include lahma bi-ajeen (a Lebanese mini-pizza with meat); tabbouleh, properly made with very little cracked wheat; and an egg-shaped meat-and-wheat kibbeh. They pleased a pair of inspectors who also enjoyed the Italian and Greek lamb dishes above, and who had the highest praise for the accompanying rice. Fish include salmon, prawns and halibut. Desserts are limited, although you may be offered green figs with yoghurt or cream. Turkish coffee is commended, and some 30 wines are decently priced from £11.95. Long-serving waiters are friendlier than they look.

CHEF: Mr Hoonanian   PROPRIETOR: Mohamed Hanni Al-Taraboulsy   OPEN: Mon to Sat D only 6 to 10.30 (11 Fri and Sat)   CLOSED: 25 Dec, 1 Jan, Good Fri, Easter Mon   MEALS: alc (main courses £10.50 to £14). Set D 6 to 7 £10.95 (2 courses)   SERVICE: not inc   CARDS: Amex, Delta, MasterCard, Switch, Visa   DETAILS: 50 seats. Private parties: 50 main room. Vegetarian meals. Children's helpings. Wheelchair access (not WC). Music. Air-conditioned

## SALFORD  Greater Manchester                                          map 8

# ▲ Lowry Hotel, River Room
# Marco Pierre White

50 Dearmans Place, Chapel Wharf,
Salford M3 5LH
TEL: (0161) 827 4000   FAX: (0161) 827 4001                     COOKING 4
EMAIL: enquiries@thelowryhotel.com                                FRENCH
WEBSITE: www.thelowryhotel.com                                   £27–£65

A staircase rises from the vast foyer to a bar and a 'five-sided aircraft hanger' of a dining room, where a wall of windows overlooks the Irwell, and another is covered in wine bottles. As in other MPW diffusion restaurants, the static carte offers a selection of carefully prepared, French-inspired, populist dishes. Among them are grilled scallops with endive Tatin, and a smooth, rich rectangle of foie gras parfait, scattered with black truffle, sitting on a plate coated with first-class jellied stock with a rich beefy flavour.

Forget innovation, surprises or seasonality (asparagus is served in October), but remember there are menus for vegetarians, vegans and children. Materials may not always be tip-top quality, and some items (such as the bread sauce with roast chicken) fail to endear, but successes have included a sliced, fanned breast of duck, accurately timed, served with a small mound of choucroute on roasting juices laced with Madeira, and a first-class sherry trifle. Staff are pleasant, competent and knowledgeable about the food. Wines are generally high in quality and carry prices to match (though the list starts at £14).

CHEF: David Woolf   PROPRIETOR: Rocco Forte   OPEN: all week 12 to 2.30 (12.30 to 3 Sun), 6 to 10 MEALS: alc (main courses £11 to £16.50). Set L £12 (2 courses) to £15, Set L Sun £15.95, Set D 6 to 7 £15 (2 courses) to £18, Set D £25 to £36 (whole table only). Bar menu also available SERVICE: 10% (optional), card slips closed   CARDS: Amex, Delta, Diners, MasterCard, Switch, Visa   DETAILS: 120 seats. 30 seats outside. Private parties: 120 main room, 8 to 20 private rooms. Car park. Vegetarian meals. Children's helpings. Wheelchair access (also WC). Music. Air-conditioned (*The Which? Hotel Guide*)   ACCOMMODATION: 165 rooms, all with bath/shower. TV. Phone. Room only £185 to £1,000. Rooms for disabled. Baby facilities

---

*'We didn't really understand the significance of the ''in-shore cod'' (thinking cod was always caught out at sea), so queried this with the ... waiter. He absolutely insisted that ''in-shore'' referred to the light crust on top of it, and wouldn't hear of it having anything to do with where it was fished.'* (On eating in the West Country)

---

map 3

# ▲ Sandgate Hotel, La Terrasse ▮ ✴

The Esplanade, Sandgate CT20 3DY                                   COOKING **7**
TEL: (01303) 220444   FAX: (01303) 220496                        MODERN FRENCH
WEBSITE: www.sandgatehotel.com                                        £38–£76

A dozen steps lead to the front door of this four-storey Victorian terraced house on the seafront, facing Samuel Gicqueau's native France. It is 'always a pleasure to visit', and comfortably furnished, with light, airy décor that suits the bright seaside location. The food is interesting, imaginative and well executed, with foie gras (from Landes) and shellfish (perhaps from Scotland) dominating first courses. Simple yet beguiling combinations include scallops with sliced potatoes and black truffle, roast langoustines with Szechuan pepper and candied lime, and duck foie gras on pain d'épice with roast pear and a ginger and orange sauce.

Main courses have a similarly sharp focus. Fish from the Folkestone trawlers might take in roast turbot with ceps and a red wine sauce, or a Mediterranean treatment of red mullet served with stuffed piquillo peppers and fried calamari with tomato, basil and black olives. Romney Marsh lamb might appear from time to time; beef is Aberdeen Angus (served simply, classically and indulgently with foie gras, truffle and Madeira sauce); and côte de veau comes with salsify and truffle shavings, all assembled by the maitre d' at table. Vegetables may not feature prominently, but then this is French cooking. Gallic farmhouse cheeses are kept in peak condition, and desserts might include a hot pistachio soufflé with bitter chocolate sorbet, and a brochette of pineapple and mango with coconut rice pudding.

Service is friendly and 'professional in the French manner' – which is to say polite and unobtrusive – and meals are well paced. Wines, a pedigree-heavy collection, are also largely from France, but with a smattering of well-chosen selections from elsewhere. Despite the preponderance of big names from Burgundy, Bordeaux, the Rhône and California, mark-ups are fair, even if bottle prices are not cheap. Those wanting to push the boat out can choose from a dozen vintages of Château d'Yquem or a number of mature Bordeaux premiers crus. Digging around will turn up some interesting selections under £20, starting at £14.

CHEF: Samuel Gicqueau   PROPRIETORS: Zara and Samuel Gicqueau   OPEN: Wed to Sun L 12.15 to 1.30, Tue to Sat D 7.15 to 9.15   CLOSED: 10 days early Oct, 4 weeks Jan   MEALS: alc (main courses £17.50 to £24). Set L Wed to Fri £24.50, Set L Sat and Sun £34, Set D Tue to Thur £24.50, Set D Fri and Sat £34   SERVICE: not inc   CARDS: Amex, Delta, Diners, MasterCard, Switch, Visa   DETAILS: 20 seats. Private parties: 26 main room. Car park. Children's helpings. No smoking in dining room. Wheelchair access (not WC). Music. No mobile phones   ACCOMMODATION: 13 rooms, all with bath/shower. TV. Phone. B&B £45 to £78. Baby facilities (*The Which? Hotel Guide*)

---

*London Round-ups listing additional restaurants that may be worth a visit can be found after the main London section.*

## SAPPERTON Gloucestershire          map 2

# Bell at Sapperton ✻          NEW ENTRY

Sapperton GL7 6LE                                          COOKING 1
TEL: (01285) 760298   FAX: (01285) 760761          MODERN EUROPEAN
                                                          £28–£50

'A very pleasant and civilised way to spend an evening,' noted one reporter after visiting this revamped old stone hostelry in a serene Cotswold hamlet. 'Walkers and horses welcome,' says a notice, and there are real ales on tap, but the place is now firmly in the fashionable gastro-pub groove. Daily fish specials are well worth considering, perhaps grilled fillet of sea bass with spiced chickpea mash, or roast monkfish wrapped in Parma ham with wild garlic leaves. The printed menu changes with the seasons: cassoulet of confit of duck with Toulouse sausage seems to be a firm favourite, otherwise expect anything from chargrilled lamb burgers to frittata of sweet peppers and spinach. Desserts such as tarte Tatin with apple and Calvados ice cream are chalked on a board. An affordable 40-bin wine list includes around a dozen or so by the glass: prices start at £11.50.

CHEF: Alyson McKenzie   PROPRIETORS: Paul Davidson and Pat Le Jeune   OPEN: all week 12 to 2, 7 to 9.30 (9 Sun)   CLOSED: 25 Dec, D 26 Dec and 31 Dec   MEALS: alc (main courses £10.50 to £17)   SERVICE: not inc, card slips closed   CARDS: MasterCard, Switch, Visa   DETAILS: 80 seats. 50 seats outside. Car park. Vegetarian meals. Children's helpings. No children under 10 at D. No smoking in 1 dining room. No music. No mobile phones

## SAWLEY Lancashire          map 8

# Spread Eagle ✻

Sawley BB7 4NH                                          COOKING 3
TEL: (01200) 441202   FAX: (01200) 441973          MODERN BRITISH
off A59, 4m NE of Clitheroe                             £22–£46

The setting is a major attraction for visitors to this cottagey seventeenth-century inn, with its views of the River Ribble and the Bowland hills beyond. Most people come here to eat in the aptly named Riverside Restaurant, where Greig Barnes produces a range of dishes with a modern international slant. Influences from the Far East, France and the Mediterranean help to give his menu a lively outlook. Seared tuna is served with wasabi-flavoured potato, sesame seeds and thread noodles; chargrilled rump of beef sits atop olive oil mash with shallot confit and an oxtail and thyme sauce; while Barbary duck breast is accompanied by a herb crumpet, slow-cooked onions and a sauce finished with elderflower cordial. Desserts are a satisfying bunch, from sticky toffee pudding to roasted pineapple with sultana pancakes and black pepper ice cream. Service is 'quick, friendly and unobtrusive'. The approachable wine list offers plenty of decent drinking at keen prices and there's a special list for whisky fans. House Dubeouf is £9.95.

CHEF: Greig Barnes   PROPRIETORS: Nigel and Ysanne Williams   OPEN: Tue to Sun L 12 to 2.30, Tue to Sat D 6 to 9   MEALS: alc exc Sun L (main courses £8 to £13.50). Set L Sun £12.50 (2 courses) to £14.95, Set L Tue to Fri and Set D Tue to Thur £8.50 (2 courses) to £11.45, Set D Fri £10.50 (2 courses) to £12.95   SERVICE: not inc   CARDS: Amex, Delta, MasterCard, Switch, Visa

DETAILS: 80 seats. Private parties: 100 main room, 10 to 100 private rooms. Car park. Vegetarian meals. Children's helpings. No smoking in dining room. Wheelchair access (also WC). Music (£5)

---

## SCARBOROUGH North Yorkshire                               map 9

# Lanterna £

33 Queen Street, Scarborough YO11 1HQ
TEL/FAX: (01723) 363616
EMAIL: ralessio@lanterna-ristorante.co.uk
WEBSITE: www.lanterna-ristorante.co.uk

COOKING 3
ITALIAN
£30–£80

In June 2003 the Alessios will be celebrating 30 years at their back-street restaurant, a well-maintained dining room with a pleasantly old-fashioned look. They have avoided the temptation to mark the anniversary by making wholesale changes to the menu, having chosen instead to highlight those dishes that have stood the test of time – chicken breast with onions, mushrooms cream and brandy, for example – while adding one or two new items to their repertoire. Fish is a highlight (Giorgio makes daily early-morning trips to the market to hand-pick the best for his kitchen), much of it simply grilled or baked, though it may also appear as tuna with butter beans, salmon ravioli in cream and caviar sauce, or pasta with cuttlefish ink and squid. Service – overseen by Rachel Alessio – is consistently praised in reports. An almost exclusively Italian wine list includes some big names alongside more humble offerings, and kicks off with Barbera del Monferrato and Piemonte Cortese at £10.50 a bottle (£2.75 a glass).

CHEF: Giorgio Alessio   PROPRIETORS: Giorgio and Rachel Alessio   OPEN: Mon to Sat D only 7 to 10.30   CLOSED: 2 weeks end Oct, 25 and 26 Dec, 1 Jan   MEALS: alc (main courses £12 to £29)   SERVICE: not inc, card slips closed   CARDS: Delta, MasterCard, Switch, Visa   DETAILS: 30 seats. Private parties: 36 main room. Vegetarian meals. Children's helpings. No children under 2. Wheelchair access (not WC). Music. Air-conditioned

---

## SEAHAM Co Durham                                           map 10

# ▲ Seaham Hall Hotel ⼂ ✴                   NEW ENTRY

Lord Byron's Walk, Seaham SR7 7AG
TEL: (0191) 5161400   FAX: (0191) 5161410
EMAIL: reservations@seaham-hall.com
WEBSITE: www.seaham-hall.com

COOKING 6
MODERN EUROPEAN
£34–£81

'This is a hotel and a half,' was the opinion of one who had braved the crashing of ten-foot-high waves along the Durham coastal path in winter, and pitched up here in some gratitude. A large hypnotic water sculpture stands before a historic building where Lord Byron too once found a retreat. Inside is a strikingly modern bar-lounge, and a demure dining room, its walls covered in 'what looks like wrinkly tissue paper', with a peaceful view on to a balustraded garden. While some of that design-consciousness seems to have rubbed off on John Connell's formidably proficient cooking, the food lacks nothing in depth or seriousness. A stone slab of half a dozen appetisers is the first indication of a kitchen hot on detail, an impression confirmed by a first-course croustade, on to which is piled a base of wild mushrooms in Madeira sauce, a piece of seared foie gras and several slices of pink-cooked pigeon breast, the whole surrounded by salad leaves and soft-boiled quails' eggs dressed in sweet balsamic.

Combinations may be familiar – roasted calamari with risotto nero, crab salad with avocado and pink grapefruit – but the quality of materials and the skill in execution are what impress. A piece of 'zingily fresh' Cornish sea bass, its skin salted, scored and crisped, is juicy and full of flavour, served with roasted vegetables, or there might be farmhouse chicken with truffle-glazed veal sweetbreads. For dessert might come chocolate and orange tart with orange salad, or (in late autumn) pain perdu made from brioche, topped with good vanilla ice cream, and surrounded by roasted apple slices and blackberries. Service is quite charming enough to be able to loosen up a bit.

The wine list, every bit as sophisticated as the surroundings, is not just a collection of big French names. Instead, there are well-chosen wines from across both Old and New Worlds which are not subject to greedy mark-ups. For those wishing to push the boat out, reds from the 'private cellar' selection – mostly comprising Bordeaux – are the place to look; there is reasonable choice under £20, with prices opening at £15.50.

CHEF: John Connell  PROPRIETORS: Tom and Jocelyn Maxfield  OPEN: all week 12 to 2, 6.30 to 9.30  MEALS: alc D (main courses £23 to £25). Set L Mon to Sat £14.50 (2 courses) to £19.50, Set L Sun alc (main courses £17 to £20). Set D £34 to £55. Light L menu also available  SERVICE: not inc  CARDS: Amex, Delta, Diners, MasterCard, Switch, Visa  DETAILS: 50 seats. 50 seats outside. Private parties: 20 main room, 10 to 120 private rooms. Car park. Vegetarian meals. Children's helpings. No smoking in dining room. Wheelchair access (also WC). Music. No mobile phones. Air-conditioned  ACCOMMODATION: 19 rooms, all with bath/shower. TV. Phone. B&B £135 to £500. Rooms for disabled. Baby facilities. Swimming pool (The Which? Hotel Guide)

## SEAVIEW  Isle of Wight                                       map 2

## ▲ Seaview Hotel 💱✕                           NEW ENTRY

High Street, Seaview PO34 5EX
TEL: (01983) 612711   FAX: (01983) 613729                         COOKING 2
EMAIL: reception@seaviewhotel.co.uk                             ANGLO-FRENCH
WEBSITE: www.seaviewhotel.co.uk                                    £26–£45

Very obviously the hub of the eponymous town, sitting rather grandly in a narrow one-way street just up from the seafront, the hotel seems all things to all patrons. There are a couple of bars, a private room, and a 'louche, sepulchrally lit' dining room with shaded candles and a big brass clock. The Haywards have been here for over 20 years, but the kitchen has recently seen the arrival of Michael Green (from the Heathcotes' empire) and Mavis Barry (from BA), who turn their hands to such local delights as Isle of Wight tomato summer pudding, salmon ceviche topped with sour shredded cucumber, and a hot ramekin of crabmeat and cream cooked under a gratinated cheesy layer.

One thing people expect, this close to the sea, is good fish, and the kitchen duly obliges with moist, well-timed monkfish wrapped in Parma ham on a russet-coloured crustacean stock, and a fish special: a generous piece of impressively fresh turbot dressed in lemon and pesto, sauced with beurre blanc. Meat works equally well, judging by shredded duck confit in a bowl of salad leaves dressed with orange and mustard, and by slices of Godshill pork tenderloin on a bed of mash impregnated with caramelised onion threads, with a rich, cream sauce of mustard and Stilton. In an attempt to dent the island's garlic mountain, regional cheeses are accompanied by an apricot and garlic chutney, or there may be poached pear, or passion-fruit crème brûlée to finish. Service can be amiably absent-minded. The wine list has a classically French bias, plenty of options under £20, and Corney & Barrow house wine at £9.95.

CHEFS: Michael Green and Mavis Barry   PROPRIETORS: Nicola and Nicholas Hayward   OPEN: all week L 12 to 1.30, Mon to Sat D 7.30 to 9.30   MEALS: alc exc Sun L (main courses £13 to £16). Set L Sun £16.95   SERVICE: not inc, card slips closed   CARDS: Amex, Delta, Diners, MasterCard, Switch, Visa   DETAILS: 70 seats. 50 seats outside. Private parties: 40 main room, 30 private room. Car park. Vegetarian meals. Children's helpings. No children under 5 at D. No smoking in dining room. Wheelchair access (not WC). No music. Air-conditioned   ACCOMMODATION: 16 rooms, all with bath/shower. TV. Phone. Room only £55 to £140. Baby facilities (*The Which? Hotel Guide*) (£5)

## SELLACK Herefordshire                                              map 5

# Lough Pool Inn ✻ 🍴 £

Sellack HR9 6LX
TEL: (01989) 730236   FAX: (01989) 730462                        COOKING 4
off A49, 3m NW of Ross-on-Wye on the Ross to            MODERN EUROPEAN
Hoarwithy road                                                  £26–£45

Part of the draw is that Lough Pool still functions as a pub (check out the real ales), including a table-strewn garden for fine weather and a flag-floored bar with a log fire, plus an informal but smart mustard-yellow dining room for those wanting to escape the smoke and sit at a proper wooden table. The food covers pub-fare bases too – a BLT doorstep, steak and kidney with Guinness, and first-class local ribeye steak with chips – and to find them done so well is a delight. But the menu has wider appeal too (daily specials are chalked on a board); ideas are straightforward yet lively, and results are pleasurable. Deep-frying (to be expected in a pub) is particularly well done, thanks to a light, crisp batter that might coat, for example, the onion rings accompanying chargrilled lamb's liver, and fish is capably handled, producing crisp-skinned sea bass on a potato and olive cake, surrounded by tomatoes and red peppers in a vibrant yellow olive oil.

Nuts are a favoured ingredient (perhaps roasted hazelnuts in the creamy sauce to accompany an unmoulded goat's cheese soufflé), cumin is likely to appear (in the side-plate carrots maybe), and orange is almost certain to turn up somewhere. Relishes make an impact too: a beetroot one with haggis fritters, and a sweet-pepper piccalilli with a first-class ham hock and foie gras terrine. Desserts tend to favour cakes and tarts, from a sticky date pudding with butterscotch sauce, via orange cake (told you) with maple syrup, to a stickily chewy pecan tart. Service is willing, and the compact wine list, starting with Chilean and French house wines at £10.50, mostly stays commendably under £20 (try the South African Merlot or Argentinian Chardonnay).

CHEF: Kevin Gauvain   PROPRIETOR: Stephen Bull   OPEN: all week 12 to 2.30, 6.30 to 9.30
CLOSED: no food 25 Dec and D 26 Dec   MEALS: alc (main courses £8.50 to £14)   SERVICE: not inc,
card slips closed   CARDS: Delta, MasterCard, Switch, Visa   DETAILS: 80 seats. 50 seats outside.
Private parties: 30 main room. Car park. Vegetarian meals. No children under 14 in bar.
Children's helpings. No smoking in dining room. Wheelchair access (not WC). No music

## SHEDFIELD Hampshire
map 2

# Wickham Vineyard ✴

NEW ENTRY

Botley Road, Shedfield SO32 2HL
TEL: (01329) 832985   FAX: (01329) 834907
EMAIL: erica@wickhamvineyard.co.uk
WEBSITE: www.wickhamvineyard.co.uk
on A334 between Botley and Shedfield

*(HANTS GFG 2003 COMMENDED)*

COOKING 5
MODERN EUROPEAN
£27–£49

From this modern brick barn, with wooden rafters and local artwork (for sale)
on its walls, a picture window overlooks serried ranks of vines. Barring the
Muzak, all is 'eminently civilised', with the chef's wife Erica Graham ('as well
informed about the food as if she'd cooked it herself') running front-of-house. A
contemporary menu conjures up some intriguing ideas, from pan-fried foie gras
with a cherry sorbet, to fillet of zander with bouillabaisse jus, and while the
kitchen follows a few fads (whipping up frothy sauces for example), its fine
ingredients and hard work combine to make this good value for money.

A main-course lamb dish – raviolo of sweetbreads, crisp-skinned confit
shoulder, herbed fillet and crusty caramelised tongue – confirms that raw
materials are good, and timing impressive. While garnishing is thankfully
limited, the kitchen sometimes over-elaborates, though there is little else to
quibble with. Highlights have included a single accurately seared scallop,
topped with langoustines (coated in light batter and deep fried), perched on a
little cake of herb-flecked risotto, with a touch of well-judged frothy butter
sauce.

Desserts are equally well constructed: a small tart of crisp, shortbread-like
pastry is covered with a fat smear of vanilla-speckled custard and a thin layer of
young, pink, stewed rhubarb, the sides buttressed by tiny sticks of crisply
cooked rhubarb. Extras show a desire to impress, from a choice of butter with the
well-made bread to an ace appetiser and pre-dessert. Seven Wickham wines
(including a red and two sparklers) open the list and are all available by the
glass, as are another dozen or so house wines. A couple of pages of pricier
offerings widen the choice.

CHEF: James Graham   PROPRIETORS: Gordon and Angela Channon   OPEN: Tue to Sun L 12 to 2,
Tue to Sat D 7 to 9   CLOSED: first 3 weeks Jan   MEALS: Set L Tue to Sat £13.50 (2 courses) to
£15.50, Set L Sun £17.50, Set D £23.50 (2 courses) to £28.50. Light L menu also available
SERVICE: not inc, card slips closed, 10% for parties of 8 or more   CARDS: Delta, MasterCard,
Switch, Visa   DETAILS: 44 seats. 18 seats outside. Private parties: 50 main room. Car park.
Vegetarian meals. Children's helpings. No smoking in dining room. Wheelchair access (also
WC). Music. No mobile phones  £5

*See inside the front cover for an explanation of the symbols used at the tops of entries.*

# Blue Room Brasserie  £                      NEW ENTRY

798 Chesterfield Road, Woodseats,
Sheffield S8 0SF                                      COOKING **4**
TEL: (0114) 255 2004   FAX: (0114) 255 1635          MODERN EUROPEAN-PLUS
WEBSITE: www.blueroombrasserie.co.uk                 £25–£49

This attractively light and airy venue in a suburb of Sheffield has quickly become a popular destination, and makes a welcome addition to the city's dining options. Eclectic is perhaps the best word to sum up the cooking style, which shows both traditional and modern influences and gets its culinary ideas from across Europe and Asia, with a particular penchant for Thai and Japanese flavours. The wide reach is demonstrated in starters such as baked feta and red onion tart, and fat juicy mussels in a 'brilliant' sauce based on coconut milk and shellfish stock.

Around a dozen main courses are on offer, taking in everything from pan-fried brill with risotto primavera, to a fine version of duck confit with impressively crisp skin, served with bubble and squeak. Sauces are a strong point: a syrupy jus accompanies succulent quail (with a fresh-tasting 'wonderfully herby' stuffing), and an equally sticky and intensely flavoured reduction comes with tender, slow-baked shoulder of lamb on a mound of garlicky mashed potatoes. Finish, perhaps, with raspberry brûlée or tiramisù. Three dozen wines offer a decent cross-section of styles and good value. House Chilean is £11.95 a bottle, £2.95 a glass.

CHEFS: Christian Kent and Christian Szurko   PROPRIETORS: Christian, Scott and Lindsay Kent   OPEN: Sun L 12 to 3, Tue to Sat D 6 to 9.45 (10 Fri, 10.30 Sat)   CLOSED: bank hol Mons   MEALS: alc D (main courses £8 to £24). Set L Sun £16.95, Set D Tue to Fri 6 to 7 £14.95   SERVICE: not inc   CARDS: Delta, Diners, MasterCard, Switch, Visa   DETAILS: 130 seats. Private parties: 100 main room, 40 private room. Car park. Vegetarian meals. Children's helpings. Wheelchair access (also WC). Music. Air-conditioned

# Carriages

289 Abbeydale Road South, Dore,
Sheffield S17 3LB                                    COOKING **3**
TEL: (0114) 2350101                                  MODERN ENGLISH
WEBSITE: www.carriagesrestaurant.co.uk               £26–£50

A converted shop in the south-west corner of Sheffield is the setting for this tastefully decorated modern restaurant. As befits such a place, the menu is short and to the point, with just five or six choices per course; fresh ingredients, contemporary flavours and wide-ranging ideas set the tone. The kitchen has some witty takes on old faithfuls, including lamb shank terrine with a mint, pea and herb dressing, and melon brûlée with mango salsa, while main courses sound a more earthy note. Roast guinea fowl comes with black pudding croquette and baby leeks, and pan-fried fillet of cod with shrimp and horseradish Yorkshire pudding and seafood gravy. Bread-and-butter pudding with butterscotch sauce is the signature dessert; otherwise try sweet lemon and mango tart, or white chocolate pot with chocolate brownie and chocolate ice cream. Old and New World wines jostle for supremacy on the carefully assembled, 50-strong wine list. House French is £11.90.

CHEF: James Riley   PROPRIETOR: Cary Brown   OPEN: Sun L 12 to 2.30, Tue to Sat D 7 to 10   MEALS: alc D (main courses £12.50 to £16). Set L Sun £17.95   SERVICE: not inc   CARDS: Delta, MasterCard, Switch, Visa   DETAILS: 50 seats. Private parties: 60 main room. Car park. Vegetarian meals. Children's helpings. Wheelchair access (also WC). Music

## Rafters

220 Oakbrook Road, Nether Green,
Sheffield S11 7ED                                                          COOKING 3
TEL: (0114) 230 4819                                                  MODERN BRITISH
WEBSITE: www.raftersrestaurant.com                                       £35–£46

Don't look for the entrance to Rafters in the row of shops on Oakbrook Road; the front door is discreetly hidden round the corner, and the restaurant itself is up a flight of stairs. Beyond the bar area is a homely, intimate dining room, where a lemon and terracotta colour scheme conveys a Mediterranean feel.

Menus offer lively, modern cooking based on classical techniques, but aiming for a lighter feel. Forthright flavours are a common trait, as in a starter of slow-roast tomatoes of 'concentrated, intense and tingly' flavour, served on herby focaccia with mushroom cream. Main courses promise similarly high impact: rack of lamb with a tart of devilled kidneys, creamed potatoes, parsnip crisps and a tomato jus, for example. A tendency to embellish dishes, however, diverts attention from the main business; one reporter's fresh, flavourful cod, of 'nacreous luminescence', had to compete with its accompanying Arran mustard sauce, potato and horseradish rösti, and crab and seafood spring roll. Less fussy dishes have been more successful, such as a dessert of poached plums in orange zest sauce with vanilla ice cream. Service is 'attentive, professional and focused'. The wine list, organised by style, stays mostly below £20, opening with house French at £10.50.

CHEFS: Jamie Bosworth and Marcus Lane   PROPRIETORS: Wayne and Joanne Bosworth   OPEN: Mon and Wed to Sat D only 7 to 10   CLOSED: 25 Dec, 1 week Jan, 2 weeks Aug, bank hols   MEALS: Set D £24.95   SERVICE: not inc, card slips closed   CARDS: Amex, Delta, MasterCard, Switch, Visa   DETAILS: 40 seats. Private parties: 40 main room. Vegetarian meals. Children's helpings. No children under 7. No cigars/pipes in dining room. Music

## Richard Smith at Thyme ▼ ✸ £

32–34 Sandygate Road, Crosspool,
Sheffield S10 5RY
TEL: (01142) 666096                                                       COOKING 5
FAX: (01142) 660279                            MODERN BRITISH/MEDIETERRANEAN
WEBSITE: www.thymeforfood.co.uk                                          £18–£63

Despite its third name change in as many years, and yet more expansion (this time to the pastry kitchen), Richard Smith's cool, modern, efficient brasserie-style operation remains focused on an appealing menu based on good supplies. The long-roll call of well-sourced ingredients includes roast Cornish monkfish, Whitby haddock (deep-fried in beer batter with chunky chips and tartare sauce), dived scallops, roast rack of Derbyshire lamb, and venison (with braised red cabbage), although the range of treatments extends to the Mediterranean and beyond.

Portions are on the large side, and dishes can be rather elaborate – for presentational rather than sound culinary reasons, reporters say – but nobody can feel short-changed by the breadth of choice. This is a place where duck still comes with orange sauce (the crisply baked leg on a separate plate from the breast), and where a meal might start with a Thai hot and sour soup, followed by a risotto flavoured with basil milkshake, and then a plate of Pontefract rhubarb turned into a crumble, a fool, a jelly and a sorbet. The emphasis is on generally sound execution rather than excitement or finesse, but successes among desserts have included a biscuit pastry case filled (just before serving) with crème pâtissière and plums. Nibbles and vegetables are charged extra, and service can be a bit zealous about topping up, but wines are taken seriously. Six house selections appear at the front (bottle prices start at £12.50) and a 'cellar selection' of pricier bottles at the back. There is a good balance between Old and New World producers, and prices are sensible enough to encourage exploration throughout.

CHEFS: Simon Wild and Tim Vincent  PROPRIETORS: Richard and Victoria Smith  OPEN: all week L 12 to 2 (3 Sun), Mon to Sat D 6 to 10  MEALS: alc exc Sun L (main courses £8 to £20). Set L Mon to Sat £12 (2 courses) to £16, Set L Sun £18.50, Set D Mon to Thur 6 to 7 £15  SERVICE: not inc, 10% for parties of 10 or more  CARDS: Amex, MasterCard, Switch, Visa  DETAILS: 90 seats. Private parties: 70 main room, 8 to 24 private rooms. Vegetarian meals. Children's helpings. No smoking in dining room. Wheelchair access (also WC). Music. No mobile phones. Air-conditioned £5

## SHELF West Yorkshire                                                    map 8

# Bentley's ⚡✳

12 Wadehouse Road, Shelf HX3 7PB
TEL: (01274) 690992   FAX: (01274) 690011                          COOKING 4
EMAIL: bentleys@btinternet.com                                MODERN BRITISH
WEBSITE: www.bentleys-foodandwine.co.uk                             £18–£46

Bentley's, ten years old in 2002, 'remains one of our best local restaurants', according to a Yorkshire-based inspector. It all fits into a compact two-up, two-down terraced house: bar area for pre-meal drinks on the ground floor, and two 'surprisingly spacious' dining rooms in the cellar. Décor is simple, and tables are laid with smart linen even at lunchtime.

The carte is listed on a blackboard, supplemented at lunchtimes by two- and three-course set menus. That overworked word 'eclectic' is nevertheless the best description of Paul Bentley's cooking style, though it is mostly based on traditional flavour combinations. French black pudding on open ravioli with prosciutto and peas, for example, might be followed by grilled sea bass with king prawns and roast vegetables dressed with aged balsamic vinegar. An inspector was suitably impressed by the lightness and fresh taste of crisply battered queen scallops (with corals), and by a main course of tasty, accurately cooked beef fillet with a generous helping of rich bourguignonne-style sauce and smooth mashed potatoes. Beware, portions are generous, so you may need to share a dessert: lemon and lime Bakewell tart, for example, with thin, light pastry and a moist, tasty filling. A short but decent wine list opens with four house selections from £9.95.

CHEFS: Paul Bentley and Anthony Bickers   PROPRIETORS: Paul and Pamela Bentley   OPEN: Tue to Fri L 12 to 2, Tue to Sat D 6.30 to 9.30   MEALS: alc (main courses £10 to £16.50). Set L £8.75 (2 courses) to £9.95   SERVICE: not inc, card slips closed   CARDS: Delta, MasterCard, Switch, Visa   DETAILS: 68 seats. Private parties: 24 main room, 8 to 24 private rooms. Vegetarian meals. No smoking in dining room. Music. Air-conditioned

## SHEPTON MALLET  Somerset                                      map 2

# ▲ Charlton House Hotel, Mulberry Restaurant  � ✳

Shepton Mallet BA4 4PR
TEL: (01749) 342008   FAX: (01749) 346362
EMAIL: enquiry@charltonhouse.com                    COOKING 6
WEBSITE: www.charltonhouse.com                   MODERN BRITISH
on A361 to Frome, 1m E of Shepton Mallet                £32–£78

The house may be an elaborate marketing ploy for Mulberry furnishings, but it is discreetly and effectively done: drapes, big settees, rag-rolled walls and fabric-covered chairs combine to make it feel both opulent and rustic. Since last year a larger kitchen has come on stream, and an eighteenth-century orangery is being restored for private dining, but the contemporary cooking style remains unaltered.

A sense of industry prevails, as the repertoire deploys a wide range of skills, and dishes are made up of several components. Quantock duck breast, for example, comes with a Jerusalem artichoke and foie gras spring roll parcel, braised Savoy cabbage and confit potato. The menu appealingly juxtaposes northern and southern European ideas – red mullet with tapénade, beside salt beef with horseradish cream – and, although there are country-house gestures (sea bass with a champagne and caviar cream sauce, for example), a preference for vinaigrettes and oils over traditional stock-based sauces has merit: perhaps in the pesto accompanying roast breast of guinea fowl with pappardelle and artichokes.

Cheeses are mostly local and, as well as a selection with plum chutney, might include a croustillant of goats' cheese with a honey- and thyme-dressed salad. Desserts embrace raspberry tart with a spicy walnut praline mousse, and combinations such as a trio of English puddings: sticky toffee, sherry trifle and pear crumble. The wine list eschews the usual country-house style, swapping long lists of Bordeaux and Burgundy for a more modern Old World-meets-New list arranged by style and price. You will need deep pockets to crack open most bottles – there is not much on offer under £20 – though sixteen table wines and six dessert wines are served by the glass, ranging from £3.95 to £8.25.

CHEF: Adam Fellows   PROPRIETORS: Mr and Mrs Roger Saul   OPEN: all week 12.30 to 2, 7 to 9.30   MEALS: Set L £14.50 (2 courses) to £18.50, Set D £42 to £54   SERVICE: not inc, card slips closed   CARDS: Amex, Delta, Diners, MasterCard, Switch, Visa   DETAILS: 90 seats. 20 seats outside. Private parties: 70 main room. Car park. Vegetarian meals. Children's helpings. No smoking in dining room. Wheelchair access (also WC). Music. No mobile phones   ACCOMMODATION: 16 rooms, all with bath/shower. TV. Phone. B&B £113 to £315. Baby facilities. Fishing (*The Which? Hotel Guide*)

## SHERBORNE CAUSEWAY Dorset                                              map 2

# ▲ Wayfarers £                                          NEW ENTRY

| | |
|---|---|
| Sherborne Causeway, Shaftesbury SP7 9PX | COOKING 4 |
| TEL/FAX: (01747) 852821 | MODERN EUROPEAN |
| on A30 2m west of Shaftesbury | £24–£50 |

This restaurant beside the A30 has low ceilings, exposed rough stone walls and 'pretty, feminine', rather cluttered décor, and is home to some accomplished cooking. Its simpler Bistrot set menu is a bargain, while the imitation parchment carte can be convoluted: a roast boned quail supposedly filled with a 'boudin' of smoked ham and pistachio, for example, turns out to be simply stuffed (no sign of sausage) but is tasty nonetheless.

Basic materials are well handled, though garnishes abound, and complexity and extras make the food more 'country-house' than one expects of a small, individually run restaurant. One assemblage involved strongly seared turbot fillets, scallops with their roe, fresh pasta, a scallop mousse, tasty mushrooms, asparagus, green beans and broad beans, all in a classically made beurre blanc flavoured with lemon grass and ginger. Despite some imbalances, the food impresses for its notable technical skills, and for its freshness throughout

Mark Newton is good at various forms of dough, including pasta, blinis, cep dumplings, and bread (including a springy, malty brown roll); one impressive dessert has been a spongy-fluffy savarin with a honey crust, filled with tiny balls of apple, topped with vanilla-speckled ice cream and garnished with spun sugar, with a toffee butterscotch sauce. Clare Newton handles front of house, and France heads a reasonably priced list that starts with six house wines under £12 (£2 a glass).

CHEF: Mark Newton   PROPRIETORS: Clare and Mark Newton   OPEN: Tue to Fri and Sun L 12 to 1.30 (bookings only), Tue to Sat D 7 to 9.15   CLOSED: 2–3 weeks from 26 Dec, 1 week end June   MEALS: alc (main courses £16 to £17). Set L and D Tue to Fri £16.95. Set L Sun £19   SERVICE: not inc, card slips closed   CARDS: Amex, Delta, Diners, MasterCard, Switch, Visa   DETAILS: 34 seats. 8 seats outside. Private parties: 34 main room. Car park. Vegetarian meals. Children's helpings. No children under 8 at D. Wheelchair access (also women's WC). No music   ACCOMMODATION: 1 room with bath/shower. B&B £55 to £70. No children under 12  (£5)

## SHERE Surrey                                                          map 3

# Kinghams ⚡✳

| | |
|---|---|
| Gomshall Lane, Shere GU5 9HE | |
| TEL: (01483) 202168 | COOKING 3 |
| WEBSITE: www.kinghams-restaurant.co.uk | MODERN ENGLISH |
| just off A25 Dorking to Guildford road | £30–£57 |

Half-timbered between its red tiles and bricks, this seriously ancient building a stone's throw from the church consists of two small rooms with tiny windows, a big communal hearth and closely packed tables. It feels 'cottagey, tea-roomy, villagey', and its strengths are admirable raw materials and accurate timing. As well as a carte and a fixed-price option, a separate fish menu, actually a 'fish board' placed on the table, might offer mussels poached in white wine and cream, grilled Dover sole, and fillet of brill with a chive and scallop butter.

Some of the more up-to-date ideas in the repertoire might include three large scallops on flat, roughly textured pea and bacon patties with a lemony dressing, or tiger prawns and crab dumplings in a broth flavoured with lemon grass, ginger and lime leaves. Meat dishes, meanwhile, have included three thick slices of first-class loin of lamb, the skin crisp, the meat pink and juicy, served with oven-dried aubergines and tomatoes with a sweet potato mash and a strongly minty sauce. Although main courses come with vegetables, more are offered (and charged extra).

Desserts take a generally traditional line, from apple and blackcurrant in filo pastry, to a creamy and artfully presented lemon mousse on a layer of sponge cake, accompanied by a scoop of sweet raspberry sorbet and a basket of berries. Service, from young women petite enough to glide under the low beams, is 'chirpy, friendly and perky', and a balanced wine list kicks off with Sicilian house varietals (Inzolia and Sangiovese) at £11.95 (£3 a glass).

CHEF/PROPRIETOR: Paul Baker   OPEN: Tue to Sun L 12 to 2, Tue to Sat D 7 to 9   CLOSED: 25 Dec to 3 Jan   MEALS: alc exc Sun L (main courses £11 to £20). Set L £13.95 (2 courses), Set D Tue to Thur £15.95 (2 courses)   SERVICE: not inc   CARDS: Amex, Delta, Diners, MasterCard, Switch, Visa   DETAILS: 50 seats. 20 seats outside. Private parties: 50 main room, 20 to 30 private rooms. Car park. Vegetarian meals. Children's helpings. No smoking in dining room. Wheelchair access (not WC). No music. No mobile phones  (£5)

---

## SHINFIELD Berkshire                                                    map 2

# L'Ortolan ♥ ⁵⁄✳

**NEW ENTRY**

Church Lane, Shinfield RG2 9BY
TEL: (0118) 988 3783   FAX: (0118) 988 9338
WEBSITE: www.lortolan.com

COOKING 7
MODERN FRENCH
£38–£80

Following in the footsteps of Nico Ladenis and John Burton-Race at this old red-brick vicarage takes a bit of nerve, but reporters are unanimously convinced that this is a worthy successor. The Grade II listed building has been given a stylish, bold and no-expense-spared makeover, producing a clubby lounge bar with suede and leather armchairs, a pale-yellow conservatory, and a sober dining room done in brown and beige. Menus are laid out in set-price format – dinner offers a choice of three or seven courses, while lunch is an undoubted bargain – and Alan Murchison's classical training at Le Manoir (see entry, Great Milton) shines through in some very fine cooking.

His trade marks include innovative combinations, thoughtful presentation (with lots of space on the plate) and clearly defined flavours, and of course first-class ingredients: two trimmed fillets of top-quality, herb-crusted halibut (served with a tomato fondue and roast baby endive), or a thick, accurately timed fillet of beef (also herb-crusted) on a bed of dauphinois potato, with a jug of rich Shiraz-based wine sauce to pour over. This is supremely confident cooking, be it a crisp breast of roast mallard wrapped around a melting core of foie gras (the star of the evening for one couple), or a ballottine of rare salmon coated in chopped herbs, decorated with a triangle of roast skin for contrast, and served with a rich potato mousse, the plate zigzagged with a mild horseradish cream.

Desserts range from a tangy lemon tart, with ultra-thin crisp pastry and a fine caramelised top, served with a well-judged honey ice cream, to an Armagnac and prune parfait topped with a juicy marinated prune, accompanied by a light, crisp, apple beignet and lightly poached plums. Appetisers, bread, pre-desserts and petits fours are of a consistently high standard, and service is attentive, efficient and knowledgeable, not least the guided tour of the cheeses: a fine selection, some unusual, in tip-top condition. The wine list is well-bred and wide-ranging; in addition to the expected French selections, there are bottles from Uruguay and Tunisia, as well as some excellent selections from Spain and the New World. Some big price-tags appear, but these are mitigated by a lively collection in the under-£20 range and a good selection of half-bottles. Eight house wines sell for £14 to £22 (£4.25 to £6).

CHEF: Alan Murchison   PROPRIETOR: Newfee Ltd   OPEN: all week L 12 to 2.15, Mon to Sat D 6.45 to 9.15   CLOSED: 24 Dec to 6 Jan, 11 to 26 Aug   MEALS: Set L £19 (2 courses) to £45, Set D £39 to £45   SERVICE: not inc   CARDS: Amex, Delta, Diners, MasterCard, Switch, Visa   DETAILS: 50 seats. 30 seats outside. Private parties: 30 main room, 6 to 24 private rooms. Car park. Vegetarian meals. Children's helpings. No smoking in dining room. Wheelchair access (not WC). No music. No mobile phones

## SHIPHAM Somerset                                                     map 2

# ▲ Daneswood House ⁵⋇

Cuck Hill, Shipham BS25 1RD
TEL: (01934) 843145   FAX: (01934) 843824
EMAIL: info@daneswoodhotel.co.uk
WEBSITE: www.daneswoodhotel.co.uk                         COOKING 3
S of Bristol off A38 towards Cheddar; hotel is on        MODERN BRITISH
left as you leave the village                            £30–£49

The change from homeopathic health hydro to hotel and restaurant has given this Edwardian building something of a quirky character, a feeling enhanced by decorative foibles such as ornate radiators and flock wallpaper, and by Muzak from Perry Como and Dean Martin. Service, overseen by the manageress in a black cocktail dress, manages to combine decorum with familiarity and efficiency.

The kitchen deals in moderately complex and ambitious food, turning out ravioli of quail and foie gras, for example, and works with prime materials such as roasted sea bass fillet, and seared loin of tuna served with salade niçoise. It takes in some local ingredients along the way, including Mendip lamb, Quantock duck (the breast roasted and served with spiced poached plums), and, of course, mature Cheddar cheese. Desserts aim to be as comforting as the rest, judging by warm brioche-and-butter pudding, and hot chocolate fondant. A largely traditional French wine list offers some relief from Burgundy and Bordeaux (in the Loire and Beaujolais) and ropes in Italy, Spain and the antipodes for a bit of extra variety, plus a useful 16 house wines under £18.

CHEFS: Heather Matthews and Elise Hodges   PROPRIETORS: David and Elise Hodges   OPEN: all week 12 to 2, 7 to 9.30   CLOSED: 25 Dec to 3 Jan   MEALS: Set L Mon to Sat £23.95 (2 courses) to £29.95, Set L Sun £15.95 (2 courses) to £19.95, Set D £23.95 (2 courses) to £29.95   SERVICE: not inc, card slips closed   CARDS: Amex, Delta, Diners, MasterCard, Switch, Visa   DETAILS: 50 seats. Private parties: 35 main room, 10 to 14 private rooms. Car park. Vegetarian meals. Children's helpings. No smoking in dining room. Wheelchair access (also WC). Music ACCOMMODATION: 17 rooms, all with bath/shower. TV. Phone. B&B £89.50 to £150. Baby facilities (*The Which? Hotel Guide*) £5

## SHIPSTON ON STOUR  Warwickshire                                    map 5

# ▲ Chavignol ♟ ✳

at The Old Mill, 8 Mill Street, Shipston on
Stour CV36 4AW
TEL: (01608) 663888   FAX: (01608) 663188                   NEW CHEF
EMAIL: chavignol@virginbiz.com                         MODERN EUROPEAN
WEBSITE: www.chavignol.co.uk                                £37–£123

Substantial changes occurred at Chavignol just as the Guide went to press. Firstly Chav Brasserie moved from Chipping Norton to join the senior restaurant here at Shipston. Paul Haywood came with it, and it has opened as a separate entity, serving up its rather more casual style of food (prawn samosa, penne with chorizo and onions, Bakewell tart and ice cream, for example). Then Chavignol's chef Marcus Ashenford left, leaving Mark Maguire in charge of the kitchen. This has always been an accomplished operation, serving up some fine (and sometimes luxury) materials in satisfying ways: roast scallops marinated in honey and orange and served on blinis, perhaps, or foie gras on a mound of mushy peas, sharing the plate with duck rillettes. Mark Maguire also made an attentive and friendly host, so quite how front-of-house will shape up with him in the kitchen is uncertain. Many of the (French) wines on the bumper list are sourced directly from the growers, which inevitably makes them better value. Bottles range from big-name classics to cult favourites such as the Grosset Polish Hill Riesling from Australia. One house red and one house white are £14, and anything up to and including £40 a bottle is sold by the glass.

CHEF/PROPRIETOR: Mark Maguire   OPEN: Tue to Sun L 12 to 2, Tue to Sat 7 to 10   MEALS: Set L £18 (2 courses) to £40, Set D £30 to £85   SERVICE: not inc   CARDS: Amex, Delta, MasterCard, Switch, Visa   DETAILS: 35 seats. 20 seats outside. Private parties: 25 main room. Car park. Vegetarian meals. Children's helpings. No smoking in dining room. Wheelchair access (also WC). No music   ACCOMMODATION: 5 rooms, all with bath/shower. TV. Phone. B&B £95 to £190 (*The Which? Hotel Guide*) £5

## SHREWSBURY  Shropshire                                             map 5

# Sol ✳

82 Wyle Cop, Shrewsbury SY1 1UT                            COOKING 5
TEL: (01743) 340560   FAX: (01743) 340552                  INTERNATIONAL
WEBSITE: www.solrestaurant.co.uk                           £30–£50/£56

A narrow shopfront opens into a long, narrow space on two distinct levels, all decorated in cheerful, warm Mexican colours. Visual impact is one of the kitchen's priorities too – the food comes on arty, rectangular plates of tinted glass with wavy rims – and dishes tend to look showy and complex: seared scallops with a spicy melon chutney and cucumber dressing, for example, consists of two parallel rows of five or six items each. Trios remain a favoured way of presenting food, as in a 'contrast of seafish' starter, incorporating a sardine fillet with a sharp relish, 'superb-quality' tuna carpaccio coated in herbs, and a 'smooth, luscious' creamy smoked haddock brandade.

John Williams is certainly not short of ideas, as he serves frogs' legs fritters with coriander aïoli, and pairs loin of Tamworth pork with truffle mash and roast scallops, although standards can be uneven: our inspector's main course of Marshbrook lamb wasn't up to much, and desserts have included a solid and unremarkable champagne and citrus jelly served with a 'terrific' tiny, thick frangipane tart and a first-class lemon-curd ice cream. Among incidentals, crisp-crusted bread is 'professionally made and very fresh'. Service is from 'well-behaved St Trinian's schoolgirls with Mexican school ties', ably supervised by Debbie Williams. Wines tend to vault over the £20 barrier with alarming ease, although house vin de pays is £12.

CHEF: John Williams   PROPRIETORS: John and Debbie Williams   OPEN: Tue to Sat 12.30 to 1.45, 7 to 9.30   CLOSED: 1 week winter, 1 week summer   MEALS: alc L (main courses £11 to £15). Set D £29.50 to £34   SERVICE: not inc, card slips closed   CARDS: Delta, MasterCard, Switch, Visa   DETAILS: 35 seats. Private parties: 20 main room, 20 private room. Vegetarian meals. No children under 8. No smoking in dining room. Wheelchair access (not WC). Music

---

**SKIPTON** North Yorkshire                                                              map 8

# Le Caveau ⅙✳ £

86 High Street, Skipton BD23 1JJ                                             COOKING 2
TEL/FAX: (01756) 794274                                                    ANGLO-FRENCH
                                                                              £23–£42

French name notwithstanding, this restaurant epitomises Yorkshire hospitality. A vaulted cellar between a bank and a building society, it has a convivial atmosphere, and the no-nonsense, seasonally changing carte is like a breath of fresh, moorland air. It offers half a dozen choices for each course, supplemented by blackboard specials. Traditional values don't preclude nods to current fashions, as in a starter of toasted goats' cheese on black pudding with plum chutney, or in Gressingham duck breast on red cabbage with red onion, apple and a hint of cinnamon. But the limits of sensible good taste are never transgressed, and on a cold November day a couple of reporters were warmed first by the welcome, then by parsnip and Parmesan soup followed by lamb casserole, and roast cod. Hot home-made puddings might include blackberry and apple crumble or a strawberry vacherin. The succinctly annotated, skilfully chosen wine list has just three bottles over £20 and offers exceptional value. Four wines are available by the glass, ranging from £2 to £2.85 (for Chilean Chardonnay and Cabernet Sauvignon), house wines are £9.50, and there are useful half-bottles.

CHEF: Richard Barker   PROPRIETORS: Brian Womersley and Richard Barker   OPEN: Tue to Sat 12 to 1.45, 7 to 9.30   CLOSED: 30 Dec to 7 Jan, 1 week May bank hol, first 2 weeks Sept   MEALS: alc (main courses £9.50 to £15). Set L £7.95 (2 courses), Set D Tue to Thur £13.95   SERVICE: not inc CARDS: Amex, Delta, MasterCard, Switch, Visa   DETAILS: 28 seats. Private parties: 28 main room, 12 to 16 private rooms. Vegetarian meals. Children's helpings. No smoking in dining room. Music (£5)

## SOUTHALL Greater London — map 3

# Brilliant ⁵✳ £

72–76 Western Road, Southall UB2 5DZ
TEL: (020) 8574 1928   FAX: (020) 8574 0276
EMAIL: brilliantrestaurant@hotmail.com
WEBSITE: www.brilliantrestaurant.com

COOKING 3
NORTH INDIAN
£24–£57

When the Anand brothers started in Southall in 1975, Brilliant seated just 36 people. Now it is a 250-seater with all the trappings, including a function room, outside catering, karaoke facilities, a wedding licence and parking for 60 cars. Big windows look out onto the street, a huge TV screen shows sport and entertainment: the whole place bustles with confidence, friendliness and fun. Not surprisingly, the owners have kept faith with their highly successful menu, and the kitchen continues to turn out accurate, keenly spiced North Indian dishes across the board. Butter chicken is a signature starter, but also look for fried masala egg, fish pakora (using Kenyan tilapia), and makkai pilli pilli (corn on the cob cooked in spices). Main courses and 'special meals' cover mostly familiar territory, whether it be methi chicken 'redolent of fenugreek', meat kofta, or king prawn biryani. Vegetables include karahi Mexican mix as well as Bombay aloo, while kulcha (rolled and fried pastry) features among the breads. Drink Kingfisher beer or lassi. House wine is £9.

CHEF: D.K. Anand   PROPRIETORS: K.K. and D.K. Anand   OPEN: Tue to Fri L 12 to 2.15, Tue to Sun D 6 to 11   CLOSED: first 3 weeks Aug   MEALS: alc (main courses £4.50 to £14). Set L and D £17.50 (min 3)   SERVICE: 10%, card slips closed   CARDS: Amex, Delta, Diners, MasterCard, Switch, Visa   DETAILS: 250 seats. Private parties: 120 main room, 80 to 120 private rooms. Car park. Vegetarian meals. Children's helpings. No smoking in 1 dining room. Music. Air-conditioned (£5)

## SOUTHPORT Merseyside — map 7

# Warehouse Brasserie £

30 West Street, Southport PR8 1QN
TEL: (01704) 544662
EMAIL: info@warehousebrasserie.co.uk
WEBSITE: www.warehousebrasserie.co.uk

COOKING 2
GLOBAL
£18–£54

On a street running between Lord Street and the promenade this contemporary, efficiently run brasserie takes up two stylishly refurbished floors of a former warehouse. Dali paintings decorate the walls, wine list and inviting modern menu, which takes in 'small dishes' of Cajun-spiced Tiger prawns, Szechuan peppered duck pancake with hoisin drizzle, and a mini Lebanese meze plate of lamb kebab, seafood vine leaf and cheese parcel. There are pasta and salad dishes (one reporter's chicken variation on Caesar salad was 'one of the nicest I've had'), as well as main courses of fish 'n' chips with mushy peas, seared calf's liver with confit onions, and maybe roast saddle of spring lamb with lemon and mint. Puddings are in traditional vein – sticky toffee, or bannoffi pie – lunch is considered a bargain, and the 40-strong, briefly annotated wine list starts with house vin de pays at £9.95.

CHEF: Marc Vérité  PROPRIETOR: Paul Adams  OPEN: Mon to Sat 12 to 2, 5.30 to 10.30  CLOSED: 25 and 26 Dec, 1 Jan  MEALS: alc (main courses L £5 to £15, D £9 to £15.50). Set L £7.95 (2 courses) to £9.95, Set D Mon 5.30 to 10.30 and Tue to Thur 5.30 to 7.30 £9.95 (2 courses) to £12.95  SERVICE: not inc, 10% for parties of 8 or more  CARDS: Amex, Delta, MasterCard, Switch, Visa  DETAILS: 110 seats. Private parties: 74 main room, 1 to 45 private rooms. Vegetarian meals. No cigars/pipes. Occasional music. Air-conditioned

## SOUTHSEA Hampshire
map 2

# Bistro Montparnasse
**NEW ENTRY**

103 Palmerston Road, Southsea PO5 3PS
TEL: (023) 9281 6754
WEBSITE: www.bistromontparnasse.co.uk

COOKING 2
MODERN EUROPEAN
£25–£43

A stone's throw from Southsea's sprawling seafront, down the quieter, more genteel end of Palmerston Road, this former private house has been revitalised by the present owners. The bright, breezy interior, its walls hung with paintings, is colourful but simple, and enlivened by candles. Service is efficient and professional with a good sense of timing.

Menus change every three weeks. Some dishes reveal oriental influences, as in a hot-and-sour prawn soup, or a starter of lime-marinated tuna with bean sprouts, white radish salad and soy vinaigrette. A main course of chargrilled Gressingham duck with rhubarb compote may be lifted by preserved ginger, while first-class sea bass has been partnered by a griddled scallop, a fishcake, and crab sauce. Desserts may not be startling, but the simple presentation showcases solid flavours, as in a sweet, crunchy crème brûlée, and in a brandy-snap basket filled with three types of chocolate ice-cream. The wine list is imaginative and fairly good value. There is choice under £20, though the majority of bottles tend to be costlier. House wines are £12, and eight wines are available by the glass.

CHEFS: Kevin Bingham and Andrew Blakeledge  PROPRIETORS: John Saunders and Kevin Bingham  OPEN: Tue to Sat 12 to 2, 7 to 9.30  CLOSED: first 2 weeks Oct, 25 and 26 Dec, 1 Jan, first 2 weeks Mar  MEALS: Set L £12 (2 courses) to £15, Set D £18.50 (2 courses) to £23.50. Light L menu Tue to Sat £7.50 (2 courses) also available  SERVICE: not inc  CARDS: Delta, MasterCard, Switch, Visa  DETAILS: 34 seats. Private parties: 34 main room, 12 to 30 private rooms. Vegetarian meals. Wheelchair access (not WC). Music

## SOUTHWOLD Suffolk
map 6

# ▲ Crown Hotel

90 High Street, Southwold IP18 6DP
TEL: (01502) 722275  FAX: (01502) 727263
EMAIL: crown.hotel@adnams.com
WEBSITE: www.adnams.co.uk

COOKING 1
MODERN BRITISH-PLUS
£30–£42

Sitting on the main street, within easy reach of miles of the Suffolk coastline, this outlet for Adnams Wine Merchants combines the roles of pub, wine bar, restaurant and small hotel. The food takes an upbeat approach, offering a varied diet of chicken liver parfait with chilli jam, marinated herrings with red onion salsa (try finding a wine to match that), and rolled loin of lamb with black pudding and tabbouleh. Seafood might take the form of smoked haddock tartlet, or sauté tiger prawns with red Thai curry, while desserts run to a hot chocolate and plum fondant, and caramelised banana with coconut bavarois. The wine list is a gem. Clearly written and sensibly ordered, it has much to delight everybody, whether their tastes run to classic claret or new-wave Spain. Sensible prices are another plus, starting at £9.50, although if you have money to spend, you can do that too: how about 1975 Pétrus for £425?

CHEF: Chris Coubrough  PROPRIETOR: Adnams Hotels  OPEN: all week 12.30 to 2, 7.30 to 9  MEALS: restaurant Set L £16.50 (2 courses) to £19.50, Set D £22 (2 courses) to £27; bar alc (main courses £9 to £13)  SERVICE: not inc, card slips closed  CARDS: Amex, Delta, Diners, MasterCard, Switch, Visa  DETAILS: 84 seats. 15 seats outside. Private parties: 80 main room. Car park. Vegetarian meals. No children under 5 after 7pm. Children's helpings. No smoking in dining room. Wheelchair access (also WC). No music. No mobile phones  ACCOMMODATION: 13 rooms, 12 with bath/shower. TV. Phone. B&B £75 to £105. Baby facilities (*The Which? Hotel Guide*)

## STADDLEBRIDGE  North Yorkshire                                    map 9

# ▲ McCoy's

The Cleveland Tontine, Staddlebridge,
Northallerton DL6 3JB
TEL: (01609) 882671  FAX: (01609) 882660
EMAIL: enquiries@mccoysatthetontine.co.uk
WEBSITE: www.mccoysatthetontine.co.uk
6m NE of Northallerton, at junction of A19 and A172

COOKING 5
BISTRO
£24–£55

There is a restaurant above McCoys, but it opens only on Saturday evenings, offering a slightly louche atmosphere of potted palms, old loose-covered sofas, parasols, fairy lights and 1930s music. The rest of the time, the basement bistro is the draw, where Marcus Bennett cooks an enterprising menu that garners ideas from all over. Elements of a dish are cleverly built up to deepen the overall impact, so that white crabmeat is rolled up in smoked salmon, then served with pickled herring, a brown crab dressing, avocado sauce and lemon oil. Another first course gives king scallops an honour guard of cauliflower purée, pancetta, a deep-fried oyster, sweet-and-sour red pepper dressing and parsley oil.

Eating in the restaurant, one pair of reporters were impressed by a well-executed saffron risotto with peppers, tomatoes and olives, while a mixed-grill main course of duck, although not very elegantly presented, delivered good flavour and careful timing. Pan-fried calf's liver served with bubble and squeak, a home-made herb sausage, and horseradish sauce sounds like a crowd-pleaser, as do desserts that extend from sticky toffee pudding, through crème brûlée flavoured with white chocolate, to rice pudding with a dollop of plum and ginger jam. The exclamation-mark that follows the announcement of a 60p charge for bread is perhaps an acknowledgement that it will take a bit of swallowing. The single-page wine list feels fairly pricey for the bistro ambience, but selections are sound, if not exactly cutting-edge. Prices start at £11.95.

CHEF: Marcus Bennett  PROPRIETORS: Tom and Eugene McCoy  OPEN: all week 12 to 2, 7 to 9.30  CLOSED: 25 and 26 Dec, 1 Jan  MEALS: alc (main courses L £9 to £13, D £15.50 £18). Set L £10.95 (2 courses) to £13.95, Set D £14.95 (2 courses) to £16.95  SERVICE: not inc  CARDS: Amex,

Delta, Diners, MasterCard, Switch, Visa   DETAILS: 70 seats. Private parties: 60 main room, 14 to 45 private rooms. Car park. Vegetarian meals. Children's helpings. Music. Air-conditioned ACCOMMODATION: 6 rooms, all with bath/shower. TV. Phone. B&B £75 to £95

## STANTON Suffolk                                                    map 6

# Leaping Hare Vineyard Restaurant  🦫 ✻ £

Wyken Vineyards, Stanton IP31 2DW
TEL: (01359) 250287                                              COOKING 2
at Ixworth, turn E off A143, and follow signs for        MODERN BRITISH
Wyken Vineyard                                                   £27–£47

This restaurant uses fine local produce in its daily-changing à la carte menus. Wyken Farmers' Market supplies many items, including fine cheeses, while meat is 'born and raised in Suffolk and Norfolk', and on 'very special days' includes Shetland lamb from the Carlisles' own flock. In the simple, well-balanced dishes Suffolk asparagus (in spring), seared scallops, and calf's liver are notable ingredients, and the new American chef does them full justice. His Californian experience is reflected in 'a real masterpiece' – Chez Panisse almond tart – but also in occasional over-reliance on citric, particularly lemon, flavours.

The restaurant occupies part of an 'exceptionally beautiful and tastefully restored' building that also accommodates a gift, food and clothes shop, and a café where the choice of drinks includes farm-pressed apple juice, exotic speciality espresso coffees, organic Moroccan mint tea, and caffeine-free Cape Malay Redbush Chai tea. Service is 'efficient, friendly and helpful'. A cider and six wines (one red) from Wyken Vineyards are available, alongside a short list of 'guest wines'; the focus is on good-value drinking, with most bottles costing less than £20.

CHEF: Nicholas Abrams   PROPRIETORS: Kenneth and Carla Carlisle   OPEN: all week L 12 to 2.30, Fri and Sat D 7 to 9.30   CLOSED: 4pm 24 Dec to 6 Jan   MEALS: alc (main courses £9 to £17). Café menu also available 12 to 4.30   SERVICE: not inc, 10% (optional) for parties of 6 or more, card slips closed   CARDS: Delta, MasterCard, Switch, Visa   DETAILS: 45 seats. 20 seats outside. Car park. Vegetarian meals. Children's helpings. No smoking in dining room. Wheelchair access (also WC). No music  £5

## STOCKBRIDGE Hampshire                                          map 2

# Greyhound �stemmed ✻                              [NEW ENTRY]

31 High Street, Stockbridge SO20 6EY                         COOKING 5
TEL: (01264) 810833   FAX: (01264) 811656       MODERN EUROPEAN
                                                                £31–£58

People travel from far and wide to Stockbridge for one reason: the Test, one of the most sought-after game rivers in the country, runs nearby. Now it seems there is another reason to visit. This traditional eighteenth-century inn has been transformed with some style into an 'informal but up-market' gastro-pub, while retaining a rustic tone and reserving space at the bar for drinkers. 'It is a class act,' thought an inspector, impressed by the skill and finesse evident in Nick Wentworth's modern cooking.

The short, weekly-changing menus show a slight preference for fish, including a starter of salmon and cod fishcake topped with a well-timed poached egg served on a chive beurre blanc. Main courses have taken in John Dory with a tempura oyster accompanied by baby leeks and champagne velouté, and roast cod with spring vegetables and caper jus. Non-fish dishes are no less appealing or impressive: asparagus risotto with lemon oil was a 'perfect portion of well-cooked rice laced with chunks of fine-quality asparagus cooked spot-on', with meaty options perhaps including roast breast of Barbary duck with sweet potato and Chinese leaves. The common characteristics running through all dishes are quality ingredients handled with care, well-judged portion control and creative and colourful presentation. This goes equally for desserts, such as blackcurrant sablé with Granny Smith sorbet. The wine list is a thoroughly modern affair, with good selections from across the wine-making globe, with France, Australia and New Zealand offering most interest. Mark-ups are sensible, and a page of 'twenty under twenty' picks out some good – and good-value – bottles. Prices start at £11.50, and eight wines are sold by the glass from £2.95 to £4.50.

CHEF: Nick Wentworth   PROPRIETOR: Barry Skarin   OPEN: all week L 12 to 2.30, Mon to Sat D 6.30 to 10   MEALS: alc (main courses £10 to £17.50). Bar menu available L   SERVICE: 12% (optional), card slips closed   CARDS: Amex, Delta, MasterCard, Switch, Visa   DETAILS: 50 seats. Private parties: 40 main room. Car park. Children's helpings. No smoking in 1 dining room. No pipes in dining room. Wheelchair access (also WC). Occasional music. Air-conditioned

## STOCKCROSS Berkshire                                                        map 2

## ▲ Vineyard at Stockcross ▮

Stockcross RG20 8JU
TEL: (01635) 528770   FAX: (01635) 528398
EMAIL: general@the-vineyard.co.uk                          COOKING 7
WEBSITE: www.the-vineyard.co.uk                         ANGLO-FRENCH
just off A4, 2m W of Newbury on B4000                        £36–£87

This slice of swank in Berkshire's rolling countryside is a sleek, modern luxury hotel, its older core skilfully wrapped around with extensions. Oddly, there is no vineyard here (it's in America, where Sir Peter Michael owns a winery), but there is an oval pond with flames appearing to rise dramatically from its surface. Vehicles are valet-parked, and it isn't too difficult to feel, momentarily, like a celebrity, as you are swept through reception into an airy, elegant split-level dining room with smartly uniformed but unstuffy, professional staff.

John Campbell came from Lords of the Manor at Upper Slaughter, and has cranked things up a gear thanks to his evident skills, innovative ideas and adventurous flavour combinations: perhaps a grain mustard sherbet on a creamy smoked haddock risotto, for example, or a slow-cooked fillet of beef nevertheless served rare, with a bourguignonne ice cream. Dishes are complex yet cohesive, and presentation is exemplary: for example, an impeccable wild mushroom risotto with truffle foam, or a moist 'tournedos' of fine organic salmon, served simply on a bed of lightly spiced Puy lentils, topped with a sliver of grilled foie gras.

Other dishes are more like variations on a well-known theme, such as the combination of pink Goosnargh duck breast and rich confit, served with a few prunes and a 'garbure' acting as a sauce, the result 'well conceived and harmonious'. Menu descriptions are understated, which can lead to the odd surprise: our inspector's praline parfait, accompanied by an orange and caramel jelly, was covered in an unannounced and overwhelming basil froth. Cheeses arrive in prime condition 'without ceremony or explanation', and the set-price daily menu is a comparative bargain.

The wine list is enormous, with a separate list for Californian wines, the Vineyard's speciality. That selection includes many producers not frequently seen in the UK, as well as 'cult Cabernet' wines such as Harlan Estate and Screaming Eagle. On the international list Oregon Pinot Noirs and Australian reds are big stories, as are Italian Super-Tuscans and Barolos, alongside more predictable Bordeaux and Burgundy offerings. A range this stellar doesn't come cheap, though. Happily, at the back of the list can be found almost 60 wines from £12 to £20 which offer interesting, good-value drinking.

CHEF: John Campbell   PROPRIETOR: Sir Peter Michael   OPEN: all week 12 to 2, 7 to 10   MEALS: Set L Mon to Sat £17 (2 courses) to £49, Set L Sun £26, Set D £17 (2 courses) to £60   SERVICE: not inc   CARDS: Amex, Delta, Diners, MasterCard, Switch, Visa   DETAILS: 74 seats. Private parties: 60 main room, 60 private room. Car park. Vegetarian meals. Children's helpings. No smoking in 1 dining room. Wheelchair access (also WC). Music. Air-conditioned ACCOMMODATION: 31 rooms, all with bath/shower. TV. Phone. B&B £219 to £550. Baby facilities. Swimming pool (*The Which? Hotel Guide*)

## STOKE BRUERNE  Northamptonshire                                         map 5

# Bruerne's Lock

5 The Canalside, Stoke Bruerne NN12 7SB
TEL: (01604) 863654   FAX: (01604) 863330
EMAIL: bruernlock@aol.com                                    COOKING 1
WEBSITE: www.bruerneslock.co.uk          TRADITIONAL ENGLISH-PLUS
off A508, 3½m from M1 junction 15                           £25–£56

The red-brick Georgian building, beside a lock on the Grand Union Canal, has a basement bar, and a ground-floor restaurant with stripy wallpaper and interesting vintage photographs of canal scenes. Ideas range from a simple (and commended) honey-glazed duck-leg confit with rocket salad, to an elaborate-sounding crépinette of chicken and crispy prawns on a mango and coconut Thai sauce with spiced apple and red cabbage.

Results may be hit and miss, and although the cooking is sometimes old-fashioned, it has its good points, not least the perfectly decent raw materials: queen scallops and mushrooms, for example, in a creamy sauce inside a pastry box, accompanied by battered crab claws. Timings may be conservative, but results are worthwhile, as in supple slices of interestingly spiced duck breast, served with a good stock-and-plum purée. Strong clear flavours and contrasting textures are evident, too, in a thin filo basket of smooth lemon mousse topped with a champagne sorbet. Wines make an effort to stay affordable.

CHEF: Pascal Bachelier   PROPRIETOR: H.F.T. Leisure Ltd   OPEN: Tue to Fri and Sun L 12 to 2, Tue to Sat D 7 to 9.30   CLOSED: 2 weeks from 26 Dec   MEALS: alc exc Sun L (main courses L £10 to £11, D £16 to £19). Set L £10.95 (2 courses) to £12.95, Set L Sun £18, Set D £17.95. Bar menu

available in summer    SERVICE: not inc    CARDS: Amex, Delta, MasterCard, Switch, Visa
DETAILS: 52 seats. 20 seats outside. Private parties: 52 main room, 10 to 14 private rooms. Car
park. Vegetarian meals. Children's helpings. No smoking in dining room. Music

## STOKE SUB HAMDON Somerset                                          map 2

# Priory House Restaurant ▼ ✼

1 High Street, Stoke sub Hamdon TA14 6PP                           COOKING 7
TEL/FAX: (01935) 822826                                     MODERN EUROPEAN
WEBSITE: www.theprioryrestaurant.co.uk                            £30–£64

Smartly decorated in blue and beige, and minimalist without seeming too bare,
Priory House conveys a 'cool, modern and very pleasing' impression. Martin
Hadden, meanwhile, appears as keen as mustard, like 'a young man hungry for
business', with a strong, contemporary style of cooking to sell. Having worked
with Nico Ladenis, his precision and clear focus are perhaps only to be expected,
and there are echoes of the master in such dishes as hot foie gras with
caramelised orange salad, and in grilled boudin blanc with cauliflower cream.

An essential simplicity runs through the cooking, producing a partnership of
salt-cod brandade with French beans and truffle oil, and of grilled skate wing
with bouillabaisse sauce. This is food that excites in a quiet and contemplative
way rather than by roping in exotic ingredients. It certainly soothes, thanks not
least to its combination of richness and soft textures, evident for example in
flavourful chicken breast well partnered by foie gras, and in a starter of artichoke
heart and glazed crab hollandaise.

Pasta is a favoured material, turning up as linguine with ceps, and as a goats'
cheese raviolo in tomato consommé, and the freshness of fish has impressed,
from red mullet to sea bass with leeks. Desserts are as well conceived and crafted
as the rest, judging by poached pear with vanilla cream and a jug of butterscotch
sauce, and by a warm chocolate tart with vanilla sauce and orange ice cream. The
varied wine list has an eye for quality at all levels and, while those with £30 to
spend will be handsomely rewarded, there is choice under £20, starting with a
handful of very acceptable house wines (from £13) and wines by the glass (from
£4).

CHEF: Martin Hadden    PROPRIETORS: Martin and Michele Hadden    OPEN: Tue to Sat 12 to 2, 7 to
9    CLOSED: 2 weeks Christmas, 2 weeks Aug, bank hols    MEALS: Set L £14 (2 courses) to
£39.50, Set D £24 (2 courses) to £39.50    SERVICE: not inc, card slips closed    CARDS: Delta,
MasterCard, Switch, Visa    DETAILS: 30 seats. Private parties: 30 main room. Vegetarian meals
available if pre-booked. Children's helpings. No smoking in dining room. Wheelchair access (not
WC). No music

---

'[Waiting staff were] perky; one of them reacted to everything, including a request for tap
water, with ''Wonderful!'', which is a lot more positive than ''No Problem'', if you ask me.'
(On eating in Surrey)

*All entries, including Round-ups, are fully indexed at the back of the Guide.*

# Fleur de Sel ✺

| | |
|---|---|
| Manleys Hill, Storrington RH20 4BT | COOKING **6** |
| TEL: (01903) 742331   FAX: (01903) 740649 | FRENCH |
| | £32–£69 |

Beamed, attractively decorated and favoured by the Sussex bourgeoisie, the Perrauds' resolutely French restaurant occupies a sixteenth-century house on the outskirts of the village. What the atmosphere may sometimes lack in *joie de vivre* it makes up for in space and elegance. The style tends to be light, turning up fragrant globe artichoke soup, and local asparagus in puff pastry with tomato sauce, but it is also capable of more substantial fare. One winter luncher began with venison and pistachio terrine, followed by braised oxtail that had been boned, shredded and formed into a ball, surrounded by sweet little onions, turned carrots and green beans, all in a rich winey sauce.

The cooking is technically proficient, aiming more for precision than excitement, with a degree of luxury manifest in, for example, warm lobster terrine with a creamed leek sauce, an escalope of foie gras, and calves' sweetbreads with spinach and artichokes. Duos and trios are much in evidence, as in an assembly of sea bass, brill and salmon in a rich cream sauce, while enterprising partnerships extend to an orange and Grand Marnier soufflé served with coffee ice cream. Service from an all-French team is both formal and assured, and wines are heavily, though not exclusively, skewed towards France, with comparatively affordable Languedoc and Gascony helping to balance the usual heavyweight regions. House wines are £12.50 (£3 per glass).

CHEF: Michel Perraud   PROPRIETORS: Michel and Bernadette Perraud   OPEN: Tue to Fri and Sun L 12 to 2, Tue to Sat D 7 to 9.30   CLOSED: 2 weeks Jan, 2 weeks Sept   MEALS: Set L Tue to Fri £15.50 (2 courses) to £19.50, Set L Sun £19.50 (2 courses) to £23.50, Set D Tue to Thur £19.50 (2 courses) to £23.50, all week L and D £29 (2 courses) to £34   SERVICE: 12.5% (optional), card slips closed   CARDS: Amex, Delta, MasterCard, Switch, Visa   DETAILS: 54 seats. Private parties: 20 main room. Car park. No children under 10. No smoking in dining room. Smoking in bar only. Wheelchair acces s (not WC). Music. No mobile phones

# Tot Hill House ✺

| | |
|---|---|
| Tot Hill, Stowmarket IP14 3QH | COOKING **2** |
| TEL/FAX: (01449) 673375 | MODERN EUROPEAN |
| | £28–£49 |

'A peaceful little oasis on the busy A14' is how one reporter described this attractive, stylish, creeper-clad country house. The dining room, framed by exposed dark-oak timbers, has a blue carpet, terracotta walls and features a collection of equine art (a theme echoed in the small lounge bar). Oval-backed dining chairs are drawn up to white linen-clad tables, while service is 'pleasant and professional'.

Appealing menus – set-price affairs of two or three courses – change with the seasons and adopt a modern approach. A starter of tomato, red onion, halloumi, mozzarella and black olive tart, 'bursting with flavour', might be followed by mignons of fillet steak with a sweetcorn fritter in a rich whisky and Worcestershire cream sauce. Fish (from Billingsgate) might appear as sea bass fillets with parsnip purée and red wine sauce, while straightforward desserts deliver the likes of Muscat crème brûlée, or strawberry and cinnamon torte with Greek yoghurt and cream. Canapés, appetisers and home-made fudge all add value, and service is friendly and professional. The annotated wine list is laid out by style, has a welcome dozen wines in halves, and starts with six house wines up to £14.95 (£4 a glass).

CHEFS: Christopher Bruce and Daniela Bruce-Foster   PROPRIETORS: Christopher and Mary Bruce   OPEN: Wed to Fri and Sun L 12 to 1.30, Wed to Sat D 7 to 8.30 (9 Sat)   CLOSED: 2 weeks early Jan, 1 week July   MEALS: Set L £22.50 (2 courses) to £27.50, Set L Sun £15.95 (2 courses) to £18.95, Set D £22.50 (2 courses) to £27.50   SERVICE: not inc   CARDS: Amex, Delta, MasterCard, Switch, Visa   DETAILS: 36 seats. Private parties: 36 main room. Car park. Children's helpings. No smoking in dining room. No music

## STOW-ON-THE-WOLD Gloucestershire                              map 5

## ▲ Kings Arms  £                                          NEW ENTRY

Market Square, Stow-on-the-Wold GL54 1AF
TEL: (01451) 830364   FAX: (01451) 830602                           COOKING 2
EMAIL: info@kingsarms.stowonthewold.co.uk                    MODERN EUROPEAN
WEBSITE: www.kingsarms.stowonthewold.co.uk                        £22–£41

This old stone pub is a no-frills establishment on two floors, with a daily-changing menu chalked on a board and a penchant for fresh materials simply and honestly prepared. The kitchen is not too ambitious, yet rings interesting changes: calf's liver with balsamic and walnuts, breast of duck with quince paste and sherry, or an open omelette scattered with sliced courgette and pine nuts, then dusted with purply sumac powder. A commendable air of restraint pervades the cooking, producing a couple of plainly grilled headless sardines on a rocket and Parmesan salad, and a whole lemon sole with a smear of well-judged pounded anchovy and rosemary, simply accompanied by spinach and waxy potatoes. Homely desserts include a summer bowl of cherries, and a cored pear, poached in gentle cinnamon and wine liquor, with a blob of clotted cream. Service is cheery, helpful and clued-up. Choose your wine not from a list but from a wall in the upstairs room: bottles are set out as if in a wine shop, and whites can be machine-cooled in a matter of moments. There is choice under £20, and house wines are £10.

CHEF: Peter Robinson   PROPRIETORS: Louise and Peter Robinson   OPEN: all week L 12 to 2.30 (3 Sat and Sun), Mon to Sat D 6 to 9.30 (10 Fri and Sat)   MEALS: alc (main courses £6 to £12)   SERVICE: not inc, card slips closed   CARDS: Delta, MasterCard, Switch, Visa   DETAILS: 60 seats. 20 seats outside. Private parties: 15 main room, 8 to 15 private rooms. Car park. Children's helpings. Music   ACCOMMODATION: 9 rooms, all with bath/shower. TV. Phone. B&B £90 to £120. Rooms for disabled

NEW CHEF *is shown instead of a cooking mark where a change of chef occurred too late for a new assessment of the cooking.*

## ▲ Royalist ▼ ✻ £

Digbeth Street, Stow-on-the-Wold GL54 1BN
TEL: (01451) 830670   FAX: (01451) 870048
EMAIL: info@theroyalisthotel.co.uk
WEBSITE: www.theroyalisthotel.co.uk

COOKING **4**
MODERN BRITISH
£43–£52

Claiming the title of England's oldest inn (dating from 947, and originally used as a hospice to shelter lepers), the Royalist in its present incarnation dates from some time later, judging by its mullioned windows, and its intriguing dining room where fireplaces seem to have been built into the walls over many ages. It is a relaxed, comfortable and smart room in which to enjoy some contemporary cooking, from quail with shallot Tatin and a plum and red wine sauce, to snail and foie gras ravioli with Puy lentils and wilted rocket.

Combinations are not outlandish, however: seared dived scallops come with watercress purée, and sea bass fillet with mussels and leek velouté. Roasting is a favoured way with main courses, applied to chump of Cotswold lamb with moussaka and champ mash, and to game such as partridge with braised red cabbage, and venison with wild mushrooms. Finish, perhaps, with a warm pear and frangipane Tatin, or a mango and creamed rice pudding charlotte with mango crisps. The wine list covers Old and New Worlds roughly equally. Although there are pricey bottles (mostly burgundy and claret), there is also good choice at the cheaper end. Prices start at £9.75 for Chilean Merlot, and six house selections are £12.95 (£2.75 a glass).

CHEF: Alan Thompson   PROPRIETORS: Alan and Georgina Thompson   OPEN: restaurant Mon to Sat D 7 to 9.30   MEALS: Set D £32.   SERVICE: 10% (optional), card slips closed   CARDS: Amex, Delta, MasterCard, Switch, Visa   DETAILS: 30 seats. Private parties: 50 main room, 8 to 16 private rooms. Car park. Vegetarian meals. Children's helpings. No smoking in dining room. Wheelchair access (not WC). Music   ACCOMMODATION: 8 rooms, all with bath/shower. TV. Phone. B&B £50 to £170 (*The Which? Hotel Guide*) **£5**

---

**STRATFORD-UPON-AVON Warwickshire**　　　　　　　map 5

## Margaux

**NEW ENTRY**

6 Union Street, Stratford-upon-Avon CV37 6QT
TEL/FAX: (01789) 269106

COOKING **3**
ENGLISH/MEDITERRANEAN
£27–£56

This town-centre bistro occupies the ground floor and basement of a small, shop-front terrace building, its unpretentious décor mixing deep blue and orange paintwork with modern wood-panelling, wooden tables and chairs and loud music. Equally colourful Maggie (née Margot) Brebner provides a theatrical touch with her ebullient front-of-house performance '... darling, sweetheart, my love ...', and is the source of the restaurant's pun: Margaux, Margot, geddit?

Meanwhile, the kitchen's sophisticated modern repertoire surprises and delights. Meals might start with a lobster and langoustine terrine with crab and spiced guacamole, or with roast quail on mushy peas and crispy pancetta. Quality raw ingredients combine with imagination, skill and sound timing to produce, for example, a 'smashing' duo of pork (confit belly and pan-fried escalope) served on an 'impeccable' Calvados jus; seasonal vegetables are another plus. Puddings are just as competently executed but more conventional in nature: fresh lemon tart perhaps, or a stalwart bread-and-butter pudding with home-made honey ice cream. There is no Margaux on the short but agreeably priced wine list, which starts with house Chilean red and white at £11.75 (£2.95 a glass).

CHEF: Shaun Brebner   PROPRIETOR: Maggie Brebner   OPEN: Mon to Sat 12 to 2, 5.30 to 10   CLOSED: 25 and 26 Dec, 1 Jan   MEALS: alc (main courses £8 to £18)   SERVICE: not inc   CARDS: Amex, Delta, MasterCard, Switch, Visa   DETAILS: 50 seats. Private parties: 30 main room. Vegetarian meals. Children's helpings. Music  (£5)

## Russons ⁵⁄⁴✳ £

8 Church Street, Stratford-upon-Avon CV37 6HB   | NEW CHEF |
TEL: (01789) 268822   GLOBAL
£25–£42

An old shop-fronted building in the heart of Stratford, with flag floors, beams decked in dried hops, and chunky pine tables, is the setting for this friendly, unpretentious bistro. Nick Watson (who has previously cooked at Charringworth Manor in Chipping Camden) arrived too late for us to inspect but early menus show that the kinds of dishes to expect are Caesar salad; roast Norfolk duck with black cherry and brandy sauce; grilled whole silver dorade with basil olive oil and served with salad niçoise; and banana banoffi cream pie. A short, globe-trotting wine list turns over every six months, but aims to stay mostly under £20. House Chilean Merlot and Sauvignon Blanc, at £10.25, are also available by the large or small glass.

CHEF: Nick Watson   PROPRIETORS: David and Sarah Russon   OPEN: Tue to Sat 11.30 to 1.45, 5.30 to 9.45   CLOSED: 25 Dec to 2 Jan   MEALS: alc (main courses £8 to £15)   SERVICE: not inc, card slips closed   CARDS: Amex, Delta, MasterCard, Switch, Visa   DETAILS: 50 seats. No children under 6 after 7pm. No smoking in 1 dining room. Music

## STUCKTON Hampshire                                           map 2

## ▲ Three Lions ♀ ⁵⁄⁴✳

Stuckton SP6 2HF
TEL: (01425) 652489   FAX: (01425) 656144
EMAIL: the3lions@btinternet.com
½m SE of Fordingbridge, off A338 but not
signposted from it: take the turn just S of   COOKING 6
Fordingbridge and follow a sign down a narrow   ANGLO-FRENCH
country lane   £32–£58

'Completely ordinary and average' outside, this two-storey brick building is filled with balustrade partitions, flock wallpaper, an exuberant carpet, gathered curtains and a copse-worth of pine, plus a 'zoo' of miniature China animals. A chalkboard in the bar succinctly lists the kitchen's current offerings, perhaps sauté scallops in citrus sauce, a farm egg, bacon and cep salad, or vine roasted partridge. This place has always had an unstuffy approach – Jayne Womersley is a lively, friendly hostess – and an ability to source unusually fine raw materials, many of them local. Michael Womersley gathers his own fungi, including St George's mushrooms (briefly available in spring), which he serves in a starter with first-class, accurately timed lamb's kidneys on potato rösti: a main course in miniature.

Actual main courses might take in grilled sea bass with star anise, wild boar with a lemon and apple sauce, or a beef tournedos – supple, marbled meat, full of flavour, accurately cooked – with a port and oxtail sauce, accompanied by a busy little 'hamburger' of oxtail meat, foie gras, sweetbreads, pork and apricots. Half a dozen vegetables (the same for all main courses) are served on a side plate (charged separately at dinner, but not at lunch). A high degree of technical competence suffuses everything, and although the food may lack a little daring and excitement, it is admirable for the simplicity of its ideas and accuracy of execution.

'Caramelised apples' is what the blackboard, rather inadequately, calls a fine, fresh-tasting tarte Tatin made with soft, luscious pastry and coated in syrup (rather than glazed), served with a scoop of 'beautifully flavoured' vanilla ice cream. Incidentals include first-class bread, and wines from the straightforward list favour France and southern Europe, with just a few selections from the New World. Eleven house wines, all under £20, start at £12.75 (five come by the glass, from £2.60).

CHEF: Michael Womersley   PROPRIETORS: Mr and Mrs Michael Womersley   OPEN: Tue to Sun L 12 to 2, Tue to Sat D 7 to 9.30 (10 Sat)   MEALS: alc (main courses £13.50 to £16.75). Set L Tue to Fri £14.75 (2 courses)   SERVICE: not inc   CARDS: Delta, MasterCard, Switch, Visa   DETAILS: 60 seats. 10 seats outside. Private parties: 60 main room, 10 to 30 private rooms. Car park. Vegetarian meals. Children's helpings. No smoking in dining room. Wheelchair access (not WC). No music. No mobile phones   ACCOMMODATION: 5 rooms, all with bath/shower. TV. B&B £49 to £85. Rooms for disabled. Baby facilities (*The Which? Hotel Guide*)  £5

---

## STURMINSTER NEWTON  Dorset                                    map 2

## ▲ Plumber Manor  ⅚✗

Sturminster Newton DT10 2AF
TEL: (01258) 472507   FAX: (01258) 473370
EMAIL: book@plumbermanor.com
WEBSITE: www.plumbermanor.com                              COOKING 2
A357 to Sturminster Newton, take first left to               ANGLO-FRENCH
Hazelbury Bryan, on left-hand side after 2m                  £29–£52

Wisteria and magnolia grace the façade of this solid, rambling house which, in the three centuries since it was built, has had just one careful owner, the Prideaux-Brune family. Its style is comfortable and unpretentious, the cooking straightforward and skilful. The menu has little truck with modern ideas, preferring time-honoured items such as grilled goats' cheese on roast peppers to start, or avocado, melon and prawns Marie Rose, but good raw materials and accurate timing are part of the appeal.

Main courses might run to loin of pork with apples and sage, or beef medallions with green peppercorn sauce, and classic sauces typically include hollandaise with grilled salmon, or béarnaise with chateaubriand. A few dishes, such as beef carpaccio with creamed horseradish, or fish of the day, attract a supplement (£3 for starters, £4 for main courses). Vegetables come in large quantities, and desserts, wheeled round on a trolley, are served from big plates or deep bowls, perhaps taking in black cherry frangipane and chocolate truffle torte. A traditional wine list (mostly French) is supplemented by a New World section mostly under £20. House Vin de Pays d'Oc is £11.50.

CHEF: Brian Prideaux-Brune  PROPRIETOR: Richard Prideaux-Brune  OPEN: Sun L 12.30 to 1.30, all week D 7.30 to 9  CLOSED: Feb  MEALS: Set L £19, Set D £21.50 (2 courses) to £24.50  SERVICE: not inc, card slips closed  CARDS: Amex, Diners, MasterCard, Switch, Visa  DETAILS: 60 seats. Private parties: 45 main room, 12 to 22 private rooms. Car park. Vegetarian meals. Children's helpings. No smoking in dining room. Wheelchair access (also WC). No music  ACCOMMODATION: 16 rooms, all with bath/shower. TV. Phone. B&B £85 to £155. Rooms for disabled. Baby facilities (The Which? Hotel Guide)

---

## SURBITON Surrey                                          map 3

# French Table                            | NEW ENTRY |

| 85 Maple Road, Surbiton KT6 4AW | COOKING 4 |
| TEL: (020) 8399 2365   FAX: (020) 8390 5353 | FRENCH/MEDITERRANEAN |
| | £26–£54 |

Sharp-eyed reporters spotted this newcomer soon after it opened, just as the last edition of the Guide was on its way to press: a simple but stylish, glass-fronted shop conversion, light and welcoming, with flag floor, pastelly turquoise walls and red banquettes. It is considered a good neighbourhood restaurant serving food that is 'up to date but not daft'. Eric Guignard's experience (he cooked at Crivelli's Garden in the National Gallery – see entry, London – and before that at White Onion) enables him to produce some imaginative, attractively presented food made with good ingredients, served up with a degree of sophistication often lacking in suburban restaurants.

With the exception of one dish – foie gras two ways, served with (if desired) a glass of Coteaux du Layon – the menu changes every few weeks, early spring and summer versions offering a brochette of tuna marinated in harissa with couscous and ratatouille, and lightly battered deep-fried scallops, on a well-made creamy risotto shot through with shafts of peeled asparagus and finely shredded lime leaf. Earthier dishes are equally well handled, judging by a 'triumphant' main course of pork belly, curled into a disc, its outside caramelised into a brown goo, on a bed of haricot beans in a cream sauce.

Desserts might include an assiette of chocolate, or a passion-fruit tart, the juice mixed into a smooth, tangy custard, placed in thin, crisp pastry, topped with sugar and grilled, accompanied by a light coconut sorbet. Sarah Guignard welcomes, looks after an informal front-of-house team, and is both knowledgeable and enthusiastic about the lively two-page wine list, which affords plenty of scope up to £30 (check out the Moroccan red at £21.50), starting with house vins de pays at £11.75.

CHEF: Eric Guignard  PROPRIETORS: Eric and Sarah Guignard  OPEN: Wed to Fri and Sun L 12 to 2.30, Tue to Sat D 7 to 10.30  CLOSED: 25 and 26 Dec, 1 week Jan, 2 weeks end Aug  MEALS: alc D (main courses £10 to £15). Set L Wed to Fri £12.50 (2 courses) to £15.50, Set L Sun £14.95  SERVICE: 12.5% (optional), card slips closed  CARDS: Delta, MasterCard, Switch, Visa  DETAILS: 48 seats. Vegetarian meals. Children's helpings. No-smoking area. Wheelchair access (not WC). Music. No mobile phones. Air-conditioned

## SUTTON GAULT Cambridgeshire                              map 6

# ▲ Anchor Inn ▼ ⅝✳

Bury Lane, Sutton Gault CB6 2BD
TEL: (01353) 778537   FAX: (01353) 776180
EMAIL: anchorinnsg@aol.com
WEBSITE: www.anchor-inn-restaurant.co.uk                    COOKING 2
off B1381 Sutton to Earith road, just S of Sutton,       MODERN BRITISH
6m W of Ely                                                  £30–£58

Inside the whitewashed inn, hidden away in the flat Fen landscape, are several small, low-ceilinged rooms with scrubbed pine tables, bench seating and an open wood-burning fire. Although some who have travelled a long way have found it disappointing, it is a favourite with locals: the draw is an informal set-up, a longish menu, and more hits than misses, including a fresh, light and tasty watercress soup, crisp-skinned yet moist salmon with tagliatelle, and a first-class smoked haddock risotto. It is the kind of place where it feels normal to eat just a starter and a pud: perhaps home-made black pudding on crushed potatoes with a poached egg, followed by apple and blackberry crumble tart. The wine list offers value and variety, and gives diners a clue as to a wine's weight or relative dryness. Prices start at £12.50, and six wines are offered by the 175ml glass from £3.50 to £3.90.

CHEFS: Martin and Zoë Russell   PROPRIETORS: Robin and Heather Moore   OPEN: all week 12 to 2, 7 to 9 (6.30 to 9.30 Sat)   CLOSED: D 25 Dec, 26 Dec   MEALS: alc exc Sun L (main courses £11 to £19.50). Set L Sun £18.50. Light L menu also available Mon to Fri   SERVICE: not inc, 10% for parties of 10 or more   CARDS: Amex, Delta, MasterCard, Switch, Visa   DETAILS: 70 seats. 20 seats outside. Private parties: 30 main room. Car park. Vegetarian meals. Children's helpings. No smoking in 1 dining room. Wheelchair access (also WC). No music. No mobile phones   ACCOMMODATION: 2 rooms, both with bath/shower. TV. Phone. B&B £50 to £95

## SUTTON-ON-THE-FOREST North Yorkshire                     map 9

# Rose & Crown ⅝✳

Main Street, Sutton-on-the-Forest YO61 1DP
TEL: (01347) 811333   FAX: (01347) 811444
EMAIL: reserve@rosecrown.co.uk                             COOKING 6
WEBSITE: www.rosecrown.co.uk                             MODERN BRITISH
on B1363, 8m N of York                                       £27–£60

'This really is a find,' reckoned one visitor. The Rose & Crown is a welcoming, homely former pub in the centre of a tidy, attractive village, its lemon-painted dining room sporting original beams, stiff white linen cloths and fresh flowers. Stephen Harper's cooking sounds deceptively easy, taking in a cream of split pea soup, or potted brown shrimps to begin, followed perhaps by roast breast of corn-fed chicken, or pan-fried tranche of salmon with spring onion risotto. But materials are first rate, and skills extend to a home-made black pudding (with crushed swede and carrots), and to a slice of moist, meaty, tasty ham hock terrine served with apple chutney.

The set lunch is considered 'fantastic value for three innovative and well-cooked courses'; at dinner, the carte might offer rabbit ravioli, a hot tart of salmon, crab and leek, or roast squab pigeon with braised Savoy cabbage and ceps. Main courses (only lamb seems to have disappointed on occasion) come with a selection of vegetables, and desserts run the gamut from sticky toffee pudding to roast peaches served with pecan and hazelnut caramel and chilled rice pudding. Loud music may not be to everyone's taste, but there is jollity (and value) in the roving 50-bottle wine list, its contents 'properly served'. Four house wines are £12.95 or less (£3.25 a large glass).

CHEF: Stephen Harper   PROPRIETOR: Ralph Magee   OPEN: Wed to Sun L 11.45 to 2 (4 Sun), Wed to Sat D 6.45 to 9   CLOSED: 25 and 26 Dec, 2 weeks Jan   MEALS: alc (main courses £14.50 to £20). Set L £9.95 (1 course) to £16.95. Sandwich menu also available Wed to Sun L   SERVICE: not inc   CARDS: MasterCard, Switch, Visa   DETAILS: 46 seats. 16 seats outside. Private parties: 46 main room. Car park. Vegetarian meals. Children's helpings. No smoking in dining room. Wheelchair access (also WC). Music. No mobile phones  (£5)

## SWAFFHAM  Norfolk                                              map 6

## ▲ Strattons  🍴

4 Ash Close, Swaffham PE37 7NH
TEL: (01760) 723845   FAX: (01760) 720458                    COOKING 4
EMAIL: strattonshotel@btinternet.com                      MODERN EUROPEAN
WEBSITE: www.strattons-hotel.co.uk                            £45–£54

Even regular shoppers in this bustling market town may have little idea of Strattons' existence: though barely 100 yards from the market square, this Palladian-style villa is hidden down an alleyway. Visitors to the Scotts' restaurant-with-rooms enjoy its peaceful gardens, the bold colours and rich fabrics of its interiors, and dine on high-quality local ingredients, sourced with conviction and care and used by the kitchen with imagination and flair. The ground-floor dining room (in contrast to the rest of the house) is cool and understated, with grey-green walls, seagrass flooring, white tablecloths and calico-covered chairs.

Vanessa Scott's fixed-price menus have much to offer, with six or seven choices at each level: perhaps starting with a terrine of organic smoked salmon and fresh salmon accompanied by local rhubarb in a champagne and vanilla jelly with a thyme and vanilla reduction. Main courses have featured a fillet of corn-fed chicken braised in lavender, accompanied by spring onion and bacon mash, while vanilla cheesecake with lavender ice cream is one way to finish. Les Scott's service is knowledgeable and relaxed, and his lengthy wine list – organised by style with handwritten notes – includes bottles from £11.50 (£3.95 a glass).

CHEFS: Vanessa Scott and Margaret Cooper   PROPRIETORS: Les and Vanessa Scott   OPEN: all week D only 7 to 9.30; closed one evening a week, phone to check   CLOSED: 24 and 25 Dec   MEALS: Set D £35   SERVICE: not inc, card slips closed   CARDS: Amex, MasterCard, Switch, Visa   DETAILS: 22 seats. 8 seats outside. Private parties: 10 main room. Car park. Vegetarian meals. Children's helpings. No smoking. Occasional music. No mobile phones   ACCOMMODATION: 7 rooms, all with bath/shower. TV. Phone. B&B £75 to £170. Baby facilities (The Which? Hotel Guide)

# Singers ⁵⁄✳

| | |
|---|---|
| 16 Westgate, Tadcaster LS24 9AB | COOKING **2** |
| TEL: (01937) 835121 | MODERN EUROPEAN |
| WEBSITE: www.singersrestaurant.co.uk | £20–£36 |

Tables with names like 'Lennon', and song sheets papering the walls, point up the theme of this musically inclined, town-centre restaurant. Early-evening deals have been given the thumbs up, while the full dinner menu runs along contemporary European lines. Grilled tuna with mango and pink grapefruit salsa drizzled with herb oil is a typically lively starter, although a tartlet of mushrooms and onions has also been enjoyed. Good raw materials are capably handled: ribeye steak is 'always so tender' and comes with bubble and squeak and green peppercorn sauce. Desserts are safe bets, along the lines of strawberries with ice cream in a brandy-snap basket. Service is friendly and 'ably masterminded' by Philip Taylor. Value for money extends to the short wine list with its soprano whites and baritone reds. House vin de pays is £9.95.

CHEFS: David Lockwood and Jonathan Wilson  PROPRIETORS: Philip Taylor and Guy Vicari  OPEN: Tue to Sat D only 6 to 9.30  CLOSED: 25 and 26 Dec, 1 Jan  MEALS: Set D Tue to Fri 6 to 7 £12.95, Set D Tue to Thur £10.95 (1 course) to £18.95, Set D Fri and Sat £18.95  SERVICE: not inc, card slips closed  CARDS: Delta, MasterCard, Switch, Visa  DETAILS: 38 seats. Private parties: 38 main room. Vegetarian meals. No smoking in dining room. Wheelchair access (not WC). Music. Air-conditioned

# Gemini ⁵⁄✳

| | |
|---|---|
| 28 Station Approach, Tadworth KT20 5AH | COOKING **3** |
| TEL/FAX: (01737) 812179 | FRENCH/MODERN EUROPEAN |
| WEBSITE: www.gemini-restaurant.com | £25–£52 |

Decorated throughout in creamy yellow, with art deco lampshades and abstract pictures, this is a comfortable restaurant with good-sized, well-spaced tables. Robert Foster's broadly European approach deals in a few classics, such as osso buco with risotto Milanese, alongside more playful combinations that might include roast rump of lamb with hummus, Mediterranean vegetables and chorizo oil, or sea bass fillets with sun-blush tomatoes, cockles and asparagus. Much of the food aims at the comfort zone, in the shape of buttered crumpets topped with rabbit rillettes, or pasta ribbons and smoked haddock with a poached egg, a theme that desserts continue. A parfait combining Ovaltine, Baileys and milk chocolate is layered with shortbread biscuits, and a variation on bread-and-butter pudding is made with croissants, white chocolate and whisky, and served with clotted cream. A short, varied wine list starts with eight house wines, including vin de pays red and white at £11.50.

CHEF/PROPRIETOR: Robert Foster  OPEN: Tue to Fri and Sun L 12 to 2.30, Tue to Sat D 7 to 9.30  CLOSED: 2 weeks Christmas  MEALS: alc Tue to Fri (main courses £15 to £17). Set L Tue to Fri £11.50 (2 courses) to £16.50, Set L Sun £19.95, Set D Tue to Thur £12 (2 courses) to £15, Set D

Sat £31.75   SERVICE: not inc   CARDS: Amex, Delta, Diners, MasterCard, Switch, Visa   DETAILS:
50 seats. 12 seats outside. Private parties: 60 main room. Vegetarian meals. Children's helpings.
No children under 12 exc Sun L. No smoking in dining room. Wheelchair access (not WC). Music

## TAPLOW  Berkshire                                                    map 3

# ▲ Cliveden, Waldo's ♥ ⅚✳

Taplow SL6 0JF
TEL: (01628) 668561   FAX: (01628) 661837
EMAIL: reservations@clivedenhouse.co.uk                          COOKING 7
WEBSITE: www.clivedenhouse.co.uk                          MODERN EUROPEAN
off A4, 2m N of Taplow on Cliveden Rd                             £91–£135

Enjoying wonderful vistas from the gardens, parterre and wooded grounds that
drop steeply to the Thames, the vast grey house, more impressive than beautiful,
is in National Trust grounds (a £4 surcharge per diner is made on their behalf).
Unlike the Terrace dining room, Waldo's – below the cavernous ground-floor
lounge, with its dark carved wood and portrait of Nancy Astor – is,
unfortunately, unable to make anything of the view, although by way of
compensation the walls of its clubby confines are covered in striking paintings.

As one might expect of Mark Dodson (who cooked for a dozen years at the
Waterside Inn, Bray; see entry), materials take in prime species and cuts, and
treatments involve some light footwork, from langoustine beignets to lobster
cannelloni, from a ballottine of foie gras to Angus beef with girolles. Apart from
a little uneven salting, technique is as honed as can be. Dishes tend to satisfy
rather than excite, but have produced excellent Bresse pigeon breast served with
thin slices of foie gras, some rather ordinary mashed potato, and a seasonal April
ragoût of morels and broad beans, plus optional red wine jus offered from a
copper skillet. Presentation is straightforward and unostentatious, for example
in a starter combining three neatly trimmed quail breasts on a bed of spinach,
and two chunks of crusty sweetbreads mixed with bits of apple coated in a
toffee-ish vinaigrette.

Among desserts, 'the hot soufflé was my best ever', according to a senior
inspector, whose previous best had also been cooked by Mark Dodson (when at
the Waterside). This was an evenly textured almond version, subtly flavoured
with Amaretto liqueur, topped with flecks of soft bitter chocolate, served with
an Amaretto ice cream (cradled in a thin strip of eggy almond biscuit), and a
sauce that was 'the most pure essence of apricot imaginable'. Top that. Nibbles
are also of impeccable quality. Service is rather stiff and formal, the paranoid
practice of requiring a credit card number to confirm a booking is not conducive
to enjoyment, and what one visitor described as 'obscene' prices are not made
any easier by a high-quality but thumpingly expensive wine list where you will
be lucky to find even a half-bottle under £20. Chilean reds, for example, begin at
£39. House Australian Pinot Noir is £29, Spanish Sauvignon Blanc £21. More
wines by the glass (a mere five are listed, from £6 to £9 for 175ml) wouldn't go
amiss on a list of this size and scope, either. That said, choices are well
considered, with one of the best selections of Austrian wines in the country and
some well-chosen New World bottles.

CHEF: Mark Dodson  PROPRIETOR: Cliveden Ltd  OPEN: Tue to Sat D only 7 to 9.30  CLOSED: Christmas to first week Feb  MEALS: Set D £69 to £89. Cover £4  SERVICE: not inc  CARDS: Amex, Delta, Diners, MasterCard, Switch, Visa  DETAILS: 24 seats. Private parties: 24 main room, 12 to 60 private rooms. Car park. No children under 12. Jacket and tie. No smoking in dining room. No music. No mobile phones. Air-conditioned  ACCOMMODATION: 39 rooms, all with bath/shower. TV. Phone. B&B £190 to £495. Rooms for disabled. Baby facilities. Swimming pool

## TAUNTON Somerset                                         map 2

# Brazz £

Castle Bow, Taunton TA1 1NF
TEL: (01823) 252000  FAX: (01823) 336066
EMAIL: enquiries@brazz.co.uk
WEBSITE: www.brazz.co.uk                                    COOKING 2
From M5, follow directions for town centre and             MODERN BRITISH
Castle Museum/Hotel                                        £20–£48

In a stunning setting that comprises a dome with fibre-optic light, an illuminated tank stocked with a shoal of silver dollar fish, and some diverting modern artwork, Brazz presses all the right trendy buttons. Even the name (for other branches in Exeter and Bristol, see entries) proclaims the lack of preciousness evident in both the unfailingly friendly service and the food. Garlic mushrooms on toast, curried chicken with spiced potato, mussels served by the kilo with Belgian wheat beer, and chocolate chip ice-cream constitute a sound interpretation of contemporary fast food. Roast vegetable soup and the house fishcake with lemon butter sauce are well-reported, and if neither steamed treacle pudding with custard nor orange sorbet appeals, then a plate of English and Irish cheeses might. Drinking is fun, too, with interesting beers and ciders, cocktails, and an enterprising list of commendable wines on offer: around 14 are available by the glass, from £2.75.

CHEF: Mark Pullman  PROPRIETOR: English Brasserie Company  OPEN: all week 12 to 3, 6 to 10.30 (11 Fri and Sat)  MEALS: alc (main courses £8 to £15). Set L and D £8.95 (2 courses) to £10.95. Bar/Graze menu also available  SERVICE: 10% (optional), card slips closed  CARDS: Amex, Delta, Diners, MasterCard, Switch, Visa  DETAILS: 80 seats. Private parties: 80 main room. Car park. Children's helpings. No-smoking area. Wheelchair access (also WC). Music

# ▲ Castle Hotel ▼ ⅝✗

Castle Green, Taunton TA1 1NF
TEL: (01823) 272671  FAX: (01823) 336066                   COOKING 6
EMAIL: reception@the-castle-hotel.com                      MODERN BRITISH
WEBSITE: www.the.castle.hotel.com                          £29–£59

This venerable site has been occupied since the eighth century, and has been a hostel or hotel since the eighteenth. Its interior variously evokes Victorian Gothic (with its solid, carved wood), and 'Camelot' (with its tassels and fleurs-de-lys), while the modern dining room's pastel colours, chandeliers and well-spaced tables induce an expansive and restful feel. Closely managed by Kit Chapman (when not rolling out the Brazz brand: see entries in Exeter, Bristol and above), this is a restaurant with a purpose, laudably updating traditional British ideas in an attempt to produce its own distinctive style.

Foremost among such dishes are a mutton and caper pudding in a suet casing (served with braised cabbage and mash), and a loyal 'Celebration of British beef' incorporating a small piece of fillet, a couple of oxtail joints, and a beef olive stuffed with ox heart, all served with roast parsnips and mash. The kitchen is no slave to principle, however, happily producing diverse and user-friendly dishes such as scrambled duck egg with smoked eel and spiced oil, sea bass with truffle macaroni cheese, and rabbit 'pie' in a filo samosa.

Desserts are just as accomplished, from a pale pink strawberry blancmange with a blob of cheesecakey ice cream, to a highly rated variation on rhubarb and custard whose rhubarb jelly, and paper-thin pieces of dried rhubarb, provide just the right degree of sweetness. Service from well-trained staff is top-notch, and wines from a well-rounded list succeed in covering just about every flavour and style, though in some areas pricing is rather stiff; the New World generally offers better value than the Old. Prices start at £12 for non-vintage Australians, and there are a few interesting bottles below £20. Six wines come by the glass (£3 to £6.50).

CHEF: Richard Guest   PROPRIETORS: the Chapman family   OPEN: all week L 12.30 to 2, Mon to Sat D 7 to 9   MEALS: set L £16.95 (2 courses) to £19.95, Set D £29.95 (2 courses) to £35. Bar light L menu also available   SERVICE: 10% (optional), card slips closed   CARDS: Amex, Delta, Diners, MasterCard, Switch, Visa   DETAILS: 65 seats. Private parties: 80 main room, 12 private room. Car park. Vegetarian meals. No smoking in dining room. Wheelchair access (not WC). No music. No mobile phones   ACCOMMODATION: 44 rooms, all with bath/shower. TV. Phone. B&B £105 to £245. Rooms for disabled. Baby facilities

---

**TAVISTOCK Devon**                                                          map 1

## ▲ Horn of Plenty ❧✱

Gulworthy, Tavistock PL19 8JD
TEL/FAX: (01822) 832528
EMAIL: enquiries@thehornofplenty.co.uk
WEBSITE: www.thehornofplenty.co.uk                          COOKING 6
3m W of Tavistock on A390, turn right at                         GLOBAL
Gulworthy Cross                                                £28–£65

The setting, in trim gardens and wild orchard overlooking the Tamar valley, is worth a detour in its own right. Opportunities for moorland and coastal walking nearby provide an excuse for pigging out at dinner, while those who get a window table in the conservatory dining room can admire the view without further effort. There has been a bit of to-ing and fro-ing in the kitchen over the past year, which may explain some of the adverse comments we have received, but the latest is that Peter Gorton is back in full charge.

Appetisers duly herald what is to come, a cappuccino cup of mushroom essence with girolles and truffle oil holding out the promise of professionally made, comforting, mainstream food. Not every dish is as uncluttered as it might be, but technical skills ensure that each element is a triumph: for example in a skewer of two fat, perfectly seared scallops, interspersed with sweet pepper squares, served with two cannelloni filled with chopped asparagus and wild mushroom duxelles. Attention to detail is sound: sliced loin of lamb gets a twice-baked parsley and garlic soufflé, a stunningly intense Madeira sauce, and a small mound of jumbled vegetables in a properly made béarnaise.

Desserts look showy too. Spun sugar spears encasing whole almonds have adorned an otherwise straightforward praline parfait with apricot coulis; or there might be a mousse of bitter Valrhona chocolate with chocolate sorbet and griottine cherries. All this comes at a price, a point insistently made in this year's reports: for best value, try lunch. Service is solicitous, if slow-paced. On the wine front, a £20 budget will leave you with little but the house selection to choose from; it isn't a bad one, though, and opens at £14 for a dry white Bordeaux or a Puglian Sangiovese.

CHEF: Peter Gorton   PROPRIETORS: Paul Roston and Peter Gorton   OPEN: Tue to Sun L 12 to 2, all week D 7 to 9   MEALS: Set L £18.50 to £23.50, Set D Mon £23.50, Set D Tue to Sat £39.50   SERVICE: not inc, 10% for parties of over 10   CARDS: Amex, Delta, MasterCard, Switch, Visa   DETAILS: 60 seats. 12 seats outside. Private parties: 60 main room, 4 to 16 private rooms. Car park. Vegetarian meals. No children under 10 at D. No smoking in dining room. Wheelchair access (also WC). Music. No mobile phones   ACCOMMODATION: 10 rooms, all with bath/shower. TV. Phone. B&B £95 to £200. Rooms for disabled. Baby facilities (*The Which? Hotel Guide*)

## TEFFONT EVIAS  Wiltshire                                                      map 2

# ▲ Howard's House ⚡✳

Teffont Evias SP3 5RJ
TEL: (01722) 716392   FAX: (01722) 716820
EMAIL: enq@howardshousehotel.com
WEBSITE: www.howardshousehotel.com                              COOKING 5
off B3089, W of Dinton and 9½m W of Salisbury,            MODERN BRITISH-PLUS
signposted Chicksgrove                                             £30–£59

A stream runs alongside the road through the picture-postcard village, placing this seventeenth-century dower house in a quintessentially English setting. Beyond the flag-floored hallway, it is warmly decorated in pastel shades, with lots of country comforts. Paul Firmin left during the course of the year, leaving Boyd McIntosh in charge of the stoves under new ownership. His accomplished modern cooking uses first-rate and notably fresh ingredients (including vegetables and herbs from the garden), presentation is colourful and sophisticated, and saucing, seasonings and timings hit the spot.

Simplicity works in the food's favour, producing three accurately seared scallops arranged around halves of sweet baked tomato, or another starter of four trimmed quail legs with a mound of truffled Puy lentils. Dishes are marked by clarity of flavour, no matter how busy they appear to be: for example, a steamed turbot fillet, topped with a ravioli of carrot and coriander, on a round of truffled mash in a foaming champagne cream sauce. Recommended desserts include a round of light puff pastry filled with caramelised pear slices, accompanied by a strongly flavoured honey and cinnamon ice cream. Service is friendly, willing and polite, and a classically oriented, French-dominated but appealingly varied wine list has a sprinkling of bottles under £20, a reasonable selection of halves, and starts with southern French house wine at £9.95.

CHEF: Boyd McIntosh   PROPRIETORS: Bill and Noële Thompson   OPEN: Sun L 12 to 2.30, all week D 7 to 9.30   CLOSED: 23 to 26 Dec   MEALS: alc D (main courses £13 to £20). Set L Sun £19.50, Set D £23.95   SERVICE: not inc   CARDS: Amex, Delta, Diners, MasterCard, Switch, Visa   DETAILS: 36 seats. 36 seats outside. Private parties: 40 main room, 140 private room. Car park.

Vegetarian meals. Children's helpings. No smoking in dining room. Wheelchair access (not WC). Occasional music ACCOMMODATION: 9 rooms, all with bath/shower. TV. Phone. B&B £80 to £170. Baby facilities. Fishing (*The Which? Hotel Guide*)

## TETBURY Gloucestershire · map 2

# Trouble House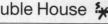

Cirencester Road, Tetbury GL8 8SG
TEL: (01666) 502206   FAX: (01666) 504508
EMAIL: enquiries@troublehouse.co.uk
WEBSITE: www.troublehouse.co.uk

COOKING 5
MODERN BRITISH
£36–£48

A simply furnished roadside pub serving honest food without pretension is many people's idea of a good find, and the description just about sums up the operation here. But if rough stone walls and pine floors convey a rustic impression, don't expect simple pub food; more likely is a fine smoked haddock risotto, a leek and blue cheese tart, or pan-fried skate with creamed Savoy cabbage. Straightforwardness is a strength – in a simple ripe Reblochon, grilled and served with roast tomatoes – and the variety that Michael Bedford packs into the carte is commendable.

Luxuries come in the shape of a foie gras and apple terrine, alongside humbler materials such as braised neck of lamb, and there are dishes that play to the gallery (ribeye steak with French fries and béarnaise sauce) as well as more unusual items such as a first-course potato and bacon cake served with truffle cream. This is intelligent cooking – using meat from a local butcher, game in season and fish from Cornwall – whose clear focus makes it particularly satisfying to eat. Finish with passion-fruit and banana soup, or a rich chocolate fondant cake with vanilla ice cream, and drink from a short wine list that starts with affordable reds and whites from France, Chile, Australia and South Africa; house wines start at £10.25.

CHEF: Michael Bedford   PROPRIETORS: Michael and Sarah Bedford   OPEN: Tue to Sun 12 to 2, Tue to Sat 7 to 9.30   CLOSED: 25 Dec, 26 Dec D, 1 Jan D   MEALS: alc (main courses £9 to £15) SERVICE: not inc   CARDS: Amex, Delta, MasterCard, Switch, Visa   DETAILS: 50 seats. 30 seats outside. Private parties: 8 main room, 20 private room. Car park. Vegetarian meals. Children's helpings. No smoking in 1 dining room. Wheelchair access (not WC). Music

## TETSWORTH Oxfordshire · map 2

# Swan at Tetsworth

High Street, Tetsworth OX9 7AB
TEL: (01844) 281182   FAX: (01844) 281770
WEBSITE: www.theswan.co.uk

COOKING 4
MODERN EUROPEAN
£29–£52

The Swan is an unusual combination of restaurant and antiques emporium, the latter being the main business of this huge old inn, which dates from the Middle Ages and is situated in a pretty hamlet. When you have done browsing the wares of the large number of dealers who operate here, the spacious dining room makes a great place in which to recuperate. Simple treatment of good ingredients sums up the kitchen's approach: dishes are not too ambitious and flavour combinations not particularly daring, but the praise heaped on it by reporters is deserved for attention to detail, precise timing, attractive presentation and some excellent raw materials. Typical of the wide-ranging style might be Gressingham duck breast with red cabbage and Madeira; Oxfordshire sausages with Meaux mustard mash; and seared scallops with black pudding and sun-blush tomatoes. Starters might include Muscovy duck egg with Parma ham and chive beurre blanc, while desserts run to bread-and-butter pudding, and pannacotta. Wines are similarly diverse, and prices are fair. The concise list opens with four house selections at £11.95.

CHEF: Naseem Salam   PROPRIETOR: Swan Holdings Ltd   OPEN: all week L 12 to 2.15 (3.30 Sun); Tue to Sat D 7 to 9.15 (9.45 Sat)   CLOSED: 25 and 26 Dec   MEALS: alc (main courses £9.50 to £17)   SERVICE: not inc, 10% for parties of 10 or more   CARDS: Delta, MasterCard, Switch, Visa DETAILS: 55 seats. 20 seats outside. Private parties: 55 main room, 14 private room. Car park. Vegetarian meals. Children's helpings. No-smoking area. No cigars/pipes in dining room. Wheelchair access (also WC). Music  £5

## THAME  Oxfordshire                                                          map 2

# ▲ Old Trout ▾ 🍷 ✣

29–30 Lower High Street, Thame OX9 2AA                       COOKING 2
TEL: (01844) 212146   FAX: (01844) 212614                   MODERN BRITISH
WEBSITE: www.theoldtrouthotel.co.uk                          £26–£64

Watch out for unexpected small steps between the floodlit paved garden and the conservatory through which you enter the relaxed, unfussy restaurant. It is modern in style, despite the low, beamed ceilings, and new owners and chefs continue to source local, organic free-range produce for their generally contemporary dishes. Despite the odd critical voice, visitors have enjoyed warm spicy beef salad with peppers in a 'nice sharp dressing' with soya sauce; and galantine of guinea fowl and chicken livers with caramelised onion and a grenadine coulis. Main dishes have included monkfish tail in a rocket crust on tomato and olive risotto, and thin-cut calf's liver on potato purée with crisped Parma ham curls. Home-made pear-liqueur-soaked sponge fingers with pear mousse and caramel sauce made a full-flavoured finale at one meal. Service is willing but not intrusive, and the wine list is brief but well-chosen, including top producers from New and Old Worlds. Fair mark-ups provide interesting drinking under £20. The list suggests 'asking for a current selection of house wines', which start at £15.

CHEFS: Philippe Fouillé and Will Bromley   PROPRIETOR: The Inn Company   OPEN: all week L 12 to 2.30, Mon to Sat D 6.30 to 10   MEALS: alc (main courses £9 to £23.50). Set L Mon to Fri £12 SERVICE: not inc, card slips closed   CARDS: Amex, Delta, MasterCard, Switch, Visa   DETAILS: 70 seats. 30 seats outside. Private parties: 30 main room, 8 to 12 private rooms. Car park. Children's helpings. Vegetarian meals. No smoking in 1 dining room. Music. No mobile phones ACCOMMODATION: 7 rooms, all with bath/shower. TV. Phone. B&B £65 to £95  £5

---

*Not inc in the details at the end of an entry indicates that no service charge is made and any tipping is at the discretion of the customer.*

## TITLEY  Herefordshire                                          map 5

# ▲ Stagg Inn  ♥ ✸  £

Titley, Nr Kington HR5 3RL
TEL: (01544) 230221   FAX: (01544) 231390
EMAIL: reservations@thestagg.co.uk
WEBSITE: www.thestagg.co.uk
on B4355 between Kington and Presteigne

COOKING 5
MODERN BRITISH
£21–£47

A tall, custard-painted brick building, the Stagg manages to retain its pubby feel – staff are 'notably helpful and friendly' – while also serving straightforward food that is cooked with intelligence and assurance. The feel of the place is very English and quite old-fashioned, but neat, with no clutter or clichés. Steve Reynolds focuses squarely on quality local ingredients and on seasonality, which he backs up with some precise cooking. In spring one may find fresh and simple pea and mint risotto, or courgette and thyme soup made lush with potatoes and cream. Herefordshire duck may be partnered by elderflower and port sauce and served with stewed pears, while fillet of Hereford beef may be more simply served, with sauté mushrooms.

Desserts tend to be traditionally English – maybe treacle tart with clotted cream, or bread-and-butter pudding with cinnamon crème Anglaise – and the cheese board homes in on Herefordshire and Wales. This emphasis on local materials extends to drinks as well, which take in a couple of good bitters on draught, regional ciders and apple juices, and an English Reichensteiner among an interesting array of Old and New World wines. The list is sensibly annotated, and there are some less usual, but food-friendly, styles and grape varieties scattered about. Mark-ups are low and much of the list is priced below £20. Six house wines sell for £10.90 (£1.90 a glass).

CHEFS: Steve Reynolds and Andrew Lynch   PROPRIETORS: Nicola and Steve Reynolds   OPEN: Tue to Sun L 12 to 2, Tue to Sat D 6.30 to 10 (9 Sun)   CLOSED: first 2 weeks Nov, 25 and 26 Dec, 1 Jan   MEALS: alc exc Sun L (main courses £10.50 to £15.50). Set L Sun £12.50. Bar menu also available   SERVICE: not inc, card slips closed   CARDS: Delta, MasterCard, Switch, Visa DETAILS: 40 seats. 16 seats outside. Private parties: 30 main room, 15 to 30 private rooms. Car park. Vegetarian meals on request. Children's helpings. No smoking in dining room. No music ACCOMMODATION: 2 rooms, all with bath/shower. TV. B&B £40 to £60

## TODMORDEN  West Yorkshire                                     map 8

# Old Hall  ✸  £

Hall Street, Todmorden OL14 7AD
TEL: (01706) 815998   FAX: (01706) 810669

COOKING 3
MODERN BRITISH
£22–£55

Situated in the centre of Todmorden is this magnificent Elizabethan manor house. The proprietors have been very clever with the interior, redesigning the two main dining rooms to give a contemporary feel, with lots of soft cream and white, though keeping the dark wood panelling and ornate fireplaces. Old Hall radiates warmth and hospitality and, as one reporter said, has a 'country-house party' feel.

Dishes tend towards comforting, tried and tested pairings, such as smoked salmon with poached eggs, or tomato and Parmesan gratinée tart with rocket for starters, and perhaps a main course of rump of English beef with pink peppercorns and red wine reduction, plus 'proper' chips. There are some culinary surprises, too, such as a 'trio' of wood pigeon, pheasant and springbok, or a starter of bang-bang chicken. Afters might include 'light as a feather' chocolate pudding with chocolate sauce or a plate of English cheeses. The short wine list is organised by price; mark-ups are fair, and there is a good balance between Old and New World selections. Bottle prices start at £9.95 for South African Chenin Blanc.

CHEF: Chris Roberts   PROPRIETORS: Nick and Madeleine Hoyle   OPEN: Tue to Sun L 12 to 2 (2.30 Sun), Tue to Sat D 7 to 9.30   CLOSED: 25 Dec, first week Jan   MEALS: alc exc Sun L (main courses £12 to £20). Set L Tue to Sat £7.50 (2 courses), Set L Sun £10.95 (2 courses) to £13.95   SERVICE: not inc, 10% for parties of 10 or more   CARDS: Diners, MasterCard, Switch, Visa   DETAILS: 70 seats. 20 seats outside. Private parties: 24 main room, 8 to 24 private rooms. Vegetarian meals. Children's helpings. No smoking in dining room. Music. No mobile phones

---

**TORQUAY** Devon                                                                                  **map 1**

# No 7 Fish Bistro  £

| | |
|---|---|
| 7 Beacon Terrace, Torquay TQ1 2BH | COOKING **1** |
| TEL:  (01803) 295055 | FISH |
| | £22–£49 |

'Some fish are seasonal and choice can be limited by adverse weather conditions,' says a note on the menu. There's no doubting the freshness of raw materials nor the honesty of the cooking at the Stacey family's friendly bistro a stone's throw from the harbour: 'Blackboard specials make up 70 per cent of our menu,' say the owners, which must surely be a reassuring indicator. Dishes could not be simpler: start with a bowl of substantial seafood broth, or pan-fried squid with garlic, before perhaps grilled wing of skate, a fish of the day deep-fried in batter, a freshly boiled crab, or something a bit more complex like baked fillet of cod with prawns thermidor. Plenty of quaffable whites show up on the wine list, which has eight, including champagne, by the glass. House wines run from £10 to £13.50.

CHEFS: Oliver and Paul Stacey   PROPRIETORS: Graham and Jill Stacey   OPEN: Wed to Sat L 12.45 to 1.45, Tue to Sat D 6 to 10.15 (7 to 9.45 winter); also open Mon D June and Oct, Sun and Mon D July to Sept   CLOSED: 1 week Nov, Christmas and New Year, 2 weeks Feb   MEALS: alc (main courses £10 to £17.50)   SERVICE: not inc   CARDS: Amex, Delta, Diners, MasterCard, Switch, Visa   DETAILS: 38 seats. Private parties: 20 main room. Vegetarian meals. Children's helpings. Wheelchair access (not WC). Music. Air-conditioned  (£5)

---

Card slips closed *in the details at the end of an entry indicates that the total on the slips of credit cards is closed when handed over for signature.*

*Subscribers to Which? Online can access* The Good Food Guide *on www.which.net.*

## TOTNES Devon

map 1

# Effings ✿ £

NEW ENTRY

50 Fore Street, Totnes TQ9 5RP
TEL: (01803) 863435

COOKING 3
MODERN EUROPEAN
£22–£44

Nigel Marriage has an impressive CV, having worked for Raymond Blanc at Le Manoir and John Burton Race at L'Ortolan. So why, wondered one visitor, is he working in the kitchen of a delicatessen, serving just four tables for lunch (more are planned) and daytime snacks only? Whatever the reason, the same visitor concluded that it was a successful arrangement and made for 'an extremely pleasant way to spend lunch'. Attention to detail is all that you would expect from a full-blown restaurant (baskets of freshly home-baked bread, nibbles and so on), and a warm, friendly atmosphere adds to the charm, but the food's true strength lies in its top-quality raw materials. The short menu has only one starter (and one pud also) – perhaps chilled cucumber and mint soup topped with flaked salmon, cucumber and lime zest – but main courses offer a good choice of meat and non-meat dishes: for example, 'moist, tender' chicken breast wrapped in basil and pancetta with a 'light, refreshing' sweet and sour sauce; or a colourful, sweet, vividly flavoured red pepper mousse with basil. Wines are few in number but high in quality; house selections are £12.95.

CHEFS: Nigel Marriage and Karl Rasmussen   PROPRIETORS: Michael Kann and Jacqueline Williams
OPEN: Mon to Sat L only 12 to 2.30   CLOSED: bank hols   MEALS: alc (main courses £9 to £17.50).
Snack and other menus available 9.30 to noon, 2.30 to 5.30   SERVICE: net prices, card slips
closed   CARDS: Amex, Delta, MasterCard, Switch, Visa   DETAILS: 15 seats. Private parties: 16
main room. Children's helpings. No smoking in dining room. Wheelchair access (also WC). No
music. No mobile phones. Air-conditioned

# Wills Restaurant ✿

NEW ENTRY

3 The Plains, Totnes TQ9 5DR
TEL: (0800) 056 3006
EMAIL: jenny@eiaddio.com
WEBSITE: wwweiaddio.com

COOKING 2
MODERN EUROPEAN
£23–£53

Easy to find, in an elegant Regency townhouse that was the birthplace of William Wills, Egyptologist and explorer, Wills (the restaurant) seems to have taken some inspiration from the man. The dining room, with its open fireplace and dark red walls, displays an amazing mixture of artefacts, prints and photographs, which gives the place a 'pleasantly dotty' effect. Dominique Prandi used to work at Maison Novelli (see London entry), and seems to have brought a few ideas with him. A selection of steamed wild mushrooms comes wrapped in a poppy-seed pancake, served in a port and Madeira reduction and dusted with cep powder (the latter a Novelli trademark). Or there might be tian of crab with pink grapefruit and a poached quail's egg.

Although over-complication can render some dishes less successful than they might otherwise be, much imagination and skill go into the cooking, and ingredients are carefully sourced, including fresh prawns and fish from Brixham (perhaps a pavé of fresh, well-timed halibut on crushed new potatoes with a lemon and vanilla reduction). Fruit and vegetables are from a nearby shop, and meat from a local supplier, perhaps turning up as a traditional steak and mushroom pudding accompanied by roasted vegetables.

Grilled pineapple on rum-flavoured crème anglaise with rum and raisin ice cream pleases for its contrasts of textures and temperatures, or you might choose a 'trio of fruit mousse' (mango, blackberry and raspberry). Service is welcoming and friendly, and the short wine list, organised by grape variety, focuses on value with its round-the-world selection. House wines start at £11. A café next door under the same ownership serves tea, coffee and lunches.

CHEF: Dominique Prandi   PROPRIETORS: Philip Silvester and Jenny Priest   OPEN: Sun L 12 to 2.30, Tue to Sat D 7 to 9.30   MEALS: alc (main courses L £6 to £11, D £15 to £19). Set D £28   SERVICE: not inc   CARDS: Amex, Delta, Diners, MasterCard, Switch, Visa   DETAILS: 50 seats. Private parties: 25 main room, 10 to 15 private rooms. Vegetarian meals. Children's helpings. No smoking in dining room. Music. Air-conditioned  (£5)

---

**TUNBRIDGE WELLS Kent**                                             map 3

# ▲ Hotel du Vin & Bistro ▮

Crescent Road, Tunbridge Wells TN1 2LY
TEL: (01892) 526455   FAX: (01892) 512044                    COOKING 4
EMAIL: reception@tunbridgewells.hotelduvin.com                   BISTRO
WEBSITE: www.hotelduvin.com                                    £32–£53

An elegant Georgian building close to the centre of genteel Tunbridge Wells is home to one of the first members of this expanding mini-chain of hotels, now with siblings in Bristol and Birmingham as well as the original in Winchester (see entries). The success of the group is down to a winning formula combining an informal atmosphere and a high comfort level, with a fair peppering of luxury touches. The food plays its part in this arrangement: the bistro-style menu makes a suitably unstuffy impression, offering a range of soothing classical dishes such as Toulouse cassoulet, skate wing with beurre noisette and capers, and pot-roast shoulder of lamb with 'petits pois à la française'. Even the more contemporary ideas have a traditional feel: stuffed pig's trotter with Clonakilty black pudding and mash, for example, or confit cod fillet with braised lentils and chorizo. Portions are generous, and desserts, if you can manage them, are mostly old favourites such as sticky toffee pudding, or rhubarb crumble with Birds custard. Waiters have occasionally shown a blasé attitude, but service is generally commended as polite and attentive.

The wine list is generous in scope, and its service is evidently taken very seriously. France – including lesser-known regions – is very strong, but wines from elsewhere in Europe (there are samples from Greece, Switzerland and Hungary) and the New World are equally well chosen. Mark-ups are commendably fair. Lovers of dessert wines will find plenty to delight, while a good selection of half-bottles rounds out the excellent list. Prices start at £11.50, and a list of wines by the glass (£4 to £6.90) is suggested on the menu.

CHEF: Graham Ball   PROPRIETOR: Hotel du Vin Ltd   OPEN: all week 12 to 1.45, 7 to 9.30   MEALS: alc (main courses £12.50 to £15). Set L Sun £23.50   SERVICE: not inc   CARDS: Amex, Delta, Diners, MasterCard, Switch, Visa   DETAILS: 85 seats. 20 seats outside. Private parties: 70 main room, 4 to 12 private rooms. Car park. Vegetarian meals. Children's helpings. No cigars/pipes in

dining room. Wheelchair access (also WC). No music  ACCOMMODATION: 36 rooms, all with bath/
shower. TV. Phone. Room only £85 to £195. Rooms for disabled. Baby facilities (*The Which?
Hotel Guide*)

# Thackeray's ⁵⧊✳

**NEW ENTRY**

85 London Road, Tunbridge Wells TN1 1EA
TEL: (01892) 511921   FAX: (01892) 527561
EMAIL: reservations@thackeraysrestaurant.co.uk
WEBSITE: www.thackeraysrestaurant.com

COOKING 5
MODERN FRENCH
£30–£75

After the departure of Bruce Wass (Thackeray's was last listed in the 2000
edition of the Guide), new owners took over the white clapper-boarded house,
refurbished it extensively inside, and reopened shortly after the last edition of
the Guide appeared. 'Dead cool' is the impression it now makes. 'I was glad I
wore a black dress with a grey jacket as I toned in beautifully,' confessed one
visitor, admiring the clean lines, oak floors, tables covered in plain white linen,
and the fish tank upstairs. Richard Phillips, who has worked for Marco Pierre
White, brings a dash of cosmopolitan vitality to the cooking. Modern
partnerships include foie gras with a potato and smoked bacon blini and wild
garlic sauce, and a small tower of creamy, lobster-topped risotto in a vanilla-
flecked butter sauce.

Artful presentation extends to a neat arrangement of pink and green in a
salmon and langoustine terrine with baby leeks and herb vinaigrette, and to an
attractively 'controlled mess' of firm-fleshed halibut fillet, crusted in wild
mushroom paste and set on spinach, served with a lightly jellied red wine and
five-spice sauce. The kitchen stops short of florid gesture, though, merely
deploying the components of a dish attractively, and concentrating on
essentials, such as quality of materials and timing: for example, of thick pieces
of brill and translucent salmon tied with a ribbon of salmon skin, served with a
fine bouillabaisse sauce.

Chocolate features prominently among desserts, for instance in a hot praline
soufflé into which the waiter pours melted chocolate: 'it was wonderful to dig
beneath the fluff to bundles of nuts swimming in chocolate sauce'. Service tends
to be slick and businesslike, and wine lovers looking for change from £20 on the
sharply chosen and well-bred list will need to choose from the house selection,
which starts with Vin de Pays d'Oc at £11.50.

CHEF: Richard Phillips   PROPRIETORS: Richard Phillips, Paul Smith and Mark Pullinger   OPEN:
Tue to Sun L 12.30 to 2.30, Tue to Sat D 6.30 to 10.30   CLOSED: 25 Dec D, 26 Dec, 1 Jan, bank
hols   MEALS: alc exc Sun L (main courses £14 to £19). Set L Tue to Sat £14.75 (2 courses) to £50,
Set L Sun £22.50, Set D £50   SERVICE: 12.5% (optional), card slips closed   CARDS: Delta,
MasterCard, Switch, Visa   DETAILS: 60 seats. 30 seats outside. Private parties: 60 main room, 8
to 16 private rooms. Vegetarian meals. Children's helpings. No smoking in dining room.
Wheelchair access (not WC). Music. Air-conditioned

---

(£5) *indicates that the restaurant has elected to participate in the* Good Food
Guide *voucher scheme. For full details, see page 6.*

---

## TWICKENHAM Greater London

map 3

# McClements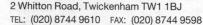

2 Whitton Road, Twickenham TW1 1BJ
TEL: (020) 8744 9610   FAX: (020) 8744 9598
EMAIL: johnmac21@aol.com
WEBSITE: www.mcclementsrestaurant.com

COOKING **6**
FRENCH
£37–£60

McClements has an 'agreeably old-fashioned, quiet and civilised atmosphere'; it is the kind of place where 'the pace is stately and unhurried, waiters are deferential and your meal is interspersed with sorbets, amuse-gueules and pre-dessert desserts'. It is also the kind of place where you can expect some seriously classy cooking that rarely fails to impress reporters, and often brings on an attack of the superlatives. All the way from mini samosa appetisers, and unsweetened truffle crème brûlée, through to petits fours that might include chilli-laced chocolates, John McClements puts a degree of care and attention into his cooking that is matched by his skill and invention and by the quality of ingredients.

His style is classically minded French, but with an innovative streak that might produce an unusual but very successful bouillabaisse en gelée: a blob of fish mousse surrounded by various other jellied fish. Another starter that has come in for plenty of praise is a raviolo filled variously with 'vibrantly fresh' langoustines or lobster and served in a 'gentle and warming' creamy truffle sauce. After an intermediary sorbet might come stuffed pig's trotter filled with a delicate mousse of chicken and ceps 'far removed from the earthy connotations of the dish'; rabbit provençale (with calamari, white beans and a rabbit kidney); or perhaps roast saddle, leg and loin of lamb 'served pink and very tender' with peeled broad beans, carrots, asparagus and a small cylinder of mash. Finish with lime and rhubarb charlotte topped with strawberry ice cream, or a straightforward but excellent pear tarte Tatin. Wines are a touch on the pricey side, but all 28 on the 'sommelier choice' list are offered by the glass, and house wines start at £14.

CHEF/PROPRIETOR: John McClements   OPEN: all week L 12 to 2.30, Mon to Sat D 6.30 to 11
MEALS: Set L £20 (2 courses) to £24, Set D £30 to £35   SERVICE: 10% (optional), card slips closed
CARDS: Amex, Delta, MasterCard, Switch, Visa   DETAILS: 40 seats. Private parties: 60 main room, 60 to 80 private rooms. Car park. Vegetarian meals. No smoking in 1 dining room. Wheelchair access (also WC). No music. Air-conditioned  (£5)

## TYNEMOUTH Tyne & Wear

map 10

# Sidney's

**NEW ENTRY**

3–5 Percy Park Road, Tynemouth NE30 4XN
TEL: (0191) 257 8500   FAX: (0191) 257 9800
EMAIL: bookings@sidneys.co.uk
WEBSITE: www.sidneys.co.uk

COOKING **3**
MODERN BRITISH-PLUS
£17–£46

An unspoiled seaside village with a medieval priory and a main street full of arts and crafts shops is not quite what one expects to encounter on Tyneside somehow, and yet that is where Sidney's is to be found. The ordinary-looking shopfront rather belies the contemporary feel of the interior, where a primary-coloured dining room with bare floorboards, and specials chalked on blackboards, locate it firmly in the twenty-first century. 'Empire food' is a new, and not altogether felicitous, coinage for the kind of modern fusion food the kitchen deals in; also on offer are themed nights, such as a highly successful Mediterranean one. The regular menu features items such as teriyaki chicken kebab with pawpaw salsa, and halibut steak with preserved lemon, roast fennel potato cake and rosemary butter, and most dishes seem to be brought off with considerable flair. Lamb shank tagine with chickpeas was given sweet contrast one night with a fig and coriander couscous. Soups are good (a red pepper version has been well spoken of), but desserts may require some explanation for the likes of peach stressel cake, or crème brûlée with buanda biscuits. A short, serviceable wine list opens with Duboeuf house wines at £10.50, or £2.95 a glass. Also run by Andy Hook is Blackfriars Café Bar and Restaurant, Friar Street, Newcastle upon Tyne; tel (0191) 261 5945.

CHEF: Sam Mowbray   PROPRIETOR: Andy Hook, Hooked On Group   OPEN: Mon to Sat 12 to 2.30, 6 to 10   CLOSED: bank hols exc Good Fri   MEALS: alc (main courses £11 to £16). Set L £5 (1 course, inc wine) to £8.95, Set D Mon to Fri 6 to 7 £8.50 (2 courses) to £10.95   SERVICE: not inc   CARDS: Amex, Delta, MasterCard, Switch, Visa   DETAILS: 50 seats. Private parties: 30 main room, 20 private room. Vegetarian meals. Children's helpings. No smoking at L, before 9pm at D. Wheelchair access (not WC). Music. Air-conditioned   (£5)

## ULLINGSWICK   Herefordshire                                       map 5

# Three Crowns                                    | NEW ENTRY |

Bleak Acre, Ullingswick HR1 3JQ
TEL: (01432) 820279
EMAIL: info@threecrownsinn.com
WEBSITE: www.threecrownsinn.com                              COOKING 4
from A417 turn E (signed Ullingswick), then          MODERN BRITISH
straight on for 1½m                                          £23–£41

Reached along winding lanes, this compact country inn has two dining rooms and a small terrace. White-painted brick, black beams and mismatched bare-wood tables emphasise the rusticity, curtains of 'grandad's shirt' material match the serviettes, and service is solicitous but easy-going. The sensible menu structure (all starters one price, all mains another) foreshadows the cooking's direct style. There is no artifice, just well-judged cooking of the main ingredients (many locally sourced), evident in an airy but crisp twice-baked Cheddar soufflé, and in a grilled sirloin of beef, rare as requested, with a well-flavoured béarnaise.

Frills are happily few, beyond a well-crafted 'restaurant presentation' of a confit shoulder of Marches lamb – boned, carefully rolled, cooked and sliced – with a tasty, tomato-sauced mix of beans and Morteau sausage. Skills extend to desserts too: a well-made version of River Cafe's chocolate nemesis with chocolate ice cream ('a week's chocolate in one hit'), and a wedge of citrus tart combining thin, friable pastry, flavourful lemon and orange filling, and a light, crisp glaze. A few Herefordshire drinks are chalked on a board, and a short, roving wine list reveals a fine Sicilian white (Regaleali from Tasca d'Almerita) and half a dozen house wines including Chilean Merlot (£14) and Italian Pinot Grigio (£14.50).

CHEF/PROPRIETOR: Brent Castle   OPEN: Wed to Mon (and Tues from Jan 2003) 12 to 2, 7 (6 July and Aug) to 9.30 (9 Sun)   CLOSED: 2 weeks from 24 Dec, Mon from Jan 2003   MEALS: alc (main courses £13). Set L (not Sun) £10 (2 courses) to £12   SERVICE: not inc, card slips closed   CARDS: Delta, MasterCard, Switch, Visa   DETAILS: 45 seats. 20 seats outside. Private parties: 45 main room. Car park. Vegetarian meals. Children's helpings. No-smoking area. Wheelchair access (also WC). No music  (£5)

## ULLSWATER Cumbria                                                    map 10

# ▲ Sharrow Bay ▮ �

Ullswater CA10 2LZ
TEL: (017684) 86301   FAX: (017684) 86349
EMAIL: enquiries@sharrow-bay.com
WEBSITE: www.sharrow-bay.com                                         COOKING 6
2m from Pooley Bridge on E side of lake, on road                    ENGLISH
signposted Howtown and Martindale                                   £39–£67

The death of Brian Sack on 1 January 2002 signalled the end of an era. His partner Francis Coulson, who died four years earlier, opened the hotel in 1948, and between them they created Britain's first and archetypal country-house hotel. In the aftermath, little has changed. The setting remains 'awesome', with views across the lake to Helvellyn so magnificent that even 'a chip butty would prove a veritable feast'. New owner Nigel Lightburn carries the mantle of continuity seriously, and even those not attuned to the country-house style find themselves willingly drawn into its enveloping luxury. It is a friendly, relaxing, even homely kind of place, despite the anachronistic regimented routine: as the clock strikes nine, regulars hurry over their last mouthful of sorbet, as main courses are served on the dot.

Dinner is six courses, two of which are intermediate, the first of these a choice of soup or fish: halibut ('quite possibly the most perfectly cooked piece of fish I have ever eaten') served with provençale vegetables for one visitor. This is followed by a sorbet that can be 'more like a dessert than a tangy refresher'. First courses are full of interest, from foie gras on a potato galette, to crab and scallops combined into a little cake. But this is also a place where starters come in the form of pig's trotter filled with pork shank, chicken and mushroom, served on pease pudding; or braised oxtail boned and filled with cabbage, bacon and mushrooms.

One of the kitchen's favourite ways with meat is to serve two contrasting cuts and treatments, perhaps fillet steak with an oxtail croquette, or a lean, tender, evenly pink rack of lamb contrasting well with a piece of fattier braised shoulder, served with impeccable, garlicky gratin dauphinois. Another is to accompany the meat with a sweet, fruity relish, maybe pink, tender breast of duck with honey and orange sauce, its sweetness tempered by a little soy in the marinade. Results vary, and 'nice but ordinary' is how the food can strike reporters, with a few dishes combining poor materials and cooking. Puddings, most laid out for inspection on entry to the dining room, have had a mixed reception over the year too, but warm cherry gâteau pithiviers comes highly recommended, as does a light, creamy, sharp-tasting iced lemon parfait. A small selection of well-researched cheeses is kept in fine condition, although few reporters have room for any by this stage.

The wine list, put together by sommelier James Payne, is encyclopedic. Although Bordeaux and Burgundy are given much space, there is plenty of room for rising stars from the New World, particularly Australia, California and New Zealand; new-wave Spain is another high point. Although mark-ups are sensible, the elevated status of many wines means that diners will have to dig around for choice under £25. All the wines in the 15-strong 'Sharrow selection' (£16.50 to £33), chosen to match the menu, are available by the glass.

CHEFS: Juan Martin and Colin Akrigg   PROPRIETOR: Nigel Lightburn   OPEN: all week 1 to 1.30, 8 to 8.30   CLOSED: early Dec to early Mar   MEALS: Set L £30 to £36.25, Set D £47.25   SERVICE: net prices, card slips closed   CARDS: Delta, MasterCard, Switch, Visa   DETAILS: 60 seats. Private parties: 35 main room. Car park. No children under 13. Jacket and tie. No smoking in dining room. Wheelchair access (also WC). No music. No mobile phones. Air-conditioned ACCOMMODATION: 26 rooms, 23 with bath/shower. TV. Phone. D,B&B £140 to £420. Rooms for disabled. No children under 13 (*The Which? Hotel Guide*)

## ULVERSTON Cumbria                                                     map 8

# ▲ Bay Horse ⁵⨯

Canal Foot, Ulverston LA12 9EL
TEL: (01229) 583972   FAX: (01229) 580502
EMAIL: reservations@thebayhorsehotel.co.uk
WEBSITE: www.thebayhorsehotel.co.uk                   COOKING 4
turn off A590 near centre of Ulverston, following     ENGLISH COUNTRY-HOUSE
signs to Canal Foot                                    £30–£58

The road from Ulverston to Canal Foot passes a chemical plant before offering a panoramic view of the Leven estuary. At the water's edge is this eighteenth-century inn (with brasses, framed fishing lures and Laurel and Hardy memorabilia), once a stop for stagecoaches from Lancaster that braved Morecambe Bay at low tide. The 'country-house' approach shows in an 8pm single-sitting dinner, and the conservatory dining room's weekly-changing menu of around five items per course takes in Aberdeen Angus fillet, rack of Welsh lamb, and Waberthwaite pork with an apple and Calvados sauce.

Good-quality seafood has included impressively fresh pan-fried monkfish tails and scallops – needing, and getting, just a quick blast of heat top and bottom – served in lemon and parsley butter: 'simplicity itself'. If the food is not grippingly exciting, neither is it dull, as the kitchen turns out a smooth cream of leek and butternut squash soup that was 'still interesting by the last mouthful'. Cheeses are worth a punt, and brown sugar meringue – powdery, nutty and toffee-flavoured – is an excellent example, served with a strawberry-filled chocolate basket. South Africa, the wine list's strongest suit, is well supported by fair choice from elsewhere, and prices (from £15.50) are not grasping.

CHEFS: Robert Lyons and Esther Parker   PROPRIETORS: John Tovey and Robert Lyons   OPEN: Tue to Sun L 12 to 1.30, all week D 7.30 for 8 (1 sitting)   MEALS: alc (main courses £21.50 to £23). Set L £17.95. Bar menu also available   SERVICE: not inc, card slips closed   CARDS: Amex, MasterCard, Switch, Visa   DETAILS: 50 seats. 20 seats outside. Private parties: 50 main room.

Car park. Vegetarian meals. No children under 12. No smoking in dining room. Wheelchair access (also WC). Music. Air-conditioned ACCOMMODATION: 9 rooms, all with bath/shower. TV. Phone. D,B&B £97.50 to £185. No children under 12 (*The Which? Hotel Guide*)

## UPPER SLAUGHTER  Gloucestershire                                    map 5

# ▲ Lords of the Manor  ♥ ⌂ ✳

Upper Slaughter GL54 2JD
TEL: (01451) 820243   FAX: (01451) 820696
EMAIL: lordsofthemanor@btinternet.com
WEBSITE: www.lordsofthemanor.com
turn W off A429, 2½m S of Stow-on-the-Wold

COOKING **6**
MODERN FRENCH
£39–£88

Pale stone walls and rich fabrics set the tone, and the prosperous feel is confirmed by deep chairs and sofas in the bar and by the smartly attired dining room overlooking a courtyard. John Campbell moved to the Vineyard at Stockcross (see entry) soon after the 2002 Guide appeared, and Toby Hill stepped into his shoes from the Box Tree (see entry, Ilkley), bringing a mature and accomplished style of cooking that suits the venue.

Dishes retain their essential simplicity, thanks to assured handling of fine raw materials: a small disc of accurately cooked wild mushroom risotto, gently infused with truffle oil, is covered with a few shards of fleshy (not fatty) duck confit, and a main course of first-class, flavourful lamb ('the best piece of rump I have tasted') comes with a rather cool purée of flageolet beans and a fine stock-based sauce. Behind the straightforwardness, though, lies a high degree of sophistication, for example in a tranche of fresh, moist cod timed to the second (crisp, salty skin, translucent centre), topped with a shellfish raviolo, served with a pile of tomato flesh 'revelatory' in its fullness of flavour, and surrounded by a sauce combining the best of both shellfish and tomato.

Direct appeal and bold simplicity characterise desserts, too: a lightly honeyed, gently flavoured goat's cheese pannacotta with sweet roast figs, say, or a dark chocolate 'saveur' (like a fondant, with crusty outside and molten interior) served with milk ice cream. Service (especially from the maitre d') is well up to the food, and wines, too, are of lofty pedigree. Classic French regions underpin the list, but there is space enough for Italy, Spain and New World countries (even a page of English wines). Prices reflect the luxurious surroundings, however, so there is little under £20. A few 'sommelier's favourites' kick off at £21, and ten wines are available by the glass (£5.50 to £7.50).

CHEF: Toby Hill  PROPRIETOR: Empire Ventures  OPEN: all week 12.30 to 2, 7 to 9.30  MEALS: alc exc Sun L (main courses £21 to £27). Set L Mon to Sat £16.95 (2 courses) to £19.95, Set L Sun £23.50, Set D £40. Bar/terrace menu also available  SERVICE: not inc at L, 12.5% at D  CARDS: Amex, Delta, Diners, MasterCard, Switch, Visa  DETAILS: 50 seats. 40 seats outside. Private parties: 50 main room, 4 to 30 private rooms. Car park. Vegetarian meals. Children's helpings No children under 7 at D. No smoking in dining room. No music. No mobile phones ACCOMMODATION: 27 rooms, all with bath/shower. TV. Phone. B&B £99 to £299. Baby facilities (*The Which? Hotel Guide*)

---

*London restaurants by cuisine are listed near the front of the book.*

# ▲ Percy's ✸

Virginstow EX21 5EA
TEL: (01409) 211236   FAX: (01409) 211275
EMAIL: info@percys.co.uk
WEBSITE: www.percys.co.uk
follow signs to Percy's at Coombeshead from                    COOKING 5
Gridley corner on A388, or from B3218 at                    MODERN BRITISH
Metherell Cross junction                                       £48–£64

Given that the house is some 400 years old, it comes as something of a surprise to
walk into the modern bar with its aquamarine- and lavender-coloured walls.
Beyond is a more understated and traditional dining room, with cream-coloured
walls and lots of wood, and beyond the house itself lie 130 acres of fields, trees,
ponds, chickens, sheep, horses and a kitchen garden. As to the food, the
watchwords are simplicity and freshness, which can make some dishes appear
disarmingly plain. In place of exotic spices and well-travelled ingredients, we
find dishes enlivened with no more than a few fresh herbs or salad leaves from
the garden. But this is more than just token use of the estate's bounty; it is a
prototype for the regeneration of country restaurants that have suffered badly
over the past couple of years, ever since the outbreak of foot-and-mouth disease.
What is more, such self-sufficiency can, in the long run, also contribute to a sense
of regional identity in cooking.

Poultry seem to supply eggs rather than meat, but home-reared lamb has
appeared on the menu, simply roast with garlic and lavender jus, and fish is well
sourced, yielding perhaps pan-fried Cornish scallops, or impeccably fresh skate
accompanied by a herby tomato sauce. Smoked eel salad has impressed, and
desserts have included lemon tart with rosemary ice cream, and caramelised
apple tart with cinnamon ice cream. Cheeses might be a little more inspiring,
service is pleasant and friendly, Muzak rather destroys the tranquil ambience,
and wines, grouped by style, offer reasonable choice at moderate prices.

CHEF: Tina Bricknell-Webb   PROPRIETORS: Tony and Tina Bricknell-Webb   OPEN: all week 12 to
1.30, 6.30 to 9.30   MEALS: Set L and D £37.50 to £42.50   SERVICE: not inc, card slips closed
CARDS: Amex, Delta, MasterCard, Switch, Visa   DETAILS: 40 seats. Private parties: 28 main
room, 9 to 12 private rooms. Car park. No children under 12. No smoking in dining room.
Wheelchair access (also WC). Music. No mobile phones   ACCOMMODATION: 8 rooms, all with
bath/shower. TV. Phone. B&B £90 to £165. Rooms for disabled. No children under 12. Fishing
(*The Which? Hotel Guide*)

---

*Restaurateurs justifiably resent no-shows. If you quote a credit card number when booking,
you may be liable for the restaurant's lost profit margin if you don't turn up. Always
phone to cancel.*

*All entries in the Guide are re-researched and rewritten every year, not least because
restaurant standards fluctuate. Don't rely on an out-of-date Guide.*

---

# Wolski's ✻ £ | NEW ENTRY

Monarch House, George Street,
Wakefield WF1 1NE
TEL: (01924) 381252   FAX: (01924) 787570
WEBSITE: www.wolskis.co.uk

COOKING 3
MODERN BRITISH/SEAFOOD
£22–£52

Adding a touch of sophistication to an unglamorous location, this multi-purpose venue housed in a former wine merchant's looks distinguished despite the neon signs that give it the appearance of a nightclub. In fact, it brings together a restaurant (dinner only) with a bar/brasserie, as well as offering conference and banqueting facilities and a licensed wedding room. Lunch in the brasserie might run to tender grilled calf's liver and bacon with mustard mash and onion gravy; crisp-skinned grilled chicken breast with field mushrooms and a well-made gravy; or a generous portion of fisherman's pie containing salmon, cod and prawns under an attractively browned potato topping. The restaurant menu has a more formal structure but offers similar food: chicken liver parfait on a toasted brioche with apple and pear chutney, for example, which might be followed by roast loin of lamb with boudin noir and rosemary jus. Fish and seafood are the kitchen's passion, fuelled by supplies from the restaurant's own boat, which operates out of Flamborough, bringing in sea bass, Dover sole, crab and lobster, the last perhaps chargrilled with chilli and garlic. The list of around 35 well-chosen wines offers plenty under £20, including house Australian red and white at £10.95.

CHEF: James Hall   PROPRIETORS: Judith Dargan, Steve Wolski and Steve Butterfield   OPEN: bar/brasserie Mon to Fri 12 to 2.30, 6 to 9.30, Sat 12 to 2.30; restaurant Sun L 12 to 6, Mon to Sat D 6.30 to 10   MEALS: alc (main courses bar/brasserie £5.50 to £8; restaurant £9 to £16). Set L Sun restaurant £11.95, Set D restaurant £14.95   SERVICE: not inc   CARDS: Diners, MasterCard, Switch, Visa   DETAILS: 100 seats. Private parties: 200 main room. Vegetarian meals. Children's helpings. No smoking in dining room. Music. Air-conditioned  £5

# ▲ Manor House ✻

Northlands, Newbold Road,
Walkington HU17 8RU
TEL: (01482) 881645   FAX: (01482) 866501
EMAIL: info@the-manor-house.co.uk
WEBSITE: www.the-manor-house.co.uk
off B1230 towards Beverley from Walkington

COOKING 1
MODERN BRITISH
£26–£70

This old ivy-clad building, set in three acres, is furnished in conventional country-house style, and dinners are taken in a 'cluttery' conservatory sporting green and yellow parasols, with fine views over well-tended grounds. The place is 'formal', 'starchy' and not without pretension, but the bottom line is that ingredients are of good quality, and properly cooked. The main menu – three courses plus a mid-meal soup or sorbet – is an expensive one (with supplements for foie gras and lobster), and the repertoire is quite narrow, but the kitchen has turned out a decent avocado salad with crispy bacon (served in a pastry basket), and well-trimmed, pink roast rack of lamb with sweet red cabbage and crunchy young carrots. The less expensive offering might take in fishcakes, and chicken breast in a pepper sauce. Finish perhaps with fresh fruit flan, or bread-and-butter pudding, and drink from a wine list that majors on France but picks up some interesting bottles from elsewhere. House wines are £13.95 and £14.95.

CHEF: Derek Baugh   PROPRIETORS: Derek and Lee Baugh   OPEN: Mon to Sat D only 7 to 9.15 CLOSED: 24 Dec to 3 Jan, bank hols   MEALS: Set D Mon to Fri £15 to £30, Set D Sat £30   SERVICE: not inc, card slips closed   CARDS: Delta, MasterCard, Switch, Visa   DETAILS: 55 seats. Private parties: 55 main room, 15 to 24 private rooms. Car park. No children under 12. No smoking in dining room. Music. No mobile phones   ACCOMMODATION: 7 rooms, all with bath/shower. TV. Phone. Room only £75 to £110  (£5)

## WARMINSTER  Wiltshire                                                              map 2

## ▲ Bishopstrow House ⚡✖

Warminster BA12 9HH
TEL: (01985) 212312   FAX: (01985) 216769                          COOKING 3
EMAIL: enquiries@bishopstrow.co.uk                    MODERN COUNTRY-HOUSE
on B3414, 1m E of Warminster                                      £32–£73

Little of the stonework is visible from outside, most of it now colonised by creepers. The rest of the operation seems to have been taken over by healthy pursuits, some more vigorous than others, as people come for a swim in one of the pools, a detoxifying algae wrap, or an Indian head massage. Some menu items are obligingly marked as low in fat and cholesterol, for example a starter of mildly chillied chargrilled squid on a pile of fine, glistening rocket leaves, with a wedge of lemon to give it a lift.

Chris Suter's country-house cooking style continues to aim for bright flavours, deploying capers, aged balsamic vinegar, truffle oil and pesto along the way. Despite the nods to healthy eating, main courses come with copious amounts of meat: for example a shank of lamb (actually two, one still on the bone) with an unctuous, olive-oily potato purée, in a pool of red wine sauce, plus a slick of salsa verde. There are several trendy gestures, including ornately decorated desserts, which, judging by our inspector's nougat glacé, are not a high point. Wine prices are geared towards expense accounts, with little choice under £20 apart from house vin de pays at £14.

CHEF: Chris Suter   PROPRIETOR: Von Essen Hotels   OPEN: all week 12.15 to 2, 7.30 to 9 (9.30 Fri to Sun)   MEALS: Set D £20 (1 course) to £38. Bar menu also available L and D   SERVICE: 15% (optional)   CARDS: Amex, Delta, Diners, MasterCard, Switch, Visa   DETAILS: 70 seats. 45 seats outside. Private parties: 70 main room, 6 to 27 private rooms. Car park. Vegetarian meals. Children's helpings. No smoking in dining room. Music   ACCOMMODATION: 32 rooms, all with bath/shower. TV. Phone. B&B £99 to £330. Baby facilities. Swimming pool. Fishing (*The Which? Hotel Guide*)  (£5)

*New main entries are listed near the front of the book. Some may have appeared in earlier years (though not in the previous edition) or as a Round-up entry last year.*

## WARWICK Warwickshire — map 5

# Findons

7 Old Square, Warwick CV34 4RA
TEL: (01926) 411755 FAX: (01926) 400453 — COOKING 2
EMAIL: rosemary@findons-restaurant.co.uk — MODERN BRITISH
WEBSITE: www.findons-restaurant.co.uk — £26–£59

On a pleasant street of Georgian houses and offices in the heart of Warwick, Findons has a warm, welcoming feel ('service with a smile' from attentive and informed staff is part of the appeal), its aspirations egged on by a band of loyal supporters. The quality of materials is top notch – a local butcher and Birmingham's fish market play their part – and timing is accurate, although a tendency to add decorative 'bits and bobs' can detract from the overall effect. Much of the cooking relies on last minute preparation, taking in scallops with apple couscous, poached sea bass with mustard and fennel, and flavourful lamb fillet (very rare, you aren't asked) with a herb crust, accompanied by a sauce of fresh peas and roast shallots. Bread-and-butter pudding comes highly rated, and a short, sensibly priced wine list, incorporating a few special clarets and Madeiras, starts with house Spanish white and French red at £10.95.

CHEFS: Michael Findon and Stuart Haste PROPRIETOR: Findon & Williams Ltd OPEN: Mon to Fri L 12 to 2, Mon to Sat 7 to 9.30 CLOSED: 26 Dec MEALS: alc (main courses £11 to £19). Set L Mon to Fri £9.95 (2 courses) SERVICE: not inc, 10% for parties of 8 or more CARDS: Amex, Delta, Diners, MasterCard, Switch, Visa DETAILS: 48 seats. 25 seats outside. Private parties: 36 main room, 8 to 12 private rooms. Vegetarian meals. No children under 8. No smoking in 1 dining room. Wheelchair access (not WC). Music (£5)

## WATERMILLOCK Cumbria — map 10

# ▲ Rampsbeck Country House Hotel

Watermillock, Ullswater CA11 0LP
TEL: (017684) 86442 FAX: (017684) 86688
EMAIL: rampsbeck@btconnect.com — COOKING 3
WEBSITE: www.hotel-lakedistrict.com — ANGLO-FRENCH
on A592 2m SW of Pooley Bridge — £35–£65

This elegant eighteenth-century country mansion sits on the shore of Ullswater surrounded by acres of park and gardens. Inside, the pastel-coloured lounge is full of knick-knacks and sofas, while the dining room sets its mood with low lights and dark curtains.

Dinner follows the well-tried Lakeland hotel formula: four courses, with coffee and petits fours included. The range of well-sourced ingredients shows in starters such as roast loin of rabbit with Cumbrian air-dried ham and balsamic dressing, or pan-fried Périgord foie gras with poached pear and cinnamon. Then a soup, such as white bean and smoked bacon velouté, precedes elaborate main courses deploying all kinds of techniques: the oven is needed for suprème of Barbary duck with braised endive, button onions and cep jus, while steaming is applied to a medley of seafood served with noodles and a frothy champagne sauce. Desserts typically range from hot prune and Armagnac pudding with butterscotch sauce to Amaretto and praline parfait with crisp nougatine;

otherwise, there are British and Irish cheeses. Light lunches are available in the bar. Wines from Greece, Israel and Lebanon rub shoulders with European classics on the wide-ranging list, organised by style. Mark-ups are fair, leaving ample room for manoeuvre under the £20 mark; 11 house wines start at £11.25.

CHEF: Andrew McGeorge   PROPRIETORS: Tom and Marion Gibb   OPEN: all week 12 to 1, 7 to 8.30 CLOSED: early Jan to mid-Feb   MEALS: Set L Mon to Sat £28, Set L Sun £26, Set D £35 to £41. Light L menu also available 12 to 1.45   SERVICE: not inc, card slips closed   CARDS: Delta, MasterCard, Switch, Visa   DETAILS: 40 seats. Private parties: 60 main room, 6 to 16 private rooms. Car park. Children by arrangement. No smoking in dining room. No music ACCOMMODATION: 20 rooms, all with bath/shower. TV. Phone. B&B £60 to £198. Fishing (*The Which? Hotel Guide*)

## WATH-IN-NIDDERDALE  North Yorkshire                    map 8

## ▲ Sportsman's Arms  ♀ ⅝✳

Wath-in-Nidderdale, Pateley Bridge HG3 5PP                      COOKING 4 TEL: (01423) 711306  FAX: (01423) 712524                        ANGLO-FRENCH off B6265, 2m NW of Pateley Bridge                              £27–£52

The uninitiated will no doubt be surprised by the unexpected formality of the dining room at what might first seem like just another remote moorland inn, especially after crossing the 'unfeasibly narrow' old packhorse bridge to reach it. However, Sportsman regulars will know that this is no ordinary seventeenth-century hostelry, but rather an attractive hotel and restaurant set among grouse moors in popular fishing and walking country. Large clocks and a dark-wood dresser are set against light, fresh paintwork with tables of crisp white linen and a delightful mismatch of chairs.

The surrounding countryside contributes to the kitchen's abundant larder, with game (in season) and fish (delivered daily from the Whitby boats) finding their place in the Carters' modern repertoire: perhaps Finnan haddock and cod fishcakes, with baby mixed leaves and sauce rémoulade. Scottish haggis (served on neeps with local black pudding and sweetbreads in a red onion sauce) may be followed by a well-balanced ballottine of stuffed best end of local lamb with asparagus and natural jus. Puddings continue to fly the flag with a tangy lemon tart, while service proves friendly, observant and efficient. The wine list is sensibly organised and sensibly priced. France has the edge over the competition from elsewhere in Europe and the New World, red and white Burgundy being particularly strong. Nine house recommendations start at £12.90.

CHEFS: Ray and Jamie Carter, and Seth Marsland   PROPRIETORS: Ray and Jane Carter   OPEN: Sun L 12 to 2, Mon to Sat D 7 to 9.30   CLOSED: 25 Dec   MEALS: alc D (main courses £13 to £16.50). Set L Sun £18.50. Bar menu available all week L and D   SERVICE: not inc, card slips closed   CARDS: MasterCard, Switch, Visa   DETAILS: 70 seats. 50 seats outside. Private parties: 50 main room, 4 to 12 private rooms. Car park. Vegetarian meals. Children's helpings. No smoking in dining room. Wheelchair access (not WC). No music. No mobile phones ACCOMMODATION: 13 rooms, 11 with bath/shower. TV. Phone. B&B £45 to £100. Fishing (*The Which? Hotel Guide*)

## WELLS Somerset                                    map 2

# Ritcher's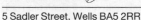

5 Sadler Street, Wells BA5 2RR
TEL: (01749) 679085   FAX: (01749) 673866                COOKING **2**
EMAIL: info@ritchers.co.uk                          MODERN BRITISH
WEBSITE: www.ritchers.co.uk                              £19–£46

'As sound as ever,' summed up one regular to this two-tier operation with its
ground-floor bistro and first-floor dining room. The cooking does not aim to be
imaginative or original, but it is both worthy and dependable. The kitchen
keeps tabs on fashionable preparation and presentation but doesn't lose sight of
the importance of good-quality materials, from a trio of English lamb (grilled
noisette, sauté sweetbreads, pot-roast shoulder) to an 'honestly grilled steak'
that comes with a kidney pudding, red wine gravy and a £5 supplement.

   First courses run from a plain goats' cheese and rocket salad, via leek and
chorizo tartlet, to a ravioli of roast quail with wild mushrooms and Madeira
sauce. Main-course vegetables typically take in mange-tout and first-rate
dauphinois potatoes, and desserts have included a fine tarte Tatin, and a
'chocolate affair' that was crisp outside and moist inside, with an admirable
sauce. Service at its best is prompt yet relaxed, although it has also been abrupt
and unhelpful. A short list of wines, grouped by grape variety and style, starts
with eight house wines under £14.

CHEF: Nick Hart   PROPRIETORS: Kate Ritcher and Nick Hart   OPEN: all week 12 to 2, 7 to 9.30
(6.30 to 10 Sat in summer)   CLOSED: 26 Dec, 1 Jan   MEALS: Set L £6.95 (1 course) to £10.95, Set
D £18.50 (2 courses) to £22.50   SERVICE: not inc, card slips closed   CARDS: MasterCard,
Switch, Visa   DETAILS: 42 seats. 12 seats outside. Private parties: 20 main room. Vegetarian
meals. No children under 10 at D. No cigars/pipes while others eat. Wheelchair access (not WC).
Music. Air-conditioned

## WELLS-NEXT-THE-SEA Norfolk                        map 6

# ▲ Rococo at the Crown ▼

The Buttlands, Wells-next-the-Sea NR23 1EX
TEL: (01328) 710209   FAX: (01328) 711432              COOKING **5**
EMAIL: reception@rococoatthecrown.co.uk             MODERN BRITISH
WEBSITE: www.rococoatthecrown.co.uk                      £33–£68

Although a large warehouse with lifting gear points to its historical role as a
port, Wells is only next-the-sea when the tide is in. Otherwise, it's a long walk
over the dunes, especially from Rococo, on the edge of a large green circled by
big old trees. Drinks are taken in an all-white Smoke Room (a remnant from its
pub days), and meals in an all-yellow dining room, both given a lift by Anne
Anderson's colourful paintings. Ideas are appealing, and luxuries such as foie
gras (perhaps in a truffled parfait) are balanced by humbler materials such as a
salad of crisp tongue (served cold) with smoky bacon, some leaves and caper-
spiked lentils. Local crab might make an appearance too, in a filo pastry stack
with tomato salsa.

   Good ingredients are generally well handled, often in simple ways: for
example in a starter of wild mushrooms on brioche with an accurately poached

duck egg, surrounded by a herby beurre blanc (a favourite saucing method). Main courses at inspection disappointed, partly for reasons of timing, but desserts are a highlight, taking in a slice of just-melting prune and Armagnac parfait with a fine crème anglaise, and an individual cooked-to-order lemon tart, made with crisp sweet shortcrust pastry and a perfectly judged filling. Wines range from well-priced selections, through steady Burgundy and Bordeaux offerings, to cultish bins from the New World. The result is plenty to choose from under £20, as well as options for those with deeper pockets. Prices start at £10.50 for Spanish white.

CHEFS: Nick Anderson and Kelly Norton   PROPRIETORS: Wells Fine Dining Company Ltd   OPEN: Sun L 12 to 2, all week D 7 to 9.30   MEALS: Set L £20, Set D £29.50 (2 courses) to £39.50; brasserie menu available all week 12 to 2, 6 to 9.30   SERVICE: not inc, card slips closed   CARDS: Amex, Delta, MasterCard, Switch, Visa   DETAILS: 50 seats. 24 seats outside. Private parties: 40 main room, 6 to 24 private rooms. Vegetarian meals. Children's helpings. No smoking while others eat. Wheelchair access (not WC). No music   ACCOMMODATION: 11 rooms, all with bath/shower. TV. Phone. B&B £85 to £120. Baby facilities (*The Which? Hotel Guide*)  £5

---

## WELWYN GARDEN CITY  Hertfordshire                                          map 3

## ▲ Auberge du Lac ▼

Brocket Hall, Lemsford, Welwyn Garden
City AL8 7XG
TEL: (01707) 368888   FAX: (01707) 368898
EMAIL: auberge@brocket-hall.co.uk
WEBSITE: www.brockethall.co.uk

| NEW CHEF |
|---|
MODERN FRENCH
£40–£92

Paul Dunstane, who has worked at cheznico in London and at Harveys in Bristol (see entry), arrived in the kitchen of this eighteenth-century former hunting lodge just as the Guide was going to press, but his cooking seems set to match the opulent surroundings. Luxuries abound – in a truffle risotto for example, and in a ham and foie gras terrine – and other materials are equally well sourced: perhaps pot roast Goosnargh chicken with truffled pomme purée, or veal sweetbreads with a fricassee of cockles, girolles and white beans. Service and wine are equally French, the list centring on Burgundy and Bordeaux (including some rare old claret vintages with four-figure price tags). Other well-chosen selections come from Spain, Italy, and the New World. There is little to be found under £25, but the value issue is mitigated somewhat by a list of 40-plus wines sold by the glass (£6 to £11.50).

CHEF: Paul Dunstane   PROPRIETOR: CCA International   OPEN: Tue to Sun L 12 to 2, Tue to Sat D 7 to 10   MEALS: Set L Tue to Sat £25 (inc wine) to £38, Set L Sun £30, Set D £38 to £45   SERVICE: 10%, card slips closed   CARDS: Amex, Delta, Diners, MasterCard, Switch, Visa   DETAILS: 70 seats. 70 seats outside. Private parties: 70 main room, 2 to 30 private rooms. Car park. Vegetarian meals. Children's helpings. No cigars/pipes in dining room. Wheelchair access (not WC). Music. No mobile phones. Air-conditioned   ACCOMMODATION: 16 rooms, all with bath/shower. TV. Phone. B&B £150 to £170. Rooms for disabled. Baby facilities

---

*If customers are asked to switch off mobile phones while in a restaurant, this is noted in the details at the end of an entry.*

---

## WEST BAY Dorset — map 2

# Riverside Restaurant 🍴

West Bay DT6 4EZ
TEL: (01308) 422011   FAX: (01308) 458808
WEBSITE: www.riverside-restaurant.co.uk
off A35, 1m S of Bridport

COOKING 1
SEAFOOD
£24–£66

Basically a neighbourhood café transported to a harbour setting, Riverside is approached along a balustraded walkway ('magical' at dusk), and makes the most of its watery views. Light, white and bright, with old board floors and bare wooden tables, it understandably concentrates on seafood. A daily menu supplements the already long regular one, perhaps listing monkfish bourride, or scallops grilled in the shell with coriander and lime butter.

Half a dozen fish are usually offered plainly grilled, and cod in Guinness batter with matchstick chips and mushy peas is well reported, although a poor shellfish risotto was one item that let down an inspection meal. Desserts run the gamut from old-fashioned banana split and knickerbocker glory to roast saffron pears with lemon and ricotta ice cream. Service is casual – 'they don't consciously rush you, but they're used to people getting on with it' – and prices on the roving wine list (including the short fine wine selection) are reasonable. If the nameless house wine at £13 a litre doesn't tempt, consider Domaine Cauhapé's Jurançon Sec at £15.50.

CHEFS: Nic Larcombe and Will Longman   PROPRIETORS: Arthur and Janet Watson   OPEN: Tue to Sun L 12 to 2.15, Tue to Sat D 6.30 to 8.45 (open Sun D and Mon L and D on bank hols; D hours vary Feb/Mar and Oct/Nov, phone to check)   CLOSED: 1 Dec to mid-Feb   MEALS: alc (main courses £10 to £25). Set L Feb to Apr and Oct to Nov £12.50 (2 courses) to £15.50 (inc wine), Set D Fri Feb and Mar and Oct to Nov £20   SERVICE: not inc, card slips closed   CARDS: Delta, MasterCard, Switch, Visa   DETAILS: 90 seats. 30 seats outside. Vegetarian meals. Children's helpings. No smoking in dining room. Wheelchair access (also women's WC). Occasional music

## WEST TANFIELD North Yorkshire — map 9

# ▲ Bruce Arms 🍴 £

Main Street, West Tanfield HG4 5JJ
TEL: (01677) 470325   FAX: (01677) 470796
EMAIL: iwanttostay@brucearms.com
WEBSITE: www.brucearms.com

COOKING 4
MODERN ENGLISH
£25–£44

Once feeling like an aspirational pub, the Bruce Arms now seems to have gone into overt bistro mode. The transformation has brought an accumulation of eye-catching decorative bric-à-brac: antique telephones, tennis racquets, oil lamps and specimens of international banknotes. Geoff Smith notes an increasing number of customers choosing fish, something he happily caters for with the likes of seared mackerel with caramelised peppers and onions, grilled sea bass with tomato compote, or roast cod with grain mustard mash. Meat cookery is good too though, as evidenced by a braised shoulder of local lamb served with mash and a red wine gravy in which the cooking juices could be positively tasted. Simpler pub-type dishes, such as chicken-liver pâté with grape, apple and brandy chutney, are tastily rendered, while soft-textured desserts – crème brûlée or cappuccino mousse served in a cup – present no challenges. 'Chatty, bubbly' service copes admirably, even when the place is packed. The wine list is an enterprising selection, with Australian Shiraz, Chilean Merlot and an Argentinian Semillon-Sauvignon supplementing European offerings; house Duboeuf is £10.

CHEF/PROPRIETOR: Geoff Smith    OPEN: Wed to Sun 12 to 2, 6.30 to 9.30    CLOSED: 2 weeks mid Feb    MEALS: alc D (main courses £9 to £16.50). Light L menu available (main courses £3.50 to £5)    SERVICE: not inc, card slips closed    CARDS: Delta, MasterCard, Switch, Visa    DETAILS: 40 seats. 16 seats outside. Private parties: 24 main room, 18 to 30 private rooms. Car park. No smoking in 1 dining room. Wheelchair access (not WC). Music    ACCOMMODATION: 3 rooms, all with bath/shower. TV. B&B £40 to £60

## WETHERSFIELD Essex      map 6

# Dicken's Brasserie 🛠 £

The Green, Wethersfield CM7 4BS
TEL: (01371) 850723    FAX: (01371) 850727      COOKING 2
EMAIL: reservations@dickensbrasserie.co.uk      MODERN BRITISH
WEBSITE: www.dickens.co.uk      £27–£55

The blue-fronted brasserie is as accommodating as can be, offering a straightforward menu of staple but appealing dishes in two sizes: £6 or £10. This makes possible the sort of flexibility that reporters regularly appreciate, allowing them to pop in for a light lunch, a weightier dinner, or sometimes the other way round. The range extends from a warm breakfast salad, via vegetable risotto, to liver and bacon with mash and gravy. On the way it takes in a hefty-sounding triple sausage and squeak, and an even more substantial house grill: 'a challenge worth taking', according to the house itself.

Puddings run from crêpes suzette to chocolate sundae, while a children's menu at £5.50 lists chicken fritters, crispy cod, or sausage and chips, plus a small pudding chosen from the regular list. Many of the wines are pegged at £15, with a short selection of more expensive ones (still not much more than £25). Six half-bottles, two house wines (£9.95), plus another eight by the glass, all confirm the customer-friendly impression.

CHEF/PROPRIETOR: John Dicken    OPEN: all week 12 to 2, 6.30 to 9.30    MEALS: alc (main courses £10 to £22)    SERVICE: not inc    CARDS: Delta, MasterCard, Switch, Visa    DETAILS: 40 seats. Private parties: 40 main room, 20 private room. Car park. Children's helpings. No smoking in dining room. Wheelchair access (not WC). Music. No mobile phones

## WHITBY North Yorkshire      map 9

# Magpie Café 🛠 £

14 Pier Road, Whitby YO21 3PU
TEL: (01947) 602058    FAX: (01947) 601801      COOKING 2
EMAIL: ian@magpiecafe.co.uk      SEAFOOD
WEBSITE: www.magpiecafe.co.uk      £19–£52

'It's worth the wait' might be the motto of this incomparable seaside café in a converted merchant's house on the harbourside opposite the fish market. The place is chock-a-block virtually throughout the year, the queues get longer and, if it rains, the owners provide umbrellas. Deliveries from the boats often arrive twice daily, so there's no doubting the freshness of raw materials. There are menus for any time of day, plus specials, children's deals and more, but the star of the show is undoubtedly fish and chips, although some have opted for a seafood hotpot (complete with plenty of ciabatta for mopping up), a splendid locally cured kipper with brown bread, and supremely fresh grilled Dover sole with lemon butter sauce. A prodigious list of desserts, including home-made cakes with cheese, rounds things off. Service runs like a dream, thanks to a bevy of well-organised and efficient ladies. House French is £8.95.

CHEFS: Ian Robson and Paul Gildroy   PROPRIETORS: Ian Robson and Alison McKenzie Robson   OPEN: all week 11.30 to 9 (6.30 Sun Nov to Mar)   CLOSED: 25 Dec, 1 Jan, mid-Jan to early Feb   MEALS: alc (main courses £5.50 to £18)   SERVICE: not inc, card slips closed   CARDS: Delta, MasterCard, Switch, Visa   DETAILS: 100 seats. Private parties: 50 main room. Vegetarian meals. Children's helpings. No smoking in dining room. Occasional music. Air-conditioned   (£5)

## WHITCHURCH  Hampshire

map 2

# Red House ⁵⁄✳ £

21 London Street, Whitchurch RG28 7LH                COOKING 2
TEL: (01256) 895558                                   GLOBAL
                                                      £22–£43

With a garden, patio and kids' play park, this long white-painted building near the town centre is obviously oriented towards families and casual eating. Although the inside is open-plan, in fact it comes in two distinct parts: a lounge-bar area, and a non-smoking dining room, both (apart from a couple of enormous mirrors) quite plainly decorated. Lighter meals are represented by pasta, wraps, melts and baguettes, while the main menu goes in for rather more ambitious offerings of chargrilled pigeon breast with haricot beans and coriander, or teriyaki venison steak with Savoy cabbage.

Flavours tend to be forthright, judging by a Cajun-spiced skate wing with crab mash and shellfish sauce, although rack of lamb might come with no more than sauté mushrooms and spinach in a red wine sauce. Homely desserts take in bread-and-butter pudding, chocolate brownies, and a toffee apple parfait, and the reasonably priced 30-strong wine list starts with house Conca de Barberá red and white at £9.95.

CHEFS: Shannon Wells and Pete Nash   PROPRIETORS: Shannon and Caroline Wells   OPEN: all week 12 to 2, 6.30 (7 Sun) to 9.30   MEALS: alc (main courses L£6 to £15, D £9 to £16)   SERVICE: not inc, card slips closed, 10% for parties of 8 or more   CARDS: MasterCard, Switch, Visa   DETAILS: 35 seats. Car park. Vegetarian meals. Children's helpings. No children under 12 at D. No smoking in dining room. Wheelchair access (also men's WC). No music

---

*Several sharp operators have tried to extort money from restaurateurs on the promise of an entry in a guidebook that has never appeared.* The Good Food Guide *makes no charge for inclusion.*

---

## WHITSTABLE Kent       map 3

# Sportsman  ✹✖

Faversham Road, Seasalter, Whitstable CT5 4BP
TEL: (01227) 273370   FAX: (01227) 262314

COOKING 3
MODERN EUROPEAN
£29–£47

Recently, the Harris brothers have been consolidating the success of their first three years in business by extending their network of local suppliers: lamb now comes from the salt marshes that surround their isolated pub, situated a short drive along the coast out of Whitstable. A local gardener has been brought on board to supply organic vegetables, and locally caught fish remains a feature. Cooking, like the décor, keeps things simple to make the best of the fine materials, but makes an impact with some robust flavour combinations: for example, crispy duck with smoked chilli salsa and sour cream, pork belly stuffed with black pudding and served with crackling, or local turbot braised in vin jaune with morels. Daubes and braises are a speciality – shin of beef in red wine, perhaps – prepared over a two-week period to allow flavours to develop. If you have room, tarte Tatin for two, served with unpasteurised Jersey cream, is the dessert to go for. A short list of wines includes five by the glass from £2.40. Bottle prices start at £9.95.

CHEFS: Stephen Harris, Dan Flavell and Jim Shave   PROPRIETORS: Stephen, Philip and Damian Harris   OPEN: Tue to Sun L 12 to 2, Tue to Sat D 7 to 9   CLOSED: 25 Dec   MEALS: alc (main courses £10 to £16)   SERVICE: not inc, card slips closed, 10% for parties of 6 or more   CARDS: Delta, Diners, MasterCard, Switch, Visa   DETAILS: 50 seats. Private parties: 20 main room. Car park. Vegetarian meals. No smoking in 1 dining room. Wheelchair access (not WC). Music. Air-conditioned

## WICKHAM Hampshire       map 2

# ▲ Old House  ✹✖

The Square, Wickham PO17 5JG
TEL: (01329) 833049   FAX: (01329) 833672
EMAIL: enq@theoldhousehotel.co.uk
2½m N of Fareham, at junction of A32 and B2177

NEW CHEF
ANGLO-FRENCH
£29–£55

The eighteenth-century building's barn-like dining room, with white walls, heavy beams and comfortably upholstered chairs, creates an old-fashioned setting, into which stepped Francis Devrianne, too late for us to receive any feedback. His menu treads familiar Old House territory, taking in a salad of sauté foie gras with truffle dressing, wild mushroom risotto, and sea bass with pesto cream butter. Wines are grouped by style, with fair choice under £20, and prices start at £10.95 (£2.75 a glass) for house South African.

CHEF: Francis Devrianne   PROPRIETORS: John and Gloria Goodacre   OPEN: Tue to Sun L 12 to 2, Mon to Sat D 7 to 9.30   CLOSED: 26 Dec to 5 Jan   MEALS: alc exc Sun L (main courses £17 to £18.50). Set L £15 (2 courses) to £18.50, Set L Sun £18.50, Set D £18.50 (2 courses) to £21.50   SERVICE: 10% (optional)   CARDS: Amex, Delta, Diners, MasterCard, Switch, Visa   DETAILS: 60 seats. Private parties: 40 main room, 8 to 14 private rooms. Car park. Vegetarian meals.

Children's helpings. No smoking in dining room. Wheelchair access (not WC). Occasional music. No mobile phones  ACCOMMODATION: 9 rooms, 8 with bath/shower. TV. Phone. B&B £65 to £90. Baby facilities  (£5)

## WILLITON Somerset                                                    map 2

## ▲ White House ▮ ⁵⅄

11 Long Street, Williton TA4 4QW                                    COOKING 6
TEL: (01984) 632306                                      ENGLISH/MEDITERRANEAN
                                                              £48–£58

The appropriately named Georgian house is in the middle of this small village, its plain frontage brightened up a little by green shutters. Behind the high white walls is a courtyard filled with plants and trees: not for outdoor eating, but visible from the peaceful dining room, which is filled with a collection of treasures accumulated over the 35 years that the Smiths have been here.

Menus make a virtue of simplicity. The Smiths are proud of their top-quality materials provided by a well-established network of suppliers, which might show up as a straightforward dish of caramelised scallops on a bed of fried samphire, or a warm tart of Gruyère and Parmesan with a lamb's lettuce salad. The choice at main course might be between grilled noisettes of local lamb with sauce paloise, lightly roasted saddle of local venison with wild rice, redcurrants and game jus, or pan-fried red mullet on marinated aubergine and tomato coulis. All dishes are served with the same generous selection of vegetables, which may seem slightly old-fashioned but it is all part of the unpretentious charm of the place. Finish perhaps with grappa-flavoured pannacotta with fresh berries, or blackcurrant sorbet with poached raspberries.

'The welcome was as warm as ever,' remarked a satisfied return visitor, appreciative of the friendly service and relaxed, informal atmosphere, and much impressed by Dick Smith's wine expertise: indeed, wines are a fundamental part of a stay here, and there is plenty on the list to tempt. They are sourced from a number of respected merchants and the care taken is evident: well-chosen bottles from throughout France, with the likes of Bandol and Provence adding breadth to Rhône, Bordeaux and Burgundy. There are a few from the New World, plus a decent selection of half-bottles. Pricing is fair; house wines start at £12 (£2.80 a glass), while two pages of selected new arrivals and old favourites provide a short-cut to interesting drinking.

CHEFS/PROPRIETORS: Dick and Kay Smith  OPEN: all week D only 7 to 8.30  CLOSED: Nov to mid-May  MEALS: Set D £36  SERVICE: not inc  CARDS: none  DETAILS: 24 seats. Car park. Children's helpings. No smoking in dining room. Wheelchair access (not WC). No music  ACCOMMODATION: 10 rooms, 9 with bath/shower. TV. Phone. B&B £49 to £112. Baby facilities

---

*The 2004 Guide will be published before Christmas 2003. Reports on meals are most welcome at any time of the year, but are particularly valuable in the spring (no later than June). Send them to* The Good Food Guide, *FREEPOST, 2 Marylebone Road, London NW1 4DF. Or email your report to* goodfoodguide@which.net

## WINCANTON Somerset                                         map 2

## ▲ Holbrook House ▼ ⅝✗                          | NEW ENTRY |

Wincanton BA9 8BS
TEL: (01963) 32377   FAX: (01963) 32681
EMAIL: reservations@holbrookhouse.co.uk                    COOKING 4
WEBSITE: www.holbrookhouse.co.uk                    MODERN EUROPEAN
on A371, approx 1m N of junction with A303                    £25–£54

Leisure and conference facilities contrast with this old manor house's surprisingly domestic interior and with the small dining room, done out in face-powder pink, with posies in stainless-steel teapots on tables. Brett Sutton arrived in late 2001, and his food adds another contrast: complex and full of effort, it includes, for example, roast boned quails with confit salsify, creamed spinach, seared foie gras, pommes mireille and sauce Albufera. But it 'eats better than the menu sounds', raw materials are very good or outstanding, and results are uncluttered and appealing: perhaps three accurately seared scallops, each atop a tiny soft potato rösti and a slice of firm chicken boudin, with skinned baby broad beans and trompette mushrooms

Individual components, and combinations of flavours and textures, are successful, as in a generous, supple, pink-roasted venison fillet, sliced thickly on to sauerkraut flecked with carrot and chorizo, surrounded by a dark, strong-flavoured bitter chocolate sauce containing roast shallots and baby beetroots. One of the best desserts is a peeled, cored whole apple, sliced into layers, on a bed of creamy, clearly spiced rice pudding, with a scoop of first-rate malt ice cream stuck with apple crisps.

Copious and fiddly extras inspire less confidence, although breads (plain and flavoured) are good. Service is courteous and 'superbly individual though pedantically formal' for one who confessed, tongue in cheek, to finding it 'a particular thrill for those of us who like to have their food served by a waiter wearing gloves'. Wines, grouped by style, don't always go for big names, but focus on sound producers, many from lesser-known regions of the winemaking globe. A selection of 13 house wines (four available by the glass) ranges from £10 to £24. Fair pricing means that there is good choice under £20, although there are pricier bottles for those who wish to push the boat out.

CHEF: Brett Sutton   PROPRIETORS: Pat and John McGinley   OPEN: all week 12.30 to 2, 7.30 to 9.30   MEALS: Set L £11.50 (2 courses) to £14.95, Set D £28 (2 courses) to £33. Bar/light meal menu available 11 to 11   SERVICE: not inc   CARDS: Amex, Delta, MasterCard, Switch, Visa DETAILS: 40 seats. 20 seats outside. Private parties: 35 to 160 in main or private rooms. Car park. Vegetarian meals. No children under 5. Children's helpings. No smoking in dining room. Wheelchair access (also women's WC). Music. No mobile phones   ACCOMMODATION: 20 rooms, all with bath/shower. TV. Phone. B&B £95 to £245. Rooms for disabled. Baby facilities. Swimming pool

---

*If a restaurant is new to the Guide this year (did not appear as a main entry in the last edition),* NEW ENTRY *appears opposite its name.*

---

**map 5**

## ▲ Wesley House ▼ ⁵✗

High Street, Winchcombe GL54 5LJ
TEL: (01242) 602366   FAX: (01242) 609046
EMAIL: reservations@wesleyhouse.co.uk
WEBSITE: www.wesleyhouse.co.uk

COOKING **2**
MODERN BRITISH
£27–£64

Leaded windows may give it the air of a tearoom, but the beams and rough exposed stone in this centuries-old building near Sudeley Castle point to more substantial business. The broad Anglo-French thrust of the menu is tempered by a smoked salmon and dill risotto here, and a chilli jam there, but the repertoire also takes in more mainstream stuffed duck leg with a port and fig reduction, and pork fillet with spiced Puy lentils and grain mustard.

Desserts span a similar range, from a lavender and almond pannacotta to passion-fruit soufflé with white chocolate sauce. Perhaps because the restaurant is open every mealtime except Sunday dinner, standards have not always held up, but incidentals (bread and the appetiser soup) are highly rated. South Africa figures prominently on the wine list, with Australia, New Zealand and California making worthwhile contributions too. France forms most of the Old World side of the equation. Mark-ups are fair, with New World wines offering best value. House South African is £14.

CHEF: Alex Breach   PROPRIETOR: Matthew Brown   OPEN: all week L 12 to 2, Mon to Sat D 6.45 to 9.15   MEALS: alc L (main courses £11 to £20). Set L Mon to Sat £10 (2 courses) to £14.50, Set L Sun £18.50 (2 courses) to £21.50, Set D Mon to Fri £26 (2 courses) to £31, Set D Sat £31   SERVICE: not inc   CARDS: Amex, Delta, MasterCard, Switch, Visa   DETAILS: 55 seats. 20 seats outside. Private parties: 65 main room. Children's helpings. No smoking in dining room. Wheelchair access (not WC). Music. No mobile phones   ACCOMMODATION: 6 rooms, all with bath/shower. TV. Phone. B&B £40 to £80. Baby facilities (*The Which? Hotel Guide*) £5

**map 2**

## Bertie's ✧

5 Jewry Street, Winchester SO23 8RZ
TEL/FAX: (01962) 860006
EMAIL: winchester@berties.co.uk
WEBSITE: www.berties.co.uk

COOKING **2**
MODERN BRITISH
£23–£47

Simon Lakey, listed as chef in last's year's Guide, has moved to Bertie's sibling in Romsey (see entry), and his place has been taken by former sous-chef Kevin Anfield. The Winchester outlet is a 'bright, breezy, very popular neighbourhood local', and it gets packed. The menu is as contemporary as the décor, and there's a lot going on in most dishes: the highlight of an inspection meal was an accurately roast duck breast with spinach purée, accompanied by a mound of lyonnaise potatoes gilded with ratatouille, all surrounded by rosemary jus. Presentation may sometimes goes over the top at the expense of flavour, but successes have included a tomato and basil tarte Tatin, sea bass with fennel and leeks, and 'a generous bowl' of passion-fruit and mango crème brûlée with almond shortbreads. Lunch is a more robust kettle of meat and fish, promising braised beef and ale casserole, and cardamom-spiced smoked haddock with champ. The 60-bottle, global wine list offers plenty of choice under £20, and the house selection starts at £12.50.

CHEF: Kevin Anfield  PROPRIETOR: David Birmingham  OPEN: Mon to Sat 12 to 2, 6 to 10 (5.30 for pre-theatre menus by arrangement)  CLOSED: 23 to 30 Dec, bank hols  MEALS: alc (main courses L £7 to £13, D £10 to £16). Set D Mon to Fri £15.95 (2 courses) to £18.95  SERVICE: not inc, 10% for parties of 6 or more  CARDS: Amex, Delta, Diners, MasterCard, Switch, Visa  DETAILS: 70 seats. Private parties: 40 main room, 10 to 28 private rooms. Vegetarian meals. No-smoking area. Wheelchair access (not WC). Music  (£5)

## WINCHESTER  Hampshire                                              map 2

# Chesil Rectory  £✷

1 Chesil Street, Winchester SO23 0HU                          COOKING 6
TEL: (01962) 851555    FAX: (01962) 869704                    MODERN BRITISH
                                                              £43–£96

The Rectory is claimed to be 'one of the least altered fifteenth-century houses in the UK', evident from the large amount of original structure still showing. Its half-timbered splendour and generously spaced tables create 'an appropriately dignified atmosphere' for a former rectory. Philip Storey's menus, meanwhile, continue to evolve, capitalising on seasonality and local supply-lines, and the style of cooking is sufficiently modern-British to include twice-baked Roquefort soufflé ('creamy and full of flavour'), and Gressingham duck breast with pak choi, fondant potato and shallots.

Certain dishes have stood the test of time: a version of tournedos Rossini, or the highly rated pork with black pudding, spinach, mustard and apple. A bed of spinach also formed the underlay for an accurately cooked skate wing at a spring dinner, and the lamb sauced with red wine and redcurrants more than passed muster too. Soft textures and gently rich flavours characterise the dessert repertoire, epitomised by three ways with caramel or a trio of crèmes brûlées. More unusual was a dish of cooked rhubarb, strained to produce a 'clear, delicate and delightful' soup, and garnished with strawberries and vanilla ice cream. Efficient, good-humoured service augments a thoroughly classy operation, although it is a shame the wine list offers so little below £20, for it is an interesting and wide-ranging selection. The house wines – half-a-dozen each of reds and whites – run from £16 for a Bordeaux Sauvignon or a Sangiovese from the Abruzzi, to £24.

CHEF: Philip Storey  PROPRIETORS: Philip Storey and Catherine Storey  OPEN: Tue to Sat 12 to 1.45, 7 to 9.15 (9.45 Sat)  MEALS: Set L £22 (2 courses) to £32, Set D £35 (2 courses) to £65  SERVICE: not inc, 12.5% for parties over 6  CARDS: Amex, Delta, Diners, MasterCard, Switch, Visa  DETAILS: 40 seats. Private parties: 40 main room, 10 to 40 private rooms. Children's helpings. No smoking in 1 dining room. Music

---

*Dining rooms where music, either live or recorded, is never played are signalled by* No music *in the details at the end of an entry.*

*indicates that there has been a change of chef since last year's Guide, and the Editor has judged that the change is of sufficient interest to merit the reader's attention.*

# ▲ Hotel du Vin & Bistro 🍷

Southgate Street, Winchester SO23 9EF
TEL: (01962) 841414   FAX: (01962) 842458
EMAIL: reservations@winchester.hotelduvin.com
WEBSITE: www.hotelduvin.com

COOKING 4
MODERN EUROPEAN
£33–£54

General enthusiasm for this chain, founded in Winchester, remains undimmed (see other entries in Birmingham, Bristol and Tunbridge Wells). It is the entire package that appeals, including a lively atmosphere, enjoyable food and a terrific wine list. Light colours, ragged-effect walls, wood panelling, antique leather chairs and white napery combine to produce an informal yet graceful background to some classic bistro cooking: from jambon persillé to pigeon breast with braised lentils, from frisée salad with lardons and poached egg to tuna niçoise. To emphasise the point even more, a short list of 'simple classics' includes Black Angus ribeye steak with frites, and cassoulet de Toulouse.

The search also takes in desserts of rhubarb and apple crumble, cherry clafoutis, and Bakewell tart with custard. It is the very straightforwardness of the food that wins friends, and of course allows the wines to shine. France figures prominently on the list, in the classic selections and in the lesser-known regions such as Corsica and Jura. New World producers are not given short shrift either, with some well-chosen examples from New Zealand, Australia and South Africa. The sommelier's suggestions by the glass appear on the menu (from around £4.50) and change daily. Reasonable mark-ups mean that there are plenty of interesting bottles to choose from at £20 or below, and house red and white start at £12.95, or £3.65 per glass.

CHEF: Gareth Longhurst   PROPRIETOR: Hotel du Vin Ltd   OPEN: all week 12 to 1.45, 7 to 9.30   MEALS: alc exc Sun L (main courses £12.50 to £15.50). Set L Sun £23.50   SERVICE: not inc   CARDS: Amex, Delta, Diners, MasterCard, Switch, Visa   DETAILS: 65 seats. 25 seats outside. Private parties: 48 main room. Car park. Vegetarian meals. Children's helpings. No cigars/pipes in dining room. Wheelchair access (not WC). No music   ACCOMMODATION: 23 rooms, all with bath/shower. TV. Phone. Room only £99 to £195. Rooms for disabled. Baby facilities (*The Which? Hotel Guide*)

---

# ▲ Wykeham Arms 🍴✶ £

75 Kingsgate Street, Winchester SO23 9PE
TEL: (01962) 853834   FAX: (01962) 854411
EMAIL: doreen@wykehamarms.fsnet.co.uk

COOKING 2
MODERN BRITISH/MEDITERRANEAN
£22–£41

Enter at the corner of the building into a pub-with-restaurant that retains, along with the name, many suggestions of its primary calling. The walls are mounted with horsy tackle and a collection of tankards, seating is on wooden settles with cushions, and there are beer mats paradoxically depicting the wines of Burgundy. Not all the cooking is as traditionally English as you might expect. One couple greatly enjoyed an oriental salad of pigeon and noodles, guinea fowl with red cabbage and sweet potato, and chicken breast on a bed of lemon and parsley couscous with a scattering of diced mango. Fish is given modern Mediterranean treatment – roast cherry tomatoes and pesto for grilled lemon sole, and a spinach and goats' cheese salad with a sun-dried tomato and basil dressing to go with baked salmon – while crowd-pleasing desserts run to chocolate parfait with white chocolate sauce, and bread-and-butter pudding made with apricot brandy. Friendly staff help to make the experience all the more enjoyable. A short, snappy wine list delivers good value, with plenty of choice from across the New and Old Worlds under £20. Prices start at £10.95, and around 20 wines are sold by the glass.

CHEFS: Nicola Saunders, Alex Jones and James Tea PROPRIETOR: George Gale & Co Ltd OPEN: all week L 12 to 2.30, Mon to Sat D 6.30 to 8.45 CLOSED: 25 Dec MEALS: alc (main courses L £6 to £6.50, D £10 to £14.50) SERVICE: not inc, card slips closed CARDS: Amex, Delta, Diners, MasterCard, Switch, Visa DETAILS: 70 seats. 45 seats outside. Car park. Vegetarian meals. No smoking in 1 dining room. No music. No mobile phones ACCOMMODATION: 14 rooms, all with bath/shower. TV. Phone. B&B £50 to £120. No children under 14 (*The Which? Hotel Guide*)

## WINDERMERE Cumbria                                                    map 8

## ▲ Gilpin Lodge ♥ ☕ ✲⚹

Crook Road, Windermere LA23 3NE
TEL: (015394) 88818 FAX: (015394) 88058
EMAIL: hotel@gilpin-lodge.co.uk
WEBSITE: www.gilpin-lodge.co.uk
on B5284, 2m SE of Windermere

COOKING 5
MODERN BRITISH
£30–£65

The lodge is a late-Victorian house, originally a private home, on a hilltop not far from Windermere. Its dense and immaculately tended gardens reinforce the feeling of a pastoral idyll, and woodland and fells crowd about. The property is extensive enough to boast four dining rooms, and conveys a conservative and slightly formal feel. After a few comings and going in the kitchen, Mark Jordan arrived from Pink Geranium (see entry, Melbourn) in the summer of 2002, the challenge of a fixed-price dinner menu of five courses allowing him the chance to shine in a number of departments.

Terrines of one sort or another are a favoured way to start, perhaps a triangular slice of a tomato version topped with a goats' cheese beignet and pesto, or a richer guinea fowl and foie gras mixture with poached quails' eggs and sauce gribiche. The second course is either soup (a generous cup of asparagus velouté with white truffle oil on a summer menu), a sorbet (claret and fig for one visitor), or something like smoked salmon mousse served in an eggcup with brown bread and butter. Main courses aim to show off local meats to their best advantage, such as Cumbrian beef fillet with dauphinois, or venison accompanied by – among other things – a small apple tarte Tatin, roast figs and a jus of Agen prunes.

Designer flair is brought to bear on desserts, such as crème brûlée surmounted by a tower of poached rhubarb and two tall almond tuiles, held together with a thread of rapidly setting chocolate. The wine list is a lively read, bringing together good producers from Old and New Worlds, giving them sensible tasting notes and refraining from applying mark-ups that sting. There is reasonable choice, especially of whites, at or under the £20 mark, particularly from New World countries. Five house wines are between £14.50 and £17.50.

CHEF: Mark Jordan PROPRIETORS: John and Christine Cunliffe OPEN: all week 12 to 2.30, 7 to 9 MEALS: alc L Mon to Sat (main courses £9 to £14.50). Set L Sun £19.50, Set D £38.50 SERVICE: not inc CARDS: Amex, Delta, Diners, MasterCard, Switch, Visa DETAILS: 55 seats. 24 seats outside. Private parties: 20 main room, 10 to 25 private rooms. Car park. Vegetarian meals. No children under 7. No smoking in dining room. Wheelchair access (not WC). Music. No mobile phones  ACCOMMODATION: 14 rooms, all with bath/shower. TV. Phone. B&B £85 to £210. Rooms for disabled. No children under 7 (*The Which? Hotel Guide*)  £5

## ▲ Holbeck Ghyll ✶✗

Holbeck Lane, Windermere LA23 1LU
TEL: (015394) 32375   FAX: (015394) 34743
EMAIL: stay@holbeckghyll.com
WEBSITE: www.holbeckghyll.com                                      COOKING 5
from A591, 3m N of Windermere, turn E (Holbeck              MODERN FRENCH
Lane, signposted Troutbeck); hotel is ½m on left                 £38–£72

Close to Windermere, and yet sufficiently far from the crowds, Holbeck Ghyll is a nineteenth-century stone-built hunting lodge in eight acres of grounds, with fine views over the lake, comfortable lounges, and an impressive panelled dining room. Quality of materials is high (although so are prices), and the cooking is self-consciously designed to impress, starting with classic French openers in which shellfish plays a significant role: cannelloni of crab and smoked salmon, or a salad of warm langoustines with lobster and celeriac rémoulade. Or there might be a rather sophisticated terrine, such as a pressing of oxtail and root vegetables with a beetroot dressing

Main courses home in on prime materials, in the shape of roast turbot (with creamed leeks and red wine sauce), or best end of lamb (with aubergine and tapénade jus), although they also find room for a slightly more rustic-sounding daube of beef. Desserts run to classical examples – cherry clafoutis perhaps – but also take the modern route, presenting several variations on a theme together: a plate of chocolate, or an assiette of apple. A showy wine list at not very friendly prices takes in some very fine wines, while ordinary drinkers need to sift through the haystack to find a few needles under £20. Half a dozen well-chosen house wines start the ball rolling at £18.50 to £22.50 (just under £5 a glass).

CHEF: David McLaughlin  PROPRIETORS: David and Patricia Nicholson  OPEN: all week 12.30 to 2, 7 to 9.30  MEALS: Set L £25, Set D £45. Light meals available all day  SERVICE: not inc, card slips closed  CARDS: Amex, Delta, Diners, MasterCard, Switch, Visa  DETAILS: 50 seats. 20 seats outside. Private parties: 65 main room, 2 to 30 private rooms. Car park. Vegetarian meals. No children under 8. No smoking in dining room. Wheelchair access (also WC). No music. No mobile phones  ACCOMMODATION: 21 rooms, all with bath/shower. TV. Phone. D,B&B £120 to £320. Rooms for disabled. Baby facilities (*The Which? Hotel Guide*)  £5

## Jerichos ✶✗

Birch Street, Windermere LA23 1EG                                COOKING 5
TEL/FAX: (015394) 42522                                           ENGLISH
EMAIL: enquiries@jerichos.co.uk                                   £31–£48

Five years on, this industrious husband and wife team, who set up in modest yet strikingly decorated premises after Chris Blaydes left Miller Howe (see entry below), continues to draw praise. Their brand of hearty brasserie-style food is grounded in local and seasonal produce – Lakeland spring lamb and Lunesdale duck among them – spiked with some bright flavours from further afield: chicken and duck liver parfait with mango chutney, for example, or pan-fried black pudding with thyme risotto. Goats' cheese pannacotta with home-cured gravlax pleased one reporter. Although meat predominates (beef fillet with French fries, pork tenderloin with a Puy lentil casserole), fish has come in for praise too: very fresh, accurately cooked cod and hake for one couple.

Desserts are more limited and may include poached spiced pear with chervil vinaigrette, but appetites by this stage tend to be satisfied anyway. Service may slow a little when the place is full, but nobody seems to mind, and a friendly atmosphere prevails thanks to Jo Blaydes. South Africa features strongly on the wine list, which is structured to give diners guidance about matching wine with food. Mark-ups are low and there's plenty of choice under £20. A house selection of four whites and four reds starts at £12.50 (£3.25 by 175ml glass).

CHEF: Chris Blaydes   PROPRIETORS: Chris and Jo Blaydes   OPEN: Tue to Sun D only 6.45 to 9.30 CLOSED: last 2 weeks Nov, first week Dec, 24 to 26 Dec, 1 Jan   MEALS: alc (main courses £13.50 to £16.50)   SERVICE: not inc   CARDS: Delta, MasterCard, Switch, Visa   DETAILS: 35 seats. Private parties: 24 main room. Vegetarian meals. No children under 12. No smoking in dining room. Music

---

## ▲ Miller Howe  ▼ ⬡ ⚡

Rayrigg Road, Windermere LA23 1EY
TEL: (015394) 42536   FAX: (015394) 45664
EMAIL: lakeview@millerhowe.com
WEBSITE: www.millerhowe.com
on A592, between Windermere and Bowness

COOKING 6
ENGLISH COUNTRY-HOUSE
£29–£64

One of the most favourably sited addresses in the Lake District overlooks Windermere in a setting of great tranquillity and comfort, and the current kitchen team has managed to maintain the formidable level of cooking that has always been associated with Miller Howe. An early-summer meal began with a warm salad of pancetta and chorizo with green beans, truffles and pecorino served with a fried quail's egg. Fish follows: perhaps a small piece of sea bass on tomato and saffron couscous, often with some kind of foaming sauce, in this case flavoured with coriander.

After the inevitable sorbet, some fine local meat is produced: Windermere black sheep and Lord Cavendish's salt-marsh lamb have been the highlights of late, the loin roasted past pink and sliced on to stewed creamed leeks. The famous cornucopia of accompanying vegetables may run the risk of muting the impact of the main dish, although there is always something worth talking about (lime and vanilla mash among recent diversions). That streak of inventiveness continues in desserts, such as red wine and fig soup with goats' cheese ice cream, or hot chocolate fondant with dark chocolate sauce and a spicy ice cream of lemongrass and black pepper. Service is said to be 'regimented'.

Unusually for an English country-house hotel, New World wines – especially those from South Africa – are the main focus of the list. 'European wines', at the back of the list, include some important producers from France and Italy, though the offerings are less impressive. There is a good selection of half-bottles, but full bottle prices don't often dip below £20, although four house wines, from Australia and the Loire, are £17.50.

CHEFS: Paul Webster and Jamie Roberts  PROPRIETOR: Charles Garside  OPEN: all week 12.30 to 1.30, 8 (1 sitting)  MEALS: Set L Mon to Sat £17.50, Set L Sun £19.95, Set D £39.50  SERVICE: not inc, card slips closed  CARDS: Amex, MasterCard, Switch, Visa  DETAILS: 60 seats. 60 seats outside. Private parties: 60 main room, 30 private room. Car park. Vegetarian meals. No children under 8. No smoking in dining room. Wheelchair access (not WC). Music. No mobile phones. Air-conditioned  ACCOMMODATION: 15 rooms, all with bath/shower. TV. Phone. B&B £95 to £350. Rooms for disabled. No children under 8. Fishing (*The Which? Hotel Guide*)  £5

## ▲ Samling ⁵⁄₄✷                                    NEW ENTRY

Ambleside Road, Windermere LA23 1LR
TEL: (015394) 31922   FAX: (015394) 31400                     COOKING 5
EMAIL: info@thesamling.com                               MODERN BRITISH
WEBSITE: www.thesamling.com                                  £39–£89

This relative newcomer to the Windermere scene does the country-house hotel thing with a light touch and a lot of imagination (as indeed does its sibling in Seaham, see entry). Up a steep drive, the white-painted building houses a comfortable sitting room with wood panelling, rattan and teak furniture and a profusion of comfortable sofas and armchairs. In contrast, the dining room is restrained and simple, with a stripped wooden floor, beige walls and seven or eight tables with white damask tablecloths.

A few luxury ingredients surface on the short menu (about five starters and five main courses): perhaps a 'stunningly successful' cauliflower soup with truffle cream, or a warm salad of lobster with roasted vegetables and asparagus purée. Main courses rely on solid flavour combinations, such as Goosnargh duck with swede fondant and confit cabbage, or brill poached in cider with mussels and apples. Attractively presented desserts might include a pear Tatin, or a first-class, light chocolate fondant with lychee sorbet. Service, by trendy-looking young staff, is helpful, friendly and efficient. An eight-course menu gourmand boasts some intriguing combinations, such as red mullet gazpacho with goats' cheese tortellini, and there is also a vegetarian menu. The wine list comes in two halves: a 'house wine' list, with around thirty bottles selling for between £15 and £25, and a shorter 'fine wine' list, with ten bottles, mostly French. Twelve wines are available by the glass.

CHEF: Chris Meredith  PROPRIETOR: Tom Maxfield  OPEN: Sun L 12 to 2, all week D 7 to 9.30  MEALS: Set L £27.50, Set D £40 to £60  SERVICE: not inc  CARDS: Amex, MasterCard, Switch, Visa  DETAILS: 20 seats. 10 seats outside. Private parties: 20 main room, 2 to 20 private rooms. Car park. Vegetarian meals. Children's helpings. No smoking in dining room. Wheelchair access (also WC). Music. No mobile phones  ACCOMMODATION: 10 rooms, all with bath/shower. TV. Phone. D,B&B £135 to £365. Rooms for disabled (*The Which? Hotel Guide*)  £5

---

▲ *means accommodation is available.*

*Prices quoted in the Guide are based on information supplied by restaurateurs. The prices quoted at the top of each entry represent a range, from the lowest meal price to the highest; the latter is inflated by 20 per cent to take account of likely price rises during the year of the Guide.*

---

## WINKLEIGH Devon
map 1

# Pophams ⁵⧸✳

Castle Street, Winkleigh EX19 8HQ
TEL: (01837) 83767

COOKING 5
MODERN BRITISH
£30–£43

This tiny restaurant in the centre of the village has to be the Guide's most minimal entry. It has only three tables and is open only two lunchtimes a week. While this reduces the chance of any feedback, it does mean that Melvyn Popham and Dennis Hawkes can manage their simple, unfussy operation by themselves. The latter is 'something of a character' and even 'has a habit of leaning over your table and trying to get a word in edgeways if he can'. Visitors can watch their food being prepared, drink their own wine (it has no licence and charges no corkage), and start with a warm crab tart, chicken liver terrine, or salmon and cod fishcake with curry cream sauce. Main courses generally bring a simple choice between meat or fish: perhaps boned best end of local lamb in puff pastry with mushroom pâté and Madeira sauce, or a seared tuna steak on a green bean and quails' egg salad. Finish with orange tart or sticky toffee pudding.

CHEF: Melvyn Popham   PROPRIETORS: Melvyn Popham and Dennis Hawkes   OPEN: Thur to Fri L 11.45 to 2.30   CLOSED: Feb   MEALS: alc (main courses £15 to £17)   SERVICE: not inc   CARDS: none   DETAILS: 10 seats. No children under 14. No smoking in dining room. Occasional music. Air-conditioned

## WINTERINGHAM North Lincolnshire
map 9

# ▲ Winteringham Fields ⸽ ⁵⧸✳

Winteringham DN15 9PF
TEL: (01724) 733096   FAX: (01724) 733898
EMAIL: wintfields@aol.com
WEBSITE: www.winteringhamfields.com

COOKING 9
PROVINCIAL FRENCH/SWISS
£43–£109

Fifteen years ago it must have taken an act of faith to open such an ambitious restaurant in a tiny village just south of the Humber. But confidence has been amply rewarded, and readers are only too happy to beat a path to its door. 'Beg, borrow, save, re-mortgage your house to eat here,' pleaded one reporter. Or as another put it: 'Expensive? Certainly. Worth it? Every penny.' It is a welcoming haven – warm, enveloping, civilised and colourful – where meals typically begin either in a homely, Victorian-style drawing room, or in the small Kew Garden-like conservatory. Black and white etchings of Swiss scenes in the peaceful and simply decorated dining room, and a cowbell over the fireplace, are the only overt signs of Germain Schwab's origins.

Value is considered good for what is some of the best cooking in the country, especially given the impeccable standard of 'extras' such as the melting balls of foie gras, the tiny cupfuls of intense soup (perhaps pineapple with a smoky bacon froth), or a cauliflower purée topped with a rich jelly containing caviar. They come seamlessly in waves, all part of the natural flow of the meal, yet by the end nobody feels too full.

The cooking is characterised by sheer skill and attention to detail, but the dedication and discipline are combined with a lively sense of fun. Reporters enjoy themselves immensely, while marvelling at the pyrotechnics: the runny egg yolk encased in thin pasta and scattered with black truffle is still making waves, served as a starter with nutty, fried veal sweetbread. Likewise a dish of halibut wrapped in thin potato scales served on a cushion of interwoven leeks (looking like a green gingham cloth) with a halibut mousse.

The kitchen runs on a 'superlative mixture of experiment and experience', equally at home with Moroccan flavours (chermoula of plaice with couscous), a comparatively straightforward but memorable dish of roast sea bass in a salt crust, or a fine starter of pan-fried langoustines accompanied by three open-ended filo pastry organ pipes filled with 'a wonderful aubergine-tasting mush'. And there is a surprise menu. 'Are you all right with sheep's eyeballs, madam?' (said with a lovely smile).

Textures throughout are a delight – for example in a baked meringue with a cold but melting filling of soft caramel and mascarpone ice cream – and presentational highlights run from a consommé appetiser with the word 'consommé' jokily stencilled in mayonnaise, to the trompe l'oeil palette of sorbets in paint pots with a miniature caramelised sugar paintbrush. Also highly praised are cheeses in perfect condition, their chariot driver (a 'knowledgeable enthusiast'), and the accompaniments.

Beyond all this you get 'outstanding' service, effortlessly sustained from greeting to departure, and variously described as faultless, unobtrusive, warm, calm, discreet and quite simply 'unmatched'. 'The message received was that these are genuinely nice people, proud of and pleased with what they do.' What you also get is the permanent and approachable presence of the owners. Germain and Annie Schwab do not spend time promoting themselves on television or opening up other branches, but devote themselves entirely to the business. And it shows. Other restaurateurs please copy.

On the wide-ranging, imaginative and clearly annotated wine list France is particularly strong, although other European countries (including Switzerland) are not ignored. There is a decent selection of half-bottles at the back and a brief list of bin-ends on the first page. Mark-ups are steep (it's a struggle to find much under £25), though no worse than at other top establishments: and at least the sommelier knows his wares and recommends wisely. The house selection starts at £17.50 for a rather unexciting Italian Pinot Grigio.

CHEF: Germain Schwab  PROPRIETORS: Germain and Annie Schwab  OPEN: Tue to Sat 12 to 1.30, 7 to 9.30  CLOSED: last week Oct, 2 weeks Christmas, last week Mar, first week Aug  MEALS: alc (main courses £27 to £30). Set L £26 to £28, Set D £36 to £66  SERVICE: net prices, card slips closed  CARDS: Amex, Delta, MasterCard, Switch, Visa  DETAILS: 42 seats. Private parties: 8 main room, 6 to 10 private rooms. Car park. Vegetarian meals. No smoking in dining room. Wheelchair access (not WC). No music. No mobile phones  ACCOMMODATION: 10 rooms, all with bath/shower. TV. Phone. B&B £75 to £185. No children under 8 (exc babes in arms) (*The Which? Hotel Guide*)

---

*The Guide always appreciates hearing about changes of chef or owner.*

*The Guide is totally independent, accepts no free hospitality, and survives on the number of copies sold each year.*

## WITCHFORD Cambridgeshire map 6

# ▲ Needhams

| | |
|---|---|
| 186 Main Street, Witchford CB6 2HT | COOKING 2 |
| TEL/FAX: (01353) 661405 | GLOBAL |
| | £25–£49 |

This is a converted brick farmhouse with pink walls, flower-patterned carpets and red tablecloths, where locals tend to dress up for a night out. Luke Pearson takes a thoroughly modern swipe at the cooking, incorporating such novelties as vanilla tobacco syrup to accompany hickory-smoked pigeon breast with herb drop scones. The carte is a generous one, with no concessions to tempt in lunchers, and leaves few culinary stones unturned. How about smoked haddock, Cheddar and spring onion spring rolls with a lemon, chervil and cream cheese dressing? Or roast sea bass fillet served with fried chervil gnocchi and queen scallops in a red wine sauce vierge? Even desserts join in the game, in the shape of warm treacle tart with saffron ice cream and passion-fruit syrup. Wines, in no particular order on the list, stay accommodatingly under £20 for the most part, starting with house South African at £9.95.

CHEF: Luke Pearson   PROPRIETORS: Luke Pearson and Verity Lowe   OPEN: Tue to Sun L 12 to 2 (2.30 Sun), 7 (6.30 Fri and Sat) to 9 (9.30 Fri and Sat)   CLOSED: first 2 weeks Jan   MEALS: alc exc Sun L (main courses £10.50 to £16.50). Set L Sun £16.25   SERVICE: not inc   CARDS: Amex, Delta, MasterCard, Switch, Visa   DETAILS: 50 seats. Private parties: 90 main room, 14 to 25 private rooms. Car park. Vegetarian meals. Children's helpings. No smoking in dining room. Wheelchair access (also WC). Music   ACCOMMODATION: 2 rooms. B&B £35 to £50

## WITHERSLACK Cumbria map 8

# ▲ Old Vicarage ♥ 🍷 ✳

| | |
|---|---|
| Church Road, Witherslack LA11 6RS | |
| TEL: (015395) 52381   FAX: (015395) 52373 | |
| EMAIL: hotel@oldvicarage.com | COOKING 2 |
| WEBSITE: www.oldvicarage.com | MODERN BRITISH/FRENCH |
| off A590, take first left in village to church | £26–£51 |

A steep hill and a narrow lane lead to this Victorian rectory next to the church, about a mile out of the hamlet. The lounge is cheery enough, and although the dark dining room is not a flattering shade of brown, its tables are well spaced and attractively laid. James Brown has left to run his own catering staff agency, but Joe Hargreaves benefits from already established supply lines, including locally produced smoked salmon and quails' eggs, pork and bacon from Woodalls of Waberthwaite, and Rough Fell lamb from a local farmers' co-operative.

Results at inspection were mixed, but highlights included a tasty rabbit and pigeon terrine spiked with pistachio nuts (served with a first-class sweet-sharp plum chutney), and fillet of bream on a powerfully flavoured spinach and basil risotto. Desserts tend to be soothing, along the lines of lemon cheesecake topped with a thin layer of hard, dark chocolate, or steamed orange and honey sponge pudding with vanilla custard. An 'early-bird' menu offers a good-value alternative to the carte. The wine list is arranged by style, placing established favourites next to rising stars and not shying away from a Greek white or a Canadian Pinot Noir. There is plenty of choice under £20, with prices starting at £10 for French country red and white. Four wines are sold by the small or large glass (£2.20 to £3.60, or £3 to £4).

CHEFS: Joe Hargreaves and Neil Smith   PROPRIETORS: Jill and Roger Brown, and Stan and Irene Reeve   OPEN: Sun L 12.30 to 1.30, all week D 6.15 to 9   MEALS: alc D (main courses £14 to £18). Set L Sun and D 6.15 to 7 £12.50 (2 courses) to £15.50   SERVICE: not inc, card slips closed   CARDS: Amex, Delta, MasterCard, Switch, Visa   DETAILS: 40 seats. Private parties: 20 main room, 8 to 12 private rooms. Car park. Vegetarian meals. Children's helpings. No smoking in dining room. Music. No mobile phones   ACCOMMODATION: 14 rooms, all with bath/shower. TV. Phone. B&B £65 to £170. Baby facilities (*The Which? Hotel Guide*) (£5)

## WITNEY Oxfordshire                                                      map 2

## ▲ Fleece Hotel and Brasserie ⅗ £   [NEW ENTRY]

11 Church Green, Witney OX28 4AZ
TEL/FAX: (01993) 892270                                          COOKING 2
EMAIL: reservations@thefleecehotelandbrasserie.co.uk    MODERN EUROPEAN
WEBSITE: www.thefleecehotelandbrasserie.co.uk                    £25–£48

On a tree-lined green with a church at the end, the Fleece's brown plaster exterior stands out from the grey Oxfordshire stone around it. Scott and Emily Hunter moved from The Harrow at West Ilsley (listed in last year's Guide) to this open-plan ground-floor brasserie, minimally decorated in muted tones, although rather spoilt by intrusive music. A prix-fixe menu offers two choices per course, and the longer carte includes a section of 'Simple Classics' from Caesar salad to sirloin steak with mushrooms, tomato and chips. Roast breast of duck (with thoroughly browned skin) comes with a tower of bubble and squeak and glazed baby onions, while vegetable accompaniments are well chosen: perhaps artichokes and new potatoes with sea bass, or broad beans and fennel with grilled sole. Trios appear – salmon to start, or lemon to finish – and caramelised lemon tart with a fine crackly top has come with a professionally made raspberry sorbet. France and the southern hemisphere account for most of the wine list; four French house wines are £11.95.

CHEFS: Scott Hunter and Simon Read   PROPRIETORS: Scott and Emily Hunter   OPEN: all week 12 to 2.15 (3 Sun), 6.30 to 10 (11 Fri and Sat)   MEALS: alc (main courses £8.50 to £15). Set L £12.50 (2 courses) to £15, Set D £12.50 (2 courses) to £15. Light L menu also available   SERVICE: not inc, card slips closed   CARDS: MasterCard, Switch, Visa   DETAILS: 90 seats. 40 seats outside. Private parties: 70 main room, 10 to 20 private rooms. Car park. Vegetarian meals. Children's helpings. No smoking in 1 dining room. Wheelchair access (also WC). Music   ACCOMMODATION: 11 rooms, all with bath/shower. TV. Phone. B&B £65 to £95. Rooms for disabled

*Several sharp operators have tried to extort money from restaurateurs on the promise of an entry in a guidebook that has never appeared.* The Good Food Guide *makes no charge for inclusion.*

## WOKINGHAM  Berkshire                                      map 3

# Rose Street ✸

6 Rose Street, Wokingham RG40 1XU                              COOKING **5**
TEL: (0118) 978 8025   FAX: (0118) 989 1314          MODERN ANGLO-FRENCH
                                                              £30–£67

This is a pretty, cottagey, sixteenth-century building with exposed beams and
four dining rooms, one of them a conservatory, where starched white cloths set
the tone for carefully presented food using sound ingredients. Generous choice
on the carte extends from confit quail on mushroom risotto, to Cornish turbot
with a tomato and basil tart, by way of a few extra daily dishes, such as a smooth
chicken liver parfait spiked with brandy, served on brioche with a piece of
lightly cooked chicken liver and a rocket salad.

Although broadly Anglo-French, the cooking also takes in a crisp, appetising
Thai fishcake served with a lightly seared scallop, a sushi roll and a small puddle
of sweet chilli relish. Dishes can be quite busy, but never overstep the mark in
terms of complexity. Gressingham duck, for example, is served three ways: a
tender, tasty, crisp-skinned breast, a confit leg, and a slice of liver on Savoy
cabbage, accompanied by a strongly flavoured sauce of blackcurrant, honey and
port, and a perfectly made fondant potato. Other interesting partnerships
include a first-class, flavourful beef fillet topped with a layer of melting cheese
and served with a puff pastry tart of white onion purée and spinach.

Recommended among desserts is a lightly crisp chocolate fondant with a
dark, rich filling that comes with sour cream ice cream, soft marinated cherries
and chocolate sauce. Service seems to have varied during the year, but at
inspection was welcoming, polished and professional. France's classic regions
dominate the wine list, with a few from elsewhere bringing down the average
price.

CHEF: Paul Scott   PROPRIETORS: Paul Scott and John Read   OPEN: Mon to Sat 12 to 2, 7 to 9.30
CLOSED: 25 and 26 Dec, 1 Jan, bank hol L   MEALS: alc (main courses £13.50 to £22.50). Set L
£12.95 (2 courses) to £16.95   SERVICE: 12.5% (optional), card slips closed   CARDS: Delta,
MasterCard, Switch, Visa   DETAILS: 44 seats. Private parties: 20 main room, 8 to 20 private
rooms. Vegetarian meals. Children's helpings. No smoking in 1 dining room. Wheelchair access
(also women's WC). Music  £5

## WOODBRIDGE  Suffolk                                        map 6

# Captain's Table ✸ £

3 Quay Street, Woodbridge IP12 1BX                            COOKING **4**
TEL: (01394) 383145   FAX: (01394) 388508            MODERN EUROPEAN
WEBSITE: www.captainstable.co.uk                              £20–£36

Woodbridge railway station, 100 yards away, makes a handy navigational
reference point and (in dry weather) a useful overspill car park. The restaurant is
sparsely but pleasingly decorated, in fact looking 'more like a pub than a
restaurant', with a walled garden for fine-weather eating. The menu also picks
up some pub-style dishes, including a home-made pork pie with cucumber and
onion pickle, and mushroom and aubergine moussaka. It is unpretentious stuff
with an understandably strong line in seafood, from a first-class mussel

chowder, via tasty 'rillettes' of trout and salmon, to a fine tuna niçoise where the fish was 'just shown the frying pan'. And there are local crabs and lobsters in summer too.

Straightforward treatments are applied to meat, from chargrilled ribeye steak with chips and grain mustard sauce, to slow-roast duck leg with apple and pear chutney. To finish, iced chocolate soufflé gets the thumbs up, or there may be hot toffee pudding, bread-and-butter pudding, or a warm Victoria plum and almond tart. Wines are varied and sensibly priced (£11.95 brings an organic Muscadet-sur-Lie 2000), starting with house vin de pays at £8.95.

CHEFS: Pascal Pommier and Olivier Galeran  PROPRIETORS: Jo and Pascal Pommier  OPEN: Tue to Sun and bank hol Mon L 12 to 2 (3 Sun high season and bank hols), Tue to Sat and bank hol Sun and Mon D 6.30 to 9.30 (10 Fri and Sat)  CLOSED: first 2 weeks Jan  MEALS: alc (main courses £6 to £11.50)  SERVICE: not inc, card slips closed  CARDS: Delta, MasterCard, Switch, Visa  DETAILS: 50 seats. 30 seats outside. Private parties: 34 main room, 19 to 34 private rooms. Car park. Vegetarian meals. Children's helpings. No smoking in dining room. No music

---

**WORCESTER** Worcestershire                                                    map 5

# Brown's ✁✗

24 Quay Street, Worcester WR1 2JJ                                        COOKING 3
TEL: (01905) 26263  FAX: (01905) 25768                               ANGLO-FRENCH
                                                                          £27–£52

Long-serving Brown's occupies a converted grain mill beside the Severn, its interior stylish, minimalist and sophisticated, with a high roof, clever spotlights, iron girders and a curved mezzanine gallery. 'This wonderful building grows on me with every visit,' noted one well-travelled reporter. The handwritten menu is fixed-price, descriptions are minimal, and soup and fish specials change daily ('delightful' kebabs of langoustines with bacon, for example). Everyone approves of the bread, and one visitor thought the 'elegant and luscious' unsalted butter some of the best she had come across. Vegetables are plentiful, and the kitchen manages to lift ordinary items such as swede and cabbage to new heights. Raw materials are notably good and handled capably. Sauté squid is precisely balanced with mild ginger and spring onion, calf's liver cooked pink and served with 'first-rate' mash, and roast rack of lamb ('an animal that had seen a lot of exercise') has been accurately timed. Desserts might range from hot chocolate pudding to home-made praline ice cream with caramelised almonds and hazelnuts. A smart, professional young team copes admirably out front. France predominates on the classically inclined wine list, but the New World does get a look in. House wine is £11.95.

CHEFS: W.R. Tansley and G. Phipps  PROPRIETORS: W.R. and P.M. Tansley  OPEN: Wed to Fri and Sun L 12.30 to 1.45, Tue to Sat D 7.30 to 9.45  CLOSED: 24 and 31 Dec, bank hol Mons  MEALS: Set L £21.50, Set L Sun £28. Set D £37.50  SERVICE: net prices, card slips closed  CARDS: Amex, Delta, MasterCard, Switch, Visa  DETAILS: 100 seats. Vegetarian meals. No children under 9. No smoking in dining room. Wheelchair access (also WC). Occasional music

---

*If 'The Which? Hotel Guide' is noted at the end of an entry, this means that the establishment is also in the 2003 edition of our sister guide, published in September 2002.*

## WORFIELD Shropshire                                         map 5

# ▲ Old Vicarage ⚑ ⅖✳

Worfield WV15 5JZ
TEL: (01746) 716497   FAX: (01746) 716552
EMAIL: admin@the-old-vicarage.demon.co.uk          COOKING 2
WEBSITE: www.oldvicarageworfield.com               MODERN BRITISH
off A454 3m E of Bridgnorth                         £32–£64

'How many children did those Edwardian vicars produce?' wondered one
visitor, struck by the size of this three-storey brick-built house. Only the
conservatory is recent, its wrought-iron frame more in keeping with the original
than the whimsical wooden birds hanging from the ceiling, which flap their
wings when a string is pulled. The rest of the rather dark house is more or less in
period: parquet floors, heavy curtains, antique tables, and walls covered in small
paintings and prints. Blaine Reed's cooking remains much as before, but the
menus have been clarified and updated: a carte is available every evening, and a
set-price menu at lunchtimes and most weekday evenings.

Carefully sourced materials range from Longhorn beef (the fillet chargrilled
and served with wild mushrooms) to loin of Bobbington boar with creamed
Savoy cabbage; seafood includes Shetland salmon, and Devon sea bass with a
pickled lemon vinaigrette. Desserts avoid the heavy English route in favour of
passion-fruit délice with oven-dried cherries, and lemon crème brûlée with
strawberry yoghurt ice cream. The wine list is refreshingly imaginative – bottles
seem to have been chosen for their quality, rather than for their marketing profile
– and mark-ups are not at all prohibitive. The ten appealing house selections,
which change 'throughout the year', range from £16 to £24 (£4.40 to £6.10 a
glass).

CHEF: Blaine Reed   PROPRIETORS: David and Sarah Blakstad   OPEN: Sun to Fri L 12 to 1.45, all
week D 7 to 8.45 (7.30 Sun)   MEALS: alc (main courses £15 to £19.50). Set L £18.50, Set D Mon to
Thu £17.50 (2 courses) to £21.50   SERVICE: not inc   CARDS: Amex, Delta, Diners, MasterCard,
Switch, Visa   DETAILS: 47 seats. Private parties: 31 main room, 10 to 14 private rooms. Car park.
Vegetarian meals. Children's helpings. No smoking in dining room. Wheelchair access (also
WC). Occasional music. No mobile phones   ACCOMMODATION: 14 rooms, all with bath/shower.
TV. Phone. B&B £75 to £175. Rooms for disabled. Baby facilities (*The Which? Hotel
Guide*) (£5)

## WORLESTON Cheshire                                         map 5

# ▲ Rookery Hall ◎ ⅖✳

Worleston CW5 6DQ
TEL: (01270) 610016   FAX: (01270) 626027
EMAIL: rookery@arcadianhotels.co.uk                COOKING 3
WEBSITE: www.rookeryhallhotel.com                  MODERN EUROPEAN
on B5074, 2½m N of Nantwich                         £31–£74

Built in 1816, the hall has extensive grounds and a serene atmosphere. In the
panelled dining room tall windows look over tree-fringed lawns, a previous
owner's arms adorn the plaster ceiling, and tables are inlaid with marquetry: a
fine setting for some ambitious cooking from a new chef.

Sourcing is a strength – judging by three big fat scallops, immaculately seared with a charcoal crust – and technical skills are considerable; everything down to the last detail is carefully, earnestly made. Some more experimental flavour combinations don't quite come off, and traditional ideas seem to work best: among these a safely classical cylinder of lamb fillet topped with basil mousse, wrapped in Parma ham, roasted pink and thickly sliced, then served with unctuous, tasty ratatouille, silky buttery spinach and fondant potato, all surrounded by a decent stock sauce.

Desserts might include an aniseed parfait, or a simple, well-risen soufflé tasting clearly of vanilla, packed with boozy cherries and served with a Kirsch ice cream. Staff are disarmingly helpful and eager to please: napkins are spread and domes still lifted (even the one covering the butter accompanying the first-class bread). The French-dominated list has comparatively few wines under £20, but those by the glass (on a separate list, from £3.25) are unusually good.

CHEF: Craig Malone   PROPRIETOR: Hand Picked Hotels   OPEN: Sun to Fri L 12 to 2.30, al week D 7 to 9.45   MEALS: alc D (main courses £15 to £24.50). Set L £14.95 (2 courses) to £16.95, Set D £32. Bar menu available   SERVICE: not inc   CARDS: Amex, Delta, Diners, MasterCard, Switch, Visa   DETAILS: 38 seats. Private parties: 40 main room, 2 to 60 private rooms. Car park. Vegetarian meals. Children's helpings. No smoking in dining room. Wheelchair access (also WC). No music. No mobile phones   ACCOMMODATION: 45 rooms, all with bath/shower. TV. Phone. B&B £95 to £170. Rooms for disabled. Baby facilities. Fishing (*The Which? Hotel Guide*)

## WRIGHTINGTON Lancashire                                    map 8

# Mulberry Tree ₤✻ £

9 Wrightington Bar, Wrightington WN6 9SE
TEL/FAX: (01257) 451400                                       COOKING **5**
take Parbold exit from M6 junction 27 then first             MODERN BRITISH
right down Mossy Lea road                                     £25–£50

Formal and casual modes are combined successfully at this former pub, where an open-plan layout gives a refreshingly contemporary feel. The atmosphere is relaxed enough to cater for those who just want to pull up at the bar for a drink, but there is also a comfortable brasserie and a more formal restaurant where some seriously good cooking is going on.

Mark Prescott's style reflects his training under the Roux brothers, and finds its roots in classical French techniques. A preference for rich, earthy flavours is apparent in a terrine of wild duck and wood pigeon with apple and red onion chutney, and in main courses of braised lamb shank with Puy lentils and thyme, or roast belly pork on 'cassoulet-style' white beans. But the scope of the menu – boosted by a daily specials list – is wide enough to take in lighter options, such as seared salmon fillet with teriyaki, spring onion and chilli glaze. Inventive dessert creations may include nougat glacé with Maltesers and caramel sauce, or oranges and raspberries set in whisky jelly with Drambuie crème anglaise. 'Friendly, efficient and knowledgeable' staff are overseen by a 'superb' maître d'. The wine list suits the setting: not too long, plenty below £20, and a few classier bottles for good measure. House wines are £10.50.

CHEFS: Mark Prescott and Michael Sindall   PROPRIETORS: James Moore and Mark Prescott   OPEN: Tue to Sun 12 to 2 (2.30 Sun), 6 to 9 (10 Fri and Sat)   CLOSED: 26 Dec to 1 Jan   MEALS: alc (main courses £9 to £18). Set L Sun £15.95. Bar menu available   SERVICE: not inc   CARDS: Delta,

MasterCard, Switch, Visa   DETAILS: 60 seats. 16 seats outside. Private parties: 50 main room. Car park. Vegetarian meals. Children's helpings. No smoking in dining room. Wheelchair access (not WC). Music

## WYE Kent                                                                map 3

## ▲ Wife of Bath

4 Upper Bridge Street, Wye TN25 5AF
TEL: (01233) 812540   FAX: (01233) 813630                    COOKING 3
EMAIL: reservations@wifeofbath.com                        MODERN EUROPEAN
WEBSITE: www.wifeofbath.com                                  £33–£53

As the Guide went to press, news reached us that John Morgan had sold his homely village restaurant and retired. The new owners have decided, on the time-honoured principle of not fixing what ain't broke, to retain the capable services of Robert Hymers. He does the simple things admirably well, making brandied chicken liver parfait profoundly rich and yet light, and, for a main course, pairing a piece of lightly smoked salmon with a crisp-skinned fillet of sea bass served with a chervil and lemon-grass sauce. Fish is well handled generally – monkfish and prawns come as a brochette with a moistening salsa of tomatoes and coriander – but it was the timing of a rack of lamb that so impressed at inspection: the noisettes were as pink and as tender as is consistent with emphasising their flavour, and the caper and parsley butter with which they were topped completed an all-round triumph. Brown bread ice cream is a house speciality, or there might be perfectly crusted crème brûlée incorporating pieces of banana. 'Well-trained, attentive and careful' staff serve it all up. The solid, fairly priced wine list opens with French house wines at £13.75 or Australian alternatives at £14.50.

CHEF: Robert Hymers   PROPRIETORS: Mr and Mrs Andrew Fraser   OPEN: Tue to Sat 12 to 2, 7 to 10   MEALS: alc L (main courses £13 to £16.50). Set L £11.50 (2 courses), Set D £25.75   SERVICE: not inc   CARDS: Amex, Delta, Diners, MasterCard, Switch, Visa   DETAILS: 52 seats. Private parties: 52 main room. Car park. Vegetarian meals. Wheelchair access (not WC). No music ACCOMMODATION: 5 rooms, all with bath/shower. TV. Phone. B&B £45 to £95. Rooms for disabled

## WYMONDHAM Leicestershire                                          map 5

## Berkeley Arms 💥 £

59 Main Street, Wymondham LE14 2AG                          COOKING 2
TEL/FAX: (01572) 787587                                  MODERN EUROPEAN
EMAIL: nick-cathy@mcgeown.fslife.co.uk                        £22–£42

Standing at the crossroads, this extended cottage of local Ancaster stone is Wymondham's only watering hole, which is effectively a pub with culinary aspirations. There are still real ales at the bar, but the main interest is in the cooking, which shows plenty of worldwide influences; portions are hearty, prices are very fair. Lunch promises various 'lite bites' built around ciabattas, crostini and open sandwiches, as well as pubby main courses such as lasagne, corned beef hash and chargrilled lamb burgers. The full dinner menu (which changes monthly) ushers in some more ambitious ideas: maybe seared salmon tartlet with basil, tomato and caramelised onion to start, then seared calf's liver served on truffled spinach with horseradish mash and truffle oil. Bringing up the rear are desserts like toasted waffle with vanilla ice cream and berry compote. House wine is £8.50.

CHEF: Nick McGeown PROPRIETORS: Nick and Cathy McGeown OPEN: Thur to Sun L 12 to 2, Tue to Sat D 7 to 9 MEALS: alc exc Sun L (main courses L £6 to £9.50, D £9.50 to £13.50). Set L Sun £6.95 (1 course) to £11.95, Set D Tue to Thur £8.95 (2 courses) SERVICE: not inc CARDS: Delta, MasterCard, Switch, Visa DETAILS: 30 seats. Private parties: 35 main room. Car park. Vegetarian meals. Children's helpings. No smoking in dining room. Wheelchair access (also WC). Music. No mobile phones

**YARM Stockton-on-Tees** **map 10**

## Chadwick's £

104B High Street, Yarm TS15 9AU — COOKING **4**
TEL: (01642) 788558 FAX: (01642) 788344 — GLOBAL
WEBSITE: www.chadwicksrestaurant.com — £23–£50

This self-styled 'Continental café' is a bustling, high-street venue, smartly turned out with plenty of indoor foliage, faux-marble pillars and bright contemporary paintings. It offers an equally topical style of cooking that refuses to settle anywhere in particular. David Brownless characterises the menus as modern British with Italian, Spanish and Greek influences, which makes one wonder how he explains the presence of satay-spiced mussels with coconut milk and peanuts, or chicken masala with pilau rice and raita. Lunch dishes sound most fun, offering black pudding rolls with pineapple chilli dunk, or corned beef hash with a fried egg and béarnaise, while evenings bring on grilled sirloin with tomato butter and mixed leaves, or salmon 'tournedos' with spiced lentils, foie gras and apple chutney. Traditional puddings bring you gently back to earth. Service is pleasingly free of airs and graces. Reds are more interesting than whites on the short wine list (there's a Peloponnese red as well as a St-Emilion grand cru). House wines from Duboeuf are £10.95.

CHEFS: David Brownless and Stephen Conyard PROPRIETOR: David Brownless OPEN: Tue to Sun L 12 (11 Sun) to 2.30, Tue to Sat D 5.30 to 9.30 CLOSED: 3rd week Oct, 25 and 26 Dec, 1 Jan MEALS: alc (main courses L £6 to £9.50, D £1.50 to £16.95). Tapas menu also available Mon to Fri 5.30 to 6.30 SERVICE: not inc CARDS: Delta, MasterCard, Switch, Visa DETAILS: 70 seats. Private parties: 70 main room. Children's helpings. No smoking in dining room. Music

**YARMOUTH Isle of Wight** **map 2**

## ▲ George, Brasserie

Quay Street, Yarmouth PO41 0PE
TEL: (01983) 760331 FAX: (01983) 760425 — COOKING **3**
EMAIL: res@thegeorge.co.uk — MODERN BRITISH
WEBSITE: www.thegeorge.co.uk — £30–£56

An imposing building on the Solent near the ferry terminal for Lymington, with commanding sea views, the George offers two dining rooms. The restaurant is small, formal, enclosed and expensive, while the brasserie is light and open with buttermilk-yellow walls, light wood tables and chairs, and the chance of al fresco eating on fine days. Its cheerful menu includes a couple of seafood dishes –

such as crab risotto, or deep-fried cod cakes with a tomato and mussel sauce – but mostly goes in for straightforward comfort in the shape of wild mushroom tart with a poached egg and hollandaise, or braised belly pork with flageolet beans. Chicken liver and foie gras terrine adds a note of luxury, but dishes don't aim too high. Grilled Aberdeen Angus ribeye with bacon, mushrooms and potatoes is about as posh as it gets. Finish with mascarpone cheesecake and peach sorbet, or a mille-feuille of chocolate with orange sorbet. The wine list is sensibly arranged by price, with a short but sweet selection of well-chosen bottles from the New and Old Worlds. In addition, there is a separate section for champagne and a number of older red Bordeaux dating back to 1937. Here, as on the main list, prices are sensible. Fifteen house wines, all £13.50, offer very good value.

CHEF: Kevin Mangeolles  PROPRIETORS: Jeremy and Amy Willcock, and John Illsley  OPEN: brasserie all week 12 to 3, 7 to 10; restaurant Tue to Sat D only 7 to 10  MEALS: brasserie alc (main courses £12 to £16). Set L £13.95 (2 courses) to £17.95; restaurant Set D from £50  SERVICE: none, card slips closed  CARDS: Amex, Diners (brasserie only), MasterCard, Switch, Visa  DETAILS: brasserie 80 seats. 150 seats outside. Private parties: 20 main room, 30 private room. Children's helpings. No music; restaurant 40 seats. Private parties 20 main room. 20 private room. No children under 10. No music. Air-conditioned  ACCOMMODATION: 17 rooms, all with bath/shower. TV. Phone. B&B £120 to £215

## YATTENDON Berkshire                                                      map 2

## ▲ Royal Oak ✦

The Square, Yattendon RG18 0UG
TEL: (01635) 201325   FAX: (01635) 201926                   COOKING 2
EMAIL: theroyaloakhotel@hotmail.com                      MODERN BRITISH
off B4009, 5m W of Pangbourne                                £27–£65

A traditional brick building on the main road through this tiny village, and reputedly visited by Cromwell, internally the Oak combines buttermilk walls with rich red and blue rugs, and green and cream swagged curtains. It consists of a bar dispensing real ales, a brasserie, and a dining room set with white napery that serves a seasonally changing carte. Few culinary stones are left unturned as the kitchen reaches for Parmesan shavings, chilli jam and countless other accompaniments.

Diverse offerings might include crispy duck spring roll on fried pak choi with a sweet-and-sour dressing; sea bass in a lemon-grass velouté; and kidneys and bacon with herbed rösti, black pudding and grain mustard sauce. Orientalism is less pronounced among desserts, exemplified by hot chocolate fondant with clotted cream; and banana and pineapple fritters with butterscotch sauce and pecan-coated vanilla ice cream. A roving wine list caters for most pockets, starting with house vin de pays at £12.

CHEF: Jason Gladwin  PROPRIETOR: Corus/Regal Hotel Group  OPEN: restaurant Sun L 12 to 2.30, Mon to Sat D 7 to 9.30; brasserie all week L and D  MEALS: alc (main courses £11 to £24.50). Set L Sun £17 to £23. Brasserie menu also available  SERVICE: 10% (optional), card slips closed  CARDS: Amex, Delta, Diners, MasterCard, Switch, Visa  DETAILS: 60 seats. 45 seats outside. Private parties: 30 main room, 10 private room. Car park. Vegetarian meals. No smoking in dining room. No music  ACCOMMODATION: 5 rooms, all with bath/shower. TV. Phone. Room only £105 to £140. Baby facilities (The Which? Hotel Guide)

## ▲ Blue Bicycle ❦ ✸                              NEW ENTRY

34 Fossgate, York YO1 9TA
TEL: (01904) 673990   FAX: (01904) 677688                    COOKING 5
EMAIL: blue.bicycle@btopenworld.com                     MODERN BRITISH
WEBSITE: www.bluebicyclerestaurant.com                        £34–£59

At one end of the Foss Bridge, the Blue Bicycle used to be what the Victorian era
would have termed a house of ill repute. A distant hint of its salacious origins is
preserved in the silent-movie image of a topless starlet on the menu cover. Now
it is a comfortably furnished and elegant restaurant with two guest rooms, and
dining at both ground-floor and basement levels. Downstairs, you eat in little
candlelit alcoves where curtained-off beds were once positioned.

Kenny Noble has some fine ideas, not the least of which appears at the outset
in the form of bread freshly baked in a 'plant-pot', together with a whole bulb of
roasted garlic. Appetite duly whetted, you might then proceed to a tortilla
basket filled with seared scallops on pea purée with smoked bacon, the shellfish
superbly timed, firm and fresh. Similarly sensitive timing distinguished a
reporter's main course of sea bass with cucumber spaghetti and a red pepper
sauce, garnished with little crayfish, while a piece of Aberdeen Angus fillet is
accompanied, traditionally but effectively, by thin chips, chopped tomato and a
creamy mustard sauce. Menus read well, maintaining interest with such
preparations as chorizo cream and beer-braised shallots with duck, and mussels
provençale and straw potatoes with seared swordfish.

'Simple but brilliant' dessert ideas include a steamed greaseproof-paper
parcel of red berries and banana flavoured with Pernod and vanilla, or blueberry
and lemon cream with a ginger-snap. The food is all delivered by 'some of the
best staff I have seen anywhere for attitude, friendliness and alertness', which
may have been how some of those Victorian patrons felt on leaving too. A lively
wine list, arranged by price, takes in some top New World producers and places
them alongside their European counterparts. Ten recommended house wines,
available by the bottle (£13 to £19.50) and glass (£3.50 to £5.20), point out the
best-value, although there are a few well-known 'names' should diners want to
push out the boat.

CHEF: Kenny Noble   PROPRIETORS: David Rose and Sarah Brownbridge   OPEN: all week 12 to
2.45, 6 to 10   CLOSED: 1 Jan   MEALS: alc (main courses £11.50 to £20)   SERVICE: 10% (optional),
card slips closed   CARDS: Amex, Delta, Diners, MasterCard, Switch, Visa   DETAILS: 86 seats.
Private parties: 20 to 30 private rooms. Vegetarian meals. No smoking in dining room.
Wheelchair access (not WC). Music   ACCOMMODATION: 2 rooms, both with bath/shower. TV.
B&B £180 (double room). Rooms for disabled

---

*Which? Online subscribers will find* The Good Food Guide *online, along with other*
*Which? guides and magazines, at* www.which.net. *Phone (08459) 830254 for*
*information on how to become a subscriber.*

---

# Melton's ▼ ✳

7 Scarcroft Road, York YO23 1ND                    COOKING **5**
TEL: (01904) 634341   FAX: (01904) 635115          MODERN BRITISH
WEBSITE: www.meltonsrestaurant.co.uk               £26–£51

Dark wood, bright murals and close-together tables contribute to the welcoming and friendly feel of what one regular describes as a 'comfortingly familiar' restaurant. After a dozen years in Scarcroft Road the Hjorts are expanding. Opening a cafe-bar and bistro (see entry below) is by no means a bad idea if you are as good at the business as they are. Feedback suggests that the original may have suffered slightly in the process, but the long-term nuts and bolts remain: fine raw materials and a sound technical grasp of essentials keep this place in pole position.

Dishes are well composed and accurately cooked, at best amounting to more than the sum of their parts. One such is a hot chicken liver parfait sandwiched between thin, crisp layers of herbed pastry, garnished with grapes, bacon and walnuts in a Madeira reduction: the result, 'autumn on a plate'. Another example of textural pleasure comes from a piece of belly pork, its crisp crackling contrasting with melting fatty meat. Alternatives might include a sunny red mullet fillet with tapénade, or earthy braised oxtail with glazed root vegetables. White chocolate parfait with lime syrup is a good way to finish. Coffee, bottled water and service are, as always, complimentary, adding to the sense of value for money.

The lengthy wine list roams the wine-making globe, rooting out an interesting collection of bottles from France to Morocco via Italy, Spain and the New World. 'Wine suggestions' at the front advise on what bottles might match various dishes. Seven house wines sell for £12.50 a bottle (£3 per glass). A number, including the house offerings, are also available by the 50cl carafe.

CHEFS: Adam Holiday and Michael Hjort   PROPRIETORS: Michael and Lucy Hjort   OPEN: Tue to Sat L 12 to 2, Mon to Sat D 5.30 to 10   CLOSED: 25 Dec to 14 Jan, 1 week Aug   MEALS: alc (main courses £12 to £18). Set L and D 5.30 to 6.15 £17   SERVICE: not inc, card slips closed   CARDS: Delta, MasterCard, Switch, Visa   DETAILS: 42 seats. Private parties: 36 main room, 12 to 18 private rooms. Vegetarian meals. Children's helpings. No smoking in 1 dining room. Wheelchair access (not WC). Music. Air-conditioned  £5

# Melton's Too ✳ £                          **NEW ENTRY**

25 Walmgate, York YO1 9TX                          COOKING **1**
TEL: (01904) 629222   FAX: (01904) 636677          MODERN EUROPEAN
WEBSITE: www.meltonstoo.co.uk                      £19–£40

The new offshoot of the long-standing Melton's (see entry above) aims to be a more relaxed and casual place (bookings are not taken), serving less complicated food in an environment of bare brick walls and plain wooden furniture. A long brasserie-style menu is divided into sections according to portion size, and a blackboard supplements this with tapas and daily specials. 'Well travelled' was how a reporter summed up the cooking: steak and kidney pie, couscous with merguez, confit de canard with mash, and Thai curries all feature. Among the tapas dishes, spicy, herby meatballs with mint and coriander in a tomato sauce, lemon and chilli chicken, and tortilla filled with mushrooms made a favourable impression at inspection. Prices on the very short wine list start at £10.50 and stay mostly under £15.

CHEF: Jason Plevey  PROPRIETORS: Michael and Lucy Hjort  OPEN: all week 10.30 to 10.30 (9.30 Sun)  CLOSED: 25 and 26 Dec, D 31 Dec, 1 Jan  MEALS: alc (main courses £6 to £12)  SERVICE: not inc  CARDS: Delta, MasterCard, Switch, Visa  DETAILS: 130 seats. Private parties: 40 main room, 15 to 25 private rooms. Vegetarian meals. Children's helpings. No smoking in dining room. Wheelchair access (also WC). Music. Air-conditioned  (£5)

## ▲ Middlethorpe Hall ♀ ⁂

Bishopthorpe Road, York YO23 2GB
TEL: (01904) 641241  FAX: (01904) 620176
EMAIL: info@middlethorpe.com
WEBSITE: www.middlethorpe.com

COOKING 3
MODERN BRITISH
£30–£56

Though too close to town to be rural, this three-storey, brick giant of a place, built in 1699, has acres of grounds and gardens with mature trees. Large portraits seek to humanise the grand scale, and the comparatively intimate dining room has antique pale oak panelling all round, 'making it feel like you are eating inside a wooden box'. Lunch offers three choices per course, dinner six, with a few interesting ideas, such as langoustine with pork cheek and lentils, or roast quail with boudin blanc and quail-egg ravioli.

Sound materials take in veal sweetbreads, rabbit, loin of lamb, and a range of fish from braised turbot to a tranche of moist, flaky cod, its crisp skin strewn with salt crystals, served with fat, glistening ceps and roasted salsify. Desserts are a distinct highlight, judging by a freshly made plum clafoutis: simple but first-class. Communication with non-English-speaking staff can be difficult, and service itself is heavy on gesturing and posturing. The wine list takes itself seriously too, with (service-inclusive) prices to prove it. The champagne, claret and burgundy sections are large; other wines are tucked away at the back, but here too mark-ups are high (£44.50 for Cloudy Bay Chardonnay 1999). Two bottles sneak under £20: house red and white at £14.50.

CHEF: Martin Barker  PROPRIETOR: Historic House Hotels  OPEN: all week 12 to 1.45, 7 to 9.45  CLOSED: 25 and 31 Dec (open for residents)  MEALS: Set L £16.50 (2 courses) to £22, Set D £36  SERVICE: net prices, card slips closed  CARDS: MasterCard, Switch, Visa  DETAILS: 60 seats. Private parties: 50 main room, 6 to 50 private rooms. Car park. Vegetarian meals. No children under 8. Jacket. No smoking in dining room. Wheelchair access (not WC). No music. No mobile phones  ACCOMMODATION: 30 rooms, all with bath/shower. TV. Phone. Room only £109 to £340. No children under 8. Swimming pool (*The Which? Hotel Guide*)

# Scotland

## Silver Darling ⅛✳

| | |
|---|---|
| Pocra Quay, North Pier, Aberdeen AB11 5DQ | COOKING **4** |
| TEL: (01224) 576229   FAX: (01224) 588119 | SEAFOOD |
| | £30–£62 |

Down by the harbour entrance, Didier Dejean continues to fly the flag for both Aberdeen and seafood. There's plenty of choice, from plain oysters with lemon and shallot dressing to fancier smoked salmon roulade with steamed asparagus, melted blue cheese and sauce vierge. Many dishes are French (perhaps fillet of rock turbot poached in red wine with a sorrel velouté), some are modern British (North Sea halibut with a macadamia nut crust, in a spicy lemon-grass and coconut emulsion), and some just straightforward: a grilled selection of whatever fish the daily market offers, perhaps with a sweet pepper coulis and basil oil.

Aberdeen's fish market is one of the UK's finest, so freshness and quality are not an issue, nor is variety: from John Dory to langoustines, from scallops to tuna and sea bass, from lemon sole to monkfish. There are token offerings for meat eaters, too, and (unusually for a fish restaurant) desserts get proper attention: witness a double chocolate mascarpone tart with a sharp berry coulis, also a warm, sweet goats' cheese and orange tart with a caramel and red wine syrup. The short wine list (naturally white-heavy) starts with an unspecified Fruits de Mer wine at £13.50, but there's not a lot under £20.

CHEF: Didier Dejean   PROPRIETORS: Didier Dejean and Ms K. Murray   OPEN: Mon to Fri L 12 to 1.45, Mon to Sat D 7 to 9.30   CLOSED: 25 Dec to first week of Jan   MEALS: alc (main courses L £9.50 to £14.50, D £16.50 to £19.50)   SERVICE: not inc, card slips closed   CARDS: Amex, Delta, Diners, MasterCard, Switch, Visa   DETAILS: 50 seats. Private parties: 50 main room, 10 to 18 private rooms. No smoking in dining room. Music

---

*The 2004 Guide will be published before Christmas 2003. Reports on meals are most welcome at any time of the year, but are particularly valuable in the spring (no later than June). Send them to* The Good Food Guide, *FREEPOST, 2 Marylebone Road, London NW1 4DF. Or email your report to goodfoodguide@which.net*

# ▲ Summer Isles Hotel ▮ ⁵⚹

Achiltibuie IV26 2YG
TEL: (01854) 622282   FAX: (01854) 622251
EMAIL: summerisleshotel@aol.com
WEBSITE: www.summerisleshotel.co.uk
take A835 to Drumrunie, 10m N of Ullapool, then          COOKING 5
single-track road for 15m; hotel 1m past          MODERN EUROPEAN
Achiltibuie on left                              £24–£60

A long, meandering single-track road leads to this relaxing and 'unstuffy yet
sophisticated' hotel, with views, walks and wildlife for diversion. It is
comfortable rather than luxurious, 'hasn't been spoilt by an interior designer',
and owes much to the warm hospitality and personal involvement of the Irvines.
Lunch is a short carte showcasing local seafood: langoustines and spiny lobsters
'beyond reproach', or an enormous platter combining Lochinver oysters
'bursting with fresh sea flavour', smoked salmon two ways, pickled herrings,
spiny lobsters and smoked haddock that 'could hardly be faulted'.

Dinner is a five-course no-choice menu with cheese bringing up the rear after
that most ancient transport of delights, a sweets trolley. Langoustines might turn
up again, in filo pastry with a tamarind sauce, followed by grilled John Dory
fillet with a caviar and vermouth sauce, and then roast duck with a spiced plum
compote. Puddings come without frills or presentational gimmicks: perhaps a
velvety chocolate mousse on a digestive biscuit base, or a light meringue case
filled with thick cream and sliced strawberries and raspberries, served with
butterscotch ice cream.

An extensive wine list favours the good and great of red Bordeaux from cru
bourgeois to premiers crus, including a number of mature bottles at prices that
are fair, if not cheap. The rest of the list concerns itself with classic regions of
France before moving on to the rest of Europe and the New World. Bottle prices
start at £9 and move up to three figures and even four, but there is plenty of
interest below £20 and poking around can reveal excellent value.

CHEF: Chris Firth-Bernard   PROPRIETORS: Mark and Gerry Irvine   OPEN: all week 12.30 to 2, 8pm
(1 sitting)   CLOSED: 13 Oct to 15 Apr   MEALS: alc L (main courses £7.50 to £25). Set D £41. Bar
menu available   SERVICE: net prices, card slips closed   CARDS: MasterCard, Switch, Visa
DETAILS: 28 seats. Private parties: 8 main room. Car park. Children's helpings. No children under
6. No smoking in dining room. No music. No mobile phones   ACCOMMODATION: 13 rooms, all with
bath/shower. Phone. B&B £69 to £228. Rooms for disabled. No children under 6. Fishing (*The
Which? Hotel Guide*)

---

*All details are as accurate as possible at the time of going to press, but chefs and owners
often change, and it is wise to check by telephone before making a special journey. Many
readers have been disappointed when set-price bargain meals are no longer available.
Ask when booking.*

## ALLOWAY  South Ayrshire

map 11

### ▲ Ivy House ✠

NEW ENTRY

Ivy House Hotel, 2 Alloway, Ayr KA7 4YL
TEL: (01292) 442336   FAX: (01292) 445572
EMAIL: enquiries@theivyhouse.uk.com
WEBSITE: www.theivyhouse.uk.com

COOKING 3
ANGLO-FRENCH
£24–£56

Ivy House is a plain, solid-looking but evidently well-cared-for hotel set amid trees at the edge of a golf course. The welcome is warm but the general feel is formal – well-spaced tables are laid with white linen and sprays of carnations – and the kitchen shows signs of lofty ambition. Four-course menus, priced according to main-course choice, include a 'palate cleanser' after the starter (cherry and gin sorbet, for example), and various other extras. Stylish presentation characterises the food, which brings a few modern influences to bear on a mainly traditional approach. A terrine of wild duck, Toulouse sausage and haricot beans with sauce vierge made a strong visual and taste impact at an inspection meal. Among main courses, roast supreme of Gressingham duck with confit Savoy cabbage, gratin of fondant potato, haricot bean and beetroot jus proved a success, and another reporter found it easy to praise loin of lamb with crushed new potatoes, seared foie gras and bourguignon jus. Finish perhaps with strawberry crème brûlée with glazed pear on an orange sorbet. A list of over 100 wines from across the world opens with nine house recommendations from £14.75 (£2.25 a glass).

CHEF: Joe Queen   PROPRIETORS: George and Eli Whillock   OPEN: Mon to Sat 12 to 2.30, 5 to 9.45, Sun 12 to 6.45   MEALS: alc (main courses £11 to £23). Set L Mon to Sat £11 (2 courses) to £14, Set L Sun £18.50 (2 courses) to £22. Set D Mon to Fri £14 (2 courses) to £18, Set D Sat £29 to £35. Café menu available 12 to 5   SERVICE: not inc, card slips closed   CARDS: Amex, Delta, MasterCard, Switch, Visa   DETAILS: 102 seats. 40 seats outside. Private parties: 65 main room, 12 to 24 private rooms. Car park. Vegetarian meals. Children's helpings. Jacket and tie at Sat D. No smoking in dining room. Wheelchair access (also WC). Music   ACCOMMODATION: 5 rooms, all with bath/shower. TV. Phone. B&B £75 to £100 (The Which? Hotel Guide)

## ANNBANK  South Ayrshire

map 11

### ▲ Enterkine House ✠

Annbank KA6 5AL
TEL: (01292) 521608 and 520580
FAX: (01292) 521582
EMAIL: mail@enterkine.com
WEBSITE: www.enterkine.com

COOKING 3
FRENCH/ITALIAN
£28–£52

Large windows in the lounge and dining room of this idiosyncratic hotel make the most of wonderful views over the Ayrshire countryside, and soothing décor adds to the relaxed ambience. The low-key feel of the place also infuses the cooking, which aims to impress without showiness. Chef Douglas Smith states that 'taste, for me, is much more important than looks', and his preferred style is rustic peasant food, though his menus also reflect his classical training: among starters may be a salad of duck with celeriac, apple and walnut, or a gratin of smoked haddock with rarebit and a tomato salad. To follow might be a soup, perhaps a velouté of celeriac with parsley and truffle oil, then a choice of main courses ranging from grilled loin of lamb with hotpot potatoes and rosemary gravy, to sea bass crusted with gremolata served with peperonata, roast tomatoes and asparagus. Finish perhaps with warm pear and almond tart with crème fraîche, or Valrhona chocolate cheesecake with orange cream. Wines are strongest in France, but the selection is varied and fairly priced. House wines are £13.95.

CHEF: Douglas Smith   PROPRIETOR: Oswald Browne   OPEN: Sun to Fri L 12 to 2.30, all week D 7 to 9.15   MEALS: Set L £18.50, Set D £32.50   SERVICE: not inc, card slips closed   CARDS: Amex, Delta, MasterCard, Switch, Visa   DETAILS: 40 seats. Private parties: 26 main room, 8 to 14 private rooms. Car park. No children under 11. No smoking in dining room. Wheelchair access (also WC). No music. No mobile phones   ACCOMMODATION: 6 rooms, all with bath/shower. TV. Phone. B&B £90 to £230. Rooms for disabled. No children under 11. Fishing  (£5)

---

**ANSTRUTHER** Fife                                                  map 11

# Cellar ▮ ⁵⁄✻

24 East Green, Anstruther KY10 3AA                           COOKING **6**
TEL: (01333) 310378   FAX: (01333) 312544                  MODERN SEAFOOD
                                                                £29–£50

Just one street back from the harbour is an arched entry to a small courtyard, which leads to the restaurant. Plain stonework is tempered by attractive fabrics, country-style furniture, low lighting from lamps and candles, and an open fire when the weather calls for it, all generating a warm and friendly atmosphere. Peter Jukes has now passed the 20-year milestone, employing a little help in the kitchen but as passionate as ever about raw materials and their seasonal availability.

His repertoire may not change particularly fast, but there are two brakes on it: customers like to eat their favourite dishes time and again, and, since the kitchen's focus is on making the best of its materials, that usually involves doing not very much to them. Hence, dressed crab arrives simply in the shell with salad leaves, lemon mayonnaise and brown bread, while finnan haddock gets classic treatment, served in a creamy omelette.

Prime-quality fish includes roast halibut, served on a bed of crisp green vegetables (beans, broccoli, asparagus), with bacon, pine kernels and a pot of hollandaise, but even non-fish dishes are highly rated. A wild mushroom risotto comes 'at the top of our risotto scale' for one couple. Desserts are as straightforward as the rest, and none the worse for that, taking in vanilla ice cream with butterscotch sauce, an iced hazelnut praline parfait with raspberry and Cassis coulis, and a slice of triple chocolate mousse terrine with orange liqueur custard. A casually handwritten list belies the seriousness of the wines therein. Bordeaux fans will be cheered by the presence of some fine first- and 'super-second' growths, while those with slimmer wallets can choose from a selection of French country whites. The Americas, and European wines from outside France, are covered in style too, while almost 30 half-bottles round out the list. Bottle prices start at £15, and there is fair choice under £20.

CHEFS: Peter Jukes and Stuart Brown   PROPRIETOR: Peter Jukes   OPEN: Wed to Sun L 12.30 for 1 (1 sitting), Tue to Sat D and Sun and Mon D Whitsun to Oct 7 to 9.30   MEALS: Set L £15.50 (2 courses) to 18.50, Set D £25 (2 courses) to £28.50   SERVICE: not inc, card slips closed   CARDS: Amex, Delta, Diners, MasterCard, Switch, Visa   DETAILS: 40 seats. Private parties: 48 main room. Children's helpings. No smoking in dining room. Wheelchair access (not WC). Music

## AUCHTERARDER Perthshire & Kinross                                   map 11

## ▲ Andrew Fairlie at Gleneagles ⚡✱

| | |
|---|---|
| Gleneagles Hotel, Auchterarder PH3 1NF | COOKING 6 |
| TEL: (01764) 694267   FAX: (01764) 694163 | MODERN FRENCH |
| EMAIL: andrew.fairlie@gleneagles.com | £82–£119 |

With its Mark Philips equestrian centre and Jackie Stewart shooting school, not to mention its golf course, Gleneagles obviously aims high, which is why Andrew Fairlie is here. Although his portraits adorn the dining room, he is not your usual celebrity chef, preferring to devote his energies to producing dinner, six days a week. His cooking is clearly focused, reflecting his training in French kitchens; and while the skills may be traditional, the outlook is contemporary. A warm salad of winter vegetables comes with beetroot essence, and sauté snails and frogs' legs appear on a pumpkin risotto.

Local materials loom large, including lamb from a Perthshire estate supplied by Andrew Fairlie's brother, though ingredients also take a cosmopolitan turn: Castelluccio lentils accompany Jura scallops, chorizo beignets partner pan-fried halibut, and Landes duckling is cooked twice for good measure. Presentation is carefully crafted, and luxuries abound: a velouté of ceps comes with truffle tortellini, and lobster is home-smoked and served with a herb and lime butter sauce.

The food's reassurance continues at dessert stage, with a hot Valrhona chocolate and orange pudding, and plum and hazelnut tart with prune and Armagnac ice cream. Anyone expecting bargains on the wine list will be disappointed: although the collection is a fine one, only a handful of bottles come in under £30, which takes the shine off.

CHEF/PROPRIETOR: Andrew Fairlie   OPEN: Mon to Sat D only 7 to 10   CLOSED: 5 Jan to 1 Feb   MEALS: alc (main courses £27). Set D £55 to £75   SERVICE: not inc   CARDS: Amex, Diners, MasterCard, Switch, Visa   DETAILS: 40 seats. Private parties: 45 main room. Car park. Vegetarian meals. No smoking in dining room. Wheelchair access (also WC). Music. No mobile phones. Air-conditioned   ACCOMMODATION: 250 rooms, all with bath/shower. TV. Phone. B&B £125 to £1,450. Rooms for disabled. Baby facilities. Swimming pool. Fishing (*The Which? Hotel Guide*)

---

*The Guide relies on feedback from its readers. Especially welcome are reports on new restaurants appearing in the book for the first time. All letters to the Guide are acknowledged.*

Not inc *in the details at the end of an entry indicates that no service charge is made and any tipping is at the discretion of the customer.*

---

# ▲ Boath House ⅍

Auldearn IV12 5TE
TEL: (01667) 454896   FAX: (01667) 455469
EMAIL: wendy@boath-house.demon.co.uk                    COOKING 5
WEBSITE: www.boath-house.com                        FRANCO-SCOTTISH
on A96, 2m E of Nairn                                    £37–£61

Boath House is an imposing Georgian mansion set in 20 acres of grounds, complete with a lake. It is a grand country-house hotel in the modern fashion, offering luxuriously appointed antique-furnished bedrooms, spa facilities and a gym, as well as a classy restaurant. The Mathesons tell us they have recently quadrupled the size of their kitchen garden, so that in summer they are now almost self-sufficient. The repertoire of this veritable cottage industry is enhanced with home-made bread and preserves and home-smoked meat and fish, all of which are put to good use by an enterprising kitchen.

Five-course dinner and three- or four-course lunch menus have a modern-classic feel, offering not too many surprises but plenty of interest: the opening 'potage' may be a velouté of celeriac with Parmesan, or smoked monkfish with salmon and langoustine tortellini, while the first course proper is usually an attractively simple-sounding dish, such as a salad of roast scallops with basil oil. The only choice comes at main course, usually between fish and meat: medallions of venison with spiced red cabbage and red wine sauce, or turbot on lemon and pea risotto, for example. A cheese course precedes dessert of perhaps chocolate tart with almond ice cream and macerated strawberries. Although most of the wines on the predominantly French list weigh in above £20, six house wines are priced from £12.50, and eight wines are offered by the glass.

CHEF: Charles Lockley   PROPRIETORS: Don and Wendy Matheson   OPEN: Thur to Sun L 12.30 to 1.45, all week D 7 to 8.45   MEALS: Set L £24.95 to £28.95, Set D £38   SERVICE: not inc   CARDS: Amex, Delta, MasterCard, Switch, Visa   DETAILS: 28 seats. Private parties: 24 main room, 6 to 10 private rooms. Car park. Children's helpings. No smoking in dining room. Wheelchair access (also WC). Occasional music. No mobile phones   ACCOMMODATION: 7 rooms, all with bath/shower. TV. Phone. B&B £95 to £200. Rooms for disabled. Baby facilities. Fishing (*The Which? Hotel Guide*)  £5

# Fouters Bistro ⅍

2A Academy Street, Ayr KA7 1HS
TEL: (01292) 261391   FAX: (01292) 619323                 COOKING 2
EMAIL: eat@fouters.co.uk                             MODERN SCOTTISH
WEBSITE: www.fouters.co.uk                              £21–£50

Occupying a narrow cellar, with a rough stone-flagged floor and close-together tables, Fouters takes its sourcing of native materials seriously. It serves smoked salmon from the Summer Isles, Carrick venison with braised cabbage, and loin of Ayrshire lamb on a Toulouse cassoulet. There is even a Taste of Scotland platter for the undecided. A daily specials board announces what's fresh in the seafood line: perhaps baked fillet of Atlantic cod with chorizo mash, or seared west coast scallops, flavoured with ginger and served on Japanese noodles. Lunch tends to be a bit less formal than dinner, offering battered haddock with chips and tartare sauce, or the 'house pasta', followed by an iced Grand Marnier soufflé, or sticky toffee pudding with hot fudge sauce. Forty-plus wines, mostly from France, stay generally under £20, starting with house vin de pays at £11.95.

CHEFS: Laurie Black and Lewis Pringle   PROPRIETORS: Laurie and Fran Black   OPEN: Tue to Sat 12 to 2, 6 to 10   CLOSED: 25 to 27 Dec, 1 to 3 Jan   MEALS: alc (main courses L £5 to £10, D £9 to £17.50). Set D exc 7.30 to 10 Sat £9.50 (2 courses)   SERVICE: not inc   CARDS: Amex, Delta, Diners, MasterCard, Switch, Visa   DETAILS: 38 seats. 12 seats outside. Private parties: 40 main room, 8 to 14 private rooms. Vegetarian meals. Children's helpings. No smoking in dining room. Occasional music. No mobile phones. Air-conditioned (£5)

## BALLATER  Aberdeenshire                                              map 11

## ▲ Balgonie ⁵⚹

Braemar Place, Ballater AB35 5NQ
TEL/FAX: (013397) 55482
EMAIL: balgoniech@aol.com
WEBSITE: www.royaldeesidehotels.com

COOKING 3
MODERN SCOTTISH
£29–£52

Peace and tranquility are among the attractions at this well-kept, creeper-clad, Edwardian-style country house. Appetites can be honed at croquet on the lawn before sitting down at a polished wooden table in the modern-looking dining room. A standard three-course format is extended to four with the aid of a fish course (perhaps grilled herrings in oatmeal), and menus are short but balanced, usually taking in a cheesy starter (say, feta salad with artichokes and black olives) alongside a soup (curried parsnip, maybe) and a fish option, such as a tian of crabmeat spiked with coriander.

So close to Balmoral, many local suppliers (including the butcher) are Royal Warrant holders. Game might take the form of roast pheasant with game chips, or a terrine accompanied by either spiced pear chutney or beetroot confit, and combinations are generally tried and tested, from roast loin of pork with prunes to Gressingham duck breast with Puy lentils. Desserts, too, are straightforward: a fig and almond tart perhaps, hot lemon sponge, or a meringue nest filled with berries and Chantilly cream. Among wines to note on the 60-strong list are a couple of Australians – d'Arenberg Shiraz 1998 and Ninth Island Sauvignon Blanc 1999 – both under £20.

CHEFS: John Finnie and Graham Stewart   PROPRIETORS: John and Priscilla Finnie   OPEN: all week 12.30 to 2 (by reservation only), 7 to 9   CLOSED: 5 Jan to 12 Feb   MEALS: Set L £19, Set D £31.50   SERVICE: not inc, card slips closed   CARDS: Amex, Delta, Diners, MasterCard, Switch, Visa   DETAILS: 30 seats. Private parties: 30 main room. Car park. Children's helpings. No smoking in dining room. Wheelchair access (also WC). Occasional music   ACCOMMODATION: 9 rooms, all with bath/shower. TV. Phone. B&B £60 to £125. Baby facilities (*The Which? Hotel Guide*) (£5)

---

*'It must take half the fun out of dome-lifting, for the staff, when there's only one diner, and synchronisation is out of the question.'* (On eating in Cheshire)

# ▲ Darroch Learg ♀ ⌘

Braemar Road, Ballater AB35 5UX
TEL: (013397) 55443  FAX: (013397) 55252
EMAIL: info@darrochlearg.co.uk
off A93 Ballater to Braemar road at W edge of
village

SCOTLAND
GFG 2003
COMMENDED

COOKING **6**
MODERN SCOTTISH
£27–£58

This is a tranquil place, with a light and tastefully decorated conservatory dining room, and a warm welcome and attentive service from members of the Franks family. The kitchen takes its supplies seriously, calling on dived scallops, and local chanterelles and soft fruits such as raspberries and strawberries. Meats from impeccable sources are treated with respect, perhaps Balmoral venison, or a fillet of Highland beef paired with sticky, deeply flavoured braised shin, served with celeriac purée and a fine stock- and wine-based sauce. Lamb is less favourably received, but duck is a winner, the breast for one visitor given earthy intensity from slices of black pudding and a truffled sauce.

Dinner, three courses, typically gets off to a flying start, perhaps featuring a terrine of tasty ham hock and creamy foie gras, the plate studded with blobs of intense, sticky, green pea purée, or an outstanding plate of pork served four ways: a succulent roast rib, a fine, lightly textured black pudding, a ravioli of confit pork, and a stuffed rib, all served with a first-rate jus and cauliflower purée. Everything stays on an even keel, right through to desserts, such as a pyramid of rich chocolate with mulled fruits and cappuccino ice cream, or a first-class vanilla parfait with hazelnut sponge and prunes, a dish notable for its successful cohesion of flavours and textures. The lengthy, annotated wine list favours Europe, although there are some carefully selected producers in the Australia, South Africa and California sections. Mark-ups are generally fair, with a bin-end section offering particularly good value. Prices start at £15.90 for Italian red, and there is plenty of interesting drinking under £20. Five wines are sold by the glass (£4 to £5).

Under the same ownership is the Station (at Station Square, Ballater), offering breakfast, light lunch, tea and dinner for about six months of the year from spring to autumn; tel (013397) 55050.

CHEF: David Mutter  PROPRIETORS: the Franks family  OPEN: all week 12.30 to 2, 7 to 9  CLOSED: Christmas, last 3 weeks Jan  MEALS: Set L Mon to Sat £19.50, Set L Sun £18.50, Set D £35. Light L available Mon to Sat  SERVICE: net prices, card slips closed  CARDS: Amex, Delta, Diners, MasterCard, Switch, Visa  DETAILS: 48 seats. 8 seats outside. Private parties: 62 main room. Car park. Vegetarian meals. Children's helpings. No smoking in dining room. Wheelchair access (not WC). No music  ACCOMMODATION: 18 rooms, all with bath/shower. TV. Phone. B&B £42 to £155. Rooms for disabled. Baby facilities (*The Which? Hotel Guide*)

---

*Prices quoted in the Guide are based on information supplied by restaurateurs. The prices quoted at the top of each entry represent a range, from the lowest meal price to the highest; the latter is inflated by 20 per cent to take account of likely price rises during the year of the Guide.*

---

## BALQUHIDDER Stirling                                    map 11

## ▲ Monachyle Mhor ⭐✳

Balquhidder FK19 8PQ
TEL: (01877) 384622   FAX: (01877) 384305
EMAIL: info@monachylemhor.com
WEBSITE: www.monachylemhor.com

COOKING 4
MODERN SCOTTISH
£25–£50

A long single-track road leads to the pink-washed house and its cluster of cottage bedrooms, where a conservatory dining room overlooks Lochs Voil and Doine. This may be a long way from anywhere, but it looks and feels modern and well cared for, and the kitchen is serious. Fresh produce is central to its aspirations, and in the Braes of Balquhidder, as in much of rural Scotland, nature's larder is a particularly handy resource: wild duck, grouse and pheasant come from a local estate, deer are shot in the Glen, mushrooms are picked nearby, while a walled kitchen garden and a local grower make their own contributions. As an example of what all this bounty adds up to on the plate, look no further than a pan-fried breast of grouse accompanied by chanterelles and a concasse of garden vegetables.

Seafood arrives from both east and west coasts, perhaps turning up in a starter as poached fillet of cod with cod's roe, poached egg and hollandaise, or in a main course of seared scallops with smoked haddock and wild rice kedgeree, accompanied by steamed greens, wasabi and cracked peppercorn butter. Tom Lewis also cures beef and pork to produce his own version of bresaola and Parma ham, puts on a vegetarian menu, and turns out desserts such as caramelised rice pudding with stewed rhubarb, and lemon and passion-fruit crème brûlée. A sensibly chosen, reasonably priced and helpfully annotated wine list adds to the appeal, starting with five house wines from £11 to £15.50.

CHEF: Tom Lewis   PROPRIETORS: Rob, Jean and Tom Lewis   OPEN: all week 12 to 1.45, 7 to 8.45   CLOSED: 5 Jan to 14 Feb   MEALS: alc (main courses £8.50 to £15.50). Set L £19, Set D £32.50   SERVICE: not inc   CARDS: MasterCard, Switch, Visa   DETAILS: 40 seats. 20 seats outside. Private parties: 24 main room, 6 to 12 private rooms. Car park. Vegetarian meals. No children under 12. No smoking in dining room. Wheelchair access (also WC). No music. No mobile phones ACCOMMODATION: 10 rooms, all with bath/shower. TV. Phone. B&B £60 to £140. No children under 12. Baby facilities. Fishing (The Which? Hotel Guide)

## BLAIRGOWRIE Perthshire & Kinross                        map 11

## ▲ Kinloch House Hotel ♟ ⭐✳

Blairgowrie PH10 6SG
TEL: (01250) 884237   FAX: (01250) 884333
EMAIL: reception@kinlochhouse.com
WEBSITE: www.kinlochhouse.com
on A923, 3m W of Blairgowrie towards Dunkeld

COOKING 4
SCOTTISH
£21–£75

Prepare to be greeted by 'a red-faced gentleman in a kilt' at this atmospheric country-house hotel, and to be waited on by similarly uniformed staff. It is all designed to create an indulgent mood, aided by wood panelling, log fires and plush furnishings. Dinner is the main business, and materials are conscientiously sourced: meat from a local butcher, vegetables from the hotel's own restored Victorian walled garden. The kitchen's priority is an interpretation of Scottish cooking that might take in anything from Shetland mussels (steamed in white wine and cream) to roast loin of venison (with a truffled game ravioli and braised red cabbage). As if three courses weren't expensive enough already, a whole page of supplements applies to fillet steaks and prawn dishes. Vegetarians get their own menu, and desserts might run to a date and vanilla pudding with butterscotch sauce and fudge ice cream. Portions are well judged, service is prompt and courteous, and wines, in keeping with the feel of the place, are suitably classic. Red Bordeaux (13 vintages of classed growths going back to 1966) gets top billing, followed by Burgundy, the Rhône and Alsace, before heading off to Italy, Germany and the New World. Own-label house wines start at £14.95, but prices rise quickly from there.

CHEF: Bill McNicoll  PROPRIETORS: David and Sarah Shentall  OPEN: all week 12.30 to 2, 7 to 9.15  CLOSED: 15 to 30 Dec  MEALS: Set L £13.50, Set D £26 (2 courses) to £35  SERVICE: none, card slips closed  CARDS: Amex, Delta, Diners, MasterCard, Switch, Visa  DETAILS: 55 seats. Private parties: 55 main room, 2 to 24 private rooms. Car park. Vegetarian meals. No children under 7 at D. Jacket and tie. No smoking in dining room. Wheelchair access (also WC). No music. No mobile phones  ACCOMMODATION: 20 rooms, all with bath/shower. TV. Phone. D,B&B £105 to £220. Rooms for disabled. Baby facilities. Swimming pool (*The Which? Hotel Guide*)

---

## CAIRNDOW Argyll & Bute                                     map 11

# Loch Fyne Oyster Bar 💤✳ £

Clachan, Cairndow PA26 8BH
TEL: (01499) 600236  FAX: (01499) 600234
EMAIL: oysterbar@loch-fyne                                    COOKING 2
WEBSITE: www.loch-fyne.com                          TRADITIONAL SEAFOOD
on A83, at head of Loch Fyne                                  £20–£70

A long, low building stands at the head of the loch, with a shop to one side, a restaurant to the other. The company has long championed the idea of fresh seafood served simply, a model with which few would quibble; branches around the country testify to its appeal. 'Environmental care', 'animal welfare' and 'sustainable resources' are watchwords when it comes to supplies, and their own oysters, mussels and smoked salmon are supplemented by a few items from local fishermen, and by Glen Fyne venison and ribeye steak. Most dishes are straightforward, and all the better for it: perhaps gravad lax with dill sauce, smoked salmon fillet sushi-style, or a plate of cold langoustines with mayonnaise. Options extend from a modest half-dozen oysters on ice to an indulgent platter of lobster, oysters, langoustines and queen scallops, while desserts take in sticky toffee pudding and crème caramel. A short list of (mainly youthful white) wines is sensibly priced, starting with house French at £9.95.

CHEF: Tracy Wyatt  PROPRIETOR: Loch Fyne Oysters Ltd  OPEN: all week 9 to 9 (closed D Mon to Thur 6 Jan to 20 Mar)  CLOSED: 25 and 26 Dec  MEALS: alc (main courses £5 to £32.50)  SERVICE: not inc  CARDS: Amex, MasterCard, Switch, Visa  DETAILS: 120 seats. 20 seats outside. Private parties: 50 main room, 20 to 60 private rooms. Car park. Vegetarian meals. Children's helpings. No smoking in dining room. Wheelchair access (also WC). No music. No mobile phones  £5

## CLACHAN-SEIL Argyll & Bute — map 11

### ▲ Willowburn Hotel

Clachan-Seil, by Oban PA34 4TJ
TEL: (01852) 300276 FAX: (01852) 300597
EMAIL: willowburn.hotel@virgin.net
WEBSITE: www.willowburn.co.uk
from Oban take A816 S for 8m; then take B844, following signs for Seil Island and Luing, for 7m; after hump-backed bridge Willowburn is approx ¼m on left

COOKING **3**
MODERN SCOTTISH/FRENCH
£38–£50

To reach the hotel, half an hour's drive south of Oban, you first need to cross Clachan Bridge, built in the late eighteenth century, which famously spans what looks like a small river, but is in fact part of the Atlantic Ocean. Wildlife abounds on Scotland's West Coast, and peace and quiet are the order of the day. Such surroundings transform the nature of shopping: Chris Mitchell's menu sets out its stall by detailing the provenance of materials. They grow their own herbs, salad leaves and soft fruit (including straw-, rasp-, goose-, blue-, and black-berries, and red and white currants), pick wild blossoms such as elderflower, and get their eggs from just down the road.

Local fishermen (one of whom doubles as the window cleaner) typically provide crab, prawns, and lobster (perhaps poached, with a red wine reduction), while other fish are landed at Oban: maybe seared halibut served with an aubergine fritter. Lamb is hill farmed, and beef is Aberdeen Angus, the fillet perhaps stuffed with walnuts and herbs. Dinner is four courses (the second a soup or sorbet), and coffee is included. Meals might start with salmon (smoked in-house), or a warm salad of asparagus with leaves, pine nuts and lemon sauce, and end with hazelnut profiteroles, or an unusual dessert of lemon, plum and white chocolate. Wines include examples from Greece, Uruguay, Austria and Switzerland, and start with four house wines at £11.75.

CHEF: Chris Mitchell PROPRIETORS: Jan Wolfe and Chris Mitchell OPEN: all week D only 7 to 8 CLOSED: Dec to 15 March MEALS: Set D £29 SERVICE: not inc, card slips closed CARDS: Delta, MasterCard, Switch, Visa DETAILS: 24 seats. Private parties: 10 main room. Car park. Vegetarian meals. Children's helpings. No smoking in dining room. Music. No mobile phones ACCOMMODATION: 7 rooms, all with bath/shower. TV. D,B&B £65 to £140 (*The Which? Hotel Guide*) (£5)

## COLBOST Highland — map 11

### ▲ Three Chimneys

Colbost, Dunvegan, Isle of Skye IV55 8ZT
TEL: (01470) 511258 FAX: (01470) 511358
EMAIL: eatandstay@threechimneys.co.uk
WEBSITE: www.threechimneys.co.uk
on B884, 4m W of Dunvegan

COOKING **5**
MODERN SCOTTISH
£34–£83

Exposed stone walls and rough plastering contribute to the 'rustic chic' feel of this brace of picturesque whitewashed crofters' cottages, reached down a single-track road by the shore of Loch Dunvegan. Apart from small improvements to seating and tableware, little changes; it remains unpretentious, relaxing, comfortable and stylish, without being in any way folksy. Seafood, much of it local, takes pride of place: from half a dozen Skye oysters, via lobster (whole, or turned into a bisque), to simply grilled West Coast cod with skirlie mash. And despite the name Dunvegan, there are some staunchly vegetarian dishes, such as a white nut loaf with spiced red cabbage and a hot plum sauce, as well as full-blooded venison collop, cooked rare, served with plain crushed potatoes and celeriac in a rich sea of fruity beetroot gravy.

The food, like the surroundings, is professional yet low key, the kitchen's 'impeccable techniques' applied to small, crisply fried, tasty crab cakes with a herby salad, and to a carrot, orange and ginger soup that 'could hardly be bettered'. A sense of restraint applies throughout, even down to the absence of squiggly sauces and fancy dustings, not least among desserts. These rely on fine craftsmanship, evident in a shortcrust pastry tart of apple and almond, and in a small pear poached in ginger wine (a pleasant change from the customary red wine), with a puddle of bitter chocolate sauce and an ice cream studded with crystallised ginger. Service is friendly but unobtrusive, and wines are equally well considered. The list kicks off with seven house selections (including champagne) available by the bottle (from £15.75) and glass (from £3.95). Although the list slightly favours France, the New World – California and Australia in particular – is well represented, too.

CHEFS: Shirley Spear and Isabel Tomlin   PROPRIETORS: Eddie and Shirley Spear   OPEN: Mon to Sat L 12.30 to 2, all week D 6.30 to 9.30   CLOSED: 6 to 24 Jan, L Nov to end Mar   MEALS: Set L £15 (2 courses) to £21, Set D £37 to £44   SERVICE: not inc   CARDS: Amex, Delta, MasterCard, Switch, Visa   DETAILS: 40 seats. 6 seats outside. Private parties: 20 main room, 20 private room. Car park. Vegetarian meals. Children's helpings. No smoking in dining room. Wheelchair access (not WC). No music   ACCOMMODATION: 6 rooms, all with bath/shower. TV. Phone. B&B £140 to £175. Rooms for disabled. Baby facilities (*The Which? Hotel Guide*)

---

**CRINAN  Argyll & Bute**                    map 11

## ▲ Crinan Hotel, Westward Restaurant

Crinan PA31 8SR
TEL: (01546) 830261   FAX: (01546) 830292
EMAIL: nryan@crinanhotel.com
WEBSITE: www.crinanhotel.com
off A816, 6m NW of Lochgilphead

COOKING 6
MODERN EUROPEAN
£51–£61

Crinan consists of two separate restaurants. Lock 16 on the top floor has traditionally been the better option, but the arrival of Ben Tish at the Westward – now refurbished, with big, passionate blue seascapes – has moved things up a gear. In fact, it is more return than arrival, since he worked here some ten years ago, filling in the time since at some good London addresses. The deal is four courses, one of them a fishy interlude after the starter (perhaps a wee lozenge of well-judged salt-cod brandade on tapénade), and modish ingredients are eschewed in favour of stalwart local produce, typified by a simple plate of freshly landed jumbo prawns from the loch.

Tish's quietly assured cooking pays proper attention to timing, seasoning and temperatures: for example, in a delicately textured but robustly flavoured ravioli of wild rabbit, with a hint of mustard and a stick of salsify; and in a full-flavoured, man-sized saddle of Argyll hill lamb, in an intense jus sharpened by pungent roast garlic, with Parmesan-gratiné asparagus and poached fennel. Seafood is deftly handled too. Squeaky roast queen scallops, 'with corals akimbo', come with lightly pickled sweet-and-sour vegetables, topped with vanilla foam, while an accurately pan-fried fillet of brill might be served with crushed white beans and a sage jus enlivened by a couple of capers.

The cheeseboard is wisely limited to two examples in peak condition – Scottish versions of Cheddar and Stilton – that come with crunchy, hand-crafted oatcakes. Desserts, meanwhile, are deceptively simple but highly accomplished: perhaps a definitive, wobbly, sheeny-white pannacotta, accompanied by strawberries poached in champagne, or a white Valrhona chocolate tart with a bitter chocolate and honey sauce. One of the few items in need of improvement is the coffee. Commendably, wines aim for interest and variety in the affordable stretches, throwing in all sort of grape varieties; but the more expensive (and comparatively conservative) options are equally tempting. Prices start at £16.

CHEF: Ben Tish   PROPRIETORS: Nicolas and Frances Ryan   OPEN: all week D only 7 to 9   CLOSED: Christmas and New Year   MEALS: Set D £40. Bar menu available   SERVICE: not inc, card slips closed   CARDS: Amex, MasterCard, Switch, Visa   DETAILS: 40 seats. 25 seats outside. Private parties: 65 main room. Car park. Vegetarian meals. Children's helpings. No smoking in dining room. Wheelchair access (also WC). No music   ACCOMMODATION: 20 rooms, all with bath/shower. TV. Phone. D,B&B £95 to £270. Rooms for disabled (*The Which? Hotel Guide*) £5

---

## CROSSMICHAEL   Dumfries & Galloway                                      map 11

# Plumed Horse ⅝✳

| | |
|---|---|
| Main Street, Crossmichael DG7 3AU | COOKING 6 |
| TEL: (01556) 670333 | MODERN EUROPEAN |
| WEBSITE: www.plumed-horse.co.uk | £27–£66 |

Nothing about the village, the small whitewashed building or the simply but tastefully decorated dining room suggests that the food here will be special. Nonetheless, it is 'worth making a long journey to enjoy a really memorable meal'. Since last year a sensible set dinner menu (three courses plus coffee) has been added to the options. Set menu choices may be limited to two items per course, and ingredients may sometimes overlap, but they are beguiling choices: perhaps including a jellied terrine of pork knuckle and foie gras to start, followed by salmon fillet with crab tortellini and saffron risotto.

Materials include free-range meats, and Kirkudbright-landed scallops and white fish, and techniques are well up to scratch: witness a small disc of truffle risotto of just the right texture, or a correctly cooked corn-fed chicken breast on shredded cabbage and bacon with a light yet intensely flavoured stock reduction. But it is the kitchen's versatility that stands out: for example in the accompaniments to roast fillet of sea bream (saffron and chilli chickpeas and a scallop and caviar fishcake), and in a dish of pork consisting of loin, honey-braised belly and tail, and sauté kidney, all served with candied turnips.

Desserts also bring a mixture of straightforwardness and invention, perhaps in the shape of banana brûlée with butterscotch sauce, or in a passion-fruit 'sausage' served with rhubarb and orange mash. The short wine list kicks off house red and white at £12.60, or £3.25 per large glass. Note that a £3 charge is levied on couples who share either a starter or dessert.

CHEFS: Tony Borthwick and James Pearce  PROPRIETOR: Tony Borthwick  OPEN: Tue to Fri and Sun L 12.30 to 1, Tue to Sat D 7 to 9  CLOSED: 2 weeks Jan, 2 weeks Sept  MEALS: alc (main courses £16 to £22). Set L Tue to Fri £15.95, Set L Sun £18.95, Set D Tue to Fri £25  SERVICE: not inc, card slips closed  CARDS: Delta, MasterCard, Switch, Visa  DETAILS: 30 seats. Private parties: 24 main room, 12 to 24 private rooms. No smoking. Wheelchair access (also WC). Music. No mobile phones. Air-conditioned

## CUPAR Fife
map 11

# Ostlers Close ▼ ✶

25 Bonnygate, Cupar KY15 4BU  
TEL: (01334) 655574  
WEBSITE: www.ostlersclose.co.uk  

COOKING 5  
MODERN SCOTTISH  
£28–£56

Hidden away down an alley off the high street in the centre of a small market town, Ostlers Close would not do well if it had to rely on passing trade. Fortunately, it has built up a devoted following over the past 20 years; don't be surprised to find that most of the clientele are regulars and well known to the Grahams, but expect just as warm and friendly a welcome if you are visiting for the first time.

'Think global, act local' might be a fitting axiom to sum up James Graham's philosophy: top-quality local produce is at the core of his cooking, although inspiration comes from far and wide, as exemplified by seared West Coast scallops with red pepper salsa, roast saddle of Shetland lamb with a lamb cassoulet, and roast duck breast with Bombay potatoes and plum sauce. The ongoing quest for quality materials has this year led the Grahams to employ a local fishmonger to make salt-cod, and lots of work goes on behind the scenes growing herbs, picking wild mushrooms, and making preserves such as pickled samphire and chilli chutney.

There are some surprises on the wine list, with Mexican Barbera and New Zealand Pinot Gris adding a *frisson* of excitement to the well-chosen offerings from France (to which the first few pages are devoted). Mark-ups throughout the eclectic, handwritten list are generally fair, leaving much to choose from under £20. House red and white are from Chile and sell for £14 and £13 respectively, or £3.50 by the glass.

CHEF: James Graham  PROPRIETORS: James and Amanda Graham  OPEN: Fri and Sat L 12.15 to 1.30, Tue to Sat D 7 to 9.30  MEALS: alc (main courses L £10.50 to £13.50, D £16.50 to £18.50)  SERVICE: not inc, card slips closed  CARDS: Amex, Delta, MasterCard, Switch, Visa  DETAILS: 26 seats. Private parties: 26 main room. Children's helpings. No smoking in dining room. No music. No mobile phones £5

*'Sorry my reports have become irregular but I spend half a year abroad. It's a pity I can't give you a report of an Albanian meal I ate recently. You would never complain about motorway service stations again.'* (From a frequent reporter to the Guide)

# Braidwoods ⚡✕

Drumastle Mill Cottage, Dalry KA24 4LN
TEL: (01294) 833544   FAX: (01294) 833553
EMAIL: keithbraidwood@btconnect
WEBSITE: www.braidwoods.co.uk
1m off A737 on Dalry to Saltcoats road

COOKING **6**
MODERN SCOTTISH
£29–£60

Braidwoods can be counted among the top dozen or so restaurants in Scotland. The long whitewashed cottage is reached down a winding path, and the setting is relaxing: 'formal but not stuffy' is how it struck one visitor, with its tasteful display of local artwork. Quite a few supplies are local too, and most of the other ingredients come from somewhere in Scotland: purposeful sourcing which gives drive and direction to Keith Braidwood's contemporary cooking.

The result is food with 'loads of character and flavours', and notable among successes has been an intensely flavoured soup of Arbroath smokie and finnan haddock, a dish of boneless quail stuffed with black pudding and served on a bed of Puy lentils, and top-quality pigeon paired with a fillet of venison. Baked fillet of west coast turbot typically comes on a risotto: for one visitor pea risotto with a surprisingly winning chicken stock sauce.

Desserts hit the comfort zone, taking in a warm dark chocolate soufflé pudding with cinnamon ice cream, bread-and-butter pudding, and banana crème brûlée with a bitter Valrhona chocolate ice cream. Nicola Braidwood dispenses friendly service, and well-chosen wines at generally sensible prices add to the appeal. There's a fair spread of half-bottles, and a quartet of house wines under £17.

CHEF: Keith Braidwood   PROPRIETORS: Keith and Nicola Braidwood   OPEN: Wed to Sun L 12 to 1.45, Tue to Sat D 7 to 9   CLOSED: 25 Dec, first 3 weeks Jan, first 2 weeks Sept   MEALS: Set L Sun £23, Set L Wed to Sat £15 (2 courses) to £18, Set D £30 to £34   SERVICE: not inc, card slips closed   CARDS: Amex, Delta, Diners, MasterCard, Switch, Visa   DETAILS: 24 seats. Private parties: 14 main room. Car park. No children under 12 at D. No smoking in dining room. No music. No mobile phones

# ▲ 2 Quail ⚡✕

Castle Street, Dornoch IV25 3SN
TEL: (01862) 811811
EMAIL: goodfood@2quail.com
WEBSITE: www.2quail.com

COOKING **4**
MODERN EUROPEAN-PLUS
£46–£55

There can't be much passing trade this far north of Inverness, so the Carrs' small restaurant with rooms sensibly sticks to dinner only, at a set price, with three choices per course. Menus may be short, but they provide a balanced and interesting selection of dishes, perhaps starting with tempura fried prawns, a cheese and chive soufflé, or lamb koftas with couscous and tsatsiki. Fish is likely to appear – perhaps as a salmon fishcake, or poached halibut with an oyster ravioli and vermouth sauce – but meat usually predominates among main courses. Gressingham duck breast might come with braised fennel, or perhaps with limes, while roast loin of lamb is typically paired with roast vegetables and thyme gravy.

If chocolate features among desserts it might be in a tart, accompanied by coconut ice cream, or as a chocolate pot flavoured with orange; otherwise there may be a rather classical 'floating islands' or vanilla bavarois. Wines are well chosen, and mostly under £30; if funds allow, consider Schloss Vollrads Riesling Spätlese 2000 (£28) or Dom. Tempier Bandol 1997 at £30. House Vin de Pays d'Oc is £13 (£2.75 a small glass).

CHEF: Michael Carr    PROPRIETORS: Michael and Kerensa Carr    OPEN: Tue to Sat D only 7.30 to 9.30    CLOSED: 2 weeks Feb/Mar, open Christmas and New Year by prior arrangement only    MEALS: Set D £35    SERVICE: not inc    CARDS: Amex, Delta, MasterCard, Switch, Visa    DETAILS: 18 seats. Private parties: 10 main room, 6 to 10 private rooms. No smoking in 1 dining room. Wheelchair access (not WC). Occasional music    ACCOMMODATION: 3 rooms, 2 with bath/shower. TV. B&B £35 to £80. No children under 8

## DUNKELD  Perthshire & Kinross                                    map 11

# ▲ Kinnaird ✸

Kinnaird Estate, by Dunkeld PH8 0LB
TEL: (01796) 482440    FAX: (01796) 482289
EMAIL: enquiry@kinnairdestate.com
WEBSITE: www.kinnairdestate.com                                    COOKING 6
from A9 2m N of Dunkeld, take B898, signposted              MODERN EUROPEAN
Kinnaird, for 4½m                                                £43–£71

As somewhere to relax and get away from it all, Kinnaird takes some beating. Its 9,000-acre estate helps, as do the sumptuously decorated rooms and the ministrations of Douglas Jack, 'the best hotel manager we have come across'. 'We are not the shooting and fishing types,' wrote one couple, who nevertheless enjoyed themselves immensely and are 'saving up to go again'.

Trevor Brooks's cooking is built on solid foundations. Abundant local produce includes game, salmon, trout, vegetables, cheese and fruit, as well as vegetables from the hotel's own walled garden, while on-site smoking takes in salmon, haddock, beef and cheese. Classical ideas and techniques underpin the repertoire and keep everything on track – roast squab pigeon comes with lentils, and breast of duck with a honey glaze – but there is enough ingenuity to keep interest on the boil. Seared red mullet is served as a starter with potato gnocchi and peas, and rabbit is subject to a number of treatments, its loin served with mushroom tortellini and truffle, or its leg stuffed with squid and perched on a vegetable and bacon risotto.

Dinner during low season (although with marginally less choice) is by no means a poor relation, and lunch offers the option of a hot salt-beef sandwich, as well as the full works, perhaps including a foie gras and smoked apple terrine, roast salt-cod with langoustine chowder, and hot prune and Armagnac soufflé. Other desserts to look out for include baked lemon tart with mascarpone sorbet, and chocolate negus with pistachio anglaise. Quality throughout the wine list is extremely high, but there are no bargains: a handful of French country wines are among the very few to make it under £20, including Vin de Pays d'Oc Syrah and Chardonnay house wines at £18.

CHEF: Trevor Brooks   PROPRIETOR: Constance Ward   OPEN: all week 12.30 to 1.45, 7 to 9.30
MEALS: Set L £30, Set D £45. Light L available   SERVICE: not inc, card slips closed   CARDS: Amex,
Delta, MasterCard, Switch, Visa   DETAILS: 35 seats. Private parties: 35 main room. Car park. No
children under 12. Jacket and tie. No smoking in dining room. Wheelchair access (also WC). No
music. No mobile phones   ACCOMMODATION: 9 rooms, all with bath/shower. TV. Phone. D,B&B
£225 to £475. Rooms for disabled. No children under 12. Fishing (The Which? Hotel Guide)

## EDINBURGH Edinburgh                                                    map 11

# Atrium ▼

| | |
|---|---|
| 10 Cambridge Street, Edinburgh EH1 2ED | COOKING 3 |
| TEL: (0131) 228 8882   FAX: (0131) 228 8808 | MODERN EUROPEAN |
| WEBSITE: www.atriumrestaurant.co.uk | £31–£63 |

Striking décor, featuring plenty of highly polished wood, canvas and wrought
metal, is bound to catch the eye at this trendy venue, sited in the heart of
Edinburgh's financial district close to several theatres. Food draws together a
mix of fashionable modern ideas, some rather ambitious-sounding, others with
more straightforward appeal. Among starters, for example, might be ragoût of
rabbit with sweet peppers, olives and potato, alongside risotto primavera with
Parmesan cracknel, or white bean soup garnished with confit duck,
demonstrating the kitchen's penchant for earthy flavours. Main courses follow
suit; typical offerings are fillet of cod with roast artichokes, wild mushrooms and
wild garlic leaves; loin of venison with pea purée, button onion and smoked
bacon sauce; and breast of maize-fed duck with fennel and onion marmalade,
fondant potato and squash purée. Finish on a rich note with tarte Tatin and
condensed milk ice cream, or perhaps chocolate pavé with cocoa sorbet and dark
chocolate sauce. The wine list throws the spotlight on some less famous (but
excellent quality) wine regions and producers around the globe. Italy, Spain
and North America are particular strengths, although the more traditional
Bordeaux, Rhône and Burgundy sections are rewarding too. Mark-ups are
sensible, while a selection at the front picks out interesting styles across the
price range. Bottle prices start at £14, with 16 wines by the glass.

CHEF: Neil Forbes   PROPRIETORS: Andrew and Lisa Radford   OPEN: Mon to Fri L 12 to 2, Mon to
Sat D 6 to 10   CLOSED: 25 and 26 Dec, New Year   MEALS: alc (main courses L £10 to £12.50, D
£14.50 to £20). Set D £25   SERVICE: not inc, 10% (optional) for parties of 6 or more   CARDS:
Amex, Delta, Diners, MasterCard, Switch, Visa   DETAILS: 70 seats. Private parties: 100 main
room. Vegetarian meals. Children's helpings. Wheelchair access (also WC). No music. Air-
conditioned

# ▲ Balmoral, Number One ⁵⋇

| | |
|---|---|
| 1 Princes Street, Edinburgh EH2 2EQ | |
| TEL: (0131) 557 6727   FAX: (0131) 557 8740 | COOKING 6 |
| EMAIL: numberone@thebalmoralhotel.com | MODERN EUROPEAN |
| WEBSITE: www.roccofortehotels.com | £31–£85 |

The bar, with its tinted mirrors, is nearly as large as the dining room of this
basement restaurant. Browns and creams predominate in the retro 1950s-style
décor, and fine materials are strewn over the menus: roast langoustine timbale,
or sauté duck foie gras to start, followed by grilled scallops, or squab pigeon. The

food is not complicated, which works very much in its favour, evident in wafer-thin circles of delicately marinated venison fillet, accompanied by a mound of earthy wild mushrooms in a pungent truffle dressing, all flavours working well together. And saucing technique is exemplary, including a straightforward yet well-judged stock-based red wine version, to go with tasty chicken, Puy lentils and 'the best creamed cabbage ever'.

The food is light and yet doesn't compromise on flavour, producing an escabeche of outstandingly fresh red mullet fillet, fragrant with saffron. Items on a plate are intelligently combined, rendering results that are greater than the sum of their parts: for example, a 'simple but wonderfully effective' dish of rich, moist, braised oxtail meat, removed from the bone and wrapped in gently salty prosciutto (osso buco is treated the same way), in a rich Madeira and stock sauce. Desserts are as enticing as the rest, taking in a hot banana and chocolate chip soufflé, and warm rice pudding with exotic fruits and a champagne sabayon.

A choice array of loaves ('wonderful walnut, excellent garlic, fine tomato') is brought to table and sliced to order. Service is affable and friendly, and anybody looking for a bargain should head straight for the set-price lunch menu: less than half the price of the same dishes at dinner. Perhaps lunch is subsidised by the wine list, which does no favours to those on a tight budget. Prices start at £18, and Viña Esmeralda from Torres, for example, which retails at around £6, here costs £30. Quality is high too, though, and the list is well chosen.

CHEF: Jeff Bland  PROPRIETOR: Rocco Forte Hotels  OPEN: Mon to Fri L 12 to 2, all week D 7 to 10 (10.30 Fri and Sat)  MEALS: alc (main courses £19.50 to £22.50). Set L £12.50 (2 courses) to £15.50, Set D £38.50 to £52.50  SERVICE: not inc  CARDS: Amex, Delta, Diners, MasterCard, Switch, Visa  DETAILS: 50 seats. Private parties: 100 main room. Children's helpings. No smoking in 1 dining room. Wheelchair access (also WC). Music. No mobile phones. Air-conditioned  ACCOMMODATION: 186 rooms, all with bath/shower. TV. Phone. Room only £115 to £275. Rooms for disabled. Baby facilities. Swimming pool

# Blue £

10 Cambridge Street, Edinburgh EH1 2ED
TEL: (0131) 221 1222  FAX: (0131) 228 8808
WEBSITE: www.bluebarcafe.com

COOKING 2
MODERN BRITISH
£23–£50

On the ground floor is Atrium (see entry), above it is this vibrant, up-to-the-minute venue. It looks the part, and slots neatly into twenty-first-century Edinburgh. Menus change monthly and, in true contemporary fashion, descriptions are pared to the ee cummings bone ('grilled mackerel, pickled vegetables', for example). Soups – such as cream of spinach, nutmeg and mascarpone – kick off proceedings, along with sandwiches and 'light blue' items such as smoked haddock and leek risotto with poached egg. Generous mains range from rump of lamb with bubble and squeak and pea purée, to roast salmon with spiced couscous. Raspberry crème brûlée and Malteser ice cream exemplify desserts. Children are well fed until 8pm, and early-evening menus suit the needs of culture vultures heading for the nearby Traverse Theatre and Usher Hall. The wine list is also minimalist – brief, crisp, unannotated – with prices from £13.10 to £28.60, and 11 wines by the glass, all under £4.

CHEF: David Haetzman   PROPRIETORS: Andrew and Lisa Radford   OPEN: Mon to Sat 12 to 3, 6 to 11   CLOSED: 25 and 26 Dec, New Year   MEALS: alc (main courses £10.50 to £13.50). Set L £9.95 (2 courses) to £12.95, Set D 6 to 7.30 £11.95 (2 courses) to £14.95   SERVICE: not inc, 10% for parties of 6 or more   CARDS: Amex, Delta, Diners, MasterCard, Switch, Visa   DETAILS: 120 seats. Private parties:120 main room. Vegetarian meals. No children after 8pm. Children's helpings. Wheelchair access (also WC). Music. Air-conditioned

## ▲ The Bonham ⚡✕

35 Drumsheugh Gardens, Edinburgh EH3 7RN
TEL: (0131) 623 9319   FAX: (0131) 226 6080                          COOKING 4
EMAIL: restaurant@thebonham.com                          MODERN EUROPEAN
WEBSITE: www.thebonham.com                                        £26–£53

The hotel aims for stylish and comfortable, while the modern dining rooms – the non-smoking one at the back abuts the kitchen – are more brasserie-like. Some think of what's on offer here as good cooking let down by poor service, others as good service let down by poor food, hence the words 'pot' and 'luck' probably best cover such inconsistencies. Either way, lunch is a bit of a steal, offering perhaps a dazzlingly bright green watercress soup, and a risotto of tiger prawns ('few but tasty'), while the slightly more ambitious dinner goes in for red mullet and potato terrine with lemon oil, and steamed sea bass fillet with pesto mash, cockles and a chive sauce.

Evident skill is brought to bear in a crisp pastry tartlet of artichokes with a light pesto dressing, and in a generous rectangle of accurately timed, crisp-skinned salmon, although rare ribeye steak comes with a rather mean portion of béarnaise. High-quality chocolate parfait of 'ethereal texture' is one star among desserts, while others have championed a rich chocolate sponge pudding with maple syrup and pecans, and tasty glazed pears with balsamic vinegar. Staff are, at best, friendly and efficient, although they are not always at their best. A compact wine list does the business (with eight by the glass from £3.50), backed up by a short list of more special bottles.

CHEF: Michel Bouyer   PROPRIETOR: Peter Taylor, The Town House Company   OPEN: all week 12 to 2.30 (12.30 to 3 Sun), 6.30 to 10   MEALS: alc D (main courses £11.50 to £18). Set L £12.50 (2 courses) to £15   SERVICE: not inc   CARDS: Amex, MasterCard, Switch, Visa   DETAILS: 60 seats. Private parties: 60 main room, 4 to 24 private rooms. Vegetarian meals. No smoking in 1 dining room. Wheelchair access (also WC). Music   ACCOMMODATION: 48 rooms, all with bath/shower. TV. Phone. B&B £140 to £325. Rooms for disabled. Baby facilities (*The Which? Hotel Guide*) £5

## Café St Honoré ⚡✕

34 NW Thistle Street Lane, Edinburgh EH2 1EA                          COOKING 2
TEL: (0131) 226 2211                                            MODERN BISTRO
WEBSITE: www.cafesthonore.com                                      £27–£50

'A pastiche French bistro with a noisy, buzzy, happy atmosphere' is how one reporter summed up this tiny atmospheric place down a cobbled lane. Aged mirrored walls, varnished brown ceilings and a bar crammed with bottles set the mood. What it offers is 'full-flavoured, not overworked food': chicken liver tartlets, smoked haddock with a poached egg, and 'great steaks', not to mention mighty helpings of boeuf bourguignonne. This is food for those with 'gargantuan capacity', and it can seem cumulatively rich, although plum tomato and fennel soup, or a warm salad of scallops, monkfish and chorizo with pine nuts, show the healthier side of things. Saddle of venison with red cabbage, bacon and wild mushrooms, and navarin of lamb with mash are immensely satisfying, and there isn't much light relief among desserts of bread-and-butter pudding with vanilla sauce, or lemon mousse in a dark chocolate cup. Service is sharp and alert, while the wine list promises plenty of affordable drinking. Ten house selections are £10.50 and £10.95.

CHEFS: Chris Colverson and Garrett O'Hanlan   PROPRIETORS: Chris and Gill Colverson   OPEN: Mon to Sat and Sun during Festival 12 to 2.15, 5 (6 Sat) to 10   CLOSED: 3 days Christmas, 3 days New Year, Apr and May bank hols   MEALS: alc (main courses L £8 to £14.50, D £13.50 to £19). Set D 5 to 7 £9 (2 courses) to £18   SERVICE: not inc, 10% for parties of 8 or more   CARDS: Amex, Delta, Diners, MasterCard, Switch, Visa   DETAILS: 45 seats. Private parties: 45 main room, 6 to 28 private rooms. Vegetarian meals. Children's helpings. No smoking in 1 dining room. Wheelchair access (not WC). Music

---

## ▲ Channings ⚡✳

**NEW ENTRY**

15 South Learmonth Gardens,
Edinburgh EH4 1EZ
TEL: (0131) 315 2225   FAX: (0131) 332 9631
EMAIL: restaurant@channings.co.uk
WEBSITE: www.channings.co.uk

COOKING 4
MODERN SCOTTISH
£29–£61

Part of a chain of small luxury hotels (The Bonham, see above, is in the same group), Channings is understated, luxurious, with a peaceful ambience and a 'Victorian feel'. Wood panelling also lends it a studious air, and although the dining room is not large, tables are well spaced. Richard Glennie works within a classical framework, yet is no slave to it, producing an impressive combination of sweet scallops with flavourful garlic cauliflower purée, well set off by its tomato and caper accompaniment, and accurately cooked and seasoned sea bass with crisp skin and moist flesh, accompanied by scallops and a sauce redolent of shellfish stock.

The food is distinguished by the integrity of its flavours: everything on the plate is there for a reason, not just added to make it look pretty, as a couple of poultry dishes confirm. A fine, tasty chicken breast, with chicken mousse stuffed under the skin, is served with herb gnocchi, leeks and broad beans, and a first-class deep-flavoured duck breast, with an even better confit encased in cabbage, comes with a rich, sticky and wonderfully complementary date and stock sauce. Intense flavours are typical of desserts, which have included an iced coconut parfait with a mango coulis, and a dark chocolate bavarois with white chocolate sorbet. Service is welcoming, friendly and efficient, while wines on the 50-strong list are classified according to style, kick off at £12, and stay mostly below £20. Seven are served by the glass at £3.50.

CHEF: Richard Glennie   PROPRIETOR: Peter Taylor, The Town House Company   OPEN: Tue to Sat 12.30 to 2, 7 to 9.30 (10 Fri and Sat)   MEALS: Set L £15 (2 courses) to £18, Set D £23 (2 courses) to £27. Gourmet menu L and D £38 (whole table only)   SERVICE: not inc   CARDS: Amex, Delta,

Diners, MasterCard, Switch, Visa   DETAILS: 34 seats. Private parties: 34 main room, 4 to 18 private rooms. Vegetarian meals. No smoking in dining room. Music   ACCOMMODATION: 46 rooms, all with bath/shower. TV. Phone. B&B £130 to £210. Baby facilities  £5

## Fishers ♥

| | |
|---|---|
| 1 Shore, Leith, Edinburgh EH6 6QW | COOKING **2** |
| TEL: (0131) 554 5666 | INTERNATIONAL SEAFOOD |
| | £26–£46 |

Fresh seafood is the main business of the day at this bustling one-time pub on the Leith waterfront. Eat casually in the crowded bar or opt for the more formal restaurant overlooking the water. The kitchen revels in kaleidoscopic flavours, and there's more than a hint of fusion about the results. Even something as simple as grilled lemon sole might surface with wasabi and samphire butter, while a salad of seared salmon sashimi contains ginger and orange aïoli, mizuna leaves and candied chillies; halibut might appear with roast pumpkin, beetroot and rocket salad. Meat eaters are not ignored, although raw materials receive similarly exotic treatment: five-spice belly pork with lime-grilled sweet potato and tamarind sauce, for example. Tingling fresh sorbets and ice creams provide a palate-cleansing finale. A second branch has opened: see entry below. Wine-wise, the short 'fine wines' section is the most interesting part of the list, offering decent value from notable producers. Mark-ups throughout are commendably low, with the majority of bottles under £20. Prices – for house red and white vins de pays – start at £9.75.

CHEFS: Sally Findlay, Glyn Sommerville, Kerr Marrion and Richard Hilton   PROPRIETORS: Graeme Lumsden and James Millar   OPEN: all week 12 to 10   CLOSED: 25 and 26 Dec, 1 Jan   MEALS: alc (main courses £9 to £17). Bar menu available   SERVICE: not inc, 10% for parties of 8 or more   CARDS: Amex, Diners, MasterCard, Switch, Visa   DETAILS: 50 seats. Private parties: 30 main room. No music. No mobile phones

## Fishers in the City ♥ ⅝ £            | NEW ENTRY |

| | |
|---|---|
| 58 Thistle Street, Edinburgh EH2 1EN | |
| TEL: (0131) 225 5109   FAX: (0131) 225 5434 | COOKING **3** |
| EMAIL: enquiries@fishersbistros.co.uk | SEAFOOD |
| WEBSITE: www.fishersbistros.co.uk | £23–£52 |

An offshoot of the Leith original (see entry above), this is a lively, congenial, unhurried, bistro-style place serving mostly fish to a largely cosmopolitan crowd. Casual at the front, more formal beyond the open-to-view kitchen, it sports black and white photographs on deep ochre walls, and the absence of either tablecloths or side plates points to its straightforward, down-to-business approach. Impressively sourced ingredients, and a broadly based menu backed up by blackboard specials (including lobster and crayfish at market prices), set the tone for some more than capable cooking, from a delicate, creamy soup of celeriac and Jerusalem artichoke, to halibut stuffed with wild mushrooms, wrapped in Bayonne ham and coated in chervil hollandaise.

Less usual offerings might include richly flavoured tuna-like Australian wild salmon, or expertly pan-fried garfish ('a meaty, white, eel-like species'), served with a potato salad incorporating wild garlic and smoked bacon in a cider and pink peppercorn dressing. Zingily sharp and precisely judged salsas add to the pleasure, carnivores might be offered lamb cutlets, and vegetables are so well treated that vegetarians might fare better than at some more specialised outlets. Desserts are not in the same class, although warm chocolate tart with vanilla ice cream is recommended. Service is knowledgeable and friendly. The wine list is a good read, with lively styles from the Old and New Worlds, particularly Australia, France and Italy (for reds). A fine wine section features some good stock, mainly from Burgundy, and there is fair choice by the glass. Prices kick off with house vin de pays at £10.95 (£2.95 a glass).

CHEFS: Brendan Sugars and Andy Bird  PROPRIETORS: J. Graeme Lumsden and James Millar  OPEN: all week 12 (12.30 Sun) to 10.30  MEALS: alc (main courses £8.50 to £19)  SERVICE: not inc, 10% for parties of 6 or more  CARDS: Amex, Delta, MasterCard, Switch, Visa  DETAILS: 90 seats. Vegetarian meals. Children's helpings. No smoking in 1 dining room. Wheelchair access (also WC). Music

# (fitz) Henry

19 Shore Place, Leith, Edinburgh EH6 6SW
TEL: (0131) 555 6625   FAX: (0131) 555 0025
EMAIL: mail@fitzhenrys.com
WEBSITE: www.fitzhenrys.com

COOKING 4
FRENCH/BRASSERIE
£28–£53

Although it calls itself a brasserie, (fitz) Henry has all the hallmarks of a serious restaurant. Walk into a welcoming, high-ceilinged bar, and then into a dining room with red upholstery and crisp white napery. Despite a vaguely medieval feel from the cast iron chandelier and stone-flagged floor, it is relaxed, well run, and combines informality with efficiency. The kitchen's contemporary French outlook embraces mainstream ideas, from a terrine of foie gras with fig chutney to artichoke barigoule with matching mousse, yet within its disciplined framework Hubert Lamort still finds room for some intriguing variety.

He serves roast cod with deep-fried chickpea cakes and wilted spinach, and accompanies a potato and onion tartlet with roast Reblochon and chicory fondue. Other materials include lamb from the Pentlands, Highland venison and west coast scallops, while desserts run to a walnut and frangipane tart, and iced banana parfait with chocolate brownie. Wine mark-ups are on the high side, but the list has an eye for both quality and diversity.

CHEF: Hubert Lamort  PROPRIETORS: Valerie Faichney and Alan Morrison  OPEN: Mon to Fri L 12 to 2.30, Mon to Sat D 6.30 to 10  CLOSED: 25 and 26 Dec, 1 to 16 Jan  MEALS: alc D (main courses £12 to £17). Set L £9.50 (1 course) to £16.  SERVICE: not inc  CARDS: Amex, Delta, MasterCard, Switch, Visa  DETAILS: 60 seats. Private parties: 40 main room, 20 to 40 private rooms. Car park. Vegetarian meals. Children's helpings. Wheelchair access (also WC). Music. No mobile phones. Air-conditioned  (£5)

---

'[Starters] were ridiculously nouvelle ... When I asked my companion if she would like to try my salad – a few twists of tomato flesh, tiny criss-crossed asparagus tips and a minute pile of salad leaves – she peered at my plate and asked, "Where is it?"'
(On eating in the West Country)

---

# Haldanes ♥ ⅝✳

39A Albany Street, Edinburgh EH1 3QY
TEL: (0131) 556 8407   FAX: (0131) 556 2662
EMAIL: dinehaldanes@aol.com
WEBSITE: www.haldanesrestaurant.com

COOKING 3
MODERN SCOTTISH
£39–£63

It is all very low key in this sedate, old-fashioned basement. One traveller relishing the squashy sofas in the lounge 'kept thinking I should curl up and read a book'. The kitchen uses traditional Scottish ingredients in sometimes innovative and interesting ways, although it seems that meat and game are treated with more respect than fish. Braised lamb shank (perhaps served with a vegetable panache and Puy lentils) has been praised, along with richly flavoured venison with a 'tartish' beetroot sauce and celeriac mash. Starters such as a crisp filo tartlet of crab and onion with smoked salmon cream sauce show a degree of culinary professionalism, and desserts have shone out: witness a delicate nougatine glacée accompanied by a raspberry coulis with 'real flavour', or 'quivery' white chocolate pannacotta with black cherries doused in rum and vanilla. Details such as home-baked rolls and the home-made fudge served with coffee add to the overall comfort. Service is affable, and the wine list is very well-chosen, with top-notch producers from Old World and New. A list of ten house selections (available by 175ml and 250ml glass from £3) starts off at £12.85 a bottle for Spanish red and white. There's a 'food with wine guide' and a nifty chart showing which claret vintages from the various communes are ready to drink and which are not.

CHEF: George Kelso   PROPRIETORS: George and Michelle Kelso   OPEN: all week D only 6 to 9 (9.30 Fri and Sat)   CLOSED: 1 Jan   MEALS: alc (main courses £17 to £21.50)   SERVICE: not inc   CARDS: Amex, Delta, Diners, MasterCard, Switch, Visa   DETAILS: 50 seats. Private parties: 50 main room, 8 to 20 private rooms. Vegetarian meals. Children's helpings. No smoking in dining room. Occasional music. No mobile phones  (£5)

# Kalpna ⅝✳ £

2–3 St Patrick Square, Edinburgh EH8 9EZ
TEL: (0131) 667 9890

COOKING 2
INDIAN VEGETARIAN
£12–£38

For two decades Ajay Bhartdwaj has been delivering a highly distinctive version of Indian vegetarian cooking in his utilitarian restaurant. The menu offers a cocktail of dishes drawn mainly from Gujarat, southern India and Rajasthan, so expect a fascinating mix of the familiar and the esoteric, from samosas and pakoras to aloo firdoshi (potato 'barrels' stuffed with pistachios, raisins and coriander) and hader chuman (a hot-and-sour combo of sun-dried tomatoes, home-made cheese, baby corn, green chillies, and vegetables). Rice includes brown as well as basmati. On Wednesday nights there is an extensive thali buffet: 'take a small amount each time with a separate helping of rice,' advised one correspondent, who sampled seve tameta (tomatoes in onion gravy), gobhi naranghi (cauliflower in orange juice with melon seeds) and more. Simpler buffets are the order of the day at lunchtime. Service can be 'cool', but the well-planned wine list is worth exploring. House wine is £9.50.

CHEF/PROPRIETOR: Ajay Bhartdwaj   OPEN: Mon to Sat L 12 to 2.30, all week D 5.30 to 10.30 (10 Sun)   CLOSED: Christmas, New Year   MEALS: alc (main courses £4.50 to £7.50). Set L £5 (2 courses) to £5.50, Set D £9.50 to £15   SERVICE: 10%, card slips closed   CARDS: MasterCard, Visa   DETAILS: 60 seats. Private parties: 65 main room. Vegetarian meals. No smoking in dining room. Wheelchair access (not WC). Occasional music

# Martins  🍷 🍴 🥖

| | |
|---|---|
| 70 Rose Street North Lane, Edinburgh EH4 3DX | COOKING 3 |
| TEL: (0131) 225 3106   FAX: (0131) 220 3403 | MEDITERRANEAN |
| EMAIL: martinirons@fsbdial.co.uk | £30–£62 |

A new team has settled into the kitchen of this rather intimate restaurant since the last edition of the Guide, and the dining room has been given a facelift with fashionable vanilla walls and green dado. Otherwise little else has changed. Martins sets its own reputable low-key standards in a 'purist' Muzak- and smoke-free atmosphere where fine food is enjoyed quietly. Menus vary from day to day and the style is fashionably Mediterranean, with emphasis on the sweetness and smoothness of roasted tomatoes and caramelised shallots; even the freshly baked bread comes with rocket vinaigrette instead of butter.

Soups have included a red pepper version with crème fraîche, and pink breast of wood pigeon has come with an ultra-silky foie gras sauce. Centrepieces show plenty of assurance, although details can let the side down: lacklustre fennel and risotto with seared fillets of sea bass, for example, or 'squishy' garlic potatoes alongside splendidly tender roast rack of lamb. Desserts might feature seasonal rhubarb tarte Tatin, or a 'triumphant marriage' of bitter espresso crème brûlée with crushed mascarpone and Amaretto cheesecake; but leave room for the impressive selection of unpasteurised Scottish cheeses. Wines are sourced from around the globe. France is quite strong, as are such food-friendly areas as Alsace (with a range of bottles from Rolly Gassmann) and Austria (wines by top producer Willi Bründlmayer). Mark-ups are erratic: fair on some, higher on others, such as a Cloudy Bay Chardonnay 1998 for £33.95. Five house wines (all £14; £2.30/£3.50 by the glass) are good value.

CHEFS: Jason Gallagher and Neil Mackenzie   PROPRIETORS: Martin and Gay Irons   OPEN: Tue to Fri L 12 to 2, Tue to Sat D 7 to 10 (6.30 to 11 during Festival)   CLOSED: 24 Dec to 21 Jan, 1 week end May, 1 week end Sept   MEALS: alc (main courses £16 to £23). Set L £13.50 (2 courses), Set D £25   SERVICE: not inc, 10% (optional) for parties of 6 or more   CARDS: Amex, Delta, Diners, MasterCard, Switch, Visa   DETAILS: 50 seats. Private parties: 30 main room, 8 to 20 private rooms. Vegetarian meals. No children under 8. No smoking in dining room. Wheelchair access (not WC). No music. No mobile phones

# Off the Wall  NEW ENTRY

| | |
|---|---|
| 105 High Street, Edinburgh EH1 1SG | COOKING 4 |
| TEL/FAX: (0131) 558 1497 | MODERN SCOTTISH |
| WEBSITE: www.off-the-wall.co.uk | £26–£60 |

'Tranquil dining in a brilliant situation' is how a reporter described this first-floor restaurant overlooking the Royal Mile just off North Bridge. Tables with white cloths are well spaced, lighting is subdued, the mood relaxed and cosmopolitan. Off the wall it's certainly not, though: this is a smooth operation with a courteous welcome, expert service and assured cooking.

Chef/proprietor David Anderson's clean and simple dishes match the surroundings, his style, classically based with modern influences, making use of skilfully selected local produce. Menus are consequently seasonally based, but Scottish beef always features, perhaps full-flavoured fillet served with red cabbage, a well-judged port sauce and 'exceptional' truffle butter mash; or saddle of spring lamb with artichoke, fine beans, tomato confit and a well-executed rosemary jus. A starter of roast cod in an intense crab broth with tiny salmon gnocchi has proved a 'triumph of flavour and texture contrast', while caramelised pineapple Tatin with crisp, buttery puff pastry and caramel sauce is typical of puddings. The discerning, keenly chosen wine list soon passes £20, but house wines start at £13.75 and £13.95 for, respectively, Chilean Sauvignon Blanc and South African Pinotage, and around half a dozen bottles are sold by the glass.

CHEF: David Anderson   PROPRIETORS: David Anderson and Aileen Wilson   OPEN: Mon to Sat 12 to 2, 5.30 to 10.30   MEALS: alc D (main courses £15 to £19). Set L £12.50 (2 courses) to £15.50 SERVICE: not inc   CARDS: Amex, Delta, MasterCard, Switch, Visa   DETAILS: 44 seats. Private parties: 44 main room. Vegetarian meals. Children's helpings. Occasional music  (£5)

# Restaurant Martin Wishart

54 The Shore, Leith, Edinburgh EH6 6RA
TEL/FAX: (0131) 553 3557
EMAIL: info@martin-wishart.co.uk
WEBSITE: www.martin-wishart.co.uk

COOKING 6
MODERN FRENCH
£27–£72

The continued popularity of this Leith waterfront venue makes it difficult to get into; you may need to book a couple of months in advance for a weekend visit, though expansion into the next-door premises, in progress as the Guide went to press, should help to make it easier to sample Martin Wishart's stylishly distinctive take on haute cuisine.

The cooking can be intricate and complex, meals are elaborated further with appetisers and pre-desserts, and luxury ingredients are to the fore: a starter assiette of oysters, for example, features them cold with smoked salmon and Muscadet jelly, poached with vermicelli pasta and champagne, and as beignets flavoured with chives and ginger. Main courses can raise the stakes further: witness roast halibut fillet with slices of glazed pig's trotter, confit tomato, braised endive, pomme galette and sauce gribiche. Simpler-sounding items are also available, however, such as braised shin of beef with celeriac purée, glazed winter vegetables, and pommes Anna with prunes.

Judging by reports – both in terms of number received and level of enthusiasm expressed – its elevated reputation is deserved, with an inspector's meal hitting some 'truly great' heights: for example, a starter of foie gras roulade formed into a conical tower surrounded by an intensely flavoured Madeira jelly and given textural contrast by a light salad of apple and hazelnuts. Fruit is used to good effect in puddings – summer berry mousse, say, or caramelised rhubarb tart – with perhaps a mille-feuille of white and dark chocolate mousse among alternatives. Slick service is overseen by an 'excellent' maître d', and a democratic wine list offers something to suit most budgets, with quality high across the board, starting with organic house wines at £13.50 to £14.50.

CHEF/PROPRIETOR: Martin Wishart   OPEN: Tue to Fri L 12 to 2, Tue to Sat D 7 to 10   CLOSED: Christmas and New Year   MEALS: alc (main courses £16.50 to £19.50). Set L £14.50 (2 courses) to £16.50, Set D £45   SERVICE: not inc, 10% for parties of 6 or more   CARDS: MasterCard, Switch, Visa   DETAILS: 45 seats. Private parties: 50 main room. Children's helpings. No smoking before 2pm and 10pm; no cigars/pipes in dining room. Wheelchair access (also WC). Occasional music. No mobile phones. Air-conditioned

## ▲ The Scotsman                                    NEW ENTRY

20 North Bridge, Edinburgh EH1 1YT
TEL: North Bridge (0131) 622 2900; Vermilion (0131) 622 2814
FAX: (0131) 652 3652                                           COOKING 2
EMAIL: northbridge@thescotsmanhotelgroup.co.uk;      BRASSERIE/MODERN
vermilion@thescotsmanhotelgroup.co.uk                    EUROPEAN
WEBSITE: www.thescotsmanhotel.co.uk                        £26–£66

Fashioned from the former offices of *The Scotsman* newspaper in the centre of Edinburgh, this is a two-pronged operation. North Bridge Brasserie occupies a high wood-panelled room dominated by four large marble pillars surrounding an island bar, with more seats on a balcony up the flight of steel stairs. It is a place to drink, watch sushi being made, and eat from a brasserie menu: half a dozen oysters, Moroccan lentil and pancetta soup with Greek yoghurt, and flavourful crab cake with mizuna salad and a chilli dip. As well as sushi and sashimi, the Japanese section also delivers tempura prawns (three for £8.50) with a dip made from bonito flakes, while the carte offers grills of fish and meat, each with a choice of six sauces, four potato and four side dishes. Among the options might be half a dozen well-cooked scallops (plus corals) with salsa verde and 'great chips', or beef fillet with a first-class béarnaise sauce and good olive mash. Finish with an unusual warm chocolate beetroot cake with mascarpone ice cream, or a selection of cheese with a purée of spiced pears and chunky oatcakes. There are formal eating times, but snack food is available throughout the day. A colourful, annotated list divides the wines into groups according to style, and aims for interest and quality rather than bargains. House wines are £13.50.

Vermilion, in the basement, is the more formal dining room, decorated in dark brown with backlit bottles in glass cases. Its three-course weekly-changing menu calls on a welter of contemporary flourishes, such as foie gras with cauliflower cream and celery jelly. Fine materials are deployed: for example, in a light-textured tian of crab and lobster with a gazpacho made from sweet peppers, and in flavourful seared tuna with accurately poached eggs and a well-judged bean salad, a dish whose whole was judged greater than the sum of its parts. Meat options, meanwhile, have embraced tender, cumin-flavoured rack of lamb, served with couscous spiked with onion and aubergine, and topped with some first-rate fried sweetbreads. Raspberry clafoutis is more of a pastry tart (with crème patissière) than a clafoutis, while banana parfait comes with a mango salsa, and warm dark chocolate tart with mascarpone sorbet. Wines are a more serious affair too, in terms of both quality and price. Very few come in under £20, which is the asking price for house Australian Chardonnay (Riddoch Estate) and South African Cabernet Sauvignon (Graham Beck).

CHEF: Jeff Balharrie   PROPRIETOR: Scotsman Hotel Group   OPEN: North Bridge all week 12.15 to 2.30, 6 to 10.30; Vermilion Tue to Sat D only 7 to 10   CLOSED: Christmas   MEALS: North Bridge alc (main courses £7.50 to £15), Set L £9.45 (2 courses), Set D £13.50 (2 courses). Vermilion Set D £39   SERVICE: not inc   CARDS: Amex, Delta, Diners, MasterCard, Switch, Visa   DETAILS: 85 seats North Bridge, 30 seats Vermilion. Private parties: 30 Vermilion. Vegetarian meals both restaurants. Children's helpings North Bridge. No smoking Vermilion. Wheelchair access (also WC), Music and air-conditioned both restaurants   ACCOMMODATION: 68 rooms, all with bath/shower. TV. Phone. Room only £175 to £950. Rooms for disabled. Baby facilities. Swimming pool (*The Which? Hotel Guide*)

## Shore ✻ £

3 Shore, Leith, Edinburgh EH6 6QW
TEL/FAX: (0131) 553 5080
EMAIL: enquiries@the.shore.ukf.net
WEBSITE: www.edinburghrestaurants.co.uk/shore.html

COOKING 2
SEAFOOD
£23–£42

Live folk music and Latin jazz regularly add to the buzz at this eighteenth-century house overlooking the Water of Leith. Even without the music, it is not short of atmosphere, being split into a bustling traditional bar and a smart but informal wood-panelled dining room, warmed by open fires in winter and festooned with potted plants and flowers. The kitchen focuses on seafood, offering a daily-changing menu that keeps a weather eye on the seasons and aims to make the most of fresh ingredients without over-elaboration. In practice, this means pan-fried squid in sun-blush tomato mayonnaise, or sardines with rosemary and balsamic vinegar, followed by chilli- and herb-crusted roast cod with orange and coriander sauce, or grilled halibut with black pudding, smoked salmon and basil oil. Appealing vegetarian and game options offer an alternative, and wines represent fair value and decent choice, including eight by the glass from £1.90. House Côtes du Roussillon is £10.40.

CHEFS: Dan Styles, Alison Bryant and Mel Prentice   PROPRIETOR: Stuart Linsley   OPEN: all week 12 to 2.30 (3 Sat and Sun), 6.30 to 10   CLOSED: 25 and 26 Dec, 1 and 2 Jan   MEALS: alc (main courses L £7.50 to £11.50, D £11 to £15)   SERVICE: not inc, 10% for parties of 8 or more   CARDS: Amex, Delta, Diners, MasterCard, Switch, Visa   DETAILS: 36 seats. 12 seats outside. Private parties: 36 main room. Vegetarian meals. Children's helpings. No smoking in dining room. Wheelchair access (not WC). Music  (£5)

## Skippers £

1A Dock Place, Leith, Edinburgh EH6 6LU
TEL: (0131) 554 1018   FAX: (0131) 553 5988
EMAIL: info@skippers.co.uk
WEBSITE: www.skippers.co.uk

COOKING 2
SEAFOOD
£22–£54

Fresh fish in unvarnished surroundings sums up this long-serving Leith bistro. A homely, welcoming atmosphere prevails, and the kitchen continues to plough its tried and trusted furrow, delivering high-quality seafood with the minimum of culinary interference. Some dishes are fixtures – home-cured gravlax, fish soup, oysters with shallot vinaigrette – but it pays to explore the list of daily specials. Buttered Finnan haddock appears with asparagus and rarebit topping for lunch, while in the evening there could be fillets of wild sea bass on tomato fondue. Meat eaters might opt for roast loin of Border lamb or ribeye steaks, and there are tarts filled with goats' cheese and pesto for vegetarians. Finish with rhubarb crème brûlée or chocolate brownie with vanilla cream. The wine list majors on Sauvignon blanc and Chardonnay, and prices are affordable. Six house wines start at £9.75.

CHEFS: Mary Walker and Matt Flintney  PROPRIETORS: Gavin and Karen Ferguson  OPEN: all week 12.30 to 2 (2.30 Sun), 7 to 10  CLOSED: 24 to 26 Dec, 31 Dec to 2 Jan  MEALS: alc (main courses L £6.50 to £17, D £12 to £20)  SERVICE: not inc, 10% for parties of 6 or more  CARDS: Amex, Delta, MasterCard, Switch, Visa  DETAILS: 66 seats. 10 seats outside. Private parties: 20 main room, 30 private room. Wheelchair access (also WC). Music

# Tower Restaurant 🍴✶

Museum of Scotland, Chambers Street,
Edinburgh EH1 1JF
TEL: (0131) 225 3003  FAX: (0131) 220 4392
EMAIL: mail@tower-restaurant.com
WEBSITE: www.tower-restaurant.com

COOKING 2
SEAFOOD/MODERN BRITISH
£33–£68

The entrance can be unwelcoming after the Museum of Scotland has closed, but the long dining room (reached by a lift) looks smart and swish, with great views of the skyline, particularly the castle. It puts out a populist menu running the gamut from pub favourites to comfort food: expect prawn cocktail, fish and chips with pea purée, and grilled calf's liver soft enough to spread on toast. Sound materials provide the foundation for light, well-made, flavourful tuna nori rolls with pickled ginger and fierce wasabi, for a satisfyingly rich duck liver pâté with a pleasing fruit chutney, and for a ribeye steak, cooked medium-rare as ordered, with potato wedges and Dijon mustard. Basic cold seafood items take in half a dozen rock oysters, and Buckie crab with mayo, while traditional puddings might take the form of glazed lemon tart, or a first-rate vanilla cheesecake with glazed plum. Service is if anything too attentive, prices are more ambitious than the food warrants, and wines favour the Old World though touch down in the New as well. The list is organised according to price, and a dozen wines by the 175ml glass range from £3.50 to £6.25.

CHEF: Steven Adair  PROPRIETOR: James Thomson  OPEN: all week 12 to 5, 5 to 11  CLOSED: 25 and 26 Dec  MEALS: alc (main courses L £8 to £18, D £12 to £24). Set D 5 to 6.30 £12 (2 courses)  SERVICE: not inc, card slips closed, 10% for parties of 6 or more  CARDS: Amex, Delta, Diners, MasterCard, Switch, Visa  DETAILS: 90 seats. 130 seats outside. Private parties: 200 main room, 20 to 90 private rooms. Vegetarian meals. No smoking in dining room. Wheelchair access (also WC). Music. Air-conditioned

*The text of entries is based on unsolicited reports sent in by readers, backed up by inspections conducted anonymously. The factual details under the text are from questionnaires the Guide sends to all restaurants that feature in the book.*

# Valvona & Crolla Caffè Bar ▮ ✶ £

19 Elm Row, Edinburgh EH7 4AA
TEL: (0131) 556 6066   FAX: (0131) 556 1668
WEBSITE: www.valvonacrolla.com

COOKING 2
ITALIAN
£23–£46

Busy, noisy, and something of an Edinburgh institution, this is 'a great place for an informal lunch'. There are no bookings, so it is best to arrive before it gets really packed; when the shutters are lifted, out comes a wonderful aroma of coffee and freshly baked bread. A shop and deli sell coffee, kitchenware, cookbooks, cutlery and casseroles, while the strength of the spacious dining area, with its tightly packed tables, is real food with a southern Italian accent, made from generally fine ingredients, typically sourced from small producers. This comes at a price, and sometimes with longer waits than such simple assemblies warrant, but that is because even the simplest items such as bruschetta are made to order.

Even though little cooking is involved, it has its off days when some materials are below par. For the most part, however, there is enthusiasm for anything from a plate of antipasti (cured meats, sausages, olives and a fistful of mizuna leaves sprinkled with mozzarella), albeit served without bread, via a thick but light-textured pizza topped with courgettes and Parmesan, to desserts of tiramisù, duomo (a maraschino-soaked sponge with a hazelnut filling), and almond and fruit tart, made with the finest of shortcrust pastry, served with crème fraîche. The full wine list (the owners are also wine merchants) has an astounding array of Italian wines, as well as a selection of good bottles from elsewhere around the world. Diners can select any bottle from the range to drink with their meal for the retail price plus a corkage charge of £4. In addition, for the daily-changing menu, a wine is selected to partner each starter and main course, available by the bottle or glass.

CHEFS: Carina and Mary Contini   PROPRIETORS: the Contini family   OPEN: Mon to Sat 8 to 6 (L 12 to 2.30) and D during Festival   CLOSED: 25 and 26 Dec, 1 and 2 Jan   MEALS: alc (main courses £7 to £13)   SERVICE: not inc   CARDS: Amex, Delta, MasterCard, Switch, Visa   DETAILS: 75 seats. Private parties: 60 main room. Vegetarian meals. Children's helpings. No smoking in dining room. Wheelchair access (also WC). Music

| EDNAM  Borders | map 11 |
|---|---|

# ▲ Edenwater House ✶

Ednam TD5 7QL
TEL: (01573) 224070   FAX: (01573) 226615)
EMAIL: relax@ edenwaterhouse.co.uk
WEBSITE: www.edenwaterhouse.co.uk
on B6461, 2m N of Kelso

COOKING 4
MODERN BRITISH
£42–£50

The Kellys' attractive and comfortable former vicarage – next to the church in a small rural village – opens its doors to non-residents for dinner on Fridays and Saturdays, with Jeff front-of-house and Jacqui in the kitchen. Tastefully decorated in warm, restful colours, Edenwater House is just the place to relax, with views over the 'lovely garden' and down to Eden Water, the river from which it takes its name. No dithering over long menus here, the format is strictly a four-course no-choice affair. Dishes are 'designed with flair but not over-elaborate' and display a sometimes adventurous use of ingredients.

A chestnut mushroom, cep and loin of rabbit tartlet glazed with goats' cheese, served with honeyed mustard and tarragon sauce and wild rocket salad shows the style; this might be followed by a soup, perhaps fennel and smoked salmon. A main-course breast of Gressingham duck on sweet potato rösti has come with a mix of Chinese leaves, spring onion and ginger, and with carrots caramelised with orange and cardamom, in a spiced plum sauce. Dessert could bring brandy towers filled with rhubarb fool accompanied by iced pineapple parfait. The annotated wine list centres on France but also spans the globe, with prices rising from £12.50 a bottle (£3 glass).

CHEF: Jacqui Kelly   PROPRIETORS: Jeff and Jacqui Kelly   OPEN: Fri and Sat D only 8 to 8.30 (all week for residents)   CLOSED: 25 and 26 Dec, first two weeks Jan   MEALS: Set D £30   SERVICE: net prices, card slips closed   CARDS: Delta, MasterCard, Switch, Visa   DETAILS: 16 seats. Private parties: 16 main room. Car park. Children's helpings. No children under 10. No smoking in dining room. No music. No mobile phones   ACCOMMODATION: 4 rooms, all with bath/shower. TV. B&B £55 to £90. No children under 10 (*The Which? Hotel Guide*)

---

**ERISKA  Argyll & Bute**                                              **map 11**

## ▲ Isle of Eriska ♥ ⅚✕

Ledaig, Eriska PA37 1SD
TEL: (01631) 720371   FAX: (01631) 720531
EMAIL: office@eriska-hotel.co.uk
WEBSITE: www.eriska-hotel.co.uk
off A828, 12m N of Oban

COOKING **6**
SCOTTISH
£48–£57

It isn't only human guests who receive the attentions of staff here: badgers come shambling on to the terrace to be fed as well, emphasising the island's status as a nature sanctuary. Lying just off the Argyll coast in Loch Linnhe, and reached by its own bridge, the island is wholly owned by the Buchanan-Smith family, and at its heart the eponymous country-house hotel is a remote retreat run with every attention to detail.

Robert MacPherson has been cooking here for half a dozen years, using fine local materials to produce robust dishes that sometimes have an unusual edge but always manage to avoid gimmickry. The six-course dinner menu offers a pair of choices for the first two courses, and then three for the main, followed by dessert, a savoury and cheese. If that sounds like quite a lot to put away, be assured that the balance is cleverly judged. A puff pastry 'casket' containing wild mushrooms in a cream sauce with garlic and sage, 'full of subtle flavours', might open a meal. Soups to follow, such as one made from roast red peppers with basil oil, are correspondingly intense, while sesame oil and ginger make up a groundswell of flavour for a tempura-battered fillet of red mullet. Roasts carved from the trolley are rightly the centrepiece of an evening, with haunch of venison, rib of beef, or ham glazed in honey and mustard among the well-reported possibilities.

Alternatively, a fish main course might be seared salmon in a herb butter sauce with freshly shelled peas and salty samphire. Pastry work is very fine, whether in the canapés or in a dessert such as rhubarb and almond tart served with superior vanilla ice cream in a nest of spun sugar. Cheeses from Scotland

and France are impeccably kept, and the full repertoire of petits fours with coffee brings on fudges, jellies and meringues. It is all served with grace and aplomb, and in enormous comfort. The wine list cunningly combines solid wines from the classic regions of France with up-and-coming names from the New World. Mark-ups are commendably low (house wines start at £9.80), leaving wide choice under £20.

CHEF: Robert MacPherson  PROPRIETORS: the Buchanan-Smith family  OPEN: all week D only 8 to 9  CLOSED: Jan  MEALS: Set D £38.50  SERVICE: not inc, card slips closed  CARDS: MasterCard, Switch, Visa  DETAILS: 40 seats. Private parties: 40 main room, 6 to 15 private rooms. Car park. Children's helpings. Jacket and tie. No smoking in dining room. Wheelchair access (not WC). No music. No mobile phones  ACCOMMODATION: 19 rooms, all with bath/shower. TV. Phone. B&B £125 to £300. Rooms for disabled. Baby facilities. Swimming pool. Fishing (*The Which? Hotel Guide*)

---

**FAIRLIE  North Ayrshire**                                                        **map 11**

## ▲ Fins ❧

Fencefoot Farm, Fairlie KA29 0EG
TEL: (01475) 568989  FAX: (01475) 568921
WEBSITE: www.fencebay.co.uk                                        COOKING 2
on A78, 1m S of Fairlie, signposted Fencefoot                      SEAFOOD
Farm                                                                £20–£51

The shop part of Fencefoot Farm features the house wine, a range of hot and cold smoked fish and crustaceans, and St Andrews pottery among its wares. All of these can also be enjoyed in the simply furnished restaurant, where a warm welcome awaits the enthusiastic crowds – mostly locals – who come for the aforementioned seafood. Portions are described as 'good old-fashioned sinkers' in the Scottish tradition, using plenty of rich, creamy and buttery sauces. Favourites such as Cullen skink feature among starters, though simple platters of smoked fish and seafood salads make lighter alternatives. Among main courses, a large piece of well-timed crisp-skinned sea bass accompanied by a Mediterranean salad has been enjoyed. If you don't have room for dessert, skip it: coffee comes with a good tablet. A pair of house wines at £10.80 a bottle, £2.50/£3.50 a glass, opens the mainly French wine list; there is also a good selection of beers.

CHEFS: Gillian Dick, Jane Burns and Jill Thain  PROPRIETORS: Jill and Bernard Thain  OPEN: Tue to Sun L 12 to 2.30, Tue to Sat D 7 to 9  CLOSED: 25 and 26 Dec, 1 and 2 Jan, 1 week Jan  MEALS: alc (main courses L £8 to £13, D £10 to £25). Set L Tue to Thur £8.50 (2 courses) to £11.50, Set D Tue to Thur £11 (2 courses) to £14  SERVICE: not inc, card slips closed  CARDS: MasterCard, Switch, Visa  DETAILS: 30 seats. Private parties: 50 main room. Car park. Vegetarian meals. Children's helpings. No young children at D. No smoking in dining room. Wheelchair access (also WC). Music. No mobile phones  ACCOMMODATION: 2 rooms. B&B £25 to £30  (£5)

---

*Restaurateurs justifiably resent no-shows. If you quote a credit card number when booking, you may be liable for the restaurant's lost profit margin if you don't turn up. Always phone to cancel.*

---

## FORT WILLIAM Highland                                        map 11

# Crannog ⅝✳

| | |
|---|---|
| Town Pier, Fort William PH33 7NG | COOKING **2** |
| TEL: (01397) 705589   FAX: (01397) 700134 | SEAFOOD |
| WEBSITE: www.crannog.net | £26–£54 |

The view is spectacular, and anyone content with just that will soon be able to peer at the website's live pictures of the loch, boats, sunsets or just plain old Fort William rain. The absence of frills at this plainly decorated lochside restaurant points to an enviable single-mindedness: links between raw material and end product could hardly be closer. Divers land scallops, a fishing boat goes out each day in Lochs Linnhe and Eil to pick up langoustines from the creels, and Crannog now has sea tanks for holding live fish and shellfish, so that they are available on a regular basis. Langoustines are typically served hot with garlic butter, oysters come plain, or grilled with a chillied herb crust, and steamed mussels with a classic sauce of white wine, parsley, garlic and cream. By way of variety there is grilled Loch Awe rainbow trout, Aberdeen Angus steak, and saddle of Highland venison, and vegetarians now have a couple of choices on the menu (instead of just blackboard pot luck as before). Traditional desserts take in a Drambuie-flavoured trifle, and sticky apricot and ginger pudding. Wines (mostly white) stay largely under £20.

CHEF: Garry Dobbie   PROPRIETORS: Finlay and Lorna Finlayson   OPEN: all week 12 to 2.30 (3 June to Aug), 6 to 9.30 (10 June to Aug)   CLOSED: 25 Dec and 1 Jan   MEALS: alc (main courses £9 to £19). Set L £10 (buffet)   SERVICE: not inc   CARDS: MasterCard, Switch, Visa   DETAILS: 65 seats. Private parties: 65 main room. Car park. Vegetarian meals. No smoking in 1 dining room. Wheelchair access (also WC). Music

# ▲ Inverlochy Castle ♥ ⅝✳

| | |
|---|---|
| Torlundy, Fort William PH33 6SN | |
| TEL: (01397) 702177   FAX: (01397) 702953 | |
| EMAIL: info@inverlochy.co.uk | COOKING **6** |
| WEBSITE: www.inverlochycastlehotel.com | MODERN EUROPEAN |
| on A82, 3m N of Fort William | £42–£78 |

Built in 1863 near the erstwhile site of a thirteenth-century fortress, Inverlochy is every inch a castle. With Ben Nevis at its back, the scenery is pretty imposing too, as was remarked on by Queen Victoria, who stayed here ten years after it was finished. Take your pick from any of three dining rooms, all of which are furnished in part by gifts from the King of Norway.

Matthew Gray, who stepped up to become head chef two years ago, has impressively maintained the formidable standards set by his predecessor. The range encompasses a good sandwich menu as well as a carte at lunchtime, and dinners of four courses plus coffee, all underpinned by good Scottish produce (Isle of Skye crab, Loch Linnhe prawns, Aberdeen Angus beef). Ideas are intriguing too: salmon carpaccio to accompany a bavarois of fennel, while the old familiar melon to start is made into a granita to go alongside marinated tuna and crab. A modernist approach to combination partners monkfish with mussels, beetroot and tomato cream, and the mashed potato with rabbit and bacon has pieces of black pudding added to it for extra depth. In between starters and mains, a no-choice soup is served (perhaps sweetcorn chowder with salt-cod), and on the home straight you may choose from a selection of cheeses with home-made walnut bread, or something like a gâteau of pain perdu with bananas and toffee sauce.

The wine list is solid, if not exactly cutting edge. Classic French regions are the main focus, with good selections of champagne and red and white Burgundy, although the red Bordeaux section favours lesser-known producers and sub-appellations over big names. New World selections, though briefer, are well chosen, and this is where the best value is found. Wines below £20 are thin on the ground, with prices starting at £14 for Spanish red.

CHEF: Matthew Gray   PROPRIETOR: Inverlochy Castle Ltd   OPEN: all week 12.30 to 1.45, 7 to 9.15   CLOSED: mid-Jan to mid-Feb   MEALS: Set L £23 (2 courses) to £28.50, Set D £49.50. Light L available   SERVICE: not inc, card slips closed   CARDS: Amex, MasterCard, Switch, Visa   DETAILS: 50 seats. 10 seats outside. Private parties: 50 main room, 2 to 16 private rooms. Car park. Vegetarian meals. Jacket and tie. No smoking in dining room. Wheelchair access (also WC). Music. No mobile phones   ACCOMMODATION: 17 rooms, all with bath/shower. TV. Phone. B&B £205 to £550. Baby facilities. Fishing (The Which? Hotel Guide)

## GLASGOW Glasgow                                        map 11

# Amaryllis

1 Devonshire Gardens, Glasgow G12 0UX
TEL: (0141) 337 3434   FAX: (0141) 339 0047                    COOKING 6
EMAIL: info@amaryllis1.demon.co.uk                      MODERN EUROPEAN
WEBSITE: www.gordonramsay.com                              £35–£80

While One Devonshire Gardens changed hands during 2002, Amaryllis, an independent entity, continues on its steadily impressive course: eating here is definitely 'a treat'. It occupies an elegant corner room on the ground floor, with high ceilings, wood panelling and comfortable chairs, and is staffed by skilled and knowledgeable professionals who are rather formal and unsmiling.

Contemporary luxury is the kitchen's stock in trade, in the shape perhaps of a pumpkin velouté (topped with a slice of truffle) over a generous sediment of roughly chopped ceps, or two pink breasts of poached and grilled Bresse pigeon, accompanied by wild mushrooms in first-rate pasta, on a bed of shredded, braised cabbage. It also does 'routine luxe' well: for example, in a slice of foie gras parfait sprinkled with sea salt and arranged on a bed of frisée and poached artichoke heart, surrounded by green beans and girolles.

Above all, it is the combination of technical skill and assertive flavours that gives the cooking its imprimatur, evident in grilled, crisp-skinned red mullet fillets, meticulously boned and timed, on a mirepoix of root vegetables, surrounded by a well-flavoured saffron and tomato sauce. Tastes and textures are carefully considered, producing among other highlights an 'impeccable' cannon of lamb: pink, flavourful slices arranged on a 'scone' of crushed new potatoes with a sticky thyme jus.

To finish, a rich and buttery apple Tatin (a dish for two) is served from a copper pan, accompanied by a smooth vanilla ice cream and a small jug of caramel sauce. Considering the amount of space, it is surprising that a non-smoking dining room cannot be engineered: wine professionals would never dream of tasting their wares in a smoke-filled room, and the very fine list deserves better. Its prices, however, put most of it beyond the reach of ordinary customers, and there are no house wines.

CHEF: David Dempsey PROPRIETOR: Gordon Ramsay OPEN: Wed to Fri and Sun L 12 to 2.30, Wed to Sun D 6.45 to 11 (10 Sun) CLOSED: 1 and 2 Jan MEALS: Set L £18 (2 courses) to £35, Set D £35 to £45 SERVICE: not inc CARDS: Amex, Delta, MasterCard, Switch, Visa DETAILS: 70 seats. Private parties: 36 main room, 12 to 24 private rooms. Children's helpings. No cigars/pipes in dining room. Wheelchair access (also men's WC). No music

## Café Gandolfi £

| | |
|---|---|
| 64 Albion Street, Glasgow G1 1NY | COOKING 2 |
| TEL: (0141) 552 6813 FAX: (0141) 552 8911 | INTERNATIONAL |
| | £18–£42 |

Gandolfi has been a fixture of the Glasgow café scene for more than two decades and it continues to pack in the crowds. Stunning interior design from Tim Stead, stained glass by John Clark and flexible all-day opening are part of the winning combination. The motto, in Gaelic, translates as 'Well fed – well blessed': so says proprietor Seumas MacInnes, and he should know. Finnan haddock with potatoes, Arbroath smokies, and Stornoway white pudding with apples and crispy onion tip their bonnet to the Scottish larder, but there's much more besides. Try eggs en cocotte for breakfast, linguine with Italian sausage at lunchtime, or chickpea dhal for refuelling in the afternoon. Otherwise the seasonal menu promises everything from pissaladière to clootie dumpling with butterscotch sauce. Drink Gandolfi lemonade, a classy beer or something from the neatly assembled wine list. House Australian is £11.20, and nine wines (including champagne) come by the glass.

CHEF: Margaret Clarence PROPRIETOR: Seumas MacInnes OPEN: all week 9am (noon Sun) to midnight CLOSED: 25 and 26 Dec, 1 and 2 Jan MEALS: alc (main courses £5 to £14) SERVICE: not inc, 10% for parties of 6 or more CARDS: Amex, Delta, MasterCard, Switch, Visa DETAILS: 65 seats. Private parties: 25 main room. Vegetarian meals. Children's helpings. No children in dining room after 8.30pm. No-smoking area. No music. Air-conditioned

## Chardon D'or ⅝✳  NEW ENTRY

| | |
|---|---|
| 176 West Regent Street, Glasgow G2 4RL | |
| TEL: (0141) 248 3801 FAX: (0141) 248 3901 | COOKING 5 |
| EMAIL: info@lechardondor.com | FRENCH/MEDITERRANEAN |
| WEBSITE: www.lechardondor.com | £28–£61 |

This Golden Thistle is a smart, elegant restaurant above an art gallery, whose spacious open-plan dining room is decorated in restrained modern style. It is a cheerful and unstuffy stage on which Brian Maule (a 33-year-old from Ayrshire who used to cook at Le Gavroche, see entry, London) has launched his solo career; the 'bm' logo stamping his identity on the operation. Raw materials are well sourced, techniques are sound and results often first class, be it in a frothy, light-textured white bean soup, or a smooth, rich ballotine of foie gras accompanied by a tasty concoction of mushrooms and crème fraîche, and by a salad with a beguilingly bitter-sweet dressing.

This is cooking of 'flair without flamboyance', evident in a main course of sea bass, the skin blistered from the grill, its simple sauce balancing gently sweet sweetcorn with lightly salty black mushrooms; and in roast pigeon in a light, clear-tasting consommé with shredded cabbage, artichoke and girolles. Desserts are equally successful, from a classical shortcrust pastry case containing a glazed and intensely lemony filling, served with a fine raspberry coulis, to apricot trifle topped with a thick layer of vanilla yoghurt, accompanied by wafer-thin bubbly shortbread biscuits. A mainly French wine list offers some classy bottles at classy prices, and some easy drinking New World wines that won't break the bank. Bottles start at £11.95 (£4 a glass).

CHEF/PROPRIETOR: Brian Maule   OPEN: Mon to Fri L 12 to 3, Mon to Sat D 6 to 10   CLOSED: bank hols, 2 weeks Jan   MEALS: alc (main courses £14.50 to £18.50). Set L and D 6 to 7 £14.50 (2 courses) to £17.50. Set L and D £38 (whole table)   SERVICE: not inc, 10% for parties of 8 or more   CARDS: Amex, Delta, MasterCard, Switch, Visa   DETAILS: 85 seats. Private parties 26 main room, 6 to 10 private rooms. Vegetarian meals. No smoking in dining room. No mobile phones

# Gamba

225A West George Street, Glasgow G2 2ND
TEL: (0141) 572 0899   FAX: (0141) 572 0896
EMAIL: info@gamba.co.uk
WEBSITE: www.gamba.co.uk

COOKING 3
SEAFOOD
£28–£63

Occupying a city-centre basement, Gamba wafts a refreshing sea breeze through Glasgow's urban and increasingly urbane heart. It owes its pleasingly relaxed atmosphere in part to smart décor, comfortably spaced tables and 'friendly and helpful' staff, but also to Derek Marshall's broad-minded fish and seafood cookery that shows imagination and creativity while remaining eminently sensible. Old-fashioned fish soup, for example, is given a twist with the addition of ginger and dumplings, yet its strength is its basis in a good, thick stock. And whether you go for grilled lemon sole with tartare sauce and chips at one end of the main-course spectrum, or Cajun-spiced red snapper with honey, cream and wild rice at the other, it's a safe bet that the fish will be fresh and the preparation careful and precise. Desserts are no afterthought – a creamy parfait with a generous slug of Auchentoshan whisky has come in for fulsome praise – and wines offer good choice in both red and white camps. Prices are mostly over £20, but four house selections open at £13.95.

CHEF: Derek Marshall   PROPRIETORS: Alan Tomkins and Derek Marshall   OPEN: Mon to Sat 12 to 2.30, 5 to 10.30   CLOSED: 25 and 26 Dec, 1 and 2 Jan   MEALS: alc (main courses £11 to £20). Set L £12.95 (2 courses) to £15.95, Set D 5 to 6.30 £10.95 (2 courses) to £13.95   SERVICE: not inc, 10% for parties of 6 or more   CARDS: Amex, Delta, MasterCard, Switch, Visa   DETAILS: 66 seats. Private parties: 70 main room. Vegetarian meals. No children under 14. Music. No mobile phones. Air-conditioned

'The waitress tried to convince me that what appeared for all the world to be a large breakfast cup full of milky instant coffee was actually an espresso. Having once been offered a ''genuine'' Rolex in Thailand for £10, I was on to this ruse in a flash. She then threw me off my stride by suggesting it was a double.' (On eating in East Anglia)

# Gordon Yuill

257 West Campbell Street, Glasgow G2 4SQ
TEL: (0141) 572 4052    FAX: (0141) 572 4050
WEBSITE: www.gordonyuillandcompany.co.uk

COOKING 2
MODERN EUROPEAN
£26–£55

The eponymous proprietor was the manager of Glasgow's historical Rogano (see entry) for 17 years. A light, airy feel by day at this place becomes slightly ecclesiastical in the evenings, with heavy white church candles illuminating plain beech-laminated tables and Venetian blinds. Cooking influences mix Far Eastern and Mediterranean modes with more obviously demotic British touches, as in deep-fried cod with pea purée and chips, braised lamb shank with colcannon and onion gravy, with perhaps clootie dumpling and custard to finish. Simple starters, such as grilled goats' cheese on a slice of grilled aubergine and a sprinkling of balsamic, may not set the world on fire for novelty, but are fresh and well prepared. Indulge yourself at the end with bread-and-butter pudding, which is made with croissants and sauced with rum and caramel. Breakfasts are especially recommended. The short wine list stays mostly under £20, starting at £10.95 a bottle or £3 a glass. There is a second branch in Glasgow's West End at 2 Byres Road, G11 6NY, tel. (0141) 337 1145.

CHEF: Ian Mackie    PROPRIETOR: Gordon Yuill    OPEN: all week 8am to 10.30pm    MEALS: alc (main courses £8 to £20)    SERVICE: not inc    CARDS: Amex, Delta, Diners, MasterCard, Switch, Visa    DETAILS: 80 seats. Vegetarian meals. Wheelchair access (also WC). Music. Air-conditioned  £5

---

# ▲ Hilton Glasgow, Cramerons 🍴✗

1 William Street, Glasgow G3 8HT
TEL: (0141) 204 5555    FAX: (0141) 204 5004
WEBSITE: www.hilton.com

COOKING 2
MODERN EUROPEAN
£39–£63

One of several restaurants on the Hilton's ground floor, Camerons is comfortable, spacious and has the air of a gentlemen's club. Scottish produce features on a series of fixed-price menus that include Vegetarian and Market versions (the latter £39.50), and fish is prominent. Lunch might offer glazed smoked haddock with Mull Cheddar and rarebit leek risotto, and dinner a herbed fillet of Mallaig turbot with chillied mushrooms. Materials are native but treatment is diverse, and the same applies to meat: say, Rannoch Moor venison with a sweet mustard crust, lentil stirfry and Asian spiced jus. The cooking's ambition may give the impression of 'trying too hard to be special', but it gets the essentials right. Finish perhaps with a dark chocolate and raspberry torte, or a trio of banoffi ice cream, sticky toffee pudding and a praline mousse. Wines, listed by style, start with four house wines at £16, and more tempting bottles start at around £25.

CHEF: James Murphy    PROPRIETOR: Hilton plc    OPEN: Mon to Fri L 12 to 1.45, Mon to Sat D 7 to 9.45    CLOSED: 31 Dec, bank hols    MEALS: Set L £22.50 (2 courses) to £27.50 (inc wine), Set D £20 (2 courses) to £39.50    SERVICE: not inc, card slips closed    CARDS: Amex, Delta, Diners, MasterCard, Switch, Visa    DETAILS: 48 seats. Vegetarian meals. No children under 12. No smoking in dining room. Wheelchair access (also WC). Music. No mobile phones. Air-conditioned    ACCOMMODATION: 319 rooms, all with bath/shower. TV. Phone. B&B £128 to £168. Rooms for disabled. Baby facilities. Swimming pool  £5

# Rogano

| | |
|---|---|
| 11 Royal Exchange Place, Glasgow G1 3AN | COOKING **4** |
| TEL: (0141) 248 4055    FAX: (0141) 248 2608 | SEAFOOD |
| WEBSITE: www.rogano.co.uk | £27–£83 |

The reporter who commented that the main dining room at Glasgow's longest-serving restaurant is 'like an old ship of state' got it spot on. Its ornate art deco interior was installed at the same time as the luxury liner *Queen Mary* was being assembled at the Clyde shipyards in 1935. Dark-tinted mirrors and Chinese-style reliefs make it a must-see, and with the return of Andrew Cummings in 2001 the cooking brings extra polish to the whole experience.

Classic haute cuisine and fish dishes are at the heart of the menus, so expect sauté foie gras with sultanas marinated in Sauternes, perhaps followed by halibut on truffled wild mushrooms with red wine sauce, or gratinated scallops Mornay. Hard-boiled quail's eggs make a touching accompaniment to superior smoked salmon, and the simplicity of top-notch ingredients handled well in both lobster béarnaise and grilled langoustines with garlic butter pleased one pair of diners. For those not fishily inclined, beef fillet Rossini, or noisettes of lamb with poached apricots might tempt, and there is a separate vegetarian menu. Portions can be on the small side, and vegetable accompaniments could do with looking at, not being at all impressive at inspection, but a dessert such as cherry and almond tart with good pastry and superb vanilla ice cream restores confidence. Alternatively, try a plated selection of Scottish and French cheeses. The wine list is as classical as the surroundings, with France leading the charge, and other countries often reduced to a single selection in each colour. Prices are high, with the starting point £15.

CHEF: Andrew Cummings    PROPRIETOR: Punch Retail    OPEN: all week 12 to 2.30, 6.30 to 10.30
CLOSED: 25 and 31 Dec, 1 and 2 Jan    MEALS: alc (main courses £18 to £33.50). Set L £16.50
SERVICE: 12.5%, card slips closed    CARDS: Amex, Delta, Diners, MasterCard, Switch, Visa
DETAILS: 70 seats. 20 seats outside. Private parties: 70 main room, 8 to 24 private rooms.
Vegetarian meals. Wheelchair access (not WC). Music. No mobile phones. Air-conditioned (£5)

# ▲ Saint Jude's

| | |
|---|---|
| 190 Bath Street, Glasgow G2 4HB | |
| TEL: (0141) 352 8800    FAX: (0141) 352 8801 | COOKING **3** |
| EMAIL: reservations@saintjudes.com | GLOBAL |
| WEBSITE: www.saintjudes.com | £20–£57 |

Looking stylish and contemporary, Saint Jude's consists of a bar downstairs and a restaurant upstairs, where cool colours and large windows help to create a light, airy feel. An Australian chef cooking contemporary Mediterranean food using oriental ingredients sounds like an interesting proposition. In fact, the culinary output from this arrangement is not as diverse or miscellaneous as the theory might lead one to predict: poached duck egg on sauté pink fir potatoes with spinach and chorizo sounds sensible enough, as do John Dory with lemon zest, asparagus, thyme and ginger, and chargrilled sirloin of Aberdeen Angus with port, baby beetroots, beer-battered onion rings and horseradish. Dishes can be quite involved, but every element seems to fit: witness a starter of whisky oak- and juniper-smoked salmon, trout and mussels with salmon caviar and horseradish crème fraîche. Desserts might include vanilla crème brûlée with figs poached in rum, or strawberry and vanilla cassata. A mixed bag of fairly priced wines opens with own-label vins de pays at £12 a bottle, £3 a glass.

CHEF: Martin Teplitsky  PROPRIETORS: Robert Paterson and Paul Wingate  OPEN: Mon to Fri L 12 to 3, all week D 6 to 10.30  CLOSED: 25 and 26 Dec, 1 and 2 Jan  MEALS: alc (main courses L £5 to £7, D £10.50 to £18.50). Set L £11.50 (2 courses) to £14.50, Set D 6 to 7.15 £11.50 (2 courses) to £14.50. Bar menu available D  SERVICE: not inc, 10% for parties of 6 or more  CARDS: Amex, Delta, Diners, MasterCard, Switch, Visa  DETAILS: 56 seats. Private parties: 66 main room, 12 to 26 private rooms. Vegetarian meals. No cigars/pipes during meals. Music. Air-conditioned  ACCOMMODATION: 6 rooms, all with bath/shower. TV. Phone. B&B £105 to £185  (£5)

## Stravaigin

28 Gibson Street, Glasgow G12 8NX
TEL: (0141) 334 2665   FAX: (0141) 334 4099
EMAIL: bookings@stravaigin.com
WEBSITE: www.stravaigin.com

COOKING 4
GLOBAL
£20–£44

This original Stravaigin (see also Stravaigin 2, below), near the university, is smart and noisy, with a bar on the ground floor and the restaurant below. Service is swift and staff hard-working, although they don't take themselves too seriously. 'Stravaigin' means 'wandering about', and that's the name of the game in this kitchen, which fuses influences from around the world with enthusiasm. Dishes may sound seriously overcomplicated, and you may need an international gastronomic dictionary to identify some ingredients, but results are spot-on. Much depends on sourcing prime raw materials, from Perthshire pigeon to plaice from the west coast.

Unusual breads in a bamboo steamer precede a tiny appetiser: perhaps a Chinese teacup of intense chicken broth spiked with lemon grass. That sets the tone. Loud, assertive flavours, tempered with delicate touches, create impressive harmonies: fillet of chermoula-marinated Argyllshire lamb served on harissa-infused molgrabh (large couscous) accompanied by roast aubergine stuffed with a purée of fennel and walnuts; or roast Barbary duck breast arranged on cubes of sweet potato with sesame, ginger and cubes of fried belly pork. To finish, ice creams come bursting with interesting flavours, and espresso is good and strong. The long international wine list has a big French contingent; house wine is £12.95.

CHEF: Alan Doig  PROPRIETOR: Colin Clydesdale  OPEN: Fri to Sun L 12 to 2.30, Tue to Sun D 5 to 11  MEALS: Set L £16.95 (2 courses) to £19.95, Set D 5 to 7 £11.95, Set D £21.95 (2 courses) to £26.95. Bar menu also available  SERVICE: not inc  CARDS: Amex, Delta, Diners, MasterCard, Switch, Visa  DETAILS: 75 seats. Private parties: 75 main room. Vegetarian meals. Children's helpings. No smoking before 11pm. Music. Air-conditioned  (£5)

*The cuisine styles noted at the tops of entries are only an approximation, often suggested to us by the restaurants themselves. Please read the entry itself to find out more about the cooking style.*

# Stravaigin 2

8 Ruthven Lane, Hillhead, Glasgow G12 9BG
TEL: (0141) 334 7165   FAX: (0141) 357 4785
EMAIL: mailbox@stravaigin2.com
WEBSITE: www.stravaigin.com

COOKING **2**
GLOBAL
£21–£51

Like the original Stravaigin (see above), this is a restaurant that takes multiculturalism seriously: fine Scottish produce, some from a dedicated local organic farmer, used in a cooking style that plucks ideas from just about every international cuisine you can think of. Ribbons of Smeeton's seared lamb on a mustard- and yoghurt-dressed salad of watercress and pine nuts is one of the more straightforward creations among starters; 'oriental-style' salmon ceviche with ginger, lemon crème fraîche and a spicy pineapple relish is from the other end of the creativity scale. The main-course range stretches all the way from the West Coast of Scotland (seared salmon on chorizo and fava bean mash with lemon-scented rocket) to Vietnam (pan-fried pork fillet on an egg noodle pancake with coriander and peanut pesto and plum sauce). There is also a 'roving tapas' menu, which puts a global spin on the Spanish format with dishes like Burmese semolina and cardamom cake with toasted sesame syrup, or Cajun-style roasted pork and sweet potato jambalaya. A short, diverse wine list opens with house wines at £12.95.

CHEF: David Damer   PROPRIETOR: Colin Clydesdale   OPEN: all week 12 (11 Sat and Sun) to 11 CLOSED: 25 Dec, 1 Jan   MEALS: alc (main courses £11 to £17). Set L £10.95   SERVICE: not inc CARDS: Amex, Delta, Diners, MasterCard, Switch, Visa   DETAILS: 75 seats. Private parties: 40 main room, 30 to 40 private rooms. Vegetarian meals. Children's helpings. No smoking between 12 and 2 and 5 and 10. Wheelchair access (also WC). Music. Air-conditioned  (£5)

---

# Ubiquitous Chip ▮

12 Ashton Lane, Glasgow G12 8SJ
TEL: (0141) 334 5007   FAX: (0141) 337 1302
EMAIL: mail@ubiquitouschip.co.uk
WEBSITE: www.ubiquitouschip.co.uk

COOKING **4**
SCOTTISH
£29–£71

'It is a privilege to eat here,' noted one visitor to this bastion of the Glasgow restaurant scene. Much of the allure of the place derives from its secluded setting and the luxuriant, white-walled courtyard. The main dining room, with its clothed tables and proper napkins, is directly adjacent, and there is a less formal brasserie-style operation upstairs: in both, the focus remains sharp.

For more than 30 years Ronnie Clydesdale has championed Scottish produce, although it often turns up in quite unexpected guises. Readers approve of the cooking's 'regional accent' – everything from Cullen skink to venison haggis – and the top-flight wine list. Passion, dedication and enthusiasm ensure that the Chip larder is copiously stocked with Orkney organic salmon, Loch Fyne herrings, scallops, West Coast squid (which might be meatily stuffed with oxtail) and even ling ('enhanced with lime-scented potatoes').

From the land and the skies come partridge and pigeons, Ayrshire bacon, Perthshire pork – perhaps stuffed with dates in a 'rich but uncloying sauce' – and Argyllshire venison with a confit of turnip, soused red cabbage and a gin and juniper sauce. Caledonian oatmeal ice cream is a signature dessert, otherwise the menu might offer iced coffee parfait with a cinnamon doughnut. Good Scottish cheeses are served with apple jelly and fruit bread. The wine list concentrates on classic areas of Europe, with mature Burgundy and classed-growth Bordeaux among the specialities, although ample room is given to the fine wines of Germany. California and Australia make up much of the New World offerings. Prices aren't cheap, but five house wines are available for £13.95 or £3.50/£4.70 per small/large glass.

CHEF/PROPRIETOR: Ronald Clydesdale  OPEN: Mon to Sat 12 to 2.30, 5.30 to 11, Sun 12.30 to 3, 6.30 to 11  CLOSED: 25 Dec, 1 Jan  MEALS: Set L Mon to Sat £19.95 (2 courses) to £24.95, Set L Sun £17.50, Set D £29.95 (2 courses) to £34.95  SERVICE: not inc  CARDS: Amex, Delta, Diners, MasterCard, Switch, Visa  DETAILS: 200 seats. Private parties: 80 main room, 20 to 40 private rooms. Vegetarian meals. Children's helpings. Wheelchair access (also WC). No music. No mobile phones. Air-conditioned

## GULLANE  East Lothian                                                    map 11

## ▲ Golf Inn  £                                                    NEW ENTRY

Main Street, Gullane EH31 2AB
TEL: (01620) 843 259   FAX: (01620) 842 006                         COOKING 2
EMAIL: info@golfinn.co.uk                                   MODERN EUROPEAN
WEBSITE: www.golfinngullane.com                                    £21–£40

What with the name, and Muirfield almost on the doorstep, there's no mistaking the theme here: a wall of golfing memorabilia and trophies lurks behind the extravagantly creeper-clad façade. Chef Neil Wright's style is as simple as can be, but the execution is effective. Grilled asparagus with a poached egg and thyme hollandaise made a well-timed lunch starter, while that old standby, toasted goats' cheese, has been lifted by imaginative juxtaposition with Puy lentils and pesto; likewise a tomato and basil vinaigrette has invigorated a crisply finished piece of salmon. Dinner menus may bring baked lamb chops with rosemary and onion 'confit', duck breast with orange and ginger, or a truffled-oiled wild mushroom risotto for vegetarians. The dessert to aim for looks like the intensely rich chocolate Nemesis. The kitchen runs at a fairly stately pace, even when not noticeably busy. A short, carefully chosen wine list opens with house varietals from Santa Rita of Chile at £10.50.

CHEFS: Neil Wright, Gavin Corbett and Brian Inglis  PROPRIETORS: Gavin and Rhona Corbett and Neil Wright  OPEN: all week 12 to 2.30, 6.30 to 9.30  CLOSED: 25 and 26 Dec, 1 and 2 Jan  MEALS: alc (main courses £6.50 to £13.50). Set L £12.50 (2 courses) to £15.50, Set D £18.50 (2 courses) to £22.50  SERVICE: not inc  CARDS: Amex, Delta, Diners, MasterCard, Switch, Visa  DETAILS: 70 seats. 25 seats outside. Private parties: 40 main room, 10 to 40 private rooms. Vegetarian meals. Children's helpings. Wheelchair access (also WC). Music  ACCOMMODATION: 14 rooms, 12 with bath/shower. TV. Phone. B&B £30 to £80. Baby facilities (The Which? Hotel Guide)

---

Occasional music *in the details at the end of an entry means live or recorded music is played in the dining room only rarely or for special events.* No music *means it is never played.*

# ▲ Greywalls ⓘ ⁵⁄✗

Muirfield, Gullane EH31 2EF
TEL: (01620) 842144   FAX: (01620) 842241
EMAIL: hotel@greywalls.co.uk                COOKING 4
WEBSITE: www.greywalls.co.uk                MODERN BRITISH
on A198, at E end of Gullane                £27–£62

Built by Lutyens in 1901, Greywalls is a splendidly elegant country hotel set in
extensive gardens designed by Gertrude Jekyll, overlooking Muirfield golf
course and the Firth of Forth. Despite this highly refined pedigree, the place has
a relaxed atmosphere. The cooking, based on quality local produce, aims to steer
a course between innovation and tradition: dinners may typically begin with
wafers of peat-smoked Shetland salmon with potato and truffle salad, or
perhaps ham hock terrine with pease pudding and parsley sauce, but there
might also be a more contemporary tartare of yellow-fin tuna with ginger oil.
Main courses have similarly broad appeal, ranging from roast halibut fillet with
coriander and mussel broth to fillet of Angus beef with chartreuse of oxtail. The
choice of 'puddings, cheese and savouries' to finish may include chocolate tart
with honeycomb ice cream, or Waterloo cheese pressed with truffle shavings on
fig salad.

The wine list favours the grand wines of France, Bordeaux in particular, with
a multitude of older vintages, such as Ch. Haut-Brion 1934 (for £1,100). The list
gestures in the direction of non-French Europe before moving on to some good
New World selections, where America, Australia and New Zealand are strong
points. For after dinner, there's a selection of older vintage ports at prices that
represent excellent value. Despite the elevated status of many of the wines, there
is reasonable choice below £20. A ten-strong 'Greywalls selection' starts at
£14.50 for red and white Bergerac.

CHEF: Simon Burns   PROPRIETORS: Giles and Ros Weaver   OPEN: all week 12.30 to 2, 7.30 to
9.15   CLOSED: late Oct to mid-Apr   MEALS: Set L £15 (2 courses) to £17.50, Set D £40. Light L
available Mon to Sat   SERVICE: not inc, card slips closed   CARDS: Amex, Delta, Diners,
MasterCard, Switch, Visa   DETAILS: 50 seats. 12 seats outside. Private parties: 35 main room, 2
to 20 private rooms. Car park. Jacket and tie. No smoking in dining room. Wheelchair access
(not WC). No music   ACCOMMODATION: 22 rooms, all with bath/shower. TV. Phone. B&B £115 to
£230. Rooms for disabled. Baby facilities (The Which? Hotel Guide)  (£5)

## INVERKEILOR Angus                                                   map 11

# ▲ Gordon's ⁵⁄✗

32 Main Street, Inverkeilor DD11 5RN
TEL/FAX: (01241) 830364                      COOKING 4
WEBSITE: www.gordonsrestaurant.co.uk         MODERN SCOTTISH
off A92 from Arbroath to Montrose            £26–£51

Consistency is a virtue of Gordon Watson's small restaurant in a quiet town close
to Lunan Bay, as a satisfied reporter testified following a return visit. The
cooking takes its cues from classical preparations and flavour combinations but
develops traditional themes with contemporary twists: pavé of white crabmeat
and ginger with crushed avocado, chive blinis and an orange, coriander and

vanilla dressing is a starter that typifies the style as much as roast quail stuffed with black pudding and served on a bed of Puy lentils. Main courses can be quite elaborate and luxurious, as in herb-crusted halibut fillet with asparagus and pea risotto, scallops and caviar beurre fondue, or Angus beef fillet with mushroom and smoked bacon ravioli, kiln-dried cherry polenta, celeriac purée and red wine jus. Reporters have been impressed by the artistic presentation and careful cooking of dishes and the evident high quality of raw materials, as well as the warm welcome from Maria Watson and the unpretentious atmosphere of the place. House wines on the reasonably priced list of around two dozen bottles are £10.95.

CHEFS: Gordon and Garry Watson   PROPRIETORS: Maria and Gordon Watson   OPEN: Wed to Fri and Sun L 12 to 1.45, Tue to Sat D 7 to 9   CLOSED: Jan   MEALS: Set L Wed to Fri £15 (2 courses) to £18, Set L Sun £22.50, Set D £30.50 to £33.50   SERVICE: not inc   CARDS: Delta, MasterCard, Switch, Visa   DETAILS: 24 seats. Private parties: 24 main room, 20 private room. Car park. No children under 12. No smoking in dining room. Wheelchair access (also WC). No music. No mobile phones   ACCOMMODATION: 3 rooms, 2 with bath/shower. TV. B&B £47 to £90. No children under 12

---

**INVERNESS Highland**                                                            map 11

# ▲ Culloden House ⅋✳

Culloden, Inverness IV2 4BF
TEL: (01463) 790461   FAX: (01463) 792181
EMAIL: info@cullodenhouse.co.uk
WEBSITE: www.cullodenhouse.co.uk                               COOKING 2
from Inverness take A96 towards Nairn, turn right            INTERNATIONAL
after 1m, then left at Culloden House Avenue                    £34–£61

Although this is not the original house in which Bonnie Prince Charlie prepared for the Battle of Culloden in 1746 – that was partially destroyed in a fire a few years later – it is an impressive, creeper-clad Georgian mansion that was built on the same site by the prominent Forbes family. High ceilings, Adam plaster reliefs, chandeliers and false marble pillars add to the sense of scale and grandeur, although service is quite ordinary and unassuming. Lunch is a carte, while the set-price dinner takes a standard three-course format and extends it to four with the aid of a mid-meal soup or sorbet.

Native materials are increasingly evident, in an Orkney crab salad (with a coriander and ginger dressing), and in a plate of Loch Fyne smoked salmon to start, followed perhaps by roast loin of Highland venison (with a wild mushroom and chicken mousse), or Scottish beef fillet with a creamed peppercorn sauce. Vegetarian options have included a red onion and goats' cheese pie, while desserts run to crème brûlée, and chocolate truffle torte. Wine coverage is extensive, although prices are skewed towards the higher end. House red and white are £15 (£3.75 a glass).

CHEF: Michael Simpson   PROPRIETOR: Edward Cunningham   OPEN: all week 12.30 to 2, 7 to 9   CLOSED: Christmas   MEALS: alc L (main courses £12 to £19.50). Set D £38   SERVICE: not inc, card slips closed   CARDS: Amex, Diners, MasterCard, Switch, Visa   DETAILS: 60 seats. Private parties: 60 main room, 15 to 40 private rooms. Car park. Vegetarian meals. Children's helpings.

No children under 10. No smoking in dining room. Occasional music. No mobile phones ACCOMMODATION: 28 rooms, all with bath/shower. TV. Phone. B&B £155 to £275. No children under 10 (£5)

## ▲ Dunain Park ♀ ⁵⁄₊

Inverness IV3 8JN
TEL: (01463) 230512   FAX: (01463) 224532
EMAIL: dunainparkhotel@btinternet.com
WEBSITE: www.dunainparkhotel.co.uk                    COOKING 2
on A82 towards Fort William, 1m from town            MODERN SCOTTISH
boundary                                             £42–£57

From the main road a winding drive leads through six-acre grounds to this Georgian mansion. Heavy drapes, paintings of lochs in large gilt frames, and a cabinet of porcelain figurines typify the décor, and well-heeled customers dine at dark wooden tables. This example of country-house hotel eating uses native ingredients – Aberdeen Angus beef from local herds (fillet or sirloin served with a choice of half a dozen sauces), fish from the north and east coasts, and west coast scallops, maybe with deep-fried courgettes and caper mash.

Ideas from further afield take in a Thai dressing here, Cajun spicing there, and such French-style dishes as Gressingham duck breast with Puy lentils. The two-acre walled garden supplies herbs, vegetables and soft fruits in season, and a local picker often delivers chanterelles and shiitake mushrooms. You help yourself to desserts from a sideboard buffet, but amiable and attentive service from the Nicoll family forms the background to the meal.

With around a hundred bins, the wine list is broad-ranging, although France gets top billing before the focus is turned to Europe and the New World. Value, rather than big names, is a priority, so there is good choice in the under-£20 range, augmented by 30 or so half-bottles. Prices start at £14.50.

CHEF: Ann Nicoll   PROPRIETORS: Edward and Ann Nicoll   OPEN: all week D only 7 to 9   MEALS: alc (main courses £17 to £19)   SERVICE: not inc, card slips closed   CARDS: Amex, Delta, Diners, MasterCard, Switch, Visa   DETAILS: 34 seats. Car park. Vegetarian meals. Children's helpings. No smoking in dining room. Wheelchair access (not WC). No music   ACCOMMODATION: 13 rooms, all with bath/shower. TV. Phone. B&B to £198 (double room). Rooms for disabled. Baby facilities. Swimming pool (The Which? Hotel Guide) (£5)

## KILCHRENAN  Argyll & Bute                                           map 11

## ▲ Taychreggan ⁵⁄₊

Kilchrenan PA35 1HQ
TEL: (01866) 833211 and 833366
FAX: (01866) 833244
EMAIL: info@taychregganhotel.co.uk              [ NEW CHEF ]
WEBSITE: www.taychregganhotel.co.uk            MODERN SCOTTISH
on B845, 7m S of Taynuilt                       £49–£59

'Awe inspiring' may be overdoing the pun a bit, but this is certainly a fine location on the edge of Loch Awe. The dining room benefits from the view, and from well-spaced tables, while the kitchen has a new incumbent. The same format obtains – five courses, one a soup or sorbet – with a choice of three items at each stage. A typical meal might start with crab cake (with a mango and pineapple salad and a sweet chilli sauce), then lemon-grass soup, followed by beef fillet with grain mustard mash, and might end with lemon tart (with chocolate and orange ice cream) and cheese. At the time of going to press bar lunches had been suspended while the bar area was being refurbished, but these were scheduled for resumption soon. A serviceable wine list is supplemented by some finer bottles, particularly claret, and house French red and Chilean white are £13.95.

CHEF: Kenneth Black   PROPRIETOR: North American Country Inns   OPEN: all week D only 7.30 to 8.45   CLOSED: 24 to 27 Dec   MEALS: Set D £37.50. Bar L menu available   SERVICE: not inc
CARDS: Amex, Delta, MasterCard, Switch, Visa   DETAILS: 40 seats. Private parties: 20 main room. Car park. Vegetarian meals. No children under 14. No smoking in dining room. Music. No mobile phones   ACCOMMODATION: 19 rooms, all with bath/shower. Phone. B&B £99 to £250. No children under 14. Fishing (*The Which? Hotel Guide*)

## KILLIECRANKIE   Perthshire & Kinross                                    map 11

## ▲ Killiecrankie Hotel ♟ �znⵓ

Killiecrankie PH16 5LG
TEL: (01796) 473220   FAX: (01796) 472451
EMAIL: enquiries@killiecrankiehotel.co.uk                            COOKING 3
WEBSITE: www.killiecrankiehotel.co.uk                                  GLOBAL
off A9, 3m N of Pitlochry                                             £43–£51

New owners took over this former dower house at the beginning of 2002; for Tim Waters, former head of wine-buying at Oddbins, it marked a career change. He has had the good sense to retain the services of Mark Easton, and one of his first jobs was to upgrade the previously poor bar food. It seems to have worked, judging by one party's 'beautifully cooked' goujons of chicken with crisp chips, Cumberland sausage and salad, and home-made ice creams. Dinner remains the main meal however (with a choice of four items per course), and the cooking is firmly based on Scottish produce, some of it local, some from the hotel's own garden.

The kitchen has its eye on the wider world, though, and there are French, Mediterranean and Eastern ideas at work: in roast loin of Perthshire lamb stuffed with a chicken and wild mushroom mousse, in grilled sea bass fillet with courgette ribbons and a caper sauce, and in grilled marinated teriyaki salmon with seared scallops, steamed vegetables and braised rice. Main course options also usually include a salad, perhaps of honey-roast ham, or smoked salmon and prawns. Finish with orange sponge pudding, or dark chocolate mousse with Agen prunes. New Zealand is a strength of the wide-ranging, well-priced wine list, with France and the Mediterranean making up the balance. Value figures large too, with a good selection of bins (many of them from areas off the beaten track) below £20. Bottle prices start at £13.90, and there is a well-rounded selection of half-bottles.

CHEF: Mark Easton   PROPRIETORS: Tim and Maillie Waters   OPEN: all week D only 7 to 8.30
CLOSED: 3 Jan to 13 Feb   MEALS: Set D £32. Bar menu also available L 12.30 to 2 and supper 6.30 to 9 (9.30 June to Sep)   SERVICE: not inc, card slips closed   CARDS: MasterCard, Switch, Visa
DETAILS: 34 seats. Private parties: 20 main room, 14 private room. Car park. No children under 9.

No smoking in dining room. Wheelchair access (not WC). No music. No mobile phones
ACCOMMODATION: 10 rooms, all with bath/shower. TV. Phone. D,B&B £75 to £210 (*The Which?
Hotel Guide*) £5

## KINCLAVEN Perthshire & Kinross map 11

## ▲ Ballathie House ♥ ⅝✗

Kinclaven, by Stanley PH1 4QN
TEL: (01250) 883268   FAX: (01250) 883396
EMAIL: email@ballathiehousehotel.com
WEBSITE: www.ballathiehousehotel.com
off B9099; take right fork 1m N of Stanley

COOKING 2
MODERN SCOTTISH
£28–£64

Expansive lawns and a Tay-side setting are part of the draw at this tranquil,
turreted baronial mansion, which rewards expectations with its attractively
furnished and decorated interior. The kitchen's contribution centres around
full-blooded roast loin of Rannoch Moor venison served with mushroom
gnocchi, or fillet of Aberdeen Angus with a brandy and peppercorn sauce. Other
native materials extend to seafood, in the shape of salmon fillet on a crab and
fennel risotto, and sauté Skye prawn tails with creamed Savoy cabbage. Start,
maybe, with a chicken and goose liver pâté, or baked goats' cheese salad, and
finish with a chilled citrus fruit tart, or warm banana fritters with coconut ice
cream.

The wine list kicks off with 15 'cellarman's choice' bottles, all under £18 (£3 to
£4.60 by the glass) before taking a well-structured tour around the wine regions
of France and the New World. Mark-ups are on the high side in some areas,
leaving limited choice under £20, although prices start at £13.50 for house
Australian red and white.

CHEF: Kevin MacGillivray   PROPRIETOR: Ballathie House Hotel Co Ltd   OPEN: all week 12.30 to
1.45, 7 to 9   MEALS: Set L Mon to Sat £15.50 (2 courses) to £18.50, Set L Sun £19.50, Set D £35
to £38.50. Bar/light L menu also available   SERVICE: not inc   CARDS: Amex, Delta, Diners,
MasterCard, Switch, Visa   DETAILS: 70 seats. Private parties: 60 main room, 10 to 32 private
rooms. Car park. Vegetarian meals. Children's helpings. Jacket and tie. No smoking in dining
room. Wheelchair access (also WC). No music   ACCOMMODATION: 42 rooms, all with bath/
shower. TV. Phone. B&B £75 to £200. Rooms for disabled. Fishing

## KINGUSSIE Highland map 11

## ▲ The Cross ▮ ⅝✗

Tweed Mill Brae, Ardbroilach Road,
Kingussie PH21 1TC
TEL: (01540) 661166   FAX: (01540) 661080
EMAIL: relax@thecross.co.uk
WEBSITE: www.thecross.co.uk

COOKING 6
MODERN SCOTTISH
£47–£56

The old mill's stonework, some of it bare, some whitewashed as in the dining
room, provides a characterful setting, emphasising the rustic charm of this long-
standing Highland favourite. At the same time, modern paintings, sculptures
and fittings – and the sharp, up-to-date Scottish menu – confirm that it is no
backwoods operation. Tony and Ruth Hadley run a very personal enterprise in

which first-class materials are treated with skill and intelligence. Nobody seems to mind the minimal choice: none at all for the first three courses, then just two main courses and desserts (or cheese).

The focus is on native produce, from dived West Coast scallops (perhaps sautéed, with an asparagus salad) to Ayrshire guinea fowl (with a tarragon mustard), and although treatments tend to be simple – beef fillet comes with ceps and a Madeira sauce – their skilful manipulation is obvious: 'we were to eat pea and mint soup many times on this holiday,' wrote one travelling couple, 'but this was the best by far.' At other times flavours can be quite vivid. Butternut squash soup, for example, is blended with coconut milk and spiked with lime leaves, while crab cakes, incorporating capers and lemon grass, might be served on a mango and sweet pepper salsa.

Like much of the cooking, desserts may sound unshowy, but their unassuming nature hides considerable skill, the options typically including a lemon cheesecake, or a plum and almond frangipane tart with vanilla ice cream. Tony Hadley is a sympathetic host whose care, understanding and enthusiasm for both food and wine contribute so much to the Cross's personality. The wine list, which describes itself as 'one person's incursions into the world of wines', includes not a single bottle from France, although there is plenty of breadth from Austria (mostly from Willi Opitz), Greece, Hungary and Israel. In the New Zealand section is a 'vertical' selection of Cloudy Bay Sauvignon Blanc with nine vintages back to 1986. There is an excellent choice of half-bottles and very reasonable mark-ups throughout. Prices start at £10.50 for Greek Retsina or Chilean Chardonnay. For 2003, Hadley is developing a 'more streamlined list'.

CHEFS: Ruth Hadley and Becca Henderson   PROPRIETORS: Tony and Ruth Hadley   OPEN: Wed to Mon D only 7 to 8.30   CLOSED: 1 Dec to 28 Feb   MEALS: Set D £37.50   SERVICE: not inc, card slips closed   CARDS: MasterCard, Switch, Visa   DETAILS: 28 seats. Private parties: 28 main room. Car park. No children under 8. No smoking in dining room. Wheelchair access (also WC). No music   ACCOMMODATION: 9 rooms, all with bath/shower. Phone. D,B&B £190 to £230. No children under 8 (The Which? Hotel Guide)

---

## LEVEN Fife                                                          map 11

# Scotland's Larder ⁵⁄✳                              | NEW ENTRY |

Upper Largo, Leven KY8 6EA
TEL: (01333) 360414   FAX: (01333) 360427                    COOKING 1
EMAIL: booking@scotland-larder.co.uk                          SCOTTISH
WEBSITE: www.scotland-larder.co.uk                           £17–£42

This unpretentious operation runs on fine Scottish produce, some of it also sold in the adjoining shop. The succinct à la carte is available from 10 to 6, and there is a set lunch menu (a set dinner too on Friday and Saturday), plus a blackboard listing daily specials, all showcasing what Christopher Trotter considers 'some of the finest produce in the world'. Crabs come from Crail, oysters from Seil Island, salmon (for gravlax) from Shetland, and fish from Pittenweem or Peterhead. Venison (farmed from Auchtermuchty, or wild from Speyside and Rannoch) might appear as a huge, tender, flavourful steak with mint butter. Also highly rated has been ham with hollandaise and poached egg, and vegetables – generally variations on mash and cabbage – are also praised. Seven wines come by the glass (£2.80), carafe or bottle (£10.50), and there is a short supplementary list for those who ask.

CHEF/PROPRIETOR: Christopher Trotter   OPEN: all week L 10 to 6, Fri and Sat D 7.30 to 9.15   MEALS: alc (main courses £5 to £15). Set L £6.95 (2 courses) to £8.95, Set D £24   SERVICE: not inc, card slips closed   CARDS: Delta, MasterCard, Switch, Visa   DETAILS: 45 seats. 20 seats outside. Private parties: 100 main room. Car park. Children's helpings. No smoking in dining room. Wheelchair access (also WC). Music. No mobile phones at D  (£5)

## LINLITHGOW  West Lothian                                        map 11

## ▲ Champany Inn  ▮

Champany Corner, Linlithgow EH49 7LU
TEL: (01506) 834532   FAX: (01506) 834302
EMAIL: reception@champany.com                          COOKING 5
WEBSITE: www.champany.com                              SCOTTISH
2m NE of Linlithgow at junction of A904 and A803       £39–£86

Dating from the seventeenth century, and once a working farm, the group of buildings includes a Chop and Ale House (try the hamburger), a bar converted from a hay loft, and a circular restaurant in what was the millhouse. Against a background of heavy furnishings, copper pans and ancestral portraits, the dining room is set with dark, polished tables and sparkling glassware, and has two priorities: steak and wine. Racks of well-hung meat (three weeks in an ionised chill room is the norm) can be spotted, the cooking is done openly on specially designed stoves, and the choice is straightforward: a hunk of striploin, ribeye, porterhouse or whatever, served with vegetables if desired. A basket of raw vegetables, sometimes including wild mushrooms, is offered round to tempt.

One who started with fresh, sweet, Loch Gruinart oysters came away well pleased, while the hot smoked salmon gets another vote, and there are diversions from chicken liver parfait to lobster and baked chicken, but it would be daft (at least for a first-timer) not to eat steak in some form. Equally, it would be a pity not to take advantage of the wine cellar, one of the most extensive in Scotland. It tends to stick to the classics – Bordeaux, Burgundy and Rhône – although Australia and California are strong too, and all bottles are aged on the premises. Mark-ups, however, are steep; even Argentina and Chile have nothing to offer below £25. Own-label South African house wines start at £14.50 (£3.65 by the glass).

CHEFS: Clive Davidson, David Gibson and Kevin Hope   PROPRIETORS: Clive and Anne Davidson   OPEN: Mon to Fri L 12.30 to 2, Mon to Sat D 7 to 10   CLOSED: 25 and 26 Dec, 1 and 2 Jan   MEALS: alc (main courses £17.50 to £32.50). Set L £16.75 (2 courses). Chop and Ale House menu available all day Sat and Sun, L and D Mon to Fri   SERVICE: 10%, card slips closed   CARDS: Amex, Delta, Diners, MasterCard, Switch, Visa   DETAILS: 50 seats. 20 seats outside. Private parties: 50 main room, 6 to 30 private rooms. Car park. No children under 8 in main restaurant; children welcome in Chop and Ale House. Wheelchair access (also WC). No music   ACCOMMODATION: 16 rooms, all with bath/shower. TV. Phone. B&B £105 to £125. Rooms for disabled (The Which? Hotel Guide)

*Subscribers to Which? Online can access* The Good Food Guide *on www.which.net.*

# ▲ Albannach ▮ ✘

Baddidarroch, Lochinver IV27 4LP
TEL: (01571) 844407   FAX: (01571) 844285
EMAIL: the.albannach@virgin.net
WEBSITE: www.thealbannach.com

COOKING **5**
MODERN SCOTTISH
£47–£57

Dinner is a no-choice five-course affair at the Albannach, a welcoming restaurant-with-rooms perched high above the busy fishing harbour. It is served with panache by the owner, who dons his kilt for the occasion. The kitchen's produce embraces local, organic, free-range and wild, with shellfish from friends' creels (crab, lobster, crayfish and langoustine), oysters from local beds, vegetables from neighbouring crofters, Morayshire beef and seasonal game. With such an abundant natural larder, there's no truck with gimmicks, just sound technique and an 'emphasis on allowing natural flavours to shine through'. An inter-course soup (perhaps well-balanced red pepper, orange and sherry) and pre-dessert cheeses (smoked Gubbeen and Cashel Blue with oatcakes, dates and grapes) wend their way between the main elements.

Starters have taken in a warm tartlet of Loch Roe crab with spiced tomato chutney, while a main course roast breast of Gressingham duck – on braised red cabbage with carrot and cardamom purée and a potato and thyme galette – has come with a 'faultless' Madeira sauce. To finish, aniseed parfait with a pastry basket of raspberries might be followed by coffee in the panelled conservatory with its spectacular views across the bay to the Assynt mountains. The wine list's focus is on France, and good producers are its main pre-occupation, but prices are low enough to encourage experimentation: if in doubt, look to the southern hemisphere for greater affordability. There is a strong half-bottle section, and house wines start at £10.

CHEFS/PROPRIETORS: Colin Craig and Lesley Crosfield   OPEN: Tue to Sun D only 8 (1 sitting) CLOSED: 1 Dec to 14 Mar   MEALS: Set D £37   SERVICE: not inc   CARDS: Delta, MasterCard, Switch, Visa   DETAILS: 16 seats. Private parties: 20 main room. Car park. No children under 12. No smoking in dining room. No music. No mobile phones   ACCOMMODATION: 5 rooms, all with bath/shower. Phone. D,B&B £87 to £190. Rooms for disabled. No children under 12 (*The Which? Hotel Guide*)

# Limetree ✘      NEW ENTRY

High Street, Moffat DG10 9HG
TEL: (01683) 221654   FAX: (01683) 221721
WEBSITE: www.limetree-restaurant.co.uk

COOKING **3**
MODERN BRITISH
£24–£34

This newcomer opened in July 2001 in a two-storey, double-fronted Georgian stone house in the middle of Moffat. The bistro-style dining room is divided into two areas and has undressed tables of light wood. The cooking – emphasising robust flavours and interesting taste combinations – at first seems simple and rustic, but the no-frills presentation is misleading: there is real sophistication here, and hearty, pleasing flavours.

The menu is short and changes frequently. Starters might include salmon cured in lime juice and sweet chilli with cucumber, spring onion and coriander; or maybe a hearty helping of fennel and saffron soup. For main courses, pink, tender rump of lamb sits atop spiced aubergine with tomato, fresh herbs and hummus, while crisp-skinned chicken breast comes with wilted spinach leaves and mushroom mash. Desserts depend on quality ingredients rather than fancy presentation: pears and plums poached in red wine, say, perhaps enhanced with lemony custard and shortbread biscuits (home-made, like the bread and ice-creams). The short wine list, divided almost evenly between Old World and New, sports a few interesting bottles; house wines are £9.50.

CHEF: Matt Seddon   PROPRIETORS: Matt and Artemis Seddon   OPEN: Mon to Sat D only 6.30 to 9.30   CLOSED: first 2 weeks Oct, 2 weeks Jan   MEALS: Set D £15.75 (2 courses) to £19.50   SERVICE: not inc, card slips closed   CARDS: Delta, MasterCard, Switch, Visa   DETAILS: 24 seats. Private parties: 16 main room. No smoking in dining room. Wheelchair access (not WC). Music

## ▲ Well View  ♟ ⚶

Ballplay Road, Moffat DG10 9JU
TEL: (01683) 220184   FAX: (01683) 220088
EMAIL: info@wellview.co.uk
WEBSITE: www.wellview.co.uk

COOKING 4
SCOTTISH-FRENCH
£26–£51

This mid-nineteenth-century house on the edge of Moffat (a spa town in Victorian times, hence the hotel's name), is a regular stop on the way to the Highlands for one couple. The generosity of Janet Schuckardt's food (lunch is three courses, dinner five plus canapés and sweetmeats) adds to the homely feel, while her accurate judgements in terms of timings and combinations of materials ensure that she gets the best from her ingredients. There is no choice before dessert, so effort is concentrated on each dish: perhaps a tartlet of white Stilton and apricots, followed by Arctic char on braised cabbage with a dill cream sauce, or, at another meal, deep fried haggis balls with a small, well-dressed salad, followed by grilled goats' cheese on a mix of Mediterranean vegetables.

After a main course of, perhaps, pan-roast duck breast with a plum and port sauce on stir-fried vegetables, comes cheese, then a choice of two desserts. A degree of indulgence is evident in chocolate chip steam pudding with custard, and in a Drambuie cream with raspberry sauce. The wine list favours Bordeaux, Burgundy and the Rhône, but there are some good selections from Australia, Italy and Spain. Mark-ups are sensible, giving diners scope for good drinking at or around the £20 mark. Five house wines start at £13 (£3 a glass).

CHEFS: Janet and Lina Schuckardt   PROPRIETORS: Janet and John Schuckardt   OPEN: Sun to Fri L 12.15 to 1.15, all week D 6.30 to 8.30   MEALS: Set L £18, Set D £32   SERVICE: none, card slips closed   CARDS: Amex, Delta, MasterCard, Switch, Visa   DETAILS: 24 seats. Private parties: 20 main room, 6 private room. Car park. No children under 6 at D. No smoking in dining room. No music. No mobile phones   ACCOMMODATION: 6 rooms, all with bath/shower. TV. B&B £60 to £108. Baby facilities (The Which? Hotel Guide)  £5

---

🍾 denotes an outstanding wine cellar; ♟ denotes a good wine list, worth travelling for.

## MUIR OF ORD  Highland                                    map 11

## ▲ Dower House ▼ ⅚✳

Highfield, Muir of Ord IV6 7XN
TEL/FAX: (01463) 870090
EMAIL: enquiries@thedowerhouse.co.uk
WEBSITE: www.thedowerhouse.co.uk

COOKING 3
MODERN BRITISH
£47–£57

This single-storey eighteenth-century building has bags of character and the
lived-in feel of a private home rather than a hotel. Log fires warm the lounge and
dining room. Self-taught Robyn Aitchison bases his cooking around decent
fresh materials: breads from a local baker, herbs and vegetables from the garden,
and reliable supplies of seafood, meat and game. Dinner is a three-course, no-
choice affair without gimmicks, and the food tastes as it should. A starter of
braised asparagus with Parma ham and shaved Parmesan couldn't be simpler,
while main courses might range from tender beef fillet, enlivened with a herb
relish and unusual salad leaves from the polytunnel, to seared scallops with
John Dory and a basil and olive oil dressing. To finish, there might be pear tarte
Tatin or grilled pineapple with lime caramel sauce 'exactly as described'.
Cheeses are well-kept, coffee comes with home-made truffles, and nettle tea is a
pleasing brew. The globe-trotting wine list is split evenly between the Old and
New Worlds, with good value and careful selection evident everywhere. Pricing
is reasonable, giving diners a good deal of choice, particularly in the £20 to £25
range. French house wines are priced at £16.

CHEF: Robyn Aitchison  PROPRIETORS: Robyn and Mena Aitchison  OPEN: all week D only 8 to
9.30 (L by arrangement)  CLOSED: 2 weeks Nov, 25 Dec  MEALS: Set L £21, Set D £35  SERVICE:
not inc, card slips closed  CARDS: MasterCard, Switch, Visa  DETAILS: 28 seats. 6 seats outside.
Private parties: 28 main room. Car park. Children's helpings. No children under 5 after 8pm in
dining room. No smoking in dining room. Wheelchair access (also WC). No music. No mobile
phones  ACCOMMODATION: 5 rooms, all with bath/shower. TV. Phone. B&B £65 to £150. Baby
facilities (The Which? Hotel Guide)

## NAIRN  Highland                                          map 11

## ▲ Clifton House ▮ ⅚✳

1 and 3 Viewfield Street, Nairn IV12 4HW
TEL: (01667) 453119  FAX: (01667) 452836
EMAIL: macintyre@clifton-hotel.co.uk
WEBSITE: www.clifton-hotel.co.uk

COOKING 4
MODERN SCOTTISH
£36–£56

From outside, the Victorian house may look like any other in the row, but once
through the door its very personal flavour becomes apparent: from the artistic
furnishings and décor, to the dozen or so concerts, plays and readings that take
place, usually between October and April. J Gordon Macintyre presides over an
old-fashioned menu, in untranslated French, that typically offers champignons
à la grecque, oeufs mayonnaise, and terrine de col vert (duck to the rest of us).
   Despite the narrow repertoire, and reliance on advance preparation for first
courses, a combination of well-sourced materials and simple treatments
produces a range of accomplished dishes. Salmon might come with beurre
blanc, chicken breast with mushrooms, and beef fillet with bordelaise sauce, to

be followed by sherry trifle, pears in vanilla syrup, or caramel custard. The wine list takes a classic approach, favouring red Bordeaux and red and white Burgundy (some excellent selections and mature vintages from both regions), and food-friendly Loire reds (served at a cool temperature) are a plus. Well-chosen New World wines round out the list, New Zealand being a particular strength. Prices aren't low, but there are a few interesting wines under £20; house claret is £12 a bottle (£2.50 a glass).

CHEFS: J. Gordon Macintyre and Charles Macintyre   PROPRIETOR: J. Gordon Macintyre   OPEN: all week 12.30 to 1.30, 7 to 9.30   CLOSED: Christmas and New Year   MEALS: alc (main courses £15 to £20)   SERVICE: none, card slips closed   CARDS: Amex, Diners, MasterCard, Visa   DETAILS: 45 seats. Private parties: 60 main room, 20 private room. Car park. Children's helpings. No smoking in 1 dining room. Music. No mobile phones   ACCOMMODATION: 12 rooms, all with bath/shower. B&B £60 to £107 (*The Which? Hotel Guide*)

---

**OBAN  Argyll & Bute**                                                      **map 11**

# Ee-Usk  £                                           | NEW ENTRY |

104 George Street, Oban PA34 5NS                              COOKING **2**
TEL: (01631) 565666   FAX: (01631) 570282                        SEAFOOD
EMAIL: eeusk.fishcafe@virgin.net                               £22–£47

The former proprietors of the Pierhouse in Port Appin (see entry) have moved here to Oban's main street (the name is a phonetic rendering of the Gaelic for fish). Inside all is bright, plain and minimalist (blue and yellow décor, blond wood tables, blue banquettes, ultra-modern pictures), with cheerful service and an informal ambience.

The menu – also chalked on a blackboard outside the door – is fish (barring steak and piri piri chicken), which is cooked with care but without overwhelming sauces. A light, creamy chowder starter is full of chunks of undyed smoked haddock; Thai fishcakes don't underplay the chillis and come with a sweet chilli sauce. Pan-fried halibut, fresh and simply cooked, may come with creamed leeks and sauté potatoes. Simple desserts include créme brûlée, sticky toffee pudding, chocolate fudge cake, and a pleasingly astringent lemon cheesecake. The short wine list, favouring fish-friendly whites, has a decent range and low prices; almost everything is under £20, and prices start at £9.95.

CHEFS: Sheila MacLeod and Dino Zavaroni   PROPRIETORS: the MacLeod family   OPEN: all week 12 to 3, 6 to 10   CLOSED: 25 and 26 Dec, 1 and 2 Jan   MEALS: alc (main courses £6 to £20) SERVICE: not inc   CARDS: Delta, MasterCard, Switch, Visa   DETAILS: 56 seats. Children's helpings. No-smoking area. Music. Air-conditioned  (£5)

---

*'So, I just had to try the lamb's testicles...didn't I! What can I say without revealing my sources? Only that they had the same texture as, well, other testicles. Dense and slightly mealy. Coarser and more granular than sweetbreads and overcooked as they were quite dry. Not a patch on the bull's testicles I once had in Madrid but then those had come from a bull who had distinguished himself in the bullring whereas I doubt this lamb had ever had that opportunity.'* (On eating in London)

---

# ▲ Peat Inn ▮ ✸

Peat Inn KY15 5LH
TEL: (01334) 840206   FAX: (01334) 840530
EMAIL: reservations@thepeatinn.co.uk
WEBSITE: www.thepeatinn.co.uk                          COOKING 4
at junction of B940 and B941, 6m SW of St              SCOTTISH
Andrews                                                £30–£70

Inside the modest-looking coaching inn, at a road junction in open countryside, is a comfortable lounge with high-quality furnishings and a few idiosyncratic decorations along the lines of candlesticks made from old cutlery. The dining room extension at the rear has big windows, high-backed chairs and well-appointed tables, where lunch – the most popularly reported meal, a single sitting with a no-choice menu of three courses – is considered good value.

David Wilson's food is as proudly Scottish as can be, with fish, fowl and game taking pride of place. His commitment to local materials and championing of native produce – scallops, salmon and prawns 'the essence of freshness', for example – have been both pioneering and unwavering. This is a restaurant that faithfully reflects its regional roots and the seasons, as it has done for the 30 years it has been in the Guide. Evident skill is also deployed much of the time, although the food too often lacks the vigour, energy and indeed judgement that made the Peat Inn's name: main-course meats in particular, such as tasty, pink roast venison, or sesame-crusted guinea fowl, invariably seem to outshine their lacklustre and sometimes undercooked vegetable accompaniments.

To finish, mango sorbet served with red berries and vanilla sauce is 'just what summer days were made for', or there may be a little pot of rosemary-flavoured chocolate. Incidentals, such as bread and the appetiser soup, are well reported, and service is affable and helpful. 'I am not a traditionalist,' states David Wilson in the introduction to his long, varied and logically compiled wine list. Nevertheless, the 'classic' areas of France – Champagne, Bordeaux, Burgundy – are well represented (helpfully, the list includes vintage charts where appropriate to indicate the quality of various vintages) but so are wines from Germany and the New World. There is also a healthy selection of half-bottles; full bottle prices start at £16.

CHEF: David Wilson   PROPRIETORS: David and Patricia Wilson   OPEN: Tue to Sat 1 (1 sitting), 7 to 9.30   CLOSED: 25 Dec, 1 Jan   MEALS: alc D (main courses £16 to £19.50). Set L £19.50, Set D £30 to £45   SERVICE: not inc, card slips closed   CARDS: Amex, Delta, MasterCard, Switch, Visa   DETAILS: 48 seats. Private parties: 24 main room, 10 to 14 private rooms. Car park. Vegetarian meals. Children's helpings. No smoking in dining room. Wheelchair access (also WC). No music. No mobile phones   ACCOMMODATION: 8 rooms, all with bath/shower. TV. Phone. B&B £75 to £155. Rooms for disabled (*The Which? Hotel Guide*)

---

*All entries in the Guide are re-researched and rewritten every year, not least because restaurant standards fluctuate. Don't rely on an out-of-date Guide.*

# Let's Eat 🕽 £

77 Kinnoull Street, Perth PH1 5EZ
TEL: (01738) 643377   FAX: (01738) 621464                    COOKING 3
EMAIL: enquiries@letseatperth.co.uk                    MODERN EUROPEAN
WEBSITE: www.letseatperth.co.uk                              £26–£50

Tony Heath and Shona Drysdale have leased their property in George Street, which used to house Let's Eat Again, to concentrate their energies on the original. As the Guide went to press a few changes to the menu, and perhaps even the style, were planned, but Tony Heath remains in charge of the kitchen, his menu's generosity matched by the food's broad appeal. On offer might be a small omelette on soft goats' cheese with tomato chutney, or wild mushroom risotto with truffle butter, followed by chicken breast with Marsala and cream.

Organic materials range from salad leaves to Tamworth pork, and a sound source of meat from an understanding butcher means that the kitchen can get a lamb shoulder stripped down, and take just the piece it needs for a long, slow, six-hour cook, the result served with braised shallots, mixed beans and mash. Beef is hung for four weeks, producing a chargrilled ribeye with French fries, and fish and shellfish (from the West Coast or Aberdeen market), might include mussels with shallots, white wine and cream, or cod fillet topped with a cumin and coriander crust. Finish with rice pudding and blueberry compote, or dark chocolate tart with white chocolate sorbet. An amenable wine list stays mostly under £20, starting with a handful of house wines from £11 to £13.

CHEF: Tony Heath   PROPRIETORS: Tony Heath and Shona Drysdale   OPEN: Tue to Sat 12 to 2, 6.30 to 9.45   CLOSED: 25 and 26 Dec, last 2 weeks Jan, last 2 weeks July   MEALS: alc (main courses L £8.50 to £11, D £9 to £17)   SERVICE: not inc, card slips closed   CARDS: Amex, Delta, MasterCard, Switch, Visa   DETAILS: 65 seats. Private parties: 70 main room. Vegetarian meals. Children's helpings. No smoking in dining room. Wheelchair access (also WC). Music  £5

# 63 Tay Street 🕽 🕽

63 Tay Street, Perth PH2 8NN                               COOKING 3
TEL: (01738) 441451   FAX: (01738) 441461              MODERN EUROPEAN
                                                             £26–£45

With cool white walls and a wooden floor, the long dining room gives an airy, light and fresh impression, its appeal enhanced by views over the River Tay and Kinnoull Hill. Jeremy Wares cooks a weekly-changing menu (all starters at one price, likewise mains and desserts) in contemporary style. A few bright-sounding flavours pop up – a chicken, paprika and Moray ham terrine with cucumber salsa, for example – but a sound grasp of essentials underpins the cooking, producing dishes that are generally interesting without being too attention-seeking. Salmon might be served three ways – smoked, tartare, and warm on avocado salsa – while scallops have come with a red wine reduction and leek risotto.

Different moods are catered for in a main course of leek and Parmesan tart with couscous salad, and another of braised lamb shank with root vegetables, while a visitor in mid-August took advantage of the first grouse of the season (roast, with a bread sauce). Finish with crème brûlée (variously flavoured with raspberries or pineapple), or a chocolate and Drambuie mousse with shortbread. Shona Wares 'makes you feel at home with wonderful friendly service', and the well-annotated wine list lends a helping hand round the vineyards of Europe and the New World. Organised by style, most wines come in under £25, with a few pricier bottles from California, Burgundy and Bordeaux. House wines start at £10.95 (£3.25 per glass).

CHEF: Jeremy Wares   PROPRIETORS: Jeremy and Shona Wares   OPEN: Tue to Sat 12 to 2, 6.30 to 9   CLOSED: first 2 weeks Jan, last 2 weeks Aug   MEALS: alc (main courses L £7.50, D £15) SERVICE: not inc, card slips closed   CARDS: Amex, Delta, MasterCard, Switch, Visa   DETAILS: 32 seats. Private parties: 32 main room. Vegetarian meals. No smoking in dining room. No music  (£5)

## PORT APPIN  Argyll & Bute                                              map 11

# ▲ Airds Hotel ♆ ✇ ⅗✳

Port Appin PA38 4DF
TEL: (01631) 730236   FAX: (01631) 730535
EMAIL: airds@airds-hotel.com                                    COOKING 6
WEBSITE: www.airds-hotel.com                               MODERN BRITISH
2m off A828, on E shore of Loch Linnhe                         £58–£70

This tranquil small hotel near the harbour has been run by the Allens for 25 years. A recent change at the stoves leaves the four-course dinner format unchanged, and raw materials are still first-class (many of them local, wild or organic). Luxuries are conspicuous by their presence: a champagne jelly accompanying lightly cooked oysters; a cep sauce with confit duck leg; and truffles that might appear with roast squab pigeon or with a whole west coast lobster.

Dishes look attractive, not because of elaborate garnishes, but because materials and composition are well judged: witness a large, wafer-thin, smooth raviolo bursting with the pink and white flesh of lobster and langoustine, on a foundation of crunchy shredded cabbage, surrounded by a frothy shellfish velouté. What the cooking may lack in flair or flamboyance it makes up for in near faultless execution, judging by a tian of fresh crab layered with tomato, served with a well-dressed herby salad, and by pink-fleshed, crisp-skinned Gressingham duck breast in a rich Kirsch sauce with cherries, smoked bacon and shallots. Accompanying vegetables are of exemplary quality and accurately timed, from tasty new potatoes to carrots, turnips and wild mushrooms.

Desserts have yielded refreshing orange and grapefruit segments in a Grand Marnier jelly, and a well-balanced coconut and cardamom mousse with pineapple and mango; appetisers and petits fours are of a high order. Service is generally friendly and professional, although a couple of reporters mention incidents best described as 'confrontational' (sending customers away with a flea in their ear is no way to earn repeat business). The wine list offers some classy bottles, particularly for lovers of fine red Burgundy. In addition to classic French regions, there are top producers from Italy and California, although better value can be found in the Australian section. Overall, prices are not cheap; five house wines range from £16 (for Australian Shiraz) to £36.50 (for white Burgundy), and there is a good selection of half-bottles, many from Burgundy.

CHEFS: Graeme Allen and Paul Burns   PROPRIETORS: the Allen family   OPEN: all week D only 7.30 to 8.30   CLOSED: 17 to 27 Dec   MEALS: Set D £45   SERVICE: not inc, card slips closed   CARDS: Delta, MasterCard, Switch, Visa   DETAILS: 32 seats. Private parties: 32 main room. Car park. No smoking in dining room. No music. No mobile phones   ACCOMMODATION: 12 rooms, all with bath/shower. TV. Phone. D,B&B £110 to £330 (*The Which? Hotel Guide*)

## ▲ Pierhouse 🍴✷

Port Appin PA38 4DE
TEL: (01631) 730302   FAX: (01631) 730400
EMAIL: pierhouse@btinternet.com
WEBSITE: www.pierhousehotel.co.uk
off A828, on E shore of Loch Linnhe, opposite
Lismore ferry

COOKING 3
SEAFOOD
£25–£57

Castle Stalker rises dramatically nearby, the ferry for Lismore departs from the end of the pier where fishermen land their catches, and the views are stunning; there is little more one could ask of the setting beside Loch Linnhe. Meanwhile, ongoing refurbishment and updating preserves the comfort factor inside. As for its food, when the criteria of simplicity and freshness are met, then it is really on song.

Go for fresh and unadulterated seafood, particularly from the loch itself: from oysters (cold or grilled) and lobster to langoustines with mayonnaise or garlic dip. Scampi tails might come in crispy batter, grilled scallops with bacon rice, and a giant platter for two (weighing in at nearly £60) showcases the lot. Don't expect too much of incidentals or desserts, but take advantage of a wine list that does its level best to stay under £20, starting with house Chardonnay and Merlot (both Vin de Pays d'Oc) at £11.

CHEF: Rita Thomson   PROPRIETORS: David and Elizabeth Hamblin   OPEN: all week 12.30 to 2.30, 6.30 to 9.30   CLOSED: 25 and 26 Dec   MEALS: alc (main courses £10 to £25)   SERVICE: not inc, card slips closed   CARDS: Delta, MasterCard, Switch, Visa   DETAILS: 70 seats. 24 seats outside. Private parties: 70 main room, 5 to 14 private rooms. Car park. Vegetarian meals. Children's helpings. No smoking in dining room. Wheelchair access (also WC). Music. No mobile phones   ACCOMMODATION: 12 rooms, all with bath/shower. TV. Phone. B&B £45 to £90. Baby facilities ⑤

### ST MARGARET'S HOPE Orkney                                    map 11

## ▲ The Creel 🍴✷

Front Road, St Margaret's Hope KW17 2SL
TEL: (01856) 831311
EMAIL: alan@thecreel.freeserve.co.uk
WEBSITE: www.thecreel.co.uk
off A961, 13m S of Kirkwall, on South Ronaldsay

COOKING 7
MODERN SCOTTISH
£37–£50

Orkney has a special magic. Huge expanses of sea curve at the horizon to meet blue sky and cotton wool clouds, and it is a great place for walking, bird-watching, world-class archaeological sites and fine fish, which is where the Creel comes in. It remains unpretentious (although the main dining room has new pine tables and high-backed chairs), and dinner typically offers three or four starters (a soup, one or two fish, and a meat dish), followed by one meat and two fish options. But if that sounds limited, think again: one couple counted seventeen different types of fish and eight varieties of shellfish on the menu during a week's stay. Among soups might be a smooth, creamy scallop and oyster version, or a rich, reddish-brown velvet crab soup, packed with flavour, containing chunks of megrim. Alternative starters are no less appealing, judging by slices of moist, steamed roulade of skate wing wrapped around a bullet of tapénade, the plate dotted with puréed wild sorrel. But this is not complicated food; its success stems from materials that are unbeatable for quality, whether in a simple crab salad, or in queen scallops with garlic butter.

Given that many popular fish are in short supply, Alan Craigie is supplementing them with less familiar but more plentiful species: sea witch (deep-fried, with a pea and mint purée and a tomato-enriched garlicky mayonnaise); tope (crisply fried and served with a salsa verde made from watercress, capers and olive oil); and torsk (or tusk; two thick, tender fillets served with half a dozen shelled langoustine tails on one occasion, with cockles, mussels and a creamy pea and spinach purée another). He might also track down coley, forkbeard, deep reds, ling and saithe.

Meat eaters should not neglect lamb, if available: braised shoulder with peas and shallots, or maybe a terrine of North Ronaldsay mutton with rhubarb chutney. Desserts tend to be modest and domestic, perhaps almond and orange cake, summer fruit soup, or a 'special' combining chocolate mousse, meringue, crème caramel and a butterscotch sauce. Reasonable mark-ups distinguish the short wine list, which opens with an Australian Cabernet at £9.50 and a New Zealand Sauvignon Blanc at £12.50.

CHEF: Alan Craigie   PROPRIETORS: Joyce and Alan Craigie   OPEN: all week D only 7 to 9   CLOSED: Nov, Jan and Feb   MEALS: alc (main courses £16 to £18)   SERVICE: not inc, card slips closed CARDS: MasterCard, Switch, Visa   DETAILS: 36 seats. Private parties: 36 main room, 12 private room. Car park. Children's helpings. No smoking in dining room. Wheelchair access (also WC). No music   ACCOMMODATION: 3 rooms, all with bath/shower. TV. B&B £45 to £75. Baby facilities (The Which? Hotel Guide)

---

**ST MONANS** Fife  map 11

# Seafood Restaurant 🍴✳

NEW ENTRY

16 West End, St Monans KY10 2BX
TEL: (01333) 730327   FAX: (01333) 730508
EMAIL: seafoodrest@aol.com
WEBSITE: www.theseafoodrestaurant.com

COOKING 5
SEAFOOD
£31–£60

Overlooking the rocky harbour entrance, with views of the village, the waves, Bass Rock and the Isle of May, this converted pub is well set up with a stylish bar and a small, bright, clean-looking, modern dining room complete with an 800-year-old freshwater well. Diligently sourced materials are at the heart of it, including live shellfish, oysters direct from the grower, and scallops delivered by the diver, a variable input that naturally results in a constantly changing menu.

Careful timing brings out the best in materials, including a main course of scallops with a herb and sweet chilli salsa, and there are some unusual but effective combinations, such as a lobster and mango salad with a beetroot and white truffle oil dressing. Dinner brings a second-course choice of perhaps half a dozen Kilbrandon oysters, or a lobster cappuccino, before cod fillet in Cajun spices, or turbot with a well-made Meaux mustard sauce.

The fare is not exclusively seafood, however. One visitor enjoyed a hearty-sounding but well-judged starter of accurately timed beef fillet, served with a herb risotto and a dressing combining orange, cardamom, vanilla and balsamic vinegar. At inspection, the only real cloud on the horizon concerned the earthy crushed potatoes that underpinned all main courses. Desserts extend from rum pannacotta to a prune and Armagnac pudding with banana ice cream and butterscotch sauce. Service is friendly and relaxed, but also attentive and efficient. Prices on the annotated wine list are quick to hop over the £20 barrier, but there are seven house wines under £15.

CHEF: Craig Millar  PROPRIETOR: Roybridge Ltd  OPEN: all week 12 to 2 (12.30 to 2.30 Sun), 7 to 9.30  CLOSED: Mon Sept to Apr, 25 and 26 Dec, 1 to 3 Jan  MEALS: Set L £16 (2 courses) to £20, Set D £25 (2 courses) to £35  SERVICE: not inc, card slips closed  CARDS: Amex, Delta, MasterCard, Switch, Visa  DETAILS: 44 seats. 32 seats outside. Private parties: 44 main room. Children's helpings. No smoking in dining room. Wheelchair access (also WC). No music. No mobile phones

## SPEAN BRIDGE Highland     map 11

## ▲ Old Pines ▐ ⁂

Spean Bridge, By Fort William PH34 4EG
TEL: (01397) 712324  FAX: (01397) 712433
EMAIL: goodfood@oldpines.co.uk
WEBSITE: www.oldpines.co.uk

COOKING 4
MODERN SCOTTISH
£37–£49

A stand of tall Scots pines marks this timbered homestead. The very casual scene – people coming and going, reading, drinking tea, playing board games, scanning the menu, studying the wine list, ready to order by 7pm – sets eating and drinking in a familial context. The dining room is open-plan, tables (and often wines) are shared, and the menu offers the Hobson's choice that most people get at home.

But just look at what goes into the menu. Isle of Muck squat lobster or crab comes with home-grown salad leaves; fish from Mallaig is made into a soup; trout (home-smoked) comes with a mustard sauce; and the wild fungi with the venison were probably picked by Bill Barber. Anyone working through the five courses will have soup and a salad under their belt before they reach the main course – perhaps John Dory with mussels in a vermouth and orange sauce – with maybe a lemon and raspberry posset plus a plate of farmhouse cheeses to come. The wine list, organised by grape variety and usefully annotated, gives good value; mark-ups are low, and there is much below £18 (one Australian bargain is Grant Burge Filsell Shiraz at £18). A frequently changing selection is offered by the glass, and bottle prices start at £10.50.

CHEF: Sukie Barber  PROPRIETORS: Bill and Sukie Barber  OPEN: Tue to Sun D 8 (7.30 in winter) CLOSED: 2 weeks Nov to Dec, 2 days Christams  MEALS: Set D £32. Light L menu also available Tue to Sun  SERVICE: not inc, card slips closed  CARDS: MasterCard, Switch, Visa  DETAILS: 30 seats. Private parties: 30 main room. Car park. Children's helpings. No smoking in dining room. Wheelchair access (also WC). No music  ACCOMMODATION: 8 rooms, all with bath/shower. D,B&B £80 to £170. Rooms for disabled. Baby facilities (The Which? Hotel Guide)

## STEIN Highland       map 11

# Lochbay ✳✻ £

1–2 Macleod Terrace, Stein, Isle of Skye IV55 8GA
TEL/FAX: (01470) 592235
EMAIL: djamwilkinson@aol.com       COOKING **2**
WEBSITE: www.lochbay-seafood-       FISH
restaurant.co.uk       £23–£60

An enviable position, no more than a stone's throw from the sea, is part of the appeal of the Wilkinsons' tiny cottage restaurant. True to its setting, it specialises in fresh seafood, cooked in the simplest ways possible without unnecessary enrichment or arty re-invention. Talisker oysters (served au naturel or grilled with garlic butter), Sconser scallops, Shetland salmon and Loch Bay king prawns are just some of the pleasures on offer. Daily specials are listed on the blackboard, otherwise the menu deals in warm salad of seared squid, medallions of monkfish with shellfish sauce, seafood platters and lobsters. Finish in traditional style with cranachan or clootie dumpling. Baguettes and light dishes are available at lunchtime. The wine list is brief and to the point, with Scottish blackberry wine tacked on for good measure. House wines, served by the carafe or glass, start at £10.50 a litre.

CHEF: David Wilkinson   PROPRIETORS: David and Alison Wilkinson   OPEN: Mon to Fri 12 to 2.30, 6.30 to 9   CLOSED: 1 Nov to 21 Dec; 25, 26 and 31 Dec; 6 Jan to Easter   MEALS: alc (main courses £9.50 to £28)   SERVICE: not inc, card slips closed   CARDS: Delta, MasterCard, Switch, Visa   DETAILS: 26 seats. 12 seats outside. Private parties: 26 main room. Car park. Children's helpings. No smoking in dining room. Wheelchair access (not WC). Occasional music

## STONEHAVEN Aberdeenshire       map 11

# Tolbooth

Old Pier, Stonehaven AB39 2JU       COOKING **3**
TEL/FAX: (01569) 762287       SEAFOOD
WEBSITE: www.tolboothrestaurant.co.uk       £28–£49

Down by the harbour of this delightful old fishing village, the single, long, first-floor room is reached up a flight of stone steps seemingly hewn from the side of the building. The kitchen's theme is seafood, its treatments varied, taking in half a dozen oysters baked with garlic, cream, herbs and Parmesan, and steamed cockles and mussels with chilli, ginger, coriander and sherry. Main courses tend to be straightforward – perhaps baked gilt-head bream, or skate wing with anchovy and caper beurre blanc – and rarely get more complicated than, say, smoked finnan haddock in a creamy tomato sauce with a poached egg and truffle oil. Finish with toasted coconut cheesecake, or a triple chocolate parfait with crème anglaise, and drink from an obligingly varied and fairly priced wine list.

CHEFS: Christopher McCarrey, Tim Kuzspit and Stuart Duncan   PROPRIETOR: Christopher McCarrey   OPEN: Tue to Sat D only 6 to 9.30 (10 Fri and Sat)   CLOSED: 3 weeks after Christmas   MEALS: alc (main courses £11 to £19)   SERVICE: not inc   CARDS: Delta, MasterCard, Switch, Visa   DETAILS: 42 seats. Private parties: 42 main room. No children under 8. No cigars/pipes in dining room. Occasional music   (£5)

## STRATHYRE Stirling

map 11

## ▲ Creagan House 👍✳

NEW ENTRY

Strathyre FK18 8ND
TEL: (01877) 384638   FAX: (01877) 384319
EMAIL: eatandstay@creaganhouse.co.uk
WEBSITE: www.creaganhouse.co.uk

COOKING 4
FRENCH/SCOTTISH
£30–£44

A welcoming restaurant-with-rooms converted from a former seventeenth-century farmhouse, Creagan House is run with 'punctilious attention to detail' by owners Gordon and Cherry Gunn. The mock-baronial dining room, with vaulted ceiling, wooden floor, grand fireplace and long, polished refectory-style tables, is the setting for Gordon's Scottish-French repertoire.

Dishes are presented with 'merciful simplicity' to allow the flavours of locally sourced meats and fresh produce to shine: 'smokie in a pokie' is an irresistible way to start, combining smoked haddock wrapped in smoked salmon, served with a classic light butter sauce. Main courses might run to collop of venison and sweet potato fondant in a well-judged Primitivo sauce enriched with chocolate, or loin of local lamb with a 'flannet' (a crisp, dainty pastry tartlet) of lambs' kidneys and a port and redcurrant sauce. The accompanying seasonal vegetables have received praise from a number of reporters, one proclaiming them the 'best I've had in a Scottish restaurant'. To finish, go for Scottish cheeses, or perhaps hazelnut and chocolate mousse cake. Cherry Gunn runs front-of-house, where service proves helpful and unobtrusive. The lengthy, annotated global wine list has a Francophile bent, plentiful drinking under £20 and a commendable range of halves. A house selection of eight bottles starts at £9.90 with seven by the glass or carafe.

CHEF: Gordon Gunn   PROPRIETORS: Gordon and Cherry Gunn   OPEN: all week D only 7.30 to 8.30   CLOSED: 1 week Oct, 26 Jan to 7 Mar   MEALS: Set D £20.75 to £24.75   SERVICE: not inc, card slips closed   CARDS: Amex, MasterCard, Visa   DETAILS: 14 seats. Private parties: 35 main room. Car park. Children's helpings. No smoking in dining room. Wheelchair access (not WC). No music. No mobile phones   ACCOMMODATION: 5 rooms, all with bath/shower. B&B £57.50 to £95. Rooms for disabled. Baby facilities   £5

## STRONTIAN Highland

map 11

## ▲ Kilcamb Lodge ♥ ✳

Strontian PH36 4HY
TEL: (01967) 402257   FAX: (01967) 402041
EMAIL: enquiries@kilcamblodge.com
WEBSITE: www.kilcamblodge.com
on A861, near head of Loch Sunart

COOKING 4
SCOTTISH-FRENCH
£27–£52

One of the oldest stone-built houses in the area, Kilcamb sits in a prime spot with exceptional views over Lake Sunart. The hotel has changed owners since last year, but it still exudes warm hospitality, and adjustments are few. Winter opening seems to have met with success, dinner is now at 8, and residents (breakfast is recommended) need to order food and drink in advance. As before, the menu offers two or four courses, but not three, which is odd given that one is a no choice mid-meal soup. Neil Mellis, meanwhile, continues to make good use of bounteous native seafood, including Loch Sunart langoustines, and seared Morar scallops perhaps served with mango and cucumber salsa.

Although the main ingredients remain much the same, their treatment is upbeat and modestly inventive, taking in pot-roast quail with black pudding and apple, and roast loin of Mingarry venison served with braised red cabbage, goats' cheese gnocchi, and a chocolate and game sauce; similarly, roast Grampian pork comes with a café-au-lait sauce. Desserts tend be more traditional, lemon curd brûlée, say, or iced lime parfait with raspberry coulis. Lunch is a less elaborate affair of hot and cold sandwiches, soup or salad. The annotated wine list, arranged by grape variety, picks out good examples of each style. Bottles come from all over the winemaking globe, although there is a slight bias towards France. Mark-ups are fair, allowing great potential for enjoyment under £20, although those who want to spend more money on something special will find a few heavyweights scattered about. Eight house wines range from £13.60 to £19.90.

CHEF: Neil Mellis   PROPRIETORS: Ian and Jenny Grant   OPEN: Sun L 12 to 2.30, all week D 8 (1 sitting)   MEALS: Set L Sun £14.95. Set D £23.50 (2 courses) to £32.50. Bar L menu available Mon to Sat   SERVICE: not inc, card slips closed   CARDS: Delta, MasterCard, Switch, Visa   DETAILS: 35 seats. 10 seats outside. Private parties: 40 main room. Car park. Vegetarian meals. Children's helpings. No smoking in dining room. Wheelchair access (not WC). No music. No mobile phones   ACCOMMODATION: 11 rooms, all with bath/shower. TV. Phone. B&B £70 to £145. Baby facilities (The Which? Hotel Guide)

## SWINTON Borders                                                        map 11

## ▲ Wheatsheaf 🍴

Main Street, Swinton TD11 3JJ
TEL: (01890) 860257   FAX: (01890) 860688
EMAIL: reception@wheatsheaf-swinton.co.uk
WEBSITE: www.wheatsheaf-swinton.co.uk
on A6112, 6m N of Coldstream

COOKING 3
MODERN SCOTTISH
£22–£50

'A useful port of call at times of culinary starvation,' admitted a reporter from the Borders who regularly trips out to this stone-built restaurant-with-rooms by the village green. There's a new lounge for pre-prandial drinks and coffee; otherwise choose to eat in the rather dark original dining room or the lighter, modern conservatory extension.

Printed menus are supplemented by blackboard specials, and the kitchen is keen on local and organic produce. Seafood from Eyemouth might appear as langoustines with garlic butter, or smoked haddock fishcakes done the Thai way, while salmon landed from the nearby Tweed could be baked and served with creamy lemon sauce. Meat is from local farms, and game gets a good look in: put it all together and you might find breast of wood pigeon on a medallion of beef and black pudding with fondant potatoes and thyme-scented juices. Reporters have also enjoyed breast of guinea fowl with apricots and a Calvados and tarragon sauce. Desserts tend to be rich (Malteser and pecan parfait with chocolate and maple syrup sauce), service is well paced, and the global wine list opens with six house selections at £11.75 a bottle, £2.85 a glass.

CHEFS: Alan Reid and John Keir  PROPRIETORS: Alan and Julie Reid  OPEN: Tue to Sun L 12 to 2, Tue to Sat D 6 to 9.30  MEALS: alc (main courses L £5 to £10, D £10 to £17)  SERVICE: not inc, card slips closed  CARDS: Delta, MasterCard, Switch, Visa  DETAILS: 44 seats. 16 seats outside. Private parties: 26 main room, 12 to 18 private rooms. Car park. Children's helpings. No smoking in dining room. No music  ACCOMMODATION: 8 rooms, all with bath/shower. TV. Phone. B&B £55 to £105. Baby facilities (*The Which? Hotel Guide*)

## TORRIDON Highland                                           map 11

# ▲ Loch Torridon Hotel 🍴✖

Torridon, by Achnasheen, IV22 2EY
TEL: (01445) 791242   FAX: (01445) 791296
EMAIL: info@lochtorridonhotel.com                    | NEW CHEF |
WEBSITE: www.lochtorridonhotel.com                   MODERN EUROPEAN
off A896 at the head of Upper Loch Torridon          £51–£61

Kevin Broome (listed last year at RSJ in London) moved up to this full-blown Scottish baronial-style hotel (which last year we plotted by error in Achnasheen, some 20 miles or so down the road) too late for us to receive any feedback. His style, however, is an appealing one, taking in starters of pan-roast ox tongue salad, and potted skate on jelly, followed by grilled cod fillet with Cullen skink mash, and ribeye of beef with caramelised shallots. Desserts include a dark chocolate and peppercorn tower, a blackcurrant delice, and a warm apple and custard crumble. Ten house wines under £18 head a largely French list (arranged by region) with a New World selection (arranged by style). Reports are particularly welcome.

CHEF: Kevin Broome  PROPRIETORS: David and Geraldine Gregory  OPEN: all week D only 7 to 8.45  CLOSED: 2 Jan to 1 Feb  MEALS: Set D £39. Light lunch menu also available 2 to 4  SERVICE: not inc, card slips closed  CARDS: Amex, Delta, Diners, MasterCard, Switch, Visa  DETAILS: 38 seats. Private parties: 16 main room. Car park. Vegetarian meals. Children's helpings. No children under 10 at D. No smoking in dining room. Wheelchair access (not WC). No music. No mobile phones  ACCOMMODATION: 20 rooms, all with bath/shower. TV. Phone. B&B £55 to £286. Rooms for disabled. Baby facilities. Fishing  (£5)

## TROON South Ayrshire                                        map 11

# ▲ Lochgreen House 🍷 🍴✖

Monktonhill Road, Southwood, Troon KA10 7EN
TEL: (01292) 313343   FAX: (01292) 318661            COOKING 5
EMAIL: lochgreen@costleyhotels.co.uk                 FRANCO-SCOTTISH
WEBSITE: www.costleyhotels.co.uk                     £30–£53

The large house (a private residence as recently as 1991) goes in for warmth and comfort in a mannerly sort of way. With its fine oak, and plush floral fabrics, it is richly appointed without being too ornate, except perhaps for the stuffed peacock on the baby grand piano, and maybe the tapestried, medieval-style dining room. If the surroundings feel like a cocoon, the food is no less cosseting: lunch might offer a whole baby sole with tartare sauce to begin, followed by medallions of beef with château potatoes and thyme jus.

Menus change monthly, but dishes soothe throughout the year, ranging from spatchcocked quail with wild mushroom risotto, via humble sardine fillets served à la Niçoise, to lightly curried scallops with crab couscous. Turbot is wild, chicken corn-fed, and if eggs feature – perhaps poached, with hollandaise, on an escalope of salmon – they will probably come from the hotel's own hens. Soft textures predominate, not least among desserts of, for example, hot chocolate and pistachio pudding, or blackcurrant cheesecake with a lemon sorbet. The wine list is solid rather than exciting, with France receiving most attention. Eight house selections mark out the best-value wines, ranging from £14.95 to £19.50 (£3.50 to £4.65 a glass), and although options under £20 are not the most imaginative, there is plenty to go at for those with a bit more spare cash.

CHEF: Andrew Costley   PROPRIETORS: William and Catherine Costley   OPEN: all week 12 to 2, 7 to 9   MEALS: alc L (main courses £11 to £13). Set L £19.95, Set D £32.50   SERVICE: not inc   CARDS: Amex, Delta, MasterCard, Switch, Visa   DETAILS: Private parties: 80 main room. Car park. Vegetarian meals. Children's helpings. No smoking in dining room. Wheelchair access (also WC). Music. Air-conditioned   ACCOMMODATION: 15 rooms, all with bath/shower. TV. Phone. B&B £99 to £160. Rooms for disabled (*The Which? Hotel Guide*)

---

# MacCallums' Oyster Bar

The Harbour, Troon KA10 6DH                                    COOKING 3
TEL: (01292) 319339                                               SEAFOOD
WEBSITE: www.maccallums.co.uk                                    £20–£53

Despite its sailing theme – with Americas Cup memorabilia everywhere – this brick and wood building is closer to the fish market and Seacat terminal than to the yachting marina. Top-quality fresh seafood is the starting point (John MacCallum runs a wet-fish shop in Glasgow), and the kitchen wisely takes a minimal approach to much of it, turning out grilled sole with parsley butter, and some of the finest langoustines, simply cooked with garlic butter: 'you get six large ones for only £6.50; very good value.'

The range takes in anything from a classic bouillabaisse with rouille, or scallops with bacon, to some upbeat Eastern flavours, such as Thai fishcakes with sweet-and-sour cucumber sauce, or monkfish tempura and stir-fried vegetables with a sweet chill sauce. A token roast chicken with black pudding might be thrown to meat eaters, while desserts have included pear in red wine with vanilla ice cream, and sticky toffee pudding with butterscotch sauce. A short list of wines, mostly white, mostly under £20, starts with house Danie de Wet Chardonnay and a French Sauvignon Blanc at £9.50.

CHEFS: Scott Keenan and Stephen Smith   PROPRIETORS: Joan and James MacCallum   OPEN: Tue to Sun L 12 to 2.30 (3.30 Sun), Tue to Sat D 7 to 9.30   MEALS: alc (main courses £10 to £20.50). Set L Tue to Sat £9.95 (2 courses) to £12.45   SERVICE: not inc, card slips closed   CARDS: Delta, MasterCard, Switch, Visa   DETAILS: 43 seats. Private parties: 43 main room. Car park. Wheelchair access (not WC). Music

---

*The Guide is totally independent, accepts no free hospitality, and survives on the number of copies sold each year.*

# Wales

## ▲ Penhelig Arms Hotel 🍷 ✳

Terrace Road, Aberdovey LL35 0LT
TEL: (01654) 767215   FAX: (01654) 767690
EMAIL: info@penheligarms.com
WEBSITE: www.penheligarms.com                          COOKING 2
on A493 Tywyn to Machynlleth road, opposite            BRITISH
Penhelig station                                       £21–£50

Only the road outside separates this old inn from the Dovey estuary. Inside, it has been redecorated, its two linked dining rooms done in restful pale grey and blue, with one wall of bare Welsh slate. The long menu features home-cooked food using good raw materials, including particularly striking fresh fish: perhaps a fritto misto of breadcrumbed whitebait, lightly spiced squid rings and a small fillet of crisply-battered sea bream, served with a large blob of well-made tartare sauce. Despite a salsa here, or a chilli relish there, much of the cooking and saucing tends to be old-fashioned: for our inspector a large chargrilled fillet steak with a roux-based mushroom and Roquefort sauce, accompanied by a dish of irregularly timed vegetables.

Desserts are in similarly traditional mould, offering banoffi pie, or a large, flat wedge of sloppy sticky toffee pudding. Service is as homely as the food: 'That'll finish you off!' accompanied one pudding order. As for wines, the quality, breadth and excellent value of this admirable selection points to a clued-up enthusiast. As an inspector said, 'Your eyes pop out when you see the prices. What other list in Britain has so much to offer for £10–£15 per bottle?' A dozen house wines (all between £10 and £12, or £2.50–£3.50 a glass) include Italians from the Inzolia grape (white, Sicily) and the Corvina (red, Veneto). There is also a decent selection of half-bottles.

CHEF: Jane Howkins   PROPRIETORS: Robert and Sally Hughes   OPEN: all week 12 to 2, 7 to 9.30 CLOSED: 25 and 26 Dec   MEALS: Set L Mon to Sat £10.95 (2 courses), Set L Sun £13.95, Set D £24. Bar menu available D   SERVICE: not inc, card slips closed   CARDS: Delta, MasterCard, Switch, Visa   DETAILS: 40 seats. 30 seats outside. Private parties: 24 main room. Car park. Children's helpings. No smoking in dining room. No music. No mobile phones. Air-conditioned ACCOMMODATION: 14 rooms, all with bath/shower. TV. Phone. B&B £39.50 to £92 (*The Which? Hotel Guide*) £5

▲ *means accommodation is available.*

## ABERSOCH Gwynedd map 7

# ▲ Porth Tocyn Hotel ⅍

Bwlch Tocyn, Abersoch LL53 7BU
TEL: (01758) 713303   FAX: (01758) 713538
EMAIL: porthtocyn.hotel@virgin.net
WEBSITE: www.porth-tocyn-hotel.co.uk   COOKING 4
on minor road 2m S of Abersoch through hamlets   MODERN EUROPEAN
of Sarn Bach and Bwlch Tocyn   £44–£53

One of the Guide's most venerable establishments, Porth Tocyn owes its longevity to several factors. First, it has evolved in small ways over the years so as not to get left behind by changing fashions. Second, and perhaps more important, it is run as it was when first opened by Nick Fletcher-Brewer's grandparents, with the personal touch of caring, hands-on proprietors giving it a comfortable, unstuffy atmosphere. Third, it has a setting overlooking Cardigan Bay that remains nothing short of spectacular.

Dinner is 'a treat to look forward to', according to a well-travelled inspector – a five-course set-price affair with soup after the starter, and cheeses and fruit to follow dessert – and the cooking style is as traditional as the format. Among highlights have been a starter of sauté pigeon breast on black pudding with caramelised apple and a cider and pear jus, a 'light and refreshing' carrot and orange soup, and an 'eye-catching' construction of duck breast layered with smooth celeriac purée and finely sliced red cabbage. The wine list has been trimmed a little this year in order to concentrate on wines with more popular appeal. Six well-chosen house selections range from £12.50 to £15.95.

CHEFS: David Carney and Louise Fletcher-Brewer   PROPRIETORS: the Fletcher-Brewer family
OPEN: Sun L 12.15 to 2, all week D 7.15 to 9 (9.30 high season)   CLOSED: most of mid-Nov to mid-Mar   MEALS: Set buffet L Sun £19, Set D £27.50 (2 courses) to £34. Light L available Mon to Sat
SERVICE: not inc, card slips closed   CARDS: MasterCard, Switch, Visa   DETAILS: 50 seats. 30 seats outside. Car park. Vegetarian meals. Children's helpings. No very young children at D. No smoking in dining room. Wheelchair access (not WC). No music. No mobile phones
ACCOMMODATION: 17 rooms, all with bath/shower. TV. Phone. B&B £56.50 to £137. Rooms for disabled. Baby facilities. Swimming pool (*The Which? Hotel Guide*)

## BASSALEG Newport map 4

# Junction 28 ▼

Station Approach, Bassaleg NP10 1LD
TEL: (01633) 891891   FAX: (01633) 895978
from M4 junction 28 take A468 towards   COOKING 1
Caerphilly, turn right at Tredegar Arms and take   MODERN BRITISH
first left   £19–£43

Appropriately named after the nearest M4 exit, this busy, bustling place inhabits a converted local railway station overlooking the lower reaches of the River Usk. A colonial, Pullman-type carriage is hooked on to one end of the dining room, although there's no fast track though the vast menu, which emphatically identifies 'Meats', 'Vegetarian' and 'Fish' in the shape of rump of lamb with provençale couscous and rosemary sauce; strudel of spinach,

Mozzarella and hazelnuts with tomato sauce; and herb-crumbed fillet of hake with tomato, saffron and tarragon sauce. Early-evening 'flyer' options (5.30 to 7pm) offer a fairly priced deal. Service is attentive and the bill can be 'a pleasant surprise'. A well-priced wine list offers sensibly priced bottles from around the world starting with three house offerings at £10.65 (£1.95 a glass).

CHEF: Jon West   PROPRIETORS: Richard Wallace and Jon West   OPEN: all week L 12 to 2 (4 Sun), Mon to Sat D 5.30 to 9.30   CLOSED: 26 Dec and 1 Jan   MEALS: alc (main courses £8 to £16). Set L Mon to Sat £6.95 (1 course) to £10.45, Set L Sun £10.95 (2 courses) to £12.95. Set D 5.30 to 7 £12.95   SERVICE: not inc, card slips closed   CARDS: Amex, Delta, MasterCard, Switch, Visa   DETAILS: 165 seats. Private parties: 60 main room, 12 to 60 private rooms. Car park. Vegetarian meals. No cigars/pipes in dining room. Wheelchair access (also WC). Occasional music. Air-conditioned

## BEAUMARIS  Isle of Anglesey                                                    map 7

# ▲ Ye Olde Bulls Head ♥ ✳

Castle Street, Beaumaris LL58 8AP
TEL: (01248) 810329   FAX: (01248) 811294                          COOKING 4
EMAIL: info@bullsheadinn.co.uk                                MODERN EUROPEAN
WEBSITE: www.bullsheadinn.co.uk                                      £43–£52

The characterful old inn, which dates back centuries and has entertained Dr Johnson and Charles Dickens, conveys a feeling of being unspoilt while still providing modern creature comforts. Its public rooms include a bar with beams and a log fire, a light and airy conservatory brasserie (with a separate chef and menu), and a more formal but comfortable and stylish upstairs dining room: essentially a long loft with sloping roof, high-backed chairs, and a generous fixed-price menu.

Fish is a strong suit, mainly from local waters but also including creditable specimens from a recently opened fish farm: for example, a sizeable, fleshy whole grilled turbot topped with flavourful crusty gremolata, a straightforward dish owing its success to good-quality raw material. Cooking techniques are sound, presentation good, and dishes are well balanced, as in a light and tasty twice-baked goats' cheese soufflé inlaid with nuts, raisins and peppercorns (served with a crisp, fresh salad), and thin slices of locally smoked beef served with pickled walnuts and preserved garlic cloves.

Cheese typically arrives as three slices (Llangollen, Shropshire Blue and a French, for one visitor) with commercial biscuits, and desserts might take in roast pistachio parfait, or a rich, dark chocolate fondant topped with a smooth and creamy mascarpone ice cream. France is the focus of the front half of the wine list, although there are some well-chosen selections from the rest of Europe and the New World, too. Mark-ups are generally fair, giving plenty of choice under £20. The list is rounded out by 22 half-bottles, and four house wines starting at £14.25 (£3.75 a glass).

CHEF: Ernst Van Halderen   PROPRIETOR: Rothwell and Robertson Ltd   OPEN: Mon to Sat D only 7 to 9.30   CLOSED: 25 and 26 Dec, 1 Jan   MEALS: Set D £29.75. Brasserie menu available all week 12 to 2, 6 to 9   SERVICE: not inc   CARDS: Amex, Delta, MasterCard, Switch, Visa   DETAILS: 45 seats. Private parties: 25 main room, 6 to 15 private rooms. Car park. Vegetarian meals. No children under 7 in dining room. No smoking in dining room. No music   ACCOMMODATION: 13 rooms, all with bath/shower. TV. Phone. B&B £64 to £100. Baby facilities (*The Which? Hotel Guide*)

## BROAD HAVEN Pembrokeshire                                          map 4

# ▲ Druidstone £

Druidston Haven, Broad Haven SA62 3NE
TEL: (01437) 781221   FAX: (01437) 781133
EMAIL: jane@druidstone.co.uk
WEBSITE: www.druidstone.co.uk

| | |
|---|---|
| from B4341 at Broad Haven turn right at sea; | COOKING 2 |
| after 1½m turn left to Druidston Haven; hotel ¾m | GLOBAL FUSION |
| on left | £20–£38 |

'An amazing one-off place to visit and savour,' noted one visitor to this stone house on the Pembrokeshire cliffs that offers 'an engaging mix where '70s hippie chic meets new-millennium liberalism'. After 30 years here the Bell family are not standing still, and *inter alia* a new Garden Room overlooking St Bride's Bay should be finished by Christmas 2002. As always, the menu is strong on local ingredients, subjected to influences garnered from around the world. Seared scallops with rocket and Carmargue rice is typical, although there is something more homespun about braised beef in a deep, rich gravy with parsley dumplings and pickled walnuts. Vegetarians are well served with asparagus, orange and pine nut salad, or roast vegetables with polenta. St Clement's soufflé is a favourite dessert, otherwise try home-made mango ice cream. Prices on the 30-strong wine list are restrained; house French is £7.50.

CHEFS: Jon Woodhouse and Angus, Rod and Jane Bell   PROPRIETORS: Rod and Jane Bell   OPEN: Sun L 1 to 2, Mon to Sat D 7.30 to 9.30   MEALS: alc (main courses £8 to £14.50). Bar menu available all week L   SERVICE: none, card slips closed   CARDS: Amex, Delta, MasterCard, Switch, Visa   DETAILS: 30 seats. 80 seats outside. Private parties: 30 main room, 1 to 12 private rooms. Car park. Vegetarian meals. Children's helpings. No smoking while others eat. Wheelchair access (also WC). No music. No mobile phones   ACCOMMODATION: 9 rooms. B&B £35 to £84 (*The Which? Hotel Guide*)

## CAPEL GARMON Conwy                                                 map 7

# ▲ Tan-y-Foel ⁵✳

Capel Garmon, Nr Betws-y-Coed LL26 0RE
TEL: (01690) 710507   FAX: (01690) 710681
EMAIL: enquiries@tyfhotel.co.uk
WEBSITE: www.tyfhotel.co.uk

| | |
|---|---|
| take turning marked Capel Garmon and Nebo | COOKING 5 |
| from A470 about halfway between Betws-y- | MODERN BRITISH-PLUS |
| Coed and Llanrwst | £43–£55 |

The Pitmans run their small, discreet and quiet country-house hotel in a highly professional manner. It is a rough, grey, bare stone building hidden away down narrow winding lanes, set in eight of its own acres, and reminding one visitor of a meditation centre. Natural colours and oriental deities predominate, and the short menu certainly gives visitors something to think about. With just two choices per course (and a wine suggestion for each) the kitchen can concentrate its energies where they are needed. Main course typically offers a straight choice between meat and fish, the former perhaps taking in fillet of Welsh Black beef with horseradish mash, caramelised onion tart and a rich beef jus. Accompaniments tend to get moved around according to circumstance: a rice cake that once accompanied steamed salmon fillet, and a carrot and ginger sauce that previously partnered marinated loin of pork, find themselves together on the same plate beside a piece of steamed halibut.

What matters, though, is the sheer pleasure that this clear-tasting cooking provides. Even such long-in-the-tooth items as Charentais melon with Parma ham excite interest, in this case due at least partly to an accompanying deep-fried fig with a sweet honey and mustard vinaigrette. Puddings are no less enticing, judging by a warm chocolate and star anise muffin with mocha ice cream and chocolate sauce, and by poached apricots with shortbread and butterscotch sauce. A roving yet compact wine list picks its way carefully through some first-class producers and starts with a handful of house wines at £15.

CHEF: Janet Pitman  PROPRIETORS: P.K. and J.C. Pitman  OPEN: all week D only 7.30 to 8.15 (booking essential)  CLOSED: 1 Dec to 1 Feb  MEALS: Set D £29 to £31  SERVICE: not inc CARDS: Amex, Delta, Diners, MasterCard, Switch, Visa  DETAILS: 12 seats. Car park. No children under 7. No smoking in dining room. Vegetarian meals with prior notice. No music. No mobile phones  ACCOMMODATION: 8 rooms, all with bath/shower. TV. Phone. D,B&B £90 to £150. No children under 7 (The Which? Hotel Guide)

## CARDIFF  Cardiff                                            map 4

# Armless Dragon ⚡✳ £

97–99 Wyeverne Road, Cathays,
Cardiff CF24 4BG                                          COOKING 1
TEL: (029) 2038 2357   FAX: (029) 2038 2055               MODERN WELSH
WEBSITE: www.thearmlessdragon.co.uk                       £17–£45

Paul Lane has plied his trade here since 1999, although the restaurant – near the university – is a long-standing Cardiff fixture. The overall impression is of unadorned simplicity; the welcome is friendly, service efficient, and the place exudes honesty and lack of pretension. Chalkboard menus are heaved around from table to table, and the repertoire suggests lively endeavour, loyalty to local ingredients and a global outlook. The upshot might be perfectly baked goats' cheese with piccalilli, or Caesar duck leg salad, to start, before best end of Brecon lamb, cooked just pink and served with a slice of potato and lamb 'pie' and an understated lentil purée. Fish also shows up in, say, monkfish with spinach and mussels in saffron sauce, while desserts have featured a silky smooth yoghurt bavarois with rhubarb compote. Sixty well-spread wines (even two from Wales) include many decent bottles under £20; house wine is £8.90.

CHEF/PROPRIETOR: Paul Lane  OPEN: Tue to Fri L 12 to 2, Tue to Sat D 7 to 9 (9.30 Fri and Sat) MEALS: alc (main courses £9 to £16). Set L £8 (2 courses) to £10  SERVICE: not inc, card slips closed  CARDS: Delta, MasterCard, Switch, Visa  DETAILS: 45 seats. Private parties: 50 main room. Vegetarian meals. Children's helpings. No smoking in dining room. Wheelchair access (not WC). Music  £5

# Da Venditto

**NEW ENTRY**

7–8 Park Place, Cardiff CF10 3DP
TEL: (029) 2023 0781  FAX: (029) 2039 9949
EMAIL: sherry@vendittogroup.co.uk
WEBSITE: www.vendittogroup.co.uk

COOKING 4
MODERN ITALIAN
£25–£68

Part of a small group that includes a wine bar and a couple of pizzerias, Da Venditto is modern and smartly decorated with a fair bit of cherry wood, glass and stainless steel surrounding its well-spaced tables. The food is modern too, some dishes more Italian than others, among them smoked haddock and potato soup with a poached egg; smoked mussel sausage with a lemon thyme risotto; and the wonderful-sounding ippoglosso (halibut) baked with lentils.

Risotti are well made (the kitchen gets a lot of practice), judging by a pink shrimp version served with well-timed small sea bass fillets. Besides a classical-sounding osso buco Milanese, there may also be a pairing of fresh-tasting seared scallops with roundels of fine black pudding on a bed of sun-dried tomato mash. Cheeses, mostly Italian, come with a pickled walnut, and desserts have included a wedge of chocolate tart (thin pastry, dense filling) served with Amaretto ice cream. Lunch is a bargain, and those seeking oils, balsamic vinegar, sauces, mostarda and the like will find a display of bottles and jars for sale by the door. A shortish, mostly Italian wine list starts with house red and white at £14.50 (£4 a glass).

CHEFS: Mark Freeman and Carl Hammett  PROPRIETOR: Toni Venditto  OPEN: Mon to Sat 12 to 2.30, 6 to 10.45  CLOSED: 25 and 26 Dec, bank hols  MEALS: Set L £12.50 (2 courses) to £16. Set D 6 to 7 and 10 to 10.45 £19.50 (2 courses), Set D £27.50 (2 courses) to £37.50  SERVICE: not inc, card slips closed  CARDS: Amex, Delta, MasterCard, Switch, Visa  DETAILS: 55 seats. Private parties: 55 main room. Car park after 5pm. Children's helpings. Wheelchair access (also WC). Music. No mobile phones. Air-conditioned  (£5)

# Le Gallois

6–10 Romilly Crescent, Canton, Cardiff CF11 9NR
TEL: (029) 2034 1264  FAX: (029) 2023 7911
EMAIL: le.gallois@virgin.net
WEBSITE: www.legallois.co.uk

COOKING 3
MODERN EUROPEAN
£27–£71

The outside is reminiscent of a modern warehouse conversion that one visitor thought 'wouldn't look amiss in London'. Inside, the split-level dining room has a sunshine yellow and blue colour scheme, with iron bars separating its different eating areas. The menu makes promising reading, with plenty of tempting options in a predominantly French style, albeit coloured by local sensibilities. Red mullet and Provence pepper terrine with fennel, orange and pesto salad, or perhaps beetroot risotto with sour cream and oscietra caviar might feature among starters, while mains take in pot-roast pig with truffle mash, crispy Alsace bacon and a honey and clove sauce, as well as roast cod with a cheese and herb crumb, served with a cockle and chive jus. Unfortunately, dishes don't invariably live up to descriptions, and shyness with herbs and seasoning and inaccurate timing, particularly of meat, were detectable at inspection; however, the same meal produced a dessert of well-made prune and Armagnac ice cream with a light prune soufflé: 'a classy little number'. The extensive wine list is predominantly French, with a good selection of regional wines; house Côtes de Gascogne red and white are £13.50.

CHEF: Padrig Jones  PROPRIETORS: the Jones and Dupuy Families  OPEN: Tue to Sat 12 to 2.30, 6.30 to 10.30  MEALS: Set L £12.95 (2 courses) to £37, Set D £20 (1 course) to £37. Gourmet menu also available £85 L and D  SERVICE: not inc, 10% for parties of 6 or more, card slips closed  CARDS: Amex, Delta, MasterCard, Switch, Visa  DETAILS: 60 seats. Private parties: 60 main room. Car park. Vegetarian meals. Children's helpings. No cigars/pipes in dining room. No-smoking area available. Wheelchair access (also WC). Occasional music. Air-conditioned

## Izakaya Japanese Tavern £

Mermaid Quay, Cardiff Bay, Cardiff CF10 5BW
TEL/FAX: (029) 2049 2939
EMAIL: ayakazi@aol.com
WEBSITE: www.izakaya-japanese-tavern.com

COOKING 4
JAPANESE
£22–£62

An East-West team fronts this enterprising venture, which stands on a first-floor balcony overlooking the rejuvenated vistas of Cardiff Bay. It was set up by Iesytn and Yoshiko Evans to provide locals and visitors with a taste of tavern-style Japanese food. In a setting of blond flooring, paintings, lanterns and high stools, customers are encouraged to order a few little dishes, as tapas, with more following later as appetite dictates. The atmosphere is informal and light-hearted. Beyond are three tatami rooms with sunken tables for traditional dining.

The 40-dish menu is emblazoned in full colour with photographs and helpful descriptions. All aspects of the cuisine seem to be covered, from easy-to-conjure tonkatsu (breaded pork cutlet) to ika natto (raw squid and fermented soy beans with wakame seaweed). There are also a few examples of sushi and sashimi, skewers of yakitori and versions of deep-fried tempura. Elsewhere, look for bowls of ramen noodles and more specialist delicacies such as saba miso ni (mackerel simmered in ginger and miso sauce), and tori bainikuae (steamed chicken breast served cold with plum sauce). Drink Japanese beer or choose from five kinds of saké. The modest list of 16 wines favours the New World, although house wines (£9.80) are French.

CHEFS: Yoshiko Evans and Peter Mansbridge  PROPRIETORS: Iestyn and Yoshiko Evans  OPEN: Mon to Sat 12 to 2, 6 to 10.30, Sun 1 to 9.30  CLOSED: Christmas and New Year  MEALS: alc (individual dishes £2 to £13.50). Set D (and sometimes L) £15 to £25  SERVICE: not inc  CARDS: Amex, Delta, Diners, MasterCard, Switch, Visa  DETAILS: 90 seats. 6 seats outside. Private parties: 80 main room. No-smoking areas. Wheelchair access (also WC). Music

---

'Pasta made by an unskilled chef can be like chewing your bottom lip.'
(On eating in the West Country)

£ means that it is possible to have a three-course meal, including coffee, half a bottle of house wine and service for £30 or less per person, at any time the restaurant is open, i.e. at dinner as well as lunch. It may be possible to spend considerably more than this, but by choosing carefully you should find £30 or less achievable.

# ▲ St David's Hotel & Spa, Tides Marco Pierre White 🍞 ✻

Havannah Street, Cardiff CF10 5SD
TEL: (029) 2045 4045   FAX: (029) 2048 7056
EMAIL: reservations@thestdavidshotel.com
WEBSITE: www.roccofortehotels.com

COOKING 3
MODERN EUROPEAN
£32–£68

Spectacular views over the bay are a big draw at this landmark hotel (in the running for the longest restaurant name in the book), and when daylight starts to go and lights come on everywhere 'the effect is quite magical'. Spacious, modern and minimalist, with much use of glass and stainless steel, it consists of a marble-tiled bar, a dining room with floor-to-ceiling windows, and a terrace for al fresco eating and drinking in fine weather, all with a decorative 'ocean liner' theme. Since Marco Pierre White took a hand in proceedings, both food and service have become more professional, and Paul Knight has shifted the cooking up a gear.

On offer is a carte in MPW mould, with omelette Arnold Bennett, parfait of foie gras en gelée, and wing of skate with winkles, while the short, set-price Market Menu puts forward dishes with less of a classical bias: perhaps a crisp filo pastry parcel of tangy goats' cheese, or a golden-fried fillet of bream with slices of aubergine, pepper and courgette. Meat options, meanwhile, might include braised shank of Welsh lamb with Puy lentils, or a tender, flavourful medallion of rare beef on a pouch of creamy potato. A warm ginger sponge with a scoop of milk ice cream and caramel sauce provided 'the best type of comfort food but in modest portions' for one visitor. A 'discretionary' service charge is added, but credit card slips are left open, and a rather self-important wine list could do a lot more for modest drinkers, although it offers a dozen by the glass up to £7.

CHEF: Paul Knight   PROPRIETOR: Rocco Forte Hotels   OPEN: all week 12.30 to 2.15, 6.30 to 10.30
MEALS: alc (main courses £13.50 to £27.50). Set L Mon to Sat £15 (2 courses) to £19, Set L Sun £23. Set D £25 (2 courses) to £29.50   SERVICE: 10% (optional)   CARDS: Amex, Delta, Diners, MasterCard, Switch, Visa   DETAILS: 110 seats. 30 seats outside. Private parties: 110 main room. Vegetarian meals. Children's helpings. No smoking in dining room. Wheelchair access (not WC). Music. Air-conditioned   ACCOMMODATION: 132 rooms, all with bath/shower. TV. Phone. B&B £110 to £210. Rooms for disabled. Baby facilities. Swimming pool (£5)

# Woods Brasserie

The Pilotage Building, Stuart Street, Cardiff Bay,
Cardiff CF10 5BW
TEL: (029) 2049 2400   FAX: (029) 2048 1998

COOKING 4
MODERN EUROPEAN
£31–£59

Occupying a fine nineteenth-century stone building with a mirrored bar and open kitchen (go upstairs to get a fine view over the bay), this ten-year-old brasserie cuts its coat according to its cloth. Simple grills, plenty of fish and a couple of vegetarian options are the mainstay of a straightforwardly presented menu, the range taking in Aberdeen Angus ribeye with chips and béarnaise, sweet potato cake with rocket and salsa, and seared salmon fillet with a couscous crust. Equally varied starters run from crab and corn chowder, via ham hock and

Puy lentil salad, to Thai fishcakes with dipping sauce. The upside of the carte is that you can make a meal from a couple of starters, the downside is that vegetables are charged extra. Finish with rice pudding and spiced plums, or caramelised bananas with ginger cream. Wines are chosen to suit the circumstances and are fairly priced, starting with a quartet of house Chilean varietals for just under £14.

CHEF: Martyn Peters   PROPRIETORS: Martyn and Deborah Peters   OPEN: Tue to Sun L 12 to 2 (Sun 11.30 to 3), Tue to Sat D 7 to 10   CLOSED: 25, 26 and 31 Dec, 1 Jan, bank hols   MEALS: alc (main courses Tue to Sat £9 to £19, Sun brunch £8 to £13)   SERVICE: not inc, 10% for parties of 6 or more   CARDS: Amex, Delta, Diners, MasterCard, Switch, Visa   DETAILS: 90 seats. 32 seats outside. Private parties: 60 main room, 1 to 36 private rooms. Vegetarian meals. Children's helpings. Wheelchair access (also WC). Music. Air-conditioned

## CLYTHA Monmouthshire                                                    map 2

# ▲ Clytha Arms ▮ ⁵✳

Clytha NP7 9BW
TEL: (01873) 840206   FAX: (01873) 840209
EMAIL: one.bev@lineone.net
WEBSITE: website.lineone.net/~one.bev                                    COOKING 3
off old Abergavenny to Raglan road, S of A40, 6m                    MODERN WELSH
E of Abergavenny                                                        £28–£50

'A superb country pub; I would love it as my local' is a typical response to this centuries-old converted dower house miles from anywhere. It feels like a traditional local – newspapers to read, table skittles and real ales and ciders on draught – although the dining room has the air of a no-nonsense French country restaurant. The message is clear: food is what counts here.

The Cannings pride themselves on using top-quality local ingredients for dishes with a modern global slant: their 'solid competent cooking without pretensions or silly frills' might produce wild boar rillettes with red onion chutney, roast duck with Shiraz and cinnamon sauce, or pan-fried brill with black pasta, before passion-fruit brûlée or Y-Fenni rarebit on walnut bread. Generally the kitchen is on top form, but Sunday lunch has disappointed more than one reporter. Affordable drinking is the key to the wine list, which scatters a few unexpected gems amid some less stellar offerings. Ten house selections kick off the list at £10.95 (£1.90 a glass), and there is wide choice under £20.

CHEFS: Andrew and Sarah Canning   PROPRIETORS: Andrew and Beverley Canning   OPEN: Tue to Sun L 12.30 to 2.15, Tue to Sat D 7 to 9.30   CLOSED: 25 Dec   MEALS: alc (main courses £12 to £17). Set L and D £15.95 (2 courses) to £17.95. Bar menu also available   SERVICE: not inc, card slips closed (unless requested otherwise)   CARDS: Amex, Delta, Diners, MasterCard, Switch, Visa   DETAILS: 60 seats. 40 seats outside. Private parties: 50 main room, 18 private room. Car park. Vegetarian meals. Children's helpings. No smoking in dining room. No music   ACCOMMODATION: 4 rooms, all with bath/shower. TV. B&B £50 to £90. Baby facilities (The Which? Hotel Guide)   (£5)

---

*The Guide's top-rated restaurants are listed near the front of the book.*

---

# Café Niçoise

124 Abergele Road, Colwyn Bay LL29 7PS　　　　　　COOKING 3
TEL/FAX: (01492) 531555　　　　　　　　　　FRENCH/MODERN EUROPEAN
　　　　　　　　　　　　　　　　　　　　　　　　£26–£46

The name should leave you in no doubt as to the intentions of this congenial
neighbourhood bistro. Originally a single-fronted shop, it now sports a split-
level dining room with contemporary plank flooring and terracotta walls.
Conwy mussels, Welsh beef and lamb suggest that there is keen local sourcing,
and menus change with the seasons. Ideas nonetheless come from near and far:
haunch of venison with red onion confit and sloe gin sauce lines up alongside
cauliflower risotto with garlic spinach. The cheeseboard has a strong Welsh
presence and desserts might feature crème brûlée with Kahlua and banana,
although the 'assiette du chef' is a fixture. One-dish lunches – chicken risotto
with Madeira, or pan-fried salmon with pasta and spinach – are good value.
Around three dozen affordable wines are organised by style, halves are well
represented, and there are six house recommendations (£9.95 per bottle, £1.95 a
glass).

CHEF: Chris Jackson　PROPRIETOR: Lynne Swift　OPEN: Wed to Sat L 12 to 2, Tue to Sat D 7 to 10
(earlier or later by prior arrangement)　MEALS: alc (main courses £6 to £14.50). Set L Wed to Sat
and D Tue to Fri £13.75 (2 courses) to £16.95　SERVICE: not inc, card slips closed　CARDS: Amex,
Delta, MasterCard, Switch, Visa　DETAILS: 32 seats. Private parties: 30 main room. Vegetarian
meals. Children's helpings. No-smoking areas. Music　£5

# Tir-a-Môr ▮

1–3 Mona Terrace, Criccieth LL52 0HG　　　　　　COOKING 4
TEL: (01766) 523084　　　　　　　　　　MODERN WELSH/SEAFOOD
　　　　　　　　　　　　　　　　　　　　　　　　£29–£45

Clare and Martin Vowell's 'gem of a little eatery' stands in the shadow of
Criccieth Castle. It looks like a converted corner shop, and inside dried flowers
and wood-carvings evoke a 'Tyrolean Bierkeller', but the food is serious. Tir-a-
Môr means 'Land and Sea', although sea provides the main inspiration. Fish
specials are listed daily on a board. What impresses is not just the freshness of
raw materials but the clear simplicity of their treatment: as in a smooth
mousseline of scallops with a coral sauce, or plump, king-sized prawns fried
with garlic and parsley. Nothing is too showy: roast cod fillet comes with
asparagus and hollandaise; Dover sole is baked with sea salt and lime.

　　Supplies from the land are resolutely local: salt-marsh lamb, Lleyn beef, and
vegetables 'of the finest quality'. From beyond Wales, there might be sauté foie
gras on an apple pancake, or Gressingham duck breast 'cooked a tad rare for
some tastes' but sympathetically paired with onion marmalade and a red berry
jus. Desserts maintain the standard, witness a tiny pyramid of home-made
vanilla ice cream with miniature pancakes and toffee sauce, or tart new season's
rhubarb with crème patissière and pastry 'cannelloni'. Service is extremely

friendly but can be on the slow side. The wine list is arranged by style and features a pick-'n-mix selection of good producers from around the world. Mark-ups are commendably low, which means there is much scope for experimentation under £20. Three house wines sell for £10.95 to £11.95, or £2.95 a glass.

CHEFS/PROPRIETORS: Clare and Martin Vowell   OPEN: Mon to Sat D only 7 to 9.30   CLOSED: Christmas, New Year, Jan   MEALS: alc (main courses £12 to £16.50)   SERVICE: not inc   CARDS: MasterCard, Switch, Visa   DETAILS: 36 seats. Private parties: 24 main room. Vegetarian meals. No children under 7. No smoking till all food service ends. Wheelchair access (not WC). Music. No mobile phones

---

**CRICKHOWELL  Powys**                                                                    **map 4**

## ▲ Bear Hotel ⁎⃗

High Street, Crickhowell NP8 1BW
TEL: (01873) 810408   FAX: (01873) 811696                                   COOKING 1
EMAIL: bearhotel@aol.com                                                 MODERN WELSH
WEBSITE: www.bearhotel.co.uk                                                   £33–£48

This fifteenth-century coaching inn, in a small rural market town in the Brecon Beacons National Park, is considered 'a good local' as well as a place for some enterprising pub food. The aftermath of foot-and-mouth disease has propelled the kitchen in the direction of local farmers' markets for more of its produce, and although it still shows a penchant for some trendy ideas and ingredients, such as Thai prawn cakes with a sweet chilli cucumber dressing, it also deploys Welsh lamb, Black beef and local venison. Results can be less consistent during busy periods, but among the niftier ideas are a simple garden pea pancake with smoked salmon and a quenelle of horseradish crème fraîche, and pan-fried loin of pork with lentil cream and a mustard and celeriac mash. The house speciality dessert is a bread-and-butter pudding made with rum and bananas, served with brown bread ice cream. Service is competent, and a varied and affordable wine list starts with house vin de pays red and white at £8.95.

CHEFS: Colin Laughton and Brian Simmons   PROPRIETORS: Judy and Stephen Hindmarsh OPEN: Sun L 12 to 2, Tue to Sat D 7 to 9.30   MEALS: alc (main courses £14 to £18). Bar menu available 12 to 3, 6 to 10   SERVICE: not inc, card slips closed   CARDS: Amex, Delta, MasterCard, Switch, Visa   DETAILS: 60 seats. 30 seats outside. Private parties: 40 main room. Car park. Vegetarian meals. No smoking in 1 dining room. Wheelchair access (also WC). No music ACCOMMODATION: 34 rooms, all with bath/shower. TV. Phone. B&B £54 to £130. Rooms for disabled. No children under 7 (*The Which? Hotel Guide*)

---

*'Bubble and squeak neither bubbled nor squeaked.'* (On eating in Cambridgeshire)

*Some restaurants leave credit card slips open even though they also make a fixed (or 'optional') service charge. The Guide strongly disapproves of this practice as it may result in consumers unknowingly paying twice for service. A list of restaurants that have told us they do this, or that were found by our inspectors to do so, can be found at the front of the book.*

---

# ▲ Nantyffin Cider Mill Inn ♀ ⅝

Brecon Road, Crickhowell NP8 1SG
TEL/FAX: (01873) 810775
EMAIL: info@cidermill.co.uk
WEBSITE: www.cidermill.co.uk
1½m NW of Crickhowell at junction of
A40 and A479

COOKING 2
MODERN WELSH-PLUS
£27–£50

'After a great walk in the mountains we were stunned to find this gem of an eatery in the heart of the Brecon Beacons,' reported a gang of ten who received nourishment for 'mind, body and soul'. In its present guise, this converted drovers' inn has been doing a great service to the region for more than a decade, and it continues to earn praise. The kitchen's commitment to local, home-grown and traditional ingredients is clear from dishes such as Pembrokeshire mussels with cider and leeks, slow-cooked confit of Welsh lamb on celeriac mash, and roast loin of Gloucester Old Spot pork topped with goats' cheese on sauté greens. In more modern vein, seared scallops with chilli jam has been spot-on, while chargrilled ribeye steak has been appreciated by 'a 12-year-old rugby player'. Portions are mighty; leave room, though, for nutmeg crème brûlée, or panettone bread-and-butter pudding. Service is speedy and efficient, and wines include a collection of interesting bins from good New World (or modern-minded European) producers. Mark-ups are fair, encouraging experimentation. Four house wines (two red, two white) are £11.95–£12.95. Separate 'connoisseurs' selections' stretch the imagination more than the wallet. (Note that the accommodation offered is in a separate building, 500 yards away.)

CHEF: Sean Gerrard   PROPRIETORS: Sean Gerrard, Glyn and Jessica Bridgeman   OPEN: Sun L 12 to 2.15, Tue to Sat D (all week D Apr to Aug) 6.30 to 9.45   CLOSED: 1 week Jan, 1 week Nov, Sun and Mon D Sept to Mar   MEALS: alc (main courses £10.50 to £16.50)   SERVICE: not inc, card slips closed   CARDS: Amex, Delta, MasterCard, Switch, Visa   DETAILS: 100 seats. 50 seats outside. Private parties: 50 main room. Car park. Vegetarian meals. Children's helpings. No smoking in dining room. Wheelchair access (also women's WC). No music   ACCOMMODATION: 22 rooms, all with bath/shower. TV. Phone. B&B £35 to £110. Swimming pool. Fishing   (£5)

## DOLGELLAU Gwynedd                                          map 7

# Dylanwad Da ♀ ⅝ £

2 Ffôs-y-Felin, Dolgellau LL40 1BS
TEL: (01341) 422870

COOKING 3
BISTRO
£23–£40

Dylan Rowlands has been nourishing locals and visitors to Snowdonia from his modest establishment since 1988. A new carpet and chairs have introduced a bit of a facelift behind the lace curtains of the old shopfront, but the food hasn't changed. Parts of the menu are bilingual, and Welsh ingredients are given a good airing: traditional faggots turn up as a starter served cold with spiced apple, the steaks are Welsh beef, and there are cheeses from the Principality to finish. Many dishes are in well-tried bistro vein, but the menu has its cosmopolitan touches too: Portuguese pork stew with olives and peppers, Sicilian caponata, Thai chicken and vegetable curry, as well as lamb casserole with root vegetables and smoked bacon. As a finale, choose, say, double chocolate roulade, or poached berries with brown sugar meringues. Dylan has recently bought an espresso machine and is now open during the day for coffee and cakes (but not full meals).

A short but sweet list of keenly priced mature red Bordeaux from the 'cellar specials' selection is at the heart of the wine list, accentuated by a number of good bottles at fair prices from elsewhere in Europe and the New World. Although house wines are not the most exciting drinking, the price of £10.50 (£2 a glass) makes them easy to swallow.

CHEF/PROPRIETOR: Dylan Rowlands OPEN: Thur to Sat D 7 to 9 (Tue to Sat in summer, all week Easter and Whitsun) CLOSED: Feb to mid-Mar MEALS: alc (main courses £9.50 to £14.50). Set D £16 SERVICE: not inc CARDS: none DETAILS: 30 seats. Private parties: 30 main room. Vegetarian meals. Children's helpings. No smoking in dining room. Wheelchair access (not WC). Music. No mobile phones (£5)

**EGLWYSFACH Powys** WALES GFG 2003 COMMENDED map 7

## ▲ Ynyshir Hall

Eglwysfach SY20 8TA
TEL: (01654) 781209 FAX: (01654) 781366
EMAIL: info@ynyshir-hall.co.uk
WEBSITE: ynyshir-hall.co.uk
turn E off A487, 6m SW of Machynlleth

COOKING 7
MODERN BRITISH
£40–£83

Personally and professionally run by the Reens, who take charge of front of house, Ynyshir is both comfortable and a 'haven of tranquility' (next door is an RSPB reserve). Seasonal ingredients, some local, play an important role, including venison, lamb from the Brecon Beacons, and lobsters and prawns from Cardigan Bay, and the bold, confident colours of Rob Reen's paintings are echoed in strong flavours that come from the kitchen. A seven-course tasting option has been added to the regular three-course menu (from which it is derived), and a prodigious amount of skill and well-rehearsed labour goes into the dishes: for example crisp, pale pink, pan-fried foie gras with gently acidic tamarind won tons on aged balsamic vinegar.

'Beguiling contrasts of colours and textures' were a feature of one visitor's three-way scallop starter comprising a mousse blended with cream and coriander, a sealed, pan-fried scallop, and one cooked in a crisp nori seaweed overcoat. Dishes are also scrupulously prepared, as in a main course of quickly seared brill fillet, served with crushed potatoes mixed with lemon and watercress, truffle-scented trompette mushrooms and a red wine sauce. Desserts are equally enticing, for example a creamy but intensely fruity passion-fruit mousse contrasting well with a small crisp disc of pineapple. Another 'stunning' combination for one visitor was of mascarpone cheesecake with white chocolate ice cream, each gently flavoured with coffee. Incidentals such as bread and appetisers are well rendered, and the wine list will delight oenophiles, particularly fans of red Bordeaux. Vintages go back to 1945, taking in some impressive names and other good vintages along the way. The choice of red and white Burgundy is also good, while Alsace, the Loire, southern France and the Rhône round out the French section before the list heads off in the direction of Australia, Italy and the New World. Value is not a high point, though, with just a smattering of wines under £20. A dozen house wines are priced between £15 and £38 (£3 to £7 by the glass).

CHEF: Les Rennie   PROPRIETORS: Rob and Joan Reen   OPEN: all week 12.30 to 1.30, 7 to 8.45 CLOSED: 5 to 25 Jan   MEALS: Set L £28.50, Set D £42 to £55. Light L menu also available SERVICE: not inc, card slips closed   CARDS: Amex, Delta, Diners, MasterCard, Switch, Visa DETAILS: 40 seats. Private parties: 25 main room, 15 private room. Car park. Vegetarian meals. No children under 9. No smoking. Occasional music. No mobile phones   ACCOMMODATION: 10 rooms, all with bath/shower. TV. Phone. B&B £95 to £275. Rooms for disabled. No children under 9 (*The Which? Hotel Guide*)

## FELIN FACH  Powys                                                                    map 4

## ▲ Felin Fach Griffin ✳

Felin Fach, Powys LD3 0UB
TEL: (01874) 620111   FAX: (01874) 620120
EMAIL: enquiries@eatdrinksleep.ltd.uk                          COOKING 3
WEBSITE: www.eatdrinksleep.ltd.uk                             MODERN BRITISH
on A470, 4½m NE of Brecon                                          £21–£40

Once a working farm/country pub in the wilds between the Black Mountains and the Brecon Beacons, this stylish venue pulls in customers from far and wide with its accomplished food. Meals kick off with freshly baked soda bread, a reminder that chef Charles Inkin trained at Ballymaloe House in Shanagarry, Republic of Ireland (see entry). The short menu is built around a network of local suppliers (beef from a neighbouring farm, organic salad leaves from a nearby grower); materials are handled sympathetically, and results are convincing. A lunchtime starter of pan-fried sweetbreads with purple sprouting broccoli and balsamic juices is typical of the kitchen's awareness of the seasons, while Middle White pork sausages with creamed mash and onion gravy suggests an eye for rare-breed meat.

Dinner (fixed-price) shows signs of confident muscle flexing. To start, there might be Polish beetroot soup with ravioli of wild mushrooms and dill, while mains range from grilled sea bass with sauté potatoes, artichokes and salsa verde to roast quail with buttered spinach, creamed lentils and pancetta. Rounding things off are chocolate mousse with Welsh clotted cream and vanilla crème brûlée. Around three dozen wines promise interesting drinking at fair prices from £9.70.

CHEFS: Charles Inkin and Konrad Ceglowski   PROPRIETORS: Huw Evans Bevan and Charles Inkin OPEN: Tue to Sun 12.30 (1 Sun) to 2.30, 7 to 9.30 (9 Sun)   CLOSED: last week Jan and first week Feb   MEALS: alc L (main courses £6.50 to £10). Set D £17.50 (2 courses) to £22   SERVICE: not inc, card slips closed   CARDS: Delta, MasterCard, Switch, Visa   DETAILS: 40 seats. Private parties: 30 main room, 12 to 20 private rooms. Car park. Vegetarian meals. Children's helpings. No smoking in dining room. Wheelchair access (also WC). Music   ACCOMMODATION: 7 rooms, all with bath/shower. Phone. B&B £47.50 to £82. Baby facilities (*The Which? Hotel Guide*)

*Which? Online subscribers will find* The Good Food Guide *online, along with other Which? guides and magazines, at* www.which.net. *Phone (08459) 830254 for information on how to become a subscriber.*

# ▲ Three Main Street ✸

3 Main Street, Fishguard SA65 9HG                        COOKING **5**
TEL: (01348) 874275   FAX: (01348) 874017          MODERN EUROPEAN
                                                              £41–£49

'Like being at a dinner party in an up-market art gallery' is how one visitor saw this fresh, inviting, and plainly but comfortably decorated grey-fronted Georgian house near a busy junction in the centre of town. The dining room is cool, uncluttered and tasteful, with bare floorboards, and contemporary paintings on white walls, while the cooking is neither fussy nor pretentious, just skilfully put together. It is a place to find summer salads given proper attention: perhaps one of neatly trimmed, moist guinea fowl leg on an assembly of leaves, tossed with croûtons and walnuts and glistening with a whole-grain mustard dressing. Another ordinary-sounding but first-class dish combines warm, sharp goats' cheese crusted with crushed hazelnuts, and sweet, sliced cold beetroot, its contrasts of flavour, texture and temperature proving 'perfectly simple, and completely effective'.

Cooking times tend to be conservative, so don't expect really pink meat or translucent fish, but good materials taste how they should, from a light, twice-baked, crab-packed soufflé with a mild sweet chilli jam, via a seafood nage of sea bass, monk, halibut and salmon (in a broth flavoured with fennel, orange, saffron and basil), to well-sourced, flavourful rack of lamb with simple accompaniments of mint and redcurrant jellies and port sauce. Vegetables, served separately, are well handled. Desserts might run to a wedge of apricot and frangipane flan, or one of lemon tart with thick pastry, and extras include moreish bread and a first-rate appetiser soup. Service under the direction of Inez Ford is charming and friendly, and fair pricing distinguishes the compact yet varied wine list. Southern French house wine is £11.95.

CHEFS: Marion Evans and Ron Smith   PROPRIETORS: Marion Evans and Inez Ford   OPEN: Tue to Sat 12 to 2 (bookings only), D 7 to 9   CLOSED: Tue in winter, Feb   MEALS: Set L and D £24 (2 courses) to £30   SERVICE: not inc   CARDS: none   DETAILS: 35 seats. Private parties: 20 main room, 15 private room. Vegetarian meals. Children's helpings. No smoking in dining room. Wheelchair access (not WC). No music. No mobile phones   ACCOMMODATION: 3 rooms, all with bath/shower. TV. B&B £50 to £80 (*The Which? Hotel Guide*)

# ▲ Plas Dolmelynllyn ▼ ✸

Ganllwyd LL40 2HP
TEL: (01341) 440273   FAX: (01341) 440640
EMAIL: info@dolly-hotel.co.uk                            COOKING **1**
WEBSITE: www.dolly-hotel.co.uk                        MODERN WELSH
on A470, 5m N of Dolgellau                                  £36–£43

A casual passer-by could miss this imposing Gothic-style building of dark stone, screened from the road by vegetation, so it helps to be in the know. Stained glass, antique furniture and richly coloured textiles provide a homely backdrop for four-course dinners that typically include a soup (wild mushroom for one visitor) or water ice (pineapple and lime perhaps) following a starter such as a leek and smoked Cheddar soufflé. Accurately cooked beef fillet and spiced breast of chicken have impressed, there is always a vegetarian option – perhaps a galette of artichoke hearts and roast red pepper with goats' cheese – and fish dishes have included fillets of hake with a Welsh rarebit crust. Finish with toffee banana cheesecake, or steamed lemon pudding with cinnamon custard. The wine list is clear and concise, with sensible tasting notes, and organic wines are picked out in green. About evenly balanced between New World and Old, it offers a wide choice under £20. House vins de pays kick off at £10.75.

CHEF: Joanna Reddicliffe   PROPRIETORS: Jonathan and Ella Barkwith, and Joanna Reddicliffe   OPEN: all week D only 7 to 8.30   CLOSED: 1 Dec to 28 Feb   MEALS: Set D £27.50   SERVICE: not inc, card slips closed   CARDS: Amex, Delta, Diners, MasterCard, Switch, Visa   DETAILS: 20 seats. Private parties: 40 main room. Car park. Vegetarian meals. No children under 10. D available 6pm for children under 10. No smoking in dining room. No music. No mobile phones   ACCOMMODATION: 10 rooms, all with bath/shower. TV. Phone. B&B £55 to £125. Fishing (*The Which? Hotel Guide*)  (£5)

## HARLECH  Gwynedd                                                    map 7

## ▲ Castle Cottage  ⅜

Y Llech, Harlech LL46 2YL
TEL: (01766) 780479   FAX: (01766) 781251                    COOKING 2
EMAIL: glyn@castlecottageharlech.co.uk                    MODERN WELSH
WEBSITE: www.castlecottageharlech.co.uk                      £33–£45

Reckoned one of the oldest houses in Harlech, this long, low sixteenth-century stone cottage rests in the shadow of the medieval castle. Glyn and Jacqueline Roberts run it as a hospitable restaurant-with-rooms: he cooks, she presides out front. The dining room feels inviting and cottagey with its beams and persistent pig images, but the cooking strikes a more contemporary chord. Resolute commitment to local produce defines the repertoire: smoked salmon is from Rhydlewis, air-dried ham from Carmarthen. Starters might include mussel, prawn and sweetcorn chowder, while mains could range from grilled Welsh Black steaks with green peppercorn and Cognac sauce, to brochette of monkfish with pesto crust and tomato sauce. Welsh rarebit with marinated anchovies is a savoury alternative to tarragon crème brûlée, or poached pear with red wine syrup and Chantilly cream. The enterprising and largely non-European wine list begins with the Roberts' personal recommendations and finishes with some affordable bin ends; prices start at £10.50.

CHEF: Glyn Roberts   PROPRIETORS: Glyn and Jacqueline Roberts   OPEN: all week D only 7 to 9   CLOSED: 3 weeks Feb   MEALS: Set D £22.50 (2 courses) to £24.50   SERVICE: not inc, card slips closed   CARDS: Delta, MasterCard, Switch, Visa   DETAILS: 45 seats. Private parties: 45 main room. Vegetarian meals. Children's helpings. No smoking in dining room. Wheelchair access (not WC). Occasional music. No mobile phones   ACCOMMODATION: 6 rooms, 4 with bath/shower. B&B £30 to £65. Baby facilities (*The Which? Hotel Guide*)  (£5)

---

*If 'The Which? Hotel Guide' is noted at the end of an entry, this means that the establishment is also in the 2003 edition of our sister guide, published in September 2002.*

---

# The Brasserie

68 The Highway, Hawarden CH5 3DH                COOKING **2**
TEL: (01244) 536353   FAX: (01244) 520867       MODERN EUROPEAN
                                                £22–£45

A refurb since last year's Guide has given this village restaurant a light and airy new look, with cream walls, navy-blue woodwork and artistically hung drapes. Mark Jones and Neal Bates continue to run this place as well as their larger venture in Chester (Brasserie 10/16, see entry), with the result that production can be patchy. Strips of honey-glazed pork on a salad of noodles, mushrooms and red onions with a soy and sesame dressing has made an appetising inspection starter, and a ribeye steak with leek and mustard crumble and tarragoned sauté potatoes has mobilised good ingredients. Adventurous fish preparations have included seared cod on pea and basil mash with roasted tomatoes and pesto. Ice creams and sorbets come from Cheshire Farm, or you could finish with chocolate sponge pudding. House wines are Italian and start at £9.95 a bottle, or £2 a glass.

CHEFS: Mark Jones and John Roberts   PROPRIETORS: Neal Bates and Mark Jones   OPEN: Tue to Fri and Sun L 12 to 2, Tue to Sun D 6.45 to 9 (9.30 Sat)   MEALS: alc (main courses £9 to £16). Set D Tue to Fri 6.45 to 9 £9.95 (2 courses). Light L menu available Tue to Fri   SERVICE: not inc   CARDS: Delta, MasterCard, Switch, Visa   DETAILS: 40 seats. Vegetarian meals. No cigars in dining room. Music. Air-conditioned   (£5)

# ▲ The Cors ⚡

Newbridge Road, Laugharne SA33 4SH              COOKING **2**
TEL: (01994) 427219                             MODERN WELSH
                                                £32–£44

Nick Priestland is head cook and gardener at this Victorian house with verandahs either side of the entrance, which now earns its keep as a restaurant with two letting rooms. The setting is magical, the three-acre gardens are kept in superb order, and the décor inside is all gilt mirrors and antique furniture. Menus are handwritten on cards or chalked on a board in the bar, choice is sensibly restricted, and the loyalty to local ingredients is impressive. Scallops from the Milford boats might be seared and served with béarnaise sauce, hot-smoked salmon from the Brechfa smokehouse is paired with wild rocket and sweet mustard sauce. Apart from fish, there is organic Welsh Black beef, salt marsh lamb and roast duck breast with plum sauce and chilli jam. Twenty wines promise impressive drinking at fair prices. House French is £9.50.

CHEF/PROPRIETOR: Nick Priestland   OPEN: Thur to Sat D only 7 to 10   MEALS: alc (main courses £13 to £17)   SERVICE: not inc   CARDS: none   DETAILS: 30 seats. 12 seats outside. Private parties: 24 main room. Car park. Vegetarian meals. No smoking in 1 dining room. Wheelchair access (not WC). Music. No mobile phones   ACCOMMODATION: 2 rooms, both with bath/shower. B&B £30 to £70   (£5)

## LLANBERIS Gwynedd        map 7

# Y Bistro ⚡

43–45 High Street, Llanberis LL55 4EU
TEL: (01286) 871278
EMAIL: ybistro@fsbdial.co.uk
WEBSITE: www.ybistro.co.uk        COOKING 2
off A4086, at foot of Mount Snowdon, in centre of        MODERN WELSH
village        £30–£47

Lace curtains, busy wallpaper, spindle-back chairs and 'doily-type' tablecloths all point to a haven from fashion. Indeed it is 'all very domestic', with comforting food to match. Good raw materials contribute to the success of simple, homespun dishes, which might range from spiced lentil and root vegetable soup, via lamb's liver with tomato sauce and garlic mash, to roast pheasant with leeks and wild mushrooms. Regional input extends to fillet of Lleyn beef, and a locally made black pudding served with apple and cider sauce. Wine and cream are typical sauce ingredients: a white Rhône sauce for locally landed baked brill, a creamy mustard one for pan-fried pork tenderloin. Vegetables are fresh and well timed, and the homely approach continues into desserts of brown sugar meringue with whipped cream, and apple and mincemeat crumble with bara brith ice cream. Some Welsh wines feature on the short reasonably priced list; house French starts at £10.

CHEF: Nerys Roberts   PROPRIETORS: Danny and Nerys Roberts   OPEN: Mon to Sat D only 7.30 to 9.45   MEALS: alc (main courses £12.50 to £17)   SERVICE: not inc, card slips closed   CARDS: Delta, MasterCard, Switch, Visa   DETAILS: 40 seats. Private parties: 42 main room. Vegetarian meals. Children's helpings. No smoking in dining room. Wheelchair access (not WC). No music (£5)

## LLANDDEINIOLEN Gwynedd        map 7

# ▲ Ty'n Rhos 🛏 ⚡ £

Seion, Llanddeiniolen LL55 3AE
TEL: (01248) 670489   FAX: (01248) 670079
EMAIL: enquiries@tynrhos.co.uk
WEBSITE: www.tynrhos.co.uk        COOKING 3
off B4366, 5m NE of Caernarfon on road        BRITISH/WELSH
signposted Seion        £24–£47

In a serene location with Snowdonia at the back and views of the Menai Strait and Anglesey out front, this one-time farmhouse is now a fully fledged country-house hotel, with manicured lawns, a pair of lakes and plenty of creature comforts. Inside, everything is impeccable, and the kitchen is up and running with a keen new brigade.

As ever, the emphasis is on local fish, meat from nearby farms and butchers, and produce from the kitchen garden, plus a fine selection of Welsh cheeses. The cooking is genuine, techniques are sound, and there are no superfluous gimmicks. Light lunches point up the straightforward approach: asparagus and smoked bacon tart with superlative shortcrust pastry, and braised shoulder of

Welsh lamb with cumin and swede mash, for example. More ambitious dinner menus promise the likes of seared gravlax with cod brandade and fennel oil, Trelough duck breast with beetroot sauce and boulangère potatoes, and warm chocolate fondant with roasted plums and mascarpone cream. Breads come fresh from the oven and coffee arrives with home-made petits fours. The wine list is a manageable and reasonably priced slate, with ten house selections at £11.50 (£4 a glass).

CHEFS: Alwyn Hughes, Jim Roberts, Alan Pope and Michelle Davies  PROPRIETORS: Lynda, Nigel and Andrew Kettle  OPEN: Tue to Sun L 12 to 1.30, Mon to Sat D 7 to 8.45  CLOSED: 22 to 31 Dec  MEALS: alc D (main courses £9.50 to £18). Set L Tue to Sat £12.95 (2 courses) to £14.50, Set L Sun £14.95, Set D £22.50  SERVICE: not inc, card slips closed  CARDS: Amex, Delta, MasterCard, Switch, Visa  DETAILS: 35 seats. Private parties: 25 main room, 15 to 30 private rooms. Car park. Vegetarian meals. Children's helpings. No children under 6. No smoking in dining room. Wheelchair access (not WC). Occasional music. Air-conditioned  ACCOMMODATION: 14 rooms, all with bath/shower. TV. Phone. B&B £59 to £118. Rooms for disabled. No children under 6 (*The Which? Hotel Guide*)

## LLANDEILO  Carmarthenshire                                           map 4

# ▲ Cawdor Arms £✳

72 Rhosmaen Street, Llandeilo SA19 6EN
TEL: (01558) 823500   FAX: (01558) 822399                              COOKING 2
EMAIL: cawdor.arms@btinternet.com                                MODERN BRITISH
WEBSITE: www.cawdorarms.com                                            £23–£45

Cawdor Arms has the air of a grand town house, with a flagstone floor in the bar, and spacious lounges populated with comfortable chesterfields. It may be a bit dark, but nobody seems to mind much. The food varies from a simple tomato and tarragon soup, to a more ambitious terrine of monkfish and bream served with ginger brioche and sweet pickled cauliflower. It takes in provincial-sounding ideas, such as a trio of rabbit with aubergine and wild mushrooms, and usually offers a couple of fish dishes: salmon with asparagus risotto, or cod with a sauté of leek and bacon. Desserts run from fig and pear custard pie with a hazelnut parfait, to a well-judged sticky toffee pudding, and four Welsh wines feature on the short, reasonably priced list. A 'special selection' deals with bottles over £20, and three house wines are £10.10 (£4 a large glass).

CHEF: Jane Silver  PROPRIETORS: Sylvia, Jane and John Silver  OPEN: all week 12 to 2, 7.15 to 8.45  CLOSED: 1 to 3 Jan  MEALS: alc exc Sun L (main courses L £3.50 to £12, D £8 to £16). Set L Sun £14.50. Light L available Mon to Sat  SERVICE: not inc, card slips closed  CARDS: Amex, Delta, MasterCard, Switch, Visa  DETAILS: 100 seats. 20 seats outside. Private parties: 100 main room, 4 to 20 private rooms. Car park. Vegetarian meals. Children's helpings. No smoking in dining room. Wheelchair access (not WC)  ACCOMMODATION: 17 rooms, all with bath/shower. TV. Phone. B&B £45 to £80. Baby facilities (*The Which? Hotel Guide*)  £5

---

*Several sharp operators have tried to extort money from restaurateurs on the promise of an entry in a guidebook that has never appeared.* The Good Food Guide *makes no charge for inclusion.*

## LLANDEWI SKIRRID  Monmouthshire

map 4

# Walnut Tree Inn

Llandewi Skirrid NP7 8AW
TEL: (01873) 852797   FAX: (01873) 859764
WEBSITE: www.thewalnuttreeinn.com
on B4521, 3m NE of Abergavenny

COOKING 5
MEDITERRANEAN/ITALIAN
£36–£64

Even 18 months on, readers are still visiting the Walnut Tree for the first time since the Taruschios left, and still comparing it with the old days, finding it fresher-looking, more spacious, less frenetic. Some things haven't changed: 'the first face we saw was a waitress we remember well from previous visits – she's been there since 1972!' And the same simple atmosphere and attitude continue. Lunch offers three or four options per course, while the carte is more than generous; it may not change much, nor be closely tied to the seasons, but dishes range from Taruschio favourites such as Lady Llanover's salt duck, to a dead simple half-dozen Irish rock oysters, to a classically Italian bollito misto with tongue, capon, pork sausage and brisket simmered in a clear broth.

Stars among starters include moist, crisp, breadcrumbed belly pork with a lemon and caper dressing, and a flavourful crab and saffron tart, followed perhaps by a first-class combination of rare, juicy, roast wild duck with blackberries. Dishes can be substantial, judging by a huge portion of tender squid, accompanied by slices of fried, ungreasy aubergine and tomatoes, although an 'alarmed vegetarian' writes that main course options appear to be limited, which is rather odd given that Mediterranean and Italian food is normally so vegetarian-friendly. Desserts might include a thin, crisp, chocolate and praline tart, and warm fresh figs in a honey and balsamic sauce. Since the restaurant has refused to furnish the Guide with any details, we are unable to consider its wine list for a 'Glass' symbol (as it had last year), nor can we confirm prices, opening times and some of the other details given below.

CHEF: Stephen Terry   PROPRIETORS: Francesco Matioli and Stephen Terry   OPEN: Tue to Sun and bank hol Mon L 12 to 3, Tue Sat D 6.30 to 11   CLOSED: D 23 Dec to 3 Jan   MEALS: alc (main courses £8.50 to £18). Set L £14.50 (2 courses) to £18   SERVICE: not inc   CARDS: MasterCard, Switch, Visa   DETAILS: 80 seats. 20 seats outside. Private parties: 40 main room. Car park. Vegetarian meals. Wheelchair access (not WC). No music. Air-conditioned

## LLANDRILLO  Denbighshire

map 7

# ▲ Tyddyn Llan ✷

Llandrillo LL21 0ST
TEL: (01490) 440264   FAX: (01490) 440414
EMAIL: tyddynllanhotel@compuserve.com
WEBSITE: www.tyddynllan.co.uk
on B4401, 4½m S of Corwen

COOKING 5
MODERN BRITISH
£26–£55

The atmosphere of this peaceful country-house hotel is always relaxed and civilised. Its dining room has been refurbished in blue and creamy yellow, although much else remains the same: it looks out over a lawn and is well stocked with paintings by that most affable and welcoming of hosts Peter Kindred (the Kindreds celebrate 20 years here in 2003).

A daily menu offers no choice (save soup or sorbet as an intermediate course), and most effort seems concentrated in the carte. Raw materials are first-class: 'I was struck by the excellence of their seafood, in this remote and landlocked part of Wales' noted an inspector. Dishes can be rather fussy and complex though, for example a 'very arty, very colourful' salad of four fat scallops, meaty and accurately timed, on a bed of well-made curried cauliflower couscous, surrounded by 15 little decorative piles: alternating almonds with chervil, potato cubes, and tiny dice of red Campari jelly topped with a blob of black caviar. If flavour combinations can trip over themselves in trying to be cutting-edge, there is nothing much wrong with technical skills. Duck, for example, has come three ways – a tasty pan-fried breast, confit drumstick, and a couple of slices of just-sealed foie gras – accompanied by a cider-flavoured fondant potato spiked with cinnamon, some fine wild mushrooms, and a fruity alcohol sauce.

Trios may also appear among desserts, including beautifully made variations on an apricot theme: a sweet soufflé, sharp sorbet and wobbly, vanilla-speckled pannacotta embedded with dried apricots. The roving wine list centres on good-value, characterful drinking, with much choice under £20. Ten house wines are priced from £13 to £17.50.

CHEF: Steven Burnham   PROPRIETORS: Peter and Bridget Kindred   OPEN: Tue to Sun L 12.30 to 2, all week D 7 to 9   CLOSED: 2 weeks Jan   MEALS: alc (main courses L £8 to £12.50, D £16.50 to £18.50). Set L £10 (2 courses), Set L Sun £17. Set D £27   SERVICE: not inc, card slips closed   CARDS: Amex, Delta, Diners, MasterCard, Switch, Visa   DETAILS: 60 seats. 15 seats outside. Private parties: 45 main room. Car park. Vegetarian meals. Children's helpings. No smoking in dining room. Wheelchair access (also WC). Music   ACCOMMODATION: 10 rooms, all with bath/shower. TV. Phone. B&B £67.50 to £140. Baby facilities. Fishing (*The Which? Hotel Guide*) (£5)

## LLANDUDNO Conwy                                          map 7

## ▲ Bodysgallen Hall ▼ ⅙✕

Llandudno LL30 1RS
TEL: (01492) 584466   FAX: (01492) 582519
EMAIL: info@bodysgallen.com                              COOKING 3
WEBSITE: www.bodysgallen.com                          COUNTRY HOUSE
off A470, 2m SE of Llandudno                              £28–£64

Part of the group that owns Middlethorpe Hall in York and Hartwell House in Aylesbury (see entries), Bodysgallen takes the country-house style in its stride. Formally laid gardens and water features come into their own in fine weather, while log fires take care of the rest of the year. David Thompson's cooking suits the setting, with some quite rich and elaborate dishes, plus a mid-meal sorbet at dinner, but, as the menu notes, simpler items are available on request. One reporter who stayed a few days was 'pleased to have plain grilled Dover sole on the final night'.

Amid the luxuries – of langoustine and scallop terrine, or foie gras boudin with braised lentils and tomato chutney – are a few brighter contemporary flavours: home-smoked cod and lobster rillettes with a green salsa, for example, or goats' cheese soufflé with rocket and sweet chilli dressing. Prime materials take in baked turbot with a shrimp and cockle nage, and poached loin of veal served with black pudding and braised Savoy cabbage, while desserts run to pineapple Tatin with aniseed sorbet. Alternatively, finish with Welsh rarebit. The wine list starts off in Australia before whizzing off to New Zealand, Chile, the US and the rest of the world via France. There are a few amusing typos, but generally the list is well-conceived, although you'll have to look hard to find much under £20. Five house recommendations, all but one French, range from £14.50 to £21.50.

CHEF: David Thompson   PROPRIETOR: Historic House Hotels   OPEN: all week 12.30 to 1.45, 7 to 9.30   MEALS: Set L £16 (2 courses) to £18, Set D £34.90   SERVICE: net prices, card slips closed   CARDS: Delta, MasterCard, Switch, Visa   DETAILS: 50 seats. Private parties: 40 main room, 10 to 40 private rooms. Car park. Vegetarian meals. No children under 8. Jacket and tie. No smoking in dining room. Wheelchair access (also WC). Occasional music. No mobile phones. Air-conditioned   ACCOMMODATION: 35 rooms, all with bath/shower. TV. Phone. Room only £109 to £260. Rooms for disabled. No children under 8. Swimming pool (*The Which? Hotel Guide*)

---

## ▲ St Tudno Hotel ▮ ⤧

Promenade, Llandudno LL30 2LP
TEL: (01492) 874411   FAX: (01492) 860407
EMAIL: sttudnohotel@btinternet.com
WEBSITE: www.st-tudno.co.uk

COOKING 4
MODERN EUROPEAN
£27–£58

Perhaps it is the views of Llandudno Bay and the long, curved promenade from the front rooms, or maybe hands-on involvement from the owners, but somehow this seaside hotel conveys a distinctly French feel. It is a relaxing and hospitable place, with plants, lattice screens and hanging baskets in the horticulturally themed dining room, and a generous seasonal carte supplemented by some daily extras. Local materials play their part, and the kitchen's broad European approach might encompass crab risotto, grilled cod with a hotpot of Conwy mussels, or saddle of Welsh lamb served with a cake of cabbage and oatmeal. Scope extends from utterly simple chilled melon and pineapple, to an indulgent foie gras and chicken sausage with wild mushrooms and truffle oil, while a 14-year-old reporter praises the 'juicy' Welsh Black beef fillet in a red wine sauce, adding 'the chefs always send me in a bowl of chips...this is my favourite hotel'.

Perhaps appropriately for a seaside resort, desserts offer plenty of ice creams and sorbets: a plate of strawberry, rhubarb and lemon ice creams, a Cointreau and orange sorbet to accompany pineapple and ginger cheesecake, or a coconut ice cream to partner warm chocolate fondant. The highly individual wine list (featuring wines from many growers that the owners have visited) is noteworthy for its range and sense of enthusiasm. Mark-ups are reasonable; 'recommended' reds and whites start at £11.50 for French Vin de Pays d'Oc but include a number of interesting bottles from Austria, Mexico and the like. Ten wines are served by the glass, plus a range of sherries from Hidalgo.

CHEFS: David Harding and Stephen Duffy   PROPRIETORS: Martin and Janette Bland   OPEN: all week 12.30 to 1.45, 7 to 9.30 (9 Sun)   MEALS: alc D (main courses £16.50 to £19.50). Set L Mon to Sat £13 (2 courses) to £16, Set L Sun £16.95   SERVICE: not inc   CARDS: Amex, Delta, Diners, MasterCard, Switch, Visa   DETAILS: 60 seats. Private parties: 50 main room. Car park. Vegetarian meals. Children's helpings. No children under 5 at D. No smoking in dining room.

Wheelchair access (not WC). Music. No mobile phones. Air-conditioned ACCOMMODATION: 18 rooms, all with bath/shower. TV. Phone. B&B £65 to £276. Baby facilities. Swimming pool (*The Which? Hotel Guide*) £5

---

## LLANFRYNACH Powys                                                     map 4

# White Swan ⊱✗

Llanfrynach LD3 7BZ
TEL: (01874) 665276   FAX: (01874) 665362
WEBSITE: www.the-white-swan.com
take A40 from Brecon 3m E towards                                   COOKING 3
Abergavenny, then B4558; follow signs to                              GLOBAL
Llanfrynach                                                        £23–£51

'A "beacon" in the Beacons,' quipped a visitor to this tastefully renovated village pub not far from Brecon. The décor is very 'clean cut', with oak beams and stone-flagged floors; there are leather seats in the reception area and real ales on handpump, although the image is now more restaurant than watering hole. Rod Lewis buys locally (organic vegetables from Hay-on-Wye, venison from a farm down the road, Trelough ducks from Herefordshire) but plunders the world – from Mediterranean to Pacific Rim – for culinary inspiration. Put everything together, and the result might be 'wet' leek and Parmesan polenta with roast Portabello mushrooms, red pepper and cumin oil; or Moroccan spiced lamb shank with Spanish mash and harissa sauce. The short printed menu changes every few weeks, while a blackboard lists seafood specials (grilled fillets of sea bass with Chinese noodles, for example) and a few other dishes. Home-made vanilla ice cream has been welcomed as a refreshingly light finale. The wine list offers around 50 bins, mostly at prices that won't drain the wallet. House Chilean is £11.95.

CHEFS: Rod Lewis and Stephen Way   PROPRIETOR: Richard Griffiths   OPEN: Wed to Sun 12 to 2 (2.30 Sun), 7 to 9.30 (9 Sun)   CLOSED: 25 and 26 Dec   MEALS: alc (main courses £7 to £12, D £10 to £17)   SERVICE: not inc, card slips closed   CARDS: Delta, MasterCard, Switch, Visa   DETAILS: 85 seats. 50 seats outside. Private parties: 60 main room, 50 private room. Car park. Vegetarian meals. Children's helpings. No smoking in dining room. Wheelchair access (also WC). Music £5

---

## LLANGAMMARCH WELLS Powys                                            map 4

# ▲ Lake Country House ♥ ⊱✗

Llangammarch Wells LD4 4BS
TEL: (01591) 620202   FAX: (01591) 620457
EMAIL: info@lakecountryhouse.co.uk
WEBSITE: www.lakecountryhouse.co.uk                               COOKING 4
at Garth, 6m W of Builth Wells, turn off B483 on to          MODERN BRITISH
B4519, then take first right                                      £29–£57

The enormous, mock half-timbered hotel is called after the lake that occupies three of its 50 acres of grounds. Inside, too, space is plentiful, and lounge and dining room are stacked to the gills with fabrics, sofas, rugs, carpets and yards of curtains; the atmosphere is 'moneyed and upper-class, on both sides of the pay desk'.

Dinner, the main meal, starts with a no-choice soup, followed perhaps by a mascarpone and tarragon soufflé, and then saddle of local venison on creamed lentils. The quality of raw materials is well above average, and – despite a country-house tendency to avoid bold flavours and incorporate lots of garnish – they are handled with great expertise: as shown by a 'beautifully wobbly' scallop mousse surrounded by orange-flavoured beurre blanc dotted with Avruga caviar. A dish of Welsh lamb has come as a trio consisting of a halved kidney, a square fat pillow of cannon, and a tiny cutlet on the bone (all pink), plus six vegetables including Thai asparagus and a scoop of basil-flavoured mash.

Finish with blackcurrant charlotte, an apple and Calvados parfait, or Welsh farmhouse cheeses. Despite an air of military precision from the boss, and trolleys for both bread and cheese, service from smiley and helpful girls is not excessively formal. The upper-crust feel of the place extends to the Franco-centric wine list, on which mature Bordeaux is particularly well represented. A more modest selection of New World wines is listed toward the back. At the front, a list of 'special recommendations' turns up some interesting bottles, many below £20. House wines start at £13.50.

CHEF: Sean Cullingford   PROPRIETORS: Mr and Mrs J.P. Mifsud   OPEN: all week 12.15 to 1.45, 7.15 to 9   MEALS: Set L £18.50, Set D £35. Afternoon tea available   SERVICE: not inc   CARDS: Amex, Delta, Diners, MasterCard, Switch, Visa   DETAILS: 50 seats. Private parties: 85 main room, 10 to 40 private rooms. Car park. Vegetarian meals. No children under 8 in dining room after 7pm. Children's helpings. Jacket and tie. No smoking in dining room. Wheelchair access (also WC). No music. No mobile phones   ACCOMMODATION: 19 rooms, all with bath/shower. TV. Phone. B&B £95 to £220. Rooms for disabled. Baby facilities. Fishing (*The Which? Hotel Guide*)  £5

---

## LLANRHIDIAN Swansea       map 4

# Welcome to Town ⚡✳     NEW ENTRY

Llanrhidian SA3 1EH
TEL/FAX: (01792) 390015            COOKING 3
EMAIL: enquiries@thewelcometotown.co.uk    CLASSICAL/MODERN WELSH
WEBSITE: www.thewelcometotown.co.uk           £21–£47

The name may seem rather odd, given that this self-styled 'country bistro' occupies a 300-year-old whitewashed inn overlooking the Bury estuary. Ian and Jay Bennett arrived here from Kirroughtree Hotel, Newton Stewart (see Round-up entry), in summer 2001 and have quickly impressed reporters with their dedication to fresh local produce, especially fish. Fixed-price lunch menus are outstanding value, although choice is pared down to just three items at each stage: even so, there is much to savour and dishes really do 'stand on their own feet'. 'Perfectly filleted' escabeche of mackerel has impressed as a starter, and the sympathetic treatment of high-class raw materials has also been evident in fillet of gilt-head bream with buttery braised leeks and sauce vierge, while there are no signs of winding down in desserts, such as a benchmark, but 'unbelievably rich', crème brûlée.

The same principles apply to the extensive evening carte, which ranges from fillet of local sewin on a pea pancake with sorrel sauce to best end of Welsh lamb with saffron sauce, grilled aubergine and pesto. Service is deft, and the short wine list has plenty of affordable drinking from around the world. House French is £10.

CHEFS: Ian Bennett and Helen Farmer   PROPRIETORS: Ian and Jay Bennett   OPEN: Tue to Sun L 12 to 2, Tue to Sat D 7 to 9.30   CLOSED: first 2 weeks Jan   MEALS: alc D (main courses £11.50 to £17). Set L £9.95 (2 courses) to £12.50   SERVICE: not inc   CARDS: MasterCard, Switch, Visa DETAILS: 38 seats. 20 seats outside. Private parties: 30 main room. Car park. Vegetarian meals. Children's helpings. No smoking in dining room. Music

## LLANSANFFRAID GLAN CONWY  Conwy                                  map 7

# ▲ Old Rectory Country House ▼ ⅝✳

Llanrwst Road, Llansanffraid Glan Conwy, Nr
Conwy LL28 5LF
TEL: (01492) 580611   FAX: (01492) 584555
EMAIL: info@oldrectorycountryhouse.co.uk
WEBSITE: www.oldrectorycountryhouse.co.uk
on A470, 1m S of junction with A55

COOKING 6
MODERN BRITISH/FRENCH
£49–£59

To the north-west is a magnificent vista over the Conwy estuary and Norman castle; to the south, Snowdon. In 2003 the Vaughans celebrate 20 years at this comfortably furnished house with its fine antiques, oil paintings and general air of opulence. Wendy Vaughan cooks a no-choice menu (likes and dislikes are handled – mostly satisfactorily – by telephone when booking), usually starting with fish (maybe gilt-head bream with a potato and artichoke ragoût), then perhaps herb-crusted fillet of Welsh Black beef with wild mushrooms. A no-choice menu needs broad appeal, but confident cooking here also adds a personal stamp: as in firm, sweet, juicy spiced monkfish with savoury vanilla risotto, a pleasantly sharp red wine sauce and fragrant basil oil.

Presentation is unfussy; a pink loin of Welsh mountain lamb in April (the meat barely hung at all) came with a Savoy cabbage parcel, a little mixture of roots, and creamy mash studded with green olives, in a light yet deep-flavoured jus. Puddings (choice of two) come with an ice – perhaps hot pine-nut tart with plums and mascarpone sorbet – and simple artistry shows in even straightforward items. Trios are popular: for one visitor a ramekin of passion-fruit mousse, a small bowl of diced tropical fruits, and a sorbet studded with whinberries provided 'an explosion of flavours'.

It is worth noting that this is a small place, and if the hotel is full there is no room for non-residents; also, there is some regimentation – dinner is at a set time, and breakfast must be booked precisely – though meals themselves can be leisurely and last all evening. Given the no-choice menu, the only decision to make is about which wine to choose from a list peopled by well-chosen producers from most of the wine world's hot-spots, though the Old World carries most weight. Burgundy and red Bordeaux are carefully selected and well-priced (although some older vintages may no longer be available), while California provides interesting drinking too. A good selection of half-bottles rounds things out. Prices start at £15.90 and reasonable mark-ups mean a wide choice at the value end of the price range.

CHEF: Wendy Vaughan  PROPRIETORS: Michael and Wendy Vaughan  OPEN: all week D only 7.30 for 8.15 (1 sitting)  CLOSED: Dec and Jan, open weekends only Nov and Feb  MEALS: Set D £34.90  SERVICE: not inc, card slips closed  CARDS: Delta, MasterCard, Switch, Visa  DETAILS: 14 seats. Car park. No children under 5. No smoking in dining room. No music  ACCOMMODATION: 6 rooms, all with bath/shower. TV. Phone. B&B £99 to £169. No children over 6 months or under 5 (*The Which? Hotel Guide*)

## LLANWRTYD WELLS  Powys    map 4

# ▲ Carlton House ✻

Dol-y-coed Road, Llanwrtyd Wells LD5 4RA

TEL: (01591) 610248   FAX: (01591) 610242                           COOKING 6

EMAIL: info@carltonrestaurant.co.uk                          MODERN BRITISH

WEBSITE: www.carltonrestaurant.co.uk                              £34–£53

'I am always looking for establishments providing some sustenance after regular thrashing of the Welsh rugby team in Cardiff on my way home to North Wales. Carlton House fits the bill admirably.' It is a small, unprepossessing town house whose bright, modern dining room, refurbished with some style, sets the tone. Meals have the relaxed feel of a private dinner party, and diners are offered a set-price menu whose only choice is at cheese or dessert stage, and a carte with no choice at all, although dishes can be replaced by those from the set-price menu.

First-rate materials, many local, provide the foundation for a simple style of cooking that might take in a slice of thick, tasty smoked salmon wrapped around spiced crab in mayonnaise, served with a straightforward salad. Goats' cheese typically features among starters, perhaps baked in a tart with onion marmalade, or layered with a crisp, deep-fried croûton and slivers of green apple, and served with dressed leaves.

Main courses are where most of the action is, and robust Mediterranean treatment is not uncommon. First-class wild sea bass from Milford Haven, with a lightly salty skin, might be set on a bed of lemony couscous with a superior ratatouille-like assortment of vegetables, surrounded by a sweet red pepper coulis. Rare, tender, tasty beef has also been given a southern French work-out, topped with tapénade and served with deep-fried capers and roast cherry tomatoes in a rich sauce with olives and pesto. Meals might finish with a strong-tasting chocolate fondant with a lively brandy-flavoured custard, or a turret of mushy pavlova with fresh raspberries clinging to the sides, in a pool of fine raspberry coulis. The short wine list goes global for inspiration, and most bottles check in at under £20. House wines from Chile start at £11.

CHEF: Mary Ann Gilchrist  PROPRIETORS: Alan and Mary Ann Gilchrist  OPEN: Mon to Sat D only 7 to 8.30  CLOSED: 15 to 30 Dec  MEALS: alc (main courses – 2 choices – £17 to £20). Set D £20 (2 courses) to £25  SERVICE: not inc, card slips closed  CARDS: Delta, MasterCard, Switch, Visa  DETAILS: 14 seats. No smoking in dining room. Wheelchair access (not WC). No music. No mobile phones  ACCOMMODATION: 6 rooms, 5 with bath/shower. TV. B&B £40 to £80 (*The Which? Hotel Guide*)  (£5)

---

✻ *indicates that smoking is either banned altogether or that a separate dining room (not just an area) is maintained for non-smokers.*

---

## MACHYNLLETH Powys

map 4

## ▲ Wynnstay ⚡✕

Maengwyn Street, Machynlleth SY20 8AE
TEL: (01654) 702941   FAX: (01654) 703884
EMAIL: info@wynnstay-hotel.com
WEBSITE: www.wynnstay-hotel.com

COOKING 4
MODERN WELSH
£19–£36

This eighteenth-century inn, near Machynlleth's Clock Tower, has a warm, yellow dining room with flagged floor and bare wooden tables. Gareth Johns has always sourced superb produce (much of it Welsh): lamb and Black beef, of course, and seasonal sewin with rhubarb, but also Gressingham duck, the sliced breast served pink and crisp-skinned on a bed of red cabbage. His appealing menus, changed daily, may include reminiscences of his days at the Red Lion in Llanfihangel-nant-Melan, such as soused mackerel, or Penrhyn mussels with leeks and Welsh white wine.

Sound skills are evident in moist salmon wrapped in Carmarthen ham and served with a saffron-scented risotto, all surrounded by a trickle of butter and fish-stock sauce. Dishes are well conceived, and extra vegetables with main courses can be excellent (albeit those on the plate may not need supplementing). A winning dessert is a ring of sweet, fresh, macerated roast pineapple in a caramel sauce flecked with rough-ground black pepper. The offered mid-meal sorbet seems out of place here, and incidentals like bread, butter, appetisers and ice creams fall below the standard of the rest, but Sheila Dark provides chatty service, and a short, fair-value wine list (lacking vintages) starts at under £11.

CHEFS: Gareth Johns and Justin Robinson   PROPRIETORS: Charles and Sheila Dark   OPEN: Sun L 12 to 2, all week D 7 to 9   MEALS: Set L Sun £6.95 (1 course) to £10.95, Set D £18 (2 courses) to £21. Bar menu also available Mon to Sat L 12 to 2 and all week D 6.30 to 9   SERVICE: not inc CARDS: Amex, Delta, Diners, MasterCard, Switch, Visa   DETAILS: 90 seats. 12 seats outside. Private parties: 60 main room. Car park. Vegetarian meals. Children's helpings. No smoking in dining room. Wheelchair access (also men's WC). Occasional music. No mobile phones. Air-conditioned   ACCOMMODATION: 23 rooms, all with bath/shower. TV. Phone. B&B £45 to £100. Baby facilities  £5

## MONTGOMERY Powys

map 7

*(seal: WALES GFG 2003 COMMENDED)*

## Bricklayers Arms ⚡✕ £

Chirbury Road, Montgomery SY15 6QQ
TEL: (01686) 668177
EMAIL: thebricklayersarms@hotmail.com
WEBSITE: www.thebricklayers.uk.com
on B4386, 1m southwest of Chirbury

COOKING 3
MODERN BRITISH
£25–£43

Decorated in warm reds and oranges, this country inn just within Wales has charm, atmosphere and an upstairs dining room complete with beams, pitched roof and bare floorboards shiny with age. Items on the printed menu include a simple but impressive starter of gravadlax of gin-soaked salmon with a fine dill crust, and a fish stew with saffron potatoes and chillies. What excites most, though, is the 'rare breeds board'. Paradoxically, the way to preserve rare breeds is to eat them, and here you can sample a range from Tamworth pork to closely textured, slightly gamy-flavoured Manx Loghtan lamb (the breeds aren't rare because they lack taste!).

The cooking seems sharper, sparer, less fussy than a year ago: a sure sign of maturity in a chef, for paring dishes down to essentials requires skill and confidence (as well as fine materials). The results include a well-balanced starter of seared, roughly chopped chicken livers strewn with bacon and capers and set on a round of toast smeared with black pudding; or pink, seared Brimford Hill wild venison marinated in Syrah and juniper – 'top-class, bursting with flavour' – on a cake of sweet potato and fennel. Vegetables are served separately and copiously, and the plate of five miniature desserts is recommended. Service is friendly and easy-going, and a dozen wines start at £9.50.

CHEF: Robert Jennings   PROPRIETOR: Sara Pezzack   OPEN: Wed to Sun L 12 to 2, Tue to Sat D 7 to 9   CLOSED: 26 Dec, 1 and 2 Jan, 2 weeks Feb, 2 weeks Sept   MEALS: alc (main courses £10 to £14.50). Bar menu available   SERVICE: not inc, card slips closed   CARDS: Delta, Switch, Visa   DETAILS: 65 seats. 12 seats outside. Private parties: 35 main room, 20 to 35 private rooms. Car park. Vegetarian meals. No smoking in dining room. Wheelchair access (also WC). No music  £5

## NANTGAREDIG  Carmarthenshire                                    map 4

## ▲ Four Seasons 🌸

Nantgaredig SA32 7NY
TEL: (01267) 290238   FAX: (01267) 290808
EMAIL: jen4seas@aol.com                                  COOKING 2
WEBSITE: www.visit-carmarthanshire.co.uk/4seasons        MODERN BRITISH
on B4310, ½m N of Nantgaredig                            £33–£44

People tend to gather in the small blue and yellow lounge until it gets full, and then go off to eat in the large, airy barn (once a milking parlour) with its black slate floors, whitewashed stone walls, and conservatory extension. For over a decade Maryann Wright and Charlotte Pasetti have applied comparatively simple techniques to both local and more far-flung ingredients, producing anything from a generous thick chunk of Black beef fillet with mustard butter, or shank of Welsh saltmarsh lamb with rosemary-flavoured roasted vegetables, to smoked Brecon venison with a balsamic- and orange-dressed Parmesan salad.

Not everything in the workmanlike repertoire is equally red-blooded, given a puff pastry circle with cherry tomatoes and pieces of smoked haddock, and a pancake filled with spinach and Teifi cheese. Finish with a raspberry variant on crème brûlée, or a warm pear and almond tart, and drink from a fairly priced wine list starting with house red and white at £10.

CHEFS/PROPRIETORS: Maryann Wright and Charlotte Pasetti   OPEN: Tue to Sat D only 7.30 to 9.30   CLOSED: Christmas   MEALS: Set D £25   SERVICE: not inc, card slips closed   CARDS: Delta, MasterCard, Switch, Visa   DETAILS: 45 seats. 8 seats outside. Private parties: 55 main room. Car park. Vegetarian meals. Children's helpings. No smoking in dining room. Wheelchair access (not WC). Music   ACCOMMODATION: 6 rooms, all with bath/shower. TV. B&B £45 to £80. Rooms for disabled. Baby facilities. Swimming pool (The Which? Hotel Guide)  £5

The Good Food Guide is a registered trade mark of Which? Ltd.

## NANT-Y-DERRY  Monmouthshire

map 2

# Foxhunter ✸

**NEW ENTRY**

Nant-y-Derry NP7 9DN

TEL: (01873) 881101  FAX: (01873) 881377

off A4042, approx 5m S of Abergavenny

COOKING **4**

MODERN BRITISH

£29–£57

Open-plan and spick and span, this tall, refurbished pub of grey-brown stone is plainly decorated with bare floorboards, beechwood tables and chairs, and a few seafood prints. Only ten miles from the Walnut Tree Inn (see entry, Llandewi Skirrid), the Foxhunter resembles it in several ways: the casual yet animated atmosphere is similar; one visitor found familiar faces among both staff and customers; and the food's rustic simplicity is reminiscent of the old Taruschio style.

Ambition is kept in check, skills are up to the job, presentation is unfussy, and the cooking is bold and generous without being complicated: one meal, for example, started with a little, flat, round omelette full of tiny, whole wild asparagus, topped with a good coat of finely grated cheese. Tebbutt gets the balance of flavours right, producing a bowl of freshly made, accurately timed spaghetti, served with slices and tentacles of squid, chopped chilli and garlic, and lots of roughly chopped flat leaf parsley, all simply warmed through. An honest and deliberately unrefined note shows up, too, in grilled rack of lamb, well crusted with lots of flavour, served with a sauce made from no more than cooking juices and a slug of port, with a scattering of well-timed vegetables.

Desserts run from spotted dick, and banana tart, to a selection of creamy ice creams, with a shortbread biscuit for contrast. The home-made focaccia dished out at the start of every meal was declared 'the best bread I've ever tasted' by an aficionado. A 60-strong wine list aims for plenty of variety while keeping prices within reason. Churton Sauvignon Blanc 2001 and Salice Salentino Riserva 1997 are both under £20, house red and white under £12.

CHEFS: Matt Tebbutt and Ricky Stephenson  PROPRIETORS: Matt and Lisa Tebbutt  OPEN: Wed to Sat 12 to 2.30, 7 to 10  CLOSED: 24 to 26 Dec, 2 weeks Feb  MEALS: alc (main courses £11 to £17).  SERVICE: not inc, 10% for parties of 8 or more  CARDS: Delta, MasterCard, Switch, Visa DETAILS: 65 seats. Private parties: 60 maain room, 20 to 40 private rooms. Car park. Vegetarian meals. Children's helpings. No smoking in dining room. Wheelchair access (also WC). Music

## NEWPORT  Pembrokeshire

map 4

# ▲ Cnapan ✸

East Street, Newport SA42 0SY

TEL: (01239) 820575

COOKING **1**

BRITISH

£20–£46

This pale pink townhouse has a family-friendly atmosphere and a 'lived-in' feel: well, it *is* run by two generations of the same family. After nearly 20 years, the Coopers and Lloyds have an established style that evolves gently, maintaining a traditional feel: starters at dinner, for example, might include smooth chicken liver and bacon paté with apple and garlic chutney, while main courses encompass marinated pork fillet with spicy pears and a creamy mushroom, pepper and herb sauce, alongside Preseli lamb marinated in Eastern spices and yoghurt with chilli and tomato salsa. With the sea on Newport's doorstep, there is an emphasis on fish and seafood, listed on a blackboard that is updated daily: lobster, sea bass and sewin all appear regularly. Desserts might include lemon and lime cream pie, or apple and apricot sticky tart. Wines are a straightforward selection; house wines are £9.75.

CHEF: Judith Cooper   PROPRIETORS: Michael and Judith Cooper, John and Eluned Lloyd   OPEN: Wed to Mon L 12 to 2, Wed to Sat and Mon D 6.30 to 8.45 (bookings preferred for D)   CLOSED: Christmas, Jan, Feb, L mid-week Nov to Easter   MEALS: alc (main courses L £6.50 to £9.50, D £13 to £18.50)   SERVICE: not inc, card slips closed   CARDS: Delta, MasterCard, Switch, Visa   DETAILS: 36 seats. 30 seats outside. Small car park. Vegetarian meals. Children's helpings at L. No smoking in dining room. Wheelchair access (not WC). Occasional music. No mobile phones   ACCOMMODATION: 5 rooms, all with bath/shower. TV. B&B £32 to £64. Baby facilities (*The Which? Hotel Guide*)

## PONTDOLGOCH Powys                                    map 7

## ▲ Talkhouse ⚡

| Pontdolgoch SY17 5JE | COOKING 2 |
|---|---|
| TEL: (01686) 688919   FAX: (01686) 689134 | MODERN BRITISH |
| on A470, about 1½m NW of Caersws | £29–£43 |

Stylishly converted from a traditional country inn to a thoroughly modern restaurant-with-rooms, the Talkhouse retains an informal atmosphere thanks to the personal attentions of chefs/proprietors Colin and Melanie Dawson. Start in the characterful bar area with a pre-prandial drink while scrutinising the long blackboard of modern British dishes that offer something for just about everyone. Chargrilled rib of Welsh Black beef with horseradish mash, mushrooms and tomatoes in red wine gravy will appeal to traditionalists; for fans of modern fish cookery there might be seared fillet of Cornish cod with baked red pepper, tapénade mash and a prawn and coriander salsa; and Roquefort soufflé with toasted pine nuts and poached pears should keep vegetarians happy. And who wouldn't go for warm chocolate mousse with wild lime and coconut ice cream to finish? Since last year, the wine list has been expanded, with the new list offering more selections from France and Italy. There's plenty to choose from under £20, with bottle prices starting at £10.60 for German white. Eleven wines are served by the small or large glass.

CHEFS/PROPRIETORS: Colin and Melanie Dawson   OPEN: Tue to Sun 12 to 1.30 (6 Sun), Tue to Sat 6 to 9   CLOSED: 1 week autumn, 25 and 26 Dec, 1 Jan, 1 week early spring (ring to check)   MEALS: alc (main courses £10.50 to £14)   SERVICE: not inc, card slips closed   CARDS: Amex, Delta, MasterCard, Switch, Visa   DETAILS: 30 seats. 8 seats outside. Private parties: 30 main room. Car park. Vegetarian meals. No children under 14 at D. No smoking in dining room. Wheelchair access (not WC). Music. No mobile phones   ACCOMMODATION: 3 rooms, all with bath/shower. TV. B&B £65 to £95. No children under 14 (*The Which? Hotel Guide*)   (£5)

🖎 indicates that there has been a change of chef since last year's Guide, and the Editor has judged that the change is of sufficient interest to merit the reader's attention.

# ▲ Tregynon Farmhouse ⅚✳

Gwaun Valley, Pontfaen SA65 9TU
TEL: (01239) 820531   FAX: (01239) 820808
EMAIL: tregynon@online-holidays.net
at junction of Narberth-to-Fishguard B4313 and                    COOKING 1
B4329, take B4313 towards Fishguard, then take                MODERN BRITISH
first right, and first right again                                  £33–£45

Hidden in the impenetrable depths of the green and rambling Gwaun Valley, this lovingly restored farmhouse dates from the sixteenth century, its log fire, large sofas and antique furniture adding up to a civilised setting. The menu (which rotates on a six-day cycle) is recited over the phone, and main courses need to be ordered the day before: perhaps chicken schnitzel, or plaice fillet with a ginger and lemon butter sauce. The only regular item (usually attracting a small supplement) is slow-cooked, herb-crusted rack of Pembrokeshire lamb. Tregynon aspires to high standards, and the Heards 'clearly know what they ought to be doing', although in the event the kitchen does not always rise to the occasion, serving some overcooked meat and fish at inspection.

Start perhaps with a 'homely' spinach crêpe, or black pudding with tomato and Welsh rarebit, and finish with a domestic selection of puddings (recited at table) that might take in pineapple with kirsch, or a brittle meringue nest with cream and raspberries. Peter Heard officiates as jovial master of ceremonies in full evening dress, and sherries and other aperitifs head up a good-value round-the-world wine selection, in turn followed by a well-chosen, lengthily annotated main list. Prices start at £11.50.

CHEFS: Peter and Jane Heard, and Gemma Cox   PROPRIETORS: Peter and Jane Heard   OPEN: Mon to Wed, Fri and Sat D only 7.30 to 8.30   MEALS: Set D £24.50 to £28; booking essential
SERVICE: not inc   CARDS: Delta, MasterCard, Switch, Visa   DETAILS: 20 seats. Private parties: 14 main room, 2 to 6 private rooms. Car park. Vegetarian meals. No children under 8. No smoking in dining room. Wheelchair access (also WC). Music   ACCOMMODATION: 3 rooms, all with bath/shower. TV. Phone. B&B £72.50 to £82.50

# Harbour Lights ⅚✳

Porthgain, nr St David's SA62 5BL
TEL: (01348) 831549   FAX: (01348) 831193
EMAIL: restaurant@art2by.com
WEBSITE: www.wales-pembs-art.com/pages/restaurant.htm              COOKING 4
off A487 at Croesgoch, 4m W of Mathry                                SEAFOOD
                                                                    £38–£47

Fronted by a large car park, Harbour Lights is a small cottage restaurant with an art gallery attached. Brightly coloured contemporary artwork helps to liven up the largely wooden surfaces, and the kitchen's preoccupation, unsurprisingly, is local fish and seafood, simply cooked. It is the combination of fresh supplies and straightforward treatment that appeals, rather than any attempt at sophisticated cooking. Things don't come much simpler than freshly potted Porthgain crab, and while a dish of laverbread, cockles, bacon and Llangoffan cheese can hardly aspire to greatness, it makes an enjoyable and distinctive starter.

Among other successes have been ultra-fresh, accurately timed, locally caught sea bass with a light beurre blanc and an oily pesto, and moist, tasty, pan-fried fillets of John Dory in a well-judged sweet pepper and chilli sauce. To finish, an exemplary banoffi pie and a blackcurrant brûlée, made with organic yoghurt, are both as light and fresh as one could ask for. Service is capable and personable, though it can lag behind when things get busy, and a short wine list starts with Côtes de Gascogne white at £10.50.

CHEFS: Anne Marie Davies and Ryan Davies   PROPRIETORS: Anne Marie and Huw Davies   OPEN: Wed to Sat and bank hol Sun D only 6.30 to 9.30   MEALS: Set D £27   SERVICE: not inc   CARDS: Delta, MasterCard, Switch, Visa   DETAILS: 30 seats. 10 seats outside. Car park. No smoking in dining room. Wheelchair access (not WC). Music

## PORTMEIRION  Gwynedd                                              map 7

## ▲ Hotel Portmeirion ▼ ⁂

Portmeirion LL48 6ET
TEL: (01766) 770000   FAX: (01766) 771331
EMAIL: hotel@portmeirion-village.com                          COOKING 2
WEBSITE: www.portmeirion.com                        MODERN WELSH-PLUS
off A487, signposted from Minffordd                              £27–£53

Built by Clough Williams-Ellis, and opened in 1926, the hotel is part of an Italianate fantasy village that was once a secluded haven for writers, and famously a film set for the TV series *The Prisoner*. Meals are taken in a curved dining room with an appealing view over the estuary, and benefit from an impressive roll call of native materials, among them seafood from Menai Straits oysters to locally farmed turbot, from Lleyn crabs and lobsters to salmon smoked at Llandudno. That doesn't stop the kitchen wheeling out Mediterranean ideas (such as a Mozzarella salad with roast cherry tomatoes, balsamic figs and a pesto dressing), nor does it forget Welsh meat: lamb of course, and perhaps a fillet of Pen Llyn beef on a woodland mushroom and leek risotto.

Puddings provide good variety, taking in anything from a thyme and black cherry parfait, via ginger and orange sponge, to spicy chocolate loaf with a Baileys sauce. The wine list focuses on France before shining a spotlight on the rest of Europe, and then heading boldly to the New World. Producers are well chosen and value for money is excellent, with mark-ups kept commendably low. Seven house wines are priced at £11 (£2.80 per glass), in addition to a Welsh house wine (£13.50 a bottle, £3 a glass).

Nearby Castell Deudraeth Bar and Grill offers a brasserie-style menu featuring local seafood, although reports so far suggest that it is not up to the standard of Portmeirion itself.

CHEFS: Colin Pritchard, Billy Taylor and Steven Rowlands   PROPRIETOR: Portmeirion Ltd   OPEN: Tue to Sun L 12 to 2, all week D 6.30 to 9.30   CLOSED: 5 Jan to 1 Feb   MEALS: Set L £11.50 to £14.50, Set L Sun £16, Set D £30 (2 courses) to £35   SERVICE: not inc, card slips closed   CARDS: Amex, Delta, Diners, MasterCard, Switch, Visa   DETAILS: 100 seats. Private parties: 100 main room, 30 private rooms. Car park. Vegetarian meals. Children's helpings. No smoking in dining room. Occasional music. No mobile phones  ACCOMMODATION: 51 rooms, all with bath/shower. TV. Phone. Room only £105 to £185. Rooms for disabled. Baby facilities. Swimming pool (*The Which? Hotel Guide*)  (£5)

## PWLLGLOYW  Powys

map 4

## ▲ Seland Newydd ⁵⅞

Pwllgloyw LD3 9PY
TEL/FAX:  (01874) 690282
EMAIL:  seland@newydd.fsbusiness.co.uk
WEBSITE:  www.selandnewydd.co.uk
on B4520, 4m N of Brecon

COOKING 4
MODERN BRITISH/FRENCH
£23–£48

On the scenic route between Brecon and Builth, this is a comfortable, informal but stylish pub and restaurant, evidently worth a detour. 'Even though it is over 40 miles from my home, I will make every effort to return,' writes one satisfied customer. Similar food is served throughout, but those in the dining room get white napery and a printed menu, perhaps offering creamy parsnip and thyme soup, followed by rump of Welsh lamb with butter beans, vegetables and rosemary-infused meat juices.

While the cooking is straightforward, it is brought up to date with a few deftly chosen ingredients: a terrine containing ham, potato, arrtichoke and carrot is set with crème fraîche and served with beetroot chutney, while Greenland halibut comes with truffle oil risotto and vermouth fish cream. Vegetables are specific to each dish (asparagus, plum tomatoes, broccoli and chicory for the halibut, for example), and desserts run from a glazed passion-fruit tart to vanilla rice pudding with plum compote and walnut ice cream. A short, serviceable wine list stays mostly under £20, starting with a trio of house wines at £9.95.

CHEF: Paul Thomasson  PROPRIETORS: Tony Savage and Paul and Margaret Thomasson  OPEN: Wed to Sun L 12 to 2.30, Tue to Sat D 7 to 9  MEALS: alc (main courses £12 to £16). Set L Sun £12.95. Bar menu also available Wed to Sat L and Tue to Thurs D  SERVICE: not inc, card slips closed  CARDS: Delta, MasterCard, Switch, Visa  DETAILS: 30 seats. 25 seats outside. Private parties: 40 main room, 8 private room. Car park. Vegetarian meals available (though not on menu). Children's helpings. No smoking in dining room. Wheelchair access (also WC). Music  ACCOMMODATION: 3 rooms, all with bath/shower. TV. B&B £42.50 to £50. Rooms for disabled. Fishing (*The Which? Hotel Guide*)

## PWLLHELI  Gwynedd

map 7

## ▲ Plas Bodegroes ▮ ⁵⅞

(WALES OF THE YEAR RESTAURANT)

Nefyn Road, Pwllheli LL53 5TH
TEL:  (01758) 612363  FAX:  (01758) 701247
EMAIL:  gunna@bodegroes.co.uk
WEBSITE:  www.bodegroes.co.uk
on A497, 1m NW of Pwllheli

COOKING 7
MODERN WELSH
£27–£57

Although the Chowns modestly see it more as a 'restaurant-with-rooms' than a country-house hotel, this is nevertheless a special place. Paintings by local artists, from unknowns to Williams Selwyn and Sir Kyffin Williams, add warmth to a sophisticated dining room with its Scandinavian style, pastel colours and sharp lighting. 'Eating here is always a civilised experience.'

Chris Chown's food has the simple stamp of confidence, evident even from the straightforwardly written menu, and dishes have a distinct character, be it a deep bowl of seafood hotpot incorporating plump mussels, prawns, scallops and white fish, spiked with chilli and coriander, or the rustic appeal of warm slices of tender, savoury pig's tongue, served with a lightly jellied brawn, full of chunky bits of meat, all pepped up by a mustard dressing. Seafood is well rendered, judging by a hearty, colourful and richly flavoured lobster risotto 'bursting with sea savour', and by a main course of turbot – a thick wedge from the shoulder – baked on the bone, the flesh floating away in firm, glutinous flakes, served with a large blob of lime hollandaise.

Above all the kitchen understands how to turn ingredients into exciting dishes without over-complication or losing the plot; it encapsulates the real taste of this richly endowed part of Wales. Welsh Black ribeye beef with oxtail sauce is a Chown classic, the rare meat rapidly seared and rested, the sauce accompanied by glazed shallots. Fierce searing and proper resting are also applied to Hereford duck breast, which is likewise contrasted with a slow-cooked leg; this may be something of a cliché these days, but here it is lifted above the norm by a chicory Tatin and an orange kick to the jus.

To finish, bara brith and butter pudding (accompanied by a whisky ice cream) is something of a Chown original, or there may be an ultra-rich chocolate soufflé with white chocolate ice cream. Meals are rounded out with fresh-tasting appetisers and good bread, and Sunday lunch is considered a bargain. Staff, led by Gunna Chown, serve without fuss yet are never far away, and the extensive wine list provides characterful drinking at a range of price levels. It covers the wine-making globe, but Italian whites and French regional wines are particularly noteworthy. Fair pricing is evident throughout, giving plenty of choice under £20. Twenty house selections start at £14.50.

CHEF: Chris Chown   PROPRIETORS: Chris and Gunna Chown   OPEN: Sun L 12 to 2, Tue to Sun D 7 to 9.30   CLOSED: 30 Nov to 14 Feb   MEALS: Set L Sun £15.50, Set D £32.50   SERVICE: not inc, card slips closed   CARDS: Delta, MasterCard, Switch, Visa   DETAILS: 40 seats. Private parties: 40 main room, 10 to 16 private rooms. Car park. No smoking in dining room. Wheelchair access (also WC). Occasional music   ACCOMMODATION: 11 rooms, all with bath/shower. TV. Phone. B&B £40 to £120. Baby facilities (*The Which? Hotel Guide*)  (£5)

## REYNOLDSTON  Swansea                                          map 4

## ▲ Fairyhill  ▮ ⅝✳

Reynoldston SA3 1BS
TEL: (01792) 390139   FAX: (01792) 391358
EMAIL: postbox@fairyhill.net
WEBSITE: www.fairyhill.net                                   COOKING 4
from B4295 going W bear left at Oldwalls;                  MODERN WELSH
Fairyhill is about 1½m along road                            £30–£59

The large terrace of this creeper-clad, eighteenth-century house overlooks woodland and meadows, making it a pleasant spot for drinks outside in summer. The house itself is a pleasing mix of styles, the cooking likewise, featuring a few native items from dry cured bacon (in a warm salad of monkfish) via grilled Black beef fillet with a steak and kidney pudding sauce, to seared loin of new season lamb, cooked pink, the finely chopped liver and kidney served in a little deep-fried potato basket, with a well-judged red wine sauce.

Seafood is a strength, raw materials well served by steaming: fillets of sewin with al dente asparagus and a lemony hollandaise, or Gower lobster with a slightly sweet stem ginger sauce. Although some disappointments have been expressed, an inspection meal confirmed the essential worthiness of the cooking. Meals might end with thin slices of apple coated with Llanboidy cheese, accompanied by a mildly spiced apple chutney, or with a hot banana soufflé pancake in a copious fudge sauce. Service is friendly and very attentive.

Strong traditional sections on the wine list are backed up by interesting showings from Austria and Wales, and a fair selection of half-bottles. A couple of domaines are singled out for special attention: an unusual claret, Ch Rousseau de Sipian (the 1999 is £22.50), and the Burgundies of Coche-Dury. User friendliness extends to a page of good-value French country wines, a selection of bottles under £20, and a half-dozen by the glass. House Vin de Pays d'Oc is £13.50 (£3.50 a large glass).

CHEFS: Adrian Coulthard and Bryony Jones    PROPRIETORS: Paul Davies and Andrew Hetherington    OPEN: all week 12.30 to 2, 7.30 to 9 (8.15 Sun)    CLOSED: 26 Dec, 1 to 16 Jan    MEALS: alc L (main courses £12 to £18.50). Set L £14.95 (2 courses) to £18.95, Set L Sun £21.50, Set D £27.50 (2 courses) to £35    SERVICE: not inc, card slips closed    CARDS: Amex, Delta, MasterCard, Switch, Visa    DETAILS: 60 seats. 20 seats outside. Private parties: 40 main room, 23 to 40 private rooms. Car park. Vegetarian meals. Children's helpings; no children under 8 at D. No smoking in dining room. Wheelchair access (not WC). Music    ACCOMMODATION: 8 rooms, all with bath/shower. TV. Phone. B&B £110 to £225. No children under 8 (*The Which? Hotel Guide*)

---

**ST DAVID'S** Pembrokeshire                                                        **map 4**

# Morgan's Brasserie ✳✻ £

20 Nun Street, St David's SA62 6NT
TEL: (01437) 720508                                                         COOKING **2**
EMAIL: morgans@stdavids.co.uk                                      FISH/MODERN BRITISH
WEBSITE: www.morgans-in-stdavids.co.uk                                    £27–£47

Occupying the downstairs room of a converted terraced house, its walls covered in prints and photographs, Morgan's has a cottagey feel. Given its location (fish is landed at Milford Haven), seafood is an understandable speciality, the daily dishes chalked up on a board: perhaps grilled Dover sole with lemon and dill butter, or a filo 'purse' containing salmon, sole and monkfish in a light sauce. Other native materials might appear in the form of Penclawdd cockles (beside a fillet of sea bass), or sewin with laverbread and orange sauce in season, and Welsh lamb and Black beef are also likely to turn up. Dishes are not complicated; indeed, they have a 'domestic simplicity' about them, from Caesar salad to a peppery, creamy wild mushroom and tarragon soup. Finish maybe with a selection of Welsh cheeses, or a creamy, brittle-topped crème brûlée. Service is a weak point, but a tolerably priced wine list (starting at £12) adds to the sense of value.

CHEF: Ceri Morgan   PROPRIETORS: Ceri and Elaine Morgan   OPEN: Tue to Sat D only 6.30 to 9 (days may vary in low season)   CLOSED: Jan and Feb   MEALS: alc (main courses £9.50 to £17) SERVICE: not inc, card slips closed   CARDS: Amex, MasterCard, Switch, Visa   DETAILS: 32 seats. Private parties: 20 main room. Vegetarian meals. Children's helpings. No smoking in dining room. Music

## SKENFRITH  Monmouthshire

map 2

# ▲ Bell at Skenfrith ✱✕

NEW ENTRY

Skenfrith NP7 8UH
TEL: (01600) 750235   FAX: (01600) 750525
EMAIL: enquiries@skenfrith.com
WEBSITE: www.skenfrith.com

COOKING 2
MODERN BRITISH
£27–£52

This seventeenth-century inn beside the Monnow has been restored with more than usual care. Externally a whitewashed, slate-roofed country pub, its inside – pale oak, mirrors and brushed chrome – betoken a city brasserie. These are early days, and as yet the restaurant menu is available only four sessions a week, although the dining room is 'a pleasure to eat in'.

The short, modern menu reads enticingly – foie gras comes with cowslip and shallot jam, as well as pear and truffle oil – and, if ambition slightly outruns skill, there have been notable successes, including four plump, juicy scallops arranged around a pile of leaves with a Parmesan wafer and rocket pesto, and a sweet red onion tart topped with melted Llanboidy cheese and anointed with beetroot and raspberry vinaigrette.

Desserts have included a creamy, wobbly pannacotta powerfully scented with lavender (served with apple sorbet, praline wafer and vin santo drizzle), and a pine nut cantucci tiramisù with espresso chocolate sauce and basil syrup. Service is attentive and amicable. Wines favour reds and span a range of styles and prices from £10 for a vin de pays to £190 for Ch. Latour: but both Ch. Beaumont 1998 and a half of Willi Opitz's Goldackerl Beerenauslese 2000 are under £20.

CHEF: Leigh Say   PROPRIETORS: William and Janet Hutchings   OPEN: all week 12 to 2.30, 7 to 9.30 (note restaurant menu available Wed to Sat D only)   MEALS: Set L Sun £13.50 (2 courses) to £17.50. Set D Wed to Sat £27 (2 courses) to £32.50. Bar menu available L (exc Sun) and D (main courses £10 to £15)   SERVICE: not inc, card slips closed   CARDS: Amex, Delta, MasterCard, Switch, Visa   DETAILS: 30 seats. 40 seats outside. Private parties: 40 main room. Car park. Vegetarian meals. No children under 8 in dining room. Children's helpings. No smoking in dining room. Wheelchair access (also WC). Music. No mobile phones   ACCOMMODATION: 8 rooms, all with bath/shower. TV. Phone. B&B £65 to £140. Baby facilities  (£5)

## SWANSEA  Swansea

map 4

# La Braseria  £

28 Wind Street, Swansea SA1 1DZ
TEL: (01792) 469683   FAX: (01792) 470816
WEBSITE: www.labraseria.com

COOKING 1
SPANISH
£19–£53

Swansea's stab at a Spanish bodega comes complete with multi-coloured glazed tiles, rough-plastered walls and a hotch-potch of wine crates, barrels and rustic plates. The procedure is simple: find a table, either upstairs or downstairs, note its number, then order at one of the two bars, with their displays of meat (anything from rump steak to crispy duck) and fish (scallops, sea bass, hake and more). Everything on offer is there, and most of it is cooked before your eyes. Chargrilling is the principal technique, and dishes usually come with light sauces, chips, jacket potatoes or salads; flavours are clear and portions generous. For dessert crème caramel, we are told, is 'made in-house fresh every day', or try torta Amaretto or lemon mousse. Lunchtime deals are some of the best in the city (no wonder the place hums with customers), and service is bright and friendly. The wine list also has a Spanish accent, though Burgundy and Bordeaux also have a firm presence; house Spanish is £10.25.

CHEF: Ian Wing   PROPRIETOR: Manuel Tercero   OPEN: Mon to Sat 12 to 2.30, 7 to 11.30   CLOSED: 25 and 31 Dec   MEALS: alc (main courses £8 to £24). Set L £7.50 (2 courses)   SERVICE: not inc, card slips closed   CARDS: Amex, Delta, Diners, MasterCard, Switch, Visa   DETAILS: 170 seats. Private parties: 100 main room. Vegetarian meals. Wheelchair access (also WC). Music. Air-conditioned

## Didier & Stephanie's

56 St Helen's Road, Swansea SA1 4BE   COOKING 2
TEL: (01792) 655603   FAX: (01792) 470563   FRENCH
EMAIL: stedanvel@hotmail.com   £21–£42

As if it weren't French enough already, live accordion music on the second Thursday of each month adds a certain *je ne sais quoi* to the atmosphere at Stephanie Danvel's and Didier Suvé's warm and friendly restaurant. Menus are bilingual, but there is no questioning the nationality of the cooking: feuilleté of snails with herbs and diced vegetables, chicken liver salad with apples, and croustillant of black pudding with onions are typical of starters, while main courses take in rabbit casserole with prunes, and confit duck with pink peppercorn sauce. That said, there are a few touches that show sympathy to local tradition: lemon sole with cockles and tarragon, for example, or roast sea bass with laverbread. Finish with nougat ice cream, vanilla crème brûlée or a selection of French farmhouse cheeses. France unsurprisingly dominates on the short wine list. House wines are £9.90 a bottle.

CHEFS/PROPRIETORS: Stephanie Danvel and Didier Suvé   OPEN: Tue to Sat 12 to 2, 7 to 9.30 CLOSED: Christmas and New Year   MEALS: alc D (main courses D £11 to £13). Set L £7.20 (1 course) to £12.20   SERVICE: not inc   CARDS: Amex, Delta, MasterCard, Switch, Visa   DETAILS: 52 seats. Private parties: 30 main room, 22 private room. Vegetarian meals. Music

## Hanson's £

Pilot House Wharf, Trawler Road, Swansea   COOKING 3
Marina, Swansea SA1 1UN   MODERN BRITISH/SEAFOOD
TEL: (01792) 466200   FAX: (01792) 201774   £22–£50

Fish is the focus at this popular restaurant in Swansea Marina, on the first floor of the Old Pilot House above a fishing tackle shop. Fishing boats land their catch on the restaurant's doorstep, and chef Andrew Hanson puts it to good use in the selections chalked up on a board. Starters might include ultra-fresh spicy deep-fried monkfish in chilli tempura batter with sauce Indienne and minted crème fraîche, or an old-fashioned baked seafood thermidor au gratin, served in a hearty portion. For a main course, silver-skinned bass may be served with Mediterranean vegetables with black olive and basil cream sauce.

There is plenty for non-piscophiles, too – such as duck liver parfait for a starter, or a generously presented roast rack of new season's lamb set on gratin potatoes with a sweet redcurrant-flavoured jus – and there is a short vegetarian menu as well. Desserts might include tiramisù accented with raspberries and strawberries, or summer-fruit crème brûlée with a crunchy topping. The list of about 30 wines includes some from well-chosen New World producers. Bottle prices start at £10.95, and most are under £20.

CHEF: Andrew Hanson   PROPRIETORS: Helen Tennant and Andrew Hanson   OPEN: all week L 12 to 2, Mon to Sat D 6.30 to 9.30   CLOSED: 24 Dec D, 25 and 26 Dec, Easter, bank hols   MEALS: alc (main courses £10 to £20). Set L £12.95   SERVICE: not inc   CARDS: Delta, Diners, MasterCard, Switch, Visa   DETAILS: 50 seats. Private parties: 50 main room. Vegetarian meals. Children's helpings. Music

---

**TALSARNAU  Gwynedd**                                                                     map 7

# ▲ Maes-y-Neuadd ▼ ✸

Talsarnau LL47 6YA
TEL: (01766) 780200   FAX: (01766) 780211
EMAIL: maes@neuadd.com                                                    COOKING 4
WEBSITE: www.neuadd.com                                              MODERN WELSH
off B4573, 1m S of Talsarnau                                               £24–£51

From its mountain setting this beautiful old mansion house overlooks Cardigan Bay. A change in ownership this year has had no apparent ill effects on the restaurant, with Peter Jackson remaining as a steadying influence. Reports are as full of superlatives as ever.

The three- or four-course dinner menu offers two choices at each stage, except dessert: there the gourmand can duck hard choices and sample the lot (one party enjoyed a selection of Welsh cheeses, then a puff-pastry case of apple and plum with thick cream, then warm pineapple with butterscotch sauce, and finally 'wonderful' ice creams such as pepper and Curaçao). Before all that, there may be pan-fried mackerel on a bed of onions and mushrooms, or a 'pretty and colourful' pressed game terrine with apple jelly; then perhaps crisp-skinned, pink-fleshed goose with mustard mash and braised shallots, or roast brill with leeks, carrots and courgettes.

Attention to detail is a virtue here: jugs of iced water on tables ('Why can't everybody do that?' mused an inspector), 'tempting' nibbles served with pre-dinner drinks, as well as an appetiser at table, and many varieties of bread made in-house. Service is knowledgeable, unobtrusive and efficient. The Franco-centric wine list opens with 16 red Bordeaux, taking in some quality crus bourgeois, but steering clear of the big guns, before moving on to Burgundy and other French regions. As with Italy and Spain, New World selections are brief and tend towards tried-and-tested styles. Three house wines (one from Wales) open the bidding at £12.95 to £14.95 (£3.30 to £3.95 a glass), but there is decent choice elsewhere on the list under £20.

CHEFS: Peter Jackson and John Owen Jones  PROPRIETORS: Peter and Lynn Jackson, and Peter and Doreen Payne  OPEN: all week 12 to 1.45, 7 to 9  MEALS: Set L Sun £15.25, Set D £28 to £32. Bar and light L menus also available Mon to Sat. Cover £3 Mon to Sat L in restaurant  SERVICE: not inc, card slips closed  CARDS: Amex, Delta, Diners, MasterCard, Switch, Visa  DETAILS: 60 seats. 16 seats outside. Private parties: 50 main room, 2 to 12 private rooms. Car park. Vegetarian meals. Children's helpings. No children under 7 in main restaurant after 7pm (family dining room available). No smoking in dining room. Wheelchair access (also women's WC). No music. No mobile phones  ACCOMMODATION: 16 rooms, all with bath/shower. TV. Phone. D,B&B £73 to £233. Rooms for disabled. Baby facilities (*The Which? Hotel Guide*)  £5

## TREDUNNOCK  Monmouthshire  map 2

## ▲ The Newbridge ♥  NEW ENTRY

Tredunnock NP15 1LY
TEL: (01633) 451000  FAX: (01633) 451001
EMAIL: thenewbridge@tinyonline.co.uk
WEBSITE: www.thenewbridge.co.uk
from Caerleon take Llangibby/Usk road;
after approx 3m turn right opposite hotel;  COOKING 2
go through village of Tredunnock and  MODERN WELSH/MEDITERRANEAN
down hill to banks of River Usk  £18–£53

Inside this big butter-yellow building on the banks of the Usk, there is a pleasantly relaxed ambience that combines country pub (black beams and steeply pitched white roof) and city wine bar. The menu has a traditional backbone but one that is tempered by modish ingredients and techniques, especially at dinner: roasted squab pigeon with wild mushrooms, foie gras and port jus, for example. A Sunday lunch party enjoyed conventional 'thick and savoury' pea and ham soup, roast leg of Hereford pork with apple sauce and 'very crisp' crackling; then a thick round of jam roly-poly that was crowned with a physalis and anointed with a light custard. Newer ideas have included onion and Brie tart with hazelnut dressing; and 'juicy, succulently fresh' roast cod with creamed potatoes, tomato compote and aïoli. Note the good-value set lunches. Service is capable and professional, while wines are a diverse bunch. Italians are particularly well chosen, with native white grape varieties providing some of the most interesting and good-value bottles on the list. Mark-ups are low, with prices starting at £9 for Australian Chardonnay, and there is plenty to choose from under £20. Eight wines are available in two glass sizes (£1.65 to £3.45 or £2.50 to £4.80).

CHEF: Andrew Reagan  PROPRIETOR: Glen Rick Court  OPEN: all week L 12 to 2.45 (4.30 Sun), Mon to Sat D 6 to 9.45  MEALS: alc D (main courses £12 to £17.50). Set L £9.95 (2 courses) to £13.95, Set L Sun 8.95 (2 courses) to £9.95. Light L menu available  SERVICE: not inc, card slips closed  CARDS: Amex, Delta, Diners, MasterCard, Switch, Visa  DETAILS: 75 seats. 20 seats outside. Private parties: 75 main room, 18 private room. Car park. Vegetarian meals. Children's helpings. Wheelchair access (also WC). Music  ACCOMMODATION: 6 rooms, all with bath/shower. TV. Phone. Prices on application  £5

*The Guide always appreciates hearing about changes of chef or owner.*

map 2

# ▲ Crown at Whitebrook 🍷 ⁵⁄✳

Whitebrook NP25 4TX
TEL: (01600) 860254    FAX: (01600) 860607
EMAIL: crown@whitebrook.demon.co.uk
WEBSITE: www.crownatwhitebrook.co.uk
leave A466 at Bigsweir bridge, 6m S of                    COOKING 4
Monmouth; follow signs to Whitebrook; hotel is      MODERN EUROPEAN
2m on left                                               £25–£50

In a narrow wooded valley a mile from the Wye on the edge of Tintern Forest, the
Crown has a pleasingly unsophisticated air about it, the dining room's crisp
napery and polished cutlery 'reminiscent of Cotswolds tea rooms' for one visitor.
The spark is in the cooking, whose individuality is evident in a pink rack of
lamb served with a fat liver and kidney sausage, accompanied by a strong, well-
reduced honey and thyme jus, and in a pairing of monkfish with foie gras in a
Sauternes butter sauce. Not all reporters are equally happy with results, but an
inspection meal showed sound judgement in contrasting colours, textures and
flavours: for example, in an appetiser of sweet onion tartlet with a salty hoisin-
type sauce, and in a tiny starter of sweet scallops with a minute pyramid of rice
and chopped quail's egg in a sharp dressing.

More contrasts are provided by a smooth, cold, intensely flavoured caraway
parfait served with a hot fig sponge in toffee sauce. Portions are not large so don't
arrive with a big appetite; main courses are 'garnished' but not with vegetables,
so an extra side plate may be advisable. Service is straightforwardly efficient, the
pace of dinner leisurely, and wines – mostly well chosen – are generally sensibly
priced. Pricier red Bordeaux (and a single Burgundy) appear on the 'Crown
specials' list, while 16 house recommendations range from £11.95 to £35.95. The
list is rounded off by a good selection of half-bottles and dessert wines, most of
the latter available by the glass.

CHEF: Mark Turton    PROPRIETORS: Angela and Elizabeth Barbara    OPEN: Tue to Sun L 12 to 1.45,
all week D 7 to 8.45    CLOSED: 22 Dec to 11 Jan    MEALS: alc L Tue to Sat (main courses £8.50 to
£11). Set L Sun £17.50, Set D £29.95    SERVICE: not inc    CARDS: Amex, Delta, Diners,
MasterCard, Switch, Visa    DETAILS: 32 seats. Private parties: 22 main room, 10 to 12 private
rooms. Car park. Vegetarian meals. No children under 12. No smoking in dining room. No music
ACCOMMODATION: 11 rooms, all with bath/shower. TV. Phone. B&B £55 to £95. No children under
12. Baby facilities (The Which? Hotel Guide)  (£5)

# Channel Islands

## Bistro Soleil ▼

La Route de la Haule, Beaumont JE3 7BA                                    COOKING **4**
TEL: (01534) 720249   FAX: (01534) 625621                              BISTRO/SEAFOOD
                                                                           £21–£48

The relaxed and sunny feeling here encapsulates summer: bare wood floors, bright colour scheme and, from the large windows with bright blue awnings, stunning views over the beach and out to sea. An outside patio is separated from the beach by a low wall.

The menu has a voguish air, with such trendy items as confit of aubergine (here served with guacamole, mozzarella and tomato salad), red mullet escabeche, or sun-blushed tomato pesto accompanying a baked goats' cheese gâteau. But there are more traditional dishes, too: a starter of oak-smoked salmon with capers, chopped onions and pink peppercorns, or a main-course roast rack of lamb with minted pea purée and rosemary jus. Given the location, it is no surprise that fresh fish looms large here: some of the best-sourced and most competently cooked in the area, with a welcome freshness and sweetness. Good supplies are treated with respect all round.

Desserts tend to the traditional, with orange sticky toffee pudding and hot fudge sauce, or coconut and mango Bakewell tart. The wine list is characterised by good choice and refreshingly low mark-ups, with almost all of the 30-plus wines coming in under the £20 mark. House red and white start at £8.50.

CHEF: Ian Jones   PROPRIETOR: Chris Power   OPEN: Tue to Sun L 12.15 to 2, Tue to Sat D 7 to 9 (9.30 Fri and Sat)   CLOSED: 25 and 26 Dec, 1 Jan   MEALS: alc (main courses £13 to £16). Set L £12.75 (2 courses) to £14.75, Set D £24   SERVICE: not inc, 10% for parties of 10 or more   CARDS: Amex, Delta, MasterCard, Switch, Visa   DETAILS: 55 seats. 40 seats outside. Private parties: 60 main room. Car park. Vegetarian meals. Children's helpings. No cigars/pipes in dining room. Wheelchair access (not WC). Music

---

*If 'vegetarian meals' is noted in the details at the end of an entry, this means that a restaurant routinely lists at least one vegetarian starter and main course on menus. Other restaurants, however, may offer good vegetarian choices if you let them know in advance, so it is worthwhile phoning to enquire.*

map 1

# Jersey Pottery, Garden Restaurant £

Gorey JE3 9EP
TEL: (01534) 851119   FAX: (01534) 856403
EMAIL: admin@jerseypottery.com
WEBSITE: www.jerseypottery.co.uk

COOKING 2
MODERN BRITISH/SEAFOOD
£25–£64

One eats in a large, glass-roofed, open-plan room trellised with lush greenery, or outside on a flower-filled patio under parasols. Despite the massive throughput, service from name-badged staff doesn't seem to miss a beat, and the kitchen caters briskly to all tastes, including those seeking generous platters of fresh seafood. A summer salad of asparagus, roast shallots, San Daniele ham and pine-nuts with Parmesan shavings shone at inspection; so did a sturdy portion of salmon, 'cooked to a salty crunch on top, perfectly pink and succulent inside', intelligently partnered with an orange and fennel salad. Choice is wide, encompassing foie gras parfait with red wine jelly; grilled brill fillet with wild mushrooms; and coriander-crusted beef fillet with horseradish mash. On the serve-yourself dessert table, among seasonal fruits, mousses, gateaux, etc., the 'exquisitely sticky and rich' chocolate tart stands out. The half-French wine list is reasonably priced, opening at £11.95.

CHEFS: Tony Dorris and Andrew Berry   PROPRIETORS: the Jones Family   OPEN: Tue to Sun L only 12 to 2.30 (3 Sun)   MEALS: alc Tue to Sat (main courses £9.50 to £28). Set L Tue to Sat £19.50, Set L Sun £17.50 to £22   SERVICE: net prices, card slips closed   CARDS: Amex, Delta, Diners, MasterCard, Switch, Visa   DETAILS: 190 seats. 60 seats outside. Private parties: 290 main room, 30 to 80 private rooms. Car park. Vegetarian meals. Children's helpings. Wheelchair access (also WC). Music (£5)

# Suma's

Gorey Hill, St Martin, Gorey JE3 6ET
TEL: (01534) 853291   FAX: (01534) 851913

COOKING 5
MODERN EUROPEAN
£25–£60

A magnificent location helps – beg for a table by the window, and watch the evening's catch being landed in the harbour – but the restaurant itself is well appointed, its light wood, white walls and stylish place settings giving it a bright and fresh feel. The food shares something of the luxury of Longueville Manor (under the same ownership; see entry, St Saviour), offering foie gras terrine with duck confit, a truffle-scented woodland mushroom tart, and half a roast lobster with Jersey crab and sauce vierge, but much of it comes in slightly jazzier vein. Grilled Jersey scallops are served with black pudding and pea purée, for example, and one visitor was impressed by his 'winning combination' of sardine and squid with chorizo on a deconstructed ratatouille.

Meat dishes range from braised pork belly with apples and buttered cabbage, to roast Gressingham duck with ginger-preserved peaches, both incidentally also served with foie gras. Puddings generally favour classical ideas, some available as a platter of five mini-desserts featuring a brûlée, an ice cream, lemon cheesecake, chocolate torte and strawberries. A short but lively wine list offers as much choice below £20 as above, starting with a brace of vins de pays below

£10. Alternatively, try Côtes de Duras Sauvignon Blanc 2000 (£12), or Best's Australian Cabernet Sauvignon 1998 (£15.50).

CHEF: Shaun Rankin   PROPRIETORS: Malcolm Lewis and Susan Dufty   OPEN: all week 12 to 2.30, 6.30 to 10 (9.30 Sun)   CLOSED: 23 Dec to 17 Jan   MEALS: alc (main courses £10.50 to £20). Set L Mon to Sat £14 (2 courses) to £18, Set L Sun £18.50   SERVICE: net prices, card slips closed   CARDS: Amex, Delta, Diners, MasterCard, Switch, Visa   DETAILS: 45 seats. 14 seats outside. Private parties: 45 main room. Vegetarian meals. Music. Air-conditioned

## ST AUBIN Jersey                                                    map 1

## ▲ Harbour View ✻ £                        NEW ENTRY

Le Boulevard, St Aubin JE3 8AB                           COOKING 3
TEL: (01534) 747306   FAX: (01534) 499460                  FRENCH
EMAIL: harbourview@localdial.com                          £24–£47

As billed, this terrace restaurant overlooks the small, pretty harbour of St Aubin. An outside seating area on wooden decking with white umbrellas leads to a glassed-in porch dining room in warm Mediterranean colours. Eric Claverie hails from Gascony, from where he draws his inspiration: salade Gascon, for instance, brings together pan-fried foie gras and Pyrenean ham on a piece of toast spread with onion purée. 'Meaty, sea-fresh and expertly cooked' prawns come with crisp leaves and a piquant dressing, and blackboard specials might include fresh crab. Among mains, grilled duck magret is given a slightly shy green peppercorn sauce, but the crisply browned sauté potatoes with it are a joy. Other seafood stars have included grilled sea bass stuffed with thyme, ingeniously accompanied by a foil parcel of ratatouille vegetables and fennel delicately seasoned with honey. Slices of apple and banana – the latter cooked in its skin – make diverting supports for an otherwise canonical crème brûlée, or try fruit clafoutis or pot au chocolat. French staff are efficient, professional and friendly. The all-French wine list has a good south-western selection, and the prices are mostly very fair, starting at £10.20 or £2.50 a glass.

CHEF: Eric Claverie   PROPRIETORS: Kelly Keadell and Eric Claverie   OPEN: all week 12 to 2.30 (3 Sat and Sun), 6.30 to 9.30   CLOSED: Nov to Apr (subject to change; phone to check)   MEALS: alc (main courses £9.50 to £15.50). Set L and D from £16.50 to £27.50   SERVICE: not inc   CARDS: Amex, MasterCard, Switch, Visa   DETAILS: 32 seats. 52 seats outside. Private parties: 20 main room. Car park. Children's helpings. No smoking in dining room. Wheelchair access (not WC). Music   ACCOMMODATION: 12 rooms, all with bath/shower. TV. B&B £28 to £70

## ST SAVIOUR Jersey                                                  map 1

## ▲ Longueville Manor ▮ ✻

St Saviour JE2 7WF
TEL: (01534) 725501   FAX: (01534) 731613              COOKING 5
EMAIL: longman@itl.net                           MODERN EUROPEAN
WEBSITE: www.longuevillemanor.com                        £33–£77

Gilt mirrors, polished wooden coffee tables, and orchids in large brass pots are the order of the day at this venerable manor house, and the panelled Oak Room, with its heavy cutlery and starched white napery, is thoughtfully reserved for non-smokers only. Staff are efficient, dedicated and friendly, and at dinner there are four different set menus – menu du jour, vegetarian menu, Taste of Jersey and 'Gourmet' menu – as well as the carte.

Understandably seafood features prominently, perhaps as a risotto of local lobster with asparagus and scallops, or sea bass fillet with sauce vierge, and luxuries are never far away: foie gras appears with roast quail and fig compote as a first course, and alongside grilled beef fillet with truffled potatoes. This is food designed for comfort, and meals end on an appropriately soothing note with prune and armagnac soufflé, or hot chocolate fondant with crispy pineapple and vanilla ice cream.

The encyclopaedic wine list kicks off in traditional territory – Bordeaux and Burgundy – before continuing through the Rhône, the Loire and Alsace, then heading off to other European countries, via a good-value list of Portuguese wines, and the wider world. Producers are well-chosen, mark-ups fair. New World sparkling wines are a bargain, and keenly-priced house wines start at £14 for Chardonnay or Cabernet Sauvignon vin de pays d'Oc.

CHEF: Andrew Baird   PROPRIETORS: Malcolm Lewis and Susan Dufty   OPEN: all week 12.30 to 2, 7 to 10   CLOSED: 3 to 17 Jan   MEALS: alc (main courses £26.50 to £29). Set L £17.50 (2 courses) to £22.50, Set D £37.50 to £57.50 (£80 inc wine)   SERVICE: net prices, card slips closed   CARDS: Amex, Delta, Diners, MasterCard, Switch, Visa   DETAILS: 65 seats. 30 seats outside. Private parties: 65 main room, 4 to 24 private rooms. Car park. Vegetarian meals. Children's helpings. No smoking in 1 dining room. Wheelchair access (also WC). No music. No mobile phones   ACCOMMODATION: 30 rooms, all with bath/shower. TV. Phone. B&B £160 to £450. Rooms for disabled. Baby facilities. Swimming pool

# Northern Ireland

## Ginger Tree  £

| | |
|---|---|
| 29 Ballyrobert Road, Ballyclare BT39 9RY | COOKING **3** |
| TEL: (028) 9084 8176   FAX: (028) 9084 4077 | JAPANESE |
| | £23–£50 |

'Without doubt an oddity, but charmingly so', felt an inspector after visiting this once grand nineteenth-century farmhouse. A Japanese garden, visible from the dining room, acts as a calming influence and also gives a clue to the cuisine; likewise the spiky flower arrangements that adorn black-clothed tables, and the décor, which has a definite Japanese feel. Various set menus take a central dish as their theme, e.g. chicken teriyaki, beef yakinikufu, or sukiyaki, and come with appetisers, soup and several other courses. You can also choose from a wide-ranging carte that offers traditional Japanese dishes such as 'meaty, succulent eel (from Lough Neagh) with kabayaki sauce, pan-fried pork fillet in ginger and teriyaki sauce, and vegetarian tempura, for example. The wine list includes saké by the large or small pot; house French wines (£11.50) open a range that trots through Europe, the Americas and the Antipodes.

CHEF: Shotaro Obana   PROPRIETORS: Elizabeth English Wylie and Shotaro Obana   OPEN: Mon to Fri L 12 to 2, Mon to Sat D 7 to 8.30   CLOSED: 24 to 26 Dec, L 1 Jan, 11 and 12 July   MEALS: alc (main courses 9.50 to £13.50). Set L £13.95, Set D £15.95 to £30   SERVICE: not inc   CARDS: Amex, Delta, Diners, MasterCard, Switch, Visa   DETAILS: 65 seats. Private parties: 75 main room, 15 to 20 private rooms. Car park. Vegetarian meals. Children's helpings. No cigars in dining room. Wheelchair access (also WC). Occasional music. Air-conditioned  (£5)

## Shanks  ♥

| | |
|---|---|
| The Blackwood Golf Centre, 150 Crawfordsburn | |
| Road, Bangor BT19 1GB | COOKING **6** |
| TEL: (028) 9185 3313   FAX: (028) 9185 2493 | MODERN EUROPEAN |
| WEBSITE: www.shanksrestaurant.com | £34–£75 |

If this restaurant's location, in the grounds of the Clandeboye estate and golf centre, suggests corporate anonymity, nothing could be less true. It uses impeccable raw materials, mostly from local organic and non-GM suppliers; game is shot on the estate; and the seafood is locally caught: prawns in Portavogie, scallops in Strangford, lobster in Dundrum. Then, in a Conran-designed interior (walls dripping with original Hockneys), or on the outdoor terrace in summer, Robbie Millar's cooking brings out the best in these fine ingredients.

Fixed-price menus give a wide choice, which sometimes show a tendency towards elaboration: seared foie gras may come with carrot purée, poached grapes and an Orange Muscat jus as well as the expected toasted brioche; curried cauliflower soup is adorned with spiced apple and coriander crème fraîche. Monkfish gets appropriately meaty treatment – potatoes, Savoy cabbage and smoked bacon join it in a fricassee dressed with lobster and garlic vinaigrette – while estate venison comes with a 'red cabbage puff', roast parsnips and chestnuts, all sauced with Madeira. Meals end on a slightly simpler note: prune and Armagnac tart with Sauternes custard, or warm apple soup with gingerbread ice cream.

The wine list starts with six interesting house bottles (£15 to £20) before taking a quick world tour. Burgundy, Bordeaux and Australia stand out, and New World selections concentrate on quality-focused 'new-wave' producers. Mark-ups aren't unduly high, with imaginative choice under £20, starting at £13 for Australian dry Muscat.

CHEF: Robbie Millar  PROPRIETORS: Robbie and Shirley Millar  OPEN: Tue to Fri L 12.30 to 2.30, Tue to Sat D 7 to 10  CLOSED: 24 to 26 Dec, 1 to 21 Jul, Easter Bank hols  MEALS: Set L £17 (2 courses) to £38, Set D £29 (2 courses) to £38  SERVICE: not inc, 10% for parties of 10 or more  CARDS: Amex, Delta, MasterCard, Switch, Visa  DETAILS: 60 seats. Private parties: 60 main room, 10 to 36 private rooms. Car park. Vegetarian meals. Children's helpings. No pipes/cigars in dining room. Wheelchair access (also WC). Air-conditioned

## BELFAST  Co Antrim                                        map 16

# Alden's

229 Upper Newtownards Road, Belfast BT4 3JF                COOKING 3
TEL: (028) 9065 0079   FAX: (028) 9065 0032            MODERN EUROPEAN
                                                            £27–£65

A former supermarket done out in a bright orange decorative theme is the setting for this modern brasserie. A bar area with comfortable sofas leads into a fashionably austere dining room with a soothing atmosphere where everyone feels at home. The cooking is characterised by carefully sourced materials, imaginatively cooked and attractively but simply presented. Cath Gradwell seeks far and wide for influences: beetroot and sweet herring salad with mustard dressing might be among the starters alongside deep-fried whitebait with chilli jam, or even foie gras terrine with a toasted brioche. Main-course options are likely to encompass pork and leek sausages with champ and onion gravy, roast fillets of Dover sole with purple-sprouting broccoli and prawn sauce, or rare-grilled venison with Parma ham butter. Finish with anything from profiteroles to baked tamarillos with vanilla ice cream. The wine list constitutes a well-thought-out international selection. Around two dozen house wines are priced from £12.50, and five are available by the glass.

CHEF: Cath Gradwell  PROPRIETOR: Jonathan Davis  OPEN: Mon to Fri L 12 to 2.30, Mon to Sat D 6 to 10 (11 Fri and Sat)  CLOSED: 2 weeks July, bank hols  MEALS: alc (main courses £8 to £20). Set L £8.95 (1 course), Set D Mon to Thur £14.95 (2 courses)  SERVICE: not inc  CARDS: Amex, Diners, MasterCard, Switch, Visa  DETAILS: 70 seats. Private parties: 80 main room. Vegetarian meals. No-smoking area. Wheelchair access (also WC). Music. Air-conditioned

# La Belle Epoque £

61 Dublin Road, Belfast BT2 7HE
TEL: (028) 9032 3244   FAX: (028) 9020 3111

COOKING 2
MODERN FRENCH
£16–£39

If you're driving up Dublin Road looking for La Belle Epoque, take it slowly. It's surprisingly easy to miss the Art Deco frontage, and if you do, a long loop round the one-way system is the penalty. The atmosphere here is of bustling informality; the clientele includes employees from the nearby BBC and students having a night off from beans on toast. French food is what it's all about, and reassuringly old-school French at that. Crab bavarois with grapefruit and orange, or queenies and mussels tossed in butter with garlic, shallots and parsley to start, perhaps followed by goose magret sauced with Dijon mustard, green peppercorns and ginger. Multi-ingredient sauces also accompany the fish, with mango, peppers, red onions and chilli going into a salsa accompanying Cajun-spiced salmon. Finish with crêpes suzette, or home-made sorbets in a brandy-snap basket. The wine list is 50:50 French and other (Spain, Chile, Australia and South Africa); prices open at £9.85.

CHEF: Alain Rousse   PROPRIETORS: Alain Rousse, Gonzalo Sanchez and J. Lindsay   OPEN: Tue to Fri 12 to 5, 5.30 to 11   CLOSED: 25 and 26 Dec, 1 Jan, 12 and 13 July   MEALS: alc (main courses £6.50 to £11.50). Set L £6.25 (2 courses), Set D Tue to Thur £15   SERVICE: not inc   CARDS: Amex, Delta, Diners, MasterCard, Switch, Visa   DETAILS: 84 seats. Private parties: 24 main room. Vegetarian meals. Wheelchair access (also WC). Music

# Cayenne

7 Ascot House, Shaftsbury Square,
Belfast BT2 7DB
TEL: (028) 9033 1532   FAX: (028) 9026 1575
EMAIL: reservations@cayennerestaurant.com
WEBSITE: www.cayennerestaurant.com

COOKING 2
FUSION
£21–£42

Discreet to the point of being difficult to spot, smart and fashionable Cayenne offers an enthusiastic welcome and a lively atmosphere. Behind its frosted-glass windows, fragments of the Belfast telephone directory decorate the walls of its long, walnut-panelled dining room, and the menu seems to recognise no boundaries. It is perfectly possible to eat and drink Italian – vegetable bruschetta, fusilli pasta with pesto and Gorgonzola, and a bottle of Valpolicella – or to go completely Asian with sushi, hotpot and Tiger beer. Some dishes such as prawn risotto with Thai green curry defy pigeon-holing, but this is not food for purists, rather for those who enjoy the vitality of fusion cooking.

The carte offers appetisers, soups (perhaps Mexican smoked chilli lime broth), salads, rice and noodle dishes, and mains of perhaps duck breast with cocotte potatoes and wasabi pepper cream. Desserts tend to be more homespun, along the lines of baked lemon cheesecake (albeit with a kiwi and passion-fruit salsa), and prices are understandably a little easier at lunchtime, when the format is a boon to snackers. An up-to-date, reasonably priced, varietally arranged wine list suits the circumstances, with around ten by the glass, plus fine wines and cocktails.

CHEF: Andy Rea   PROPRIETORS: Paul and Jeanne Rankin   OPEN: Mon to Fri L 12 to 2.30, Mon to Sat D 6 to 11.15   CLOSED: 25 and 26 Dec, 1 Jan, Easter Mon and Tue, 12 and 13 July   MEALS: alc (main courses L £5 to £10, D £8.50 to £13.50). Set L £10.50 (2 courses) to £13.50, Set D Mon to Thur 6 to 6.45 and 10 to 11 £10.50 (2 courses)   SERVICE: not inc, 10% for parties of six or more   CARDS: Amex, Delta, Diners, MasterCard, Switch, Visa   DETAILS: 95 seats. Private parties: 80 main room. Vegetarian meals. Children's helpings. No-smoking area. Wheelchair access (also WC). Music. Air-conditioned

## ▲ Metro Brasserie £

13 Lower Crescent, Belfast BT7 1NR
TEL: (028) 9032 3349   FAX: (028) 9032 0646
EMAIL: info@crescenttownhouse.com
WEBSITE: www.crescenttownhouse.com

COOKING 2
MODERN EUROPEAN
£21–£46

There is a pleasing oxymoron in this establishment's self-description as 'modern classic', a notion borne out by the daily-changing menus. They show influences from all corners of the globe, as well as an effort to search out fine local products. The early-bird menu, two courses for £9.95, might offer penne pasta with aubergine, tomato and olive oil, or honey-roast pork fillet with glazed carrots and champ. This 'home and away' theme is even more evident in the à la carte with a starter of caramelised onion, chicken, smoked Gubbeen cheese tart with truffled rosemary oil and crème fraîche, followed perhaps by fillet of salmon with fragrant rice, Asian greens and a ginger and sesame dressing. Afterwards stay near home with Irish cheeses or go supranational with mint chocolate cheesecake and crème de menthe cream. The short, eclectic wine list starts with Californians at £11, and most bottles are under £20.

CHEF: Aaron Loughran   PROPRIETOR: Wine Inns Ltd   OPEN: Mon to Sat D only 6 to 9.30 (10 Fri and Sat)   CLOSED: 25 Dec   MEALS: alc (main courses £9 to £15.50). Set D 6 to 7.30 £9.95 (2 courses) to £12.50   SERVICE: not inc, card slips closed   CARDS: Amex, Delta, Diners, MasterCard, Switch, Visa   DETAILS: 72 seats. 12 seats outside. Vegetarian meals. Wheelchair access (also WC). Music. No mobile phones. Air-conditioned   ACCOMMODATION: 11 rooms, all with bath/shower. TV. Phone. B&B £50 to £100

## Nick's Warehouse ▼ £

35–39 Hill Street, Belfast BT1 2LB
TEL: (028) 9043 9690   FAX: (028) 9023 0514
WEBSITE: www.nickswarehouse.co.uk

COOKING 5
MODERN IRISH
£22–£46

Nick's Warehouse was indeed originally a warehouse, owned by the Bushmills Whiskey Company. Nowadays, eclectic modern paintings line the bare brick walls, and a lively bar area and open-plan kitchen give the place a real buzz. Menus are as free-spirited as the setting, the cooking style loosely described as 'modern Irish' but taking in a wide variety of influences. Eat in the 'Anix', the bar or the upstairs restaurant. In the Anix, a typical meal might feature crumbed deep-fried crab claws with a pair of dips (basil and Parmesan, chilli), followed by grilled turbot fillets on pan-fried asparagus with sun-dried tomato dressing. A lighter lunch menu deals in unusual salads, sandwiches and a selection of cheaper hot dishes. In the restaurant proper, green pea and ham soup, or spiced fried squid salad with chilli dressing, may be among starters, while main courses range from loin of lamb on mash with Guinness and mushroom gravy to roast fillet of salmon on fennel and Parmesan risotto with salsa verde.

To round things off, choices might include morello cherry pannacotta with Malteser ice cream, or the intriguing-sounding warm chocolate and Guinness cake with crème fraîche, and for those without a sweet tooth there are Irish cheeses. The wine list is quirky, with the 'normal' list supplemented by a short grouping of 'fine wines' and a brief but very well-chosen page of offerings from Spain's up-and-coming regions. All bottles on the main list are under £20, and mark-ups on the fine and Spanish selections are low. Eight house wines are £11.50 (£2.95 per glass).

CHEFS: Nick Price, Alan Higginson and Gerrard Sands   PROPRIETORS: Nick and Kathy Price   OPEN: Mon to Fri L 12 to 3, Tue to Sat D 6 to 9.30 (10 Fri and Sat)   CLOSED: 25 and 26 Dec, 1 Jan, Easter Mon and Tue, May bank hol, 12 July   MEALS: alc (main courses £7 to £14)   SERVICE: 10% (optional), card slips closed   CARDS: Amex, Delta, Diners, MasterCard, Switch, Visa   DETAILS: 185 seats. Private parties: 10 to 50 private rooms. Vegetarian meals. Children's helpings. Wheelchair access (also WC). Music. Air-conditioned

# Restaurant Michael Deane

34–40 Howard Street, Belfast BT1 6PF   COOKING 6
TEL: (028) 9033 1134   FAX: (028) 9056 0001   MODERN EUROPEAN-PLUS
£39–£82

The setting downstairs in the brasserie is reminiscent of a classical gentlemen's club, though the atmosphere is lively, with cheerful, informal service. Upstairs, the restaurant proper has a more refined atmosphere, as characterised by the quaint practice of spelling out prices on the menu. But this is a restaurant with a prestigious name.

Michael Deane's style is broad-mindedly modern European, founded on classical techniques but bringing them up to date with plenty of contemporary ideas. Among starters, spiced beef carpaccio with cucumber and curry is one of the more unusual choices you are likely to encounter, but no less appealing are brandade of cod with 'green vegetable' and smoked salmon, or open pasta of goats' cheese, salami and tomato. Main courses continue in similar vein: breast of duck with pomme fondant, black pudding and foie gras is typically earthy and rustic sounding, though the execution and presentation of dishes aim for a degree of elegance and style. Other options might include roast monkfish with creamed artichoke and crisp pancetta, or local salmon with cabbage, vanilla, asparagus and tomato. Finish perhaps with banana parfait with glazed bananas and a rum and raisin syrup. The wine list is a weighty tome featuring plenty of high-rolling French classics. Those with more modest drinking budgets will appreciate the house selections from £14.50.

CHEF/PROPRIETOR: Michael Deane   OPEN: restaurant Fri L 12.15 to 2, Wed to Sat D 7 to 9.30; brasserie Mon to Sat 12 to 2.30, 5.30 to 11   CLOSED: Christmas, Easter, first 2 weeks July, bank hols   MEALS: Set L £19 (2 courses) to £25, Set D £31 (2 courses) to £55   SERVICE: not inc, 10% for parties of 6 or more   CARDS: Amex, Delta, MasterCard, Switch, Visa   DETAILS: 35 seats. Private parties: 35 main room. Vegetarian meals. No cigars/pipes in dining room. Music. No mobile phones. Air-conditioned

# Ta Tu

701 Lisburn Road, Belfast BT9 7GU
TEL: (028) 9038 0818   FAX: (028) 9038 0828
WEBSITE: www.ta-tu.com

COOKING **2**
MODERN EUROPEAN
£23–£45

Billed emphatically as a 'Bar and Grill', this minimalist venue seeks to provide Belfast's south side with a touch of fashionable chic. The design is ultra-modern and it's a crowd-puller: expect fancy drinks and high decibels in the trendy bar. Beyond is a more sedate, but relaxed dining room, where the food shows serious intent: organic produce is supported and the menu fizzes with voguish ideas. Chef Neil Bradley earned his stripes at Roscoff (now Cayenne; see entry) and there's hardly a dish that doesn't have some kind of eclectic tag. Beef carpaccio is jazzed up with Asian spices, while pale smoked salmon comes with toasted coconut and curried potatoes. If you are looking for traditional comfort, there's also lamb hotpot with roasted vegetables and onion rings. Desserts veer between apple crumble and wacky-sounding Malteser semifreddo. An all-day bistro menu adds to the flexible, cosmopolitan mood of the place. The wine list is a global selection with plenty by the glass (from £2.75), and house wines start at £9.95.

CHEF: Neil Bradley   PROPRIETOR: Bill Wolsey   OPEN: all week 12 to 6, 6 to 9.45 (8.45 Sun) CLOSED: 25 and 26 Dec, 12 July   MEALS: alc (main courses L 12 to 6 £5.50 to £9.50, D after 6 £11 to £14). Bar and bistro menu also available   SERVICE: 10% for parties of six or more   CARDS: Amex, Delta, MasterCard, Switch, Visa   DETAILS: 90 seats. 24 seats outside. Private parties: 50 main room. Vegetarian meals. Children's helpings. Wheelchair access (also WC). Music. Air-conditioned (£5)

## LIMAVADY  Co Londonderry                                          map 16

# Lime Tree  £

60 Catherine Street, Limavady BT49 9DB
TEL: (028) 7776 4300
WEBSITE: www.limetreerest.com

COOKING **2**
MODERN EUROPEAN
£15–£46

A set-price dinner menu might have been introduced, but little else has changed at this charming family-run restaurant in the centre of the small market town of Limavady. The food is largely traditional in style and broadly European in nature. Meals typically open with game terrine with Cumberland sauce, or perhaps pasta ribbons in a chicken, tomato and herb sauce, while main courses range from minute steak with peppercorn sauce to fresh Donegal fish crêpe, or poached cod fillet with parsley sauce. To finish, lemon and lime cheesecake, and steamed orange marmalade sponge with custard are likely to be among the options. Early-bird and business lunch menus offer particularly good value. The short wine list opens with a handful of house selections at £9.95.

CHEF: Stanley Matthews   PROPRIETORS: Stanley and Maria Matthews   OPEN: Wed to Fri and Sun L 12 to 2, Wed to Sun D 6 to 9 (9.30 Fri and Sat, 8.30 Sun)   CLOSED: 1 week Nov, 25 and 26 Dec, 1 week end Jan, 1 week from 12 July   MEALS: alc (main courses L £6 to £7.50, D £12 to £16.50). Set L Wed to Fri £6.95 (2 courses) to £7.95, Set L Sun £13.75, Set D Wed to Fri and Sun 6 to 7 £9.95 (2 courses) to £12.95, Set D Wed to Sun £19.50   SERVICE: not inc   CARDS: Amex, Delta, MasterCard, Switch, Visa   DETAILS: 30 seats. Private parties: 36 main room. Vegetarian meals. Children's helpings. No cigars/pipes in dining room. Wheelchair access (also WC). Music

# Republic of Ireland

We have not given marks for cooking for the Republic of Ireland entries because of a shortage of reports; please do give us feedback should you visit. To telephone the Republic from mainland Britain, dial 00 353 followed by the number listed, but dropping the initial 0. Prices are given in euros throughout this section.

## BALLYDEHOB  Co Cork                                               map 16

## Annie's ✶✕

Main Street, Ballydehob
TEL: (028) 37292                                                    EUROPEAN
€51–€67

Anne Barry's approach to running a restaurant is founded on the core values of 'consistency and the personal touch': must be a good formula, as her eponymous restaurant celebrates its twentieth anniversary in 2003. Menus offer plenty of choice, with roughly half a dozen each of fish and meat main courses and almost as many starters, plus an optional intermediary course of soup or sorbet. The cooking has broad scope within a somewhat old-fashioned remit: sauté lambs' kidneys in a filo pastry case, and mussels stuffed with garlic butter and breadcrumbs are typical starters, while main courses range from roast rack of lamb with mint chutney and a mild mustard sauce to pan-fried monkfish with a bacon and spring onion sauce. The carefully chosen wine list opens with six house offerings at €16.

CHEFS/PROPRIETORS: Dano and Anne Barry   OPEN: Tue to Sat D only 6.30 to 10   CLOSED: Nov, 24 to 26 Dec, bank hols   MEALS: alc (main courses €24 to €25). Set D €38 to €42   SERVICE: not inc   CARDS: MasterCard, Visa   DETAILS: 44 seats. Vegetarian meals. Children's helpings. No smoking in 1 dining room. Wheelchair access (also WC). Occasional music. No mobile phones. Air-conditioned

---

*If customers are asked to switch off mobile phones while in a restaurant, this is noted in the details at the end of an entry.*

*The 2004 Guide will be published before Christmas 2003. Reports on meals are most welcome at any time of the year, but are particularly valuable in the spring (no later than June). Send them to* The Good Food Guide, FREEPOST, 2 Marylebone Road, London NW1 4DF. Or email your report to goodfoodguide@which.net

**BALLYLICKEY Co Cork** map 16

## ▲ Ballylickey Manor House

Ballylickey, Bantry Bay
TEL: (027) 50071 FAX: (027) 50124
EMAIL: ballymh@eircom.net
WEBSITE: www.ballylickeymanorhouse.com

FRENCH
€74–€91

There are plenty of places in rural Ireland that are beautifully sited, but the attractions for visitors here are gardens full of mature trees, informal riverside walks and the views across Bantry Bay to the mountains beyond. Dinner, in a handsome room with open wood fires in cold weather, is a stylish affair, beginning with complimentary appetisers such as cauliflower soup served in a doll's-house tureen. Commended dishes this year have been toasted goats' cheese salad, highly moreish beef carpaccio, fillet of black sole with aubergines and honey served with diced potato, and apple crumble with vanilla ice cream. Duck breast is well reported, and there is a table of well-kept Irish and French cheeses to ponder too. Wines are French or Italian with many imported direct from the growers. Prices start at €28.

CHEF: Marie Dwyer PROPRIETORS: George and Christiane Graves OPEN: Mon to Sat D only 7 to 9 CLOSED: Nov to Mar MEALS: Set D €50 to €52 SERVICE: not inc CARDS: Amex, MasterCard, Visa DETAILS: 35 seats. 25 seats outside. Private parties: 35 main room, 30 to 40 private rooms. Car park. Children's helpings (residents only). No children under 4. Jacket and tie. No smoking in dining room. No music ACCOMMODATION: 12 rooms, all with bath/shower. TV. Phone. B&B €220 to €340. Rooms for disabled. Baby facilities. Swimming pool. Fishing

**BALLYVAUGHAN Co Clare** map 16

## ▲ Gregans Castle Hotel

Ballyvaughan
TEL: (065) 7077 005 FAX: (065) 7077 111
EMAIL: res@gregans.ie
WEBSITE: www.gregans.ie
on N67, 3½m S of Ballyvaughan

MODERN IRISH/FRENCH
€52–€68

The Haden family extends a warm welcome in this comfortable, creeper-clad country house under Corkscrew Hill. Besides majestic views over the Burren and Galway Bay, it offers the highly accomplished cooking of Régis Herviaux, who brings a touch of French classical style to dishes such as roast stuffed poussin with sun-dried tomatoes and wholegrain mustard sauce, and baked cod fillet wrapped in Kinvara organic smoked salmon and sauced with lemon butter. Layered meringue filled with passion-fruit and almond mousseline garnished with strawberries makes a good way to end. The wine list splits fairly evenly between Old and New Worlds: there are strong New Zealand selections, and a focus on Bordeaux, Burgundy and the Rhône. Prices are fair and organic/biodynamic wines are highlighted. Six house selections range from €19 to €25.

CHEF: Régis Herviaux PROPRIETORS: the Haden family OPEN: all week D only 7 to 8.30 CLOSED: 22 Dec to 13 Feb MEALS: alc D (main courses €20 to €23). Set D €26 (2 courses) to €41. Bar L menu also available 12 to 3 SERVICE: not inc, card slips closed CARDS: Amex, MasterCard,

Visa   DETAILS: 50 seats. Private parties: 70 main room, 15 to 30 private rooms. Car park.
Children's helpings. No smoking in dining room. Music. No mobile phones   ACCOMMODATION: 22
rooms, all with bath/shower. Phone. B&B €176 to €400. Rooms for disabled. Baby facilities

## BANTRY  Co Cork                                                                        map 16

## ▲ Larchwood House ⁵⚹

Pearsons Bridge, Bantry
TEL: (027) 66181                                                          MODERN IRISH
                                                                          €50–€60

The creeper-clad house has magnificent gardens with tropical shrubs and
flowers and cultivated 'wild' flora flourishing in glades by the river. At Sheila
Vaughan's fixed-price dinners the first and main courses are separated by not
one intermediate but two: the first a soup, say carrot and orange, the second a
fruity creation like pear and peach parfait. Before them might come a warm salad
of duck and ginger, or stuffed mushrooms with garlic and cheese, while the
main course might be a generous serving of fat, juicy scallops with basil and
lemon, or accurately cooked beef fillet in red wine sauce. Puddings – bread-and-
butter pudding, or praline ice cream with butterscotch sauce – come elaborately
garnished. Breakfasts, for sensible overnighters, are pronounced 'excellent'. The
wine list is largely French, with brief forays elsewhere, and prices look
reasonable. House bottles – white Côtes du Lubéron and red Côtes du Ventoux –
are €19.

CHEF/PROPRIETOR: Sheila Vaughan   OPEN: Mon to Sat D only 7 to 9.30   CLOSED: Christmas week
MEALS: Set D €36   SERVICE: not inc, card slips closed   CARDS: Amex, Diners, MasterCard, Visa
DETAILS: 25 seats. Private parties: 13 main room. Car park. Children's helpings. No smoking in 1
dining room. Wheelchair access (not WC). Music.   ACCOMMODATION: 4 rooms, all with bath/
shower. B&B €40 to €80. Fishing

## BLACKLION  Co Cavan                                                                    map 16

## ▲ MacNean Bistro ⁵⚹

Main Street, Blacklion
TEL: (072) 53022   FAX: (072) 53404                                       MODERN IRISH
                                                                          €33–€69

The Bistro provides an appealing menu that combines top-quality local produce
with modern ideas about cooking. Among starters, tempura of lemon sole with
basil mayonnaise and chilli jam should get the message across that this is
cooking that happily crosses frontiers, as should cinnamon-grilled quail on pea
risotto with balsamic lentils and a crispy fried egg. Main courses, meanwhile,
range from steamed hake on a saffron and chorizo risotto with a lobster and
coconut cream to a more traditional-sounding, though not entirely conventional,
beef fillet with Parmesan crust on red onion and bacon rösti. End with a pudding
along the lines of passion-fruit cream with berries, or vanilla and coconut crème
brûlée with honeycomb ice cream. Five house wines of each colour open a varied
international list. Prices start at €15.95.

CHEFS/PROPRIETORS: Neven and Vera Maguire OPEN: Sun L 12.30 to 3.15, Thur to Sun D 6 to 9 (9.30 Sat, 8 Sun) CLOSED: 1 week Christmas MEALS: alc D (main courses €18.50 to €20). Set L Sun €22, Set D €50 SERVICE: not inc CARDS: MasterCard, Visa DETAILS: 40 seats. Private parties: 40 main room, 10 to 15 private rooms. Vegetarian meals. Children's helpings. No smoking in dining room. Wheelchair access (not WC). Music. Air-conditioned ACCOMMODATION: 5 rooms, all with bath/shower. TV. Phone. B&B €33 to €66. Baby facilities

## CASHEL  Co Tipperary                                                 map 16

# Chez Hans

Moor Lane, Cashel
TEL: (062) 61177                                                MODERN EUROPEAN
                                                                      €43–€78

This rural retreat has been run by the expatriate Matthia family since the late 1960s. Jason's style of cooking is informed by Mediterranean lightness and vividness, so expect tagliatelle with smoked salmon and crab, grilled Rossmore mussels under a garlic crumb, and then cassolette of seafood in a chive velouté, or chargrilled veal cutlet with tomato compote and béarnaise to follow. The local Cashel Blue cheese is wholeheartedly supported, turning up in a salad of marinated chicken with new potatoes and bacon, or by itself at the meal's end. The sweet alternative might be iced nougat with raspberry sauce. A French-based wine list has shorter selections from elsewhere, the bidding opening at €20.95.

CHEF: Jason Matthia PROPRIETORS: Hans-Peter and Jason Matthia OPEN: Tue to Sat D only 6 to 10 CLOSED: 1 week Christmas, last 2 weeks Jan, first week Sept MEALS: alc (main courses €22 to €26). Set D Tue to Fri 6 to 7.30 €21 (2 courses) to €27, Set D €40 SERVICE: not inc CARDS: MasterCard, Visa DETAILS: 70 seats. Private parties: 70 main room. Car park. Vegetarian meals. Children's helpings. Music

## CASTLEBALDWIN  Co Sligo                                               map 16

# ▲ Cromleach Lodge 🌿✳

Castlebaldwin, Via Boyle
TEL: (071) 65155   FAX: (071) 65455
EMAIL: info@cromleach.com
WEBSITE: www.cromleach.com                                        MODERN IRISH
signposted from Castlebaldwin on the N4                              €73–€87

After nine years, one reader found 'the quality, ambience and friendliness still of the highest'. For those staying the night, a room with a view over Lough Arrow may complement Moira Tighe's first-rate modern Irish dinner, offering four or five choices per course. Starters could encompass a traditional confit duck leg on crisp potato galette alongside contemporary creations like spiced lamb in a filo parcel with a yoghurt and chive dressing. After an intermediary sorbet, main courses typically run to Sligo beef fillet with bacon and onions, or wild salmon escalope on creamed spring onions. Desserts have included marbled chocolate mousse gâteau with Baileys crème anglaise. The wine list, diverse but largely French, opens at €21.95.

CHEF: Moira Tighe    PROPRIETORS: Christy and Moira Tighe    OPEN: all week D only 6.30 to 8.30
CLOSED: Nov to Jan    MEALS: Set D €55    SERVICE: not inc    CARDS: Amex, MasterCard, Visa
DETAILS: 55 seats. Private parties: 25 main room, 2 to 25 private rooms. Car park. Vegetarian
meals. Children's helpings. No smoking in dining room. Wheelchair access (not WC). Music. No
mobile phones    ACCOMMODATION: 10 rooms, all with bath/shower. TV. Phone. B&B €145 to
€330. Rooms for disabled. Baby facilities

## CORK  Co Cork
map 16

# Crawford Gallery Café 🍞

Emmet Place, Cork
TEL: (021) 4274415
IRISH/BRITISH
€28–€46

Isaac Allen, from the family that run Ballymaloe House in Shanagarry (see
entry), is now chef/proprietor of this 'modern Irish bistro' attached to an art
gallery on the ground floor of Cork's one-time Custom House. Breakfast includes
Ballymaloe breads and home-made preserves, while lunch menus broaden the
repertoire, moving quickly from open sandwiches and salads to steak with chips
and béarnaise, chicken baked with mushrooms and home-grown marjoram, and
glazed loin of bacon with summer cabbage purée and Irish Mist sauce. A
handful of reasonably priced wines starts at €16.50.

CHEF/PROPRIETOR: Isaac Allen    OPEN: Mon to Sat 12.30 to 2.30 (3 Sat)    MEALS: alc (main courses
€8 to €12). Set L €18    SERVICE: not inc    CARDS: MasterCard, Switch, Visa    DETAILS: 60 seats.
Private parties: 60 main room, 60 to 200 private rooms. Vegetarian meals. No-smoking area.
Wheelchair access (also WC). Occasional music  (£5)

## CROOKHAVEN  Co Cork
map 16

# Out of the Blue 🍴
**NEW ENTRY**

Crookhaven
TEL: (028) 35929
MODERN EUROPEAN-PLUS
€48–€70

Burvill Evans's latest venture gazes into the blue too, for his restaurant overlooks
the waterfront. Uncovered tables, plain white crockery, and pastel walls hung
with old black and white prints, together with 'solicitous and pleasant service',
provide the setting for 'cooking worth travelling for'. The carte, divided between
'filler' and 'fuller' dishes (and 'fulfilled' desserts), offers half a dozen choices at
each course. Start with 'neatly timed' grilled scallops in a won ton case, served
on a mild avocado salsa with chilli oil, tandoori duck pâté, or wild mushroom
risotto topped with smoked Gubbeen. Crispy duck, the house speciality, off the
bone in a gentle ginger and apricot glaze, is highly commended, as is fillet of
crisp-skinned sea bass baked in salt, served on a bed of onion, garlic, tomato and
thyme. Three Irish cheeses may divert attention from 'good-looking, gooey'
crème brûlée, or chocolate marquise. House wines, a Chianti and a Riesling, are
€17.

CHEF/PROPRIETOR: Burvill Evans    OPEN: Wed to Sun D only 6.15 to 9.45    MEALS: alc (main
courses €20 to €26)    SERVICE: not inc    CARDS: MasterCard, Visa    DETAILS: 42 seats. Private
parties: 18 main room. Children's helpings. No smoking in 1 dining room. Music

## DINGLE  Co Kerry                                                          map 16

# Half Door ▮ ⁂

3 John Street, Dingle
TEL: (066) 9151600   FAX: (066) 9151883
EMAIL: halfdoor@iol.ie                                    MODERN IRISH/SEAFOOD
WEBSITE: www.halfdoor@iol.ie                                        €45–€100

Given its location on a finger of south-west Ireland that juts into the Atlantic this restaurant naturally specialises in seafood, though carnivores will find beef, chicken and duck are on the à la carte menu, and roast rack of lamb among the specials. Otherwise, centre stage is taken by seafood chowder, medallions of monkfish, salmon-and-sole paupiettes, and lobster (Thermidor, or taken from the tank and boiled). A few dishes are lifted by concessions to metropolitan modernity: blackened filet of salmon, garlic and mango duo; or peppered pineapple sauce with a roast half-duckling. Old-style desserts might take in home-made chocolate fudge cake. The wine list favours France, with some good selections from the Loire and the Rhône, but also gathers together interesting selections from elsewhere in Europe and the New World. Fourteen house wines (from €18 to €28) represent, like the list as a whole, very good value.

CHEF: Teresa O'Connor   PROPRIETORS: Denis and Teresa O'Connor   OPEN: Tue to Sat L 12.30 to 2, Mon to Sat D 6 to 10   MEALS: alc (main courses €10 to €45)   SERVICE: not inc   CARDS: Amex, MasterCard, Visa   DETAILS: 50 seats. Private parties: 20 main room. No children after 7pm. Children's helpings. No smoking in 1 dining room. Wheelchair access (not WC). No music. Air-conditioned

## DONEGAL  Co Donegal                                                       map 16

# ▲ Harvey's Point ⁂

Lough Eske, Donegal
TEL: (073) 22208   FAX: (073) 22352
EMAIL: info@harveyspoint.com                              MODERN EUROPEAN
WEBSITE: www.harveyspoint.com                                        €40–€73

This sprawling Swiss chalet-style hotel has an enviable setting on the shores of Lough Eske, with the Blue Stack Mountains for a dramatic backdrop. It aspires to offer 'an island of serenity' through providing lavish hospitality and a high degree of luxury in every respect, not least the food. New chef Martin Lynch was due to start just as the Guide went to press and, assuming he will continue in similar style as his predecessor, will deliver set menus with a slightly conservative feel. Expect dishes such as tournedos Rossini with Madeira sauce and truffled mash, pan-fried Dover sole meunière, and medallions of venison with celeriac purée and game sauce, with perhaps tiramasù to finish. The brief wine list features some good names, mainly from Europe, with a separate 'prestige' list. Twenty-four house wines start at €18.50.

CHEF: Martin Lynch   PROPRIETORS: Marc Gysling and Deirdre Mc Glone   OPEN: all week 12.30 to 2.30, 6.30 to 9.30   CLOSED: Sun D, Mon and Tues from Nov to Easter (open Christmas)   MEALS: Set L €20 (2 courses) to €25, Set D €27 (main course only) to €44. Bar snacks also available to 5.30   SERVICE: not inc   CARDS: Amex, Diners, MasterCard, Visa   DETAILS: 100 seats. Private parties: 100 main room, 20 to 200 private rooms. Car park. Vegetarian meals. No children. Jacket and tie. No smoking in dining room. Wheelchair access (also WC). Occasional music. Air-conditioned   ACCOMMODATION: 20 rooms, all with bath/shower. TV. Phone. No children. B&B €98 to €178

## DOOLIN  Co Clare                                              map 16

# ▲ Ballinalacken Castle ⅚✳

Coast Road, Doolin
TEL/FAX:  (065) 707 4025                                    MODERN IRISH
WEBSITE: www.ballinalackencastle.com                        €45–€75

The tortuous road winds through magically named places – Kinvarra and Ballyvaughan, the Burren and Corkscrew Hill – before reaching this Victorian house beside a castle that overlooks the Atlantic and the Cliffs of Moher. Here Frank Sheedy's enticing contemporary cooking takes in smoked salmon blinis with avocado cream and sweet-and-sour red onion, or goats' cheese fritters on beetroot 'carpaccio' with raspberry vinaigrette to start, and main courses like fillets of John Dory with mustard cabbage, or duck – confit leg and honey-glazed breast – with balsamic and pineapple jus. In between comes a nightly-changing soup or the fixture seafood chowder, and at the end Irish cheeses, or the likes of caramelised plums with ginger ice cream in rum custard. House French varietals at €16.50 head a list that darts around the globe.

CHEF: Frank Sheedy  PROPRIETORS: Denis and Mary O'Callaghan  OPEN: Wed to Mon D only 6.45 to 8.45  CLOSED: early Oct to late Apr  MEALS: alc (main courses €17 to €29)  SERVICE: not inc  CARDS: Amex, MasterCard, Visa  DETAILS: 40 seats. Private parties: 40 main room. Car park. Vegetarian meals. No smoking in dining room. Music  ACCOMMODATION: 12 rooms, all with bath/shower. TV. Phone. B&B €100 to €176. Baby facilities

## DOUGLAS  Co Cork                                             map 16

# Lovetts ♥ ⅚✳

Churchyard Lane, Well Road, Douglas
TEL: (021) 4294909   FAX: (021) 294024                       MODERN EUROPEAN
                                                             €41–€73

There have been kitchen renovations since last year and a second private dining room has been added; unchanged is Lovetts' commitment to outstanding local produce, cooked sensitively and imaginatively. A brasserie menu provides simpler choices – like moules marinière, or crisp chicken confit on leek and potato hash – while the main restaurant offers roast rack of spring lamb with wholegrain mustard mash, venison medallions with red cabbage, pancetta and pine nuts, or several daily blackboard fish specials. Vegetarians have their own menu. Puds number steamed ginger and lemon pudding, or a filo stack of caramelised apples and hazelnuts. The wine list combines bottles from classic French regions with a selection from southern France, before touring the rest of Europe. Spanish reds are well chosen, and the list is rounded out by a selection from the New World. Pricing is generally fair; five house wines cost €17.75 to €24.

CHEF: Marie Harding   PROPRIETORS: Niamh Lovett and Marie Harding   OPEN: Tue to Sat D only 6.30 to 9.30   CLOSED: 1 week Christmas, 1 week Aug bank hol   MEALS: alc (main courses €18 to €24). Vegetarian Set D €20 (2 courses). Brasserie menu also available   SERVICE: not inc, 10% for parties of 5 or more, card slips closed   CARDS: Amex, Diners, MasterCard, Visa   DETAILS: 40 seats. Private parties: 48 main room, 12 to 24 private rooms. Car park. Vegetarian meals. Children's helpings. No smoking in dining room. Wheelchair access (not WC). Music. No mobile phones

## DUBLIN  Co Dublin                                                           map 16

## ▲ Browne's Brasserie ⚡✶                    NEW ENTRY

22 St Stephen's Green, Dublin 2
TEL: (01) 638 3939   FAX: (01) 638 3900
EMAIL: info@brownesdublin.com                    MODERN EUROPEAN
WEBSITE: www.brownesdublin.com                    €42–€80

Browne's Brasserie is set in a grand building on the north side of the square, overlooking St Stephen's Green. High ceilings, varnished wood floors and sombre colours prevail in the sitting room, where diners are encouraged to enjoy a drink before making their way through to the cream-coloured dining room; here, a profusion of crisp linen and candles sets the tone. The menu gathers together some eclectic flavourings: Piquillo peppers stuffed with crabmeat and salmon with salsa verde and curry oil, for example, or fishcakes served with pickled lime, sweet potato salad and chilli jam. Other main courses may run to 'stunning' chargrilled rack of veal with white asparagus, croquette potatoes and sauce Foyot, and desserts might include rhubarb and strawberry pavlova. The wine list is fairly short but takes in selections from around the globe, starting with five house wines (€19 to €21.75) and finishing with some well-selected Bordeaux and burgundies.

CHEF: Sebastian Scheer   PROPRIETOR: Barry Canny   OPEN: Sun to Fri L 12.30 to 2.30, all week D 6.30 to 11 (10 Sun and bank hols)   CLOSED: D 24 Dec to 3 Jan   MEALS: alc exc Sun L (main courses L €13 to €18.50, D €18 to €29.50). Set L Sun €27   SERVICE: not inc, card slips closed, 12.5% for parties of 6 or more   CARDS: Amex, Diners, MasterCard, Visa   DETAILS: 70 seats. Private parties: 70 main room, 38 private room. Vegetarian meals. Children's helpings. No smoking in 1 dining room. Music. Air-conditioned   ACCOMMODATION: 12 rooms, all with bath/ shower. TV. Phone. B&B €170 to €235. Rooms for disabled. Baby facilities

## Chapter One ⟟ ⚡✶                    NEW ENTRY

18–19 Parnell Square, Dublin 1
TEL: (01) 873 2266   FAX: (01) 873 2330
EMAIL: info@chapteronerestaurant.com                    MODERN IRISH/EUROPEAN
WEBSITE: www.chapteronerestaurant.com                    €40–€88

Down a flight of steps beneath the Writers' Museum on this dramatic central Dublin square is this spacious, sophisticated restaurant. Two rooms connected by an archway are set with large tables, a pianist plays discreetly, and the welcome is warm. Ross Lewis cooks with inspiration and elegance, pairing breaded lambs' sweetbreads and deep-fried tongue in a salad with gribiche dressing, and adding a well-judged portion of fondant potato to braised guinea fowl with a morel and tarragon cream sauce. Desserts run to crème brûlée with rhubarb, or chocolate fondant with peaches and ginger anglaise. The wine list gathers together a wide variety of styles from around the globe and has sensible tasting notes and food pairing suggestions. A selection of fine red wines focuses on Bordeaux, along with bottles from Burgundy, Italy, Spain and Australia. House red and white are €18.50 (€4 a glass).

CHEF: Ross Lewis   PROPRIETORS: Ross Lewis and Martin Corbett   OPEN: Tue to Fri L 12.30 to 2.30, Tue to Sat D 6 to 10.45   CLOSED: 2 weeks Christmas   MEALS: alc D (main courses €24.50 to €29). Set L and D 6 to 7 €27.50   SERVICE: 10%   CARDS: Amex, Diners, MasterCard, Visa DETAILS: 85 seats. Private parties: 85 main room, 14 to 20 private rooms. No smoking in 1 dining room. Music. No mobile phones. Air-conditioned

## ▲ Clarence Hotel, Tea Room ▼ ✖

6–8 Wellington Quay, Dublin 2
TEL: (01) 407 0813   FAX: (01) 407 0818
EMAIL: reservations@theclarence.ie
WEBSITE: www.theclarence.ie

MODERN EUROPEAN
€48–€81

This Liffey-side building reflects both 1850s origins and 1996 refurbishment, with high coved ceilings, curious wood-framed windows, and a panelled dado in the Tea Room restaurant. Menus are seasonal and use local produce. The set lunch might include pork fillet and belly with crushed parsnips, turnip and orange jus, or Earl Grey crème brûlée with lemon fizz and mini hot cross bun. A dinner starter of shellfish lasagne with langoustine bisque, roast scallop and Avruga caviar could be followed by crisp roast sea bass accompanied by a tarte fine of ceps, roast artichokes and salsify, or pot roast squab with choucroute, fondant potato, roast foie gras and Madeira sauce. The long wine list starts with 20 by the glass (from €6.50), and includes classic bottles from France, the USA and the southern hemisphere, plus a few distinguished examples from elsewhere; bottle prices start at €23.

CHEF: Anthony Ely   PROPRIETORS: Bono and The Edge   OPEN: Sun to Fri L 12.30 to 2.30 (12 to 3 Sun brunch), 6.30 to 10.30   CLOSED: 23 to 27 Dec   MEALS: alc (main courses €18 to €22). Set L €24 to €50, Set L Sun €18 to €24, Set D €39.50 (2 courses) to €50   SERVICE: not inc, 12.5% for parties of 8 or more   CARDS: Amex, Delta, Diners, MasterCard, Visa   DETAILS: 80 seats. Private parties: 16 main room, 12 to 70 private rooms. Vegetarian meals. No smoking in 1 dining room. No pipes in dining room. Wheelchair access (also WC). Music   ACCOMMODATION: 48 rooms, all with bath/shower. TV. Phone. Room only €285 to €2,000. Rooms for disabled. Baby facilities

## Commons

Newman House, 85–86 St Stephen's
Green, Dublin 2
TEL: (01) 478 0530   FAX: (01) 478 0551
EMAIL: sales@thecommonsrestaurant.ie
WEBSITE: www.thecommonsrestaurant.ie

MODERN IRISH/FRENCH
€47–€122

A distinguished address, this: the Commons is in a Georgian house that was the original home of University College. A south-facing terrace is used for summer dining and pre-dinner drinks, while the stylish dining room is adorned with specially commissioned paintings on a James Joyce theme by some of Ireland's top artists. The inventive, upmarket cooking lives up to the setting: warm pressed and braised pig's head with gribiche mayonnaise, roasted turbot with cep casserole and pomme purée, or loin of rabbit with braised baby squid and confit cherry tomatoes. Dish prices are 'expensive but worth it', in the view of one who enjoyed 'meltingly succulent' Cork scallops and the bread selection, which 'could have constituted a meal in itself'. Elaborate desserts have included 'pure chocolate and chestnut', comprising a soufflé, a mousseline, iced white chocolate and chestnut Maxim, and a chocolate spiral. Big names from France dominate the wine list, which starts with a page of ten house selections from €22.

CHEF: Aiden Byrne   PROPRIETOR: Mike Fitzgerald   OPEN: Mon to Fri L 12.30 to 2.15, Mon to Sat D 7 to 10.30   CLOSED: 25 Dec to second week Jan, 2 weeks Aug, bank hols   MEALS: alc D (main courses €31 to €41). Set L €32, Set D €85   SERVICE: not inc   CARDS: Amex, Diners, MasterCard, Visa   DETAILS: 74 seats. 24 seats outside. Private parties: 80 main room, 26 to 60 private rooms. Vegetarian meals. Children's helpings. No-smoking area. Music

## L'Ecrivain 🍷✳

109A Lower Baggot Street, Dublin 2
TEL: (01) 661 1919   FAX: (01) 661 0617          MODERN IRISH/FRENCH
WEBSITE: www.lecrivain.com                              €48–€116

This city-centre stalwart welcomes all and sundry with its lack of pretension: 'no jacket and tie nonsense' here, said one. Derry Clarke strives to use the finest of local produce, put together by 'classically French-trained chefs'. House specialities include baked rock oysters, smoked bacon and cabbage, and Guinness sabayon, but there are some wider influences too. An assiette of wild Irish salmon combines a chilled ballottine, salmon cured with dill and mustard, and seared salmon teriyaki, while a main course of baked fillet of halibut may come with chorizo, Thai basil orzo, a froth of star anise and lime, and pine nut gremolata. Finish with something like lemon parfait. The Franco-centric wine list aims high, and value is not a high point. House wines start at €25 (€6.25 a glass).

CHEF: Derry Clarke   PROPRIETORS: Derry and Sally-Anne Clarke   OPEN: Mon to Fri L 12.30 to 2.30, Mon to Sat D 7 to 11   CLOSED: 24 Dec to 4 Jan, bank hols   MEALS: alc D (main courses €36 to €38). Set L €27 (2 courses) to €38, Set D €50   SERVICE: 10%   CARDS: Amex, MasterCard, Visa   DETAILS: 100 seats. 20 seats outside. Private parties: 30 main room, 18 to 20 private rooms. Vegetarian meals. Children's helpings. No children under 8. No smoking in 1 dining room. Occasional music. No mobile phones. Air-conditioned

## Les Frères Jacques

74 Dame Street, Dublin 2
TEL: (01) 679 4555   FAX: (01) 679 4725
EMAIL: info@lesfreresjacques.com                        FRENCH
WEBSITE: www.lesfreresjacques.co.ie                    €35–€103

Reporters have conflicting opinions of the service here, but the table d'hôte dinner (€34), is praised for its traditional French character. There may be celeriac soup with truffle oil and chives, followed perhaps by terrine of chicken with Bayonne ham and sauce Gribiche, then seared salmon escalope with ratatouille and soy olive oil, plus blancmange scented with Kirsch, crème anglaise and chocolate sauce to finish. The à la carte may open with the simplicity of native or rock oysters, or a snail-filled brioche with garlic brûlée topping and meat glaze juices. Lobster is usually on the menu, as is Wicklow lamb, perhaps as noisettes with gratin Dauphinoise and thyme, and fish and game, in season, are key ingredients. Farm cheeses, French and Irish, compete against warm chocolate fondant with white chocolate sauce with crushed hazelnuts. The long wine list is mostly French classics, with some appealingly mature reds. House selections are €17.15, and there are useful half- and quarter-bottles.

CHEF: Richard Réau   PROPRIETOR: Jean-Jacques Caillabet   OPEN: Mon to Fri L 12.30 to 2.30, Mon to Sat D 7 to 11   CLOSED: D 24 Dec to 2 Jan, bank hol Mons   MEALS: alc D (main courses €27 to €35.50). Set L €20, Set D €34   SERVICE: 12.5%, card slips closed   CARDS: Amex, Delta, MasterCard, Visa   DETAILS: 60 seats. Private parties: 45 main room, 6 to 20 private rooms. No smoking in 1 dining room. Music. Air-conditioned  (£5)

## Jacob's Ladder 🍴✳

4–5 Nassau Street, Dublin 2
TEL: (01) 670 3865   FAX: (01) 670 3868
WEBSITE: www.jacobsladder.ie

MODERN IRISH
€39–€105

From the windows of this first-floor restaurant you can look over the lawns of Trinity College. The simple wood-floored dining room now boasts linen tablecloths; also new since last year is an eight-course tasting menu, based around seasonal produce, which shows off the kitchen's scope and ambitions. On the carte, starters like guinea-fowl parfait with watercress, blueberry and apple compote, or warm white asparagus and leek tart with rocket pesto and tomato dressing, might be followed by roast loin of veal with confit potato, cauliflower, mousserons and mushroom fumet, or fillet of cod with scallops, scallion risotto, young vegetables, ginger and lime. There's also a lot going on in desserts, such as passion-fruit brûlée with glazed pineapple, Kirsch sabayon and coconut sorbet. The short, fixed-price dinner menu follows a similar path, and there are some simpler alternatives at lunchtime. The New World dominates the short wine list, which kicks off with seven house selections at €19.50 (€4.75 a glass).

CHEF: Adrian Roche   PROPRIETORS: Adrian and Bernie Roche   OPEN: Tue to Sat 12.30 to 2.30 (2 Sat), 6 to 10   CLOSED: 2 weeks Christmas, 17 Mar, 6 to 13 Aug   MEALS: alc (main courses €13 to €29). Set D Tue to Fri 6 to 7 €19 (2 courses) to €24.75, Set D €31.74. Tasting menu available D €70 (min 2)   SERVICE: not inc   CARDS: Amex, Diners, MasterCard, Visa   DETAILS: 80 seats. Private parties: 50 main room, 10 to 50 private rooms. Vegetarian meals. Children's helpings. No smoking in 1 dining room. Music  (£5)

*The Guide office can quickly spot when a restaurateur is encouraging customers to write recommending inclusion. Such reports do not further a restaurant's cause. Please tell us if a restaurateur invites you to write to the Guide.*

# Mermaid Café

69–70 Dame Street, Dublin 2
TEL: (01) 670 8236   FAX: (01) 670 8205
EMAIL: mermaid@iol.ie
WEBSITE: www.mermaid.ie

MODERN EUROPEAN
€35–€79

Very relaxed, very Dublin: the Mermaid doesn't pretend to be anything other than a café, offering robust and colourful cooking in an appropriately down-to-earth setting. The weekly-changing menu is broad in its scope and modern in its tastes: peppered seared salmon with orange, fennel and chilli might appear alongside chunky pork terrine with horseradish cream on toast; while main courses run the gamut from roast venison loin with red cabbage, roast carrots, mash and cranberry gravy, to slow-cooked lamb shank with mild green Kashmiri curry and honey roast squash. Value is unquestionable and the brunch menu looks like a pleasant way to start a Sunday. Four house wines open at €17.50, and the short main list offers good choice for those with a little more money to spend.

CHEF: Temple Garner   PROPRIETORS: Mark Harrell and Ben Gorman   OPEN: all week 12.30 to 2.30, 6 to 11, Sun brunch 12 to 3.30   CLOSED: 24 to 26 Dec and 31 Dec, 1 Jan, Good Fri   MEALS: alc D (€18 to €28). Set L €13.95 (1 course) to €21.95. Sun brunch (€8 to €14)   SERVICE: not inc, 12.5% for parties of 5 or more   CARDS: MasterCard, Visa   DETAILS: 65 seats. Private parties: 30 main room. Vegetarian meals. No-smoking area. Wheelchair access (also WC). Music. Air-conditioned  £5

# ▲ Merrion Hotel, Morningtons Brasserie

Upper Merrion Street, Dublin 2
TEL: (01) 603 0600   FAX: (01) 603 0700
EMAIL: info@merrionhotel.com
WEBSITE: www.merrionhotel.com

MODERN IRISH
€43–€87

Mornington's offers a 'contemporary Irish cuisine' that shows strong Italian influence and some from Asia, but favours classic flavour combinations. Typical starters are leek and potato soup with smoked salmon crème fraîche, or for vegetarians, aubergine and three cheese gâteau, tomato coulis and crisp fennel bread croûte. You might then choose something traditional (fish and chips with mushy peas) or sophisticated (seared soya duck, stir-fried baby corn, pak choi and shiitake mushrooms with chilli and soya dressing). For desserts, you might choose warm hazelnut and chocolate ravioli on poached pears. House wines from €23 start a well-balanced transnational list that has 18 half-bottles, a dozen by the glass and a leaning to famous names.

CHEF: Ed Cooney   PROPRIETOR: Landmark Investments   OPEN: Mon to Fri L 12.30 to 2, all week D 6 to 10   MEALS: alc D (main courses €18 to €25). Set L €23 (2 courses) to €28. Snack and light L and D menus also available   SERVICE: not inc   CARDS: Amex, Delta, Diners, MasterCard, Visa   DETAILS: 60 seats. Vegetarian meals. Children's helpings. Wheelchair access (also WC). Music. Air-conditioned   ACCOMMODATION: 145 rooms, all with bath/shower. TV. Phone. Room only €280 to €950. Rooms for disabled. Baby facilities. Swimming pool

# One Pico ✱

**NEW ENTRY**

5–6 Molesworth Place, Dublin 2
TEL: (01) 676 0300   FAX: (01) 676 0411
EMAIL: eamonnoreilly@ireland.com
WEBSITE: www.onepico.com

MODERN IRISH-PLUS
€46–€115

This comfortable, contemporary dining room close to St Stephen's Green has managed to have been around for a few years before coming to the Guide's attention. At least this means it is unlikely to be a flash in the pan, having had time to put down some roots. Eamonn O'Reilly's cooking is modern Irish, which is to say that some traditional ideas feature but the scope is wide enough to take in king scallops with herb risotto, roast beetroot, Puy lentils and a veal jus; and crisp duck spring roll with chilli jam. Dishes tend to be complicated, although technique is sound enough. A main course of rack of lamb, for instance, is accompanied by pomme écrasé, pipérade, onion confit, and a tomato and basil jus, while a pea risotto comes with asparagus and Parmesan, a poached egg and caramelised onions. Desserts are no more straightforward, although île flottante with crème anglaise, Valrhona chocolate salad and mint oil proved a 'surprisingly good combination of flavours'. The wine list offers good range in both Old and New Worlds. Prices start at €25.

CHEF/PROPRIETOR: Eamonn O'Reilly   OPEN: Mon to Sat 12 to 3, 6 to 11   CLOSED: 2 weeks from 25 Dec, 2 weeks from 4 Aug   MEALS: alc D (main courses €18 to €27). Set L €22.50 (2 courses) to €26.50, Set D €70   SERVICE: 10%, card slips closed   CARDS: Amex, Diners, MasterCard, Visa   DETAILS: 75 seats. Private parties: 90 main room, 10 to 46 private rooms. Vegetarian meals. No smoking in 1 dining room. Music. No mobile phones. Air-conditioned

# Restaurant Patrick Guilbaud

21 Upper Merrion Street, Dublin 2
TEL: (01) 676 4192   FAX: (01) 661 0052

MODERN IRISH/FRENCH
€47–€174

One of Dublin's top restaurants, this is next door to the Merrion Hotel, itself housed in a Georgian terrace. The dining room has a glass wall overlooking a charming courtyard, there are green tablecloths, heavy silver and crystal glasses, and this is the sort of restaurant that does all the extras, including amuse-gueules. If portions appear small, the cuisine's richness and complexity renders them more than adequate. A starter of three thick, juicy slices of scallop may come with cauliflower mousseline, bittersweet Muscavado caramel and almond milk. Irish crubbeen (pig's trotters) is here served as a 'carpaccio': the meat pressed into a terrine, sliced thinly and served with Puy lentils, walnut and sherry dressing and iced mustard cream. Main-course John Dory may partner earthy duck confit flavoured with walnut 'wine' and chilled oyster cream. Service is reliable and formal, and the wine list is extensive, if rather pricey, with house wines starting at €27.

CHEF: Guillaume Lebrun   PROPRIETOR: Patrick Guilbaud   OPEN: Tue to Sat 12.30 to 2.15, 7 to 10.15   CLOSED: two weeks from 24 Dec, Irish bank hols   MEALS: alc (main courses €40 to €53). Set L €28   SERVICE: not inc   CARDS: Amex, Diners, MasterCard, Visa   DETAILS: 80 seats. 20 seats outside. Private parties: 85 main room, 2 to 25 private rooms. Vegetarian meals. No music. No mobile phones. Air-conditioned

# Roly's Bistro &#x1F374;&#x2716;

7 Ballsbridge Terrace, Dublin 4
TEL: (01) 668 2611   FAX: (01) 660 8535
EMAIL: ireland@rolysbistro.ie
WEBSITE: www.rolysbistro.ie

IRISH/FRENCH
€29–€74

'Bistro' may not be the most appropriate designation for this venue, which is more of a smart and fairly large restaurant, albeit with an informal atmosphere. Some old-fashioned ideas hold sway in the kitchen, though these are not always rendered in traditional ways. Starters might include rocket salad with puff pastry twirls, shallot and truffle dressing, or venison terrine with pickled vegetables and a toasted brioche. Main courses might take in roast cod fillet with buttered scallions and rocket, a balsamic reduction and apple and horseradish cream, or wild Irish game pie with roasted chestnuts and cranberries. Desserts are indulgent-sounding creations like spiced pear and mincemeat strudel with vanilla ice cream and maple fudge sauce. The succinct wine list features ten house selections at €17.70 and eight more at €19.70.

CHEF: Paul Cartwright   PROPRIETORS: John and Angela O'Sullivan, and Colin O'Daly   OPEN: all week 12 to 3, 6 to 10   CLOSED: 25 and 26 Dec   MEALS: alc D (main courses €16.50 to €24.50). Set L €17.71, Set D Mon to Thur 6 to 6.45 €18.75 (2 courses) to €21.25   SERVICE: 10%   CARDS: Amex, Diners, MasterCard, Visa   DETAILS: 150 seats. Private parties: 60 main room. Vegetarian meals. No smoking in 1 dining room. Wheelchair access (also WC). Occasional music. Air-conditioned

---

# Shanahan's on the Green &#x1F37D;&#x1F374;&#x2716;   **NEW ENTRY**

119 St Stephen's Green, Dublin 2
TEL: (01) 407 0939   FAX: (01) 407 0940
WEBSITE: www.shanahans.ie

STEAK AND SEAFOOD
€75–€139

Shanahan's spreads across two floors, the ground floor decked out with cream walls and red carpet and plenty of mirrors. The menu reads a bit like that at an American steak house, although Irish produce (west coast mussels, Galway oysters, etc.) is picked out in italics. Steaks – cooked on a special super-hot grill – are the speciality here. The meat comes from certified Irish Angus beef, ranging from 'sensational' petite filet (8 ounces) to 'gloriously moist and succulent' bone-in ribeye (24 ounces). For those not besotted with beef, there are other meaty and fishy main courses and a variety of side orders. Staff are well trained and ultra-efficient. Wines, arranged by style, are a good mix of European and New World bottles. The 'interesting reds' selection is just that, with cleverly chosen – if not cheap – wines from around the globe. Prices start at €23, with eight wines by the glass from €8.

CHEF: Leo Small   PROPRIETOR: John Shanahan   OPEN: all week D only 6 to 10.30 (11 Fri and Sat) CLOSED: 1 week Christmas, bank hols   MEALS: alc (main courses €27.50 to €39.50). Bar menu available   SERVICE: not inc, 15% for parties of 6 or more   CARDS: Amex, Delta, Diners, MasterCard, Visa   DETAILS: 100 seats. Private parties: 60 main room. Vegetarian meals. No smoking in 1 dining room. No cigars/pipes in dining room. Music. No mobile phones. Air-conditioned

# Thornton's ♥ ✄

1 Portobello Road, Dublin 8
TEL: (01) 454 9067   FAX: (01) 453 2947
EMAIL: thornton.m@iolfree.ie

MODERN IRISH
€56–€152

A move was planned for Kevin Thornton's restaurant, from just off Dublin's main drag alongside the Grand Canal in Portobello to the Fitzwilliam Hotel at 128 St Stephen's Green, shortly after the Guide was about to go to press (details, such as the new telephone number, were not available). Assuming the move goes ahead, and that continuity prevails in terms of staff and format, expect to find modern-style treatment of upmarket ingredients in the new setting. There might be red mullet wrapped in nori on a bed of prawn jelly; foie gras sautéed with scallops or fashioned into a terrine with rabbit and served with leek purée; or sea bass served truffle sauce. Desserts might take in tarte Tatin with butterscotch ice cream, and there is a selection of top-quality Irish and French cheeses. Mark-ups on the extensive wine list are high; though house wines start at €23, prices rise like a well-cooked soufflé thereafter. That said, producers are top-notch and the focus is on food-friendly styles, with mature Bordeaux leading the way. Prices and some other information listed below may not apply to the new location.

CHEF: Kevin Thornton   PROPRIETORS: Kevin and Muriel Thornton   OPEN: Fri L 12 to 2.45, Tue to Sat D 7 to 10.30   MEALS: alc (main courses €38 to €44). Set L €36, Set D €100   SERVICE: not inc CARDS: Amex, Diners, MasterCard, Visa   DETAILS: 40 seats. Private parties: 40 main room. Vegetarian meals. Children's helpings. No smoking in 1 dining room. Music. Air-conditioned

---

**GALWAY  Co Galway**　　　　　　　　　　　　　　　　　　　　　**map 16**

# Archway ✄　　　　　　　　　　　　　　　　　　　　| NEW ENTRY |

Victoria Place, Galway
TEL: (091) 563693   FAX: (091) 563074
WEBSITE: www.archway.ie

MODERN FRENCH
€34–€94

The archway itself is no more than a name-board through which you pass on the way to the first-floor restaurant, with its white-stone walls, black ceiling beams and soft French-style music playing in the background. Tableware on linen-covered tables is elegant and unfussy, and staff, dressed in black and white, are 'helpful and friendly rather than formal'. 'Assured cooking' has produced an amuse-gueule of white-bean mousse with a 'well-judged' foil of mustard sauce, a fine fennel soup with delicate gnocchi, and 'perfectly cooked' squab pigeon with foie gras and artichoke. Excellent French cheeses compete with smooth mango mousse, or crème brûlée, while coffee with 'moreish' petits fours has also been judged first class. Wines are mainly French classics, with a decent showing of half-bottles. House wines are €23.50.

CHEF: Brendan O'Sullivan   PROPRIETORS: Brendan O'Sullivan and Caroline Barry   OPEN: Tue to Fri L 12.30 to 1.45, Tue to Sat D 7 to 9.30   CLOSED: 24 Dec to 9 Jan   MEALS: alc (main courses L €10, D €20 to €33). Set L €9.50 (1 course) to €19.50, Set D €38   SERVICE: not inc, 10% for parties of 6 or more   CARDS: Amex, Delta, Diners, MasterCard, Visa   DETAILS: 30 seats. Private parties: 34 main room. Vegetarian meals. Children's helpings. No smoking in dining room. Music. Air-conditioned

## ▲ Marlfield House ₷✳

Courtown Road, Gorey
TEL: (055) 21124   FAX: (055) 21572
EMAIL: info@marlfieldhouse.ie                        MODERN FRENCH
WEBSITE: www.marlfieldhouse.com                        €53–€90

Marlfield is a country house on a grand scale, complete with woodland walks, a
rose garden and much more besides. Seasonal pickings from the hotel's kitchen
garden liven up Henry Stone's thoroughly modern cooking. Influences from
Europe and beyond are evident in starters of marinated beef fillet with rocket
and Parmesan shavings, or confit of Barbary duck leg with braised Puy lentils
and lime sherry dressing. Dinner proceeds with a soup or sorbet, before main
courses ranging from fillet of turbot with provençale vegetables, dill and lemon-
grass sauce to guinea fowl with a ragout of smoked bacon, leeks and oyster
mushrooms. As a finale, there might be classic lemon tart or poached pears with
almond and Amaretto ice cream. The monumental wine list is loaded with
serious French vintages at serious prices.

CHEF: Henry Stone   PROPRIETOR: Mary and Ray Bowe   OPEN: Sun L 12.30 to 1.45, all week D 7
to 9 (9.30 Sat)   CLOSED: Mid-Dec to 1 Feb   MEALS: Set L Sun €36, Set D €56. Bar menu also
available   SERVICE: not inc   CARDS: Amex, Diners, MasterCard, Switch, Visa   DETAILS: 65 seats.
Private parties: 20 main room, 20 to 30 private rooms. Car park. Vegetarian meals. No children
under 10 at D. No smoking in dining room. Wheelchair access (also WC). No music. No mobile
phones. Air-conditioned   ACCOMMODATION: 20 rooms, all with bath/shower. TV. Phone. B&B
€110 to €750. Baby facilities

## ▲ Assolas Country House ₷✳

Kanturk
TEL: (029) 50015   FAX: (029) 50795
EMAIL: assolas@eircom.net
WEBSITE: www.assolas.com
signposted from N72, NE of Kanturk, 8m W of              MODERN IRISH
Mallow                                                    €55–€66

This seventeenth-century manor house is run in a very hands-on way by the
Bourke family, and though standards of comfort and cooking are high, the
atmosphere is homely and welcoming. (Note that dinner is served to residents
only.) An unfussy style of cooking allows the 'well-nigh perfect' quality of the
materials – plenty of herbs, fruit and vegetables from their own walled gardens,
and first-rate produce from local suppliers – to shine through. Kinsale mussels
simmered in olive oil and herbs, and creamy yet slightly rough-textured chicken
liver pâté have been impressive starters, while a main course of roast Kanturk
lamb with redcurrant sauce has featured 'very tender' meat. A fish alternative
might be brill fillet with béarnaise. Finish perhaps with strawberry shortcake
with raspberry sorbet. Wines are exclusively European, many from family-
owned vineyards; house Côtes du Rhône from Guigal is €20.

CHEF: Hazel Bourke   PROPRIETORS: the Bourke family   OPEN: all week D only 7 to 8 (residents only)   CLOSED: 1 Nov to 16 Mar   MEALS: Set D €45   SERVICE: none, card slips closed   CARDS: MasterCard, Visa   DETAILS: 20 seats. Private parties: 20 main room. Car park. Children's helpings. No children under 6 at D. No smoking in dining room. No music. No mobile phones   ACCOMMODATION: 9 rooms, all with bath/shower. Phone. B&B €95 to €240. Baby facilities. Fishing

## KENMARE  Co Kerry                                                        map 16

# ▲ Park Hotel Kenmare  ▮ ⅀

Kenmare
TEL: (064) 41200   FAX: (064) 41402
EMAIL: info@parkkenmare.com                                    MODERN IRISH
WEBSITE: www.parkkenmare.com                                    €85–€124

A touch of opulence infuses this grand Victorian country house set in idyllic countryside overlooking Kenmare Bay, with grand views from the dining room across the Beara peninsula to the Caha Mountains beyond. Luxury shows up in the cooking, too, along with a sense of ambition and complexity: for example, in a starter of pan-fried escalope of duck foie gras with Sneem black pudding, Granny Smith sorbet, rhubarb chutney and truffle jus. Main courses might take in poached turbot fillet on celeriac purée, braised cabbage, blue cheese ravioli and a mustard sauce; or herb-crusted loin of Kerry lamb with chargrilled aubergine, sauté spinach, potato galette and a thyme and tomato jus. A warm brioche box of caramelised fruit with lemon curd and Amaretto ice cream maintains the pace into desserts. The encyclopaedic wine list gives red Bordeaux and white Burgundy the largest spaces in the cellar, but attention goes on the New World too, particularly California and Australia. Best value can be found in the 'limited' section; otherwise, prices tend to be steep. House wines are around €30.

CHEF: Joe Ryan   PROPRIETOR: Francis Brennan   OPEN: all week D only 7 to 9   CLOSED: 28 Oct to 23 Dec, 2 Jan to mid-Apr   MEALS: alc (main courses €30 to €35). Set D €58   SERVICE: not inc   CARDS: Amex, Diners, MasterCard, Visa   DETAILS: 120 seats. 30 seats outside. Private parties: 60 main room, 10 to 60 private rooms. Car park. Vegetarian meals. No children under 6 after 8pm. Jacket and tie. No smoking in dining room. Wheelchair access (not WC). No music. No mobile phones   ACCOMMODATION: 46 rooms, all with bath/shower. TV. Phone. B&B €198 to €698. Rooms for disabled. Baby facilities

# ▲ Sheen Falls Lodge, La Cascade  ▮

Kenmare
TEL: (064) 41600   FAX: (064) 41386
EMAIL: info@sheenfallslodge.ie
WEBSITE: www.sheenfallslodge.ie
follow signs for Glengariff from Kenmare; hotel            MODERN IRISH
signposted after about ½m                                    €85–€102

Quality local ingredients figure large at La Cascade, the fine-dining restaurant at this hotel set on a 300-acre estate, and include game and lamb, as well as chanterelles (from the grounds) and local lettuces and herbs. Chris Farrell's menu pleasingly blends classic and fashionable, taking in a smattering of luxury ingredients (viz. a starter of ravioli of rabbit with morel consommé and foie gras). Native oysters may come with a champagne sabayon, cucumber, pear and caviar, while loin of venison, 'grilled perfect pink', may be served with braised lettuce, celeriac and baby leek and finished with a bitter chocolate sauce. For dessert there may be poached black figs with blackcurrants, blueberry compote and fennel ice cream, and it's all finished off with 'unhurried' and 'quietly proficient' service. The 'sommelier's selection' offers a short-cut on the 1,000-strong wine list, where France is the main focus – besides burgundy and claret, the Loire's light reds are a welcome feature – Italy is well represented, and there's reasonable New World coverage. Six house wines start at €27.

CHEF: Chris Farrell   PROPRIETOR: Bent Hoyer   OPEN: all week D only 7.15 to 9.30   CLOSED: 2 Jan to 1 Feb   MEALS: Set D €60. Light L and bistro D menus also available   SERVICE: not inc, card slips closed   CARDS: Amex, Diners, MasterCard, Visa   DETAILS: 120 seats. Private parties: 120 main room, 2 to 20 private rooms. Car park. Vegetarian meals. Children's helpings. No cigars/pipes in restaurant. Wheelchair access (also WC). Music. No mobile phones   ACCOMMODATION: 61 rooms, all with bath/shower. TV. Phone. Room only €210 to €380. Rooms for disabled. Baby facilities. Swimming pool. Fishing

## LISDOONVARNA  Co Clare                                      map 16

# ▲ Sheedy's ⁵⚹

Lisdoonvarna
TEL: (065) 707 4026   FAX: (065) 707 4555
EMAIL: enquiries@sheedyscountryhouse.com                    MODERN IRISH
WEBSITE: www.sheedyscountryhouse.com                        €47–€80

Set in a Georgian house in the centre of a small town, the restaurant of this 'superb small hotel' brings together a fusion of decorative styles, setting off original features, such as fireplaces, with modern fittings and colour schemes, purple and terracotta among them. Local ingredients give an Irish flavour to John Sheedy's cooking, though a broad range of influences informs his style: try grilled St Tola goats' cheese on roasted pumpkin with home-made crab apple jelly and pine kernels for a starter, or perhaps well-presented steamed asparagus wrapped in smoked salmon, served with a thin hollandaise. Fish dishes come in for special praise: 'perfectly seared' salmon fillet in a buttery stew of peas and baby onions, or 'thick, moist' fillet of hake with tapénade crust and provençale vegetables. Meat eaters might opt for slow-roasted duck breast with a confit of its leg, potato stuffing and herb gravy, or simply grilled ribeye with baked mushrooms and Café de Paris sauce. A fairly short, international wine list offers fair value, prices starting at €18.

CHEF: John Sheedy   PROPRIETORS: John and Martina Sheedy   OPEN: all week D only 6.45 to 8.30   CLOSED: 15 Oct to 15 Mar   MEALS: alc (main courses €18 to €32). Bar menu available D   SERVICE: not inc, card slips closed   CARDS: Amex, MasterCard, Visa   DETAILS: 28 seats. Private parties: 28 main room. Car park. Vegetarian meals. Children's helpings. No children under 10 after 7.30pm. No smoking in dining room. Wheelchair access (also WC). Music. No mobile phones   ACCOMMODATION: 11 rooms, all with bath/shower. TV. Phone. B&B €60 to €80. Rooms for disabled

## MALLOW  Co Cork                                               map 16

# ▲ Longueville House 🍴

Mallow
TEL: (022) 47156   FAX: (022) 47459
EMAIL: info@longuevillehouse.ie
WEBSITE: www.longuevillehouse.ie
3m W of Mallow on N72 Killarney road turn right          MODERN IRISH/FRENCH
on to Ballyclough road                                            €64–€77

Built in 1720, with extra wings and a conservatory added in the nineteenth century, Longueville is a vision of Georgian grandeur to delight the eye. The River Blackwater runs through the property and supplies salmon and trout to the kitchens, and the estate also provides lamb – all of which is grist to William O'Callaghan's industrious mill. In the Presidents' Restaurant, beneath portraits of Irish presidents gone by, the set dinner may include the likes of ballottine of wild pigeon with mushrooms and foie gras dressed in Black Muscat and white currants, or roast tuna with oregano, lemon and olive oil, or that lamb, herb-crusted and roasted on the bone, served with barley risotto. Finish perhaps with tropical fruit mousse and a berry coulis. Wines are drawn largely from classical and southern France, with forays further afield, and house vins de pays are €22.

CHEF: William O'Callaghan   PROPRIETORS: the O'Callaghan family   OPEN: all week D only 6.30 to 9.30   CLOSED: mid-Dec to early Mar   MEALS: Set D €47. Tasting menu €61 (whole table). Bar menu also available to 5pm   SERVICE: not inc, card slips closed   CARDS: Amex, Diners, MasterCard, Visa   DETAILS: 70 seats. Private parties: 40 main room, 14 to 18 private rooms. Car park. Vegetarian meals. Children's helpings. No smoking in dining room. Wheelchair access (also men's WC). Occasional music. No mobile phones   ACCOMMODATION: 21 rooms, all with bath/shower. TV. Phone. B&B €135 to €336. Baby facilities. Fishing

## NEWPORT  Co Mayo                                              map 16

# ▲ Newport House 🍾 🍴

Newport
TEL: (098) 41222   FAX: (098) 41613
EMAIL: info@newporthouse.ie                                     IRISH/FRENCH
WEBSITE: www.newporthouse.ie                                     €66–€101

This historic Georgian country house has its own salmon fishing and, inevitably, some of the catch appears on the dinner menu: perhaps in a terrine with sole and monkfish with a white wine, tomato and chive butter sauce, or maybe smoked in-house and served au naturel. Dinner is six courses, taking in soup or sorbet, salad after the main course, and Irish farmhouse cheeses before dessert. The cooking may not be innovative, but focuses on top-quality materials available locally: roast rack of lamb with sauce paloise, Connemara scallops with creamed leeks and Vermouth sauce, and poached turbot fillet with julienne vegetables. The wine list majors on classic France, taking in mature vintages of top red Bordeaux dating back to 1966 (plus a lone wine from the fabled 1961 vintage). Given the age of many of these bottles and the fact that service is included, prices are quite fair, although those on the lookout for bargain bottles would do well to look at the range from Australia, or house French, priced at €24.

CHEF: John Gavin   PROPRIETORS: Thelma and Kieran Thompson   OPEN: all week D only 7 to 9.30
CLOSED: 8 Oct to 18 Mar   MEALS: Set D €46   SERVICE: not inc, card slips closed   CARDS: Amex,
Diners, MasterCard, Visa   DETAILS: 35 seats. Private parties: 12 main room. Car park. Children's
helpings. No smoking in dining room. No music. No mobile phones   ACCOMMODATION: 18 rooms,
all with bath/shower. Phone. B&B €117 to €252. Baby facilities. Fishing

## OUGHTERARD  Co Galway                                                                 map 16

# ▲ Currarevagh House ⁵✳

Oughterard, Connemara
TEL: (091) 552312   FAX: (091) 552731
EMAIL: currarevagh@ireland.com
WEBSITE: www.currarevagh.com
4m NW of Oughterard on Hill of Doon lakeshore        IRISH COUNTRY-HOUSE
road                                                                         €43–€52

This Victorian house is set deep in the Connemara countryside, by the shore of
Loch Corrib. Harry and June Hodgson are untroubled by the whims of fashion,
sticking to what they know and trust: old-fashioned dinner-party cooking, five-
course no-choice menus, everyone sitting down to eat together at 8pm. A typical
day's menu might open with carrot and cumin soup, followed by a fish course,
often featuring Corrib trout, perhaps as a mousseline with green peppercorn
sauce. Then comes a main course of roast leg of lamb with mint sauce, stuffed
potatoes, chicory and leeks, or perhaps duck breast with game sauce, Anna
potatoes and spinach. Meals are rounded off with dessert of grilled fruits with
cider sabayon, or baked Alaska, then Irish cheeses. French classics dominate the
wine list, though it opens with a pair of house Chileans at €15.

CHEFS: June and Henry Hodgson   PROPRIETORS: Harry and June Hodgson   OPEN: all week D
only 8pm (1 sitting)   CLOSED: 20 Oct to Mar   MEALS: Set D €32   SERVICE: 10%, card slips closed
CARDS: MasterCard, Visa   DETAILS: 30 seats. Private parties: 15 main room. Car park. Children's
helpings. No non-resident children under 6. No smoking in dining room. No music. No mobile
phones   ACCOMMODATION: 15 rooms, all with bath/shower. B&B €80 to €188. Fishing

## RATHMULLAN  Co Donegal                                                                map 16

# ▲ Rathmullan House ⁵✳                              NEW ENTRY

Rathmullan
TEL: (074) 58188   FAX: (074) 58200
EMAIL: info@rathmullanhouse                                          MODERN IRISH
WEBSITE: www.rathmullanhouse.com                                      €57–€68

The Wheeler family have run this country-house hotel on Lough Swilly for 40
years. There's a well-kept garden outside, a plethora of antiques inside, and a
Bedouin-style dining-room where diners may enjoy the best local produce,
including organic fruit and vegetables from the hotel's walled garden. Seamus
Douglas cooks up some bright, modern dishes such as white pudding with a
Cashel Blue tartlet and mustard sauce, followed by, say, baked brill with pea
purée, Parma ham and lemon butter. Rathmullan lamb, particularly well
reported, may come as a roast loin with boulangère potatoes, cabbage, roast
garlic and redcurrant sauce. The mid-meal sorbet – a memorable gooseberry

version at a spring dinner – is also singled out. Finish with chocolate marquise, or hot banana and coconut pudding with caramel sauce. A good wine list starting at €18.50 covers the conventional European and New World bases, and is supplemented by a 'Connoisseurs' Corner' list of classy/pricey bottles.

CHEF: Seamus Douglas   PROPRIETORS: the Wheeler family   OPEN: all week D only 7.30 to 8.45
CLOSED: 23 to 26 Dec, Jan to 14 Feb   MEALS: Set D €42.50. Bar/light L menu also available
SERVICE: 10%, card slips closed   CARDS: Amex, Diners, MasterCard, Visa   DETAILS: 70 seats.
Private parties: 100 main room. Car park. Vegetarian meals. Children's helpings. No smoking in
dining room. No music. No mobile phones   ACCOMMODATION: 24 rooms, all with bath/shower.
TV. Phone. B&B €80 to €110. Rooms for disabled. Baby facilities. Swimming pool (£5)

## SHANAGARRY  Co Cork                                              map 16

## ▲ Ballymaloe House

Shanagarry, Midleton
TEL: (021) 4652531   FAX: (021) 4652021
EMAIL: res@ballymaloe.ie
WEBSITE: www.ballymaloe.com                                  IRISH/INTERNATIONAL
2m outside Cloyne on Ballycotton road                            €46–€85

Despite being a fairly large-scale operation, there is a pleasing degree of intimacy to this place, engendered by the Allen family's warm-hearted approach. It is represented not least in the care that goes in to growing their own produce in their gardens and in sourcing the finest fish from Ballycotton. The modern country-house style of cooking is another attraction, bringing together classical techniques and understanding with some gently innovative ideas: chilled avocado soup with sweet pepper and coriander salsa, for example, or roast haunch of peppered venison with horseradish cream and roast Jerusalem artichokes. A lengthy, France-orientated wine list offers fair value, opening with house wines from €19.

CHEF: Rory O'Connell   PROPRIETORS: the Allen family   OPEN: all week L 1pm (1 sitting), 7 to 9.30
CLOSED: 23 to 28 Dec   MEALS: Set L €25 to €32, Set D €55   SERVICE: not inc, card slips closed
CARDS: Amex, Diners, MasterCard, Switch, Visa   DETAILS: 120 seats. Private parties: 20 to 50
private rooms. Car park. Vegetarian meals. Children's helpings. No children under 7 at D. No
music. No mobile phones   ACCOMMODATION: 34 rooms, all with bath/shower. Phone. B&B €105
to €260. Swimming pool

## WATERFORD  Co Waterford                                         map 16

## Dwyers £

8 Mary Street, Waterford
TEL: (051) 877478   FAX: (051) 877480
EMAIL: info@dwyersrestaurant.com                          FRENCH-MODERN IRISH
WEBSITE: www.dwyersrestaurant.com                              €37–€70

The building that houses Martin Dwyer's long-running restaurant was once a police barracks, but is now the scene of some very decent cooking where some modern sensibilities have recently crept in. This might translate into a starter of turkey and pheasant sausage with satay sauce, or one of lettuce and scallion soup. Main courses typically include one fish, one meat and one vegetarian option: the fish will depend on what is available at nightly auctions, but might be done up with crisp olive oil crumb and served with anchovy-flavoured mayonnaise. Otherwise, there might champ potato cakes with toasted Knockalara cheese and peperonata. The short wine list starts at €14.

CHEFS: Martin Dwyer and Declan Coughlan   PROPRIETORS: Martin and Sile Dwyer   OPEN: Mon to Sat D 6 to 10   CLOSED: 1 week Christmas   MEALS: alc (main courses €16.50 to €25.50). Set D 6 to 7 €25   SERVICE: not inc   CARDS: Amex, Diners, MasterCard, Visa   DETAILS: 32 seats. Private parties: 24 main room, 4 to 8 private rooms. Vegetarian meals. Children's helpings. No-smoking area. Wheelchair access (also WC). Music  £5

## WEXFORD  Co Wexford                                            map 16

# La Riva                                          NEW ENTRY

Crescent Quay, Wexford
TEL/FAX: (053) 24330                           MODERN EUROPEAN/IRISH
EMAIL: warrengillen@aol.ie                              €31–€69

Go at lunchtime or on a summer's evening to admire the views over the Slaney estuary from the Georgian windows of this 'pleasant, Mediterranean-style, first-floor restaurant'. Warren Gillen has given the cooking a blast of modern fusion, with special menus for the Wexford Opera Festival producing deep-fried oysters and zucchini with paprika aïoli, and five-spice monkfish with lemon and orange couscous and chilli jam. The kitchen is also at home with European tradition: witness a warm salad of Mediterranean vegetables, or a classy risotto of oyster mushrooms, spinach, tarragon and mascarpone. To finish, apple and pecan crumble is a 'concentrated affair', set off with rich vanilla ice cream. Service is cheerful, and prices on the short and sharp wine list start at €15.20.

CHEF/PROPRIETOR: Warren Gillen   OPEN: L June to Sept, Oct and Dec, all week 12.30 to 2.30, D all week 6 (5.30 June to Sept) to 10 (11 Sat, 1am during Festival)   MEALS: alc (main courses €10 to €24)   SERVICE: 10%   CARDS: MasterCard, Visa   DETAILS: 50 seats. Private parties: 40 main room. Vegetarian meals. Children's helpings. No children under 6 after 8pm. Music. No mobile phones. Air-conditioned

# Round-ups

Looking for a suitable place to eat can be a lottery, especially if you are travelling around the country with no set plans in mind. The Round-up section is intended to provide some interesting gastronomic possibilities, whether you find yourself in an unfamiliar city centre or a rural outpost. Pubs are becoming increasingly valuable as sources of high-quality food, but the listings below also include modest family-run enterprises in country towns, racy café/bars and ethnic restaurants in big cities, and a sprinkling of hotel dining rooms in all parts of the land. Dip into this section and you are almost bound to find somewhere that suits your needs and pocket. Entries are based mainly on readers' recommendations, supported where appropriate by inspectors' reports. Sometimes restaurants appear in the Round-ups instead of the main entry section because seasonal closures or weekly openings limit their usefulness, or because late changes in the kitchen or to ownership have occurred, or because feedback this year has been thin on the ground. Reports on these are especially welcome, as they help to broaden our coverage of good eating places in Britain. Round-up entries (outside London) are arranged alphabetically by locality within England, Scotland, Wales, Channel Islands and Northern Ireland.

## England

● **ALDEBURGH** (Suffolk)
*Café 152*   152 High Street, (01728) 454152. 'A much loved and frequented restaurant,' confirmed a local fan of this bright and breezy seaside café-cum-deli. The kitchen makes ample use of local fish for Aldeburgh crab gratin with chilli and lemon, lobster with samphire and mayonnaise, and well-reported scallops with crispy leeks. Alternatively, opt for something meaty like potted duck with spiced oranges (£5.25) or best end of lamb with pea purée (£12.25). Desserts are many and varied, from rhubarb crumble tart to lime mousse (£3.95). Sit outside when the weather allows. Wines are a keenly chosen bunch from Adnams; prices start at £9.95. Closed Tue.

● **AMERSHAM** (Buckinghamshire)
*Gilbey's*   1 Market Square, (01494) 727242. A garden for al fresco meals is a bonus at this popular wine bar/restaurant with another branch in Ealing (see London Round-ups). The efficient staff help create the 'pleasant ambience'. Well-reported dishes have included smoked haddock and sorrel fishcakes, Caesar salad with bacon, calf's liver with caramelised onions, and moist guinea fowl with parsnip and celeriac mousse. Lunchtime set menus are good value £10.95 (2 courses). Much of Gilbey's fame rests on the fact that the owners are importers of French wines, so many are cheaper than you might find elsewhere: house wines start at £8.25. Open all week.

*Kings Arms*   30 High Street, (01494) 726333. John Jennison's venerable timbered inn remains a notable landmark in Old Amersham. Beams abound in the dining room, although the kitchen is firmly in touch with today's trends, making much use of wasabi, couscous and pancetta. Typical dishes from the carte (main courses £13–£16) might include breast of duck with strawberry and green peppercorn sauce, or brochette of salmon and monkfish with tomato and ginger dressing, before Mascarpone cheesecake. Some simpler ideas appear on the set menus (£15.50 L, £19 D). Wines are grouped by style and the list kicks off with a 16-strong 'Cellar Selection'; prices begin at £11.90. Closed all day Mon, and Sun D.

● **BARNARD CASTLE** (Co Durham)
*Blagraves House* 30 The Bank, (01833)
637668. Reputedly the oldest house in the
town, this 'most beautiful' Grade I listed
dwelling continues to do sterling service as
a family-run restaurant. The location may
be historic, but the owners' cooking has a
modern slant and reporters are eager to
sing its praises: marinated anchovies on
crostini, ragoût of seafood with tapénade
sauce, and guinea fowl stuffed with apples
have all been applauded, while the star
dessert seems to be home-made 'cinder
toffee' ice cream. Main courses £10 to £16,
and set D Mon to Fri £15.95. Service is
'swift, welcoming and efficient', and the
60-strong wine list opens with six by the
glass; house wine is £10.25. Open Tue to
Sat D.

● **BARTON UPON HUMBER** (North
Lincolnshire)
*Elio's* 11 Market Place, (01652) 635147.
Elio Grossi has been running this reliable
trattoria since 1983, and it pleases the
punters with bread and tomato soup ('a
tasty bargain'), pizzas, pastas and old
faithfuls like bistecca alla pizzaiola.
However, the real gems are the 'brilliant'
fish specials, perhaps poached halibut
Mornay, or chargrilled tuna steak with
roast peppers. Sweets get mixed reports,
although Italian chocolate trifle and
cheesecake have been enjoyed.
Affordable Italian wines, with house red
and white at £9.25 a litre. Main courses
£7–£21.50, plus a set price lunch and early
evening menu. Accommodation
available. Open Tue to Fri L, and Mon to
Sat D.

● **BATH** (Bath & N. E. Somerset)
*Dukes Hotel* Great Pulteney Street,
(01225) 787960. The hotel is a swish
Grade I, Palladian-style mansion on to
which has been tacked Fitzroy's Brasserie;
a busy room full of elephant logos and
artefacts as well as prints of hippos and
zebras. Menus offer salads, pasta and
risottos alongside stir-fried mussels with
chilli, coconut and coriander; chargrilled
lamb neck fillet with pea purée; and
honey-glazed duck with truffled mash.
Desserts could range from passion-fruit

and Pimm's cheesecake to hot chocolate
cup with fresh raspberries. Main courses
£12.50–£14.50. France dominates the
wine list, which includes a handful of
house selections from £14 a bottle (£3.50 a
glass). Open all week.

*Firehouse Rotisserie* 2 John Street,
(01225) 482070. Crowds pack into this
lively joint for sharp cooking with a
Californian accent. The brick-fired oven
delivers pizzas (£9.95) with toppings such
as spicy chicken with avocado, salsa fresca,
coriander and sour cream, while the
rotisserie and grill do their work on Pacific
crab and smoked salmon cakes (£11.95),
and five-spice glazed duck with seared
Szechuan pak choi, ginger, scallions and
toasted sesame seeds ('the best duck dish
I've had in years', admitted a regular). The
wine list is 'good value and imaginative'.
Open Mon to Sat. There is a branch in
Anchor Square, Bristol, tel. (0117) 9157
323.

*Woods* 9–13 Alfred Street, (01225)
314812. Two-course, fixed-price lunches
are the real bargain at this long-standing
brasserie opposite the Assembly Rooms.
For £9.50 you can enjoy, say, marinated
fillet of mackerel with pickled vegetables,
followed by lamb casserole with roasted
garlic and rosemary. Daily specials add
some spice to the carte: sauté of tiger
prawns and scallops with chilli, lemon
grass and saffron; and confit of duck on
braised Puy lentils with thyme and
pancetta, for example. Main courses
£9.50–£18. Ten wines by the glass are
worth checking out on the fairly priced,
40-strong list. Open all week.

● **BIRKENHEAD** (Merseyside)
*The Station* 24–28 Hamilton Street,
(0151) 647 1047. Billed as an organic
bakery, food store and deli with a
restaurant and five bedrooms, this
enterprising venture, adjacent to
Hamilton Square station, aims to please all
comers. At lunchtime it functions as a
café/brasserie, but puts on its glad rags in
the evening, when customers can sample
Thai fishcakes with chilli jam and crème
fraîche, rack of lamb with an olive crust,
followed by chocolate fondant with

banana ice cream. Main courses £6.50–£12. The wine list offers plenty of sound drinking under £20: house wines are £12 (£2.85 a glass). Closed Sun D.

● **BIRMINGHAM** (West Midlands)

*Birmingham Marriot, West 12* 12 Hagley Road, Five Ways, (0121) 452 1144. The sumptuous restaurant in this swish hotel was about to be re-launched as the Guide went to press. What was once the Sir Edward Elgar is now called West 12, while Langtry's Brasserie is scheduled to become the bar. New chef Nigel Parnaby, from the Randolph Hotel in Oxford, was about to take charge of the kitchen, but no menus or wine list were available before our deadline. Reports on the new regime, please. Open all week.

*Cafe Ikon* Ikon Gallery, 1 Oozells Square, Brindleyplace, (0121) 248 3226. On the ground floor of the Ikon Gallery, this café makes one of the best lunchtime destinations in the city. The décor suits the airy modern surroundings and the menu focuses on tapas and their larger cousins, raciones. Nibbles range from toasted hazelnuts with paprika to Manchego cheese with quince paste, while more substantial offerings come in the shape of higado de pollo al jerez (chicken livers with capers, sage, sherry and cream), or sardines al ajillo (grilled with garlic and lemon). There are also five versions of paella and a few desserts such as traditional baked custard. Drink Spanish wines, beers or sherries. Closed all day Mon and Sun D.

*Denial* 120–122 Wharfside Street, (0121) 643 3080. In a prime site by the canal, right next to The Mailbox (Birmingham's swanky new designer shopping complex), this new kid on the block is already beginning to make waves. Forget the jokey name ('Hi, I'm in Denial!'), this place looks the part, and the kitchen has serious intentions. The cooking may not be mould-breaking, but it knows what it's about: starters of red snapper escabeche, or smoked quail salad with Cabernet Sauvignon dressing, might precede baby halibut with crushed lemon confit potato and fennel nage, or goats' cheese and leek

risotto, while desserts could take in frozen tarragon mousse with marinated strawberries. Main courses £14.95, plus weekend brunch and bar snacks. Well-chosen wines from £10. More reports, please. Closed Sun D.

*Hyatt Regency Hotel, Court Café* 2 Bridge Street, (0121) 643 1234. This towering glass monolith stands within walking distance of the International Convention Centre and Symphony Hall and does its work as a business hotel. The Court Café in the foyer is a useful venue for 'snacking': salads and pasta are light options (£4.50–£11). Otherwise go for something more substantial like chargrilled peppered tuna with oriental noodles (£14), or pot-roast chicken with creamed leeks and fondant potatoes (£12.50). Coconut brûlée with star anise ice cream (£5) is a typical dessert. A globetrotting wine list offers plenty by the glass although mark-ups may seem steep. Open all week.

*Maharaja* 23–25 Hurst Street, (0121) 622 2641. 'One of the most enduring and endearing Indian restaurants in central Birmingham,' commented a reporter about this old-stager close to the Hippodrome. The décor has been given a makeover but not much changes on the short menu, which majors in familiar Punjabi/Muglai dishes. Tandooris are a feature, and there's generally a daily special, as well as the likes of chicken sagwala with spinach (£7.20), and lamb pasanda (£7.20). Decent vegetables include lotus roots with peas (£4.95). Service is keen and the short wine list has house selections at £8.25. Closed Sun.

*San Carlo* 4 Temple Street, (0121) 633 0251. Up a side street a few minutes' walk from New Street station, this modern-looking Italian continues to pack in the crowds. Scores of pizzas and pastas of every description dominate the long menu, and there are also plenty of old faithfuls in the shape of veal Marsala, bistecca alla Romana, and calf's liver with sage. Added to this are antipasti aplenty, bruschettas and a blackboard focusing on well-handled fish specials. Main courses £5–£13. Service is effusively Italian and there are some decent regional wines to choose from. Open noon to 11pm all week.

**Thai Edge** 7 Oozells Square, (0121) 643 3993. A cool, very contemporary and smart venue in a square crowded with gastronomic competition. Acres of white space are broken up by wall-to-ceiling glass panels and huge structures of interwoven wood; otherwise the colour purple prevails. Two-course 'express' lunches (£9.90) live up to their name, and the 160-dish menu covers a lot of ground, from chicken soup with bean curd, glass noodles and seaweed (£5), to rice with minced pork and snake beans (£6.50). In between are most of the staples of the Thai repertoire, including fishcakes, green papaya salad (£7.50), Mussaman curry (£10.80) and deep-fried pomfret (£15.80). Service is 'benign and gracious'. Drink Singha Thai beer or dip into the short wine list. Open all week.

**Wing Wah** The Wing Yip Centre, 278 Thimblemill Lane, Nechells, (0121) 327 7879. Quite a way out of the city and its Chinese Quarter, Wing Wah is linked to the Wing Yip Centre (of supermarket fame), and offers genuine cooking, backed up by service that scores points for pleasantness and good manners. Braised oysters with belly pork and Chinese mushrooms has been a winner, likewise shredded beef with onions and dried chilli. Soups such as shark's fin with crabmeat have been spot-on, and egg-fried rice has been pleasant enough 'to eat on its own'. Help-yourself, buffet-style lunches are served in an area adjacent to the main restaurant. Reports please. Open all week.

● **BISHOP'S STORTFORD** (Hertfordshire)
**Lemon Tree** Water Lane, (01279) 757788. Handily situated in the centre of town – with an equally useful car park – this relaxed restaurant is ideal for a quick lunch, and there's no pressure to have the full works, despite the fixed-price format (two/three courses £15.50/£19.50; main course only £11.50, starter and dessert £9.50). Start with pressed country terrine with pickled wild mushrooms, or seared squid in Indian spices before moving on to

roast cod with Puy lentils and red onion relish, or grilled calf's liver with bacon, parsnip purée and Pommery mustard sauce. Milk chocolate tart and sticky toffee pudding have been recommended desserts. 'Very good wine by the glass,' according to one reporter. Open all week, exc Sun D.

● **BISHOP'S WALTHAM** (Hampshire)
**Wine Bar** 6–8 High Street, (01489) 894476. Brick walls, brick-clad pillars and a wooden walkway round the bar characterise this modern wine bar and restaurant's separate seating areas. The emphasis is on presentation, and ingredients are from the Mediterranean. A plate of cured meats may include salami, prosciutto, bresaola and chorizo with roasted beetroot and red onion jam, but starters also include French onion soup and Thai crab cakes. Grilled ribeye steak with salad and French fries might pacify those who find crispy confit of duck with sesame oiled noodles and lemon-grass pak choi just too far out. Main courses £9–£16. A selection of 60 wines start at £10.95 for house red and white. Open all week.

● **BLACKMORE** (Essex)
**Epicurus at the Leather Bottle** The Green, (01277) 823538. Gary Witchalls gave up his post as deputy director of the Butlers Wharf Chef School, did a spell at the Millennium Dome and has now settled at this country pub/restaurant with aspirations in a busy Essex village. Bangers and mash (£7.50) caters for the traditionalists, but the menu zooms swiftly into the realms of marinated red mullet and roast pepper salad with crab mayonnaise (£5.25), and slow-cooked belly pork with mushroom dauphinoise and glazed red cabbage (£11.95). Round things off with grilled pineapple and coconut ice cream (£4.95). Service is cheerful and the short wine list does its job affordably. Open all week.

● **BLACKPOOL** (Lancashire)
**Kwizeen** 47–49 King Street, (01253) 290045. Marco Calle-Calatayud's bistro re-invented itself with 'a complete dining room makeover' early in 2002. Reports suggest that the smart décor is a great

improvement, with lots of modern stainless steel and a new suspended ceiling. Printed menus are supplemented by blackboard specials, including pheasant with chocolate and chilli sauce, or 'Snow Shoes' (huge Dover soles). Recent successes have included veal sweetbreads with red wine sauce, and lamb pie on bubble and squeak, while desserts might run to rum-roasted pineapple with mango sorbet. Main courses £10, two-course lunches £5.95. The wine list has also been re-vamped: three dozen bottles start at £9.50. Closed Sun.

● **BOUGHTON LEES** (Kent)
*Eastwell Manor* Eastwell Park, (01233) 213000. In the South-east there are few grander places than this immaculate stone pile to eat and live it up with style. Chef Giles Stonehouse left as the Guide was going to press and a successor was yet to be appointed. No doubt the cooking will continue to suit the surroundings and the wine cellar will take Bordeaux and Burgundy seriously: prices are also serious, although there are some less heavyweight bottles for more affordable drinking; house selections start at £13. Reports, please. Open all week.

● **BOURNEMOUTH** (Dorset)
*Westbeach* Pier Approach, 01202 587785. A buzzy, youthful and modern eating house that reverberates with the sights and sounds of the seaside: there are great views over the sands and it's a must for people-watching. The décor reflects the beach atmosphere and the menu offers a decent choice of modern British dishes with the emphasis on fish: roast Cornish hake with tomato, wild mushrooms and shallots, perhaps. Meaty alternatives might be sauté black pudding with chorizo and goats' cheese, or chargrilled ribeye steak, while desserts run to orange tarts with pineapple salsa. Set menu £16.95 (2 courses) to £19.95. Hard-working staff, live jazz on Thursdays and some quaffable wines from £9.95. Open all week.

● **BRIGHTON** (East Sussex)
*Moshi Moshi Sushi* Bartholomew Square, (01273) 719195. It was Moshi Moshi that introduced us to the kaiten back in 1994, and although these conveyor-belt restaurants have been springing up all around London, they are still a novelty outside the capital. Sit at tables or next to the counter and watch the colour-coded plates pass by – take whatever catches your eye. Nigiri, maki and sashimi are made with good-quality fish, while specials and 'Japanese tapas', ordered at the counter, include crispy-grilled salmon temaki, gyoza, and excellent tempura. Teriyaki unagi (eel) donburi proved a satisfying and good-value lunch for one visitor. Vegetarian options are always available. House wine is £11.50. Plate prices £1.20 to £3.50, sushi sets £5.90 to £11.50. Open all week.

● **BRISTOL** (Bristol)
*Glassboat* Welsh Back, (0117) 929 0704. Breakfast (from 7am, Mon to Fri) opens proceedings on this converted barge berthed in the historic dock overlooking Bristol's waterside developments. Lunches are fair value (starter £2.50, main £5.95), while the full evening repertoire is cosmopolitan through and through, taking in, perhaps, celeriac fries with truffle aïoli; crispy chicken suprême with vanilla risotto and chorizo; and deep-fried cinnamon ice cream with tropical fruit salsa. Main courses £12–£17. Service has been 'exemplary'. The wine list runs to 240 bins from around the world, with nine by the glass; prices from £11. Closed Sat L and all day Sun.

● **BROADWAY** (Worcestershire)
*Oliver's* High Street, (01386) 854418. Decorated with prints of, and named after, the Lord Protector, this stepsister of the Lygon Arms has forsworn oriental incursions, and its menus are now wholly European, indeed mainly British. Starters that can also be taken as main courses include crab and Gruyère tart with asparagus, baked English goats' cheese with beetroot and orange relish, and grilled mackerel with gooseberry chutney. Mains (£9.50 to £11.50), some doubling as

starters, take in Torbay sole in beer batter with tartare sauce, Cotswold sausage and mash, and slow-cooked lamb with roast potatoes. All the wines on the short list are sold by the glass from £3.25; bottle prices start at £12.50. Open all week.

● **BROCKENHURST** (Hampshire)
*Thatched Cottage* 16 Brookley Road, (01590) 623090. An eye-catching thatched roof does, indeed, grace this 400-year-old cottage deep in the New Forest. Inside, it is quaintly appointed and diners can watch their food being prepared in the open kitchen. Luxury, elaboration and florid descriptions abound on the set dinner menus, £35 to £52, which might advertise seafood sausage in a mustard cream with lentil 'confetti'; roast Quantock duck with vegetable 'bouquet', pease pudding and basil-infused duck consommé; and soufflé of rum-marinated strawberries with avocado sauce. There's an à la carte menu too. France is a big player on the upper-crust wine list, with prices starting at £12.50. Accommodation available. Closed all day Mon and Sun D.

● **BROME** (Suffolk)
*Cornwallis Country Hotel* Brome, (01379) 870326. Pass through the huge gates and up the tree-lined drive to find this 'lovely yellow slumbering Elizabethan building', which now functions as a rather grand country hotel with a restaurant and bar. In the long, dark dining room, reporters have enjoyed fashionable offerings such as crab and samphire risotto; cod, salmon and coriander fishcakes with pineapple salsa and chilli syrup; and roast fillet of salmon with bubble and squeak, cucumber and caper berry pickle. Main courses £9–£14; set menus also available. To finish, there's 'Cornwallis 1861' trifle, served in a wineglass. A list of some 160 wines includes almost 30 by the glass: prices from £11.50 a bottle. Open all week.

● **BROMFIELD** (Shropshire)
*Cookhouse* Bromfield, (01584) 856565. Clive of India was once resident in this old farmhouse, although these days it serves as a handy pit stop for travellers on the A49. The lounge bar and courtyard are useful for a reviving drink and a snack, but the best deals are to be had in the café bar (Caesar salad, smoked haddock fishcakes, pizzas and the like, around the £7 mark). Alternatively opt for the more formal restaurant if you fancy, say, king prawns with aïoli, venison with green peppercorn and raisin sauce (£14.95), or sticky toffee pudding. House wines from £9.75. Hot food is served all day at weekends, but it's drinks and cakes only in the afternoon Mon to Fri. Open all week 11 to 11.

● **BROXTON** (Cheshire)
*Frogg Manor* Nantwich Road, (01829) 782629. In 2002, John Sykes celebrated 15 years in residence at this mildly eccentric Georgian manor house. His dinner menu is priced at '30 guineas' (£31.50), although there's nothing antiquated about the globally inclined repertoire: Java seafood vol-au-vent, medallions of lamb Orleans (in red wine gravy flavoured with French lavender honey), chicken 'Charlee Chan' (poached and served with lime and apricots) or Greenland plum duck. The 70-strong wine list kicks off with three house wines at £12.95. Accommodation available. Open all week.

● **BURGH lE MARSH** (Lincolnshire)
*Windmill* 46 High Street, (01754) 810281. Standing in the shadow of the windmill that provides flour for its bread, this country restaurant is prized for its cosy atmosphere and personal touches. Fish is a good choice: Mediterranean seafood soup, and sea bass cooked in foil with tarragon, have been praised. Other promising ideas might be crispy roast duckling with Victoria plum sauce, and pigeon breast on creamed celeriac with Madeira sauce; there are also some star turns among the desserts, notably 'fluffy' brioche bread-and-butter pudding with whisky and marmalade ice cream. Main course prices (£19 to £21) include a starter and dessert, while Sun L is £13.50. Ports aplenty, and a decent list of around 70 wines from £9.95. Open Sun L and Tue to Sat D.

● **BURPHAM** (West Sussex)
*George and Dragon* Burpham, (01903) 883131. Set on the fringes of the South

Downs is this eighteenth-century inn offering light snacks in the bar and more elaborate meals in the separate restaurant. The latter might feature mille-feuille of curried mussels and spinach, then breast of corn-fed chicken with morel and foie gras farce and sauce poivrade, followed by prune and Armagnac tart with cinnamon ice cream. Set dinner menus start at £19.95 (two courses). The compact list of 30-odd wines has plenty of sound drinking for around £15 and starts at £12.50. Open Mon to Sat D.

● **BURY ST EDMUNDS** (Suffolk)
*Angel Hotel, Abbeygate Restaurant*
Angel Hill, (01284) 714000. There are views of the historic Norman gates from the windows of this traditional hotel dining room, where oil paintings hang on navy blue walls. Fixed-price menus (three courses £23.50) are reckoned to be 'pretty good value' for cooking that is modern without being radically innovative. Guinea-fowl terrine; seared monkfish with coriander, lime and garlic; and suprême of chicken with creamy wild mushroom sauce show the style. Successful desserts have included tartlet of mascarpone with warm balsamic vinegar strawberries, and prune and Armagnac ice cream. Service is not always great, but the wine list is solidly reliable. Open all week.
*Maison Bleue* 30–31 Churchgate Street, (01284) 760 623. 'A jaunty little French seafood restaurant' is how one reporter summed up this charming, quite chic place. The best advice is to go for the lunchtime plat du jour (£7.95) or one of several set menus (£9.95–£19.95). Dishes range from 'moules poulettes', via poached salmon with coriander hollandaise, to grilled monkfish with mash and basil sauce; meat eaters might prefer foie gras with roasted fig, or lamb shank in red wine. Desserts could include honey and saffron parfait. The affordable wine list starts with house French at £9.95. Closed all day Mon and Sun.
*Priory Hotel, Garden Restaurant*
Tollgate, (01284) 766181. The Garden Restaurant makes a comfortable place to eat in this impressive Georgian building

behind a high flint wall. Fixed-price menus (lunch: two/three courses £15.50/£19.95; dinner: three courses £24.95) deliver classic hotel cooking in the shape of fillet of red mullet with cucumber 'spaghetti' and plum sauce; braised lamb shank with spring onion mash and redcurrant jus; and seared salmon with sun-blush tomato couscous and dill cream. The line-up of desserts might feature treacle tart with vanilla ice cream or milk chocolate and pecan nut terrine. House wines are £12.50 a bottle (£2.25/£4.50 a glass).

● **BUXTON** (Derbyshire)
*Columbine* 7 Hall Bank, (01298) 78752. A converted Georgian terraced house on two floors is the setting for Steve and Kim McNally's relaxed restaurant-with-cellars. Local produce shows up well in best end of Derbyshire lamb with rosemary and garlic gravy (£11.65), and on the creditable cheeseboard; other attractions are Cullen skink; salad of crispy 'picked' duck with oranges, spring onions and plum dressing; and free-range chicken breast stuffed with banana and air-dried ham with curried coconut cream sauce (£10.85); vegetarians have their own menu. Finish with pear and almond tart or stem ginger ice cream. House Duboeuf is £7.95. Open Mon to Sat D, Thur to Fri L June to July; closed Tue D Nov to April.

● **CAMBRIDGE** (Cambridgeshire)
*Loch Fyne* The Little Rose, 37 Trumpington Street, (01223) 362433. In a converted pub opposite the Fitzwilliam Museum, this East Anglian branch of the burgeoning Loch Fyne chain (see main entry Cairndow, Scotland) is a welcoming place with pleasing décor and friendly service. Fish soup (£3.95), gravadlax (£5.95/£8.95) and whole grilled lemon sole have been favourably reported, but the menu also features pots of mussels (£8.45), langoustine salad, and seared tuna on a bed of chilled noodles with chilli dressing (£12.95), not to mention oysters every which way. Grilled pork and herb sausages are one of the few carnivorous alternatives, and you can finish with, say,

lemon posset. Affordable, fish-friendly wines from £9.95. Open all week.

**Sala Thong** 35 Newnham Road, (01223) 323178. The river, as seen from the restaurant's chauffeured punt, offers more visual pleasures than the interior décor, and the menu has few surprises for carnivores. But vegetarians have a wide choice, including soups such as bamboo shoot and shiitake mushroom, or hot-and-sour with oyster and button mushrooms. Other starters include mung bean toast, or vegetarian spring rolls, followed perhaps by a lentil or vegetable curry (£6–£8), or a stir-fry of tofu with vegetables or with chilli and basil. Vegetarian spicy salad, tempura, pad Thai and fried rice complete the picture, and the two house wines (the whole list) are £7.95. Closed all day Mon.

● **CHEAM** (Surrey)

**Bay Tree** 22 Ewell Road, (020) 8643 8838. Michael and Gill Andrews do just about everything in this attractive restaurant, which was formerly a shop. The cooking might be described as Mediterranean with additions, offering gazpacho with coriander yoghurt dressing (£5), pan-fried salmon fillet with lime polenta chips, herb salad and chilli mayonnaise (£8), and rump of lamb with pesto mash and garlic-roasted aubergine (£12.75). Menus change regularly, as does the modest wine list (bottles from £12 to £22.50). Open Tue, Fri and Sun L, and Tue to Sat D.

● **CHICHELEY** (Buckinghamshire)

**Chester Arms** Chicheley, (01234) 391214. Motorists seeking an alternative to Newport Pagnell services on the nearby M1 could do worse than make a detour to this handsome, rural pub. It offers a friendly welcome, and simple food at fair prices (main courses £9.25–£15.20), with fish and beef at the top of the list: chargrilled sea bream perhaps, or sirloin steak with a peppercorn sauce. Start with an impeccably fresh crab salad (£5.50), and finish with a fine Bakewell tart (£3.25). Portions are generous, and a roving wine list starts with three house wines at £10.40.

● **CHICHESTER** (West Sussex)

**Comme Ça** 67 Broyle Road, (01243) 788724. Décor and menus at this popular former pub are resolutely old-style French. Le saumon fumé comes with whisky sauce; the tartelette is à la mascarpone et au crabe from Selsey; sole is Douvres not Dover. Prices, however, are in pounds not euros (main courses £11.85–£12.95). Unusual salads might include chicory with blue cheese and pecan nuts, and desserts take in 'fine, juicy' summer pudding and mint chocolate ice cream in a brandy-snap basket. Wines are decently priced, with some interesting half-bottles and a few New World representatives. Closed Sun D and Mon.

● **CLIFFORD'S MESNE** (Gloucestershire)

**Yew Tree Inn** Clifford's Mesne, (01531) 820719. Set on a hillside in lovely country close to the Forest of Dean, this converted sixteenth-century cider house is now a family-run pub/restaurant. Anna Hackett looks after front-of-house, while husband Paul heads the kitchen. Home-grown and local produce are used to good effect in ambitious-sounding dishes such as tartare of crab, smoked salmon prawns and crème fraîche, and loin of Old Spot pork with prune stuffing and Pommery mustard cream. Home-baked breads are praised, while desserts could feature rich chocolate tart with orange mousseline. Main courses £11–£15. A well-chosen slate of around 80 wines (from £10.50), plus a 'private cellar', includes 16 by the glass from £2.50. Accommodation available. Closed Sun D and Mon.

● **CONSTANTINE** (Cornwall)

**Trengilly Wartha** Nancenoy, (01326) 340332. The remote setting in deepest Cornwall is irresistible, but you may need to check directions with the owners. This highly popular pub/restaurant boasts a huge list of some 250 enthusiastically chosen wines from just about every corner of the globe, along with real ales and a prodigious choice of malt whiskies. The cooking also takes a world view of things, offering ceviche, three-cheese ravioli with plum tomato and herb compote, and salmon fillet with spiced crab wrapped in filo with lemon-grass butter sauce, followed by nectarine tarte Tatin and West Country cheeses. Set menus £21.50 (2 courses) to £27. Accommodation available. Open all week.

● **CROUCH** (Kent)

*Chequers Inn* Basted Lane, (01732) 884829. Take a detour south of the A25 to find the tiny hamlet of Crouch and its white-painted local pub – which seems quite modern, with its pine floors and large 3D paintings on lime-green walls. The kitchen delivers upmarket pub dishes along the lines of smoked haddock fritters with spring onion and caper mayonnaise (£5.50), grilled monkfish with mustard mash and Dijon cream sauce (£13.95), and ribeye steak with horseradish dauphinoise, ratatouille stuffed mushroom and red wine jus (£14.50). Grand Marnier crème brûlée (£4.25) is a typical dessert. Service runs at top speed and there are few wines to choose from. Open Tue to Sat L and D, Sun noon to 4pm.

● **DARTMOUTH** (Devon)

*Hooked* 5 Higher Street, (01803) 832022. Fish, the whole fish and nothing but the fish is what to expect in this 'fabulous' looking medieval building, which has been neatly converted into a relaxed restaurant. Terracotta walls are bedecked with seafaring prints and there are piscine ceramics dotted around the room. Daily supplies of seafood are used for such dishes as chilled English pea soup with smoked trout and horseradish dumpling with a Parmesan lid (that's one dish), and pesto roasted hake, chorizo crisp, paella risotto, pea velouté and saffron tomato sauce (that's another). Organic vegetables are cooked to a tee. Finish with, say, fresh fruits in Chambery syrup with home-made sorbets. Open Tue to Sat L, Mon to Sat D.

● **DENMEAD** (Hampshire)

*Barnard's* Hambledon Road, (023) 9225 7788. 'Competent, straightforward cooking with good ingredients' is what you can expect at David and Sandie Barnard's restaurant in a parade of shops.

Menus change regularly, and dinner might kick off with rillettes of duck confit or tartare of tuna before roast guinea fowl with caramelised lime sauce or pea and mint risotto with battered spicy courgettes, while desserts could include peach Alaska or baked white chocolate cheesecake. Some simpler ideas, like stir-fried chicken with sweet-and-sour sauce, appear at lunchtime. Main courses L £7 to £7.50, and D £11.50 to £15. The short, global wine list kicks off with Australian house selections at £11. Open Tue to Fri L and Tue to Sat D.

● **DODDISCOMBSLEIGH** (Devon)

*Nobody Inn* Doddiscombsleigh, (01647) 252394. An idyllic setting in a quiet Devon valley draws punters to this renowned and archetypal country pub. Bar food is robust home-cooking: trout and horseradish pâté, steak and kidney pudding, and rhubarb crumble. Moving up a gear, the restaurant menu promises wild mushroom risotto, quail stuffed with rice and apricots (£8.90), and herb-crusted marlin (£9.40). The breathtaking selection of West Country cheeses continues to grow, as does the monumental 800-strong wine list which has something for all pockets (prices start at £7); 'top notch' real ales, too. Accommodation available. Open all week (restaurant Tue to Sat D only).

● **EMSWORTH** (Hampshire)

*Fat Olives* 30 South Street, (01243) 377914. Friendly, straightforward restaurant in a former fisherman's cottage close to the shore. Evening à la carte starters might include confit duck salad with cashew nuts and honey dressing (£5.25); in main dishes, pork fillet comes with black pudding mousse (£12.95); John Dory with black olive potato cake and red pepper coulis (£13.50). This lively imagination extends to desserts such as pecan nut, maple syrup and date pie with vanilla sauce (£4.95); while original twists in the simpler lunch menu (one to three courses, £9.50–£15.50) might include griddled aubergine, fennel and pesto salad, or rabbit rillettes with redcurrant sauce. Closed Sun and Mon.

● **EVERSHOT** (Dorset)
*Acorn Inn* Fore Street, (01935) 83228.
Renowned as 'The Sow and Acorn' in
Thomas Hardy's *Tess of the d'Urbervilles*,
this sixteenth-century pub wears its
beams and oak panelling well. It is under
the same ownership as the Fox Inn,
Corscombe (see England, main entry) and
the culinary approach is similar. Fish from
West Bay might appear as Parmesan-
crusted sea bass with tomato and juniper
sauce, game from a nearby estate is
casseroled (£10.85), while duck breast is
served on stir-fried courgettes with
raspberry vinaigrette (£14.50). Conclude
with lemon syllabub or crème brûlée.
Decent beers and wines; house wines from
£10.50. Accommodation available. Open
all week.

● **EVESHAM** (Worcestershire)
*Evesham Hotel* Coopers Lane, (01386)
765566. John Jenkinson and family have
been running the show at this
'delightfully idiosyncratic' hotel for some
37 years and show no signs of calling it a
day. The cooking revolves around menus
that are full of quirky names and wordy
descriptions, but reporters like the results.
One satisfactory meal took in Fasganeoin
Toast (chicken livers with cashew-nut
sauce and orange segments), and pan-
fried pork with sliced apple and a host of
vegetables, before Turkish flan (crème
caramel with burnt sugar sauce). Main
courses £10–£18.50. The drinks list is a
vast catalogue of 700 wines ('housed in
five photo albums') and specialist
beverages. Accommodation available.
Open all week for L and D.

*Riverside* The Parks, (01386) 446200.
Very much a home-from-home, this
family-run hotel boasts a dreamy setting
alongside the banks of the Avon in
Evesham Abbey's historic Deer Park.
'Particularly good' bar meals are served on
the terrace (weather permitting),
otherwise Rosemary Willmott works to an
extensive fixed-price menu (L £19.95, D
£29.95) with an international flavour.
Stuffed vine leaves with tomato sauce or
Thai-spiced mussels might precede
chargrilled goose breast on potato and leek

mash, or roast fillet of sea bream with
wilted spinach. Finish with organic coffee
ice cream or hot baked banana. The 60-
strong wine list includes six by the glass.
Closed all day Mon and Sun D.

● **EXETER** (Devon)
*Carved Angel Café* 21A Cathedral Yard,
(01392) 210303. Breakfast, light lunches
and dinners make this café facing the
Cathedral green a useful destination for
informal eating in the city. Specials such as
tempura prawns with sweet chilli sauce or
loin of pork with grain mustard sauce flesh
out the repertoire, which also takes in
goats' cheese pithiviers, grilled sea bass
with sweet-and-sour leeks, and pan-fried
calf's liver with mash and smoked bacon
sauce. Chocolate mille-feuille and
pannacotta with fresh raspberries are
typical desserts. Main courses £5–£7 L,
£9–£13 D; house wine £9.95. Related to
the Carved Angel in Dartmouth (see main
entry). Closed Sun D.

*Galley* 41 Fore Street, Topsham, (01392)
876078. Paul Da-Costa-Greaves' passion is
fish and he goes about his trade with
almost missionary zeal. The setting is a
converted 300-year-old cottage in a town
just outside Exeter, and supplies arrive
daily from the local boats or from
Brixham. Menus are peppered with exotic
ideas: for example, John Dory with
Bombay potatoes, or wok-fried tiger
prawns, scallops and octopus with
Chinese spices, ginseng and more.
Desserts might feature popcorn served
with pecan pie. A sprinkling of organic
wines adds interest to the list, and there
are also organic beers and local drinks.
Main courses £16–£23. Accommodation
available in 'nautical cabins'. Closed Mon
to Wed L.

● **FERNHURST** (Surrey)
*King's Arms* Midhurst Road, (01428)
652005. Out in the middle of nowhere,
this old country pub certainly looks the
part, with its walls of Sussex stone,
hanging baskets and beams. The kitchen
tries hard, although results have been
inconsistent of late. A short printed menu
is bolstered by blackboard specials and it's
a mix of traditional pub grub (corned beef

hash, beer-battered cod and chips) plus more up-beat offerings (fillets of sea bass with caramelised chicory, for example). Sweets include home-made ice creams and tarte Tatin. Main courses £8–£14.50. Service is unpretentious, and the wine list is a thoughtfully assembled slate; house French is £9.85. Closed Sun D.

● **FLETCHING** (East Sussex)
*Griffin Inn* Fletching, (01825) 722890. For more than four centuries this inn has been a focal point of village life, although it now draws custom from much further afield. The kitchen cares about ingredients (free-range pork, Sussex lamb), and fish from Newhaven is showcased every Thursday evening. Dishes have a contemporary flavour, as in marinated squid with couscous, seared fillet of organic salmon with pea and mint mash (£14.50), or chargrilled beef with red chilli and rocket butter (£17.95). Desserts might include coconut pannacotta with 'poire de menthe'. The well-constructed wine list has 12 by the glass, with prices from £9.80. Bar food is also top-quality and can be enjoyed while taking in the great view from the garden. Accommodation available. Open all week.

● **FLITWICK** (Bedfordshire)
*Flitwick Manor* Church Road, (01525) 712242. Centuries of history surround this rather grand-looking manor set in manicured grounds complete with a croquet lawn. Chef Richard Walker cooks in the country-house style; luxury ingredients abound, and prices are not cheap. Dinner might begin with pan-fried scallops and black pudding with chive purée and truffle jus, before braised lamb shank with thyme juices or roast breast of guinea fowl with rösti potatoes and tarragon jus. Hot clementine soufflé served with a sorbet is a decent way to finish. Meals are set price: lunch £19.50–£24.50, dinner £43. The long wine list is for those with deep pockets; house wine is £19.50. Accommodation available. Open all week.

● **FOLKESTONE** (Kent)
*Pauls* 2A Bouverie Road West, (01303) 259697. 'Jovial' Paul Hagger's informal bistro pulls in the crowds with its keenly priced food and friendly buzz: a 'very jolly experience', concluded one happy soul. The kitchen casts its net far and wide for 'wok-tossed' squid with coconut and lemon grass, wild boar sausages, and sauté strips of fillet steak with paprika, garlic and Dry Martini sauce. Vegetarians also have plenty of choice. Lunch and supper 'clubs' (no membership required) are good-value deals, while on Sundays a carvery (£11.95) replaces the main menu (booking essential). More than 100 wines start at £9.65. Closed Sun D.

● **FORTON** (Lancashire)
*Bay Horse Inn* Bay Horse, (01524) 791204. It may look like just another village pub, but this black-and-white hostelry now serves up interesting renditions of dishes old and new. Potted Morecambe Bay Shrimps and slow-cooked Goosnargh duck with potato purée, elderberry wine and honey give a North Country twist to the menu, which also takes in smoked chicken Caesar salad, braised lamb shank with grain-mustard mash, ale and thyme sauce, followed by poached pear in red wine. Main courses £9–£16. Around 40 well-spread wines, including ten by the glass; prices start at £10.95. Closed all day Mon and Sun D.

*El Nido* Whinney Brow Lane, (01524) 791254. International cooking with a Spanish slant is the order of the day at this long-serving Lancashire venue. Denizens of the North-west and beyond can dine on paella, 'bistec diane', and merzula verde (halibut with prawns and cucumber sauce), before rounding things off with pineapple, coconut and pina colada. The table d'hote (£14.95) is a good-value fiesta, likewise the early-bird menu (main course £10.95), where you will find things like smooth chicken liver pâté, and roasted daube of salmon with 'a light dill drizzle'. Forty wines start at £9.75, with six by the glass. Open Sun L and Tue to Sat D.

● **GATESHEAD** Tyne & Wear
*McCoy's at the Baltic* The Centre for Contemporary Art, South Shore Road, (0191) 440 4949. It is good to see th Gateshead's new contempora

venue has taken food seriously. The McCoy brothers (see main entry, McCoy's in Staddlebridge) have been brought in to run the three food and drink venues on the site: the Riverside Café/Bar, the Riverside Restaurant, and the Rooftop Restaurant. A meal at the Riverside Restaurant (described as serving brasserie-style meals) produced an 'excellent' knuckle of ham terrine with a home-made chutney, asparagus in a lemon cream mayonnaise, and fresh scallops and chorizo salad. 'A great venue and great food,' commented one early visitor. The Baltic can be reached from Newcastle quayside via the Gateshead Millenium Bridge. Reports, please. Open all week.

● **GEDNEY DYKE** (Lincolnshire)
*Chequers* Main Street, (01406) 362666. 'A little oasis' is how one reporter described this Fenland pub where carefully sourced ingredients are used in blackboard menus listing intriguing contrasts of ancient and modern. Boston oysters (£5.95), Gloucester Old Spot pork chop with grain mustard sauce (£11.95), steaks of Lincoln red beef, and treacle tart with custard represent tradition; and now rare jugged hare is a chef's special. More contemporary are prawn and smoked salmon in a filo basket; Gressingham duck breast with blueberry sauce; and lemon and cardamom crème brûlée. Short, modestly priced wine-list. Open all week.

● **GILLAN** (Cornwall)
*Tregildry Hotel* Gillan, (01326) 231378. Splendid views over Falmouth Bay are one of the big attractions at this family-run clifftop hotel approached along a narrow lane. Dinner menus change daily, although chargrilled ribeye steak with French fries is a fixture. Otherwise start with sweet potato and lentil soup, or a gâteau of avocado, smoked salmon and prawns, before roast monkfish with rosemary, saffron aïoli and paprika potato wedges, or lamb steaks with orange and oriental spices on a bed of noodles. Puddings include locally made ice creams, treacle tart with clotted cream and West Country cheeses. Meals are set price (£25 for four courses). House wine is £11.75.

Accommodation available. Open all week D Mar to Oct.

● **GOOSNARGH** (Lancashire)
*Solo* Goosnargh, (01772) 865206. 'A country restaurant with lots of well-chosen ornamentation and a very comfortable feel' is how one reporter described this detached house on the edge of the village. The owner is Italian, although the menu quickly moves beyond cannelloni into a broad international repertoire spanning everything from 'prawn cocktail 2001' to chicken korma with fine noodles – taking in chicken breast stuffed with Lancashire garlic cheese in a saffron and white wine sauce along the way. Beautifully presented desserts range from sticky toffee pudding to wobbly pannacotta with red berries. Service runs like clockwork. Dinner is £25.90 for four courses. Open Tue to Sat L and D, Sun L.

● **GREAT HINTON** (Wiltshire)
*The Linnet* Great Hinton, (01380) 870354. After a serious re-vamp, this village inn is now an open-plan pub/restaurant, emphatically geared to eating, with low beamed ceilings and deep-peach-coloured walls. Chef/landlord Jonathan Furby produces bistro-style dishes along the lines of smoked salmon and lemon sole terrine with caper and herb dressing (£5.25), grilled ribeye steak with braised baby faggots and sage sauce (£11.95), and milk chocolate and cappuccino mousse (£4.50). Reporters have also praised his home-made breads and ice creams. Bright, attentive and very relaxed service. Open Tue to Sun, L and D.

● **GREAT WHITTINGTON** (Northumberland)
*Queens Head* Great Whittington, (01434) 672267. Three centuries old, but in the business of serving contemporary food, this remote hostelry serves up the likes of pan-seared scallops on a fine bean and tomato salad (£6.95), pork tenderloin with onion marmalade and black pudding fritters (£10.95), and vegetable strudel with black-bean and ginger sauce (£9.95), with bread-and-butter pudding (£4.95) to finish. Also look for chef's specialities such

as seared fillet of halibut with a ragoût of asparagus and prawns and herb beurre blanc. The wine list embraces Old and New World producers, with prices from £12.50. Open Tue to Sun L and D.

● **GREAT YARMOUTH** (Norfolk)
*Seafood Restaurant* 85 North Quay, (01493) 856009. The Kikis family have been delivering old-school fish cookery in this converted pub since 1979. Echoes of their native Greece can be found in taramasalata, baklava and the like, but the thrust of the menu is spanking-fresh seafood – although it may appear with enveloping cream-based sauces. The printed menu spans everything from prawns in garlic butter (£7.95) to fillets of Dover sole with Dijon mustard and ham sauce (£17.75), but look out also for more ambitious specials such as tuna teriyaki. Service is charmingly mature. To drink, there's champagne by the glass and a substantial wine list from £10.95. Closed Sat L and all day Sun.

● **HADDENHAM** (Buckinghamshire)
*Green Dragon* 8 Church Way, (01844) 291403. Once a simple village pub, the Green Dragon has been given a fresh identity as a fully fledged restaurant by its new owners – although the 'homely and homespun feel' remains and the whole place is extremely chatty. The son-of-the-house delivers some creditable versions of modern pub dishes: salmon and crab fishcakes with mango and papaya salsa is a pleasing starter (£6), while mains run from Gressingham duck breast with port and ginger sauce (£13) to steak and kidney pudding laced with ale (£9.50). Desserts range from treacle tart to Tuscany orange cake. Excellent cut-price deals on Tues and Thur (£10.95 for three courses). Open all week.

● **HARROGATE** (North Yorkshire)
*Bettys* 1 Parliament Street, (01423) 502746. The first-born of a near-legendary mini-chain of North Country tearooms, opened by a Swiss confectioner in 1919. What you get in all the outlets is a cross between a European pâtisserie and a traditional Yorkshire tea-shop, with a few eclectic savouries such as warm lemon

chicken served with spring herb salad (£8.50) tossed in for good measure. Toasts, breads, cakes and sandwiches (£1–£7) are its stock in trade. To drink, there are innumerable teas, coffees, chocolate and wines: the house selection – Swiss, of course – comes in at £13.20 a bottle (£3.35 a glass). Open all week. There are branches in Ilkey, Northallerton and York.

● **HARROW** (Greater London)
*Ram's* 203 Kenton Road, (020) 8907 2022. 'What a really honest, likeable restaurant,' enthused a visitor to this newcomer, a short walk from Kenton Tube station. Inside, it is smart, modern and minimalist; diners keep company with prints of sacred cows and Hindu gods. The menu focuses exclusively on the vegetarian Surti cuisine of Gujarat. Good home-made chutneys point up kachori and vengan na bhartu (mashed roasted aubergine with a sour citrus edge), breads are fascinating, and prices are 'ridiculously cheap' (starters £1.50–£3.60, mains £3–£4.50). 'Staff are a dream', enthusiasm and gracious serenity abound. Lime soda is the drink of choice; otherwise lassi or beer might do the trick; there are also a couple of wines by the glass. More reports, please. Closed Mon, exc bank hols.

● **HARVINGTON** (Worcestershire)
*Mill at Harvington* Anchor Lane, (01386) 870688. It may be 'remote', but this skilfully extended mill by the River Avon (just outside the village) makes the perfect setting for a decent local country restaurant-with-rooms. The kitchen delivers accurate, unpretentious cooking along the lines of baked marinated goats' cheese with an aubergine blini, and sea bass on shellfish risotto with langoustine and brandy jus, plus home-made coconut ice cream with spiced pecan nuts to finish. Five-course meals range from £27 to £37 according to which main course is chosen. Casual meals are also available in the Chestnut Tree bistro (£7 to £8). Service is young and enthusiastic, and the inexpensive wine list should 'appeal to most tastes'. Open all week.

● **HEREFORD** (Herefordshire)
*Café @ All Saints* All Saints Church, High Street, (01432) 370415. All profits from this café go towards the upkeep of the Grade I listed medieval church in which it is housed. The setting may be unassuming but the kitchen has serious intentions, delivering lunchtime specials (around £5.50) such as pasta with purple sprouting broccoli and garlic cream sauce, plus daily soups (butternut squash and lentil, £2.10), quiches (roast sweet potato with spinach and Hereford Hop cheese, £4.20) and salads (£2.95). Grilled sandwiches are available throughout the afternoon. Organic tea, apple juice and cider, as well as Chilean house wine at £8.75 a bottle. Open Mon to Sat 8.30am to 5.30pm, plus occasional evenings.

● **HEYTESBURY** (Wiltshire)
*Angel* High Street, (01985) 840330. Once a coaching stop on the road to Salisbury, this seventeenth-century inn is still in the business of providing sustenance and overnight shelter for travellers. The menu leaps back-and-forth from fashion to tradition, taking in risotto of chorizo, basil and sun-dried tomatoes, and chicken breast with lemon pepper sauce and a sauté of oyster mushrooms and Savoy cabbage (£9.95); as well as grilled plaice with tomato and chive sauce (£9.50), and wild boar sausages with grain mustard mash (£7.95). Tarts, hot puddings and crumbles conclude proceedings on a comforting note. House wines from £11.50. Accommodation available. Open all week.

● **HOUGHTON CONQUEST** (Bedfordshire)
*Knife & Cleaver* The Grove, Houghton Conquest, (01234) 740387. Originally a village pub, this stone-built inn off the B530 south of Bedford now functions as a restaurant-with-rooms, complete with a courtyard, orchard garden and conservatory dining room. Daily fish specials might include lobsters, oysters, moules marinière (£5.75) and rich crab cakes (£5.95), while meat eaters might opt for rack of Welsh lamb with mash (main courses £10–£17). Desserts might feature 'densely satisfying' chocolate pot, or poached plums in a plum 'soup' with balls of 'crumble' ice cream (desserts £4.50). Impeccable cheeses, too. Service is smartly attentive and the wine list is a reputable slate; house wines are £11 a bottle (£1.80 to £2.50 a glass). Accommodation available. Open L all week and Mon to Sat, D.

● **HOVINGHAM** (North Yorkshire)
*Worsley Arms* Hovingham, (01653) 628234. A honey-coloured coaching inn in a village a few miles from the North York Moors. Fixed-price restaurant menus (three courses £25) run along the lines of deep-fried ricotta and spinach goujons with spicy tomato sauce, followed by seared salmon with crushed new potatoes and chive cream, before lemon posset; pay a supplement and you might get roast saddle of wild rabbit stuffed with wild mushrooms, celeriac purée and broad beans. Simpler food is served in the Cricketers' Bar. Proprietor Anthony Finn's wine list bears all the hallmarks of a passionate enthusiast: prices start at £12 and there is plenty of quaffable stuff under £20. Accommodation available. Open all week.

● **ILMINGTON** (Warwickshire)
*Howard Arms* Lower Green, (01608) 682226. Prosperity and stylishness sum up this stone-built pub/restaurant by the village green. Inside, it feels like a 'generously spacious old family home' and everything runs impeccably. Menus are on blackboards around the place, and there's plenty of choice, from seared scallops with sweet chilli sauce and crème fraîche (£6.50) via sauté of lambs' kidneys with shallots and 'sherry Dijon' sauce (£9.50) to Mrs G's toffee meringue (£5), or vanilla pannacotta with spiced plums (£4.50). Prices on the short wine list start at £10.50 a bottle, £2.75 a glass. Open all week.

● **IPSWICH** (Suffolk)
*Il Punto* Neptune Quay, (01473) 289748. If you fancy dining aboard ship, this converted Belgian gun boat moored next to the Customs House might be just the thing. The main business happens in the

restaurant with its varnished floorboards and brass railings, where both the food – and most of the staff – have a French accent. Typical dishes might range from straightforward Dover sole meunière to garlic and herb-crusted rack of lamb with an aromatic jus. The kitchen also makes a few detours for carpaccio of tuna and fillet of pork with pineapple chutney and curry sauce. Main courses £8 to £18. Snacks and light lunches are served in the Top Deck Wine Bar. Open Tue to Fri L, Tue to Sat D.

*Scott's Brasserie*   4A Orwell Place, (01473) 230254. Scott Davidson's eponymous brasserie close to the town centre is a handy choice for eating out in Ipswich. His mixed hors d'oeuvre plate (£11.50 for two people) offers the chance to work your way through appetisers like Stilton and port pâté, duck and spring onion samosas, and filo-wrapped king prawns. Main courses follow a similarly eclectic path with venison sausages on a spring onion rösti, and Thai crab cakes with sweet chilli sauce (£10.25), while desserts could feature Bramley apple fritters with Bermuda black rum sauce. Thirty wines include seven by the glass; prices from £9.95. Closed Sat L and all day Sun.

● KING'S LYNN   (Norfolk)

*Riverside*   27 King Street, (01553) 773134. A trusted network of local producers and smallholders supplies the kitchen at this converted 500-year-old timbered building with great riverside views. Creamed Arbroath smokies is a signature dish (£6.95), but the choice extends to roast vegetable tarte Tatin (£14.95), and sauté fillets of black bream on tapénade mash with coriander sauce (£15.95). Light lunches are well reported, and a long-serving pastry chef produces desserts such as prune and Armagnac tart or marmalade bread-and-butter pudding. Around 65 wines offer plenty of decent drinking at fair prices; house wine is £10.95. Closed Sun.

● KINTBURY   (Berkshire)

*Dundas Arms*   53 Station Road, (01488) 658263. David Dalzell-Piper has been at the helm of this pub/restaurant for 35 years and continues to run the place in true and steady fashion. The setting, on a little island between the canal and river, is one major attraction; another is the magisterial wine cellar that holds some 150 top-quality bins (with prices from £13 to £150). On the food front, the kitchen delivers a mixed bag of dishes old and new, from celeriac soup and calf's liver with bacon, to Thai fishcakes, and roast monkfish with capers and sun-dried tomatoes. Finish with, say, iced orange soufflé. Main courses £12.50–£15. Accommodation available. Closed Mon D and all day Sun.

● LEEDS   (West Yorkshire)

*Brio*   40 Great George Street, (0113) 246 5225. Smoked haddock and smoked salmon are now the only interlopers on the menu of this unwaveringly Italian ristorante. Minestrone della casa, bresaola with rocket and Parmesan, and calamari fritti are typical starters. Pasta runs from classic ravioli with asparagus and ricotta, to farfalline (butterflies) with smoked bacon sautéed with Savoy cabbage and fagioli beans. Main dishes (£9.95–£15.50), all accompanied by baby roast potatoes with rosemary, include three ways with sirloin steak, veal fricassee with thyme and cream, and dishes of the day. Closed Sun.

*Bryans*   9 Weetwood Lane, (0113) 278 5679. Fish and chips washed down with champagne is one way of enjoying yourself at this legendary venue close to Headingley Cricket Ground. Since 1934, the owners have been delivering the real McCoy, fried the Yorkshire way in beef dripping. Haddock is king in these parts and you can choose your own size ('regular', 'baby' or 'jumbo'); otherwise ring the changes with hake or halibut. Kick off with breaded mushrooms and finish with peach Melba. 'Senior citizen' deals are served each day and there is live jazz on alternate Saturdays. House wine is £2.10 a glass, £11.50 a litre. Open all week.

*Cactus Lounge*   St Peter's Square, (0113) 243 6553. Pre-theatre deals (£9.95) are a good bet at this Mexican joint, handily situated close to the West Yorkshire

Playhouse and the School of Music. The full menu is a classic run through tacos in various guises, burritos, chimichangas, plus some less familiar items such as turtle bean and prawn soup, pan-fried black-bean cakes with coriander cream, and pescado (fillet of cod simmered with coriander, olives and capers). Main courses £6.50–£12. To drink, there are plenty of bottled beers, or dip into the minuscule wine list: house wine is a bargain at £8.45 a bottle, £1.95 a glass. Closed Sat.

*Olive Tree*   Oaklands (0113) 256 9283. 'The atmosphere is reminiscent of Greek holidays but with better food!' observed a fan of George and Vasoulla Psarias' long-serving restaurant a few miles from Leeds city centre. The place really hums when there's live music and dancing, but it attracts praise at any time. Meze remains a favourite and it's worth noting some of the specials, such as octopus in red wine with baby onions, yiovvetsi (a classic dish of lamb cooked in the oven with orso pasta), and chicken stuffed with feta cheese, spinach and dill. Interesting desserts, too. Main courses £9–£13.50. The updated wine list also has some intriguing modern Greek names: prices start at £11.95. Open all week L and D.

*Salvo's*   115 Otley Road, (0113) 275 5017. A venerable Leeds institution, owned and run by the Dammone family since 1976. It's loud and noisy, queues are frequent and there are no bookings for dinner. The mainstays are pasta and pizzas with some odd-sounding toppings ('michuru' includes Japanese glazed chicken and spring onions). Otherwise, braised lamb shank with gremolata and crushed potatoes has been liked (£12.50), and the specials list extends to king prawns with salsa verde and black noodles (£14.50). Set lunches for £5 and early-bird menus (£10 to £12.95) are ace deals. Hard-working staff and 'absolutely excellent' espresso. House wine is £10.50. Open Mon to Sat L and D.

● LEICESTER   (Leicestershire)
*Opera House*   10 Guildhall Lane, (0116) 223 6666. Originally the Opera House

Hotel, these two old buildings next to the cathedral have been given a new lease of life as an ambitious modern restaurant. Fish shows up on the regularly changing menus (set lunch is £13.50; dinner is à la carte, main courses £16.50 to £19.50), which might promise anything from a 'splendid' salad of crayfish and gravlax with pesto to whole roast sea bass with rosemary, braised Cos lettuce, ratatouille and tapénade sauce. Elsewhere, reporters have endorsed collop of veal with shallots, and duck breast with beetroot and orange marmalade. Figs roasted with port and honey served with a lemon crème brûlée is a good finale. House wines from £11.25. More reports, please. Closed Sun.

● LEYBURN   (North Yorkshire)
*Sandpiper Inn*   Market Place, (01969) 622206. The stone-built old pub run by the Harrison family has two double rooms, and a pleasant little garden. Dinner à la carte is a nice blend of traditional and modern, so kidneys in wild mushroom sauce, or melon, avocado and grapefruit, might be followed by lamb with blueberry and mint, or pork fillet wrapped in Parma ham with roast peppers, sun-dried tomatoes and Parmesan macaroni; then summer fruit pudding, or summer vacherin. Lighter dishes available at lunch include sausage and mash, and omelette Arnold Bennet. Prices L £3–£10.50, D main courses £9–£13.50. Wines from £10.50, only six of the 30 offered are over £20. Closed all day Mon.

● LICHFIELD   (Staffordshire)
*Chandlers*   Corn Exchange, (01543) 416 688. Billed as a 'Grande Brasserie', this converted corn exchange has high, vaulted ceilings, stained-glass windows and a circular gallery. Output from the cosmopolitan kitchen ranges from corned beef hash to crispy duck confit with stir-fried noodles, taking in lamb kebabs with couscous and tsatsiki along the way. Fish specials – sea bass with wild mushrooms and wilted spinach, perhaps – are listed separately and there are useful fixed-price deals for lunch (£5.75 to £8.75) and supper (£11.75 to £15). Desserts might

run to vanilla-poached pear with mandarin sorbet. Ten wines by the glass head a short, sharp list starting at £10.95 a bottle. Open all week.

● **LIDGATE** (Suffolk)
*Star Inn* The Street, (01638) 500275. Since 1993 Maria-Teresa Axon has brought a touch of Mediterranean sun to this out-of-the-way Suffolk watering hole. Catalan, Italian and French dishes jostle for the limelight with more traditional pub grub on the long blackboard menu: grilled squid, paella Valenciana and salmon à la Gallega stand alongside lasagne, venison in port and daube of beef. Main courses £11.50–£13.50. To drink, there are real ales and a decent contingent of Spanish bottles; house wine is £12. Closed Sun D.

● **LOWER ODDINGTON** (Gloucestershire)
*Fox Inn* Lower Oddington, (01451) 870555. A cottage garden with its own heated terrace adds to the pleasure of this 'good-looking' pub in a delightful Cotswold village. Tuesday is 'fish day' and reports have praised seared scallops with mizuna and ginger and 'just perfect' sea bass. Elsewhere, there have been votes for fresh sardines and shoulder of lamb in tomato and basil sauce. Desserts have also been applauded: iced chocolate terrine with Cointreau rounded off one dinner 'with a little decadence'. The pub holds a good stock of malt whiskies, and the wine list is bolstered by a 'hidden cellar' of more exclusive bottles. Main courses £7.50–£10.95. Accommodation available. Open all week L and D.

● **MAIDEN NEWTON** (Dorset)
*Le Petit Canard* Dorchester Road, (01300) 320536. Once a coaching inn, this attractive Dorset cottage now earns its living as a modest country restaurant. Sunday lunches (£19.50) are available twice-monthly, but the main business is dinner. Menus are fixed-price for two or three courses (£22.50 to £26): begin with asparagus wrapped in Parma ham with hollandaise, before guinea fowl with tarragon, cream and wild mushroom sauce or breast of Gressingham duck with

an oriental five-spice jus. Desserts could include Tia Maria crème brûlée and dark chocolate mousse torte. Decent sherries, plus around 40 fairly priced wines, including six by the glass. Open Tue to Sat D and every first and third Sun L.

● **MALVERN WELLS** (Worcestershire)
*Planters* 191–193 Wells Road, (01684) 575065. South-east Asian home-cooking in the shadow of the Malvern Hills is an unlikely prospect, but Sandra Pegg and chef Chandra de Alwis carry on regardless. Their short menu spans Indonesia, Thailand, India and elsewhere for satays, hot and sour chicken soup, well-received vadays (lentil rissoles with yoghurt and coconut dip), and 'classic' nasi goreng (starters around £5, mains around £9). Recent reports suggest that the cooking does not always live up to expectations, but this remains a useful local address. The set 'rijstafel' (rice table) will provide you with the full works. House wine is fairly priced at £9.50. Open Wed to Sat D.

● **MANCHESTER** (Greater Manchester)
*Bridgewater Hall, Charles Hallé Restaurant* Lower Mosley Street, (0161) 950 0000. This appendage to the concert hall is open only on concert nights for meals before and after the event, and offers a menu du jour at £15.50 for two courses, £19.50 for three. Start with the fixture, potage Yehudi Menuhin, or perhaps a salad of mango and crayfish tails. Mains could include skate wing with crispy Morecambe Bay shrimps, or more exotic Chinese-style confit duck with hoi sin syrup and noodles. Cheeses have included fourme d'Ambert and some lesser-known British varieties. The short varied wine list starts at £11.95 for house selections.

*Market Restaurant* 104 High Street, (0161) 834 3743. For more than 20 years, this quirkily decorated restaurant has been plying its trade just off Piccadilly. Menus change monthly and the repertoire is an intriguingly mixed bag (main courses £11–£16) that caters equally well for carnivores and vegetarians. Smoked chicken with guacamole, and herb-crusted salmon on braised aubergines with red pepper dressing, share the billing with 'patatas bravas' (deep-fried potatoes with spiced tomato sauce), and parsnips 'Molly Parkin'. Bringing up the rear might be old-fashioned rhubarb trifle or English farmhouse cheeses. Thirty wines include six by the glass; prices start at £7.95. Open Fri and Sat D only.

**Palmiro**  197 Upper Chorlton Road, (0161) 860 7330. Once an end-of-terrace shop, this is now an ultra-modern Italian establishment catering for a young crowd. Service is sharp and eager, and the sensibly concise, seasonally changing menu avoids trattoria clichés; it might offer seared pigeon breast on fruit polenta, followed by fish bollito misto with pear pumpkin salad (£10.95), or rabbit with baby onions in agrodolce (£9.95). To finish, choose between Venetian rice budino with roast plum, Grappa and blood orange sorbet, or 'artisan' Italian cheeses. The 60-strong wine list is peppered with decent drinking from classy Italian producers; house wine is £8.75. Open Sun L and all week D.

**Stock**  Stock Exchange, 4 Norfolk Street, (0161) 839 6644. Reading menu prices makes a change for brokers in the handsome Stock Exchange building. A satisfied reporter found 'first-class' service and noted the fresh ingredients and 'positive but balanced seasoning'. Choose your antipasti from the buffet or succumb to such temptations as stuffed aubergine, or bresaola with marinated grilled vegetables. Pasta may come with stinging nettle and courgette sauce, while main courses take in roast pigeon on a bed of leek and potato (£11.50), and ostrich fillets in a creamy port sauce (£16) – plus more conventional meats. A daily choice of fish specials might include halibut in champagne sauce. An all-Italian wine list kicks off at £13.50.

**Tai Pan**  Brunswick House, (0161) 273 2798. Located above a supermarket, this substantial Chinese eating house puts great store by its dim sum (£2–£2.80), and regulars have singled out char sui cheung fun, war tip, and scallop dumplings as exemplary versions of the genre. Roast duck (£8.20) is 'superbly authentic' with caramelised skin, creamy fat and silkily tender flesh, and one-plate rice and noodle dishes (£5.80–£9.80) have also been well received. Several banquet menus are aimed mainly at Western customers. There have been some changes in management of late, which could account for fluctuating standards noted by reporters. Open all week.

**That Café**  1031 Stockport Road, (0161) 432 4672. It may not be the most desirable district of Manchester, but Alison Eason and co are doing well in this 'interesting conversion of an ordinary terrace house'. The menu changes weekly and has pleased visitors with asparagus and herb pots (£5.75), monkfish with a cumin and coriander crust and a coconut, chilli and lime sauce (£14.25), followed by buttered Brazil nut and toffee parfait (£3.95). The owners provide 'friendly, personal attention', there's live jazz on the first Wednesday of each month, and the short wine list opens with house selections from £9.95. Open Sun L, Tue to Sat D.

● **MELMERBY** (Cumbria)

**Village Bakery**  Melmerby, (01768) 881515. When Andrew Whitely started this organic bakery in 1976, it seemed like a blueprint for the ecologically minded enterprise of the future. Twenty-five years on, the place is still true to its principles. The hub of the restaurant is the wood-fired oven that is used for everything from breads to pies and cakes. But there's a full-blooded approach to things here: you can get home-cured bacon sandwiches (£3.50) and full fry-ups for breakfast (served until 11am), plus snacks including Cumberland sausage rolls and pasties, and lunch dishes ranging from Thai fishcakes (£3.25) to pork tenderloin with mushroom sauce (£9.50). Beers, ciders and wines are 100 per cent organic. Open all week for breakfast and lunch.

● **MOUSEHOLE** (Cornwall)

**Cornish Range**  6 Chapel Street, (01736) 731488. Situated in one of the narrow lanes that meander through this quintessentially Cornish harbourside village, this restaurant sticks to its allegiances: fish comes from Newlyn just down the road, lamb and beef are from local farmers, and leaves and herbs are from a local nursery. Chef Adam Ashbourne turns these fruits of the land and sea into pan-fried scallops with salsa verde, or Stilton and endive salad as starters, and main courses of rack of lamb with mustard and herb crust, or pan-fried monkfish with a tomato, thyme and garlic dressing. The summer seafood platter (£39.95 for two) is especially popular. House Australian is £10.95. Three tastefully decorated bedrooms are available. Main courses £11.95 to £15.95.

● **NAILSWORTH** (Gloucestershire)
*Mad Hatters* 3 Cossack Square, (01453) 832615. This organic restaurant is run with great commitment by the owners: they grow many of the herbs and vegetables themselves, and would appear to have a loyal following among the local community. The handwritten menu offers dishes featuring some classical flourishes: emince of pork zurichoise might follow a Taleggio and red onion tartlet, or oxtail soup. Duck breast with sour cherry sauce was a highlight of one meal. Puddings have included a pistachio meringue with red fruits. Main courses from £14.50 to £16.50. The organic ethos extends to the drinks list. Closed all day Mon and Tue, Sun D.

● **NEWARK** (Nottinghamshire)
*Café Bleu* 14 Castle Gate, (01636) 610141. Huge canvases line the walls of this flamboyantly designed venue close to the castle ruins. It all looks very arty, with ornate gilt mirrors, clear glass vases filled with pebbles, and tiny spotlights arranged on rails against the orange ceiling. The kitchen goes in for elaborate brasserie ideas like roast wood pigeon with sauté caraway noodles, wild mushrooms and baby spinach (£4.95), then poached monkfish 'pot au feu' with steamed potatoes and smoked salmon tortellini (£13.95), followed by desserts such as lime cheesecake with bitter chocolate sorbet (£4.50). House wines range between £10 and £12. Live jazz four nights a week. Open all week L, Mon to Sat D.

● **NEWCASTLE UPON TYNE** (Tyne & Wear)
*Treacle Moon* 5–7 The Side, (0191) 232 5537. Taking its title from the name Lord Byron gave to his honeymoon, this neat minimalist restaurant by the Quayside promises to be a boon to Newcastle's burgeoning eating scene. A new chef arrived after our inspection deadline, but the cooking seems set to continue along the contemporary British path, offering the likes of wild mushroom cappuccino; honey-roast duck breast with leek and shallot mash and redcurrant sauce; and iced strawberry parfait with cracked pepper shortbread. Main courses £12–£19. The 40-strong wine list includes six by the glass; bottle prices start at £13.50. Reports, please. Open Mon to Sat D.

● **NEWENT** (Gloucestershire)
*Three Choirs Vineyards Restaurant* Newent, (01531) 890223. Seventy acres of cultivated vines, a visitor centre and shop are just part of the package at this Cotswold success story. There's also a restaurant offering dishes such as warm salad of queenie scallops, mushrooms and pine kernels (£6.50), grilled fillet of local pork with apple purée and cider sauce (£13.75), and praline parfait with mango coulis and red wine syrup (£4.75). The full range of Three Choirs wines (20 in all) is available by the glass, otherwise the list has plenty of interesting stuff from elsewhere; prices start at £8.50. Acccommodation available. Open Tue to Sun L, Tue to Sat D.

● **NEWMILLERDAM** (West Yorkshire)
*On the Edge* Newmillerdam, (01924) 253310. On the edge of Newmillerdam Country Park, this café-style restaurant in a stone cottage offers good value across the board. The short dinner menu runs along the lines of prawns in filo pastry with chilli sauce, lamb shank marinated with mint and rosemary (£11.95), and Cajun-style salmon with tomato and lime salsa (£10.95), while one reporter was particularly pleased to round things off with 'Yorkshire' rice pudding. Choice may be rather limited at lunchtime. The list of around two dozen wines includes four by

the glass. Accommodation available. Closed all day Mon, Sat L and Sun D.

● **NORTH BOVEY** (Devon)

*Blackaller Hotel* North Bovey, (01647) 440322. Down by the banks of the Bovey River, this converted three-centuries-old woollen mill surrounded by woods and moorland is now a charming country hotel. Devon produce is used emphatically for the daily-changing dinner menu, which is fixed price for four courses (£24). Begin with sauté field mushrooms in herb and garlic cream sauce before roasted tomato and harissa soup. Main courses might be rack of local lamb with red wine and rosemary sauce, or roast salmon fillet with a Parmesan crust, while desserts could include warm prune and chocolate torte with clotted cream. House wine is £9.50. Open Tue to Sat D.

● **NORTON** (Wiltshire)

*Vine Tree* Foxley Road, (01666) 837654. This south Cotswold village inn has a pleasant ambience and a short main menu supplemented by daily-changing fish specials, plus steaks for carnivores. Imaginative, and ambitious piscine offerings might be lightly spiced red snapper with a pea and coriander foam; yellow fin tuna with seaweed and Chinese egg noodles; or pan-fried monkfish cheeks with Parma ham, roasted peppers and cherry tomatoes (all £12.95). Service is friendly and there are over 60 interesting wines mostly below £20; of these, 15 Vine Tree Favourites are offered by the large glass.

● **NORWICH** (Norfolk)

*By Appointment* 25–29 St Georges Street, (01603) 630730. An extremely welcoming proprietor greets guests to this sixteenth-century building, where the tone is one of cosy comfort. The gilt-framed blackboard that proclaims the dinner menu may offer coriander-marinated salmon with pineapple, mango and red pepper salsa, then rack of lamb with apricot and pistachio stuffing, and banana rum brûlée – all of which have pleased reporters. There are also plenty of alternatives for vegetarians and vegans, who have their own menus. Main courses

around £16. A well-spread list of 65 wines kicks off with house French at £9.75. Accommodation available. Open Tue to Sat D.

● **OXFORD** (Oxfordshire)

*Fishers* 36–37 St Clements, (01865) 243003. Aptly named, this restaurant just off Magdalen Bridge is wholeheartedly dedicated to fish cookery, with supplies from the market dictating the daily-changing menu. Traditions are upheld with baked Dover sole (£18.50) and haddock and chips (£9.50), but the repertoire takes off rapidly into the realms of grilled scallops with sesame, soy and spring onion dressing (£6.95); and seared yellow fin tuna with chorizo, fine bean and tomato salad (£13.50). Confit of duck for carnivores, chargrilled aubergines for vegetarians. House wine is £9.95. Closed L Mon and Tue.

*White House* 2 Botley Road, (01865) 242823. Expect a mixed crowd in the bar of this large pub close to the railway station, although the atmosphere in the adjoining restaurant has a more refined character. The menu is long, portions are hearty, and presentation catches the eye. Components sometimes don't gel, but there are some good things to be had, such as fillet of sea bass on tagliatelle, alongside medallions of beef with chilli sauce, and cod with garlic and walnut butter. Roasted vegetables have been praised, and tarte Tatin makes an impressive finish. Main courses £9.50–£15.95. Fairly priced wines with plenty of choice between £10 and £20. Open all week.

● **PLUMTREE** (Nottinghamshire)

*Perkins* Old Railway Station, (0115) 937 3695. Nostalgia for the railway station it once was is part of the charm of this blackened red-brick building and its non-smoking conservatory overlooking the old track. Attentive, friendly service is attractively old-fashioned too, and the menu offers retro ideas such as paupiettes of lemon sole stuffed with crab mousse and glazed with sauce Dugléré (£9.75). Otherwise find marinated rack of lamb in smoked garlic with port jus (£11.50), or Toulouse sausage, avocado and cherry tomato compote. Set lunch menu available, including Sundays. House wines from £10.75, others modestly priced, and useful half-bottles too. Closed all day Mon and Sun D.

● **POLPERRO** (Cornwall)
*Kitchen* The Coombes, (01503) 272780. Local crab (when available) is a speciality at this modest family-run village restaurant, while other fish specials have included Cajun-style lemon sole, or sea bass with Muscadet and chive cream sauce. Ian and Vanessa Bateson draw inspiration from near and far: Caesar salad with coriander chicken, prawns in tempura batter, and Goan-style lamb xacuti, for example – plus good choice for vegetarians. Sweets might take in ginger brioche pudding or 'Gina's treacle tart'. Main courses around £10–£15, and cheap-and-cheerful wines offer four by the glass at £3. Note, no cheques. Closed Oct to Easter; phone to check for opening times.

● **OSWESTRY** (Shropshire)
*The Lime Kiln* Porth-y-Waen, (01691) 831550. Ian and Jayne Whyte moved to this unassuming roadside pub on the A495 after making their name as restaurateurs in Brighton. They have opted for a less ambitious approach here, providing everything for everybody in the shape of baguettes, summertime barbecues and boules in the beer garden – not to mention catering for kids. Typical dishes on their blackboard menus might be warm salad of pigeon breast with black pudding and chorizo; braised lamb shank on spring onion mash; poached smoked haddock with Welsh rarebit; and to finish apple and cinnamon crumble. Open Tue to Sun L and D.

● **READING** (Berkshire)
*London Street Brasserie* 2–4 London Street, (01189) 505036. The al fresco dining terrace of chef-patron Paul Clerehugh's restaurant overlooks the River Kennet. Indoors is agreeable too: 'simple uncluttered design' and 'willing, very helpful service' make a pleasant background for a long, 'modern eclectic' menu. Modernity doesn't exclude

tradition: oysters are served *nature*, or 'Benedict' (baked over spinach with Bayonne ham and hollandaise), for £7.50 a half dozen. Oriental and Italian notes resound in seared blue fin tuna with pak choi and noodles (£12.80), and rabbit with pancetta, pasta, black pudding and tarragon mustard dressing (£14.95). Local cheeses compete with desserts and 50 wines rise from £12.50. Open all week noon to 7.

● **RICHMOND** (Surrey)
*Canyon* The Tow Path, (020) 8948 2944. Here is a little piece of California close to the towpath by Richmond Bridge. The place buzzes, service is slick and the menu makes spicy reading. Starters (£5–£7) of smoked duck salad with chorizo and grapefruit, or lime and coconut crab cakes, might be followed by grilled leg of lamb with chickpea fritters and flat bread (£16), or grilled monkfish with broad beans, bacon, mint, lemon and garlic (£16). Weekend brunch is worth knowing about. There are some decent New World bottles on the well-spread wine list: house French is £12. Open Mon to Fri L and D, and Sat and Sun brunch.

*Petersham Hotel, Nightingales*
Nightingale Lane, (020) 8939 1090. In this huge Victorian mansion with 60 bedrooms, on a hill overlooking the Thames, chef Andy Johns's dinner menus achieve some interesting contrasts with ingredients: witness artichokes with glazed chicken livers; mustard lentils with roast cod and crisp potatoes; vodka orange granité on passion-fruit tart. Lunches might offer pan-fried skate on hot-and-sour red cabbage, or cod again, this time Gruyère-crusted, with mustard velouté and tomato fondue (£17.50). Two-course set dinners are £19.50. A hundred wines rise quickly from £14.50.

● **ROCK** (Cornwall)
*Alwyn's Pavilion* Rock Road, (01208) 862622. A converted shop bedecked with paintings is the setting for Alwyn and Jenny Evans' bistro-style restaurant. Fresh fish plus herbs, salad leaves and vegetables from the allotment are the cornerstones of their short blackboard

menu, which might promise cream of sorrel soup, pan-fried fillets of sea bass with lemon thyme and capers, or fillet of turbot meunière with sunblush tomatoes and basil. A separate list of desserts could feature Bakewell tart with clotted cream or kiwi fruit Pavlova. Main courses £14.50–£17. Seven 'everyday' wines from £9.95 head the short, mainly French list. Open Mon to Sat D only.

● ROCKBEARE (Devon)

*Jack in the Green* London Road, (01404) 822240. In 2002, Paul Parnell celebrated a decade at the helm of this popular roadside pub. Food is the main business, and you can eat in the bar from a menu that runs from smoked haddock fishcakes (£8.95) to wild mushroom risotto (£7.95). Things move up a gear in the restaurant (three courses at dinner £21, two £17.25), where the repertoire brings into play confit of belly pork with boudin blanc, roast guinea fowl with grapes and Chardonnay, and fillet of salmon with sauerkraut. Service is generally fine, and the lengthy wine list offers plenty of decent drinking by the glass. Open all week.

● ROYDHOUSE (West Yorkshire)

*Three Acres Inn* Roydhouse, (01484) 602606. Three acres of grounds (with 'great views on a fine day') do indeed surround this huge inn, which now functions as restaurant, food shop and hotel. The owners have been in residence for over 30 years and are not about to change their highly successful formula. A vast menu scours the globe for hot-and-sour duck broth, home-made Toulouse sausages with olive oil and garlic mash, pot-roast lamb shank in Moroccan spices (£12.95), and Whitby lobster thermidor (half £16.95, whole £29), while puddings might include brown bread ice cream. The fairly priced, 80-bin wine list includes ten by the glass; house wines from £10.95. Open all week.

● ST ALBANS (Hertfordshire)

*Sukiyaki* 6 Spencer Street, (01727) 865009. A likeable little Japanese restaurant just off the market place. Despite the absence of raw fish (the owners have been unable to find a supplier who will guarantee the necessary freshness), the menu promises simple, straightforward home-cooking. Set lunches are excellent value (£7–£9.50); otherwise dip into the short carte (starters around £4, mains £8–£13.50), which offers starters of agedashi dofu (deep-fried bean curd), ebi fry (deep-fried king prawns in breadcrumbs), before tonkatsu, grilled salmon with teriyaki sauce and – of course – sukiyaki cooked and served at the table. Drink tea or beer, or both. Open Tue to Sat L and D.

● ST IVES (Cornwall)

*Tides Cafe* 6 The Digey, (01736) 799600. Tucked away down a side street, this one-time shop is now a 'trendy' café/restaurant with slate floors, driftwood-framed mirrors and metal tables with mosaic tops. The food has strong Mediterranean and Australian overtones and the blackboard typically advertises starters of thick onion and vine tomato soup (£3.95), and king prawn kebabs with a mango, chilli and coriander dip (£6.95), before pan-fried ostrich with grilled polenta (£13.95), and sole with pea cream sauce, mash and crispy pancetta (£14.95). Greek yoghurt with honey and kiwi fruit (£3.95) makes a refreshing finale. Service is informal and the short wine list has plenty under £20; house Australian is £10.95. Open Mon to Sat L and D (closed Mon between Nov and Mar).

● SALISBURY (Wiltshire)

*LXIX* 69 New Street, (01722) 340000. Latin scholars should have no difficulty in deciphering the name of this light, airy restaurant with a bistro next door. Clever lighting and modern artwork set the tone, and the kitchen works to a brasserie-style menu along the lines of tartlet of goats' cheese and red onion marmalade, fillet of hake with mash and caper butter, and mille-feuille of wild mushrooms. Desserts have included a well-made rum pannacotta. Main courses £12–£19. The wine list favours France, with house wine at £9.95 a bottle (£2.95 a glass). Open Mon to Sat L and D.

● **SHAFTESBURY** (Dorset)
*Fleur De Lys* 25 Salisbury Street, (01747) 853717. This comfortable, traditional restaurant on the first floor of a town house provides 'attentive' service. Rare twenty-first-century touches include grilled brill fillets topped with roast scallops on wilted watercress with a coriander sauce (£15.75). More typical are simple grilled Dover sole fillets (£20), pan-fried calf's liver on rösti with caramelised onions (£15.75), and warm Dorset apple cake with clotted cream (£5.50). The long, fully priced and eccentrically annotated wine list opens at £12.50. Closed Mon D in winter, Mon L and Sun D.

● **SHEFFIELD** (South Yorkshire)
*Greenhead House* 84 Burncross Road, (0114) 246 9004. Opening times are limited, but this modest family-run set-up continues to serve Sheffield well. Reporters have approved of the light lunch menu, with its three-fish gravadlax served with warm blinis and a cucumber and yoghurt salad (£4/£7.50), as well as rillettes of rabbit with honey-pickled grapes (£4/£7.50), before sauté strips of beef served in a puff pastry case with a red wine and green peppercorn sauce (£8.25). To finish, prune and Armagnac tart, and coffee pannacotta with 'cat's tongue' biscuits (£4.25), have also received the thumbs-up. Service has been 'excellent'. Open Thur to Fri L, Wed to Sat D.

*Mediterranean* 271 Sharrow Vale Road, (0114) 266 1069. Tapas and fresh fish share top billing in this 'good-humoured' restaurant away from the city centre. If you fancy grazing, pick the tapas menu (not available Fri and Sat D), with merguez sausages, marinated anchovies, or stuffed baby aubergines. Otherwise, the full menu will take you from pan-fried quail salad and deep-fried squid, to lemon tart, via chargrilled salmon with pesto (£11.95) and fillet of snapper with tarragon beurre blanc (£12.50). Daily specials offer further variety in the shape of, say, venison sausages, vegetarian parcels, and roast brill with mushrooms and shallots. A Braille menu is available,

and service receives lots of plaudits. Closed all day Sun.

● **SHEPTON MALLET** (Somerset)
*Blostin's* 29–33 Waterloo Road, (01749) 343648. Since 1985, Nick and Lynne Reed have developed Blostin's into a sound and reliable neighbourhood restaurant. Their supplies of local produce have improved over the years, although menus don't seem to change a great deal. Dinner is fixed-price (£15–£17) and vegetarians have a full menu to themselves. Warm salad of chicken and smoked bacon is a typical starter, while main courses might run to honey-roasted loin of pork or salmon in filo pastry. Finish with, say, iced ginger meringue. The wine list offers what the owners' call 'a spread of world favourites'; house wines are £9.95 and £10.50. Open Tue to Sat D.

● **SINNINGTON** (North Yorkshire)
*Fox and Hounds* Main Street, (01751) 431577. The setting – on the fringes of the North Yorks Moors – may be dyed-in-the-wool traditional, but the food in this country pub/restaurant zings with fashionable flourishes. Caper berries, chorizo and polenta add a touch of modernism to the long menus, which are bolstered by weekly specials. Away from deep-fried smoked fish risotto balls, or oven-roasted sea bass with salsa verde, you can also get a jazzed-up version of toad-in-the-hole, steamed venison and pheasant pudding, and hazelnut treacle tart with bourbon biscuit ice cream. Main courses £8.50–£15.50. Around two dozen wines from £8.95. Accommodation available. Open all week.

● **SOUTHALL** (Greater London)
*Gifto's Lahore Karahi* 162–164 The Broadway, (020) 8813 8669. A great crowd-pleaser on Broadway, this huge ground-floor arena now has the look of a minimalist canteen – and a furiously busy one, too. The cooking is Pakistani, and the action centres on the tandoor, which delivers everything from chicken and seekh kebabs, to quails and pomfret. Pani puri and other vegetarian chaat snacks are also available (£1.20 to £2.50), along with tawa specials cooked on hot plates (note

the 'takka tak' liver and kidney) and a handful of intriguing curries: lamb with tinda (baby pumpkin), for example (£6.20). Unlicensed but you can bring your own drink. Open all week.

● **STAITHES** (North Yorkshire)
*Endeavour* 1 High Street, (01947) 840825. New owners Brian Kay and Charlotte Willoughby are making a name for themselves in this cottagey restaurant-with-rooms by the sea. Locally landed fish is their main endeavour and reporters have been pleased with an 'unusual' watercress pancake topped with turbot and smoked salmon mousse (£4.95), 'proper' prawn cocktail (£4.65) and fillets of sea bass with a rosemary and anchovy crust (£12.25). Meat eaters are also well served with the likes of lamb tagine (£10.95), breads are home-baked and vegetables receive some unlikely twists (baby leeks with prunes, for example). Finish perhaps with crème brûlée (£4.75). House wine is £10.50. More reports, please. Open Sun L, Tue to Sat D.

● **STOKE HOLY CROSS** (Norfolk)
*Wildebeest Arms* 82–86 Norwich Road, (01508) 492497. Hanging carpets, African spears and masks set the tone in this pub/restaurant a few miles south of Norwich. The kitchen takes a modern view of things, offering the likes of warm Parma ham and Parmesan salad with truffle oil and hazelnuts (£6.25), grilled sea bass with tarragon risotto, wilted spinach and sauce vierge (£12.95), and passion-fruit tart with rhubarb sorbet (£5.25). Service is from attentive, young staff. The lengthy wine list scours the globe and includes 20 by the glass; prices start at £10.95. Open all week. There is a sister pub, The Mad Moose, at 2 Warwick Street, Norwich, tel. (01603) 627687.

● **STOKE PRIOR** (Worcestershire)
*Epic' Bar Brasserie* 68 Hanbury Road, (01527) 871929. The name is short for epicurean, rather than a reflection on how long meals take; it is a fitting aspiration for this bright, modern, busy casual place, the first of many planned outlets in the West Midlands. Staff compensated for any lack of experience with an 'observant, willing

and altogether nice' attitude towards our inspector. The five soups (£3.25–£4) take in Italian, Thai and Moroccan elements as well as English (smoked haddock, potato and parsley). The rest of the menu is similarly balanced, with some more domestic main dishes such as skate and chips (£11.50), and slow-roasted duck (£13.75). Thirty reasonably priced wines with twelve by the glass; Italian house selections £10.50. Open all week.

● **STOKE ROW** (Oxfordshire)
*Crooked Billet* Newlands Lane, (01491) 681048. 'Magical atmosphere, romantic, sexy, low lights': no wonder crowds make the tortuous trek to this high-profile country pub/restaurant in an 'impossible location'. But there's more. The kitchen has bags of ambition, offering elaborate-sounding dishes like cumin-seared veal fillet with cucumber, coriander and chilli noodles, mizuna, wood mushrooms and mild wasabi (£16.80), or 'line-caught' sea bass with sauté squid, grilled Mediterranean vegetables, salsa verde and basil oil dressing (£14.95). Service is very youthful and very good. The wine list is a global selection, with seven by the glass. Open Mon to Sat L and D, all day Sun.

● **STOW ON THE WOLD** (Gloucestershire)
*Hamiltons Brasserie* Park Street, (01451) 831700. The look of the place ('a Cotswold version of Scandinavian modern brasserie décor') and the newspapers supplied for patrons have been considered pleasing elements. 'Very good, attentive service' brings imaginative starters (around £5.50) such as smoked haddock and spring onion risotto with lemon and vanilla oil; and asparagus with Parma ham, lemon and sorrel dressing. Main dishes (£11–£13) might add tomato and basil sauce to calf's liver, bacon and onion, or citrus couscous and salsa verde to steamed sea trout. Equally inventive desserts (£4.50) include blueberry Bakewell tart. Short diverse wine list from £11.

● **STRATFORD-UPON-AVON** (Warwickshire)
*Desports* 13–14 Meer Street, (01789) 269304. Novelty looms large in this restaurant on the first floor of a centuries-

old half-timbered house. Most dishes come in two sizes – as starters or mains – and are divided up by origin: 'from the earth' (vegetarian dishes such as sweet potato, lentil and chickpea cakes), 'from the land' (meat, including crispy belly pork on sweet-and-sour noodles) and 'from the sea' (devilled cod on wilted spinach). Desserts (say, tarte Tatin) are 'from Heaven'. Main courses range from £12 to £16, and the short wine list includes house Bourgency at £10.95. Closed all day Mon and Sun.

● **SUDBURY** (Suffolk)
*Red Onion Bistro* 57 Ballingdon Street, (01787) 376777. A new team is now installed in the kitchen of this pleasantly jolly bistro with red-checked curtains at the windows and posters on the walls. There's no doubting the value for money (especially the set menus, £8 to £10), but results have been a touch uneven. On the plus side, reporters have enjoyed home-made game terrine with – of course – red onion jam (£3.95), chicken breast on tagliatelle (£9.25), and baked salmon fillet with sun-ripened tomato crust (£8.95). Ice creams and sorbets are the best bets for dessert. House wine is £9. There are branches in Bury St Edmunds and Colchester. Closed Sun D.

● **SWANAGE** (Dorset)
*Cauldron Bistro* 5 High Street, (01929) 422671. Fish from the local boats is the prime reason for plotting a course to Terry Flenley's south coast bistro. Scallops might be given the classic 'coquilles St Jacques' treatment or they might be put into a salad with bamboo shoots. Dover sole is grilled with olive oil and served with hand-cut chips (£16.50), and there might be blackened chicken with lime and ginger sauce for carnivores (£12.50). Finish with chocolate truffle cake or water ices. Light lunches of local crab or wild boar and apple sausages are served Thur to Sun (main courses £5–£7). Service is 'enthusiastic'. House wine is £10.95. Also open for D Tue to Sun.

● **TADCASTER** (North Yorkshire)
*Hazlewood Castle, Restaurant 1086* Paradise Lane, (01937) 535353.

'Restaurant 1086' refers to the fact that this ancient castle was mentioned in the Domesday Book; now it is a luxury hotel with its own cookery school. John Benson-Smith's extravagant-sounding menus marry dishes with suitable wines, and his repertoire takes in everything from 'Parmesan doodled sea scallops with a roast tomato and bacon stew' to roast duck breast with 'parsnip purée, roast salsify veggies and a slight tasting of intriguing and addictive blackcurrant and liquorice syrup'. To finish, there might be chilled vanilla risotto. L £12 one course, £19.50 for three; three-course D £35. House wine is £15.95. Accommodation available. Open Sun L and Tue to Sat D.

● **TADPOLE BRIDGE** (Oxfordshire)
*Trout* Tadpole Bridge, (01367) 870382. Situated in a tiny hamlet by a bridge over the Thames, this is very much an unadorned village pub. Chef Neil Hougardy's menus bristle with interesting ideas: a ragoût of snails is served on a grilled black mushroom with Stilton hollandaise (£5.95), while Singapore chicken and noodle laksa (£11.95) turns up next to roast guinea fowl with a chestnut farce on a bed of roasted vegetables (£14.95). Finish with chocolate and date bread and butter pudding (£4.75). The substantial wine list includes nine by the glass. Accommodation available. Closed Sun D.

● **TETBURY** (Gloucestershire)
*Calcot Manor* Tetbury, (01666) 890391. Occupying a converted Cotswold farmhouse built around a courtyard with barns and stables is this attractive country hotel with two distinct eating venues: the Gumstool Inn offers straightforward brasserie cooking, while the Conservatory Restaurant takes a more serious view of things. Here you might find seared monkfish in Thai mussel broth (£15.50), as well as chargrilled calf's liver and bacon (£13.50), or roast rack of local lamb with garlic and parsley crust (£17.50). Most starters, such as tagliolini with langoustine tails, can also be eaten as light main courses. A substantial list of 150 wines starts at £14. Open all week.

*Close Hotel*  8 Long Street, (01666) 502272. Daren Bale runs a tight ship in the kitchen of this Cotswold country-house hotel, and his menus are ardently modern in outlook. As well as fixed-price menus (dinner £35, lunch £12.50/£16.50), there is a carte (starters £8.50, mains £22.50) that promises the likes of ballottine of confit belly pork with wild mushroom and white bean broth, followed by wild salmon with sorrel, artichoke and Parmesan, finishing with chocolate and cardamom mousse with caramelised pear (£7.50). There's also a full selection for vegetarians, who might opt for sweet potato and courgette lasagne with tomato concassé and poached egg. Open all week.

● **TEWKESBURY** (Gloucestershire)
*Aubergine Caffe Bar*  73 Church Street, (01684) 292703. 'A decent pit stop if you happen to be in the area,' noted one traveller who lunched at this wooden-floored café/bar. Informality reigns, and you can choose anything from a light snack to a full meal. Chicken liver pâté (£4.65) and 'golf ball' fishcakes (£6.50) have been well received, likewise prawn won tons with sweet jam (£7.50). If you're looking for something more substantial, the menu also promises Moroccan lamb tagine (£7.75), pork and cider casserole (£6.75) and Thai green chicken curry (£7.50), before sweets like tiramisù terrine (£3.75). Service is swift and very pleasant. Teas, coffees and juices to drink; otherwise prices on the modest wine list start at £9.50. Closed Sun D and Mon.

● **TORQUAY** (Devon)
*Mulberry House*  1 Scarborough Road, (01803) 213639. In this Victorian terrace house near the seafront and town centre, you must book to lunch, dine or stay in one of the three rooms. Chef and owner Lesley Cooper's five choices in each course of the daily menu offer imaginative home-cooking. Typical starters are chicken, lemon and parsley mousse with mayonnaise; or rabbit sausage with orange and grain mustard dressing. Brixham skate wing, or braised leg of organic lamb with butter beans, tomato and rosemary, might follow, then

chocolate cream bombe with crystallised fruits. Main courses £8.50–£12.50. Short, interesting wine list from independent merchants with house wines £10. Accommodation available. Open Fri to Sun L and Wed to Sat D (residents only Mon and Tue D).

● **TREEN** (Cornwall)
*Gurnard's Head*  Treen, (01736) 796928. Gurnard naturally figures on the menu of this Cornish pub/restaurant from time to time, along with other fish specials including grey mullet (with garlic, thyme and pickled lemon, £12.95) and codling (with mussels in white wine sauce, £12.50). Meaty alternatives might include plump chicken cooked Normandy-style with apples and a Calvados sauce (£10.95). Sweet-toothed puds could take in pistachio and almond baklava (£3.95) or baked pear with a red wine and caramel syrup (£3.50). Staff are cheerful, real ales are kept in tip-top condition and there are some quaffable wines to choose from: house vin de pays is £12. Open all week.

● **TRESCO** (Isles of Scilly)
*Island Hotel*  Tresco, (01720) 422883. Everyone on the Island of Flowers 'greets you with a smile', according to one traveller who greatly enjoyed this delightful hotel. Dinner one night produced a multi-coloured crab mousse with creamy brandy sauce, 'dark green' leek and potato soup, and guinea fowl with a crisp rösti followed by vanilla-pod cheesecake with blackcurrant ice cream. Fish and seafood get prime billing on the menu: say, Tresco lobster, Bryher crab, or seared Cornish scallops with black pudding. Service is willing and courteous. The 'cellar list' is a mighty tome with prices from £15 upwards. Open all week.

● **TWICKENHAM** (Greater London)
*Brula*  43 Crown Road, (020) 8892 0602. Chef Bruce Duckett and co-owner Lawrence Hartley lent part of their names to this curiously titled neighbourhood bistro, which is pleasingly decked out with Victorian stained glass panels and padded church pews. Fixed-price lunches (£8 to £10) are excellent value for, say, beetroot and cumin soup followed by fish of the day

with grilled courgettes and shrimp butter. In the evening, a carte comes into play with the likes of pissaladière, navarin of lamb, or saddle of rabbit with apricots, almonds and spinach (£13.50). House wine is £10. No credit cards, but Switch accepted. Closed Sun.

*Loch Fyne Restaurant* 175 Hampton Road, (020) 8255 6222. One of many branches spawned by the original in Cairndow (see main entry, Scotland), this outlet in a converted pub follows the formula to the letter. Pots of mussels, Loch Fyne oysters (£1 each) and smoked salmon (£5.95) are backed up by dishes such as marinated red mullet with fennel and coriander (£5.95), poached smoked haddock with creamed spinach and peas (£7.50), and fillet of bass with roasted artichokes and rosemary (£12.95). Meat eaters are offered smoked venison and ribeye steaks. Whites dominate the short modern wine list; house French is £9.95. Open all week.

● **WESTFIELD** (East Sussex)
*Wild Mushroom* Westfield Lane, (01424) 751137. Fixed-price lunches have been deemed 'excellent value'(£12.95 to £15.95) at this 'most pleasant' Victorian house with a conservatory/bar overlooking the garden. One well-reported meal began promisingly with a pre-starter of pork rillettes, before seafood tempura with Thai dressing, pigeon breasts on mash with parsnip chips, then bread-and-butter pudding with Amaretto ice cream. In the evening, the kitchen cranks up a gear for, say, seared Rye Bay scallops with chive Vermouth sauce, pancetta and caramelised onion (£14.50). The lengthy wine list includes representatives from the nearby Carr Taylor vineyard; house wines start at £10.50. Open Tue to Fri and Sun L and Tue to Sat D.

● **WEYBOURNE** (Norfolk)
*Gasche's* The Street, (01263) 588220. Eat inside this thatched cottage restaurant, or on its patio, from menus contrasting retro dishes against others bringing modern twists to sound classic bases. On the one hand, avocado with prawns in Marie Rose sauce, pâté maison, and grilled Dover sole. On the other, duck and oriental vegetables in filo pastry with Thai dip, baked chicken breast with mango and mint salsa, or perhaps a compromise in roast pork stuffed with prunes and hazelnuts, with red wine and sage sauce. Set L £13.25, set D £24.50. House wines are £10, most of the other 40 are under £20, and there are interesting halves and sweet wines. Open Wed to Sun L, Wed to Sat D.

● **WEYMOUTH** (Dorset)
*Abbotsbury Seafood Bar* Abbotsbury Oyster Farm, (01305) 788867. This off-shoot of Abbotsbury Oyster Farm keeps live mussels, oysters and scallops in its tanks, and gets all fish from a 'day boat' so it is really fresh, with no overnight storage at sea. The day's catch is posted on a blackboard, and plaice, Dover sole, lemon sole, gurnard and brill may be available; but note that in bad weather there might be none at all. The oysters and mussels may be enjoyed au naturel or grilled, and there are sandwiches, salads and platters too. Dissenting carnivores may choose steak. Main courses £7–£12.50. House white is £8, house red £9. Open Tue to Sat L, Thur to Sun D.

*Perry's* 4 Trinity Road, (01305) 785799. Fresh seafood and harbour views win the day in this established restaurant overlooking the water. Fish dishes are chalked on blackboards, and you can expect anything from Loch Fyne mussels and Portland crab claw salad to whole roast sea bass with citrus and olive oil dressing (£16.50). Otherwise, there's a printed menu that caters for all tastes with feta cheese salad, confit of duck on noodles with honey and ginger (£12.50), and toffee mousse with apple and butterscotch. The substantial list of 65 wines has plenty of fish-friendly whites; house wine is £9.95. Open Tue to Fri and Sun L, all week D (Sun D Easter to Sept only).

● **WHITSTABLE** (Kent)
*Whitstable Oyster Fishery Co* Royal Native Oyster Stores, (01227) 276856. A stone's throw from the beach, this converted warehouse makes a clean,

unfussy setting for some decently handled fresh seafood. Apart from the eponymous bi-valves, the menu includes plenty of good things: reporters have praised warm Norfolk shrimps with toast, chargrilled slip sole, monster cock crab with mayonnaise, and scallops in cream and mushroom sauce. Freshly baked French bread to start, 'exceptionally good' maple crème brûlée, or ice cream to finish. Staff are friendly, and the modest wine list has lots of fish-friendly whites. Main courses £8.50–£18. Accommodation available, and a cinema. Closed all day Mon, Sun D in winter.

● **WOBURN** (Bedfordshire)
*Paris House* Woburn Park, (01525) 290692. Woburn Park is 'stunning, even in March, and is ideal for a post-prandial ramble', noted visitors to this historic half-timbered house on the Duke of Bedford's estate. Peter Chandler has been plying his trade here since 1983; there is ability and ambition at work – although it comes at a price (Set L £30 to £35, Set D £50 to £55). The repertoire is classic French all the way, from truffled duck foie gras, via fillet of beef in red wine and shallot sauce, to sablé of pears with poire William sabayon. Service is smartly attentive and the lengthy wine list targets those with deep pockets. House wine is £15. Closed all day Mon and Sun D.

● **WOLVERHAMPTON** (West Midlands)
*Bilash Tandoori* 2 Cheapside, (01902) 427762. Situated in the centre of town opposite the Civic Centre, this long-serving Indian offers a wide-ranging menu of dishes that are just a bit different. Pickles are freshly made and the proceedings kick off with some unexpected starters such as pancake roll stuffed with shredded chicken, and vegetable-stuffed peppers. There are the usual tandooris and biryanis, but the kitchen scores with its specials: mirchwangan korma (a red hot chilli version made with lamb) comes highly recommended, also note maacher tok (fish cooked with tropical Bangladeshi fruit) and mulli diya murghi (marinated chicken with white radish). Lunch specials are good value. Open Mon to Sat.

# *Scotland*

● **ARCHIESTOWN** (Moray)
*Archiestown Hotel* Archiestown, (01340) 810218. On the village square, this hotel has been the hub of local life for a goodly length of time, and new incumbents have given it a lift. Food is served in the recently re-vamped bistro and the menu takes a 'home-and-away' view of things, from local rump steak (£11) and west coast scallops meunière (£14.50), to wild mushroom risotto with shaved Parmesan. Duck foie gras is produced on the premises, and reporters have also appreciated a 'wee' haggis parcel laced with whisky, and langoustines with garlic butter. Finish with, say, summer fruit terrine. House wine is £12.50. Open all week L and D.

● **AYR** (South Ayrshire)
*Fruits De Mer* North Harbour Street, 01292 282962. Fruits of the sea are the main attraction in this converted chandler's shop beside the River Ayr.

Sound ingredients are often given creamy, old-school treatment, as in steamed mussels with leeks in cider cream sauce, or baked queen scallops with smoked salmon sauce topped with Black Forest ham. A non-seafood menu runs in tandem, promising the likes of sirloin steak with brandy and green peppercorn sauce, and chicken breast with lemon and tarragon. Main courses £6–£17. Finish with lemon cheesecake, or saffron-poached pear with berry compote. Wines are a cheap-and-cheerful bunch starting at £9.50. Open Fri and Sat L, Tue to Sun D.

● **BOWMORE** (Argyll & Bute, Islay)
*Harbour Inn* The Square, (01496) 810330. Shellfish from the quayside, plus beef, lamb and game from Jura and Islay show Scott and Wendy Chance's commitment to local produce – and you can sample the results in their whitewashed inn on the village square. Lagavulin scallops and Loch Gruinart

oysters share the billing with Bruichladdich smoked beef (served with wild mushroom vol-au-vent, £6.95), a mixed grill of Islay lamb with wholegrain mustard sauce (£14.70), and fillet steak served with haggis, parsnip chips and a sauce laced with Bowmore whisky (£17.20). Apart from some splendid malts, there's also a bargain-price, global wine list, with house wines setting the ball rolling at £10.50. Accommodation available. Closed Sun L.

● **CRIEFF** (Perthshire & Kinross)

*Bank Restaurant* 32 High Street, (01764) 656575. Housed in the former British Linen Bank (now Grade I listed), the McGuigans' town-centre bistro is a hive of activity where the owners now hold wine tastings and cookery workshops. A network of local suppliers (some organic) provide the raw materials for dishes like a Pittenweem lobster and langoustine broth infused with saffron and fennel (£3.50), or fillet of Tibbermore beef with morels, roasted shallots and port jus (£15.50). Desserts might run to pistachio parfait with poached baby pear and dark chocolate sauce. Around three dozen affordable wines include six by the glass. Accommodation is planned. Closed all day Mon and Sun D.

● **DERVAIG** (Argyll & Bute, Mull)

*Druimard Country House* Dervaig, (01688) 400345. The nearby Mull theatre pulls in the crowds, and the kitchen of this restored Victorian manse provides sustenance when it is needed. Fixed-price dinners might begin with courgette and mint soup glazed with Parmesan cream, then a sorbet, before a medley of local fish on saffron mash with a Noilly Prat and chive sauce, or loin of Scottish lamb on 'Irish' cabbage with parsley purée. Desserts such as chilled caramelised rice pudding with blueberry compote precede Scottish cheeses with oatcakes. The well-spread, global wine list begins with French house wines at £10.25. Menus are set price £29.50, accommodation available. Open all week D (L for residents only).

● **GATTONSIDE** (Borders)

*Hoebridge Inn* Gattonside, (01896) 823082. Tony and Maureen Rennie continue to please all comers at this converted coaching inn by the banks of the Tweed. Their regularly changing, global menu spans everything from Cullen skink (£3.95) to Asian-inspired chicken tortellini with a carrot and coconut infused broth (£4.95) among starters, while mains take in chargrilled fillet of Aberdeen Angus beef (£14.95), and crispy duck breast with 'drunken raisins', onion won tons and soy glaze (£11.95). Unusual ice creams and sorbets to finish (£3–£4). The comprehensive wine list has been strengthened with a New World contingent and remains 'exceptional value'. Open Tue to Sun D.

● **GLASGOW** (Glasgow)

*Air Organic* 36 Kelvingrove Street, (0141) 564 5200. As you might expect, there's a noticeable organic presence on the menu at this first-floor venue with a pavement area for al fresco dining. The food is an eclectic mix, although Japan is the main player, closely followed by Thailand and Italy. From the section headed 'air ocean' you might find peppered blue fin tuna salad with creamed balsamic and croûtons (£13), while 'air carnivore' offers saddle of Scotch lamb with Parmesan mash, roasted peppers, olive pâté and rosemary oil (£15.50). There are salads and bento boxes, as well as fixed-price deals (£15 and £20). The wine list features a number of organic bottles. Open all week.

*Lux* 1051 Great Western Road, (0141) 576 7576. Lux is on the upper floor of a late Victorian former railway station, designed by J.J. Burnett. Chargrilled ostrich steak on traditional skirlie with cracked peppercorn sauce, and fillet of Scotch beef brushed with red Thai paste on bean sprouts and coriander sour cream show how the kitchen blends local ingredients with exotic flavours. Fish dishes depend on the market, while desserts might include saffron-poached pear on Drambuie ice cream, or passion-fruit crème fraîche. Set-price menu £24.50

(2 courses) to £28.50. Around 50 wines include plenty by the glass; house is £14.50. Downstairs is Stazione, a Mediterranean restaurant and bar. Open Tue to Sat D.

*Rococo* 202 West George Street, (0141) 221 5004. Décor and music are equally uninhibited in this spectacular basement café-cum-bar, justifying its name. Dishes, fittingly, take in the likes of lobster oil with a starter paulette of smoked salmon and salad; seared scallops with gazpacho sauce and black olive dressing; or guinea fowl with sage café au lait sauce. Prices range from £14 (two-course L and pre-theatre) to £33.50-plus (three-course D). Four hundred wines start at £16 and rise to great heights. Closed all day Sun.

*78 St Vincent* 78 St Vincent Street, (0141) 248 7878. 'The setting and general ambience had an almost Parisian air,' felt one visitor to this town-centre venue in a former bank. Chef Stuart Wilson left as the Guide was about to go to press and no successor had yet been appointed, if things stay on course, there will be a brasserie-style menu with a strong Scottish vein running through it, backed up by a list of more than 40 wines, including several by the glass; house French is £13.95. Reports, please.

● **GLENLIVET** (Moray)
*Minmore House* Glenlivet, nr Ballindalloch, (01807) 590378. Set in the heart of Glenlivet Crown Estate, this stone-built country house is making its mark in the area. Four-course dinner menus (£30) change daily, there's no choice, and we've had good reports on Victor Janssen's cooking. Meals begin with soup (perhaps butternut squash and orange) before, say, seared king scallops baked in prawn sauce, while mains could include grilled rack of lamb with white beans, roasted fennel and dauphinois; desserts are the likes of iced apricot soufflé. The wine cellar is substantial and there are excellent breakfasts for those staying in the hotel. Open all week.

● **INVERNESS** (Highland)
*Glenmoriston Town House Hotel* 20 Ness Bank, (01463) 223777. The Italian-born owner of this hotel on a leafy bank of the River Ness has created his own brand of fusion food: Scottish produce given an Italian treatment. Gently pungent tortelloni of potato and truffle, and rack of lamb on fennel dauphinois with red wine sauce both impressed one visitor. The hotel is decorated in vibrant colours, with La Riviera dining room attractively painted in shades of blue and white. Set L £6.50 to £12, set D £19.50 to £24.50. Open all week. Reports, please.

● **KINFAUNS** (Perthshire & Kinross)
*Kinfauns Castle* by Perth, (01738) 620777. This grand 'baronial pile' makes much of its history and heritage, and has awesome views to match. The interior is resplendent with tartans, coats-of-arms and panelling, while the kitchen exploits Scotland's larder for its modern-accented menus. The fixed-price dinners (£35 to £38) might begin with honey-roast duck breast with herb risotto before fillet of Highland beef with julienne of mange-tout and basil jus, or seared halibut and scallops with savoury couscous. Desserts are equally vibrant, as in glazed lemon and passion-fruit tart. The wine list is a mammoth collection of 270 bins, with house wines from £15. Accommodation available. Open all week.

● **MELROSE** (Borders)
*Burt's Hotel* Market Square, (01896) 822285. A fixture of the Melrose social scene for many years, the Hendersons' family-run hotel continues to tick over, and the food served in the slightly dark, pubby bar has been well received: home-made parfait, salmon fishcakes, and chocolate brûlée have all been endorsed. Otherwise, the comfortably appointed restaurant offers Scottish hotel cooking along the lines of smoked pigeon and quail egg salad; a trio of Border lamb chops with redcurrant jelly and mint sauce; and 'moreish' banoffi tart. The global wine list is organised by grape variety; house wines start at £11.95. Open all week.

● **NEWTON STEWART** (Dumfries & Galloway)
*Kirroughtree Hotel* Newton Stewart, (01671) 402141. Built in 1719, this

imposing country mansion stands proudly in grounds ablaze with rhododendrons and swathes of azaleas. Dinner is a formal affair, centring on an elaborate four-course menu (£32.50). Buffalo mozzarella with tomato and basil oil might open the account, before smoked sea trout bavarois; for main course you might choose fillet of turbot on sweetcorn couscous with braised fennel, asparagus and Vermouth sauce before finishing with, say, walnut and Amaretto parfait, or a selection of five Scottish cheeses. The heavyweight wine list shoots skywards from house wine at £14.95. Open all week.

● **OBAN** (Argyll & Bute)
*Waterfront* 1 The Pier, (01631) 563110. 'From the pier to the pan ... as fast as we can!' is the motto of this fish restaurant in a former seamen's mission: watch ferries landing from the spacious first-floor dining room. Coffee and sandwiches are served from 10.30am, but the main business is locally caught fresh seafood: expect prawn and monkfish noodle soup (£6.25), pan-fried sea bass with prawn rice and mild tomato and chilli cream (£14.95), and deep-fried haddock with chips (£95). There are T-bone steaks for carnivores, and desserts include home-made passion-fruit cheesecake (£4.25), as well as Orkney ice creams. Straightforward, reasonably priced wines from £11.50. Open all week.

● **PLOCKTON** (Highland)
*Plockton Inn* Innes Street, (01599) 544222. 'What a really high-class seaside village pub/hotel should be,' enthused one reporter. There is local beer on tap and the owners try to ensure that ingredients for the kitchen are also as local as possible. Fish comes from the harbour 100 yards away and it might show up as mussels in white wine, king scallops with fennel and Pernod, or skate with black butter; the inn's smokehouse also makes a sizeable contribution. Sirloin steaks, haggis and lemon chicken satisfy the carnivores. Finish with brown sugar meringues or Scottish cheeses. Main courses £8.50–£13.50. Fifty malt whiskies and two dozen

affordable wines from £9.50. Open all week.

● **ST ANDREWS** (Fife)
*Catch Seafood Bistro* St Andrews Aquarium, The Scores, (01334) 477470. Adjacent to the St Andrews Aquarium, this bistro on two levels enjoys an enviable position right on the shore: large windows make the most of the view. It's an intimate place, with lots of bare wood giving the dining areas a Scandinavian feel, while pictures of fishing scenes reinforce the piscatorial theme. A new chef donned his whites as the Guide was going to press, but seafood is likely to remain the main theme. The short wine list keeps prices in check with house selections at £11.95. Reports, please. Closed Mon.

● **STROMNESS** (Orkney)
*Hamnavoe* 35 Graham Place, (01856) 850606. Finstown Bay mussels, organic salmon with smoked paprika crust, and white crab in Highland Park whisky sauce are typical of the local seafood specialities on offer in this cosy little place. Chris and Shelagh Thomas also seek out Orkney steaks (perhaps stuffed with sauté scallops), and vegetarians could be treated to provençale vegetable tarte Tatin with grilled goats' cheese and beetroot caviar. Round things off in traditional Scottish style with Eccelfechan tart or clootie dumpling with brandy. Main courses £9–£20, desserts £3.50. House wine is £9. No credit cards. Open Mon to Sat D only from mid-May to late Sept.

● **WALLS** (Shetland)
*Burrastow House* Burrastow, (01595) 809307. Bo Simmons and Henry Anderton now run Burrastow as a guesthouse rather than a hotel, but non-residents are still welcome if they book in advance. The setting is an eighteenth-century residence by the water's edge and fishing is one of its major attractions. Fruits of the sea also appear on the no-choice dinner menu (£25 for non-residents), which might offer Shetland mussels in red Thai sauce, and breast of duck with cranberries and port, before Normandy apple flan. Several organic wines grace the well-spread list, which

begins with 'proprietor's selections' at £9.25 a bottle (£2 a glass). D,B&B from £60 per person.

● **WEST LINTON** (Borders)
*Old Bakehouse* Main Street, (01968) 660830. Scottish produce shows strongly on the menus offered at this converted bakery (which still has the original ovens built into the walls). Starters might include potted Eyemouth shrimps, or a terrine of Perthshire wild boar, while main courses run to braised shank of Yarrow Valley lamb, and roast medallions of salmon with spring onion butter sauce. Cheeses are also from north of the border; otherwise choose a dessert such as white chocolate cheesecake with Mars Bar ice cream. Coffee is served with a traditional 'tablet'. Open Wed to Sun L and D.

# *Wales*

● **ABERYSTWYTH** (Ceredigion)
*Conrah Country House* Chancery, (01970) 617941. Set in a 22-acre estate with landscaped gardens and views towards the mountains of Cader Idris, this country hotel makes a useful getaway in the coastal hills of mid-Wales. The kitchen makes productive use of regional ingredients and the pickings from the kitchen garden for a salad of smoked chicken, prawns and crispy Carmarthen ham with hazelnut vinaigrette, or ragoût of monkfish, smoked haddock and vegetables with laverbread and saffron cream. Desserts might include apple fritters with fruit confit and balsamic vinegar, or pear and dark chocolate tart. Main courses L £6 to £12.50 and set D £24 (2 courses) to £27. Eight house wines start at £12. Open all week (phone to check Sun D).

● **CARDIFF** (Cardiff)
*Buffs* 8 Mount Stuart Square, (029) 2046 4628. Part wine bar, part restaurant, this venue does a busy lunch and supper trade. Lunches are a mixed bag: smoked mackerel pâté (£3.95), salt beef with dill pickles and potato salad (£5.95), venison sausages with mash (£6.25), backed up by blackboard specials. The full restaurant menu scours the globe for baked laverbread and bacon (£4.95), Thai prawns with a 'parcel' of rice and dipping sauces (£12.95), and tandoori vegetables (£7.95), taking in chargrilled steak, and calf's liver with creamed leeks along the way. Open L only, Mon to Fri, and Sun.

*Le Monde* 60 St Mary Street, (029) 2038 7376. Right in the centre of the city, close to the Millennium Stadium, is this lively joint with its own way of doing things. The rules are as follows: stand in the queue (there are no bookings except for large parties), head for the display counters of meat and fish, choose what you want and how you want it cooked, then find a table. Chargrilling is applied to everything from salmon steaks to Scotch beef fillet; otherwise expect baked crawfish tails, venison with port sauce and more. Main courses £9–£20. House wines start at £9.95. On the same site and under the same ownership are La Brasserie, tel. (029) 2037 2164; and Champers, tel. (029) 2037 3363. Closed all day Sun.

● **HAY-ON-WYE** (Powys)
*Tipple 'n Tiffin* The Pavement, (01497) 821932. Informality rules in this casual place, where you can eat in the airy ground-floor room or sink into deep sofas in the basement bar. The short menu is built around plates and bowls to share: home-smoked fish, Celtic mussels, 'shards' to dip in molten Welsh cheeses and laverbread, plus a few larger dishes like slow-roast, marinated ribs of Tamworth pork with chilli noodles. Prices range from £6 to £8. Salads, freshly baked breads and a few home-made puddings complete the picture. The excellent value for money extends to the short, sharp wine list; prices from £10 a bottle (£2.50 a glass). Open Tue to Sat.

● **LLANARMON DYFFRYN CEIRIOG**
(Wrexham)
*West Arms Hotel* Llanarmon Dyffryn
Ceiriog, (01691) 600665. Once a shooting
inn, this isolated rough-stone hostelry, set
in the Ceiriog Valley in the foothills of the
Berwyn Mountains, has apparently
dispensed hospitality and sustenance
since 1670. Standard pub grub is served in
the heavily beamed bar, while meals in
the dining room are noticeably more
ambitious. Local produce shows up well in
pheasant breast wrapped in bacon on
herbs and baby leaves, or fillet of Welsh
beef on rösti potatoes with a peppercorn
sauce, while to finish you could choose
between devilled kidneys or mango crème
brûlée. Set dinner menu £19.90 to £24.90.
Service is very 'smiley'. House wines are
£11.95. Open Sun L and all week D.

● **LLANFYLLIN** (Powys)
*Seeds* 5 Pen Y Bryn Cottages, (01691)
648604. 'Good food, produced simply in a
minuscule kitchen' is how fans sum up the
appeal of Mark and Felicity Seager's
cottage restaurant. Bistro-style, fixed-
priced dinners (around £21 for three
courses) could take in home-potted
shrimps, and sauté lambs' kidneys with
grain mustard sauce, before comforting
puddings such as treacle tart or chocolate
and rum mousse. The atmosphere is
'excellent' and the substantial list of over
160 wines is 'modestly priced'; six are
available by the glass. Open Wed to Sun L,
Tue to Sat D.

● **LLANWDDYN** (Powys)
*Lake Vyrnwy Hotel* Lake Vyrnwy,
(01691) 870692. The very model of a
sporting country house, this hotel stands
high on the hillside of the Berwyn range
with views of the lake and the mountains
beyond. Fixed-price dinner menus
(£29.50) provide a whirlwind tour of just
about every major cuisine, cruising
though risotto of pancetta and shiitake
mushrooms, Moroccan couscous with
caramelised vegetables, and Asian
poached chicken breast with lemon grass
and ginger broth, before touching down
with Welsh cheeses and vanilla-poached
rhubarb cheesecake. Open all week.

● **PEMBROKE** (Pembrokeshire)
*Old Kings Arms* Main Street, (01646)
683611. Tradition looms large in this old-
fashioned hotel with its oak beams, dark
panelled walls and rural bric-à-brac. Chef
Taffy Woolles has a keen eye for local
produce, whether it be fish, organic meats
or cheese, and his menus (main courses
£10.95–£13.75) show some neat up-to-
date touches. Straightforward dishes such
as grilled Dover sole or Welsh Black fillet
au poivre are done to perfection, and there
are more intricate ideas such as chicken
breast stuffed with cheese, Carmarthen
ham and sage, or confit of duck on juniper
cabbage. Decent desserts range from
lemon posset to 'hefty, unctuous' toffee
pudding. The wine list has many
respectable bottles under £15. Open all
week.

● **RUTHIN** (Denbighshire)
*Da Vincis* 7 Upper Clwyd Street, (01824)
702200. 'Leonardo's' chicken liver pâté
(£3.95) is among starters on the menu in
this airy, split-level restaurant. The Italian
theme continues with roast duck breast
cooked with fennel, raisins and Barolo
(£13.50), as well as salmon fillet wrapped
in Parma ham with roasted peppers
(£12.50). Wales also has its say in the
shape of leek tartlet topped with smoked
salmon (£4.95), and loin of lamb in
laverbread and red wine sauce (£14.95).
Desserts (£3.50) are a mixed bag, ranging
from lemon tart with raspberry coulis to
strawberry meringues. Presentation is
well above average and the wine list has
house French at £5.50 per half-litre, £9.95
a litre, or £2.25 a glass. Closed Sun and
Mon.

*Off the Square at the Castle Hotel* St
Peter's Square, (01824) 702479. Leopard-
skin wall panels and imitation gargoyles
add a touch of interest to this
neighbourhood eating place. Prices are
low, children are welcome, and the menu
shows signs of ambition. Warm Roquefort
soufflé on a honeyed pecan nut and
poached pear is an intriguing starter,
while mains could run from chargrilled
chicken with papaya salad to pan-fried
salmon on bubble and squeak with

creamed leek sauce. Sticky toffee pudding with warm butterscotch sauce looks like the star dessert: 'once eaten never forgotten'. Main courses £8.50–£15; light lunch menu also available. House wines at £8.50 kick off an affordable list. Open all week.

● **SOLVA** (Pembrokeshire)
*The Old Pharmacy* 5 Main Street, (01437) 720005. The Lawton brothers continue on their way at this bistro-style restaurant in a one-time chemist's shop. Daily supplies of fish from the local boats, or nearby Milford Haven, might appear as Cajun-style fillet of halibut, or whole sea bass baked with chilli, ginger and lemon grass (both dishes £16.50). The rest of the menu globetrots for bouillabaisse (£6.50), Caribbean king prawns (£15.50), and saddle of Welsh lamb with mint and pine kernel stuffing and Cumberland sauce (£16). Finish with, say, French crêpes, tiramisù or white chocolate and Cointreau crème brûlée (desserts £4.50). Ten house wines from £10.95 (£2.60 a glass). Open all week D.

● **SWANSEA** (Swansea)
*Knights* 614–616 Mumbles Road, (01792) 363184. There are views over the wide sweep of Swansea Bay from the windows of this stylish, light and airy restaurant. One and two-course lunches are excellent value, fresh fish gets its own daily menu, and the evening carte shows plenty of ambition: deep-fried sea bass 'soufflés' come with lobster and crab sauce (£5.45), while sauté kangaroo steak is served with pak choi, beansprouts and black-bean sauce (£13.25). By contrast, desserts (£3.40) are good old-fashioned offerings like summer pudding or rhubarb and gooseberry crumble. Around four dozen wines offer plenty of sound drinking for under £20; house wine is £10.40. Closed Sun D.

*P.A.'s* 95 Newton Road, (01792) 367723. The daily-changing fish menu at this lively spot in Mumbles might include simply grilled lemon sole, or more elaborate monkfish medallions with king prawns, smoked bacon and garlic (both dishes £13.95). The local speciality, wild sewin (Welsh salmon trout), might come as a cutlet with orange and basil butter sauce (£12.25). On the two-course lunch menu (£8.95), sauté sardines might precede pork tenderloin with a sage, onion and brandy sauce. Home-made desserts embrace summer fruit cheesecake. Dinner dishes are more elaborate, including perhaps beef medallions with gooseberry compote and a red wine and mint jus. Forty wines, with house selections £8.95. Closed Sun D.

● **WELSH HOOK** (Pembrokeshire)
*Stone Hall* Welsh Hook, (01348) 840212. Secret, secluded and rather private, this 600-year-old country hotel actually feels like 'a little piece of France transplanted into Wales'. The cuisine is authentically Gallic, service is impeccable and the place has bags of style. The menu du jour is £21 for four courses; the carte is more expensive (main courses around £15). Expect a repertoire that runs from escargots and Flemish leek and blue cheese tartlet to flambéed breast of duck with orange peel and Cognac, cassoulet and – in more modern vein – 'fantastic' turbot in a vanilla and red peppercorn sauce. Desserts have included 'delicate' chilled nougat studded with nuts. The short wine rarely strays beyond the French borders; house selections are £12.20. Open Tue to Sat D.

● **WOLF'S CASTLE** (Pembrokeshire)
*The Wolfe* Wolf's Castle, (01437) 741662. Well-kept, picturesque and built of grey stone, this old inn now functions as bar, brasserie and restaurant, with menus to suit each area. Welsh produce has its say on chef Simon Periam's carte (main courses £9.50–£16.75), which might offer goats' cheese and Carmarthen ham brioche with onion and Grenadine marmalade before, say, steamed fillet of brill, with cockle and laverbread cream, or something more exotic like cutlet of wild boar with black cherries and kumquats. Desserts could include chocolate Amaretto terrine. Around 30 decent wines are bolstered by owner Gianni di Lorenzo's 'personal collection'. Accommodation available. Open all week.

# Channel Islands

● ST BRELADE (Jersey)
*Sea Crest Hotel* La Route du Petit Port,
(01534) 746353. The sands of St Ouen's
Bay are just a stroll away from this
roadside restaurant, which also boasts
views of La Poulente headland. The
kitchen makes good use of locally landed
fish for dishes such as roast monkfish
rolled in brioche crumbs with chargrilled
vegetables and tapénade, and fillet of brill
with a crab cake, pak choi and mussel and
saffron sauce. There's also plenty for meat
eaters (spiced rump of lamb with
couscous), while desserts take in
everything from 'surprise' banana split to
zabaglione. Menu options include set-
price deals at £10 or £17.50, and a carte
(starters £6.50–£8.50, mains £12.50–
£18.50). France dominates the lengthy
wine list; house selections from £10.85.
Closed Mon and Sun D.

● ST PETER PORT (Guernsey)
*La Frégate* Les Cotils, (01481) 724624.
An idyllic setting overlooking the harbour
is one of the main attractions at this
luxurious hotel, which has been
redecorated in 'nihilistic style' (or 'neutral
colours', as another put it). The cooking
receives good reports: mussel soup
(£5.95), brill on spinach with lobster sauce
(£14.75), and lime and lemon tart (£4.95)
have been endorsed, and the kitchen also
ventures further afield for spiced tempura
of plaice (from the three-course table
d'hote menu, £15.95), and vegetable
couscous with goats' cheese and red
pepper coulis (£9.95). There are some
'beautiful' wines on the predominantly
French list, which opens with house
selections at £11.50. Open all week.

# Northern Ireland

● LONDONDERRY (Co Londonderry)
*Beech Hill Hotel, Ardmore Restaurant* 32
Ardmore Road, (028) 7134 9279. Beech
trees do indeed grow in the landscaped
grounds outside this impressive
eighteenth-century country mansion. The
food served in the Ardmore Restaurant
strikes a more modern note, flamboyant
ideas rubbing shoulders with a few more
homely creations. Confit of rabbit leg
comes with vanilla seed risotto and vanilla
sauce, pan-seared sea bass is paired with
fennel purée and a fennel confit, while
noisettes of lamb are cooked 'en
crépinette' and served with a fettuccine of
vegetables and tarragon jus. Two/three
course lunch is £14.95/£17.95, dinner is
£19.95/£27.95; there is also a carte (main
courses £10–£15) and separate menus of

'lighter options' and vegetarian dishes.
House wines from £12.50.
● PORTSTEWART (Co Londonderry)
*Smyths Restaurant* 2–4 Lever Road,
(028) 7083 3564. Originally a cobbler's,
this pebble-dashed building has been
neatly converted into a homely,
comfortable restaurant with a very jolly
atmosphere. The cooking is bistro style
(starters £3–£4.75, mains £9.75–£13.75)
with mussels in white wine and garlic, or
wild mushroom en croûte, preceding
guinea fowl with a herbed potato cake and
courgette ribbons, or chargrilled chicken
with aubergine and spicy couscous.
Desserts (£3.95) might include rhubarb
syllabub and almond mille-feuille. Live
music in the bar area on Wednesdays and
Sundays. Open Tue to Sun L and D.

# The Good Food Club 2002

Many thanks to all the following people who contributed to this year's Guide...

Russell and Irene
  Abrahams
Dr Sidney Abrahams
David Adam
Jan Adams
Mr and Mrs J.G.
  Adams
Stephen Adams
Mr D.E. Addison
Martin Ainsworth
John and Leslie Aird
Mrs S. Albinson
Mr and Mrs
  Alexander
Dr and Mrs A.A.
  Alibhai
Alexander Allcock-
  Rouse
M. Allen
Sir Anthony Alment
Catherine Althaus
Mr and Mrs
  Angelrath
Sir Michael Angus
Mr H. Arbuthnott
Cynthia Archer
Michael Armstrong
Dr Sidney Arnott
Brian Ashby
Dr Robert Asher
V. Ashworth
Mr C. Aspin
D. and D. Astle
Mr P.D. Atkins
Nicholas Atkinson
David Atwell
Mr and Mrs D.G.
  Austin
Mrs C.S. Avery
  Jones
Mr and Mrs I.M.
  Bacon
Roger Baggallay
Jane and Martin
  Bailey
Iain Baillie
Mr W.H. Baily
Audrey Bainbridge
Mr and Mrs J. Baird
Mr R.W. Baker

Richard Balkwill
Dr C.B. Ballinger
Hilary Bammer
John Barker
Glenice Barnard
Mr and Mrs B.J.
  Barry
Jane Barry
Mr M.D. Bartlett
Alan and Lisa Barton
Mr P. Basterra
Mrs M.A. Batchelor
Romney Bathurst
Mrs J.B. Battersby
Lindsay Baugh
Conrad Bayliss
T.H. Beale
Valerie Beck
Ms E. Becker
Mr F.R. Beckett
Prof J. Belchem
C.J. Bell
George Bell
John Bence
John Bennett
Mr and Mrs J.
  Bentley
Peter Bentley
W.M. Bentsen
Mr C.K. Beresford
Lucy Beresford
Gabriele Berneck
Patrick Best
Paul Betts
P.L. Bevis
Mrs L.M Bhgelmi
Dr Delia Bickerton
Betty and Chris Birch
Ken Bird
Mr R.G. Birt
Dr. J. Bisdee
Mr C.T. Blackburn
Trevor and Ann
  Blackburn
Mrs V. Blackburn
Mrs J.H. Blake
Mr P. Blake
Mrs J.A. Blanks
Edward Blincoe
Mr and Mrs S. Bliss

C.C. Bonwick
Alistair Booth
Dr Ben Booth
Michel Boulesteix
Canon and Mrs
  Bourdeaux
Mr A.J. Bowen
Rosemary Bowen
George and
  Garnette Bowler
John Boyd
Simon Boyd
Lorraine Boyle
Anthony Bradbury
Barry Brahams
Beatrice Brandon
Chris Bray
Mr and Mrs Edwin
  Brew
Alex Bridgeman
Kenneth Brightman
Hazel Broadbent
Bob Broadhead
Mrs P.J. Broadhurst
Andrew Broche
Roy Bromell
Alan Brooker
Dr David Brooks
Douglas Brooks
Col J.M. Browell
Dr and Mrs D.G.
  Brown
David and Jackum
  Brown
Graham Brown
Kaye Brown
Mr N. Browne
Mr and Mrs S.G.
  Brunning
William Bruton
M. Bryden
Mr and Mrs Bryson-
  Edwards
Mike Buchanan
R.W. Buckle
Alan Buckuz
Jeremy Budden
Alan Bullock
Daphne Bullock
David Bultitude

Michael Bunce
Mr and Mrs A.G.M.
  Burge
Mr W.W. Burke
Renee and Gareth
  Burn
Michael Burns
Mr M.H. Burr
T. Burton
Mrs J. Bush
Richard Bush
Paul and Chris
  Butler
Peter Byworth
Dr Anne Calder
Roger Calverley
Mrs C. Campbell
Mr J. Campos
Jane Carroll
Dr John Carroll
Mr K. Carslaw
Brian Carson
Tracy Carville
Richard Cashmore
Holger Castenskiold
Dr R.E. Catlow
Mr and Mrs M.
  Cavaghan-Pack
Susan Chait
Richard Chapman
S. Charles
Mr N. Charnock
Mr B.A. Chatwin
Peter Cheetham
David Chol-
  mondeley
Mr and Mrs K.M.
  Choy
Mr and Mrs J.
  Clapham
Mrs A. Colbatch
  Clark
David Clarke
Mr P.K. Clarke
William Clarke and
  Myra Drake
K. Cleveland
Doug and Ruth
  Clunie
Roger Cockbill

Michael Codron
Ann Cohen
Mr and Mrs Cole
K.J. Coleman
Sara Colville
Mr R.T. Combe
Mr W. Combe
Michael Comninos
Michael Connolly
Sean Connolly
Michelle Cook
Ronald Cook
Peter Coombes
Mr B.A. Cooper
Peter Cooper
Prof Alex Coram
Ron and Sheila
  Corbett
Brian Cornwell
Mr and Mrs Corrie
  Hill
Mr and Mrs A.
  Cotcher
Stephen Court
N.A. Coussmaker
Mr T. Simon
  Couzens
Pamela Cowen
G. Craig
Gordon Craig
Mr and Mrs Peter
  Crane
Nigel Crapper
Mr J. Crisp
Mr A. Cross
Neil Croucher
Doreen Cun-
  ningham
Mr and Mrs Dalzell
Mr M. Daneshvar
Dr Stan Da Prato
Patricia Darby
Michael Darin
Peter and Jane
  Davey
Mr and Mrs D.W.M.
  Davidson
Alun Davies
Beatrix Davies
Brian and Sue
  Davies
Duncan Davies
John Davies
Margaret Davies
R. Davies
Brian Davis
D.S. Davis
N. Davis
Roger Davis

Dr and Mrs R.P.R.
  Dawber
Prof Alan Day
Mr M.J. Day
Ms N.C. Dee
James Delahooke
Timothy James De
  Lay
Sarah De Lisle
Mr and Mrs F.C. de
  Paula
T. Delay
Hugh Dempster
Mr and Mrs Dewar
Mrs K. Diamond
Fiona Dick
Ms E. Dickinson and
  Mr R. Seddon
Alex Dickson
Mellanie Dixon-Peel
Mr G.M. Dobbie
Mr and Mrs James
  Douglas
Mr A.J. Dourleyn
Fergus Dowding
Hilary and Mike
  Downes
Barrie Drewitt
Mr D.R. Drucquer
Robin Drummond
Laleh Dubash
John Ducker
Sally Duckham
Mr and Mrs L.S.
  Dunbar
Prof John Duncan
Nigel Duncan
Paul Dunmore
Dr Andrew Dunn
Ryan Dutton
Claude Duval
Mr R.S. Eades
John Earthy
Dr and Mrs Lindsay
  Easton
Mr and Mrs K. Eckett
Mrs N. Eden
Dr S. Eden
Aileen Edwards
Anthony and Beth
  Edwards
Malcolm Edwards
Mark Edwards
Mr R.C. Edwards
John Elder
Mr G. Elflett
Mrs C.M. Elkington
Derrick and
  Margaret Elliot

Mr I.R. Elliott
David Ellis
Dr and Mrs R.A.
  Emmott
D.J. Endersby
Mr H.M. Escolme
Maurice Escow
David Etherington
Mrs A.M. Evans
D. Evans
Mr and Mrs M.
  Everard
Jed Falby
E.R. Farmer
T. Farrell
Mr and Mrs Farrell
Ann Farrow
Mrs E.A. Faulkner
Dr Philip Feldman
Mr G.A. Fenn
Brian Ferms
Stephanie Fierz
John Finlayson
Julie Fisher
Sir Richard Fitz-
  herbert
Mr A.T.R. Fletcher
Clare Fletcher
G.E Fletcher
Anthea Forbes
Dr E.A. Foreman
Christopher Forman
Mrs P.L. Forrest
Mr and Mrs R.E.
  Forrest
G.L. Forster
Mr A. Foster
Mr R.J.N. Fowler
Linda Frain
Daphne Francis
Graham Franses
R.S. and S. Frapwell
Mr R.L. Fraser
Ann and Don French
Joy French
Mr C.W. Freyer
Mr A. Furness
Mr R. Fuse
Mr Gamitcheson
Paul Gane
R.J. Garlick
Amanda Garrett
Dr Ian Gavin
Mr K. Geenwell
Patricia Gerrard
Mr P. Gibbs
Richard Gibson
Anthony Gilbey
Elizabeth Gilmore

John Glaze
P.M. Glover
Christopher Godber
Mr and Mrs Jim
  Godfrey
Maria Goldberg
Dr Lawrence Goldie
Joy and Raymond
  Goldman
Linda and Susie
  Goldschmidt
Corinne Golightly
Mr R.F. Gompertz
Tom Gondris
Kate Goodchild
Mrs J. Gooding
Joan Goodrum
Larry and Pauline
  Goodson
Kate Gordon
Mr R.L. Gorick
Terry Gorman
Mr and Mrs A.
  Gough
Mr C. Gould
Mrs J.B. Gould
Amanda Gourlay
Mr M.B. Gowers
Mr and Mrs J.W.L.
  Graham
John Graham
Mr R. Graham
David Grant
Mrs M. Granzon
Jean Gray
Monique Gray
Mr M.C. Green
Mr T.G. Green
Richard Greenwell
Jim Greenwood
Conal Gregory
Mrs J. Gregory
Dr P.R. Gregory
E.J. Gribbon
Mr R.F. Grieve
Edward Griffin
Mr E.F. Griffin
Ffion Griffith
Mr R.F.B Grimble
Mr and Mrs Jim
  Grimes
Nigel Grimweed
Mr N.M. Grimwood
Richard Grosby
Dr K. Grove
Lieut K.R. Groves
Jayne Guest
Stuart Guntzenbach
Alice Gwinnell

Michelle and
Spencer Hagard
Joy Haigh
Dr Bryan Hall
C.J. Hall
Ian Hall
Dr J.M. Hall
Marlene Hall
Prof Peter Hall
Tom Halsall
Dr B. Hamilton
Matthew Hamlyn
John Hammond
Tony Hampton
Mr C. Hancock
Gordon Hands
Mr F.G. Hankins
Ian Hannah
Mr S. Hanney
David Hansen
Mr J.G. Hanson
Mr F. Hardy
Mr J. Harison
Christopher Harlowe
Tim Harper
Dr and Mrs J.A.
Harrington
Raymond Harris
Rita Harris
Dr B.D.W. Harrison
Howard Harrison
Nigel Harte
Mr J.D. Hartley
Ben and Valerie
Hartman
C.I. Harvey
Julian Harvey
Peter Harvey
Mr I.H. Haste
Mrs S.D. Hayes
Vivian Hayter
Lydia Heah
T.P. Heavisides
Mr H. Hedworth
A.J.A. Helme
Pat and Roger
Heminway
Mr J.F. Hemmings
Mr P.R. Hemsley
Dr Ann Henderson
Mr N.F. Henshaw
Drs Geoffrey and
Joselen Heron
Dr Andrew
Herxheimer
Mrs V. Heseltine
John Heskell
D. Hew
Allan Hewitt

James Hewlett
John Hicks
Russell Hilborne
Mr A. Hill
D.R. Hill
Jennifer Hill
Wendy Hillary
Mr E. Hinds
Mr and Mrs P.A.
Hoare
Mrs L. Hodge
Ian Hollows
Frank Hoppe
Betty Hooper
Ralph Hopton
Alistair Horne
Chris Horner
Capt Vincent
Howard
Mr D.M. Howarth
Lydia and Julian
Howarth
Alan Howe
D.P. Howell
Timothy Howram
David Hudson
Katherine Hughes
N. and M. Hull
Mr and Mrs E. Hume
Dr Tim Hunt
Mr T.J. Hypher
Fred Inglis
Mrs H.E. Ingmire
Dr Sheila Innes
K.G. Isaacson
Mrs B.W. Jack
Dr P. Jacques
Sally Jaine
Gareth James
Mrs R.G. James
J.R. Jameson
Bruce Jamieson
Robert Jamieson
Anthony Jay
Brenda Jeeves
M.F. Jeeves
Mary Jefferies
Alan Jefferson
Sarah Jeffery
A.B. Jenkins
Sir Elgar Jenkins
Valerie Jenkins
F.G. Jennings
Kathy Jenson
Paul Jerome
David Jervois
Stephen Jessel
Mr B.M. Joce
Robert John

Ron Johns
Dr Paddy Johnson
R.T. Johnson
Alexander
Johnstone
Mrs M. Johnston
Jones
Benita and Ian
Jones
Douglas Jones
Ian Jones
Mrs J. Jones
L. Jones
Mel Jones
Paul Joslin
Peter Jowitt
Mr M.R. Judd
Mr R. Karpinski
Dr Leon Kaufman
Mr M.M. Keir
Allan Kelly
Geoffrey Kemp
Henry Kemp
C.N. Kendall
Rosalind Kent
Mrs J.M. Kenwand
Anne Kerr
Rev Peter Kettle
Elizabeth Key
Mr and Mrs J.H.
Kilby
Peter Kilfoyle
John Kimble
Mr and Mrs Michael
Kirk
Mr R.N. Kirk
C. Kitchen
Carol Kite
John Kleeman
Sylvia Knapp
Dr E.B. Knight-
Jones
R.G.A. Knott
Peter Knowes
Chris Kong
Wendy Kramer
Peter Kromes
Mr W.F. Lahaise
Mr I. Laidlaw-
Dickson
Mr S.H. Lait
Christine Lakic
R. Lambert
Michael Launder
Mr and Mrs Kevan
Lavender
Dr and Mrs J.
Lawrence
Richard Lawrence

Mr A. Lawson
Dr and Mrs L.
Leaston
Mr and Mrs G.H.
Ledbury
Adrian Lee
Mr M.P. Lee
Patricia Lee
Lt Col M.I. Leese
Mrs J.M. Lefeaux
Mike Lefroy
P.L. Leonard
Dr Michael Lerner
Mr D.J. Lethem
O. Levinson
Mike Levy
Alan Lewis
Mr and Mrs E. Lewis
Susan Lewis
Mr and Mrs Leonard
Licht
Mr B.N. Liddiard
Mr J.R. Liddiard
Mr and Mrs R.G.
Lightwood
Mrs Lincoln
Keith and Katherine
Lindop
Katherine Lindsay
Prof P.A. Lindsay
Ian Lipton
Mr V.C.M. Lister
Mrs B. Littlefair
Dr David Lloyd
James Lloyd
Andrew Lobbenberg
Brigitta Lock
Victoria Lodge
Ian Logan
Paul Lomas
Sheila Longbottom
Zara Longlands
Mr and Mrs
Lourenco
Deborah Loveluck
M. Lowden
Mr G.S. Lowth
Jeremy Lucas
Mr P.S. Luckin
David Lymer
Dr and Mrs A.J.
Macdonald
Dr and Mrs I.S.
Macdonald
Robert Macgregor
Mr A.J. Macintosh
C.H.N. Mackey
Mrs A. Mackinnon

Prof Margaret Maden
Sean Magee
Peter Mair
Mr J.P. Malon
Jan Manning
David Mariano
Dr C. Markus
J.P. Marland
Philippa Marnham
Christine Marris
June Marsden
Mrs M. Marsh
R.O. Marshall
Mr and Mrs Roger Marshall
Mr and Mrs T.F. Marshall
Mr and Mrs St John Marston
Alex Martin
Mr and Mrs G.D. Martin
Roger and Joan Martin
Donald Massey
Victoria Matthern
Mr J. Maxim
Dr Victor Maxwell
C.J. May
Elspeth May
Ian May
Mr and Mrs Kenneth May
Doug Mayman
Fiona Maynard
J. Mcarthur
Kevin and Margaret Mcbrien
Colin Mccarty
Thomas Mccourt
John McCracken
Michael Mcevoy
Charles McFeeters
Colin and Lilian McGhee
Jennifer Mcintosh
Mr and Mrs Maurice Mckee
Dr John Mckenzie
Mr J.A. McKinnell
Barbara Mcleish
Mr J.P. Mcmahon
Anthony Meekin
Sally Melling
A. Melnikoff
Mr and Mrs D. Melzack
Mrs E. Merriam

Harold Michaels
Dr Guy Michell
Robin Middleton
Mr and Mrs J.D. Miles
Jean and Iain Millar
Christine Miller
Mr T.W. Miller-Jones
Mrs S.B. Milne
Chris Milton
Dr Philip Mitchell
Wendy Montague
Mr A.J.R. Moon
Ms R.D. Moon
Barry Moorcroft
Mrs C.M. Moreton
John Morgan
Malcolm and Catherine Morrell
Mr N. Mountjoy
Gillian Moussa
Sandy and Lorna Muir
Patrick Murphy
Mr G.R. Murray
Sara Nathan
Mr and Mrs Natton
Dr Malcolm Nattrass
Mr C.H. Naylor
Chris and Vicki Naylor
Julia Neuberger
Max Newfeld
B. Newman
Brian and Tessa Newman
F.S. Newman
Mr J. Newman
Dr John Newton
Mr and Mrs Nichollsen
Mr C.C. Nichols
Frank Nicol
Ann and Edward Nicoll
Brian Norbury
J.G. Norris
Bruce and Kate Nottage
Dr Ian Nussey
David Nutt
Lucy O'Leary
Neal O'Leary
Mr K.P. O'Mahoney
Gregg O'Reilly
Anthony Ogden
Prof Robert Orledge
Mr and Mrs R.E. Osborne

Dr Elizabeth Owen
Patricia Owers
William Pack
Stephen Page
Dr Kelvin Palmer
Dennis Parker
Mr J.R. Parker
Richard and Andrea Parker
Karly Parrett
John Richard Parry
Owen Parry
Dr C.J. Parsons
Greg Parsons
Mr and Mrs John Parsons
Steven Parsons
N. Partelle
Lt Col H.C. Paterson
Bridget Patterson
Paul Patterson
Michael Pattison
Michael Perkins
Debra Perry
Keith Perry
B. Perryman
P. Peterson
Mr B.W.B. Pettifer
Joanna Phillips
Dr Alex Phipps
A.M. Pickup
Dr A.D. Picton
Richard Pierce
David Pilling
Hugh Pitt
Prof Peter Plesch
Simon Pollentime
K.W. Prescot
Arthur Price
Mrs L. Price
R.S. Price
Mr and Mrs Jeremy Prideaux-Jackson
Edwin Prince
M.E.G. Prince
J. Procter
Andrew Putnam
Jack Raeburn
Jim Railton
Anne-Marie Ralston
A. and S. Randall
Julie Randall
T.A. Rankin
Dr and Mrs Raphael
Caroline Raphael
Gerald Ratzin
Phillip Rayner
Mrs A. Redfern
Shirley Redpath

Mrs B. Reedman
Dave and Daphne Reesor
Paul Reeve
Prof and Mrs G. Reeves
Mr and Mrs J. Reeves
David Reid
Pat and Derek Rendell
John Reuter
Mr B.W. Reynolds
John Reynolds
Anne Rhodes
Mr and Mrs G. Rhodes
Lewis Rich
Mr D.L. Richards
Mr and Mrs W. Richards
Mr C.J. Richardson
Heather Richardson
Mr C. Ridley
Bryan Rigby
Gordon Ringrose
B.J. Ripley
Dr B. Ritson
Mrs L. Roberts
Mark Roberts
Mr A.J. Robertson
Ronald and Rosemary Robertson
Alan Robinson
Mr D.R. Robinson
Harry Robinson
John Robinson
Sarah Robinson
Mr and Mrs M. Roche
Mr J. Rochelle
Sir Frank Rogers
F. Rogers
Margaret Rogers
Joanne Rose
Maureen Rothstein
Mr P.G. Row
Michael Rowland
Mr and Mrs D. Rowlands
Robin Roy
Mr and Mrs Ian Royle
Stephen Rudge
Mr D. Russell
Sally Russell
Mr J.S. Rutter
Ilse Ryder

Penny Ryder
Miss N. Sacchetti
L. and J. Saferoni
Mr L. Saffron
Keith Salway
Peter and Aileen
    Salway
Mrs K.A.R.
    Saunders
Mr and Mrs J.A.
    Savage
Emma Scammell
Chrisopher Scarles
Michael Schofield
Jeremey Scholes
Howard Schuman
Julian Schwar-
    zenbach
Esme Scott
John Scott
Elenor Sebastian
E.J. Seddon
David Sefton
Paul and Stewart
    Sempile
Chris Serjeant
Cliff and Ann-Marie
    Sharp
John Sharpe
Bryan Sharratt
J.D. Sheffield
Mrs E. Silverwood
Giles Sim
Sue Simon
Audrey and David
    Simpson
Penny Simpson
Paula Sinberg
Mr C.T. Sinclair-
    Stevenson
Mr T.R.H. Sizer
Mrs J. Skilbeck
Peter Skinnard
Mr D.A. Slade
Kevin Sloane
Gillian Smale
Simon Small
Mark Smee and
    Fiona Clifton
Mr and Mrs C.M.
    Smith
Frances Smith
John Smith
Julie Smith
Kenneth Smith
Paul and Yvonne
    Smith
John Smither
Mr A.J. Smithson

Julie Smullen
Mr G. Smyth
Mr and Mrs G.H.
    Snell
Stephen and Helen
    Solley
D.J. Solomon
Mr and Mrs W.A.
    Somers
John Sparrow
Alan Spedding
Dr Lian Spencer
Mrs Stainforth
Gaile Stanley
Mr K.R. Stanley
Mr J. Stanley-Smith
Derek St Clair-
    Stannard
John Steadman
P.M. Steeples
Mrs G.M. Stein
Mrs Stephens
Mrs J. Stephens
Anthony Stern
Will Stevens
Alastair Stevenson
Dr Andrew
    Stevenson
John Stevenson
Dr and Mrs James
    Stewart
Capt and Mrs J.S.
    Stewart
Mr P.N. Stoakley
Neville Stock
F.M. Stockdale
Lynda Stockdale
David Stoddart and
    K. Bertrand
Mr and Mrs C.M.
    Stooke
Dr D.W. Stooke
C.W.R. Storey
J.C. Stot
John Stott
Mary Stow
Alastair Streatfield
Pamela Stringer
Julian Struthers
    Danskin
Neil Stuart
Mr and Mrs N.
    Stupple
Diane Summer
Jill Sumner
Michael Sutcliffe
Mrs C.M. Sutton
A.M. Sutton-Scott-
    Tucker

Margaret Swain
Mrs A.J.G.
    Swainson
Mr T. Swallow
Ray Sweby
Brenda Symes
Richard Tabor
Anne Tait
Simon Tanlaw
John Tarrant
Mr and Mrs Tate
Evelyn Tawell
Mrs A.C. Taylor
Prof David Taylor
George Taylor
Jean Taylor
Mrs J.L. Taylor
M.L. Taylor
Peter Taylor
Mrs J.E. Terrington
Peter Terrington
Dr B. Tha-
    layasingam
Russell Thersby
Alan Thomas
J.E. Thomas
Mrs J.M. Thomas
Sue Thompson
Mrs D.M. Thomson
Elaine Thomspon
J.E. Thornell
Mr and Mrs G.N.
    Thornton
Michael Thrusfield
Mr and Mrs Thurlow
John Tipton
Alison Todd
Mr H. Tomlinson
John Tovey
Elizabeth Towns
Steven Trembath
Sylvia Trench
Dr P.E. Trier
Mr and Mrs J.C.M.
    Troughton
Mrs B.R. Turnbull
W. Turnbull
Iain Tyson
Charles Ullmann
Adrian Underwood
Roger Utley
Mary Jane S. Van
    Meter Johnson
Mr J. Vanderbilt-
    Sloane
Anthony Verdin
Dr P.J. Verrill
Mrs S. Vicar
Mr M.S. Viner

Mitesh Visaria
Dr A. Voller
Michael Wace
Mr P.H. Wainman
Lilian Wakefield
Mrs A.M. Walden
Ted Walken Hansen
Chris Walker
Drs John and
    Maureen Walker
Mr and Mrs R.
    Walker
Val Walker-Dendle
Beryl Waller
Dr Graham Wallis
Inez and Kees
    Walraven
Capt P.J. Walsh
Mr and Mrs J. Ward
Mrs O.M. Ward
S. Ward
Mr A.J. Wardrop
Mr R.A. Wartnaby
John Warwick
Mr and Mrs J.S.
    Waters
Frank Watkin
Dr W.P. Watson
Mrs J. Watt
John Weaver
John Webb
Don Webber
Ethel Webster
Dr I. Webster
Marcia Webster
Roger Weldhen
R. Wells
I.E. West
Mr J.F.M. West
M.J. West
T.J.M. Weston
Mrs M. Weston-
    Smith
Dr and Mrs E.J.
    Wharton
Stacey Whatling
Mr and Mrs John
    Wheeler
Dr G.T. Whitaker
Liz White
Martin White
N.H. White
Mrs S.S. White
John Whiteley
Paul Whiteley
Paul Whittard
Mr and Mrs S.
    Whittle
Barry Whyman

John Wilkin
Mr J.B. Wilkins
Mr P. Willer
Mrs A. Williams
Mr D. Williams
Dick Williams
Mr and Mrs G.
  Williams
Mr M.K. Williams
J.W.M. Wilsom

Drs A. and C. Wilson
Kate Wilson
Prof P.N. Wilson
Lesley and Bernd
  Wilson-Goellnitz
Paul Windle-Taylor
Stuart Winter
Prof Richard Wise
G.M. Wisenfeld
Mr G.W. Wood

David Woods
Barbara Wooldridge
J.L. Wormald
Mr and Mrs C. Worth
J.A. Wotley
John and Rachel
  Wren
Dr A.P. Wright
Dr J.D. Wright
Keith Wright

R.A. Wyld
Mr and Mrs J
  Wyndham
Bruce Yardley
John Yeudall
Camilla Youde
John Zimbler
Hindle Zinkin

# Index of entries

# Index of entries

Names in bold are main entries. Names in italics are Round-ups.

# Report Form                                    2003

To the Editor *The Good Food Guide*
FREEPOST, 2 Marylebone Road, London NW1 4DF

Or send your report by electronic mail to: *goodfoodguide@which.net*

From my personal experience the following establishment should/should not be included in the Guide (please print in BLOCK CAPITALS):

_____

_____

Telephone_____

I had lunch/dinner/stayed there on (date) _____

I would rate this establishment _____ out of ten.

*please continue overleaf*

My meal for ___ people cost £_____ *attach bill where possible*

☐ Please tick if you would like more report forms

Reports received up to the end of **May 2003** will be used in the research of the 2004 edition.

I am not connected in any way with management or proprietors, and have not been asked by them to write to the Guide.
Name and address (BLOCK CAPITALS, please)

_____

_____

Signed _____

As a result of your sending us this report form, we may send you information on *The Good Food Guide* and *The Which? Hotel Guide* in the future. If you would prefer not to receive such information, please tick this box ☐.

To the Editor *The Good Food Guide*
FREEPOST, 2 Marylebone Road, London NW1 4DF

Or send your report by electronic mail to: *goodfoodguide@which.net*

From my personal experience the following establishment should/should not be included in the Guide (please print in BLOCK CAPITALS):

_____

_____

Telephone_____

I had lunch/dinner/stayed there on (date) _____

I would rate this establishment _____ out of ten.

*please continue overleaf*

My meal for ___ people cost £_____ *attach bill where possible*

☐ Please tick if you would like more report forms

Reports received up to the end of **May 2003** will be used in the research of the 2004 edition.

I am not connected in any way with management or proprietors, and have not been asked by them to write to the Guide.
Name and address (BLOCK CAPITALS, please)

_____

_____

Signed _____

As a result of your sending us this report form, we may send you information on *The Good Food Guide* and *The Which? Hotel Guide* in the future. If you would prefer not to receive such information, please tick this box ☐.

# Report Form

To the Editor *The Good Food Guide*
FREEPOST, 2 Marylebone Road, London NW1 4DF

Or send your report by electronic mail to: *goodfoodguide@which.net*

From my personal experience the following establishment should/should not be included in the Guide (please print in BLOCK CAPITALS):

_____

_____

Telephone_____

I had lunch/dinner/stayed there on (date) _____

I would rate this establishment _____ out of ten.

*please continue overleaf*

My meal for ___ people cost £_____ *attach bill where possible*

☐ Please tick if you would like more report forms

Reports received up to the end of **May 2003** will be used in the research of the 2004 edition.

I am not connected in any way with management or proprietors, and have not been asked by them to write to the Guide.
Name and address (BLOCK CAPITALS, please)

_____

_____

Signed _____

As a result of your sending us this report form, we may send you information on *The Good Food Guide* and *The Which? Hotel Guide* in the future. If you would prefer not to receive such information, please tick this box ☐.

# Report Form                                    2003

To the Editor *The Good Food Guide*
FREEPOST, 2 Marylebone Road, London NW1 4DF

Or send your report by electronic mail to: *goodfoodguide@which.net*

From my personal experience the following establishment should/should not be included in the Guide (please print in BLOCK CAPITALS):

_____

_____

                                Telephone_____

I had lunch/dinner/stayed there on (date) _____

I would rate this establishment _____ out of ten.

*please continue overleaf*

My meal for ___ people cost £_____ *attach bill where possible*

☐ Please tick if you would like more report forms

Reports received up to the end of **May 2003** will be used in the research of the 2004 edition.

I am not connected in any way with management or proprietors, and have not been asked by them to write to the Guide.
Name and address (BLOCK CAPITALS, please)

_____

_____

Signed _____

As a result of your sending us this report form, we may send you information on *The Good Food Guide* and *The Which? Hotel Guide* in the future. If you would prefer not to receive such information, please tick this box ☐.